THE ARAB-ISRAELI CONFLICT

The Arab-Israeli Conflict
Readings and Documents
Abridged and Revised Edition

EDITED BY

JOHN NORTON MOORE

SPONSORED BY THE

American Society of
International Law

Princeton University Press
Princeton, New Jersey
1977

Copyright © 1977 by Princeton University Press

Published by Princeton University Press, Princeton, New Jersey
In the United Kingdom: Princeton University Press, Guildford, Surrey

All Rights Reserved

Library of Congress Cataloging in Publication Data will
be found on the last printed page of this book

Printed in the United States of America
by Princeton University Press, Princeton, New Jersey

Acknowledgments

THE PRINCIPAL PURPOSE of this abridged edition of *The Arab-Israeli Conflict* is to promote greater understanding of one of the most persistent and explosive challenges to world order of our time. It has been reassuring to see the enthusiasm from all quarters with which the project has been greeted. The very enthusiasm of the response, however, makes it impossible to thank adequately all who assisted in the preparation of the reader. Among the special debts which stand out, I should particularly like to thank the authors and publishers who made this project possible by generously giving permission to reprint their work and the American Society of International Law under whose auspices the reader has been published. A list of contributors and a list of individual permissions appear in the back of this volume.

In selecting readings and documents for inclusion, every effort has been made to achieve balance on the issues and presentation of the principal viewpoints. To facilitate this balance and to ensure inclusion of as wide as possible a range of materials, a draft table of contents and introduction were circulated to the members of the American Society of International Law Panel on the Role of International Law in Civil Wars as well as a number of other scholars and statesmen familiar with the issues. Responses to these drafts were most helpful. I am particularly grateful for the suggestions of Professor M. Cherif Bassiouni of De Paul University College of Law, Dr. Yehuda Z. Blum, Senior Lecturer in International Law at the Hebrew University of Jerusalem, Stephen M. Boyd, the Assistant Legal Adviser for Near Eastern and South Asian Affairs of the Department of State, Professor John Claydon of the Queens University Faculty of Law, Professor Irwin Cotler of the Osgoode Hall Law School, His Excellency Dr. Abdullah El-Erian, Ambassador of the United Arab Republic to France and formerly Deputy Permanent Representative of the United Arab Republic to the United Nations, Professor Roger Fisher of the Harvard Law School, Burhan W. Hammad, the Deputy Permanent Observer of the League of Arab States to the United Nations, Dr. Rosalyn Higgins of the Royal Institute of International Affairs, Professor Majid Khadduri of The Johns Hopkins School of Advanced International Studies, Professor W. T. Mallison, Jr., of George Washington University National Law Center, Professor Rouhollah K. Ramazani of the University of Virginia Department of Government and Foreign Affairs, Professor Michael Reisman of the Yale Law School, Stephen M. Schwebel, Executive Vice President of the American Society of International Law, Dr. Amos Shapira,

Senior Lecturer in Law at the Tel Aviv University, Professor Julius Stone of the University of Sydney Faculty of Law, and Dr. Yaacov S. Zemach, Lecturer in Law at the Hebrew University of Jerusalem.

A very special debt is owed the American Society of International Law for its commitment to scholarly integrity and the free interchange of ideas, which continues to serve as an inspiration. I should especially like to thank Stephen M. Schwebel, the Executive Vice President of the Society, for his early encouragement and continuing assistance. The members of the Society's Civil War Panel have also assisted with helpful suggestions throughout the project. The members of the Panel are: Thomas Ehrlich, Dean of the Stanford Law School, Richard A. Falk, Milbank Professor of International Law and Practice at Princeton University and past Chairman of the Panel, Tom J. Farer, Professor of Law at Rutgers University, Edwin Brown Firmage, Professor of Law at the University of Utah, Wolfgang Friedmann, Professor of Law at Columbia University and Chairman of the Panel, G. W. Haight of the New York Bar, Eliot D. Hawkins of the New York Bar, Brunson MacChesney, Professor of Law at Northwestern University and former President of the American Society of International Law, Myres S. McDougal, Sterling Professor of Law at Yale and former President of the American Society of International Law, John Norton Moore, Professor of Law and Director of the Graduate Program at the University of Virginia School of Law and Rapporteur of the Panel, Stephen M. Schwebel, Executive Vice President of the American Society of International Law and Professor of International Law at the School of Advanced International Studies of The Johns Hopkins University, Louis B. Sohn, Bemis Professor of International Law at Harvard and formerly Counselor on International Law of the Department of State, Howard J. Taubenfeld, Professor of Law at Southern Methodist University, Lawrence R. Velvel, Professor of Law at the Catholic University of America, and Burns H. Weston, Professor of Law at the University of Iowa.

John E. Claydon, now Assistant Professor of International Law at Queens University, did a significant amount of the work involved in compiling the volume while he was my research assistant at the University of Virginia, and I am much indebted to him. Mr. Stephen M. Dichter, Mr. Fred Tipson, and Mrs. Karen M. Yates also helped in innumerable ways as research assistants. Sir John Wheeler-Bennett aided in obtaining from the British Museum a photostat of the original Balfour Declaration, which has contributed a touch of historical excitement to the reader. Finally, I wish to thank Sanford G. Thatcher, Social Science Editor of the Princeton University Press, for his continuing assistance throughout the project.

The selection of readings and documents in this volume does not imply endorsement of any article or position by the American Society of International Law. Nor does assistance in the preparation of the reader or authorship by a government official imply official endorsement either of the reader or of the viewpoint expressed by the author. The final responsibility for the reader and any errors and infelicities it may contain is my own.

JOHN NORTON MOORE*

*This volume was submitted for publication prior to the Editor's leave of absence from the University of Virginia to serve as the Counselor on International Law to the Department of State and subsequently as the Chairman of the National Security Council Interagency Task Force on the Law of the Sea and Deputy Special Representative of the President for the Law of the Sea Conference. The views expressed by the Editor are his personal views and do not necessarily represent the views of the United States Government or any agency thereof.

Contents

B. *The United Nations Emergency Force and Its Withdrawal*

IV. THOUGHTS ON SETTLEMENT

Introduction
THE CONTINUING MIDDLE EAST CRISIS

THIS IS an abridged edition of a three-volume compilation of readings and documents on the Arab-Israeli conflict published under the auspices of the American Society of International Law. A principal purpose of this compilation is to promote wider understanding of one of the most persistent and explosive international problems of our time. United States Under Secretary of State Joseph J. Sisco has warned that "the Middle East ... holds greater ... risks for world peace than any other area in the world." The warning should be heeded. The Arab-Israeli conflict is one that has defied solution since the commencement of the British Mandate for Palestine in 1922, and since the termination of that Mandate in 1948 it has precipitated four wars – once in 1948, again in 1956 and 1967, and still again in 1973. In the aftermath of the third Arab-Israeli War of June 1967 and the October War of 1973 the conflict has become enormously more volatile. The main factors responsible for this increased volatility have been a more active Soviet and American involvement, particularly an increased sophistication of weapons systems on both sides, the growth of the Palestine liberation organizations, the joining of new Arab states in the conflict, the destabilizing effect of the withdrawal of the United Nations Emergency Force, and the territorial dislocations of the Six-Day War. Events during the past five years, including the Egyptian "war of attrition" against Israeli positions in the Suez Canal area, Israeli bombing raids against Egypt, the introduction in an operational capacity of Soviet military personnel into Egypt, the internal conflict in Jordan in which Syria militarily intervened on behalf of Palestinian insurgents and the United States considered counterintervention, intensified bombings, kidnappings, and the hijackings of commercial aircraft in international flight by the Popular Front for the Liberation of Palestine, and finally the resumption of full-scale hostilities in the October War of 1973 and the resulting oil embargo have underscored the crisis proportions of the Middle Eastern threat to world order.

The Arab-Israeli conflict, like all major world-order disputes, has its own unique background and issues. Efforts at containment and conciliation of the conflict will have a better chance for success to the extent that they are informed on these issues. Sometimes, of course, apparent issues may conceal more fundamental disagreement. But usually there is at least a sufficient relation between what the parties claim and their perceptions about the dispute to make an understanding of competing claims useful in efforts at settlement. An understanding of opposing arguments is also useful in shedding parochial identifications and in recognizing reasonable and unreasonable contentions in one's own and opposing positions. In appraising complex issues of world order there is no escape from the necessity for in-depth familiarity with the circumstances of the conflict and the competing claims of the belligerents.

It is also hoped that this compilation will serve as a catalyst for further development of a range of important international problems raised by the Arab-Israeli conflict. Among other issues in need of development are the principle of self-determination, the law of reprisal in settings of continued belligerency, the legal effects of cease-fire and armistice agreements, the meaning of "no acquisition of territory by war" and its interrelation with the Charter principle permitting defense against an armed attack, the identification and utilization of international straits and waterways, the constitutional nature of and most effective structure for United Nations peacekeeping forces, the constitutional authority of the General Assembly, Security Council, and Secretary-General in recommending, guaranteeing, and enforcing plans for settlement, the structure of international fact-finding machinery, criteria for appraisal of the obligation to pursue peaceful settlement of international disputes, and the perennial problem of distinguishing permissible from impermissible coercion. Many of the readings brought together in this volume make substantial contributions in one or more of these areas.

A Brief Historical Overview of the Arab-Israeli Conflict[1]

The Arab-Israeli conflict has been one of the most persistent world-order disputes of the contemporary international system. Prior to the October War there had been three Arab-Israeli wars in twenty-three years, and until the cease-fire of August 7, 1970, the level of hostilities at Suez was such as to suggest a description of it as "the fourth Arab-Israeli War."[2] Accordingly,

[1]For an excellent summary of the history of the Arab-Israeli conflict through July 1967 and an introduction to the United Nations role in the conflict, see LOUIS B. SOHN, CASES ON UNITED NATIONS LAW 416-74, 527-634 (2nd rev. edn., 1967). This introductory overview draws heavily on Professor Sohn's work.

[2]The level of continuing hostilities has been such that some observers on both sides view the conflict as one war. Whether it is viewed as one, four, or five wars, the essential points about the conflict are that there have been four to five outbreaks of relatively more intense coercion during its history and that claims to continuing belligerency should be subjected to appraisal under the United Nations Charter and other applicable legal regimes.

it may be helpful in assimilating the range of readings in this volume to set out briefly a historical overview of the conflict. The reader should be careful, however, not to uncritically accept a historical framework as the only or even the most important framework for appraisal. The United Nations Charter embodies the judgment that unilateral coercion against the territorial integrity or political independence of any state may not be used even to redress circumstances which are perceived by the belligerents as major wrongs. Instead, major unilateral coercion may be lawfully employed only in defense and only "until the Security Council has taken measures necessary to maintain international peace and security." Similarly, the Charter focus on fundamental human rights and self-determination of peoples is most meaningfully a focus on present rather than past circumstances.

The latter part of the nineteenth and early part of the twentieth century witnessed a dramatic growth in both Arab and Jewish nationalism. Arab nationalism sought independent Arab states free from Turkish and later British and French control. Jewish nationalism sought a homeland for the Jews. Both were destined to collide over the territory of Palestine. During World War I Great Britain made a series of ambiguous and, by some interpretations, contradictory promises to both Arabs and Jews in support of their national aspirations. In the Balfour Declaration, a letter of November 2, 1917, from Lord Balfour, the British Foreign Secretary, to Lord Rothschild, the British government announced that it viewed "with favour the establishment in Palestine of a national home for the Jewish people ... ." It went on to say, however, "... it being clearly understood that nothing shall be done which may prejudice the civil and religious rights of existing non-Jewish communities in Palestine ... ." The British militarily occupied Palestine during 1917-18, and by an agreement between the Allied Powers Palestine was placed under British Mandate. The complementary terms of the Balfour Declaration were incorporated in the British Mandate for Palestine, which was confirmed by the Council of the League of Nations on July 24, 1922. At the commencement of the Mandate there were approximately 486,000 Moslems, 84,000 Jews, and 71,000 Christians in Palestine.[3]

[3] The Report of the United Nations Special Committee on Palestine provides perhaps the most detailed figures. It states that in 1922 there were 486,177 Moslems, 83,790 Jews, 71,464 Christians, and 7,616 others in Palestine. See the *Report to the General Assembly of the United Nations Special Committee on Palestine*, 2 U.N. GAOR, Supp. #11, at 11, U.N. Doc. A/364 (Sept. 3, 1947). Some other sources give a slightly higher figure for Moslems or Arabs in Palestine at the commencement of the Mandate. Professor Quincy Wright maintains that the 1922 population of Palestine consisted of "600,000 Moslems, 73,000 Christians and 84,000 Jews." Wright, "The Middle East Crisis," in THE MIDDLE EAST: PROSPECTS FOR PEACE, BACK-GROUND PAPERS AND PROCEEDINGS OF THE THIRTEENTH HAMMARSKJOLD FORUM 1, 4 (The Association of the Bar of the City of New York, 1969). See also L. SOHN, CASES ON UNITED NATIONS LAW 417 (2nd rev. edn., 1967).

The ambiguity of the Balfour Declaration and League Mandate and the factual setting to which they were applied led to increasing strife between Arab and Jewish communities in Palestine, each of which interpreted the ambiguities to support its vision of the future of Palestine. Jews interpreted the mandatory obligation as leading toward a Jewish state. Arabs, on the other hand, interpreted the obligation as creating only a Jewish National Home within Palestine. These differences and resentment of continued Jewish immigration and settlement in Palestine provoked Arab riots in Palestine in 1920-21, 1929, 1933 and 1936-38. A Royal Commission chaired by Lord Peel was appointed in 1936 in response to the Arab revolt earlier that year. Its report in 1937 contended that the Arab desire for national independence and their opposition to the establishment of a Jewish National Home in Palestine were the principal causes of the rioting. Finding the Arab and Jewish positions irreconcilable under the terms of the Mandate, it recommended the partition of Palestine into separate Arab and Jewish states. The Peel Commission plan was opposed by the Arabs, and although the Jewish Agency approved the fundament of partition, it opposed the particulars of the Peel plan. With the opposition of both Arabs and Jews, the plan was not adopted.

Following the failure of the Peel plan and a London Conference of 1939 called to work out agreement between the parties, the British Government adopted a more restrictive policy toward Jewish immigration and announced its policy to be the creation of an independent Palestine State within ten years. The Jewish community opposed this shift in British policy, which had been announced in a White Paper of May 17, 1939, particularly in view of events in Germany, which lent a special urgency to efforts for the establishment of a Jewish National Home.

The assumption of power by the Nazi Party in Germany in 1933 and the subsequent genocide of European Jews during World War II prompted Jews to immigrate to Palestine in ever greater numbers, particularly after the end of the war in 1945. As Jewish immigration accelerated following the war, conflicts between the Arab and Jewish communities and the Jewish community and restrictive British immigration policy gave rise to increased terrorism and civil strife. During this postwar period, several additional British proposals for a compromise plan were rejected by both sides.

By April 2, 1947, the British Government had had enough of the situation and requested the General Assembly "to make recommendations, under Article 10 of the Charter, concerning the future government of Palestine...." The General Assembly considered the British request at a Special Session of the Assembly held in 1947. During the session the General Committee of the

Assembly refused to include on the agenda a request by five Arab states that the Assembly also consider "the termination of the Mandate over Palestine and the declaration of its independence." Subsequently, the General Assembly appointed a Special Committee on Palestine to investigate and report to the Assembly. The Assembly also called on all governments and peoples to refrain from the use of force pending action by the General Assembly on the report of the Special Committee.

In August 1947 the majority of the United Nations Special Committee on Palestine recommended a plan of partition with economic union. The plan was to partition Palestine into an Arab state, a Jewish state, and an international trusteeship for the City of Jerusalem, with some degree of economic and other union between the successor states and Jerusalem. The Special Committee plan was approved by the General Assembly with only minor changes. The vote on November 29, 1947, was 33 to 13 with 10 abstentions. Although the Jewish Agency accepted the plan, it was rejected by the Arab states, which denied the authority of the General Assembly to partition Palestine. An Arab-supported draft resolution to refer the legality of the partition plan to the International Court of Justice was rejected by the General Assembly *Ad Hoc* Committee on the Palestinian Question.

After General Assembly approval of the partition plan, disorder and terrorism in Palestine grew rapidly. Despite this accelerated collapse of order, the Security Council refused to take action on the recommendations of the General Assembly concerning implementation of the plan. On March 5, 1948, however, the Security Council appealed "to all governments and peoples ... to take all possible action to prevent or reduce such disorders as are now occurring in Palestine," and on April 1 the Council called upon "the Arab and Jewish armed groups in Palestine to cease acts of violence immediately." Subsequently, on April 17, the Council called upon "all persons and organizations in Palestine and especially upon the Arab Higher Committee and the Jewish Agency" to cease military activities immediately. On April 23 the Security Council established a Truce Commission for Palestine, and in May the General Assembly adopted a resolution authorizing the appointment of a United Nations Mediator in Palestine. Count Folke Bernadotte of Sweden, then Vice-President of the International Red Cross, was appointed on May 20 as the United Nations Mediator.

The Palestine Mandate was terminated at midnight on May 14, 1948. The Jewish community immediately proclaimed the State of Israel within the territorial boundaries of the partition plan and the new state was quickly recognized by a number of states, including the United States and the Soviet

Union. Almost immediately Egypt, Syria, Transjordan, Lebanon, and other Arab states intervened, in the words of a cablegram of May 15 from the Secretary-General of the League of Arab States to the United Nations Secretary-General, "to restore law and order and to prevent disturbances prevailing in Palestine from spreading into their territories and to check further bloodshed." The first Arab-Israeli War had begun. A Security Council call for a four-week cease-fire produced a short-lived truce which went into effect on June 11, 1948. The Arab states rejected a Security Council appeal for an extension of the cease-fire, and, following the resumption of hostilities, Israel secured substantially greater territory than it was initially allotted under the 1947 partition plan. A Security Council Resolution of July 15, 1948, determined that "the situation in Palestine constitutes a threat to the peace" and ordered the governments concerned "to desist from further military action." Both sides complied with the resolution, and an uneasy cease-fire began on July 18, 1948. Following negotiations on the Island of Rhodes with respect to the settlement with Egypt and Jordan and in no man's land at the front itself with respect to the settlement with Syria and Lebanon, armistice agreements went into force between Israel and Egypt, Lebanon, Jordan, and Syria in February, March, April, and July of 1949 respectively. The Armistice Agreements were concluded through the mediation of Dr. Ralph J. Bunche, who had been appointed Count Bernadotte's successor after the Count was assassinated by Jewish terrorists in the summer of 1948. Under the terms of the Armistice Agreements a United Nations Truce Supervision Organization was to observe and maintain the Armistice arrangements. Though little noticed, UNTS observers continued to function in the Syrian and Suez sectors even after the withdrawal in 1967 of the United Nations Emergency Force. On May 11, 1949, Israel was admitted to membership in the United Nations.

One of the tragic consequences of the 1948 war was the displacement of a large number of refugees. It has been estimated that there were approximately 726,000 Arab refugees who fled from Israel during the first Arab-Israeli War.[4] In December of 1948 the General Assembly established a Conciliation Commission for Palestine which was charged with assisting the parties to achieve a final settlement, with preparing a proposal for an international regime for the Jerusalem area, and with facilitating the repatriation, resettlement, and economic and social rehabilitation of refugees. The Commission was also charged with assisting the parties to achieve a final settlement

[4]See L. Holborn, *The Palestine Arab Refugee Problem*, 23 INT'L JOURNAL 82, 88 (1968).

and with preparing a proposal for an international regime for the Jerusalem area under effective United Nations control. The Resolution which created the Conciliation Commission provided with respect to the refugees that "the refugees wishing to return to their homes and live at peace with their neighbors should be permitted to do so at the earliest practicable date, and ... compensation should be paid for the property of those choosing not to return and for loss of or damage to property which, under principles of international law or in equity, should be made good by the Governments or authorities responsible...."[5] In December 1949 the United Nations Relief and Works Agency (UNRWA) was created to assist in carrying out a relief and works program. UNRWA subsequently assumed responsibility for the refugee assistance programs. Although there have been a number of proposals made by Israel and the Arab states toward solution of the refugee problem, to date it has not been solved. Rather, each successive war, particularly the Six-Day War, has increased the number of refugees. According to the Annual Report of UNRWA, on the eve of the Six-Day War there were 1,344,576 refugees registered with UNRWA and living in the Gaza Strip, Jordan, Lebanon, and Syria.[6] It has been estimated that the Six-Day War created approximately 234,000 new Arab refugees as well as again displacing a substantial number of the earlier refugees.[7]

Although Israel regarded the Armistice Agreements of 1949 as creating an obligation to effect transition to a permanent peace, the Arab states did not regard the agreements as a final peace terminating the state of belligerency with Israel. One consequence of this continuing state of belligerency was the imposition by Egypt of restrictions on passage through the Suez Canal of Israeli ships and cargo bound for Israel. In response to these restrictions and the claim to maintain continuing belligerency, on September 1, 1951, the Security Council called upon Egypt to terminate restrictions on the passage

[5] G. A. Res. 194(111), U.N. DOC. A/810 at 21 (1948).

[6] See Holborn, *The Palestine Arab Refugee Problem*, 23 INT'L JOURNAL 82, 88 n. 9 (1968). Any estimate of the number of refugees is fraught with dangers, including a threshold problem of who is a Palestinian refugee. See *ibid.* at 88-90.

[7] According to a 1967 Report of the Commissioner-General of UNRWA, approximately 100,000 persons who were not previously registered as UNRWA refugees fled from the West Bank to the East Bank, over 99,000 nonregistered persons living in Syria moved northwards and eastwards from the area occupied by Israel, and approximately 35,000 persons moved from the Sinai Peninsula to the United Arab Republic in the months immediately following the June War. In addition, over 116,000 UNRWA-registered refugees were displaced from these areas. See the *Report of the Commissioner-General of the United Nations Relief and Works Agency for Palestine Refugees in the Near East, 1 July 1966 – 30 June 1967*, 22 U.N. GAOR, Supp. 13, at 11-14, U.N. DOC. A/6713 (1967).

of goods through the Suez Canal to Israel ports and considered that, "since the Armistice regime ... is of a permanent character, neither party can reasonably assert that it is actively a belligerent ... ."[8]

Though marred by numerous violations, the Armistice regime prevented major hostilities until 1956. In July 1956 Egypt nationalized the Suez Canal Company. After Egypt rejected the proposals of a London Conference of Canal Users, France and Britain informed the Security Council that the Egyptian action constituted a threat to peace and security. France and Britain were principally concerned with Egyptian nationalization and management of the Canal. Israel was primarily concerned with stepped up *fedayeen* raids from Gaza and Sinai, intensified raids from Jordan, Egyptian harassment of Israeli shipping in the Strait of Tiran, and a tripartite military alliance concluded on October 23 between Egypt, Syria, and Jordan. On October 29 Israeli armor invaded the Sinai and raced to the Canal and the Southern tip of Sinai at Sharm El-Sheikh. The Israeli strike was supported by a delayed joint French-British airborne attack on the Canal area allegedly to restore the security of the area.

Because of the negative votes of France and Great Britain, both permanent members of the Council, the Security Council was unable to reach agreement on a resolution calling for an immediate cease-fire in this second Arab-Israeli War. This inability to reach agreement because of the negative vote of a permanent member set the stage for a subsequent Council vote on October 31 to summon the first Emergency Special Session of the General Assembly under the machinery of the Uniting for Peace Resolution. Subsequently, the Assembly adopted a series of resolutions calling for a cease-fire and return to armistice lines and creating a United Nations Emergency Force in the Middle East (UNEF). Under the combined pressure of the United Nations, the United States, and the Soviet Union, Britain, France, and Israel agreed to a cease-fire and on the arrival of UNEF French and British troops began withdrawing. French and British withdrawal was completed by December 22, 1956. Israeli withdrawal, particularly from Gaza and the strategic Sharm El-Sheikh area which dominated the Strait of Tiran, was slower. After receiving assurance in an *aide-mémoire* of February 11, 1957, that the United States viewed the Gulf of Aqaba and the Strait giving access thereto as international waterways and that it would be prepared "to join with others to secure general recognition of this right," Israeli forces withdrew on March 8, leaving the area in the control of UNEF forces. Since Israel had refused

[8] 6 U.N. SCOR, 558th meeting 2-3, U.N. DOC. 5/2322 (1951).

permission for the stationing of UNEF forces on Israeli territory, UNEF forces were stationed solely on Egyptian territory.

Though disturbed by repeated violations and in later years by a pattern of repeated Arab *fedayeen* raids from the territory of neighboring Arab states followed by larger-scale Israeli reprisal raids, the 1956 cease-fire and UNEF presence contributed to preventing the outbreak of major hostilities for over ten years. In May and June of 1967, however, an escalating series of threats and counterthreats culminating in the withdrawal of UNEF at Egyptian request and Egyptian reimposition of the blockade against Israeli shipping in the Strait of Tiran and massing of Egyptian forces in Sinai led to the third or "Six-Day" Arab-Israeli War. On June 5, 1967, the Israeli air force attacked Egyptian military airfields. The war quickly enlarged to include Syrian, Jordanian, and other Arab forces, but within six days Israel had occupied large areas of territory including the Gaza Strip, the Sinai, the Golan Heights, East Jerusalem, and the West Bank of Jordan.

For a variety of reasons, including the threat of a Soviet veto, the Security Council was unable to act prior to the Six-Day War. But after the outbreak of fighting the Security Council passed a series of four resolutions from June 6 through June 12 calling for a cease-fire. Shortly thereafter a cease-fire went into effect. During 1967 the General Assembly and the Security Council also passed several resolutions concerning humanitarian assistance to civilians and prisoners of war and calling on Israel not to take unilateral measures to alter the status of the City of Jerusalem. The Security Council later re-emphasized, in both 1968 and 1969, its call to Israel not to take measures to change the status of the City of Jerusalem.

After prolonged diplomatic effort, on November 22, 1967, the Security Council unanimously adopted Resolution 242 affirming a package basis for settlement of the Arab-Israeli conflict. The Resolution affirmed "that the fulfillment of Charter principles requires the establishment of a just and lasting peace" which should include "[w]ithdrawal of Israel armed forces from territories occupied in the recent conflict" and "[t]ermination of all claims or states of belligerency and respect for and acknowledgement of the sovereignty, territorial integrity and political independence of every State in the area and their right to live in peace within secure and recognized boundaries free from threats or acts of force." The Resolution also affirmed the necessity "for guaranteeing freedom of navigation through international waterways in the area," "for achieving a just settlement of the refugee problem," and "for guaranteeing the territorial inviolability and political independence of every State in the area, through measures including the establishment of demilitarized zones," and requested "the Secretary-General to designate a Special Representative to... maintain contacts with the States concerned in order to promote agreement and assist efforts to achieve a peaceful and accepted settlement in accordance with... this resolution." Pursuant to Resolution 242, Secretary-General U Thant appointed Dr. Gunnar Jarring, Swedish Ambassador to the Soviet Union, as his Special Representative. Initial efforts of Dr. Jarring, and subsequent bilateral Soviet-United States and four-power British-French-Soviet-United States talks, failed to produce an agreement within the framework of Resolution 242 acceptable to both Arabs and Israelis.

In the years following the passage of Resolution 242 the cease-fire steadily deteriorated. One incident which illustrated the trend was the Israeli raid on December 28, 1968, on the Beirut International Airport. The precisely executed commando raid resulted in the destruction of thirteen Arab commerical aircraft of an estimated value of approximately $44 million but did not cause loss of life. Israel announced that the raid was in retaliation for an attack two days earlier by members of the Popular Front for the Liberation of Palestine upon an El Al passenger plane in Athens, in which an Israeli passenger had been killed when the airplane was machine-gunned as it was preparing to take off. On December 31 the Security Council unanimously adopted a resolution condemning Israel for the Beirut raid.

Fearing that prolonged Israeli occupation of the territories seized in the Six-Day War would lead to legitimation of the *de facto* borders, President Gamal Abdel Nasser of Egypt announced in the spring of 1969 that the cease-fire with Israel was no longer valid, and thereupon Egyptian armed forces began a "war of attrition" against Israeli defenses along the Suez Canal. Heavy artillery exchanges along the Canal led to an acceleration of air activity, and during January and February of 1970 the Israelis conducted deep penetration bombing raids against targets in Egypt. In response to the raids a secret trip by Nasser to Moscow led to the introduction on Egyptian territory of Soviet SA-3 ground-to-air missiles. During the spring of 1970 the situation deteriorated further with the introduction of Soviet military advisers into Egypt in an operational capacity, an intensification of the war along the Suez Canal, and a rise in the pattern of Palestinian guerrilla raids on Israeli settlements launched from within Jordan and Lebanon and Israeli responses against the guerrilla encampments within those countries.

In June of 1970 United States Secretary of State William P. Rogers negotiated an "at least" 90-day standstill cease-fire between Israel, Egypt, and Jordan, which went into effect on August 7. Under the terms of the agree-

ment between Israel and Egypt, both sides were to "stop all incursions and
all firing, on the ground and in the air, across the cease-fire line," and to
"refrain from changing the military status quo within zones extending 50
kilometers to the east and the west of the ceasefire line." In order to verify
observance, each side was permitted to "rely on its own national means, including reconnaissance aircraft, which will be free to operate without interference up to 10 kilometers from the cease-fire line on its own side of that
line."[9] Ambassador Jarring then invited them to take part in discussions
opening in New York on August 25. On September 6 Israel informed Dr.
Jarring that, because of Egyptian violation of the standstill cease-fire by
continuing construction and emplacement of Soviet anti-aircraft missiles in
the Suez cease-fire zone, Israel was suspending participation in the talks
until the missiles installed in violation of the cease-fire were withdrawn.
For its part, Egypt charged Israel with violations of the cease-fire in the
form of overflights west of the Canal into the Egyptian sector of the cease-
fire zone.

The Rogers initiative for an "at least" 90-day standstill cease-fire was
followed by a rash of hijackings and attacks on commercial aircraft by the
Popular Front for the Liberation of Palestine, which opposed the cease-fire.
Jordanian acceptance of the Rogers initiative and the hijackings by the
Popular Front in turn triggered a series of major clashes between Palestine
Liberation Organization forces in Jordan and the army of King Hussein,
culminating in an abortive Syrian intervention on behalf of the Palestinian
guerrillas and a threatened United States counterintervention. Although the
level of external intervention in Jordan quickly receded, military clashes
have continued between Jordanian troops and Palestinian guerrilla forces,
and the tension on the Jordan-Syria border has remained high.

President Nasser died on September 28, 1970. He was succeeded as
President of the United Arab Republic by Anwar el-Sadat. On November 4,
1970, the General Assembly passed a resolution requesting an additional
three-month extension of the cease-fire. Subsequently, on December 30, 1970,
Abba Eban, the Foreign Minister of Israel, informed Ambassador Jarring that
in view of "present political and military conditions" Israel was willing to
resume talks. During January and February of 1971 an exchange of views
between Egypt, Israel, and Jordan through Ambassador Jarring seemed to
narrow the gap between them only slightly. The most significant exchange

[9] Cease-Fire-Standstill Agreement Between Israel and the United Arab Republic
Effective August 7, 1970, obtained from the United States Department of State. See
also 63 DEP'T STATE BULLETIN 178-79 (1970).

was occasioned by an *aide mémoire* of February 8 from Ambassador Jarring to Israel and the United Arab Republic. The replies of the United Arab Republic on February 15 and Israel on February 26 indicated substantial continuing disagreement over the interpretation of Resolution 242, particularly whether it required territorial withdrawal from all the occupied territories or a negotiated withdrawal to "secure and recognized boundaries." The United Arab Republic reply, however, did for the first time indicate willingness to enter into a peace agreement with Israel if other differences could be resolved.

Diplomatic efforts since the Jarring initiatives of January and February focused on United States efforts to negotiate an interim settlement centering on a reopened Suez Canal. Although by August 1971 no such agreement had been reached, the Rogers initiated cease-fire had survived its first anniversary.

In October 1973 the world was again rudely reminded of the continuing tragedy of the Arab-Israeli conflict. At 2:00 p.m. on the afternoon of October 6, 1973, the High Holy Day of Yom Kippur in the Jewish community, Egyptian and Syrian armies attacked Israeli military forces along the Suez Canal and in the Golan Heights. The Egyptian army crossed the Canal in force and quickly achieved a bridgehead on the East Bank. Simultaneously, the Syrian army attacked Israeli forces on the Golan Heights and penetrated Israeli defenses. As Israel mobilized, Israeli forces counterattacked. After fierce fighting and extremely heavy casualties on both sides, the Israelis made their way to within twenty-two miles of Damascus. And on the Egyptian front, the Israelis penetrated the Egyptian bridgehead on the East Bank of the Canal and established a bridgehead of their own west of the Canal behind the Egyptian lines, some fifty miles from Cairo.

Though the Jordanian front did not become actively involved, Jordan and other Arab states sent military forces to Syria to assist it. The fighting also resulted in an alert of United States forces as the United States and the Soviet Union exchanged stern diplomatic notes, and it resulted too in the use of the "oil weapon" as Arab states acted in concert to cut off oil shipments to the United States and the Netherlands.

As the situation deteriorated, Secretary General Brezhnev of the USSR invited urgent consultations with the United States. In response, United States Secretary of State Henry Kissinger flew to Moscow for discussions. As a result of these discussions, the United States and the Soviet Union agreed on a draft Security Council resolution calling for an immediate cease-fire, immediate implementation of Security Council Resolution 242 of

1967, and immediate negotiations between the parties. The resolution was adopted on October 22 by the Security Council. During the following week, the Security Council passed three additional resolutions confirming the cease-fire, urging that the forces of the two sides be returned to the positions they occupied when the cease-fire became effective, strengthening the body of United Nations observers to supervise the cease-fire, and establishing a new United Nations Emergency Force.

Subsequent diplomatic activities have centered on efforts by Secretary Kissinger to mediate a stable cease-fire and a more durable peace. On September 1, 1975, these efforts bore fruit as the Arab Republic of Egypt and Israel signed an interim agreement on the Sinai. Though the agreement is not a final peace agreement, it was a significant step by both Egypt and Israel and has permitted the reopening of the Suez Canal to nonmilitary cargoes bound for Israel.

The Principal Issues in the Conflict

The issues raised by the continuing Arab-Israeli conflict are as diverse as might be expected from the prolonged history of the conflict. The principal issues, however, are grouped around six major clusters of problems. First, the establishment of the State of Israel, the human rights of Arab and Jewish refugees of the repeated conflicts, and, closely related, the claim to self-determination of the Palestinian people. Second, freedom of navigation through waterways in the area, including the Strait of Tiran, the Gulf of Aqaba, and the Suez Canal. Third, the status of the City of Jerusalem and protection of and access to the Holy Places. Fourth, utilization of the Jordan waters by riparian states. This seems to be one of the few issues in the conflict which may have become less intractable following the 1967 war. Fifth, issues relating to the permissibility of resort to coercion and the consequences of such resort. Among others, these issues include the effect of an armistice regime, the legality under the United Nations Charter of a continuing state of belligerency, the lawfulness of the belligerents' use of force in each of the Arab-Israeli wars, the extent of the duty for surrounding states to prevent *fedayeen* raids against Israel launched from their territory, the legality of Israeli raids and other actions against guerrilla bases in neighboring Arab states, the meaning of no acquisition of territory by war and the interrelation with the Charter principle proscribing aggressive coercion and permitting defense against an armed attack, and the scope and applicability of the Geneva Conventions of 1949 for the humanitarian protection of civilians and prisoners of war. Finally, the Arab-Israeli conflict raises a series of issues concerning the authority and structure of the United Nations. These issues include among others the authority of the General Assembly and the Security Council to recommend and enforce settlement of international disputes (such as the General Assembly recommendation concerning partition of Palestine and the more recent Security Council Resolutions 242 and 338), the structure of and basis for United Nations peacekeeping in the light of the UNEF withdrawal, the credibility gap with respect to United Nations fact-finding and resolutions concerning the Middle East and the need to depoliticize such proceedings, and the perennial problem of increasing the effectiveness of the United Nations as an agency for promoting justice and managing international conflict.

Appraisal of the Issues in the Conflict

The readings selected for this volume are, in general, careful and scholarly. Nevertheless, it should not be assumed that merely because an argument is made it has merit. A careful comparison of the opposing arguments is usually the safest guide to appraisal. Perhaps more importantly, not all of the issues raised are of equal importance in analyzing the conflict. Development of a hierachy of issues is a critical task in appraisal.[10] In weighing individual selections it is also useful to keep in mind the principal elements of choice which account for different conclusions. They are: first, a differing emphasis on the descriptive (roughly, what the law is) and prescriptive (roughly, what the author believes the law ought to be) intellectual tasks; second, in carrying out the descriptive task, differing fact selection, rule selection (and interpretation), and application of the rule (or principle or standard) to the facts; and third, in carrying out the prescriptive task, differing goal selection and varying assessment of the impact of alternative actions on postulated goals. Most disagreement about "the facts" of world-order disputes is less disagreement about whether a particular event occurred than it is selection from a complex context of those events which support the world-view of the writer. Accordingly, the reader should ask why the author selected the events he did and what criteria the author used consciously or unconsciously to determine which of the "facts" were most relevant. Similarly, in most scholarly dialogue it is important to ask why a particular rule or principle is selected as determinative in a particular context as well as whether the rule is authoritative. In this regard it is particularly important to keep in mind that Article 103 of the United Nations Charter provides: "[i]n the event of a conflict between the obligations of the

---

[10] And, of course, legal issues are not the only considerations relevant for appraisal.

Members of the United Nations under the present Charter and their obligations under any other international agreement, their obligations under the present Charter shall prevail." Thus, since all of the states parties to the Arab-Israeli conflict are bound by the Charter, the obligations of the Charter are the most important source of legal rights and duties in appraising the conflict.

A Few Words of Caution in Using Documents

A few words of caution may be helpful in using the documents in this compilation. First, overreliance on historical documents for analysis of world-order disputes may lead to excessive emphasis on historical conditions at the expense of present reality. Although a knowledge of past experience is indispensible for understanding the present, to be most useful appraisal must ultimately be focused on present circumstances and conditions. Moreover, history alone does not provide a sufficient basis for normative appraisal. One of the most important principles of the United Nations Charter is that past grievances, no matter how deeply felt, may not be the basis for unilateral coercion to right the perceived wrong. Lawful unilateral coercion is restricted to individual and collective defense. The Charter thus rightly incorporates the present behavioral understanding that perceptions usually differ about the justice or injustice of particular events. The Charter also embodies the judgment that war always has been a destructive mode of change but that in the present international system it flirts with global catastrophe. Accordingly, the Charter principle that force should not be used as an instrument of national policy except in defense must be considered in any thoughtful appraisal of international disputes.[11]

Secondly, documents are merely the tip of an iceberg of an ongoing process of social interaction. Each document simultaneously represents the outcome of a complex process of interaction and is in turn an influence on subsequent processes. Context, including temporal setting, then, may play an important role in interpretation or understanding. One example is that documents and agreements of the colonial period should be interpreted with an awareness of the quite different perspectives about principal international actors and the reality of colonial agreements which characterized the period. Similarly, it would be a mistake simply to add up the General Assembly and Security Council resolutions favoring the Israeli position and those favoring the Arab position as a basis for judgment about comparative fault. Such an

[11] Because of its general availability the United Nations Charter has not been included in this compilation. Articles 1, 2(3), 2(4), 33, and 51 are of particular relevance.

effort is of little value without an awareness of the so-called automatic majority for the United States position in the General Assembly in the early years of the United Nations and of the radical shift in General Assembly alignment since 1960 toward a Third World "automatic majority." One should also be aware that, beginning about 1953, the Soviet veto has been regularly applied in support of the Arab position in the Security Council and that particularly in the last few years Arab influence has risen dramatically within the United Nations.

Lastly, the inclusion of a large selection of documents and materials may obscure the greater or lesser relative importance of the various documents. The importance and legal significance of the documents included in this volume vary widely. Those which are particularly fundamental include the Balfour Declaration, the League of Nations Mandate for Palestine, the General Assembly recommendation concerning the plan of partition with economic union for Palestine, General Assembly Resolution 194 (III) concerning the Palestine Conciliation Commission, Jerusalem, and the status of the Palestinian refugees, the 1949 Armistice Agreements between Israel and Egypt, Jordan, Syria, and Lebanon, Security Council Resolution 242 of November 22, 1967, setting forth principles for settlement and requesting the Secretary-General to designate a Special Representative to assist in achieving peaceful settlement, Security Council Resolution 338 of October 22, 1973, calling for immediate implementation of Resolution 242 and immediate negotiations between the parties, and the September 1975 interim agreement between Egypt and Israel.

Arrangement of the Volume

Part One leads off with an analysis of underlying issues in the conflict, taking up in turn Arab and Jewish nationalism and the rights of refugees, freedom of navigation through the Strait of Tiran, the Gulf of Aqaba, and the Suez Canal, and the status of Jerusalem and the Holy Places. The section on Arab and Jewish nationalism and the rights of refugees includes articles on both the self-determination and refugee issues. Although a separate focus on these issues would have been at least equally plausible, they were combined because articles concerning one also frequently concern the other and because from a Palestinian perspective these issues are frequently viewed as congruent. There is a great deal of writing available on utilization of the Jordan waters, but space considerations precluded its inclusion. The omission reflects the lesser importance of this issue in the hierarchy of underlying issues. Territorial issues, particularly Israeli withdrawal from the occupied territories and the establishment of "secure and recognized boundaries," are certainly major issues in the conflict, but for the most part they are dealt with in articles concerning the aftermath of the Six-Day War, the October War, and efforts at settlement. Accordingly, they have been left to Parts Two and Four dealing with continued hostilities and efforts at settlement.

Part Two begins with a section on the Six-Day War, the October War, and continued hostilities, which examines in turn the background and setting of recent hostilities, legal issues concerning the use of force and its consequences, and the applicability and implementation of the Geneva Conventions for the protection of civilians and prisoners of war. Part Three emphasizes the role of the United Nations and surveys the general historical and constitutional aspects of the United Nations role in the Arab-Israeli conflict and issues raised by the withdrawal of the United Nations Emergency Force prior to the Six-Day War. Part Four concludes the readings with a section on settlement. This section includes a variety of private perspectives on settlement in addition to some of the more complete statements of governmental positions. The section on settlement is particularly useful in demonstrating that a range of positive solutions is available if the parties can be persuaded to undertake meaningful negotiations. Part Five then concludes the volume with a compilation of major documents relevant to the conflict. As these documents indicate, there have been a variety of efforts at conflict management in the region spanning more than fifty years. A thorough grounding in the strengths and weaknesses of these past efforts is an indispensible tool for anyone seriously concerned with promoting peaceful settlement. The documents in Part Five have in general been arranged in chronological sequence. It has seemed more appropriate, however, for the Constantinople Suez Canal Convention of 1888 to be placed with the materials on the Suez Crisis rather than with those on the origins of the conflict.

In selecting and organizing articles in the reader, it has not always been possible to divide the articles neatly according to the organizational framework of the reader. When minor overlap between sections has occurred, it has been felt preferable to accept rather than to edit the articles too severely, which might result in a strained presentation of the author's major points. In general, editing of articles and documents has been resorted to only where necessary to delete obviously repetitious or extraneous materials or to meet overall page limitations for publication. Consequently, most selections have been printed in full. Where editing has been necessary, the usual scholarly conventions have been followed. Citations to source are footnoted for all documents. And for articles citations are provided in the list of permissions in the back of the volume.

One of the pleasant aspects of editing *The Arab-Israeli Conflict* has been the opportunity to review the voluminous scholarly literature and documentation on the conflict. Unfortunately, the relevant material is so extensive that it could not be included even in an extensive three-volume reader. The historical sweep of the Arab-Israeli conflict has generated a staggering quantity of articles, documents, and official statements. United Nations materials alone would fill a number of volumes if all of the Security Council and General Assembly debates, reports of the Secretary-General, and other United Nations proposals, recommendations, and reports were included. Inevitably, then, it has been necessary to make hard judgments about which articles among those available should be included and which excluded in the abridged edition. Regrettably, some essays which merited republication could not be included because of lack of space.[12] In making these selections, a cardinal principle has been to make as balanced a presentation on each issue and on the conflict as a whole as the range of the existing scholarly material would permit. An effort has also been made to include the leading articles and principal documents as well as a representative sample of the major positions.[13] For reference to additional materials, the volume includes a bibliography prepared by Mrs. Helen Philos, Librarian of the American Society of International Law.

[12] For example, space limitations prevented the inclusion of Dr. Rosalyn Higgins's definitive study of the creation and withdrawal of the United Nations Emergency Force. See I R. HIGGINS, UNITED NATIONS PEACEKEEPING 1946-1967: DOCUMENTS AND COMMENTARY 221-78, 335-415 (1969). They also precluded the inclusion of the Armistice Agreements between Israel and Lebanon, Jordan, and Syria, the record of the Security Council debates on the important Resolution 242, and a number of useful reports of the Secretary-General.

[13] Naturally, the three-volume compilation includes a substantially larger selection. By way of comparison, the larger compilation includes 98 articles and 189 documents.

THE ARAB-ISRAELI CONFLICT

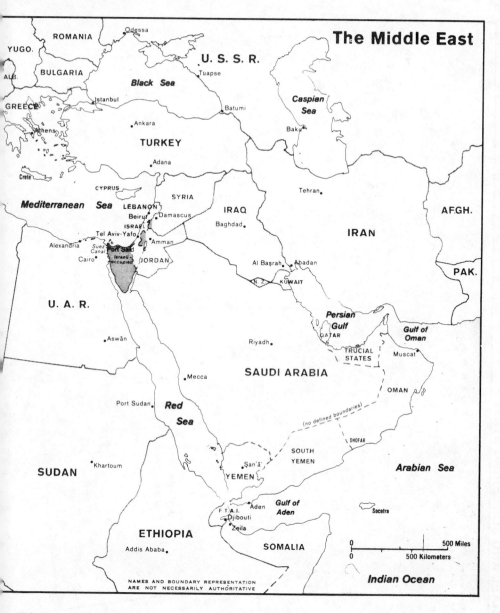

The Middle East

Ed. Note: The first three maps represent the situation after the Six-Day War but before the October War.

ISRAEL AND BORDERING STATES

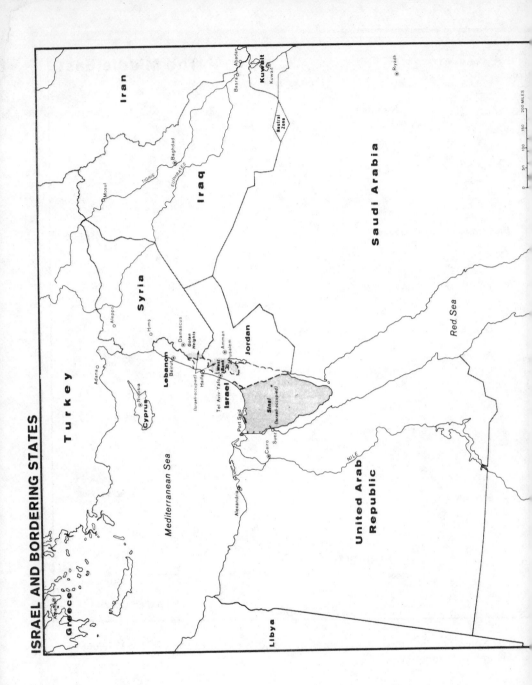

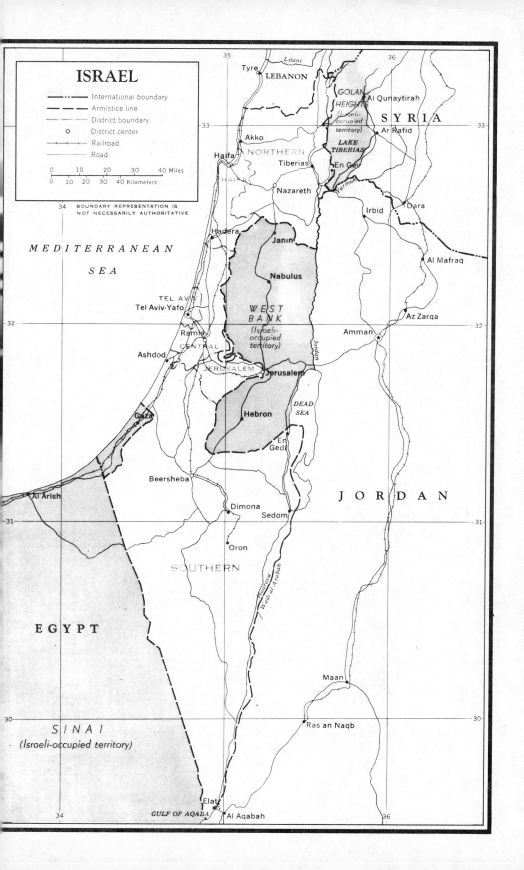

ISRAEL

- ·–··– International boundary
- – – – Armistice line
- ·–·–·– District boundary
- ○ District center
- ┼┼┼┼ Railroad
- ——— Road

0 10 20 30 40 Miles
0 10 20 30 40 Kilometers

BOUNDARY REPRESENTATION IS
NOT NECESSARILY AUTHORITATIVE

MEDITERRANEAN

SEA

Tyre
LEBANON
Litani

GOLAN
HEIGHTS
(Israeli-occupied territory)
Al Qunaytirah

S Y R I A

Akko
NORTHERN
Ar Rafid
LAKE
TIBERIAS
Haifa
HAIFA
Tiberias
En Gev
Nazareth
Yarmuk
Irbid
Dara

Hadera
Janin
Al Mafraq

Nabulus

TEL AVIV
Tel Aviv-Yafo
WEST BANK
(Israeli-occupied territory)
Amman
Az Zarqa

Ramla
CENTRAL
Ashdod
JERUSALEM
Jerusalem

DEAD SEA
Hebron

Gaza
En Gedi

Beersheba

J O R D A N

Al Arish

Dimona
Sedom

Oron

SOUTHERN

Wadi al Arabah

E G Y P T

Maan

Ras an Naqb

S I N A I
(Israeli-occupied territory)

Elat
GULF OF AQABA
Al Aqabah

The Israeli-Syrian Disengagement Lines

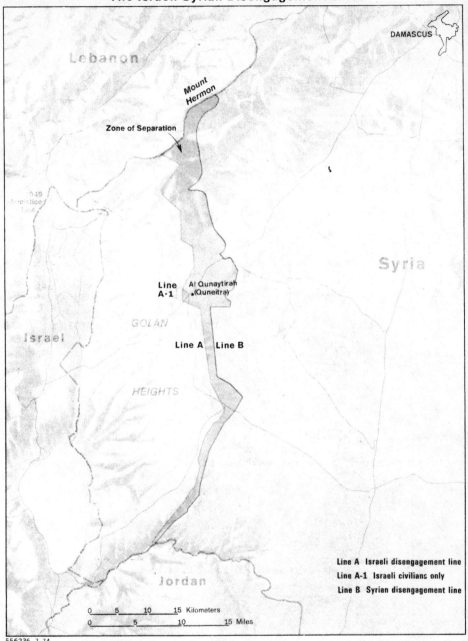

556236 7-74

Ed. Note: This map represents the first U.N. disengagement agreement for the Golan Heights following the October War.

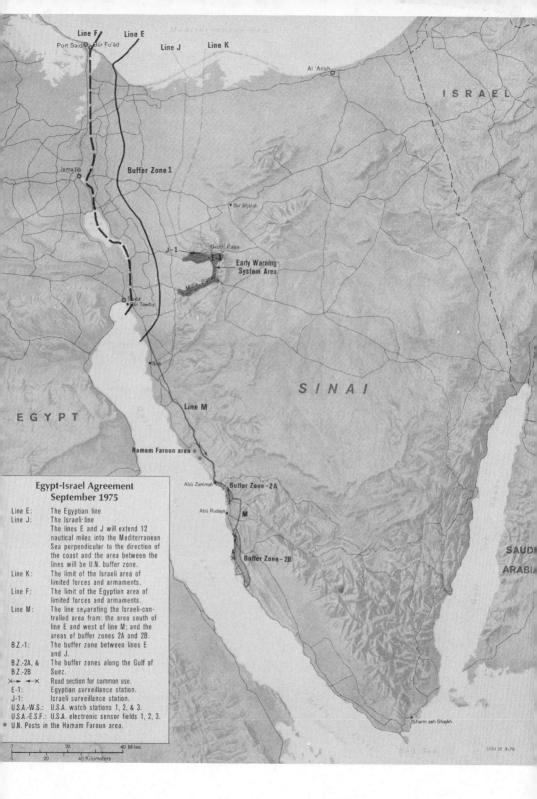

Line F Line E

Port Said Būr Fu'ād

Line J Line K

Al 'Arīsh

ISRAEL

Ismāʻīlia

Buffer Zone 1

Bīr Jifjāfah

Giddi Pass

J-1 E-1

Early Warning
System Area

Mitla Pass

Suez Būr Tawfīq

Sidr

SINAI

EGYPT

Line M

Hamam Faroun area

Abū Zanīmah Buffer Zone-2A

Abū Rudays M

SAUDI
ARABIA

Buffer Zone-2B

Sharm ash Shaykh

Egypt-Israel Agreement
September 1975

Line E: The Egyptian line
Line J: The Israeli line
            The lines E and J will extend 12
            nautical miles into the Mediterranean
            Sea perpendicular to the direction of
            the coast and the area between the
            lines will be U.N. buffer zone.
Line K: The limit of the Israeli area of
            limited forces and armaments.
Line F: The limit of the Egyptian area of
            limited forces and armaments.
Line M: The line separating the Israeli-con-
            trolled area from: the area south of
            line E and west of line M; and the
            areas of buffer zones 2A and 2B.
B.Z.-1:   The buffer zone between lines E
            and J.
B.Z.-2A, & The buffer zones along the Gulf of
B.Z.-2B   Suez.
×–► ◄–×   Road section for common use.
E-1:   Egyptian surveillance station.
J-1:   Israeli surveillance station.
U.S.A.-W.S.: U.S.A. watch stations 1, 2, & 3.
U.S.A.-E.S.F.: U.S.A. electronic sensor fields 1, 2, 3.
● U.N. Posts in the Hamam Faroun area.

0   20   40 Miles
0   20   40 Kilometers

558432 9-75

I. UNDERLYING ISSUES

A. *Arab and Jewish Nationalism and the Rights of Refugees*

Sovereignty over Palestine

HENRY CATTAN

The territories which are now occupied by Israel are the following:

the territory which was envisaged for the Jewish state in accordance with General Assembly resolution 181 (II) of November 29 1947 and

the various territories which Israel has seized in excess of the General Assembly resolution. These territories comprise:

i. More than half the areas which General Assembly resolution 181 (II) of November 29 1947 had reserved for the Arabs of Palestine and which were to constitute the territory of the proposed Arab state. These additional areas were occupied by Israel in 1948 and 1949.[1]

ii. The City of Jerusalem, which under the same General Assembly resolution was to have been subject to an international regime administered by the United Nations. Israel occupied the New City of Jerusalem in 1948 and the Old City of Jerusalem in 1967.

iii. The West Bank of Jordan, the Sinai Peninsula and the Golan Heights—being territories of Jordan, Egypt and Syria respectively. Israel seized these territories in June 1967.

iv. The Gaza Strip was also seized by Israel in June 1967.

The above-mentioned territories are shown in Appendix VII.

It is proposed to examine here the question of sovereignty over such territories and the legal status of Israel in regard to such territories. This legal question may not be of much interest to the layman but it has an important bearing upon the eventual solution.

In its common usage, the term sovereignty means the supreme power of a state over a certain territory and its people regardless of the legitimacy of its origin. But sovereignty involves also a broader and more fundamental concept: the legal and inalienable title of a king or a nation to a territory. It was on the basis of this concept of legitimacy of title that the pre-Napoleonic sovereigns were restored to power and

[1] See Section 2 of Part I.

Europe was reconstructed after 1815.[2] It is on the basis of the same concept that the nationhood of Poland was preserved during the long interregnum between 1795 and 1919 until it finally triumphed with the restoration of its international personality. The same broad concept explains the survival of Austria's sovereignty during the period of its forced union with Germany in 1938 until its formal re-establishment in 1945. In all these cases, sovereignty was not extinguished by the forceful occupation of territory or by conquest. Consequently, a distinction exists between legal and political sovereignty, the latter meaning factual dominion and control and the former signifying the rightful and inalienable title of a people to a territory. Such a distinction corresponds to the difference that is made between sovereignty in law and sovereignty in fact.[3] Professor Schwarzenberger has made the distinction between legal and political sovereignty as follows: 'The last word is still not with law, but power. On such a level, the counterpart to legal sovereignty is political sovereignty.'[4] Mr. Ian Brownlie has made the same distinction by contrasting the 'assumption of the powers of government' with '*de jure* sovereignty'.[5] It is in the sense of legal sovereignty that the term sovereignty is used hereinafter.

I SOVEREIGNTY OF THE ORIGINAL INHABITANTS OF PALESTINE

Notwithstanding the political vicissitudes in Palestine during the last fifty years, legal sovereignty still lies today in the original inhabitants of the country as they existed at the time of the detachment of Palestine from Turkey at the end of the First World War.

Prior to the occupation of Palestine by the British Army in 1917 during the First World War, Palestine formed an integral part of Turkey, which was a sovereign and independent state. The inhabitants of Palestine, Moslems, Christians and Jews, all Arabic-speaking peoples, were then Turkish citizens and enjoyed, as we have already seen, equal rights

[2] See Guglielmo Ferrero, *The Reconstruction of Europe* (translation by Jaeckel, New York, 1941), and C-M. de Talleyrand, *Mémoires*, Vol. II.

[3] As to this distinction, see Gaston Jèze, *Etude Théorique et Pratique sur l'Occupation* (Paris, 1896), p. 46.

[4] G. Schwarzenberger, *The Fundamental Principles of International Law* (Hague Recueil, 1955), p. 215.

[5] Ian Brownlie, *Principles of Public International Law* (Oxford 1966), pp. 100–102.

with the Turks in government and administration.[6] The Turkish constitution made no distinction between Turk or Arab or between Moslem or Christian or Jew. Turks and Arabs, therefore, shared sovereignty over all the territories of the Turkish Empire regardless as to whether such territories were Turkish or Arab provinces. This situation continued until the detachment of the Arab provinces, including Palestine, from Turkey at the end of the First World War. Such detachment was at first *de facto*, and resulted from the military occupation of Palestine by the British Army in 1917 and then became *de jure* by Turkey's renunciation of its sovereignty over the Arab territories in accordance with the Treaty of Lausanne of July 24 1923.

The British military occupation of Palestine in 1917 did not give sovereignty to the occupying power nor take away the sovereignty of the inhabitants. Apart from the fact that under international law the military occupation of enemy territory does not give the occupier a territorial title, it was clear that the avowed objective of the Allied Powers during the First World War was not the acquisition of territory in the Middle East. This is evident from the various pledges and formal assurances given to the Arabs by Great Britain and its Allies between 1915 and 1918 regarding the future of the Arab territories. These pledges and assurances were mentioned in Section 1 (1) of Part I.[7] It should be remarked that the reference to the British pledges and assurances given to the Arabs during the First World War does not signify that such pledges and assurances are made a foundation for the Arab claim to Palestine. The title of the Palestinian Arabs to Palestine does not, and cannot, depend upon the pledges and assurances of a third Power which, moreover, possessed neither sovereignty nor dominion nor any right whatsoever over the country. Their title rests upon their ownership of the country from time immemorial. That the title of the Palestinians to Palestine dates from time immemorial is literally true, not a figure of speech. Frequently, the date of the Arab occupation of Palestine is related back to the Moslem Arab conquest of the country some thirteen centuries ago. This is not historically accurate. The Moslem conquest of Palestine in A.D. 637 was not the starting-point of the occu-

[6] See Section 1 (1), of Part I, *ante*.

[7] For the text of these pledges and assurances see the Report of the Committee set up by the British Government to consider the McMahon-Hussein Correspondence and statements made on behalf of His Majesty's Government in 1918, *Cmd.* 5964, and George Antonius, *The Arab Awakening* (Khayats, Beirut).

pation of the country by the Palestinians. The Arabs, including the Palestinians, are a pre-Islamic people. They lived in Palestine and other parts of the Middle East before the advent of Islam and the Moslem conquest. As we have seen earlier in Part I, the Palestinians were the descendants of the Philistines and Canaanites, and have lived continuously in Palestine since the dawn of history, even long before the ancient Hebrews set foot in the country.

The Covenant of the League of Nations, approved by the Paris Peace Conference on April 28 1919, and incorporated into the Treaty of Versailles on June 28 1919, also discarded any idea of annexation by the occupying powers of the territories seized from Turkey and Germany during the First World War. The Covenant dealt in Article 22 with the future of the Arab communities and territories of the Turkish Empire and also with the future of the former German Colonies. Article 22 of the Covenant established a new status under international law for the Arab communities detached from the Turkish Empire and, it is important to note, recognized their 'existence as independent nations'. Article 22 began with the statement:

> To those colonies and territories which as a consequence of the late war have ceased to be under the sovereignty of the States which formerly governed them. . . .[8]

Its fourth paragraph stated:

> Certain communities formerly belonging to the Turkish Empire have reached a stage of development where their existence as independent nations can be provisionally recognized subject to the rendering of administrative advice and assistance by a mandatory until such time as they are able to stand alone.[9]

Mr. Duncan Hall has observed: 'Underlying Article 22 was the assumption of independent national sovereignty for mandates. The

---

[8] See Appendix I. The term 'colonies', as distinct from 'territories', must be understood to refer to the former German colonies in Africa. The Arab provinces of the Turkish Empire were not colonies, as already noted, since they formed an integral part of Turkey.

[9] The use of the expression 'communities belonging to the Turkish Empire' is misleading. The Arab provinces 'belonged' to the Turkish Empire in the sense that they formed part of this country, but not in the sense in which a colony 'belongs' to the mother country. It has been made amply clear that Arabs and Turks enjoyed equal rights and shared sovereignty over the whole Turkish Empire.

drafters of the Covenant took as their starting-point the general notions of "no annexation" and "self-determination".' [10] In the case concerning the International Status of South-West Africa (1950) the Court held that in Article 22 of the Covenant of the League of Nations 'two principles were considered to be of paramount importance: the principle of non-annexation and the principle that the well-being and development of such peoples form a sacred trust of civilization'.[11] The inhabitants of the mandated territories were the beneficiaries of this trust.[12]

The legal effect under international law of the detachment of Palestine from the Turkish Empire and of the recognition by the League of Nations of the community inhabiting it as an independent nation was to make of this country a separate, independent and international political entity. The community which then inhabited Palestine thus became a subject of international law in which was vested the legal sovereignty over the territory in which it lived.

But although Palestine acquired its own sovereignty as a result of its detachment *de facto* from Turkey and the recognition of its people as an independent nation by the Covenant of the League of Nations, the formal renunciation by Turkey of its sovereignty over its former Arab provinces occurred only some time later. The Supreme Council of the Principal Allied Powers sought to impose upon Turkey the Treaty of Sèvres of August 10 1920. This Treaty, however, was not ratified by the Turkish Government, which objected to some of its provisions. Ultimately, the Allied Powers had to negotiate with the Turkish nationalists, who had abolished in 1922 the Sultanate and declared the Ottoman Government to be no longer in existence. The Turkish nationalists accepted the separation of the Arab provinces and concluded with the Allied Powers the Treaty of Lausanne of July 24 1923 after certain provisions of the abortive Treaty of Sèvres had been withdrawn and abandoned. Among the provisions of the abortive Treaty of Sèvres to which the Turkish authorities had taken objection and which were abandoned was the provision concerning the Jewish national home. The Treaty of Sèvres had provided in Article 95 that the parties agreed to entrust, by application of Article 22 of the Covenant of the League of Nations, the

[10] H. Duncan Hall, *Mandates, Dependencies and Trusteeships* (Carnegie Endowment for International Peace, Washington, 1948), p. 80.
[11] *I.C.J. Reports*, 1950, p. 131.
[12] *Ibid.*, p. 132.

administration of Palestine to a Mandatory to be selected by the Principal Allied Powers, and that the Mandatory would be responsible for putting into effect the declaration made on November 2 1917 by the British Government in favour of the establishment in Palestine of a national home for the Jewish people.[13] Turkey refused to subscribe to this provision. Instead, Article 16 of the Treaty of Lausanne provided as follows:

> Art. 16. Turkey hereby renounces all rights and title whatsoever over or respecting the territories situated outside the frontiers laid down in the present Treaty and the islands other than those over which her sovereignty is recognized by the said Treaty, the future of these territories and islands being settled or to be settled by the parties concerned.

It is significant that by excluding any reference in the Treaty of Lausanne to the declaration of November 2 1917, Turkey, as the state which had possessed sovereignty over Palestine in the past, did not, upon renunciation of such sovereignty, mortgage the future of Palestine with any obligation relating to the establishment of a Jewish national home. The Treaty left the future of Palestine, and other Arab territories, to be decided by 'the parties concerned'. This expression was not defined, but it can only mean the communities which inhabited these territories, since they were the parties primarily concerned.

It is also significant that the renunciation by Turkey of 'all rights and title' over the Arab territories detached from it was not made in favour of the signatory Powers or of any Power in particular. This is in contrast with Article 15 in the same Treaty wherein 'Turkey renounces in favour of Italy all rights and title' over certain specified islands. The difference between the two renunciation provisions can be ascribed to two reasons: first, it was not the intention that the Principal Allied Powers or any one of them should acquire sovereignty over the Arab provinces; secondly, the Arab communities in the provinces detached from Turkey were the original inhabitants and already possessed sovereignty over their own territories. Hence they were not in need of any renunciation to be made in their favour, in contrast with Italy, which needed a renunciation of sovereignty in its favour to enable it to acquire sovereignty over the islands which came under its occupation. In this regard Turkey's

---

[13] See the text of Article 95 of the Treaty of Sèvres in Hurewitz, *Diplomacy in the Near and Middle East* (D. Van Nostrand, New Jersey, 1956), Vol. II, p. 84.

renunciation by the Treaty of Lausanne of its sovereignty over the Arab territories is comparable to Spain's relinquishment of its sovereignty over Cuba by the Treaty of Paris, 1898. In both cases the renunciation of sovereignty was not made in favour of the occupying Power. In the case of Cuba Spain's renunciation was held to vest sovereignty in the inhabitants:

> In the present case, as the United States expressly disclaimed any intention to exercise sovereignty, jurisdiction, or control over the island, 'except for the pacification thereof', the ownership of the island, upon the relinquishment by Spain of her sovereignty over it, immediately passed to the inhabitants of Cuba, who, in the resolutions referred to, were declared to be free and independent, and in whom, therefore, abstractly considered, sovereignty resided.

> Had the language been 'Spain cedes to the United States the island of Cuba' as by Article II she did Porto Rico, that would have divested her of all title to and, by consequence, all sovereignty over Cuba, both of which would then immediately have passed to the United States, as they did in the case of Porto Rico; subject, however, to the rights of the people. True, when, pursuant to the treaty, the United States occupied the island, the inhabitants thereof during such occupancy undoubtedly owed allegiance to the United States, i.e., fidelity and obedience for the protection they received, but that did not divest them of their inherent rights. (*Galban and Company, A Corporation* v. *the United States*, 40 Ct. Cls. (1905), 495, 506–507.)[14]

Although Palestine had as a result of these developments become a separate and independent political entity, distinct from the political entity of which it previously formed part, and possessed of its own sovereignty, its people were prevented from the exercise of full and effective sovereignty as a result of two circumstances: the existence of a military occupier, and subsequently the grant in 1922 by the Council of the League of Nations of a mandate to the British Government to administer Palestine.

It is necessary, therefore, to consider whether the grant to the British Government of a mandate over Palestine affected the sovereignty of its inhabitants.

Conflicting views have been expressed in the past as to who possessed sovereignty in the case of a mandated territory. Some have argued that

[14] Hackworth, *Digest of International Law*, Vol. I, page 425.

sovereignty lay in the Principal Allied Powers[15] or in the League of Nations[16] or in the mandatory[17] or jointly in the League of Nations and the mandatory[18] or in the inhabitants of the mandated territory.[19] All the various views which have been expressed on the point—except that which considers sovereignty to reside in the inhabitants of the mandated territory—have now been abandoned or discredited. None of the views that sought to vest sovereignty elsewhere than in the inhabitants of the mandated territory appears to rest on an acceptable legal or logical basis.

It is obvious, on the one hand, that the Peace Treaties concluded with Germany and Turkey at the end of the First World War did not embody any renunciation by these states of their sovereignty over the territories detached from them in favour of the principal Allied Powers or the League of Nations or the mandatory Power. It is equally obvious, on the other hand, that it was not the intention of the Covenant of the League of Nations or the mandates that the principal Allied Powers or the League of Nations or the mandatory Power should acquire sovereignty over the mandated territories. The terms of the mandates granted by the League of Nations in respect of former Turkish and German territories did not involve any cession of territory or transfer of sovereignty to the mandatory Power. The International Court of Justice has recently confirmed this principle with regard to the mandate for South-West Africa. The Court said:

> The terms of this Mandate, as well as the provisions of Article 22 of the Covenant and the principles embodied therein, show that the creation of this new international institution (i.e., the mandate) did not involve any cession of territory or transfer of sovereignty to the Union of South Africa. The Union Government was to exercise an international function of administration on behalf of the League, with the object of promoting the well-being and development of the inhabitants.[20]

[15] Hoijer, Le Pacte de la Société des Nations (1926) (Spes, Paris, 1926), p. 374.

[16] Redslob, Le Système des Mandats Internationaux, p. 196.

[17] H. Rolin, Le Système des Mandats Internationaux, Revue de Droit International et de Législation Comparée (1920), p. 302.

[18] Quincy Wright, Sovereignty of the Mandates, AJIL (1923), p. 698.

[19] P. Pic, Le Régime du Mandat d'après le Traité de Versailles, RGDIP, Vol. 30, 1923, p. 334; Millot, Les Mandats Internationaux, p. 91; Stoyanovsky, La Théorie Générale des Mandats Internationaux, p. 92.

[20] Advisory Opinion of the International Court of Justice regarding the Status of South-West Africa, I.C.J. Reports (1950), p. 132.

The view that sovereignty over a mandated territory lies in its inhabitants received the support of several writers, and was summarized by Mr. Van Rees, Vice-President of the Permanent Mandates Commission, as follows:

> Enfin, un dernier groupe d'auteurs—divisé en deux fractions—le seul groupe qui a tenu compte du principe de non-annexion adopté par la Conférence de la Paix, soutient que les auteurs du Pacte ont voulu tenir en suspens ou bien la souveraineté elle-même sur les territoires sous mandat pour une période équivalente à la durée des mandats respectifs (Lee D. Campbell, *The Mandate for Mesopotamia and the principle of trusteeship in English law*, p. 19; A. Mendelssohn Bartholdi, *Les Mandats africains* (traduction), Archiv für politik und Geschite, Hamburg, 1925) ou bien *l'exercice* des pouvoirs souverains dont furent provisoirement chargées certaines nations en qualité de tuteurs. D'après ce dernier point de vue la souveraineté elle-même serait détenue, depuis la renonciation des anciens Empires, par les communautés et les populations autochtones des différents territoires. En d'autres termes, les anciens Empires ayant renoncé à leurs droits et titres sur les territoires en question sans qu'il y ait eu transfert de ces droits et titres à d'autres Puissances, la souveraineté, qui appartient à ces divers peuples et communautés jusqu'au moment de leur soumission à l'Allemagne et à la Turquie, renaît automatiquement du fait de la renonciation susdite. (Paul Pic, *Le régime des mandats d'après le Traité de Versailles*, RGDIP, Paris, 1923, p. 14; Albert Millot, *Les mandats internationaux*, Paris, 1924, pp. 114–118; J. Stoyanovski, *La théorie générale des mandats internationaux*, Paris, pp. 83 and 86.)[21]

The same author pointed out that the view which held that sovereignty lies in the indigenous communities and populations of the mandated territory 'is the only one which at least takes into account the principle of non-annexation unanimously adopted by the Peace Conference'.[22]

The concept of sovereignty is not strained by recognizing the attribute of sovereignty to the inhabitants of mandated territories. Westlake has said: 'The duties and rights of States are only the duties and rights of the men who compose them.'[23] Article 22 of the Covenant of the League of Nations specifically recognized, as we have seen, the existence

[21] D. F. W. Van Rees, *Les Mandats Internationaux* (Rousseau, Paris, 1927), p. 20.
[22] Translation from D. F. W. Van Rees, *Certains Aspects du Régime des Mandats Internationaux* (Bibliotheca Visseriana, 1931), p. 21.
[23] Westlake, *Collected Papers*, p. 78.

of certain communities as independent nations. Independence implies sovereignty. In its resolution adopted in 1931 the Institute of International Law described the communities under mandate as subjects of international law.[24] The international personality of communities under mandate first recognized by the Covenant of the League of Nations has now come to be accepted as a principle of international law.[25] Pélichet has observed:

> La personnalité internationale ne fut longtemps reconnue qu'aux Etats. Ce n'est qu'à la fin du XIXe siècle, sous l'influence de Mancini et de l'école italienne, qu'on admit que certaines collectivités, étrangères aux Etats, pouvaient relever du droit des Gens et en devenir des sujets. Cette opinion a de plus en plus prévalu.[26]

One of the first writers who proclaimed the principle that sovereignty lies in the inhabitants of the mandated territory was Professor Pic. He said:

> Les rédacteurs du Traité de Versailles, s'inspirant avant tout d'un droit pour les peuples de disposer d'eux-mêmes, ont formellement proclamé qu'il n'y aurait *aucune annexion* des territoires sous mandat par une puissance quelconque, pas plus par la collectivité des Etats ayant nom Société des Nations et siègeant à Genève, que par tel ou tel Etat particulier. Ces territoires appartiennent virtuellement aux populations ou communautés autochtones, dont la Société des Nations s'est constituée le défenseur, et au regard desquelles elle joue un peu le rôle d'un conseil de famille. Or, en droit interne, un conseil de famille n'a, pas plus que le tuteur qu'il désigne, et dont il controle les actes, de droit privatif sur les biens du pupille.[27]

A somewhat similar view was held by Professor Quincy Wright with respect to the 'A' mandates. He observed:

> Communities under 'A' mandates doubtless approach very close to sovereignty.[28]

[24] *AJIL* (1932), p. 91.

[25] See in this regard E. Pélichet, *La Personnalité internationale distincte des collectivités sous mandat* (Rousseau, Paris, 1932), p. 183.

[26] E. Pélichet, *op. cit.*, p. 51.

[27] Professor P. Pic, *op. cit.*, p. 334.

[28] Quincy Wright, *Sovereignty of the Mandates*, AJIL, Vol. 17, 1923, p. 696. Mandates were classified into three types: 'A', 'B' and 'C'. This classification was made in a 'descending order of political individuality' according to their international status and the degree of authority given to the mandatory. The 'A' mandates applied to Iraq, Palestine, Syria and Lebanon. The 'B' mandates applied to German possessions in West

The Earl of Birkenhead thought that the 'A' mandated territories had a close similarity to protected States. He observed:

> The question as to the sovereignty of the mandated territory raises difficulties. It may lie in the League of Nations, in the mandatory State or in the mandated territory. With regard to the 'A' territories their close similarity to protected States would suggest a solution; but ... the 'B' and 'C' territories may have to await the happening of some crucial event ... before its juristic position can be unquestionably defined.[29]

Referring to Palestine and Syria in particular, the same author said:

> The position of Palestine and Syria is that they were integral portions of the Turkish Empire (which has renounced all right or title to them: Article 16 of the Treaty of Lausanne, 1923), they have become, administratively, partially dependent now upon an appointed mandatory State, but they are acknowledged—in the terms of Article 22 of the Covenant—to be entitled to provisional recognition of independence. .... The status of Palestine and Syria resembles very closely that of States under suzerainty.[30]

Millot also vested sovereignty in the inhabitants of the mandated territory. He based his view upon Article 22 of the Covenant of the League of Nations and the intention of the Peace Conference which ended the First World War. Regarding the Arab territories detached from the Turkish Empire he said that Article 22 of the Covenant has declared these territories to be provisionally independent States and remarked that 'independent' means 'sovereign'.[31]

Stoyanovsky has argued that the people of a mandated territory are not deprived of the right of sovereignty but are deprived only temporarily of its *exercise*. The right of sovereignty belongs to the inhabitants of the mandated territory 'by virtue of the principles of nationality and self-determination which are the foundations of modern international law'.[32] The distinction between sovereignty and its exercise in the case of mandated territories is comparable to the distinction made

---

Africa. The 'C' mandates related to German possessions in South-West Africa and to certain South Pacific Islands. It is to be remarked that only in the case of 'A' mandates were the communities concerned recognized by Article 22 of the Covenant as independent nations.

[29] Earl of Birkenhead, *International Law*, 6th ed., p. 99.

[30] Earl of Birkenhead, *op. cit.*, p. 40.

[31] Millot, *Les Mandats Internationaux*, pp. 91 et 115.

[32] Stoyanovsky, *La Théorie Générale des Mandats Internationaux*, p. 83.

under private law between ownership and its exercise in cases of guardianship, curatorship or other forms of tutelage.

Pélichet has advanced the view that communities under mandate enjoy real, not only virtual, sovereignty:

> La jouissance des droits de souveraineté est détenue réellement, et non point virtuellement par les collectivités.[33]

In regard to Palestine, Pélichet pointed out that the United Kingdom, as the mandatory Power, has concluded agreements with Palestine, as the mandated territory. Thus a community under a mandate can acquire rights, conclude agreements and assume international obligations. In consequence, he concluded:

> Nous estimons que la théorie de la souveraineté des peuples sous mandat est celle qui convient le mieux à l'esprit comme à la lettre de l'article 22.[34]

In his separate opinion concerning the International Status of South-West Africa, Lord McNair expressed the opinion that the mandate system does not fit into the old conceptions of sovereignty. According to Lord McNair sovereignty over a mandated territory is 'in abeyance'.[35]

The principle that sovereignty lies in the people of the mandated territory itself was recently applied to territories held under trusteeship in accordance with the Charter of the United Nations. Mandates and trusteeships possess the same legal affiliation. In the case of Società A.B.C. v. Fontana and Della Rocca, the Italian Court of Cassation held that 'sovereignty over the territory of Somaliland is vested in its population, although, under Article 2 of the Trusteeship Agreement, the administration of the territory, for the period specified in the Agreement, has been entrusted to Italy'.[36] The same view was expressed by Oppenheim, who observed:

> In considering the question of sovereignty over trust territories—a question which is by no means of mere academic importance—the distinction must be borne in mind between sovereignty as such (or what may be described as residuary sovereignty) and the exercise of sovereignty. The latter

---

[33] E. Pélichet, *op. cit.*, p. 100.

[34] E. Pélichet, *op. cit.*, p. 108.

[35] Advisory Opinion of the International Court of Justice regarding the Status of South-West Africa, *I.C.J. Reports* (1950), p. 150.

[36] Decision dated August 10 1954, *International Law Reports* (1955), Vol. 22, p. 77.

is clearly vested with the trustee powers subject to supervision by and accountability to the United Nations.[37]

We can, therefore, conclude this inquiry by remarking that the grant by the Council of the League of Nations of a mandate to the British Government to administer Palestine did not deprive its people of their right of sovereignty. The legal status of Palestine under international law during the British mandate and upon its termination on May 15 1948 can, therefore, be summarized as follows: during the currency of the mandate the people of Palestine enjoyed an independent international status and possessed sovereignty over their land; Palestine possessed its own identity, which was distinct from that of the mandatory power; its administration was theoretically its own though, in fact, it was in the hands of the mandatory; the Government of Palestine, as representative of the people of Palestine, concluded agreements with the mandatory power and became party, through the instrumentality of the mandatory, to a number of international treaties and conventions; however, the full exercise of sovereignty by the people of Palestine was restricted in certain respects by the powers of administration entrusted to the mandatory power by the League of Nations; upon the termination of the mandate the mandatory's powers of administration came to an end and, as a result, the restrictions upon exercise of full sovereignty by the people of Palestine ceased, so that by virtue of this right as well as by virtue of their right of self-determination they became entitled to govern themselves and to determine their future in accordance with normal democratic principles and procedures. The first and fundamental rule in any democracy is the rule of the majority. This rule, however, was not respected by the General Assembly of the United Nations, which recommended in 1947, in circumstances and under political pressures already mentioned, the partition of the country between Arab and Jewish states. The events which followed and the emergence of Israel have prevented the Palestinian people from exercising their right of sovereignty over their own land. The question which we have now to consider is whether the emergence of Israel and its occupation in 1948 and 1949 of various territories of Palestine did deprive the people of Palestine of their sovereignty. In other words, did Israel acquire legal sovereignty over such territories? For reasons of

[37] Oppenheim, *International Law* (Longmans, London, 1955), Vol. I, 8th ed., p. 236.

clarity in the discussion rather than because of any difference in conclusions, this inquiry into the legitimacy or illegitimacy of Israel's title will be made separately in respect of the territory destined for the Jewish state by the United Nations partition resolution and of the other territories which Israel seized in excess of the same resolution.

2 HAS ISRAEL ACQUIRED LEGAL SOVEREIGNTY OVER THE TERRITORY ALLOCATED TO THE JEWISH STATE BY THE PARTITION RESOLUTION?

The question as to whether Israel has acquired sovereignty over the territory which was allocated to the Jewish state by the partition resolution can be examined in the light of three political developments with a view to determining whether any one of them could have conferred title or sovereignty upon Israel. These three developments are: the Balfour Declaration of November 2 1917; the United Nations resolution on the partition of Palestine of November 29 1947, and the forcible occupation by Israel in 1948 and in 1949 of the territory earmarked for the proposed Jewish state by the said resolution.

a   *No grant of sovereignty was or could have been involved in the Balfour Declaration*

The Balfour Declaration, which the Zionists have utilized almost as a document of title for the establishment of a Jewish state in Palestine, never possessed any juridical value. At no time did the British Government as the author of such declaration possess any right of sovereignty over Palestine, whether on the date on which the Balfour Declaration was made or at any time thereafter, which could have enabled it to recognize any rights in favour of the Jewish people in or over Palestine. Hence the British Government was not in a position validly to grant any title or any rights to the Jews over Palestine because a donor cannot give away what does not belong to him. Professor W. T. Mallison, Jr., has observed:

Perhaps even more fundamental than analysis of the Balfour Declaration agreement is the issue of the juridical authority of the British Government to make a promise of political support in favor of Zionist nationalism.[38]

It has also been remarked that,

The most significant and incontrovertible fact is, however, that by itself the (Balfour) Declaration was legally impotent. For Great Britain had no sovereign rights over Palestine; it had no proprietary interest; it had no authority to dispose of the land. The Declaration was merely a statement of British intentions and no more.[39]

Moreover, neither party to the Declaration, namely, the Zionist Jews and the British Government, intended that it should convey any territorial rights to the Jews or result in their acquisition of sovereignty over Palestine. On the one hand, the Zionists, at least outwardly, emphatically denied that the Jewish national home mentioned in the Balfour Declaration did envisage the establishment of a Jewish state or the grant of sovereignty to the Jews. Writing in 1919, Sokolow, who is the Zionist historian, stated:

It has been said, and is still being obstinately repeated by anti-Zionists again and again, that Zionism aims at the creation of an independent 'Jewish State'. But this is wholly fallacious. The 'Jewish State' was never a part of the Zionist programme.[40]

Mr. Norman Bentwich, a Zionist Jew who held for several years the office of Attorney-General of Palestine during the British Mandate, has declared on a number of occasions that sovereignty was no part of the Jewish national home. He said:

State sovereignty is not essential to the Jewish national ideal. Freedom for the Jew to develop according to his own tradition, in his own environment, is the main, if not the whole demand.[41]

He also wrote:

It has often been made an objection to Zionist hopes that the Moslem Arabs now in possession of Palestine lands, already numbering more than a

[38] W. T. Mallison, Jr., The Zionist—Israel Juridical Claims to Constitute the 'Jewish People' Nationality Entity and to Confer Membership in it: Appraisal in International Law, *The George Washington Law Review*, Vol. 32, p. 1002, June 1964.
[39] Sol M. Linowitz, Analysis of a Tinderbox: The Legal Basis for the State of Israel, *American Bar Association Journal*, Vol. 43, 1957, pp. 522–523.
[40] Sokolow, *History of Zionism*, xxiv.
[41] Norman Bentwich, *Palestine of the Jews* (London, 1919), p. 195.

quarter of a million, cannot be ejected. . . . But it is neither to be expected, nor is it desired, that the Jews should occupy and appropriate the whole country.[42]

Mr. Bentwich defined the concept of the Jewish national home as not implying the grant of rights of political sovereignty but as offering the opportunity for cultural development. He said:

The idea of a national home for a homeless people is now embodied in this single mandate (The Mandate for Palestine). . . . It signifies a territory in which a people, without receiving rights of political sovereignty, has, nevertheless, a recognized legal position and the opportunity of developing its moral, social and intellectual ideas.[43]

In 1934, Mr. Bentwich distinguished between a national home and a state in the following terms:

A national home, as distinguished from a state, is a country where a people are acknowledged as having a recognized legal position and the opportunity of developing their cultural, social and intellectual ideals without receiving political sovereignty.[44]

Mr. Bentwich thought that the Jews should integrate within Palestine together with the Arab inhabitants:

The Jewish people on their side do not ask for political power or national sovereignty. . . . They have no need or desire to rule over others. Ultimately, they would ask within the territory to form an integral part of the government of the land, together with the Arab inhabitants.[45]

On the other hand, the British Government as author of the Balfour Declaration did not intend to grant any political sovereignty to the Jewish people in Palestine. In its Statement of Policy of 1922, the British Government declared that the interpretation which His Majesty's Government place upon the Declaration of 1917, 'need not cause alarm to the Arab population of Palestine. . . . His Majesty's Government

---

[42] *Ibid.*, pp. 206–207. It may be remarked in passing that his reference to the Moslem Arabs numbering 'more than a quarter of a million' was a gross underestimate of the number of Moslem Arabs who inhabited Palestine at the time.

[43] Norman Bentwich, *The Mandates System* (Longmans, London, 1930), p. 24.

[44] Norman Bentwich, *Palestine* (E. Benn, London, 1934), p. 101.

[45] *Ibid.*, p. 288.

have not contemplated . . . the disappearance or the subordination of the Arabic population. . . . They would draw attention to the fact that the terms of the (Balfour) Declaration referred to do not contemplate that Palestine as a whole should be converted into a Jewish National Home, but that such a Home should be founded in Palestine.'[46] This interpretation of the Jewish National Home was again confirmed in the Statement of Policy issued by the British Government in October 1930.[47] In the Statement of Policy of May 1939 the British Government dealt at length with the meaning it attributed to the Jewish national home:

> 3. The Royal Commission and previous Commissions of Enquiry have drawn attention to the ambiguity of certain expressions in the Mandate, such as the expression 'a national home for the Jewish people', and they have found in this ambiguity and the resulting uncertainty as to the objectives of policy a fundamental cause of unrest and hostility between Arabs and Jews. . . .
>
> 4. It has been urged that the expression 'a national home for the Jewish people' offered a prospect that Palestine might in due course become a Jewish State or Commonwealth. His Majesty's Government do not wish to contest the view, which was expressed by the Royal Commission, that the Zionist leaders at the time of the issue of the Balfour Declaration recognized that an ultimate Jewish State was not precluded by the terms of the Declaration. But, with the Royal Commission, His Majesty's Government believe that the framers of the Mandate in which the Balfour Declaration was embodied could not have intended that Palestine should be converted into a Jewish State against the will of the Arab population of the country. That Palestine was not to be converted into a Jewish State might be held to be implied in the passage from the Command Paper of 1922, which reads as follows:
>
>> Unauthorized statements have been made to the effect that the purpose in view is to create a wholly Jewish Palestine. Phrases have been used such as that 'Palestine is to become as Jewish as England is English'. His Majesty's Government regard any such expectation as impracticable and have no such aim in view. Nor have they at any time contemplated . . . the disappearance or the subordination of the Arabic population, language or culture in Palestine. They would draw attention to the fact that the terms of the (Balfour) Declaration referred to do not contemplate that

[46] *Cmd.* 1700, p. 18.
[47] *Cmd.* 3692.

Palestine as a whole should be converted into a Jewish National Home, but that such a home should be founded in Palestine.

But this statement has not removed doubts, and His Majesty's Government therefore now declare unequivocally that it is not part of their policy that Palestine should become a Jewish State. They would indeed regard it as contrary to their obligations to the Arabs under the Mandate, as well as to the assurances which have been given to the Arab people in the past, that the Arab population of Palestine should be made the subjects of a Jewish State against their will.[48]

Finally—and this is the most important consideration—whatever may have been the meaning and intention of the Balfour Declaration—the people of Palestine, who were the party most directly concerned as the owners of the country, were not consulted about the British promise to the Jews. They never gave their consent to the establishment of a Jewish national home in Palestine and never accepted the British Declaration. Neither did the other Arabs accept the Balfour Declaration. The Agreement made between Emir Faisal and Dr. Chaim Weizmann on January 3 1919 regarding the carrying into effect of the Declaration of November 2 1917 might appear to be an exception. It should be observed, however, that Emir Faisal possessed no representative capacity that entitled him to speak on behalf of the Arabs of Palestine or of the Arabs generally, or to commit the Arabs to an acceptance of the Balfour Declaration. Emir Faisal was then attending the Peace Conference at Paris in 1919 to secure political support for the claims of the Kingdom of Hejaz. In the so-called Faisal–Weizmann Agreement he is described as 'representing and acting on behalf of the Arab Kingdom of Hejaz'. He did not represent or act on behalf of the Arabs of Palestine or the Arabs generally. Mr. George E. Kirk has observed,

> At this stage the Palestine Arabs had never been consulted; they had given no mandate to Faisal to negotiate on their behalf; and his agreement with the Zionist leader could not be considered binding on anyone but himself and his father.[49]

Faisal's Agreement with Weizmann was repudiated by the Syro-Palestinian Congress of 1921. Even as regards Emir Faisal himself, the

---

[48] *Cmd.*, 6019, pp. 3 and 4.
[49] George E. Kirk, *A Short History of the Middle East* (Methuen and Co., London, 1948), p. 151.

Agreement lapsed in accordance with its own terms on the strength of a condition therein included by Emir Faisal that if the Arabs did not obtain their independence as demanded by him or if the slightest modification or departure were made to his demands the Agreement would be 'void and of no account or validity'. Since the conditions which he attached were not fulfilled, the Agreement never acquired validity.[50]

At the Anglo-Arab Conference of London in 1939, the Committee set up to consider the McMahon-Hussein Correspondence (1915–1918) came to the conclusion that it was evident from the statements made during and after the war that 'His Majesty's Government were not free to dispose of Palestine without regard for the wishes and interests of the inhabitants of Palestine, and that these statements must all be taken into account in any attempt to estimate the responsibilities which—upon any interpretation of the Correspondence—His Majesty's Government have incurred towards those inhabitants as a result of the Correspondence'.[51]

The Arabs have continuously protested against the Balfour Declaration from the first day it came to their knowledge. The Palestine Arabs have strenuously fought the Declaration. There cannot be the least doubt that their rights are not and cannot be impaired, diminished or in any way affected by a Declaration made by a third party against their interests. It is equally clear that the Jews did not gain any title or other right whatsoever in Palestine on the basis of the Declaration. From the juridical standpoint, therefore, any claim by the Jews to Palestine on the basis of the Balfour Declaration is entirely groundless, if not plainly nonsensical.

b   *No title was derived by Israel under the resolution on the partition of Palestine adopted by the General Assembly of the United Nations on November 29 1947*

We now turn to consider whether Israel has or could have acquired any title or sovereignty over the territory earmarked for the Jewish state by virtue of the resolution of November 29 1947, which recommended

[50] George Antonius, *The Arab Awakening* (Khayats, Beirut), pp. 285 and 286. George Antonius remarks that the main interest of the Faisal–Weizmann Agreement 'is in the evidence it affords of the lengths to which Faisal was prepared to go in the sense of Arab–Jewish co-operation so long as that did not conflict with Arab independence': p. 286.

[51] Report of the Committee, March 16 1939, *Cmd.* 5974, p. 11.

the partition of Palestine between Arab and Jewish states. This inquiry does not concern the wisdom or justice of partition or the circumstances of political pressure and undue influence by which the resolution was obtained. These aspects were considered earlier in Section 1 (3) of Part I. The present inquiry will be limited to an examination of the legal effect of the resolution and, in particular, of the question whether the General Assembly of the United Nations could juridically give any title to the Jews or to a Jewish State over any part of the territory of Palestine.

The legal position in this regard is quite clear and obvious. The United Nations are an organization of States which was formed for certain purposes mentioned in the Charter. At no time did this organization possess any sovereignty or other power in or over Palestine. The United Nations could not give what they did not possess. Neither individually nor collectively could the members of the United Nations alienate, reduce or otherwise affect the sovereignty of the people of Palestine, nor dispose of their territory, whether by partition or otherwise. Nor could the United Nations in any way impair or diminish the political rights of the original inhabitants or grant to alien immigrants any territorial or political rights in Palestine. Not only did the United Nations possess no sovereignty over Palestine but they did not even possess any power to administer the country. The League of Nations had assumed the power to supervise the administration of mandates established after the First World War in accordance with Article 22 of the Covenant. With the dissolution of the League of Nations the power of supervision which it possessed over mandates came to an end. Such a result was recognized by the resolution adopted at the last meeting of the League of Nations held on April 18 1946. The resolution stated that 'on the termination of the League's existence, its functions with respect to the mandated territories will come to an end'.[52] At the same meeting the Chinese delegate pointed out that the Charter of the United Nations made no provision for the assumption by the United Nations of the functions of the League with respect to mandates.[53] The Trusteeship system envisaged by Article 77 of the Charter of the United Nations did not apply to territories held under mandate except to the extent that they might be placed

[52] Twenty-first Ordinary Session of the Assembly of the League of Nations, *Document* A.33, 1946, pp 5–6.
[53] *Ibid.*, p. 3.

thereunder by means of trusteeship agreements. Mr. Duncan Hall has summarized the position in these words:

> In the case of mandates, the League died without a testament. . . . There was no transfer of sovereignty to the United Nations. . . . Sovereignty, wherever it might lie, certainly did not lie in the United Nations.[54]

Not possessing any sovereignty or any right of administration or any other right whatsoever over Palestine, the United Nations could not legally determine, as they sought to do in 1947, the future government of Palestine by recommending the partition of the country between Arab and Jewish states. Such action completely lacked any juridical basis. The Palestine Question was brought on the agenda of the General Assembly of the United Nations as a result of a request made by the mandatory power to the Assembly for a recommendation to be made under Article 10 of the Charter concerning the future government of Palestine. Article 10 provides as follows:

> The General Assembly may discuss any questions or any matters within the scope of the present Charter . . . and, except as provided in Article 12, may make recommendations to the Members of the United Nations or to the Security Council or to both on any such questions or matters.

On the assumption that the Palestine Question was one of 'the questions or matters within the scope of the Charter' within the meaning of Article 10, and that consequently the General Assembly could discuss such a question or matter and make a recommendation to Members of the United Nations or to the Security Council, it is clear that the General Assembly had no power to make any recommendation that would be incompatible with the rights of the people of the country. In particular, the General Assembly did not possess the power to decide, impose or recommend the future form of Government of the country or to decide its partition between its original inhabitants and foreign immigrants, or otherwise to interfere with the sovereignty of its inhabitants. The question of the future government of Palestine was a matter which fell within the exclusive competence of its people and had to be decided in accordance with ordinary democratic principles and procedures. Any recommendation made by the General Assembly to the mandatory power whose functions were about to terminate could not

[54] H. Duncan Hall, op. cit., p. 274.

affect the mandated territory, its integrity or the rights of its people. Any such recommendation, unless accepted by the original inhabitants of the country, had no value, either in law or in fact. Mr. P. B. Potter has observed that:

> The United Nations has no right to dictate a solution in Palestine unless a basis for such authority can be worked out such as has not been done thus far.
>
> Such a basis might be found by holding that sovereignty over Palestine, relinquished by Turkey in the Treaty of Lausanne, passed to the League of Nations, and has been inherited by the United Nations, a proposition which involves two hazardous steps. Or it might be held that the Mandate is still in force and that supervision thereof has passed to the United Nations, which is much more realistic but still somewhat hazardous juridically. The Arabs deny the binding force of the Mandate, now or ever, as they deny the validity of the Balfour Declaration on which it was based, and again they are probably quite correct juridically.[55]

Professor Quincy Wright has recently expressed the view that 'The legality of the General Assembly's recommendation for partition of Palestine was doubtful.'[56]

The same view was expressed by Professor I. Brownlie who said:

> It is doubtful if the United Nations 'has a capacity to convey title', *inter alia* because the Organization cannot assume the role of territorial sovereign . . . Thus the resolution of 1947 containing a Partition plan for Palestine was probably *ultra vires* (outside the competence of the United Nations), and, if it was not, was not binding on member states in any case.[57]

The Palestinian Arabs questioned in 1947 the competence of the United Nations to recommend the partition of Palestine or otherwise prescribe the manner of its future government. In this regard, Sub-Committee 2 to the Ad Hoc Committee on the Palestine Question stated in its report dated November 11 1947 as follows:

> 15 (c) Before considering the effect of the provisions of the United Nations Charter on the Mandate, it should be pointed out that the United

---

55 Pitman B. Potter, The Palestine Problem Before the United Nations, *AJIL* (1948), Vol. 42, p. 860.
56 Quincy Wright, *The Middle Eastern Crisis*, an address to the Association of the Bar of the City of New York, November 1968.
57 I. Brownlie: *Principles of Public International Law* (Clarendon Press, Oxford, 1966), pp. 161–162.

Nations Organization has not inherited the constitutional and political powers and functions of the League of Nations, that it cannot be treated in any way as the successor of the League of Nations in so far as the administration of mandates is concerned, and that such powers as the United Nations may exercise with respect to mandated territories are strictly limited and defined by the specific provisions of the Charter in this regard.

Competence of the United Nations

16. A study of Chapter XII of the United Nations Charter leaves no room for doubt that unless and until the Mandatory Power negotiates a trusteeship agreement in accordance with Article 79 and presents it to the General Assembly for approval, neither the General Assembly nor any other organ of the United Nations is competent to entertain, still less to recommend or enforce, any solution with regard to a mandated territory. Paragraph 1 of Article 80 is quite clear on this point, and runs as follows:

'Except as may be agreed upon in individual trusteeship agreements, made under Articles 77, 79, and 81, placing each territory under the trusteeship system, and until such agreements have been concluded, nothing in this Chapter shall be construed in or of itself to alter in any manner the rights whatsoever of any States or any peoples or the terms of existing international instruments to which Members of the United Nations may respectively be parties.'

18. In the case of Palestine, the Mandatory Power has not negotiated or presented a trusteeship agreement for the approval of the General Assembly. The question, therefore, of replacing the Mandate by trusteeship does not arise, quite apart from the obvious fact alluded to above that the people of Palestine are ripe for self-government and that it has been agreed on all hands that they should be made independent at the earliest possible date. It also follows from what has been said above, that the General Assembly is not competent to recommend, still less to enforce, any solution other than the recognition of the independence of Palestine, and that the settlement of the future government of Palestine is a matter solely for the people of Palestine.[58]

As previously observed in Section 1 (3) of Part I, all the requests which were made in 1947 by the Arabs at the United Nations for an advisory opinion by the International Court of Justice on the legal issues, including the question of competence of the General Assembly

[58] Document A/AC 14/32, November 11 1947, *Official Records of the Second Session of the General Assembly, AD HOC Committee on the Palestine Question*, pp. 276–277.

to recommend or implement partition, were turned down as a result of the political pressures exercised in favour of partition.

In adopting the resolution of November 29 1947 the General Assembly completely ignored the wishes of the people of Palestine and acted contrary to the will of the majority of the population. The principle of majority rule, which is one of the dogmas of modern civilization, was utterly ignored in 1947 in the case of Palestine. The partition resolution was pre-eminently a political decision which was engineered by Zionism and its friends in violation of the principles of law, justice and democracy. At no time was the partition resolution accepted by the Palestinians or by the Arab states. The partition resolution, therefore, lacked all juridical basis, was not within the powers of the General Assembly, and could not confer any valid title upon Israel over such part of Palestine as was earmarked for the Jewish state.

The conclusion herein reached that Israel cannot derive any valid title under the partition resolution is further strengthened by the consideration that, as previously mentioned, the Jewish state which emerged in 1948 and assumed the name of Israel was not established in conformity with the partition resolution. The manner of establishment of Israel and its organic structure have deviated in every material respect from the basic provisions of the United Nations resolution, whether they be territorial, demographic, political or constitutional. By forcibly displacing the Arab inhabitants of the Jewish state and by usurping a large part of the territory of the proposed Arab state, the Jews have created in Palestine something entirely and radically different from what the United Nations had contemplated in 1947. Territorially, Israel is not the Jewish state which was envisaged by the resolution of the United Nations. Demographically, Israel is not the Jewish state which was contemplated by the United Nations. Politically and constitutionally also, Israel cannot be considered to be the Jewish state envisaged by the United Nations. The Jewish state as envisaged by the General Assembly resolution was Jewish only in name, for in fact, as previously noted, it would have had an Arab majority.[59] Israel, as formed in 1948 and as it exists today, is a racist state in which its Arab population was reduced by

[59] The proposed Jewish state would have had a total population of 1,008,800 consisting of 509,780 Arabs and 499,020 Jews: U.N. Document A/AC 14/32 November 11 1947, Official Records of the 2nd session of the General Assembly, Ad Hoc Committee, 1947, p. 291. See also Section 1 (3) of Part I, *ante*.

methods already considered to about ten per cent of its original number. Thus, by its seizure of a large part of the territory of the proposed Arab state and by displacing the majority of its Arab population, Israel has completely distorted the concept of the Jewish state as originally envisaged by the United Nations. It is evident that the United Nations never intended to create a racist and theocratic state from which the original inhabitants of the country, both Moslems and Christians, would be ousted. Organically, Israel is not, and cannot be considered to constitute, the Jewish state whose creation was proposed by the United Nations in 1947, and hence cannot lay claim to the territorial and other rights, whatever their value, which were intended by the partition resolution for a materially different political and demographic entity.

c   *No title was gained by Israel as a result of conquest or occupation*

Before May 14 1948 the state of Israel did not exist. On that date, a number of Jews—largely of foreign origin and most of them not even possessing the nationality of the country—proclaimed the existence of the state of Israel and proceeded by force of arms to seize a substantial area of Palestine after driving away its Arab inhabitants. Can such seizure give a legal title to Israel? The answer is obvious. Israel cannot under international law claim title to the territories which it seized in 1948 and 1949 either by conquest or by occupation.

The right of conquest does not exist any more. It is now established by the consensus of the civilized community that military conquest is not a ground of acquisition of territory. War cannot give title. This principle, which was recognized by Article 22 of the Covenant of the League of Nations, was expressed in no uncertain terms by the United Nations during the fifth emergency special session of the General Assembly which was convened in the summer of 1967 following Israel's aggression. The same principle was also reaffirmed by the Security Council in its resolutions of November 22 1967 and May 21 1968, both of which emphasized 'the inadmissibility of the acquisition of territory by war' (Appendices VIII and IX).

Neither can Israel derive any title by occupation. Several considerations relating to the nature of the territory which was seized, the identity of the occupiers and the circumstances of the occupation negate the acquisition by Israel of any legal title to such territory.

In accordance with accepted principles of international law, occupation as a means of acquiring territory can only be conceived in the case of a *terra nullius*. 'Occupation can only come into play when there is a *res nullius* to be occupied.'[60] Palestine was at no time *terra nullius*, so that it was not open for occupation nor capable of acquisition by any state or any group of alien settlers. Palestine belonged to the Palestinians, i.e., its original inhabitants who had been established there for centuries.

Turning to the identity of the occupiers, it has already been observed that they were mainly aliens—both in origin and nationality. The bulk of the Jews who seized a large area of Palestine and proclaimed the State of Israel on May 14 1948 were foreign immigrants—some of whom had been admitted by the mandatory power as 'legal immigrants' while others had penetrated the country illegally[61]—and who in all cases had entered the country against the wishes of its original inhabitants.[62] Only a small number of the Jews who lived in Palestine in 1948 were indigenous inhabitants, and these were mostly opposed to the concept and establishment of a Jewish State. Moreover, the majority of the Jews who proclaimed the state of Israel in 1948 were not even citizens of Palestine. Although the mandatory power facilitated the acquisition of Palestinian citizenship by Jewish immigrants and did not require more than two years' residence in order to give them the country's nationality, the total number of certificates of naturalization granted by the Government of Palestine between 1925 and 1945 to all categories of immigrants—Jews and others—did not exceed 91,350.[63] The number of Jewish immigrants who had acquired Palestinian citizenship up to 1945 was 132,616 persons.[64] Thus the total number of Jews who possessed Palestinian citizenship in 1948—comprising both the original Jewish inhabitants of

---

[60] Earl of Birkenhead, *International Law*, 6th ed., p. 93; Oppenheim, *op. cit.*, p. 555.

[61] The Palestine Government estimated the number of Jewish illegal immigrants in 1945 to have been between 50,000 and 60,000: Government of Palestine, *A Survey of Palestine*, Vol. I, p. 210.

[62] Most of Israel's political leaders, past and present, have come from Russia, Poland, South Africa and other countries, and cannot even claim to belong to the country by birth on its soil. Mr. Ben Gurion, Israel's former Prime Minister, has taken pride in asserting that he came to Palestine in 1906 as a Russian tourist on a three-months' visa and simply overstayed: Ben-Gurion, *Israel, Années de Lutte* (Flammarion, Paris, 1964), p. 9.

[63] Government of Palestine, *A Survey of Palestine*, Vol. I, p. 208; Government of Palestine, *Statistical Abstract*, 1944–1945, pp. 36 and 46.

[64] Government of Palestine, *A Survey of Palestine*, Vol. I, p. 208.

Palestine and naturalized Jewish immigrants—hardly reached one-third of the Jewish population[65] or one-ninth of the total population. In these circumstances, the establishment of Israel by a minority group of foreign settlers who in the main did not even possess the citizenship of the country cannot be viewed as the act of a section of the original inhabitants seceding from the mother country. It would be a ludicrous situation under international law if a minority of alien settlers owning no more than 6 per cent of the land should, by reason of a successful military seizure of 80 per cent of the area of the country, be deemed to have acquired title and sovereignty over the territory which they have usurped.

The circumstances of the occupation also negate the acquisition of any valid title by Israel to the territory which it has seized. The territory of Palestine was wrested from its owners by violence exercised by a small but strongly organized alien minority which displaced by terrorism, expulsions and fear the majority of the original inhabitants. Thus, the very origin of Israel's occupation was wrongful and illegitimate and its seizure of Palestine territory was a usurpation of a land that does not belong to it. Oppenheim points out that where an act alleged to be creative of a new right is done in violation of an existing rule of international law, it 'is tainted with illegality and incapable of producing legal results beneficial to the wrongdoer in the form of a new title or otherwise'.[66] Oppenheim further mentions that the Permanent Court of International Justice has repeatedly held that an act which is not in accordance with law cannot confer upon a state a legal right.[67]

3 HAS ISRAEL ACQUIRED LEGAL SOVEREIGNTY OVER TERRITORIES SEIZED IN EXCESS OF THE PARTITION RESOLUTION?

The legal position with respect to the territories which Israel seized in 1948 and 1949 in excess of the territorial limits of the Jewish state as

[65] Official Records of the 3rd Session of the General Assembly, First Committee, Part I, p. 849.

[66] Oppenheim, op. cit., pp. 141–142.

[67] Order of December 6 1930 in the case of the *Free Zones of Upper Savoy and the District of Gex* (2nd phase): *P.C.I.J.*, series A, No. 24; Order of August 3 1932, concerning the *South-Eastern Territory of Greenland*, *ibid.*, series A/B, No. 48, p. 285; Advisory Opinion of March 3 1928, the case of the *Jurisdiction of the Courts of Danzig*, *ibid.*, series B, No. 15, p. 26.

fixed by General Assembly resolution 181 (II) of November 29 1947 is also quite obvious.[68] On the one hand, the considerations already discussed that preclude the acquisition of legal sovereignty by Israel over the territory envisaged by the partition resolution for the Jewish state apply with equal force to the areas which Israel has seized in excess of the said resolution. Neither conquest nor occupation can give Israel any valid legal title to such territories. On the other hand, Israel's seizure of territories earmarked for the Arab state and the New City of Jerusalem can give it no title for the reason that such seizure is not only incompatible with international law but also constitutes a violation of General Assembly resolution 181 (II) of November 29 1947 which fixed and defined the geographical limits of the Jewish state, the Arab state and the City of Jerusalem. Juridically, therefore, Israel can have no possible claim to the territories which it seized in excess of the partition resolution, for it is inconceivable that it could acquire rights by violating a General Assembly resolution.

Israel has in turn invoked the partition resolution to justify its occupation of the territory envisaged for the Jewish state, and rejected and violated the same resolution by its seizure of territories earmarked for the Arab state.[69] In 1948 Count Bernadotte made it plain that Israel was not entitled to consider provisions of the partition resolution which are in its favour as effective and treat certain others of its provisions which are not in its favour as ineffective. In his reply dated July 6 1948 to the Israeli Government's letter of the preceding day wherein it objected to the Mediator's suggestions for a peaceful settlement of the Palestine Question on the ground of their 'deviations from the General Assembly resolution of November 29 1947',[70] Count Bernadotte stated as follows:

> 2. . . . You have not taken advantage of my invitation to offer counter-suggestions, unless I am to understand that your reference in Paragraphs 1 and 2 of your letter to the resolution of the General Assembly of November 29 1947 implies that you will be unwilling to consider any suggestions which do not correspond to the provisions of that resolution.
>
> 3. In paragraph 1 of your letter it is stated that my suggestions 'appear to ignore the resolution of the General Assembly of November 29 1947'. . . .

[68] The territories which Israel seized in excess of the partition resolution were described in Sections 2 and 3 (3) of Part I and are shown in Appendix VII.

[69] See Ben-Gurion, *Israel, Années de Lutte* (Flammarion, Paris, 1964), pp. 59 and 61.

[70] U.N. Document A/648, p. 9.

6. As regards paragraph 4 of your letter, I note that your Government no longer considers itself bound by the provisions for Economic Union set forth in the November 29 resolution for the reason that the Arab State envisaged by that resolution has not been established. In paragraphs 1 and 2, however, the same resolution is taken as your basic position. Whatever may be the precise legal significance and status of the November 29 resolution, it would seem quite clear to me that the situation is not of such a nature as to entitle either party to act on the assumption that such parts of the resolution as may be favourable to it may be regarded as effective, while those parts which may, by reason of changes in circumstances, be regarded as unfavourable are to be considered as ineffective.[71]

Israel may not blow hot and cold. It is elementary that Israel cannot claim title to the territory envisaged for the Jewish state under the General Assembly resolution and deny the title of the Palestinians to the territories envisaged for the Arab state under the same resolution. Such an attitude is tantamount to a denial by Israel of its birth certificate. In his Progress Report to the General Assembly of the United Nations, Count Bernadotte took the position, almost as a matter of course, that Israel is not entitled to retain the areas which it had occupied in excess of the partition resolution. He said in his Progress Report:

(C) The disposition of the territory of Palestine not included within the boundaries of the Jewish State should be left to the Governments of the Arab States in full consultation with the Arab inhabitants of Palestine, with the recommendation, however, that in view of the historical connexion and common interests of Transjordan and Palestine, there would be compelling reasons for merging the Arab territory of Palestine with the territory of Transjordan. . . .[72]

Count Bernadotte's view that Israel was not entitled to retain the areas which it seized in excess of the General Assembly's resolution was shared by the U.S. representatives at the third session of the General Assembly of the United Nations held at Paris in 1948. Dr. Philip C. Jessup, then U.S. representative, indicated the position of the United States as being that if Israel desired additions to the boundaries set forth

---

[71] Count Bernadotte's Progress Report to the General Assembly dated September 16 1948 (U.N. Document A/648) contains extracts only from the said letter. However, the full text of Count Bernadotte's letter to the Provisional Government of Israel dated July 6 1948 which contains the passages quoted above is set out in his diary published under the title *To Jerusalem* by Hodder and Stoughton, London, 1951, pp. 153–158.

[72] U.N. Document A/648, p. 18.

in the resolution of November 29 1947 'it would have to offer an appropriate exchange, acceptable to the Arabs, through negotiation'.[73] Similarly, Mr. Rusk for the United States declared at the same session that 'any modifications in the boundaries fixed by the resolution of 29 November 1947 could only be made if acceptable to the state of Israel. That meant that the territory allocated to the State of Israel could not be reduced without its consent. If, on the other hand, Israel wished to enlarge that territory, it would have to offer an exchange through negotiation.'[74]

The U.S. Government maintained its view that Israel cannot keep territory seized in excess of the partition resolution when it appeared during the meetings of the Conciliation Commission for Palestine held in Lausanne in 1949 that Israel's obdurate attitude regarding territory and refugees was preventing any settlement on the basis of the Lausanne Protocol. On May 29 1949 the U.S. Government addressed through its Ambassador, Mr. James G. McDonald, a note to Israel which:

> Expressed disappointment at the failure of Eytan (Israel's representative) at Lausanne to make any of the desired concessions on refugees and boundaries; interpreted Israel's attitude as dangerous to peace and as indicating disregard of the U.N. General Assembly resolutions of November 29 1947 (partition and frontiers), and December 11 1948 (refugees and internationalization of Jerusalem); reaffirmed insistence that territorial compensation should be made for territory taken in excess of November 29 resolution and that tangible refugee concessions should be made now as essential preliminary to any prospect for general settlement.[75]

During the debate in 1949 on Israel's application for admission to membership of the United Nations, Israel explained the discrepancy between the territory which it held at that time and the territory envisaged for the Jewish state by the resolution of November 29 1947 as follows:

> All the areas occupied by Israel's forces at this time are so occupied with the agreement concluded with Arab States under the resolution of November 16.[76]

---

[73] Official Records of the 3rd Session of the General Assembly, Part I, 1948, First Committee, pp. 682 and 727.

[74] Official Records of the 3rd Session of the General Assembly, 1948, *supra*, p. 836.

[75] James G. McDonald, *My Mission to Israel* (Simon and Schuster, New York, 1951), pp. 181–182.

[76] Official Records of the 3rd Session of the General Assembly, 1949, Part II, p. 347.

The 'resolution of 16 November' to which reference is made in the aforementioned statement was resolution No. 62 of the Security Council dated November 16 1948. This resolution took note that 'the General Assembly is continuing its consideration of the future Government of Palestine in response to the request of the Security Council in its resolution 44 (1948) of April 1 1948' and called upon the parties involved in the conflict to seek agreement with a view to the immediate establishment of the armistice. The 'agreement' mentioned by Israel's representative as a basis for its occupation can, therefore, only refer to the Armistice Agreements which had then been concluded with Egypt, Lebanon and Jordan under a resolution of the Security Council which envisaged that 'the future Government of Palestine' was still under consideration by the United Nations. This can only mean that the whole question of Palestine was in suspension. Furthermore, Israel's occupation of Palestinian territory under the Armistice Agreements is not and cannot be a source of title. In fact, the Armistice Agreements specifically provided that the armistice lines are not to be construed as political or territorial boundaries and are delineated 'without prejudice to the ultimate settlement of the Palestine Question'.

In order to justify the seizure of various areas falling outside the boundaries of the proposed Jewish state, Israel has suggested that it did not limit itself to the territorial boundaries of the partition resolution because the Arabs themselves had rejected the partition plan. According to Israel, the Arab refusal to accept partition and the military intervention of the Arab states have rendered the partition resolution null and void. This, in its view, opened the way for Israel to grab as much territory as it could. Israel's argument is specious and, of course, devoid of any legal basis. The Arabs had a perfect legal right to oppose the dismemberment of their country and to defend the territorial integrity of their homeland. The Arab refusal to accept partition and the ensuing strife between Arabs and Jews could in no way confer upon Israel the right to seize any part of the territory of Palestine and much less to usurp the territories reserved by the United Nations for the original people of Palestine. The fact that the latter were aggrieved by the partition resolution and considered it to be null and void and not binding upon them cannot be invoked by the Jews as an excuse for aggravating the wrong and usurping the remainder of Palestine. The Arab–Israeli conflict of 1948 did not take away, diminish or affect the rights of the Palestine Arabs nor enlarge the rights of the Jews. As regards the intervention of the Arab states, it was proclaimed in 1948 that the object of their intervention was to go to the help of the Palestinians who were the victims of Jewish terrorism and were threatened by the superior military force of the Jews. Lieutenant-General Burns has remarked that the Arabs outside Palestine had as much right to come to the assistance of Arabs in Palestine as Jews outside Palestine to come to the assistance of Jews within.[77] Israel's seizure in 1948 and 1949 of territories outside the geographical limits of the Jewish state as fixed by the partition resolution is a clear and obvious usurpation committed in violation of the General Assembly resolution. The United Nations did not consider that the Arab–Israeli conflict of 1948 affected in any way their resolutions on Palestine or that the results of the conflict enlarged the rights of the Jews in Palestine, for, as noted earlier, the General Assembly accepted Israel into the fold of the United Nations only after 'recalling its resolutions of November 29 1947 and December 11 1948 and taking note of the declarations and explanations made by the representative of the Government of Israel before the Ad Hoc Committee in respect of the implementation of the said resolutions'.[78] This took place on May 11 1949 long after the end of the 1948 conflict. Furthermore, as already mentioned in Section 2 of Part I, the Jews themselves have largely contributed to the defeat of the partition resolution by their seizure before the end of the mandate of the greater part of the territories reserved for the Palestine Arabs by such resolution. Hence, they cannot, in order to justify their seizure of territories in excess of the partition resolution, say that such resolution has lapsed as a result of the armed conflict of 1948.

In the light of the preceding considerations it is safe to say that Israel did not and could not gain title either to the territory which, as a result of an excess of competence and authority, the General Assembly designated as the area of the proposed Jewish state or to the territories which the General Assembly designated as the area of the proposed Arab state. The legal status of Israel in relation to the entirety of the territory which it occupied prior to June 5 1967 is identical with its status in relation to the territories which it seized since June 5 1967: it is the status of a belligerent occupier. And it is indifferent whether Israel is considered a

[77] E. L. M. Burns, *Between Arab and Israeli* (George G. Harrap & Co., London, 1962), p. 127.
[78] Resolution No. 273 (III) of May 11 1949. See Section 3 (2) of Part IV.

belligerent occupier or a conqueror. In neither case can it acquire sovereignty. 'Israel, alone among all the countries of the world, possesses not a single square inch of territory which she could assuredly proclaim to be her own in perpetuity.'[79] Israel does not possess any recognized frontiers but only armistice lines. Its relationship with its neighbours is still technically today a state of war suspended by the Armistice Agreements of 1949 and the cease-fire resolutions of the Security Council of June 1967. It is settled under international law that a belligerent occupier does not acquire sovereignty.[80] The legitimate sovereign, though prevented from exercising his authority, retains legal sovereignty. Professor Jèze has pointed out that the belligerent occupier acquires a 'sovereignty in fact but not in law':

> Cette prise de possession, qui repose exclusivement sur la force, n'entraine pas au profit du vainqueur l'acquisition du territoire occupé. . . . Supposons d'abord que l'Etat dont le territoire est envahi se refuse à traiter, et que le vainqueur maintienne son occupation. La domination de l'Etat victorieux sera une souveraineté de fait et non de droit. . . . Tant que des protestations se feront entendre, il y aura bien une domination de fait, mais non un état de droit.[81]

The basic attributes of sovereignty were set out in the French Constitution of September 3 1791 which declared: 'sovereignty is one, indivisible, inalienable and imprescriptible'. Title over Palestine lies in its original inhabitants, in whom sovereignty vested upon detachment of the country from Turkey. Their sovereignty over their ancestral land is 'one, indivisible, inalienable and imprescriptible' and extends to the whole territory of Palestine regardless of any partition, occupation, usurpation or lapse of time.

The people of Palestine have never given their consent to any transfer of title over their country nor have they recognized any sovereignty in the occupier. 'In present day international law', observes Professor Schwarzenberger, 'it is by itself not sufficient to transform wartime occupation into a transfer of sovereignty. Even in the relations between

---

[79] Hedley V. Cooke, *Israel, A Blessing and a Curse* (Stevens and Sons, London, 1960), p. 186.

[80] Oppenheim, *International Law* (Longmans, London, 1963), 7th ed., Vol. II, p. 618.

[81] Gaston Jèze, *Etude Théorique et Pratique sur l'Occupation* (Paris, 1896), pp. 44–46. See also Ian Brownlie, *Principles of Public International Law* (Oxford, 1966) who refers to the continued existence of legal personality under international law despite that the process of government in an area falls into the hands of another state, pp. 100–102.

belligerents, not to speak of third States, the title requires to be consolidated by positive acts of recognition or consent or, at least, by acquiescence of the former territorial sovereign.'[82]

It might perhaps be argued that Israel is a state which is recognized by a large number of other states. Such recognition, however, is not general. Israel is not recognized by the Arab states nor by a large number of other states. More important still, Israel is not recognized by the original people of Palestine in whom sovereignty lies. The fact of recognition by other states cannot give to Israel what it lacks: legal sovereignty. Under international law recognition does not confer sovereignty. The recognition or non-recognition of a state is not determined at present under international law by considerations relating to its legitimacy or regularity of origin. Professor Philip C. Jessup has observed that the practice of basing recognition on constitutional legitimacy instead of on actual existence and control of the country has not as yet been widely enough accepted to be acknowledged as having the force of customary law.[83] Recognition by other states does not remove the vice with which an occupation is tainted:

> La reconnaissance par les Puissances ne peut avoir au point de vue juridique aucune influence sur la validité de l'occupation. . . . La reconnaissance du fait accompli par les Puissances civilisées est impuissante à couvrir le vice qui entache la prise de possession.[84]

Nor does lapse of time make legitimate Israel's wrongful occupation of Palestine. Professor Giraud has observed that in contrast to private law, no prescription is envisaged by international law to regularize irregular situations.[85]

---

[82] G. Schwarzenberger, *International Law*, 3rd ed., p. 302.

[83] *AJIL* (1931), p. 721.

[84] Gaston Jèze, *Etude Théorique et Pratique sur l'Occupation* (Paris, 1896), p. 298.

[85] E. Giraud, *Le Droit International et la Politique*, Académie de Droit International, *Recueil des Cours*, 1963, Vol. III, p. 425.

The Question of Sovereignty over Palestine

NATHAN FEINBERG

If I were asked to sum up the contents of Henry Cattan's book "Palestine, The Arab and Israel, The Search for Justice" [1] in a few sentences, I believe that the best way of doing so would be to quote a number of the author's contentions and statements in his own words. "Israel", he writes, "is an illegitimate and unnatural creation" [2]; "the essence of the [Arab–Israel] conflict... is the basic injustice of 1948" [3]; "the first misconception concerns the possibility of acceptance by the Arabs of the factual situation created by Israel in 1948" [4]; "the liquidation of the consequences of the conflict of June 1967 alone will not solve the basic issues involved in the Palestine Question" [5]; "the establishment of a just and lasting peace requires much more than the withdrawal of Israeli forces from the territories occupied during the recent conflict [of 1967]" [6]; "the people of Palestine have never given their consent to any transfer of title over their territory nor have they recognized any sovereignty in the occupier" [7]; "the Palestine injustice cannot be buried under

1. Henry Cattan, *Palestine, The Arabs and Israel, The Search for Justice* (hereafter quoted as Cattan, *Palestine*) (London, 1969).
2. *Ibid.*, p. 138.
3. *Ibid.*, p. 139.
4. *Ibid.*, p. 140.
5. *Ibid.*, pp. 181—182.
6. *Ibid.*, p. 182.
7. *Ibid.*, p. 274.

a *fait accompli*" [8]; "Israel has often said that 'the clock cannot be turned back'.... But... history shows that many a time the clock was, in fact, turned back to redress a glaring injustice or to remove a colonialist implantation. If justice is to be done in Palestine and peace to be restored to the Middle East the clock must be turned back." [9]

Yet the question arises: how does one turn back the clock of history? Nor is the question pertinent only today, twenty three years after the establishment of the State of Israel. The United Nations Mediator, Count Bernadotte, asked the very same thing just seven weeks after Israel came into being. In his reply of 5 July 1948 to a letter in which the Arab League had proposed the elimination of Israel as an independent political entity and the establishment of a unitary Arab State in Palestine, with full rights and guarantees for the Jewish minority, Bernadotte put the grave counter-question: how could this be done by peaceful means? "I am fully convinced", he wrote, "that there is no possibility whatever of persuading or inducing the Jews to give up their present separate cultural and political existence and accept merging in a unitary Palestine in which they would be a permanent minority. The alternative method of achieving the Arab objective would be to wipe out the Jewish State and its Provisional Government by force. This course as Mediator, I obviously cannot recommend." [10]

8. *Ibid.*, p. 141.   9. *Ibid.*
10. U.N. Doc. A/648, *Progress Report of the United Nations Mediator on Palestine* (1948), p. 24.

Cattan's book, as its contents indicate, is aimed, first and foremost, at the law-abiding and peace-loving reader, who cannot be won over to the Arab cause by advocacy of the use of force.[11] Accordingly, the author finds it necessary to adopt other means of achieving his purpose and, to this end, formulates two legal propositions, on the basis of which he seeks to show that "turning the clock back" is both lawful and possible. The first of his propositions is that, despite the decisions on Palestine taken by international bodies and despite the establishment of the State of Israel, the Arabs of the former British Mandated territory still hold sovereign rights over Palestine today. The second is that, in view of the special circumstances in which the State of Israel came into being and the undertakings that it assumed on becoming a member of the United Nations, the latter Organization is competent to reexamine the Partition Plan of 1947 and impose on Israel any settlement which the United Nations may deem proper to redress the injustice suffered by the Arabs in consequence of the Plan.

Let us begin then by examining these two propositions, which constitute the central theme of Cattan's book. After that, a number of the other questions raised will be considered.

11. In Cattan's book one does not find the routine accusations made in the Arab literature that Israel is "a colonial fact", "a colonial phenomenon", "a beach-head of the capitalist world", "the ally of the capitalist Powers". See, for example: *Colloque de Juristes Arabes sur la Palestine — La Question Palestinienne, Alger 22-27 Juillet 1967* (hereafter quoted as *Colloque*) (Alger, 1968), pp. 44, 57, 110.

I. The Question of Sovereignty over Palestine

Cattan devotes a special appendix to the subject of sovereignty. He is right in saying that "the question of sovereignty over Palestine is of a strictly juridical nature"[12] and that it "has an important bearing upon the eventual solution [of the Arab–Israel conflict]"[13]. However, his conclusions on this matter are extremely arbitrary and without any foundation in current international law.

1. *"Legal sovereignty" and "political sovereignty"*

In his book, Cattan draws a distinction between "legal sovereignty" and "political sovereignty". According to his definition, the latter means "factual dominion and control" over a certain area of land, whereas the former is "the legal and inalienable title... of a nation to a territory"[14]. "Notwithstanding the political vicissitudes in Palestine during the last fifty years", he holds, "legal sovereignty still lies today in the original inhabitants of the country as they existed at the time of the detachment of Palestine from Turkey at the end of the First World War."[15]

The first point to make in this connection is that "legal sovereignty" and "political sovereignty" are not accepted terms in public international law. To the best of my knowledge they do not appear in any of the many textbooks on this branch of the law; nor are they mentioned in the *Dictionnaire de la terminologie du droit interna-*

---

12. Cattan, *Palestine,* p. 183.   13. *Ibid.,* p. 242.
14. *Ibid.,* pp. 242, 243.   15. *Ibid.*

tional — published in 1960 under the auspices of Professor Basdevant — where all the various meanings of the term "sovereignty" are clarified and defined [16]. Professor Schwarzenberger did, it is true, resort to these two terms some years ago in his lectures at the Hague Academy of International Law — and it is on these lectures that Cattan bases himself. But Schwarzenberger used the terms in a completely different sense from that which Cattan seeks to give them. For Schwarzenberger, political sovereignty is not the antithesis of legal sovereignty; his contention is that, in the atomic age, not all of the States which enjoy legal sovereignty are equally sovereign in the political sense. "At present", he writes, "[only the States] which are able to produce the superweapons of our age or are relatively immune against their application... have freedom of decision in situations in which, owing to lack of such weapons or means of effective protection against their application, other States may consider it advisable to act differently from how they would if they were sovereign in the political sense." [17] Cattan also cites the jurist

16. See : *Dictionnaire de la terminologie du droit international* (Paris, 1960), pp. 573—579.
17. G. Schwarzenberger, "The Fundamental Principles of International Law", *Recueil des Cours de l'Academie de Droit International* (hereafter quoted as *R.A.D.I.*), tome 87 (Paris, 1956), p. 215.
   The sentence cited by Cattan from Schwarzenberger's lectures ... "the last word is still not with law, but power" (Cattan, *Palestine*, p. 243) — does not appear in the lectures as a general statement in an independent sentence. It expressly relates to the differences of opinion between the two existing blocs and is preceded by the words : "It would mean to ignore

Brownlie on this point [18]; but the two terms in question do not appear either in the pages of Brownlie's book to which he refers the reader [19], or on the following page where the same subject is dealt with [20]. Nor do I find any authority there for the substantive meaning which Cattan attributes to those terms. Moreover, Cattan's attempt to weave into the present context the question of the conquest of one State by another — such as the conquest of Austria by Nazi Germany — is quite irrelevant [21]. The conquering State does not acquire sovereignty — not even "political sovereignty", to use Cattan's terminology — but "authority", as provided by Article 42 of the Annex to the Fourth Hague Convention of 1907, respecting the laws and customs of war on land.

Yet a further indication of the extent to which Cattan's use of the concept of sovereignty is arbitrary is to be found in the following passage from his own book: "Prior to the occupation of Palestine by the British Army in 1917, during the First World War, Palestine formed an integral part of Turkey.... The Turkish constitution made no distinction between Turk or Arab or between Moslem or Christian or Jew. Turks and Arabs, therefore, shared sovereignty over all of the territories of the Turkish Empire regardless as to whether such territories were Turkish or Arab provinces." [22] And a few pages

that, at least in the overall relations between West and East" (Schwarzenberger, *op. cit.*, p. 215).

18. Ian Brownlie, *Principles of Public International Law* (Oxford, 1966), pp. 100—102.

19. Cattan, *Palestine*, p. 243.   20. Brownlie, *op. cit.*, p. 103.

21. Cattan, *Palestine*, p. 243.   22. *Ibid.*, pp. 243—244.

further on, he reiterates this point in these words: "It has been made amply clear that Arabs and Turks enjoyed equal rights and shared sovereignty over the whole Turkish Empire." [23] Is it really possible to contend, in all seriousness, that the Arabs shared with the Turks — in the time of the Sultan Abdul Hamid, or under the Young Turks — sovereignty over the whole of the Ottoman Empire?

Whatever the terminology that Cattan may choose to employ, it can be assumed that, in using the phrase "legal sovereignty", he had in mind what it is usual to call "self-determination", or in French — "droit des peuples à disposer d'eux-mêmes". I have already taken the opportunity in an earlier publication [24] of discussing in some detail the place of the question of self-determination in the Arab–Israel conflict, both from a legal point of view and from political and moral points of view. Accordingly, I can confine my remarks here to a summary of the main conclusions [25]. In that earlier work, I stressed the fact that right up to the present day there are differences of opinion as to whether self-determination of peoples is a binding rule of positive international law, or merely a political principle or moral postulate. But one point is clear beyond any doubt: it was not a binding rule of law

23. *Ibid.*, p. 245, note 9.
24. N. Feinberg, *The Arab-Israel Conflict in International Law, A Critical Analysis of the Colloquium of Arab Jurists in Algiers* (Jerusalem, 1970), pp. 44—55.
25. I shall adopt the same course in the case of other arguments in Cattan's book on which I have already expressed my views in my book on the *Colloque*.

at any of the many stages on the road towards the emergence of the State of Israel — neither on 2 November
1917, the date of the Balfour Declaration; nor on 24
July 1922, when the Palestine Mandate was finally defined by the Council of the League of Nations; nor on
29 November 1947, when the General Assembly of the
United Nations passed its Resolution on the partition of
Palestine; nor on 15 May 1948, the date of the establishment of the State of Israel. Support for this conclusion
can even be found in the work of the Algerian jurist
Mohammed Bedjaoui [26], who opened and closed the Colloquium of Arab jurists in Algiers and whose views —
one may assume — will not be without weight among
advocates of the Arab case. It would seem to follow, then,
that the distinction and terms underlying Cattan's discussion of the question of sovereignty have no basis whatsoever in international law; and, if our assumption is correct that by "legal sovereignty" Cattan meant the right
of self-determination, then neither on the day of the establishment of the State of Israel, nor in the period preceding that event, was that principle recognized as a
binding rule of positive international law.

2. *Turkey's views on the Jewish National Home and the Treaty of Lausanne*

Cattan contends that Turkey opposed the setting up of
the Jewish national home and that in Article 16 of the
Treaty of Lausanne, which it signed in 1923, it renounced

26. See: Mohammed Bedjaoui, *Law and the Algerian Revolution*
(Brussels, 1961), pp. 241—243.

its rights over Palestine to the Arabs [27]. These claims are without any foundation in law or in fact.

(a) *The Treaty of Sèvres*. Because the Balfour Declaration is mentioned in the Treaty of Sèvres (which remained unratified), but not in the Treaty of Lausanne, Cattan draws the conclusion that "Turkey refused to subscribe to... [the] provision [regarding the national home]" [28]. But this is completely to ignore the fact that the Treaty of Sèvres was signed two years before the confirmation of the Palestine Mandate by the Council of the League of Nations, whereas the Treaty of Lausanne was signed exactly one year after its confirmation. In the circumstances, it was quite logical and reasonable for those who drafted the Treaty of Lausanne to refer, in Article 16, to "the future of these territories [that Turkey renounced] being settled or to be settled by the parties concerned"; and, in so far as Palestine is concerned, it is the words "being settled", not "to be settled", that apply, for — as we have already seen — the decision on the settlement had already been taken on 24 July 1922, with the final drafting of the Palestine Mandate by the League of Nations [29].

27. Cattan, *Palestine,* pp. 246—247; and see *ibid.,* p. 18.
28. *Ibid.,* p. 247.
29. The fact that the Palestine Mandate only came into force fourteen months after its confirmation by the Council of the League of Nations is attributed by Cattan to Turkey's objection to the Jewish national home (*ibid.,* p. 18). But this is not the case. The real reason for the delay was the dispute between France and Italy as to certain provisions of the Mandate for Syria and the Lebanon, and France's demand that the latter Mandate come into force at the same time as the Palestine

(b) *Article 16 of the Treaty of Lausanne.* In Cattan's opinion, "the parties concerned" referred to in Article 16 are "the communities which inhabited these territories, since they were the parties primarily concerned" [30]. This interpretation is unconvincing. The words "the parties concerned" were used in Article 16 because it was impossible to resort to the usual term "the Contracting Parties", since that included not only the Principal Allied Powers, but also Greece, Romania and Yugoslavia. Nor was it possible to use the term "the Governments concerned" — as was done, for example, in Articles 49 and 92 of the Treaty — for the Covenant of the League of Nations, which was already in force at the time when the Treaty was being drafted, entrusted the Council with an important — and even decisive — role in the framing of the Mandates. Clearly, then, the words "the parties concerned" can in no way be regarded as referring to the Arabs [31].

Mandate. On 29 September 1923 the French and Italian representatives notified the League of Nations that the differences between their two countries had been reconciled, and on the very same day the Mandates came into force. See: *League of Nations, The Mandates System, Origin—Principles—Application* (Geneva, 1945), pp. 20-21; *League of Nations, Permanent Mandates Commission* (hereafter quoted as *P.M.C.*) *Minutes of the Second Session* (Geneva, 1922), p. 10.

30. Cattan, *Palestine,* p. 247.
31. Cattan also dwells on a difference in the wording of Articles 15 and 16: whereas in Article 15 Turkey renounces certain territories "in favour of Italy", there is no indication in Article 16 in whose favour it renounced. On the strength of this difference, he draws the conclusion that, in the case of Palestine, there was no need for any clarification, since "the original in-

(c) *The provisions as to Palestinian nationality.* There
is yet another point which proves that Turkey had no
objection to the establishment of the Jewish national
home in Palestine. In the draft of the Treaty presented
to the Turkish delegation on 31 January 1923, it was
provided — in Article 35 — that "Jews of other than
Turkish nationality who are habitually resident in Palestine on the coming into force of the present Treaty
will have the right to become citizens of Palestine by
making a declaration in such form and under such conditions as may be prescribed by law" [32]. And in the letter
sent from Ankara on 4 February 1923 to the heads of
the British, French and Italian delegations, Ismet Pasha,

habitants ... already possessed sovereignty over their own territories" (*ibid.*). If the position with regard to Palestine were
really as Cattan presents it, there would have been no point
at all in speaking of "the future of the territories ... being
settled", for sovereignty — according to his approach — was
automatically vested in the Arab inhabitants of Palestine. In fact,
Cattan himself points out the true reason why Article 16 makes
no mention of the entity in whose favour the territories are
renounced when he writes: "it was not the intention that the
Principal Allied Powers or any one of them should acquire
sovereignty over the Arab provinces" (*ibid.*). Nor does Cattan's
reference, in this context, to a judgment given in the United
States in 1905, in connection with the treaty on Cuba between
the United States and Spain, support his argument. In that
case the Court was concerned with the transfer of sovereignty
to the inhabitants of Cuba who "were declared to be free and
independent" (*ibid.*, p. 248), whereas Palestine was placed
under a Mandatory regime and the Mandatory was expressly
bound to set up a Jewish national home there.

32. *Cmd. 1814, Turkey No. 1 (1923), Lausanne Conference on
Near Eastern Affairs, 1922—1923* (London, 1923), pp. 697—
698.

head of the Turkish delegation, declared, *inter alia,* that
Turkey unreservedly accepts the proposed arrangement
as to citizenship [33]. The said provision of Article 35 was,
it is true, eventually omitted from the final text of the
Treaty of Lausanne; this, however, was not because
Turkey changed its mind about accepting the arrangement, but because of certain misgivings from the point
of view of the French law on citizenship, raised at the
Conference by the French representative, who, by the
way, took the opportunity of pointing out that, in principle, he had no objection to the provision in question [34].

3. *The "sovereignty" of the original inhabitants of Palestine by virtue of the Mandates system*

Cattan seeks to base the "legal sovereignty" — to use his
terminology — of the original inhabitants of Palestine
over this territory on the international Mandates system,
too. To this end, he relies on one of the many doctrines
as to the question of sovereignty over Mandated territories
prevalent in the period of the League of Nations. According to this doctrine, sovereignty over such a territory
did not reside in the Principal Allied and Associated
Powers, or in the Mandatory Power or the League of Na-

---

33. *Ibid.,* pp. 837–841.
34. *Conférence de Lausanne sur les affaires du Proche Orient
(1922–1923), Recueil des Actes de la Conférence, deuxiéme
série, tome 1er, Procès-verbaux et documents relatifs à la seconde
partie de la Conférence* (Paris, 1923), p. 23; see also N. Feinberg, "The Principles of Palestinian Citizenship as laid down
by International Law", *Some Problems of the Palestine
Mandate* (Tel Aviv, 1936), pp. 47–64.

tions, but in the inhabitants themselves. Cattan's contention is that "all these various views... — except that which considers sovereignty to reside in the inhabitants of the Mandated territories — have now been abandoned or discredited. None of the [others]... appears to rest on an acceptable legal or logical basis." [35]

It is worth making quite clear at the outset that Cattan's claim, that the doctrines which he dismisses have been abandoned, is unfounded. In 1950, Kerno, addressing the International Court of Justice on behalf of the Secretariat of the United Nations Organization, stressed, in the course of his survey of the various doctrines as to sovereignty over Mandated territories, that despite the abundance of legal theories "there exists no consensus, nor even a clearly discernible preponderance of opinion" [36]. This is not the occasion to establish which of these doctrines was, and is now, the correct one. For the purposes of the present discussion I am prepared to accept the one adopted by Cattan; but, even so, this does not prove the accuracy of his thesis. By Article 22, paragraph 8, of the Covenant of the League of Nations, the terms of the Mandates were to be "explicitly defined" in each case by the Council of the League [37]. Cattan has taken the easy way out and completely ignored the provisions of the Palestine Mandate. But, of course, he cannot by doing so eradicate the following facts: the second

35. Cattan, *Palestine,* p. 249.
36. *International Court of Justice, Pleadings, Oral Arguments, Documents, International Status of South West Africa, Advisory Opinion of July 11th, 1950,* p. 192.
37. *Ibid.,* p. 191.

paragraph of the preamble to the Palestine Mandate —
the international constitution, in accordance with whose
provisions the Mandated territory of Palestine was to be
administered — embodies the Balfour Declaration [38]; in
the second Article, the Mandatory was made "responsible
for placing the country under such political, administrative
and economic conditions as will secure the establishment
of the Jewish national home"; the sixth Article called
on the Mandatory to "facilitate Jewish immigration under suitable conditions and encourage... close settlement
by Jews on the land"; the seventh requires the Mandatory
to "facilitate the acquisition of Palestine citizenship by
Jews who take up their permanent residence in Palestine";
and in the White Paper of 1922, published by the British
Government as a definition of its future policy in Palestine
immediately prior to the confirmation of the Mandate, we
find this statement — "it is essential that it [the Jewish
people] should know that it is in Palestine as of right

---

38. The Spanish member of the Permanent Mandates Commission,
Professor L. Palacios, defined the Balfour Declaration as "the
very soul of the Mandate" (*P.M.C., Minutes of the Twenty-
Seventh Session*, Geneva, 1935, p. 198). And the British Royal
Commission of 1936, too, under the chairmanship of Lord Peel,
held that "unquestionably, ... the primary purpose of the
Mandate ... is to promote the establishment of the Jewish
National Home" (*Cmd. 5479, Palestine Royal Commission
Report*, London, 1937, p. 39). Again, in 1946, the Anglo-
American Committee of Enquiry of that year also came to the
conclusion that "though extensive safeguards were provided
for the non-Jewish peoples, the Mandate was framed primarily
in the Jewish interest" (*Cmd. 6808, Report of the Anglo-
American Committee of Enquiry regarding the Problems of
European Jewry and Palestine*, London, 1946, p. 61).

and not on sufferance" [39]. In the face of these clear and express provisions, what possible legal significance is to be attributed to Cattan's claim that the Jews who immigrated to Palestine during the Mandate were "mainly aliens — both in origin and nationality" [40], or that "Ben Gurion... came to Palestine... as a Russian tourist" [41], or there was an "implantation in Palestine of a foreign people" [42]. In support of his case, Cattan cites extensive passages from the book of van Rees, Vice-Chairman of the Permanent Mandates Commission [43]. But surely, in reading that book he cannot have failed to notice the following words on the Palestine Mandate and the return of the Jews to Palestine: "In virtue of the Balfour Declaration, brought in the opening passage of the Mandate, [the Jewish people] is — in effect — a part of the inhabitants of Palestine." [44] And some two years later, at one of the sessions of the Permanent Mandates Commission, van Rees declared: "[the Jewish] people would not enter the country as foreigners... ." [45]

---

39. Cmd. 1700, Palestine, Correspondence with the Palestine Arab Delegation and the Zionist Organization (London, 1922), p. 19.
40. Cattan, Palestine, p. 267.
41. Ibid., p. 267, note 62.
42. Ibid., p. 25. See also, in the same vein, pp. 28, 39, 266, 268.
43. Ibid., p. 250.
44. D.F.W. Van Rees, Les mandats internationaux, Les principes généraux du régime des Mandats, tome 1 (Paris, 1928), p. 100. The passage cited here and subsequent passages cited in English from works in French or other languages are in the writer's own translation.
45. P.M.C., Minutes of the Seventeenth (Extraordinary) Session (Geneva, 1930), p. 39. Cattan also refers to a resolution, adopted in 1931 by the Institute of International Law, which

4. *The Balfour Declaration and the Palestine Mandate*

Turning to the question "whether Israel has acquired sovereignty over the territory which was allocated to the Jewish State by the partition resolution", Cattan remarks that it "can be examined in the light of three political developments... . These three developments are : the Balfour Declaration of November 2, 1917; the United Nations resolution on the partition of Palestine of November 29, 1947, and the forcible occupation [sic!] in 1948 and 1949 of the territory earmarked for the proposed state by the said resolution." [46]

I find it difficult to understand why Cattan includes the Balfour Declaration in that list and not the Palestine Mandate. He may have done so because it is so much easier to treat the Declaration as if it claimed a legal significance, which it does not have, and then proceed to prove that it lacks that significance, than to put for-

"described the Communities under the Mandate as subjects of international law" (Cattan, *Palestine,* p. 251). But that resolution is no authority for his thesis as to the "legal sovereignty" of the Arabs over Palestine, for what it said, *inter alia,* was this: "the Mandate is created in each case by act of the Council of the League of Nations" and "that act of Mandate defines the obligations of the Mandatory Power" (H. Wehberg, *Institut de Droit International, Tableau général des résolutions, 1873-1956,* Bâle, 1957, p. 18). And, as already pointed out, the Palestine Mandate imposed on the Mandatory Power the task of setting up a Jewish national home in Palestine. Moreover, throughout the years of its existence, the League of Nations fully exercised its supervisory powers to ensure that this obligation was faithfully carried out.

46. Cattan, *Palestine,* p. 255.

ward any persuasive legal arguments against the validity of the Palestine Mandate.

At all events, Cattan reiterates the old Arab contention that "at no time did the British Government as the author of such declaration possess any right of sovereignty over Palestine, whether on the date on which the Balfour Declaration was made or at any time thereafter, which could have enabled it to recognize any rights in favour of the Jewish people in or over Palestine" [47], and that "from the juridical standpoint, therefore, any claim by the Jews to Palestine on the basis of the Balfour Declaration is entirely groundless, if not plainly nonsensical" [48]. "The Balfour Declaration", he adds, "... never possessed any juridical value." [49]

This line of argument is pointless. The Balfour Declaration was never intended to determine the fate and future of Palestine. All that that document provided was that "His Majesty's Government *view with favour* [50] the es-

47. *Ibid.*   48. *Ibid.,* p. 260.

49. *Ibid.,* p. 255. It is surprising that Cattan also sees fit to rely on Professor Mallison's article (Cattan, *ibid.,* p. 256), for in it Mallison specifically expresses the view that "the Balfour Declaration is now a part of customary international law" and that while "the Anglo-American Convention on Palestine, 1924, is no longer in effect, as such, ... the Balfour Declaration included in it is valid as customary law ...". See: W. T. Mallison Jr., "The Zionist-Israel Juridical Claims to Constitute 'The Jewish People' Nationality Entity and to Confer Membership in it: Appraisal in Public International Law", *The George Washington Law Review,* vol. 32 (Washington 1964), p. 1030 and p. 1035, note 230. I confess that it is difficult to grasp the full meaning of this statement; but one thing is clear — it can hardly be said to add to the force of Cattan's case.

50. Italics added.

tablishment in Palestine of a national home for the Jewish people and *will use its best endeavours* [51] to facilitate the achievement of this object..." [52]. There was nothing at all wrong in giving such a promise. It was no more an infringement of international law than was giving pro-mises to the Arabs and other nations during the War. The Balfour Declaration became a binding and unchallenge-able international obligation from the moment when it was embodied in the Palestine Mandate, which the dis-tinguished judge, Moore, went so far as to define — in his opinion in the Permanent Court of International Justice in the Mavrommatis Case — as "in a sense an [international] legislative act of the Council" [53]. That the Palestine Mandate was *sui generis* in so far as interna-tional Mandates are concerned in no way detracts from its legality [54]. Cattan's constant reference to the Balfour Declaration, while intentionally ignoring the fact that it

51. Italics added.
52. By the way, the Balfour Declaration was not the first to be issued in support of Zionist aspirations. It was preceded by the declaration given on 4 June 1917 by Jules Cambon, Secretary-General of the French Foreign Office, to Nahum Sokolow, one of the leaders of the World Zionist Organization, in these words: "The French Government, which entered this present war to defend a people wrongfully attacked, and which continues to struggle to assure the victory of right over might, can but feel sympathy for your cause ['the renaissance of the Jewish nationality in the land from which the people of Israel were exiled so many centuries ago'], the triumph of which is bound up with that of the Allies." See: N. Sokolow, *History of Zionism, 1600—1918,* vol. II (London, 1919), p. 53.
53. *Permanent Court of International Justice, Series A, No. 2, The Mavrommatis Palestine Concessions* (1924), p. 69.
54. See Feinberg, *The Arab-Israel Conflict,* pp. 38–44.

formed part of the Mandate, makes his case meaningless
from a legal point of view.

5. *The power of the General Assembly of the United
Nations in respect of the Resolution on the partition
of Palestine*

Cattan stresses that his "inquiry does not concern the
wisdom or justice of partition...", but whether the Partition Resolution was within the Assembly's powers at all.
In his opinion, "the legal position in this regard is quite
clear and obvious [55].... . The partition resolution... lacked
all juridical basis, was not within the powers of the General Assembly, and could not confer any valid title upon
Israel over such part of Palestine as was earmarked for
the Jewish state [56].... . The Arabs had a perfect legal right
to oppose the dismemberment of their country and to
defend the territorial integrity of their homeland." [57]

55. Cattan, *Palestine,* p. 261. See also: *ibid.,* p. 262.
56. *Ibid.,* p. 265. See also: *ibid.,* pp. 268, 269.
57. On this point, Cattan rests his case on passages from the report
    of Sub-Committee II of the 1947 Assembly's Ad Hoc Com-
    mittee on the Palestine Question (*ibid.,* pp. 263–264). He
    also draws on the Sub-Committee's conclusions on a number
    of other occasions (*ibid.,* pp. 28, 29) and even introduced,
    in an appendix to his book, a map prepared by it on land-
    ownership in Palestine in 1945 (*ibid.,* p. 210). It is per-
    tinent to remark here that Sub-Committee II was composed
    solely of representatives of those States which, in principle,
    opposed the partition plan, as put forward by the majority of
    the members of U.N.S.C.O.P. (United Nations Special Com-
    mittee on Palestine), and favoured the establishment of "an
    independent, unitary State", as put forward by a minority.
    On the Sub-Committee were the representatives of six Arab
    States and of Pakistan, Afghanistan and Colombia. There was

It is surprising that Cattan — like certain other jurists — resorts to this argument that the Assembly exceeded its powers, for, already in 1950, the International
Court of Justice, in its Advisory Opinion on South West
Africa, unanimously held that "the competence to determine and modify the international status... [of a Mandated territory]" rests with the Mandatory, acting with
the consent of the United Nations Assembly [58]. Cattan
cites the statement made by the Chinese representative, at
the winding up session of the League of Nations in 1946,
that the Charter of the United Nations contains no provision for the assumption by the United Nations of the
League's functions with regard to Mandates [59]. But,
whatever weight Cattan may attribute to the opinion of
China's representative, the fact remains that the International Court has held otherwise. "The Court", writes
Professor Bastid, "... has held that the Assembly of the
United Nations replaces the organs of control already
existing as part of the machinery of the League of Na-

a feeling that, to avoid the appearance of one-sidedness, its
composition should be altered, and the representatives of two
Arab States were prepared to vacate their places in favour of
neutrals or of countries which had not definitely committed
themselves to any particular solution of the Palestine Question.
The Chairman of the Sub-Committee, Colombia's representative, did not see fit to accede to the proposal made in this
connection and, in consequence of this refusal, he resigned.
The representative of Pakistan was elected in his place. See:
Yearbook of the United Nations, 1947—1948 (New York,
1949), p. 240.

58. *International Status of South-West Africa, Advisory Opinion*:
I.C.J. Reports 1950, p. 144.

59. Cattan, *Palestine,* p. 261.

tions" [60]; and she then goes on to say: "The Court has equally recognized [the Assembly's] power to modify the international status [of a Mandated territory]." [61] This includes the power to change the status of a Mandated territory by setting up two States. Thus, for example, the Mandate for Syria and the Lebanon of 1922 expressly provided that, on its termination, two separate States would be set up — not a single unitary State. Moreover, when — in 1937 — the British Royal Commission voiced the possibility of the partition of Palestine, and the Council of the League of Nations and the Permanent Mandates Commission were asked to consider that proposal, no questions at all were raised as to the illegality of partition. Nor did the United Nations regard itself as incompetent to approve the partition of the trust territory of Ruanda-Urundi into two States — Rwanda and Burundi — despite the fact that the trusteeship agreement of 1946 contained no express or implied authority for partition of the territory. And, in 1962, the Assembly of the United Nations felt under no obligation to reject *a limine*, on grounds of illegality, the plan for the partition of South West Africa, but went on to discuss the substantive merits of that plan [62].

60. S. Bastid, "La jurisprudence de la Cour Internationale de Justice", *R.A.D.I.*, tome 78 (Paris, 1952), p. 665.
61. *Ibid.*, p. 667.
62. For details on this question see: Feinberg, *The Arab-Israel Conflict*, pp. 55—71.

6. *The status of Israel's territory under the Armistice Agreements*

Since, as we have seen, Cattan denies Israel's sovereignty even over the territory allotted to it in the Partition Resolution, it goes without saying that he does not recognize its right to territories beyond the boundaries provided for in that Resolution but included within its boundaries under the Armistice Agreements [63]. In addition to his general arguments in support of his thesis, he invokes — in the present context — yet another reason: "Israel's occupation of the Palestinian Territory under the Armistice Agreements" "is not and cannot be a source of title" [64], for in each of them (with Egypt, Jordan, the Lebanon and Syria) it is "specifically provided that the armistice lines are not to be construed as political or territorial boundaries and are delineated 'without prejudice to the ultimate settlement of the Palestine Question' " [65]. The first point to make here is that in the above sentence, cited by Cattan from the text of the Armistice Agreements, the word "peaceful" is omitted between the words "ultimate" and "settlement", without this omission being indicated, as is customary, by a dotted line or dashes. Moreover, each of the four Agreements stipulates that "no provision... shall in any way prejudice the rights, claims and positions of either Party", words which constitute an unequivocal acknowledgement of the fact that Israel, too, has rights, claims, and so on. Secondly, it is

63. Cattan, *Palestine,* pp. 157, 160.
64. *Ibid.,* p. 272.   65. *Ibid.*

difficult to understand why Cattan ignores the many other provisions of the Armistice Agreements which are of so much greater significance than the one that he refers to. Thus, each of the Agreements states that its purpose is "to facilitate the transition from the present truce to permanent peace in Palestine"; that "the right of each Party to its security and freedom from fear of attack by the armed forces of the other shall be fully respected"; that "no aggressive action by the armed forces... of either Party shall be undertaken, planned or threatened against the people or the armed forces of the other"; that neither Party shall "... advance beyond or pass over for any purpose whatsoever the Armistice Demarcation Lines"; and that the Parties are not "to revise or to suspend the application" of the provisions forbidding the use of force, even by mutual consent. In the light of these perfectly clear provisions, there is only one possible answer to the question of the legal status of the territories outside the boundaries delineated by the Partition Resolution: the Arab States undertook to respect the armistice lines and refrain from revising them unless Israel give its consent to such revision in the course of the drafting of a "permanent peace settlement" [66]. I should add that, even if this prohibition were not expressly included in the Armistice Agreements, it would apply by virtue of Article 2, paragraph 4, of the Charter of the United Nations, which forbids the threat or use of force against "the territorial integrity or political independence of any State" [67].

66. See: Feinberg, *The Arab-Israel Conflict,* pp. 76–79.
67. In a textbook on international law published in the Soviet

And those who in 1970 drafted the "Declaration on Principles of International Law concerning Friendly Relations and Cooperation among States in accordance with the Charter of the United Nations", formally and unanimously adopted by the twenty-fifth General Assembly, saw fit to declare in express terms that the prohibition against the threat or use of force also applies to "international lines of demarcation such as armistice lines" [68].

7. The contention that Israel has no claim to sovereignty over a single square inch of Palestinian soil

Cattan concludes his discussion of the question of sovereignty with the following statement: "The legal status of Israel in relation to the entirety of the territory which it occupied prior to June 5, 1967 is identical with the status in relation to the territories which it seized since June 5, 1967: it is the status of a belligerent occupier. And it is indifferent whether Israel is considered a belligerent occupier or a conqueror. In neither case can

Union in 1969, we read: "In so far as a general armistice is a decisive step towards the restoration of peace — and that is the only normal position from the point of view of international law — every attempt to evade the armistice and renew hostilities ... must be regarded as constituting an act of aggression ... . A general armistice cannot, therefore, be cancelled and is, in principle, to be considered to be of unlimited duration". See: *The Academy of Sciences of the Soviet Union, Course of International Law*, vol. 5, (Moscow, 1969), p. 405 (Russian).

68. Resolution 2625 (XXV), U.N., *General Assembly, Official Records, Twenty-Fifth Session*, Suppl. No. 28 (17/8028), 1970, p. 122.

it acquire sovereignty." [69] Here, again, Cattan seeks to strengthen his general legal thesis by adducing additional arguments. One is that "Israel does not possess any recognized frontiers" and, in this connection, he cites the following sentence from H. O. Cooke's book — "Israel a Blessing and a Curse": "Israel, alone among all the countries of the world, possesses not a single square inch of territory which she could assuredly proclaim to be her own in perpetuity." [70] But the absence of permanent frontiers does not detract from the status of a State as a sovereign State. In December 1920, Albania became a member of the League of Nations, as a sovereign and independent State, even though it had no fixed boundaries at that time [71], a fact which the Permanent Court of International Justice referred to in one of its opinions without comment or reservation [72]. And in 1921, Lithuania became a member of the League despite its boundary dispute with Poland [73]. "Both reason and history demonstrate", stressed Professor Jessup, in the course of the Security Council meeting at which Israel's application for admission to the United Nations was debated, "that

69. Cattan, *Palestine,* pp. 273–274.
70. *Ibid.,* p. 274.
71. See: F. P. Walters, *A History of the League of Nations* (Oxford, 1960), p. 123, where it is said: "As for Albania [when it became a member of the League], her frontiers were still undefined ... ."
72. *P.C.I.J., Series B, No. 9, Question of the Monastery of Saint Nahum* (1924), p. 10.
73. See: N. Feinberg, "L'admission de nouveaux membres à la Société des Nations et à l'Organisation des Nations Unies", *R.A.D.I.,* tome 80 (Paris, 1953), p. 329.

the concept of territory does not necessarily include precise delimitation of the boundaries of that territory." [74] And Professor Guggenheim justly remarks that, "bearing in mind the principle of effectiveness, it is not necessary that the law of nations establish rules of an imperative nature regarding the need to demarcate the territory of the State.... New States can, therefore, be recognized in international law even if their frontiers have not yet been definitively settled." [75]

The second reason adduced by Cattan is that "Israel is not recognized by the Arab States nor by a large number of other States. More important still, Israel is not recognized by the original people of Palestine in whom sovereignty lies." [76] Here, too, the non-recognition of Israel by the Arab States, and by a number of other States supporting them [77], cannot derogate from Israel's status as a sovereign State or impair its rights as a legal international entity. The Institute of International Law — the highest

74. U.N. Doc. S/PV. 383, 2 December 1948, p. 11.
75. See: P. Guggenheim, *Traité de droit international public*, tome I (Genève, 1953), pp. 379—380. See also: *North Sea Continental Shelf, Judgment, I.C.J. Reports 1969*, p. 32.
76. Cattan, *Palestine*, p. 275.
77. Cattan's claim is that the number of States which have not recognized Israel is "large" (*ibid.*, p. 275). But Professor Quincy Wright describes the position far more accurately when he speaks of "its [Israel's] recognition by most States" and goes on to point out that even the Arab States recognized Israel, with qualifications, in a declaration to the United Nations Conciliation Commission on May 12, 1949; by this he means the Protocol signed on that date, to which we shall refer, later on, in a different context. See: Quincy Wright, "The Middle East Problem", *American Journal of International Law*, vol. 64, No. 2 (1970), p. 271.

scientific body in this branch of law — has held that "the existence of a new State, and all the juridical consequences of such existence, are not affected by the refusal of one, or more States, to recognize it" [78]. And this same principle was embodied in the Charter of the Organization of American States, confirmed in 1948 at the Bogota Conference, in these words: "The political existence of the State is independent of recognition by other States. Even before being recognized, the State has the right to defend its integrity and independence, to provide for its preservation and prosperity and consequently to organize itself as it sees fit... ." [79] In his lectures at the Hague Academy of International Law, Professor Rousseau dwells on the illogical and inconsistent nature of current international practice, whereby one State withholds its recognition from another, despite the collective recognition extended to the other State by its very admission as a member of the United Nations. In this context he refers to the non-recognition of Israel by the Arab States and criticizes the Secretariat of the United Nations for having yielded to this practice and even upheld it. Indeed, he goes on to define the resultant situation as "the contamination of legal principles by political opportunism" [80]. It

78. H. Wehberg, *op. cit.*, p. 11.
79. "Charter of the Organization of American States, Bogotá, April 30, 1948", *American Journal of International Law,* vol. 46, No. 2, Official Documents (1952), p. 46.
80. Ch. Rousseau, "Principes de droit international public", *R.A.D.I.,* tome 93 (Leyde, 1958), p. 457. Professor Rolin, too, in his lectures at the Hague Academy of International Law, has expressed the view that, once a State has been admitted to the United Nations, "old Members must no longer contest

seems clear, then, that Cattan's argument, that Israel has
no permanent boundaries and is not recognized by a number of States, is of no significance in so far as its status as
an independent State is concerned and does not detract,
in any way, from the rights that it enjoys as such.

the international personality of the new Member .... The new
State can claim the protection extended to it by the general
international law, in particular — respect for its independence,
inviolability of its territory, the right to a flag. All that can be
denied it is the active or passive exercise of the *jus legationis*"
or, in other words, the other States cannot be compelled to
enter into diplomatic relations with it. See: H. Rolin, "Les
principes de droit international public", *R.A.D.I.* tome 77
(Paris, 1951), pp. 332–333. And Brownlie writes: "Few would
take the view that the Arab neighbours of Israel can afford
to treat her as a nonentity: the responsible United Nations
organs and the individual States have taken the view that
Israel is protected, and bound, by the principles of the United
Nations Charter governing the use of force" (Brownlie, *op. cit.,*
p. 85). See also: Feinberg, *The Arab-Israel Conflict,* pp. 71—79.

Arab Palestine: Phoenix or Phantom?

DON PERETZ

BECAUSE many Palestine Arabs are stateless under international law, their importance has frequently been overlooked in the numerous parleys and in the skein of complex international negotiations over the Middle East crisis. The Palestine dispute, as it is euphemistically labeled in the United Nations, has appeared on the annual agenda of the U. N. General Assembly for over twenty years, generally under the guise of assistance to refugees. Neither the principal antagonists nor the major powers officially acknowledge existence of the Palestinians as a nation-party to the dispute.

In a recent interview Israeli Prime Minister Golda Meir emphasized that there is no such thing as either a Palestinian nation or people. Palestine Arabs are considered by the Government of Israel as little different from those of the surrounding Arab states. When queried about creation of a new Arab Palestine on the West Bank, Prime Minister Meir pointed out that it would be too small; only if it were part of Jordan or Israel could the area remain viable. Furthermore, she emphasized, there is no representative body speaking for the so-called Palestinians. Had the Arabs who fled in 1948 not urged Jordan's King Hussein into the June 1967 war the Hashemite Kingdom might well have become the successor state to Palestine. Israel's experience with the already existing fourteen Arab states discourages it from supporting the creation of still another. Furthermore, to treat the Palestinians as a political entity would be inconsistent with Israel's internal and external policies. At present the Israeli Government considers its principal antagonists to be the Arab states of Jordan, Syria, Iraq and, to a greater extent, the United Arab Republic. The major goal of Israel's Arab policy is to reach agreement with the U.A.R., whose President Nasser is considered the chief obstacle to peace. The Israelis believe that only after he has been convinced of the need to come to terms with Israel will other Arab nations follow suit.

The reluctance of Israel and the major powers to recognize the Palestinians only inflames the latters' already deep hostility toward the West. Their situation is not unlike that of other self-identified national groups in the Middle East which sought international recognition during this century—such as the Armenians, the Jews and the Kurds.

The national identity of the Palestine Arabs has gone through a cycle of: discovery in the 1920s, political failure in the 1930s, near abandonment in the 1940s, disillusionment in the 1950s and '60s, and rebirth, rediscovery and new expectations since 1967.

II

Prior to establishment of the British Mandate at the end of World War I, there was no distinctive Palestinian people, nor political entity. The land and its inhabitants were considered backwater regions of the less developed Ottoman Syrian provinces. Only after establishment of the British Mandate in 1920, and the rise of Jewish nationalism in the country, did a distinctive Palestinian Arab consciousness emerge in response to the challenge of these two forms of European intrusion. In that era Palestinian Arab nationalism, led by a coalition of Muslim landed gentry and upper-middle-class Christian Arab families, resembled nationalist movements then emerging elsewhere in the Arab East. Some 80 percent of its constituency was a politically unsophisticated rural peasantry. There was little if any ideology, and that little was devoid of social content. Major emphasis was on elimination of foreign control and influence—in the case of Palestine, British controls and European Jewish influences. The Palestinian Arab national effort culminated in the abortive rebellion between 1936 and 1939; it failed because of massive use of British armed force and lack of internal cohesion among nationalist leaders. Nevertheless, heroes of this rebellion are still eulogized by the new nationalist organizations; their military failures and inability to form a cohesive political movement are overlooked.

The major revision of Great Britain's policies in Palestine, embodied in the 1939 White Paper, was a great victory for Palestine-Arab nationalism since it made an independent Arab state seem inevitable. Nevertheless, most of the country's Arab leaders slipped into lethargy and paralysis of action which was to last nearly thirty years. By the end of World War II, Jewish nationalism in Palestine was much more dynamic, well organized and politically effective. Both within the country and abroad, Zionists and their supporters surpassed the Palestine-

Arab nationalists in militant political activity, finally voiding
the White Paper and achieving their goal of statehood. The
disjointed and inchoate Palestine-Arab nationalist movement
reached its nadir in 1947–48 with defeat and exodus of the Arab
population from Jewish-held areas.

Until termination of the Mandate in 1948, both Arab and
Jewish residents of the country were identified as British subjects, although they did not hold British citizenship. When Israel
was established, its Jewish and some of its Arab inhabitants became citizens of the new state. More than one million Palestine
Arabs were left in an international limbo, with no recognized
citizenship status. Within the next decade, Palestinians who remained in the Hashemite Kingdom and in those parts of Palestine annexed to it acquired Jordanian citizenship; a small number of Christian Palestinians qualified for Lebanese citizenship,
and the others—some 700,000—have remained stateless persons until today. Syria, while refusing citizenship to Palestine
refugees, granted them most, but not all, citizenship rights.
Lebanon was reluctant to offer citizenship to the large number of
Muslim Palestine refugees it harbored for fear they would destroy the delicate balance between the country's Christians and
Muslims. Egypt, already one of the world's most overpopulated
nations, kept most of the Palestinians under its jurisdiction
penned up in the tiny Gaza enclave, which was governed as
though it were still a separate country rather than part of the
U. A. R.

During the next two decades "Palestinian Arab" became
synonymous with "Palestine refugee" in international consciousness. Even in Arab countries and among the Palestinians themselves there was little distinction, and annual debates over the
refugees at the United Nations and the activities of UNRWA
further blurred any clear difference. The most visible evidence
of Palestinian existence was the network of refugee camps where
tensions between the inhabitants and natives of host countries
forcefully delineated the occupants from other Arabs.

Jordan needed its Palestinians as a population base for the new
Hashemite Kingdom, but all the other Arab states encouraged
the displaced Arabs to retain their national identity. This was
not difficult since few were socially accepted in the host countries
and many non-Palestinian Arabs regarded the outsiders as a disruptive and troublesome element. Palestinians therefore main-

tained their old social structure and family ties, formed their
own political groups, intermarried with each other and continued to regard themselves as a distinctive national group.
Recognition of this identity was further encouraged by the
United Nations through the network of relief, social and particularly educational services provided to Palestine refugees
through UNRWA. In the UNRWA schools, where refugee
children were educated by Palestinian teachers, a new generation of ardent Palestine patriots was raised. The most zealous
proponent of militant activism against the "intruder state" of
Israel was this new generation of U.N.-educated youth.

Various Arab governments attempted to exploit the distinctive
character of the Palestine Arab community before 1967. Jordan,
Iraq, Syria and Egypt encouraged and gave sustenance to Palestine Arab nationalist groups of one type or another. Usually
these groups were instruments of national policy of various Arab
governments, which provided them with political and material
support, including arms for so-called commando organizations
which supposedly operated independently. Inter-Arab efforts to
give political respectability and national élan to the Palestinian
movement resulted in formal recognition of the Palestine Liberation Organization at the 1964 summit meeting of Arab leaders in Cairo. While Ahmed Shukairy, recognized by the conference as leader of the PLO, led it through a maze of verbal
pyrotechnics, up to 1967 it had failed to gain real political autonomy or to galvanize strong popular support. In effect, it remained an instrument of inter-Arab policy manœuvres.

After the 1967 fiasco, Palestinians were disillusioned with
nearly all the established leadership, organizations and governments; Shukairy and the old-line leadership associated with him
were discredited. Wherever there were large concentrations of
Palestinians, diverse new groups emerged, led by a younger
generation unfettered by the political and social commitments
of its elders. The new leadership reflected the transformation of
the Palestine Arab community that had occurred during the
"lost" generation. Living in or near to urban areas, most Palestinians had lost their peasant skills and outlook, acquiring many
of the views and sophistications of town and city. Several hundred thousand were employed in urban trade, commerce, industry and ancillary occupations. More than one hundred thousand
had developed skills in the Arabian oil states. In two decades,

approximately 50,000 Palestinians attended universities, nearly equaling the number of young professionals trained by Israel during this period. The new generation of Palestinians had all the attributes of a displaced minority group, including great ✓ aspirations for upward mobility, political restiveness, and a core of revolutionary-minded young men who aspired to "reëstablish the homeland."

Several dozen new Palestinian organizations were created within two years of the 1967 defeat. By far their greatest emphasis was on military or paramilitary activity aimed at Israel. Disillusioned with failures of conventional tactics against Israel and with Arab government fiascos, most of the new groups drew inspiration from guerrilla techniques and activities modeled on those of Algeria, North Viet Nam and Latin American revolutionaries. The objective was no longer that of Arab governments such as the U.A.R. or Jordan—to achieve Israel's withdrawal from the occupied territories and to circumscribe and delimit ✓ its frontiers—but to obliterate completely the Jewish state.

In the ebb and flow of inter-Arab politics since 1967, the new Palestinian groups have merged, subdivided, reunited and again fragmented, finally organizing themselves into three or four principal political-military organizations: the Palestine Liberation Organization; *Fatah;* the Popular Front for the Liberation of Palestine; and *Saiqa.* While there are political differences and diversities in the type of commando or terrorist activity each advocates, personality clashes rather than ideology often account for the variety of organizations. They differ generally from the pre-1967 groups in their asserted independence from Arab governments, in the growing number of young intellectuals and professionals they have enlisted in their ranks, and in the extent of support they have received from Arabs generally and from Palestinians in particular. While most of the organizations indirectly draw subsidies from Arab governments, including Kuwait and Libya, they have also succeeded in rallying substantial private contributions from wealthy Palestinians and other zealous supporters throughout the Arab world.

The reliability of commando communiqués is highly questionable, but their political effect throughout the Arab East is becoming increasingly obvious. Within the last two years they have created a new identity for the Palestinians. "Refugee" is no longer synonymous with "Palestine Arab." Increasingly, "Palestinian" is identified with the commando warrior rather than with the downtrodden displaced person. This is evident among Arab students, intellectuals, professionals and the man in the street, from Casablanca to Kuwait. While much commando activity is exaggerated if not entirely fictitious, there is sufficient substance to their achievements to have created a commando mystique. Posters on university campuses and in government offices and shopping centers; the daily radio bulletins and pronouncements by commando leaders; and the Arabic press—all have created in Arab consciousness the image of a new Palestinian who, unlike the traditional and now aging military leadership, is young, vigorous, intelligent, self-sacrificing, intensely patriotic and single-mindedly dedicated to reëstablishment of Arab Palestine. This image pervades even the thinking of commando critics such as Lebanese and Jordanian officials, who recognize that fedayeen terrorism in Israel serves only to weaken their own stability.

Not only Israel but several Arab governments are targets of commando activities. Some leaders of the organizations aim to overthrow any politician who might interfere with their guerrilla strategy against Israel; others have set their sights on total revolution of Arab political life. Among the former are leaders of Fatah and PLO who can coöperate with conservative monarchs or with radical socialists. Within the past year these two less revolutionary-minded groups have been involved in machinations behind the scenes to topple the ruling establishments of Jordan, Lebanon, Saudi Arabia and Libya. In Jordan and Lebanon, commando leaders have sought, with some success, to gain control of strategically located territories for training recruits, or for striking across the Israeli border. The commandos are reported to have taken over fourteen of the fiftcen refugee camps in Lebanon and to have free access to most camps in Jordan. This has led to a de facto partition in which King Hussein's government has been forced to acquiesce. Because of the wide support enjoyed by the commandos among Jordan's largely Palestine Arab population, the Hashemite Kingdom has found it impossible to repress them and on occasion it even coöperates in providing covering fire for their movements across the frontier. Consequently Jordan has become the recipient of nearly daily artillery and air strikes, which have leveled towns, disrupted agricultural life in the river valley and threatened both political and economic stability.

In Lebanon, where Palestinians are a small minority but have considerable support among the population, the commandos threaten to end the country's relative isolation from direct military confrontation with Israel. Since the first Arab-Israeli war of 1948 the Lebanese-Israeli border has been more or less free of the military clashes that have periodically erupted between Israel and Syria, Jordan and Egypt. While willing to permit the organizations free movement, fund raising and propaganda activity within its borders, the Lebanese Government has been reluctant to countenance establishment of guerrilla enclaves. The dilemma has torn the government apart, divided the population into pro and anti commandos, and led to threats of both Syrian and Israeli intervention on behalf of or against the Palestinians. But now the commandos are asserting themselves in all areas they deem vital—including the Lebanese frontier. They recognize no right of withdrawal from confrontation with Israel, insisting that every Arab and Arab state has an obligation to join the "War of Liberation."

Members of even the "conservative" organizations were involved in an aborted coup in Saudi Arabia this fall resulting in arrest and imprisonment of several score high-ranking Saudi army officers. In Libya, where hundreds of Palestinians have found niches as teachers, physicians and professionals, they played a role in the successful overthrow of the monarchy. The new Libyan Republic's first civilian Prime Minister is a Haifa native whose family left when clashes between Jews and Arabs made life in Palestine difficult. He has asserted his and his government's full support for liberation of his former homeland.

Public approval of the commandos has become so widespread that Egypt's President Nasser has been placed in the ambiguous position of offering them his blessings at the same time that he calls for implementation of the U.N. November 1967 resolution. More recently, the Soviet Union has also withdrawn its disapproval of the commandos as a reactionary and disruptive element. Now they have been awarded Soviet accolades as fighters for independence of the people of Palestine.

The most wide-ranging goals have been stated by the small but influential and hyper-activist Popular Front for the Liberation of Palestine. Led by a zealous Christian Palestinian, George Habash, the PFLP emerged from the militant Arab Nationalist Movement, an organization of intellectuals whose goals were considered so revolutionary that it was banned in most Arab nations after its creation several years before the 1967 débâcle. Although it now concentrates its activities on the Palestine issue, its goals encompass the Arab world. The PFLP is splintered into Marxist and more Marxist factions. The most zealous would, with the aid of the Chinese Communists or any other equally revolutionary group, strive now for total revolution throughout the Arab world using any tactic necessary to bring down the political and social structure of all "corrupt" Arab states.

Attacks by the Front on commercial aircraft and civilian centers within Israel and abroad are an embarrassment to less zealous compatriots and to Arab governments. It was a PFLP attack on an Israeli commercial airliner that precipitated the raid on the Beirut airport last year, followed by dissolution of the Lebanese Government and continued internal political crisis. Since the Israeli Government holds accountable Arab countries from which such attacks are planned or undertaken, PFLP tactics threaten continued political crisis in the Arab world. At parleys between the Lebanese Government and various commando leaders conducted last summer in Beirut, the Front openly stated its aim to bring down the country's "reactionary" communal political system.

III

It is increasingly evident that instead of being a tool of Arab governmental policies, the new Palestine organizations are striving to reverse the pattern of control and to exercise strong influence on those governments which at one time controlled Palestinian destinies. The commandos have in effect become an instrument of pressure for more militant action by governments such as Lebanon, Jordan and the U.A.R. The support that commandos have rallied among university students and other leaders of Arab opinion has undermined the few voices of moderation existing prior to 1967.

The commando mystique clearly extends to Arab citizens of Israel and those in the occupied territories. A survey conducted in 1968 by Hebrew University sociologists indicated that Arab defeat in the Six Day War increased respect for the state among Israeli Arab schoolchildren but also greatly intensified feelings of hatred toward Israel, deepened Arab consciousness and made more determined than ever before the resolve to wage still another war against the Jewish state. With each passing month of Israeli occupation, the number of young Arab Israeli supporters of the commando movement grows. During the first half of 1969, the number of youths who were apprehended for supporting commando activities was nearly one hundred. While small in relation to the Arab population of Israel, the number exceeds the total of Israeli Arabs arrested for such activities since the state was established twenty years ago.

One of the most serious aspects of this phenomenon is that it threatens to undermine relationships laboriously built up since 1949 between the Government of Israel and its Arab minority. Though not ideal, relations had slowly become tolerable. Israeli Arabs had come to be recognized as citizens and many had voluntarily, even willingly, accepted this status. During the past twenty years Israel's universities have graduated several hundred Arabs. While many have been dissatisfied with their minority position, a considerable number found a place in Israeli society. Arabs worked in lower- and middle-level government posts and a few rose to become police officers. However, with increased commando activity, there is growing apprehension among both Israeli Arabs and Jews about the future of amicable relationships between the communities. After every incident the arrest of scores of Arabs and destruction of suspected terrorist homes by Israeli security authorities embitter feelings in both communities. Those who for twenty years strove to liberalize Israel's policies toward its Arab minority find themselves increasingly isolated; this is reflected in the recent election results, which increased by a substantial percentage the number of Knesset members favoring a hard line toward the Arabs.

So far, commando military escapades along the frontiers and terrorist activities within Israel have failed to disrupt life or to have a serious impact on its ever increasing military capacity. The border fighting has claimed 80 percent of the more than 2,000 casualties sustained by Israel since the 1967 War (nearly 500 of them fatal); 10 percent were inside the occupied areas and 10 percent in pre-1967 Israel. This fall Defense Minister Moshe Dayan noted that casualty figures had increased from an average of 50 a month in the year after the war to an average of 157 in the third postwar year. While the casualty rate from Arab confrontations is still less than the number suffered in automobile accidents in Israel, it has an obvious impact on public attitudes and further explains the turn toward militancy evident in the 1969 elections.

Indirectly the economy has been affected by the labor shortages caused by the large number of men under arms and by the need for reservists to serve up to age 55. Nevertheless, the economy is booming again, though foreign currency reserves are falling to a dangerously low level and the military budget eats up to 21 percent of Israel's GNP—three times more than in most modern nations.

There is also fear among civil libertarians that security restrictions in the Arab community could lead to increasingly restrictive measures against all dissidents, including Jews. While the vast majority of Israelis support their government's internal and external Arab policies, the small critical minority feels that it may be threatened if commando activities lead to expanded interference by security authorities in Israel's internal life.

IV

In recent months some commando intellectuals have become aware of the importance of winning over potential Jewish dissidents within Israel as well as gaining support in the West. Policy-planning groups in the high command of PLO, now recognized as the representative body of most commando organizations with the exception of the PFLP, have opened discussions about long-range plans in the occupied territories. However, they have failed to come forward with a program that would elicit support or even interest among any substantial number of Israelis or their supporters. At best their political goals are vague and ill-defined.

The commandos state categorically that they seek to destroy the government and state of Israel, its Zionist institutions and its exclusive Jewish character; they brook no compromise based on the pre-1967 borders or even the 1947 U. N. partition resolution. Some leaders have indicated that Palestine would become an Arab state; others have been more ambiguous. None has publically recognized the possibility of coexistence between Arab and Hebrew nationalism, both of which have the identical attributes of a linguistic base, a rich cultural and historical heritage and deeply instilled popular consciousness, and both of which derive from a major religio-national ethos.

Hebrew broadcasts of the commando organizations directed

to Israel are listened to with derision rather than fear or hope of discovering any serious political intent. The recently announced objective of converting Palestine into a democratic secular state ✓ in which all Jews, Muslims and Christians will live in equity is not believed because of the long years in which the people as well as the state of Israel were threatened. The organizations have yet to define clearly the kind of government they propose, the status of minority groups, whether or not the country is to be an Arab state, or what is to become of its Hebrew-speaking residents who retain an attachment to their language and cultural, social and political institutions. The tragedy in this situation—and the root of conflict—is that each group denies the other the right of such identity and strives to assert exclusive control over the area that each believes to be the essential heartland of its national life.

The Palestine Arab nationalist movement represented in the varied groups that have been created since 1967 is still run through with many of the difficulties and shortcomings that have characterized modern Arab politics. The mystique and slogans full of emotional overtones tend to vitiate clear-cut, well-defined policy goals. The tendency to rely on exaggerated battle communiqués, while fortifying their image and mystique, undermines political credibility among those whom the commandos seek most to influence—the Jews of Israel, as well as influential outsiders. Above all there is lack of cohesive leadership. While the Fatah commando and PLO leader, Yasir Arafat, is the most visible and most colorful personality, he still lacks the charisma that Egypt's President Nasser so successfully capitalized on to become the pre-1967 leader of Arab nationalism. During the past two years there have been several instances in which members of one commando group have sought to undermine competing organizations. Yet despite these shortcomings the Palestine movement and the new organizations have become a factor of significance which cannot be ignored in any settlement of the Middle East crisis.

As the more militant groups strike out with increasing frequency at targets such as American oil companies, they threaten to sever the supply of oil to the West. The Front and other commando organizations have threatened to extend their attacks against other Western "imperialist" targets in the Middle East, but if they do so they will merely weaken further the already tenuous relations between the United States and the few remaining friendly Arab governments in the region.

Some Palestinians have demanded that they be represented in the deliberations convened to deal with the crisis. This presents an international dilemma. Although some Third World nations are moving toward recognition of a Palestine entity, so far even the U.A.R. has dragged its feet on clarification of long-range policy toward Palestine. Jordan hesitates, since recognition of the Palestine entity would give approval to partition of the Hashemite Kingdom. Neither the United States nor Great Britain can sanction territorial fragmentation of one of their chief Arab allies in the area.

Yet it would be in the interest of all parties concerned if the Palestinians had a recognized voice in negotiations. There are a number of issues in the dispute that are of only indirect concern to the non-Palestinian Arab states, but must sooner or later result in direct contacts between Israelis and Palestine Arabs. These include the return or compensation for Palestine Arab property now held by Israel; the future of Jerusalem, which is not only a Jewish but a Palestinian Arab city; and the status of several hundred thousand stateless persons who left Israeli-held territory in 1948 and 1967. While Israel wants to negotiate with states as far removed from these issues as the U.A.R. or Syria, negotiations would be much more likely to succeed if they were carried on between those whose vital interests are most involved. As for the United States, it will find American interests and American friendships in the area becoming increasingly endangered if steps are not taken soon to reach an accord with what is now the most disruptive element in Middle East politics—the Arabs of Palestine.

The Position of the Palestinians in the Israeli-Arab Conflict and Their National Covenant (1968)

Y. HARKABI

Part I

THE PALESTINIANS IN THE ISRAEL-ARAB CONFLICT*

These days a sharp controversy is raging among us concerning the place of the Palestinians in the conflict, their collective identity and the question whether they are the party with whom Israel can negotiate a peace settlement.

Their self-definition as Palestinians gives them a strong sense of common identity. The overwhelming majority of them preserved their identity and attachment to Palestine despite the passage of time, their hardships and dispersion. This is also true of the period which preceded the Six Day War. Children who were born to Palestinian parents in other countries did not identify themselves to foreigners in terms of the country where they were born; they said rather, "I am from Haifa" or "I am from Jaffa," thus demonstrating their Palestinianism in a specific and concrete way.

It is true that states like the UAR and Iraq evoked the idea of "the Palestinian entity" in meetings of the Arab League from 1959 on, doing so for tactical reasons within inter-Arab rivalries, and the Palestine Liberation Organization was established by a decision of the Arab rulers at their First Summit Conference. However, the call for the Palestinians to organize themselves and assume the central role in the struggle against Israel came *also* from within the ranks of the Palestinians themselves. Such ideas recur with great forcefulness in the writings of Palestinians at the beginning of the sixties. This applies also to the fedayeen organizations. Though most of them were formed and continued to exist owing to the support of

---

3. By Y. Harkabi, Lecturer in Int'l Affairs, Hebrew Univ., formerly Brig. General and Head of the Strategic Research Dept. of the Ministry of Defense of Israel. This document was obtained through the courtesy of the Consulate Genera of Israel. (Translated by Y. Karmi.)

* Revised text of a lecture given at Tel-Aviv University on May 18, 1969 in memory of Moshe Haviv. Appeared in *Ma'ariv* November 21, 1969.

one or another Arab state, it would be a mistake to regard the Palestinian organizations as mere pawns that serve the aims of the Arab states.

A number of factors contributed to this feeling of identity and attachment to Palestine. First and foremost, the factor of a common place of origin, shared experiences, and common fate and suffering in the past and present. Another factor was the difficulty of absorption into Arab countries economically and, no less, socially. Despite the common language and cultural background, and notwithstanding Arab nationalism, the Palestinians felt like strangers in Arab countries and expressed this in their poetry. It is significant that one collection of poems was called "Hymns of the Strangers."* Their admission to feeling like strangers in Arab countries contradicts the basic conception of Arab nationalism, which has emphasized Arab unity, manifested in the feeling of being at home in every Arab country. In this matter, as in others, Arab nationalist ideology is not in tune with the feelings of the individual. The fact that a considerable segment of the Palestinians has been living *en masse* in refugee camps has also contributed to their preservation of group identity. The Zionist example may also have had some influence. A conflict is a competitive situation, and the preservation by the Jews of their attachment to Palestine served as an example to be emulated. It is as though the Palestinians said, "We are no less than the Jews, who preserved a tie to this country for a long period of time." Tibawi notes that "a new Zionism" was formed among the refugees.

Among the refugees a state of mind developed which stigmatized assimilation into Arab societies as an act of disloyalty. A committee of the Norwegian Institute for the Study of Peace, which investigated the situation in the Gaza Strip in 1964, was impressed by the unity of presentation and consensus in the argumentation of the refugees. They noted in this respect: "It is difficult to imagine a social group with a more homogeneous perception and definition of the past and the present than the refugees in the Gaza Strip. Regardless of age, income or educational level and the social status in general of the men we spoke with, the definition seemed to be the same—at least in so far as they wanted to present it to foreigners." Their report relates that among the refugees there was even a prevailing tendency to disparage efforts at improving living conditions in the camps, lest this imply the admission that these were permanent living places. The report notes that Palestinians tended to

---

* A. L. Tibawi, "Visions of the Return: The Palestine Refugees in Arabic Poetry and Art," *The Middle East Journal,* 17 (1963), pp. 507-526.

prefer short-term work contracts in Arab countries, again lest they be considered of little faith regarding the anticipated imminent "return." A need was generated to demonstrate a faith that, indeed, they soon would return to "the homeland." The refugees began calling themselves officially "returnees" (*'ā'idûn*) instead of "refugees," in accordance with a decision of the First Congress of the Palestine Liberation Organization. There may have been an expectation that the psychological mechanism of "self-fulfilling prophecy" would operate, that is, the very name "returnees" assures not only that the hope would not fade but more, that it would be realised. The word *'awda*, "return," or "repatriation," was made a principal slogan. In the recesses of their heart many refugees probably doubted that hope for "the return" would materialize in the near, or even distant, future. But, according to the report of the Norwegians, the mechanism of "pluralistic ignorance" operated among them; that is, each one was apprehensive that only he was of little faith, as though the others were wholly confident in an early return, and as a result no one dared make his doubts public. Ideas that are repeated, even if not believed at first, are slowly assimilated in human consciousness, for otherwise a "cognitive dissonance" is created. It is uncomfortable to live in two different conceptual frameworks, what is said and what is believed, and ultimately belief is adjusted to what is said. Because of the stigma of absorption into Arab countries it was presumably easier for a Palestinian to become assimilated before 1948 than afterwards. Nevertheless, many were absorbed in Arab and other countries.

In their preservation of group attachment there was also an element of protest and negation of their situation as refugees, which is translated into the hope that one day redemption would come and they would return to their land. The return is seen as a collective salvation and messianic vision. Tibawi speaks of "the mystique of the return."

The form of attachment to Palestine varies with the generations. In the attachment of the *older generation* to the country there was a concrete factor: longing for property they left and their former way of life. Among the older generation a process of "idylization" of the way of life before "the disaster" operated against the background of negating life in the present. By selective memory, the shadows of Arab life in the land were forgotten, and the village house expanded with the passage of time and became a palace. In their stories to their children the parents probably described their life before the war in 1948 as a period of glory and a heroic struggle.

There may have been in this an element of apology by the father
before his son, to this effect: "Don't look at me in my decline, for
the life of the camp has destroyed me. Once I was a man." It is
significant that 'Arif al-'Arif entitles his book, *al-Firdaws al-Mafqûd*
(*Paradise Lost*).

Among the *younger generation*, which constitutes the majority
of the Palestinians, the attachment is not directly experiential. The
younger generation did not experience the hardships of the 1948
war and the exodus. Their quest to return does not stem from longing for some property, as in their parents' case, but from negation
of their present life and from an *ideological* position: the wrong
that was inflicted on the Palestinians, Israel's aggressiveness, and the
requirement that justice be done and Israel liquidated. The education that the youth received brought them to the point where the
village life of most of the parents ceased to enchant them. The return does not appear as a return to the village of their parents but
as a political act in which the Palestinians become the sovereigns
over Palestine and all their problems, as it were, are solved.

Paradoxically, the ideological attachment of the youth, though
indirect, is by no means weaker than the concrete, direct attachment
of the parents. The vehemence of the ideological and learned attachment can be much stronger than that of the concrete and direct
attachment.

The Six Day War, and the possibility given to many Palestinians to see Israel, and even to visit their place of origin, could impair
the concrete attachment, for it became clear to the visitors that the
property for which they longed, and in whose imagined existence
they sought consolation, was no longer. The concrete attachment
to the country is more vulnerable to the concrete reality expressed
in changes that took place in the scenery and the consolidation of
the State of Israel, while the ideological attachment of the younger
generation is more immune to these facts.

Illusion ultimately disappoints. This applies to us also. It is
best for us to acknowledge facts of reality without attempting to
deny them. An acknowledgment that the Palestinians have an attachment to Palestine need not produce in us a state of anxiety. The
conflict is also a contest of attachments. Our awareness that the
Arabs also have an attachment to the country need not impair our
own. I emphasize this because I have found that there is among us
a degree of fainthearted reluctance to see some of the facts of the
Arab-Israeli conflict as they are. An example of this is the reaction

I have found in Israeli audiences to evidences of Arab attachment to Palestine.

In lectures before an Israeli audience I sometimes read a paragraph from Nasir ad-Din an-Nashashibi's book, *Return Ticket* (Beirut, 1962). Toward the end of the book (p. 205) the author says:

> Every year I shall say to my little son: "We shall return my son, and you will be with me; we shall return; we shall return to our land and walk there barefoot. We'll remove our shoes so that we may feel the holiness of the ground beneath us. We'll blend our souls with its air and earth. We'll walk till we come to the orange trees; we'll feel the sand and water; we'll kiss seed and fruit; we'll sleep in the shade of the first tree we meet; we'll pay homage to the first martyr's grave we come across. We'll turn here and there to trace our lives. Where are they? Here with this village square, with this mosque's minaret, with the beloved field, the desolate wall, with the remains of a tottering fence and a building whose traces have been erased. Here are our lives. Each grain of sand teaches us about our life. Do you not remember Jaffa and its delightful shore, Haifa and its lofty mountain, Beth Shean and the fields of crops and fruit, Nazareth and the Christians' bells, Acre and the memories of al-Jazzar, Ibrahim Pasha, Napoleon and the fortress, the streets of Jerusalem, my dear Jerusalem, Tiberias and its peaceful shore with the golden waves, Majdal and the remnant of my kin in its land?"

When one reads this paragraph, even if he be poisoned by the abundant words of abuse and calumny against Israel found in Nashashibi's book which preceded this paragraph, he will admit, even if reluctantly, that there is here an expression of genuine longing and love for the country.

I found that an older audience, upon hearing this, would be moved. The divulgence that an Arab too may have an emotional attachment to this country was a confusing and ominous surprise. In a younger audience the reaction was different. Among them the prevailing tendency was to accept the plain meaning of the words as something natural and understandable. In their reaction the youth said, in effect, "If the author wishes to run barefoot, let him run and get himself stuck by thorns." I think that, despite its frivolousness, such a reaction is more healthy.

Whoever is moved by these manifestations of human longing for this country, and whose heart is touched by this phenomenon, should have no illusions concerning its significance for us. The refinement expressed in feelings of yearning does not, by any means, become refinement toward the Israelis. On the contrary, on the following page Nashashibi describes the effect his words will have on his son:

> I shall see the hatred in the eyes of my son and your sons. I shall see how they take revenge. If they do not know how to take revenge, I shall teach them. And if they agree to a truce or peace, I shall fight against them as I fight against my enemy and theirs. I want them to be callous, to be ruthless, to take revenge. I want them to wash away the disaster of 1948 with the blood of those who prevent them from entering their land. Their homeland is dear to them, but revenge is dearer. We'll enter their lairs in Tel-Aviv. We'll smash Tel-Aviv with axes, guns, hands, fingernails and teeth, while singing the songs of Qibiya, Dir Yasin and Nasir ad-Din.* We shall sing the hymns of the triumphant, avenging return. . . .

Truly, it is a tragic complication in which we are enmeshed. In the presence of the intention of annihilation we cannot permit ourselves to become soft, and at times not even to assume a humanistic stance, for this may imply responsiveness to the quest of our annihilation, and this is a self-contradiction.

The leaders of the Palestinians made special efforts to preserve the Palestinian attachment of the members of their flock and to nurture it by means of education, writing of history, collection of folklore, and the like. In brief, efforts were made to mould a Palestinian people although it had no territory. In this also the Jews, as a people without territory and government, served as an example. It was easy for the Palestinian leadership and intelligentsia to find work and become absorbed in Arab countries. But for the sake of the political goal they were callous to the suffering of their people and exerted pressure upon them not to become absorbed but to remain in their camps. This duplicity was not hidden from the refugees, who regarded the Palestinian leadership with a great deal of reservation. It is difficult to place trust in a leadership which establishes itself in convenient positions and leads a normal way of life while at the same time demanding of its flock that it live wretchedly. This may have been one of reasons why the tendency among the refugees to organize themselves was late in coming.

It is understandable that among the Palestinians especially,

---

* A village east of Tiberias which is frequently mentioned in Arabic literature as an example of Jewish terrorism. 'Arif al-'Arif relates that ten Arabs were killed there (an-Nakba, Vol. I, p. 205).

along with their attachment to Palestine, pan-Arab sentiments would be more prevalent than among other Arab groups. Through their dispersion and wanderings many of the Palestinians became acquainted with Arab countries and sometimes even attached to them, whereas Egyptian, Syrian and Lebanese Arabs tend to know one country, and patriotism toward their homeland predominates pan-Arab sentiments.* In this also they can draw an analogy with Jews. Just as the Jews, owing to their dispersion, tended toward cosmopolitanism, so the Palestinians tended toward pan-Arabism. It is not accidental that the Qawmiyyûn al-'Arab movement, which so emphasized the idea of Arab unity, emerged from amid the Palestinians.

Acquaintance with the Arab states did not always endear these states to the Palestinians, for they indeed had their fill of bitters with them. Their loyalty to ideas of pan-Arabism may have arisen among them as a compensation for the grievances they had against the individual Arab countries. The Palestinians had complaints against the Arab countries for several reasons: they did not fulfill their obligations to the Palestinians, imposed discriminatory restrictions upon them, and manipulated the Palestinian problem within their own rivalries. The Palestinians were a fermenting factor in the Arab countries. Several of the Arab states were apprehensive about their influence and consequently clipped their wings. The Palestinians have also had many grievances on the social level, for many Arabs were indifferent to their suffering and did not treat them as brethren in distress.

The Palestinians gave vent to their grievances in their literature (Ghassan Kanafani's novels for example). But it would be simplistic to conclude from these literary accounts that, because of their resentment of Arab countries, they will be amenable to agreement with us. The heart of man is sufficiently wide to encompass hostility toward more than one enemy, and the enemy of his enemy does not automatically become his friend. Along with grievances toward the Arab countries the Palestinians also have feelings of gratitude, for they did derive benefits from these countries. Even if they experienced difficulties of absorption, they could find work and send their chil-

---

* Arab ideologues tend now to distinguish between the one Arab "nation" and the many Arab "peoples," such as the Egyptians, Iraqis and so on. They call attachment to the nation *qawmiyya*, "nationalism," whereas attachment to the people, and especially its land, they call *waṭaniyya*, which recently took on the sense of "patriotism." Correspondingly, there are also those who distinguish between the general homeland of all the Arabs, *al-waṭan al-'âmm*, and the homeland of a specific people, which is called *al-waṭan al-khâss*.

dren to to study in their colleges. The recognition that in the confrontation against Israel they ultimately depend on the support of the Arab countries, especially in the military struggle, is another factor which inhibits the development of enmity toward them. The result, therefore, is not dissociation from the Arab countries but a complex attitude that contains an element of ambivalence: friendship and distrust at the same time.

Arabic belles-lettres are certainly a more faithful mirror of what is happening in the public than the political literature written according to the dictate of rulers. There is more spontaneity in its expressiveness than there is in publicistic writing   [sic]. However, in evaluating political positions one should distinguish well between the position on the popular level and the one on the government level. For example, in the literary depiction of English life in the years 1938-1939 enmity toward the Germans was not at all conspicuous, but an inference from this to England's position as a state would be misleading. From literary descriptions of the life of the Japanese farmer it was probably impossible to infer that there existed a conflict between Japan and the United States critical enough to produce an explosion as great as the attack on Pearl Harbor. In general, the individual is not preoccupied in his private life with a national conflict. He worries about his personal problems, first and foremost his daily bread, especially in countries where poverty prevails. Therefore, it would also be an error to derive lessons concerning the political position of a group of Palestinians or Egyptians from literary descriptions of the life of the individual in that group. If the conflict preoccupies the Egyptian as an individual slightly, this by no means implies that it is marginal to Egypt as a state. If the average Egyptian is not filled with enmity toward Jews and Israel, this is not translatable into political terms. Egypt as a state may be bitterly hostile toward Israel. Political leadership determines political objectives, and it is not necessarily influenced daily by popular conceptions. The direction of influence is generally the opposite, for recognized and accepted leaders, even if they are not helmsmen of the state, influence their people more than their people influence them. Political opinions and views among the public are not formed spontaneously as much as they are the effect of influence by that circle called "the moulders of public opinion": local leaders, journalists, authors and, at their head, the political leadership. Popular emotions do not create an international conflict. For the most part, people do not make war because they hate; they hate because they make war. It is political conflict that incites hatred. Notions that are current among the people may have significance in so far as they bear upon their support of the government. But again, this requires qualification, especially as regards Arab countries. Regimes did not come to power in Arab countries because they had popular support necessarily, but having achieved power they could create it. The regimes in Arab countries can be unpopular, or become unpopular, and nevertheless retain their position for a long time.

A question that is being argued with great fervor is whether the Palestinians are a people or nation. But there is no accepted criterion or definition by which to decide who is a people or nation. It cannot be determined, for example, what the necessary components are which form a nation. Neither territory nor language are a necessary criterion. The Jews, for example, had no territory, and there are nations which have no language of their own, or which speak a number of languages. It was not without reason that Ernest Renan defined the nation subjectively as "a daily plebiscite." That is, the human group determines according to its feelings and mutual attachment whether it is a nation or not. The argument that the Palestinians are not a nation because such a nation has not existed in the past is not persuasive. No nation existed primordially, and all were the product of an historical process, generally by affiliation to a governmental center. The distinction between people and nation on the one hand, and non-people and non-nation on the other, is not a dichotomous division. It seems better to view nationhood as a continuum, on the one side of which there is a group of people among whom there is no cohesion, and on the other side of which there is a group whose cohesion has been realized. This continuum implies that the existence of the nation is relative. For example, the Swedes, if it is possible to say so, are "more a nation" than the Turks, the Turks more a nation than the Pakistanis, the Pakistanis more a nation than the Tanzanians, and so on. The Palestinians are found somewhere on this continuum, and their national status will be determined by what happens to them. If at some point a Palestinian state is created, this status will reach maturity and be reflected also in subjective feelings.

Until 1948 the conflict was basically between Israel and the Palestinians. The intervention of the Arab states caused the role of the Palestinians to diminish. After May, 1948 their position in the conflict became marginal. The pendulum swings back in the first half of the sixties, when the Palestinians again gain prominence. It should be noted that this emergence parallels a process of *rad-*

icalization in the concept of the form of warfare against Israel. Ideas appear to the effect that the conflict involves "a war of national liberation," in which the Palestinians will be the vanguard, and the war, at least in its early stages, will take on the form of guerrilla warfare. It should be remembered that, in the meantime, changes of the guard had started in the Palestinian leadership, and a younger generation emerged, of a predominantly Leftist state of mind, which advocated activism in the struggle with Israel and disparaged the "passivity" (ṣalbiyya) of the previous generation. This state of mind of the younger generation was first given a literary expression. The younger generation deliberated and expressed thoughts in periodicals and books concerning the most efficient form of combatting Israel. Only afterwards were these ideas given organizational form in the shape of the fedayeen groups, the chief of them being Fatah.

A great change took place in the status of the Palestinians as a result of the Six Day War. The stature of the Palestinians, which was bowed by their defeat in 1948 and their exile, was raised, for after the downfall of the Arab armies the fedayeen actions gained renown for them in Arab countries and outside, and the Palestinians were transformed from an inferior factor into standard-bearers of Arab nationalism and a source of pride. Again, this is not always translated into the concrete, practical attitude of the population in Arab countries toward them. Their support remains on a national and political level and is not always expressed in real action to mitigate the suffering of the Palestinian refugees.

In the past the conflict was presented as though it had two levels: the first, the national-geopolitical antagonism between Israel and Arab nationalism; and the second, the problem of the Palestinians. Arab ideologues emphasized that the antagonism on the national level was the principal one, and that even if the issue of the Palestinians were solved and the refugees settled, still the principal antagonism between Israel and Arabdom would remain.

As a result of the war the situation has been reversed and, according to current fashion, the contradiction with the Palestinians is presented as the essence of the conflict, for this is allegedly a struggle for national liberation. Arabs explain, especially to foreigners, that the antagonism is not that of the large Arab states versus a small state like Israel but of an oppressed people against a strong, colonialistic, oppressive state. David has become Goliath. It is maintained that the antagonism of the rest of the Arab states is a by-product of the Palestinian cause. Thus, the geopolitical issue is demoted, if only temporarily and for purposes of presentation. The ecology of the conflict is shifted. It is not between states but between a government and a people struggling for its liberation, and by definition a just war that deserves support. The "liberation" of the Palestinians is not the elimination of their subjugation but the establishment of their sovereignty over Palestine.

The paradox in this switch is that when the conflict was marginal for public opinion in Arab countries it was represented as a conflict between the Arab states and Israel, while precisely when the importance and saliency of the conflict increased in the national life of neighboring states it is not represented as a conflict between them and Israel but between the Palestinians and Israel.

Since the importance of the Palestinians in the conflict has grown, the question arises: can a settlement emerge from them?

The Palestinians are divided into two main groups. The first consists of those who live in the West Bank (Judah and Samaria) and the Gaza Strip. Many in this group are apprehensive about a renewal of the war, for they may assume by extrapolation that in the contest between Israel and the Arabs they are liable to be the principal victims. For this reason, it is no wonder that these people would want a settlement which might prevent a renewed eruption of the war. They could also explain to the Arab countries that such a settlement with Israel will benefit the Arabs, for it would bring about withdrawal of the Israeli military presence from the territories that are occupied. This settlement, they could contend, is not the final word, and would not be a barrier when the Arab states regain their strength, making it possible for them to reopen the war. In fact, the idea of a Palestinian state arose in Arab countries. It was brought up by the Egyptian journalist, Ahmad Baha' ad-Din (in his book, *The Proposal for a State of Palestine and the Controversy Surrounding It*). However, he did not intend a state that would make peace with Israel but "a confrontation state" that would include Jordan. This state would make a military pact with the other Arab states and serve as the base for the onslaught against Israel. It should be noted that the idea is not new; it is merely the metamorphosis of an idea that arose previously concerning the establishment of "The Republic of Palestine." The issue was brought up by General Qassem in 1959 and arose again during the first stages in the establishment of the Palestine Liberation Organization at the beginning of 1964, and then afterwards when relations between the organization and the Jordanian rulers became strained.

The leaders of the Arab states, including the leaders of the Palestinian organizations, took a strong, unequivocal stand against a Palestinian state in any agreement with Israel. Most of those who debated the proposal of Baha' ad-Din, whose articles he includes in his book, rejected it. They pointed out that the present time is not appropriate for this proposal because the establishment of a Palestinian state would arouse opposition among circles close to the government of Jordan and thus produce an internal rift, weakening the front against Israel.

An agreement by the Palestinians of the West Bank to a settlement with Israel in face of opposition by the Arab rulers would brand them as traitors. One must not underestimate the deterrent force of this stigma for them. More serious from their point of view is the fear that a settlement with Israel would cut them off from the places of dispersion where their families are—from sons, daughters and relatives in Arab countries. This is how the Arab countries might penalize them. The Palestinians on the West Bank cannot, therefore, allow themselves a settlement for human and family reasons. It is no surprise that so few expressed support for the idea of a Palestinian state.

The Palestinians of the West Bank want two things; the catch is that they are incompatible. It is possible that many of them wish a settlement with Israel, but on condition that the Arab League and the Arab states endorse it. They face the dilemma: on the one hand, fear of war and the desire for a settlement that would prevent it; and on the other, apprehension of separation from their families and national ostracism. It is no wonder that, when they are forced to choose between leaving the situation as is with all its dangers and a settlement in defiance of the Arab countries, they tend to elect the first alternative.

A strong stand against the idea of a Palestinian state on the West Bank was taken by the Palestinian National Council in its Fourth Congress, which took place in Cairo beginning on July 10, 1968.* Among its political resolutions, under the heading, "The Dubious Calls for Creation of a Fraudulent Palestinian Entity," it is stated:

> The Zionist movement, imperialism and the tool of both, Israel, are making efforts to reinforce the Zionist aggression against Palestine and to strengthen the Israeli military victory of 1948 and of 1967 by establishing a Palestinian entity in the territory conquered after the aggression of June 5th, an entity

---

* The Palestinian National Council is the highest institution of the Palestine Liberation Organization, which now amalgamates virtually all the Palestinian organizations.

which will bestow legality and permanence on the State of Israel. This is an act which entirely contradicts the right of the Palestinian Arab people to the whole of its homeland of Palestine. This fraudulent entity is actually an Israeli colony which will finally liquidate to Israel's advantage the Palestinian problem. At the same time, it will be a temporary stage which will enable Zionism to evacuate the Arab inhabitants from the Palestinian territories which were conquered after the aggression of June 5th. Moreover, there will be the possibility of setting up a vassal (*'amil*) Palestinian Arab administration, upon which Israel will depend in its contest with the Palestinian revolution. There also enter into this framework the imperialist and Zionist programs to place the Palestinian territories conquered after June 5th under international administration and protection.* Whence the National Council declares its absolute denunciation of the idea of the fraudulent Palestinian entity in the territories of Palestine conquered after June 5th and, together with this, denunciation of every form of international protection. Likewise, it declares that every Arab individual or group, Palestinian or non-Palestinian, calling for the vassal entity and international protection, or supporting it, is the enemy of the Palestinian Arab people and the Arab nation. (The official report of the Congress, pp. 39-40.)

The declaration concerning "the enemy of the people" is, in effect, a threat against life.

Presenting the problem as though what is required for a settlement with the Palestinians is Israel's recognition of them is a distortion. This indictment on the tongue of Israelis only abets [sic] the slander against Israel, that it is the principal barrier to peace. If among some circles in the world our image has become tarnished, not only the extremists among us, but even many of those who claim to be men of peace, are responsible. Israel, in fact, has already recognized a Palestinian entity, as implied in its very acceptance of the Partition Resolution in 1947, which determined the establishment of a Palestinian Arab state in our neighborhood. The problem was, and remains, quite the opposite: not recognition on our part of their right to a section of this country but the non-recognition on the part of the Palestinians and the Arabs of our national right to a separate national existence of our own. In the Palestinian position there was a consistent totalistic demand for exclusive possession.

---

* This has to do with the idea of demilitarizing the West Bank for a number of years under UN protection. It was suggested by foreign consuls in conversations with men of the West Bank and was considered by its leaders.

This appeared in the form of opposition to the Partition Plan, and
appears today in the demand for "general liberation" and sovereignty over the whole territory of Palestine. (The reader will find
documentation of this in the version of the Palestinian National
Covenant in Part II.) Our declaration from morning to evening that
we recognize the Palestinians is entirely irrelevant to the possibility
of establishing a Palestinian state through an agreement with us,
even within the Armistice demarcation lines.

The second Palestinian group consists of those found outside
the present boundaries. They have nothing to lose from the continuation of the conflict, as do the Arabs of the West Bank. Their
leaders have capitalized on the conflict and thrive on it. Men like
Yassir Arafat and George Habash acquired a high status only owing
to the conflict. In their case there is rabid opposition to a compromise solution. They vehemently oppose any political settlement,
regardless of boundaries or conditions, because their opposition is
to the principle of a Jewish state in any size or shape. They formulated this opposition to a political settlement in their "National·
Covenant," in its new version adopted by their Congress in Cairo of
July, 1968 and reinforced it with explicit resolutions. The National
Covenant is the Palestinians' basic political document and it was
approved by most of the terrorist organizations.* Concurrence with
it is a condition for joining the "Command of Armed Struggle,"
which now makes joint announcements for most of the terrorist
organizations. What is said in it has more weight and importance
than the declaration of any Palestinian spokesman. For understanding the Arab position, especially that of the Palestinians, there is
not a more important document. Article 21 of this charter asserts:
"The Palestinian Arab people, in expressing itself through the
armed Palestinian revolution,** rejects every solution that is a substitute for the complete liberation of Palestine. . . ." The right of
self-determination becomes the right of "restoring" the whole territory of Palestine. The Jews now living in the country have no
right of national self-determination. Many Palestinian leaders outside the country affirm that they do not fear another war, nor even
another defeat of the Arab states. On the contrary, it appears that
they are interested in embroiling the Arab states in the conflict as
much as possible. The position of the Palestinians toward us is

---

* See below, Part II.
** "The armed Palestinian revolution" is an idiom from the lexicon of
Fatah. It is expressed in the fact that the Palestinians take upon themselves the
chief role in the struggle against Israel by undertaking fedayeen actions.

polarized. Their hostility toward Israel is much more central in their world-view than was the hostility of the Nazis to Jews. However, they now choose to hide their aim of destroying Israel in euphemistic expressions, such as, "the dezionization of Israel," or "the restoration of the rights of the Arabs in Palestine," which does not alter the basic meaning, namely, the annihilation of Israel.

Even though the Arabs' confidence in their ability to achieve their aim was shaken by the Six Day War, the radicalism of the Palestinian leadership outside the country increased as a result of the war. This can be deduced from comparison of the Covenant in its first version of May, 1964, from the time of Shukeiry, with the version adopted under the influence of Yahya Hamuda and Yassir Arafat concerning the fate of the Jews in the free Palestinian Arab state after it is "liberated" and Israel annihilated. The former version can be interpreted to the effect that the Jews who lived in Palestine in 1947 would be recognized as Palestinians, that is, would be able to remain; whereas in the new text, as revised in the fourth session of the National Council (July, 1968), it is explicitly stated that only Jews who lived permanently in Palestine before 1917 would be recognized as Palestinians. This implies that the rest are aliens and must leave. It is indeed difficult to agree with the claim of some people, that the Arabs have become more realistic and their position more moderate, if a hallowed and authoritative document like the National Covenant specifies the aim of banishing almost two and a half million Jews.

What can be a more flagrant contradiction of the slogan they brandish today concerning a "pluralistic society"? It should be mentioned that the representatives of all the Palestinian organizations participated in the Congress, including the principal fedayeen groups. The Popular Front for the Liberation of Palestine, which is critical of the Palestine Liberation Organization, did not criticize this article. The importance of such articles in the Covenant is not in their practical value but in the state of mind reflected in them. Shukeiry did speak of throwing the Jews into the sea and used many vilifying expressions, but his position was in principle less radical. In view of the extremism of the official Palestinian and Arab position, what value is there to the words of an Arab student outside the country who tries to lend moderation to his remarks, whether out of false piety or an effort to conform to the general atmosphere and find favor in foreigners' eyes, while in closed gatherings of Arab students he holds the official position, and upon returning to his country shows the same tendency to conform to the radical atmosphere of the Arab countries? Even if we assume that he was sincere in his remarks, their value is nil over against the collective position. Moreover, there is no sign of any dissociation from this formulation of the Covenant by any Arab group, including Arab student organizations abroad. In no Arab newspaper or other publication was there even the slightest afterthought about the wisdom of this formulation. In the meantime, another two Congresses were held and the Covenant was not amended. It seems that there is no more decisive evidence regarding the essence of the Palestinian Arab position.

One may ponder what induced the Palestinian Congress which assembled in Cairo on July 10, 1968 to introduce this change which is so radical regarding the Jews "who would be permitted" to remain in a Palestinian state. We shall probably have to wait for solid information until clarifications are published by the participants in the Congress, or until its minutes or those of the Covenant Committee appointed to formulate it become known. In the meantime, it is possible to guess what factors prompted this. It may be that the very emphasis by Palestinian spokesmen that the state will be "democratic" necessitates the reduction of the number of Jews to a small minority. It is also possible that the radicalization of their position as result of Fatah's gaining control of the Palestine Liberation Organization produces greater doctrinal consistency: since Zionism is despicable, it is necessary to purge the country of all the Jews who came after the first political recognition that was granted to Zionism in the Balfour Declaration. Fatah defines the purpose of the war thus: "The action of liberation is not only the liquidation of an imperialistic base but the obliteration of a society" (Fatah pamphlet, *Taḥrîr al-Aqtâr al-Muḥtalla wa-Uslûb al-Kifâḥ ḍidd al-Istiʿmâr al-Mubâshir* [*The Liberation of the Occupied Territories and the Means of Combatting Direct Colonialism*], new edition, September, 1967, p. 16; Fatah Yearbook, 1968, p. 39). It may also be that the qualitative superiority of the Israeli and Israeli society, which was conspicuous in the Six Day War, in contrast to Arab individual and societal weakness, engenders apprehensions about living together with a significant Jewish minority; hence the need that it be small. Reduction of the number of Jews in Palestine is inherent in the Arab position. If to the outside world they now prudently avoid specifying that it will be done by violent means, as a compensation, the dimensions of the reduction have increased.

The Palestinian Arab position, as expressed in pronouncements of Palestinian spokesmen, is not only a demand to return to Palestine as its sovereigns but that Palestine should return to the Arabs as Arab, that is, after its foreign population is purged from it. It is not accidental that in their descriptions of its "liberation" they frequently use the verb "purify." Professor Fayez Sayegh, the chief Arab propagandist in the United States, who was a member of the Executive Committee of the Palestine Liberation Organization and the founder of the Palestine Research Organization, formulates the position in the following words: "Peace in the land of Palestine and its neighbors is our fondest desire. The primary condition for this is the liberation of Palestine, that is, the condition is our return to an Arab Palestine and the restoration of Palestine to us *as Arab*" (Emphasis added. *Ḥafna min Ḍabâb* [*A Handful of Mist*], PLO Research Center, Beirut, July, 1966, p. 19), Shafiq al-Hut, the head of the Beirut branch of the Palestine Liberation Organization, writes in the same spirit: "Disregarding the Palestinian entity is only a part of the Zionist imperialist plot, the aim of which is the liquidation of the people of Palestine and prevention of its attaining its right in the struggle for liberation of its usurped country, restoration of it as free and Arab, and returning its people to it as free and sovereign, abounding with honor and glory" (Haqâ'iq *'alâ Ṭarîq at-Taḥrîr* [*Truths on the Way to Liberation*], PLO Research Center, Beirut, November, 1966, p. 6). Publications of Fatah usually end with the motto, "Long live a free Arab Palestine," emphasizing the Arab character the population must have.

Among the Arabs the Palestinians outside the country are the most radical and uncompromising group. Their leaders and intellectuals acquired positions and influence in Arab public life, and they are the chief inciters against Israel. These Palestinians are not hostile to Israel on account of the hostility of the Arab states but the opposite: the hostility of the Arab states is caused to a great degree by the hostility of the Palestinians. Nasser reiterates the statement, "We shall not concede the rights of the Palestinians," that is, he presents himself as fighting their war. Nasser repeatedly defines the Palestinian problem as one of "a people" and its "fatherland," that is, the people must become sovereign over its fatherland. Nasser indicated that he would agree to a peace settlement after a just solution from the point of view of the Palestinians was found. He could agree to the Security Council Resolution of November 22, 1967 because this condition was included in it. The problem is that according to his interpretation this justice means the sovereignty of the Palestinians over their homeland. The injustice inflicted on the Palestinians is not only in their loss of property but is implicit in the circumstance that their homeland and sovereignty were taken from them. Less than restoration of sovereignty is not "just," and a partial justice is a self-contradiction because it permits the injustice to remain. Thus, the use of the language current among the Arabs, "a just solution of the problem of the Palestinians," is actually a euphemism for the destruction of Israel. The existence of Israel and a just solution of the problem of the Palestinians, as the Palestinians and Arabs define it, are thus incompatible.

A complication is created which is the essence of the Arab-Israeli conflict at the present stage. The Palestinians on the West Bank can hardly allow themselves to reach a settlement with us on account of the Arab states. The Arab states are bound to a degree that should not be minimized [sic] by their commitment to the Palestinians, especially those outside our borders. In this triangle, therefore, the Palestinian leadership outside our borders is the principal barrier to a settlement.

At the present stage the Palestinians outside the country are more influential than those of the West Bank. The relationship is asymmetrical. The Palestinian leaders outside the country have influence over the Palestinians of the West Bank, but it is doubtful if the leaders of the West Bank could influence the Palestinians outside to change their position. This change is possible only by means of the suppression of their organizations by the Arab states. Indeed, between them and the Arab states there are seeds of antagonisms which may develop into a confrontation.

One should not overlook the status and influence this Palestinian leadership outside the country has. However, when it becomes clear to what extent it has failed, especially in relying on fedayeenism, when this does not produce the anticipated results, its status is bound to be weakened. When the Arab states discover to what extent continuation of the conflict is destructive from their aspect, draws them into political disintegration, and denies them any possibility of national progress and recovery, they may take action against the Palestinian organizations outside the country. Then there will be an opening for negotiation and a settlement between Israel and the Palestinians nearby, and between Israel and the Arab countries.

WORKS CITED

al-'Arif, 'Arif. an-Nakba: Nakbat Bayt al-Maqdis wal-Firdaws al-Mafqûd (The Disaster: The Disaster of Palestine and the Paradise Lost). 5 vols. Sidon-Beirut: al-Maktaba al-'Asriyya, 1947-1955.

Baha' ad-Din, Ahmad. Iqtirâh *Dawlat Filasṭin wa-mā Dâra ḥawlahâ min Mu-nâqashât (The Proposal for a State of Palestine and the Controversy Sur-rounding It).* Beirut: Dar al-Adab, 1968.

Galtung, I. and J. *A Pilot Project from Gaza.* Peace Research Institute, Oslo, February, 1964.

al-Hut, Shafiq. *Ḥaqâ'iq 'alâ Ṭarîq at-Taḥrîr (Truths on the Way to Liberation).* PLO Research Center. Beirut, November, 1966.

Munazzamat at-Taḥrîr al-Filasṭîniyya (PLO). al-Majlis al-Waṭanî al-Filasṭînî al-Mun'aqad fî al-Qâhira fî 10-17 Tammûz (Yûliyô), 1968 (The Palestinian National Council, which Convened in Cairo July 10-17, 1968). Official Report.

an-Nashashibi, Nasir ad-Din. *Tadhkirat 'Awda (Return Ticket).* Beirut: al-Maktab at-Tijari, 1962.

Sayegh, Fayez. Hafna *min Ḍabâb (A Handful of Mist).* PLO Research Center. Beirut, July, 1966.

Tibawi, A. L. "Visions of the Return: The Palestine Refugees in Arabic Poetry and Art," *The Middle East Journal,* 17 (1963), pp. 507-526.

Part II

THE PALESTINIAN NATIONAL COVENANT*

The Palestinian National Covenant is perhaps the most important document of this stage of the Israel-Arab conflict, especially with regard to the Arab side. It represents a summation of the official position of the Palestinian organizations in the conflict.

The previous version of the Covenant was adopted by the First Palestinian Congress, which convened in Jerusalem in May, 1964 at the time of the establishment of the Palestine Liberation Organization. In the official English translation of the previous version it was called "Covenant" and not "Charter," in order to emphasize its national sanctity, and the introductory words to the Covenant conclude with an oath to implement it. The Congress stipulated that a Palestinian National Council, the highest institution of the Palestinian organizations, would meet periodically, and that a two-thirds majority of the Council members would be required to amend the Covenant. As a result of the changes which came about in the Palestine Liberation Organization after the Six Day War the Palestinian National Council convened in Cairo for its fourth session on July 10-17, 1968 and amended the Covenant. It should be noted that representatives of almost all the Palestinian

---

* Appeared in *Maariv* December 12, 1969.

organizations existing in Arab countries participated in this session, including all the fedayeen organizations. Fatah and the fedayeen organizations under its influence had thirty-seven representatives in the National Council of one hundred members and the Popular Front had ten. Fatah's style is recognizable in the new Covenant. This amended version was certainly not formulated casually; it represents a position that was seriously considered and weighed. The amended version is here presented. In order to highlight the changes we shall compare this version with its predecessor.

The main principles which were set down in the Covenant are:

In the Palestinian State only Jews who lived in Palestine before 1917 will be recognized as citizens (Article 6).

Only the Palestinian Arabs possess the right of self-determination, and the entire country belongs to them (Articles 3 and 21).

Any solution that does not involve total liberation of the country is rejected. This aim cannot be achieved politically; it can only be accomplished militarily (Articles 9 and 21).

Warfare against Israel is legal, whereas Israel's self-defense is illegal (Article 18).

For the sake of completeness the Covenant is presented here in its entirety.

THE PALESTINIAN NATIONAL COVENANT*

THIS COVENANT WILL BE CALLED "THE PALESTINIAN NATIONAL COVENANT" (*AL-MÎTHÂQ AL-WAṬANÎ AL-FILASṬÎNÎ*).

In the previous version of the Covenant of May, 1964 the adjective "national" was rendered by *qawmî*, the usual meaning of which in modern Arabic is pan-Arab and ethnic nationalism, whereas here they use the adjective *waṭanî*, which signifies nationalism in its narrow, territorialistic sense as patriotism toward a specific country. This change intends to stress Palestinian patriotism.

---

* The body of the document is translated from the Arabic original. Articles of the 1964 Covenant repeated here are rendered on the basis of the official English translation of that Covenant but with alterations of style and terminology. The same procedure is followed in translating quotations from the earlier Covenant cited in the commentary (Y.K.)

ARTICLES OF THE COVENANT[4]

ARTICLE 1) PALESTINE IS THE HOMELAND OF THE PALESTINIAN ARAB PEOPLE AND AN INTEGRAL PART OF THE GREAT ARAB HOMELAND, AND THE PEOPLE OF PALESTINE IS A PART OF THE ARAB NATION.

In most Arab constitutions it is simply stipulated that the people of that country constitutes an integral part of the Arab nation. Here, because of the special problem of territory, it is also stressed that the land is an integral part of the general Arab homeland. The previous version in the Covenant of 1964 was more vague: "Palestine is an Arab homeland bound by strong Arab national ties to the rest of the Arab countries which together form the Great Arab Homeland." The combination "the Palestinian Arab people" recurs often in the Covenant and is also intended to stress the special status of the Palestinians, though as Arabs.

ARTICLE 2) PALESTINE WITH ITS BOUNDARIES THAT EXISTED AT THE TIME OF THE BRITISH MANDATE IS AN INTEGRAL REGIONAL UNIT.

The same formulation as in the previous version. It is implied that Palestine should not be divided into a Jewish and an Arab state. Although it is an accepted tenet of Arab nationalism that existing boundaries should be abolished, since they were artificially delineated by the imperialist powers, here they are sanctified. The expression "that existed at the time of the British Mandate" is vague. The article is subject to two interpretations: 1) The Palestinian State includes also Jordan and thus supersedes [sic] it; 2) The West Bank is detached from Jordan.

ARTICLE 3) THE PALESTINIAN ARAB PEOPLE POSSESSES THE LEGAL RIGHT TO ITS HOMELAND, AND WHEN THE LIBERATION OF ITS HOMELAND IS COMPLETED IT WILL EXERCISE SELF-DETERMINATION SOLELY ACCORDING TO ITS OWN WILL AND CHOICE.

The decision concerning the problem of the internal regime is deferred until after the liberation. The crux of this article is to postpone the decision concerning the relation to the Kingdom of

---

4. Text of the Covenant is printed in all upper case type. Commentary by Y. Harkabi appears in upper and lower case type.

Jordan and Hashemite rule. There is also the emphasis here that only the Palestinian Arabs possess a national legal right, excluding of course the Jews, to whom a special article is devoted below.

ARTICLE 4) THE PALESTINIAN PERSONALITY IS AN IN-NATE, PERSISTENT CHARACTERISTIC THAT DOES NOT DISAPPEAR, AND IT IS TRANSFERRED FROM FATHERS TO SONS. THE ZIONIST OCCUPATION, AND THE DIS-PERSAL OF THE PALESTINIAN ARAB PEOPLE AS RESULT OF THE DISASTERS WHICH CAME OVER IT, DO NOT DE-PRIVE IT OF ITS PALESTINIAN PERSONALITY AND AF-FILIATION AND DO NOT NULLIFY THEM.

The Palestinian, therefore, cannot cease being a Palestinian. Palestinianism is not citizenship but an eternal characteristic that comes from birth. The Jew is a Jew through the maternal line, and the Palestinian a Palestinian through the paternal line. The Pales-tinians, consequently, cannot be assimilated. This article implies that Palestinian citizenship follows from the Palestinian character-istic. This is the Palestinian counterpart to the Law of Return.

ARTICLE 5) THE PALESTINIANS ARE THE ARAB CIT-IZENS WHO WERE LIVING PERMANENTLY IN PALESTINE UNTIL 1947, WHETHER THEY WERE EXPELLED FROM THERE OR REMAINED. WHOEVER IS BORN TO A PALES-TINIAN ARAB FATHER AFTER THIS DATE, WITHIN PALESTINE OR OUTSIDE IT, IS A PALESTINIAN.

A reinforcement of the previous article. This definition refers solely to the Arabs. With reference to the Jews the matter is dif-ferent. This is because being Palestinian is basically equivalent to being Arab.

ARTICLE 6) JEWS WHO WERE LIVING PERMANENTLY IN PALESTINE UNTIL THE BEGINNING OF THE ZIONIST INVASION WILL BE CONSIDERED PALESTINIANS.

In the section on resolutions of the Congress, in the chapter entitled "The International Palestinian Struggle" (p. 51), it is stated: "Likewise, the National Council affirms that the aggression against the Arab nation and its land began with the Zionist invasion of Palestine in 1917. Therefore, the meaning of "removal of the traces of the aggression" must be removal of the traces of the aggression which came into effect from the beginning of the Zionist invasion and not from the war of June, 1967. . . ."

"The beginning of the Zionist invasion" is therefore at the time of the Balfour Declaration. This conception is current in Arab political literature. In the 1964 version the corresponding article was: "Jews of Palestinian origin will be considered Palestinians if they are willing to endeavor to live in loyalty and peace in Palestine." The expression "of Palestinian origin" is vague, for the article does not specify which Jews are to be considered of Palestinian origin. Since in the previous article (5 in the new version, 6 in the old) the date which determines being Palestinian is set at 1947, the implication could be that this applies also to the Jews. Since the aim is the return of the Arab Palestinians, it is necessary to make room for them. However, in the meantime, Jews have taken up residence in Arab dwelling-places, especially those Jews who immigrated after 1947; hence also from a practical aspect it is necessary to remove these Jews in particular.

The Jews who will not be recognized as Palestinians are therefore aliens who have no right of residence and must leave.

The National Covenant is a public document intended for general distribution. The Executive Committee of the Palestine Liberation Organization specified in its introduction to the official report of the proceedings of the Congress as follows: "In view of the importance of the resolutions of the Palestinian National Council in its session convened in Cairo from July 10 to 17, 1968, we published them in this booklet so that the Palestinians in every place may read them and find in them a policy and a program. . . ." (pp. 17-18).

One might expect that those hundred members of the National Council would have recoiled from adopting such an extreme position which could serve as a weapon against the Palestinians. The fact that they did not is itself of great significance and testifies to the severity of the Palestinian Arab position.

A year and a half has elapsed since the Covenant was amended, sufficient time to raise criticism against this manifestation of extremism. However, until now no Arab body, including the Popular Front for the Liberation of Palestine, which is usually critical of the Palestine Liberation Organization and Fatah, has dissociated itself from the position presented in this article. To the best of my knowledge, no article has been published in an Arab newspaper that raises criticism against it. This silence is also highly significant.

The amended version of this article points to a radicalization of the Palestinian Arab position. It contains decisive evidence as to the nature of the slogan Arab leaders brandish concerning a "pluralistic, democratic state." Pluralism that is expressed in the elimination of two million four hundred thousand Israeli Jews is nothing but throwing dust in the eyes.

Arab spokesmen add that the aim is for the Palestinian state to be secular, as opposed to Israel, which they condemn as an anachronistic state founded upon a religious principle. It should be noted, however, that in all the constitutions of the Arab states (except Lebanon) Islam is explicitly established as the state religion. The Syrian constitution of 1964 stipulates that the president of the state must be a Muslim. In most of the constitutions it is also emphasized that the *Shari'a* (Islamic Law) is the source of the laws of the state. Fatah appealed to a congress held in al-Azhar University in September, 1968 to consider contributions to the fedayeen *Zakât* (a religious alms tax) and warfare against Israel, *Jihâd*. Thus they wage a religious war in order to establish a secular state. The crown of democracy, with which Palestinian spokesmen adorn the Palestinian state, also arouses scepticism in view of the Arabs' failure to set up democratic regimes.

Even if the Palestinians, realizing how this article damages their cause, amend it, such an amendment would be tactical and reactive, a response to foreign criticism, while the 1968 version reflects the more spontaneous mood.

ARTICLE 7) THE PALESTINIAN AFFILIATION AND THE MATERIAL, SPIRITUAL AND HISTORICAL TIE WITH PALESTINE ARE PERMANENT REALITIES. THE UPBRINGING OF THE PALESTINIAN INDIVIDUAL IN AN ARAB AND REVOLUTIONARY FASHION, THE UNDERTAKING OF ALL MEANS OF FORGING CONSCIOUSNESS AND TRAINING THE PALESTINIAN, IN ORDER TO ACQUAINT HIM PROFOUNDLY WITH HIS HOMELAND, SPIRITUALLY AND MATERIALLY, AND PREPARING HIM FOR THE CONFLICT AND THE ARMED STRUGGLE, AS WELL AS FOR THE SACRIFICE OF HIS PROPERTY AND HIS LIFE TO RESTORE HIS HOMELAND, UNTIL THE LIBERATION—ALL THIS IS A NATIONAL DUTY.

The second part, the preparation for the struggle, is new and was formulated under the influence of the special place that is now given to fedayeenism.

ARTICLE 8) THE PHASE IN WHICH THE PEOPLE OF PAL-
ESTINE IS LIVING IS THAT OF THE NATIONAL (*WAṬANĪ*)
STRUGGLE FOR THE LIBERATION OF PALESTINE.
THEREFORE, THE CONTRADICTIONS AMONG THE PAL-
ESTINIAN NATIONAL FORCES ARE OF A SECONDARY
ORDER WHICH MUST BE SUSPENDED IN THE INTEREST
OF THE FUNDAMENTAL CONTRADICTION BETWEEN
ZIONISM AND COLONIALISM ON THE ONE SIDE AND THE
PALESTINIAN ARAB PEOPLE ON THE OTHER. ON THIS
BASIS, THE PALESTINIAN MASSES, WHETHER IN THE
HOMELAND OR IN PLACES OF EXILE (*MAHĀJIR*), ORGA-
NIZATIONS AND INDIVIDUALS, COMPRISE ONE NA-
TIONAL FRONT WHICH ACTS TO RESTORE PALESTINE
AND LIBERATE IT THROUGH ARMED STRUGGLE.

It is necessary to postpone internal disputes and concentrate on
warfare against Israel. The style of "secondary contradictions" and
"fundamental contradictions" is influenced by the language of Fatah
and the younger circles. In the previous corresponding article it is
stated: "Doctrines, whether political, social or economic, shall not
divert the people of Palestine from their primary duty of liberating
their homeland. . . ."

ARTICLE 9) ARMED STRUGGLE IS THE ONLY WAY TO
LIBERATE PALESTINE AND IS THEREFORE A STRATEGY
AND NOT TACTICS. THE PALESTINIAN ARAB PEOPLE
AFFIRMS ITS ABSOLUTE RESOLUTION AND ABIDING DE-
TERMINATION TO PURSUE THE ARMED STRUGGLE AND
TO MARCH FORWARD TOWARD THE ARMED POPULAR
REVOLUTION, TO LIBERATE ITS HOMELAND AND RE-
TURN TO IT, [TO MAINTAIN] ITS RIGHT TO A NATURAL
LIFE IN IT, AND TO EXERCISE ITS RIGHT OF SELF-
DETERMINATION IN IT AND SOVEREIGNTY OVER IT.

The expression "a strategy and not tactics" is from the lexicon
of Fatah expressions (see Y. Harkabi) *Fedayeen Action and Arab
Strategy* [Adelphi Papers, No. 53, The Institute for Strategic Studies,
London, 1968], p. 8). They use it with reference to fedayeen activities: they are not a support weapon but the essence of the war.
"The armed struggle" is a broader concept, but here too stress is
placed on action of the fedayeen variety. "The armed popular revolution" signifies the participation of the entire people in the war

against Israel. It is depicted as a stage that will be reached by means of broadening the activity of the fedayeen. They are merely the vanguard whose role is to produce a "detonation" of the revolution until it embraces all levels of the people.

The radicalism in the aim of annihilation of the State of Israel and the "liberation" of all its territory eliminates the possibility of a political solution, which is by nature a compromise settlement. Such is the reasoning in this article and in Article 21. There remains only the way of violence.

ARTICLE 10) FEDAYEEN ACTION FORMS THE NUCLEUS OF THE POPULAR PALESTINIAN WAR OF LIBERATION. THIS DEMANDS ITS PROMOTION, EXTENSION AND PROTECTION, AND THE MOBILIZATION OF ALL THE MASS AND SCIENTIFIC CAPACITIES OF THE PALESTINIANS, THEIR ORGANIZATION AND INVOLVEMENT IN THE ARMED PALESTINIAN REVOLUTION, AND COHESION IN THE NATIONAL (*WAṬANĪ*) STRUGGLE AMONG THE VARIOUS GROUPS OF THE PEOPLE OF PALESTINE, AND BETWEEN THEM AND THE ARAB MASSES, TO GUARANTEE THE CONTINUATION OF THE REVOLUTION, ITS ADVANCEMENT AND VICTORY.

·   This article is new. It describes the "alchemy" of fedayeenism, how its activity broadens and eventually sweeps the entire people. The masses in Arab countries are described in the language of Fatah as constituting "the supportive Arab front," the role of which is not only to offer aid but to assure that the Arab states will not deviate, on account of local interests and pressures, from their obligation to support the Palestinian revolution.

ARTICLE 11) THE PALESTINIANS WILL HAVE THREE MOTTOES: NATIONAL (*WAṬANIYYA*) UNITY, NATIONAL (*QAWMIYYA*) MOBILIZATION AND LIBERATION.

Here there is no change. These mottoes are inscribed above the publications of the Palestine Liberation Organization.

ARTICLE 12) THE PALESTINIAN ARAB PEOPLE BELIEVES IN ARAB UNITY. IN ORDER TO FULFILL ITS ROLE IN REALIZING THIS, IT MUST PRESERVE, IN THIS PHASE OF ITS NATIONAL (*WAṬANĪ*) STRUGGLE, ITS PALESTINIAN PERSONALITY AND THE CONSTITUENTS THEREOF, IN-

CREASE CONSCIOUSNESS OF ITS EXISTENCE AND RESIST
ANY PLAN THAT TENDS TO DISINTEGRATE OR WEAKEN
IT.

The idea of Arab unity requires giving priority to the pan-Arab
character over the local character. From the aspect of a consistent
doctrine of unity, stressing local character or distinctiveness is divisive because it strengthens difference, whereas unity rests on what is
common and uniform. The issue of the relation between local
distinctiveness and pan-Arab unity has much preoccupied the ideologues of Arab nationalism. The conservative circles tend to stress
the need for preserving local character even after unity has been
achieved. By this means Arab unity will be enriched through
variegation. The revolutionary circles, on the other hand, stress
unity and homogeneity. This is based either on a practical consideration, that internal consolidation will be reinforced in proportion to the reduction of distinctive factors, or on the view that the
local character is part of the heritage they wish to change. The
controversy between distinctiveness and unity is also reflected in
the conception of the structure of unity. Those who seek to preserve
distinctiveness deem it necessary to conserve the existing political
frameworks in a loosely confederated unified structure. Those who
stress unity tend to try and obliterate the existing political frameworks, along with their boundaries, which were merely the adjunct
of a colonial system, with the object of achieving a more consolidated political structure. This controversy may be represented as
an antinomy in which Arab nationalism is caught: Unity which
tries to suppress the distinctive character of its parts will arouse
local opposition; unity which conserves the local distinctive character may abet [sic] divisive tendencies.

This article intends to answer the charge that stressing Palestinian distinctiveness is an objective that conflicts with Arab unity
(in the language of Arab nationalism, the sin of Shu'ûbiyya or
Iqlîmiyya). This charge was heard, for example, from within circles
of the Qawmiyyûn al-'Arab movement, who were dedicated to the
idea of Arab unity. Previous to the Six Day War this charge also had
a practical aspect, namely, the assessment that excessive stress on the
Palestinianism of the struggle against Israel diminished the role of
the Arab states as direct participants in this confrontation. The
response to this charge is, therefore, that preservation of Palestinian
distinctiveness is merely a temporary necessity, to be transcended in
favor of Arab unity. There is, however, a contradiction between

this contention and the previous assertion of the eternity of the Palestinian personality.

ARTICLE 13) ARAB UNITY AND THE LIBERATION OF PALESTINE ARE TWO COMPLEMENTARY AIMS. EACH ONE PAVES THE WAY FOR REALIZATION OF THE OTHER. ARAB UNITY LEADS TO THE LIBERATION OF PALES-TINE, AND THE LIBERATION OF PALESTINE LEADS TO ARAB UNITY. WORKING FOR BOTH GOES HAND IN HAND.

This again is an antinomy. Victory over Israel requires concentration of all Arab forces upon the struggle, a concentration made possible only by the establishment of a supra-state authority to control all these forces, that is, a common government. Nasser repeatedly warned that unity is a precondition for initiating war against Israel. But attaining unity is a long-range affair. Consequently, war against Israel is deferred until a remote time, because undertaking a war without unity would only lead to defeat. On the other hand, unity can be attained only by the detonation of a spectacular event, like victory over Israel. The ideologues of Fatah were much preoccupied with this issue (see *Fedayeen Action and Arab Strategy*, p. 9). Their response is contained in their slogan: "The liberation of Palestine is the road to unity, and this is the right substitute for the slogan, 'unity is the road to the liberation of Palestine.' " Actually, this article offers a verbal solution, circumventing the problem of priority by characterizing both events as contemporary, just as in the previous version of the Covenant.

ARTICLE 14) THE DESTINY OF THE ARAB NATION, IN-DEED THE VERY ARAB EXISTENCE, DEPENDS UPON THE DESTINY OF THE PALESTINE ISSUE. THE ENDEAVOR AND EFFORT OF THE ARAB NATION TO LIBERATE PALES-TINE FOLLOWS FROM THIS CONNECTION. THE PEOPLE OF PALESTINE ASSUMES ITS VANGUARD ROLE IN REAL-IZING THIS SACRED NATIONAL (*QAWMI*) AIM.

This is a common notion in the Arab position. It is often stated in Arab political literature that the Palestine issue is *fateful* for the very Arab existence. It is maintained that the existence of Israel prevents the Arabs from achieving their national goal. Furthermore, the existence of Israel necessarily leads to its expansion and the liquidation of the Arabness of additional Arab lands. The Palestinians have an interest in stressing the fatefulness of the struggle against Israel and its centrality for the whole Arab world. They thus spur on the others to take an active role in the struggle against Israel. It may be that there is also hidden here the intention to lend symmetry to the conflict. Thus, both sides threaten each other with extinction, and the Arabs are not alone in this. A formula for division of labor is also presented here. The Palestinians will be the vanguard marching before the Arab camp.

ARTICLE 15) THE LIBERATION OF PALESTINE, FROM AN ARAB VIEWPOINT, IS A NATIONAL (*QAWMĪ*) DUTY TO REPULSE THE ZIONIST, IMPERIALIST INVASION FROM THE GREAT ARAB HOMELAND AND TO PURGE THE ZIONIST PRESENCE FROM PALESTINE. ITS FULL RESPONSIBILITIES FALL UPON THE ARAB NATION, PEOPLES AND GOVERNMENTS, WITH THE PALESTINIAN ARAB PEOPLE AT THEIR HEAD.

The goal is, therefore, twofold: defense of the rest of the Arab countries and removal of Zionism from Palestine.

FOR THIS PURPOSE, THE ARAB NATION MUST MOBILIZE ALL ITS MILITARY, HUMAN, MATERIAL AND SPIRITUAL CAPABILITIES TO PARTICIPATE ACTIVELY WITH THE PEOPLE OF PALESTINE IN THE LIBERATION OF PALESTINE. THEY MUST, ESPECIALLY IN THE PRESENT STAGE OF ARMED PALESTINIAN REVOLUTION, GRANT AND OFFER THE PEOPLE OR PALESTINE ALL POSSIBLE HELP AND EVERY MATERIAL AND HUMAN SUPPORT, AND AFFORD IT EVERY SURE MEANS AND OPPORTUNITY ENABLING IT TO CONTINUE TO ASSUME ITS VANGUARD ROLE IN PURSUING ITS ARMED REVOLUTION UNTIL THE LIBERATION OF ITS HOMELAND.

There is the implied concern lest, without the support of the Arab states, the drive of "the Palestinian revolution" will dissipate. The distinction of this version as compared with its predecessor, is mainly in the accentuation of "the active participation" of the Arab states and the issue of "the armed Palestinian revolution," which is certainly to be attributed to Fatah's ideological influence upon the Palestine Liberation Organization.

ARTICLE 16) THE LIBERATION OF PALESTINE, FROM A SPIRITUAL VIEWPOINT, WILL PREPARE AN ATMOS-

PHERE OF TRANQUILITY AND PEACE FOR THE HOLY
LAND, IN THE SHADE OF WHICH ALL THE HOLY PLACES
WILL BE SAFEGUARDED, AND FREEDOM OF WORSHIP
AND VISITATION TO ALL WILL BE GUARANTEED, WITH-
OUT DISTINCTION OR DISCRIMINATION OF RACE,
COLOR, LANGUAGE OR RELIGION. FOR THIS REASON,
THE PEOPLE OF PALESTINE LOOKS TO THE SUPPORT OF
ALL THE SPIRITUAL FORCES IN THE WORLD.

ARTICLE 17) THE LIBERATION OF PALESTINE, FROM A
HUMAN VIEWPOINT, WILL RESTORE TO THE PALES-
TINIAN MAN HIS DIGNITY, GLORY AND FREEDOM. FOR
THIS, THE PALESTINIAN ARAB PEOPLE LOOKS TO THE
SUPPORT OF THOSE IN THE WORLD WHO BELIEVE IN
THE DIGNITY AND FREEDOM OF MAN.

The very existence of Israel and the lack of a Palestinian homeland create alienation in the Palestinian, for these deprive him of
his dignity and bring him to a state of subservience. As long as Israel
exists the Palestinian's personality is flawed. This is an addition in
the spirit of Fatah which was not in the previous version, and it is
probably influenced by recent revolutionary literature, such as the
teaching of Franz Fanon.

ARTICLE 18) THE LIBERATION OF PALESTINE, FROM AN
INTERNATIONAL VIEWPOINT, IS A DEFENSIVE ACT NE-
CESSITATED BY THE REQUIREMENTS OF SELF-DEFENSE.
FOR THIS REASON, THE PEOPLE OF PALESTINE, DESIR-
ING TO BEFRIEND ALL PEOPLES, LOOKS TO THE SUP-
PORT OF THE STATES WHICH LOVE FREEDOM, JUSTICE
AND PEACE IN RESTORING THE LEGAL SITUATION TO
PALESTINE, ESTABLISHING SECURITY AND PEACE IN ITS
TERRITORY, AND ENABLING ITS PEOPLE TO EXERCISE
NATIONAL (*WATANIYYA*) SOVEREIGNTY AND NATIONAL
(*QAWMIYYA*) FREEDOM.

As in the previous version, the existence of Israel is illegal;
therefore war against it is legal. In Palestinian literature there is a
frequent claim that the fedayeen assaults against Israel are legal,
while the self-defense and reactions of Israel are illegal, for their
aim is to perpetuate the state which embodies aggression in its very
establishment and existence. To the foreign observer this distinction
between the legality of attacking Israel and the illegality of the response may appear as sham innocence that is indeed even ludicrous.

Nevertheless, it may be assumed that there are Arabs for whom this is not only a matter of formal argument but a belief.

Ibrahim al-'Abid, in an article entitled "The Reasons for the Latest Israeli Aggression" (The Six Day War), writes: "Fedayeen action is a right of the people of Palestine because the right of national liberation is an extension of the right of peoples to self-defense, and it is the right which the United Nations Charter affirmed as an original natural right" (Anis Sayegh, ed., *Filastīniyyāt*, PLO Center for Research, Beirut, 1968, p. 107).

ARTICLE 19) THE PARTITIONING OF PALESTINE IN 1947 AND THE ESTABLISHMENT OF ISRAEL IS FUNDAMENTALLY NULL AND VOID, WHATEVER TIME HAS ELAPSED, BECAUSE IT WAS CONTRARY TO THE WISH OF THE PEOPLE OF PALESTINE AND ITS NATURAL RIGHT TO ITS HOMELAND, AND CONTRADICTS THE PRINCIPLES EMBODIED IN THE CHARTER OF THE UNITED NATIONS, THE FIRST OF WHICH IS THE RIGHT OF SELF-DETERMINATION.

It is often found in Arab literature that the Mandate and the Partition Resolution, though accepted by the League of Nations and the United Nations Organization, have no legal force. They represent an aberration and not a norm of international law. The reason for this is that they contradicted the fundamental principle of the right of self-determination. This article is copied from the previous version.

ARTICLE 20) THE BALFOUR DECLARATION, THE MANDATE DOCUMENT, AND WHAT HAS BEEN BASED UPON THEM ARE CONSIDERED NULL AND VOID. THE CLAIM OF A HISTORICAL OR SPIRITUAL TIE BETWEEN JEWS AND PALESTINE DOES NOT TALLY WITH HISTORICAL REALITIES NOR WITH THE CONSTITUENTS OF STATEHOOD IN THEIR TRUE SENSE. JUDAISM, IN ITS CHARACTER AS A RELIGION OF REVELATION, IS NOT A NATIONALITY WITH AN INDEPENDENT EXISTENCE. LIKEWISE, THE JEWS ARE NOT ONE PEOPLE WITH AN INDEPENDENT PERSONALITY. THEY ARE RATHER CITIZENS OF THE STATES TO WHICH THEY BELONG.

Again an identical formulation. This article incorporates the principal claims concerning historical right: The Jews lived in Palestine for only a brief time; their sovereignty over it was not exclusive; the Arabs did not conquer it from them and need not restore it to them; and the Arabs remained in the country longer than the Jews. Moreover, a state embodies a national, not a religious, principle. The Jews, as having merely religious distinctiveness, do not need a state at all, and a Jewish state that makes of Judaism a nationalism is a historcial and political aberration. Therefore, Zionism, as a manifestation of Jewish nationalism, distorts Judaism.

Since the State of Israel is not based on a true nationalism, it is very often described in Arabic as "an artificial entity." This is also brought as proof that Israel can be destroyed. This conception is also at the basis of fedayeen theory: since the Jews have no real nationalism, terror will cause their disintegration to the point that they will consent to relinquish Jewish statehood.

The conception that the Jews do not constitute a national entity is a vital principle for the Arab position. For if the Israelis are a nation, then they have the right of self-determination, and the claim that only the Palestinian Arabs have the right of self-determination, and that only they must decide the national character of the country, is not valid. Moreover, the Arab claim for exclusive national self-determination appears in all its starkness as chauvinism that demands rights for itself while denying the same rights to the other.

ARTICLE 21) THE PALESTINIAN ARAB PEOPLE, IN EX-PRESSING ITSELF THROUGH THE ARMED PALESTINIAN REVOLUTION, REJECTS EVERY SOLUTION THAT IS A SUBSTITUTE FOR A COMPLETE LIBERATION OF PALESTINE, AND REJECTS ALL PLANS THAT AIM AT THE SETTLEMENT OF THE PALESTINE ISSUE OR ITS INTERNATIONALIZATION.

This rejection of any compromise settlement is an addition to the previous version. In the resolutions of the fourth session of the Palestinian National Council a long and detailed section is devoted to the rejection of the Security Council Resolution of November 22, 1967 and any peaceful solution, with insistence upon the intention to undermine any attempt in this direction.

ARTICLE 22) ZIONISM IS A POLITICAL MOVEMENT ORGANICALLY RELATED TO WORLD IMPERIALISM AND HOSTILE TO ALL MOVEMENTS OF LIBERATION AND PROGRESS IN THE WORLD. IT IS A RACIST AND FANATICAL MOVEMENT IN ITS FORMATION; AGGRESSIVE,

EXPANSIONIST AND COLONIALIST IN ITS AIMS; AND
FASCIST AND NAZI IN ITS MEANS. ISRAEL IS THE TOOL
OF THE ZIONIST MOVEMENT AND A HUMAN AND GEO-
GRAPHICAL BASE FOR WORLD IMPERIALISM. IT IS A
CONCENTRATION AND JUMPING-OFF POINT FOR IM-
PERIALISM IN THE HEART OF THE ARAB HOMELAND,
TO STRIKE AT THE HOPES OF THE ARAB NATION FOR
LIBERATION, UNITY AND PROGRESS.

In this new version there is an accentuation of Israel's relation
to world imperialism and intensification of its denunciation. This is
in the spirit of the Leftist sentiments that prevail among the up-and-
coming Arab generation. The claim that the hostility of Zionism is
directed, not only against the Arabs, but against all that is good in
the world, is also an addition. Thus, warfare against Israel is ele-
vated from an Arab interest to a universal humanistic mission.

ISRAEL IS A CONSTANT THREAT TO PEACE IN THE
MIDDLE EAST AND THE ENTIRE WORLD. SINCE THE
LIBERATION OF PALESTINE WILL LIQUIDATE THE ZION-
IST AND IMPERIALIST PRESENCE AND BRING ABOUT
THE STABLILIZATION OF PEACE IN THE MIDDLE EAST,
THE PEOPLE OF PALESTINE LOOKS TO THE SUPPORT OF
ALL LIBERAL MEN OF THE WORD AND ALL THE FORCES
OF GOOD, PROGRESS AND PEACE; AND IMPLORES ALL OF
THEM, REGARDLESS OF THEIR DIFFERENT LEANINGS
AND ORIENTATIONS, TO OFFER ALL HELP AND SUP-
PORT TO THE PEOPLE OF PALESTINE IN ITS JUST AND
LEGAL STRUGGLE TO LIBERATE ITS HOMELAND.

ARTICLE 23) THE DEMANDS OF SECURITY AND PEACE
AND THE REQUIREMENTS OF TRUTH AND JUSTICE
OBLIGE ALL STATES THAT PRESERVE FRIENDLY RELA-
TIONS AMONG PEOPLES AND MAINTAIN THE LOYALTY
OF CITIZENS TO THEIR HOMELANDS TO CONSIDER
ZIONISM AN ILLEGITIMATE MOVEMENT AND TO PRO-
HIBIT ITS EXISTENCE AND ACTIVITY.

The attachment of Jews to Israel expressed in Zionism creates
dual-nationality and political chaos. Arabs apparently do not sense
the contradiction in this claim. Despite the prevalence of supra-
national tendencies among circles in the progressive world, with
which the Palestinians claim to have an affinity, a narrow, formal

nationalistic approach is stressed here, which maintains that a man cannot cherish a loyal attachment to any factor apart from his own state.

ARTICLE 24) THE PALESTINIAN ARAB PEOPLE BELIEVES IN THE PRINCIPLES OF JUSTICE, FREEDOM, SOVEREIGNTY, SELF-DETERMINATION, HUMAN DIGNITY AND THE RIGHT OF PEOPLES TO EXERCISE THEM.

ARTICLE 25) TO REALIZE THE AIMS OF THIS COVENANT AND ITS PRINCIPLES THE PALESTINE LIBERATION ORGANIZATION WILL UNDERTAKE ITS FULL ROLE IN LIBERATING PALESTINE.

This article (with the omission of the conclusion, "in accordance with the fundamental law of this organization") is identical to the previous version. In this and the next article the Palestine Liberation Organization is presented as the umbrella organization bearing the general responsibility for the struggle of all the Palestinians against Israel.

ARTICLE 26) THE PALESTINE LIBERATION ORGANIZATION, WHICH REPRESENTS THE FORCES OF THE PALESTINIAN REVOLUTION, IS RESPONSIBLE FOR THE MOVEMENT OF THE PALESTINIAN ARAB PEOPLE IN ITS STRUGGLE TO RESTORE ITS HOMELAND, LIBERATE IT, RETURN TO IT AND EXERCISE THE RIGHT OF SELF-DETERMINATION IN IT. THIS RESPONSIBILITY EXTENDS TO ALL MILITARY, POLITICAL AND FINANCIAL MATTERS, AND ALL ELSE THAT THE PALESTINE ISSUE REQUIRES IN THE ARAB AND INTERNATIONAL SPHERES.

The addition here, as compared with the previous version, is that the organization assumes also the role of bringing into effect the regime it prefers after the victory.

ARTICLE 27) THE PALESTINE LIBERATION ORGANIZATION WILL COOPERATE WITH ALL ARAB STATES, EACH ACCORDING TO ITS CAPACITIES, AND WILL MAINTAIN NEUTRALITY IN THEIR MUTUAL RELATIONS IN THE LIGHT OF, AND ON THE BASIS OF, THE REQUIREMENTS OF THE BATTLE OF LIBERATION, AND WILL NOT IN-

TERFERE IN THE INTERNAL AFFAIRS OF ANY ARAB
STATE.

The obligation of neutrality, therefore, is not absolute but is
qualified by the requirements of the battle of liberation.

ARTICLE 28) THE PALESTINIAN ARAB PEOPLE INSISTS
UPON THE ORIGINALITY AND INDEPENDENCE OF ITS
NATIONAL (*WAṬANIYYA*) REVOLUTION AND REJECTS
EVERY MANNER OF INTERFERENCE, GUARDIANSHIP
AND SUBORDINATION.

The Palestinian movement is not the tool for any Arab state
and does not accept orders from any outside authority.

ARTICLE 29) THE PALESTINIAN ARAB PEOPLE POSSESSES
THE PRIOR AND ORIGINAL RIGHT IN LIBERATING AND
RESTORING ITS HOMELAND AND WILL DEFINE ITS POSI-
TION WITH REFERENCE TO ALL STATES AND POWERS
ON THE BASIS OF THEIR POSITIONS WITH REFERENCE
TO THE ISSUE [OF PALESTINE] AND THE EXTENT OF
THEIR SUPPORT FOR [THE PALESTINIAN ARAB PEOPLE]
IN ITS REVOLUTION TO REALIZE ITS AIMS.

This is a new article, which includes a threat that the friendship of any state toward Israel will entail the enmity of the organization. A similar principle was established in the First Arab Summit
Conference.

ARTICLE 30) THE FIGHTERS AND BEARERS OF ARMS IN
THE BATTLE OF LIBERATION ARE THE NUCLEUS OF
THE POPULAR ARMY, WHICH WILL BE THE PROTECT-
ING ARM OF THE PALESTINIAN ARAB PEOPLE.

In other words, there is a future in the fedayeen or military
career.

ARTICLE 31) THIS ORGANIZATION SHALL HAVE A FLAG,
OATH AND ANTHEM, ALL OF WHICH WILL BE DETER-
MINED IN ACCORDANCE WITH A SPECIAL SYSTEM.

ARTICLE 32) TO THIS COVENANT IS ATTACHED A LAW
KNOWN AS THE FUNDAMENTAL LAW OF THE PALES-

TINE LIBERATION ORGANIZATION, IN WHICH IS DE-
TERMINED THE MANNER OF THE ORGANIZATION'S
FORMATION, ITS COMMITTEES, INSTITUTIONS, THE
SPECIAL FUNCTIONS OF EVERY ONE OF THEM AND ALL
THE REQUISITE DUTIES ASSOCIATED WITH THEM IN
ACCORDANCE WITH THIS COVENANT.

ARTICLE 33) THIS COVENANT CANNOT BE AMENDED EX-
CEPT BY A TWO-THIRDS MAJORITY OF ALL THE MEM-
BERS OF THE NATIONAL COUNCIL OF THE PALESTINE
LIBERATION ORGANIZATION IN A SPECIAL SESSION
CALLED FOR THIS PURPOSE.

The Liberation of Palestine Is Supported by International Law and Justice

ISSA NAKHLEH

In 1919 Palestine, Iraq, Lebanon and Transjordan were recognized as independent states by all the nations assembled in Paris for the Versailles Peace Conference, and at the same time they were temporarily placed under Mandates of the League of Nations.

The Mandate for Palestine was entrusted to Great Britain. The population of Palestine in 1919 was 95% Moslem and Christian Arabs and 5% Jews.

The Mandate system was created by Article XXII of the Covenant of the League of Nations for the administration of the non-Turkish provinces of the Ottoman Empire and former German colonies. The States placed under Mandates fell into three classes: Class "A" included Palestine, Iraq, Syria, Lebanon and Transjordan; Class "B" comprised Togoland, the Cameroons, Tanganyika and Ruanda; Class "C" included Southwest Africa, German Samoa, New Guinea and others.

According to Article XXII of the Covenant of the League of Nations the countries of the Class "A" Mandate, which included Palestine, "were recognized as provisionally independent nations, subject to the rendering of administrative advice and assistance by a Mandatory until such time as they are able to stand alone."

Under international law Palestine was recognized as a State, with territory, with fixed boundaries and with a population "whose wellbeing and development formed a sacred trust of civilization." The British Mandatory organized a civil administration which it called the Government of Palestine. That Government consisted of an Executive, a Judiciary and ten Departments, which administered the affairs of the country. The Government of Palestine was headed by a High Commissioner and a Chief Secretary, aided by various Assistant Secretaries. Palestine citizenship was created by the Palestine Citizenship Order-in-Council which defined who were to be considered citizens of Palestine. Palestine passports were issued to citizens. The Government of Palestine took part ir

many important international conferences and became a member
of several international agencies.

These facts are proof that Palestine had all the qualifications of
a State under international law. However the indigenous population of Palestine were unable to exercise their sovereignty due
to the presence there of the British High Commissioner and other
British officials.

Britain Denies Palestine Self-Determination

All countries placed under Mandates have become independent
and are now members of the United Nations with the exception
of Palestine and a few others.

In the 29 years following 1919 the British Mandatory failed to
carry out its mandate to give the population of Palestine independence and self-determination. Throughout that period Great
Britain continued dumping alien Jews into an Arab country and
using the Balfour Declaration as justification.

The Balfour Declaration confirmed the infamous and perfidious
conspiracy by which in 1916 Great Britain betrayed her Arab
allies in World War I by promising world-wide alien Jews "a Jewish
national home in Palestine" as the price the Zionist Jews demanded for using their influence to railroad the United States into
World War I as Great Britain's ally. Samuel Landman, a London
solicitor and legal adviser to the World Zionist Organization, described, in his *Great Britain, the Jews and Palestine* (London,
1936), the Balfour Declaration as follows: " . . . the best and perhaps the only way (which proved so to be) to induce the American
President to come into the War was to secure the co-operation of
Zionist Jews by promising them Palestine, and thus enlist and
mobilise the hitherto unsuspectedly powerful forces of Zionist
Jews in America and elsewhere in favour of the Allies on a *quid
pro quo* contract basis."

As soon as this conspiracy became known to the Arabs they
protested vigorously, demonstrated and demanded their liberty

and independence. From 1919 to 1939 many Arab uprisings took place. British military forces, reaching 200,000 British troops in 1936–1939, crushed Arab resistance using the most unjustified and ruthless methods. More than 50,000 Palestinian Arabs were killed during the 29 years of British rule in Palestine. More than 100,000 Palestinian Arab nationalists were imprisoned or thrown into concentration camps. Many British Commissions were sent from London to investigate the situation in Palestine. Each and every one of them came to the identical conclusion – that the Mandate was "unworkable because there existed two incompatible obligations, one to the indigenous Arab population and the other to Jews."

Jews Resort to Terrorism

Ultimately the British Government issued the 1939 White Paper, promising Palestine self-determination and limiting the further immigration of Jews to Palestine. This White Paper enraged the international Jewish Agency and Zionists throughout the world. While Great Britain was engaged in a life and death struggle in World War II, terrorist gangs of Jews in Palestine – the Hagana, the Irgun and the Stern gangs – waged an armed insurrection, committing the most barbaric atrocities and acts of terrorism against the British forces, the Government of Palestine and the civilian Arab population. Many thousand victims were killed, maimed or wounded. According to official British documentary evidence David Ben-Gurion and his Jewish Agency colleagues plotted, planned and ordered the execution of these crimes and atrocities.

Palestine Question Submitted to United Nations

In 1947 the Government of the United Kingdom decided it could no longer handle the situation in Palestine and referred the problem to the United Nations. When the General Assembly of the United Nations met in a special session in April 1947, there were

in Palestine 1,350,000 Moslem and Christian Arabs who were
Palestine citizens by birth, about 200,000 Jews naturalized Pales-
stine citizens and about 450,000 alien Jews, mostly illegal immigrants.

A United Nations Special Committee on Palestine was appointed
to investigate the problem and make recommendations for political settlement. The influence of the Western Powers and Zionist
machinations produced a "majority plan" for partitioning Palestine. The "minority plan" proposed a Federal State.

By pressure, undue influence and power politics a resolution
proposing reference of the Palestine issue to the International
Court of Justice to determine whether the United Nations had
authority to partition Palestine or any other country was rejected
in the General Assembly.

As the result of pressure and improper manipulation by the
Western Powers the General Assembly of the United Nations
adopted the resolution of November 29, 1947, recommending the
"partition" of Palestine into an Arab State, a "Jewish State" and
an International Zone for the Jerusalem-Bethlehem area.

Civil War broke out in Palestine immediately after the adoption
of the United Nations "partition resolution." The Security Council
discussed the situation in Palestine and considered it a threat to
international peace, adopting resolutions for a cease fire and truce.
It recommended a special session of the General Assembly to
"consider further the future Government of Palestine." The Second Special Session of the General Assembly convened on April
16, 1948. The United States submitted proposals for placing Palestine under Trusteeship, whereby the Trusteeship Council would
exercise supervisory powers over Palestine, appointing a Governor-
General.

While the United Nations was in session searching for a peaceful
solution to this problem, the minority of Jews in Palestine by
force and violence, aided and abetted by British troops, expelled
more than one million Moslem and Christian citizens from Palestine from their ancestral homeland, occupying their homes and

properties, robbing them of all their personal possessions. Jews owned less than 1% of Palestine, yet they plundered and occupied all private and public property in 80% of Palestine. The minority of Jews in Palestine was about 30% of the total population, less than one-half were naturalized Palestine citizens and the balance illegal alien immigrants.

British-Zionist Conspiracy

It is an historic fact that prior to the month of April, 1948, Palestine Arabs were winning the fight against the Jews throughout the country. Arabs dominated more than 82% of the area of Palestine. Jews were unable to travel on highways between important cities. All Jewish quarters in Jerusalem were about to surrender. Jews lost every battle they fought against Palestine Arabs. In the 1951 *Year Book* of occupied Palestine, pages 44–45, David Ben-Gurion confirms the victories of Palestine Arabs, stating "by March [1948] anyone without faith could find ample justification for believing the end was near . . . This last week in March was the black week."

The massacre of Arabs in Deir Yasin occurred on April 10, 1948. Terrorist Jews massacred more than 350 aged Arab men, women and children with barbarism exceeding that of the Nazis. Terrorist Jews stripped ten Arab women naked, forced them into a truck, displaying them in a victory parade throughout the Jewish quarters, later turning them loose in the outskirts of the Arab quarters.

The British then carried out their part of the bargain by supplying Jews with all types of the most modern weapons, including Centurian tanks. British forces disarmed Arabs in every city, town and village throughout Palestine. The British military forces took part in battles between Jews and Arabs, insuring victory for the Jews. This British-Zionist conspiracy resulted in the expulsion of Arabs from Tiberias, Haifa, Jaffa, Acre, Safad, Beisan, modern Jerusalem and all villages surrounding these towns. When the disarmed Arab civilian population were threatened with massacre by the terrorist Jews, the British military forces, representing the British Mandatory Power and as such responsible for law and order, were considerate enough to urge the Arabs to surrender and generous enough to offer army trucks and lorries to evacuate Arab civilians to enable them to take refuge in neighboring Arab countries!

Could there have been a more honorable way by which Great Britain, the Mandatory Power, fulfilled her obligation to lead Palestinians to independence and self-determination? Zionist claims of victory were made to deceive world public opinion. Zionists know they did not win a war honorably on the field of battle. It was a "British-made" victory. British armed forces aided and abetted Jews, enabling them to win the second round against the Palestine Arabs after April 1948. Great Britain used her then powerful influence in the Arab world to prevent Palestine Arabs from taking part in the war after May 15, 1948.

Zionists Defy United Nations

In spite of the fact that the United Nations General Assembly was still meeting in the Special Session called to search for a peaceful solution of the Palestine problem, the international Jewish Agency on May 14, 1948, proclaimed their so-called "Declaration of Independence."

The Jews in occupation of Palestine called themselves the so-called "State of Israel" and organized a so-called "Provisional Government." The international Zionist gangsters believed they could thus wipe the State of Palestine off the face of the map by a stroke of their pen and by "proclaiming" their "Declaration of Independence." The Jews, a minority in Palestine, by force and violence violated the territorial integrity of Palestine and the political independence of the Moslem and Christian Arab majority of Palestine. The Jews expelled more than one million Arab citizens from their ancestral homeland in defiance of Article 2, Paragraph 4, of the United Nations Charter which "forbids the threat or use of force against the *territorial integrity or political independence of any State,* or in any other manner inconsistent with the purpose of the United Nations."

Points of International Law

These are the facts of the Palestine tragedy. But what is the position according to international law, the United Nations Charter and the Charter of Human Rights? Can a naturalized Palestine citizen who is a Jew expel a native Palestine citizen who is a Moslem or a Christian? If not, can a Jew, who is an alien illegal immigrant in Palestine, do so? If a minority of Jews by force and violence occupied 80% of Palestine, what right do these Jews have in Palestine as occupants under international law? Can these Jews legally claim they are a "Jewish State"? Can these Jews claim sovereignty in Palestine under international law?

Citizens Cannot Expel Citizens

A citizen of a State cannot expel another citizen. A State cannot expel or exile a native citizen. Since the First World War the international community has endeavored to lay rules for the protection of minorities and safeguarding their rights to life, liberty and religious freedom. The maxim adopted was that all citizens were to be equal before the law, enjoy the same civil and political rights without any distinction due to race, language or religion. It also provided that minorities or any State could petition the League of Nations if these rights were violated.

The preamble of the United Nations Charter reaffirms faith in fundamental human rights, in the dignity and worth of the human person, in the equal rights of men and women, of nations large and small. The Declaration of Human Rights guarantees against violation of the rights of the individual. These principles of international law support our contention that the minority of the naturalized Palestine Jews could not expel the majority of the

citizens of Palestine from their ancestral homeland and deprive
them of their citizenship, their political, religious and civil rights,
and their right to political independence and self-determination.

If international law affords protection to minorities and guarantees their rights and freedom, is it not legal and logical to assume
that the same protection of the law is afforded to the majority
against the minority? What would be the position under international law if the 3,500,000 Jews in New York State expelled the
13,500,000 Christians and proclaimed themselves "Israel-on-the-
Hudson"? What would be the position under international law if
the 7,000,000 French Canadians expelled the 12,000,000 British
Canadians and proclaimed themselves the "State of Joan of Arc"?
What would be the position under international law if the colored
minority of Georgia expelled the white majority and proclaimed
themselves the "Republic of Ham"?

Aliens Cannot Expel Citizens

If naturalized Jews in Palestine cannot deprive Palestine Arabs
of their rights, under what principle of international law and
justice can alien Jews, legal or illegal residents in Palestine, deprive
the indigenous Arab Palestine population of sovereignty and birth-
right in their homeland?

According to the principles of international law, "the natural
home and field of activity of every human being is his home State.
He cannot claim any right to be admitted to, or settle in, foreign
States. If admitted, he is merely a guest who must put up with the
conditions offered him. He must obey the general laws of the land.
Being a foreigner he must put up with the lack of many advantages
conferred on the natives. If he is not satisfied, he can leave the
country."(Ross: *A Textbook of International Law*). In the present
case alien Jews illegally in occupation of Palestine claim every
right and deny the lawful indigenous population all their rights.

Jews Used Force in Defiance of the United Nations

Commenting on the use of force and any change that might take place in Palestine, Senator Warren Austin, United States Ambassador to the United Nations, in a statement to the Security Council on April 1, 1948, described the legal position in Palestine as follows: "So long as there is a Mandate no other country or people has a right to use military force in Palestine. Until an agreement is entered into which transmits this responsibility from the United Kingdom to its successor, or until an agreement is made with the United Nations, the Security Council has the responsibility of trying to maintain order and peace in Palestine." (Security Council official records).

Yet, by an armed insurrection and in defiance of the General Assembly of the United Nations and the Security Council, Jews occupied 80% of Palestine and "proclaimed" themselves the counterfeit so-called "State of Israel."

Occupants Acquire No Rights or Sovereignty

The rules of war in international law deal with the occupation by one State of the territory of another State. At the same time it considers the occupation by armed insurrection as a military occupation to which the principles of international law apply. The concensus of opinion of international lawyers confirms the following principles:

1. "Insofar as the Covenant of the League of Nations, the Charter of the United Nations and the General Treaty for the Renunciation of War prohibit war, they probably render invalid conquest on the part of the State which has resorted to war." (Lauterpacht: *Oppenheim's International Law*).

2. "The occupant does not in any way acquire sovereign rights in the occupied territory but exercises a temporary right of administration on a trustee basis. . . . The legitimate government of the territory retains its sovereignty but . . . the

latter is suspended during the period of belligerent occupation." (von Glahn: *Occupation of Enemy Territory*).

3. "Military occupation does not confer title or extinguish a nation. As long as the people of the occupied country do not accept military conquest, so long as they can manifest, in one way or another, their inalterable will to regain freedom, their sovereignty even though flouted, restricted and sent into exile still persists." (Philip Marshall Brown, in: *American Journal of International Law,* Volume 35).

4. "Mere seizure of territory does not extinguish the legal existence of a government." (Charles Cheney Hyde: *International Law as Applied by the United States*).

5. "The occupant is not entitled to alter the existing form of government, to upset the constitution and domestic laws of the territory occupied or set aside the rights of the inhabitants." (War Office [London], *Manual of Military Law*).

6. "The most important principle of law is that occupation does not displace or transfer sovereignty." (McNair: *Legal Effects of War*).

7. "The rights of the inhabitants of an occupied territory are also safeguarded against abuse and violation. They owe no allegiance of any sort to the occupying power. Their family honor and rights, and private property, must be protected. Individual or mass forcible transfers, as well as deportation of the inhabitants from occupied territory to the territory of the occupying power or that of any other country, are prohibited regardless of their motive." (von Glahn: *Occupation of Enemy Territory*).

The *Manual of Military Law,* published by the British War Office, and Professor von Glahn in his book *Occupation of Enemy Territory,* sum up what an occupant may or may not do in the occupied territory as follows: "It would be unlawful to change the constitution or form of government of the occupied territory, or replace the existing language of the occupied area with the language of the occupant. The nationality of the inhabitants of the occupied area does not change. *The occupant is forbidden to change the internal administration of the area or establish a new State or assist in the maturing of plans to do so."*

Occupation of Palestine by Jews Illegal

These principles of international law establish beyond any shadow of doubt that the occupation of 80% of Palestine by a minority of Jews was illegal. Under international law Jews could not establish a State in Palestine. They could not change the internal administration in the country. They could not substitute a new governmental structure. They could not change the nationality of the inhabitants. They could not replace the Arabic language. They could not expel, exile or forcibly transfer the population of Government of Palestine or occupy, appropriate, dispose of, or use the private property of the inhabitants of the country. They could not commit outrageous acts, atrocities and massacres against the inhabitants.

The international Zionist leaders led by David Ben Gurion and his associates committed in Palestine "war crimes and crimes against humanity" as defined by Article 6 of the Nuremberg Charter, of which Nazi leaders were convicted by the International Military Tribunal and hanged.

Admission to United Nations Cannot Legalize Occupation

When confronted with these cogent arguments some people ask, "What about the admission of the so-called 'State of Israel' to the United Nations?"

We maintain that such admission cannot give the minority of Jews in Palestine, the occupants by force of 80% of Palestine, any right or sovereignty because the United Nations has no authority to do so. One of the purposes of the United Nations in Article 1 of the Charter is *"to bring about by peaceful means and in confor-*

mity with the principles of justice and international law, adjustment or settlement of international disputes or situations which might lead to a breach of the peace."

The words "by peaceful means" and "in conformity with justice and international law" are imperative. The United Nations cannot contravene, violate or ignore the principles of international law and justice. The occupation of Palestine by force and violence by alien Jews and the expulsion of more than one million inhabitants can hardly be said to have beert accomplished by "peaceful means," or are consistent with the principles of justice and international law.

The United Nations, as well as all its members, are bound by the doctrine of non-recognition and therefore cannot recognize in any way the illegal occupation of Palestine by Jews. Lauterpacht in his book *Recognition in International Law* and McMahon in his book *Conquest and Modern International Law* state: "The doctrine of non-recognition is based on the view that acts contrary to international law are invalid and cannot become a source of legal rights to the wrongdoer. That view applies to international law, one of the general principles of law recognized by civilized nations. The principle *ex injuria jus non oritur* is one of the fundamental maxims of jurisprudence. An illegality cannot, as a rule, become a source of legal right to the wrongdoer."

"After the end of hostilities there is full room for the application of the principle that no rights and benefits can accrue to the aggressor from his unlawful act." (Lauterpacht: *Oppenheim's International Law*).

Dr. T. C. Chen in his book *International Law of Recognition* states the position clearly as follows: "It is generally believed that the duty of non-recognition is implied in the Covenant of the League of Nations, Article 10 of which reads 'The members of the League undertake to respect and preserve as against external aggression the territorial integrity and existing political independence of all members of the League.' The refusal to treat a violation as legal seems to be the minimum exertion that ought to be required from other members consistent with their obligations under the Article. The Charter of the United Nations does not contain a guarantee clause similar to Article 10 of the Covenant, yet members of the United Nations have pledged themselves to the purposes and obligations enumerated in Articles 1 and 2 of the Charter. It is hardly possible that recognition of illegal acquisitions could be compatible with these obligations."

Therefore the resolution of the General Assembly of the United Nations had no effect under international law and did not legalize the unlawful occupation of Palestine by Jews.

Admission of So-Called "Israel" to United Nations Illegal

The admission of so-called "Israel" to the United Nations was contrary to international law and to the letter and spirit of the United Nations Charter. A so-called "State of Israel" never existed in fact or in law. It was nothing but an illegal "proclamation" and illegal occupation by a minority of Jews. Furthermore, such admission was obtained by undue pressure and deceit and therefore it is void. This so-called "Provisional Government of Israel," which consisted of international Zionist gangsters, aliens from many foreign lands, representing Zionists throughout the world, submitted an application for membership in the United Nations! On December 17, 1948, the Security Council rejected that application.

The Western Powers submitted the application to the General Assembly in April 1949 and was referred to the Political Committee for further discussion. Many delegates questioned Zionist representatives whether they intended to abide by resolutions of the General Assembly regarding Palestine. The Committee was given affirmative assurance by Abba Eban, a citizen of the Union of South Africa who had no relation to Palestine. His answers were misleading. He gave the impression that Jews intended to abide by United Nations resolutions on Palestine. The Western Powers exerted strong pressure upon delegates in the Political Committee for the admission of the so-called "State of Israel."

Strong pressure by the Western Powers was again exerted in the General Assembly for adopting the resolution of May 11, 1949, for admitting the so-called "State of Israel" to the United Nations.

The General Assembly recalled "its resolution of 29 November 1947 and 11 December 1948 and took note of the declarations and explanations made by the Representative of the Government of Israel [a citizen of the Union of South Africa] before the *Ad Hoc* Political Committee in respect of the implementation of the said resolutions."

Therefore the admission of the so-called "State of Israel" for membership in the United Nations was a qualified admission. Furthermore, Article 4 of the United Nations Charter provides that the United Nations can only admit as a member "a peace-loving State which accepts the obligations of the Charter and able and willing to carry out these obligations."

The so-called "State of Israel" never was a State. It consisted of a minority of Jews, alien illegal immigrants, transplanted into Palestine, who, by an armed insurrection, in violation of international law, expelled more than one million citizens from Palestine and stole all their assets. How could they be a "peace-loving" nation? How could they carry out obligations under the United Nations Charter when their very existence, their occupation of 80% of Palestine and the crimes committed by them against its inhabitants are the greatest mockery of the United Nations Charter?

For these cogent reasons, it is submitted that the admission of these international Zionist gangsters to the United Nations was void *ab initio* and had no validity under international law. It could not possibly convert robbery and looting into an act of benevolence nor transmit crimes into acts of decency nor transform aggression into "peace-loving."

vs Have No Rights or Sovereignty in Palestine

principles of international law to the present

position of the Jews in Palestine, their presence there is nothing but illegal occupation. Unlawful occupation cannot give Jews rights or sovereignty in Palestine. "Sovereignty-in-Exile" is still vested in the 2,000,000 Moslem and Christian indigenous citizens of Palestine.

The Palestine Arabs never have accepted and never will recognize the "British-made" conquest of Palestine by Jews. In the words of a great American scholar and lawyer, Philip Marshall Brown, expressed in Volume 35 of the *American Journal of International Law:* "As long as they [the Arabs of Palestine] do not accept military conquest, as long as they can manifest, in one way or another, their inalterable will to regain freedom, their sovereignty, even though flouted, restricted and sent into exile, still persists. A nation is much more than outward form of territory and government. It consists of the men and women in whom sovereignty resides. So long as they cherish sovereignty in their hearts their nation is not dead. It is not to be denied the symbols and forms of sovereignty on foreign soil or diplomatic relations with other nations."

Italy occupied Ethiopia in 1936. The King of Italy was proclaimed the Emperor of Ethiopia. Eight nations in Europe were occupied by the Nazis in World War II. Their inhabitants were subjected to Nazi rule. Their Governments fled. These eight nations established Governments-in-Exile in London. After many years they regained their sovereignty and independence when the illegal occupation of their respective countries terminated. The fate of aggressors is well known – no matter how long their aggression endures. It will not be long before the Arabs of Palestine liberate their motherland.

The illegal occupation of Palestine by Jews will soon come to an end. The right and the obligation of Moslem and Christian Arabs of Palestine to liberate their ancestral homeland are supported both by international law and well-established precedents.

Peace and the Palestinians

JULIUS STONE

I. INTRODUCTION

The idea of a "Palestinian Entity," articulated concurrently among the Arab States and the Palestinian refugees, is a creature of the past decade. The establishment of a Palestine Arab State had been proposed long ago, of course, in the Partition Resolution of 1947[1] and accepted on behalf of the future state of Israel.[2] The subsequent invasion of the newly formed Israeli state by six Arab countries thwarted its establishment. Although condemned even by the Soviets,[3] the invasion left Jordan and Egypt in military occupation of substantial parts of the abortive Palestine Arab State: the West Bank of the Jordan River, the Gaza Strip and East Jerusalem. Had the concept of a Palestine Arab State not thus come to grief, the specific "nationhood" of its population, scarcely manifest at the time, would perhaps have grown with the responsibility and experience of statehood. That possibility did not materialize. It was not until the decade of the 1960's, and probably not until after the 1967 war, that "Palestinianism" in the specific sense made its entrance on the international stage. The fact that this entry was made in an explosive context of political passion and armed violence should not cloud the long term issue which it raises.

The notion of a "Palestinian Entity" was invoked by Arab States at Arab League meetings in 1959[4] against a background of

* S.J.D., Harvard University; D.C.L., Oxford University. Challis Professor of International Law and Jurisprudence, University of Sydney. This article was prepared during a visit by the author to the Hebrew University of Jerusalem in ____ ng of 1970. Later developments, such as the stand of Egypt and the "liberation terrorist groups in relation to the U.S." peace ccessive crises between Jordan and these groups and the Jor- he Syrian intervention, illustrate the main theme.

II), U.N. Doc. A/519, at 131 (1947).
Ad Hoc Comm. on the Partition of Palestine (1947). The the meetings was the Jewish Agency for Palestine.
meeting 7 (1948). Remarks of the Ukrainian delegate.
1959, at 3, col. 1; id., Sept. 4, 1959, at 3, col. 2; id.,

mutual quarrels as well as the struggle against Israel, the ultimate goal being Israel's dismemberment.[5] Since the 1967 war, the claims of this "entity" have evolved into a central factor offered as material to the current Middle East conflict.[6] Clearly, very substantial preliminary questions arise as to the relevance of such an "entity" to the merits of the conflict. At the outset, one may challenge the genuineness of the supposed association of Palestinian "people" or "nation" with this "entity" in the sense that those are symbols which today imply entitlement to political independence.[7] The second major question concerns what bearing the "entity" could have at this stage of history on the military and political facts or moral issues which characterize the present Arab-Israeli conflict. This article will discuss both questions with primary focus on the latter.

II. Palestinian "Entity" and "Nationhood"

Even scholars rather sympathetic to Arab claims have pointed out that when the British White Paper of 1939[8] had apparently made an independent Arab State inevitable, "most of the country's Arab leaders slipped into lethargy and paralysis of action which was [sic] to last nearly thirty years."[9] Therefore, whatever interpretation might be given to the sporadic and mostly localized attacks by Arabs on Jews in 1920, 1929 and 1936 to 1939,[10] it still remains a puzzle how and why Palestinian Arab nationalism, had it already existed, could have remained inert and passive during the critical years which followed 1939. As late as 1948, the main role of the Palestinians during the Arab States' attack against the new State of Israel was either to accept life under the new State or to leave

---

Sept. 6, 1959, at 24, col. 3; id., Sept. 7, 1959, at 3, col. 1; id., Sept. 9, 1959, at 8, col. 3. A complete account of the issues at the Conference is noted in the referenced N.Y. Times articles.

5. Id.

6. See S. Shamir, The Attitude of Arab Intellectuals, in The Anatomy of Peace in the Middle East 5, 21 (1969). On the role of the new elites among the Palestinians, see Harkabi, The Position of the Palestinians in the Israel-Arab Conflict and Their National Covenant, 3 N.Y.U.J. Int'l L. & Pol. 209 (1970).

7. The attempt at association lies behind the deliberate use of the Arabic term for "nation" to symbolize Pan-Arab nationalism (qawniyya) and the term for "peoplehood" to represent the several independent Arab countries (wataniyya). See The Palestinian National Covenant, 3 N.Y.U.J. Int'l L. & Pol. 228 (1970) and commentary thereon by Harkabi, note 6 supra.

8. Parliamentary Papers 1939, Cmd. No. 6019.

9. Peretz, Arab Palestine, Phoenix or Phantom?, 48 Foreign Affairs 322, 323-24 (1970).

10. See generally C. Sykes, Crossroads to Israel (1965).

their homes to seek shelter with the Arab States and their armies. Pending more persuasive historical studies, these facts seem to point to a movement merely stirred and manipulated, and then only sporadically, by forces outside Palestine.

III. THE "ENTITY" AS A FACTOR IN THE PRESENT CONFLICT

Assuming, however, that either in 1960, 1967 or 1970 the demand for a Palestinian "entity" has acquired a genuine relation to the notion of a Palestinian Arab "peoplehood," a second question arises. What bearing would this assumed fact have on the present military and political situation or the moral position of each side? The answer is neither simple nor easily determined.

Obviously, a specific Palestinian consciousness associated with the idea of establishing a Palestinian "entity" which emerged in the 1960's must, in some sense, be a factor in the present stage of the Middle East conflict. Yet chronology does not allow this factor to be decisive in judging events which took place a half century or even a generation before, in 1917, or 1922, or 1948. An emergent nationalism cannot be treated as if it had developed decades before for purposes of facilely ignoring entitlements previously fixed and acted upon. Thus to ignore chronology would result in an arbitrary reconstruction of both events and rights of peoples, as they presented themselves after World War I, to claim a share in the distribution of the territories of the defeated Turkish Empire.

A. *After World War I*

As a matter of historical fact, the principal claimants in the distribution of the vast, formerly Turkish territories embracing the whole of the Near and Middle East were the Arab and Jewish peoples.[11] The Arabs, of course, were dispersed over the entire area with a number of cultural and political centers, but no particular center in Palestine. One scholar[12] has observed that during this period "there was no distinctive Palestine people, nor political entity." He adds that "the land and its inhabitants were considered backwater regions of the less developed Ottoman Syrian provinces."[13] Another scholar[14] has recalled that even at the height of

---

11. See S. Hadawi, Bitter Harvest—Palestine Between 1914-1967 (1967).
12. Peretz, supra note 9, at 323.
13. Id.
14. J. Parkes, History of Palestine from 135 A.D. to Modern Times (1949).

Arab, and later Turkish, hegemony over the area, Palestine was never exclusively Arab or Moslem anymore than it was exclusively Jewish or Christian, either in population or in cultural and religious concerns. The departure or re-entry of Jews and Christians reflected the degrees of persecution or tolerance of successive local rulers. A part of the Jewish people, driven from Palestine by invading conquerors, remained as dispersed communities throughout the Middle East. Another part ventured into Europe and North Africa. Still another remained in Palestine. But for Jews everywhere Palestine continued into the modern era to be the focus of religious and national life, just as it had also been the center of Jewish political life during the earlier millenium of the kingdoms of David and Solomon and, later, of the Hasmoneans.[15]

This perspective clearly indicates that Jewish and Arab nationalisms, each embracing its own cluster of scattered populations, each sharing specific cultural, religious and historical experiences deeply rooted in the Middle East region, simultaneously claimed the territories liberated during World War I from Turkish sway. Modern concepts of national self-determination necessitate careful identification of claimants to post-war distributions of territory.[16] This point is particularly valid when applied to the assumed recent emergence of a Palestinian "peoplehood." For the assertion that Israel came into existence on the basis of injustice to the Palestinian people distorts historical fact. The Arab claimant after World War I included Arabs throughout the entire area. The Palestinian Arabs were merely a peripheral rather than a distinctive segment whose interests as such were taken into account. Consequently, to present a Palestinian "entity" and people, presumably emergent in the 1960's, as a claimant against Israel now, is an unwarranted and dubious game with history.

The following conclusions about the distribution of territory after World War I and the implementation of the distribution during succeeding decades are in order. First, Jewish and Arab claims in this vast area came to the forum of justice together, not by way of Jewish encroachment upon an already vested and exclusive Arab domain. Second, the allocation made to the Arabs, as implemented by the creation of the existing Arab sovereignties, was markedly greater in area and vastly richer in resources than the "Palestine" designated as the "Jewish National Home." Third,

---

15. M. Louvish, Challenge of Israel 16 (1968).
16. Examples of previous instances are discussed in J. Kunz, The Changing Law of Nations 180, 217 (1968).

by successive steps thereafter, the initially penurious satisfaction of Jewish claims was further reduced. A portion of the original allocation was cut away in 1922 (some 70,000 of 96,000 square kilometers, including the more sparsely populated regions) to establish the State of Transjordan,[17] now renamed Jordan. The partition proposal of 1947[18] included further excisions to establish the Palestine Arab State.[19] Most of the areas designated for that Arab State were in fact seized, and thereafter held until 1967, by Egypt and Jordan in the course of the first armed attack against Israel in 1948.

Contemporary idealogues have attempted to tear the Palestine refugee question from this checkered context of history. Yet it twists and parodies both history and justice to present the Palestine issue as a struggle between the Jews of the world on one hand and the Arabs *of Palestine* on the other in which the Jews seized the major share. The struggle was rather between the Arabs of the Middle East region, including some hundreds of thousands living in Palestine, and the Jews of the world in which the Arabs took a lion's share and from which more than a dozen Arab States emerged. Neither at the time of distribution nor during later decades, moreover, was there any identifiable *Palestinian* Arab people, much less any center of Arab cultural or political life in Palestine.[20] There were Arabs who had lived in Palestine for centuries just as there were Jews who had lived in Iraq, Yemen and other parts of the region for centuries. All were to pay a price for the inheritances their respective nations received.

B. *Aftermath to the Distribution: Refugees*

In the aftermath of these allocations, some 500,000 Arabs were said to have been forced to leave their homes in Palestine.[21] An equal number of Jews were also coerced into leaving their homes and property throughout the various Arab dominions.[22] Marginal interests among major claimants often suffer some degree of wrong even in the course of a just distribution. However, the duty of redress for such wronged marginal interests generally attaches to those who benefit from the overall distribution. The measure of that duty should be gauged according to a rational and proportional division

---

17. A. Reversky, Jews in Palestine 340 (1935).

18. G.A. Res. 181(II), U.N. Doc. A/519, at 131 (1947).

19. Id.

20. Peretz, supra note 9, at 323.

21. Israel Ministry of Foreign Affairs, The Arabs in Israel 89 (1958).

22. Israel Office of Information (New York), Israel's Struggle for Peace 106 (1960).

of responsibilities. The wrong in the Middle East resulted from the initial territorial settlement and continued in a process as drawn out as that from which *all the Arab States, as well as* Israel, emerged. Correctly seen, any injustice which the Arabs of Palestine suffered was as much a function of the creation of the present Arab States as it was a direct result of the establishment of Israel.

Israel, in any case, accepted the responsibility to resettle and rehabilitate fully one half of the one million displaced persons involved, namely the Jews from Arab lands.[23] In addition, she offered to accept a similar responsibility for a significant number of displaced Arabs and offered, as part of a settlement, to receive back some 100,000 Palestinian refugees.[24] The Arab States, with vastly greater areas and resources, have not accepted responsibility to assist in the resettlement of Jewish refugees displaced in the course of the Arab-Israeli conflict. Only a few, moreover, undertook any substantial resettling of displaced Arabs.[25] Instead, the Arabs have sought to keep the "refugee" question alive as a political weapon against Israel, sometimes, as with the U.A.R. in Gaza, by confining the refugees in virtual concentration areas on the borders of Israel.[26] The notion of a Palestinian "entity" derives much of its artificiality from cold calculation in the use of this weapon.

The context in which the burden of making amends to Arabs and Jews displaced as a consequence of the post World War I distribution must be approached is that very distribution itself. As demonstrated above, the distribution overwhelmingly favored the Arabs. The moral principle involved is clear: marginal wrongs occurring in the course of a distribution should be righted by those who benefited from the distribution in proportion to that

23. A. Eban, My People, The Story of the Jews 488-93 (1968).

24. Despite the fact that Israel's offer was never acted upon, Israel reports to have allowed back 48,500 Arabs from divided families as of 1960. Israel Office of Information (New York), supra note 22, at 107.

25. H. Cook, Israel: A Blessing and a Curse 200 (1960). A certain number of the Arab refugees have also been absorbed into some Arab states, notably Lebanon and Jordan. This merely highlights the default of the other Arab states. Egypt, for example, literally confined its displaced kindred in Gaza, left the responsibility of their subsistence with U.N. agencies and concerned itself mainly, for twenty years, with channeling refugee resentment against Israel. Even in Jordan, where some assistance has been provided, there has been a willingness to place the heavy burden for refugee operations on the United Nations. See 55 Palestinian Refugees Today 4 (1968). The anti-Government activity by Palestine liberation groups in Lebanon and particularly Jordan is, in part, the fruit of neglect.

26. At least the Israelis view its use as political. See Discussion, Arab-Israel Parley: Step Toward a Political Settlement, in A Middle East Reader 430 (I. Gendzier ed. 1969).

benefit. It applies equally to Jews and Arabs regardless of whether the controlling assumption is that Arab refugees fled from Palestine as a result of intimidation by Israelis during the 1948 Arab invasion[27] or, as the Israelis assert, because they chose to join the invaders in hope of securing personal safety, possessions and perhaps even some spoils in the event of an Arab dismemberment of Israel.[28] Any final share of responsibility imputed to Israel to aid the half million Arab refugees must necessarily make allowance for the heavy burdens she assumed toward a half million Jewish refugees from Arab countries, particularly in view of the small share of resources allotted to her in the post-war distribution.

The enunciation of this principle does not mean that the international community has no role to play in refugee resettlement and rehabilitation in the area. Obviously, the international community has its own interest in fostering reconciliation and in easing tensions. However, prior standards set within the international community merely highlight the default in the duty to insure that justice is done with respect to the refugee problem in the Middle East. The record since World War II shows a remarkable recognition of the duty to resettle and rehabilitate refugees,[29] stimulated no doubt by international concern for the stabilization of frontiers and the reduction of tensions. These standards are even more plainly drawn when circumstances permit exchanges of populations.[30] The Arab-Israeli impasse would seem to be exactly such a case. But significantly, the Arab position has been characterized by motives which run counter to those of the international community: to increase tension with Israel and undermine the stability of frontiers.

C. *Title by Conquest*

Those who support the Arab cause assert that the claims of Palestinian Arabs do not rest merely on their displacement. A

---

27. The Institute for Palestine Studies (Beirut), The Palestine Question 53 (1968).

28. Israel Ministry of Foreign Affairs, supra note 21, at 7.

29. Since World War II, there have been numerous instances of massive resettlements of refugee populations. See L. Holborn, World Refugees (1960) in regard to West Germany; E. Rees, Century of the Homeless Man (1957) in regard to Austria; Balogh, World Peace and the Refugee Problem, 75 Recueil des Cours Academie de Droit International 363, 396-405 (1949).

30. The standards of civilized duty are even plainer when circumstances permit exchanges of population which will ease majority-minority relations and, therefore, tensions across new frontiers. See e.g., the Greco-Turkish exchange of population after World War I or the less orderly Hindu-Moslem exchanges in the Indo-Pakistani partition of 1948.

second ground offered for the validity of the claims is the seventh century Arab conquest of Palestine.[31] That conquest is juxtaposed against the fact that Jews displaced from Iraq and Yemen had never conquered Iraq or Yemen. The argument raises the important question of whether a military victory in the course of an ancestral incursion thirteen centuries ago is entitled to some moral priority over Israeli victories in two wars of self-defense in this century and, if so, on what grounds.

First, the seventh century Arab conquest is antedated by the older Israelite conquest of the same area from the Hittites and Philistines in the thirteenth century B.C. and the undoubted governance of the land by a succession of Jewish judges and kings for many centuries thereafter.[32] Therefore, those beguiled by claims of title based on ancient Arab conquest cannot consistently dismiss the even more ancient Jewish conquest. And those who place emphasis on more recent Arab conquests must recognize the present State of Israel by its even more recent military ability repeatedly to defeat the neighboring Arab States of the region.

It is, of course, absurd to attribute moral value to either the modernity or antiquity of conquest, as such. Title based on ancient conquest no longer supported by possession is doubly absurd. Such a concept would call for the dismemberment of many existing states in the event descendants of their earliest known conquerors could be found. An intriguing choice of claimants might be presented for the right to displace the English in the United Kingdom or to take title in the various states of North and South America. Israel's possession, based on rightful entry under international law[33] and twice successfully sustained, does not rest on such questionable grounds.

Indeed, according to the more advanced anticolonialist ideas of our age, it is Arab claims in Palestine which require justification. For instance, application of Alexandrowicz's thesis concerning "reversion to sovereignty" of peoples overrun by foreign dominators[34] to the Palestine question would render the Arab position rather threadbare. Alexandrowicz took the view that the descendants of an ancient civilization, which formerly controlled its own affairs but was subsequently submerged under foreign domination, must be regarded as having maintained their sovereignty throughout.

31. Hadawi, supra note 11, at 37-39.
32. See generally A. Sachar, History of the Jews (5th ed. 1968).
33. G.A. Res. 181(II), U.N. Doc. A/519, at 131 (1947).
34. Alexandrowicz, New and Original States: The Issue of Reversion to Sovereignty, 45 Int'l Affairs 465 (1969).

Therefore, when restored to their original land, they join the international community as an old state, reverting as of right to its former sovereignty, rather than as a new state seeking recognition.[35]

This theory is quite obviously responsive to the spirit of decolonization. It expresses a principle of morality and justice more surely, perhaps, than it expresses an established technical doctrine of international law. In any case, its application to the Arab-Israeli conflict is most interesting. For it is clear that no identifiable people now survives which can demonstrate any special relation to Palestine prior to the centuries of Jewish statehood there. The Palestinian Arabs, from the standpoint of history, were but colonists under the wing of imperial conquerors. As indicated before, they never established any specific local civilization or independent political life. Even in terms of advanced anticolonialist concepts therefore, the Palestinian claims remain unconvincing.

D. The Issue of "Majorities."

The Palestinian Arabs have commonly argued that the fact that more Arabs than Jews lived in the area that was designated as the "Jewish National Home" in 1917[36] is decisive. A majority which controls a state often does assert a right to forbid access by others which might disturb its predominance. Conceivably, one could extend some analogous right to a majority which, though not in control, has built a distinctive national life. However, as already discussed, the Arabs of Palestine did not show any specific national distinctiveness at any relevant time. Until recently, they identified themselves as residents of particular cities or districts rather than as Palestinians.

Moreover, the Arab claim to exclude Jews after World War I on the basis of their own numerical majority and currently, in the Palestinian National Covenant,[37] retrospectively to expel all those who entered thereafter is both unrealistic and inconsistent. If applied to present times, when Jews predominate numerically in Palestine, the claim would result in vesting exclusive control in the Jewish majority. Nor does it make any sense to proceed in terms of power to exclude new entries but not to include re-entries. For a significant number of those currently enrolled as "Palestine

---

35. Id. at 478-80.

36. Hussein, My War with Israel 131 (1969); A. Nutting, The Tragedy of Palestine from the Balfour Declaration to Today, in The Arab-Israeli Impasse 54 (M. Khadduri ed. 1968).

37. The Palestinian National Covenant, art. 6, supra note 7, at 230.

refugees" with UNRWA have never lived in that part of Palestine which is now Israel.[38]

In the past, the Arabs did succeed by putting pressure on the former British Mandatory in limiting re-entry of Jews to the mandate-declared "Jewish National Home."[39] Tests of "economic absorptive capacity"[40] were then imposed against the Jews and restrictive estimates, which history has since shown to have been quite arbitrary, were made. The tests were based on the assumption that Jewish entry would result in Arab displacement. But it is clear that Jewish re-entry and settlement did not create an Arab refugee problem.[41] For during the critical years of World War II, the Mandatory Power continued to hold a considerable reserve of public lands, accesss to which was barred to Jewish settlement.[42] This policy, in turn, created a seller's market in land which enabled Palestinian Arabs to reap high profits. Indeed, it was common knowledge, noted by Royal Commissions prior to the institution of restrictions on Jewish landholding, that the reactivation of the land by Jewish resettlement was accompanied by substantial immigration from surrounding Arab countries and increased rather than diminished the local Arab population.[43]

The problem of displaced Arabs, now part of the hard core of the Arab-Israeli problem, was therefore not a product of Jewish re-entry but a by-product of Arab resort to military force in 1948.[44] The validity of this conclusion is not affected by the outcome of the debate as to whether the displacement of Arabs was voluntary or as a result of Israeli pressure.[45] An assessment of the evidence

---

38. The numbers have grown so quickly that the UNRWA has reported difficulty in distributing food due to the large number of third generation refugees. 43 Palestinian Refugees Today 5-6 (1965).

39. Parliamentary Papers 1939, Cmd. No. 6019.

40. Royal Institute of Int'l Affairs, Great Britain and Palestine 1915-1945 60 (1946).

41. It is significant in this regard that art. 5 of the Covenant admits as Arab citizens of the proposed Palestine Arab State only those Arabs living permanently there until 1947 even though art. 6 dates "the Zionist invasion" from 1917. Even in the Arab version of history, then, it is assumed that. no substantial number of Arabs were displaced before 1947.

42. D. Peretz, The Middle East Today 270 (1963).

43. Peel Royal Comm'n, Cmd. No. 5479, at 241-42 (1937).

44. The official Israeli view is somewhat harsher. See speech of A. Eban, 8 U.N. GAOR 215 (1953): "Can Governments really create a vast human problem by their aggression, possess the full capacity to solve it, receive international aid toward its solution and then, with all that accumulation of responsibility upon their hands, refuse to join in the acceptance of any permanent responsibility for the faith and future of their own kith and kin?"

45. Notes 27 and 28 supra.

relating to the major movements, for example of the Arab community from Haifa, indicates that they were inspired by feelings of solidarity with the advancing Arab forces. Those feelings were accompanied, no doubt, by a general fear of impending hostilities in some cases and, in others, by hopes of gain after an Arab victory.[46] Such movements should be regarded as voluntary even though those who left naturally hoped to return either as adherents and followers or as beneficiaries of the invading armies. The choice made by these Arab refugees is easy to understand. Correspondingly, it is difficult to see how Israel, or any other state in a similar situation, having repelled the Arab attack, could be expected to invite their wholesale return. Adherence to the enemy in time of war is not easily countenanced anywhere. Israel's offer to readmit and resettle 100,000 refugees (about 20% of the total) and acceptance of 28,000 returnees whose status was legalized may be regarded as a fair response.[47] But whether an Arab from Haifa, who in 1948 deliberately chose to leave his home and his Jewish fellow citizens in obedience to the call of Arab armies, now manifests painful personal nostalgia or real feelings of "national" resurgence, is a difficult judgment to make. Fanatical campaigns to inculcate hatred against Israel among the refugees do not render the task easier.

E. *In Summary*

In light of the history sketched above, Arab claims of a "Palestinian entity" are unconvincing. If some notion of a Palestinian peoplehood is accepted as a present fact, it would certainly become relevant to the present prospects of an eventual peace among the Arabs themselves and between the Arabs and Israel. However, that notion did not justify the destruction of the 1947 partition

---

46. Statement of Valid al-Qamhawi, in Disaster in the Arab Fatherland, quoted in T. Harkabi, Time Bomb in the Middle East 20 (1970): "These factors, the collective fear, moral disintegration and chaos in every domain were what displaced the Arabs from Tiberias, Haifa, Jaffa and tens of cities and villages." Harkabi claims that the supposed massacre of Arabs at the village of Dir Yassin in Apr., 1948, later alleged to have triggered the flight, was scarcely mentioned in the contemporary reporting and only began to be offered as an explanation many months later.

47. See U.N. Conciliation Comm'n General Progress Rep., 5 U.N. GAOR, Supp. 18, U.N. Doc. A/1367/Rev. 1 (1950). Between 1952 and 1954, all outstanding balances and safe custody articles of refugees in Israeli banks were agreed to be released. Israel also helped to identify and assess refugee land holdings. The Arabs have, of course, insisted from the beginning that no consideration of Israel's security could be taken into account as regards repatriation of all refugees. Id.

plan by military aggression. Nor does it justify the larger design of destroying Israel's existence. Lastly, the inculcation of hatred and lust for revenge in younger generations who probably do not share feelings of nostalgia for a lost homeland, must negate, if unchecked, whatever possibilities remain for a lasting peace in the future.

II. JORDAN AS THE PALESTINIAN ARAB STATE

A. *Masking the Real Issues*

An important part of the present conflict arises precisely from a desperate search to find scapegoats for mistakes and failures. One might expect that the refugees as well as the Arab States should seek to project onto Israel the blame for their own failures and for the frustrations occasioned by mutual rivalries. However, the Arabs have also found a number of other objects of wrath in addition to Israel: imperialism, an Arab-Soviet invention entitled "Nazi-Zionism" and, at critical moments, the United States and United Kingdom.[48] But the difficulties of the Palestinians in fixing their group identity and in defining their homeland are at least in part due to their reluctance to face the fact that it is the existence of Jordan rather than of Israel which results in a deprivation of their claimed rights.

The Palestine promised to the Jewish people in 1917 embraced both Cisiordan and Transiordan.[49] This area lay on both sides of the Jordan River and was within the mandate requested by Britain and granted by the League of Nations in 1922.[50] At that time, however, at Britain's insistence and over the protest of Jewish organizations, Transiordan was taken out of the mandate provision for the establishment of a "Jewish National Home" and allocated to the creation within Palestine of the Emirate of Transiordan.[51] Therefore, when Transiordan became independent in 1946, this state, under the name of Jordan, was then and is now the Arab State within Palestine. The area currently called the West Bank and Gaza and Jerusalem remained within the confines provided for the "Jewish National Home" until 1948 when the State of Israel was established. The subsequent Arab attack resulted in the Jordanian seizure of the West Bank and East Jerusalem,

---

48. The Palestinian National Covenant, art. 22, supra note 7, at 241.
49. C. Weizman, Trial and Error 208 (1949).
50. 3 League of Nations Off. J. 1007 (1922).
51. Id.

while Egypt helped itself to Gaza. This territorial expansion by Jordan, whatever its international standing,[52] only reconfirmed Jordan's character as an Arab State within Palestine. The fact that it was not called the Palestine Arab State was either a semantic evasion or an idiosyncracy of the Hashemite monarch, for neither of which Israel could be held responsible.

It is noteworthy in this regard that as early as 1937 the Peel Commission considered the potential capacity of Transjordan to receive immigrants. The Commission Report noted that the area allotted to Transjordan was nearly two and a half times as large as the residual area of Palestine and contained only about a quarter of its population. It expressed the hope that, if fully developed, Transjordan could hold a much larger population. However, proposals for immigration into Transjordan were dismissed on the ground that Arab antagonism to Jewish immigration was as bitter there as in residual Palestine.[53] Accordingly, in 1937 also, it was apparent that in reality Jordan was the Palestinian Arab State.

Transjordan, then, on its creation in 1922 either had the function of a Palestinian Arab State or of simply another throne for a Hashemite to sit upon. The latter function ceased to suffice after 1948 when Palestinians constituted sixty percent of Jordan's population.[54] It is even less compelling when Palestinian "peoplehood" is assumed to be a present reality in search of a homeland. The available rational solution is for Jordan, with or without the West Bank and Gaza, to *be* the Palestinian Arab State. King Hussein's regime has rejected this solution even during its military occupation and attempted annexation of the West Bank prior to 1967.[55] For the Arabs, turning the demand for self-determination into a demand for the dismantling of Israel, in which Jordan and other Arab States could join, has had the attraction of avoiding, or at least postponing, the day when the Palestinians and the Jordanian Government must settle the real issue between themselves. It also has had the advantage of deflecting attention from the divisive ambitions of Syria, Iraq and Egypt in the ultimate fate of both

---

52. G.A. Res. 181(II), U.N. Doc. A/519, at 131 (1947).

53. Peel Royal Comm'n, supra note 43, at ch. 11.

54. Peretz, supra note 42, at 262, 293.

55. According to the Al Fatah spokesman in Cairo, on Sept. 24, 1970, "the only solution to the Jordan crisis is for the King to abdicate and leave the country." The Australian, Sept. 25, 1970. Conversely, for an account of the Bedouin royalist position, see the report filed by the correspondent of The Guardian, London, The Australian, Sept. 25, 1970.

the West and East Banks of the Jordan River which a Jordanian-Palestinian Arab settlement would bring to a head.[56] In this situation all parties concerned, but especially the Palestinian groups in their relative weakness, find it easier to join a common campaign of hate against Israel than face their internecine disagreements, the solution of which must precede an Arab-Israeli settlement.

Presently, the Arab accusations focus on the charge that Israel's refusal to recognize the claims of Palestinian Arabs blocks the emergence of "Palestinian consciousness" into Palestinian statehood.[57] A segment of Israeli public opinion also advocates that Israel should immediately declare its recognition of a Palestinian Arab right of self-determination.[58] The argument proceeds not upon the assumption that such recognition requires the dismantling of Israel but in the hope of hastening the development of favorable conditions for Palestinian political emancipation in Jordan and the territory of the West Bank. An Israeli reaffirmation of this sort would serve to re-emphasize Israel's continued support for the principle of self-determination in these waning days of the age of decolonization. It might also turn the attention of the Arab States and Palestinians to the real issues which they must first adjust among themselves.

An Israeli reaffirmation of a Palestinian right of self-determination should not, however, lead anyone to the delusion that it could be at all decisive for peace. For Israel's *further* recognition of a Palestinian right of self-determination is, in the existing situation, probably redundant. As already observed, the real question of self-determination centers on the *raison d'être* of the Kingdom of Jordan if not as the Palestine Arab State. People living in Jordan should be permitted to decide that question for themselves.

B. *The Palestinian National Covenant*

It appears clear, especially after the 1968 revision[59] of the Palestinian National Covenant, that the course chosen by the Palestinian groups and the Arab States to avoid facing the issues dividing them is to target demands against Israel which, on their face, are a plain call for Israel's destruction. The 1964 version of what

---

56. M. Kerr, The Arab Cold War 151 (2d ed. 1967).
57. Peretz, supra note 9, at 323-24.
58. See V. Avineri, Israel Without Zionists (1968).
59. The Palestinian National Covenant, note 7 supra.

is presently Article 6 of the Covenant[60] stated that "Jews of Palestinian origin will be considered Palestinians if they are willing to endeavor to live in loyalty and peace in Palestine." This was a theoretically conceivable basis for negotiating a "truly binational" state. In the 1968 amended version, however, only "Jews living permanently in Palestine until the beginning of the Zionist invasion will be considered Palestinians."[61] The Conference[62] made clear that for this and other purposes "the Zionist invasion" was deemed to have begun in 1917.[63] The path chosen by the Palestinian groups renders *any* peaceful settlement with Israel impossible. For it demands, as a precondition, the liquidation of Israel in the form of the expulsion of more than two million of its present citizens. The Covenant makes no reference, moreover, to the need for an asylum for these prospective refugees.

The added difficulties in achieving peace created by this intransigent call for Israel's dismemberment are not eased by skepticism that it represents the views of Palestinians generally. Important differences exist in the claims and postures of Palestinians living in the administered territories and those outside. Perhaps those now living side by side with the Israelis would conform with varying degrees of sincerity, if publicly questioned, to the views expressed in the Covenant. Most Arabs in the Israeli administered territories, however, are concerned with living their daily lives free from terrorist violence and from the Israeli authorities' countermeasures or from guerrilla reprisals for collaboration with Israel. The degree of cooperation with terrorist groups is not significant.[64] The violence which the terrorists find necessary to exert even against the strongly anti-Israel Gaza Arabs suggests, conversely, that there may be some willingness to cooperate with the Israelis.[65]

---

60. The Palestinian National Covenant, 1964 Version, art. 6, 3 N.Y.U.J. Int'l L. & Pol. 199, 200 (1970).

61. The Palestinian National Covenant, art. 6, supra note 7, at 230.

62. Harkabi, supra note 7, at 230.

63. Id.

64. Peretz, supra note 9, at 330. There are serious attempts now being made by both the Israelis and the Palestinians to induce the Arabs living in Israel to support each side. Id.

65. According to a report in the Jerusalem Post, Apr. 6, 1970, at 3, ". . . the main purpose of these terror acts is to prevent the local population from cooperating with the occupying power . . . . At present the terror acts are directed mostly against Gaza Strip citizens who are employed in Israel." In Mar., 1970 alone, 103 Gaza inhabitants were wounded and seven killed by Arab terrorist attacks, five killings being deliberate murders. According to reports of Aug., 1970, there had been 15 political murders by terrorists between mid-July

On the other hand, uncertainty as to a future territorial settlement also deters such cooperation with the Israelis as might result in exposure to the malice of a future Arab regime.

By way of contrast, Palestinians living outside the administered territories lack, as the account of Article 6 of the Covenant indicates, any motives of restraint. Their leaders have a stake in encouraging irresponsibility and in sharpening and widening the conflict. They are rabidly opposed to what Article 21 of the Covenant expresses as "all plans that aim at the settlement of the Palestine issue."[66] Article 21 rejects every solution that is a substitute for "a complete liberation" of Palestine.[67]

IV. CONCLUSION

The Arab States will block the road to a peaceful settlement as long as they continue to endorse the claimed "vanguard" role of the Palestine "liberation" groups.[68] While this position has had the effect of diverting attention from military setbacks, it is an expediency which results in the avoidance of the real issue that must be resolved between Jordan and the Palestine Arabs. The fact remains that it is Jordan which historically and demographically holds the key to the solution of the Palestinian question. By evading this issue, the Arab States are committed to military efforts going well beyond their vital concerns.

This situation represents a fatal circle not only of Arab defeat and frustration in war, but also of the defeat and frustration of long term Arab interests, not to mention those of the Palestinians or of the rest of the world. Until some degree of "self-liberation" is achieved by the Arab States from the more impossible demands of the leadership of the Palestine "liberation" groups, no Israeli initiative can release West Bank and Gaza Arabs from the pressures of terrorism and manipulation so that fruitful negotiations might begin. Peace ultimately will come, if at all, from the self-interested recognition by Jordan or Egypt, or both, that the aims of the present Palestinian leadership cannot succeed in the forseeable future. In the meantime, the price will be paid primarily by the Arab States in terms of the welfare of their people and the stability of their governments.

---

and mid-August, "apparently trying to liquidate Arabs suspected of collaborating with the Israel authorities." The Australian, Aug. 13, 1970.

66. The Palestinian National Covenant, art. 21, supra note 7, at 240.

67. Id.

68. Peretz, supra note 9, at 325.

The Palestine Arab Refugee Problem

LOUISE W. HOLBORN*

In the tangled Middle East situation, one of the most sensitive issues has been the situation of the Palestine Arab refugees.[1] A broad humanitarian but also highly political problem with deep emotional underpinnings, the more than a million Arab refugees remain a major factor in the tension between the Arab states and Israel. This has been the case since, with the creation of the State of Israel in 1948 and the subsequent war between Israel and her Arab neighbours, thousands of Arabs fled their former homeland. The problem was intensified by the conflict of 1956. It reached still more threatening dimensions with Israel's lightning victory in June 1967, which brought under her control large new areas including the Gaza Strip, Jerusalem, the Jordanian West Bank, and the Ali Qunaytirah section in Syria, and thus caused a further flight of refugees from these territories.

At the root of the Arab refugee problem is the continuing state of war, actual or tacit, between Israel and the United Arab Republic, Syria, Jordan and Lebanon, which have never accepted Israel's existence. The refugees have thus been kept in a continual state of expectation that at some future date there will be a return to the territory that was once called Palestine. From the point of view of the Arab

* Professor of Government, Radcliffe Institute, Cambridge, Mass.

[1] Of the extensive writings on the problem, the following general sources may be cited: John Campbell, *Defense in the Middle East* (rev. ed., New York, 1960). Roney Gabbey, *A Political Study of the Arab-Jewish Conflict: The Arab Refugee Problem* (Geneva, 1959). Frank Gervasi, *The Case for Israel* (New York, 1967). Sami Hadawi, *Palestine in the United Nations* (The Arab Information Center, 1964). Manfred Halpern, *The Politics of Social Change in the Middle East and North Africa* (Princeton, N.J., 1963). Robert W. Macdonald, *The League of Arab States* (Princeton, N.J., 1965). Don Peretz, *Israel and the Palestine Arabs* (Washington, D.C., 1958). Benjamin Rivlin and Joseph S. Szyliowicz, *The Contemporary Middle East* (New York, 1965). Nadav Safran, *The United States and Israel* (Cambridge, Mass., 1963). Fayez A. Sayegh, *The Arab-Israeli Conflict* (The Arab Information Center, 1964). Georgianna G. Stevens (ed.), *The United States and the Middle East* (Englewood Cliffs, N.J., 1964). Basic U.N. Documents are listed in U.N. General Assembly, Official Records, Twenty-second Session, Supplement No. 13, Doc. A/6713. *Report of the Commissioner-General of the United Nations Relief and Works Agency for Palestine Refugees in the Middle East*, 1 July, 1966-30 June, 1967 (cited as UNRWA *Annual Report, 1967*), pp. 1-2. For recent developments and resolutions of the General Assembly and Security Council, see *UN Monthly Chronicle*, Vol. 4, Nos. 6-9, June-October 1967.

states, to accept the refugees as integrated members of their communities, even when the refugees have secured jobs and have produced second and even third generations within Arab territories, would be a denial of this objective. For Israel, which already has a settled Arab population of more than a quarter of a million, and which has welcomed Jewish refugees from many of the Arab countries into its own community, the continued insistence that the refugees should be allowed back into the Jewish state is felt to be both irrational and a threat to its survival.[2]

Confronted with this intractable situation, Western nations, and particularly the United States, Great Britain, Canada and France have sought through U.N. agencies, in particular the U. N. Relief and Works Agency for Palestine Refugees in the Near East (UNRWA), and periodic special conferences and/or mediations, to lessen the tension not only by extending emergency relief to the Arab refugees in their camps and makeshift villages but also by providing the kind of economic and educational aid that could enable these people, and particularly the young, to develop skills useful to themselves and to others. Today the problem has become still more acute because of its newly extended dimensions and the heightened political antagonisms resulting from the June war.

Although the flight of the Arab refugees during the June war and its aftermath was not different in kind from earlier outward movements, it formed a high watermark both in numbers and in the extent of territory into which the refugees flooded. Prior to the June war two-thirds of all the refugees under the care of the UNRWA lived in the Gaza Strip and on the West Bank of the Jordan River where fighting occurred. Many more refugees were created as thousands crossed the Jordan to the East Bank with the advance of the Israeli army. Although the Israeli government maintained that its forces would refrain from acts of coercion, and would permit the refugees to remain where

[2] By the end of the British mandate in 1948 an estimated 900,000 Palestine Arabs lived in the territory which became the state of Israel. About 170,000 Arabs stayed after the first Arab-Israeli war. See Peretz, *Israel and the Palestine Arabs*, p. 95. By the end of 1966 the Arab population of Israel had increased to 313,000 through the return of some refugees and natural increase. See Walter Pinner, *The Legend of Arab Refugees* (Tel Aviv, 1967), p. 66; and for Jewish refugees from Arab states see F.T.H. Witkamp, "The Refugee Problem in the Middle East," in Research Group for European Migration Problems, *Bulletin* (The Hague), Vol. 5, No. 1, January/March 1965, p. 26; and Harry B. Ellis, "The Arab-Israel Conflict Today," in Stevens, *The United States and the Middle East*, p. 142.

they were, there were many reasons for this mass flight which has been estimated to include 350,000 new refugees.[3] Probably the most powerful incentive was fear of being caught in Israeli-controlled territory. This fear affected not only the refugees or pre-1967 vintage, but also many Jordanian officials and soldiers who were caught behind the advancing Israeli forces. In addition many fled for economic reasons, either out of fear of losing their UNRWA rations, or of being separated from the monthly remittances sent from relatives working and living in Kuwait or other countries.

Flight also occurred from other areas in which major hostilities took place. UNRWA's Commissioner-General reported that within Syria 115,000 people took flight, 35,000 fled from the Sinai Peninsula to Egypt, and 3-4,000 soldiers of the Palestine Liberation Army also fled to Egypt.[4]

At the specific request of the government, UNRWA began for the first time to operate in the U.A.R., where the problem assumed new dimensions. Many Egyptians had moved from the east bank of the Suez Canal, which was occupied by Israeli forces, and on government initiative large groups also moved from the west bank of the Canal into the interior. In addition, some 1,000 Palestinians from Gaza and Jordan, who were in the U.A.R. for educational and other reasons and were stranded, have been aided by international voluntary agencies.

Although the fighting temporarily dislocated UNRWA's work and facilities, it was possible to reestablish them quickly in large measure because of the relations long existing with the relevant governments and non-governmental organizations. By mid-July new camps had been established, new supply routes were open, and many schools

---

[3] U.N. General Assembly, Official Records, Fifth Emergency Special Session, Doc. A/6787, *Report by the Secretary-General under General Assembly Resolution 2252 (ES-V) and Security Council Resolution 237 (1967)*, August 18, 1967; *U.N. Monthly Chronicle*, Vol. 4, No. 8, August-September, 1967, p. 31; and United Nations General Assembly, Official Documents, Twenty-second session, Special Political Committee, *Report of the Commissioner-General of the United Nations Relief and Works Agency for Palestine Refugees in the Near East*, Doc. A/SPC/121, 13 December 1967, p. 1.

[4] U.N. General Assembly, Official Records, Fifth Emergency Special Session, Doc. A/6723, *Note by the Secretary-General submitting a report of the Commissioner General of the United Nations Relief and Works Agency for Palestine Refugees in the Near East*, June 19, 1967; *ibid.*, Doc. A6723/Add. 1, July 4, 1967; and the reports by the Secretary-General's special representative, Mr. Nils Göran Gussing in U.N. General Assembly, Official Records, Fifth Emergency Special Session, Doc. A/6797, *Report by the Secretary-General under General Assembly Resolution 2252 (ES-V) and Security Council Resolution 237 (1967)*, September 15, 1967.

were in operation once more. While widespread dislocation continued, the worst emergency needs were met. Unfortunately, the agreement painstakingly achieved by the International Red Cross with both sides for the return of large numbers of refugees to the West Bank of the Jordan, where UNRWA had the necessary camps, installations and other facilities, had relatively little effect.[4a] That only fourteen thousand of the 100,000 specified in the agreement took advantage of it was perhaps partly due to the fact that the Israeli government had reserved the right to pass on all applications as security risks, but probably more to the general fear or unwillingness to live under Israeli control. Both sentiments were openly encouraged by the Jordanian government.

In the June crisis the United Nations was constantly concerned with the humanitarian aspects of the situation. On June 14 the Security Council called upon the government of Israel "to ensure the safety, welfare and security of the inhabitants of the area where military operations had taken place and to facilitate the return of those inhabitants who had fled since the outbreak of hostilities." The Council also recommended to the governments concerned "the scrupulous respect of the humanitarian principles governing the treatment of prisoners of war and the protection of civilians and persons in time of war contained in the Geneva Convention of August 12, 1949."[5] On June 26 the President of the General Assembly appealed to all members, both as signatories of the Charter and morally obliged "human beings," to make contributions to ease the suffering and misery of the refugees. On July 4 the Assembly, welcoming the Security Council resolution, unanimously endorsed the efforts of UNRWA, "to provide humanitarian assistance . . ." on an emergency basis and as a temporary measure, "to other persons in the area who are at present displaced and are in serious need of assistance as a result of the recent hostilities."[6] Governments and organizations have contributed money as well as food, medical supplies, tents, blankets. Some assistance was on a bilateral

[4a] For the text of the Agreement (dated June 14, 1967), see UNRWA *Annual Report, 1967*, Annex III, p. 99.

[5] The text of Resolution S/RES/237 (1967) is reproduced in *UN Monthly Chronicle*, Vol. 4, No. 7, July 1967, p. 32.

[6] U.N. General Assembly, Official Records, Fifth Emergency Special Session, Supplement No. 1, Doc. A/6798, *Resolutions adopted by the General Assembly during its Fifth Emergency Special Session 17 June-18 September 1967, Resolution 2252 (ES-V). Humanitarian Assistance*, p. 3.

basis, some was channelled through UNRWA, the Red Cross and Red Crescent organizations, some through other voluntary agencies. Major aid in feeding persons not registered with UNRWA was provided by F.A.O., the World Food Program, and UNICEF. Voluntary agencies have and are playing an important part, not only in supplies and contributions, but also in helping the staff to run some of the facilities.[7]

Thus the emergency measures have been a combined operation of governments directly concerned, other governments, national and international voluntary agencies, and many individuals in many parts of the world. UNRWA, long established in the area and closely connected with the refugees, coordinated these relief works and was also able to provide information of general concern. However, its greatest burden was to continue the activities of the Agency in the difficult situation with respect to all persons within its mandate.

* * * *

In the light of this highly complicated and tense situation what hope for a long-term solution can be found in looking back at earlier efforts and proposals? From the earliest days of the Arab-Israeli conflict the United Nations, which had been so closely connected with the creation of Israel, has been concerned with the refugee situation. Count Folke Bernadotte, the U.N. Mediator appointed in 1948, first brought the refugee problem officially to world attention. Everything that has been done subsequently through the United Nations and its established agencies has its foundations in the key Resolution 194 of December 11, 1948, in which the General Assembly established a Conciliation Commission (C.C.P.) and instructed it to take "steps to assist the governments and authorities concerned to achieve a final settlement of all questions outstanding between them." Although a "final settlement" has not yet been reached, much has been attempted to ameliorate not only the situation of the refugees but also that of the area as a whole.

The guidelines laid down in the 1948 resolution focused on the economic development of the area as well as on the particular needs of the refugees. It instructed the Conciliation Commission "to seek arrangements which will facilitate the economic development of the area, including arrangements for access to ports and airfields and the use of

7 UNRWA Annual Report, 1967, p. 16: and International Council of Voluntary Agencies, Surveys (Geneva, 1967).

transportation and communication facilities." It was also declared that "Refugees wishing to return to their homes and live in peace with their neighbours should be permitted to do so at the earliest practicable date, and that compensation should be paid for the property of those choosing not to return and for loss of or damage to property which, under the principles of international law, or in equity, should be made good by the governments or authorities responsible." The Conciliation Commission was "to facilitate the repatriation, resettlement and economic and social rehabilitation of the refugees and the payment of compensation, and to maintain close relations with the Director of Relief for Palestine Refugees and through him, with the appropriate organs and agencies of the United Nations." These last two paragraphs form the basis for the Arab claim that Israel has never lived up to the basic U.N. pronouncement of this issue.[8]

To aid in implementing these resolutions UNRWA was established in December 1949, directed "to carry out in collaboration with local governments the direct relief and works programs as recommended by the economic survey commission," and "to consult with the interested Near Eastern governments concerning measures to be taken by them preparatory to the time when international assistance for relief and works project is no longer available." The latter provision proved a dead letter, but in response to the former UNRWA assumed the responsibility for providing the Arab refugees with relief, health and medical services, housing, clothing, child care and educational and vocational training. Despite the great physical and political difficulties, it has conducted its huge operation with an impressive combination of humanity and efficiency. Indeed, many of the young people under its care have received better schooling, medical attention and social welfare than ordinary residents of the states in which UNRWA has operated.

That there have been major problems both of administration and of financial obligations is unquestionable. The staff of UNRWA, whose lower ranks are drawn to a large extent from the Arab refugee community, has always had to work within the limits set by the Arab states—the "host countries": Egypt, Syria, Lebanon and Jordan—within which their operations took place. No less serious is the steady increase in the numbers of those listed as refugees for whom UNRWA is

[8] For the Arab point of view, see Gabbey, *A Political Study of the Arab-Jewish Problem*; Pevity, *Israel and the Palestine Arabs*; and Macdonald, *The League of Arab States*, p. 90.

responsible. The original number of refugees who fled from the State of Israel was estimated at 726,000, but by May 31, 1967, 1,344,576 persons were registered with UNRWA.[9] By the eve of the June war about 70 per cent of the total population of the Gaza Strip (then administered by Egypt), more than 36 per cent of Jordan's population, nearly 8 per cent of the Lebanese and 2 per cent of the Syrian population. About 80 per cent of the refugees were farmers, unskilled workers, the aged, the sick, and their families. The other 20 per cent were business and professional men, property owners, skilled labourers and their families. About nine-tenths of the refugees were Moslem, the rest Christian.[10]

The rather startling increase in the number of refugees is owed to a number of causes. The initial working definition of a refugee eligible for relief was: "A person normally resident in Palestine who has lost his home and his livelihood as a result of the hostilities and who is in need." UNRWA changed this definition to: "A person whose normal

---

[9] The 1949 estimate is found in U.N. Conciliation Commission for Palestine, *Final Report of the United Nations Economic Survey Mission for the Middle East*, United Nations Publications, 28 December 1949, Part I, p. 18; see also UNRWA *Annual Report, 1967*, Tables 1 and 2, pp. 59-60. The following table illustrates the refugees in all four host countries who were registered with UNRWA (Source: UNRWA *Annual Report, 1967*, p. 59, Table 1):

June 30, 1950	June 30, 1958	May 31, 1967
960,021	1,053,628	1,344,576

The May 31, 1967, figures involve 254,247 families, of whom 95,031 families (39.6 per cent) lived in 54 camps. *Ibid.*, Tables 4 and 8, pp. 62 and 66.

The following table illustrates the number of Palestine Arab Refugees resettled by 1965, as reported in the Jordan Arabic daily, *Falastin*, September 28, 1965:

Kuwait	50,000
South Arabian Peninsula	26,000
Iraq	9,000
Egypt	8,000
Total	93,000

[10] The following table shows the age distribution of UNRWA registered refugees at May 31, 1967 (Source: UNRWA *Annual Report, 1967*, Table 2, p. 60):

Country	Below 1 year	1-15 years	15 years and over	Total
Jordan	11,993	255,985	454,709	722,687
Gaza	8,984	120,941	186,851	316,776
Lebanon	3,481	64,432	92,810	160,723
Syria	3,794	59,620	80,976	144,390
Total	28,252	500,978	815,346	1,344,576

residence was Palestine for a minimum of two years immediately preceding the outbreak of the conflict in 1948, and who, as a result of this conflict, has lost both his home and means of livelihood."[11] This definition has since been extended to cover the children of such persons. To be eligible for assistance a refugee must reside in one of the four host countries in which UNRWA operates and must be in need.

It has been very difficult, however, to adhere rigidly to these definitions. People who, living right on the border, might still have their home but were cut off from their land, had to be included. There were numerous Bedouins whose place of residence could not be clearly established, but who were in need. There were also refugees who had some money at the outset but who later became destitute and had to be rehabilitated.

Moreover, as was also experienced with displaced persons living for long in camps in Europe, the phenomenon of "being a refugee" has become institutionalized. Even if refugees found adequate economic opportunities they became reluctant to turn in their UNRWA cards which for many years had been the only source for a sense of security. With this card, "real hunger" was practically excluded. One could send one's children to school with it; one obtained free medical aid with it, and exemption from taxes as well. UNRWA itself reported that "The ration card has become, in fact, so much a part of the lives and economy of the refugees that it is not at all unusual for it to be used as a tangible asset upon the strength of which substantial sums can be borrowed."[12]

There were also false registrations and concealment of family deaths. When refugees became self-supporting, there was a reluctance to make this fact known. Testifying before the Senate Sub-Committee on Refugees and Escapees on July 14, 1966, Secretary of State Dean Rusk declared, "There are almost half a million refugees who have registered refugee status but who, in fact, have jobs, and some of them at some distance from the camps, living reasonably normal lives. They want to retain their registered status, yet we would like to see con-

---

[11] U.N. General Assembly, Official Records, Ninth Session, Supplement No. 17A, Doc. A/2717/Add. 1, *Special Report of the Director and the Advisory Commission of the United Nations Relief and Works Agency for Palestine Refugees in the Near East*, p. 2, para. 19.

[12] U.N. General Assembly, Official Records, Ninth Session, Supplement No. 17, Doc. A/2717, *Annual Report of the Director of the United Nations Relief and Works Agency for Palestine Refugees in the Near East, 1 July 1953-30 June 1954*, p. 3, para. 16; and Witkamp, "The Refugee Problem in the Middle East," p. 12.

tinuation of the rectification of the roles, so that the funds that are available will be used as wisely as possible."

The Arab position on repatriation has been from the first to demand that all refugees, who once lived in Palestine, should be accepted, and that establishment of the right of repatriation must precede discussion of all other facets of their dispute with Israel. At the Lausanne Conference held in the spring of 1949, in response to Resolution 194, the Israelis made a slight move away from their otherwise intransigent position that the refugees must be "resettled in Arab lands," by offering to accept 100,000 of the refugees (including in that number 10,000 women and minors to be reunited with their families domiciled in Israel) but only if they had the right to determine the location of their settlement, and whether they were security risks. This proposal was not accepted and the conference broke up.[13] The Arabs had refused to talk directly to the Israelis on the ground that face-to-face negotiations were tantamount to diplomatic recognition, and the positions of the two sides became increasingly rigid.

On acceptable compensation, the two parties have also been unable to agree. Under great international pressure, the Israelis agreed theoretically to consider the question of compensation outside the framework of a general peace settlement, although in general they have insisted that the refugee problem must be dealt with as part of an overall peace settlement. The Israelis also released most Arab refugee funds that had been frozen in Israeli banks. Neither move was accepted on the part of the other side as an acceptable means of opening negotiations.

The third, and ultimately most hopeful approach to a solution of the Arab refugee problem, has been large-scale economic development of Arab lands. In mid 1949 the Technical Committee on Refugees of the Conciliation Commission, after examining the economic situation in those countries of the Middle East affected by the Palestine war of 1948-49, advanced a comprehensive plan to enable the relevant governments to undertake development programmes to overcome the dislocation created by the war, to integrate the refugees into the economic life of the area on a self-sustaining basis within a short period of time, and to promote economic conditions that would be conducive to the maintenance of peace and stability in the area. It recommended

---

[13] For further agreements on the reunion of broken families, see Peretz, *Israel and the Palestine Arabs*, pp. 50f.

the reduction of the Arab refugee relief rolls from 940,000 to 625,000 by January 1950, and proposed gradually replacing relief by a series of works projects through which refugees could be gainfully employed. It estimated that a total of $54.9 million would be needed for relief and works projects for the eighteen-month period within which the Commission believed it would be possible to solve the refugee problem.

These recommendations were accepted by the Fourth General Assembly. The initial relief agency, U.N. Relief for Palestine Refugees, was succeeded by UNRWA, which was established in the hope of bringing both the political and the practical aspects of the refugee problem into a single focus through economic means.[14] Works programmes were developed but had almost no long range effect. Basically, the Arab governments believed that their support of this programme would undermine the right of the refugees to return to their former homes in Israel. The latter contributed almost nothing to the cost of UNRWA projects from which they greatly benefited. At the end of 1952 UNRWA reported to the General Assembly that "the Agency found itself financing and operating labor camps to build public works which the governments themselves would have built the following year." Moreover, when the projects were finished, the refugees returned to their tents and ration lines. None of them was economically integrated. When its public works fund began to run out, UNRWA decided to bring that part of its programme to a close. These works had created neither permanent benefit for the refugees nor financial relief for the United Nations. Instead they had cost five times the amount necessary for simple relief.

The Arab states then requested financial support for a new three-year programme designed to reintegrate the refugees into the economic life of the Middle East, either by repatriation or resettlement. This plan also failed. In February 1957 the Director of UNRWA, reporting to the U.N. General Assembly that little change had occurred in the refugee situation, stated that:

> The reason lies in the realm of politics, and in deep-seated human emotions. It does not lie simply in the field of economics. UNRWA can

---

[14] See the U.N. Conciliation Commission for Palestine, *Final Report of the United Nations Economic Survey Mission for the Middle East*, Parts I and II; and for the text of Resolution 302 (IV), December 8, 1949, U.N. General Assembly, Official Records, Fourth Session, 1949, *Resolutions*, pp. 23-25.

enable some hundreds of refugees to become self-supporting each year through small agricultural development projects, grants to establish small businesses and the like, but it cannot overcome the fact that refugees as a whole insist upon the choice provided for them in the General Assembly Resolution 194 that is, repatriation or compensation.

In an effort to resolve the conflicting claims, President Eisenhower in 1953 sent Eric E. Johnston as his personal representative to the Middle East.[15] Johnston's compromise plan, which won the approval of both Arab and Israeli engineers, was to allocate 60 per cent of Jordan River waters to Lebanon, Syria, and Jordan and 40 per cent to Israel. The Arab technicians' acceptance of the sharing of riparian rights represented a first tacit recognition of Israel's existence, yet at the political level neither side agreed to the implementation of the plan.

At the United Nations the United States, Britain and France submitted a resolution favouring the diversion project, if the rights of all parties could be safeguarded. It was vetoed by the Soviet Union on January 22, 1954. Since that time the diversion issue has been unresolved in both the United Nations and the Middle East.

In 1959 Secretary-General Dag Hammarskjöld was asked by the General Assembly to make recommendations for the "reintegration of the refugees into the economic life of the Near East, either by repatriation or resettlement." He reported that reintegration of Palestine refugees would be possible only "within the context of general economic development."[16] He suggested that outside capital assistance to the Arab countries would be needed in the amount of $1.5 billion between 1960 and 1965. The cost of providing jobs for an additional refugee labour force of some 380,000 persons (as of 1959) would require a further $1.5 billion of external capital investment. The magnitude of this cost of integration effectively cooled international enthusiasm, but his estimate remains a realistic evaluation of the cost of future efforts toward either repatriation or resettlement.

In 1961, at the request of the Conciliation Commission, Dr. Joseph E. Johnson, President of the Carnegie Endowment for International

[15] See Georgianna G. Stevens, *Jordan River Partition* (Stanford 1965).

[16] U.N. General Assembly, Official Records, Fourteenth Session, Doc. A/4121, *Proposals for the continuation of United Nations assistance to Palestine, 15 June 1959.*

Peace, made a new study of the refugee problem.[17] He proposed that "refugee heads of families, insulated by the United Nations from pressure from any source, should be allowed to choose voluntarily between a return to Palestine and compensation." The United States and other members of the United Nations, including Israel, were to contribute to this compensation. Israel was to have the right to run a security check on each refugee opting for return. "Those refugees who had lacked property in Palestine," he suggested, "would receive a reintegration allowance, wherever they might choose to go. Such allowances would be administered through the United Nations, which also would act as a cushion between the two sides during the long process of settlement."[18]

Mr. Johnson's proposals were rejected by the Israel government in January 1962 with a reiteration of a Knesset resolution of November 1961, which asserted that Arab refugees could not return to Israel and that the only solution to the problem was thus in settlement in the Arab states.[19] From their side the Arab governments did not openly reject the proposals but reasserted their persistent stand that Israel must first accept in principle the provisions of Resolution 194.

*   *   *   *

As the handling of the Arab refugee problem has thus been left chiefly to UNRWA, it is particularly important to examine in more detail both UNRWA's organization and its work.

UNRWA was set up as a temporary non-political organ of the U.N. General Assembly, and its existence has been extended several times by it, the last extension being to June 30, 1969. As of December 31, 1966, it had a staff of 11,516 persons, of whom 112 were international staff and 11,404 locally recruited, virtually all Arab refugees. By the end of 1967 it had received total contributions amounting to $590,975,149, from more than 40 nations. About 98 per cent were pledges by the United States, Great Britain, Canada, and France. The

[17] He served as Special Representative of the Commission from August 1961 to January 1963. See Joseph E. Johnson, "Arab versus Israel, A pertinent challenge to Americans," an address delivered to the 24th American Assembly, New York, October 23, 1963.

[18] Harry B. Ellis, "The Arab Israeli Conflict Today," in Stevens, *The United States and the Middle East*, pp. 142-43.

[19] Mrs. Golda Meir, Israeli Minister for Foreign Affairs, before the Special Political Committee, December 14, 1962. U.N. General Assembly, Official Records, Seventeenth Session, Special Political Committee, pp. 240-42.

host countries contributed $10,821,324. The Soviet Union, which had voted for the establishment of UNRWA, has never contributed to its expenditures.[20]

In providing food, shelter, preventive and curative health services, social measures, and educational and vocation training for the refugees, UNRWA has received valuable cooperation and aid from U.N. Specialized Agencies, especially I.R.O., W.H.O., F.A.O. and the World Food Program, UNICEF and UNESCO. In his 1962 Annual Report, Dr. John Davis, then Commissioner General, pointed out the critical needs of refugee youth and UNRWA's important role in satisfying those needs. From that time on UNRWA put its emphasis on further expansion of its educational and vocational programmes in close cooperation and guidance by UNESCO. The achievements in this regard are suggested by the numbers involved. From 1951-1967 the number of elementary and secondary school pupils attending UNRWA-UNESCO schools rose from 43,112 to 186,967. By May 31, 1967, 246,451 refugee pupils were enrolled in 440 UNRWA-UNESCO schools. In addition, a further 47,993 refugee boys and girls attended government and private schools to which UNRWA paid subsidies. 1,855 men and 237 women were enrolled in UNRWA-UNESCO vocational and technical education centres during the 1966-67 school year. Since the training programme

[20] The following table shows the main government contributions, May 1, 1950-December 31, 1967 (Source: UNRWA *Annual Report, 1967*, Table 20, pp. 77-82):

I. Western Countries

United States	$411,218,069
United Kingdom	100,524,004
Canada	21,039,426
France	13,714,303
Sweden	6,619,064
Germany	4,388,021
Australia	3,583,103
New Zealand	2,380,000
Switzerland	1,448,814
Netherlands	1,198,509
Italy	1,141,326
Norway	1,089,066
Israel	406,547

II. Arab Host Countries

United Arab Republic	5,471,162
Gaza Authorities	1,199,919
Jordan	1,891,833
Lebanon	728,967
Syrian Arab Republic	1,529,443

began in 1953 there have been nearly 7,500 graduates, most of whom are now at work throughout the Middle East in the host as well as in other countries. Thus UNRWA's training programme to provide skilled workers and technicians has become a significant channel of technical assistance to the area.

The agency has a staff of 4,640 teachers, 207 handicraft instructors and, in Syria, 56 home economic instructresses. Increasing emphasis has been placed on teacher training to raise the standard of instruction in UNRWA schools. Three UNRWA/UNESCO teacher training institutions are in operation, and in 1964 the UNRWA-UNESCO Institute of Education established its programme of in-service training of teachers with the aim of improving the qualifications of teachers in UNRWA schools without interrupting the teaching. UNRWA also awards university scholarships to specially qualified students. During the 1965-66 academic year 621 scholarships were granted to refugees to attend universities. Thus a pool of training and experience is being established which can have long term consequences for the Middle East.

The Arab-Israeli conflict in June 1967 vastly complicated all these efforts in the short run, but awakened hopes that the very decisiveness of the military victory might create a new climate of opinion within which genuine solutions could be sought. The objective must be to help the Arab refugees to become productive and fully accepted citizens. Their greatest need is for political identity, economic security, and social acceptance.

The West, under the leadership of the United States, has been searching for a comprehensive settlement. In President Johnson's five principles for peace of June 19, 1967, the second is "justice for refugees."[21] The Soviet Union and the Arab countries have been adamant in their demand for the withdrawal of the Israeli armies from the occupied territories before any decisions in regard to refugees would be made.

However, on November 22 the Security Council unanimously adopted a British resolution which parallels to a certain degree President Johnson's five principles and which "affirms the necessity for achieving a just settlement of the refugee problem,"[22] and approved the appoint-

---

[21] "Principles for Peace in the Middle East," *Department of State Bulletin*, Vol. VII, No. 1463, July 10, 1967, pp. 33-34. See also Ambassador Goldberg's reiteration of the same points, *ibid.*, p. 49.

[22] For full text, see *New York Times*, November 23, 1967.

ment of a mediator, the Swedish diplomat, Mr. Gunnar Jarring. If a political settlement is reached through his efforts, the refugee problem will be tackled along with it.[23] This will require both the collective responsibility and cooperation of the Israeli and Arab governments. It would mean giving equal political and civil rights to the refugees wherever they reside, a cessation of anti-Israeli propaganda and a freeing of UNRWA to operate according to its own principles and without the political influence of local governments which have hamstrung it in the past.[24]

The way will then be open for massive economic and educational aid to the whole Middle East. A special co-ordinating role in the solution of this problem will inevitably be played by UNRWA with its knowledge and far-reaching experience. Its general educational and vocational programme should be expanded with the aim of integrating the younger generation into the overall programmes of economic development.

These developments can be stimulated both bilaterally and internally. The United Nations and its various agencies can contribute not only to the integration of the refugees in their territories but also to the accelerated modernization of the Arab countries. Such agencies can assist in the solution of the manifold problems of the area within the framework of regional and international planning. Donor countries, both Western and Communist, could then concentrate upon construction rather than relief and makeshift plans.

[23] U.N. General Assembly, Official Records, Twenty-second Session, Supplement No. 1A, A/6701/Add 1, *Introduction to the Annual Report of the Secretary-General on the Work of the Organization 16 June 1966-15 June 1967*, pp. 6-8. See also Don Peretz, "The Arab Refugees: A Changing Problem," *Foreign Affairs*, Vol. 41, No. 3, April 1963, pp. 558-70; and Cecil Hourani, "The Moment of Truth," *Encounter*, Vol. XXIX, No. 5, November 1967, pp. 3-14.

[24] One of the restraining factors on the planning of the UNRWA has been the fact that prior to submission to the General Assembly the Commissioner-General's Annual Reports have had to be discussed by the Advisory Commission, established by the Assembly (Resolution 302 (IV) paragraph 8) that consists of the principal contributing governments (the United States, Great Britain, France, Belgium and Turkey) and of the four host countries.

Legal Status of Arab Refugees

GEORGE J. TOMEH

INTRODUCTION

It is a source of special gratification to participate in a symposium on the Middle East Crisis, in which not only is attention focused on the basic legal issues but in which these issues are considered as a test of international law. If in the course of the last fifty or even the last twenty years the underlying legal principles had been observed—respect for the rights of peoples, the duties and responsibilities of states, and the sanctity of international pledges and undertakings—the recent history of the Middle East would not have been the tragic sequence we have witnessed. Now, in this moment of anxiety and concern experienced by the Arab states, it is understandable that the Arabs should plead unremittingly for their usurped rights. They expect to make this plea in an environment of understanding for the great issues of mankind, the issues of war and peace, of equity, of sovereign and human rights—the environment of our world's faltering steps toward international law and under such law.

I

SCOPE OF THE PROBLEM

The problem of the legal status of the Arab refugees involves the issue of their rights, the basis of these rights, how these rights have been affirmed or denied, what recourse is open to the refugees and what recourse is open to those concerned on their behalf, against the denial of their rights.

A. Definition and Number of Refugees

The Palestinian Arab refugees are primarily those victims of the 1947-48 tragedy, resulting in a mass exodus of the Arabs of Palestine, who have been living in exile since then. These are the *old refugees*. They number 1,344,576 registered with the United Nations Relief and Works Agency for Palestine Refugees (UNRWA) according to the last census, with 722,687 in Jordan, 316,776 in Gaza, 160,723 in Lebanon, and 144,390 in Syria.[1] There is a second generation of refugees, children of parents themselves born after May 1948. These and the inhabitants of border villages who lost their property or their livelihood, or both, but did not lose the bare walls of their homes, have been ineligible for UNRWA assistance, despite ex-

* M.A. 1944, American University, Beirut; Ph.D. 1951, Georgetown University. Ambassador Extraordinary and Plenipotentiary, Permanent Representative of the Syrian Arab Republic to the United Nations.
[1] Report of the Commissioner-General of the United Nations Relief and Works Agency, 22 U.N. GAOR, Supp. 13, tables 1 and 2, at 59, 60, U.N. Doc. A/6713 (1967).

treme need.[2] UNRWA relief has always been withheld from 282,000 in villages on the Jordan frontier and in the Gaza Strip. Unquestionably, any Palestinian shut out from his homeland and stripped of money and property falls within the category of refugee. Half a million Palestinian Arabs, however, in addition to the numbers above given, have migrated and are self-supporting in the Arab states, the United States, Canada, South America, and other countries.

A second category of *intermediate refugees* includes over 11,000 Arab inhabitants of the Demilitarized Zones between Israel and the neighboring Arab countries and other areas who were made refugees without provision for help from UNRWA because they were expelled by Israel after July 1, 1952, the deadline for eligibility.[3]

The *new Arab refugees* are the victims of the June 5 war. According to the Report of the Commissioner-General of UNRWA submitted to the Twenty-second Session of the U.N. General Assembly, 234,000 Arabs were refugees from Jordan, Syria, and the Sinai Peninsula following the crisis of June 5, 1967, in addition to 100,000 "old" refugees who fled their refugee camps (where they were registered with UNRWA) when these were overrun by the Israeli army.[4] These numbers are on the increase day by day while the Israelis, systematically as in the past, apply terrorist methods to empty the Arab lands of their Arab inhabitants.

II

RIGHTS OF THE REFUGEES

A. Basic Human Rights

Since the events of the June 5 war, which are still fresh in our minds, the rights of the new refugees have been definitely defined. The Security Council on June 14, 1967 adopted Resolution 237,[5] and the General Assembly reaffirmed it by an overwhelming majority on July 4.[6] The Security Council Resolution specifically calls upon the Government of Israel "to ensure the safety, welfare and security of the inhabitants of the areas where military operations have taken place and to facilitate the return of those inhabitants who have fled the areas since the outbreak of hostilities." Both resolutions requested the Secretary-General to follow their effective implementation and to report thereon. The Secretary-General did report on these matters on September 15, 1967, after having sent a Special Representative, Nils Gussing, to the Middle East.[7] As therein reported and subsequently up until the present time, Israel has persistently refused to implement the two resolutions and

---

[2] Report of the Commissioner-General of the United Nations Relief and Works Agency, 20 U.N. GAOR, Supp. 13, at 4-5, U.N. Doc. A/6013 (1965).

[3] *Id.* at 4.

[4] Report of the Commissioner-General, *supra* note 1, at 11.

[5] 22 U.N. SCOR, 1361st meeting 1 (1967).

[6] G.A. Res. 2252, U.N. GAOR, 5th Emer. Spec. Sess., Supp. 1, at 3, U.N. Doc. A/6798 (1967).

[7] U.N. Doc. A/6797, Sept. 15, 1967.

has adopted further illegitimate measures against the civilian population left in the occupied territories.

We submit it is clear that the Palestinian Arab refugees have certain inalienable rights:

1. the right of sovereignty over Palestine
2. the right to nationality—the Palestinian nationality
3. the right to individual property, together with the right to compensation for property arbitrarily expropriated or taken by force
4. the right of return
5. civil and religious rights
6. the right of visitation to the Holy Places
7. the rights of Palestinians inside Palestine

These rights are not mere claims. There are international documents to validate them—treaties, statements, declarations, pledges, and scores of U.N. resolutions. The denial of these rights constitutes, in essence, what is referred to as the Problem of the Palestine Arab Refugees, which has been and will continue to be the powderkeg of the Middle East. The first such transgression of these rights was the Balfour Declaration,[8] which Henry Cattan has denounced in the following words:

> The Balfour Declaration of 1917 which the Zionists have utilized almost as a document of title for the establishment of a national home in Palestine has never possessed any juridical value. Emanating from the British Government which at no moment possessed any right of sovereignty over Palestine the Balfour Declaration could not validly recognize a right of sovereignty in favour of the Jews because a donor can not dispose of what does not belong to him.[9]

Historically, Syria, an integral part of the Arab world, stretched from the Taurus mountains on the north to Egypt on the south, with no intervening linguistic, natural, or racial boundaries of importance, and unbroken, in the nineteenth century, by any national frontier. The sea on the west, the mountains on the north, the desert south and east gave it unity. But by 1922 this area had been carved up in the interests of power politics. Palestine was one of the fragments, created to implement the Balfour Declaration and satisfy World Zionism. The official report of the Shaw Commission, which the British sent to Palestine in 1929, contained the comment: "Viewed in the light of the history of at least the last six centuries, Palestine is an artificial conception."[10]

In spite of these transgressions, pledges came from the Great Powers to safeguard Arab rights. One could cite the safeguard clause of the Balfour Declaration itself: ". . . it being clearly understood that nothing shall be done which may prejudice the

---

[8] The text is officially quoted in CMD. No. 5479, at 22 (1937).
[9] H. CATTAN, TO WHOM DOES PALESTINE BELONG? 5 (1967).
[10] CMD. No. 3530 (1930), reprinted in J.M.N. JEFFRIES, PALESTINE, THE REALITY 2 (1939).

civil and religious rights of existing non-Jewish communities in Palestine." The Anglo-French Declaration to the Arabs of (undivided) Syria and Mesopotamia on November 7, 1918 is explicit: "The object aimed at by France and Great Britain . . . is . . . the establishment of National Governments and administrations deriving their authority from the initiative and free choice of the indigenous populations."[11]

The King-Crane Commission, which was dispatched to the area by President Wilson so that he could ascertain the wishes of the population, recommended, in its report issued June 29, 1919, "that the unity of Syria be preserved, in accordance with the earnest petition of the great majority of the people of Syria." In the words of the report:

> The Commissioners began their study of Zionism with minds predisposed in its favour, but the actual facts in Palestine coupled with the force of the general principles proclaimed by the Allies and accepted by the Syrians have driven them to the recommendation here made.
>
> . . . .
>
> . . . For "a national home for the Jewish people" is not equivalent to making Palestine into a Jewish State; nor can the erection of such a Jewish State be accomplished without the gravest trespass upon the "civil and religious rights of existing non-Jewish communities in Palestine . . . ."[12]

Article 22 of the Covenant of the League of Nations signed on June 22, 1919 is of particular importance, because it was the basis of what later came to be known as the "A" Mandates over Palestine, Transjordan, Iraq, Lebanon, and Syria: "there should be applied the principle that the well-being and development of such peoples form a sacred trust of civilization and that securities for the performance of this trust should be embodied in this Covenant."[13]

Remembering the rights of the Palestine Arab refugees claimed above, let us very briefly look into the Palestine Mandate itself. Article 5 stipulated that "The Mandatory shall be responsible for seeing that no Palestine territory shall be ceded or leased to, or in any way placed under control of, the Government of any foreign Power"; article 7 stated that "The Administration of Palestine shall be responsible for enacting a nationality law. There shall be included in this law provisions framed so as to facilitate the acquisition of Palestine citizenship by Jews who take up their permanent residence in Palestine."[14]

Specific attention should be paid to article 7, because of the right of the refugees to Palestinian nationality, which has been referred to above. The article is unequivocal that the nationality is the Palestinian nationality, that the Jews who take up their permanent residence in Palestine may take up this nationality. Now this

---

[11] Joint Anglo-French Declaration, Nov. 7, 1918, reprinted in CMD. No. 5479, at 25 (1937).

[12] [1919] 12 FOREIGN REL. U.S. 745, 792 (1949), reprinted in 2 J. HUREWITZ, DIPLOMACY IN THE MIDDLE EAST—A DOCUMENTARY RECORD 1914-1956, at 66, 69, 70 (1956).

[13] 3 TREATIES, CONVENTIONS, INTERNATIONAL ACTS, PROTOCOLS AND AGREEMENTS BETWEEN THE UNITED STATES AND OTHER POWERS 1910-1923, at 3336, 3342 (Redmond ed. 1923).

[14] CMD. No. 1785 (1922), reprinted in 2 J. HUREWITZ, supra note 12, at 106, 108.

same nationality is denied to the people who comprised, when that article was formulated, ninety-eight per cent of the total population of Palestine, namely, the Arabs.

The history of Palestine from the institution of the Mandate until 1939 was the history of an Arab people in almost continuous armed rebellion as they saw themselves gradually subjugated by piecemeal conquest which became full conquest in 1947. They saw their right to self-determination being denied and minority status imposed upon them.

Meanwhile, the British government realized the conflict of interests between Arabs and Jews in Palestine. It would be cumbersome to discuss all the British statements of policy issued during this period affirming, time after time, Arab rights under the Mandate. Only two will be mentioned here. First, the Churchill Memorandum or "White Paper" of 1922, which states:

> Unauthorized statements have been made to the effect that the purpose in view is to create a wholly Jewish Palestine. Phrases have been used such as that Palestine is to become "as Jewish as England is English." His Majesty's Government regard any such expectation as impracticable and have no such aim in view. Nor have they at any time contemplated, as appears to be feared by the Arab Delegation, the disappearance or the subordination of the Arabic population, language or culture in Palestine. They would draw attention to the fact that the terms of the Declaration referred to do not contemplate that Palestine as a whole should be converted into a Jewish National Home, but that such a Home should be founded *in Palestine.*[15]

Second, the British statement of May 1939, known as the MacDonald "White Paper," reaffirmed the obligation under the Mandate "to safeguard the civil and religious rights of all the inhabitants of Palestine," and asserted that "His Majesty's Government believe that the framers of the Mandate in which the Balfour Declaration was embodied could not have intended that Palestine should be converted into a Jewish State against the will of the Arab population of the country."[16]

These documents and pledges are not obsolete—not matters of academic interest only. They are ineradicable facts, to be reckoned with in assessing later events, and the denial to the Arab people of Palestine, by the act of the Great Powers in backing Zionist nationality claims and institutions, of their right to self-determination. That was the "original sin." One has to remember that Syria, Lebanon, Transjordan, and Iraq all became independent states. Palestine alone, of the "A" Mandate countries, did not, and this was not a mere accident of history.

Even fifty years ago, according to the pronouncements of the Great Powers, the indissoluble, immutable character of fundamental human rights and the concept

---

[15] BRITISH POLICY IN PALESTINE, CMD. No. 1700, at 18 (1922), reprinted in 2 J. HUREWITZ, *supra* note 12, at 103, 104.

[16] PALESTINE: STATEMENT OF POLICY, CMD. No. 6019, at 2, 3 (1939), reprinted in 2 J. HUREWITZ, *supra* note 12, at 218, 219, 220.

of right could not be altered by any act of man. If legality and ethics have not been dissipated in the interval, we must observe that the Zionist state of Israel, the aggressor in the June 5 war, had dubious rights to be in Palestine in the first place. Small wonder, then, that in the League of Nations and now in the United Nations the Palestine problem with its derivative disputes has been interminably on their agenda.

B. Rights as Recognized by United Nations

We turn now to the present, to see in what manner Israel has acted while the United Nations attempts, in debate and through processes of law, to adjudicate the derivative disputes.

The birth certificate of the State of Israel was General Assembly Resolution 181 of November 29, 1947,[17] recommending the annexed Plan of Partition with Economic Union.[18] Political forces were then at play to secure a favorable vote on Partition, at any cost and by any means. The Arab delegations requested that legal aspects of the Palestine question be referred to the International Court of Justice,[19] as the recourse provided by article 36 of the U.N. Charter, and by article 26 of the Mandate, which provided:

> The Mandatory agrees that if any dispute whatever should arise between the Mandatory and another Member of the League of Nations relating to the interpretation or the application of the provisions of the mandate, such dispute, if it cannot be settled by negotiation, shall be submitted to the Permanent Court of International Justice . . . .

It should be noted that Egypt and Iraq, which were among the sponsors of this request, had been members of the League of Nations, which made the provision just quoted unequivocal in its application. When the most important of these requests for adjudication was voted on, however, the count was 20 for, 21 against.[20] One vote decided the fate of Palestine.

This same birth certificate outlined the provisions of the declaration of independence of Israel. Article 10 of Part I of the Plan of Partition stipulated that "The Constituent Assembly of each State [*i.e.*, the proposed Jewish and Arab states] shall draft a democratic constitution for its State and choose a provisional government to succeed the Provisional Council of Government appointed by the [U.N. Palestine] Commission." The constitution, according to paragraph (d) of this article, was to guarantee "equal and non-discriminatory rights in civil, political, economic and religious matters and the enjoyment of human rights and fundamental freedoms."

---

[17] 2 U.N. GAOR, Resolutions, at 131 (1947).

[18] *Id.* at 132.

[19] 2 U.N. GAOR, Ad Hoc Comm. on the Palestinian Question 299-300 (1947).

[20] *Id.* at 203.

On May 14, 1948 Count Folke Bernadotte was appointed Mediator[21] pursuant to a resolution of the General Assembly.[22] In his report to the Third Session of the General Assembly, he stated:

> 6. [N]o settlement can be just and complete if recognition is not accorded to the right of the Arab refugee to return to the home from which he has been dislodged by the hazards and strategy of the armed conflict between Arabs and Jews in Palestine. The majority of these refugees have come from territory which, under the Assembly resolution of 29 November, was to be included in the Jewish State. . . . It would be an offence against the principles of elemental justice if these innocent victims of the conflict were denied the right to return to their homes while Jewish immigrants flow into Palestine, and, indeed, at least offer the threat of permanent replacement of the Arab refugees who have been rooted in the land for centuries.[23]

Obviously the Zionists, who wanted a state as Jewish as England is English, could not have kept the Arabs in their state, since they would have constituted a majority in that state. Count Bernadotte goes on to affirm the large-scale looting, pillaging, plundering, and the destruction of villages without apparent military necessity. He states further: "The liability of the Provisional Government of Israel to restore private property to its Arab owners and to indemnify those owners for property wantonly destroyed is clear, irrespective of any indemnities which the Provisional Government may claim from the Arab States."[24]

But Count Bernadotte was assassinated, with one of his aides, in September 1948, in the holy city of Jerusalem, and the Security Council could only express shock at the "cowardly act" of a "criminal group of terrorists."[25] A month later the Security Council noted with concern "that the Provisional Government of Israel has to date submitted no report to the Security Council or to the Acting Mediator regarding the progress of the investigation into the assassinations," and reminded ". . . the Governments and authorities concerned that all the obligations and responsibilities set forth are to be discharged fully and in good faith."[26]

On December 11, 1948 the United Nations General Assembly adopted Resolution 194, paragraph 11 of which

> . . . *resolves* that the refugees wishing to return to their homes and live at peace with their neighbors should be permitted to do so at the earliest practicable date, and that compensation should be paid for the property of those choosing not to return and for loss of or damage to property which, under principles of international law or in equity, should be made good by the governments or authorities responsible.[27]

[21] 3 U.N. SCOR, 299th meeting 4 (1948).

[22] G.A. Res. 186, U.N. GAOR, 2d Spec. Sess., Supp. 2, at 5 (1948).

[23] Progress Report of the United Nations Mediator on Palestine, 3 U.N. GAOR, Supp. 11, at 14, U.N. Doc. A/648 (1948).

[24] *Id.*

[25] S.C. Res. 57 (1948).

[26] S.C. Res. 59 (1948).

[27] 3 U.N. GAOR, Resolutions, at 21, 24 (1948).

The same resolution established a Conciliation Commission with the purpose of implementing the above-quoted paragraph.

On May 11, 1949, the General Assembly voted to accept Israel as a member of the United Nations. Paragraph 4 of the preamble to this resolution took note of "the declaration by the State of Israel that it 'unreservedly accepts the obligations of the United Nations Charter and undertakes to honour them from the day when it becomes a Member of the United Nations.' "[28]

On May 12, 1949, under the auspices of the U.N. Conciliation Commission, the Lausanne Protocol was signed.[29]   In the text it is stated that

> The United Nations Conciliation Commission for Palestine, anxious to achieve as quickly as possible the objectives of the General Assembly resolution of December 11, 1948, regarding refugees, the respect for their rights and the preservation of their property, as well as territorial and other questions, has proposed to the delegation of Israel and to the delegations of the Arab States that the "working documents" attached hereto be taken as basis for discussion with the Commission.[30]

To this document was annexed a map on which were indicated the boundaries defined in the General Assembly Resolution 181(II) of November 29, 1947, which was taken as the basis of discussion with the Commission.[31]

What took place later is described by the Conciliation Commission in paragraph 23 of the Third Progress Report: "The signing of the Protocol of 12 May 1949 provided both a starting-point and framework for the discussion of territorial questions."[32]   The delegation of Israel submitted proposals regarding the territorial questions, demanding that the international frontiers of Mandatory Palestine be considered the frontiers of Israel. When the Arab delegations protested that these proposals constituted a repudiation by Israel of the terms of the Protocol signed on May 12, the Israeli delegation replied that "it could not accept a certain proportionate distribution of territory agreed upon in 1947 as a criterion for a territorial settlement in present circumstances."[33]

When the Israeli army stands where it stands today, in occupied territories of three Arab states, members of the United Nations, and makes the withdrawal of its troops conditional on having "secure and agreed upon borders," one can, ironically, see how history repeats itself.

---

[28] G.A. Res. 273, 3 U.N. GAOR, pt. 2, Resolutions, at 18 (1949). The quoted words are those of the Foreign Minister on behalf of the Israeli State Council. 3 U.N. SCOR, Supp. Dec. 1948, at 118, U.N. Doc. S/1093 (1948).

[29] Third Progress Report of the Palestine Conciliation Commission, 4 U.N. GAOR, Ad Hoc Pol. Comm., Annex, vol. II, at 6, U.N. Doc. A/927 (1949).

[30] Id. at 9.

[31] G.A. Res. 181, supra note 17, at 150.

[32] Third Progress Report of the Palestine Conciliation Commission, supra note 29, at 7.

[33] Id. at 8.

C. Legal Implications of Paragraph 11 of Resolution 194 of December 11, 1948

The provisions of pargraph 11, sub-paragraph 1, of the General Assembly Resolution 194 of December 11, 1948 affirm the right of the refugees to return to their homes and their right to compensation, classified as compensation to refugees *not* choosing to return, and compensation to refugees for loss of or damage to property.[34] These rights, according to paragraph 11, are to be implemented "under principles of international law or in equity." What is involved here?

In a working paper prepared by the Legal Department of the U.N. Secretariat in March 1950 for the guidance of the Conciliation Commission on the implementation of paragraph 11 of Resolution 194,[35] the principles of repatriation and compensation were dealt with at length and many precedents cited, from the periods before and after the Second World War. It points out that in the former Axis and Axis-occupied countries—France, Rumania, Italy, Bulgaria, Czechoslovakia, Holland, and Yugoslavia—various laws were passed between November 1944 and May 1945 for restitution or compensation to the victims of Nazi action. In the United States occupied zone of Germany a General Claims law was passed in 1949 for restitution to those Nazi victims who had "suffered damage to life and limb, health, liberty, possessions, property or economic advancement."

It further points out that during the Second World War the Institute of Jewish Affairs of the World Jewish Congress took up the question of compensation for Jewish refugees and in 1944 published a book, *Indemnities and Reparations*, by Nehemiah Robinson.[36] The thesis was that great injustice would result from following the general rule that states may seek indemnification from foreign nations only on behalf of their own citizens who were also their citizens at the time the injury occurred. Victims of Axis countries who later acquired the citizenship of these states or merely became residents there would be excluded. As to victims who remained in or would be willing to return to their homeland, the author makes a strong case that the United Nations must intervene on their behalf.

The working paper also refers to a refugee problem of comparatively recent date which presents some similarity with the problem of the Palestine refugees:

> The Pakistan and India Governments agreed on the principle that the ownership of refugees' property, movable as well as immovable, should remain vested in the refugees. Custodians were appointed to look after and manage such property on behalf of the owners. Similarly, registrars of claims were appointed and instructed to make records of the property left behind by the evacuees.[37]

[34] 3 U.N. GAOR, Resolutions, at 21, 24 (1948).
[35] Historical Survey of Efforts of the United Nations Conciliation Commission for Palestine to Secure Implementation of Paragraph 11 of G.A. Res. 194(III), U.N. Doc. A/AC.25/W81/Rev. 2 (1961).
[36] N. ROBINSON, INDEMNITIES AND REPARATIONS (1944).
[37] Historical Survey of Efforts, *supra* note 35.

In contrast to all this, and the fact that Israeli, Zionist and Jewish organizations and Jewish individuals have had over a billion dollars in reparations from Germany,[38] we find Israeli legislation providing for confiscation of lands of "absentee" Arab owners. In three laws passed in 1948-49 (the Abandoned Areas Ordinance, the Absentee Property Regulations, and the Emergency Cultivation of Waste Lands Regulations) an "absentee" is defined as any person who was, on or after November 29, 1947 (the date of the General Assembly Resolution concerning partition of Palestine)—

    (a) a citizen or subject of any of the Arab states
    (b) in any of these states, for any length of time
    (c) in any part of Palestine outside the Israeli-occupied area
    (d) in any place other than his habitual residence, even if such place as well as his habitual abode were within Israeli-occupied territory.[39]

A conquered, surrendered, or deserted area was declared to be abandoned and sold by the Israeli Custodian to a Development Authority.[40]

Enquiry into this matter from the standpoint of the ownership of land in Palestine shows the unbelievable dimensions and grave iniquity of the liquidation of Arab rights and interests. It is established by official statistics of the Mandatory Government of Palestine,[41] submitted to the United Nations in 1947, that Jewish property in Palestine did not exceed a proportion of 5.66 per cent of the total area of the country. The document contains a breakdown of the areas owned in each district. In 1948, in violation of the territorial limits proposed by the U.N. Partition Resolution, and in 1949, in violation of the armistice agreements concluded with the neighboring countries, Israel seized another 1,400 square miles of the territory of Palestine, gaining control over seventy-one per cent of the total area of the country. Under the Israeli legislation referred to, the Israeli authorities have legalized the seizure of Arab refugee property and assets and provided for the subsequent wholesale confiscation of further property belonging to Arabs, whether refugees or not.

For twenty years now the Conciliation Commission has failed to secure legitimate Arab rights. Nineteen resolutions passed from 1949 up till now, affirming and reaffirming those rights, regretting or deploring the non-implementation by Israel of previous resolutions, have been completely disregarded.

As to the rights of the "intermediate" refugees, article V of the General Armistice Agreement with Syria provided for the "return of civilians to villages and settlements in the Demilitarized Zone"[42] and Security Council resolutions have urged

---

[38] Selzer, The Diplomacy of Atonement: Germany, Israel and the Jews, ISSUES, Summer 1967, at 23.

[39] Absentees' Property Law, [1950] Laws of the State of Israel, vol. 4, p. 68; reprinted in FUNDAMENTAL LAWS OF THE STATE OF ISRAEL 129 (J. Badi ed. 1961).

[40] See S. HADAWI, PALESTINE, LOSS OF A HERITAGE 52 (1963).

[41] 2 U.N. GAOR, Ad Hoc Comm. on the Palestinian Question, Annex 25, at 270, 292-93; Appendix VI, at 307, U.N. Doc. A/AC.14/32 (1947).

[42] 4 U.N. SCOR, Spec. Supp. 2, at 4 (1949).

on Israel their return forthwith. We get a picture of the situation from the Secretary-General's Report on the Present Status of the Demilitarized Zone Set Up by the General Armistice Agreement Between Israel and Syria:

> 16. The part of the central sector of the D/Zone which is on the eastern bank of the Jordan River is a narrow strip of land, generally controlled by Syria, while the western bank, generally controlled by Israel, is a large area. On the western bank Arab villages have been demolished, their inhabitants evacuated. The inhabitants of the villages of Baqqara and Ghanname returned following the Security Council resolution of 18 May 1951 (S/2517). They were later (on 30 October 1956) forced to cross into Syria where they are still living. Their lands on the western bank of the river, and Khoury Farm in the same area, are cultivated by Israel nationals.[43]

The question duly arises here: Does the rule of force or a political decision terminate a legal right? Does conquest give the conqueror legal title to an occupied territory? Philip Marshal Brown has given one answer: "Military occupation by itself does not confer title or extinguish a nation. . . . [S]o long as a people do not accept military conquest; so long as they can manifest, in one way or another, their inalterable will to regain freedom, their sovereignty even though flouted, restricted, and sent in exile still persists."[44]

III

RESPONSIBILITY FOR INITIATION OF HOSTILITIES

Now, it is widely assumed that the Arabs themselves were responsible for the misfortunes that befell them, because they were the ones who defied the U.N. Partition Resolution, and that all went peacefully in Palestine from November 29, 1947 until May 14, 1948, when the establishment of Israel was declared, with the Arabs attacking the new state. It has been concluded that the Arabs brought about the loss of their own rights through their aggression. Such is not the case. Emphasis on the real facts of the history of this period is not only relevant but necessary in the assessment of Arab claims.

To put the matter in perspective, I cite two official communications, one a letter sent by Brigadier General Patrick J. Hurley, Personal Representative of President Roosevelt, to the President from Cairo on May 5, 1943:[45]

> For its part, the Zionist organization in Palestine has indicated its commitment to an enlarged program for (1) a sovereign Jewish State which would embrace Palestine and probably Transjordania, (2) an eventual transfer of the Arab population from Palestine to Iraq, and (3) Jewish leadership for the whole Middle East in the fields of economic development and control.

---

[43] U.N. Doc. S/7573, at 4-5, Nov. 2, 1966.

[44] Brown, *Sovereignty in Exile*, 35 AM. J. INT'L L. 666, 667 (1941).

[45] Letter from Brig. Gen. Patrick Hurley to President Roosevelt, [1943] 4 FOREIGN REL. U.S. 776, 777 (1964).

The other was a telegram sent from Cairo by U.S. Minister Kirk in Egypt to the Secretary of State on January 23, 1943:

> On the Jewish side I have found Zionist officials of the Jewish Agency uncompromisingly outspoken in their determination that Palestine at end of this war shall become not merely a national home for the Jews, but a Jewish state despite any opposition from the 1,000,000 Arabs living there. In various ways main result of many of their efforts seems to be to goad Palestinian Arabs into breaking informal truce that has existed since war began. . . .
> It is no secret that the Hagana, their secret Jewish military organization, has plans fully made and is well equipped not only with small arms, but also with tommy-guns and machine guns many of them purchased from Vichy French forces in Syria and smuggled into Palestine during past 2 years.[46]

As to what really happened, rather than the propagandized version, we have the aid of I. F. Stone, American author of *Underground to Palestine* and *This is Israel*, who tells us that he

> first arrived in Palestine on Balfour Day, Nov. 2, 1945, the day the Haganah blew up bridges and watch towers to begin its struggle against the British and immigration restrictions. The following spring I was the first newspaperman to travel with illegal Jewish immigrants from the Polish-Czech border through the British blockade. In 1947 I celebrated Passover in the British detention camps in Cyprus and in 1948 I covered the Arab-Jewish war.[47]

In an article published August 3, 1967 he goes on to say:

> Jewish terrorism, not only by the Irgun, in such savage massacres as Deir Yassin, but in milder form by the Haganah, itself "encouraged" Arabs to leave areas the Jews wished to take over for strategic or demographic reasons. They tried to make as much of Israel as free of Arabs as possible.[48]

He also points out that:

> The myth that the Arab refugees fled because the Arab radios urged them to do so was analyzed by Erskine B. Childers in the London *Spectator* May 12, 1961. An examination of British and U.S. radio monitoring records turned up no such appeals and "even orders to the civilians of Palestine, to stay put."[49]

Irrefutable proof that the Zionists were the first aggressors in the war of 1947-48 is given by Menachem Begin, the   perpetrator of the Deir Yassin massacre, in his book *The Revolt*.[50] He tells us how the Haganah, the recognized "defense" force of the Zionist establishment in Palestine, having gone over to the principle of "offensive defense," joined forces with the Irgun, the terrorist group, and of the

---

[46] Letter from Minister Kirk to Secretary of State, [1943] 4 FOREIGN REL. U.S. 747-48 (1964).

[47] I.F. Stone, in review of special issue of *Les Temps Moderne* entitled *Le Conflict Israélo-Arabe*, The New York Review of Books, Aug. 3, 1967, at 12, col. 4.

[48] *Id.* at 10, col. 3.

[49] *Id.* at 10, col. 2.

[50] M. BEGIN, THE REVOLT, STORY OF THE IRGUN (1951).

signing of a secret agreement between the Jewish Agency, as the supreme authority over the Haganah, and the Irgun Zvai Leumi for attack on the Arabs. This was in January 1948, while the duly constituted Commission of the United Nations was still seeking a peaceful implementation of the General Assembly's recommendation. In a chapter entitled "The Conquest of Jaffa" he states:

> In the months preceding the Arab invasion . . . we continued to make sallies into the Arab area. In the early days of 1948, we were explaining to our officers and men, however, that this was not enough. Attacks of this nature carried out by any Jewish forces were indeed of great psychological importance; and their military effect, to the extent that they widened the Arab front and forced the enemies on to the defensive, was not without value. But it was clear to us that even most daring sallies carried out by partisan troops would never be able to decide the issue. Our hope lay in gaining control of territory.
>
> At the end of January, 1948, at a meeting of the Command of the Irgun in which the Planning Section participated, we outlined four strategic objectives: (1) Jerusalem; (2) Jaffa; (3) the Lydda-Ramleh plain; and (4) the Triangle.[51]

(According to the Partition plan, Jerusalem was to be a *corpus separatum*, and Jaffa was definitely to be part of the Arab state.) On April 25, 1948 (three weeks before the alleged Arab initiation of hostilities), Begin addressed his troops, en route to Jaffa: "Men of the Irgun! We are going out to conquer Jaffa. We are going into one of the decisive battles for the independence of Israel."[52] After an account of the battle, he assures us that "The conquest of Jaffa was one of the fateful events in the Hebrew war of independence."[53]

Thus the Palestine refugee problem originated, for Jaffa was practically all Arab in population. Before any Arab soldier set foot on the soil of Palestine, 400,000 Arabs had fled their Palestinian homeland in terror.

Of course, the Zionists had their own view of activities such as this, expressed by a member of the Haganah, Munya M. Mardor (now Director-General of the Israel Weapons Research and Development Authority) in a book entitled *Haganah*.[54] He tells of secret arms purchases in foreign countries: "We were conspirators, outside the law, and yet obeying what to us was a higher law."[55]

In the name of compromise, realism, and *fait accompli*, the Arabs are asked to recognize these achievements "outside the law" and admit the "conspirators" as lawful and legal successors to their land and rights.

CONCLUSION

It must have become clear that the legal imperatives affirming Arab rights in Palestine are firm and unequivocal, but that Israel and World Zionism have been

---

[51] *Id.* at 348.
[52] *Id.* at 354.
[53] *Id.* at 371.
[54] M. MARDOR, HAGANAH (1957).
[55] *Id.* at 230.

able to flout them and disregard not only all international safeguards and guarantees prior to 1947, but also the scores of U.N. resolutions concerning Arab rights.

The argument has time and again been made that the Arabs should accept the *fait accompli* established by Israel, but between 1947 and today there has been not one but several *fait accompli* to subvert Arab rights.

The Arabs prefer to see not only what is, but what ought to be and what might be, and agree with U.S. Secretary of Labor W. Willard Wirtz when he told the Labor Ministers' Conference in Venezuela: "Change is our ally, and we face squarely those who fight change because the status quo has been good to them. The divine right of the successful is as false a notion as the divine right of kings."[56]

Does a *fait accompli* constitute a norm for international law and behavior—since we are dealing with basic legal considerations? We hold, with the two American legal authorities quoted below, that no *fait accompli* can establish a precedent to be accepted in international law so long as the victims of the *fait accompli* object to it.

In 1954 the Legal Adviser of the State Department, Mr. Herman Phleger, made this statement:

> International law has been defined as those rules for international conduct which have met general acceptance among the community of nations . . . .
> . . . .
> But there is such a thing as international law. It has had a long and honorable, though chequered, career. I predict that it will play an even more important part in world affairs in the future than it has in the past. Indeed, in this rapidly shrinking world, it becomes increasingly evident that our survival may depend upon our success in substituting the rule of law for the rule of force.[57]

From the American Law Institute comes a *Restatement of the Foreign Relations Law of the United States*, which contains the following:

> e. *Objection to practice as means of preventing its acceptance as rule of law.* The growth of practice into a rule of international law depends on the degree of its acceptance by the international community. If a state initiates a practice for which there is no precedent in international law, the fact that other states do not object to it is significant evidence that they do not regard it as illegal. If this practice becomes more general without objections from other states, the practice may give rise to a rule of international law. Because failure to object to practice may amount to recognition of it, the objection by a state to a practice of another is an important means of preventing or controlling in some degree the development of rules of international law.[58]

The *fait accompli* of Israel, doing away with Arab rights, has been objected to, not only by the Arab states, but by the majority of Members of the United Nations, who throughout twenty years past have affirmed and reaffirmed the rights of Arab

---

[56] N.Y. Times, May 11, 1966, at 18, col. 2.

[57] 1 M. WHITEMAN, DIGEST OF INTERNATIONAL LAW 2 (1963).

[58] RESTATEMENT (SECOND) OF FOREIGN RELATIONS LAW OF THE UNITED STATES § 1, comment *e* (1965).

refugees for return or compensation. The United States Government has voted consistently in favor of those resolutions, while regrettably opposing draft resolutions designed to safeguard Arab property rights.

The most succinct and telling objection to Israel's *fait accompli* that I call to mind is implicit in the words of Secretary-General U Thant, in his Annual Report to the 22nd Session of the General Assembly: "People everywhere, and this certainly applies to the Palestinian refugees, have a natural right to be in their homeland and to have a future."[59]

---

[59] 22 U.N. GAOR, Supp. 1A, at 7, U.N. Doc. A/6701/Add. 1 (1967).

I. UNDERLYING ISSUES

B. *Freedom of Navigation Through the Strait of Tiran, the Gulf of Aqaba, and the Suez Canal*

Gulf of Aqaba and Strait of Tiran: Troubled Waters

CARL F. SALANS

On 23 May 1967, President Gamel Abdel Nasser of the United Arab Republic announced to the world that the Strait of Tiran and the Gulf of Aqaba would be closed to Israeli flag vessels and to vessels of other countries carrying strategic cargoes, including oil, to Israel. It was largely out of that decision that the Arab-Israeli war of June 1967 developed.

The Gulf of Aqaba is 98 miles long and varies in width from 7 to 15 miles. The United Arab Republic, Israel, Jordan, and Saudi Arabia all border on the Gulf.

The Strait of Tiran connects the Gulf of Aqaba with the Red Sea. At its narrowest point, the Strait of Tiran is about four miles wide. It has only two navigable channels, Enterprise Passage and Grafton Passage, both of which are within three miles of the U.A.R. coast and therefore within Egyptian waters. The two islands of Tiran and Sanafir, which lie athwart the Strait, have been claimed by both Egypt and Saudi Arabia, and have been occupied from time to time by Egyptian forces.

The Strait of Tiran forms the necessary passageway for access to the Israeli port of Elath at the head of the Gulf. It also provides access to Jordan's only outlet to the sea, the port of Aqaba some five miles from Elath.

The United States has for many years taken the position that the Gulf of Aqaba "comprehends"—i.e., includes or embraces—international waters and that there is a right of free and innocent passage through the Strait of Tiran and in the Gulf of Aqaba. In an aide memoire to the Israeli Embassy dated 11 February 1957, the Department of State set forth this position:

> With respect to (a) the Gulf of Aqaba and access thereto—the United States believes that the Gulf comprehends international waters and that no nation has the right to prevent free and innocent passage in the Gulf and through the Straits giving access thereto. . . .

President Dwight D. Eisenhower repeated this view in an address to the nation on 27 February 1957:

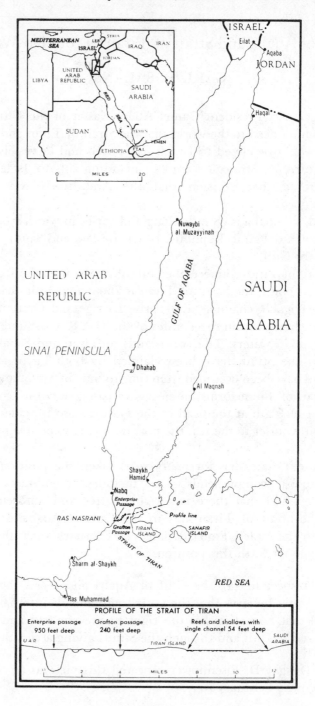

With reference to the passage into and through the Gulf of Aqaba, we expressed the conviction that the gulf constitutes international waters and that no nation has the right to prevent free and innocent passage in the gulf. . . .

We should not assume that . . . Egypt will prevent Israeli shipping from using the . . . Gulf of Aqaba. If, unhappily, Egypt does here-after violate the Armistice Agreement or other international obliga-tions, then this should be dealt with firmly by the society of nations.

In part, the United States bases its contention that the Gulf of Aqaba comprehends international waters on the fact that the United States recognizes only a three-mile territorial sea. Thus, because the Gulf varies in width from 7 to 15 miles, a stretch of water in the Gulf has the character of high seas.

But, more basically, the international character of the Gulf derives from the fact that four countries share its coastline. No one of these nations, or even a majority of them, can decide that the Gulf belongs to it, or to them, alone.

The Arab States, nevertheless, have argued that the Gulf consists of "Arab territorial waters" and that passage through it and through the Strait of Tiran cannot be undertaken without the consent of the Arab States. This position was asserted, for example, in a written representa-tion made by the Arab Missions in Washington to Secretary of State John Foster Dulles on 24 May 1957:

It is evident that due to the fact that the Gulf of Aqaba is a narrow, closed Gulf covered by Arab territorial waters, and that entrance to it is also territorial water, the Gulf is by no means, physically or legally, an open sea, whereby ships of any flag can sail as on open seas, nor is the entrance to it a matter of passage, to be undertaken without the consent of the Arab States concerned.

As for the Strait of Tiran, U.A.R. President Nasser stated his govern-ment's position at a press conference held in Cairo on 28 May 1967:

The Tiran Straits are Egyptian territorial waters over which Egypt has exercised her sovereignty rights. No power whatever its might can infringe upon Egyptian sovereignty rights and any such attempt shall be regarded as aggression against the Egyptian people and the Arab nation at large. . . .

The claim of the Arab States that the Gulf of Aqaba is "Arab territorial waters" cannot be substantiated. It has not been so treated historically, nor can it logically be so viewed today. During the Ottoman Empire and up to 1914, the Gulf was surrounded by Ottoman—not Arab—territory. Egypt, at that time, was under Ottoman suzerainty. Following the dissolution of the Ottoman Empire after 1914, the area now comprising Israel and Jordan became part of the British mandate under the League of Nations. While there was probably little international shipping in the Gulf of Aqaba during these periods, there is no indication that the waters were regarded as closed seas. At the same time, it is true that the Gulf of Aqaba has historically been a route of pilgrimage to Moslem Holy Places. Apparently some pilgrims used to travel by land to the head of the Gulf and then by ship through the Gulf and the Red Sea to Jidda. Thus, the "Arab Sea" argument has emotional appeal, even though the Gulf has lost much of its significance as a pilgrimage route. As pointed out earlier, the very fact that today four countries border on the Gulf, one of which, Israel, would not admit of its closed character, belies the Arab contention that its waters are closed.

In fact, Eygpt herself has explicitly recognized the right of free navigation through the Strait of Tiran and the Gulf. In an aide memoire of 28 January 1950, the Egyptian Ministry of Foreign Affairs explained to the U. S. Embassy at Cairo that Egypt's occupation of the two islands of Tiran and Sanafir at the entrance of the Gulf of Aqaba was only to protect the islands against damage and that

> . . . this occupation being in no way conceived in a spirit of obstructing in any way innocent passage through the stretch of water separating these two islands from the Egyptian coast of Sinai, it follows that this passage, the only practicable one, will remain free as in the past, in conformity with the international practice and recognized principles of the law of nations.

U.A.R. representative to the United Nations, Ambassador El Kony, in a speech before the U. N. Security Council on 29 May 1967, argued that the 1950 Egyptian aide memoire was not intended to guarantee free and innocent passage "to an enemy during a state of war." In fact, early in 1951, Egypt promulgated regulations requiring vessels transiting the Strait of Tiran to notify Egyptian authorities and to submit to inspection. Egypt stated it did not intend to prohibit innocent passage of warships or commercial vessels of friendly countries through the Strait of Tiran. But this was without prejudice to Egypt's "legitimate right of control as a riparian power nor to the exercise of its exceptional rights of visit and seizure of contraband. . . ." Egypt declared that "enemy" warships were forbidden access to and passage through Egyptian territorial waters, including the Strait, while "enemy" commercial vessels could have access only at the risk of seizure and detention.

While the U. S. government did not recognize the validity of the Egyptian position or the Egyptian instructions for notification of passage through the Strait of Tiran, these instructions were printed in the *Sailing Directions for the Red Sea and the Gulf of Aden* issued by the U. S. Hydrographic Office as instructions to U. S. masters and shipping companies. And presumably ships complied with these instructions on many occasions.

From the facts available, it appears that Egyptian enforcement of their policies on transit through the Strait during the early 1950s was rather spotty. There were several incidents involving detention of vessels during this period, although they were few in number, principally because of the limited traffic to the Israeli port of Elath. It was not until June 1952 that construction of the port at Elath was completed, and it was only in March 1956 that oceangoing vessels were first able to use it. Nor were there shipments of oil to Elath during this period, the oil pipeline from Elath to refineries in Haifa having been constructed in 1957-58.

In January 1957, U. N. Secretary-General Dag Hammarskjöld, in his report to the General Assembly, took the position that, while there was a right of innocent passage through the Strait, the extent of this right was subject to legal controversy:

> As stated in the previous report (A/3500), the international significance of the Gulf of Aqaba may be considered to justify the right of innocent passage through the Straits of Tiran and the Gulf in accordance with recognized rules of international law. However, . . . the International Law Commission reserved consideration of the question "What would be the legal position of straits forming part of the territorial sea of one or more States and constituting the sole means of access to the port of another state." This description applies to the Gulf of Aqaba and the Straits of Tiran. A legal controversy

exists as to the extent of the right of innocent passage through these waters.

The following year, the Geneva Conference on the Law of the Sea took up the very issue described by Secretary-General Hammarskjöld in his report to the General Assembly. The Conference adopted a Convention on the Territorial Sea and the Contiguous Zone, Article 16, paragraph 4, of which provides as follows:

> There shall be no suspension of the innocent passage of foreign ships through straits which are used for international navigation between one part of the high seas and another part of the high seas or the territorial sea of a foreign State.

This article ensures a right of innocent passage through an international strait even when the strait lies wholly within the coastal state's territorial waters. This provision clearly applies to the Gulf of Aqaba and the Strait of Tiran, either on the view that the Gulf comprehends international waters and therefore the Strait of Tiran connects two parts of the high seas or on the view that the Strait connects one part of the high seas (i.e., the Red Sea) with the territorial sea of the four riparian Gulf states, including Israel.

The United States, the United Kingdom, the Soviet Union, and 30 other countries are parties to this 1958 Convention. None of the Arab States have become parties, probably because of the Convention's implications for the Gulf of Aqaba and the Strait of Tiran. There is some question whether the last part of Article 16, paragraph 4, of the Convention, establishing the rule of innocent passage between one part of the high seas and the *territorial sea* of a foreign state, is a codification of existing customary international law already binding on states or is creative of a new rule of law not necessarily binding on non-signatories. This is a significant issue bearing on the rights of navigation through these waterways, but in the absence of a ruling by the International Court of Justice, it will probably remain a lawyer's debating point for years to come.

The International Court of Justice did decide a case in 1949 called the *Corfu Channel* case which supports the right of passage through international straits. In that case, brought by the United Kingdom against Albania, two British warships attempting to pass through the strait known as the Corfu Channel, between Albania and Greece, were damaged by mines laid in the channel. The Court said:

It is, in the opinion of the Court, generally recognized and in accordance with international custom that States in time of peace have a right to send their warships through straits used for international navigation between two parts of the high seas without the previous authorization of a coastal State, provided that the passage is innocent. Unless otherwise prescribed in an international convention, there is no right for a coastal State to prohibit such passage through straits in time of peace.

Both the 1958 Geneva Convention and the International Court opinion in the *Corfu Channel* case speak in terms of a right of "innocent passage" through international straits. What passage is "innocent"? Who is to determine whether passage is innocent?

Article 14(4) of the 1958 Geneva Convention on the Territorial Sea and the Contiguous Zone states a definition of innocent passage:

> Passage is innocent so long as it is not prejudicial to the peace, good order, or security of the coastal state. . . .

Some light is thrown on the meaning of this definition by the World Court's decision in the *Corfu Channel* case. In that case, the Court decided that the passage of a warship was innocent if her actions did not threaten the security of the coastal state. The warships in question were British naval vessels. Great Britain was at the time an ally of Greece, which had declared itself to be in a technical state of war with Albania, the coastal state. The Court looked at the character of the *passage*, and not the character of the *vessel* as a warship, as the determinative factor in deciding whether the passage was innocent; and it found that the manner of the passage of the British warships through the Corfu Channel was such as to make that passage innocent.

Moreover, the Court made it clear in the *Corfu Channel* case that determination of innocence was not a subjective decision to be made unilaterally by the coastal state. Albania had contended that the passage of the British warships was carried out in a threatening manner and that the ship's orders were to return any fire from the Albanian coast. The Court did not accept this characterization by the Albanian government, but itself considered the behavior of the British warships in the strait and found it not to have threatened the security of Albania.

The negotiating history of the 1958 Geneva Conventions on the Law of the Sea does not indicate an intention to modify the rules regarding innocent passage established by the International Court of Justice in the *Corfu* case. It therefore seems that—to use the terms of Article 14, paragraph 4, of the 1958 Convention—the question of whether passage is prejudicial to the peace, good order, or security of the coastal state is to be determined objectively from the conduct of a particular vessel in transit and not on the basis of a subjective judgment by the coastal state concerning the character of the vessel or her cargo. Applying this test to the specific question that was raised by the Egyptian closure of the Strait of Tiran to strategic cargoes, including oil, bound for Israel, it follows that the passage through the Strait of Tiran of a merchant vessel carrying oil to Israel would be "innocent" and entitled to free passage.

The United Arab Republic, however, advanced a further argument in support of its right to close the Strait of Tiran to Israeli shipping. It asserted that it was in a state of war with Israel and that innocent passage through the Strait legitimately could be suspended by a belligerent in time of war. In its announcement at Cairo on 23 May 1967, Egypt said:

> There is a state of war between us and Israel. International law gives us the right to ban the passage of Israeli ships through our territorial waters. U. S. and British talk about innocent passage is unacceptable in a state of war.

It is fair to say that the right of innocent passage through international straits guaranteed under the 1958 Convention is a peacetime right. While the Geneva Convention does not say this in so many words, passage of an enemy vessel in time of war could hardly be considered innocent except in the most unusual circumstances.

In dealing with the assertion of belligerent rights, one has to consider, at the outset, the effect of the U. N. Charter on traditional international law concepts of belligerency. Since the coming into force of the Charter, belligerent rights are available only to a state engaged in a use of armed force that is lawful under the Charter. It is lawful, for example, for one state to use force against another state pursuant to a U. N. Security Council decision or a General Assembly decision under the Uniting for Peace Resolution, or in the exercise of the right of self-defense against armed attack, or pursuant to a decision of a regional organization for the maintenance of peace and security in the region.

None of these bases were relied upon by the United Arab Republic in closing the Strait of Tiran to Israeli shipping.

Quite apart from this, however, the United States and many other nations have considered that neither the Arab States nor Israel have been entitled to exercise belligerent rights since 1949 when they entered into General Armistice Agreements. Those four agreements, between Israel and Egypt, Israel and Jordan, Israel and Lebanon, and Israel and Syria ended the state of belligerency between the respective parties. While they were not peace treaties, the armistice agreements were intended to prohibit the parties from resorting to belligerent acts against one another during the period until permanent political settlements could be reached between Israel and the Arab States.

This view is supported by Resolution 95 of the U. N. Security Council adopted 1 September 1951, calling upon Egypt to terminate restrictions on passage of Israeli shipping through the Suez Canal. That resolution contained the following passage:

> Considering that since the Armistice regime, which has been in existence for nearly two and a half years, is of a permanent character, neither party can reasonably assert that it is actively a belligerent or requires to exercise the right of visit, search and seizure for any legitimate purpose of defense.

In his report to the U. N. General Assembly of 24 January 1957, Secretary-General Hammarskjöld confirmed this view:

> It follows from the finding of the Security Council in 1951 that . . . the parties to the Armistice Agreements may be considered as not entitled to claim any belligerent rights . . . it may be held that, in a situation where the Armistice regime is partly operative by observance of the provisions of the Armistice Agreements concerning the armistice lines, possible claims to rights of belligerency would be at least so much in doubt that, having regard for the general international interest at stake, no such claim should be exercised in the Gulf of Aqaba and the Straits of Tiran. . . .

The settlement of the Tiran-Aqaba issue made in 1957 by the United Nations in the wake of the Suez conflict supports the conclusion that the United Arab Republic could not assert a state of belligerency as a basis for closing these waterways to Israeli shipping. That settlement placed a United Nations Emergency Force (UNEF) at Sharm-el-

Sheikh, at the tip of the Sinai Peninsula overlooking the Strait of Tiran, which left the Strait and Gulf open to navigation; and rights of passage through those waters were thereafter exercised until President Nasser's announcement on 23 May 1967.

Thus, as a legal matter, the United States concluded in May-June 1967 that the United Arab Republic could not rely on belligerent rights as a basis for interfering with the Israeli right of innocent passage through the Strait of Tiran and the Gulf of Aqaba. The United States has also felt that as a practical matter it did not make much sense for the Arabs to assert this right, for they could hardly maintain the right to exercise belligerent rights vis-à-vis Israel and at the same time deny Israel's right to resort to belligerent action against the Arab States.

The various legal considerations regarding freedom of passage through the Strait of Tiran and the Gulf of Aqaba that were important in determining the United States attitude toward Egyptian closure of these waterways to Israeli shipping in May 1967 are also relevant to the efforts that are now underway to reach understandings among the parties that will ensure a lasting peace in the Middle East.

Resolution of the Middle Eastern situation will require solutions to a broad range of questions that affect Israel and the Arab States. On 22 November 1967, the United Nations Security Council adopted a resolution containing an agreed set of principles for settlement, including: withdrawal of Israeli armed forces from territories occupied in the conflict; termination of all claims or states of belligerency; respect for and acknowledgement of the sovereignty, territorial integrity and political independence of every state in the area and their right to live in peace within secure and recognized boundaries free from threats or acts of force; the achievement of a just settlement of the refugee problem; and some guaranty of the territorial inviolability and political independence of every state in the area, through measures including the establishment of demilitarized zones. The U. N. Secretary-General, pursuant to that Security Council resolution, has designated a Special Representative, Ambassador Gunnar Jarring of Sweden, "to proceed to the Middle East, to establish and maintain contacts with the States concerned in order to promote agreement and assist efforts to achieve a peaceful and accepted settlement in accordance with the provisions and principles in this resolution." In addition to the principles listed above, the Security Council Resolution singles out "the necessity for guaranteeing freedom of navigation through international waterways in the area." The history of the Arab-Israeli crisis of May-June 1967 and the negotiation of the Security Council resolution can leave no doubt that the resolution refers not only to the Strait of Tiran and the Gulf of Aqaba but to the Suez Canal as well. The resolution, adopted unanimously by the Security Council, indicates a recognition of the necessity to preserve freedom of navigation through these waterways if a recurrence of the June 1967 hostilities is to be avoided and if there is to be peace in the Middle East. It also recognizes, concomitantly, that there must be a renunciation of all claims to exercise belligerent rights if the principles of free navigation are to be protected.

The United States, of course, has been a staunch supporter of the principle of freedom of navigation through the Strait of Tiran and the Gulf of Aqaba as an essential element in a solution to the Middle East situation. On 23 May 1967, following President Nasser's closure of the Strait and Gulf to Israeli shipping, President Lyndon B. Johnson stated:

> . . . the purported closing of the Gulf of Aqaba to Israeli shipping has brought a new and very grave dimension to the crisis. The United States considers the Gulf to be an international waterway and feels that a blockade of Israeli shipping is illegal and potentially disastrous to the cause of peace. The right of free, innocent passage of the international waterways is a vital interest of the entire international community.

After the hostilities, in an address to a Department of State foreign policy conference on 19 June 1967, President Johnson outlined five basic principles for peace in the Middle East. One of these he described in the following words:

> A third lesson from this last month is that maritime rights must be respected. Our nation has long been committed to free maritime passage through international waterways; and we, along with other nations, were taking the necessary steps to implement this principle when hostilities exploded. If a single act of folly was more responsible for this explosion than any other, I think it was the arbitrary and dangerous announced decision that the Strait of Tiran would be closed. The right of innocent maritime passage must be preserved for all nations.

Although the U. S. government's immediate concern with these issues of maritime rights has been centered on the Middle East and on efforts to seek a permanent resolution of tensions in the area, the legal and political importance of the questions involved in the Middle East transcend regional boundaries. The U. S. government must also bear in mind the implications of any attempt by the United Arab Republic to close international waterways to Israeli shipping and the implications of any settlement involving this issue for broader U. S. strategic and commercial interests. The international law principles of the right of innocent passage through international straits, even when those straits consist wholly of territorial waters, is of the utmost importance to the security of the United States and to the role which the U. S. Navy plays in guaranteeing that security. U. S. defensive capabilities would be profoundly jeopardized by any erosion of the principle of freedom of innocent passage through these straits.

While the United States recognizes only a three-mile territorial sea limit, a growing number of states around the world are claiming greater areas of territorial sea. Claims have been made to four miles, twelve miles, and as much as 200 miles. Indonesia and the Philippines claim that all the waters of their respective archipelagoes are territorial in nature. If these extensive claims to territorial sea were to become established, a large number of international straits throughout the world would become subject to national sovereignty—the greater the distance claimed for territorial seas, the more straits that would be affected. The importance, therefore, of preserving the rule of international law that innocent passage through international straits may not be denied is obvious.

As Ambassador Arthur Dean, who served as Chairman of the American Delegation to the 1958 Geneva Conference on the Law of the Sea, testified before the Senate Foreign Relations Committee on 20 January 1960, "The primary danger to continuance of the ability of our warships and supporting aircraft to move, unhampered, to wherever they may be needed to support American foreign policy presents itself in the great international straits of the world—the narrows which lie athwart the sea routes which connect us with our widely scattered friends and allies and admit us to the strategic materials we do not ourselves possess."

At the same time, the United States is a major trading nation whose commercial interests are vitally linked to continued freedom of the seas. U. S. exports in 1967, for example, totaled nearly 31 billion dollars, while U. S. imports amounted to almost 27 billion. World trade was valued at approximately 200 billion dollars, in that year. This trade, which is increasing rapidly each year, and which is not only of importance to the welfare of the United States and its citizens, but also is essential to the economic development and well-being of nations and peoples around the world, depends largely on the ability of vessels of all flags to pass freely through international waterways.

Thus, the Arab-Israeli conflict, and the involvement in that conflict of the principle of freedom of passage through international straits, is of far-reaching consequence for the United States. Protection of the right of free transit through international waterways is important to the preservation of peace in the Middle East—as the events of May-June 1967 attest. But also at stake are the worldwide operations of the military forces of the United States, as well as the continued flow of international trade and commerce upon which the economic prosperity of this country and virtually every other nation of the world depends. As the United States works toward a Middle East settlement, it will have both of these interests very much in mind.

Some Legal Problems of International Waterways, with Particular Reference to the Straits of Tiran and the Suez Canal

D. H. N. JOHNSON

THE fact that the recent " six-day war " in the Middle East began with an attempt to close the Straits of Tiran and ended with those Straits re-opened to shipping, but the Suez Canal closed for the second time in eleven years, has drawn attention once again to the law affecting international waterways. Because the problem is less well known, this article will concentrate for the most part on the Straits of Tiran. A few remarks will, however, be made about the Suez Canal towards the end of the article.

INTERNATIONAL WATERWAYS—GENERAL REMARKS

What is an international waterway? The question is not easy to answer. According to the leading authority,

> " For purposes of analysis, international waterways must be considered to be those rivers, canals, and straits which are used to a substantial extent by the commercial shipping or warships belonging to States other than the riparian nation or nations. . . . The international character of a waterway, thus conceived, rests upon factual considerations, for it is only by examination of the actualities of international usage that any conclusions about the requisites of international character become possible." [1]

Nevertheless, the term " international waterway " appears to be one to which the British Government attaches significance. Speaking in the General Assembly of the United Nations on March 4, 1957, the British delegate stated:

> " It is the view of Her Majesty's Government in the United Kingdom that the Straits of Tiran must be regarded as an international waterway through which the vessels of all nations have a right of passage." [2]

This view was endorsed by the Prime Minister, during the recent Arab-Israeli crisis, when he told the House of Commons on May 31 that " the Gulf of Aqaba is an international waterway and that the Straits of Tiran do provide an international waterway into which and through which the vessels of all nations have a right of passage." [3]

[1] R. R. Baxter, *The Law of International Waterways* (1964), p. 3.
[2] 667th Plenary Meetings, p. 1284.
[3] H.C.Deb., Vol. 747, No. 200, cols. 205–206.

The starting point for any consideration of this branch of the international law of the sea must be the conventions adopted at the Geneva Conference on the Law of the Sea 1958—particularly the Convention on the Territorial Sea and the Contiguous Zone and the Convention on the High Seas.[4] Behind these conventions lay not less than seven years' preparatory work by the International Law Commission, during which the views of governments were repeatedly taken into account and culminating in seventy-three draft articles prepared by the Commission in the summer of 1956 [5]; a protracted debate in the Sixth Committee of the General Assembly of the United Nations in the autumn of 1956; and certain further preparatory work conducted by or on behalf of the Secretariat of the United Nations during the period 1956–58.[6]

As part of the preparatory work just referred to, the Secretariat of the United Nations requested Commander R. H. Kennedy, O.B.E., R.N. (Retd.) to undertake two studies. The first, Preparatory Document No. 6, was " A Brief Geographical and Hydrographical Study of Straits which constitute Routes for International Traffic." [7] The second, Preparatory Document No. 12, was " A Brief Geographical and Hydrographical Study of Bays and Estuaries, the Coasts of which belong to Different States." [8] The Secretariat itself also prepared, as Preparatory Document No. 11, a " Guide to Instruments affecting the Legal Status of Straits." [9] These studies are invaluable to an elucidation of the problems now to be considered.

Generally speaking, the Geneva codification of 1958 eschewed unnecessary definitions. The following key provisions must, however, be noted.

From the Convention on the Territorial Sea and the Contiguous Zone

Article 1

1. The sovereignty of a State extends, beyond its land territory and its internal waters, to a belt of sea adjacent to its coast, described as the territorial sea.

---

[4] Cmnd. 584. The other two conventions, dealing respectively with Fishing and Conservation of the Living Resources of the High Seas, and the Continental Shelf, are not immediately relevant. All four conventions are now in force.

[5] " Report of the International Law Commission covering the Work of its Eighth Session." *General Assembly Official Records: Eleventh Session.* Supplement No. 9 (A/3159).

[6] See the article by the present writer, " The Preparation of the 1958 Geneva Conference on the Law of the Sea " (1959) 8 I.C.L.Q. 122.

[7] A/Conf. 13/6.

[8] A/Conf. 13/15.

[9] A/Conf. 13/14. Attention should also be drawn to two other studies, namely, Preparatory Document No. 1, " Memorandum concerning Historic Bays," prepared by the Secretariat itself (A/Conf. 13/1), and Preparatory Document No. 15, a paper on " Certain Legal Aspects concerning the Delimitation of the Territorial Waters of Archipelagos," prepared at the request of the Secretariat by Mr. Jens Evensen, Advocate at the Supreme Court of Norway.

Article 2
> The sovereignty of a coastal State extends to the air space over the territorial sea as well as to its bed and subsoil.

Article 5
> 1. Waters on the landward side of the baseline of the territorial sea form part of the internal waters of the State.

Articles 3 and 4 laid down technical rules concerning the drawing of base lines. It is these base lines which separate " internal waters " from " territorial sea." The legal difference is that, whereas a coastal state is entitled to exclude foreign shipping from its internal waters,[10] it must afford to such shipping a right of innocent passage through its territorial sea.

Article 7 was a lengthy article concerning bays. It defined a bay as " a well-marked indentation whose penetration is in such proportion to the width of its mouth as to contain landlocked waters and constitute more than a mere curvature of the coast." It also provided that " if the distance between the low-water marks of the natural entrance points of a bay does not exceed twenty-four miles, a closing line may be drawn between these two low-water marks, and the waters enclosed thereby shall be considered as internal waters "; and further that " where the distance between the low-water marks of the natural entrance points of a bay exceeds twenty-four miles, a straight base line of twenty-four miles shall be drawn within the bay in such a manner as to enclose the maximum area of water that is possible with a line of that length." However, Article 7 related " only to bays the coasts of which belong to a single State "; whilst its provisions were not to apply to " historic bays "[11] or to bays where, for the reasons given in Article 4, a " straight baseline system " along an entire coast, as opposed to closing lines across the mouths of individual bays, was envisaged. The implication of this was presumably that (i) where there is a bay the coasts of which belong to more than one state, a closing

---

[10] Save for one exception provided for in Art. 5 (2).

[11] No agreed list of " historic bays " has ever been drawn up, although a fairly clear example is Conception Bay in Newfoundland. See *Direct U.S. Cable Co.* v. *Anglo-American Telegraph Co.* (1877) 2 App. Cas. 394. An example—and possibly the only example—of a " historic bay " the coasts of which belong to more than one state is the Gulf of Fonseca. In a judgment given on March 9, 1917, in a case brought by El Salvador against Nicaragua, the Central American Court of Justice held that the Gulf of Fonseca was " an historic bay possessed of the characteristics of a closed sea " and that El Salvador, Honduras and Nicaragua were co-owners of its waters, except as to the littoral marine league which was the exclusive property of each (*American Journal of International Law*, 11 (1917), p. 693). With regard to " historic bays " it may be pointed out that, at a time when three miles was generally considered the maximum breadth of the territorial sea and six miles (or at the most 10) as the permissible length of closing lines across bays, the notion of a " historic bay " as a special category exempted from any restriction as to the length of the closing line was considerably more important that it now is if the 24 mile closing lines allowed by Art. 7 of the Geneva Convention are to become the general rule. The International Law Commission had recommended a maximum closing line of 15 miles.

line may not be drawn at all, except in the case of a " historic bay "; and (ii) in the case of " historic bays," whether the coasts of such bays belong to one or more states, the closing line is not restricted to twenty-four miles.

Articles 14 to 23 wrestled with the difficult problem of innocent passage. Although these articles bravely attempted to define both " innocent " and " passage," it cannot be said that any unambiguous conclusion emerges as to what constitutes an " innocent passage." If the coastal state and the state of the vessel concerned differ as to whether a particular passage is innocent or not, belated reference to international adjudication is always possible, if both sides agree. But clearly this is one of the most difficult issues in international law today, quite apart from the problem which arises if one or more of the states involved is, or claims to be, at war. If the coastal state is at war, it enjoys " belligerent rights " under which it may take certain steps against its enemy's ships, as well as neutral ships carrying cargoes to or from enemy ports.[12] These rights may be exercised even on the high seas; *a fortiori* they may also be exercised in the coastal state's own territorial sea. If, on the other hand, the coastal state is neutral, it may close its territorial sea to belligerent warships and their prizes, but it is not bound to do so.

The following further points need to be made on the Convention on the Territorial Sea and the Contiguous Zone.

(i) The convention is completely silent on the breadth of the territorial sea. An attempt was made to remedy this defect at a second conference held in Geneva in 1960, but this too failed.[13] On this critical point all that the International Law Commission had been able to say was that " international law does not permit an extension of the territorial sea beyond twelve miles " and that " the Commission, without taking any decision as to the breadth of the territorial sea up to that limit, notes, on the one hand, that many states have fixed a breadth greater than three miles and, on the other hand, that many states do not recognise such a breadth when that of their own territorial sea is less." It remains broadly true that a claim to more than twelve miles has no hope of meeting with general acceptance. A considerable number of claims up to twelve miles are put forward, but except where a claim can be justified on historic grounds (*e.g.,* Norway's claim to four miles) the states favouring three miles decline to accept such claims.

(ii) The convention has no general article on the question of straits. This is remarkable considering the attention devoted to

---

12 This statement is made on the assumption that, despite the Charter of the United Nations, it is still possible for states to be engaged in " war " and to enjoy " belligerent rights." This assumption is doubtful, but that question is too large to be discussed here.

13 D. W. Bowett, " The Second United Nations Conference on the Law of the Sea " (1960) 9 I.C.L.Q. 415.

straits in the literature of international law. Article 16 (4) does, however, provide the following:

> " There shall be no suspension of the innocent passage of foreign ships through straits which are used for international navigation between one part of the high seas and another part of the high seas or the territorial sea of a foreign State." [14]

There can be no doubt that the Conference had the Straits of Tiran very much in mind when it adopted this provision and that its adoption was sufficient to explain the refusal of the Arab states to sign the convention.

According to the leading authority mentioned above, " in geographic terms, a strait is normally a narrow passage connecting two sections of the high seas." [15] Legally, the régime of a strait is affected by its breadth, in particular by the fact whether or not passage through it is possible without passing through the territorial waters of one or other of the littoral states. Thus, on the assumption that the maximum breadth of territorial waters is three miles, no special régime will in principle be required if a strait is more than six miles wide.[16] Indeed, it may be asked why, even in the case of a narrow strait, a special régime is necessary seeing that the waters in such a strait are territorial waters and that there is an undoubted right of innocent passage through such waters. The idea of a special régime for straits seems first to have arisen through the claim of littoral states to regard some straits that were more than six miles wide as territorial." Now, however, the question is seen more from the opposite point of view, namely, the right of warships of non-littoral states to pass through narrow straits. Thus, in the *Corfu Channel* case, the International Court of Justice affirmed that " States in time of peace have a right to send their warships through straits used for international navigation between two parts of the high seas without the previous authorisation of a coastal State, provided that the passage is *innocent*." [17] The Court evaded in that case the question whether there is a similar right for foreign warships to pass through the territorial sea as such, even where there is no strait. Hence the importance in certain circumstances of determining whether there is a strait or not.

There was bitter controversy at the Geneva Conference of 1958 on the question whether warships have a right to pass through the territorial sea. On that question Professor Sorensen comments:

> " The actual text of the Convention would . . . warrant the conclusion that warships have the same right in this respect

---

[14] Art. 16 (4) follows immediately after Art. 16 (3) which permits a coastal state in certain circumstances to suspend " temporarily in specified areas of its territorial sea the innocent passage of foreign ships." Such suspension, however, must be " without discrimination amongst foreign ships."

[15] Baxter, *op. cit.*, p. 3.

[16] Of course it is not as simple as that. Navigational considerations may make it necessary to keep close to one or other shore.

[17] *I.C.J. Reports 1949*, p. 4 at p. 28. Italics in original.

as other ships, but the proceedings of the Conference leave no room for doubt that this was not the intention of the majority of delegations." [18]

Because of this uncertainty it may, as already stated, be important to decide whether a particular stretch of water is a strait or not. In talking of a special régime for straits, however, it is necessary to guard against a further confusion. Some straits have been subjected to a " special régime " in the sense of a régime actually laid down by treaty. But there are very few of these. Indeed the Secretariat's Guide, referred to above (Preparatory Document No. 11), mentions only five. These are (a) the Straits of the Dardanelles, the Sea of Marmora and the Bosphorus; (b) the Straits of Gibraltar; (c) Fuca's Straits; (d) the Straits of Magellan; and (e) the Danish Straits. The special régime—such as it is— envisaged by the International Court of Justice in the *Corfu Channel* case depends solely upon factual considerations, namely, that the straits in question are " used for international navigation between two parts of the high seas."

From the Convention on the High Seas

Article 1 defines the high seas as " all parts of the sea that are not included in the territorial sea or in the internal waters of a State." Article 2 mentions " freedom of navigation " as one of the freedoms of the high seas.

During the course of the discussions at the Geneva Conference the Israeli delegate in the Second Committee (which was dealing with the régime of the high seas) advanced certain general criticisms of the manner in which the International Law Commission had approached its task. The Commission, he felt, had maintained an unduly rigid distinction between the régime of the territorial sea and that of the high seas. Its draft articles " should be redrafted or regrouped so as to include both innocent passage and passage on the high seas within the framework of freedom of navigation." To over-emphasise the distinction between the territorial sea and the high seas was to assume that

" when a ship sailed from one port to another it crossed an invisible frontier, some miles from the shore, beyond which freedom of navigation existed. In actual fact, however, a ship

---

[18] *Law of the Sea* (International Conciliation, No. 520, November 1958), p. 235. This curious result arose in this way. The International Law Commission had proposed that coastal states might require notification of the passage of warships or even make it subject to previous authorisation. In the First Committee of the Geneva Conference the I.L.C. draft was adopted, but in plenary the Western Powers succeeded in securing the deletion of the require-ment of prior *authorisation*. A number of delegations were not content with prior *notification* only, and the entire article was lost. As Arts. 14 to 17 (the general articles concerned with the right of innocent passage) appear under a subsection entitled " Rules applicable to All Ships," it is argued that warships enjoy exactly the same rights as merchant ships.

passing through the territorial sea enjoyed the right of innocent passage, which was independent of the sovereignty of the coastal state and which formed an integral part of freedom of navigation. The fact that passage through the territorial sea might be subject to qualifications did not alter the basic fact that innocent passage was exercised as a right, and not on sufferance; suspension of such passage within the territorial sea could not be arbitrary, even as a state could not arbitrarily interfere with freedom of navigation on the high seas. Moreover, qualifications of the right of innocent passage did not always exist, as in the case of international straits and bays and free access to ports."

Rather, in the Israeli delegate's view, one should lay stress on " the concept of the unity of the voyage." [19]

THE STRAITS OF TIRAN AND THE GULF OF AQABA

The description that follows is taken from the Secretariat Study of " Bays and Estuaries, the Coasts of Which belong to Different States " referred to above.[20]

" The Gulf of Aqaba is a long narrow gulf on the eastern side of the Sinai Peninsula. The western shore is Egyptian,[21] the eastern shore is Saudi Arabian and the head of the Gulf is Israeli and Jordanian territory. The islands of Tiran and Sinafar front the entrance. The length of the gulf is about ninety-six miles."

The Study goes on to explain that the breadth of the Gulf at the entrance is five and three-quarter miles; that at its widest part the Gulf is fourteen and a half miles wide but that further up the average breadth is between eight and a half and eleven miles; and that the Gulf narrows to between three and four miles wide towards the head. There are two feasible passages. One of these is the Enterprise Passage, 1,800 yards wide, between the Sinai coast and a

---

[19] Official Records of the Second Committee (A/Conf. 13/40), Twelfth Meeting, paragraphs 5–8. Similar views were expressed by the Netherlands delegate when he said: " The right to use the high seas for purposes of navigation had legal consequences that went beyond the concept of the high seas in the geographical sense of the term. No purpose would be served by proclaiming freedom of navigation on the high seas if that freedom could be enjoyed only in the geographical area of the high seas to the exclusion of territorial and internal waters. The ' freedom of navigation ' concept should imply the right of ships of all flags to engage in international trade, because in principle it covered the right to carry goods and passengers between various ports throughout the world." (Fourth Meeting, para. 10.)

[20] p. 154, *supra.* The description of the Straits of Tiran and the Gulf of Aqaba is a combined description appearing in this Study (*i.e.*, Preparatory Document No. 12). The Study covers no fewer than 48 such bays and estuaries, including Lough Carlingford and Lough Foyle. In the other Study (Preparatory Document No. 6), devoted to " Straits which constitute Routes for International Traffic," 33 straits are described.

[21] At the time of writing Israel is in possession of the Sinai Peninsula. At this time, however, her rights and duties are those of a military occupant, not a sovereign.

line of drying coral reefs. The other is the Grafton Passage, 950 yards wide, between these reefs and Tiran island.

The legal position of Tiran and Sinafar is obscure. It appears that Egypt occupied these islands in 1950 with Saudi Arabian consent. The Egyptian delegate informed the Security Council on February 15, 1954, that the two islands had constituted Egyptian territory since 1906. But in a memorandum attached to a letter dated April 12, 1957, from the Permanent Representative of Saudi Arabia to the United Nations to the Secretary-General, it was stated that " these two islands are Saudi Arabian "; and Egypt apparently raised no objection.[22]

Having regard to the width of the Gulf, and having regard also to the dispute over the breadth of territorial waters, it is not clear whether there are any high seas inside the Straits of Tiran. Obviously, if international law imposes a maximum breadth of three miles for the territorial sea, quite a considerable part of the Gulf of Aqaba constitutes high seas. If, on the other hand, international law accepts as valid claims to a territorial sea of twelve miles, as formulated by the Arab states and many others, then no part of the Gulf of Aqaba constitutes " high seas," and the status of the Straits of Tiran is affected too, since it can no longer be said of those Straits that they " connect two sections of the high seas." In that eventuality, on whatever theory any right to enter the Gulf of Aqaba—and in particular to reach the Israeli port of Eilath—may rest, it can no longer rest on the proposition that the " Straits of Tiran " are a strait in the sense of " a narrow passage connecting two sections of the high seas."

It may be necessary to draw a distinction between merely entering the Gulf of Aqaba on the one hand and navigating as far as Eilath—or for that matter the Jordanian port of Aqaba—on the other hand. If, for example, the Gulf of Aqaba constitutes " high seas," then there would be no reason why a foreign warship, enjoying its right of innocent passage through the Straits of Tiran under the *Corfu Channel* decision, should not enter the Gulf and stay for some time therein on a surveillance mission, without ever intending to reach Eilath or Aqaba. If, on the other hand, there are no high seas within the Gulf, then a mission of that kind would seem to be excluded, but it would not necessarily follow that a foreign merchant ship would not be entitled to pass through the Straits of Tiran, sail up the Gulf, and dock at Eilath or Aqaba despite any objection by the main littoral states, Egypt and Saudi Arabia.

Leaving aside the problem of defining " innocence," Article 14 of the Geneva Convention on the Territorial Sea and the Contiguous Zone states that " Passage means navigation through the territorial

---

[22] See C. B. Selak, " A Consideration of the Legal Status of the Gulf of Aqaba," *American Journal of International Law*, 52 (1958), p. 660; and also L. Gross, " The Geneva Conference on the Law of the Sea and the Right of Innocent Passage through the Gulf of Aqaba," *ibid.* 53 (1959), p. 564.

sea for the purpose either of traversing that sea without entering internal waters, or of proceeding to internal waters, or of making for the high seas from internal waters." Vessels bound to or from Eilath could therefore be said to be exercising the right of passage not merely through the Straits of Tiran but also through the Egyptian and/or Saudi Arabian portions of the Gulf of Aqaba. Under the general rules of international law these states would be entitled to regulate such shipping, and possibly on occasions to suspend it temporarily, although the fact has to be faced that Israel will always tend to regard any such suspension as a threat to her security warranting an armed response in self-defence. But it is difficult to see how under general international law Egypt and Saudi Arabia could claim any permanent right to exclude such shipping altogether.

That the Arab claim to exclude ships bound to and from Eilath is weak under general international law is no more convincingly evidenced than by the heavy reliance placed on such other Arab claims as that Israel has no right to exist as a state or that the Arab states are at war with Israel.[23] Moreover, if the Arab claim were good under general international law, there might be serious repercussion upon the right of navigation in other areas where international boundaries converge, such as the Shatt Al Arab, the Gulf of Trieste and the Rio de la Plata, to mention only a few.

It may be as well also to comment upon the Israeli contention that the principle of the freedom of the seas implies in itself the right to navigate to and from the Israeli port of Eilath. This contention sounds plausible because it is certainly true that, for Israel, the freedom of the seas would be a much diminished prize if navigation were excluded from the Gulf of Aqaba. Nevertheless, it is doubtful if one principle of international law, the freedom of the seas, is of itself sufficient to generate rights that are entitled to take precedence over rights enjoyed under another principle of international law, in this case the principle of the territorial sovereignty of the intervening coastal states. This question of freedom of the seas versus territorial sovereignty was much discussed at Geneva in 1958 in relation to the problem of landlocked states. On that question Article 3 of the Convention on the High Seas asserted that " States having no sea coast should have free access to the sea." But, even in the case of landlocked states, such access was made dependent upon agreements with the intervening coastal states. Whatever geographical disadvantages she may suffer from in the Gulf of Aqaba, Israel has a Mediterranean coast as well. She cannot therefore claim any special privilege as a landlocked

---

23 There is a certain inconsistency between the refusal of the Arab states to recognise Israel and their claim to be at war with Israel nonetheless. The inconsistency is, however, not absolute because international law admits of the possibility of belligerent communities not recognised as states (e.g., the Confederacy in the American Civil War).

state. In practice, Israel must like all other states take her geo-graphical position as she finds it. She is entitled to the benefits of the general rules of international law, no more and no less. So far as Israel's rights in the Gulf of Aqaba are concerned, these rules are the rules relating to bays, straits and passage through the territorial sea which it has been attempted to elucidate above.

There is one other question relating to the Gulf of Aqaba which needs to be considered. This is whether the littoral states, acting in agreement, are entitled to close the Gulf to foreign shipping. The question is of course academic since the littoral states are not likely to agree on such a course, Israel in particular being determined to keep the Gulf open. Nevertheless it is necessary to consider this matter as part of the general Arab contention that the Gulf of Aqaba is an " Arab Sea " on which Israel, even if it is entitled to exist at all, has no right to maintain a presence.[24]

As already indicated, Article 7 of the Geneva Convention on the Territorial Sea and the Contiguous Zone suggests that a closing line—which has the effect of turning the waters inside it into internal waters from which foreign shipping may be totally excluded—may not be drawn at all across the mouth of a bay the coasts of which belong to more than one state, unless the bay is an " historic bay." It is doubtful, however, if this restriction would apply in the case of a bay with as narrow an entrance as the Gulf of Aqaba. On any conceivable view of the breadth of territorial waters, the Gulf of Aqaba, if it belonged to a single state, could be closed. In principle, then, it would seem that the littoral states of the Gulf of Aqaba, provided they are all acting in agreement, can do what any one of them could do if it controlled the whole area—that is, close the Gulf to foreign shipping.

This being so, it is scarcely necessary to consider the Arab claim that the Gulf of Aqaba is an " historic bay." The claim rests on the long period of Arab domination of the area between 700 and 1517 and on its control by the Ottoman Empire between 1517 and 1917. But the essence of any claim on historical grounds is lack of interruption, and the sequence of events since 1917 has been too chequered to permit of the continued recognition of any historic right. (To mention only a few of these events, the Treaty of San Remo of April 25, 1920, awarded to Great Britain a Mandate for Palestine, which then included Transjordan. In 1922 a separate Mandate was created for Transjordan, which was placed under the Amir Abdullah. In 1924 Abdullah's father, King Husayn of the Hejaz, was forced to abdicate by the King of Nejd, Ibn Saud, who

---

24 This particular Arab contention appears to be that, although Eilath was in the mandated territory of Palestine and although Eilath was also in the area awarded to the Jewish State under the United Nations Partition Plan of 1947, the Israeli occupation of Eilath was illegal because it took place on March 11, 1949, after the Israeli-Egyptian Armistice Agreement (February 24, 1949) though before the signature of the Israeli-Jordan Armistice Agreement (April 3, 1949).

in 1926 incorporated the Hejaz into his dominions, forming the present Kingdom of Saudi Arabia in 1932. As for Egypt, having been a vassal state of Turkey, she became a protectorate of Great Britain in 1914. Her independence was recognised in 1922 by Great Britain, whilst in 1923 Turkey by the Treaty of Lausanne renounced all her rights and titles over Egypt as from November 5, 1914.)

THE SUEZ CANAL [25]

Apart from the familiar contention that Israel has no right to exist, Egypt's claim to close the Suez Canal at all times to Israeli ships and cargoes destined to Israel, and from time to time to ships of all nations, rests essentially on the thesis that Egypt is at war with Israel and is entitled to take these measures in self-defence. Article I of the Constantinople Convention of October 29, 1888, respecting the Free Navigation of the Suez Maritime Canal states that " The Suez Maritime Canal shall always be free and open, in time of war as in time of peace, to every vessel of commerce or of war, without distinction of flag." Obviously this principle could not always be carried out in so bold a form, and in fact Articles IV, V, VII and VIII impose certain restrictions upon maritime belligerent Powers. Article X, however, states that " the provisions of Articles IV, V, VII and VIII shall not interfere with the measures which His Majesty the Sultan and His Highness the Khedive,[26] in the name of His Imperial Majesty, and within the limits of the Firmans granted, might find it necessary to take for securing by their own forces the defence of Egypt and the maintenance of public order." Article X also provided that " It is likewise understood that the provisions of the four Articles aforesaid shall in no case occasion any obstacle to the measures which the Imperial Ottoman Government may think it necessary to take in order to insure by its own forces *the defence of its other possessions situated on the eastern coast of the Red Sea.*" From the passage in italics it seems possible to deduce that the Constantinople Convention, although primarily concerned with the Suez Canal, might have some bearing upon the Gulf of Aqaba problem as well.

On April 24, 1957, Egypt made a Declaration, deposited with

---

25 The reader is referred to the following: L. Gross, " Passage through the Suez Canal of Israel-Bound Cargo and Israel Ships," *American Journal of International Law,* 51 (1957), p. 530; " The Suez Canal," A Selection of Documents relating to the International Status of the Suez Canal and the Position of the Suez Canal Company, November 30, 1854–July 26, 1956, published under the auspices of the Society of Comparative Legislation and International Law (London, Stevens, 1956) and to " The Suez Canal Settlement," A Selection of Documents relating to the Settlement of the Suez Canal Dispute, the Clearance of the Suez Canal and the Settlement of Disputes between the United Kingdom, France and the United Arab Republic, October 1956–March 1959, published under the auspices of the British Institute of International and Comparative Law (London, Stevens, 1960).

26 In 1888 Egypt was a vassal state of the Ottoman Empire, although under military occupation by Great Britain.

the United Nations, in which she undertook " to respect the terms and the spirit of the Constantinople Convention of 1888 and the rights and obligations arising therefrom." She further undertook that " differences arising between the parties to the said convention in respect of the interpretation or the applicability of its provisions, if not otherwise resolved, will be referred to the International Court of Justice." A Declaration in furtherance of this obligation was made on July 18, 1957. The possibility therefore exists of bringing before the International Court of Justice at least some of the legal issues arising from the present closing of the Suez Canal. The right to seize the Court is, however, carefully limited in the Egyptian Declarations to the parties to the Constantinople Convention and further to states who have made declarations under Article 36 (2) of the Statute of the International Court of Justice (*i.e.*, the Optional Clause). The parties to the Constantinople Convention were Great Britain, Germany, Austria, Hungary, Spain, France, Italy, Netherlands, Russia and the Ottoman Empire. Of these, the following only have made declarations under Article 36 (2): Great Britain, France, Netherlands, Turkey.

D. H. N. JOHNSON.*

* M.A.; LL.B.; Professor of International and Air Law, University of London.

Closure of the Suez Canal to Israeli Shipping

MAJID KHADDURI

Introduction

The Arab-Israeli war of June 1967 has again raised the question as to whether Egypt can lawfully close the Suez Canal to Israeli shipping. Israel, since its establishment, has repeatedly demanded the same right of free passage accorded to other nations, but Egypt has insisted on denying her such a right despite resolutions of the United Nations Security Council calling on Egypt to terminate the restrictions imposed on the passage of Israeli shipping and goods through the Suez Canal.[1] The six-day war gave Israel the opportunity to demand again the opening of the Canal to her shipping;[2] but President Nasir, in his speech on November 24, 1967, two days after the Security Council's resolution 242 had been adopted, calling for withdrawal from occupied territory and termination of belligerency, declared in no uncertain terms that "we shall never allow Israeli ships, whatever the cost, to pass through the Suez Canal."[3] Israel's demand and Nasir's rejection call for a reconsideration of the question in the light of the new circumstances brought about by the June war and the Security Council's resolution of November 22, 1967. It is not my purpose to review the arguments of the two parties relative to the conditions preceding the June war, except in so far as they relate to the conditions after the war, since they have been thoroughly scrutinized by a number of scholars from the two opposing viewpoints.[4] In order to examine the legal aspect of the closure of the Canal specifically to Israeli shipping, I propose to deal with the question under three headings: (1) the fundamental principles governing the present legal status of the Suez Canal; (2) Israel's claim to the right of free passage; (3) Egypt's right to control of the Canal.

---

[*]B.A. 1932, American University, Beirut; Ph.D. 1938, University of Chicago. Director of the Center for Middle East Studies, and Professor, The School of Advanced International Studies, The Johns Hopkins University. Author, Independent Iraq (1951); War and Peace in the Law of Islam (1955); Islamic Jurisprudence (1961); Modern Libya (1963).

[1] The most important resolution was, of course, S.C. Res. 95 (1951). It cited S.C. Res. 73 (1949) and other resolutions and acts calling for the cessation of hostile acts and the resolution of outstanding issues between the parties.

[2] See Abba Eban's speech at the Emergency Session of the General Assembly of the United Nations on June 19, 1967, U.N. Doc. A/PV.1526 (1967) and subsequent declarations.

[3] For full text of the speech, see al-Ahram, Cairo, Nov. 25, 1967. See also N.Y. Times, Nov. 24, 1967, at 13, col. 1.

[4] Two books might be cited which deal with the divergent views in detail: B. Avram, The Evolution of the Suez Canal Status from 1869 up to 1956 (1958), and J. Obieta, The International Status of the Suez Canal (1960).

I

Fundamental Principles Governing the Legal Status of the Suez Canal

When the Suez Canal was opened in 1869, Egypt had not yet attained independence. Its territory was part of the Ottoman Empire. The Khedive of Egypt, one of the Sultan's principal governors, had no power to act in entering into agreements relating to foreign affairs without the approval of the Sultan. Thus, the acts of concession issued by the Khedive in 1854, 1856, and 1866, granting the right to connect the Mediterranean and the Red Seas by a canal and to operate it, had to be ratified by the Sultan's firman (decree), issued on March 19, 1866, in order to be valid under the Ottoman law in force in Egypt.[5] However, no rights were derived from the concession by any third party nor was any surrender of the Sultan's sovereignty over the Canal ever intended. On the contrary, the acts of concession stressed Egypt's right to supervise the Canal, to enforce law and public order, and to occupy any point on the borders of the Canal whenever this was deemed necessary for the defense of the country, as a manifestation of sovereignty over the territory of the Canal. But the intent of throwing open the Canal to the free navigation of all nations without distinction of flag was made abundantly clear.

Nor was the Sultan's sovereignty over the Canal's territory restricted by the provisions of the Convention regulating the use of the Canal signed in Constantinople on October 29, 1888. The Convention of 1888 aimed at confirming the practices that had developed concerning free navigation for all nations, but no surrender of any sovereign rights was ever contemplated. For if the Sultan had given away any of his sovereign rights, he would have committed an act of servitude in derogation of his sovereignty over Egypt. The first principle governing the present status of the Suez Canal is, therefore, the principle of territorial sovereignty which was recognized by the signatories of the Convention of 1888. But to the manner in which the rights of sovereignty were to be exercised, we shall return later.

Next to the principle of territorial sovereignty is the principle that the Suez Canal is an "international waterway." This "internationality" was the product of a voluntary act on the part of the Ottoman Sultan in an effort to extend the benefits of free passage through the Canal to all nations without qualifying his sovereign rights. Even before the construction of the Canal was completed, the intent was, both in

---

[5] The concession, concluded with a private company, did not imply an international obligation on Egypt's behalf and could have been signed by the Khedive without the approval of the Sultan in accordance with the firman of appointment of the Khedive of 1841. But since the concession contained an obligation assumed by the two parties toward each other affecting third parties in their undertaking that they would not discriminate against other parties, and Article 14 of the 1866 concession provided that the canal and its ports would always be open as a neutral passage, the Sultan's approval became necessary. In the concession of 1866, it was stipulated that the Sultan's ratification was necessary. For texts of the acts of concession and the firmans of ratification, *see* U.S. Dep't of State, Pub. No. 6392, The Suez Canal Problem: A Documentary Publication 1-16 (1956); B. Boutros-Ghali, Le Canal de Suez, 1854-1957: Chronologie Document 10 (1958); 1 J. Hurewitz, Diplomacy in the Near and Middle East 146-49 (1956).

the acts of concession as well as in unilateral declarations, to grant the right of free navigation to all nations. Article 14 of the Concession of 1856 reads:

> We solemnly declare, for ourselves and our successors, subject to ratification by His Imperial Majesty the Sultan, that the great maritime canal from Suez to Pelusium and the ports belonging to it shall be open forever, as neutral passages, to every merchant vessel crossing from one sea to the other, without any distinction, exclusion, or preference with respect to persons or nationalities, in consideration of the payment of the fees, and compliance with the regulations established by the universal company, the concession-holder, for the use of the said canal and its appurtenances.[6]

In this, as well as in other relevant declarations of unilateral nature, the purpose was to assure the company and all nations that the canal would always be open to free navigation. Notwithstanding these declarations, as one Israeli writer stated, "[t]he passage of ships was not a right but a privilege granted by the Ottoman Empire to other nations."[7] It is also questionable that a right was established by the Sultan's declaration made at a conference held in Constantinople, in 1873, to deal with technical matters, in which he said:

> It is understood that no modification, for the future, of the conditions for the passage through the Canal shall be permitted, whether in regard to the navigation toll or the dues for towage, anchorage, pilotage, etc., except with the consent of the Sublime Porte, which will not take any decision on the subject without previously coming to an understanding with the principal Powers interested therein.[8]

Some writers have argued, on the analogy of the *Eastern Greenland Case,* that the unilateral declaration of a Foreign Minister on behalf of his country, would be "binding upon the country to which the Minister belongs."[9] Such a declaration was, in that case, held by the Permanent Court of International Justice to be binding on the country making it. The so-called "Ihlen doctrine" may or may not be accepted, but it is of no great significance to our discussion, since an internationally binding act had been accepted by the Ottoman Porte in 1888 which established beyond any doubt the international character of the Suez Canal.

In the preamble of the Constantinople Convention[10] (October 29, 1888), the nine signatory Powers[11] stated that their intention was to establish "a definitive system intended to guarantee, at all times and to all the Powers, the free use of the Suez Maritime Canal, and thus to complete the system under which the navigation of

---

[6] THE SUEZ CANAL PROBLEM, *supra* note 5, at 7; B. BOUTROS-GHALI, *supra* note 5, at 6; and 1 J. HUREWITZ, *supra* note 5, at 148.

[7] B. AVRAM, *supra* note 4, at 31.

[8] Great Britain, *Parliamentary Papers*, Commercial 19, C. 1075, at 319.

[9] [1933] P.C.I.J., ser. A/B, No. 53, at 21, 71.

[10] For English text of the Convention, *see* Great Britain, *Parliamentary Papers*, Commercial, No. 2, Suez Canal, C. 5623 (1889); THE SUEZ CANAL PROBLEM, *supra* note 5, at 16-20; B. BOUTROS-GHALI, *supra* note 5, at 16; 1 J. HUREWITZ, *supra* note 5, at 202-05.

[11] They were Great Britain, Austria-Hungary, France, Germany, Italy, The Netherlands, Russia, Spain, and Turkey.

this Canal had been placed by the Firman of His Imperial Majesty the Sultan, dated February 22, 1866 . . . ."

Moreover, the preamble indicates the principle of "internationality" as having evolved from the inception of the Canal and that the Convention was to "complete" the legal status envisioned in early declarations. As a legal obligation, however, it is Article 1, specifying free navigation to all nations, which established the principle of internationality to include freedom of passage in time of war and peace. Article 1 reads: "The Suez Maritime Canal shall always be free and open, in time of war as in time of peace, to every vessel of commerce or of war, without distinction of flag. Consequently, the High Contracting Parties agree not in any way to interfere with the free use of the canal, in time of war as in time of peace."

In order to insure "free navigation," it was realized that a "guarantee," as stated in the preamble, was necessary. To achieve such a guarantee, the signatories provided, under Article 2, that: "They undertake not to interfere in any way with security of that Canal and its branches, the working of which shall not be the object of any attempt at obstruction."

This "security" of the Canal was to be guaranteed by the acceptance of another principle, already stated in earlier declarations, that the Canal would be neutral, although the term *neutrality* is not used in the text of the Convention. Article 4 reads:

> The Maritime Canal remaining open in time of war as a free passage . . . , no right of war, act of hostility or act having for its purpose to interfere with the free navigation of the Canal, shall be committed in the Canal and its ports . . . even though the Ottoman Empire should be one of the belligerent Powers.

All other acts on the part of belligerent Powers were forbidden in the Canal and its ports. Moreover, the Canal, as Article 1 further states, "shall never be submitted to the exercise of the right of blockade." The legal consequence of these stipulations is that the Canal, in time of war, shall be excluded from the area of warfare.[12] Thus, the neutrality of the Suez Canal, even if the Ottoman Empire were one of the belligerent Powers, is the third principle governing the present legal status of the Canal. Various terms have been used to characterize this neutral regime, from "inviolability" to "neutralization," but this should be distinguished from the neutralization of states.[13]

The three principles of territorial sovereignty, internationality, and neutrality

---

[12] This means that the neutral zone should be excluded from the region where war can lawfully be prepared or waged.

[13] *See* J. OBIETA, *supra* note 4, at 68-69. Colombos, however, held a different point of view on the Canal's neutrality. He said: ". . . the Suez Canal is not neutralized in the proper sense of the term, since neutrality does not admit the passage of belligerent forces across a territory . . . . It is only subject to a particular regime for the purpose of withdrawing it from all acts of hostility within its waters and protecting it from any damage or any attempt to close it to the detriment of the World's navigation." C. COLOMBOS, THE INTERNATIONAL LAW OF THE SEA 175 (4th ed. 1961).

have been assessed differently by various writers. Some, stressing internationality and neutrality, have maintained that sovereignty was restricted by the Convention of 1888 which imposed a "perpetual servitude" over Egypt in the area of the Suez Canal.[14] Others, rejecting the imposition of an international servitude, stressed the overriding principle of territorial sovereignty and recognize neither an international character for the Canal nor an implied neutrality in its zone.[15] The latter position has been maintained by writers who either tried to defend Egypt's position on the closure of the Canal against Israel or pushed to the extreme the doctrine of territorial sovereignty in the relationship among states. On the other hand, the writers who argued the case of Israel's claim to free passage have stressed Egypt's international obligations under the Convention of 1888 without qualifications. A third position, however, may be maintained in which Egypt's contractual obligations may be respected without compromising the doctrine of sovereignty. This is the position taken in this paper.

II
Israel's Claim to the Right of Free Passage
Through the Suez Canal

Since its establishment more than two decades ago, Israel has repeatedly demanded the same right of free passage through the Suez Canal enjoyed by other nations, and has claimed that Egypt's closure of the Canal to its shipping had been done in violation of the general principles of international law, of the Convention of 1888, and of the Armistice Agreement of 1949. Let us examine Israel's complaints from these three legal angles.

Under the general principles of international law, according to Israel, all nations possess the right to navigate freely on the high seas, through international waterways that connect high seas, and through international rivers. This right, according to Israel, is "a cornerstone" of international law, and, therefore, cannot be denied to her as one of the members of the international community.

In the specific case of the Suez Canal, the right of free passage, clearly stated in the Constantinople Convention of 1888, was, in this area, to be enjoyed by all nations without distinction of flag. Israel, as one of the nations presumably included under the general term "without distinction of flag," was therefore entitled to enjoy the same right as other nations, but Egypt is alleged to have denied Israel such right in violation of the general principle of international law and of her obligations under the Convention of 1888.

Moreover, Egypt's restrictive measures, according to Israel, constitute an act of war in the Canal waters contrary to Articles 1 and 4 of the Convention of 1888, on

---

[14] See B. Avram, supra note 4, at 48-50.

[15] See Huang, Some International and Legal Aspects of the Suez Canal Question, 51 Am. J. Int'l L. 300-03 (1957).

the ground that Egypt possessed no right to take defensive measures in the Canal Zone.[16] Egypt proceeded to act on the assumption that she was at war with Israel, but this assumption was not justified, according to Israel, because no state—other than the Arab states—recognized such a state of war to have existed. On the contrary, the United Nations had on more than one occasion called on Egypt to open the Suez Canal presumably on the assumption that Egypt and Israel, as peace-loving members of that Organization, can no longer remain at war with one another. If they had ever been at war, as the Arab states held, such a state of war must be superseded by membership in the United Nations.[17]

Finally, the Armistice Agreement between Egypt and Israel (February 24, 1949)[18] has prohibited hostile acts. According to Israel, not only war in the military sense, but also the state of war between her and Egypt had been terminated. As stated by an Israeli jurist, the Agreement was intended to achieve four aims:

1. To facilitate the transition from the present truce to permanent peace and bring all hostilities to an end.

2. To fulfill the obligation of the Security Council to act with respect to threats to the peace, breaches of the peace and acts of aggression.

3. To delineate permanent demarcation lines beyond which the armed forces of the respective parties should not move.

4. To provide for the withdrawal and reduction of armed forces in order to insure the maintenance of the armistice during the transition to permanent peace.[19]

These aims, intended to establish eventual peace between Egypt and Israel, have been endorsed by the United Nations resolutions of 1949 and of 1951, which explicitly called upon Egypt to open the Suez Canal. Egypt's refusal to open the Canal, according to Israel, was a violation of both the Armistice Agreement and the United Nations Security Council resolutions of 1949 and 1951.[20]

Egypt, however, has refused to accept the charge that she has denied Israel's right of free passage in violation of international law. Israel has put forth a claim to free passage under international law on the ground that the Suez Canal—like any other strait—is an international waterway and, therefore, according to her, should be open to free navigation. But should the Suez Canal, even if regarded as an international waterway, be treated as other waterways, like straits, and, therefore, as subject to the same rules of international law? Straits, as "natural" waterways provided

[16] 9 U.N. SCOR, 658th meeting 1-25 (1954). *See also* B. AVRAM, *supra* note 4, at 119-21.

[17] This viewpoint is based on the assumption that members of the United Nations are peace-loving members and therefore no one can be at war with another member without violating the Charter of this organization. *See* H. KELSEN, THE LAW AND THE UNITED NATIONS 69 (1950); AND L.M. BLOOMFIELD, EGYPT, ISRAEL AND THE GULF OF AQABA IN INTERNATIONAL LAW 164 (1957).

[18] 42 U.N.T.S. 251, no. 654. *See also* 2 J. HUREWITZ, *supra* note 5, at 299-304.

[19] S. ROSENNE, ISRAEL'S ARMISTICE AGREEMENTS WITH THE ARAB STATES 33 (1951).

[20] *See* note 1 *supra*. For an interpretation of these views, *see* Gross, *Passage Through the Suez Canal of Israel-Bound Cargo and Israel Ships*, 51 AM. J. INT'L L. 530-68 (1957).

by nature, have existed from time immemorial and, therefore, the free passage enjoyed by all nations must be distinguished from free passage through canals which have been artificially constructed. Before a canal is opened, its territory must be under the control of some state sovereignty. Canals must, therefore, fall in a different category from straits, because they are artificial waterways opened by the express or tacit approval of the sovereign power and, *ipso jure*, the consent of the sovereign power must be first obtained. If the sovereign grants free passage by an express declaration or by an obligation under a treaty or an international agreement, it is the legal obligation undertaken by the sovereign which entitles other nations to enjoy free passage, rather than the geographical analogy with natural waterways.[21]

In the case of the Suez Canal, it was the Convention of 1888 rather than the general principles of international law that granted the right of free passage to other nations. If Israel possesses any right to enjoy free passage through the canal, such right must be derived from the aggregate right granted to other nations and not by an analogy with natural waterways which nations ordinarily enjoy under international law.

The Convention of 1888 merely confirmed the right of free passage already recognized by the Ottoman Porte before 1888 and the powers that signed this convention acquired such rights both in time of peace and war. At the time of signature, other nations were invited to adhere to the Convention, but failed to do so. With regard to non-signatory states, the question whether the Convention is obligatory on them is an open one. Israel may be said to fall in a different category of non-signatory states. As a successor state, would she not, like Egypt, be entitled to special rights?

There is no question that Egypt, already mentioned in the Convention, was granted special rights as the country immediately connected with the canal, and certain obligations were imposed on her.[22] Egypt, according to the general principles of international law, must also accept the obligations already undertaken on her behalf by the former sovereign power. Moreover, Egypt has formally declared its acceptance of the obligations under the Convention of 1888 after independence on more than one occasion.[23]

---

[21] "Unlike international rivers and straits, which are natural waterways, international canals are artificially constructed. This essentially differentiating factor has been overlooked by a number of writers who, misled by the similarity of regimes to which both international canals as well as rivers and straits are subject, have tried to find, by an analogy to the latter, a geographical or physical criterion which would serve to define an international canal."
J. OBIETA, *supra* note 4, at 24.

[22] *See* Articles 8, 9, 10, and 14 of the Convention of 1888. *Cf. supra* note 11.

[23] From 1938 in formal statements concerning the Canal following the declaration of independence to 1954, the year of signature of the treaty with Britain for evacuation of the Canal Zone. *See, e.g.,* letter from Mustafa al Sadik Bey to Lord Perth, April 16, 1938, 195 L.N.T.S. 108 (1939); Agreement between . . . Egypt and the . . . United Kingdom, October 19, 1954, 210 U.N.T.S. 1 (1955); Letter from the Minister for Foreign Affairs to Egypt to the Secretary-General . . . 24 April 1957, 12 U.N. SCOR, Supp. April-June 1957, at 8, 9, U.N. Doc. S/3818/Add. 1 (1957); statement by Egyptian Representative in Security Council, 2 U.N. SCOR 1756 (1947).

Unlike Egypt, however, Israel falls in a special category. First, she has not adhered to the Convention of 1888, which has an accession clause, and therefore may enjoy the right of free passage in time of peace like other non-signatory states to whom the right of free passage was granted before 1888, but not the right of free passage in time of war which was granted under the Convention of that year. Second, if Israel may be considered to have adhered tacitly, she must have acquired not only the right to enjoy the right of free passage, but also the obligations of the Convention. Such obligations, for instance, require that the Canal must remain neutral and not involved in the area in which war is lawfully waged, and that the Canal should not be subject to blockade. Obviously Israel has neither declared her acceptance of such obligations nor, since she carried her military operations to its very eastern bank, has she respected the neutralization of the Suez Canal.[24] Third, Egypt's territory has become the subject of an Israeli attack in 1967, which raises the question of Egypt's right to take defensive measures irrespective of whether Israel possesses the right of free passage or not. This latter point, so significantly affecting the status of the Canal, deserves to be treated separately in the following section, concerned with Egypt's right to control the Canal.

It follows from our foregoing argument that if Israel were not involved in a war with Egypt—a war in which Egypt closed the Canal as a defensive measure—Israel would be entitled to the right of free passage. There can be no doubt that Israel's attack on Egyptian territory on June 5, 1967, presumably to settle a dispute by force rather than by peaceful methods as provided by the Charter of the United Nations, was an act of war which justified Egypt's position concerning the security of the Suez Canal, since, as noted above, Israel was not entitled to enjoy the same rights and obligations as a signatory of the Convention of 1888. As a third party beneficiary, a right concerning which jurists are not all in agreement,[25] Israel might claim to enjoy certain rights to use the Canal. But in a war which Israel initiated, and in which it attacked the territorial Zone of the Canal, Egypt would be empowered to close the Canal in self-defense, no less by general law than by the very provisions of the Convention of 1888 which obligate Egypt to take measures to prohibit any state from conducting war in the Canal Zone.[26]

A controversy has raged among several writers as to whether a state of war existed between Egypt and Israel before June 5, 1967. Those who defend Israel's right to free passage through the Canal hold that belligerency between the two states created by the Palestine war of 1948-49 was terminated by the Armistice

---

[24] Although Israel did not reach the Canal Zone in the invasion of Sinai in 1956, in the June war she reached and asserted control over the eastern bank of the Canal in violation of Articles 1 and 4 of the Convention. See notes 11 and 12 *supra*.

[25] *See* LORD McNAIR, LAW OF TREATIES 309-21 (1961); HARVARD RESEARCH IN INTERNATIONAL LAW: LAW OF TREATIES 924 (J. Garner ed. 1935).

[26] In practice this seems to have been the position maintained by the Ottoman Porte and later Egypt since 1888. See J. OBIETA, *supra* note 4, at 79-87.

Agreement of February 28, 1949.[27] Moreover, the Security Council resolution of September 1, 1951, calling upon Egypt to open the Canal to Israeli shipping on the ground that hostilities had been terminated by the armistice of 1949, was asserted by some to be binding on Egypt. Egypt, according to those who supported this viewpoint, has violated the Convention of 1888 and ignored the resolution of the Security Council.[28] Those who hold an opposing viewpoint argue that the Armistice Agreement of 1949 did not terminate the state of war, since an armistice puts an end to fighting but does not establish peace. Only a peace treaty can terminate the state of war and establish peace.[29] Moreover, the Security Council resolution, based on the assumption that the intent of the Armistice Agreement was to establish peace, cannot be regarded as binding on Egypt without her consent, because the resolution was recommendatory and not mandatory in nature.[30]

The controversy between these opposing viewpoints is deemed outside the scope of this paper, which deals with the problem of the closure of the Suez Canal in the circumstances created by the war of 1967. Even if a state of war had not existed before June 5, 1967, Egypt's decision to keep the Canal closed to Israeli shipping after the June war would be justified by the measures necessary for self-defense against sudden attack on the ground that the closure of the Canal against a non-signatory to the Convention falls within Egypt's sovereign rights.

Finally, it may be asked to what extent Egypt's obligations under the Convention of 1888 have restricted her sovereign rights over the Canal? This raises the question of Egypt's right to control the Canal, which falls under the third heading of our discussion.

III

EGYPT'S RIGHT TO CONTROL OF THE CANAL

The control of the Suez Canal raises the question of the relevance of territorial sovereignty to the status of the Canal and to what extent it was restricted by an international agreement. As already stated, the internationality of the Canal may be regarded as a balancing principle between the doctrine of sovereignty and the binding obligations of an international agreement. It is in the light of this balance that Egypt's right of the control of the Canal should be assessed.

---

[27] See S. ROSENNE, supra note 19, at 82.

[28] See B. AVRAM, supra note 4, at 119.

[29] For a summary of the Egyptian point of view, see id. at 122-27.

[30] For a discussion on the nature of the U.N. resolution, see Halderman, Some International Constitutional Aspects of the Palestine Case, in this symposium, p. 78. Colonel Howard S. Levie makes the following remarks on the Security Council resolution of 1951:

"It is considered more likely that the Security Council's action was based upon a desire to bring to an end a situation fraught with potential danger to peace than that it was attempting to change a long established rule of international law. By now it has surely become fairly obvious that the Israeli-Arab General Armistice Agreements did not create even a de facto termination of the war between those states."

Levie, The Nature and Scope of the Armistice Agreement, 50 AM. J. INT'L L. 880, 886 (1956). See 2 L. OPPENHEIM, INTERNATIONAL LAW 546-51 (7th ed. H. Lauterpacht 1952).

Admitting her obligations under the Convention of 1888, Egypt has held that she has not violated Article 1 concerning "free passage" through the Canal, because the measures taken in time of war were "reasonable and necessary measures" for defense purposes, as the Egyptian Prize Court of Alexandria states.[31] It might be argued that even "reasonable" and "necessary" measures might be restricted by the Convention of 1888, since Articles 10 and 11 prohibited Egypt from actions, even for the defense of her territory, because they might interfere with the free use of the Canal. It is also argued that, as held by the World Court in the *Wimbledon* case,[32] the Canal should remain permanently free as an international waterway.

Egypt's insistence on her right to close the Canal against Israeli shipping in time of war has naturally raised the question as to whether she can close the Canal during war against any other nations including signatory powers. This seems to be different from closing the Canal against a country that had attacked Egyptian territory, including the Canal Zone. It was in the exercise of her inherent right of self-defense that Egypt denied free passage to Israel.[33] Such a situation seems either to have been taken for granted by the Convention of 1888, because it falls within the rights of sovereignty, or left undecided. Egypt's actions might, however, be justified even if the Convention is held binding upon it to grant free passage to all nations, including Israel, on the ground of the internationality of the Canal. Any such obligation would necessarily entail the reciprocal obligation on the part of Israel to respect the neutrality of the Canal and the territorial sovereignty of Egypt. It cannot be claimed that Egypt is bound by the Convention *in toto* regardless of whether Israel accepts the obligations imposed on the nine signatory powers. Such a rule would clearly be imposing an international servitude over Egypt in order to grant to Israel the right of free passage in time of peace and war and denying Egypt the right of self-defense in case of an attack on her territory. If we take this position, the purposes of the Convention would be inconsistent with the general principles of international law which recognize Egypt's right to repudiate restrictive measures on her sovereignty imposed without her consent. Nor would the Ottoman Porte have agreed to sign the Convention and acquiesce in such a servitude, because it had consistently declared before 1888 that its control over the Canal was not to be restricted by throwing the Canal's doors open to other nations.[34]

A balancing view of the principle of internationality seems to restrict Egypt's right to close the Canal in time of peace against any nation including Israel if Egypt's security were not involved. So long as Israel insists on a right of free passage under the Convention of 1888 by threatening Egypt's security, Israel seems to pursue a

---

[31] The Flying Trader, [1950] Ann. Dig. 440, 446-47 (No. 149) (Prize Court of Alexandria), 7 REV. ÉGYPTIENNE DE DROIT INTERNATIONAL 127 (1951).

[32] [1923] P.C.I.J., ser. A, No. 1.

[33] *See* Baxter, *Passage of Ships Through International Waterways in Time of War*, 31 BRIT. YB. INT'L L. 208 (1954).

[34] *See* J. OBIETA, *supra* note 4, at 78-87.

contradictory legal position by invoking one article of the Convention (Article 1) while denying Egypt's right to invoke another (Article 10).[35]

In 1956, when Egypt nationalized the Suez Canal, the Security Council passed a six-point resolution on October 13, 1956, in which it was affirmed that any settlement of the Suez Canal question should, *inter alia*, meet the following requirements: (1) free and open transit through the Canal, and (2) respect for Egypt's sovereignty.[36]

This resolution seems to embody the balancing principle of internationality by proposing to grant freedom of navigation without compromising Egypt's sovereignty. Thus, the balancing principle of internationality must be considered with due respect to Egypt's sovereignty. The principle of internationality would cease to be a balancing principle if Egypt were to be denied the right to close the Canal, as a measure of self-defense, in case of an attack. Israel can claim the right to be a beneficiary of the principle of internationality if she ceases to present a threat to Egypt's security, one of her sovereign rights.

Conclusion

From the time of the nationalization of the Canal, Egypt has not only reiterated her affirmation of the binding obligations of the Convention of 1888 and her respect of the principle of free navigation, but also declared that any dispute or disagreements which may arise in respect of that Convention would be settled in accordance with the Charter of the United Nations, and that any differences that may arise concerning the interpretation of that Convention would be referred to the International Court of Justice. In a letter dated July 18, 1957, addressed to the Secretary-General of the United Nations, Egypt accepted the compulsory jurisdiction of the International Court in all legal disputes that may arise from the application of the Convention of 1888.[37] Since Egypt has accepted the compulsory jurisdiction of the International Court on all legal disputes relating to the Suez Canal, Israel's claim to the right of free passage through the Canal might well be an appropriate case to be brought to the International Court for adjudication and might be regarded as an example for solving other Arab-Israeli issues on the basis of law and justice rather than force or diplomatic pressures.[38]

---

[35] Article 10, paragraph 1, of the Convention of 1888 provides:

"Similarly, the provisions of Articles IV, V, VII, and VIII shall not stand in the way of any measures which His Majesty the Sultan and His Highness the Khedive in the name of His Imperial Majesty, and within the limits of the Firmans granted, might find it necessary to take to assure by their own forces the defence of Egypt and the maintenance of public order."

Supra note 11.

[36] S.C. Res. 118.

[37] [1956-1957] I.C.J.Y.B. 213-14, 241. *Cf.* U.N. Doc. S/3818/Add. 1, *supra* note 23.

[38] One of the states which supported Security Council resolution 95 (1951), calling on Egypt to open the Suez to Israeli shipping, might either voluntarily or upon Israel's request refer the Suez Canal dispute to the International Court of Justice in accordance with article 36, para. 1, of the statute of that Court. Article 36, paragraph 1, provides: "The jurisdiction of the Court comprises all cases which the parties refer to it and all matters specially provided for in the Charter of the United Nations or in treaties and conventions in force."

I. UNDERLYING ISSUES
C. *The Status of Jerusalem and the Holy Places*

The Status of Jerusalem:
Some National and International Aspects

S. SHEPARD JONES

I
Scope and Purpose

If a genuine Arab-Israeli peace settlement is to be achieved as an aftermath to the 1967 war and the subsequent diplomatic efforts of the United Nations in 1967 and 1968, some understanding must be reached on the future status of Jerusalem. Of course, this is only one of many troublesome questions that evoke political malaise. The purpose of this short essay is to put the problem of Jerusalem in perspective by drawing attention to some of the background considerations that shed light on the present situation. These considerations are as much political as legal; they are both national and international, religious and secular. While the purpose is primarily to provide perspective, not to argue for a particular resolution of the future status of Jerusalem, this article does conclude with an indication of the direction and spirit within which a settlement might be sought, if the interests of all the parties are to be protected. These interests are complex and varied, and it is assumed that the cause of international peace and justice demands respect for the interests of all concerned and therefore not the complete triumph of the purposes of any one nation or religious community. The multiple interests in Jerusalem suggest the wisdom of redefining national purposes to the higher good.

II
The Nature of "The Question of Jerusalem, 1967-68"

The more restricted "problem of Jerusalem" in its present context arises out of the suddenly upset military balance and the emotional shock produced by the lightning-like war of June 1967. A part of that reality—but not its beginning[1]—was the attack by Jordanian forces on Israel on June 5, following the outbreak of war on the Egyptian-Israeli front earlier the same day. After hard fighting there followed, on June 7, the capture of Arab Jerusalem, governed by Jordan since 1948, and Israel's announcement of June 28[2] that "the law, jurisdiction and administration of the

---

* A.B. 1930, Georgetown College; A.M. 1931, University of Kentucky; Ph.D. (Rhodes Scholar) 1936, Oxford University. Burton Craige Professor of Political Science, University of North Carolina. Author, THE SCANDINAVIAN STATES AND THE LEAGUE OF NATIONS (1939); co-editor [with D. P. Myers], DOCUMENTS ON AMERICAN FOREIGN RELATIONS (vols. I-III (1939, 1940, 1941); AMERICA'S ROLE IN THE MIDDLE EAST (1958).

[1] M. HOWARD & R. HUNTER, ISRAEL AND THE ARAB WORLD: THE CRISIS OF 1967 (Adelphi Papers, no. 41, October 1967); Yost, *The Arab-Israeli War: How It Began*, 46 FOREIGN AFF. 304-06 (1968).

[2] Under ordinance of the preceding day. Summaries at p. 8 of the Report of the Secretary-General under General Assembly resolution 2254(ES-I), U.N. Doc. A/6793, Sept. 12, 1967. Also issued as U.N. Doc. S/8146.

State of Israel" were being applied to the Old City and to an enlarged East Jerusalem, as Arab Jerusalem is now designated.

Bitter protest came from Jordan[3] and other Arab states and from non-Arab states including the United States,[4] and allegations that international law had been violated by Israel. Israel asserted that Jordan was responsible for initiating the attack on Jerusalem and must accept the consequences.[5]

The United Nations General Assembly adopted two resolutions without opposition on July 4 and 14, 1967 (the latter by a vote of one hundred to zero, with eighteen abstentions, including that of the United States[6]), declaring Israel's action "invalid," and calling upon Israel "to rescind all measures already taken and desist forthwith from taking any action which would alter the status of Jerusalem."[7] Israel refused to comply, contending that "no international or other interest would be served by the institution of divisions and barriers which would only sharpen tension and generate discrimination." The claim was made that Israel was responding to "the intrinsic necessity of ensuring equal rights and opportunities to all the city's residents."[8] This answer did not meet the major issue at stake, as the General Assembly debate made clear.[9]

Looking ahead, the Israeli Government stated that its policy of integrating all of Jerusalem "does not foreclose the final settlement of certain important aspects of the Jerusalem situation which lie at the origin of the international interest in the city." Reference was made to "the need to secure appropriate expression of the special interest of the three great religions in Jerusalem." But this statement seemed to acknowledge the concerns and interests of others as something to be considered in the future, since the Foreign Minister added: "I am confident that in an atmosphere of international tranquility substantial progress could be made toward this aim, which has hitherto had no concrete fulfillment."[10] Reference was here made,

---

[3] See, e.g., remarks of King Hussein, U.N. Doc. A/PV. 1536, June 26, 1967, at 11.

[4] See, e.g., remarks of U.S. Delegation, U.N. Doc. A/PV. 1546, July 3, 1967, at 8-10.

[5] The Israeli Foreign Minister stated to the General Assembly on June 19, 1967:

"While fighting raged on the Egyptian-Israel frontier and on the Syrian front, we still hoped to contain the conflict. Jordan was given every chance to remain outside the struggle. Even after Jordan had bombarded and bombed Israel territory at several points, we still proposed to the Jordanian monarch that he abstain from any continuing hostilities . . . .

". . . Jordan's responsibility for the second phase of the concerted aggression is established beyond doubt. Surely this responsibility cannot fail to have its consequences in the peace settlement. As death and injury rained on the city, Jordan had become the source and origin of Jerusalem's fierce ordeal. The inhabitants of that city can never forget this fact, or fail to draw its conclusions." U.N. Doc. A/PV. 1526, June 19, at 50-51.

[6] U.N. Doc. A/PV. 1554, at 41.

[7] G.A. Resolutions 2253 and 2254, U.N. GAOR, 5th Emer. Spec. Sess., Supp. 1, at 4, U.N. Doc. A/6798 (1967).

[8] Exchange of letters between the Secretary-General of the U.N. and the Israeli Foreign Minister, July 15, 1967, and Sept. 11, 1967, published in U.N. Doc. A/6793, supra note 2, at 29, 30.

[9] See, e.g., Docs. A/6743, July 3, 1967, and A/6774, July 25, 1967. See also remarks of Iraqi Delegation, U.N. Doc. A/PV. 1559, Sept. 18, 1967, at 6-16.

[10] U.N. Doc. A/6793, supra note 2, at 30.

apparently, to deprivation of access to Holy Places in the Old City of almost all citizens of Israel from 1949 to 1967, for instance to the Wailing Wall, and to acts of desecration of Jewish cemeteries.[11]

This reply should be viewed in the light of the conclusion of the United Nations Secretary-General, based on information supplied by his Personal Representative in Jerusalem,[12] that it has been "made clear beyond any doubt that Israel was taking every step to place under its sovereignty those parts of the city" not previously controlled by Israel.[13] Ambassador Thalmann reported that "The Israel authorities stated unequivocally that the process of integration was irreversible and not negotiable."[14]

The Personal Representative reported that he was told that "the Arabs recognize a military occupation régime as such and were ready to co-operate with such a régime in dealing with current questions of administration and public welfare. However, they were opposed to civil incorporation into the Israel State System," which action they regarded "as a violation of the acknowledged rule of international law which prohibited an occupying Power from changing the legal and administrative structure in the occuppied territory." The population of East Jerusalem "was given no opportunity to state for itself whether it was willing to live in the Israel State community." It was claimed that the right of self-determination, in accordance with the United Nations Charter and the Universal Declaration of Human Rights, had therefore been violated.[15]

The report of the Secretary-General dated September 12, 1967 indicates that "most of the Arabs interviewed" by the Personal Representative—Arab notables in Jerusalem, both governmental and religious—stated that the Muslim population "was shocked by Israel acts which violated the sanctity of Muslim Shrines."[16]

Muslim leaders informed the Personal Representative that statements by Israeli officials and Jewish personalities "concerning Jewish claims and plans in the Temple area had had an alarming effect" on Muslim opinion.[17] The dynamiting and bull-dozing of 135 houses in the Maghrabi quarter (in front of the Wailing Wall) had also aroused strong feelings. This action involved "the expulsion of 650 poor and pious Muslims from their homes in the immediate vicinity of the Mosque of Omar and the Aksa Mosque."[18]

In a letter of July 24, 1967 the Israeli Military Governor for the West Bank was

---

[11] *See* U.N. Docs. A/7064 and A/7064/Add. 1, March 6, 1968, a distribution of a pictorial document entitled "Desecration," issued by the Israeli Ministry of Foreign Affairs, Information Division, Jerusalem, November 1967 and transmitted to the Secretary-General of the U.N., March 5, 1968.

[12] Ambassador Thalmann, a Swiss national. He arrived in Jerusalem on August 21, 1967, and departed on September 3, 1967.

[13] U.N. Doc. A/6793, *supra* note 2, at 7.

[14] *Id.*

[15] *Id.* at 24.

[16] *Id.* at 21.

[17] *Id.*

[18] *Id.*

informed that the twenty-four signatories of the letter "had constituted themselves as the Muslim body in charge of Muslim affairs on the West Bank, including Jerusalem."[19] "This 'Higher Muslim Council,' as it is also called, designated four Arab personalities to carry out the responsibilities of public administration . . . on the West Bank, including East Jerusalem, in accordance with the applicable Jordanian law." But the decisions of the "Higher Muslim Council" were not recognized by the Israeli authorities, although publicized to the Arab population through Amman radio.[20]

The Secretary-General's Personal Representative in Jerusalem also reported the text of the statement issued June 27, 1967 by the Prime Minister of Israel concerning access to the Holy Places of Jerusalem and their administration.[21] Also reported was the "Protection of the Holy Places Law," passed by the Knesset the same day,[22] as well as the Prime Minister's statement of June 7, 1967 to spiritual leaders of all communities.[23] The statement of June 27 indicated that the Holy Places in Jerusalem "are now open to all who wish to worship at them—members of all faiths, without discrimination. The Government of Israel has made it a cardinal principle of its policy to preserve the Holy Places, to ensure their religious and universal character, and to guarantee free access." It was indicated that the policy would be carried out in consultation with representatives of the religious communities. The statutory measures provided for protection of the Holy Places from desecration and other violations.

The Personal Representative reported that these measures "were very favorably received," although some took a "wait and see" attitude.[24] The Muslim reaction has been indicated above. The Catholic Church was reported as having essentially a divergent attitude to various other Christian denominations. The Holy See remained convinced that "the only solution which offers a sufficient guarantee for the protection of Jerusalem and of its Holy Places is to place that city and its vicinity under an international régime in the form of a *corpus separatum*."[25]

III

The United States and the Question of Jerusalem, 1967-68

On June 19, 1967 the President of the United States said there must be "adequate recognition of the special interest of three great religions in the holy places of Jerusalem."[26] On June 27, 1967 the Israeli Parliament approved legislation authorizing the Government to extend Israel's laws, jurisdiction and administration over addi-

---

[19] *Id*. at 44, 46.
[20] *Id*. at 22-23.
[21] *Id*. at 26..
[22] No. 5727-1967. Text printed in English, *id*.
[23] *Id*. at 25-26.
[24] *Id*. at 27.
[25] *Id*.
[26] 57 Dep't State Bull. 33 (1967).

tional territory of *Eretz* Israel ("the Land of Israel"). On June 28 the Government of Israel defined the Old City of Jerusalem and certain other territory of the former mandate of Palestine which had been under the control of Jordan since 1948 as territory to be incorporated into an enlarged city of Jerusalem.[27] On June 28 the White House indicated that the President "assumes" that "before any unilateral action is taken on the status of Jerusalem there will be appropriate consultation with religious leaders and others who are deeply concerned" and that "the world must find an answer that is fair and recognized to be fair."[28] On June 28, the Government of Israel took administrative action under the new legislation to extend its municipal services and controls over the entire city of Jerusalem.[29] Later on that day a State Department press release[30] read:

> The hasty administrative action taken [by Israel] today cannot be regarded as determining the future of the holy places or the status of Jerusalem in relation to them.
>
> The United States has never recognized such unilateral actions by any of the states in the area as governing the international status of Jerusalem . . . .

On July 3, the United States Representative to the General Assembly said that "the safeguarding of the Holy Places, and freedom of access to them for all, should be internationally guaranteed."[31]

On July 7, 1967 the Executive Committee of the National Council of Churches of Christ in the United States of America adopted a resolution[32] which, in part, read:

> With due consideration for the right of nations to defend themselves, the National Council of Churches cannot condone by silence territorial expansion by armed force. Israel's unilateral retention of the lands she has occupied since June 5 will only deepen the divisions and antagonisms which separate her from those neighbors in the midst of whom she must dwell.
>
> The territorial frontiers of the states of the Middle East should now be definitely established by negotiation in treaties of peace and the integrity of such frontiers should be assured by international protection.

More specifically, on the issue of Jerusalem, the resolution of the National Council of Churches states:

> We support the *establishment of an international presence* in the hitherto divided city of Jerusalem which will preserve the peace and integrity of the city, foster the welfare of its inhabitants, and protect its holy shrines with full rights of

---

[27] Measures summarized in U.N. Doc. A/6793, *supra* note 2, at 8.

[28] 57 DEP'T STATE BULL. 60 (1967).

[29] *See* note 27 *supra*.

[30] 57 DEP'T STATE BULL. 60 (1967).

[31] U.N. Doc. A/PV. 1546, July 3, 1967, at 3-5.

[32] Memorandum entitled "Resolution on the Crisis in the Middle East." *See* N.Y. Times, July 15, 1967, at 28, col. 1.

access to all. We encourage the earliest possible advancement of U.N. proposals to make such arrangements practicable.

We cannot approve Israel's unilateral annexation of the Jordanian portions of Jerusalem. This historic city is sacred not only to Judaism but also to Christianity and Islam.

On July 14, Ambassador Goldberg, speaking for the United States Delegation to the Fifth Emergency Special Session of the U.N. General Assembly, reiterated that "the United States does not accept or recognize . . . as altering the status of Jerusalem" the measures taken by the Israeli government on June 28. He said further that the United States did not recognize that these measures

> can be regarded as the last word on the matter, and we regret that they were taken. We insist that the measures taken cannot be considered as other than interim and provisional, and not as prejudging the final and permanent status of Jerusalem. Unfortunately, and regrettably, the statements of the Government of Israel on this matter have thus far, in our view, not adequately dealt with this situation.[33]

Nevertheless, the United States abstained from voting on General Assembly resolution A/2254,[34] the resolution not fully corresponding to United States government views, particularly since, even as revised

> it appears to accept, by its call for rescission of measures, that the administrative measures which were taken constitute annexation of Jerusalem by Israel, and because we do not believe that the problem of Jerusalem can realistically be solved apart from the other related aspects of the Middle Eastern situation.

There are, it was said, important practical issues in addition to "transcendent spiritual interests" that must be resolved. The United States representative implied that the Assembly should have gone no further than to declare itself against any unilateral change in the status of Jerusalem.[35]

Following reports in January 1968 of Israeli plans for development of certain areas of the occupied sector of Jerusalem—being between Mt. Scopus and the former armistice line—a State Department spokesman reiterated that the United States does not recognize "any unilateral actions affecting the status of Jerusalem."[36] The United States position is that Arab territories now administered by Israel as a result of the six-day war should be administered under the law of occupation as recognized by international law, not under a right of conquest. The Department of State apparently regards the Hague Convention of 1907 as applicable to the existing situation.[37]

---

[33] U.N. Doc. A/PV. 1554, July 14, 1967, at 48.

[34] Note 6 *supra* and accompanying text.

[35] U.N. Doc. A/PV. 1554, *supra* note 33, at 48, 51.

[36] N.Y. Times, Jan. 16, 1968, at 16, col. 6.

[37] For some recent statements as to rules considered applicable, see 1 M. WHITEMAN, DIGEST OF INTERNATIONAL LAW 946-52 (1963).

IV

Some Legal and Political Questions

A question has been raised as to whether acquisition of territory by conquest is valid in the light of the United Nations Charter obligations accepted by both sides. Press reports frequently refer to "territory conquered," but the Israeli government has apparently avoided making a claim on that basis. Does the integration of Arab Jerusalem by Israel hurt the prospects for an agreed settlement of larger aspects of the Arab-Israeli confrontation? What is the legal meaning and the political effect of Israel's contention that the future of Arab Jerusalem is not negotiable? Have Israel's leaders concluded that the prospects for a settlement with the Arab states are so unlikely, because of Arab intransigence; that the integration or annexation of Jerusalem does not actually endanger prospects for a peace settlement, because the prospects for the foreseeable future, despite efforts of the Secretary-General's Special Representative, Dr. Gunnar Jarring, are hopelessly dim?

It may be useful to divide the Jerusalem question into three major aspects: (1) *who* will govern Jerusalem—*i.e.*, whose "law, jurisdiction and administration" will prevail in the future? Will the city remain unified as it was prior to 1948 and in 1967-68 or again be divided? Or will it be managed in a third way? And will the determination be made by unilateral action or by agreement? (2) What arrangements can be made to assure "adequate recognition of the special interest of three great religions in the holy places of Jerusalem," *i.e.*, to guarantee the protection of the Holy Places within and outside Jerusalem and for assurance of access thereto? (3) Should an *international presence* be maintained in Jerusalem with functions broader than that of protecting the holy places? What practical proposals can be agreed to and maintained in the face of diverging interests? These are difficult political questions which confront or may confront the interested governments. The answers can best be found through the process of negotiation. Recognizing that such negotiations must inevitably be affected by other questions lying beyond the scope of this paper, let us consider certain background facts that help put the present situation in perspective.

A. Political

How does the experience of history relate to these questions? A quick look may give a distorted image, but hopefully may suggest essential reality if only approximate. Who has governed Jerusalem and how was title gained? In the past 3500 years the city has changed hands more than twenty-five times.[38] We can begin with David who about 1000 B.C. captured the old Jebusite Town and claimed it as the City of David. Later it was conquered by one empire after another—Babylonian,

---

[38] S. Perowne, The One Remains 11 (1954). *See also* Report of the Commission appointed by His Majesty's Government . . . to determine the rights and claims . . . in connection with the Western or Wailing Wall at Jerusalem: December 1930, at 9-15 (1931). Distributed as U.N. Docs. A/7057/Add. 1 and S/8427/Add. 1, Feb. 23, 1968.

Persian, Macedonian, Ptolemy, Selucid, and Roman. In 638 A.D. the Caliph Omar captured Jerusalem for Islam. Later it was held by Seljuk Turks, by Christian Crusaders, and by Egyptian Mameluks. From 1517 to 1917 Jerusalem was ruled by the Ottoman Turks, who then gave way to General Allenby of Great Britain. Following World War I, the Principal Allied Powers decided that Palestine should be a League of Nations mandate assigned to Great Britain. On July 24, 1922 the Council of the League of Nations confirmed and defined the terms of the Mandate for Palestine, with Great Britain as the Mandatory Power. The Palestine Mandate went into effect September 29, 1923.[39] When it terminated on May 15, 1948 Arabs and Jews of Palestine, and Arab armies from without, fought for possession of Jerusalem and of Palestine. The outcome confirmed the reality of what actually had already become a divided city, now occupied by Israeli and Jordan authorities,[40] with a set of conflicting claims, which, in turn, conflicted with plans and proposals of the United Nations to establish Jerusalem as a *corpus separatum* under an international régime. This proposal was part of the Plan of Partition with Economic Union, which was recommended by the General Assembly on November 29, 1947[41] in an effort to provide for the future government of Palestine, upon the termination of the British Mandate. This Plan was never fully implemented.[42]

At no time did the international community acting through the United Nations recommend that the City of Jerusalem or a portion of it be assigned to either Israel or Jordan. The claims of those two countries that they were rightful sovereigns of their parts of Jerusalem, while recognized by some states, have not been recognized by others, including the United States, the United Kingdom, France, and the Soviet Union, all of which continued to maintain embassies in Tel-Aviv and Amman.[43]

During 3000 years of history, control over Jerusalem has been almost invariably acquired by conquest.

B. Protection of and Access to the Holy Places

The historical record shows that Jerusalem has long been regarded as a place of religious significance to the adherents of three world religions all of which seek protection of their interests. Jerusalem has been revered by Jews for 3000 years, by Christians for nearly 2000, and by Moslems for more than 1300 years. Many of the shrines represent a common inheritance of three religions. Even the name of the city in Arabic (*Al-Quds*) means "The Sanctuary."[44] Although it has been said

---

[39] For text see CMD. No. 1785 (1923).

[40] P. DE AZCARATE, MISSION IN PALESTINE 1948-1952, at 182 (1966).

[41] G.A. Res. 181, 2 U.N. GAOR, Resolutions 131, 132 (1947).

[42] *See* 1 M. WHITEMAN, *supra* note 37, at 699, 701, 703.

[43] *Id.* at 594, 595, 699.

[44] P. MOHN, JERUSALEM AND THE UNITED NATIONS 427 (International Conciliation pamphlet no. 464, October 1950).

that "the business of Jerusalem is eternity,"[45] regrettably, through much of history, its spiritual significance as a city of God, of peace and of brotherly love, has been sadly tarnished by bloodshed, political intrigue and bitter rivalry for the privilege of protecting or adminstering the holy places and shrines. Religious emotion or even fanaticism has at times been exploited by temporal rulers who sought exclusive advantages not primarily those of spiritual uplift or human betterment. The diversity of religious interests—Moslem, Catholic, Jewish, Orthodox, Armenian, Coptic, Abyssinian, Syrian, Anglican and other Protestant, and with institutions established by religious bodies in Europe, Asia, Africa, and the Americas—called for some system of order and protection. In 1757 the so-called *Status Quo* was established to this end. Thereafter, Moslem *temporal* power, on the whole, did not interfere with the management of the Holy Places, but there were claims and counter-claims.[46] The system did not change greatly under the British Mandate, which in Article 13 specified that the Mandatory should preserve existing rights in connection with the Holy Places. But at times, such as 1929, there was serious rioting.[47]

C. Proposals for International Régime

When on November 29, 1947 the United Nations General Assembly recommended partition of Palestine into a Jewish state and an Arab state with Economic Union, it was recommended that the city of Jerusalem (including the existing municipality plus the surrounding villages and towns such as Bethlehem) be established as a *corpus separatum*, under a special international régime, to be administered by the Trusteeship Council on behalf of the United Nations. This régime was to include the appointment of a Governor, responsible to the Trusteeship Council, the establishment of a special police force whose members were to be recruited from *outside* of Palestine, the election of a legislative Council, and the demilitarization of the city.[48] "Jerusalem was envisaged as a *model city*, a *spiritual center*, a *seat of learning*, the influence of which could help to overcome the national and religious animosities and prejudices which for so many years have poisoned the atmosphere of the Holy Land."[49] The proposal for a *corpus separatum* seemed sensible since the General Assembly's Plan of 1947 separated Jerusalem from the proposed Jewish state by a strip of intervening Arab territory assigned to the proposed Arab state. Jerusalem under the 1947 Plan would have been a city of approximately equal Arab and Jewish population, with the Moslem Arabs somewhat more numerous than the Christian Arabs.

---

[45] Perowne, *supra* note 38, at 13.

[46] Report of the Commission . . . , *supra* note 38, at 15-22; W. Eytan, The First Ten Years 66 (1958); Mohn, *supra* note 44, at 433-38.

[47] C. Sykes, Crossroads to Israel 108-11 (1965).

[48] *See* Part III of the Plan, *supra* note 41; Eytan, *supra* note 46, at 68-69. For map showing the proposed boundaries of Jerusalem, see annex B attached to the Plan.

[49] Mohn, *supra* note 44, at 451. (Emphasis added.)

A statute for Jerusalem had been drafted by the Trusteeship Council in the spring of 1948,[50] but formal adoption was postponed owing to the state of confusion into which the larger question of Palestine had been thrown by the fighting already in progress and uncertainty as to whether the November 29, 1947 Plan could be implemented.[51] The Arab Higher Committee had rejected the Partition Plan in its entirety; the Jewish Agency accepted it under protest. No international authority had been created to take the place of the British Mandatory authority in Jerusalem which had been supported by British troops for twenty-five years. These were about to depart on May 14, 1948 as the British Government had repeatedly affirmed. Yet it had been clear for months that the Partition Plan with Economic Union could not be implemented by agreement, and it could not be implemented by force alone, since it called for economic cooperation. The Plan was clearly unworkable in the light of political realities.

The divergent policies of the Powers blocked agreement in the United Nations, not of a "definition of the International interest" in Jerusalem, but of a concerted will to implement internationally-defined policy against firm resistance. International policy, defined and redefined by the General Assembly resolutions in 1947,[52] 1948[53] and 1949[54] but not consistently supported by necessary action, was brushed aside by the national policy of a few states with clear goals. Christopher Sykes aptly refers to the "melee of conflicting British and American attempts at policy."[55] The draft statutes of an international régime in Jerusalem, although at least in one case directed to be put into effect despite opposition of Israel and Jordan, were not put into effect, and "came to nothing" in the world of action. Jordanian and Israeli armed forces took and retained control of their respective parts of Jerusalem filling a vacuum with national power. A new kind of *status quo* was maintained in Jerusalem, following the Israeli-Jordan Armistice Agreement of 1949,[56] until it was again upset by force in June 1967.

When the United Nations Conciliation Commission for Palestine[57] realized the impossibility of setting up a genuine international régime (based on the idea of a *corpus separatum*) and drafted a modified statute in 1949[58] compatible with the *fait accompli* of the partition of Jerusalem between Israel and Jordan, it remained

[50] 3 U.N. TCOR, 2d Sess., pt. 3, Annex, at 4, U.N. Doc. T/118/Rev. 2 (1948).

[51] Proceedings summarized in Annual Report of the Secretary-General on the Work of the Organization, 1 July 1947-30 June 1948, 3 U.N. GAOR, Supp. 1, at 4-5, U.N. Doc. A/565 (1948). *See also* MOHN, *supra* note 44, at 455-56; EYTAN, *supra* note 46, at 70; AZCARATE, *supra* note 40, at 184-85.

[52] G.A. Res. 181, *supra* note 41.

[53] G.A. Res. 194, para. 8, 3 U.N. GAOR, pt. 1, Resolutions 21, 23, U.N. Doc. A/810 (1948).

[54] G.A. Res. 303, 4 *id.*, Resolutions 25, U.N. Doc. A/1251 (1949).

[55] SYKES, *supra* note 47, at 357. *See also* Report of the Trusteeship Council entitled "Question of an International Regime for the Jerusalem Area and the Protection of the Holy Places," 5 U.N. GAOR, Supp. 9, U.N. Doc. A/1286 (1950).

[56] 42 U.N.T.S. 303, no. 656; 4 U.N. SCOR, Spec. Supp. 1, U.N. Doc. S/1302/Rev. 1 (1949).

[57] Established by G.A. Res. 194, *supra* note 53.

[58] 4 U.N. GAOR, Ad Hoc Pol. Comm., Annex., vol. 1, at 10, U.N. Doc. A/973 (1949).

only a "blue-print," although one worthy of study both then and now. The draft sent to the General Assembly September 1, 1949 was "pigeon-holed without even being accorded the honor of a debate," as a result of the pressure of various delegations. Some, sympathetic with the Vatican's point of view, "were not prepared to accept anything less than integral and complete internationalization."[59] All of the Arab states except Jordan also sought a more thorough-going internationalization.

Israel, on the other hand, was antagonistic because the Conciliation Commission's plan involved too much international control. The Israeli government argued that the plan ignored the "physical facts" and "deeper truths of sentiment and allegiance," adding that "For the first time in modern history, political authority in the greater part of Jerusalem rests not on military conquest but on the will and consent of the population of the city."[60] The crux of the matter was that the Conciliation Commission was responding to the General Assembly's Resolution 194(III) of December 11, 1948 wherein the General Assembly had decided that the Jerusalem area should be accorded "special and separate treatment from the rest of Palestine" and that it should be placed "under effective United Nations control." Israel's policy did not support that objective: it favored national control of Jerusalem, its new capital, in a nation re-created after decades of struggle under Zionist leadership, catapulted to birth by the agony produced by the Nazi slaughter of millions of European Jews.

V

REFLECTIONS ON THE PRESENT
INTERNATIONAL SYSTEM AND JERUSALEM'S FUTURE

The future status of Jerusalem is obviously related to the larger question of the fundamental characteristics of the future international system of the Middle East. As for the international system of the past two decades, of which international law is only a part, if we judge it primarily by the *practice* of states rather than by *proclaimed principles* which states affirm as principles that ought to be applied, we can only conclude that the use of force in pursuit of national policy is not altogether ruled out. Almost invariably when force is used, the claim of the exercise of the right of self-defense is asserted, and sometimes justified. The Arabs of Palestine asserted the right of self-defense in 1948 against the Partition Plan, adopted as a recommendation of the General Assembly. They regarded the Plan as immoral and illegal.[61] The Israeli Government asserted the right of self-defense to maintain

---

[59] AZCARATE, *supra* note 40, at 184. *See also* remarks of the Lebanese Delegation (Malik) to a committee of the General Assembly on May 5, 1949, 3 U.N. GAOR, pt. 2, Ad Hoc Pol. Comm. 219-26.

[60] Memorandum on the Future of Jerusalem, prepared by the Israeli Delegation, Nov. 15, 1949, at 2, U.N. Doc. A/AC.31/L. 34. *See also* remarks by the Israeli Delegation (Eban), 3 U.N. GAOR, pt. 2, Ad Hoc Pol. Comm. 230-37 (1949).

[61] The Arab Higher Commitee contended, at the 2d Special Session of the General Assembly, in April 1949, that the Mandate for Palestine disregarded the right to self-determination, and that the Arabs had no alternative but "to resort to the sacred right of self-defense." The Arabs had done "'what any

national identity threatened by Arab governments in 1948, in 1956, and again in 1967.[62] The United Nations did not clarify the legal situation that existed.

In this existing international system—this system more political than juridical, this system that does not assure the rule of law or international security by collective measures to frustrate a breach of the peace—perhaps the best hope for progress towards peace and security must rest with the policies of states which surely must increasingly understand the unwisdom of continued belligerency and war. While some wars can be deterred by threat of force or reprisal, the basic Middle East problem calls for other approaches. The great imperative is for a changed approach, a new attitude on both sides, which will permit the leaders of both sides to show greater understanding of the fears, the needs, and the legitimate interests of other states. This line of thinking brings us back to the idea that governments as well as leaders of public opinion should respond to the over-riding need for national self-restraint, fairness to others, and for easing tensions between nations, thereby assisting the growth of a new spirit of confidence that men can act more wisely in the future for peace and justice. It is a new vision of the practical advantages that will accrue to those who accept a community of mutual rights and responsibilities that is needed, not a continued devotion to political myths that insist on national or group exclusiveness and enmity. On what other basis can we hope for a solid political foundation on which to develop a more adequate international law?

Surely the present need is for a more realistic understanding by peoples generally of their national and regional interests. Hostility, belligerence, non-recognition of the right of neighboring states to exist, and disregard of the rights of others to territorial integrity are basic causes of insecurity for all. Perhaps it would help in resolving the problem of Jerusalem if the parties most concerned would not overemphasize the importance of political images of Jerusalem formed centuries ago in a very different age. Historic national dreams, perhaps vital in ages past, may need updating if the fundamental interests of the peoples of our time are to be advanced. Imagine the benefits that would flow if nations would discard from national myths that which is provocative and unjust to others, thereby facilitating the growth of the more constructive aspects of nationalism and encouraging healthy international cooperation. The Jerusalem question, if viewed with this spirit, with everyone avoiding malice and vituperation, might gradually be transformed to more optimistic proportions, with reduced likelihood that Jerusalem will be in the future, as it has been all too often in the past, a center for pathetic rivalry and a continuing object of re-conquest, perhaps headed once again for destruction.

---

other Member State would have done" fought in self-defense. The Partition resolution was "ill-advised," "illegal," and "could not be carried out." U.N. GAOR, 2d Spec. Sess., vol. II, Main Committees 93 (1948).

[62] See remarks by the Israeli Minister for Foreign Affairs (Eban) to the Security Council, U.N. Doc. S/PV. 1375, Nov. 13, 1967, at 6-36; ISRAEL'S STRUGGLE FOR PEACE, chs. VIII, IX and X (Israel Office of Information, New York, 1960).

This is the time for states generally to support the efforts of the United Nations Special Representative, Dr. Jarring, as he explores with the parties most directly concerned the broader dimensions of peace-making in the Middle East.[63] Will the Arab states and Israel work to establish the foundations for peace in the spirit of that resolution? Or will shortsighted, particularistic interests of states sidetrack progress toward an agreed settlement by inducing them to nullify one or the other of the basic principles adopted unanimously in the Security Council resolution of November 22, 1967?[64] It is acceptance of the entire package which is a valid test of one's interest in peace with justice. At least this seems to have been the view of the Security Council.

One would hope that the world will not experience disappointment similar to that of 1947-1952, when an opportunity for a peaceful resolution of the Arab-Israel problem foundered. Every nation's stake in moving toward peace based on agreement is enormous. This is the prerequisite for strengthening international law in the Middle East, in view of such conflicting definitions of justice as have been spread on the United Nations record for the past twenty years.

If a new appreciation of national self-interest can be developed in the months ahead, based on a wider recognition of the futility of Middle Eastern politics of recent years, presumably some agreements would become possible. It should then become possible to agree on an acceptable formula of "the national and international interest" in Jerusalem, which could then be guaranteed by the principal Powers. The balancing of interests and claims in the Middle East becomes an imperative, in view of the uncertainties of law and the facts of power, if some tolerable stability is to be achieved. The definition of justice in such a politically divided area could hardly be expected to conform to the fullest expression of national aspirations and national morality—either Arab or Israeli. A rational solution calls for a negotiated settlement (sooner rather than later) under the auspices of a third party utilizing any arrangement agreeable to the parties most concerned, and, failing that, under an arrangement determined by the Security Council.

In the interest of long-run cooperation among the peoples and nations of the Middle East, it is believed that the advantages of a *corpus separatum* for the walled City of Jerusalem could be a desirable goal for the overwhelming majority of the members of the United Nations, and would probably serve the higher, long-range interests of Israel and Jordan. To achieve this objective, it might become desirable for the states of the world to recognize West Jerusalem as the capital of the state of Israel. So much of Israeli nationalism is centered on Jerusalem as a focal point in national political life that it would seem practical to accept this reality. However,

---

[63] A recent statement of relevant U.S. policy was made on Dec. 8, 1967, by the Under Secretary of State for Political Affairs, Eugene V. Rostow, 58 DEP'T STATE BULL. 41 (1968).

[64] For text of Resolution 242, see Rosenne, in this symposium, pp. 44, 56.

this line of thinking would reserve the walled city as an International Zone—a *corpus separatum*, but would not necessarily be restricted to it.[65]

These concluding ideas do not constitute a proposal for the future status of Jerusalem. They are suggested only as possible ideas for consideration by those concerned. Both a *national* and an *international* presence would be embraced in a greater Jerusalem. An international statute would once again be drafted, and would constitute a part of the peace settlement hopefully to grow out of Ambassador Jarring's step by step efforts to build a peace on the principles of the Security Council's Resolution 242 of November 22, 1967.

But are these ideas practical? They could become practical, when carefully re-vamped by legal and political experts—if, but only if, the parties most concerned will re-evaluate their national interests in harmony with the greater need for genuine peace. The future of Jerusalem is inevitably entwined with the larger aspects of Arab-Israeli relations. In March 1968 serious violations of the cease-fire which brought renewed consideration by the Security Council confirmed earlier impressions that the prospect for genuine peace and for a rule of law in the Middle East seemed as elusive as ever. In the interest of international peace and security, perhaps the time is near when the Security Council will act to assert its authority under the Charter.[66] If not, the outlook seems one of continued belligerency, bitterness, and danger. The Middle East is faced with important choices in 1968. We can do no other than to hope for a new vision grounded in justice and focusing on a better day.

---

[65] *See* proceedings regarding Jerusalem in the Trusteeship Council 1949-1950, summarized in the special report cited *supra* note 55. *See especially* Private Memorandum from the Archbishop of Canterbury, Oct. 31, 1949, *id.* at 9-11. The Statute for the City of Jerusalem approved by the Council, April 4, 1950, is set forth *id.* at 19. *See also* Darin-Drabkin, *Jerusalem—City of Dissension or Peace?*, NEW OUT-LOOK: MIDDLE EAST MONTHLY, Jan. 1968, at 12, for an Israeli interpretation.

[66] On May 21, 1968 the U.N. Security Council adopted Resolution 252 on Jerusalem; for text, see El-Farra, in this symposium, pp. 68, 73.

Jerusalem: Keystone of an Arab-Israeli Settlement

RICHARD H. PFAFF

For the past two years, Israel has ruled over the Jordanian sector of Jerusalem. In the face of concern by the world community that Israel is altering the status of the Jordanian sector of the holy city, or "East Jerusalem" as it is now termed, the Jewish state has continued to implement its political, legal, economic, and demographic plans to integrate this part of occupied Jordan with the State of Israel.

Of all the outstanding issues of the Arab-Israeli conflict, that of East Jerusalem may well prove to be the most difficult of all to resolve. The Arab states are adamant that East Jerusalem be returned to the Arabs;[1] the Muslim community, representing one-fifth of all mankind, has vigorously expressed its opposition to Israeli "unification" of East and West Jerusalem;[2] the Roman Catholic church stands opposed to the unilateral action of Israel with regard to East Jerusalem;[3] the National Council of Churches has expressed its opposition to this action by Israel;[4] and the United Nations has repeatedly called upon Israel to rescind its action relative to East Jerusalem.[5] Furthermore, not one country has recognized this unilateral action taken by Israel. Nevertheless, Israel has not found it compatible with her interests to heed these calls from abroad. In fact, Israeli political leaders simply refuse to discuss the matter, declaring that the question of Jerusalem is not negotiable.

Since the framework of proposed settlement of the Arab-Israeli dispute is the Security Council's unanimous resolution of November 22, 1967, the Israeli position makes the prospects for peace in the Middle East difficult to envisage, for the first point of the U.N. resolution calls for "withdrawal of Israeli armed forces from territories occupied in the recent conflict." [6]

---

1. In March, 1968, for example, King Faisal of Saudi Arabia called for a "jihad" or holy war, in the defense of East Jerusalem; King Hussein of Jordan has repeatedly stressed that no peace settlement is conceivable without the return of East Jerusalem to the Arabs. See *New York Times*, March 7, 1968, for King Faisal's statement and the *New York Times*, February 17, 1968, December 21, 1968, and April 11, 1969, for references to King Hussein's position.

2. See part IV of this study.

3. *Ibid.*

4. *Ibid.*

5. *Ibid.*

6. For complete text of this resolution, see *ibid.*

The several other issues that make up the Arab-Israeli conflict are also important: Recognition of Israel's right of sovereign existence; withdrawal of Israeli armed forces from the Golan Heights, the West Bank, the Gaza Strip, and the Sinai Peninsula; the cessation of belligerency; secure boundaries for all parties; freedom of navigation; a just settlement of the Arab refugee problem; and the establishment of demilitarized zones are all matters that will require extensive negotiations. The issue of East Jerusalem, however, may prove decisive for success or failure in the quest for a peaceful and enduring solution of the Arab-Israeli problem; Jerusalem is of deep symbolic significance to the entire world, a holy city which is the source of emotional involvement for hundreds of millions of mankind.

It is the purpose of this study to examine Jerusalem, not only as the keystone of an Arab-Israeli settlement, but as a spiritual center of the three great monotheistic faiths: Christianity, Islam, and Judaism. While the analysis is primarily concerned with the political events that have marked the recent history of this holy city, its spiritual importance must also be briefly discussed. Because the "business of Jerusalem is eternity," the holy character of the city constitutes the basis for much of the political controversy over that city. The study begins, therefore, with an examination of Jerusalem's religious meaning.

I. THE CITY OF PEACE

Unique among the cities of this world, Jerusalem links the past with the present, man with his creator. For over 1.5 billion people, this holy city is a major, if not the major, geographical locus of their religious faith. The sacred books of Christianity, Judaism, and Islam speak of Jerusalem as a city apart from others, as a city of God.

One of the oldest cities in the world, Jerusalem has been a spiritual, as well as urban center for millenia. Egyptian sources dating from 1400 B.C. speak of this city as "Uru-Salim," or City of Peace. Even during the Bronze Age, this city flourished through its command over the commerce flowing between Pharaonic Egypt and Asia Minor. As civilized man expanded his domain from the eastern Mediterranean to encompass the globe, Jerusalem's importance as a metropolis waned, but as a religious center, its influence became universal.

Stripped of this spiritual dimension, Jerusalem is an uninviting place. Standing upon the summit of the Judean ridge, the sterile plateau of limestone upon which it rests presents an appearance that is both dreary and desolate. The Jerusalem area is cleft by deep ravines such as the Valley of Kidron and the Valley of Hinnom which descend rapidly to lower elevations. Some of Jerusalem's plateaus have rounded summits which have been dubbed, rather generously, as mounts: the Mount of Olives, Mount Zion, and Mount Scopus.

From this lofty, but sterile location, the descent to the Mediterranean is almost precipitous. The road to Tel Aviv, 33 miles away, has a drop of 2,485 feet which occurs almost entirely in the first few miles. Equally sharp is the drop from Jerusalem to Jericho toward the east. From the holy city southeast to the Dead Sea—a distance of only 15 miles—there is a descent of 3,870 feet.

The geographical location of Jerusalem, a boon when cities prospered behind the security of stone walls and narrow defiles, severely limits its economic utility today. Tourism, the sale of religious souvenirs, governmental administration, a small shoe factory in West Jerusalem, and a small but growing textile industry in East Jerusalem are features of the economic life of the city. Although both Israel and Jordan were giving special attention to the economic growth of those parts of Jerusalem under each country's control prior to June, 1967, it is still the Holy Places that sustain the Jerusalem economy.

Jerusalem, as with other Middle Eastern cities, is a composite of diverse ethnic and religious communities, for the most part clustered in discrete residential quarters. Because of Jerusalem's unique religious significance, the composition of the city reflects more sharply than other places the various religious communities that make it up.

The citizens of Jerusalem also may be separated in terms of certain spatial characteristics. The holy city has three parts. First, there is the walled city, the religious focus. Within the walled city are the three edifices that most link each of the three great monotheistic religions to the holy city: the Church of the Holy Sepulchre, the Haram esh-Sharif, and the Wailing Wall.

The walled city is an extremely small area. The walls, erected by the Ottoman Sultan Suleiman in 1542, are 38½ feet high and have a circumference of only 2.5 miles. The area they encompass is less than one-half a square mile. Within this area live—or did so prior to June, 1967—some 20,000 Arabs. This walled city of stone buildings, holy sites, and extremely narrow streets is one of the most densely populated areas in the Holy Land.

The walls form an irregular rectangle and are broken by six ancient gates. Running clockwise from the northeast corner these gates are: (1) St. Stephen's Gate (also called the Lion's Gate or Bab al-Asbat); (2) Dung Gate (Bab al-Magharabeh); (3) Zion Gate (Bab an-Nabi al-Daoud); (4) Jaffa Gate (The Hebron Gate or Bab al-Khalil); (5) Damascus Gate (Gate of the Columns, Bab al-Amud); and (6) Herod's Gate (Bab al-Zahar).

The streets of the walled city, running from the gates to the interior, divide it into four uneven quarters. The largest is the Muslim quarter, embracing over half of the city (including the Haram esh-Sharif) of the northeast and eastern parts. In the northwestern area, between Damascus Gate and Jaffa Gate, is the Christian quarter. In the southwestern corner is the Armenian quarter. And along the southern edge of the walled city, between the Armenian quarter and the Haram esh-Sharif is the Jewish quarter.

The population within the walled city, excluding ecclesiastics servicing the Holy Places, has been almost entirely Arab for over a thousand years. The British Mandatory Government's census for 1931 counted 25,183 people living within the walled city at that time.[1] Of this total some 20,000 were Arabs (both Christian and Muslim), about 5,000 were Jews, and a handful Armenians. Subsequent to that date, there was a steady decline in the Jewish population within the walled city, accounting for only 4,000 in 1946, and only about 2,000 in April, 1948. Among the Arab community, Muslims outnumbered Christians (1946: 10,000 Muslims to 7,000 Christians), but if one adds ecclesiastics and Armenians, the ratio of Christians to Muslims has tended to be even over past years.

Outside the walled city, generally running north of the walls is an area populated almost entirely by Arabs. To the west of the walled city is the New City, by far the more populous section, and predominantly Jewish. Beginning in the mid-nineteenth century, a number of rich American Jews sent sizable contributions to foster a Jewish community in the Jerusalem area. In the early 1850s the North

---

1. *U.N. General Assembly, Official Records (V), Suppl. 9, Question of an International Regime for the Jerusalem Area and Protection of the Holy Places.* Doc. A/1286, p. 17.

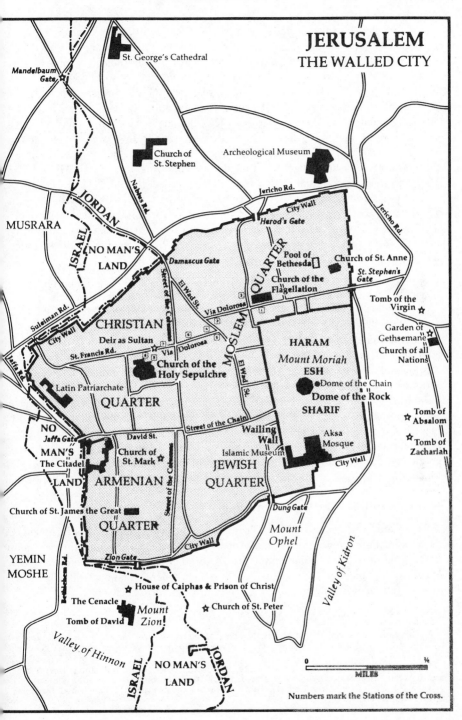

JERUSALEM
THE WALLED CITY

St. George's Cathedral

Mandelbaum
Gate

Church of
St. Stephen

Archeological Museum

Jericho Rd.

MUSRARA

JORDAN

ISRAEL

NO MAN'S
LAND

Nablus Rd.

City Wall

Harod's Gate

Jericho Rd.

Damascus Gate

QUARTER

Pool of
Bethesda

Church of St. Anne

St. Stephen's
Gate

Street of the Ca

El Wad St.

Church of the
Flagellation

CHRISTIAN

Via Dolorosa

MOSLEM

Tomb of the
Virgin

Garden of
Gethsemane

Deir as Sultan

Via Dolorosa

St. Francis Rd.

City Wall

Suleiman Rd.

Church of the
Holy Sepulchre

El Wad St.

HARAM

Mount Moriah
ESH

Church of all
Nations

Jaffa Rd.

Latin Patriarchate

QUARTER

Dome of the Chain
Dome of the Rock

SHARIF

Tomb of
Absalom

NO

Jaffa Gate

MAN'S

The Citadel

LAND

David St.

Church of
St. Mark

ARMENIAN

Street of the Chain

Wailing
Wall

Islamic Museum

JEWISH

Aksa
Mosque

City Wall

Tomb of
Zachariah

QUARTER

QUARTER

Church of St. James the Great

City Wall

Dung Gate

Mount
Ophel

YEMIN
MOSHE

Zion Gate

Valley of Kidron

House of Caiphas & Prison of Christ

The Cenacle

Mount
Zion

Tomb of David

Church of St. Peter

Valley of Hinnon

ISRAEL

NO MAN'S
LAND

JORDAN

Kidron Rd.

0   ¼

MILES

Numbers mark the Stations of the Cross.

American Relief Society for the Indigent Jews of Jerusalem was founded. A major contributor to this society was a New Orleans Jew, Judah Touro.[2] In 1854 he donated funds for the establishment of a housing project near the walled city for Jews. This project was established near Zion Gate and named Yemin Moshe, or the "right hand of Moses." From this nucleus the New City grew slowly north and west of the walled city. The great bulk of the Jewish population of Jerusalem is, however, of recent vintage. Only after the establishment of the British Mandate over Palestine in the 1920s did the Jewish community in Jerusalem grow to significant size. By 1931 some 46,000 Jews were living in the New City, and by 1946 the number had grown to 95,000, the increase primarily the result of Jewish immigration to Palestine following the rise of Hitler.[3] By 1948 the Jewish population in the New City exceeded 100,000.

The rapid growth of the Jewish community upset the ecological balance in Jerusalem. There was little economic opportunity for this expanded community and the New City, or West Jerusalem, became less a part of the corporate structure of Jerusalem than an extension of the Jewish community of Palestine into the holy city. As one official Israeli statement concludes,

> The City [i.e., Israeli Jerusalem] is not even remotely self-supporting, either agriculturally or industrially, and would never have been able to maintain its population, except as part of a wider and more productive unit in the resources of which it could proportionately share.[4]

East Jerusalem, embracing the walled city and the Arab quarters north of it, grew more slowly over the decades. In 1967 the population of East Jerusalem was only 90,000 (including Arab refugees from 1948-49), while that of West Jerusalem numbered over 180,000.

In brief, Jerusalem is two cities: an Arab East Jerusalem and a Jewish West Jerusalem. It is within East Jerusalem that one finds virtually all of the Holy Places; this is, in fact, the "Jerusalem" of religious significance.[5] In contrast, West Jerusalem is modern, more expressive of Western culture, and linked politically, economically, and ideologically with the Israeli community along the Mediterranean littoral rather than with the immediate hinterland of the holy city.

Jerusalem: Holy City of Christendom

There are close to one billion Christians in the world today. They constitute the dominant religious groups in Europe, both North and South America, and in the English-speaking commonwealths. Altogether, Christians account for about one-third of mankind. While divided into many denominations, all Christians look to Jerusalem as the site where Christ's mission was concluded.

2. J. C. Hurewitz, *Middle East Dilemmas* (N.Y.: Harper & Bros., 1953), p. 107.

3. Doc. A/1286, *loc. cit.*

4. Delegation of Israel to the United Nations, *Memorandum on the Question of Jerusalem Submitted to the Trusteeship Council of the United Nations*, Seventh Session. Lake Success, May, 1950, p. 7.

5. According to United Nations Map 229, dated November, 1949, only three Holy Places are in West Jerusalem: the Tomb of David, Ein Karim (the birthplace of John the Baptist) and the Cenacle. Part of the Cenacle is in No Man's Land between the Israeli and Jordanian sectors of the holy city.

The United Nations lists the following Christian Holy Places in the Jerusalem area:

1) Basilica of the Holy Sepulchre
2) Bethany
3) Cenacle
4) Church of St. Anne
5) Church of St. James the Great
6) Church of St. Mark
7) Deir as-Sultan
8) Tomb of the Virgin
9) House of Caiphas and Prison of Christ
10) Sanctuary of the Ascension
11) Pool of Bethesda
12) Birthplace of John the Baptist
13) Basilica of the Nativity
14) Milk Grotto
15) Shepherds Field
16) The Nine Stations of the Cross, collectively also known as the Via Dolorosa.[6]

A few miles south of the walled city is the village of Bethlehem, where three of the Holy Places cited above are found. Here, where Christ was born, is the Basilica of the Nativity, the Milk Grotto, and Shepherds Field. Every Christmas, the Christian world celebrates the event that took place in this tiny village 1969 years ago.

To the east of the walled city, on the opposite side of the Valley of Kidron, is the Garden of Gethsemane, a favorite spot, the Gospel according to St. Luke tells us, to which Christ frequently retired. Here on the slopes of the Mount of Olives, He prayed the night before His crucifixion, sweated His tears of blood, was given the kiss of betrayal by Judas, and was arrested (Luke 22:39 ff). In these same gardens is located the tomb of the Virgin Mary, and a few hundred feet away the Sanctuary of the Ascension, marking the spot from which "he was parted from them, and carried up into heaven." (Luke 23:51.)

Just outside Zion Gate is the Cenacle, the forerunner of all Christian churches. This is the site of the Last Supper and the institution of the Blessed Sacrament. Here, too, Jesus appeared to the Apostles after His Resurrection, standing in their midst and saying, "Peace be unto you." (John 20:19.)

Within the walled city, the holy sites of the Christian faith are ubiquitous. Along the Via Dolorosa, a narrow zigzag alley running from the site of Pilate's house to the Holy Sepulchre, are marked the Stations of the Cross,[7] with the final Station the Holy Sepulchre itself. This is Calvary, the site of Christ's crucifixion. Here, too, within the walls of biblical Jerusalem, is the Church of St. Anne, the Church of St. James the Great, the Church of St. Mark, the Deir as-Sultan, and

---

6. *Loc. cit.*

7. The several stations indicate the spot where Jesus is condemned, His first fall, His meeting of Mary, Simon carries His cross, His second fall, etc. The present path is much higher, of course, than the original. At the convent of the Sisters of Zion, one may descend to the ancient level where the Sisters will point out to the visitor the scratches on the pavement marking the game the Roman soldiers played for Christ's robe.

the Pool of Bethesda. In addition to these recognized Holy Places within the walled city, there are also many religious sites (shrines, churches, convents, and sanctuaries) which various Christian denominations consider especially sacred. Thus, there are more than 30 Christian Communities and the Church bodies in the walled city, representing Catholic, Orthodox, Monophysite, and Protestant sects. The Catholic Church has more than 35 orders and congregations within the walled city and in other sections of East Jerusalem.

The large number of Christian groups represented in the holy city, together with the intense devotion Jerusalem evokes from all Christendom, has frequently led to ugly sectarian disputes which challenge the sacred character of this city.[8] These very disputes, however, serve to underscore the significance of Jerusalem to Christianity. The history of Christianity and the holy city of Jerusalem also reflects this admixture of the baseness of man with his search for spiritual communion. The Crusades, noble in thought, but often marked by bloodshed, were demonstrative of this contradiction in feeling and action.

For all Christianity, the Holy Places of Jerusalem assume particular importance because of this very reason; they symbolize the teachings of Christ—teachings which sought to free man from his base emotions. To Christianity, then, Jerusalem is the city where all the 'moral aspirations of man are brought into sharp focus.

Al-Quds: Sanctuary of Islam

For the 500,000,000 Muslims of the world, Jerusalem is also a particularly holy site, subordinate only to the cities of Mecca and Medina. It is a consecrated place and is known in Arabic (the language of Islam as well as the language of Arabs) as al-Quds, or "The Sanctuary." To the Muslim, the religion of Islam *is* the religion of Abraham, Isaac, Moses, and Jesus, all recognized as prophets of the one God (Allah). Muhammad is merely the last of God's messengers. All the apostles of God are accepted; to reject the prophets of Judaism and Christianity dooms the Muslim to everlasting hell.[9] While,

> To those who believe
> In God and His apostles
> And make no distinction
> Between any of the apostles,
> We shall soon give
> Their (due) rewards:
> For God is Oft-forgiving,
> Most Merciful.[10]

To the Muslim, both Christians and Jews are *Ahl al-Kitab,* or "People of the Book." As such they are "believers" and hold juridical right under Islamic law to live as "protected peoples" within the Islamic world. The whole corpus of Islamic dogma links the three great monotheistic faiths together. Because of the

---

8. The latest took place only two years ago. See Evan M. Wilson, "The Internationalization of Jerusalem," *Middle East Journal,* XXIII (Winter, 1969), pp. 1-13. The author of this study was witness to one such melee in 1955 when a young priest of one sect held mass during a period assigned to a different sect.

9. The Quran, Surah IV: 150-151.

10. Surah IV: 152.

incorporation of Judaic and Christian religious traditions into Islam, the city of Jerusalem has been a Muslim holy city from the very beginning of Muhammad's prophetic call.

In fact, the *giblah,* or direction of prayer, was initially toward Jerusalem, not Mecca. The Muslim *giblah* was not switched from Jerusalem until 624 A.D., more than a decade after Muhammad began preaching.[11]

Jerusalem, records the Kuran, is also the site of Muhammad's "ascent" (Miradj) at the time of his "nocturnal journey" (Isra). This was a particularly important episode in Muhammad's life, one of the rare times that his life transcended the mundane. The Kuran describes this journey as follows:

> Glory to God
> Who did take His Servant
> For a journey by night
> From the Sacred Mosque
> To the Farthest Mosque
> Whose precincts we did
> Bless in order that We
> Might show him some
> Of our signs: for He
> Is the One who heareth
> And seeth (all things).[12]

The Sacred Mosque refers to the Kaba at Mecca (Masjid al-Haram) while the Farthest Mosque (Masjil al-Aqsa) refers to the Temple of Solomon in Jerusalem.

Islamic tradition, or *hadith,* has greatly embellished this journey of Muhammad, detailing the miraculous character of the event, his ascension from Jerusalem to heaven, even his conversation with God. A summary of the Islamic traditions dealing with this journey runs as follows:

The angel Gabriel escorted Muhammad one night from Mecca to Jerusalem. Muhammad made this journey mounted on a winged horse called al-Buraq. En route to Jerusalem, Muhammad stopped to pray at Bethlehem, "where was born Jesus the Messiah, son of Mary." [13] From there Muhammad went on to Jerusalem, tethering al-Buraq against the Temple Wall. Thus, the opposite side of the Wailing Wall, *the* holy site in Jerusalem for Jews, is also a holy site to Muslims. In fact, the very same wall is known to Muslims as the "Wall of al-Buraq."

After praying at the "Farthest Mosque," Muhammad stood upon a rock (*sakhra*) from which he then ascended to heaven. Muslims consider this rock second only to the Kaba itself, in order of sanctity. It is over this rock that the Islamic Caliph, Abd-al-Malik, built a shrine in 688-691 A.D. This shrine is the Dome of the Rock, popularly known as the Mosque of Omar. The Dome of the Rock, the al-Aqsa Mosque, and the "Wall of al-Buraq" are enclosed in an area known as the Haram esh-Sharif (Noble Enclosure).

---

11. For an analysis of this switch in the Islam *giblah* from Jerusalem to Mecca, see W. Montgomery Watt, *Muhammad at Medina* (Oxford: Clarendon Press, 1956), pp. 198-202.

12. Surah XVII: 1.

13. Imam al-Beihaqi, *Dalail an-Nubuwah,* on the authority of Shaddad ibn Aux, as cited in Charles D. Matthews, *Palestine-Mohammedan Holy Land* (New Haven: Yale University Press, 1949), p. 8.

After speaking with God, Muhammad returned to Mecca. According to Islamic tradition, it was during this visit to heaven that the obligation of prayer five times each day was established for Muslims.[14]

A number of other Islamic traditions deal with Jerusalem, too. Thus al-Bukhari states in his canonical collection of traditions that the Mosque al-Aqsa (i.e., the Farthest Mosque—Solomon's Temple) was the second mosque ever created. He further relates such traditions as "whosoever makes a pilgrimage to Jerusalem . . . God will give him a reward of a thousand martyrs," "whoever gives alms in Jerusalem to the value of a dirbum, it is his ransom from the Fire," or "God said to Jerusalem, Thou art My paradise and My sanctuary, and My choice of the lands! Who dwelleth in thee, it is a blessing (to him) from Me; and who is outside thee without just reason, it is from Mine anger at him." [15]

It is no wonder that the founder of the second caliphate, Muawiyah the Umayyad, proclaimed himself caliph in Jerusalem (661 A.D.) rather than Damascus, his capital.[16]

For more than a thousand years Muslim rule prevailed over Jerusalem. Only during three periods since 638 A.D. has sovereignty over the holy city been lost. The first time was during the Crusades, when Jerusalem fell under Christian rule following its capture on July 15, 1099. The Muslims recaptured the holy city in 1187, but lost it again to the Christians in 1229. Muslim rule was finally reestablished, however, some 15 years later.

The second period Jerusalem was lost to the Muslims followed General Allenby's expulsion of the Turks from that city in 1918. Muslim rule was restored to East Jerusalem between 1948 and 1967, but now, again, no Muslim flag flies over Jerusalem. For the tradition-minded Muslim, to whom the spiritual and the temporal aspects of life are closely interwoven, the loss of al-Quds—the Sanctuary—is more than a military or political event. It is a phenomenon of deep spiritual significance.

Judaism and the City of David

On June 7, 1967, Major General Moshe Dayan and other leaders of the Israeli army entered the walled city through St. Stephen's Gate. Without delay they proceeded directly to the Wailing Wall, where, after praying before this last remnant of the Temple, Dayan left a note that read "let peace prevail in Israel." Within a few days thousands of Jews streamed into the walled city to pray before the wall. For 14,000,000 Jews scattered throughout the world, this act marked the climax of a mission over 1800 years old, for the Jews prayed before the wall, not as tolerated subjects of another people, but as masters of all Jerusalem. Not since Rome put an end to the Second Jewish Commonwealth (70 A.D.) have Jews ruled over the walled city.[17]

The Wailing Wall, which more secularly-minded Palestinian Jews 30 years

---

14. Cf. *Shorter Encyclopaedia of Islam* (Ithaca: Cornell University Press, 1961), article on "Miradj."
15. These selections are from Matthews, *op. cit.*
16. Philip K. Hitti, *History of the Arabs* (New York: Macmillan, 1951), p. 189.
17. Excepting the ephemeral rule of Bar Kochba 117-135 A.D. during the Jewish revolt against Hadrian.

years earlier once dismissed as a "worthless pile of stones in a dirty Arab alley," [18] now symbolized the final return of the Jew to the Jerusalem of his forefathers.

In a sense, the entire history of Judaism these past 18 centuries has focused on the holy city. Few Jews cannot recite the psalm:

> If I forget thee, O Jerusalem
> Let my right hand forget its cunning;
> Let my tongue cleave to the roof of my mouth
> If I remember thee not,
> If I recall not Jerusalem
> On the day of my chiefest joy.
>   (CXXXVII)

The words of the great Jewish poet, Judah Halevi, reaffirm this devotion of the Jew to the holy city,

> Could I but kiss thy dust,
> So would I fain expire;
> As sweet as honey then
> My longing, my desire. [19]

Since the year 135 A.D. the basic condition of Jewry was set by its exile from Jerusalem. This exile was manifested in the scattering (diaspora) of Jews throughout the world. But despite the centrifugal forces acting upon the Diaspora Jews, a unity of the Jewish spirit has been retained. In no small way, this unity has been maintained because of the deep prophetic, literary, and liturgical relationship of Judaism to Jerusalem—City of David and site of the Temple.

To Judaism, Jerusalem is more than a holy city. It is the epicenter of the Promised Land. The writings of Judaism are replete with references to the promise God made to Abraham that the land of Canaan would ultimately belong to His chosen People. [20] So to the Jews the Land of Zion has always been home, either as apocalyptic vision, or reality. Thus immigration to Israel is termed "in-gathering"; thus General Dayan could announce that June day, 1967, that Israel had "liberated" Jerusalem.

But if Zion is "home" to the Jew, then Jerusalem is even more so:

> Jerusalem is at the center of the Land of Israel, the Temple is at the center of Jerusalem, the Holy of Holies is at the center of the Temple, the Ark is at the center of the Holy of Holies and the Foundation Stone is in front of the Ark, which point is the foundation of the world. [21]

To the Jew, all Palestine is holy, with Jerusalem the very center of this Promised Land. There is hardly a square foot of Jerusalem that does not hold historical or religious significance for Judaism. The cemeteries, particularly that on the Mount of Olives, the synagogues, particularly those that were located within the walled city, the Tomb of Absalom, the Tomb of David, the Tomb of

---

18. John Gunther, "The Realities of Zionism," *Harper's Magazine*, CLXI (July, 1930), p. 207.
19. As cited in Abram L. Sachar, *A History of the Jews* (N.Y.: Alfred A. Knopf, 1965), p. 175.
20. Genesis 17:1-8.
21. Tanhuma (Kedoshin), as cited in Arthur Hertzberg, *Judaism* (N.Y.: George Braziller, 1963), p. 150.

Simon the Just, the Tomb of Zachariah, and the several other Tombs in the Valley of Kidron—all these are but a sampling of the revered sites in the Jerusalem area for Jews.

Three great religions—all focused on a specific geographical site: For hundreds of millions this is testimony that Jerusalem must be considered apart from all other cities. Each faith makes its claim to Jerusalem; each claim is valid. To a Christian, Muslim, or Jew, Jerusalem is a point of contact between the individual and his creator. But the City of Peace is a city of people—people who serve the god of nationalism as faithfully, if not more so, than the God of Abraham. In the service of nationalism, the City of Peace becomes the city of conflict. It is to this aspect of the Jerusalem problem that we must now turn.

II. JERUSALEM UNDER THE MANDATE

At the outbreak of World War I the Ottoman Empire was but a shadow of its former greatness. Most of its Balkan and African territories had been lost and the secular power of the Sultan had been made nominal, at best, by the Young Turk revolution in 1908. Although the Empire still ruled over most of the Arab World in Asia, including the Holy Land, the stirrings of Arab nationalism in this area before 1914 suggested that they, too, would soon seek a separate political destiny. Therefore, when the Ottoman Empire joined with the Central Powers in October, 1914, Arab nationalists turned to the British for support of Arab political aspirations.

Events in Constantinople at the beginning of the war made the British more receptive to the Arabs than might otherwise have been the case. The Ottoman Sultan was also Caliph, or spiritual leader, of the Sunni (orthodox) Muslims, the dominant sect of Islam. On November 14, 1914, the Sultan-Caliph declared a *jihad* or "holy war," against the Allies. To the British who ruled over millions of Sunni Muslims in Egypt, British India, and elsewhere, the Sultan-Caliph's call was a source of potential danger, for, if heeded, widespread colonial disturbances might ensue.

To counteract the effects of this move by the Sultan-Caliph, the British needed the support of an Islamic leader whose influence would undermine the religious importance of the Caliph. They found this individual in Sherif Hussein, lineal descendant of the Prophet Muhammad and traditional custodian of the Islamic holy places in Mecca. Early in 1914 Hussein's second son, Abdullah, had already hinted to the British that Sherif Hussein might rebel against the Turks if British support were assured. So with the advent of the war and the Sultan-Caliph's call for a "holy war," the British High Commissioner for Egypt and the Sudan, Sir Henry McMahon, began negotiations by means of a series of letters with Sherif Hussein preparatory to the latter's launching an Arab revolt against the Ottoman Turks.

For the British, three major benefits could be seen in their support of Sherif Hussein. First, the call for a "holy war" by the Sultan-Caliph would lose much of its meaning; second, Arab nationalists would rally to the support of the Allies in expectation of a separate state for Arabs following the war; and third, the

Arabs would be valuable in providing military support along the desert flank in the anticipated march of General Allenby from Egypt into the Holy Land.

Before launching the 1916 Arab Revolt in support of Great Britain, Sherif Hussein of Mecca sought an understanding with the British relative to the geographical scope of the Arab State to be brought into being under British auspices subsequent to the dismemberment of the Ottoman Empire. It was Hussein's initial understanding that *all* of the area now made up of Syria, Lebanon, Jordan, Israel, Iraq, Saudi Arabia, and the sheikhdoms of the Arabian Peninsula (but excluding the Aden protectorate) would be included in this independent Arab State.[1]

The British responded by suggesting that to discuss this matter "would appear to be premature . . . in the heat of war." [2] Sherif Hussein was dissatisfied with this diplomatic hedging and continued to press Great Britain for some agreement on the area of the postwar Arab state, and,[3] under this pressure, Great Britain agreed to recognize the Arab claims, but with two important reservations. First, the Ottoman administrative districts *(vilayets)* of Baghdad and Basra would require "special administrative arrangements" (they would later become part of Iraq); and, second, that "portions of Syria lying to the west of the districts of Damascus, Homs, Hama, and Aleppo . . . should be excluded from the limits demanded." [4]

The Ottoman Empire in Asia was divided, for administrative purposes, into various *vilayets*. Each *vilayet*, in turn, was further subdivided into *sanjaks*. The *vilayet* of Syria was composed of four *sanjaks:* Hama, Damascus, Hauran, and Maan. The most southern *sanjak* in the *vilayet* of Aleppo was the *sanjak* of of Aleppo itself. The British-Arab discussions up to this point agreed that the *sanjaks* of Aleppo, Hama (which included Homs), and Damascus would go to the Arabs. It was further agreed that the *sanjaks* of Hauran and Maan would go to the Arabs. What was in dispute were the three administrative units along the Mediterranean littoral: the *vilayet* of Beirut (including the *sanjaks* of Latakia, Tripoli, Beirut, Acre, and Balqa), the quasi-independent Province of Lebanon, and the independent s*anjak* of Jerusalem. The latter, established as an independent *sanjak* in the 1880s, was not included in a larger *vilayet*, but was directly under the supervision of the Porte.

What is important to note is that neither Great Britain nor Sherif Hussein made specific reference to the proposed disposition of the *sanjak* of Jerusalem. A literal reading of the relevant correspondence would assign that *sanjak* to the Arabs. But Great Britain also suggested guaranteeing "the Holy Places against all external aggression" and that they would "recognize their inviolability." This would imply that the Jerusalem s*anjak* might have some special status even if it were to be placed within the proposed Arab state.

Sherif Hussein agreed to a temporary British administration of the *vilayets* of

1. Cmd 5957, *Correspondence between Sir Henry McMahon and The Sherif Hussein of Mecca*, July 1915-March 1916 (London: H.M.S.O., 1939), letter from Sherif Hussein to Sir Henry McMahon, July 14, 1915.

2. *Ibid.*, letter from McMahon to Hussein, dated August 30, 1915.

3. *Ibid.*, Hussein-McMahon letter of September 9, 1915.

4. *Ibid.*, McMahon-Hussein letter of October 24, 1915.

Baghdad and Basra, but insisted that the Mediterranean littoral be included in the proposed Arab State.[5] To this persistence, the British could only respond that the matter would "require careful consideration" and that "the interests of our ally, France, are involved." [6]

Once again Hussein capitulated and agreed that "the northern parts and their coasts . . . we now leave to France." [7] But by this diplomatic concession, Hussein did not give up his claim to the "southern" parts, i.e., the independent *sanjak* of Jerusalem. It was on this unsettled issue that the British-Arab negotiations ended.[8]

While Sir Henry McMahon and Sherif Hussein were exchanging these letters, Sir Mark Sykes of Great Britain had visited Cairo and was privy to this correspondence. Only later Sir Henry McMahon would be aware of what Sykes was doing. In any case, Sykes and the French diplomat Georges Picot concluded the so-called Sykes-Picot agreement of May, 1916, with full knowledge of the contents of the McMahon-Hussein correspondence.[9]

The Sykes-Picot Agreement

The 1916 Sykes-Picot Agreement consists of a series of letters between Great Britain, France, and Russia concerning the period April 26 through October 23, 1916.[10] Under the terms of this agreement it was established, *inter alia,* that:

> With a view to securing the religious interests of the Entente Powers, Palestine, with the Holy Places, is to be separated from Turkish territory and subjected to a special regime to be determined by agreement between Russia, France and Great Britain.[11]

On November 2, 1917, Lord Balfour, then Britain's Secretary of State for Foreign Affairs, published a statement of policy in the form of a letter to Baron Rothschild which stated that:

> His Majesty's Government view with favour the establishment in Palestine of a National Home for the Jewish people, and will use their best endeavours to facilitate the achievement of this object, it being clearly understood that nothing shall be done which may prejudice the civil and religious rights of existing non-Jewish communities in Palestine, or the rights and political status enjoyed by Jews in any other country.[12]

Thus, when Jerusalem fell to General Allenby in December, 1917, the Arabs were under the impression it would become part of an independent Arab state,

---

5. *Ibid,* Hussein-McMahon letter, November 9, 1915.

6. *Ibid.,* McMahon-Hussein letter, December 14, 1915.

7. *Ibid.,* Hussein-McMahon letter, January 1, 1916.

8. There was some additional correspondence, but these letters deal only with military preparations then underway.

9. Elizabeth Monroe, *Britain's Moment in the Middle East, 1914-1956* (Baltimore: Johns-Hopkins Press, 1963), p. 32.

10. The text of this agreement may be found in J. C. Hurewitz, *Diplomacy in the Near and Middle East, 1914-1965,* volume II (N.Y.: W. Van Nostrand, 1956), pp. 18-22. However the preliminary accord was concluded in May, 1916.

11. As cited in Cmd. 5479, *Palestine Royal Commission Report,* July, 1937 (London: H.M.S.O., 1937), p. 21.

12. For the text of this "Balfour Declaration" see Hurewitz, *op. cit.,* p. 26.

the Jews assumed it would be part of a British-administered Palestine until unrestricted Jewish immigration into the Holy Land allowed greater Jewish political autonomy,[13] and everyone else assumed Jerusalem would be part of an internationalized zone—everyone except President Wilson of the United States who thought that the people of Palestine should have the right to determine their own political future.[14]

The post-World War I formula for Palestine was a blow to the incipient Arab nationalist movement. After fighting alongside the British for two years, they felt a British administration of Palestine as a cover for the establishment of a Jewish National Home in that area was a dubious reward for Arab efforts.

For the Zionists, the postwar settlement, while not entirely meeting their wishes, was a wedge into Palestine. Symbolic of their intention to establish a truly National Home in Palestine was their founding of the Hebrew University. On July 14, 1918, before General Allenby had fully established his administration in Jerusalem, Dr. Chaim Weizmann (then a leader of British Zionists and later to be the first president of Israel) laid the foundation stone of the new university on Mt. Scopus.[15]

Even before the British military and administrative control of Palestine was formalized as a Mandate, Arabs and Jews began to clash in Jerusalem. In April, 1,920 riots broke out within the holy city in the course of which over 230 inhabitants were either killed or wounded. The clash was quickly suppressed by British military forces, but it served as a harbinger of things to come. The differences between the Arabs and the handful of oriental Jews who lived in Jerusalem before World War I were minimal. But now Arab-Jewish differences were assuming a cultural and intellectual character that would make their future coexistence virtually impossible. The Arabs, and to a considerable extent the oriental Jews of that time,[16] were steeped in the Eastern way of life. Their traditionalist outlook, their lack of familiarity with modern science, their emphasis on status—even their perceptions of space and time—set them off sharply from the immigrant Jews, more Western in outlook, more attuned to modern perceptions of reality, better organized and financed, and with invaluable political connections in London, Paris, and Washington, D.C. The British found themselves in the role of referee for this clash of two peoples. But the clash was not a matter of peoples divided by religion, for religious differences had existed in Jerusalem for centuries, between Christian Arab and Muslim Arab, as with these groups and

13. This point was made clear by the contents of a Zionist draft submitted to the British government on July 18, 1917 to be considered for future declaration as official British policy. The draft declaration states, *inter alia*, that the British regard "as essential . . . the grant of internal autonomy to the Jewish nationality in Palestine, freedom of immigration for Jews, and the establishment of a Jewish National Colonising Corporation for the resettlement and economic development of the country" (Hurewitz, *loc. cit.*). There is no mention made in the Zionist draft to either the civil or religious rights of the indigenous population.

14. Wilson's Twelfth Point of his 14-point address to Congress January 8, 1918, states in part, that ". . . nationalities which are now under Turkish rule should be assured . . . unmolested opportunity of autonomous development."

15. The university was moved to West Jerusalem following the 1948-49 Arab-Israeli war. Since the June, 1967, occupation of East Jerusalem, selected sections of the university have been returned to the Mt. Scopus site.

16. Particularly the *Nturei Karta* (Guardians of the City), who opposed Zionist aims in Palestine on the grounds only the Messiah can bring about the legitimate return of the Jew to Zion.

Jews; instead it was a clash between two political movements, Zionism and Arab nationalism. Both sides would use religion, the question of Holy Places, Jerusalem itself, as weapons in their struggle.

The British Mandate

On July 24, 1922, the League of Nations officially designated Great Britain as Mandatory Power in Palestine.[17] The Preamble to the Palestine Mandate specifically identified as one purpose of this Mandate "putting into effect . . . the establishment in Palestine of a National home for the Jewish people." Article 2 repeats this charge to Great Britain, while Article 4 recognizes the Zionist organization as the appropriate Jewish agency to advise the Mandatory Power. Furthermore, Article 6 calls upon the British to "facilitate Jewish immigration." To the Palestinian Arabs, all their fears seemed to be justified: the Mandate was to be merely a cover for the progressive transformation of an Arab Palestine into an essentially Jewish Palestine. Although Great Britain was made responsible for "Holy Places and religious buildings or sites in Palestine" (Article 13), it was obvious that the political struggle invited by the Mandate would, by the nature of the Zionist movement, involve these Holy Places, particularly in Jerusalem. If the site of the Holy Places, i.e., Jerusalem, represented the focal point of Zionist aspirations, then where else but in the holy city would the confrontation between Zionist and Arab take place? As noted above, such a confrontation had already taken place in Jerusalem even before the mandate was formally established.

The Wailing Wall Incident

By August, 1929, the demographic character of Palestine had been sufficiently altered so that an Arab-Jewish clash awaited only the appropriate incident. In the period 1920-29, alone, 99,805 Jews had been admitted into Palestine. Many of them had taken up residence in the New City, or West Jerusalem.[18] As might have been expected, the incident arose over one of the Holy Places in Jerusalem. Throughout 1928 and into the summer of 1929, the capacity of the Arab and the Zionist Jew to coexist peacefully in the holy city became increasingly more difficult to maintain. Emotions were becoming charged, as each group found the grounds of common discourse more difficult to discover. The bulk of the immigrant Jews were coming from Poland, Russia, and Lithuania—and they found little cultural relationship with the Arab community of Jerusalem. The exact point where the emotional fervor of the Zionist Jew and the Muslim Arab came into contact was the Wailing Wall or the Wall of al-Buraq. As early as 1925, one small incident had already occurred in connection with this Holy Place.[19] Under a Turkish decree (*firman*) of 1852 (reaffirming the position taken by the Sultan earlier, in 1757), the Holy Places of Jerusalem were subject to a rigorously-

17. For the text of the Palestine Mandate, see Cmd. 1785, *Parliamentary Papers, 1922* (London: H.M.S.O., 1923).

18. Cmd. 5479 *Palestine Royal Commission Report*, July, 1937 (London: H.M.S.O., 1937), p. 279 (Peel Report).

19. F. A. Andrews, *The Holy Land Under Mandate*, volume II (N.Y.: Houghton Mifflin Co., 1931), pp. 225-26.

enforced status quo, which Great Britain sought also to continue.[20] In 1925 the Jews sought to modify this status quo by bringing benches to the Wall to be used on the Jewish Day of Atonement. The Muslim Arabs protested immediately and these benches were removed. The Muslim Arab, however, was now suspicious of the Jewish community and its intentions with regard to the Wall—a site also holy to Muslims. The Wall was recognized Muslim property, to which Jews had customary rights, but only if used in accordance with the status quo.[21] No change could be made in this status quo without the consent of both Muslims and Jews. The implications of this point will be further drawn when the post-1967 actions of the Israeli government are analyzed in this connection.

A more serious incident occurred September 24, 1928, when Jews sought to set up a screen by the Wall to divide men and women. When ordered to remove the screen by the British, the Jews refused. The screen was eventually removed by force. The Jewish authorities protested vigorously, contending the screen was not designed "to menace the inviolability of the Muslim Holy Place." The Muslim Arabs, however, took the position that these recent efforts to break the long-established status quo governing the Wall represented "the Jews' aim . . . to take possession of the Mosque of al-Aqsa gradually." [22]

In the following months, this tension was further inflamed, as both Zionists and Arab nationalists made the Wall a political as well as religious issue.

The Zionist Jews were the first to trigger the new outbreak of violence. On August 15, 1929, the day of *Tisha B'Av*, a Jewish holy day in memory of the destruction of the Temple, a number of Zionist youths marched to the Wall, made political speeches, and sang the *Hatikvah*, or Jewish National Anthem. On the following day Arab nationalists put on a counterdemonstration. Rumor and fact, the trivial and the significant—all were fused into an inseparable pattern. To the Arabs the "provocative demonstration" [23] of the Zionist Jews confirmed their fears and dictated a violent response. A week later the "fire which had so long been kindling burst into flame." [24] From August 23-29 Arab-Jewish battles erupted throughout the Holy Land. By the time peace was restored, some 472 Jews and 348 Arabs had been killed or wounded.[25]

The Royal Commission of Inquiry (Shaw Report), which investigated this incident, succinctly summarized the basic reason why a conflict over the Wall could rapidly envelop all Palestine and involve Christian Arab, as well as Muslim Arab, in bloody conflict with the Jewish community:

> A National Home for the Jews, in the sense in which it was widely understood, was inconsistent with the demands of Arab nationalists while the claims of Arab nationalism, if admitted, would have rendered impossible the fulfillment of the pledge to the Jews.[26]

20. *Report of the Commission appointed by His Majesty's Government in the United Kingdom of Great Britain and Northern Ireland, with the approval of the Council of the League of Nations, to determine the rights and claims of Moslems and Jews in connection with the Western or Wailing Wall at Jerusalem*, December, 1930 (Hereafter referred to as Report, 1930) (London: H.M.S.O., 1931), p. 36.
21. Cmd. 5479, p. 66.
22. *Ibid.*, p. 67.
23. The phrase is that used by the Royal Commission, *loc. cit.*
24. *Loc. cit.*
25. *Ibid.*, p. 68.
26. As cited in *loc. cit.*

Two political movements were in conflict, and the focus of that conflict was the holy city itself.

The specific disputes arising out of the Wailing Wall incident led, after extensive British investigation, to the Mandatory Government of Palestine issuing detailed instructions in regard to the use of the Wall: Jews were to have access to the Wall at all times; no objects of a permanent character were to be placed by the Wall and nothing affixed to either the Wall or adjoining buildings; on specific Jewish holy days, a portable stand for use in prayer would be allowed, but this would have to be removed at the end of the holy day involved. It was further ordered that "no benches, chairs, or stools shall be brought to or placed on the pavement before the Wailing Wall" and that "no screen or curtain shall be placed on the Wall or on the pavement, for the purpose of separating men and women or for any other purpose." The maximum size of each portable object allowed was included in these instructions.[27]

The Wailing Wall incident could be resolved by such detailed instructions; the political question that led to this incident would prove to be far more impervious to administrative resolution.

The 1936 Riots

The Arabs of Palestine were concerned from the very beginning of the Mandate that British support of Jewish immigration, under the provisions of Article 6 of the Mandate, would eventually lead to Jewish community gaining demographic hegemony over the Holy Land. By the year 1936 this concern had assumed the character of panic because, with the rise of Nazi Germany in Europe, there followed a veritable quantum jump of Jewish immigration into Palestine. During the four-year period 1929-32, some 23,821 Jews had immigrated into Palestine. Between 1933 and 1936, however, Jewish immigration totaled 164,267.[28] One by-product of this rapid increase in Jewish immigration was that an Arab Jerusalem of 49,000 now faced a Jewish Jerusalem on the slopes rising westward from the walled city of more than 76,000, whose cultural and political orientation was alien to the Jerusalem across the Valley of Hinnom.

Although Jews constituted only 30 percent of the total population of 1936 Palestine, the danger of being overwhelmed by Jewish refugees from Europe now appeared real and immediate. The Royal Commission Report of 1937 (i.e., the Peel Report) suggested that Palestine could become predominantly Jewish in only a decade if the rate of immigration continued at its post-1933 rate.[29] It was this specter of Jewish inundation of Arab Palestine that brought forth in 1936 the most violent clash between Arab and Jew in the history of the Mandate up to that date.

The riots, which started in April, 1936, in Tel Aviv and Jaffa, soon spread across the Holy Land. A newly-formed Arab National Committee called for a general strike in Palestine on April 20 until "the British Government changes its

27. Report, 1930, *op. cit.*, pp. 70-71.

28. Cmd. 5479, p. 279.

29. *Ibid.*, p. 281. The total population of Palestine in 1936 numbered 1,336,518, of which 370,483 were Jewish. The Commission estimated that both Arab and Jewish populations would equal 1,210,000 by 1947, assuming an immigration rate of 60,000 per annum.

present policy . . . the beginning of which is the stoppage of Jewish immigration."[30] By May the strike brought the Arab part of the Palestinian economy to a virtual standstill. Sporadic attacks, indiscriminate sniping, and destruction of public property rapidly escalated the disturbance into incipient civil war. Throughout the summer Arab unrest continued its violent expression. By September the British had brought in more than 20,000 troops to contain the Arab community.

The 1936 riots were more than just another Arab-Jewish "disturbance"; they were a definite move on the part of the Arabs to challenge the legitimacy of British Mandatory rule. The conflict was directed as much against the British government of Palestine as against the Jewish community. This is reflected in the casualty figures for the 1936 riots: Arabs killed or wounded, over 1,000; Jews killed or wounded, 388; Mandatory Government casualties (including police), 243.[31]

As a result of the 1936 riots the Peel Report recommended that Palestine be partitioned into an Arab state that would include Trans-Jordan and a Jewish state in those areas of Palestine where the Jews already made up a clear majority of the population. In addition, it was recommended that, separate from both the proposed Jewish and Arab states, there would be a Jerusalem enclave which would include the holy city with its immediate hinterland and a corridor to the sea terminating at Jaffa.[32]

This partition scheme was never implemented, of course, although it did influence the subsequent United Nations partition plan. The justification cited in the Peel Report for proposing an enclave for Jerusalem was as follows:

> The partition of Palestine is subject to the overriding necessity of keep-
> ing the sanctity of Jerusalem and Bethlehem inviolate and of ensuring free
> and safe access to them for all the world. That, in the fullest sense of the
> mandatory phrase, is "a sacred trust of civilization"—a trust on behalf not
> merely of the peoples of Palestine but of multitudes in other lands to
> whom those places, one or both, are Holy Places.[33]

The 1936 riots posed a threat to the holy city, the fate of which was of concern to "multitudes in other lands." But the riots were only symptoms of a condition that made the whole Mandate system seem unworkable and partition inevitable: just as Jerusalem must be viewed as two cities, one Jewish and one Arab, so too was Palestine two countries, one Jewish and one Arab. The British Mandate for Palestine provided the juridical framework within the context of which this bi-national character of Palestine and its holiest site, Jerusalem, came into being. At the close of World War II, the clamor by Jewish refugees in Europe to emigrate to Palestine, coupled with a resurgence of Arab sentiment that Palestine should be freed of Mandatory rule, made continuation of such bi-nationalism in Palestine virtually intolerable. Could the inviolability of the holy city be pre-served against this background? If the Mandate system were a failure, then what system could take its place which could at once satisfy both Jews and Arabs, yet still leave Jerusalem secure as "a sacred trust of civilization"? For the British only one thing was certain—they did not have the answer.

30. *Ibid.*, p. 97.
31. *Ibid.*, pp. 105-06.
32. *Ibid.*, pp. 380-93.
33. *Ibid.*, p. 381.

III. SEARCH FOR AN INTERNATIONAL FORMULA

With the dissolution of the League of Nations in 1946, Great Britain had no international authority to which it might report on Palestine pending the establishment of an appropriate organ by the newly-established United Nations. The creation on December 10, 1945 of the Anglo-American Inquiry Committee, however, clearly indicated that Great Britain was either unable, or did not wish, to assume sole responsibility for the problem of Palestine. When the Inquiry Committee recommended that Palestine be neither a Jewish nor an Arab state, but that "the Government of Palestine be continued as at present under mandate pending the execution of a Trusteeship Agreement under the United Nations," it did so because of what it considered "the depth of political antagonism beween Arab and Jew." [1]

Great Britain, however, did not want further responsibility for Palestine and on February 14, 1947, declared that it would refer the question of Palestine to the United Nations.[2] On April 28, 1947, the General Assembly convened in special session to consider this question. A United Nations Special Committee on Palestine (UNSCOP) was established to "report on the question of Palestine" [3] at the next regular session of the General Assembly. UNSCOP was further instructed "to give most careful consideration to the religious interests in Palestine of Islam, Judaism, and Christianity." [4]

In September, 1947, UNSCOP reported back with both a majority and minority report. In addition, the Committee submitted several recommendations approved unanimously. Among these it was recommended (V) that:

> The sacred character of the Holy Places shall be preserved and access to the Holy Places for purposes of worship and pilgrimage shall be ensured in accordance with existing rights, in recognition of the proper interest of millions of Christians, Jews and Moslems abroad as well as the residents of Palestine in the care of sites and buildings associated with the origin and history of their faiths.[5]

---

1. United Nations Special Committee on Palestine, *Report to the General Assembly*, Volume I, Doc. A/364, dated 1947, p. 27.
2. *Loc. cit.*
3. *Ibid.*, p. 2.
4. *Ibid.*, p. 36.
5. *Ibid.*, p. 44.

The Minority Report

The minority report called for a federal state with Jerusalem as its capital. It further recommended that the Holy Places in Jerusalem, Bethlehem, etc., be placed under the supervision and protection of the United Nations. Thus Jerusalem would remain an integral part of an all-Palestine political system, but there would be functional internationalization of the Holy Places.

The minority report also recommended that for purposes of local administration, Jerusalem would consist of two separate municipalities, one Arab (including "that part of the city within the walls") and one Jewish. These two municipalities would jointly provide for such common public services as sewage, fire protection, telephones, water supply, etc.[6]

While the minority report was never adopted by the General Assembly, it is instructive to note two points raised in this report. First, that the city of Jerusalem could not be considered as either a demographic or a political entity. At best, Jerusalem could be treated as an entity only for certain public services. Second, that sovereignty over Jerusalem was a separate problem from sovereignty over the Holy Places. The latter, by virtue of their international significance to members of all three monotheistic faiths, could only be properly dealt with when placed under international jurisdiction.

The Majority Report

The majority report recommended that Palestine be partitioned into an Arab state and a Jewish state, and that Jerusalem be placed under the international trusteeship system of the United Nations. It was recommended that:

> The city of Jerusalem . . . include the present municipality of Jerusalem plus the surrounding villages and towns, the most eastern of which to be Abu Dis; the most southern Bethlehem; the most Western Ein Karim and the most northern Shn'fat. . . .[7]

The report further recommended that Jerusalem be demilitarized, "its neutrality shall be declared and preserved, and no para-military formations, exercises or activities . . . be permitted within its borders." [8]

On November 29, 1947, the General Assembly recommended the partition of Palestine along the lines suggested by the majority report.[9] Under part III of the partition resolution it was stated that:

> The City of Jerusalem shall be established as a *corpus separatum* under a special international regime and shall be administered by the United Nations. The Trusteeship Council shall be designated to discharge the responsibilities of the Administering Authority on behalf of the United Nations.

The boundaries of the Jerusalem area were to be the same as recommended by UNSCOP except that the built-up area of Motsa was included along with Ein Karim.

---

6. *Ibid.,* p. 63.
7. *Ibid.,* p. 57.
8. *Loc. cit.*
9. United Nations General Assembly Resolution 181 (II), Doc. A/519 (1947).

In this same resolution, the General Assembly called upon the Trusteeship Council to draft a detailed Statute for Jerusalem designed, in part, "to protect and to preserve the unique spiritual and religious interest located in the city of the three great monotheistic faiths throughout the world" (section C1). The Statute was to come into force not later than October 1, 1948.

Finally, the resolution created the United Nations Palestine Commission and charged it with the task of implementing the partition of Palestine. Events in Palestine, however, soon made it impossible for the Commission even to begin operations in the Holy Land. First, Great Britain refused to transfer authority to the Commission until its mandate officially terminated (May 15, 1948); it even indicated it did not want the Commission on Palestinian soil before May 1, 1948.[10] Second, the partition resolution sparked what the Commission identified as "virtual civil war" in Palestine.[11] British forces could maintain, at best, only nominal control over Palestine. Within days after the partition resolution guerrilla warfare erupted throughout the Holy Land.

The Jewish community in Palestine was reluctantly prepared to accept the internationalization of Jerusalem as the price for obtaining an independent Jewish state under the partition resolution.[12] The Arabs, however, opposed both the partition of Palestine and the internationalization of Jerusalem. In the face of Arab resistance, the Jews armed themselves for the forthcoming struggle. Even before the mandate ended, Jewish military forces (i.e., the Haganah) seized the cities of Tiberias, Safed, Jaffa, and Haifa.[13] Within Jerusalem also battle lines were being drawn.

The Statute for Jerusalem

Seemingly unperturbed that the fate of Jerusalem was being determined by force of arms rather than international compact, the Trusteeship Council began sitting on February 18, 1948, for the purpose of drafting a Statute for an international regime in Jerusalem.[14] On April 21 this Statute was completed, but formal approval was postponed pending receipt of further advice from the General Assembly.

The Statute repeated the statement of the partition resolution that the City of Jerusalem be established as a *corpus separatum* under the United Nations. It also stated the general purposes of internationalization (protection of Holy Places, etc.).

Article 5 of the Statute, as in the partition resolution, states that Jerusalem shall be demilitarized and that no para-military formations shall be permitted

---

10. United Nations Palestine Commission, *Report to the General Assembly,* Doc. A/532 dated April 10, 1948, p. 3.

11. *Loc. cit.* The Commission reported (p. 12) that there were 6,187 casualties in Palestine between November 30, 1947 and April 3, 1948, including 430 British, 2,977 Arab, and 2,733 Jews, as well as 47 civilians of foreign nationality.

12. Government of Israel, Office of Information, *Jerusalem and the United Nations* (Washington, D.C., July, 1953), p. 1.

13. David Ben-Gurion, *Rebirth and Destiny of Israel* (N.Y.: Philosophical Library, 1954), pp. 530-31.

14. For the text of this Statute see Trusteeship Council, *Official Records (II), Annex,* Doc. T/118/Rn.2, dated April 21, 1948.

within its boundaries. The police force envisaged for Jerusalem (Article 14) would *not* be recruited from among either Jews or Arabs.

The governor of Jerusalem would be appointed by the Trusteeship Council to which he would be responsible. He could not be, however, a citizen of either Jerusalem, the Arab state, or the Jewish state (Article 10).

Under the governor, there was to be a unicameral Legislative Council made up of 40 members, 18 of whom would be Jews, 18 Arabs, and one or two representing groups neither Arab nor Jew (e.g., Armenian) and the remainder representatives-at-large (Article 20).

Under the provisions of Articles 36 and 37 of the Statute, the governor was made responsible for the Holy Places, not only within Jerusalem, but also within the Jewish and Arab states resulting from partition. He would therefore wield territorial authority over Jerusalem and functional authority over the Holy Places beyond the boundaries of the international regime.

Finally, an opportunity was included in the Statute (Article 44) for the residents of Jerusalem, after a period of ten years, to decide by referendum what modification of the international regime they might wish to have brought about. The Statute did not deny the principle of self-determination to the residents of the holy city; it merely deferred that right for ten years. Considering the previous (and subsequent) decades of deep, ofttimes violent, political antagonism between Jews and Arabs, stemming from fundamental religious, cultural, and ideological differences, the eventual partition of the holy city might have come about by the self-determination route, even had Jerusalem been made a separate city. As Lord MacDonald, speaking in behalf of the United Kingdom before the United Nations, contended in 1949, "if the people of Jerusalem were given normal democratic liberties, their first action would be to vote the international regime out of existence." [15] The factors that caused the partition of Palestine as a whole were present in the holy city as well.

The Partition of Jerusalem

The 1948-49 Arab-Israeli war led to a *de facto* partition of Jerusalem. At precisely 4:06 p.m. on May 14, 1948, the independent State of Israel was proclaimed. The Arab community, less organized and anticipating early destruction of the new Jewish polity by the several neighboring Arab states following the evacuation of British troops from Palestine, made no similar proclamation of independence until October 1, 1948.[16] By that date, the proclamation was of neither juridical nor political significance.[17]

On May 15 Egyptian troops entered Palestine and the first Arab-Israeli war began. For the Jews and Arabs in Jerusalem, however, this conflict was already over five months old. The fight for Jerusalem had broken out within days after the partition resolution was passed. With minor exceptions the battle line—and,

---

15. U.N. Doc. A/AC 38/SR75.

16. *Proclamation of the Independence of Palestine by the Higher Arab Committee and the Representatives of Palestine Meeting in Congress,* dated October 1, 1948. For text see Muhamma Khalil, comp. *The Arab States and the Arab League: A Documentary Record,* vol. II (Beirut: Khayates, 1962), p. 579.

17. See below page 28.

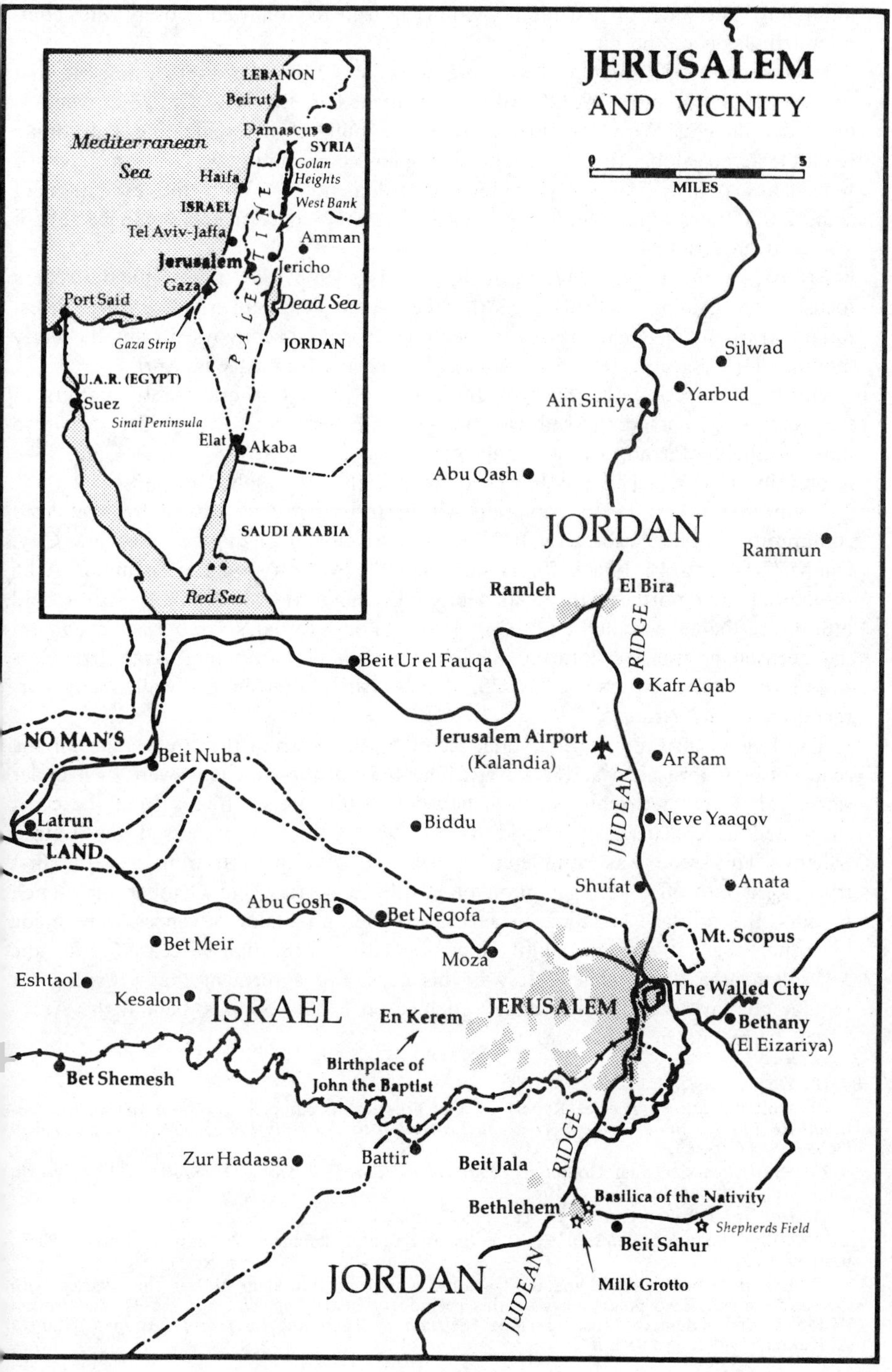
JERUSALEM
AND VICINITY
0
5
MILES
LEBANON
Beirut
Damascus
SYRIA
Mediterranean
Sea
Haifa
Golan
Heights
ISRAEL
West Bank
Tel Aviv-Jaffa
Amman
Jerusalem
Jericho
Gaza
Port Said
Dead Sea
PALESTINE
Gaza Strip
JORDAN
U.A.R. (EGYPT)
Suez
Sinai Peninsula
Elat
Akaba
SAUDI ARABIA
Red Sea
Silwad
Yarbud
Ain Siniya
Abu Qash
JORDAN
Rammun
Ramleh
El Bira
RIDGE
Beit Ur el Fauqa
Kafr Aqab
NO MAN'S
Jerusalem Airport
(Kalandia)
Ar Ram
Beit Nuba
Latrun
Biddu
JUDEAN
Neve Yaaqov
LAND
Shufat
Anata
Abu Gosh
Bet Neqofa
Mt. Scopus
Bet Meir
Moza
Eshtaol
The Walled City
Kesalon
ISRAEL
En Kerem
JERUSALEM
Bethany
(El Eizariya)
Birthplace of
John the Baptist
Bet Shemesh
RIDGE
Zur Hadassa
Battir
Beit Jala
Basilica of the Nativity
Bethlehem
Shepherds Field
Beit Sahur
JORDAN
JUDEAN
Milk Grotto

ultimately, the line of partition—within Jerusalem followed closely the communal division of the city.

According to the 1946 census there were 608,225 Jews in Palestine at that time.[18] Of these, some 99,320 were concentrated in the New City,[19] or what is now identified as West Jerusalem. With the bulk of the remaining Palestinian Jews clustered along the coast, the Jerusalem community was, as one Jewish writer has put it, "an outlying Jewish settlement." [20] With the exception of some 2,000 Jews living within the walled city, they constituted a compact Jewish island in an Arab sea.

From November 29, 1947, through May 14, 1948, the contest for Jerusalem focused on gaining control over the Tel Aviv-Jerusalem road. While Palestinian Arabs managed to blockade the road to Jewish convoys during the early months of 1948, large Jewish convoys did reach the New City in April.[21]

During this period the Jews of Jerusalem occupied several Arab quarters of the New City, including Talbiya, Bakaa, and Katamon. They also occupied most of Sheikh Jarrah, a large Arab quarter ranging north of Herod's Gate. The Arabs, in turn, attacked the Jewish quarter within the walled city.[22]

From May 14 to 18 the situation within Jerusalem was critical for the Arab community.[23] The Arabs already had been driven out of most of the New City. On May 14 and 15 Israeli forces occupied the Musrara quarter, a major Arab residential area north of the walled city. In the next two days the Arabs held little more than the walled city. On May 18 Trans-Jordan's Arab Legion entered the Jerusalem area, recapturing Sheikh Jarrah and reinforcing Arab irregulars within the walled city. On May 28, the Jewish quarter in the walled city surrendered to the Arabs.

The Legion also took over Lydda, Ramleh, and Latrun, thereby sealing off the road between Jerusalem and Tel Aviv. The Jews of the New City were then under siege. They retained their position, however, while Israeli forces from the coast succeeded in constructing a road to the New City that by-passed the Latrun Salient. This road was completed on June 9. On the following day the first truce went into effect. Resumption of hostilities in July and October threatened to alter the military situation in Jerusalem, but no major advances were made by either side. It was not until November 30, 1948, that a cease-fire in the Jerusalem area was reached. It was this cease-fire agreement that provided for regular convoy service to the Israeli enclave on Mount Scopus, behind the Arab-Israeli truce line in Jerusalem.

---

18. Doc. A/364, p. 11.

19. United Nations, Special Report of the Trusteeship Council, *Question of an International Regime for the Jerusalem Area and Protection of the Holy Places,* GAPR (v) Suppl. 9 Doc. A/1286, p. 17.

20. Rufus Learsi (Israel Goldberg), *Fulfillment: The Epic Story of Zionism* (N.Y.: World Publishing Company, 1951), p. 368.

21. *Ibid.,* p. 369; Ben Gurion, *op. cit.,* pp. 291-92.

22. Millar Burrows, *Palestine Is Our Business* (Philadelphia: Westminster Press, 1945), p. 107.

23. Exactly who was "holding out" against whom in Jerusalem at this time varies with the source cited. Two polar views on this period are Learsi, *op. cit.,* pp. 366-97, and Munib Al-Mahdi and Suleiman Musa, *Tarikh Al'Urdan fi Al-Qaran Al Ashrin* (Amman: Jamiya Al-Hakud, 1959), pp. 491 ff.

Peace Efforts at the United Nations

Even before the British mandate ended, violence and anarchy prevailing in Palestine led the United Nations to take steps to stop, or at least control, the Arab-Jewish conflict in that country. In February, March, and April the Security Council called several times for a truce in Palestine.[24] On April 23, the Security Council established a Palestine Truce Commission consisting of the Security Council members' consular officers in Jerusalem.[25] Three days later, the General Assembly passed a "Resolution for the Protection of the City of Jerusalem and Its Inhabitants" calling upon "the Trusteeship Council to study, with the Mandatory Power and the interested parties, suitable measures for the protection of the city and its inhabitants, and to submit within the shortest possible time proposals to the General Assembly to that effect." [26]

On May 14, with partition now being a product of warfare, the General Assembly adopted a resolution providing for a U.N. Mediator for Palestine.[27] Count Folke Bernadotte assumed this post May 20.

On September 16, just before he was assassinated, Count Bernadotte submitted a progress report on his work in Palestine.[28] The Mediator reported that "the City of Jerusalem, because of its religious and international significance and the complexity of interests involved, should be accorded special and separate treatment," and that, in view of this, Jerusalem should "be placed under effective United Nations control with maximum feasible local autonomy for its Arab and Jewish communities, with full safeguards for the protection of the Holy Places and sites and free access to them, and for religious freedom."

While Bernadotte was filing his report, Israel was moving toward making the part of Jerusalem under its control an integral part of the new Jewish state. In September the Israeli Supreme Court was established in the New City. A few months later, in February, 1949, the first meeting of the Israeli Knesset (parliament) convened in the New City and in that same month the first president of Israel, Dr. Chaim Weizmann, took his oath of office in Israeli Jerusalem. On January 23, 1950, the Knesset proclaimed Jerusalem (i.e., Israeli-held, or West Jerusalem) the capital of Israel. In the following year virtually all Israeli ministries were moved to West Jerusalem.

East Jerusalem, or that part of the city under military control of the Arab Legion, eventually was absorbed by Trans-Jordan, although the complexities and political machinations of inter-Arab politics delayed any move in this direction until late 1950. Even before the British withdrew from Palestine, it was tacitly understood by London that King Abdullah of Trans-Jordan would bring the Arab state proposed by the partition resolution under his wing.[29] In early 1948 negotiations were held on a new Anglo-Jordanian treaty and this assumption was necessary in order to spell out the precise juridical obligations Great Britain

24. United Nations Security Council, *Official Records* (III), pp. 295 ff.
25. United Nations Doc. S/727, dated April 23, 1948.
26. United Nations Doc. A/543, dated April 26, 1948.
27. United Nations General Assembly Resolution 187 (5-2).
28. United Nations General Assembly Official Records (III) suppl. 11. *Progress Report of the U.N. Mediator on Palestine.*
29. Benjamin Shwadran, *Jordan: A State of Tension* (New York: Council for Middle Eastern Affairs Press, 1959), p. 245.

would assume under a new treaty. To prevent either a Jewish occupation of Arab Palestine, or the rise of the Mufti of Jerusalem, Haj Amin al Husseini, as ruler over the proposed Arab state, Great Britain supported the idea of Arab Legion occupation of those areas contiguous to Trans-Jordan which had been allotted to the Arabs by the partition resolution. The British Foreign Secretary's only admonition in this regard was "do not go and invade the areas allotted to the Jews." [30] Since any discussion of formal annexation of the West Bank area occupied by Jordan during 1948 generated violent protest in other Arab states, King Abdullah moved slowly and cautiously in this direction. The Higher Arab Committee's proclamation of Palestine's independence on October 1, 1948, must be viewed as an attempt to block Trans-Jordanian annexation schemes, as much as a reaffirmation of opposition to the new Israeli state. [31] By the end of 1948, however, it was apparent that neither the rise of Israel as an independent state, nor Abdullah's annexation of the West Bank, could be reversed by the other Arab states.

In fact, the Bernadotte plan, although never adopted, did accord Trans-Jordan some juridical support for annexation by recommending that Arab Palestine be united with Trans-Jordan. [32]

In any case, Abdullah proceeded to alter his juridical position in the West Bank, including East Jerusalem. On October 1, 1948, the same day that the Higher Arab Committee was proclaiming the independence of Palestine from the Gaza Strip, [33] some 5,000 Palestinian notables met in Amman. They repudiated the Gaza proclamation and called on King Abdullah to take the West Bank under his protection. [34]

On December 1, 1948, a second meeting of this "Palestine Congress" was convened in Jericho. At this congress Abdullah was proclaimed "King of Trans-Jordan and All Palestine." [35] The Jericho Congress proclamation was subsequently approved by the Trans-Jordanian government. In April, 1949, Great Britain, with reservations over the future status of Jerusalem, approved the annexation more. [36] Formal annexation of the West Bank region, however, did not take place until December 30, 1949, [37] although military rule over the occupied areas of Arab Palestine included in the annexation scheme was ended March 17, 1949, and civil rule established.

While Abdullah was maneuvering to annex the West Bank, he also signed, on April 3, 1949, a General Armistice Agreement with Israel. [38] Under this armistice agreement, the demarcation line in Jerusalem was set as that defined by the November 30, 1948, cease-fire agreement (Article V 1 (b) of Armistice Agreement).

30. *Ibid.,* p. 246.
31. See *supra* n. 13.
32. But Jerusalem would still be given "separate treatment." See above p. 6.
33. See *supra* n. 13.
34. Shwadran, *op. cit.,* p. 280.
35. Esmond Wright, "Abdullah's Jordan: 1947-1951," *Middle East Journal,* V (Autumn, 1951), p. 456; *New York Times,* December 14, 1948.
36. *Ibid.,* p. 457.
37. *New York Times,* December 31, 1949.
38. U.N. Security Council. *Official Records,* special suppl. No. 1. U.N. Doc. S/1302/Rw. 1., dated April 3, 1949. One of the signatories was an Israeli Lt. Colonel by the name of Moshe Dayan.

The armistice also called for "free access to the Holy Places and the use of the cemetery on the Mount of Olives" (Article VIII 2). Under this armistice, it was also agreed (Annex II) that neither side would keep more than two battalions of infantry in the Jerusalem sector and no armored vehicles of any type would be allowed there.

Further Moves to Internationalize Jerusalem

While Jordan and Israel were taking steps to formalize their respective control over East and West Jerusalem, the United Nations continued to discuss the internationalization of the holy city. On December 11, 1948, the General Assembly asked the Palestine Conciliation Commission to present "detailed proposals for a permanent international regime for the Jerusalem area." [39] In the same resolution (194) the General Assembly again affirmed its position that the Holy Places "be under effective United Nations supervision."

The Commission under these instructions established a special Committee on Jerusalem and its Holy Places.[40] The Committee on Jerusalem considered acceptance by Israel and the several Arab states a prerequisite to formulating any proposal for the internationalization of the holy city. The government of Israel, however, "declared itself unable to accept the establishment of an international regime for the city of Jerusalem" but it was prepared to accept "without reservation an international regime for, or the international control of, the Holy Places in the City." [41] Almost all these places were under Jordanian control. Israel apparently was not prepared to give up the New City, but was ready to support an international regime over the Holy Places that were in Jordan.

The several Arab states, excepting Jordan, then reversed their previous opposition to internationalization and indicated to the Commission their support of such a plan. They too were generous in ceding what they did not control. In October, 1949, the Arab League Council even adopted a resolution in favor of internationalization of Jerusalem.[42] In the wake of this shift in Arab policy (again excepting Jordan), coupled with growing world support for internationalization of Jerusalem, Israel and Jordan found themselves strange allies in resisting territorial internationalization. Jordan stood alone in resisting a strictly functional internationalization of the Holy Places.

On September 1, 1949, the Commission approved a new arrangement for Jerusalem.[43] Under this plan Jerusalem would be divided into an Arab and a Jewish zone, each independent except in international matters, which would be under the jurisdiction of the United Nations Commissioner.

The U.N. Commissioner would have authority over the Holy Places, and would supervise the permanent demilitarization of Jerusalem. There would be

39. U.N. General Assembly, *Official Records (III)* pt. 2. U.N. Doc. A/810, dated December 11, 1948.

40. U.N. General Assembly, *Official Records (V) Suppl. 18*. U.N. Doc. A/1367/Rw. 1, p. 10.

41. *Loc. cit.*

42. Shwadran, *op. cit.*, p. 286.

43. U.N. General Assembly, *Official Records, Ad Hoc Political Committee Annex*, Vol. I. U.N. Doc. A/973.

a General Council composed of both Arab and Jewish representatives, and a mixed international tribunal to handle cases involving both Jews and Arabs.

In effect, this plan accepted the partition of Jerusalem as a *fait accompli* and restricted itself primarily to the internationalization of the Holy Places. As one writer has noted, this plan, which was submitted to the General Assembly in the fall of 1949, was "pigeonholed without even being accorded the honor of a debate." [44] Instead, the General Assembly passed resolution 303 (IV) charging the Trusteeship Council to revise its earlier Statute for Jerusalem and implement it immediately.[45] The Assembly emphatically instructed the Trusteeship Council not to "allow any actions taken by any interested Government or Governments to divert it from adopting and implementing the Statute of Jerusalem." [46] How this was to be done without coercive power was not indicated in the resolution.

At the same time, the General Assembly again affirmed its intention to establish an international regime for Jerusalem as a *corpus separatum*, rather than in the modified form proposed by the Committee on Jerusalem.

The Trusteeship Council, in response to the Assembly's instructions, convened in special session from December 8 to 20, 1949. It expressed concern that Israel's transfer of governmental ministries to West Jerusalem was "likely to render more difficult the implementation of the Statute" and requested Israel to "revoke the measures which it had taken." [47] Israel, on the contrary, proclaimed West Jerusalem its capital on January 23, 1950. As Prime Minister David Ben-Gurion himself admitted, "our rebuttal (to resolution 303 and the Statute of Jerusalem) . . . was unequivocal and resolute: the Government and Knesset at once moved their seat to Jerusalem." [48] Israel had made it clear from the start that she would resist any plan of territorial internationalization that would involve West Jerusalem, although "willing to accept the principle of direct United Nations responsibility for the Holy Places," which, as noted above, were virtually all in East Jerusalem. Jordan, for its part, "would not discuss any plan for the internationalization of Jerusalem." [49]

Roger Garreau, then President of the Trusteeship Council, sought to reach a compromise solution to the Jerusalem question by broadly interpreting that part of resolution 303 (IV) of December 9, 1949, allowing the Council to modify the Statute for Jerusalem drafted in 1948. Mr. Garreau's plan would have divided Jerusalem into three parts: an Israeli zone "under the authority and administration of the State of Israel"; a Jordanian zone "under the authority and administration of the Hashimite Kingdom of the Jordan"; and an "International City" under the collective sovereignty of the United Nations. Under this plan West Jerusalem would remain under the sovereignty of Israel. The International City would include all the Holy Places covered by the status quo of 1757, meaning,

44. P. De Azcarate, as cited in S. Shepard Jones, "The Status of Jerusalem: Some National and International Aspects," *Law and Contemporary Problems*, XXXIII (Winter, 1968), p. 179.

45. U.N. General Assembly, *Official Records V Suppl 4.* Doc. A/1306, dated December 7, 1949.

46. *Ibid.*, part I 2.

47. U.N. General Assembly, *Official Records, Suppl. 9. Question of an International Regime for the Jerusalem Area and Protection of the Holy Places.* Doc. A/1286, p. 1.

48. *Op. cit.*, p. 362.

49. Doc. A/1286, p. 2.

in effect, the walled city, minus the Haram esh-Sharif. The governor of the International City would exercise authority over Holy Places in any part of Palestine, in addition to governing the international zone.[50]

The plan of the Trusteeship Council's president, as so many others presented earlier, was rejected without further ado.

One year later the General Assembly tabled discussion of the Trusteeship Council's Statute of 1948, as amended, and, instead, took under consideration two draft resolutions. The first, submitted by Belgium, would have had the United Nations, "considering that, for lack of the necessary cooperation by the States concerned, the Trusteeship Council has been unable to give effect to the Statute (of Jerusalem)," set up a study group to investigate "the conditions of a settlement capable of ensuring the effective protection, under the supervision of the United Nations, of the Holy Places and of spiritual and religious interests in the Holy Land." [51] An alternative resolution, sponsored by Sweden, would have established a "United Nations Representative to represent the interests of the United Nations in the Holy City." [52] The Belgian draft resolution did not pass when submitted to a vote of the General Assembly December 15, 1950, while the Swedish Draft resolution never came up for a vote. For the next 17 years, the question of Jerusalem lay dormant, only to erupt again after June, 1967.

---

50. *Ibid.,* pp. 3-4.
51. U.N. Ad Hoc Political Committee Doc. A/AC 38/SR 73, dated December 7, 1950.
52. U.N. Ad Hoc Political Committee Doc. A/AC 38/L 73 Rw. 2, dated December 13, 1950.

IV. THE CONTINUING CRISIS

The *de facto* partition of Jerusalem lasted 19 years. The line of partition, al-though technically only a cease-fire line, was one solution to a complex political, economic, and sociological problem—it divided two peoples who never did con-stitute a single community. During the 19 years that Jerusalem was partitioned, the factors which divided these peoples initially became even more pronounced. No common municipal charter could bridge the cultural, economic, and ideological gap between the Israeli of West Jerusalem and the Arab of East Jerusalem.

Earlier this had not been so. For centuries, the Jew could coexist with his Muslim and Christian neighbors in Jerusalem because all three subscribed to the life styles of a single culture.[1] But the West Jerusalem of the twentieth century was made up largely of European Jews, whose culture was totally different from the Jerusalem Jew of yesteryear. The formalism of East Jerusalem culture con-trasted sharply with the exaggerated informalism of West Jerusalem culture. In East Jerusalem political, economic, and social relationships were marked by face-to-face relationships that seldom suggested the impersonalism of Western culture. The daily behavior of the Israeli, despite the egalitarianism, by com-parison reflected more of the bureaucratic style of the West. Whether it was a matter of selecting a bride or conducting a business transaction, East and West Jerusalem have not been culturally a single community since the Western, or Ashkenazi, Jew made his culture the dominant culture of Israel. The modernized Arab adhered to a version of Western culture that was not shared by the Israeli.

The partition of Jerusalem also reflected the diverse economic orientations of these two communities, West and East Jerusalem. The latter, linked to the agri-cultural communities of the West Bank, remained a typical Middle Eastern market town. Only that part of the economy associated with servicing the Holy Places distinguished East Jerusalem from dozens of similar market towns in the Middle East.

However, East Jerusalem remained the nexus linking the northern and southern parts of the West Bank. The commercial, communications, and transportation links of these two areas focused on East Jerusalem. In fact, Jerusalem remained

---

1. In fact, the Jew was even closer to the Muslim than was the Christian in that the Jew frequently secluded women, accepted polygamy, etc. Cf. Raphael Patai, *Golden River to Golden Road* (Philadelphia: University of Pennsylvania Press, 1962), *passim*.

at the apex of highways leading north to Ramallah, south to Hebron, and east to Jericho. Thus, East Jerusalem was a vital part of the economic structure of the West Bank, as was the West Bank to the economy of Jordan, itself. East Jerusalem, the district of Nablus, the district of Hebron, and Jordan east of the Jordan River constituted before 1967 an integrated economic unit.

By contrast, West Jerusalem was not in ecological relationship with its hinterland. It became an urban complex located without regard to ordinary economic facts of life. From the functional point of view, West Jerusalem could have been located in Galilee, the Negev, or as a suburb of Haifa. West Jerusalem was an extension of Israel into the Judean Hills, just as Israel had become an extension into the Holy Land of Diaspora Jewry. The administrative offices of the government of Israel, the Hebrew University,[2] or the various administrative branches of world Jewry were located in West Jerusalem by choice, not economic imperative.

Ideologically, the gap between West and East Jerusalem appeared irreconcilable. The Arab of East Jerusalem was precisely that—an Arab. His entire identity was derived from his "Arabism." The *umma al-arabiyyah,* or community of the Arabs, was his national referent. No matter how virulent may have been the character of inter-Arab squabbles, Arab nationalism was the source to which Arabs, whether in Amman, Beirut, or East Jerusalem, had to turn for a "definition of the situation." To the Arab of East Jerusalem, as to Arabs elsewhere, Israel was the expression of Zionism in the Middle East. The aims of Zionism were not compatible with the aims of Arab nationalism. For 19 years the Arab of East Jerusalem lived within the Arab world, not only geographically, but culturally and practically as well.

The Zionist Jew of West Jerusalem, on the other hand, was a part of a political movement that was more than just Israel; it was a movement that was in constant and significant relationship with all of world Jewry. The Jew of West Jerusalem looked westward; the Arab of East Jerusalem looked to the other parts of the Arab world. Ideologically, West and East Jerusalem stood back-to-back. The line of partition did not divide Jerusalem; it only affirmed a division that had characterized the holy city for half a century. It is against this backdrop that the events subsequent to June, 1967, must be viewed.

The Capture of East Jerusalem

Early on the morning of June 5, 1967, full-scale war broke out between Israel and four of her Arab neighbors, Egypt (i.e., the UAR), Jordan, Syria, and Iraq.[3] The Israelis' first move in the conflict was to mount air strikes against 18 Egyptian air bases. Within minutes of the Israeli attack on Egypt, Jordan's jets were attacking Israel. It had been hoped in West Jerusalem that King Hussein would limit his participation in this war to symbolic air and artillery attacks, which

---

2. The Hebrew University is a case in point. Originally located on Mt. Scopus, the campus was moved to Givat Ram in West Jerusalem following the Arab-Israeli war in 1948. The 12,000 students enrolled at the Hebrew University came from 50 different countries. The Honorary President of the American Friends of the Hebrew University is Arthur J. Goldberg, U.S. delegate to the Security Council when the critical debates on Israeli occupation of East Jerusalem were taking place, 1967-68. The Chairman of the Advisory Board is Senator Jacob K. Javits of New York.

3. Iraqi troops operated from Jordan.

could have been pictured as fulfilling his obligations to Nasser under the terms of the May 30 UAR-Jordan military alliance.[4]

In fact, Israel communicated with King Hussein through Lt. General Odd Bull, head of the U.N. Truce Supervision Organization on the morning the war started, promising not to attack Jordan if that country would stay out of the combat. This Jordan did not do and hostilities began at 10:30 a.m. all along the partition line separating West and East Jerusalem. The point to be stressed here is that Israel appeared prepared to leave East Jerusalem in the hands of Jordan as late as June 6, 1967. It was only *after* the capture of East Jerusalem that the ancient city assumed, retroactively, the status of *terra irredenta* for Israel.

The 1967 battle for Jerusalem lasted almost three days. According to Israeli military sources, the Jordanians fought tenaciously to hold East Jerusalem and Israeli forces succeeded in capturing this area only after suffering comparatively heavy casualties.[5] However, by June 7 East Jerusalem was firmly in the hands of the Israeli army. On that afternoon General Moshe Dayan and other Israeli military leaders passed through St. Stephen's Gate of the walled city and proceeded directly to the Wailing Wall where, as noted earlier, General Dayan and his party stopped to pray.[6]

Before leaving the Wailing Wall, General Dayan made a public statement marking him as the first Israeli leader to reopen the problem of Jerusalem. The General declared:

> The Israeli Defense Forces liberated Jerusalem. We have reunited the torn city, the capital of Israel. We have returned to this most sacred shrine, *never to part from it again.* (Emphasis added.)[7]

The Annexation of the Jordanian Sector

On the day the Jordanian sector of Jerusalem was brought under Israeli military control, Mayor Teddy Kollek of West Jerusalem put forward a plan to extend Israeli municipal services to the captured sector.[8]

On the following day, the Jerusalem Municipal Council (Israel) approved a $5,000,000 Jerusalem Fund for the restoration of the Wailing Wall and other religious sites in the Jordanian sector. Approval was also given by the Council that day for expansion of the Jerusalem Master Plan to include East Jerusalem. The water system of West Jerusalem was connected with that of East Jerusalem, also on June 8. Then quickly the Israelis united the sanitation, telephone, and electrical systems of the two sectors. The municipal bus service (Egged) extended its routes into East Jerusalem, street signs in both Arabic and Hebrew

---

4. Statement by Aluf (Brigadier General) Uzzi Narkis, Commander, Central Command at a press conference, Tel Aviv, June 13, 1967 in *Central Front,* Israeli Defense Force Spokesman's Office, July, 1967, P/R 111A.

5. See particularly the account of the battle for East Jerusalem given by Aluf Mishne (Colonel) Mordechai Gur, Commander of the paratroops that took East Jerusalem in *ibid.,* P/R 102.

6. It is to be noted, however, that this event would have been much less significant had Jordan permitted Israelis access to the Wailing Wall during the previous 19 years.

7. *Facts on File,* XXVII, June 7, 1967.

8. *Jerusalem Post,* June 8, 1967.

were posted, and the barriers once separating East from West Jerusalem were removed. Extensive plans were also prepared during these first few days to modernize the street lighting, to re-pave the roads, and to design future parks for the Jordanian sector.[9]

The pace of political unification was equally swift. On June 15 the Israeli Cabinet was called into session to study a bill that would enable Israel to annex East Jerusalem. On June 27 the Knesset approved a series of enabling laws for the "fusion" of East and West Jerusalem. Under the basic law, the Law and Administration Ordinance (Amendment No. 11) Law of June 27, 1967, the law, jurisdiction, and administration of the State of Israel could be extended to any area designated by the Israeli government by order.[10] On the following day, June 28, 1967, Israeli law and administration was applied to an expanded East Jerusalem that included the walled city, Sur Bahir, Sheikh Harrah, Kalandia Airport, Mount Scopus, and the vicinity of Shufat[11] (see map).

The "unified" Jerusalem then embraced over 100 square kilometers and included a population of at least 260,000, some 70,000 of whom, according to Israel, were Arabs.[12] In 1967 East Jerusalem had a population of 70,000 and the reconstituted Jerusalem encompassed several other Jordanian villages near Jerusalem. Apparently from 20,000 to 30,000 Arabs had left the Jerusalem area for eastern Jordan.

The 70,000 Arabs who remained in East Jerusalem posed an interesting problem for Israel. It was the Israeli Foreign Minister, Abba Eban, who had argued in 1950 that U.N. proposals for internationalizing Jerusalem, if implemented, would deprive 110,000 Jews of their right to belong to Israel and that, therefore, such action on the part of the U.N. would be morally incorrect, politically unwise, and a violation of U.N. principles.[13] This line of argument could also have been applied to the case of the 70,000 Arabs, who by Israeli action were deprived of their freedom to belong to the Arab community.

The actions taken by Israel with regard to East Jerusalem after its early annexation moves suggested that the problems of Arabs in East Jerusalem might only be viewed as a temporary situation by the Jewish state. Within a week after the capture of East Jerusalem by Israel some 100 homes near the Wailing Wall were razed.[14] A month later another 100 homes were destroyed in the same area.[15] Robert C. Toth of the *Washington Post* reported that according to local eyewitnesses several hundred Arab families were ousted from the Jewish Quarter in the early days after the capture of East Jerusalem. He wrote that there were "busses and trucks at the Damascus Gate waiting to take the displaced Arabs

---

9. U.N. Security Council, *Official Records, Supplement for July, August, and September, 1967.* Doc. S/8146.

10. *Ibid.*

11. *Ibid.*

12. *Ibid.*

13. Delegation of Israel to the United Nations, *Memorandum on the Question of Jerusalem Submitted to the Trusteeship Council of the United Nations,* Seventh Session, Lake Success, May, 1950.

14. *New York Times,* June 19, 1967.

15. *New Outlook* (Israel) September, 1968, p. 39.

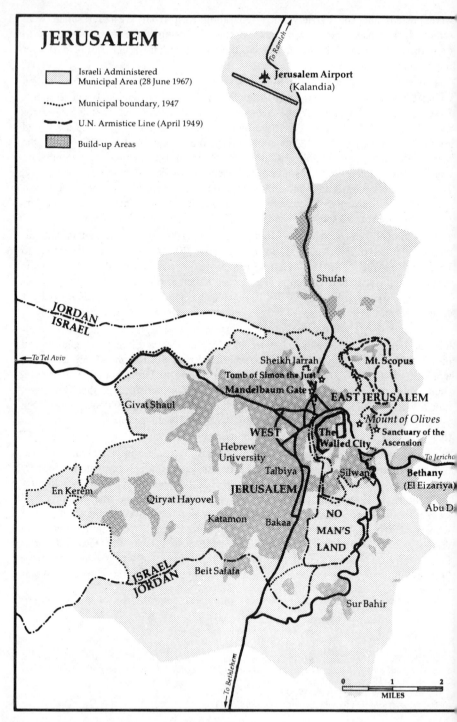

JERUSALEM

Israeli Administered
Municipal Area (28 June 1967)

Municipal boundary, 1947

U.N. Armistice Line (April 1949)

Build-up Areas

To Ramleh

Jerusalem Airport
(Kalandia)

Shufat

JORDAN
ISRAEL

To Tel Aviv

Sheikh Jarrah
Tomb of Simon the Just
Mandelbaum Gate

Mt. Scopus

EAST JERUSALEM

Givat Shaul

WEST

Hebrew
University

Talbiya

JERUSALEM

The
Walled City

Mount of Olives
Sanctuary of the
Ascension

To Jericho

Silwan   Bethany
(El Eizariya)

En Kerem

Qiryat Hayovel

Katamon   Bakaa

Abu D

NO
MAN'S
LAND

ISRAEL
JORDAN   Beit Safafa

Sur Bahir

To Bethlehem

0   1   2

MILES

Jericho and beyond."[16] At the same time the *Jerusalem Post* was urging that Israelis move into the walled city.[17]

Since June, 1967, Israel has sequestered large sections of East Jerusalem, dynamited and razed scores of Arab homes, and "encouraged" the departure from Jerusalem of their inhabitants.[18] On November 23, 1967, the Israeli National Police confiscated the unfinished Muslim hospital on the Mount of Olives to use as their new headquarters, despite vigorous protests from the Muslim Council of East Jerusalem.[19] In January, 1968, the Israeli government expropriated some 838 acres of East Jerusalem to be used for Jewish settlers.[20] And in June, 1968, the expropriation by Israel of land and buildings within the walled city between the Haram esh-Sherif and the Armenian quarter, including part of the site of al-Buraq, resulted in a strong letter of protest by the government of Jordan to the U.N. Secretary-General. In this action, more than 700 buildings, about 50 acres of land, 437 shops, and 1,048 apartments housing more than 5,000 Arabs were taken over by Israel.[21] The Arabs of East Jerusalem were seriously disturbed that Israel might intend to alter the demographic character of East Jerusalem to make all Jerusalem a Jewish city.

Annexation—The U.N. Response

On June 13, 1967, the Soviet Union requested, under the provisions of Article 1 of the U.N. Charter, an emergency special session of the U.N. General Assembly to debate the Middle East crisis. Once again the question of Jerusalem was to come before the community of nations. This time the debate on the holy city was initiated by the USSR, the bastion of atheism and international communism.

The General Assembly convened on June 17, 1967, and, after extensive debate, approved resolution 2253 (ES-V) on July 4:

The General Assembly
Deeply Concerned at the situation prevailing in Jerusalem as a result of the measures taken by Israel to change the status of the City,
1. *Considers* that these measures are invalid;
2. *Calls upon* Israel to rescind all measures already taken and to desist forthwith from taking any action which would alter the status of Jerusalem;
3. *Requests* the Secretary-General to report to the General Assembly and the Security Council on the situation and on the implementation of the present resolution not later than one week from its adoption.[22]

16. *Washington Post,* June 20, 1967.
17. *Jerusalem Post,* June 19, 1967. See also the August 1, 1967, issue of this newspaper, wherein former Israeli prime minister Ben-Gurion argued that all of Jerusalem rehabilitate and settle as quickly as possible, with the resettling of 20,000 Jewish families in East Jerusalem, and the *New York Times* of June 18 and July 3, 1968, for a report on "settlement" plans to populate East Jerusalem with Israeli families.
18. See *New York Times,* January 16, 1968; March 8, 1968; September 19, 1968; *New Outlook II* (Israel) March-April, 1968; September, 1968.
19. *New York Times,* November 24, 1967.
20. *Ibid.,* January 16, 1968.
21. U.N. Doc. A/7107 (S/8634).
22. U.N. General Assembly, *Official Records, 5th Emer. Spec. Sess., Suppl. 1,* p. 4.

This resolution was adopted by a vote of 99 to 0 with 20 abstentions (including the United States).

Ten days later the General Assembly, "taking note with the deepest regret and concern of the non-compliance by Israel with resolution 2253," reiterated its call to Israel "to rescind all measures already taken and to desist forthwith from taking any action which would alter the status of Jerusalem." (Resolution 2254 (ES-V)).

These two resolutions (2253 and 2254) of the General Assembly reflected a widespread sentiment within the United Nations: territorial aggrandizement cannot be the product of conquest by force. Secretary-General U Thant, in discussing the operations of the United Nations during the period 1966-67, stated it this way:

> It is indispensable to an international community of states—if it is not to follow the law of the jungle—that the territorial integrity of every state be respected and the occupation of one state cannot be condoned.[23]

The territorial integrity of the State of Israel was recognized by the the United Nations when it became a member of that international organization. At the same time, the State of Israel accepted the territorial integrity of the other member states of the U.N. If the United Nations were to grant juridical validity to Israeli annexation of any Arab land, this would violate its charter.

The resolutions invalidating Israeli annexation of East Jerusalem evolved out of earlier proposals that Israel withdraw from *all* occupied areas. On June 28, 1967, a 17-power draft resolution was submitted by Yugoslavia calling upon Israel immediately to withdraw its forces behind the armistice lines established by the General Armistice Agreements.[24] This draft resolution, while it received a majority, failed to obtain the requisite two-thirds majority. In addition to Yugoslavia, this draft resolution was co-sponsored by Indonesia, Cambodia, Malaysia, India, Pakistan, Ceylon, Afghanistan, Cyprus, Somalia, Tanzania, Zambia, Congo (Brazzaville), Burundi, Mali, Guinea, and Senegal. These states, ranging from southeast Asia to West Africa, made up a significant part of the underdeveloped world, the so-called Third World.

Two days later, June 30, another draft resolution was submitted, this time by 20 other members of the Third World.[25] Formally presented by Trinidad and Tobago, the draft resolution was co-sponsored by Argentina, Barbados, Bolivia, Brazil, Chile, Colombia, Costa Rica, The Dominican Republic, Ecuador, El Salvador, Guatemala, Guyana, Honduras, Jamaica, Mexico, Nicaragua, Panama, Paraguay, and Venezuela—in brief, virtually all of Latin America. This draft resolution called upon Israel to "withdraw all its forces from all the territories occupied by it as a result of the recent conflict." This proposal, while it received a majority, also failed for lack of the requisite two-thirds majority.

If one combines the 37 states supporting these two resolutions, together with

---

23. U.N. General Assembly, *Official Records, Introduction to the Annual Report of the Secretary-General on the Work of the Organization,* June 16, 1966-June 15, 1967. Doc. A/6701/Add. 1, p. 6.

24. U.N. General Assembly, *Official Records, Suppl. 1, Annual Report of the Secretary-General on the Work of the Organization,* June 16, 1967-June 15, 1968. Doc. A/7201, p. 5.

25. *Loc. cit.*

the 14 Arab states, it becomes clear that the countries of the Third World are opposed to Israeli occupation of Arab territory. In terms of the Israeli occupation of East Jerusalem, the sentiment of the community of nations extended even beyond the Third World, because as noted above, resolution 2253 (ES-V) was adopted without dissenting vote.[26]

Even before the General Assembly convened its emergency special session, the Security Council had acted on the matter of Israeli occupation of Arab territory. On June 14, 1967, resolution 237 was adopted calling upon Israel to give scrupulous respect to the provisions of the Geneva Conventions of August 12, 1949, relative to the treatment of civilian persons in occupied areas. Although rejected by Israel, this resolution was "welcomed with great satisfaction by the General Assembly" (Resolution 2252 (ES-V), July 4, 1967).[27]

The Gussing Report

Under the provisions of the Security Council resolution, Mr. Nils-Göran Gussing was appointed on July 6 the Secretary-General's Special Representative in the Middle East. A few weeks later U Thant appointed Mr. Ernesto A. Thalmann of Switzerland as his Personal Representative in Jerusalem under the provisions of the General Assembly's resolutions 2253 and 2254. While Mr. Gussing did not include Jerusalem in his own report because of Mr. Thalmann's assignment, two aspects of the Gussing report bear upon the Jerusalem question.

First, the Special Representative noted that various kinds of pressure were exerted by Israel to get Arabs to leave their villages on the West Bank for unoccupied Jordan. While there was no evidence that physical force was used, in the words of the report, "there are persistent reports of acts of intimidation by Israel armed forces and of Israel attempts to suggest to the population, by loudspeakers mounted on cars, that they might be better off on the east bank." Moreover, continued the report, "there have also been reports that in several localities buses and trucks were put at the disposal of the population for travel to the east bank." [28]

Second, there was widespread destruction of homes in occupied Jordan. Much of this, of course, was the result of the war itself. However, a number of homes in several West Bank villages were destroyed by dynamite subsequent to the cease-fire. According to Israeli sources, the homes were destroyed by dynamite in the village of Qalqilya either because of "safety" or "sanitary" reasons. In the Latrun area the Israeli Minister of Defense told Gussing that the villages of Imwas, Yalu, and Beit Nuba were destroyed by dynamiting "for strategic and

---

26. Israel did not vote on this resolution on the grounds that the issue of Jerusalem was "outside the legal competence of the General Assembly," *New York Times*, July 5, 1967.

27. U.N. Security Council, Official Records, *Supplement for October, November, and December, 1967*, Doc. 3/8158, p. 81. Israel is also bound as a U.N. member by the obligations imposed under U.N. General Assembly resolutions 95(I) of December 11, 1946 which accepted as binding on the United Nations the Charter of Nuremburg, Article 6B of which proscribes looting and seizure of public property. See also U.N. General Assembly resolution 177(II) of November 21, 1947 and the Report of the International Law Commission to the General Assembly, dated December 12, 1950.

28. *Ibid.*, p. 92.

security reasons." In the Hebron area several Arab villages were similarl
destroyed or damaged by dynamite.[29]

Israel followed similar procedures in Jerusalem. The Gussing report thus is o
value here in giving emphasis to a pattern of occupation administration that botl
alarmed the Arab with respect to the holy city and stiffened his resistance t
making lasting peace with the Jewish state. The annexation of Jerusalem an
the occupation policy of Israel in other Arab territories were perceived togethe
by the Arab as evidence of Israeli expansionism. Israeli political leaders hav
on occasion advocated expansion of Israeli territory as a national goal.[30]

Thus, for example, in April, 1969, the former Israeli prime minister and on
of that state's founding fathers, David Ben-Gurion, presented his formula fo
Arab-Israeli peace in an interview with Eric Rouleau of the French paper L
Monde.[31] He first said that "in exchange for peace . . . I would return all th
territory conquered in June 1967." When asked if this would include Eas
Jerusalem, Ben-Gurion answered, "certainly not." Moreover, he added, "after m
recent visit to the region, I realize that we will also be obliged to keep the Gola
Heights for strict security reasons."

The Thalmann Report

The report submitted by Ambassador Thalmann on East Jerusalem noted th
changing landscape.[32] "To the destruction of the war" commented the Person
Representative, "new destruction had been added." Bulldozers had cleared th
walls which had separated the firing lines, as well as many houses in the are
of the former no man's land. Also in "the walled city one could see the debris c
levelled houses." This destruction of homes within the walled city included th
dynamiting and bulldozing of some 135 homes in the Maghrebi quarter and tw
mosques.[33] After noting the juridical and technical steps taken by Israel to "unify
East Jerusalem with West Jerusalem, Ambassador Thalmann records that:

> From the cultural standpoint, the fear was expressed that the Arab way
> of life, Arab traditions and the Arabic language would suffer permanent
> damage under the influence of the Israel majority. It was also pointed
> out in this connection that . . . the Israel community . . . might have an
> adverse effect on strict Arab morals.[34]

---

29. *Ibid.,* pp. 93-96.

30. In October, 1967, Israel renamed the occupied Nablus District of Jordan "Shomror
(Samaria) and the Hebron District "Yehuda" (Judea). See *Jerusalem Post,* October 2, 196
On February 29, 1968, Israel issued a decree to the effect that occupied Arab territories wer
no longer to be regarded as "enemy territory." The decree established customs and civilia
control points for official entry or exit from "Israel." Reference might also be given here t
the rather broad guidelines used by Israeli authorities in expelling the political leadership c
the Arab community from the occupied territories on the charge that they are guilty c
"inciting subversion." See here *New York Times,* August 1, 1967; and on Israel, refusal t
allow U.N. investigation of occupied areas in 1968, see U.N. Doc. S/8699, dated June 2
1968.

31. *Le Monde, Weekly Selection,* April 23, 1969, p. 4.

32. U.N. Security Council, *Official Records, Supplement for July, August, and Septembe
1967.* Doc. S/8146.

33. *Ibid.,* p. 250.

34. *Ibid.,* p. 252.

Also, Ambassador Thalmann said, Muslims were shocked when the "Chief
Rabbi of the Israeli Army, with others of his faith, conducted prayers in the
area of the Haram esh-Sharif." [35] Muslim sensitivity to the treatment of their holy
sites was also registered in their complaint to the Personal Representative that
Israel was allowing visitors, "men and women, to enter the al-Aqsa Mosque while
unsuitably dressed and in a manner which is inconsistent with religious belief
and Arab and Islamic traditions." [36]

The Thalmann report also noted that East Jerusalem, as reconstituted within
the expanded municipal area of unified Jerusalem, included almost 130,000 Arabs,
all of whom are currently governed by a Municipal Council, "which is composed
of twenty-one members all Israelis." [37]

Events of 1968 and 1969 confirmed the Thalmann report. The dynamiting and
the bulldozing continued; further legal and administrative steps were taken to
integrate East Jerusalem into the Jewish state; the Israelis continued to state
unequivocally that the process of integration [is] irreversible and not negotiable"; [38]
and the differences between Israeli and Arab remained implacable. As the Israeli
mayor of Jerusalem, Teddy Kollek, complained, in February, 1968, efforts to
integrate the two sectors of Jerusalem "had been a total failure" because Israel
had failed to recognize the cultural and psychological patterns of the Arabs and
that the Israeli government ". . . cannot automatically impose on [the Arabs]
the approach and procedures used in Tel Aviv." [39]

Israeli Foreign Minister Abba Eban continued to suggest that "where there
has been hostile separation there is now harmonious union" and "where there
has been constant threat of violence there is now civic peace." [40] But growing
Arab resistance to Israeli occupation expressed in individual and group attacks
on Israeli civilian and military targets (including a bomb explosion in a crowded
Israeli market in Jerusalem on November 22, 1968) was difficult to reconcile
with this claim.[41]

Security Council Resolution 242 (1967)

Although Israel moved rapidly to unify Jerusalem and refused to acknowledge
the General Assembly's resolutions on the holy city, the United Nations has
continued to express itself on the subject of Israeli occupation of any part of
the Arab territories. On July 14, 1967, the United States refused to accept or
recognize the steps taken by Israel on June 28 to alter the status of Jerusalem

35. *Ibid.,* p. 250.
36. *Ibid.,* p. 267.
37. *Ibid.,* p. 237.
38. *Ibid.,* p. 238.
39. As cited in *Facts on File,* XXVIII, p. 99.
40. Israeli Information Services, *Text of Mr. Eban's Letter to the U.N. Secretary-General on
the holding of a parade in Jerusalem . . . ,* dated May 1, 1968.
41. *New York Times,* November 23, 1968. Some examples of Arab resistance would include
the general strike in East Jerusalem protesting Israeli occupation (August, 1967), an East
Jerusalem school strike (September, 1967), Arab riots protesting the first anniversary of the
Israeli annexation move (June, 1968), a strike by shopkeepers in East Jerusalem (August,
1968), bomb explosions and riots in Jerusalem (August, 1968), a hunger strike by the Arab
women of East Jerusalem protesting the Israeli annexation (January, 1969), a bombing incident in a Jerusalem bus station (February, 1969), and a bomb explosion in a Jerusalem
cafeteria (March, 1969).

and took the position "that the measures taken cannot be considered as other than interim and provisional, and not as prejudicing the final and permanent status of Jerusalem." [42]

In accordance with this sentiment the United States, on November 7, 1967, submitted a draft resolution in the Security Council, Article 1 of which included as one provision of a "just and lasting peace in the Middle East" the "withdrawal of armed forces from occupied territories." Since the American draft resolution related this condition to the commitment of member states "tc act in accordance with Article 2 of the Charter," it must be assumed that "occupied territories" included East Jerusalem. [43]

At that same meeting, India also submitted a draft resolution, co-sponsored by Mali and Nigeria, calling for Israeli withdrawal from the occupied territories. The Indian resolution was cast in stronger language than the American proposal. [44]

Neither the American nor the Indian resolution was accepted. Instead, on November 22, 1967, the Security Council accepted a draft resolution submitted by the British representative to the Council, Lord Caradon. This resolution 242 (1967) was adopted unanimously by the Council. In view of the fact that the vast majority of members in the General Assembly not represented on the Security Council had favored even stronger resolutions, resolution 242 (1967) constitutes the near unanimous position of the international community on the Arab-Israeli problem. The resolution, in full, reads as follows:

> The Security Council,
>
> Expressing its continuing concern with the grave situation in the Middle East,
>
> Emphasizing the inadmissibility of the acquisition of territory by war and the need to work for a just and lasting peace in which every State in the area can live in security,
>
> Emphasizing further that all Member States in their acceptance of the Charter of the United Nations have undertaken a commitment to act in accordance with Article 2 of the Charter.
>
> 1. Affirms that the fulfillment of Charter principles requires the establishment of a just and lasting peace in the Middle East which should include the application of both the following principles:
>
> (i) Withdrawal of Israel armed forces from territories occupied in the recent conflict;
>
> (ii) Termination of all claims or states of belligerency and respect for and acknowledgement of the sovereignty, territorial integrity and political independence of every State in the area and their right to live in peace within secure and recognized boundaries free from threats or acts of force;
>
> 2. Affirms further the necessity
>
> (a) For guaranteeing freedom of navigation through international waterways in the area;
>
> (b) For achieving a just settlement of the refugee problem;

---

42. U.N. Doc. A/PV. 1554, dated July 14, 1967.
43. See supra, note 9, Doc. S/8229.
44. U.N. General Assembly, Official Records, 23rd Session, Suppl. 2, p. 19, Doc. A/7202.

(c) For guaranteeing the territorial inviolability and political independence of every State in the area, through measures including the establishment of demilitarized zones;

3. *Requests* the Secretary-General to designate a Special Representative to proceed to the Middle East to establish and maintain contacts with the States concerned in order to promote agreement and assist efforts to achieve a peaceful and accepted settlement in accordance with the provisions and principles in this resolution;

4. *Requests* the Secretary-General to report to the Security Council on the progress of the efforts of the Special Representative as soon as possible.[45]

The day after this resolution was adopted, Secretary-General U Thant dispatched Dr. Gunnar Jarring of Sweden to the Middle East as the U.N.'s Special Envoy. Further Security Council resolutions,[46] as well as Dr. Jarring's peripatetic diplomacy, however, produced little resu't up to 1969.

On May 2, 1968, Israel held a military parade in the holy city.[47] For a number of years both Israel and Jordan had conducted military parades in their respective sectors, although such parades violated Article VII of the Jordanian-Israeli General Armistice Agreement of April 3, 1949. This time, however, Israel paraded her forces through the Arab, as well as through her own sector. Israel explained its decision to route this parade into the Jordanian sector with three points: (1) Jerusalem had become a unified city, (2) The General Armistice Agreement "was finally destroyed by Jordan on June 5, 1967," and (3) within the cease-fire area established after the June, 1967, war, the Israelis "are free to move, to act and to parade as they see fit." [48] Therefore the parade was held as planned, in the face of a specific request made by the Security Council of the United Nations in April, 1968, that Israel not route any military parade through the Arab sector of Jerusalem.[49]

The United Nations has been demonstrably unable to induce Israel to halt her annexation of East Jerusalem.

The United Nations' failure in this respect was ascribed by some observers to the absence of wholehearted support by the United States. In fact, Washington's policies toward Jerusalem was viewed by some critics as incompatible with its sponsorship of the principle of military withdrawal contained in the November, 1967, United Nations Resolution and as lacking sincerity and consistency.

---

45. See *supra*, note 6, Doc. S/8247.

46. Particularly U.N. Security Council resolution 252 (1968) of May 21, 1968, which "deplores the failure of Israel to comply" with G.A. resolutions 2253 (ES-V) and 2254 (ES-V) of July, 1967, Council resolution 258 (1968) of September 18, 1968, which "reaffirms" the position of the Council as expressed in resolution 242 (1967) of November 22, 1967, and Council resolution 259 (1968) of September 28, 1968, which "deplores the delay in the implementation" of resolution 237 (1967) of June 14, 1967, which called upon Israel to ensure the safety, welfare, and security of the inhabitants of the occupied areas. Resolution 252 (1968) was submitted by Pakistan and Senegal. The only two countries opposed to the resolution were Canada and the United States. *Cahiers de l'Orient Contemporain,* LXXII (October, 1968), p. 43.

47. *New York Times,* May 3, 1968.

48. Yosef Tekoah (Israeli Ambassador to the United Nations), *Barbed Wire Shall Not Return to Jerusalem* (N.Y.: Israel Information Services, n.d.), p. 42.

49. *New York Times,* April 28, 1968.

Care of the Holy Places

The Israelis have complained that Jewish cemeteries in East Jerusalem were desecrated, torn up, or destroyed. The Arabs, both Christians and Muslims, counter that the Holy Places at Ein Karim and the cemetery of Mamillah were subjected to similar desecration at the hands of the Israelis.

The Israelis also complain that they were denied access to the Wailing Wall for 19 years. While this grievance is based on fact and cannot be dismissed in considering alternatives for solution, it should be pointed out that the Wailing Wall was a casualty of a chain of events which began with the proclamation of the State of Israel and culminated, via the subsequent Arab-Jewish war of 1948, in the division of the city of Jerusalem, a division to which both parties have contributed through their military actions and their refusal to accept internationalization. On the other hand, under the post-1967 conditions, Muslim Arabs from the several Arab states have been denied access to their principal holy place, the Harem est-Sherif, which had been open to their pilgrimage and worship under Jordanian sovereignty. Similarly, with the present occupation of Jerusalem by Israel, Christian Arabs from most of the Arab countries have lost access to the Holy Sepulchure and other Christian shrines.

The Israelis contended that a slum area was permitted to grow adjacent to the Wailing Wall. The Arabs argued that the inhabitants of this area were Arab refugees from the Israeli section of Palestine and that, in any case, ousting poor Arab families and razing their homes would have been a dubious application of slum clearance.

The Israelis said that they would repair, restore, and maintain the Holy Places of all three faiths, as they did with the Wailing Wall. The Christian Arab, however, complained that reports of smoking, loud talk, improper dress, and dogs in the Church of the Holy Sepulchre were not compatible with the sacred character of this site; and the Muslim Arab complained that mini-skirts, embraces between the sexes, and holding a fashion show against the background of al-Aqsa Mosque were not in keeping with the character of their Holy Place.

Muslims safeguarded and respected the Holy Places of Christianity in Palestine for centuries without complaint. The controversy over the custodianship of the Holy Places centered, then, on the conflicting claims made by Israelis and Muslim Arabs on behalf of their respective religious supporters. As for the Christian community, one may note two alternate positions relative to the Holy Places.

The first position was that emanating from the Vatican: Jerusalem should be internationalized.[50] Since June 7, 1967, the Pope has continued to press for internationalization of the holy city. On June 26, 1967, Pope Paul contended "the holy city of Jerusalem must always remain that which it represents—the city of God, a free oasis of peace and prayer, a place of encounter, of elevation, of accord for all, with its own international status guaranteed." [51] In brief, the

---

50. The Vatican's position has been consistent since 1948, particularly as outlined in the encyclical letter (*In Multiplicibus*) of October 23 of that year. See *New York Times,* January 20, 1949.

51. As quoted in *Facts on File,* XXVII, June 29, 1967. See also the Pope's proposal for internationalizing Jerusalem, *New York Times,* June 19, 1967.

Vatican would like to see Jerusalem established as a *corpus separatum*, as originally envisaged under the 1947 U.N. partition resolution.

The second position was that advanced by the National Council of Churches. The Executive Committee of that organization adopted a resolution on July 7, 1967, which read, in part,

> We support the establishment of an international presence in the hitherto divided city of Jerusalem which will preserve the peace and integrity of the city, foster the welfare of its inhabitants, and protect its holy shrines with full rights of access to all. We encourage the earliest possible advancement of U.N. proposals to make such. arrangement practicable.
>
> We cannot approve Israel's unilateral annexation of the Jordanian portions of Jerusalem. This historic city is sacred not only to Judaism but also to Christianity and Islam.[52]

Islamic conferences, whether held in Kuala Lumpur (Malaysia), Amman, or Mecca all voiced strong objections to the present status of East Jerusalem. The tone of the resolution on Jerusalem adopted by the World Muslim League at its October, 1967, meeting in Mecca was indicative of this attitude:

> The Muslims must realize that the problem of Jerusalem and the territory usurped in Palestine is a general Islamic problem, and a sacred problem, and that struggle (jihad) in the cause of God for the liberation of al-Masjid al-Aqsa and the occupied lands from the grasp of the aggressors is a sacred duty imposed upon all the Muslims, and not merely upon any one Muslim people.
>
> . . . no solution or settlement will be acceptable if it does not involve the restoration of Jerusalem to its previous status.[53]

The Muslims called for a return of East Jerusalem and the Holy Places located therein to Jordan; the National Council of Churches called for the return of East Jerusalem to Jordan and the establishment of an "international presence" in the holy city to "protect the holy shrines"; the Roman Catholic Church called for the internationalization of all Jerusalem. Most of the Jewish community around the world supported the proposition that Israel should be the custodian of the Holy Places of both Christianity and Islam.

But It's My House!

One theme recurrent in this study is that the inhabitants of Arab Jerusalem subscribe to a culture markedly different from that of West Jerusalem. This was apparent to casual visitors to the holy city. The culture of the Israelis reflected greater technological sophistication, organizational capacity, and know-how than the prevailing culture of the Arabs, Christian or Muslim. The culture of Arab

---

52. Although adopted July 7, 1967, and issued to the press, the resolution was not published in any newspaper within the greater New York area until it appeared one year later in the *New York Times,* January 14, 1968.

53. As quoted in *Islamic Review and Arab Affairs* (January, 1968), p. 11.

Jerusalem was not the culture of the Organization Man; it was the culture of a society steeped in tradition, spiritual in character.[54]

The impact of this Arab culture on East Jerusalem has been marked. East Jerusalem has been a city of open hospitality, rosary beads, and tranquility. The calls of the muezzin from the minaret of the Muslim mosque and the bells ringing out from the Christian church are constant reminders that East Jerusalem is a place of prayer. The social behavior of the East Jerusalem Arab expresses the timelessness of his culture, the depth of his religious feelings. Living conditions in East Jerusalem are almost Biblical; the life-style creates an atmosphere appropriate to the sacred character of the surrounding Holy Places.

All this was changing in 1969. Certain Arabs of East Jerusalem appeared to be better off in a material sense than they were two years before. Before 1967 East Jerusalem received water only three days a week; in 1969 fresh water was available daily.[55] The electrical system of the Jordanian sector was also being modernized and its capacity increased.[56] In short, the city was being modernized. To the Arab of East Jerusalem, however, this modernization was a shock. It meant not only better municipal services, health facilities, and public schools; it also meant neon lights, cabarets, Western music, and the end of a life-style he cherished.[57]

The development of East Jerusalem from 1967 to 1969 thus reflected a subordination of Arab culture to Israeli culture. The Arabs feared that this cultural interaction would lead to a decay in their moral standards. And after economic conditions in East Jerusalem were improved under Israeli tutelage,[58] the Arabs feared that they would be forced out. The Peel Report figuratively expressed the 1969 Arab attitude some 30 years earlier:

> You say we are better off: you say my house has been enriched by the strangers who have entered it. But it is *my* house, and I did not invite the strangers in, or ask them to enrich it, and I do not care how poor or bare it is if only I am master in it.[59]

---

54. A recent description of the contrast between West and East Jerusalem is presented in Ada L. Hustable's article "Jerusalem: Vista of Two Worlds," *New York Times,* May 12, 1969.

55. Israeli water lines were connected to the lines of East Jerusalem almost immediately after the sector was captured.

56. Suggestive of the pre-modern conditions prevailing in East Jerusalem prior to June, 1967 is the fact that the electrical plant capacity for this sector of the holy city was 3,000 KW. An American city of comparable size, Boulder, Colorado, has an electrical plant capacity of 120,000 KW.

57. One of the many examples of this culture change is the "modernization" of the 130-year-old Turkish Khan (rest house) located just outside the walled city. This old site was taken over by the Corporation for the Development of Eastern Jerusalem and made into a theater-cabaret, with most of the financing provided by Henry Gestetner of London. The site was formerly owned by the Greek Orthodox Church, *Jerusalem Post,* October 27, 1967.

58. It should be noted here, however, that the Arabs of East Jerusalem were enjoying a rate of economic growth even greater than Israel prior to June, 1967. Per capita agricultural production in Jordan, for example, reached an index of 193 (1957-59 = 100) just before the war, compared to only 146 for Israel. The overall rate of growth for Israel between 1958 and 1966 averaged 9.3 percent annually, while for Jordan it was almost 9.7 percent. Moreover, Israel has been the recipient since 1948 of almost $5,000,000,000 in outside financing, while capital inflow into Jordan was much more modest during this same period. George Lenczowski, ed., *United States Interests in the Middle East* (Washington: American Enterprise Institute, 1968), pp. 64 and 73.

59. Cmd. 5479 *Palestine Royal Commission Report,* July, 1937 (London: H.M.S.O., 1937), p. 131.

Others claim that, in time, no one will want to see Jerusalem divided again. Israeli Foreign Minister Abba Eban, in a press conference given September 6, 1967, mused:

> I think as more and more people come to compare the present unity of Jerusalem with its previous division, they will become convinced that the new unity is preferable to the old devision.[60]

These people, however, were not a majority in the United Nations, in the world Muslim community, or in the Christian churches, for they had resolved otherwise. The Arabs of East Jerusalem repeatedly protested the Israeli annexation of their sector and continued to resist this action.[61]

Former President Johnson remarked in a speech delivered on September 10, 1968, that "no one wishes to see the holy city again divided by barbed wire and by machine guns." [62] While the military methods of safeguarding the division might appear out of tune with the sacred character of the city, the principle of division itself has not been rejected as unanimously as Mr. Johnson tried to affirm. Invariably, that part of the population which is coerced by military means into subjection to an alien power would prefer the division to an enforced unity. This would seem to hold true of the Arab position in the post-1967 period; and it would undoubtedly apply to Israeli attitudes had the roles of victory and vanquished been reversed.

As a matter of historical record, it may be pointed out that Jerusalem is not the only place where division has been favored by the parties directly concerned over a wrong kind of unity. The United States and other Western powers have preferred partition of Germany, Korea, and Vietnam to their unification under Communist auspices. By the same token, for a quarter of a century Berlin has been a divided city; the Berlin airlift of 1948 proved the American determination to maintain the divided status quo rather than to accept unification under Soviet control.

Four-Power Talks

The question of Jerusalem is inextricably interwoven with the other issues of the Arab-Israeli conflict. This conflict has been a central feature of international relations for decades. Three times since Israel came into being full-scale war between the Jewish state and her Arab neighbors has taken place. Moreover, since June, 1967, there have been repeated violations of the cease-fire agreement by both sides; and the prospects for peace appeared less likely than a "fourth round" between Israel and the Arab states.

60. Consulate General of the State of Israel, Los Angeles, California, *Foreign Minister Abba Eban's Press Conference of September 6, 1967*, typescript, p. 16.
61. In August, 1967, Arabs staged a general strike in protest of Israeli occupation *(New York Times,* August 8, 1967); in September, 1967, there was a school strike in East Jerusalem *New York Times,* September 19, 1967); in January of 1968 Arab women went on a hunger strike protesting Israeli annexation of East Jerusalem (*New York Times,* January 28, 1968); in November, 1968, Arab merchants in East Jerusalem went on strike protesting Israeli seizure of Arab shops (*New York Times,* November 24, 1968), and throughout 1968 and 1969 Arabs resorted to intermittent violence to underscore their hostility to Israeli occupation of East Jerusalem.
62. For the text of this speech see Lenczowski, *op. cit.,* pp. 122-26.

Both the Arab states and Israel agree that the Security Council resolution of November 22, 1967, formed the basis for an eventual peace treaty. The Israelis insisted, however, that the implementation of this resolution and the establishment of a just and lasting peace be the product of direct negotiations between the Jewish state and the Arab states.[63] Pending such direct negotiations, the Israelis were not prepared to withdraw from the occupied territories. As the late Israeli premier, Levi Eshkol, put it "our reply [to the Arabs] is that we are here." [64] The Arabs in turn, insisted that Israel first withdraw from the occupied territories before further moves toward peace could take place. Although the basis of a peace treaty existed in the form of the November 22, 1967, resolution, dispute over the procedure for implementing this resolution brought about a stalemate; a stalemate fraught with danger, not only for the parties to the dispute, but for the Great Powers too.

It was this recognition that the Arab-Israeli dispute could be a tinderbox for a more widespread conflagration which led the United States, France, Great Britain, and the Soviet Union in early 1969 to begin negotiations among themselves on the Arab-Israeli dispute. The talks were not designed to obviate Dr. Jarring's efforts to bring peace in the Middle East, but only to strengthen his hand by providing a framework within the context of which the Security Council resolution might be implemented.[65] Even before the talks began, Israel rejected this approach to reaching peace in the Middle East on the grounds that anything the Soviet Union and France agreed to would be "inimical to Israel's vital interests." [66]

Despite this, the talks between the four Great Powers opened on April 2, 1969. While the details of these talks are outside the scope of this study, certain developments concerning the city of Jerusalem are worth mentioning: At the beginning of the talks it was reported that the United States "indicated support for continued unification of the city, but with a statute providing Jordan with religious, economic and civic interests." [67] The American position, according to Ambassador Charles W. Yost, United States delegate to these talks, was that Israel should withdraw "to secure and recognized boundaries in the context of a peace settlement achieved by negotiation," with the implication that such "secure and recognized boundaries" need not be those existing prior to June 5, 1967.[68]

The general position of the United States toward the Arab-Israeli conflict has been stated on several occasions since 1967. On May 23, 1967, former President Johnson declared that "the United States is firmly committed to the support of the

---

63. On September 18, 1967, Israel rejected "foreign guarantees" of her security and reiterated her position that peace could only come about through direct negotiations with the Arab states. *Washington Post,* September 9, 1967. Israel has held to this demand for direct negotiations ever since.

64. *New York Times,* September 7, 1967.

65. *Ibid.,* April 1, 1969.

66. *Ibid.,* April 4, 1969, citing Yosef Tekoah, Israeli Ambassador to the United Nations See also *New York Times,* April 1, 1969.

67. *New York Times,* April 3, 1969.

68. *Ibid.,* May 7, 1967.

political independence and territorial integrity of all nations of [the Middle East]." [69] The former President affirmed this position on June 19, 1967 (after the six-day war had ended) by saying "the crisis underlines the importance of respect for political independence and territorial integrity of all the states of the area." [70]

The American position in this regard was reaffirmed again on November 22, 1967, when the United States supported the Security Council resolution "*emphasizing* the inadmissibility of the acquisition of territory by war" and calling for the "withdrawal of Israeli armed forces from the territories occupied in the recent conflict." [71]

On September 10, 1968, addressing a Jewish audience in the United States, President Johnson stated with reference to the Arab-Israeli conflict that "boundaries cannot and should not reflect the weight of conquest." A few weeks later he repeated the American position that "the political independence and territorial integrity of all the states in the area must be assured." [72]

The election of a new President has not altered the American attitude relative to supporting the "political independence and territorial integrity" of the states of the Middle East. On March 27, 1969, Secretary of State Rogers, speaking before the Senate Foreign Relations Committee, outlined President Nixon's position: "a just and lasting peace will require . . . withdrawal of Israeli armed forces from territories occupied in the Arab-Israeli war of 1967." [73]

The United States' policy stand toward the Israeli annexation of East Jerusalem may be logically derived from the United States' general concern with the matter of territorial integrity of the state of Jordan. Washington has refused to recognize the validity of this annexation move by Israel [74] and has contended that "the measures taken [by Israel] cannot be considered as other than interim and provisional, and not as prejudging the final and permanent status of Jerusalem." [75]

Admittedly, our policy position on this issue has not always been clear cut. Two weeks after former President Johnson's speech of June 19, 1967, the United States refused to support a General Assembly resolution calling upon Israel to refrain from annexing East Jerusalem. [76] In explaining its abstention on the July 4, 1967, resolution on the status of Jerusalem, the United States delegation emphasized its preference for language that "no unilateral action should be taken that might prejudice the future of Jerusalem." The United States would have supported a resolution to that effect, a July 4 press release stated. [77] The resolution which passed

69. U.S. Senate, Committee on Foreign Relations, *A Select Chronology and Background Documents Relating to the Middle East* (Washington: Government Printing Office, 1967), p. 135.

70. United States Department of State *Bulletin,* July 10, 1967, p. 33.

71. Security Council resolution 242 (1967). See Section IV.

72. As cited in Lenczowski, *op. cit.,* p. 124.

73. As quoted in a speech delivered by Joseph J. Sisco, Assistant Secretary of State for Near East and South Asian Affairs, before the American Israel Public Affairs Committee at Washington, D.C., April 23, 1969.

74. No other nation has recognized this action by Israel either.

75. From a speech delivered by Ambassador Goldberg on July 14, 1967, before the U.N. General Assembly during its Fifth Emergency Special Session. Doc. A/PV. 1554, dated July 14, 1967, p. 48.

76. The United States abstained. This was resolution 2253 (ES-V), dated July 4, 1967. See section IV.

77. U.S., Department of State Bulletin, July 24, 1967, Vol. LVII, No. 1465, pp. 112, 113.

99-0, with 20 abstentions, singled out Israel for censure on grounds her moves to change the status of Jerusalem were invalid; it called upon Israel to rescind measures already taken and to desist from others planned. Almost two years later it was reported by a newsletter that "on one major and crucial issue, the Administration *appears to accept Israel's position:* Jerusalem should remain a unified city" [78] (emphasis added). Richard Scott, reporting from Washington to *The Guardian* (London), also noted this apparent deviation from United States established policy relative to "territorial integrity of all states." [79] Scott wrote that Jordan would "trade" East Jerusalem for some right of access to the Mediterranean through Israel. The Arab states, however, refused to modify their position calling for the complete withdrawal by Israel to her territorial possessions prior to the June, 1967, war; while Israel, in turn, refused to withdraw from the occupied areas prior to a peace settlement and appeared to consider her "unification" of Jerusalem an accomplished fact, and outside the framework of *any* negotiated peace.[80] Thus the stalemate continued.

On May 29, 1969, the four-power conference reconvened at United Nations headquarters in New York to draft a communiqué on their progress. They adjourned that same day, however, without issuing a communiqué, suggesting that the four-power conference had also reached a stalemate.

An Arab Proposal

On April 10, 1969, in a speech delivered before the National Press Club in Washington, D.C., King Hussein of Jordan outlined the Arab formula for peace in the Middle East.[81] He also stated that he was speaking on behalf of President Nasser of the UAR.

After referring to the Security Council resolution of November 22, 1967, King Hussein said that the Arabs would agree "to terminate the state of belligerency with Israel, to provide her with guaranteed access to Sharm al-Sheik and the Suez Canal, to recognize her right to live in peace and security, and to agree to provisions which would finally solve the refugee problem." The Jordanian king thus indicated that the Arabs would agree to virtually all the demands put forward by the State of Israel before June 5, 1967.

King Hussein further noted that if a peace settlement did not come "within the next very few months" then "no outside force, even with the best of intentions, will be able to divert the area from permanent conflict and eventual war."

Turning to the issue of Jerusalem, King Hussein remarked:

> Moreover, our plan for withdrawal must include our greatest city—our spiritual capital, the holy city of Jerusalem. To us—Christian and Muslim Arab alike—Jerusalem is as sacred as it is to the Jews. And we cannot envision any settlement that does not include the return of the Arab part of the city of Jerusalem to us with all our holy places.

---

78. *Near East Report,* May 14, 1969.
79. *The Guardian,* April 9, 1969.
80. *Ibid.,* May 8, 1969.
81. For the text of this speech see the article covering the king's visit to the United States in the *New York Times,* April 11, 1969.

In return for meeting all the Israeli demands of pre-June, 1967, King Hussein declared:

> Our sole demand upon Israel is the withdrawal of its armed forces from all territories occupied in the June, 1967 war, and the implementation of all the other provisions of the Security Council resolutions.
> The challenge that these principles present is that Israel may have either peace or territory—but she can never have both.

In a joint statement issued at the conclusion of King Hussein's visit to the United States, Washington reaffirmed its support of the territorial integrity of the Hashemite Kingdom of Jordan.[82]

Policy Alternatives

The number of juridical and administrative arrangements that could be applied to the holy city far exceed the limited number of available political options. For the United States, with multifarious interests in the Middle East,[83] which political option to favor is a matter of importance. United States policy toward Jerusalem should, of course, be designed to strengthen American interests in this part of the world. This means American policy on Jerusalem should contribute to general policies of maximizing peace and stability in the Middle East, facilitating peaceful economic growth of this area, and supporting moderate and democratic political elements where they exist. With these general objectives in mind, the following policy alternatives on Jerusalem [84] may be considered:

Alternative 1: Support the Israeli annexation of East Jerusalem. This gain for Israel might facilitate negotiation of Israeli withdrawals from Syria, the West Bank, Sinai, and Sharm El-sheik; and conceivably Israel might be prevailed upon to establish an administration in Jerusalem which would properly respect the shrines of Islam and Christianity. On the other hand, by supporting (or not opposing) annexation, the United States might jeopardize its military, political, and economic interests throughout the Arab world. It would strengthen the Soviet presence in the Arab world by weakening the countervailing influence of the United States in the more moderate Arab regimes. It could seriously undermine the authority of King Hussein of Jordan and encourage extremist trends in the Arab world. It could generate adverse political consequences in Pakistan, Nigeria, Indonesia, and other countries with significant Muslim populations. By defying the nearly unanimous Jerusalem resolution, it would deal a blow to the United Nations; and it would be a repudiation of the United States' position which supports the political independence and territorial integrity of all countries in the Middle East. Of greatest importance, this alternative might weaken, rather than strengthen, the hope for a "just and lasting peace" in this area.

Alternative 2: Support the Israeli annexation of East Jerusalem with some symbolic gesture made to Jordan to allow that Arab state to exercise a form of jurisdiction over the Muslim Holy Places in Jerusalem. To adopt this policy might

---

82. *Ibid.*
83. For a comprehensive analysis of United States interests in the Middle East, see Lenczowski, *op. cit.*
84. For another discussion of alternatives see Evan M. Wilson, "The Internationalization of Jerusalem," *The Middle East Journal,* Winter, 1969, Volume 23, No. 1.

induce the adverse effects to the United States position in the Middle East noted under Alternative 1. The principal advantage to this alternative is that the Muslim community might feel more at ease to have the Holy Places of Islam under Jordanian rather than Israeli control.

Alternative 3: Support the creation of an Arab Palestine from the West Bank and the Gaza Strip, but exclude Jerusalem. Under this plan, the Arabs of Jerusalem could be citizens of the Arab state while the city of Jerusalem would be Israeli. One modification of this plan would be to establish a federal political system for Palestine with Israel and Arab Palestine federal units of the system, with Jerusalem the capital of the combined federal state. Jewish residents of Jerusalem would be Israeli citizens and Arab residents would be citizens of the Arab state. This alternative would reduce Jordan to the territorial scope of pre-1948 Trans-Jordan. It could affect adversely the position of King Hussein of Jordan. Also the Arab state in Palestine might become a virtual client state of Israel. A degree of political cooperation between Arabs and Israelis appears to be implied here which would be inconsistent with the history of their relationships over the past several decades. Finally, the plan would only promote peace and stability in the Middle East if the Arabs could be induced to accept such a plan. Under present conditions, this possibility appears remote. The two advantages of this plan are (a) it would permit a greater degree of regional economic development than would be the case if the Arab sections of Palestine were returned to their pre-June, 1967, condition; and (b) Jerusalem would technically be unified, yet under neither Israeli nor Jordanian sovereignty.

Alternative 4: Support the internationalization of Jerusalem (including both the West and East sectors). This has been the position of the Roman Catholic Church. To support this alternative would generate less hostility within the Arab world than any of the previously mentioned alternatives. It appears difficult to achieve Israeli acceptance of this alternative, however. If such internationalization were made permanent, it would deny the principle of self-determination to the inhabitants of the city. If internationalization were made temporary as under the 1948 U.N. Statute of Jerusalem, it might invite subsequent partition of the city into its respective sectors at some later date. A plan of internationalization would also invite major economic problems, particularly with regard to West Jerusalem. The advantage of such territorial internationalization is that it would extricate, to a limited degree, the holy city from the arena of Arab-Israeli nationalist conflict.

Alternative 5: Support the internationalization of the Holy Places. This alternative is similar to Alternative 2, with the United Nations substituted for Jordan and all the Holy Places substituted for Muslim Holy Places. It would suffer from weaknesses similar to those in Alternative No. 2, primarily because the Arabs would feel resentful at leaving the general area of Jerusalem under Israeli sovereignty. However, this alternative would be preferable even from the Arab point of view to total annexation of Jerusalem by Israel.

Alternative 6: Support the internationalization of the walled city only. Depending upon the position taken by the United States with regard to the rest of Jerusalem, internationalization of only the walled city would probably not be disadvantageous in terms of the United States' general interests in the Middle East. It would bring under international jurisdiction the main Holy Places of the three monotheistic faiths. It would not, however, include the Holy Places that lie outside the walled city. It would still deny the inhabitants of the walled city the right of self-determination. Finally, it would necessitate an involved administrative arrangement with the state (or states) having sovereignty over the surrounding area. The great advantages of this plan are that it would establish a U.N. presence of some size in the holy city and would give assurance to members of all three faiths that access to the Holy Places within the walled city would be guaranteed by the United Nation..

Alternative 7: Support the return of East Jerusalem to Jordanian control. Given the United States' support of the November 22, 1967, resolution, as well as later official statements from Washington, it would appear that this is United States policy in principle. As noted earlier, however, there is sufficient ambiguity in the Washington position regarding Jerusalem to raise doubt as to whether the United States interprets Israeli withdrawal from occupied territories to include· East Jerusalem or not. If the United States chose to pursue a policy designed to support the return of East Jerusalem to Jordan it would (1) reaffirm its position that political independence and territorial integrity are principles that are not tailored to fit each situation as a given administration may see fit; (2) strengthen the position of moderate pro-American Arab leaders; (3) strengthen the United States' political and economic position within the Arab world; (4) weaken any Soviet attempt to capitalize on anti-American feelings among Arab masses. Moreover, support of the return of East Jerusalem to Jordanian control would assure the Third World that the United States continues to reject any territorial aggrandizement by the use of force. Finally, such a policy would be compatible with the widespread feeling of the comity of nations as expressed in the several United Nations resolutions regarding Jerusalem.

The difficulties of taking this policy position are that (1) Israel is firmly committed to the retention of East Jerusalem and it would require much pressure (or persuasion) if the United States were to try to induce Israel to return this sector of the holy city to Jordan; (2) adoption of this policy position would generate domestic opposition, particularly among Zionist-influenced groups; (3) the Israelis would expect a guarantee in which they could have faith that they would have access to the Wailing Wall, one far stronger than a United Nations resolution; and (4) in all likelihood, some form of demilitarization of East and West Jerusalem would be necessary to provide a measure of security for the Israeli and Arab inhabitants of the city.

These difficulties, however, are not insurmountable. The principal merit of this alternative would be its conformity with the clearly articulated will of the overwhelming majority of nations, as expressed by the U.N. resolutions of July 4 and November 22, 1967, as well as with the basic American position that the peace settlement must not "reflect the weight of conquest."

The challenge for the United States is to adopt a policy on Jerusalem that would be compatible with the preservation of American interests in the Middle East within the larger context of Afro-Asia and that would prevent the City of Peace from becoming a source of a future war.

II. THE SIX-DAY WAR, THE OCTOBER WAR, AND CONTINUED HOSTILITIES

A. *Issues Concerning the Use of Force and Its Consequences*

The Arab-Israeli War: How it Began

CHARLES W. YOST

THE recent Six Day War in the Middle East grew out of the sterile confrontation to which the peoples of the region had committed themselves over the past twenty years. Both parties had frequently proclaimed their intention to go to war under certain circumstances. It seems unlikely, however, that any of them plotted and planned war for 1967. It seems more likely that they blundered into it.

Both sides might on many occasions have moved to end their confrontation by compromise, but this neither side showed the slightest willingness to do. The Israelis, feeling themselves beleaguered by fifty million hostile neighbors, acutely conscious of the recent fate of six million Jews in Europe, believed any significant concession would merely whet insatiable Arab appetites and start Israel down the slippery slope to extinction. The Arabs, looking upon the establishment of Israel as the latest in a series of imperialist occupations of their homeland, of which the presence of a million Palestine refugees was a constant reminder, found it emotionally and politically impossible to accept Israel as a permanent fact of life or to forego harassing it and conspiring against it.

This common intolerance and mutual harassment had brought on war in 1956. It is pertinent to note that, in his "Diary of the Sinai Campaign" published in 1966, General Dayan wrote that the three major objects of that campaign from the Israeli point of view were "freedom of shipping for Israeli vessels in the Gulf of Aqaba; an end to the Feydayen terrorism; and a neutralization of the threat of attack on Israel by the joint Egypt-Syria-Jordan military command." With slight variations, these were the issues that brought on war again eleven years later.

II

Through the latter part of 1966, so-called "El Fatah" incursions into Israel, sometimes carried out by Palestinian refugees, sometimes moving through Jordan or Lebanon, but for the most part mounted in Syria, grew in numbers and intensity. In October two particularly serious incidents in which several Israelis were killed caused Israel to appeal, as it often had before, to the U.N. Security Council. However, a relatively mild resolution proposed by six of its members, calling on Syria to take stronger measures to prevent such incidents, was, as on previous occasions, vetoed by the Soviet Union in the supposed interests of its Arab friends.

A new and more radical Syrian government had come to power by coup d'état earlier that year. It enthusiastically supported the claims and machinations of the so-called Palestine Liberation Army which mobilized and inflamed the refugees and carried out some of the raids. The Syrian Prime Minister declared in a press conference in October: "We are not sentinels over Israel's security and are not the leash that restrains the revolution of the displaced and persecuted Palestinian people." Early in November, moreover, a "defense agreement" was concluded between Syria and the United Arab Republic, involving a joint military command and other measures of "coördination and integration" between the two countries.

It had long been Israel's practice, whenever it judged that Arab raids had reached an intolerable level, to retaliate massively. It did so on November 13 against Es Samu in Jordan where, according to U.N. observers, eighteen Jordanian soldiers and civilians were killed and fifty-four wounded. The fact that moderate Jordan rather than extremist Syria was the target of retaliation seemed ill-judged to most of the world but was excused by Israel on grounds that there had recently been thirteen acts of sabotage committed on Israeli territory from Jordanian bases. Be that as it may, the consequences, in and out of the region, of this disproportionate and misplaced retaliation were considerable.

The U.N. Security Council, by a vote of fourteen to one abstention (New Zealand), censured Israel "for this large-scale military action in violation of the U.N. Charter and of the General Armistice Agreement between Israel and Jordan" and emphasized to Israel "that actions of military reprisal cannot be tolerated and that if they are repeated, the Security Council will have to consider further and more effective steps as envisaged in the Charter to ensure against the repetition of such acts."

Perhaps more important in its effect on subsequent events, the Jordanian Prime Minister in a press conference charged the U.A.R. and Syria, which had been denouncing King Hussein's government, with failing to bear their share of the confrontation against Israel. He accused the U.A.R. of failing to supply promised air cover and urged that Egyptian troops be withdrawn from Yemen and sent to Sinai on Israel's southern flank. The U.A.R. Commander-in-Chief of the Arab Command replied publicly with similar recriminations but the charges must have struck home to a régime so peculiarly sensitive to face and prestige.

From January to April 1967 the Syrian-Israeli frontier was agitated by an ascending series of clashes ranging from potshots at tractors plowing to exchanges of fire between tanks, artillery and aircraft. These clashes were primarily caused by the refusal of both sides, at different times, to permit the U.N. Mixed Armistice Commission even to mark the armistice line at disputed points and the insistence of both parties on farming and patrolling disputed areas.

On April 7, 1967, one of these clashes escalated into what in retrospect appears to have been the curtain-raiser to the six-day war. An exchange of fire between tanks gave rise to intervention first by Israeli and then by Syrian aircraft. This led by the end of the day to the appearance of Israeli planes over the outskirts of Damascus and to the shooting down of six Syrian planes.

The most serious aspect of this affair was that for the second time in six months Arab forces suffered a very bloody nose at the hands of Israel without the "unified Arab Command" in Cairo lifting a finger. President Nasser, who aspired to be leader of the Arab world and who had formally established a military apparatus at least for the containment of Israel, had sat quietly by while first his rival and then his ally had been conspicuously and roundly chastised. Neither the rival nor the ally hesitated publicly and privately to point out this dereliction. Nasser could of course reply, and perhaps did, that the El Fatah raids were excessive and untimely, that the Arabs must not be provoked into fighting before they were ready, and that the U.N. Emergency Force standing between his army and Israel blocked its coming to the rescue of his Arab allies. These excuses, however genuine and well-founded they may have been, were quite clearly wearing thin in the eyes of the Arabs after the April 7 affair. Those knowing President Nasser's temperament could hardly have felt any assurance that he would hold aloof a third time.

III

Yet the respite was brief. A month later, on May 11, the U.N. Secretary-General declared at a press luncheon: "I must say that,

in the last few days, the El Fatah type of incidents have increased, unfortunately. Those incidents have occurred in the
vicinity of the Lebanese and Syrian lines and are very deplorable,
especially because, by their nature, they seem to indicate that
the individuals who committed them have had more specialized
training than has usually been evidenced in El Fatah incidents
in the past. That type of activity is insidious, is contrary to the
letter and spirit of the Armistice Agreements and menaces the
peace of the area."

On the same day, May 11, Israeli Prime Minister Eshkol was
saying in a public speech in Tel Aviv that his government regarded this wave of sabotage and infiltration gravely. "In view of
the fourteen incidents of the past month alone," he said, "we
may have to adopt measures no less drastic than those of April
7." In a radio interview two days later he declared: "It is quite
clear to the Israeli Government that the focal point of the terrorists is in Syria, but we have laid down the principle that we shall
choose the time, the place and the means to counter the aggressor." Eshkol went on to say that he intended to make Israeli
defense forces powerful enough to deter aggression, to repel it and
to strike a decisive blow within enemy territory.

It would appear that a senior Israeli military officer also made
a public comment on or about May 12, the exact text of which it
has not been possible to find but which, whether or not correctly
understood, significantly contributed to Arab apprehensions.
President Nasser referred to it in a speech on May 23, saying, "On
May 12 a very important statement was made. . . . The statement said that the Israeli commanders have announced they
would carry out military operations against Syria in order to occupy Damascus and overthrow the Syrian Government."

These Israeli exercises in verbal escalation provoked far more
serious repercussions than they were no doubt intended to do and,
far from sobering the exuberant Syrians and their allies, raised
probably genuine fears in Damascus, Cairo and Moscow to a level
which brought about the fatal decisions and events of the following week. Indeed the Secretary-General, disturbed that his statement of May 11 on the El Fatah raids might stimulate Israeli
military action, announced on May 13 that that statement "cannot be interpreted as condoning resort to force by any party."

On the same day the Syrian Foreign Ministry summoned ambassadors from countries which were members of the Security

Council and told them that a plot against Syria was being concocted by "imperialist and Zionist quarters." The Ministry described "the prearranged aggressive role Israel is preparing to play within the framework of this plot" which, it declared, "began with the abortive April 7 aggression" and was revealed by "statements of Zionist Chief of Staff Rabin."

Another component in the accumulating mass of explosive elements was mentioned by President Nasser in the famous speech of June 9 in which he offered to resign. He declared at that time: "We all know how the crisis began in the first half of last May. There was a plan by the enemy to invade Syria, and the statements by his politicians and his military commanders declared that frankly. The evidence was ample. The sources of our Syrian brothers and our own reliable information were categorical on this. Even our friends in the Soviet Union told the parliamentary delegation which was visiting Moscow last month that there was a calculated intention."

There seems little doubt that the Soviets did transmit warnings along these lines to the Syrian and Egyptian governments. Eastern European sources have justified these warnings on the grounds that the Israeli Government itself advised Soviet representatives that, if the El Fatah raids continued, it would take drastic punitive action against Syria. This was of course no more than they were saying publicly, but the Israelis may have hoped that direct notice to the Soviets might induce them to persuade their Syrian friends to stop the raids.

Indeed there is evidence that Israeli officials were at this time disseminating their warnings rather widely. *The New York Times* correspondent, James Feron, in Tel Aviv reported on May 12: "Some Israeli leaders have decided that the use of force against Syria may be the only way to curtail increasing terrorism. Any such Israeli reaction to continued infiltration would be of considerable strength but of short duration and limited in area. This has become apparent in talks with highly qualified and informed Israelis who have spoken in recent days against a background of mounting border violence."

However, these private warnings, coupled with the provocative pronouncements by Eshkol and others, would seem to have backfired by convincing the Soviets, Syrians and Egyptians that a major retaliatory strike against Syria was fixed and imminent. In a speech to the United Nations on June 19 Premier Kosygin declared: "In those days, the Soviet Government, and I believe others too, began receiving information to the effect that the Israeli Government had timed for the end of May a swift strike at Syria in order to crush it and then carry the fighting over into the territory of the United Arab Republic."

On the other hand, the Israelis state that on May 12 the Director General of the Israeli Foreign Ministry, on May 19 the Foreign Minister and on May 29 the Prime Minister each invited Soviet Ambassador Chuvakhin, who had accused Israel of massing forces on the Syrian border, to visit the area and see for himself, but that in each case he refused to do so. Furthermore, in his report to the Security Council on May 19, Secretary-General Thant had referred to allegations about troop movements and concentrations on the Israeli side of the Syrian border but concluded: "Reports from UNTSO observers have confirmed the absence of troop concentrations and significant troop movements on both sides of the line." U.S. representatives in Israel at the time also saw no evidence of the alleged troop concentrations. Moreover, on May 15 the Israeli Government, observing that Egyptian forces were crossing the Suez Canal into Sinai in considerable strength, instructed its Representative at the U.N., Ambassador Rafael, to request the Secretary-General to assure Cairo on its behalf that it had no intention of initiating any military action. The Secretary-General immediately complied with the request.

Nevertheless, it should also be noted that in the May 19 report referred to above the Secretary-General remarked: "Intemperate and bellicose utterances ... are unfortunately more or less routine on both sides of the lines in the Near East. In recent weeks, however, reports emanating from Israel have attributed to some high officials in that state statements so threatening as to be particularly inflammatory in the sense that they could only heighten emotions and thereby increase tensions on the other side of the lines." Press accounts of these statements also seemed so inflammatory to U.S. State Department officials that they expressed concern to Israeli authorities.

The situation in mid-May was therefore the following: The aggravation of the El Fatah raids originating in Syria would seem to have brought the Israeli Government to the decision, announced publicly in general terms by responsible officials and confided in more specific terms to journalists and perhaps to foreign diplomats including the Soviets, to retaliate sharply and substantially if the raids continued. There is no solid evidence, however, that they intended anything so massive as a drive on Damascus. Nevertheless, this prospect had in both Moscow and Cairo an impact which the Israelis probably did not fully anticipate or correctly assess.

The Soviets had particular reason for not wishing to see the Syrian Government humiliated, defeated and perhaps overthrown. The increasingly radical Syrian governments which had assumed power during the previous eighteen months, though they were far from being communist (the Communist Party was and still is banned), had come to rely more and more on Soviet military and economic aid, to permit increasing numbers of Soviet advisers to be stationed in the country, and all in all to offer the most promising field for Soviet penetration and influence to be found anywhere in the Middle East. The particular Soviet concern for Syria was dramatically shown at the end of the six-day war when the prospect that Israeli forces might then drive to Damascus caused the Soviets suddenly to join in a demand, which they had up to that point stubbornly opposed, that U.N. observers police the cease-fire. It may well have been that by mid-May they genuinely feared massive Israeli retaliation which might topple the Syrian Government and that they therefore spurred the Egyptians on to vigorous counteraction, the full repercussions of which they did not foresee. In fear of "losing" Syria they overreached themselves and urged the Arabs to take action which resulted in much more disastrous losses for their side.

Nasser, for his part, saddled with responsibility for the unified Arab Command which was supposed to protect all the Arab states from Israel, jealous of his already damaged position as would-be leader of the Arab world, having been ridiculed by his allies and rivals for his failure to stir at the time of the Es Samu and April 7 affairs, categorically assured by Syrians and Soviets that Israel was about to attack Syria, for which public statements by Israeli leaders seemed to give warrant, may well have felt that he could no longer stand aside without fatal loss to his prestige and authority.

Israeli public statements between May 11 and 13, therefore, regardless of how they may have been intended, may well have been the spark that ignited the long accumulating tinder. On May 14 the Egyptian Chief of Staff flew to Damascus and, according to the Syrian official spokesman, discussed with Syrian officials "important matters concerning joint defense against Israel." On May 16 the Cairo radio announced that the United Arab Republic had declared a state of emergency for its armed forces because of "the tense situation on the Syrian-Israeli armistice lines, Israel's large military concentrations, its threats and its open demands for an attack on Damascus." On that same day, according to the Cairo radio, Foreign Minister Riad received the Soviet, Syrian and Iraqi Ambassadors in separate audiences and Minister of War Badran received the Soviet Ambassador accompanied by his military attaché. The fourth act of the tragedy was about to begin.

IV

At 2200 hours local time that evening, May 16, General Rikhye, Commander of the U.N. Emergency Force in Sinai, was handed the following letter from General Fawzi, Chief of Staff of the Egyptian Armed Forces: "To your information, I gave my instructions to all U.A.R. Armed Forces to be ready for action against Israel the moment it might carry out an aggressive action against any Arab country. Due to these instructions our troops are already concentrated in Sinai on our eastern borders. For the sake of complete security of all U.N. troops which install O.P.s along our border, I request that you issue your orders to withdraw all these troops immediately. I have given my instructions to our Commander of the eastern zone concerning this subject. Inform back the fulfillment of this request."

Secretary-General Thant received General Rikhye's report at 1730 hours New York time that same evening and an hour and a quarter later (at 1845 hours) at his urgent request received the U.A.R. representative to the U.N., Ambassador El Kony, to whom he presented the following views: (1) General Rikhye could not take orders from anyone but the Secretary-General; (2) if General Fawzi was asking for a temporary withdrawal of UNEF from the Line this was unacceptable because UNEF "cannot be asked to stand aside in order to enable the two sides to resume fighting"; (3) if General Fawzi was asking for a general withdrawal of UNEF from Gaza and Sinai the request should have been addressed by the U.A.R. Government to the Secretary-General; (4) the U.A.R. Government had the right "to withdraw the consent which it gave in 1956 for the stationing of

UNEF on the territory of the U.A.R."; (5) if the U.A.R. Government addressed such a request to the Secretary-General he "would order the withdrawal of all UNEF troops from Gaza and Sinai, simultaneously informing the General Assembly of what he was doing and why"; (6) a U.A.R. request for a temporary withdrawal of UNEF from the Line would be considered by the Secretary-General "as tantamount to a request for the complete withdrawal of UNEF from Gaza and Sinai, since this would reduce UNEF to ineffectiveness."

Early the next morning, May 17, Egyptian troops began to move into and beyond some UNEF positions along the Armistice Line. At noon G.M.T. that day General Fawzi conveyed to General Rikhye a request that the Jugoslav detachments of UNEF (which occupied the main portion of the Sinai Armistice Line) be withdrawn within 24 hours, adding, however, that the UNEF Commander might take "24 hours or so" to withdraw the UNEF detachment from Sharm el Sheikh (which commands the Straits of Tiran but is far distant from the Armistice Line).

Space permits only the briefest summary of the events which followed in rapid succession. On the afternoon of May 17 in New York the Secretary-General consulted with representatives of countries providing contingents to UNEF (Brazil, Canada, Denmark, India, Jugoslavia, Norway and Sweden). According to his subsequent report to the General Assembly, two of them expressed serious doubts about complying with "a peremptory request" for withdrawal and suggested reference to the Assembly, whereas two others maintained the United Arab Republic had the right to request withdrawal at any time and that request would have to be respected regardless of what the Assembly might say. Later that afternoon the Secretary-General presented to the U.A.R. Representative an aide-memoire reiterating the points he had made the previous evening and concluding that, if Egyptian troop movements up to the Line were maintained, he would "have no choice but to order the withdrawal of UNEF from Gaza and Sinai as expeditiously as possible."

The next morning, May 18, Foreign Minister Riad informed representatives in Cairo of nations with troops in UNEF that "UNEF had terminated its tasks in the U.A.R. and in the Gaza Strip and must depart from the above territory forthwith." At noon New York time the Secretary-General received a formal request from the Egyptian Foreign Minister to the same effect.

That afternoon he met with the UNEF Advisory Committee where he encountered the same divergence of views as at the meeting the previous day but where the members finally acquiesced in his belief that, in the absence of any proposal to convene the Assembly, he "had no alternative other than to comply with the U.A.R.'s demand." He did so that same evening by a message to Foreign Minister Riad and by instructions to the UNEF Commander.

The immediate reaction of Israel also deserves mention. On the morning of May 18 the Secretary-General received the Israeli representative who presented his Government's view "that the UNEF withdrawal should not be achieved by a unilateral U.A.R. request alone and asserting Israel's right to a voice in the matter." When, however, the Secretary-General raised the possibility of stationing UNEF on the Israeli side of the line, the Representative replied that this would be "entirely unacceptable to his Government," thus reaffirming the position in regard to UNEF which Israel had taken ever since the establishment of the Force in 1956.

The intent and rationale of the decisions taken in Cairo during those critical days in mid-May are still shrouded in obscurity, while those taken in response in New York are still bedeviled by controversy. What seems reasonably clear is that, as so often in the prelude to war, the control of events slipped from everyone's hands and limited decisions hastily taken had sweeping consequences no one desired.

No doubt the Egyptian Government decided sometime between May 13 and 16 that, in view of its assessment of the threat to Syria, it must move some of its armed forces up to the Sinai Armistice Line in order either to deter Israel or to come to Syria's assistance if deterrence failed. Reliable Arab sources maintain that: (1) the U.A.R. Government had as late as May 16 no intention to request the withdrawal of UNEF; (2) it desired merely the removal of several UNEF posts along the Sinai Line which would inhibit the contemplated redeployment of Egyptian forces; (3) it saw no incompatibility between this redeployment and the continuance of UNEF in its other positions *including* Sharm el Sheikh; (4) the implementation of the redeployment was left to the military leaders who failed to consult the civilian authorities, including the President, about either the scope of the redeployment they intended to carry out or the demand addressed to General Rikhye on May 16; (5) when the Secretary-General confronted the U.A.R. Government with the naked choice between reversing the redeployment, to which its military leaders had publicly committed it, and requesting the withdrawal of UNEF, it felt obliged to choose the latter; (6) furthermore, when it unexpectedly found its forces once more in possession of Sharm el Sheikh, it felt it could not fail to exercise, as it had from 1954 to 1956, its "belligerent right" to forbid the passage of Israeli vessels and "war material" through the Strait.

As to the decisions taken in New York, the U.N. authorities have maintained that: (1) the indicated redeployment of U.A.R. forces *was* incompatible with the continuance of UNEF since it deprived UNEF of its essential function as a buffer between Egyptian and Israeli forces; (2) UNEF had hitherto been able to function effectively only because of an informal U.A.R. agreement that its forces would be held 2000 meters back from the Armistice Line in Sinai (Israeli forces patrolled right up to the Line); (3) once confrontation between the two forces was re-established, conflict between them was, in the existing state of tension, very probable and UNEF units scattered among them would be wholly unable to prevent it; (4) two of the troop-contributing states, India and Jugoslavia, had made clear their intention to withdraw their contingents whatever the Secretary-General decided and others were likely to follow suit, with the probable result that UNEF would disintegrate in a disordered and ignominious fashion; (5) the U.A.R. Government had the legal right both to move its troops where it wished in its own territory and to insist on the withdrawal of UNEF at any time, just as Israel had the right to refuse it admittance; (6) if the U.N. contested that right, peacekeeping would become "occupation" and other governments would not in the future admit U.N. peacekeeping forces to their territories; (7) a reference of the Egyptian request to the Security Council or the Assembly would merely have produced, as subsequent events proved, a prolonged debate during which UNEF would have either disintegrated or been helplessly involved in war.

No conclusive judgment can be pronounced on these two lines of argument. What does seem apparent is that both the U.A.R. and the U.N., like Israel a few days before, acted precipitately and with little resort to diplomacy. If the Egyptian account is accurate, temporization on the part of the U.N. might conceivably have led to some modification in U.A.R. military dispositions which had not been authorized by its own government. It seems very doubtful, however, that in the prevailing state of emotion dispositions once taken, even without full authorization, could have been reversed. By May 17 the crisis had already acquired a momentum which seemed inexorably to sweep all parties toward and over the brink.

Nevertheless, we can hardly fail to note parenthetically the serious shortcomings of a peacekeeping procedure whereby, as in this case, a U.N. force can be ordered out of a critical area at the very moment when the danger of war, which it is stationed there to prevent, becomes most acute. The fault, however, lies not with the U.N. but with the great powers whose rivalries ever since 1945 have blocked the application of the enforcement procedures provided by Chapter VII of the Charter, under which a U.N. military force could be, for example, interposed between two prospective combatants regardless of the objections of either or both. In the absence of great-power willingness to permit the Security Council to apply compulsion of that type, the U.N. has been obliged for many years to rely on a much more fragile form of peacekeeping whereunder a U.N. force, whatever may have been the arrangements under which it entered the territory of a state, can in practice remain there only so long as its government consents. Such was the situation in Sinai before May 16.

v

To return to the concluding events of that month: President Nasser on May 22 announced his intention to reinstitute the blockade against Israel in the Strait of Tiran. This was the final fatal step. Whether, in whatever advance planning did take place, it was contemplated that Sharm el Sheikh would be reoccupied and the blockade reimposed, or whether the military exceeded their orders and one step led to another in dizzy and unpremeditated succession, is not certain. There can hardly have been any doubt at any time, however, about the grave risks involved in restoring the blockade. It seems probable that the Russians were consulted about the redeployment of Egyptian forces and perhaps the subsequent request for the withdrawal of UNEF. Reliable Soviet sources have claimed, however, that they were not informed in advance of the reimposition of the blockade, implying that they would have objected had they known.

In any case, the reaction in Israel and elsewhere was immediate. On May 23 Prime Minister Eshkol declared in parliament: "The Knesset knows that any interference with freedom of shipping in the Gulf and in the Straits constitutes a flagrant violation of international law. . . . It constitutes an act of aggression against Israel." On the same day President Johnson declared in Washington: "The United States considers the Gulf to be an international waterway and feels that a blockade of Israeli shipping is illegal and potentially disastrous to the cause of peace. The right of free, innocent passage of the international waterway is a vital interest of the international community."

Unavailing efforts were made to persuade President Nasser to revoke, suspend or moderate the blockade but, the action once taken, he did not feel politically free to reverse it, even had he so desired. Equally unavailing were efforts made to forestall a unilateral Israeli response by organizing a group of maritime powers to issue a declaration reaffirming the right of free passage through the Strait and presumably, if passage continued to be denied, to take effective multilateral action to reopen it. Very few maritime powers showed any interest in participating in a confrontation with Nasser and the Arab world, nor did members of the U.S. Congress who were consulted manifest any enthusiasm for risking another conflict in addition to Viet Nam. The exploratory dialogue between the U.S. and the U.A.R., however, continued up until the outbreak of war; as late as June 4 an agreement was announced that U.A.R. Vice President Mohieddin would visit Washington within the next few days and Vice President Humphrey would later return the visit.

In the meantime, however, the crisis had assumed proportions far beyond an argument over maritime rights. The advance of the Egyptian forces to the Armistice Line, the ouster of UNEF and the reimposition of the blockade were received with enormous enthusiasm throughout the Arab world. All the pent-up emotions which had been accumulating for twenty years, and which were continually refreshed by armed clashes, inflammatory propaganda and the presence of a million refugees, erupted in pæans of triumph from Baghdad to Marrakesh.

Nasser's prestige, which had been falling for some time, rebounded overnight. Expressions of solidarity poured in. Iraq, Algeria, Kuwait and Sudan promised troops. In a startling reversal of long-standing hostility, King Hussein of Jordan appeared in

Cairo on May 30 and concluded a mutual defense pact with the U.A.R. which a few days later was extended to Iraq. The armed forces of Egypt, Jordan and Syria were more and more concentrated around Israel's frontiers and there seemed every likelihood they would soon be reinforced by other Arab states.

This Arab euphoria, moreover, led also to verbal exaltation which could not have been without its effect on Israel. For instance, the Syrian Chief of State, Dr. Al-Atasi, said in a speech on May 22: "Arab Palestinians who were expelled from their homeland now realize that armed struggle is the only way to regain their homeland. . . . The state of gangs [Israel] will not benefit by blaming others for inciting fedayeen activities. The cause of these activities is the aggressive Zionist existence itself. Let Israel know that the Palestinian fedayeen activities will continue until they liberate their homeland." In a speech addressed on June 1 to troops departing for the "frontlines" in Jordan, President Arif of Iraq declared: "It was treason and politics that brought about the creation of Israel. Brethren and sons, this is the day of the battle to revenge your martyred brethren who fell in 1948. It is the day to wash away the stigma. We shall, God willing, meet in Tel Aviv and Haifa."

Yet even at this late date, despite all these verbal pyrotechnics and concentrations of force, there does not seem to have been any intention in Cairo to initiate a war. In reply to a question by British M. P. Christopher Mayhew interviewing Nasser on June 2, "And if they do not attack, will you let them alone?", the President said, "Yes, we will leave them alone. We have no intention of attacking Israel." Similar assurances were repeatedly given the United States by the highest Egyptian authorities.

There seems little reason to doubt them. Nasser had up to that point achieved a spectacular victory. Arab unity seemed closer to reality than it had ever been. Israel had suffered a serious setback in prestige, power and security. The mood in Cairo was an odd mixture of exaltation and fatalism, exaltation over what had been achieved, fatalism before the inescapable realization that Israel might prefer war to a political defeat of this magnitude. There was a clear understanding that Israel might attack at any time, no overweening confidence as to the outcome, but a determination to defend, whatever the costs, the intoxicating gains which had been won. Whether this determination might have been overcome by negotiation over a period of time, for example by the visits of the Vice Presidents between Cairo and Washington, cannot be known for certain. In view of the support which the Soviet Union was providing its Arab friends, this seems unlikely.

In any case the Israeli Government obviously decided that it could not wait. All the factors which had induced it to go to war in 1956—a multiplication of raids into its territory, a substantial build-up of Egyptian and other hostile forces on its borders, the blockade of the Strait—had reappeared in even more aggravated form. Efforts of the U.N. and the U.S. to relieve them by international action seemed unavailing. On May 30 Foreign Minister Eban said in a press conference in Jerusalem: "Less than two weeks ago a change took place in the security balance in this region. The two most spectacular signs of this change were the illegal attempt to blockade the international passageway at the Strait of Tiran and the Gulf of Aqaba and the abnormal buildup of Egyptian troops on the Israeli frontier. The Government and people of Israel intend to insure that these two changes are rescinded, and in the shortest possible time." Six days later Israel struck with this end in view; twelve days later it had achieved its objective, and much more beside.

VI

It is not difficult in retrospect to identify the ventures and responses on both sides which over preceding months and weeks, compounding the hatreds which had been allowed to fester for twenty years, led almost inevitably to war.

First were the El Fatah raids, organized from Syria, involving the "Palestine Liberation Army," subjecting peaceful Israeli villages to recurrent jeopardy and terror, building up through the months from October to May, unpunished and, because of the Soviet veto, even uncensured by the U.N. Security Council. Remembering the history of the previous twelve years, it is difficult to see how any Arab or Soviet leader could have failed to realize that this murderous campaign would eventually bring forth a murderous response.

Second were the Israeli "massive retaliations" at Es Samu in November and in the air over Syria and Jordan in April, designed to punish and deter, but disproportionate in size, visibility and political impact, causing also the death of innocent people, condemned by the Security Council in the strongest terms in November, as similar disproportionate retaliations had been repeatedly condemned in the past. It is difficult to see how any Israeli leader could have failed to foresee that such repeated massive reprisals must eventually place the leader of the Arab coalition in a position where he would have to respond.

Third were the public and private statements by high Israeli authorities in mid-May which indicated the probability of even more drastic retaliation against Syria in the near future if the El Fatah raids continued. These statements, even though no doubt designed to deter the raids, almost certainly convinced the Syrian and U.A.R. Governments that such retaliation was definitely projected and may well have persuaded them and the Soviets that the Syrian régime itself was in jeopardy.

Fourth was the decision by the U.A.R. Government, presumably encouraged by Soviets and Syrians, to move its armed forces up to the Sinai Armistice Line, thus reëstablishing at a moment of acute tension the direct Egyptian-Israeli military confrontation which had been the major immediate cause of the 1956 war. This redeployment of Egyptian forces was under the circumstances critical whether or not it was originally intended to be accompanied by a demand that UNEF be withdrawn.

Fifth and finally was the decision of the U.A.R. Government, finding itself whether by intent or accident once more in command of the Strait of Tiran, to exercise its "belligerent rights" by reimposing the blockade, thus reproducing the third of the elements which had brought on the 1956 war. The likely consequences of this step were indeed foreseen but, in the climate of fear, passion and "national honor" which by then prevailed, were faced with fatalism and desperation.

It remains, however, the thesis of this article that no government plotted or intended to start a war in the Middle East in the spring of 1967. Syria mounted raids against Israel as it had been doing for years, but more intensively and effectively; Israel retaliated disproportionately as it often had before, but in more rapid succession and in a way that seemed to threaten the existence of the Arab government; Nasser felt his responsibilities and ambitions in the Arab world did not permit him again to stand aside in such a contingency and took hasty and ill-calculated measures which made major conflict, already probable, practically certain. All concerned overreacted outrageously. Yet there is no evidence—quite the contrary—that either Nasser or the Israeli Government or even the Syrian Government wanted and sought a major war at this juncture.

Of course the fault of all of them, and indeed of the great powers and the United Nations, lay not so much in their actions or omissions in May and June 1967 as in their failure, indeed their common blunt refusal, to face the facts of life in the Middle East during the twenty years before that date.

There will be no peace there, no security for its inhabitants or for the great powers involved there, until the Arabs recognize that Israel, however unjust its creation appears to them, is a fact of life, that it has as much right to exist as they have, that to threaten and harass it, to arouse among their people false hopes about its dissolution, is actually as much a threat to Arab as to Israeli security, that the two equally have more to gain than lose by peaceful coexistence. On the other hand, there will also be no peace in the Middle East until the Israelis recognize that the condition of their long-term survival as a nation is reconciliation with their much more numerous Arab neighbors, that survival cannot indefinitely be preserved by military force or territorial expansion, that displays of inflexibility and arrogance are not effective modes of international intercourse, and that in particular there will be no security for Israel until, whatever the political and financial cost, the million or more Palestine refugees have been compensated, resettled and restored to dignity.

No Peace – No War in the Middle East

JULIUS STONE

I. BACKGROUND AND OUTLINE OF THE LEGAL PROBLEMS

A year of Middle East tension and conflict has passed, happily short of war, but short of peace also, since I delivered to this Branch of the International Law Association the address published as *The Middle East Under Cease-Fire*.* Interestingly enough, too, this day, November 22, 1968, is the first anniversary of the main sign of hope for Middle East peoples, namely the Security Council Resolution of November 22, 1967. It may be appropriate, therefore, if I take this opportunity of reviewing, not, indeed, all the legal problems of the Middle East, but those which have come to prominence since my last analysis. (See the Bibliography (including abbreviations) following the text, especially paragraph 3.) At the end of my address tonight, I shall have to return to a main conclusion of last year's study; for further development has made it even more important than I then thought it was.

Egypt and Syria, with massive Soviet support, have restored their armaments virtually to pre-June 1967 levels. The Arab States have encouraged terrorist organisations and incursions against Israel, despite the cease-fire. Their diplomatic harassment of Israel has been aided by the present constellation of non-permanent members of the Security Council. Still denying Israel's "right to exist", they have continued after Khartoum to insist on no recognition, no negotiation, no peace, demanding complete Israel withdrawal (sometimes even beyond the June frontiers) as a first step in any process of implementing the November Resolution. This substantial demand in whatever form I shall refer to as the Arab "threshold" demand. It is closely juxtaposed with an Israel "threshold" demand that the Arab States must recognise and accept as the objective of such implementation, the attainment of a genuine peace settlement, without reserving continued designs of destroying Israel as and when they can. I shall examine the legal aspects of both these threshold claims below, in Sections XI-XIII.

On the other side of the cease-fire lines, the State of Israel, despite its military success (or perhaps because of this), has been much put on the defensive in relation to its military administration of the territories, and to the achievement of peace. It has had to find its way among many political, economic and legal problems, the last here to be examined, touching the security and welfare of its own people and of inhabitants of the occupied territories. These have not been much lightened, as yet, by the Security Council Resolution of November 22, 1967, affirming certain principles for "the establishment of a just and lasting peace" in the Middle East, or

---

* Meeting of October 18, 1967, printed in the periodical *The Bridge*, Box 4074, G.P.O. Sydney, November 1967. The present address was delivered to the Annual Meeting of the Branch on November 22, 1968, presided over by its President, H. A. R. Snelling, Q.C., Solicitor-General of New South Wales. The presentation, of course, is of the views of the Author, which are not necessarily shared by that Association Branch or its Members. (In this 1970 Printing some printer's errors have been corrected, and lines 36-46 on p. 29 have been redrafted for clarity.)

Dr. Jarring's mission under it. The government of Israel has had also to take account of domestic public opinion which is intensely sensitive, as that of any people of like experience would be, to threats of military attack and even of future genocide, now betokened by indiscriminate terrorist assaults despite the cease-fire on civilian men, women and children, as well as on defence personnel. Problems of the legal limits of self-defence are particularly difficult in cases of State-fostered terrorist attacks. These also complicate the questions, in any case rather difficult under modern conditions, concerning the military occupant's powers over the life of the local population. And here, too, public opinion in Israel has naturally resisted one-sided U.N. surveillance there while Arab States are left free to oppress their Jewish populations unchecked, despite the fact that the governing Resolution 237 of 1967, is addressed to the "governments" concerned, so that it cannot be that *only* Israel was embraced within it. All these latter problems are over-laid, and may indeed be quite transformed, by the doubts later to be considered affecting the standing of Egypt and Jordan in certain of the territories even before the June War.

I propose to address myself here to the following principal legal issues newly thrown up by the year's events and debates.

First, I shall look at the conduct of the two sides *inter se* as regards the military aspects of the cease-fire itself. Insofar as violations are found, these questions will entail inquiries as to the lawfulness of responses thereto of the party aggrieved by the alleged violation. (Sections II-III.)

Second, I shall examine the conduct of the State of Israel in relation to the inhabitants of the territories under its control, and in particular, certain Arab charges in relation to this. (Sections IV-VI.)

Third, the religious, historical and strategic concern of both sides with East Jerusalem produces a whole group of legal problems of its own. These affect not only the post-war conduct of Israel, but the pre-war conduct of Jordan in East Jerusalem. Notably relevant here, apart from the Jordanian seizure of the city in 1948 and her abortive attempt to annex it, are Jordan's refusal to honour the provisions of the Jordan-Israel Armistice Agreement, 1949, as regards free access to the Hadassah Hospital and the University on Mount Scopus and to holy places in East Jerusalem, and the desecration of some of these last. Difficult preliminary questions arise as to the legal effects on the status of East Jerusalem, not only of the conduct of the Parties, but also of the relevant General Assembly and Security Council resolutions. (Sections VII-VIII.)

Fourth, whatever the legal force of the Security Council Resolution of November 22, 1967, many difficulties arise as to its meaning. Central to these is the question whether any priority, whether of time or of importance, attaches to the order in which the obligations and desiderata of a just and lasting peace are there set out, on which the Special Representative is "to promote agreement". The answer to this should illuminate which side, if any, is "refusing" to "implement" the Resolution. We shall also, of course, consider the legal nature (as regards its binding force) of this much discussed and much obfuscated "November Resolution". (Sections IX-XIII.)

Finally, I shall develop further last year's outline of the framework of legal relations between Israel, the Arab States, and the territories which have come under Israel control, pending agreement on a peace treaty. This will require us to consider the effect on this framework of the rather questionable titles of Egypt and Jordan to the territories concerned. (Section XIV.)

II. MILITARY OBSERVANCE OF
THE CEASE-FIRES

The study in *The Middle East Under Cease-Fire* was not centred on the *merely* military obligations under the cease-fires, which have since become as controversial as the political and the territorial.

Cease-fire agreements of the instant kind, unlimited as to time, fighting arm or sphere, mean exactly what their name conveys. They forbid all hostilities across the lines. Conceivably they *could* create other prohibitions, for instance, as to standstill of armaments or forces. But the 1967 agreements contained no such clauses. Israel, therefore, can have no legal complaint under them against the Soviet massive rearmament of Egypt and Syria, however justified its complaints on other grounds. Nor, conversely, can Egypt complain of increase or new deployment of Israel forces, in Sinai or elsewhere. Her openly declared policy of "preventive defence", that is (according to the Deputy Foreign Minister on October 27, 1968) of opening fire across the Canal by way of reaction to some increase or new deployment, is therefore an open repudiation of the cease-fire. And her attack of October 26, 1968, pursuant to this policy, was a correspondingly grave breach. What are clearly violations, are any kind of hostilities by or on behalf of or with the support of the States Parties, whether on land, at sea, or in the air, and whether they involve moving troops or aircraft, or merely shooting with guns, mortars or rockets, or sending patrols across the line. Nor does it matter whether the targets are military or civilian personnel, and whether the actors are the State's official forces, or organised armed bands, harboured or assisted by it. Furthermore, the mere lending of its territory to such activities by such bands, or by other States (whether these are bound by the cease-fire or not, and whether by intent, or by failure to use the means to prevent) is also a violation. *A fortiori* when such activities are advocated or supported by the Government of the host State. And as regards any joint planning, or joint activity of these natures, the legal responsibilities of all the States concerned must be regarded as joint and several. Egypt cannot (for example), merely by projecting the jointly promoted delinquent activity against the Jordan-Israel line, give immunity to its own line from justified counter-measures of Israel.

Some authorities, indeed, think that legal responsibility is thus to be imputed, and may amount to aggression, even if the host State is physically unable to prevent the activities. (See, for example, M. R. Garcia-Mora, *International Responsibility for Hostile Acts of Private Persons against Foreign States* (1962) 30-33. *Cf.* on the less stern rule above, Q. Wright, "The Prevention of Aggression" (1956) 50 *A.J.I.L.* 514, 527.) Interestingly here, too, as to armed bands, the Soviet Union's past diplomatic positions rather charmingly support present positions of the State of Israel. Her claims in 1929 to take military action across the Soviet-Manchurian frontier, as "counter-measures" and "legitimate defence", against Russian counter-revolutionary bands operating "in accord" with units of the Nanking Government's army from Chinese territory, are staple textbook material. (See I. Brownlie, *International Law and the Use of Force by States* (1963) 241-42; Soviet Note, Dec. 5(3), 1929, in *U.S. Foreign Relations*, 1929, ii, pp. 404-406). In 1933 she led in incorporating references to support for such armed bands, or failure to deprive them of all assistance and protection, into definitions of aggression. (Draft of League of Nations Committee on Security Questions, 193, and various Conventions Defining Aggression, on which see (1933) *A.J.I.L. Supplement* 193.) These Soviet views were maintained into the work of the U.N. Special Committee on the definition of aggression of the 'fifties, as well as in the relevant Article 2(4) of the preceding Draft Code of Offences against the Peace and Security of Mankind of the International Law Commission. (See Stone, *Aggression and World Order* (1958) 3, 115, 135, 150, 205-206, 211.)

By these widely accepted standards, Soviet-sponsored for nearly two generations, there have obviously been a good many "aggressions" and *a fortiori* cease-fire breaches by Arab States.

As to the simpler matter, first, of shootings across the cease-fire lines each side has, of course, often accused the other of opening first. No doubt, *some* instances must have arisen from local and isolated initiatives of individual soldiers. There may, too, have been cases of *bona fide* mistake, for instance of detonated mines being mistaken for hostile activity by the other side. It seems likely, however, that the great bulk of firing activity, *prima facie* violating the cease-fire, emanated from the Arab side; and this for three reasons. One is the number of instances in which the Arab Government concerned or a terrorist organisation operating under its protection, has openly claimed the "credit". Other reasons arise from the obvious interest of the Arab States in promoting such activity, and the obvious lack of Israel interest. It is difficult to see what the State of Israel stands to gain from such cross-line hostilities and very easy to see that she has much to lose. The idea that she seeks pretexts for false complaints to the United Nations is scarcely credible. Everyone knows that too many present Security Council Members are committed to voting on the Arab side, for pro-Israel resolutions to be adopted, no less than five of these Members refusing even to maintain diplomatic relations with her. Even the laying of an ambush by Egyptian forces on the Israel side of Suez in October 1968, confirmed though it was by United Nations Observers, was not visited by any Security Council condemnation. Moreover, diversionary fire is an obvious way of assisting terrorist incursions and withdrawals, and it is clear that the Arab States rather than Israel support such incursions. According to the Israel Defence Minister, there had been, up to October 29, 1968, no less than 119 cease-fire violations by Egypt. And the Egyptian declaration that its attack of October 26, 1968, inaugurated a new policy of "preventive defence" brings the fact of Egyptian initiative in military activity across the cease-fire lines quite into the open.

As to support of terrorist bands, as well as firing across the cease-fire line, Jordan's record is clearly the heaviest. First, she has failed to use means within her power to prevent systematic recruitment of terrorists, and terrorist attacks on Israel from her territory, of a scale, purposiveness and overtness clearly not dismissible as casual "frontier incidents". Only once (after the Karameh incident) and then only momentarily, has the Jordan Government made any serious effort to end this harbouring. Second, she has even allowed control of parts of her territory along the Jordan River to become full-scale bases for such hostile activity, and even sheltered terrorist units within her army bases. Third, Jordan has officially declared (both separately and jointly with Egypt and other Arab States) her encouragement and support for such hostilities and her hospitality to some of the terrorist headquarters involved. Fourth, Jordan military forces have directly co-operated with sponsored terrorist action against Israel, for instance, by diversionary firing to cover their incursions, or withdrawals. Further, Jordan has continued, after the cease-fire, to provide hospitality for forces of Iraq, which in turn helps to organise, train and despatch terrorist units against Israel. As already seen, a cease-fire does not (without more) forbid reinforcement of a Party bound. But this cannot legalise the maintenance on such a Party's territory of forces of an allied State which continues the original intent to conduct hostilities across the lines.

Egypt's military record after the cease-fire includes the unprovoked rocket attack which sank the Israel destroyer *Elath* in 1967, and is accordingly a grave one. Charges have been made from time to time of her opening fire across the Suez cease-fire line, and there was a clear finding of the U.N. Observers in October, 1968. In recent months it seems clear that she has sent patrols across the cease-fire line to lay mines and commit other hostile acts in occupied Sinai, covering such activities by diversionary firing across the lines. What has been said above as to responsibility for joint planning, joint activity, and the affording of hospitality, systematic training and other aid to terrorist groups by Jordan with Egypt and Syria, obviously applies also to these latter States as well. The Egyptian army trains terrorist personnel and its air force conveys them via Syria to Jordan. Fedayeen Battalion 141 of the Egyptian army was actually stationed in Jordan to join in terrorism and sabotage against Israel. Syria herself, though in the forefront of advocacy of renewed hostilities, has lacked either the capacity or the will (apart from promotion of terrorism) much further to match words with delinquent deeds. Lebanon, though she has occasionally associated herself with the support of terrorist organisations, and is delinquent in affording hospitality and support to various terrorist organisations, has only rarely become involved with the actual conduct of their hostile activities. (These and other complaints by Israel are elaborated in an address of the Israel representative in the Security Council (S/PV 1401, S/PV 1404, S/PV 1407, S/PV 1409-1412).) The main gist (though not of course every detail) seems admitted by public statements of the Governments concerned.

It conforms to the above analysis that the relevant occasions on which the Security Council has censured Israel involved measures of openly announced defence by Israel against currently proceeding violations from the Arab side. On March 25, 1968, the Security Council "condemned" the Israel action to destroy the terrorist base at Karameh, taken after a long series of terrorist incursions which had culminated in the blowing up of a bus-load of children and teachers, of whom 29 children were injured and two adults killed. And there was also a resolution of August 11, 1968, following upon the Israel air reprisals against the terrorist base at Es-Salt. Judgment in such cases should perhaps weigh the losses inflicted by a single Israel raid of this kind against the scores of preceding attacks to which it reacted. In the month preceding the Karameh action, Israel had sustained 37 sabotage raids, killing six persons and wounding 44. Between the June war and early April 1968, terrorists had perpetrated 53 road minings, seven acts of railway sabotage, 20 attacks on dwellings, 28 attacks on factories and public utilities, 26 shooting attacks on villages and 19 grenade attacks. From June 12, 1967, to November 9, 1968, according to Israel figures there had been no less than 963 incidents of violence or sabotage at or across the cease-fire line. (Of these 150 were in the Egyptian sector, 758 in the Jordanian, 34 in the Syrian and 21 in the Lebanese.) The Israel casualties, mainly in the Egyptian and Jordanian sectors, were 32 civilians killed and 246 wounded, and 228 soldiers killed and 759 wounded.

If, reads the standard British work on international law, appeal to the harbouring State to remove the danger of operation of armed bands from the territory "is fruitless or not possible . . . a case of necessity arises, and the threatened State is justified in invading the neighbouring country and sarming the intending raiders." (Oppenheim-Lauterpacht, *International Law,* ol. i, § 130 (6 ed., p. 266).   And see the official and semi-official state- ents and facsimiles of captured secret documents of Arab States, implicating em in what are primarily treacherous attacks on helpless civilians, Israelis nd Arabs, collected in *War By Terror,* Israel Ministry of Foreign Affairs, ctober 1968.)

If, on the above basis, the response is not seriously disproportionate to e preceding wrongs, and yet the Security Council proceeds to condemn e response rather than the wrongs, the effect must be to encourage escalation y affording initial violators continuing United Nations immunity.   The nly plausible ground for such one-sidedness would be that an organised ilitary action, however limited to avoid civilian casualties, is more likely) lead to a threat to the peace than scores of terrorist raids.   But this is rather deceptive plausibility when the official involvement of the Arab tates concerned with the terrorist activities and organisations is recalled. s has been pointed out in a related context, the Soviet Union long ago ok the view, on her borders with China, that operations of counter- volutionary bands from a neighbouring State's territory "in accord" with at State's army units, grounds military action in response by way of "counter- easures" and "legitimate defence".   (See Soviet Note, Dec. 5(3), 1929, .S. Foreign Relations, 1929, vol. ii, 405.)

I may add, finally, here, that grave breaches by one side may, under ternational law, release the wronged party from the bonds of the cease-fire; ough this rule is modified insofar as the Security Council exercises its ompetence under Chapter 7 to act in face of a renewed threat to the peace. ince, however, neither Israel nor the Arab States have claimed to be eleased from their obligations under the cease-fire, this matter need not be rther pursued.

. ARAB STATES STILL REJECTING HE CEASE-FIRE

The Arab States which participated by declaration, military action or ther support in the action against Israel in May-June 1967, included, besides gypt, Jordan, Syria and Iraq, also Algeria, Kuwait, Lebanon, Libya, lorocco, Mauritania, Saudi Arabia, Sudan, Tunisia, and Yemen.   Of ese, the first three formally accepted the cease-fire resolutions (Docs. /7947, S/7953, S/7958, S/7985); Iraq stated on June 15, 1967 (S/7990), repeated Nov. 8, 1968 (S/8894)), that its forces were under the joint ommand in Jordan implying (but not without some ambiguity) that Iraq so accepted the cease-fire.   The Government of Kuwait declined to accept e cease-fire.   Algeria and the other States named above have not yet ccepted the cease-fire.   (See Doc. S/8279, of Nov. 24, 1967.)

The Algerian forces did not engage those of Israel in the June War, but eir involvement in hostilities thereafter from Egyptian territory was com- lained of by Israel on July 17, 1967 (A/6761).   Algeria seems to be aiming a position of active belligerence despite the cease-fire.   The official lgerian News Agency openly claimed that Algerian forces joined with the gyptian in the heavy bombardment of October 26, 1968, across the Suez ne, for which the United Nations Observers with virtual unanimity placed esponsibility on the Egyptian side.   The Iraqi air force attacked Israel and in particular Lydda airport and Natanya) and its land forces attempted cross the frontier in the June War. Iraqi forces have remained in Jordan nce that time, joining allegedly with Jordanian forces in support of terrorist activities shortly to be mentioned, and the Iraqi camp at Mafrak being a main centre for these purposes. An Israel letter of November 5, 1968, to the Security Council charged that Iraqi forces in Jordan participated in the bombardment of Ashdot-Yaacov on 16-17 October, 1968. Iraq is also expressing her belligerence by suppression and ill-treatment of her Jewish citizens in Iraq, despite Security Council Resolution 237 of 1967.

However understandable the initial failure to insist on acceptance of the cease-fire by Algeria and the other belligerent Arab States, the tolerance of this situation to the present time is legally curious. Even more curious i Algeria's role in the Security Council in charging Israel with cease-fire breaches and drafting condemnation and "sanctions" proposals, when she herself is thus chronically contumelious with regard to the cease-fire resolutions. In these circumstances, far from being allowed a role of leadership in the Security Council, Algeria is legally disqualified, under Article 27(3) of the Charter from voting on all substantive Chapter VI matters touching the Arab-Israel dispute. (Cf. the view in Lall, 279.) Council debates cannot, of course be free of "politics". Yet such activity by a State itself openly flouting both the Charter and cease-fire, seems to mock even "political" principles; i matches the harsh fact, already noted, that no less than a third of the Members of the Security Council ostensibly pass on the merits of the case of the State of Israel, even while they refuse to maintain diplomatic relations with her In any case the flouting of the cease-fire order amounts legally at the leas to a threat of force against a Member State which is not committing any armed attack against the threatening State. It continues Algeria's fervent complicity in the major assault on Israel as designed with other Arab State in May-June 1967. Moreover, her former partner States being now bound by the cease-fire, Algeria cerainly cannot now claim to be engaged in hostilities by virtue of "collective self-defence" with them.

The relations of peace and war being necessarily reciprocal, this situation probably entitles Israel, despite the cease-fires with Egypt, Syria and Jordan to respond to any physical hostilities from Iraqi or Algerian forces with measures of self-defence against both the delinquent activities and the respective bases of operations in Jordan and Egypt.

VII. INTERNATIONAL STATUS OF EAST JERUSALEM

The Government of Israel gave assurances to Amman on the mornin of June 5, 1967, after hostilities with Egypt began, that hostilities would nc be extended against Jordan (despite the latter's alliance with Egypt). Never theless, Jordan thereafter began a heavy bombardment of West Jerusalem from gun emplacements in the Old City, some in the shelter of places of religion there. The East Jerusalem issue has come to appear to be a distinct issu since the reaction of the Fifth Emergency Special Session of the Genera Assembly in July 1967 to measures taken by Israel to deal with the pligh of the inhabitants of Jerusalem in the aftermath of the hostilities initiated b Jordan, and the Jordanian defeat. These measures were primarily designe to meet responsibilities which then suddenly fell on the authorities of th Israel Municipality of Jerusalem, by the additional needs of 60,000 inhabitant of the Old City, with services rather inadequate even before the war, and no collapsed under war conditions. Difficulties were aggravated by communica tions between East and West Jerusalem being still blocked by the ugly make shift walls of division thrown up after the Jordanian seizure of the Old Cit in 1948. In the nature of the situation, the requisite measures for restorin and maintaining normal life could only come from the municipal authorities of the City of Jerusalem, and then only by first removing the barriers, and extending an orderly chain of municipal authority, along with substantial means, to the Old City.

For these last purposes the necessarily first step was to bring East Jerusalem within the boundaries of the Municipality of Jerusalem. It is obvious that without this the municipal authorities could not legally provide required aid and services, which would involve use of its budget. With only one or two exceptions to be mentioned, all the steps taken before the first General Assembly resolution on the matter consisted (apart from measures to ensure free and safe access to Holy Places) of extensions of the water, garbage collection, sanitary, educational, banking, transport and telephone, public health (and specially child health) services to the Arab citizens of the Old City. These various steps, then, were basically not concerned with the legal status of Jerusalem *under international law,* but with the provision of a framework *within Israel law* to allow the only municipal authorities capable of doing so to restore, maintain, and increase the services and welfare entitlements of the local inhabitants. The Secretary-General's Personal Representative, Dr. Gussing, indeed, reported to him in September that the Israel measures were directed to equalising the legal and administrative status of all residents of the city. (S/8158, A/6797; and see S/8699, A/7149.) By that time, however, the two censuring resolutions based on contrary assumptions had been adopted.

The first of these, of July 4, 1967 (Resolution 2253 (ES-V)), expressed concern at "measures taken by Israel to change" the status of East Jerusalem, declared these measures invalid, and called on Israel to rescind them. The second, of July 17, 1967 (Resolution 2254 (ES-V)), deplored Israel's failure to "implement" the above resolution, reiterated the above call, and called on Israel to desist "from taking any action which would alter the status of Jerusalem." The Security Council in a resolution of May 21, 1968, on the status of East Jerusalem, treated the main issue before it as identical with that which had been before the General Assembly in the above two resolutions, though it added a phrase on acts of land requisition of later occurrence. These later acts will be considered separately. It seems better, for the sake of clarity, to deal with the main legal questions raised on the basis of the two Assembly resolutions of July 1967, as now endorsed by the above Security Council resolution.

On this basis the following points emerge. Let it be supposed that the 'status of Jerusalem" sought to be preserved by the resolutions is its status *under international law.* It is then difficult to see why the General Assembly did not welcome the Israel reply of July 10, 1967, to the first resolution, stating that "the term 'annexation' used by the supporters of the resolution is out of place". It is also difficult to see how the measures concerned in July 1967, either by their terms or necessary effects, could change this *international* legal status. If, on the other hand, the "status of Jerusalem" referred to is not its *international* status, what the resolution means is even more perplexing. Presumably the reference would be to the extension of the authority of the Municipality of Jerusalem to the Old City, in replacement of the authorities existing under Jordanian occupation. Yet it is clear that the former Arab Mayor and several councillors of Old Jerusalem were invited to participate through a "Greater Jerusalem" Council, and refused to do so. It also seems clear that the Jerusalem municipality could not use its budget for the benefit of Old Jerusalem without the requisite administrative control. It is also clear that so far as functionaries of the former Old City government were willing to act, they have been continued in their duties. And even if there were some ground for criticism beneath the surface of these facts, they scarcely seem sufficiently serious to warrant such strong resolutions of the General Assembly and, later, of the Security Council. (On the rather natural Israel refusal to recognise the claims of the *ad hoc* self-constituted "Higher Muslim Council" to administer the West Bank and East Jerusalem, see S. S. Jones, "The Status of Jerusalem" in J. W. Halderman (ed.), *Symposium* 169, 171-72.)

The strangeness of such a meaning emerges when we ask what would have been the effect on the inhabitants of the Old City if Israel had complied with the call on July 4, 1967, to rescind the measures which it had passed. For if the Secretary-General's Representative was right in September to think that the substantial purpose of these measures was to upgrade the services for the Old City's inhabitants to equal those for West Jerusalem's inhabitants, then the effect of rescission would be to downgrade them back to inequality. Or, testing the matter by the law of military occupation, the resolutions would be suggesting that it is *un*lawful for an occupying authority to treat the local inhabitants more favourably than at the minimum standard set by international law. (This would be only slightly less perverse than claiming that Israel has a duty to levy contributions on the local inhabitants because the law of military occupation permits this.) And in concrete terms, rescission of the Israel measures would reintroduce rationing of water in the Old City, cut down garbage collections, close newly-opened child welfare clinics and the like. Obviously, this would relieve Israel from great economic burdens; but by the same token, it would gravely prejudice the position of the Arabs of East Jerusalem, a gravity which would increase with the deferment of peace.

Yet, returning to the meaning that it is the *international* status of Jerusalem which is involved, the problems are almost as great. How, in any case, can such measures of improvement of the conditions of the local inhabitants, be said to change the *international* status of the city? And how could rescission of them affect *this* status, either way? Remembering that Jerusalem has long been a single city, that its Jewish and Arab inhabitants all live nearer to each other than Hampstead is to Charing Cross or Morningten Heights to 42nd Street, would not Israel have been subjected to censure no less severe (if more sensible) if it had perpetuated the inferior Arab entitlements arising from Jordanian seizure of East Jerusalem in 1948?

I suggested in *The Middle East Under Cease-Fire,* in October 1967, that some main operative factors in this situation were perhaps not articulated in the resolutions. One was the deep religious, and historical emotions stirred in Israel and its people by renewed access to the ancient City of David and the Temple Mount, on which their daily prayers during 2,000 years of exile had centred, and from which Jordan had illegally barred them during its 20 years of occupation. Statements of Israel's intention not again to allow division of Jerusalem can be read by this light, rather than as directed to the future international law arrangements for the city. (International law, for example, certainly imposes no duty to restore the physical walls of division or the Jordanian illegal exclusions, in place of the regime of free access for all religious communities to their Holy Places at present assured by Israel. This, together with Israel's notable avoidance of language of "annexation" might have indicated the prudence of merely noting that no change in the international legal status of Jerusalem was intended. This Israel restraint was, after all, very significant, in view of the fact that, quite apart from ancient history, Jews have always exceeded Arabs in Jerusalem in modern times. In 1844 there were 7,120 Jews to 5,000 Moslems; in 1876, 12,000 Jews to 7,560 Moslems; in 1896, 28,112 Jews to 8,560 Moslems; in 1910

47,000 Jews to 9,800 Moslems; in 1931, 51,222 Jews to 19,894 Moslems; in 1948, 100,000 Jews to 40,000 Moslems, in 1967, 200,000 Jews to 54,903 Moslems.   This restraint betokened Israel's refusal, even at a moment of military success, to resort to simplistic exploitation of the ambiguous self-determination principle.   It is even more significant in view of the fact that some international lawyers of standing see recent events as establishing Israel's sovereign title to East Jerusalem, some on grounds of lawful annexation (e.g. M. Greenspan in *Los Angeles Times,* Nov. 17, 1968, Sect. 9, 3), some on other grounds of international law (e.g. E. Lauterpacht, *Jerusalem and the Holy Places* (1968)).

So that it remains a puzzle why United Nations organs should have taken positions on the status of Jerusalem which impute to Israel claims which she has not made, and then proceed to censure such non-existing claims.   (It is no less puzzling to find learned writers following this error so unquestioningly: see e.g. Q. Wright, N. H. El-Farra, and S. S. Jones, all in J. W. Halderman (ed.), *Symposium,* respectively at 29, 72, 175.)   If the resolutions be intended as precautionary admonitions against any such claims in the future, their censorial form is surely wrong and unjust.   Neither a State, nor anyone, for that matter, should be condemned for offences which they have not committed.   But even read as mere admonitions and not censures, these resolutions are beclouded with doubt as to their meaning and propriety under international law.   As is well known, Jordan's position in East Jerusalem from 1948 to 1967 was itself based on military seizure after her unlawful resort to war in 1948; Jordan herself, when she was thus an unlawful military occupant, did in fact without being censured *openly* (but abortively) attempt to annex East Jerusalem.   By contrast Israel entered East Jerusalem lawfully in defending herself against an attack launched by Jordan from East Jerusalem, and she has not purported to annex it under international law.

Whatever international law may in future prescribe for East Jerusalem, this cannot be restoration of a Jordanian occupation illegal in its origins, and in much of its administration. As will be seen in Section XIV, international law does not attribute reversionary rights to an ousted belligerent occupant, but only to an ousted Sovereign.   Much less does it attribute them to an occupant whose original entry was unlawful.

I have reserved from consideration until now those measures charged as affecting the "status" of East Jerusalem which might be regarded as pre-judicing rather than benefiting the local inhabitants.   These, which I now approach, all appear to be related to measures of expropriation of sections of land in East Jerusalem for certain public purposes, in themselves quite various.   The earliest was the clearance from around the West Wall of the ancient Jewish Temple Mount (known as the "Wailing Wall") of slum dwellings and latrines which Jordan, deliberately or not, had allowed to obstruct access to this holiest of holy places of the Jewish faith.   Another was the requisition with compensation of land in "the Jewish Quarter" of the Old City, for the purpose again of "cleaning up" the lamentable condition into which this historic area had been allowed to come under Jordanian occupation. (See the end of Section IV, above.) The problems there are somewhat complicated by the fact that some of this land, though under perpetual lease to the Jewish owners, was *Wafk* land.   A third was the requisition, with compensation, of land at Sheik Jarrah, some of Jewish, but most of Arab ownership, for housing development between the old and new cities.

The areas involved are small, and the number of cases few. Nevertheless, they do raise important and sometimes intricate questions as to their legality, and (depending on this) as to possible liability of Israel to displaced owners.

Most of them occurred after the General Assembly resolutions, but before the Security Council resolution, which incorporated a brief reference to them into general endorsement of the two General Assembly resolutions. At the present point, I assume, for purposes of this discussion, that they might be among the kinds of measures of which all those resolutions complained.

Even on this assumption, however, it would still seem erroneous to regard the status of East Jerusalem under international law as affected by these measures. If they were lawful, *cadit quaestio*. If they were unlawful, then the State of Israel would have incurred liabilities to the owners which in due course she should be required to discharge. But it is difficult to see in either case how such acts *could prejudice the international status* of Jerusalem. The correct legal analysis is rather that the international status of Jerusalem will be an element to be weighed, in due course, in determining whether Israel has incurred such liabilities. And the same is to be said as to liabilities which Israel may have incurred by reason of other changes in the legal system generally, introduced by Israel in East Jerusalem.

VIII. LEGAL STANDING OF THE GENERAL ASSEMBLY'S RESOLUTIONS ON EAST JERUSALEM

So far I have sought the meaning of the General Assembly's resolutions on Jerusalem, on the assumption that these are in some sense operative and binding on Israel. Such an assumption itself, however, requires examination. In particular, interesting questions arise as to the nature of the Fifth Emergency Special Session itself; as to its competence to deal with matters on which the Security Council is exercising its functions; as to the competence of even a duly convoked General Assembly even when not encroaching on Security Council functions, to lay down terms for settlement of a dispute other than as mere recommendations; and as to the effect generally of resolutions of the General Assembly.

The summoning of the Fifth Emergency Special Session was initiated by request of a Soviet Union dissatisfied by the refusal of most Members of the Security Council to support its demand for Israel to be declared an aggressor, and ordered to withdraw from all occupied territories. A majority of United Nations Members supporting the Soviet Union's request, the Special Session might be thought to have been convoked under Article 20, paragraph 2, of the Charter. The title "Emergency Special Session" given to it, however, implies that it was summoned under the Uniting for Peace Resolutions. It is to be pointed out at the outset, therefore, that under the applicable Uniting for Peace Resolution A, paragraph 1, this convocation was wholly irregular. For, under that paragraph, the Uniting for Peace procedure is only applicable where "because of lack of unanimity of the permanent members" (that is, a Great Power veto) the Security Council "fails to exercise its primary responsibility for the maintenance of international peace and security." In the instant situation, this condition was simply not fulfilled. The Security Council already had, *with unanimity of its Permanent Members*, exercised this responsibility by ordering cease-fires without withdrawal of forces, these had been obeyed, and fighting had ceased. In these circumstances it is dubious whether there was any serious task within Resolution A, paragraph 1, to be performed by the General Assembly.

Legally, therefore, the basis of the Fifth "Emergency" Special Session must be sought in the more general provision of Article 20, paragraph 2, by which a majority of Members may summon a special session. Such a special session though not limited as to business by the Uniting for Peace

Resolutions, is still of course subject to the limits set by the Charter on General Assembly business.   In particular, it is subject to Article 12(1) forbidding the General Assembly to "make any recommendation with regard to a dispute or situation in respect of which the Security Council is exercising . . . the functions assigned to it".   Yet throughout the duration of the Special Session the Security Council was continuing to exercise its functions in the Arab-Israel conflict as, indeed, is indicated by the Special Session's own final resolution of July 21, 1967, which recited that "the Security Council continues to be seized" of that conflict.   The only exception to the prohibition of Article 12(1) is on the Security Council's own request; but it is of course clear that there was no such request. Moreover, the legal irregularity of this entire Soviet initiative is increased by its repugnance also to Uniting for Peace Resolution B, enjoining the Security Council to perform its functions under Chapters 6 and 7. This, after all, is exactly what the Security Council *was* doing.   And its strangeness is sharpened by the Soviet Union's almost traditional stance up to that time against what it called "usurpation" by the General Assembly of the peace enforcement powers of the Security Council.

The above are doubts raised by the business of the Fifth Emergency Special Session as a whole.   The East Jerusalem resolutions perhaps also face another problem, that even if they are *valid* resolutions, any call they make upon Members still has *no binding legal force* upon Members. They are "non-magisterial", of the nature of mere recommendations.   (*Cf.* L. Gross, "Voting in the Security Council. . ." (1968) 62 *A.J.I.L.* 315, 330-331.)   For the General Assembly's powers with regard to the maintenance of international peace and security, including the formulation of the terms of settlement of disputes between States, do not extend beyond the making of recommendations. And, indeed, since the Security Council's own powers in this regard under Article 37 are so limited, the General Assembly's could not be expected to go further. Yet Resolutions 2253 (ES-V) and 2254 (ES-V) are in most peremptory terms, "calling" on Israel to rescind or desist from certain measures in one segment of a dispute between that State and certain Arab States.   And the rather arbitrary separation of this segment from the rest of the dispute over the protest of one disputant, raises a further doubt as to the propriety of these resolutions, pressed by the United States and Canadian representatives in the Security Council on May 21, 1968.

Obviously, the General Assembly controls its own internal procedure. This does not mean, however, that the law which it transgresses ceases to be law, or that its resolutions not conforming to law can be legally binding. Certainly, peremptory language in a resolution cannot convert a mere recommendation which Member States may or may not accept, into a decision legally binding on them.   Article 25 makes it quite clear that "decisions of the Security Council in accordance with the present Charter" are binding on Members.   (On the limits now even here, see L. Gross, "Voting in the Security Council. . ." (1968 62 *A.J.I.L.* 315-334.)   But there is no corresponding general accreditation even of General Assembly "decisions", much less of its recommendations.   This would be true for even the clearest, wisest and most prudent General Assembly resolution.   It is no less true for resolutions like those on East Jerusalem, surrounded as they are by a swarm of legal and factual dubieties.   Supposed exceptional cases where some authorities impute or concede some law-making force to General Assembly resolutions, have no application to the instant problems.   They pertain mostly to resolutions which declare existing obligations of members, or in which Members' votes manifest attitudes of States evidencing the growth of a new customary principle.

The Special Session's Jerusalem resolutions, therefore, whatever their terms mean, are at most hortatory and recommendatory to Members, including the State of Israel. Loose contrary statements will no doubt continue in partisan political warfare. And, as already seen, it even proved possible in the current membership of the Security Council for that body to be induced to adopt, on May 21, 1968, by 13 votes to nil (Canada and the United States abstaining after vigorous statements of objection) its own resolution endorsing the General Assembly's positions. (This later resolution added a censure of later Israel measures requisitioning certain lands which has already been mentioned.) It becomes legally important, therefore, to ask how far the above conclusions as to regularity of the General Assembly's resolutions also apply to their endorsement by the Security Council.

The Security Council action, of course, faces no difficulties as to the regularity of its convocation to discuss this question; nor obviously are there any problems of intrusion on the exclusive jurisdiction of any other organ. On the other hand, the problem of what sensible meaning, consistent with the welfare of the Arab inhabitants of East Jerusalem, can be given to the earlier resolutions, does apply also to the Security Council's endorsement of them. The most critical point, however, is as to what operation and legal effects flow from the Security Council action. On this, it is vital to ask whether the resolution was adopted as a decision on peace enforcement under Chapter 7, or as a recommendation of terms of settlement under Article 37 of Chapter 6. From the absence even of any reference to Chapter 7, it seems clear that the latter is the case. And this is confirmed by the fact that the main issue between the majority and minority in the debate was as to whether separate handling of the Jerusalem issue would help or hinder Dr. Jarring's efforts to promote a settlement based on the Security Council's resolution of November 22, 1967. Clearly, of course, this last resolution was based on Chapter 6. (See the U.K. representative's introduction of the resolution at the 1379th Meeting, Nov. 16, 1967, S/PV 1379, p. 6; and see Section X below.)

All this being so, and the Security Council having no legal power to *impose* terms of settlement, no resolution on such a matter can be a "decision" "binding" on Members under Article 25. (*Cf.* L. Gross, *op. cit.* (1968) 315, 330-331.) In short, resolutions stating terms of settlement under Chapter 6 can be only hortatory and recommendatory, just as with General Assembly action of the same purport. Or, in terms I have elsewhere put into use, the Jerusalem resolution of May 21, 1968, must be regarded as an exercise of the Security Council's "non-magisterial" powers under Chapter 6, and not of its "magisterial" powers under Chapter 7. Nor can the Security Council, any more than the General Assembly, convert what are mere recommendations into legal dispositions binding on the disputant States. The Statement of the Sponsoring Powers at San Francisco, asserting each organ's right to interpret the Charter as to its own function, was careful to add that "if an interpretation made by any organan. . . is not generally acceptable, it will be without binding force. . .". (UNCIO Documents 703, at 710, quoted L. Gross, "Voting in the Security Council. . ." (1968) 62 *A.J.I.L.* 315, 319, and *cf.* the discussion *id.* 315-328, 334. And see on the same point in the overall United Nations system, J. W. Halderman, ". . .Constitutional Aspects of the Palestine Case" in the *Symposium* edited by him, 79 at 84-85; S. Rosenne, ". . .Middle East Settlement. . ." in the same *Symposium* 44, 57-59.)

Without derogating from any of the above reasons for regarding the Security Council's Jerusalem Resolution of May 21, 1968, as not legally binding Israel to any action, a word may be added here as to the cogent general thesis recently offered by Professor Gross, it being recalled that the United States abstained from voting on that resolution. The joint effect (Professor Gross thinks) of the practice as to abstentions by permanent members, of the increase in the number of non-permanent members of the Security Council, and of the General Assembly's emphasis in elections of these latter not on contribution to maintenance of peace and security, but on equitable geographical distribution, may require limits to be recognised on the legal force even of substantive resolutions adopted by the Security Council under Chapter 7 of the Charter. For otherwise there would be the practical absurdity that resolutions for enforcement action could be "validly" adopted by nine votes, despite the abstention of some or even all of the permanent members. To avoid this absurdity, it is necessary to conclude that such resolutions are only legally valid under Article 25 as decisions imposing on members binding obligations to act or submit to action under the resolutions if concurred in by all permanent members as required by Article 27(3). Insofar as not so concurred in (for instance because of abstentions) they are "legally valid" only in the sense that they can *authorise* members to take indicated action. But even this authorisation could not be resorted to by members to justify violation of any obligations to other States or to international organisations pre-existing it. (L. Gross, *op. cit.* at 331; Sir Gerald Fitzmaurice, "The Law and Procedure of the International Court. . ." (1968) 34 *B.Y.B. of Int.L.* 1, 5.)

XIV. "THE MISSING REVERSIONERS" AND THE NEED FOR A PEACE TREATY

The legal problems of the past year are, of course, set within the framework of the legal relations of the various States following the cease-fires. That legal framework 1 described in *The Middle East Under Cease-Fire* as at October 1967. It rested on the finding that Israel's response on June 5 was lawful on grounds of self-defence against various warlike acts, including the naval blockade of the Straits of Tiran, and the overwhelming offensive forces mounted against her, and that it respected the limits of proportionality. I note that, since then, other authorities, and notably Professor Quincy Wright, have also arrived at the conclusion that the Arab States' actions against Israel immediately preceding the June war amounted to "armed attack". (Q. Wright, "Legal Aspects of the Middle East Situation" (1968) 33 *Law & Contemporary Problems* 5, 27), and that Israel's action was within the privilege of self-defence (W. V. O'Brien, "International Law and the Outbreak of War in the Middle East, 1967" (1967) 11 *Orbis* 692, 722-723). For the self-defence provision of Article 51 does not compel a State to remain a "sitting duck", when (as in this case) its neighbours have deliberately set up a military situation in which its only options are either to defend itself immediately or to submit to certain destruction. (I may add here the point that the Toyko International Military Tribunal held that The Netherlands' declaration of war on Japan on December 8, 1941, was lawful as having been made in "self-defence", in view of the imminence of a Japanese invasion of Dutch territories, even though no actual Japanese invasion had begun. (Judgment. . . , Nov. 4-12, 1948, pp. 994-95, quoted S. Horwitz, The Toyko Trial (1950, *International Conciliation* 560).)

I also pointed out last year that the same results followed on principle, even if one proceeded according to the international law defining aggression as the Soviet Union has long expounded it: various acts of Egypt and Syria preceding June 5, 1967, falling clearly within the Soviet criteria of aggression. It also followed from the positions of a substantial majority of the Security Council, including four of the Permanent Members, and from the attitudes of most United Nations Members, which declined to endorse the Arab and Soviet demands that Israel be declared an aggressor and ordered to withdraw. Ironically the Soviet Union has now added its own confirmation to the Israel side, at the opening of the current General Assembly. She solemnly claimed on October 5, 1968, that the Soviet invasion of Czechoslovakia in August 1968 was in "self-defence" against an attempt by western States to "snatch a link" from "the Socialist Commonwealth". This, of course, was before even any hostile mobilisation began, let alone any such besieging of all frontiers by vastly superior forces which faced Israel the year before. This Soviet claim, however extravagantly wrong it was for the Czechoslovak case, certainly shows that the Soviet Union recognises that international law may, in extreme situations like that facing Israel, sanction self-defence against an enemy's armed attack, even before he actually crosses the frontier.

It followed from this analysis that Israel's status in the occupied territories was that of a lawful occupant, entitled to stay under the rule *uti possidetis* until a peace is concluded. Furthermore, insofar as Egypt in Gaza, and Jordan on the West Bank and in East Jerusalem, were themselves merely military occupants, following their attacks of 1948, it became questionable whether they were entitled to those reversionary rights which ordinarily remain in a sovereign temporarily ousted by a military occupation. In the present discussion of the legal problems of the past year, I have assumed that Israel's rights and powers in the territories concerned were those *merely* of a military occupant. It becomes, therefore, important to develop further my conclusions of last year, and to ask whether this assumption is not unjust to Israel, since her legal status is in law less limited than this.

For this inquiry I take the West Bank as typical also for cases of East Jerusalem and (*vis-à-vis* Egypt) for Gaza, and for certain small border areas of former Palestine seized by Syria in 1948.

Further learned work since *The Middle East Under Cease-Fire* has documented a number of other propositions related to Jordan's status as merely a military occupant after the seizure in 1948. First, at the time of the Arab States' attacks on Israel in 1948, the West Bank could not be regarded as *res nullius* open to acquisitive occupation. Second, the entry of Transjordan onto the West Bank was described in the Security Council as an "unlawful invasion" (Ukrainian delegate Taresenko, S.C.O.R. 306th Meeting, May 27, 1948, p. 7) and an "aggression" (U.S. delegate Austin, S.C.O.R. 302nd Meeting, May 22, 1948, pp. 41-42), for which the pretexts offered were shifting and legally insufficient. Third, even the other Arab States denied the permissibility of Jordan's abortive annexation. Fourth, this annexation was, in any case, invalid as against the "freezing" provisions of the Armistice Agreement. (Jordan's delegate El Farra himself declared in the Security Council immediately before the June war: "I know of no boundary; I know of a situation frozen by an Armistice Agreement" (U.N. Doc. S/PV 1345, May 31, 1967, p. 47).) Fifth, the principle *ex iniuria non oritur ius* and related rules as to unlawful resort to war beclouded even Jordan's limited status of Military Occupant. (*Cf.* Y. Z. Blum, "The Missing Reversioner; Reflections on the Status of Judea and Samaria" (1968) 3 *Israel Law Review* 279-302, esp. 281-295.)

It was clear, even last year, that Israel's status on the West Bank under the cease-fire, after her lawful entry during hostilities, certainly displaced Jordan's military occupation. The new question, which I am now asking, is whether these facts do not vastly enlarge Israel's rights under international law beyond the status merely of a military occupant? To answer it we must look to the foundations of the law of military occupation.

One main objective of this law has been much canvassed in the present study, namely, that of protecting the local population while enabling the Occupant to protect his forces during his administration. The other main objective is concerned with the legal relations between the Occupant *and the ousted sovereign.* In other words, the whole law of military occupation proceeds on the double assumption: first, that it was a legitimate sovereign which was ousted from the territory by the Occupant; second, that the ousting power qualifies as a military occupant of it. (*Cf.* Glahn, *The Occupation of Enemy Territory* (1957) 245.) The assumption that there are such concurrent legal interests in the same territory lies at the root of all this body of rules of international law. Its rules here are designed to sanction the Occupant's administration *ad interim* as limited by the future reversionary rights, that is, the right of re-entry, of the ousted sovereign. But if this is so (and it is difficult to see how it can be otherwise), it would seem to follow that where the ousted State never was the legitimate sovereign, the rules to assure the reversion of the legitimate sovereign do not operate in his favour. (*Cf.* Blum, *op. cit.* 293.)

Once this position is reached, and it is remembered that neither Jordan nor any other State is a sovereign reversioner entitled to re-enter the West Bank, the legal standing of Israel takes on new aspects. She is a State in lawful control of territory in respect of which no other State can show a better title. The general principles of international law applicable to such a situation, moreover, are rather well established. The International Court of Justice, when called upon to adjudicate in territorial disputes, for instance in the *Minquiers* and *Echrehos* Case between the United Kingdom and France, proceeded "to appraise the relative strength of the opposing claims to. . .sovereignty." (I.C.J. *Reports,* 1953, p. 67; emphasis supplied.) Since title to territory is thus based on a claim not of *absolute,* but only of *relative,* validity, the result here seems decisive. No other State having a legal claim even equal to that of Israel under the cease-fire and the rule of *uti possidetis,* this relative superiority of title would seem to assimilate Israel's possession under international law to an absolute title, valid *erga omnes.*

This is the analysis, of course, only of the legal position which would remain in case of a final breakdown of efforts to secure a genuinely agreed peace. That its effect is so unexpectedly decisive should not conceal the cogency of the legal principles which support it. And all this underscores how vital it is that agreed terms of settlement be reached and embodied in treaties of peace or other appropriate agreements between the States so long and so tragically in conflict.

*   *   *

Scepticism about the effectiveness of international law cannot brush aside this present legal position in the Middle East. Israel in 1969 is no mere suppliant for her rights under international law, pitting legal entitlements against superior physical power of a transgressing adversary. Rather, after a victorious self-defence ending in lawful possession of territories over some of which no other State has as good a title, Israel also maintains the military capacity to maintain her hold on these. Such possession, amounting actually (or potentially, by some formal step which Israel is entitled to take) to sovereign title, faces us with one of those rare (but not unique) situations in which legal rights and actual power march together for one contestant. Short of a direct Soviet military assault on Israel, involving risks of major war which the Soviet Union has no sensible motive of self-interest to incur, Soviet partisanship can protract but cannot basically change this situation. To change it, Arab adversaries must be strong enough to subvert the rights thus vested in Israel under international law, as well as to defeat her citizen forces. Or they must join with Israel in agreeing mutual boundaries and other terms within which each can live in peace and reasonable security, and (we may even hope) in co-operative dedication to the common tasks facing all the peoples of the region.

The "Middle East": The Misunderstood Conflict

M. CHERIF BASSIOUNI

To many an observer of events in the "Middle East" the constant state of war and confrontation of the last quarter century is bewildering. The most perplexing aspect of the question to the American observer is the almost instant failure of every proposed "peace plan." This presentation will attempt to touch upon the reasons for this phenomenon.

A basic premise of this presentation is that "peace efforts," whether they came from the United Nations, the United States, or nongovernmental sources, have failed almost simultaneously with their tender because they were based on misunderstandings of Arab perceptions of the situation. Understanding Arab perceptions of the various facets of all issues and their significance is indispensable to full realization of the potential for peaceful resolution by the proper application and implementation of international law in general and the United Nations Charter in particular. Too often international law and the United Nations Charter—themselves the product of Western European and American thought—have been indiscriminately interpreted and applied with a Western perspective to events taking place in non-Western European civilization areas of the world and to their people. These people in turn see this process as a covert extension of Western hegemony over them.

Let us consider some of the more serious of these misunderstandings and the unfortunate effects they have had on efforts to bring about peaceful resolution of conflicts in the "Middle East," with emphasis on the Arab perspective.

I. Some Definitional Problems

A. *The "Middle East," The "Arab World," and "The Arabs"*

The most obvious example of Western European and American "misunderstanding" is exhibited by the recurring use of the term "Middle East" in reference to that part of the world. The description is neither correct geographically nor apt politically. The Arab world may be in relationship to Europe mid-way to what Western Europe calls the "East." The Arab world is, however, by the same rationale, the "Middle West" in relationship to India. It all depends in which direction the beholder looks. According to many geographic definitions of the "Middle East" Iran is encompassed therein, even though that country has, for all practical purposes, no relationship to the Arab-Israeli conflict. Accordingly, the Sudan, for that matter, is excluded from the "Middle East," since it is in Africa. The Sudan, however, is a member of the

---

* Professor of Law, De Paul University, College of Law. 1970 Fulbright-Hays Professor of International Criminal Law and Visiting Professor of Law, The University of Freiburg, Germany. A.B. 1955, Coll. of the Holy Family; LL.B. 1961, Cairo, Univ.; J.D. 1964, Indiana (Indianapolis); LL.M. 1966, John Marshall.

League of Arab States, is considering becoming a member of the newly contemplated Federation of the United Arab Republic, Libya, and Syria, and is very much involved in the "conflict." One should also, by that same generally accepted definition of the "Middle East," exclude the North African states of Lybia, Tunisia, Algeria, and Morocco, even though they are members of the League of Arab States, and to varying degrees of involvement, parties to the Arab-Israeli conflict.

The area within which the "conflict" is taking place, by Arab perception, is the "Arab World." The Arab world is defined by the geo-political conceptual link of Arab nationalism. This concept encompasses the land of the Arabs (including those people within their geographic midst whom the Arabs presently consider their adversaries, the Zionists of Israel) and the people who call themselves "Arabs." From various sources of contemporary Arab political doctrine, the following definition is proposed: The Arabs are those people who regardless of their religion or faith originate from an Arab state, or a member state of the League of Arab States, or who inhabit any Arab territory that was part of the Islamic nation; who are Arab-speaking people; who share the common culture and tradition of the Arabic-speaking people; who as people through their historical development experienced in varying degrees the effects of imperialism-colonialism; who as members of different political entities aspire either to unification, integration, or coordination of their national goals and policies; and who as individuals believe they are Arabs.

B. *Palestine and the Palestinians*

The area known as Palestine is bordered by the Mediterranean on the east, the Jordan River on the west, the Golan Mountains and the Sea of Galilee on the north, and the Negev and Sinai Deserts on the south. The Palestinians, Arabs because they are descendants of Abraham and Semites by race, have inhabited the same area since time immemorial and have lived continuously in the region known as Palestine from the seventh century until the twentieth century. Since 1947-48, however, after the creation of the State of Israel on that same territory, they have been living in forced exile. Semites have always inhabited that area of the world whether they were Atheists, Jews, Christians, or Muslims.

In 634 A.D., Semitic Arabs incorporated Palestine in the Islamic nation, and its people were overwhelmingly Muslims and Christians. Few Jews had remained after the Romans occupied the land in the first century and forcefully dispersed the Semitic Jewish tribes, specifically issuing a decree banishing them from Jerusalem. That signaled the start of the Jewish Diaspora. Not all Palestinians were Jews and not all left Palestine—some remained. When the Semitic tribes who lived south of Palestine in the Arabian peninsula drove the Romans out in 634, they rescinded the decree of banishment, but few Jews returned.[1]

---

[1] A. TIBAWI, JERUSALEM: ITS PLACE IN ISLAM AND ARAB HISTORY IN THE ARAB-ISRAELI CONFRONTATION OF JUNE 1967, at 10 (ed. I. Abu Lughod 1970).

The population of Roman Palestine and then of Muslim Palestine remained fairly identifiable from the rest of either empire. Through both eras a proconsul or governor ruled the area, his authority extending to all or part of the territory described above. Throughout the entire Islamic era preceding the creation of the Turkish Ottoman empire, Palestine remained an identifiable region with more or less autonomous local government and administration. This system was not only continued but in fact markedly increased under Turkish rule. Palestine remained, with its people, an identifiable part of the Islamic nation as well as of the Turkish Ottoman empire as did other regions, such as Egypt.[2] When the Turks were driven out of Jerusalem in World War I by Arab and British forces, England perfidiously established, with the help of the League of Nations, a protectorate over Palestine. However, even that colonial device, the mandate system, spoke of the "provisionally independent state of Palestine," further underlining the identifiable character of the territory and its inhabitants as a clearly distinguishable group of people. The mandate system was predicated on the existence of a Palestinian entity, which under the mandator's administration was to blossom into complete independence. The administration of Palestine under the mandate reinforced that fact through the establishment of legislative, executive, and judicial bodies. Palestine had a flag, and its nationals carried passports recognized abroad. In effect, with the exception of foreign affairs and subject to the internal limitations imposed by Great Britain, which acted in the same manner as it had in Egypt or India, Palestine had all the characteristics of a soverign state.

In 1947-48, however, the Palestinians ceased to be a "people" and became refugees just as Palestine ceased to exist as an identifiable region. Between 1948 and 1969, Palestinians were almost uniformly treated by Western European and American spokesmen as "refugees," and from that time on the "misunderstanding" was perpetuated. Even the United Nations in its annually reaffirmed resolution granting the "refugees" a right to return to their former homeland and to compensation for their lost property did not admit to the reality that these refugees constitute a "people."[3] It was not until December 1969 that a General Assembly resolution finally recognized this fact and spoke of the "alienable rights of the Palestinian people."[4] thus it can be stated that

---

[2] Id.

[3] Bassiouni, *The Palestinians: Refugees or a People, The Catholic World* 257-62 (Sept. 1970). *See also* G.A. Res. 194, III U.N. Doc. A/810 at 21 (1948); M. BASSIOUNI, SOME LEGAL ASPECTS OF THE ARAB-ISRAELI CONFLICT IN THE ARAB-ISRAELI CONFRONTATION OF JUNE 1967, at 91, 101-03 (ed. I. Abu-Lughod 1970).

[4] G.A. Res. 2535 (xxiv), which states:
Part B. *The General Assembly,*
   Recognizing that the problem of the Palestine Arab refugees has arisen from the denial of their inalienable rights under the Charter of the United Nations and the Universal Declaration of Human Rights.
   Gravely concerned that the denial of their rights has been aggravated by the reported acts of collective punishment, arbitrary detention, curfews, destruction of homes and property, deportation and other repressive acts against the refugees and other inhabitants of the occupied territories,
   Recalling Security Council resolution 237 (1967) of 14 June 1967,
   Recalling also its resolutions 2252 (ES-V) of 4 July 1967, and 2452 A (XXIII) of 19 December 1968 calling upon "the Government of Israel to take effective and immediate steps for the return without delay of those inhabitants who have fled the areas since the outbreak of hostilities,"

the Palestinians are: Those individuals who as part of the Palestinian people entity inhabited that region of Palestine which since 1922 has been the "provisionally independent state of Palestine" (as described by the League of Nations mandate) and who are now in forced exile seeking to return to their homeland.

It must be noted that Israeli officials have publicly and officially rejected any notion that the Palestinians exist as a people or otherwise except as refugees. Their official position is that the question is only one of refugees in need of a humanitarian solution and no more. One need only point to Prime Minister Golda Meir's statement to the *Times* of London (June 15, 1969, at 1, col. 3): "There was no such thing as Palestinians . . . . They did not exist."

C. *Jews, Zionists, and Israelis*

It is of utmost importance to distinguish between (a) *Israelis* (nationals of the State of Israel), (b) *Zionists* (adherents and supporters of the political doctrine called "Zionism") and (c) *Jews* (adherents to the religious faith of Judaism).

A *Jew* is a person of the Jewish faith but can be a national of any state other than Israel and does not have to be a Zionist by reason of his faith. In fact, Orthodox Jews are strongly anti-Zionists, as are many Jews who are not (religiously) Orthodox. Sephardim Jews are Arabs while Ashkenazi Jews are European even though they claim to have maintained a link to their Semitic origin by intermarriage in Europe over the last two thousand years. This claim is highly debatable and rejected by Arabs who see in ethnicity more than a high percentage of intermarriage. Many Jewish communities, like the one in Russia, are descendants of the Khazass who are not Semites but rather are Caucasians (or of other stock) who merely converted to the Hebraic Faith. Arabs point to the notorious disparity in Israel between Arab and non-Arab Jews as an indication that even in the integrated Israeli society Arab Jews (Sephardim) are less equal than European Jews (Ashkenazi).

A *Zionist* is an adherent or supporter of the political doctrine of programs of Zionist organizations and need be neither an Israeli national nor a Jew. Many staunch Zionists live outside Israel, and many politically and financially influential supporters of Zionism are not Jews.

This article will not deal with the significance of Zionism or its implications as the subject was covered in an earlier definitive study by Professor W. T.

Desirous of giving effect to its resolutions for relieving the plight of the displaced persons and the refugees,

1. *Reaffirms* the inalienable rights of the people of Palestine;

2. *Draws the attention* of the Security Council to the grave situation resulting from Israeli policies and practices in the occupied territories and Israel's refusal to implement the above resolutions;

3. *Requests* the Security Council to take effective measures in accordance with the relevant provisions of the Charter of the United Nations to ensure the implementation of these resolutions.

1827th plenary meeting,
10 December 1969.

Mallison, Jr.[5] It must be stated, however, that American Zionists are part of the intricate organizational structure of the World Zionist Organization-American Section, which is registered with the United States Department of Justice as an "agent for a foreign government."[6] Interestingly enough, the United Jewish Appeal, which is part of this organizational and interlocking corporate structure, is a United States tax-exempt organization despite being part of a structure that is an admitted and registered agency of a foreign government and that channels its collected funds to Israel. Zionist organizations throughout the world expect to raise one billion dollars for Israel in 1971—the major portion to come from the United States.[7] This, among other manifestations of support, evidences the relationship between World Zionism and the State of Israel.

A very important consequence of Zionism is its direct financial and political support of Israel regardless of the nationality of the Zionists themselves. The Arab perception of United States policy is that it is clearly influenced by Zionist and Zionist-supporting pressure groups. The allowance of internal advantages such as the tax-exempt status granted to Zionist affiliated organizations while such advantages are denied to all others underlies this perception. The continuous political support given Israel by prominent public figures plagues even the pretense of American "even handedness" and creates a great barrier of distrust due in large part to the actual political power of Zionists in America, which is used so effectively in favor of Israel.

An *Israeli* is a citizen of Israel who nominally may be neither a Jew nor a Zionist. This distinction holds true even though Zionism makes a "claim" on all Jews of the world and "Israel" constitutes the political embodiment of the "Jewish People" doctrine relied upon by Zionism. This discriminatory doctrine is implemented in a variety of ways, the most significant of which is the Israeli "Law of Return" granting all Jews (and only Jews) a right to Israeli citizenship.[8] Not unique as a discriminatory device, its use is all too obvious to the Palestinians. This doctrine of the "Jewish People" was clearly enunciated in *Attorney General of Israel v. Eichmann,* wherein the Israeli Supreme Court held: "The connection between Jewish people and the State of Israel constitutes an integral part of the law of nations . . . ."[9] The State of Israel prosecuted

---

[5] Mallison, *Legal Problems Concerning the Juridical States and Political Activities of the Zionist Organization; Jewish Agency: A Study of International and United States Law* 19 WM. & MARY L. REV. 556 (1968); Mallison, *infra,* note 10.

[6] *See* U.S. DEPT. OF JUSTICE, FOREIGN AGENTS REGISTRATION SECTION, *The Covenant between the Government of Israel and the Zionist Executive of the Jewish Agency* (July 28, 1969); SUPPLEMENTAL REGISTRATION, *Appendix to the Covenant between the Government and the Executive of the Jewish Agency* (June 8, 1970), outlining the relationship of the public status of the Zionist organization to the Government of Israel. To illustrate the degree of the Israeli Government's control over such organizations as the B'Nai B'Rith, see Joftes v. Kaufman, Civil Action No. 3271-67 (1969), U.S. District Court, District of Columbia, wherein Mr. Joftes, the International Secretary of the B'Nai B'Rith, showed that that organization fell under Israeli control.

[7] Le Monde, Jan. 7, 1971, at 4, col. 6.

[8] Law of July 5, 1950, 4 LAWS OF THE STATE OF ISRAEL 114, *as amended,* 8 ISRAEL LAWS 114.

[9] Sup. Ct. of Israel, Crim. App. No. 336/61 (May 29, 1962).

Adolf Eichmann for crimes committed against the "Jewish People,"[10] whom the State of Israel purported to represent even though the said crimes were committed prior to the existence of the State (May 15, 1948). It was this same rationale on which Israel relied to collect war reparations and compensation from the Federal Republic of Germany for acts of the Nazi regime of Germany against European Jews during World War II, regardless of their nationality. Parenthetically, it must be noted that discrimination breeds but the same even in the reverse. The "Jewish People" doctrine arose as a consequence of its imposition on Jews by anti-Semites. Even in the U.S.S.R. Jews are presently considered a "people" except that the distinction is used as a pretense for anti-Semitism. The "Jewish People" doctrine finds its greatest support among anti-Semites who seek to perpetuate distinctions between Jews and non-Jews.

A juridically novel device is the distinction in Israeli municipal law between "nationality" reserved to Jews and "citizenship" for Israelis who may also be non-Jews. This distinction appears in identification documents released in Israel by the Ministry of Interior and was brought to world attention by the famed *Shalit* case where the children of Commander Shalit of the Israeli Navy, an Israeli and a Jew, were denied Jewish nationality because their mother was a Christian.[11] Arabs point to that fact as further evidence of Israeli discrimination. Indeed, a case can be made against Israel since the enactment of the law of return and other legal and administrative practices are violative of Article 1 and 55 of the United Nations Charter, which guarantees "respect for human rights and for fundamental freedoms for all without distinction as to race, sex, language or religion." Such practices are also in violation of the covenants for the protection of civil, political, social, and economic rights, as well as, of course, the Universal Declaration of Human Rights.[12]

II. Conflicts in The Arab World

To most Western observers, the central, if not the only, conflict in the "Middle East" is the war between Israel and some Arab states. Only recently has attention focused on the existence of the Palestinian people who were previously considered merely as refugees. There are, however, at least five different sources of conflict in the Arab World. They are:

1. The war for Palestine.
2. The territorial war between Israel and some neighboring Arab states.
3. The ideological conflict between Zionism and Arabism.
4. Conflicts within the Arab World and within Israel:
   a. The Arab Revolution.
   b. The demographic and ideological transformation of Israel.

---

[10] Mallison, *The Zionist-Israel Juridical Claims To Constitute "the Jewish People" Nationality Entity and to Confer Membership in It: Appraisals in Public International Law*, 32 Geo. Wash. L. Rev. 983, 1050 (1964).

[11] Shalit v. Minister of Interior, 23 P.D. 477-608 (1969), *noted* in Israel L. Rev. 259-263 (1970).

[12] *See also* Report of the Special Committee To Investigate Israeli Practices Affecting the Human Rights of the Population of the Occupied Territories, U.N. Doc. A/8089 (1970), which condemned Israel for human rights violations.

5. The "Cold War" in the "Middle East":
   a. United States interests and policies.
   b. U.S.S.R. interests and policies.
   c. Western European interests and policies.
   d. The Afro-Asian nonaligned states' interests and policies.

This paper will cover essentially the first two of these conflicts, touching upon the others only for illustrative purposes.

A. *The War for Palestine*

Prior to 1947, this war was primarily a civil war between Palestinians and Zionist occupiers of their lands. After the Palestinian Diaspora in 1947-48, it became a war between exiled Palestinians and those who constituted the State of Israel. That which was a civil conflict was transformed into an international war by Israel's removal of the Palestinians from the territory in contention. What makes any armed conflict a war in the sense of international law is that at least one of the parties is a state. As stated by one author: "While it takes two to make a quarrel, it takes only one government to make a war."[13] Thus, the effective exclusion of Palestinians from the territory of Palestine and the transformation of the legal and political structures of that state altered the nature of the conflict. Military operations by Palestinians subsequent to the creation of the State of Israel were claimed to be acts of terrorism within the meaning of international law. States aiding and abetting Palestinians outside Israel were held responsible by Israel for such acts, which were said to justify Israeli reprisals.[14] Assistance by Arab states to Palestinian exiles active in their "war of liberation" was even considered (by Israel) to be aggression against Israel.

What was a civil conflict became an international war solely because some of the people (the Jews in Palestine) created a new political entity (Israel) to replace another one (the provisionally independent state of Palestine under mandate) on the same territory (Palestine), excluding from that new entity and expelling from that territory those people who challenged its creation and existence (the non-Jews of Palestine).

What, then, if any, are the rights under international law of the Palestinians in this new situation? International law developed historically as the law of nations predicated on a body of customs and practice between soverign states that generated structures and rules designed to insure the safeguard of its subjects, *i.e.,* states. Nonsubjects, especially individuals, were left outside the protective scheme and right-duty relationship set by international law. Only recently has this classical notion been challenged, most especially in the human rights field.[15] It is advanced that the rights of the Palestinians are: (a) the right of self-determination and (b) the right of self-defense.

---

[13] J. Stone, Legal Controls of International Conflicts 305 (1954).
[14] Falk, *The Beyrouth Raid and the International Law of Retaliation,* 63 Am. J. Int'l L. 415 (1969); Blum, *The Beirut Raid and the International Double Standard, A Reply to Professor Richard A. Falk,* 64 Am. J. Int'l L. 73 (1970).
[15] I M. Whitman, Digest of International Law 50-58 (1963).

1. *The Palestinians' Right of Self-Determination.* a. *Nature of the Right.*[16] Self-determination as a political doctrine first manifested itself in the French and American Revolutions. It refers, in its political context, to the free and genuine expression of the will of the people, and accordingly includes the right of the people to determine their own political, economic, and cultural status, together with what form of government shall attain permanent sovereignty over their territory, natural wealth, and resources.[17]

There has been considerable disagreement as to what groups may invoke the right of self-determination. It has been said that every ethno-cultural group that constitutes the majority in a cultural area has the right to create a national state of its own. On the other hand, the theory has been advanced that the right of self-determination does not apply to such majority-minority divisions but only to nations. The term "nation" connotes large groups of people inhabiting and identified with a particular territory, sharing common historical traditions, normally speaking a common tongue, and who *feel* that they form a single and exclusive community, sharing compatible views as to their future political and civil association. Finally, it has been contended that the right of self-determination applies to any reasonably designated group. This is the crux of the problem. It is not that individuals ask to form an independent state; it is that there are several groups of people in the world who may or may not be "nations," but who are demanding the right of self-determination and its corollary, political independence. There is no agreement on where to draw the line, and thus the political doctrine has failed to find a juridical foundation that lends itself to legal implementation without resort to insurrection or a "war of liberation."

Essentially the doctrine of self-determination gained recognition as a principle of international law after World War I; indeed, procedures for the realization of this right were incorporated into the mandate system itself. It is clear, however, that under Article 22 of the League of Nations Covenant, the right of self-determination was reserved to non-self-governing territories. The mandate system was thus justified as a means of aiding the establishment of self-governing institutions in the mandate countries. Therefore, to the extent that the mandate country was subject to the "tutelage" of the Mandatory Power, the right of self-determination was reserved for the people of the mandated territory. To facilitate the eventual creation of a Jewish National Home, however, stringent restrictions upon the right of self-determination were imposed by the mandate controlling the Palestinian people. To the extent that this attempted reconciliation of such antagonistic goals placed *greater* restrictions upon the right of self-government, the establishment of the Jewish National Home conflicted with the right of self-determination.

---

[16] The discussion below on the nature of the right of self-determination is from Bassiouni & Fisher, *The Arab-Israeli Conflict—Real and Apparent Issues: An Insight into Its Future from the Lessons of the Past*, 44 St. John's L. Rev. 399-465, 448-52 (1970).

[17] *See generally* Bos, *Self-Determination by the Grace of History*, 15 Netherlands Int'l L. Rev. 362 (1968).

Although Article 2, which enumerates the principles of the United Nations, does not specifically refer to the right of self-determination, the doctrine was in fact incorporated into the United Nations Charter. Article 1(2) declares that the purpose of the United Nations is to develop friendly relations among nations "based on respect for the principle of equal rights and self-determination of peoples." Clearly the use of the singular noun "principle" indicates that "equal rights and self-determination of peoples" are considered elements of a single principle. The same phrase occurs in Article 55, which deals not with political but with social and economic matters. Many scholars feel, however, that the enunciation of the principle of self-determination in the Charter is not the embodiment *in toto* of the positive aspects of that concept.[18] For example, Hans Kelsen in *The Law of the United Nations* has stated: "If the 'peoples' in Article 1, paragraph 2 means the same as 'nations' in the Preamble then 'equal rights and self-determination of peoples' in Article I, paragraph 2 can only refer to the sovereignty of states."[19] Therefore, although not establishing self-determination of peoples in the ethno-political sense as a principle of the organizational structure of the United Nations, the Charter does, by incorporating it in the material sense, at least provide a general and recognized principle of international law.[20] Implied references to self-determination also appear in scattered articles in Chapter XII (International Trusteeship System) of the Charter. These articles refer to self-government and independence though not specifically to self-determination, and are the counterparts of Article 22 of the Covenant of the League of Nations. Other provisions of the Charter also evidence this principle. Article 73 (referring to trusteeship obligations) clearly imposes a duty, deemed "a sacred trust," to "insure, with due respect for the

---

[18] L. BLOOMFIELD, EVOLUTION OR REVOLUTION? THE UNITED NATIONS AND THE PROBLEM OF PEACEFUL CHANGE (1957); H. LAUTERPACHT, INTERNATIONAL LAW AND HUMAN RIGHTS (1950); A. ROLING, INTERNATIONAL LAW IN AN EXPANDED WORLD (1960); F. SAYEGH, THE ARAB-ISRAELI CONFLICT 9 (N.Y. Arab Information Center, 1964); G. SCELLE, QUELQUES REFLEXIONS SUR LE DROIT DES PEUPLES À DISPOSER D'EUX MEMES (1957); Bowett & Emerson, *Self-Determination*, 1966 PROCEEDINGS AM. SOC'Y INT'L L. 130, 138; de Nova, *The International Protection of National Minorities and Human Rights*, 11 HOW. L.J. 275-76 (1965); Lauterpacht, *Règles Générales du Droit de la Paix*, HAGUE REC. 1937—IV; *From Protection of Minorities to Promotion of Human Rights*, 1948 JEWISH Y.B. INT'L L. 119.

[19] H. KELSEN, THE LAW OF THE UNITED NATIONS (1950).

[20] See M. SHUKRI, THE CONCEPT OF SELF-DETERMINATION IN THE UNITED NATIONS (1965); Bowett, *Self-Determination and Political Rights in Developing Countries*, 1966 PROCEEDINGS AM. SOC'Y INT'L L. 129. The subsequent history of the United Nations corroborates the proposition that it is more than a recognized concept and has become a general principle of international law. See, e.g., the General Assembly's request of the Commission on Human Rights to study ways and means "which would ensure the right of peoples and nations to self-determination." G.A. Res. 421, 5 U.N. GAOR Supp. 20, at 43, U.N. Doc. A/1775 (1950). At its Seventh Session the General Assembly stated that "all peoples shall have the right of self determination." G.A. Res. 545, 7 U.N. GAOR Supp. 20, at —, U.N. Doc. A/2361 (1952). The Commission on Human Rights prepared several resolutions on the matter that were adopted by the General Assembly, G.A. Res. 837, 9 U.N. GAOR Supp. 21, at 21, U.N. Doc. A/2890 (1954); G.A. Res. 9 U.N. GAOR Supp. 21, at 20, U.N. Doc. A/2890 (1954); G.A. Res. 738, 8 U.N. GAOR Supp. 17, at 18, U.N. Doc. A/2630 (1953); G.A. Res. 612, 7 U.N. GAOR Supp. 20, at 5, U.N. Doc. A/2361 (1952); G.A. Res. 611, 7 U.N. GAOR Supp. 20, at 5, U.N. Doc. A/2361 (1952); G.A. Res. 648, 7 U.N. GAOR Supp. 20, at 33, U.N. Doc. A/2361 (1952); G.A. Res. 637, 7 U.N. GAOR Supp. 20, at 26, U.N. Doc. A/2361 (1952). See also Colonial Resolution, G.A. Res. 1514, 15 U.N. GAOR Supp. 16, at 66, U.N. Doc. A/L. 323 (1960). At its Tenth Session the General Assembly examined the draft articles of the Covenant on Civil and Political Rights and the Covenant on Economic, Social, and Cultural Rights, which were subsequently adopted on Dec. 16, 1966. G.A. Res. 2200, 21 U.N. GAOR Supp. 16, at 49, U.N. Doc. A/6546 (1966). See also Eagleton, *Self-Determination in the United Nations*, 47 AM. J. INT'L L. 88 (1953).

culture of the peoples concerned, their political, economic, social, and educational advancement, their just treatment, and their protection against abuses; *[t]o develop self-government, to take due account of the political aspirations of the peoples . . . ."*[21] In addition, Article 76, which sets forth the basic objectives of the trusteeship system, states:

> To promote the political, economic, social, and educational advancement of the inhabitants of the trust territories, and their progressive development towards self-government or independence as may be appropriate to the particular circumstances of each territory and its peoples and the freely expressed wishes of the peoples concerned, and as may be provided by the terms of each trusteeship agreement . . . .[22]

Finally, Article 21 of the Universal Declaration of Human Rights adopted by the General Assembly provides that "[t]he will of the people shall be the basis of the authority of government . . . ."[23]

The United Nations has indeed a prolific history of resolutions seeking to uphold and implement the principle of self-determination. Notwithstanding these pronouncements, Professor Sohn states:

> With regard to the principle of self-determination, although international recognition was extended to this principle at the end of the First World War and it was adhered to with regard to the other Arab territories, at the time of the creation of the "A" Mandates, it was not applied to Palestine, obviously because of the intention to make possible the creation of the Jewish National Home there. Actually, it may well be said that the Jewish National Home and the *sui generis* Mandate for Palestine run counter to that principle.[24]

The American position is theoretically in full support of self-determination. Professor Moore quotes Thomas Jefferson who, as Secretary of State in 1792, with reference to the recognition of France's revolutionary government, stated: "It accords with our principles to acknowledge any government to be rightful which is formed by *the will of the nation, substantially declared.*"[25] Less remote is the particular significance that the doctrine has assumed with the international dislocation of the present century. In a 1917 speech, President Wilson proposed that "no nation should seek to extend its polity over any other nation or people, but that every people should be left free to determine its own polity, its own way of development, unhindered, unthreatened, unafraid, the little along with the great and powerful."[26] Reminiscent of the Wilsonian philosophy is the Atlantic Charter, which, in expressing the ideals of the United States and Great Britain, established that they "respect the right of all peoples to choose the form of government under which they will live;

---

[21] U.N. CHARTER art. 73(a)-(b) (emphasis added).

[22] U.N. CHARTER art. 76(b).

[23] G.A. Res. 217, U.N. Doc. A/555 at 71 (1948).

[24] L. SOHN, CASES AND MATERIALS ON UNITED NATIONS LAW 429 (1967).

[25] I J. MOORE, DIGEST OF INTERNATIONAL LAW 120 (1906) (emphasis added).

[26] S. Doc. No. 685, 64th Cong., 2d Sess. 8 (1917).

and they wish to see sovereign rights and self-government restored to those who have been forcibly deprived of them . . . ."[27]

The same principle was embodied in the Declaration of Yalta on February 11, 1945, with respect to Europe; and what had been the position of the United States and France became that of the Allies and a cornerstone of the United Nations principles.

A central question remains to be answered with respect to the nature of such a right: Is it a peoples' right or is it a territorial right exercisable by those within its confines? In abstract theory, people determine their goals regardless of geographic limitations; however, in realistic theory it is exercisable only when it can be actuated within a given territory susceptible of acquiring the characteristics of sovereignty, a prerequisite for acquiring membership in the community of nations. To understand the implications of this proposition one must consider the historical development of the State of Israel as it arose out of the "provisionally independent State of Palestine" through a forceful and imposed demographic transformation.

b. *The Demographic Context of the Right of Self-Determination in Palestine and the United Nation's Partition Plan.* At the time Lord Balfour responded to a letter from Baron Rothschild in 1917, in which he made a "declaration" known since as the "Balfour Declaration," the population of Palestine was approximately 90 percent Arab. The "Balfour Declaration," mindful of the Arab character of Palestine, promised to facilitate the establishment of a "National Jewish Homeland in *Palestine*" (emphasis added) to

---

[27] S. Doc. No. 123, 81st Cong., 1st Sess. 1 (1950). *See also* Kunz, *The Present Status of the International Law for the Protection of Minorities*, 48 Am. J. Int'l L. 282 (1954).

Although some scholars have questioned the existence of the right of self-determination as a general principle of international law, this view seems insupportable. An historical review of the right as applicable to religious freedom of choice indicates a custom evidenced by some practice. Certainly, the history of colonialism-imperialism cannot sustain such a questionable proposition. If self-determination refers to a given peoples's right to choose its form of government and institutions and to control its resources, such a right is enshrined in the Charter (art. 1, ¶ 2; art. 55), and nowhere is the Charter principle more explicitly stated than in article 1 of the International Covenant on Civil and Political Rights of 1966: "All peoples have the right of self-determination. By virtue of the right they freely determine their political status and freely pursue their economic, social and cultural development . . . [and] freely dispose of their natural wealth and resources." G.A. Res. 2200, 21 U.N. GAOR, Supp. 16, at 52-58, U.N. Doc. A/6316 (1966); *see generally* H. Johnson, Self-Determination Within the Community of Nations (1967). The practice of the United Nations and its agencies is replete with examples and precedents of adhering to the right of self-determination and its implementation. The General Assembly has a prolific history of resolutions on the point. *See, e.g.,* G.A. Res. 2372, 22 U.N. GAOR, Supp. 16A, at 1-2, U.N. Doc. A/6716/Add.1 (1968) (South-West Africa). As applicable to the Palestinians, the right of self-determination was expressed by the General Assembly of December 1970 as follows:

The General Assembly,

Recognizing that the problem of the Palestinian Arab refugees has arisen from the denial of their inalienable rights under the Charter of the United Nations and the Universal Declaration of Human Rights,

Recalling its resolution 2535B (XXIV) of 10 December 1969, in which it reaffirmed the inalienable rights of the people of Palestine,

Bearing in mind the principle of equal rights and self-determination of peoples enshrined in Articles 1 and 55 of the Charter of the United Nations and concerning Friendly Relations and Cooperation among States in accordance with the Charter of the United Nations [GAOR 2625 (XXV)]:

1. *Recognizes* that the people of Palestine are entitled to equal rights and self-determination, in accordance with the Charter of the United Nations;

2. *Declares* that full respect for the inalienable rights of the people of Palestine is an indispensable element in the establishment of a just and lasting peace in the Middle East.

U.N. GAOR 2672 (XXV) (A/8013), at 4.

Jews willing to immigrate to Palestine, but also sought to safeguard the rights of the Arabs by these terms: "It being clearly understood that nothing shall be done which may prejudice the civil and religious rights of non-Jewish communities in Palestine, or the rights and political status enjoyed by Jews in any other country."[28]

A Jewish national home was contemplated then by all parties concerned as the establishment of a Jewish minority, endowed with the right to pursue its religious and cultural heritage in freedom and peace. The outcome was to be quite different. Immigration quotas were imposed by the colonial power (Great Britain), then increased by political pressure from Zionists and sympathizers as well as anti-Semites who saw in the contemplated "National Jewish Homeland" a way to rid themselves of Jewish minorities. Great Britain in 1922 and 1939, specifically rejected the notion that Jewish immigration could be allowed against the will of the Arab inhabitants when it reached such proportions as to change the Arab character of Palestine.[29] The entire population ratio was to be kept at one-third Jewish and two-thirds non-Jewish Arabs. By 1947, after an onslaught of post-World War II illegal immigration the Jewish population was estimated at about 700,000 to 900,000 non-Jewish Arabs. In some 25 years, Arabs who had constituted 90 percent of the people of Palestine comprised only 55 percent of the new total; however, they still owned over 80 percent of the land. Consider two factors: (1) the demographic transformation imposed by Great Britain and abused by illegal entry, and (2) the head count based on physical presence in Palestine without distinction as to the juridical status of those persons who could have been immigrants, deportable aliens, tourists, foreign citizens, and nationals. Notwithstanding these two factors, the United Nations decreed the partition of Palestine into a Jewish and Arab State. The Jewish State was given approximately 56 percent of the territory of Palestine, soon to be enlarged after the 1948 war to include another 23 percent (that portion of Palestine that the Partition Plan had allotted the contemplated Palestinian Arab State).[30]

The United Nations considered in the formulation of the Partition Plan two factors: (1) the inhabitants of Palestine could no longer coexist in peace and (2) there was roughly a 55 percent to 45 percent ratio between Jews and non-Jews in Palestine. On this basis, the United Nations could be said to have adhered to some form of self-determination when it imposed its Solomonian justice of splitting the territory roughly in two halves for what was approximately equal proportions of the population. Furthermore, the Palestinian

---

[28] STEIN, THE BALFOUR DECLARATION (1961).

[29] At that time, the British believed that the Balfour Declaration did not contemplate the disappearance or subordination of the Arabic population, language, or customs in Palestine or the imposition of the Jewish nationality upon Palestinian Arabs. GREAT BRITAIN FOREIGN OFFICE, DOCUMENTS ON BRITISH FOREIGN POLICY 1919-1939 (ed. Woodward & Butler 1946). This position was reconfirmed in the 1939 white paper that limited Jewish immigration to 75,000 over the following 5 years; in actuality, however an estimated 250,000 entered during the following 7 years. See also M. BASSIOUNI, supra note 3, at 93; Bassiouni & Fisher, supra note 16, at 402. See generally Mallison, supra note 5.

[30] See Wright, Legal Aspects of the Middle East Situation, 33 LAW & CONTEMP. PROB. 5 (1968).

were subsequently given the right to return in peace to where they had lived (if it had become part of the territory allotted the Jewish State) if they desired and in any event, to be compensated for their property. The only fallacy in his approach to the right of self-determination is that not all people have a right of self-determination anywhere—only those people who have a legitimate right to claim self-determination on a given territory can exercise it on that same territory. The right of self-determination accrues to the people of the territory upon which their future political expectations can be realized. Therefore, some legitimate criteria for the determination of those who constitute this group called "people" must be established.

It is estimated that over one-half of the 700,000 persons of the Jewish faith present in Palestine in 1947 who were estimated to constitute some 45 percent of the entire population of Palestine were not Palestinian nationals. Palestinian nationality did not exist and was so recorded on official documents including passports, which were issued only to nationals. The Palestine national entity was recognized by the international community by member states of the League of Nations and the then member states of the United Nations as well as other states. Assuming, therefore, the validity of the estimate that only one-half or approximately 350,000 persons of the Jewish faith were Palestinian nationals (this estimate includes those who completed immigration requirements and were eligible for Palestinian nationality), less than one-third of the entire population dictated the outcome of the future of Palestine against the express will of two-thirds of the remaining nationals. That cannot be considered a valid expression of self-determination (even less justifiable is the territorial apportionment of 56 percent to the Jewish State). This assertion is predicated, however, on the choice of a nationality criterion for the exercise of the right of self-determination. Assuming the validity of that criterion, the *de facto* presence of individuals who are nonnationals cannot be given *de jure* recognition by the United Nations in its partition plan predicated on the basis of a semblance of application of a right of self-determination. In effect, the United Nations foreclosed the Palestinians' right of self-determination by including in the category of "people" eligible to vote persons who did not qualify under a nationality criterion. This criterion is obviously not the only one that could be devised, but certainly physical presence alone would not suffice. Suppose the absurd hypothesis of ten million Arabs, unarmed and without belligerent intentions walking across the present boundaries of the State of Israel, sitting down, and asking for a head count; would that satisfy the requirement of the General Assembly's view of the right of people to self-determination and suffice to transform Israel back into an Arab state? The conclusion is inescapable in both cases but all too often leads to an erroneous framing of the issue as one involving a clash of rights. The idea of two opposing and conflicting "rights" requiring a "solution" based on pragmatic considerations resulted in the Partition Plan. The propagation of that notion is likely to lead to more misconceived peace plans. One factor invariably lacking in every exposé of the situation is the legitimacy factor. To recognize a "right" on the Israeli side equal in dignity to the Palestinians' "right" presupposes that the Israel "right" is equally legitimate. It is precisely that point which Palestinians and all Arabs challenge most vehemently, and their challenge has yet to be answered. Israel has not answered it by disclosing documentation on (1) the number of nationals in Palestine in 1947, Jewish and non-Jewish, or the proportion of nationals-nonnationals, (2) the registered and nonregistered land owners, and (3) the expropriated and seized property of the non-Jewish Palestinians, even though such records are available in Israel.[31] That people of the Jewish Faith can claim a debt owed by Europe is patent, that it collects it from the Palestinians does not follow. That is why Israel, rather than argue its legitimacy, seeks to trade its military supremacy for recognition that impliedly would give it a color of legitimacy by condonation.

Another often overlooked argument that would restrict the exercise of the right of self-determination to the population of Palestine prior to its radical demographic transformation between 1922 and 1947 lies in the mandate system and its successor, the trusteeship system of the United Nations. These systems did not envision, nor do they permit, a trust territory to be so administered by a trustee as to allow an imposed or forceful demographic transformation designed to alter the indigenous character of that territory and change its population. To allow a trustee to inject aliens into the population of trust territories against the will of the original people and to subsequently recognize in these aliens the same rights as in the original people is a flagrant violation of the trusteeship system. For the United Nations to then act on the basis of these imposed conditions is in manifest derogation of its obligations to the original indigenous population and their legitimate rights, which were to be protected as a "sacred trust." To be in accordance with legitimate criteria determined by the rights and obligations arising out of the trusteeship system and its stated purposes to which it was morally and legally bound the right of self-determination in this case should have been considered by the General Assembly when it decided on partition.[32]

c. *The Right of Self-Determination and the Relationship between People and Territory.* The right of self-determination as stated above presupposes the existence of two interrelated factors: people and territory. The Palestinians are no longer physically present on the territory with respect to which they claim a right of self-determination. The two elements of territory and population have been severed by the displacement of the Palestinian population from that territory. Does that fact extinguish the right? It should be noted that what the Palestinians claim is not a right of self-determination that arises now

---

[31] On the present condition of Palestinians in Israel in terms of wholesale confiscation and appropriation of their property, their personal removal, and the removal of their villages by force see PALESTINE STUDIES INSTITUTE, THE ARABS IN ISRAEL (Beyrouth 1968).

[32] *See* Wright, *The Middle East Problem,* 64 AM. J. INT'L L. 270 (1970).

or after their displacement in 1948 from Palestine, but is rather a right that existed then and never terminated. The main tenet of this position is that legitimate rights such as that of self-determination are not extinguishable by the coercive displacement (or preventing the return) of the "people" from the territory after the right has accrued to this very "people."

This proposition rejects a post-1948 right of self-determination that would link the Palestinian people to territory other than that which Israel carved out of Palestine. It rests instead on the existence of a pre-1947 right, preceding the Partition Plan, that was violated by an indiscriminate and arbitrary head count of persons who entered Palestine after 1923 by imposition of the colonial power in control, Great Britain. This is the position of the Palestine Liberation Organization as expressed in Article 6 of the 1948 Palestinian National Covenant: "Jews who were living permanently in Palestine until the beginning of the Zionist invasion will be considered Palestinians."

The choice of the cut-off year of 1923 was made by the P.L.O. in clarification of the meaning of the commencement of Zionist invasion. That cut-off date is, however, debatable since Palestinian Arab representatives agreed in the ensuing years to an immigration quota that allowed for the lawful entry of many European Jews. The population of Palestine was admittedly one-third Jewish, consisting of nationals and immigrants who had been admitted with the intention of becoming nationals; all such persons must be taken into account. Assuming that one-third of the population consisted of Jews eligible to choose partition on the basis of the dual criteria of nationality and lawful immigration with intent to acquire nationality, the Partition Plan, as it relates to territorial apportionment, is also patently unjustifiable since it gave the Jewish State 56 percent of Palestine. This leaves a final question: can the General Assembly partition a trust territory under any circumstances? The theoretical answer is "no," unless the "people" so choose, which again demonstrates that we invariably revert to the right of self-determination. What then of the one-third of the population unable to coexist with the remaining two-thirds? The answer to this is that it is purely an internal question subject only to the secure guarantees of the human rights of the minority under the principles of the Universal Declaration of Human Rights, the Human Rights Convention, and the various covenants. In no event can the situation give rise to an internationally cognizable right of cessation and the imposed establishment of a new state populated with nationals from a multitude of other states to the exclusion of the original nationals of the existing state.

What then is the remedy for a "people" whose right of self-determination has been violated? A right to return—this was indeed established, but only by a United Nations General Assembly Resolution that was never enforced and which remains unrealized. Is there then a method under the Charter whereby a "people," collectively, can peacefully and by lawful process claim their rights and seek redress of wrong? The answer remains unfortunately in the negative, as a collectivity of individuals are not proper subjects of international law and under the Charter have no standing vis-à-vis sovereign states. This leads to the inescapable conclusion that the efforts of any legal system that offers no means of redress of wrongs will be rejected by the aggrieved party, who is therefore left with no other alternative but to operate outside its confines.

B. *The Palestinians' Right of Self-Defense*

Before discussing this question, certain facts must be established:

1. The Palestinians are either wards of the United Nations or illegally displaced persons or both.

2. The Palestinians are not nationals of any Palestinian state, whether the one contemplated by the Partition Plan or any other subsequently created state.

3. From 1948 to date, the United Nations has confined its efforts on behalf of the Palestinians to the reiteration of the original resolution, granting them a right to return and to compensation, but without implementation, enforcement, or sanction against Israel for her failure and refusal to abide by these United Nations decisions (this is not to overlook the humanitarian efforts of UNRWA, which must be acknowledged with all due deference and regard).

4. The State of Israel in 1948-1949 occupied 23 percent more, and in 1967, 100 percent more of the Palestinian territory allotted to the Arab state than was contemplated by the Partition Plan, thereby precluding the creation of the Arab state contemplated by the Plan.

5. The Palestinians individually and collectively have no standing in international law vis-à-vis Israel, a sovereign state, and therefore cannot claim or enforce their rights as decreed by the General Assembly or recognized by international law.

The outcome of this self-defense theory depends upon the choice of either of the following assumptions:

1. The Partition Plan is invalid (a) because the Palestinians were denied the right of self-determination (as discussed above), a right arising under general principles of international law, the law of the Charter, and the practice of the United Nations, and (b) particularly because of the denial of their rights arising out of the special status of Palestine and the Palestinians under the trusteeship system; or

2. The Partition Plan is valid because the General Assembly did not violate the Palestinians' right to self-determination nor did it act in derogation of its trusteeship obligations; rather, it provided for the creation of an Arab state of Palestine while imposing upon the Jewish state of Palestine an obligation in the nature of a condition subsequent to return the Palestinians wishing to live in peace in that state and to compensate all Palestinians for the loss of property in that state.

Assumption 1: The Invalidity of the Partition Plan. The first assumption preserves the right of self-defense under general principles of international law and the Charter, specifically Article 51, which authorizes the use of force in case of an "armed attack." The Charter does not define an "armed attack." However, it could be advanced that foreign nationals who entered Palestine illegally and took arms against the majority of the nationals while acting as agents of a public body recognized by the international community constituted an "armed attack" warranting self-defense. The right is not extinguished by the success of the aggressor who manages to take control of the territory and expel or prevent the return of the original nationals.

An interesting parallel between self-determination and self-defense is that both are predicated on the same two interrelated factors of territory and people. Self-defense, however it is advanced, is the right to defend territory as well as people. The Charter's self-defense provisions embody more than a right to territorial self-defense; if this were not the case, self-defense would terminate as a matter of right by alien occupation of the territory. The right of self-defense is available to people who may exercise it first on their territory but who do not lose that right solely because they are forcefully removed from that territory. To hold otherwise would be to sanction the successful use of force and recognize that it can extinguish legitimate rights. The establishment of governments in exile in England during World War II is evidence that the framers of the Charter did not anticipate Article 51 changing the principle that people can continue their defense even after being militarily defeated, having their territory occupied, having some of their "people" coercively prevented from returning to their homeland, and having all of their people deprived of the liberation of that homeland from the foreign occupation.

The protection of people is surely as essential as that of territory. Self-defense is not a right limited to the defense of that abstraction called "sovereignty" but assumes as a main tenet the safeguard of people (within the sovereign, within the territory) from the effects of harm resulting from external "armed attack." Consider the modern technological devices that can harm, destroy, or annihilate people without literally any territorial invasion occurring. Would that be any less of an armed attack? Although it is true that the self-defense scheme of the Charter was originally predicated on the notion of armed men physically crossing a border, it nonetheless was written in the shadow of Hiroshima and Nagasaki. The conclusion is that unless Article 51 was obsolete from the date it was drafted, it must have meant and still means a form of attack *vi et armis* and all other forms of technological devices capable of harming people and destroying property, even if not carried out by individuals who physically cross the border of one state into another, so long as the harmful or destructive devices are an intentional extension of what would otherwise require a physical trespass.[33]

The meaning of self-defense is also to be read *in pari materia* with the Preamble of the Charter, which refers to "people" rather than to states, terri-

---

[33] *See* Franck, *Who Killed Article 2(4)?*, 64 AM. J. INT'L L. 809 (1970).

tories, or other political organs or juridical abstractions. The "armed attack" in the case of Palestine came from foreign nationals as well as local nonnationals and nationals of Palestine who were directed by the Jewish Agency and its affiliated organizations. The majority of these armed attackers (in this theory) were not nationals of Palestine, but nationals of other states (even though some were displaced persons). The moving organ, the Jewish Agency, was a public body, so recognized under international law when it claimed to be the recipient of the Balfour Declaration and had its name inserted in the mandate administration of the League of Nations. That it was a public body so recognized by the international community is established, although admittedly it was not a state. The question then becomes, must an "armed attack" come from a "state" or is it sufficient that it emanates from a public body drawing its membership from many states? Suppose that a hypothetical group of people belonging to organization "X" stole an atomic bomb and then sought to drop it on a particular state and its people. Would this not be an armed attack warranting self-defense within the meaning of Article 51? If an "armed attack" can be effectuated only by a state, could there be a valid system of reprisals against terrorism? Israel has certainly relied on the assumption that only tacit approval by an Arab state allowing Palestinian commandos to operate from its territory against Israel warrants reprisals against that very state from which the "armed attack" originated, even though the state proper did not commit the "armed attack."

If one accepts the invalidity of the Partition Plan, the conclusion is inescapable that the Palestinians' right of self-defense is not extinguished and that their actions against the original and successor armed attackers who occupied their land by force of arms are justifiable defensive actions. That is essentially the position of the Palestine Liberation Organization.

Probably the most interesting paradox is that Israel relies primarily on the right of self-defense under Article 51 to ward off Palestinian attacks, even going so far as to act preventively before an "armed attack" actually occurs.

Thus, the so-called clash of "rights" continues unabated. Yet the world community fails to develop structures capable of resolving even those conflicts predicated on legal claims. The lack of compulsory adjudication and the lack of standing for people or individuals as proper subjects of international law reveals the weakness of present international structures.

Assumption 2: The Validity of the Partition Plan. Consider the following facts and issues:

1. The Plan was rejected by the non-Jewish population of Palestine.

2. It was enforced by Israel in reliance upon a doctrine of self-defense even before the formal creation of the state.

3. The Jewish population of Palestine created Israel, but the Arab population failed to do the same. Did this political fact alter the legal relationship

between the two groups of people and did it affect their respective rights, duties, and obligations?

4. Was Israel's occupation of 23 percent more of the territory of Palestine an act of aggression against the contemplated Palestinian state and against the United Nations, which was still discharging its trusteeship obligation vis-à-vis the Palestinians? In general, what rights were violated and what duties did Israel fail to abide by?

5. Was the annually reiterated Resolution 194 of 1948, granting a right to return to Palestinians willing to live in peace in the Israeli state and a right to be compensated for their property regardless of their return, a condition subsequent that clouds the legitimacy of the State of Israel?

6. Does the refusal or failure of Israel to carry out the obligation to return and compensate (as well as its additionally occupied territory of Palestine) still leave the whole question within the jurisdiction of the United Nations under its trusteeship obligations?

7. Is Israel in continuous violation of international law by its failure to comply with the condition subsequently placed upon its creation and does this violation or refusal to abide by United Nations decisions and fulfill international obligations place some disability on that state's claim to act within the law of the Charter and international law in general and with respect to the self-defense issue in particular?

The so-called moderate Arab position that seeks to accept the validity of the Partition Plan has the following perception of the issues at hand:

1. Israel is an aggressor with respect to the territory it took by force of arms in 1948-49 beyond the allotment it received from the Partition Plan; Israel foreclosed by such aggression and forceful occupation the establishment of the Arab state of Palestine.

2. Self-defense is available to the Palestinians and those wishing to support their legitimate claim to regain that territory.

3. Israel has no right to self-defense while occupying that land by force of arms and refusing to yield it.

4. The United Nations has a continuing duty under its trusteeship obligations to enforce its decision in toto.

5. Israel is in perpetual violation of the Partition Plan by its failure to return and compensate Palestinians and is in violation of its duty as a member of the United Nations to carry out its international obligations.

There is no right of self-defense *stricto sensu* for the Palestinians individually or collectively because they are not a state and hence do not enjoy the privilege of the protective scheme that the Charter envisioned and which is embodied in Article 51. There is, of course, little to rely upon in the general concepts of self-defense as developed in international law and practice prior to the Charter in order to assert such a right for people who lack statehood. The argument in this case must therefore rest on the assumption that Israel's forceful prevention of the establishment of an Arab state of Palestine through occupation of a portion of that territory warrants the Palestinians' reliance on the self-defense theory. This theory would have been valid had that contemplated Arab state of Palestine been established even on a portion of the remaining territory and if its people, the Palestinians, thereafter sought to regain the balance of their territory occupied by Israel. This is not the case, however, as the balance of the territory of Palestine, which was destined for the creation of the Arab state of Palestine, was in part incorporated into Jordan (the West Bank) and in part administered by Egypt (Gaza).

This leaves only a self-defense argument for forcing the "return" of the Palestinians in the territory allotted the Jewish state which became Israel. This argument, however, fails for two reasons: first, no such right exists in international law, and second, the original resolution (194) was predicated on the return of those wishing to live in peace in that Jewish state. Therefore, the use of force in enforcing return by the Palestinians negates that which appears to be a condition precedent to return, *i.e.,* peaceful return. That argument, however, is a vicious circle because Palestinians claim Israel's refusal to allow return precludes peaceful return and hence vitiates that condition.

Palestinian Alternatives. The Palestinians are wards of the United Nations, and that organization's stake in enforcing the decision to establish an Arab state in a described portion of Palestine still leaves them with a right, but without a remedy. Thus, the acceptance of the validity of the Partition Plan without enforcement by the United Nations leaves the Palestinians without any legally enforceable remedy. Little wonder that the Plan is rejected and challenged by Palestinians. They argue that the Plan's invalidity gives them at least the right to rely on the violation of their right of self-determination, thereby making available some argument for a right of self-defense. By the United Nations' failure to enforce and supervise the implementation of its imposed solution of 1947 and because international law and the Charter leaves no legal alternative to the Palestinian people, force of arms became the only, and inevitable, avenue of redress available to them.

The Palestine Liberation Organization insists on the invalidity of the Partition and seeks the return of all Palestinians in a totally reconstituted State of Palestine. Neither Israel nor Jordan could accept the Palestine Liberation Organization plan; Jordan would lose the West Bank Valley of the River Jordan, which was incorporated into its own territory, and Israel fears the loss of its Jewish-Zionist identity. Egypt would be the only state willing to relinquish control of the Gaza area if a solution could be found that would satisfy the Palestinians.

Part of the blame for the present impasse must be squarely placed on the shoulders of the United Nations, which failed to enforce its own plan, thereby leaving the parties with no alternative to the collision course they have been on since 1947. And the War for Palestine is continued by Palestinians who disclaim anyone's right to dispose of them and their destiny. For half a century, they (and their land) were pawns manipulated first by colonial powers, then by world power politics, and finally abandoned to their own selfless lot as refugees. They took to arms, and their objective, regardless of its merits or feasibility, remains the reconstitution of what was the State of Palestine before 1947 and the establishment of a secular state with equal rights for Jews, Christians, and Muslims.

Further evidence of continued "misunderstanding" is the United Nations' purported perception of the nature of the problem. In the famed Resolution 242 of November 1967, the Palestinian people rated only one line and the undignified label of "refugee problem." The war for Palestine is not recognized even though scores of Palestinians have died for it since 1967, as have other Israelis and Arabs who supported the Palestinians. The Jarring mission to implement Resolution 242 is oblivious to the Palestinians and their war. Perhaps this explains why Israel's Foreign Minister Eban, when asked about the Palestinians' role in a peace settlement, replied: "They have no role to play."[34]

B. *The Territorial War Between Israel and Some Neighboring Arab States*

1. *The 1967 War.* Insofar as the war for Palestine is concerned, Egypt, Jordan, Syria, Iraq, and Lebanon are third-party intervenors. Their intervention assumed a military character in 1948, but since then has been limited to threats, albeit appearing at times serious. In 1956, Israel joined France and Great Britain in aggression within the meaning of the Charter against Egypt. They engaged in an "armed attack" and the Security Council ordered the aggressor's complete and unconditional withdrawal. To these surrounding Arab states, Israel's territorial expansion is a real threat. Israel's representation that it is the state of the "Jewish people," potentially some 11 to 16 million Jews, coupled with a flexible notion of boundaries (subject to expansion) causes apprehension among neighboring Arab states.

To understand these feelings one need only review recent history: consider first the Zionist quest for a "national home" under the Balfour Declaration (not a state); then the establishment of a Jewish state under the 1947 partition plan, which took over half of Palestine; thereafter in 1948-49 the acquisition by force of arms of an additional one-fourth of the Arab State of Palestine; then in 1956, aggression against Egypt throughout which avowed public pronouncements were made by Israeli officials claiming the whole of *Eretz Israel* from the Nile to the Euphrates; finally, Israel's swift and surprising blitzkrieg of 1967, which netted that state large chunks of Arab territory without any apparent intentions of returning all or any of it. This Israel *lebensraum,* its implied claims thereto, (*Eretz Israel* and the return of all Jews of the world thereto), and corroborating conduct provide the basis for neighboring states' apprehension of expansionism and aggression. This is a very real Arab fear,

---

[34] Le Monde, Jan. 20, 1969, at 2, col. 3.

and unfortunately one that finds too many supporting facts to make it mere misapprehension.

In almost every analysis available in the United States, writers presuppose either that Israel was fully justified in 1967 in the use of force against Egypt, Syria, and Jordan or was at least sufficiently justified to attack first. Thus, on the assumption that Israel acted in self-defense, its occupation of the Arab territory becomes justifiable. It is established beyond doubt that Israel attacked Egypt first and clearly within the meaning of an "armed attack" on another sovereign state. The United Nations Charter, unlike earlier doctrine of international law, was intended to repudiate the notion that imminent threat of force authorizes pre-emptive use of force in self-defense. The reason was obviously to reduce opportunities for conflict arising by "jumping the gun."[35] Notwithstanding threats in the form of speeches, there was no "armed attack" on Israel in June 1967 by any Arab state until Israel attacked Egypt. While it is interesting to speculate and assess the degree of imminence of armed attack by Egypt against Israel, as proponents of Israel claim, the fact remains that the United Nations has no permanent machinery to evaluate the seriousness or imminence of threats of armed attack. Nor does the United Nations have the machinery for a prompt evaluation of who (what state) committed an "armed attack" upon another.[36]

During and after the "six-day war," Israel consistently claimed to have been "attacked" first. Because Israel's attack was successful, however, the question of who did what to whom first was relegated until after the fact. In the meantime, there was only one witness whose proof could have been irrefutable, the U.S.S. Liberty. That American electronic surveillance vessel located in international waters monitored Israel's air sorties and could have provided the data that might have branded Israel as an aggressor and deprived it of the fruits of its victory. Israel destroyed that evidence as it bombed and strafed the upper decks of that vessel where the data and equipment was stored, killing 34 and wounding 166 American Navy men. A naval board of inquiry concluded shortly after the incident that it was a deliberate, unprovoked attack, that Israeli planes and torpedo boats could not have failed to identify the ship as an American vessel in international waters, and that the attack was intentional.[37] The report of the board of inquiry was ordered to be kept secret, presumably by the White House, because of its political implications. The fact remains that Israel, with its support in Western European countries, conducted a massive propaganda campaign to indict Egypt as an aggressor before the facts were even presented. Israel at first succeeded, but in time the man-made fog lifted, and no one now questions, not even Israel, who started the *shooting*. Israel does, however, disclaim starting the *war*, which is an interesting

[35] *See* Franck, *supra* note 33.

[36] *See* Franck & Cherkis, *The Problem of Fact-Finding in International Disputes*, 18 W. Res. L. Rev. 1483 (1967).

[37] *See* Anderson, Confirm or Deny (1969). It is interesting to note that Israel agreed upon a $3,300,000 damage claim by the United States for the attack on the Liberty.

euphemism. Israel claims that Egypt's closing of the Gulf of Aqaba, its request
for withdrawal of UNEF forces from the Sinai, and the massing of 60,000 to
80,000 men on that border constituted with respect to the closing of the Gulf
a *casus belli* and with respect to the troops' movement coupled with public ✓
speeches made by political leaders an imminent threat of "armed attack" that
justified its preventive strike.

Consider, however, these observations:

1. The blockade of the Gulf, which Israel claimed to be a *casus belli*, was
not an "armed attack" and is therefore not, as claimed by Israel, sufficient
justification to attack Egypt.[38] Furthermore, the blockade was not put into
effect since a German freighter passed through it to Eilath.

2. The late President Nasser advised Secretary General U Thant that his
request for withdrawal of UNEF Forces and the massing of Egyptian forces
on its borders was in response to Israeli attacks on Syria (April 7, 1967) and
threats of invasion of Syria.

3. Egypt's request for the withdrawal of UNEF troops was wholly consonant with the original agreement to have them quartered in Egypt only as
long as Egypt would authorize their presence.

4. Israel consistently refused to allow UNEF troops on its territory, even
after they were asked in May 1967 to leave Egypt and could have merely crossed
the border into Israel.

5. Egypt's conduct, as reported to the Security Council by Secretary General
U Thant's reports of May 19 and May 26, was predicated on her honest belief
that Israel was about to invade Syria, with whom Egypt had a mutual defense
treaty.

6. Finally, Egypt's regular army then was estimated at 150,000 men, some
50,000 of whom were in Yemen. The troops sent by Egypt to its Siani boundaries were estimated at 60,000. Considering the normal ratio of combat to
support personnel of 4 to 2, Egypt could at best have had 40,000 combatants
massed at its borders. Israel's forces were estimated at over 320,000 soldiers.
There is ample indication that Israel's intelligence services knew that Egypt was
not going to attack, but the political and military opportunity coincided.
Politically, Egypt could be made to appear the aggressor, allowing Israel to
deal a surprise military defeat while appearing to be the victim.

Considering all of these factors, the fact remains that the United Nations
was required to act without independent knowledge of the facts and relied
upon propaganda-oriented statements and manipulated factual presentations
by the news media. This is but another illustration of the necessity for the ✓
United Nations to establish a permanent fact-finding apparatus to be dispatched
anywhere in the world to report to the Secretary General on the imminence
of threats of armed attack and their source. Notwithstanding these considera-

---

[38] Mallison, *Limited Naval Blockade or Quarantine Interdiction: National and Collective Defense
Claims Valid Under International Law*, 31 GEO. WASH. L. REV. 335 (1968).

tions and in the absence of a factual determination, the United Nations in November 1967 passed its famed Resolution 242, the "cornerstone of peace."

2. *Resolution 242: The Other Side of the Coin.*[39] This catch-all resolution was intended to reiterate several Charter principles and was designed to serve as a basic framework for the solution of the "conflict." Organically divided in two parts, it separates substantive from procedural matters. Conceptually, it linked all pertinent issues into a single indivisible bundle and framed them in terms susceptible of contrasting perceptions of the proposed settlement.

The principles reiterated are so intertwined with the substantive issues, and even to some extent with those of procedure, that misconceptions were bound to develop. The form of the document attempts to segregate principles from substantive issues, but read as a whole the document remains a monumental juxtaposition of inherent paradox, as will be demonstrated in the following observations.

1. The resolution emphasizes the "inadmissibility of the acquisition of territory by war." This principle is then applied in the statement of substantive issue as follows: "Withdrawal of Israel armed forces from territories occupied in the recent conflict." Note the use of words "recent conflict," thereby excluding consideration of any territory Israel acquired by war after 1947 over and beyond the territory allotted Israel by the United Nations 1947 Partition Plan. Note also the ambiguity arising out of the absence of the word "the" before "territories occupied." Thus, the principle, although absolute on its face, is contemplated as less than absolute when applied to a substantive issue. The principle emphasized the rejection of the notion of conquest by war, but at the same time the Resolution mitigated its impact by a purposeful and latent ambiguity that encouraged territorial by one belligerent over the other's territory. To this date, Israel claims that "withdrawal" does not include *all* territories occupied, while Arab states insist that it does. Israel relies on the ambiguity arising out of the absence of the word "the" before "territories" while the Arab states insist on the principle of "inadmissibility of acquisition of territory by war" as absolute. Nowhere does the document attempt to draw a distinction between occupation of territory as a consequence of aggression and occupation of territory resulting from legitimate self-defense. Thus, two competing claims are left open: (a) Israel asserts that its occupation is legitimated because it acted in self-defense and therefore insists on preconditions to withdrawal—these would be to secure Israel from further acts by Arab states that presumably necessitated its original defensive action; (b) Arab states insist that Israel's occupation was due to aggression and cannot be condoned by allowing it the privilege of imposing preconditions of annexing any portion of Arab territory. That two such divergent claims can arise from a document intended to be the basis of peaceful resolution is incredible.

2. The second principle enunciated in the Resolution is the renunciation

---

[39] *See* Bassiouni, *The Middle East in Transition: From War to War, A Proposed Solution,* 4 INT'L LAW, 379 (1970).

of force as a means of resolving conflicts between members of the United Nations and is in keeping with Article 2 of the Charter. The Resolution applies the principle to a substantive issue in this manner: (a) termination of all claims or states of belligerency, (b) respect for and acknowledgement of the sovereignty, territorial integrity, and political independence of every state in the area, and (c) the right to live in peace within secure and recognized boundaries free from the threats or acts of force. Nowhere in the statement of these substantive issues does the question of the Palestinian people and their rights under the Charter arise. In effect, the implementation of these substantive issues would foreclose the Palestinians' claim definitively.

3. Procedurally, the scheme of the resolution was to unfold through peaceful methods of resolution, including direct or indirect negotiations, mediation, conciliation, and even adjudication or arbitration. The ultimate choice was indirect negotiation through Gunnar Jarring, acting as the Secretary General's representative. Even that, however, was attained only after two years of Israeli insistence on direct negotiations. Because there was nothing to clarify the document's position on the subject, the parties were left to their own willingness to choose an appropriate method at a time when they all were deadlocked in a hopeless ceasefire. The absence of meaningful directives afforded an opportunity to delay further the prospects of peaceful resolution. Of more serious consequence to the prospects of any peace is the Resolution's failure to establish or foresee a graduated or tiered approach to the proposed settlement. Hence, Arab states insist on Israel's fulfillment of withdrawal first, while Israel maintains that withdrawal is only one factor in the total scheme and cannot take place without a total agreement. There being no determination whether Israel is occupying Arab territory justifiably (self-defense) or unjustifiably (aggression), each side can insist on its perception of the question and interpret the Resolution accordingly. Assuming, however, the acceptance of the Israeli position that a complete settlement of all pending issues must precede any withdrawal, what is the effect of an agreement entered into (regardless of its form) by a state (Egypt or Jordan) while a portion of its national territory is occupied? The conclusion is that such an agreement would be challengeable as made under duress. Dr. Hargrove covers that point most effectively among others in his presentation. It is the contention of this writer that if a treaty is signed under present conditions and if such treaty would cede to Israel Egyptian territory (especially territory deep within Egypt such as Sharm-el-Sheikh), such a cession would give rise to two arguments against the treaty: (1) duress and (2) a possible subsequent application of the *rebus sic stantibus* doctrine. As to duress, Egypt could correctly argue that it was compelled to relinquish such territory and that it did not do so to serve any national interest. As to *rebus sic stantibus,* once the material conditions under which such an agreement would be entered into had changed, Egypt could invoke this theory to challenge the continued validity of the cession

clause. One should also contemplate that a treaty under the compulsion of military occupation for the cession of national territory, particularly in light of Resolution 242, which emphatically rejects acquisition of territory by use of force, would be a covert way of doing just what the resolution condemns. Can that which is expressly forbidden in one form be accomplished by an obvious subterfuge camouflaged under the guise of a treaty? If the answer is "yes," then such sophisticated hypocrisy is yet another proof of the triumph of coercion over principle.

4. As discussed above, the Palestinian people's question is wholly ignored by the Resolution, and no representative of the Palestinian people has even been consulted by the Jarring mission, let alone been made a party to the indirect talks under way.

5. Glaringly absent from the settlement scheme is the future status of Jerusalem, a most serious issue in contention. Israel superseded the question by "administratively annexing" Jerusalem, and notwithstanding unanimous United Nations condemnation of the fact, it remains a reality that Israel is unlikely to change except for minor modifications of form.

The Arab states' position concerning Israel is that there are essentially two sets of issues at stake: (1) the Palestinian question to which Arab states are secondary parties (the Palestinian people being the primary party) and, therefore, as to which no Arab state can compromise or even purport to represent the Palestinians, and (2) the aggressive expansionism of Zionism that is manifested by the territorial war between these Arab states and Israel. The latter is, of course, an iceberg-type issue, there being more beneath its surface than that which appears; it calls into question the ideological conflict of Zionism versus Arab nationalism.[40]

Resolution 242 ignores the first of these two sets of conflict-creating issues while failing to resolve or at least determine the second set of issues. Since the two Arab states (Egypt and Jordan) who have accepted the Resolution and are engaged in the Jarring talks cannot and will not represent the Palestinians, they are left with the issues of territoriality and state of belligerence with Israel. But these questions did not arise from the 1967 war, and they fail to characterize Israel's conduct. Thus, each state, armed with its own perceptions, molded its official position accordingly, which resulted in a conflicting dual claim of righteousness left to subside with the knowledge that it can only set the opposing parties on another conflict-collision course.

As stated by this author in another forum:

> The night of November 22, 1967, witnessed the relief of those who in New York had diligently worked out the drafting and adoption of U.N. Res. 242. It was theoretically the beginning of peace; in fact it marked the transition between blitzkreig-like war and war of attrition. It was thought of by its framers as a cut-off point so as to serve as a new plateau from which to start substantive peaceful settlement. It was indeed a new departure point; but like many paradoxes in

---

[40] *See* Bassiouni & Fisher, *supra* note 16.

history, it was the start of something wholly different from its originally intended purpose.

As most U.N. products, this one was the off-spring of political compromise hammered out by multiple parties who pursued varying purposes. As such, it fed with a measured dose of equanimity the opposing contentions it was to resolve. Unavoidably, it enunciated irreconcilable propositions and, thus, bore the seeds of its own ill fate.

The value-oriented goal which characterized this crisis-product is two-fold:
1. It was designed to demonstrate the role and ability of the U.N. in peace-keeping.
2. It was aimed at creating a spirit of world moral sanction which through the marshalling of world public opinion would lead to a world societal pressure on the parties concerned to achieve a peaceful settlement.

This approach has also characterized many a similar product of world political compromise. The discerning reader of the 1954 Geneva Accords could see that it was a "rain check" and foresee that it was not an end but a transition to the Viet Nam of today, which found its new plateau in the terms of the Geneva Accords; that much is true about Resolution 242. If we examine the resumption of military activities in the Middle East, we can observe the correlation between the ever-increasing tempo of hostilities and the gradual realization by the parties of the failure of Resolution 242. On both sides hostilities are not yet in the nature of all-out war, but they pursue a strategy of attrition which will last and escalate until full-fledged warring operations resume more decisively. Interestingly enough, neither Viet Nam nor the Middle East has reverted to nonpeaceful means on the basis of their historical arguments, but on the grounds that the conditions or terms of the "new plateau," i.e., the Geneva Accords in one case and Resolution 242 in the other, have not been complied with or have been violated. Each side, of course, accusing the other of the same and traditional arguments, fades away in light of the new declarations.

Conflicts are not resolved by emphasizing the rights or righteousness of the opposing parties, but by drawing distinction between them. Furthermore, those distinctions must rest on the relatively impartial and objective Rule of Law. Political compromises are only a substitute for a legally based determination of the respective rights and duties of any opposing parties when they themselves are parties to the compromising process and their acceptance thereof takes the place of the legal determination. Where mutual consent and voluntariness lacks, there is no substitute for the Rule of Law. The remaining alternative is the Rule of Force. Failure to accept this premise will further the perpetuation of such pronouncements as Resolution 242, which in seeking to declare has avoided to resolve, and in arriving at its compromise has evaded to determine the respective rights and duties of all parties concerned. At best it has armed them with renewed justification while putting another nail to the coffin of the peaceful resolution of this conflict.[41]

III. Conclusion

The failure of attempts at peaceful resolution of the Arab-Israeli confrontation is due in part to "misunderstandings" of Arab perceptions of the issues, be they terminological, conceptual, or procedural. The sense of fairness and justice as conceived by the Arabs is ignored and in its stead is offered a sense

---

[41] Bassiouni, *supra* note 39, at .....

of Western pragmatism wholly inconsistent with Arab culture and tradition. Necessity may force Egypt and Jordan to accept today's proffered pragmatic solution, but it will remain a palliative of unlikely substance and doubtful duration. Scholars, politicians, and laymen speculate on the right approach and balanced solution, but this writer believes that an inexorable force of events will ultimately cause the "conflict" as it is now conceived to wither away. The prediction is predicated on two observations discussed in detail in another forum.[42] They are: (1) that transformation of Israel ideologically, politically, and demographically will in time de-Zionize Israel while at the same time Arabize it in the sense of making it part of the Arab world; and (2) that rapid political transformation taking place in the Arab world will shift the emphasis from an "Israel-is-the-most-important" policy to an "internal-matters-first" policy. This in turn will be due to several factors, the most important of which are:

1. Israel's close links with world Zionism will be weakened by rising Israeli nationalism.

2. Israelis' consciousness of their responsibilities and obligations towards Palestinians will help transform that state (at least partially) so as to allow for some form of a bi-national state to exist. These two factors will be due to: (a) the increase in Sabra population and their corresponding gain in political power; (b) the presence of over 500,000 Arab Jews now in Israel; and (c) the increasing number of non-Jews living in Israel.

3. The emerging concern and struggle of Arab masses with their internal socio-economic condition will overshadow their concern with the existence of Israel.

4. The Palestinian revolutionary movement will turn inwardly rather than outwardly and will direct its efforts against established Arab governments that it considers reactionary. It will find support from emerging leftist Arab groups who will welcome the opportunity to further local revolutionary movements.

For the development of these circumstances, time is of the essence, that is, time out from actual warring operations. This projection also presupposes that no external forces will be brought to bear on either of the parties, thereby causing a posture different than the present one.

The United States and the U.S.S.R., whose individual and combined role in the Arab-Israeli conflict have had the most nefarious effects, seem willing to put that new pawn of the cold war on ice for the time being. It seems that this area of the world, which was destined to fight a surrogate cold war, will benefit from the respite that the task masters of the East and the West may be willing to temporarily grant them. Who brought the United States and the U.S.S.R. into this arena and why is not as difficult a question as one might think. Israel commenced a polarization policy when it attempted to isolate

---

[42] *Id.* at 380.

Arab states from the United States by getting the latter to be more vocally committed to its cause.[43] The result was anticipated and rather obvious to any student of Arab affairs. The Arabs soon found a friendly protector in the U.S.S.R. who saw a golden opportunity to enter the Mediterranean.

The results were more than gratifying to Israel, who anticipated that the Soviets could only give hardware and advice to the Arab states. With the United States escalating its assistance and support of Israel while the process of polarization was gradually taking place, Israel was confident it could cope with the situation. The United States fell for it and no matter how hard it now tries to balance its position, the die is cast and the political wheels in America have been set in motion to prevent a halt in that escalating process. In 1971, Israel is expected to receive 500 million dollars of military and economic aid, partly payable through long-range credit, mostly free, compliments of the United States Senate, which refused in 1970 to put a rider on a bill to preclude the use of United States armed forces in Israel. The message reads loud and clear—although the United States is not likely to embark on another Viet Nam, the events in Jordan of September 1970 raise the specter of yet another United States military intervention should the wheels of military fortune ever turn against Israel. It appears that the Nixon administration is earnestly seeking to prevent the outbreak of war, but at what internal political price is the question. The Soviet Union has heavily invested in Egypt without getting returns, as Nasser's succession brought a clearly "Egypt first" oriented government. There is no communist party in Egypt, and those of Syria and Iraq are outlawed and their members tracked down and jailed. The communization of the Arab world is not taking place—rhetoric notwithstanding. Socialism will be the way of life of those states and other economically less developed countries, but that is no premium to communism since in the case of the Arab states there is a strongly imbedded individualistic culture coupled with nationalistic tendencies that go from local and tribal allegiances to Pan-Arabism. The U.S.S.R. has, however, achieved a foothold in the Mediterranean, the Red Sea, and the Indian Ocean; tactically, this is a gain; strategically, it is very doubtful. History has a strange way of repeating itself. As the outposts of the British Empire in the form of bases were closed down one by one, and as the United States failed in its clumsy attempt to substitute its influence, so will the presence of the Soviet Union in the Arab world be subject to the same frailty of all such grandoise imperial designs. Strategically, the Soviet Union has its aims on the control of Europe, and to succeed it must be militarily, even though only symbolically, present in Western Europe's backyard, the Mediterranean. The Soviet Union could attempt, though it would not succeed, to control Arab-produced oil, thereby putting an economic squeeze on Europe, the prime consumer. But that is a double-edge sword that cannot be used without seriously affecting the economic well being of the European proletariat,

---

[43] See Bassiouni & Fisher, *supra* note 16.

upon which the Soviet Union must ultimately depend to push European governments to pursue an anti-American policy. The United States and the U.S.S.R. are therefore re-evaluating their objectives and the means to attain them with respect to the role of the Arab-Israeli conflict in their respective grand schemes. This then may be the moment for the Arabs and Israelis to look at their confrontation as would the inhabitants of a small island who were thrown together by destiny and who can either live or perish by their own doing. If that opportunity is seized, regardless of its form and apparent immediate significance, it could be that first step necessary to set in motion a whole trend of irreversible events and circumstances. This substantiates the earlier conclusion that left to themselves, given time and but one positive opportunity such as the implementation in good faith of Resolution 242, the Arab-Israeli conflict may gradually wither away. In time, the Arab world with a non-Zionist Arabized Israel as an integral part thereof may become one of the most blossoming areas in the world.

What Weight to Conquest?

STEPHEN M. SCHWEBEL

In his admirable address of December 9, 1969, on the situation in the Middle East, Secretary of State William P. Rogers took two positions of particular international legal interest, one implicit and the other explicit.[1] Secretary Rogers called upon the Arab states and Israel to establish "a state of peace . . . instead of the state of belligerency, which has characterized relations for over 20 years." Applying this and other elements of the American approach to the United Arab Republic and Israel, the Secretary of State suggested that, "in the context of peace and agreement [between the UAR and Israel] on specific security safeguards, withdrawal of Israeli forces from Egyptian territory would be required."[2]

Secretary Rogers accordingly inferred that, in the absence of such peace and agreement, withdrawal of Israeli forces from Egyptian territory would not be required. That is to say, he appeared to uphold the legality of continued Israeli occupation of Arab territory pending "the establishment of a state of peace between the parties instead of the state of belligerency. . . ."[3] In this Secretary Rogers is on sound ground. That ground may well be based on appreciation of the fact that Israel's action in 1967 was defensive, and on the theory that, since the danger in response to which defensive action was taken remains, occupation—though not annexation— is justified, pending a peace settlement. But Mr. Rogers' conclusion may be simply a pragmatic judgment (indeed, certain other permanent members of the Security Council, which are not likely to share the foregoing legal perception, are not now pressing for Israeli withdrawal except as an element of a settlement).

More questionable, however, is the Secretary of State's explicit conclusion on a key question of the law and politics of the Middle East dispute: that "any changes in the pre-existing [1949 armistice] lines should not reflect the weight of conquest and should be confined to insubstantial alterations required for mutual security. We do not support expansionism." Secretary Rogers referred approvingly in this regard to the Security Council's resolution of November, 1967, which,

> Emphasizing the inadmissibility of the acquisition of territory by war [4] and the need to work for a just and lasting peace in which every State in the area can live in security,

[1] The text is published in full in the New York Times, Dec. 11, 1969, p. 16.
[2] Ibid.   [3] Ibid.
[4] The resolution's use of the word "war" is of interest. The June, 1967, hostilities were not marked by a declaration of war. Certain Arab states have regarded themselves at war with Israel—or, at any rate, in a state of belligerency—since 1948, a questionable position under the law of the Charter. In view of the defeat in the United Nations organs of resolutions holding Israel to have been the aggressor in 1967, presumably the use of the word "war" was not meant to indicate that Israel's action was not in exercise of self-defense. It may be added that territory would not in any event be acquired by war, but, if at all, by the force of treaties of peace.

Emphasizing further that all Member States in their acceptance of the Charter of the United Nations have undertaken a commitment to act in accordance with Article 2 of the Charter.

1. Affirms that the fulfilment of Charter principles requires the establishment of a just and lasting peace in the Middle East which should include the application of both the following principles:

(i) Withdrawal of Israeli armed forces from territories occupied in the recent conflict; [5]

(ii) Termination of all claims or states of belligerency and respect for and acknowledgement of the sovereignty, territorial integrity and political independence of every State in the area and their right to live in peace within secure and recognized boundaries free from threats or acts of force; . . . .[6]

It is submitted that the Secretary's conclusion is open to question on two grounds: first, that it fails to distinguish between aggressive conquest and defensive conquest; second, that it fails to distinguish between the taking of territory which the prior holder held lawfully and that which it held unlawfully. These contentions share common ground.

As a general principle of international law, as that law has been reformed since the League, particularly by the Charter, it is both vital and correct to say that there shall be no weight to conquest, that the acquisition of territory by war is inadmissible.[7] But that principle must be read in particular cases together with other general principles, among them the still more general principle of which it is an application, namely, that no legal right shall spring from a wrong, and the Charter principle that the Members of the United Nations shall refrain in their international relations from the threat or use of force against the territorial integrity or political independence of any state. So read, the distinctions between aggressive conquest and defensive conquest, between the taking of territory legally held and the taking of territory illegally held, become no less vital and correct than the central principle itself.

Those distinctions may be summarized as follows: (a) A state acting in lawful exercise of its right of self-defense may seize and occupy foreign territory as long as such seizure and occupation are necessary to its self-defense. (b) As a condition of its withdrawal from such territory, that state may require the institution of security measures reasonably designed to ensure that that territory shall not again be used to mount a threat or

[5] It should be noted that the resolution does not specify "all territories" or "the territories" but "territories." The subparagraph immediately following is, by way of contrast, more comprehensively cast, specifying "all claims or states of belligerency."

[6] Res. 242 (1967) of Nov. 22, 1967; 62 A.J.I.L. 482 (1968). President Johnson, in an address of Sept. 10, 1968, declared:

"We are not the ones to say where other nations should draw the lines between them that will assure each the greatest security. It is clear, however, that a return to the situation of June 4, 1967, will not bring peace. There must be secure and there must be recognized borders . . .

"At the same time, it should be equally clear that boundaries cannot and should not reflect the weight of conquest. Each change must have a reason which each side, in honest negotiation, can accept as part of a just compromise." (59 Department of State Bulletin 348 (1968).)

[7] See, however, Kelsen, Principles of International Law 420–433 (2nd ed. by Tucker, 1967).

use of force against it of such a nature as to justify exercise of self-defense. (c) Where the prior holder of territory had seized that territory unlawfully, the state which subsequently takes that territory in the lawful exercise of self-defense has, against that prior holder, better title.

The facts of the June, 1967, "Six Day War" demonstrate that Israel reacted defensively against the threat and use of force against her by her Arab neighbors. This is indicated by the fact that Israel responded to Egypt's prior closure of the Straits of Tiran, its proclamation of a blockade of the Israeli port of Elath, and the manifest threat of the U.A.R.'s use of force inherent in its massing of troops in Sinai, coupled with its ejection of UNEF. It is indicated by the fact that, upon Israeli responsive action against the U.A.R., Jordan initiated hostilities against Israel. It is suggested as well by the fact that, despite the most intense efforts by the Arab states and their supporters, led by the Premier of the Soviet Union, to gain condemnation of Israel as an aggressor by the hospitable organs of the United Nations, those efforts were decisively defeated. The conclusion to which these facts lead is that the Israeli conquest of Arab and Arab-held territory was defensive rather than aggressive conquest.

The facts of the 1948 hostilities between the Arab invaders of Palestine and the nascent state of Israel further demonstrate that Egypt's seizure of the Gaza strip, and Jordan's seizure and subsequent annexation of the West Bank and the old city of Jerusalem, were unlawful. Israel was proclaimed to be an independent state within the boundaries allotted to her by the General Assembly's partition resolution. The Arabs of Palestine and of neighboring Arab states rejected that resolution. But that rejection was no warrant for the invasion by those Arab states of Palestine, whether of territory allotted to Israel, to the projected, stillborn Arab state or to the projected, internationalized city of Jerusalem. It was no warrant for attack by the armed forces of neighboring Arab states upon the Jews of Palestine, whether they resided within or without Israel. But that attack did justify Israeli defensive measures, both within and, as necessary, without the boundaries allotted her by the partition plan (as in the new city of Jerusalem). It follows that the Egyptian occupation of Gaza, and the Jordanian annexation of the West Bank and Jerusalem, could not vest in Egypt and Jordan lawful, indefinite control, whether as occupying Power or sovereign: *ex injuria jus non oritur*.

If the foregoing conclusions that (a) Israeli action in 1967 was defensive and (b) Arab action in 1948, being aggressive, was inadequate to legalize Egyptian and Jordanian taking of Palestinian territory, are correct, what follows?

It follows that the application of the doctrine of according no weight to conquest requires modification in double measure. In the first place, having regard to the consideration that, as between Israel, acting defensively in 1948 and 1967, on the one hand, and her Arab neighbors, acting aggressively in 1948 and 1967, on the other, Israel has better title in the territory of what was Palestine, including the whole of Jerusalem, than do Jordan and Egypt (the U.A.R. indeed has, unlike Jordan, not asserted sovereign title), it follows that modifications of the 1949 armistice lines among those states within former Palestinian territory are lawful (if not necessarily desirable), whether those modifications are, in Secretary Rogers' words, "insubstantial alterations required for mutual security" or more substantial alterations—such as recognition of Israeli sovereignty over the whole of Jerusalem.[8] In the second place, as regards territory bordering Palestine, and under unquestioned Arab sovereignty in 1949 and thereafter, such as Sinai and the Golan Heights, it follows not that no weight shall be given to conquest, but that such weight shall be given to defensive action as is reasonably required to ensure that such Arab territory will not again be used for aggressive purposes against Israel. For example—and this appears to be envisaged both by the Secretary of State's address and the resolution of the Security Council—free navigation through the Straits of Tiran shall be effectively guaranteed and demilitarized zones shall be established.

The foregoing analysis accords not only with the terms of the United Nations Charter, notably Article 2, paragraph 4, and Article 51, but law and practice as they have developed since the Charter's conclusion. In point of practice, it is instructive to recall that the Republic of Korea and indeed the United Nations itself have given considerable weight to conquest in Korea, to the extent of that substantial territory north of the 38th parallel from which the aggressor was driven and remains excluded—a territory which, if the full will of the United Nations had prevailed, would have been much larger (indeed, perhaps the whole of North Korea). In point of law, provisions of the Vienna Convention on the Law of Treaties are pertinent. Article 52 provides that "A treaty is void if its conclusion has been procured by the threat or use of force in violation of the principles of international law embodied in the Charter of the United Nations"—a provision which clearly does not debar conclusion of a treaty where force has been applied, as in self-defense, in accordance with the Charter. And Article 75 provides that "The provisions of the present Convention are without prejudice to any obligation in relation to a treaty which may arise for an aggressor State in consequence of measures taken in conformity with the Charter of the United Nations with reference to that State's aggression."

The state of the law has been correctly summarized by Elihu Lauterpacht, who points out that

> territorial change cannot properly take place as a result of the *unlawful* use of force. But to omit the word "unlawful" is to change the substantive content of the rule and to turn an important safeguard of legal principle into an aggressor's charter. For if force can never be used to effect lawful territorial change, then, if territory has once changed hands as a result of the unlawful use of force, the illegitimacy of the position thus established is sterilized by the prohibition upon the use of force to restore the lawful sovereign. This cannot be regarded as reasonable or correct.[9]

STEPHEN M. SCHWEBEL

[8] It should be added that the armistice agreements of 1949 expressly preserved the territorial claims of all parties and did not purport to establish definitive boundaries between them.

[9] Elihu Lauterpacht, Jerusalem and the Holy Places, Anglo-Israel Association, Pamphlet No. 19 (1968), p. 52.

Abating the Middle East Crisis Through the United Nations (and Vice Versa)

JOHN LAWRENCE HARGROVE

It is a sad fact that the United Nations and the Arab-Israeli conflict, which grew up together, have in the last three and a half years contributed reciprocally to their mutual decline. As to both, the frontiers of thinkability have progressively and dangerously expanded. The conflict itself, under the catalytic influence of the June war, quickly outgrew its sporadic character and mutated into a continuing and technologically sophisticated contest in killing and destruction across the Suez, involving ever more intimately and substantially the weaponry of the world's major and antagonistic military machines and the men of one of them. Elsewhere in the Arab east, Palestinian insurgents have by fits and starts so consolidated their position as to call into question the capacity of local political establishments—so long as they survive at all—to carry any real authority to a negotiating table. And the world's mightiest military power was recently willing to congratulate itself on having made clear its willingness to use force in the Middle East in order to check an outbreak of this endemic instability.

The United Nations has played out its complementary role. It labored for six months to produce even a general statement of the principles of settlement, while the new lines of crisis hardened. The Security Council in due course ceased to go through even the forms of considering each fresh outburst of violence across the Suez, but perforce settled into the role of passive observer of an active war. Over many months its appointed conciliator shuttled fruitlessly from capital to capital. Private talks organized under a United Nations aegis among the four permanent members of the Security Council, entered only reluctantly by the United States in the first place, saw the opportunity to work out an agreed recommended settlement slip by as they awaited the results of equally abortive talks between the two great powers in Washington. Most fundamentally, the organization now approaches the end of the fourth year of a major conflict among various of its members involving massive occupation of foreign territory, which it appears powerless to abate and as to which it lacks any face-saving alibis—like those in the case of Southeast Asia—about the impossibility of United Nations involvement. The United Nations *is* involved, and has been from the start.

The present cease-fire over Suez has provided at least the appearance of a momentary respite in the cycle of deterioration and has in any event abated the killing and destruction. But the dynamics of the conflict are not changed, and everyone knows what catastrophe it threatens, and why: We have erected

* Director of Studies, American Society of International Law; formerly Senior Adviser for International Law, United States Mission to the United Nations. The following was an address delivered before a Regional Meeting of the American Society of International Law at the University of Kansas, Lawrence, Kansas, on November 20-21, 1970. Views expressed herein are the author's own.

in the Middle East, piece by piece, the machinery of great power conflict, and it remains only for the gears at some point to be engaged. This is the foremost reason for concern with the Middle East at the moment. But the role of the continuing crisis there in the progressive atrophy of the United Nations security system could turn out to be an equal and more enduring, if subtler, danger.

Certainly we are entitled to ask, without any overly reverent deference to established dogma, what went wrong as the international community grappled with this old conflict's newest phase, which erupted in the spring of 1967. As international lawyers, we are entitled to ask how, if in any way, the resources of international law and in particular the United Nations Charter might have been brought to bear in some way differently, and whether such possibilities yet exist. And we are entitled to ask conversely what the Middle East crisis has done to the system embodied in the Charter, and what repercussions it may yet have upon that system, whether by continuation or by settlement. I suggest we seek answers first by a reappraisal of the events within the United Nations in early June 1967, following the outbreak of fighting—before the Four Power talks, before Jarring, and before Security Council Resolution 242.

The United Nations Security Council was already seized of the Middle East problem when Israel crossed the border into Sinai; in fact, the United States had been trying for some days—in vain—to instill in it the sense of urgency that we rightly felt was warranted by the withdrawal of UNEF, the closure of Tiran, and the mobilization in the Sinai. As the territory under Israeli control expanded, first in the Sinai, then—following Israel's abortive effort to keep Jordan out of the war—in the West Bank, and finally on the Golan Heights, there was agreement on all sides that the Council should order a cease-fire, or at least a readiness to acquiesce in such an order. The issue that balked Council action was whether it should simultaneously call for the withdrawal of Israeli forces to their own territory. To have done so would have been to follow the pattern of the Suez crisis in 1956, and the Arab states, strongly backed by the Soviet Union, insisted that this be done. The United States equally firmly insisted on a simple cease-fire, publicly on the ground that the first order of business was to put an end to the violence and that the particulars of settlement could be attended to later. In the end the Arabs were compelled to accept the United States position, not by its intrinsic logic but by military necessity. The Council called simply for a cease-fire. The cease-fire in due course became reasonably effective, and it was not until over six months later that the Council addressed itself in any form to those further particulars of settlement. Let us look first at the legal significance of the situation that prevailed on the ground during those six months, and then at the action that the Council eventually took in Resolution 242 on November 22, 1967.

On the ground, Israel found itself in massive occupation of Arab territory, with her Arab opponents rendered, for the moment at least, effectively incapable of resistance. The occupation had come about by means of an invasion that Israel claimed to have been in self-defense, but which, although by no means unprovoked, did amount to a first use of force by Israel. Many words have been uttered, at both public and private expense, in arguing the correctness of Israel's claim to have been acting in self-defense notwithstanding the explicit qualification in Article 51 of the United Nations Charter, which recognizes the right to use force in self-defense "if an armed attack occurs." I will not reargue the question here, but will simply state the personal view that, in our primordial international community, an exception to the prohibition of violence that legitimizes such a first strike would make the world a substantially more dangerous place in which to live, and that this is not the sort of world envisaged in the United Nations Charter.[1] So far as I am aware, Israel stands alone among governments in espousing her position on this point.

The reason I do not dwell on this issue is that, legally, nothing much of current interest follows from it. In particular, nothing follows from it that bears on the legitimacy of the continuing Israeli occupation of foreign territory. This is largely because it is a part of the law of self-defense that a use of force in the exercise of that right must be no more than is necessary to put an end to the injury being inflicted by force against the defender and must be proportionate to that injury. Whatever were the actions of the UAR on June 3 (the closing of Tiran? the amassing of forces in the Sinai?) on the basis of which Israel claims to have had the right to act in self-defense on June 4, by no stretch of the imagination can the invasion be said to have been less than proportionate to those injuries or to have failed to put an end to them within a very short time. When this occurred, if Israel had had any right to be present on foreign territory in order to defend herself, that right ceased and she was obligated by the Charter's prohibition on the use of force against territorial integrity to withdraw. The United Nations, as a result of the position taken by the United States, was unable to assert that obligation when it called for a cease-fire. And of course Israel did not withdraw and has not done so.

Now this legal analysis has of course not been universally accepted. I think there are two arguments that have been made against it. The first is that once a state has entered the territory of another in the legally justified use of force in self-defense, it is entitled to remain there until it assures itself that the injuries that gave rise to its right in the first place will not recur. After all, it is argued, the Allied forces occupied Germany and Japan for many years after the actual cessation of hostilities in World War II.

This argument is particularly difficult to apply in the case of the June war, since it is not altogether clear what were the injuries being inflicted upon Israel that we would be willing to say would in all cases give rise to a right of armed invasion in self-defense. But leaving this aside, I think the reply is

---

[1] Two United Nations legal bodies have given rise in recent years to a good deal of discussion on this point. These are the Special Committee on Principles of International Law Concerning Friendly Relations and Cooperation Among States in Accordance with the Charter, and the Special Committee on the Question of Defining Aggression. The overwhelming majority of Member States that have addressed the point in these two bodies have taken the position that a genuine "armed attack" must indeed occur before defensive force can legitimately be used. I know of no Member that has expressly argued that Article 51 could justify a "pre-emptive" attack.

simply that, although it would not have been beyond the wit of man to have devised a system in which such a rule was the operative rule, this was in fact not the system built into the Charter, with its recognition of the right of self-defense "if an armed attack occurs." Indeed, in my view it was in part the former sort of system that the Charter was intended to replace: the sort of system in which the victor, like Rome salting the ruins of Carthage, is free to take whatever measures he is capable of in pursuit of the elusive certainty that the original injury will never in the future be repeated. As to the conduct of the victorious Allies after World War II, it is not at all clear that the fundamental principles of the Charter would have permitted occupation of indefinite duration. This in part explains the presence in the Charter of Article 107, which has the effect of excepting from the other provisions of that instrument arrangements made with respect to the defeated Axis powers after World War II.

The second argument is an extension of the first. It runs to the effect that once one has legitimately seized another's territory he may hold it for an unspecified length of time in order to assure himself of the nonrecurrence not only of those specific serious injuries that originally legitimated his own use of force, but also of a collection of lesser illegalities that ought to be included in a comprehensive settlement of outstanding differences even though they admittedly would not themselves have justified the use of force. Examples, in the present case, would presumably be the illegal blocking of Israeli passage through the Suez Canal, and the lawless (and foolish) bellicosity of the Arab states over many years in threatening the use of force against a fellow member of the United Nations. Although such an argument has great appeal to hardheaded diplomats, I am afraid that it fails doubly by the tests of the Charter. Not only does it envisage the forcible occupation of foreign territory for purposes that are by hypothesis outside the scope of the right of self-defense, but it also reads out of the Charter the principle embodied in Articles 2(3) and 33, which enjoin states to settle their disputes by peaceful rather than forcible means.

All of this makes unhappily clear the real nature of the decisions being taken with regard to the security system embodied in the United Nations Charter in the days during which the positions of the United Nations and its Members with respect to Israeli occupation were being formulated. Individual governments, and the United Nations itself, were in fact making hard policy choices as to the scope and future viability of certain fundamental principles of the Charter—albeit, as in the case of the United States, decisions that frequently were not explicitly acknowledged to be legal ones at all. The United States, for example, implicitly but vigorously pressed both of the positions just described. It did so, however, not because it felt these positions to be an accurate reflection either of existing law or the way law should soundly develop, but because it had become convinced that the remarkable windfall represented by the Israeli military advantage should be exploited to achieve a comprehensive and reliable peace settlement, and incidentally because domestically it did not seem a propitious time to be convinced otherwise.

These positions were the underlying philosophy reflected in the action that the Security Council finally did take in Resolution 242 of November 22, 1967. The call for Israeli withdrawal from occupied territories, which in June was almost instinctively felt by most governments involved in New York to flow quite plainly from the Charter, had by November become a major concession on the part of Israel and the United States—and even at that a concession qualified by the absence of the definite article "the" before "territories," which was intended to leave open all arguments on whether the Security Council envisaged withdrawal from all territory occupied after June 4. In return for the principle of withdrawal, the Arabs were required to accept the principles of termination of any claims of belligerency, respect for and acknowledgment of Israel's right to the basic security protections of the Charter, and free navigation through international waterways. Israel in turn was required to accept the principle of a "just settlement of the refugee problem," and both were required to sign on to the principle of guarantee arrangements such as demilitarized zones. The effect was clear: by making Israel's obligation to relinquish militarily occupied territory conditional upon Arab agreement to a comprehensive settlement, the United Nations—physically (and some would say legally) impotent to effect a settlement itself by force—gave its endorsement to the achievement of a settlement by Israeli force.[2]

This action by the United Nations was a considerable achievement for United States multilateral diplomacy, and the United States position had a certain ring of plausibility to it. Twenty years after Israel's inception, and notwithstanding her membership in the United Nations, the Arab states persisted in the most extravagant and outlandish claims of right to destroy her by force. There had been episodic outbursts of violence during the whole period, with one major eruption in 1956. The jerry-made arrangements constructed thereafter, although they had provided ten years of relative tranquility, had broken down at the instance of one of the Arab parties. In the localized episodes of violence that pervaded the whole period, the Soviets saw to it that the Security Council was, as a general rule, substantially readier to condemn Israeli force than to chastise or admonish the Arabs with respect to the acts of indirect force emanating from them. Navigation rights, long denied Israel through the Suez, were now denied her through the Strait of Tiran as well. No conclusive settlement, as envisaged by the 1949 Armistice Agreements, was in sight. The impulse to seize a unique opportunity to "have this thing settled *our* way," once and for all, was virtually irresistible. It was, we might say, the

---

[2] Resolution 2628 (XXV), recently adopted by the General Assembly, placed more emphasis on the principle of withdrawal by *"reaffirming* that no territorial acquisition resulting from the threat or use of force shall be recognized." It did not, however, alter the basic bargain struck by Resolution 242 except in one respect not material here, namely, the introduction of "respect for the rights of the Palestinians" as a new and "indispensable" element of a settlement.

Consciousness I of international affairs asserting itself, and as a result we calculated the costs much too narrowly.

What have been the costs? First, as to the United Nations security system and the principles which it seeks to enforce, we have put the United Nations on record, at least tentatively, in favor of the proposition that if you have a powerful enough patron you *can* use force to settle your international disputes, notwithstanding the Charter's prohibition of force and its requirement to settle disputes peacefully, by means going well beyond the limits of force in self-defense permitted by Article 51. This much can be said about the effect on legal principle.

In the particular case in question, in sanctioning the continued occupation of a territory as a means of exacting settlement, we have endorsed a state of affairs having its own built-in tendencies toward violence and perhaps global catastrophe. This is essentially because, notwithstanding Resolution 242 to the contrary, we live in a world in which the Charter standards rule out acquisition or even occupation of foreign territory simply as a means of achieving one's political objectives, however justly entitled to those objectives one may be. This may be of small comfort to the Arabs by themselves, militarily impotent to give it effect. But it becomes an inescapable reality of the situation in the Middle East when the Arabs are backed by a major power possessing massive military resources and passionately intent on achieving military and political dominance in the area. It is one of the great ironies of this episode that in the Middle East the Soviet Union could so effectively have exploited to its own political ends the Charter's prohibitions on the use of force against territorial integrity, during the same period in which it invaded its own small Czechoslovak neighbor and suppressed it with a vast exercise of military might.

There have been additional costs, as the foregoing clearly indicates, from the more parochial point of view of the position of power and influence of the United States in the area—measured either absolutely, in its relationships with the states of the area, or relatively by comparison to the position of the Soviet Union. These costs have been enormous.

Finally, as to the chances of an early return to some semblance of a peaceful life for the area, no assessment can be made that does not make that period of relative, if interrupted, tranquility in the decade preceding the June war look very, very good by comparison. The least that can be said is that by taking the position we did with respect to the principle of withdrawal, we greatly compounded the difficulty of the task we alone will have to perform in due course if there is ever to be a return to peace: getting the Israelis in fact to withdraw.

One should of course be under no illusions that, had our position on the question of withdrawal been different from the outset, the situation in the Middle East would have achieved some reasonable settlement by now. Nor can it reasonably be said that Israel would have promptly withdrawn. A more reasonable hypothesis is that, had a framework of settlement been adopted from the outset acknowledging withdrawal as an imperative flowing from the Charter, there would have been, as in 1956 and 1957, a period of protracted negotiations resulting eventually in withdrawal and a variety of improvised arrangements for ensuring relative tranquility, encompassing some of the elements now regarded as essential to a comprehensive settlement. Even had this not been achieved, we could hardly be farther from settlement than we are now, and it is fair to say that other of the costs exacted by the course we pursued, against the viability of the United Nations security system and against our own position in the Middle East, would have been substantially reduced.

There remains to be said only a brief word about the law of the United Nations Charter and a future settlement. The final, net effect of the June war and its aftermath upon the United Nations security system and the principles upon which it rests will depend heavily upon the kind of deal that is struck in settlement. The question is whether the process that the United Nations has set in train, if it eventuates in settlement at all, will produce one in which the Arab states will in fact have been compelled by force to give up substantial rights recognized in them by the international community before the conflict began. The Arab states, of course, had no right to threaten Israel with force and hardly a stronger claim of right to close off navigation through the Suez Canal. Even though such lawless actions would not have justified the use of force by Israel, the Arabs are clearly not in a very good position to complain about being compelled to give them up as a part of a settlement. The relinquishment of territorial rights, however, is an altogether different matter, and it is for this reason that the insubstantiality of "rectifications" from the 1949 Armistice Lines is crucial if the settlement is not to do further violence to the law of the Charter. And here, with the single exception of Jerusalem (which is a genuinely special case), it makes little difference whether the territory in question is in the Sinai, the Golan Heights, or the West Bank. For what counts is the fact that for twenty years the international community treated the 1949 Armistice Lines as definitive of the rights and obligations under Article 2, Paragraph 4, of the Charter of the parties concerned—even though they were explicitly not to be regarded as permanent territorial boundaries in and of themselves.[3] It repeatedly rejected or ignored claims that these lines had become ineffective for that fundamental purpose by reason, for example, of the hostilities in 1956 or by reason of their express disavowal by the Arabs. For the international community now to reward the exercise of force by altering that position would be to confirm a grave injury to the principles of peaceful settlement of disputes and nonuse of force against the territory of another. It would, moreover, be fundamentally imprudent as regards the durability of the settlement itself. For what is envisaged is an *agreement* of settlement, and the language of agreement has been used by governments concerned (especially

---

[3] This was the position forcefully espoused by President Eisenhower in the Suez crisis.

the United States) with particular explicitness in discussing the territorial aspects of a future settlement. International agreements extorted by force are illegal, as the recently concluded Vienna Convention on the Law of Treaties has confirmed. More to the point, they will be *regarded* as illegal by the *next*, perhaps more radical, generation of Arab leadership if a peace settlement furnishes any reasonable ground for saying that, in order to get Israel out, the *present* Arab leadership was compelled by force to relinquish substantial rights possessed by the Arab States before the June war. And they will be supported in this position by whatever outside major power regards influence in the Middle East as sufficiently worth competing for.

In short, the United Nations Charter tells us a good bit about how to abate the Middle East crisis and how not to. And on the future treatment of that crisis a good deal depends as to the future of that organization. There are a variety of ways in which the United Nations can fail the charge given it in 1945 (we and a good many of the Members seem to be trying all of them simultaneously and impartially). It can fail from a continued lack of political commitment to its use—the *will* to genuine participation in the global system for controlling conflict that its Charter envisages. Or it can fail by allowing the principles of that system to be so bent by the diehard imperatives of the old international politics that, if and when that will evolves, there will no longer be much point in it, and a fresh start will be required.

The War and the Future
of the Arab-Israeli Conflict

NADAV SAFRAN

THE 1973 War has had an enormous impact on all the complex of factors that enter into the Arab-Israeli conflict. The study of these changes will take many years and many hands. In this article, an attempt is made to examine that impact in several areas that seem to have a particular bearing on the immediate future.

The war has brought into full view what some specialists had long been pointing out: that the Arab-Israeli conflict is actually a complex network of which Arab-Israeli relations (so far, alas, mainly military) have only been one segment. Feeding into this network, in addition, have been the changing pattern of antagonism and association that makes up inter-Arab relations, the fluctuating rivalries among the big powers with interests in the area, and many features of the internal life of the antagonistic countries. This essay will touch upon each of the preceding dimensions of the conflict.

II

The military dimension of the 1973 War provides ample material for study and reflection at all levels—from tactics to strategy and from grand strategy all the way to the level where war merges into policy. Among the lessons, the following seem to stand out:

First, the Arabs were able to achieve virtually complete surprise for their initial thrust, and this in turn had crucial consequences. It gave them the initiative for a while, dictated to the Israelis the kind of war to be fought at least at several stages, caused the war to be costly and prolonged, made outside intervention necessary and possible, and in all these ways and others determined the general outcome of the war. It has already been pointed out that the failure of Israeli and American intelligence was due not to any dearth of information about the Arabs' war preparations, but to an incorrect evaluation of that information. Israeli analysts started from the premise that Sadat was convinced that Israel enjoyed a great margin of military superiority over any military coalition he could form; consequently, they could only view the vast ostensible war preparations as an attempt to bluff Israel and the United States, and/or to force Israel into going through the psychological strain, trouble and cost of mobilization as a means of pressure on it. Such a conclusion appeared all the more plausible since Egypt and Syria had gone through similar military motions several times in the past. However, had the analysts started from a different—a political—premise, they might well have reached different conclusions. They might then have seen that, given the predicament in which Sadat found himself, any war short of one that was certain to end in quick and total disaster would be preferable to staying still. This observation may sound like wisdom after the fact, but at least one observer proceeding in the latter way had publicly anticipated the probability of war. At any rate, the point of the observation is that the faulty evaluation may well have had a structural rather than an accidental basis—the absence of appropriate or sufficient representation of political analysts in the intelligence-evaluation apparatus concerned.

Next to the general surprise at the fact that the Arabs chose to go to war when they did, people profess to be most surprised by the quality of the Arabs' performance. Conclusions have been drawn to the effect that, in the brief lapse of time since 1967, the Arabs have greatly narrowed the "technology gap" and the "quality gap" between them and Israel and have learned to fight well in a modern war.

This observer has no doubt that the Arabs did indeed fight much better in 1973 than in 1967, but he is inclined to attribute the difference to other reasons. The Arabs were no worse soldiers in 1967 than in 1973, but they fought better in the latter war because they did so under better strategic conditions. Granted that they did learn a few things from the 1967 experience, the most important by far was the necessity for them to preëmpt the initiative and to dictate to the enemy conditions for the battle that were most favorable to themselves. More specifically, they forced the enemy to fight a set battle, where the undoubted courage of their own fighting men and their numerical superiority in manpower and equipment could be used to best effect; and they denied him, at least for a crucial period, the option of fighting the kind of war he favored, and at which he was best, namely a war of rapid movement and envelopment.

Liddell Hart, the outstanding modern student of strategy, spent a lifetime propounding the thesis that creating the right strategic conditions is a much more critical consideration than the quality of the fighters. This was brilliantly confirmed in the record of the fighting in the Western Desert in World War II, where basically the same kind of forces on either side, as far as quality is concerned, experienced dramatic and repeated fluctuations of fortune, depending mainly on the conditions of fighting that their commanders succeeded or failed to create for them. In the end the point was demonstrated on both sides in the 1973 War, for the tide seems to have decisively turned once the Israeli breakthrough to the west bank of the Canal created conditions for a war of maneuver that threatened to pull down the entire Egyptian front.

Thirdly, because the Arabs were able to dictate a slugging type of war, this turned out to be extremely costly in men and especially in equipment to both sides. Indeed, in terms of continuity of action and ratio of forces to battle space, the 1973 War was one of the most intensely fought contests in history.

The intensity of the war, with the resultant rapid running down of stocks of hardware, was one of the main reasons why first one superpower and then the other intervened in the war as equipment supplier. At the same time, the rapid depletion of equipment is certain to impel the parties, if the conflict is not resolved, to seek to provide against such an occurrence in the future by accumulating equipment in much larger quantities than in the past. This means that the arms race could accelerate even more than in the past, with all sorts of deleterious consequences. One is that future wars might be even more destructive. Another is that, as one party or the other fails to keep up with the arms race (which in the key countries has already passed the ruinous levels of 20–25 percent of GNP in cost), it might be tempted to launch a preëmptive war before the odds turn further against it.

Still another possible consequence is that the number of parties involved in the conflict and the degree of their involvement are apt to increase, as the present belligerents are forced to seek more assistance from outside sources. The acceleration of the arms race is apt to involve the superpowers in the conflict even more deeply than they have been in the past. If this should give them a greater measure of control over their respective clients, the latter's independence will have been impaired. If it should not, then the chances of the superpowers becoming directly involved in a future explosion will have greatly increased.

Finally, the war did not involve much transfer of territory, nor did it change fundamentally the relative strategic posture of the parties. But it did make a political stalemate much more difficult to sustain militarily. In the north, the Israelis have improved their prewar positions somewhat, by gaining territorial depth and deploying themselves closer to Damascus and the crucial junction of the borders between Syria, Jordan and Iraq. In the south, however, although the ceasefire left forward Israeli forces in a much more threatening position than forward Egyptian forces in the short term, the underlying positions are less favorable to Israel over any sustained period than the prewar situation.

The explanation for this paradox lies in the vast difference between the normal readiness state of the two armies. The ceasefire left each side with a substantial bridgehead across the Canal and into territory formerly held by the other. The Israeli bridgehead on the west bank is more substantial, deeper and closer to vital enemy targets than the Egyptian bridgehead on the east bank. On the other hand, Israel's capacity to hold the present lines is much more limited than Egypt's. The lines are long and vulnerable for both sides, with each sitting at the other's flank and able to threaten its rear. However, Egypt can use its predominantly standing army to buttress its lines, whereas if Israel wants to do the same on its side, it will have to maintain a high level of mobilization which would get ever more ruinous with time. Gone is the neat Suez Canal line which (barring a repetition of total surprise) could be maintained by small forces in an only slightly strengthened version of the Bar-Lev line.

It follows that unless the present lines are made more "rational" by mutual agreement, they will most probably have to be changed by either war or peace before long. And as of late November the chances of their being made more "rational" by any early agreement are not too good. Israel has, of course, offered to "straighten" them out by proposing a return to the pre-war Canal line. However, although this proposal would relieve the beleaguered III Corps, Egypt is not likely to accept it. Not only would it nullify the bridgehead that Egypt gained at such great cost; not only would it make the war appear to have been in vain by restoring exactly the prewar lines; but also, by so doing, it would facilitate the restoration of the political stalemate Egypt had gone to war to break, and broke.

III

One of the most important features of the 1973 War has been the new pattern of Arab solidarity that manifested itself. A superficial look may take that solidarity to be no different from that manifested in the 1967 War. A more careful examination would quickly show some basic differences, which have very far-reaching implications for the future.

One of the differences between 1973 and 1967 is that whereas one "first-circle" Arab country—Jordan—participated only nominally this time, countries in the "second circle" around Israel played a much more meaningful role. Iraq sent very substantial forces to the front, as it did in 1967, only this time they took an active part in the fighting. Kuwait and Saudi Arabia contributed vast amounts to the war chest, while Libya contributed money as well as Mirages acquired from France. In addition, the three Maghreb countries contributed small contingents, Morocco's being the most substantial.

A second and much more important difference is that Saudi Arabia took the lead in putting the Arab "oil weapon" into play. Of course, in 1967, it and other oil-rich countries did the same, and even seemingly went farther by placing a total embargo on oil shipments to the United States and Britain. However, we know that in 1967 Saudi Arabia cut the flow of oil involuntarily, under pressure by Nasser, and therefore did not enforce the measure strictly and cancelled it as soon as possible. In 1973, on the other hand, it introduced the weapon of its own accord, in advance of the war, and has now set up a staff and adopted a systematic, subtle, long-term strategy in order to maximize its effect in direct and indirect ways.

What accounts for these two phenomena? And what are their principal implications for the future of the Arab-Israeli conflict? The first phenomenon—the more active role assumed by countries of the "second circle" around Israel—is probably the consequence of the vast growth of Israeli power in the years since 1967. As the military capabilities of Israel multiplied in these years, the "radiation" of that power began to be felt directly by these countries for the first time. As long as Israel had been hemmed in within the pre-1967 boundaries, surrounded by a ring of Arab states that contained it and threatened to roll it back, countries like Saudi Arabia, Kuwait and Iraq could feel completely safe from any Israeli threat. Whatever contribution they made to the Arab cause against Israel was made purely on the grounds of pan-Arab considerations. But as Israel overwhelmingly defeated the countries of the "first circle" in 1967 and effectively neutralized them since, it demonstrated a previously unsuspected capacity to hurt them in a significant way. From that moment, their concern with Israel began to rest no longer solely on pan-Arab considerations, but also on considerations of precaution; and their support for countries of the "first circle" became an investment in their own security.

Attentive students of the Arab-Israeli conflict will have noticed that what has just been described is merely a continuation of a process that goes back to the very beginning of the Zionist endeavor in Palestine. The Zionist movement and then Israel have had to cope with an ever-expanding combination of Arab forces opposing them and trying to push them back. Each time they defeated one combination, the power they mustered appeared menacing to Arab forces that had previously been on the periphery and impelled them to join the defeated forces in a new combination, and so on. Thus the overcoming of sporadic Palestinian Arab outbursts by the Jewish settlers helped bring about the great Arab revolt of 1936–39. The insufficiency of this revolt brought the general resistance supported by Arab League volunteers and funds in 1947–48. The collapse of that brought the intervention of the surrounding Arab states in 1948. The defeat of that combination in 1967 has brought, in 1973, the coalition of "first-circle" countries backed by countries of the "second circle."

The second phenomenon—Saudi Arabia's use of the "oil weapon"—is explicable in part by its enhanced concern about Israel. But to understand why the expression of that concern was not confined, for example, to helping Sadat finance the war requires further explanation. Indeed, throughout the years since

1967, and even before, Saudi Arabia had staunchly turned down repeated pleas by Nasser and Arab radicals to use oil as an instrument in the service of the Arab cause. King Faisal, in particular, had flatly ruled that "oil and politics should not be mixed." Why then has he changed his policy now?

The answer is that the reasons that had restrained King Faisal in the past have been removed in recent years, while the factors in favor of using oil as a weapon have been enhanced. Previously, Faisal feared that once he had sprung the "oil weapon," others, particularly Nasser, might be able to arrogate to themselves the right to decide when and how it was to be used. Moreover, since Saudi Arabia itself depended on all the revenues it was getting at the time for its own needs, the "oil weapon" was only of very limited use and could indeed be turned around by others to hurt the Saudi regime itself. In recent years, the enormous increase in oil revenues, far beyond current needs, gave the Saudi ruler much more leeway in handling the oil weapon, while the disappearance of Nasser and the failure of a comparable personality to emerge in the Arab world has meant that King Faisal could be sure to retain control of the weapon himself. The one possible exception has been Colonel Qaddafi of Libya, who considers himself to be Nasser's heir and the custodian of Arab nationalism and the pan-Arab cause; but Qaddafi would become a real threat only if he could succeed in his endeavor to extend his base so as to include Egypt. By using the "oil weapon" now and supporting Egypt financially on a large scale, Faisal hopes to minimize the principal appeal that Qaddafi and the prospect of union with Libya have had for Sadat and many Egyptians.

Two crucial implications flow from these developments in the inter-Arab arena. The first is that the greater involvement in the Arab-Israeli conflict of countries that had previously been only marginally concerned with it will make it much more difficult, if not impossible, in the future for the United States to try to contain the Arab-Israeli conflict, if it is not resolved, by means of a "balance of force" between the parties.

Until the war, the United States had viewed the Middle East in terms of two distinct constellations having only limited effect on one another—one centered on the Persian Gulf and one centered on the Arab-Israeli area. Now that concept of balance will have to be drastically revised. The Arab side in the Arab-Israeli equation will need to be expanded so as to include Arab countries of the "second circle," and even of the Maghreb—perhaps not by adding up all their military capabilities but by counting different proportions of various elements of their forces. In the area of air power, for example, where the capacity of even the remotest Arab country can be relevant to the Arab-Israeli situation, any attempt to achieve a balance—given the aroused desire of the Arab countries to acquire substantial air forces and the availability of means and suppliers—would require bringing the Israeli air force before too long close to American and Soviet levels, at least with respect to some weapon systems! Such a trend might encourage the development of a false or exaggerated sense of power on the part of Israel and tempt it to adopt rigid positions or engage in hasty action in local disputes. And if the whole balance collapses once more, as it already did twice—in 1967 and 1973—then the ensuing war would be so destructive, and its ramifications would reach so far, that the chances of the superpowers staying out of it would be practically nil.

However, the greater involvement of previously marginally concerned Arab countries, while it has certainly added to the complexity of the conflict, need not make it less susceptible to settlement, and may indeed make it more so. Countries like Iraq and Libya may exert pressure in the direction of extremism; but this pressure is apt to be more than offset by pressure toward resolving the conflict on the part of countries like Saudi Arabia and Kuwait. For if the conflict is not resolved now, these countries may find themselves in the position of having to finance much of the ongoing confrontation on the Arab side amidst a rapidly accelerating arms race with Israel—while at the same time holding back oil production, thus forfeiting revenue, in connection with the effort to influence the United States and Europe. Five or ten years from now, these countries may have enough reserves to do both and also meet their own needs. Right now, their resources would be severely taxed before long by such a double effort. Hence, as they look at the prospects facing them, they are likely to apply their weight in the direction of a reasonable and prompt settlement.

IV

Secretary of State Kissinger said that one of the principal lessons of the 1973 War was that the superpowers could not keep out of a violent explosion of the Arab-Israeli conflict. For Western Europe as a whole—one does not know about Eastern Europe —the war showed that they too could not remain unaffected in very crucial ways. The consequences in both instances are of momentous significance.

Implicit in the statement of the Secretary of State was an admission of the failure of previously held contrary expectations. These expectations had been based, among other things, on vows that the superpowers had made to each other at the highest levels in Moscow and Washington to avoid any involvement in the Middle East that would endanger their détente; and on the fact that in the interim between the 1972 and 1973 summits the Soviet military presence in Egypt had been all but eliminated.

The expectations of the Europeans, on the other hand, had been based on a sense that they had actually worked out a modus vivendi with respect to the conflict that was apt to shield them from any serious repercussions in case it exploded. That modus vivendi consisted of their deliberately abstracting themselves from any significant practical role in the conflict (leaving matters mainly to the superpowers), and then granting to the Arab side all the political and symbolic support it asked for. In this way the Europeans thought they would protect their interest in Arab oil without hurting Israel too much.

The course of events after the outbreak of the 1973 War did at first appear to conform to the previous expectations of the superpowers and Europeans. Indeed, it seemed for a while that the most important characteristic of the war, apart from the surprise of its advent and the initial course of the military operations, was going to be precisely the fact that the outside world did not seem to care much about it. In contrast to the 1967 crisis, for example, nobody issued, at first, any momentous declarations, violent condemnations, or solemn warnings; nobody alerted or moved forces for a while; and nobody even submitted a ceasefire resolution of any sort to the Security Council for two full weeks after the start of hostilities. It looked as if superpower and West European endeavors to "quarantine" the conflict and insulate themselves from its dangers were working out.

But the European expectation had rested implicitly on one unrecognized assumption, that (as the United States itself expected) the superpowers would stay out. The assumption proved wrong when the United States felt compelled to resupply Israel with arms on a massive scale, and sought to use stocks it kept in Europe and some NATO facilities for this purpose. The Europeans suddenly found themselves confronting a very painful choice they had not anticipated: whether to permit the United States to do so and thus become its accomplices and risk Arab oil sanctions, or to oppose it and put an immense added strain on already difficult NATO relationships. In varying degrees and at a different pace, they all chose the latter. As if that were not enough cause for strain, the United States then proceeded first to "settle" the war with the Soviet Union, and next to engage with it in a confrontation on a global scale, without consulting its allies.

It thus became suddenly apparent to Europe that the Middle East conflict could not be "managed" by evasive tactics and policies, and that unless it was resolved it was bound to place before the European nations truly fateful dilemmas involving, on the one hand, the very foundations of their security since World War II, and, on the other hand, the stuff of their economic existence.

As far as the superpowers were concerned, their involvement in the conflict, contrary to their anticipation, was the result of an effort on the part of the Soviets to take advantage of an unsuspected opportunity, followed by an American effort to ward off the consequences. The process began with the Soviet Union's resupplying the belligerent Arab states with arms and ammunition on a large scale and urging non-belligerent Arab states to join in the war. Why the Soviet Union chose to do so is not quite clear as yet, but a plausible explanation has to do with fluctuating coalitions in Soviet ruling councils. With respect to the Middle East, it seems that these councils had been more or less evenly divided for quite some time between those who urged support for the Arabs' war plans and those who deemed that course too dangerous for superpower relations, and futile because of the demonstrated ineffectiveness of the Arabs in war. The latter view, it seems, had the upper hand at a crucial moment in the late spring of 1972, which led the Egyptians to react by terminating the Soviet military presence in their country in July of that year. Now, as the war broke out and the Arabs, contrary to the "soft-liners'" thesis, appeared to be doing quite well, and as it appeared that the extent of possible Soviet involvement could remain under control of the Soviets themselves rather than the Egyptians, the "hard-liners" were able to win the day with a decision to help the Arabs in various ways, thereby trying to regain the position previously lost through excessive pessimism and caution.

Whether this view of the process by which the Soviets became involved is true or not, the United States sought, at first, to stop the Soviets by means of diplomatic representations, arguments about the future of détente, and perhaps promises to work together on a Middle East settlement. However, in the face of Soviet reticence, and since the intense, slugging character of the fighting meant that the overall outcome of the war could well depend on the quantities of equipment and ammunition available to the belligerents, the United States felt compelled to launch its own massive emergency resupply operation to Israel.

As the fighting ground on indecisively and as the superpowers kept feeding the contending war machines, there emerged for a moment the horrifying prospect of a prolonged war sustained by the superpowers—becoming ever more violent, sucking in ever more belligerents, extending to ever wider areas, and involving ever more destructive weapons. Since Israel, because of its relative size, could withstand this process much less than its opponents, there also loomed the possibility that it might, in a moment of despair, spring the nuclear "last resort" weapon it is supposed to possess.

Fortunately that moment did not last long, because the war suddenly changed character as a result of Israeli initiatives. The success of Israeli forces in breaking through the Egyptian lines to the west bank of the Suez Canal and then launching a wide enveloping operation against vast Egyptian forces gave the war a new, mobile character much favored by the Israelis and opened up at least a substantial probability of a rapid, 1967-type consummation. This was enough to break the deadlock between the superpowers and to lead them to agree urgently on a project for a Security Council resolution enjoining a ceasefire in place and immediate negotiations between the parties on the basis of Resolution 242 of November 1967. Thus, after starting as bystanders and proceeding to become "partners" to the opposing sides, the superpowers went on to become for a time joint arbiters, deciding on the moment and the conditions for the termination of hostilities.

The next step in the superpowers' involvement was as dramatic and grave as it was inconsistent with the one that preceded it. The form it took is well known: a worldwide alert of American forces in the face of alleged preparations made by the Soviet Union for an immediate massive military intervention in the Middle East. The exact chain of events that brought this about is not known at the time of writing, but circumstantial evidence suggests that the following elements may not be too far wrong:

(1) Somewhere along the line, in the course of the consultations between the superpowers that went on throughout the war, the United States assured the Soviets that it did not seek a total victory for Israel and wished to avoid humiliation for the Arabs in· order to maximize the chances of a peace agreement, which was the principal objective it had set for itself.

(2) As the tide of the war turned and the Israeli operations on the west bank of the Canal appeared to the Soviets to threaten total disaster for the Egyptians, the Soviets urgently invited Secretary of State Kissinger to Moscow, where General Secretary Brezhnev personally called on him to act in accordance with the assurances given. Kissinger agreed to have the fighting stop before the Israelis utterly defeated the Egyptians, but he insisted upon, and obtained in exchange, Soviet, and ostensibly Arab, agreement to the negotiation clause.

(3) As Kissinger left for home by way of Tel Aviv, the Soviets learned that fighting was continuing beyond the ceasefire deadline and that the Israelis had completed the encirclement of the Egyptian III Corps. Not only was that corps now in danger of imminent destruction, but its collapse could bring down the entire Egyptian front.

(4) The Soviets suspected at this point either that Kissinger had deceived them, or that the United States was unable to control Israel. The fact that the United States agreed to a second ceasefire resolution that enjoined a return to the first ceasefire lines suggested that the latter was probably the case. But this made it all the more necessary, and all the more seemingly safe, for the Soviets to react strongly.

(5) Just then President Sadat, worried about the fate of his entire army, issued a call to the United States as well as the Soviet Union to send in troops to enforce the ceasefire. The Soviets took advantage of the occasion and, apparently, notified the United States in a belligerently worded note that they were about to

send troops to respond to the Egyptians' call.

(6) It was now Washington's turn to suspect that the Soviets had deceived it and had engineered Sadat's invitation as well as other conditions to justify the introduction of large Soviet forces into the area. Even if these forces were not to intervene in the fighting, it was thought that their presence would create an entirely new situation in the area, one which, among other things, was not conducive to peace. Since the Soviets notified the United States prior to taking action, it was thought that they were probing for its probable reaction, and the decision was therefore made to respond in the manner most likely to discourage them.

(7) The crisis was over when the Soviets agreed in the Security Council that a newly formed U.N. peace force should not include troops from the "big five." A decision authorizing the Soviet Union and the United States to send in a small number of unarmed "observers" helped salvage Soviet prestige; at the same time a superfluous threat to have the Soviet air force supply the beleaguered III Corps if the Israelis refused to let supplies reach it by land helped preserve the image of determined defenders of Arab interests which the Soviets tried to project.

The involvement of the superpowers in the war and the forms it took showed that détente had not denoted as much of a change in superpower relations as its advocates had led everyone to believe. Even Secretary of State Kissinger, the architect of détente on the American side, admitted, as we have seen, that his expectations had been disappointed by the turn that events took. The fact that the two giants were drawn into the role of feeders of the opposed war machines could perhaps be offset by the fact that they eventually agreed on ceasefire terms that broke new ground for the prospects of peace in the area. But the confrontation at daggers drawn that followed shortly thereafter has no parallel in the history of the superpowers' involvement in the Middle East, even at the height of the cold war. Possibly that experience will prove to have been a necessary prelude to a real joint effort to bring the Arab-Israeli conflict under control, just as the 1962 Cuba missile crisis turned out to be such a prelude for several other crucial issues in the relations between the superpowers. Whether or not this will prove to be the case will, at any rate, become quite clear before very long because of the other feature of big power relations revealed by the war.

The war, we have seen, demonstrated the existence of a critical triangle between the superpowers, the Arab-Israeli conflict, and Europe. This triangle seemingly gives the Soviets an undreamt-of opportunity to score enormous gains at the expense of the United States. By encouraging Arab intransigence and doing what they can to perpetuate the Arab-Israeli conflict, they could hope to force the United States to reassociate itself fully with Israel; force Europe, worried about its very livelihood, to dissociate itself definitely from the United States; and establish for themselves a position from which they would have remote and indirect control over the flow of oil and could use that control to "Finlandize" Europe and keep it so.

Adopting such a course, however, would entail enormous costs. It would definitely mean the end of détente and everything it portended for the Soviet Union—American trade, technological assistance, investments, arms reduction and so on. It would entail the revival of the cold war in a more virulent form than ever, with all its attendant dangers. It is very likely, judging by some statements made by President Nixon, that the sharpness of the American reaction to the prospect of the Soviets' sending troops to the Middle East was prompted in substantial measure, at least, by fears and suspicions that the Soviets might have been working for that kind of consummation. But whether that is true or not, it is certain that the Soviets' embarking on the kind of course outlined would at one and the same time give many occasions for superpower confrontation and immensely enhance the chances that these would actually take place. Finally, the United States would almost certainly seek to restore the balance on the Eurasian landmass by moving much more closely to China and, together with her, trying to tilt the situation at the other end of the landmass. These are the most important implications of the alternative courses that have been revealed by the 1973 War. Which one the Soviets will choose and which way the world might be heading should become apparent before long from Soviet actions.

V

In no other domain is the war apt to have a more extensive effect than in that of the internal life of the belligerent countries. Yet, for our present purpose, we shall only look at a few aspects of the internal front and will confine ourselves to the key countries. How has the war affected the balance of considerations and forces inside Israel and Egypt, in favor of peace, war or stalemate?

The impact of the war on Israel may be understood in terms of a contest between two currents that have not only divided different groups but also made for strongly ambivalent leanings within individual Israelis.

The first current has tended to draw lessons from events as they actually happened, in order to break previous rigidities and look to new approaches that give compromise and peace a much better chance. The second has tended to dwell on preconceived notions as to how events should have and might have unfolded, and to wish to redo realities in order to bring them into conformity with these preconceptions.

Immediately after the war, the latter current, militant and belligerent, appeared to prevail; but as time went on, the former, more moderate and accommodating, appeared to be gaining ground. As of the time of writing, this trend was increasingly asserting itself. However, it was clear that the process could be interrupted and perhaps even reversed because of a breakdown of the ceasefire. The same could ensue if the pivotal Labor Party were to break up just before the forthcoming national elections, as a result of the post-mortem discussions that were beginning to take place, or because of ill-timed external pressures.

The primary source of the militant current lay in the prewar expectations universally entertained by Israelis that a war on the scale of the one that happened was just "impossible," in view of the overwhelming military superiority of Israel, repeatedly acknowledged by the Arabs themselves. War having nonetheless broken out, presumably because of some irrational, "suicidal," urge of the Arabs, all Israelis were certain of a total, fast, and cheap victory. In reality, of course, the Israelis had to fight extremely hard for 16 days and suffer, for them, enormous losses in order to score a partial victory. But all Israelis felt that this course of events was unwarranted and "unfair." It began with a series of mistakes on the Israeli side; then, when these were finally corrected and Israel was on the verge of achieving complete victory, outside powers intervened. Moreover, these outside powers contrived, after the fighting ceased, to reduce the scope of even the limited victory that Israel achieved, by pressuring it to allow supplies to go to the encircled Egyptian III Corps and trying to force Israeli forces to withdraw to a more confined perimeter.

The result of all this was an attitude that nurtured hopes for a breakdown of the ceasefire and looked for excuses to break it in order to complete the job of winning that was left undone. More important, the result was a mental disposition that resisted any idea or suggestion that did not conform with preconceived notions.

This attitude began to break down enough to give a chance for a countervailing current to start, when it became apparent that Israel was not nearly as free to act as most Israelis supposed. One of the crucial agents of the change was none other than Defense Minister Moshe Dayan, a reputedly tough man who still enjoys immense authority despite some recent setbacks. In his typical no-nonsense way, Dayan answered the leader of the opposition in the Knesset, who had said that the soldiers were very unhappy that Israel was yielding to American pressure to allow supplies to III Corps, by saying that the soldiers did not know that the shells they disposed of today were not there two weeks before, and wouldn't have been there but for the goodwill of the United States.

Once the hope of radically changing the existing state of things began to recede, reality and its lessons began to sink in. A crucial factor was the one major positive feature in the situation—the commitment assumed by the Arab side as well as the Soviet Union to enter immediately into peace negotiations.

One important lesson the Israelis began to learn is that even a militarily inferior opponent might find it advantageous to go to war if he is left with no better options. Israelis had deemed war "impossible" because they thought Sadat could not possibly hope to win. They did not realize that it might pay him to go to war if he had reasonable chances of not suffering a crushing defeat very quickly. Another lesson the Israelis began to learn—one that eminent students of war never tire of preaching—is that war is par excellence the domain of *fortuna,* a notion that had been utterly alien to Israelis, accustomed to think that their brilliant past victories had been the inevitable outcome of "scientific" preparation.

The significance of these lessons may be better appreciated if we recall that Israelis had been strongly divided before the war in their views as to what the minimal aims of their country should be in connection with the post-1967 situation. Among the considerations determining the various positions, the Arab capacity to wage war and inflict damage on Israel was initially an important factor. Evaluations of that capacity on the part of the different groups fluctuated in the course of the fighting that followed the 1967 war; but by 1970–71, when a ceasefire became firmly established, a consensus about the "impossibility" of war and about Israel's chances if it nonetheless happened had begun to prevail. Henceforth, the arguments between the upholders of different positions centered on weighing the costs and benefits of the various courses, without the prospect of war and its possible costs entering into the picture at all. Naturally, this tended to push the entire spectrum of positions in a more demanding, "hawkish" direction. Now that war—costly, cruel, and susceptible of complications—injected itself into the picture, the whole spectrum of positions could not but move, in time, in an opposite, more accommodating, direction.

Another lesson, implicit in what has just been said but worthy of specification because of its importance, consisted of the exploding of the position of those who wanted, and thought it possible, to prolong indefinitely the stalemate that came to prevail after 1970, either in order to avoid having to make choices that could precipitate undesired political splits or in the hope that time would give some kind of legitimacy to Israel's retention of the conquered territories. The war and the events accompanying it showed that the Arab-Israeli conflict had just become too complex—involving too many interests and having too many ramifications—to be susceptible of being kept indefinitely in stalemate.

But probably the most specific, important, and hopeful lesson of the war has been that centering on the relationship between territory and security—the rock on which past efforts at peace have foundered. Immediately after the war, at the height of what we called the "militant" current, Israelis argued that the war demonstrated how vital the territorial factor was and how right Israel has been in insisting on very substantial modifications of the 1967 territorial setup. Where, it was asked, would Israel be today if it did not have the buffer of the Golan and Sinai—if, for example, the enemy had been able to score an initial advance of 15 kilometers not at Khushniyya in the Golan but toward Natanya at the "waist" of pre-1967 Israel?

Since then, Israelis have continued to hold on to this argument, but have simultaneously begun to confront the inescapable paradox that in 1967 their country did infinitely better with its "insecure" boundaries than in 1973 with its "ideal" boundaries. It can, of course, be argued—and it is—that in 1973 Israel had fallen victim to a "Maginot-line mentality," that there had been an unwarranted failure of intelligence, that the Soviets had given the Arabs weapons that allowed them to achieve several tactical surprises, that they went on to replenish their arsenal as fast as Israel destroyed it, and that in the final account Israel would have still won a decisive victory but for the intervention of the United States and the Soviet Union. However, each additional explanation or excuse could only point out more and more factors relevant to security, and thus drive an additional nail in the coffin of the previous Israeli attitude that had made a fetish out of territory. The sum total of the explanations could only underscore the truth that security is a product of a multitude of factors of which geography is one, but which also comprises technology, friendships and alliances, relative size of forces and so on—including alertness and aspects of the opponent's state of mind that can be reached. The explanations would also reveal that there is a measure of interchangeability between these factors, so that one could have less of one and more of another and end up being no worse off than before, if not better.

There are signs that this kind of lesson is being learned in Israel along with others we mentioned, all of which make for the erosion of rigidities that have stood in the way of peace in the past. Given a chance, this sober, moderate current is most likely to prevail, if not throughout Israel, then at least among the majority of the ruling coalition. But there is a danger that this chance may be denied to it by one of two developments: (1) a breakdown of the ceasefire; or (2) a breakup of the Labor Party's own coalition of "hawks," "moderates" and "doves." The former development could result from some breakdown in the fragile agreements that have been reached concerning exchange of prisoners, supply to III Corps, definition of ceasefire lines, blockade of the Bab el-Mandeb Strait, and so on. The latter development might come about as a result of an internal explosion, triggered by mutual recriminations among the various segments of the party over the management of the crisis; or it could be precipitated from the outside, by prematurely putting before the party the necessity to make choices about critical issues.

The impact of the war on Egypt, too, may be viewed in terms of two competing currents, moderate and militant, opposing different segments of the power elite and feeding ambivalent inclinations in individual members of it. In contrast to Israel, both currents in Egypt, while being rooted in the prewar situation, have been shaped mainly by the course of the war and associated events. One current tends to view the outcome of the war as placing Egypt in the best bargaining position it could hope to achieve, and is therefore eager to capitalize on it in order to try to reach a settlement now. The other current believes that the war has shown that Egyptians themselves had underestimated their military capabilities and the outside support they could command, and is therefore inclined to be more reticent and insist on more demanding terms. Both currents are, to be sure, already committed to entering peace negotiations with Israel without insisting on prior Israeli withdrawal. However, the former is likely to be accommodating in order not to forfeit the present opportunity, while the latter is likely to seek a much harder bargain, even at the risk of a breakdown of the peace talks.

At the root of the more conciliatory tendency is the bitter memory of the post-1967 era. After years of struggle to eliminate the consequences of defeat, which saw Egypt's options evaporate or end in frustration one after the other, a stalemate set in that was even more oppressive than the repeated failures. For Egyptian society resembles nothing more than a vast bureaucratic enterprise, which depends entirely on impulses imparted to it from the top to operate with any degree of efficiency. Such impulses had not been forthcoming because the top leadership had been completely preoccupied with the Israeli question. President Nasser might have, had he so chosen, ignored that question for some time, but Sadat did not even have that choice; lacking any previous credit, his tenure of the presidency depended for its legitimation in a very large measure on his being able to resolve that problem. The result of all this was that by 1973 Egypt's economy had been stagnant for many years, Egypt's society was completely demoralized, its polity was a seething cauldron, the credibility of the government had sunk to zero, and Sadat and his entourage had their hands full just trying to survive from month to month.

It was in this context that Sadat was finally persuaded by the military chiefs to go to war. The aim he had set for Egypt was not total victory, which he realized was unattainable. At the very most he hoped to seize a strip along the east bank of the canal reaching out to the passes, which would represent the beginning of the process of liberating the occupied territories, put Egypt in a position to press for the evacuation of the rest, and permit the reopening of the Suez Canal and the resettling of the desolate cities of the west bank. The minimal objective, which made the whole enterprise justifiable, was to stave off total defeat long enough to provoke great-power intervention and international initiatives that would break the stalemate.

When the war ended, Egypt, to the surprise of vast segments of the power elite, had achieved considerably more than its minimal objective, though much less than its maximal objective. The fact that utter defeat in the last days of the war was averted only by a hair's breadth did not detract from the accomplishment. However, it made the moderates feel that Egypt had attained the best possible position from which to bargain for ending the stalemate on reasonable terms.

As for the militants, they had shared with everyone else the frustrations of stalemate, only they had tired first of the diplomatic efforts to break it and had urged military action sooner. In the end it was they who prevailed upon Sadat to go to war, by laying out before him the specter of greater trouble, especially the breakdown of military discipline, if he did not. The course of the war—the ease with which the Egyptian forces overran the Bar-Lev line and established a bridgehead, the very heavy casualties they inflicted upon Israel and especially their success in denying supremacy to the Israeli air force over the battle zone—appeared to the militants to vindicate their erstwhile claims, and to give Egypt some highly credible military options. On that basis, as well as on the basis of the recommitment of the Soviet Union to the Arab cause, the seemingly miraculous effectiveness of the "oil weapon" in neutralizing Europe and setting it at odds with the United States, and the evident eagerness of the United States to seek points of contact with the Arabs, they have argued that Egypt now has ample room for maneuver and substantial prospects of further enhancing it. Therefore, they conclude that Egypt need not settle for anything less than total Israeli withdrawal from all Arab territories and "justice for the Palestinians."

   It seems evident from the fact that Egypt agreed to the negotiation clause of the ceasefire resolution, and made no serious
attempts to break the encirclement of the III Corps by force, that
so far it has been the moderate current that has prevailed. However, it is equally evident that the other, more militant current
cannot be ignored and could come to prevail should there be a
breakdown of the ceasefire or should the anticipated negotiations
tarry too long in coming or give signs of inconclusiveness.

VI

   Our panoramic survey of the impact and lessons of the 1973
War shows that a resolution of the Arab-Israeli conflict has at last
become a real possibility for the parties directly concerned, and
an imperative necessity for all the outsiders that have been involved in it. It is completely understandable, therefore, that outsiders should try to exert all the influence and pressure they can
in order to bring about a peace settlement; but these outsiders
must beware of defeating their own purpose through misapplied
zeal. There are forces on either side of the Arab-Israeli front-
line, we have seen, that are inclined in directions favorable to
peace—as there are forces that are swayed by considerations that
would inhibit the give-and-take necessary for settlement. The
involved outsiders should be wary of allowing the latter to prevail *on either side of the fence,* through their pressing on either
party formulas that do violence to deeply felt and widely shared
concerns, or even through pressing any formula too soon or too
late.
   Clearly, the most fundamental concern of Israel is ensuring
its security; that of the Arabs, safeguarding their sovereignty.
The two need not be as incompatible as they were felt to be
before the war, if sufficient imagination is applied to the search
for a solution and to the conception of the resources that might
be used. This is not the place to suggest any specific plan that
does so; but we might point out in a general way, and by way of
illustrating rather than exhausting the possibilities, that the two
concerns can be reconciled in one or more of the following ways:
   (1) By bringing in an outside factor to enhance Israel's security enough to have it relax its demands for territorial modifications. One such factor might be a U.S.-Israel mutual defense
pact. A few years ago, the author made a proposal to this effect
which evoked some weighty objections on the part of Americans

and elicited skeptical reactions from Israelis.[1] Now that the United States has confirmed once more its abiding unwritten commitment to Israel's security, now that it has demonstrated its capacity to uphold that commitment in the most dramatic and effective way, and now that the Arabs have shown in many ways that they accept that commitment as legitimate, providing it does not extend to protecting Israel's conquests, most of the previously expressed concerns should cease to be relevant.

(2) By introducing a flexible time factor into an effort to reconcile the two. For example, starting from a formal recognition by Israel of Arab sovereignty, and Arab recognition of Israeli security concerns, a plan might be agreed upon whereby the actual return of the territories is accomplished in a gradual way. This would be conditioned by the establishment and consolidation of normal neighborly relations, which is deemed by the Israelis to be the best security.[2]

(3) By broadening the conception of boundaries to be settled. For example, in exchange for the Arabs' ceding sovereignty over part of their territories to meet Israeli security needs, Israel might relinquish sovereignty over some of its pre-1967 territory to meet such crucial Arab needs as the establishment of territorial contiguity between Egypt and the Fertile Crescent countries. Alternatively, a similar arrangement might be made that is based on the right of use, while sovereignty is retained intact.

Certainly many additional approaches can be developed. But even the best-worked-out plan can fail if it is not presented at the appropriate time. And right timing is not something that can be planned, but must depend on the intuition and experience of the statesmen.

[1] See Nadav Safran, "Middle East; The Fleeting Opportunity," *The Nation*, April 5, 1971, pp. 425–28.

[2] For one model of such a plan, see Nadav Safran, "U.S. Policy, Israel's Security, and Middle East Peace," Hearings before the Subcommittee on the Near East of the House Committee on Foreign Affairs, 92nd Congress, 1st session, July–October 1971.

The Arab Oil Weapon—A Threat to International Peace

JORDAN J. PAUST AND ALBERT P. BLAUSTEIN

The month of October, 1973, brought with it Arab coercion in two forms: the first was the military attack against Israeli forces begun on October 6; [1] the second was the use of economic coercion against countries that, in Arab eyes, either supported Israel or did not support the Arabs in their present quests (which include the return of claimed "Arab" lands, favorable settlement of the Palestinian peoples' claim for self-determination, and other political and military objectives).

On October 18, just twelve days after the joint Arab initiation of war against Israel, Saudi Arabia, the world's largest oil-exporting state, announced immediate cuts in oil production in an attempt to pressure the United States to reduce support for the state of Israel and also threatened to cut off all oil trade with the United States, if Arab demands were not met. By January, 1974, that trade had dried up completely. [2] On that same day in October, the Persian gulf state of Abu Dhabi announced that it was stopping all oil exports to the United States and would act similarly against any other country that supported Israel.

* J.S.D. Candidate, Yale University.
** Professor of Law, Rutgers University, Camden.
The authors are grateful for the comments and criticism offered by Myres S. McDougal, W. Michael Reisman, Eugene V. Rostow, Julius Stone, and Sidney Liskofsky. Of course, the views expressed and errors or imperfections are our own.

[1] We offer no detailed inquiry here into whether the joint Arab attack on Israeli forces violated UN S.C. Res. 242 and Article 2(4) of the UN Charter as amplified by UN G.A. Res. 2625, Declaration on Principles of International Law Concerning Friendly Relations and Co-operation Among States in Accordance with the Charter of the United Nations, 25 UN GAOR, Supp. 18, at 122–24, UN Doc. A/8028 (1970), *reprinted at* 65 AJIL 243 (1971). Readers are referred to E. V. Rostow, THE MIDDLE EAST CONFLICT IN PERSPECTIVE (1973); and J. Stone, letter, Washington Post, Dec. 8, 1973. *See also* UN CHARTER, preamble and Arts. 1 and 2; W. M. REISMAN, NULLITY AND REVISION 842–43 (1971); and E. V. Rostow, *Legal Aspects of the Search for Peace in the Middle East*, PROC. AMER. SOC. INT. LAW, 64 AJIL 64 (No. 4, 1970) and remarks at 78–87.

[2] *See* N.Y. Times, Oct. 19, 1973, at 1, col. 6. On January 12, 1974, the Saudi Minister of Petroleum Affairs stated that his country was by then not supplying "a drop of oil" to the United States or to "any refinery that supplies petroleum products to the United States," *see* N.Y. Times, Jan. 13, 1974, at 14, col. 4. It has been alleged that President Nixon's October 17 request of $2.2-billion in military aid to Israel directly contributed to King Faisal's decision to use the oil weapon. *See* E. Sheehan, N.Y. Times, Magazine, Mar. 24, 1974, at 13, 54, col. 1. *Cf.* I. Sus, *Western Europe and the October War*, 3 J. OF PALESTINE STUDIES 65, 75 (1974).

Some six weeks later, the use and impact of this form of economic coercion had broadened and intensified. Amid an aura of proclaimed unity, Arab leaders adopted a joint resolution calling for the continued "use of oil as an economic weapon."[3] Already, the Netherlands had been boycotted and all other European Common Market countries and Japan had been placed under a 25 percent oil cut.[4] As part of this mounting coercion, a new "Arab solidarity," and the joint military attack against the state of Israel, this November resolution called for: (1) a continuation of an oil embargo against countries "supporting Israel"; (2) the continued reduction of oil production in any event; and (3) the creation of a joint Arab committee to categorize states as "friendly," "neutral," and "supporting Israel" so that implementation of the Arab objectives could be carried out.[5] In addition, periodic cuts in the oil trade were threatened with targeted countries that did not change their policies or engage in certain pro-Arab conduct—a sort of periodic intensification of the coercion. Interrelated with these threats were additional Saudi Arabian claims "to cut oil production by 80 percent if the United States, Europe or Japan took measures to counter current Arab oil boycotts and reductions" in production.[6] It was made quite clear that the Arabs would decide who was to get what amount of oil, when, and for what reasons. It was also made clear that general production was going to be cut in any event;[7] and, further, if any joint or unilateral resistance were made to this approach to energy production and trade, those who resisted would be made to suffer the consequences.

Despite the conclusion of a cease-fire agreement and a "six-point" disengagement agreement between Israel and Egypt by January 18, 1974, the attempts to initiate a more comprehensive Geneva conference for settlement of Middle East problems, and the partial withdrawal of Israeli forces from post-1967 positions under UN force supervision, no reduction

---

[3] See "Arabs Halt Oil Shipments to 3 Countries," N.Y. Times, Nov. 29, 1973, at 16, col. 6. The use of an oil boycott had first occurred in the 1967 war and was directed against the United States for about one month with little effect. See J. E. Akins, *The Oil Crisis: This Time the Wolf Is Here*, 51 FOREIGN AFFAIRS 462, 468 (1973).

[4] See N.Y. Times, Nov. 23, 1973, at 1, col. 6, quoting the Saudi Arabian Oil Minister, Ahmed Zaki al-Yamani.   [5] See *supra* note 3.

[6] See *supra* note 4.

[7] Here, much broader questions are raised, such as the permissibility of increases in oil prices by oil producers; they are related to the whole process of coercion but will not be discussed here in great detail. Professor Rostow had insightfully suggested that an issue is raised as to whether Article 2(4) of the UN Charter is "the Sherman Act in disguise" in connection with the community regulation of a coercive and monopolistic manipulation of resources. The price increases can also be analyzed in terms of breach of contract or as a form of wealth deprivation and control in a global arena. See B. H. Weston, *International Law and the Deprivation of Foreign Wealth: A Framework for Future Inquiry*, 2 THE FUTURE OF THE INTERNATIONAL LEGAL ORDER: WEALTH AND RESOURCES 36, 38 n. 10, 79, *passim* (Falk and Black eds. 1970).

had occurred in the then total embargo of oil to the United States.[8] This situation continued for some five months after the initiation of the first cut in oil exports and states like France, Italy, Japan, the Philippines, and the United Kingdom lined up to trade guns and technology for oil under the pressure of economic coercion and new Arab strength.[9] A 25 percent cut in overall oil production in Arab states continued into mid March. Oil prices soared to record highs, while Europe continued under a 10–15 percent ban and many countries in the Third World experienced a loss of 25–35 percent of normal oil flow.

On March 18, five months after the initiation of the embargo by Saudi Arabia and Abu Dhabi, most of the Arab states announced in Vienna their decision to end the oil embargo against the United States and certain other countries. However, Iraq had refused to attend the meeting, and Libya and Syria refused to give their "assent" to the lifting of the embargo or to any increase in overall production. Moreover, Algeria stated that it was only lifting the embargo provisionally until June 1. The "ending" of the use of the oil weapon against the United States by participating Arab states [10] had occurred with a lingering threat to re-employ it. Additionally, there was no ending of the oil embargo against the Netherlands, Denmark, South Africa, Rhodesia, and Portugal.

This Arab strategy constitutes the deliberate employment of an economic instrument of coercion (the oil "weapon") against other states and peoples in order to place intense pressure upon their freedom of choice. Although this strategy is primarily dependent upon the use of an economic instrument of coercion, the full dimension of the coercive process has involved the interrelated use of diplomatic and ideological instruments as well as the coordinate use of military forces against the state of Israel. As such, the Arab oil embargo is in violation of international law, as formulated in the United Nations Charter and key supporting documents.

AN APPROACH TO DECISION

At times we will merely refer to this overall process of coercion as the oil "weapon" or as the Arab economic coercion or oil embargo, but the full range of Arab effort should be kept in mind. We do not find it useful to classify the entire coercive process in terms of rigid, past categories—such as embargo, boycott, reprisal, or act of "blackmail." Nor do we find it useful to consider the coercive process merely in terms of "economic warfare" or "economic aggression." Not only are these terms generally too confining for a proper focus, but some are merely conclu-

---

[8] See, e.g., "Kissinger Says a Continuation of the Arab Oil Embargo Would Be 'Blackmail'," N.Y. Times, Feb. 7, 1974, at 1, col. 4.

[9] Europe remained under an "officially" disclosed cut of 15% in oil imports from the Middle East through March 10, 1974, despite notable changes in positions and significant agreements to supply arms and technology to Arab states. See N.Y. Times, Mar. 9, 1974, at 5, col. 1.

[10] See N.Y. Times, Mar. 19, 1974, at 1, col. 1, and at 20, cols. 3–8.

sions that may be attached to a particular coercive process after fact and law have been fully considered.

Indeed, it is too simplistic to categorize events as acts of "war" or "peace," since coercion between states and peoples is continuous through time and space in differing types and levels of intensity. Far more is proscribed under international law than coercive acts which amount to acts of "war." Moreover, a great deal of coercion is "normal" or permissible in day to day relations.[11] International law takes cognizance, however, of the greater need for the regulation of varied types and intensities of coercion in this increasingly interdependent world.[12] The main concern is for a rational, policy-serving distinction between forms of permissible and impermissible coercion.

Does the conduct conform to legal policies (goal-values)[13] that the accepted prescriptions against the use of coercion seek to serve? Where a set of prescriptions discloses a complimentarity of purpose, as is often the case, and the conduct in question seems to serve certain community policies while impairing others, how is rational and policy-serving decision best promoted?[14] It is clear that rigid categories such as "embargo" or economic "war" are insufficient in reference to the full range of legal policy that is relevant or to the myriad of contextual factors that may usefully be considered in making a rational, realistic choice concerning the legality of the Arab coercive process. Similarly, it is clear that a mere reference to one set of the complementary goal-values (e.g., norms of self-defense) without reference to the other (e.g., proscriptions against certain forms of coercion) is insufficient.

Depending upon degrees of intent, intensities of impact, and a number of other factors, the use of the Arab coercive strategy may be found to constitute such a substantial impairment of the goals articulated in the United Nations Charter that decisionmakers can authoritatively characterize the use of the oil "weapon" as a violation of that instrument. The United Nations, for example, could declare that there has been a violation of those provisions dealing with the use of coercion, the promotion of friendly relations, the promotion of self-determination, the promotion of equal rights of nations large and small, the promotion of social progress and better standards of life in larger freedom, the peaceful settlement of

---

[11] For a useful example of this sort of recognition by a non-McDougalian and a related intellectual groping for distinctions, see D. Bowett, Economic Coercion and Reprisals By States, 13 VA. J. INT. L. 1, 2–5 (1972).

[12] See M. McDougal and F. Feliciano, Law and Minimum World Public Order 11–39 and 97 ff. (1961); and M. McDougal, Peace and War: Factual Continuum with Multiple Legal Consequences, 49 AJIL 63 (1955).

[13] Throughout this article we refer to the policies behind legal rules (or those documented in constitutive instruments and elsewhere) as legal policies, goal-values, or community goals.

[14] On the problem of complimentarity and the need for responsive decisionmaking which is rational and policy-serving see McDougal and Feliciano, supra note 12, at 57.

disputes, and the maintenance of international peace and security.[15]   In certain situations, the use of any economic coercion could constitute a form of "economic aggression."[16]   And where the impact of economic coercion upon the target group results in intense fear or anxiety (not at all demonstrable in this case), the use of economic coercion could constitute a form of impermissible terroristic strategy.[17]

Here we cannot provide the ultimate, detailed analysis of the use of this economic instrument of coercion which is a necessary prerequisite to a comprehensive consideration of the full range of relevant legal policies, in this case or in any future inquiry into the legality of economic coercion.   Our purpose here lies more in the disclosure of probable violations of international law and the danger to those legal policies that the international community seeks to effectuate than in a final characterization of certain Arab states as violators of the law.   For the latter purpose, it is hoped that a comprehensive analysis by appropriate community decision-makers will be initiated and will involve a detailed inquiry into all aspects of the situation—participants in the coercive process (initiators, instrumental targets, primary targets, spillover victims), the objectives of the Arabs (and all other perspectives), actual arenas of interaction (Middle East and global), resources available to all participants, elements of the strategy, actual outcomes, and probable long-term effects.[18]   Instead, we focus on the types of general community policy (goal-values) at stake, and briefly explore some of the features of context in order to demonstrate our concern and to outline factors that seem important both to facilitate the identification and clarification of policy and for the comprehensive assessment of the necessity and proportionality of the use of this particular strategy of coercion in actual context.

In any future inquiry, the important factors would include: (a) the objectives of the Arab initiators of the coercive strategy; (b) the number of

[15] See UN Charter, preamble and Arts. 1, 2, and 56.   See also McDougal and Feliciano, supra note 12, at 177–206, passim, and references cited.

[16] See, e.g., L. Chen, The Legal Regulation of Minor International Coercion 131–210 (1964), unpublished dissertation, Yale Law School.   See also McDougal and Feliciano, supra note 12, at 30–32, 194–202, 325–29, and references cited; B. Ferencz, Defining Aggression: Where It Stands and Where It's Going, 66 AJIL 491 (1972); R. Falk, Quincy Wright: On Legal Tests of Aggressive War, id., 560; and R. Tucker, Reprisals and Self-Defense: The Customary Law, id., 586.   On the related matter of justifiable "self-defense" responses to "economic aggression," see infra notes 24–27.

[17] On the legal regulation of international terroristic strategy see, e.g., J. Paust, Some Terroristic Claims Arising from the Arab-Israeli Context, Symposium, International Terrorism: Mid East, 7 Akron L. Rev. (1974); and Terrorism and the International Law of War, 64 Mil. L. Rev. 1 (1974), reprinted in 13 Revue de Droit Penal Militaire et de Droit de la Guerre (1974).   Also, compare T. M. Franck, B. B. Lockwood, Preliminary Thoughts towards an International Convention on Terrorism, 68 AJIL 69 (1974) with J. Paust supra and references cited; and J. Paust, Letter, 68 AJIL 502–03 (1974).

[18] See generally, McDougal and Feliciano, supra note 12.

participants affected; (c) the number and types of Charter goals affected; and (d) the extent to which Charter goals are affected.[19]

TRADITIONAL RULES AND THE POLICIES AT STAKE

The UN Charter.

Almost all states and peoples have pledged to each other and to all mankind their continued effort to practice tolerance; to develop friendly relations among nations based on respect for equal rights and self-determination; to cooperate in an effort to solve international economic and other problems; to live together in peace; and to settle disputes by peaceful means in such a manner that international peace, security, and justice are not endangered.[20] Article 2(4) of the Charter, containing the important pledge of all members to refrain from certain forms of impermissible coercion, provides:

> All Members shall refrain in their international relations from the threat or use of force against the territorial integrity or political independence of any state, or in any other manner inconsistent with the Purposes of the United Nations.

Thus, if the threat or use of force is against the "territorial integrity" or "political independence" of another state, Article 2(4) of the Charter has been violated. Additionally, the goal-values of Article 2(4) are impaired if the threat or use of force is "in any other manner inconsistent with the Purposes of the United Nations," many of which, as outlined above, are expressed in Article 1 and the preamble of the Charter. Thus, the substantial impairment of goals of the international community as articulated in the Charter through the deliberate use of coercion against other states, not counterbalanced by complementary policies relating to legitimate self-defense or the sanctioning of UN decisions, constitutes a violation of Article 2(4) as well as of other provisions of the Charter.[21]

What is the meaning of the word "force" in Article 2(4)? Does the Charter prohibit economic forms of coercion? It has been stated in the past that the type of "force" contemplated in Article 2(4) was "armed force." Some writers have even read into Article 2(4) the restrictive word "armed," which does not appear in the text and was not contemplated as a restriction in pre-Charter norms or in the drafting of the Charter it-

---

[19] *See* L. Chen, *supra* note 16, at 136–38, 159, *passim*; and McDOUGAL and FELICIANO, *supra* note 12, at 14–19, 30–32, *passim*.

[20] *See supra* note 15. It is significant that the preamble of the Charter begins with: "We the peoples of the United Nations . . ."

[21] *See, e.g.,* McDOUGAL and FELICIANO, *supra* note 12, at 178–79; J. PAUST and A. BLAUSTEIN, JURISDICTION AND DUE PROCESS: THE CASE OF BANGLADESH (1974); J. Paust, *A Survey of Possible Legal Responses to International Terrorism: Prevention, Punishment and Cooperative Action,* forthcoming; I. BROWNLIE, INTERNATIONAL LAW AND THE USE OF FORCE BY STATES 266–68 (1963); and 2 OPPENHEIM's INTERNATIONAL LAW 154 (H. Lauterpacht, *ed.,* 7th ed., 1952). *See also* UN G.A. Res. 2625, *supra* note 1.

self. They merely assume that, since the preamble of the Charter is more specific in stating that "armed force shall not be used save in the common interest," other forms of coercion (economic, diplomatic, ideological) were to go unregulated, despite the articulation of other Charter objectives concerning world public order and human dignity and the concomitant pledge of members in Article 56.[22] Moreover, they never fully explain, in terms of the fulfillment of Charter goals, the desirability of allowing "economic aggression" to remain unregulated, especially when such a mode of coercion can be of such significant intensity and impact that it is comparable to an armed attack upon another state.

Those writers who favor this myopic and restrictive approach to the regulation of coercion often maintain that to prohibit other forms of coercion would allow a state to exercise the right of self-defense in response to "economic aggression," "diplomatic aggression," impermissible propaganda, and so forth. Actually, such a conclusion would depend upon one's interpretation of the phrase "armed attack" in Article 51 of the Charter[23] and upon a contextual analysis that would disclose whether the actual "economic aggression," diplomatic coercion, and so forth were of such an intensity, efficacy, and magnitude as to threaten the security of another state significantly and, thus, properly justify the exercise of the right of "self-defense."[24] Here, we merely note that although Articles 2(4) and 51 are usually "complementary opposites" in terms of the basic policies at stake,[25] they do not exhaust the complementarity of norms that are relevant today.[26] Once it is realized that Article 2(4) proscribes much more than a use of force against the territorial integrity, political independence, or security interests of another state, it should also be realized that all violations of Article 2(4) do not automatically threaten the security interests of another state in a significant way or reach such an intensity

---

[22] See 2 Oppenheim, supra note 21, at 153; Goodrich, Hambro, Charter of the United Nations 104 (2d ed. 1949); Brierly, The Law of Nations 415 (6th ed. 1963). Cf. Brownlie, supra note 21, at 361–62 and 365–66; and Bowett, Self-Defense in International Law 54 and 119 (1958). Contra McDougal and Feliciano, supra note 12, at 177–202 and 240–41; Kelsen, The Law of the United Nations 915 (1951); and Paust and Blaustein, supra note 26.

[23] Compare the cogent analysis in McDougal and Feliciano, supra note 12, at 233–41 with the far less comprehensive approach and forecast offered in S. M. Schwebel, "A Takeover of Kuwait?," Washington Post, June 26, 1973, nearly four months before the actual use of the oil "weapon." See also Reisman, supra note 1, at 839 n. 6 and 849–50.

[24] See McDougal and Feliciano, supra note 12, at 179 n. 142, 200, 231–32, 235 and 240–41 and Reisman, supra note 1, at 839 n. 6. For those who think that claims to use responsive coercion in "self-defense" are not relevant to the case of the oil weapon, see remarks of Secretary of Defense Schlesinger as reported in N.Y. Times, Jan. 12, 1974, at 3, col. 1.

[25] See McDougal and Feliciano, supra note 12, at 57, 123, 126–27. Cf. Reisman, supra note 1, at 839 n. 6 and 849–50; Professor McDougal's introduction in J. N. Moore, Law and the Indo-China War viii–ix (1972); and his remarks in Paust and Blaustein, supra note 21, at 44, n. 95.

[26] See Reisman, supra note 1, at 836–51; and infra note 28.

and magnitude in that regard as to create the "condition of necessity" for a response under Article 51.[27] Although coercion not involving the use of armed force can violate Article 2(4) and result in UN action, it does not follow automatically that states may unilaterally respond as well under Article 51 of the Charter. Similarly, the reverse is true. Although a state may not properly respond under Article 51, this does not mean that Article 2(4) has not been violated.[28] It is by no means clear that the Arab coercive process does not also involve an armed attack and an intense coercion of the type contemplated under Article 51, for the oil "weapon" was employed in the context of an armed attack upon the state of Israel and its use was intended to supplement that effort.

In any event, Article 2(4) prohibits more than the threat or use of "armed" force.[29] This has been clearly articulated in a series of United Nations instruments supplementary to the Charter—documents which spell out the goal-values generally shared by the international community. Chronologically, they include:

(a) The Draft Declaration on Rights and Duties of States, 1949,[30]

(b) The Essentials of Peace resolution, 1949,[31]

(c) The Peace Through Deeds resolution, 1950,[32]

(d) The Draft Code of Offences Against the Peace and Security of Mankind, 1954,[33]

[27] See McDougal and Feliciano, supra note 12, at 179, 237, and 240. Nor must they constitute an "aggression" to be proscribed under Article 2(4). See also Reisman, supra note 1, at 838–39, 842–43 and 849–50.

[28] If coercive conduct is proscribed under Article 2(4) but does not reach levels of intensity and magnitude such as to justify responsive coercion under Article 51 (or even Article 52), the permissible response would be a community response within the relevant Charter provisions. For comment on the situation where the UN machinery is ineffective, see, e.g., Paust and Blaustein, supra note 21, at 9 n. 22, 10–11 n. 25, 22–23, 25 n. 54, and 42–44: Moore, supra note 25, at viii–ix, 183, and 185, and authorities cited; J. Paust, remarks, Conference on The Legal Regulation of the Use of Force, 2 Ga. J. Int. & Comp. L., Supp. 1, at 121–22 (1972); Reisman, supra note 1, at 836–58; J. E. Bond, A Survey of the Normative Rules of Intervention, 52 Mil. L. Rev. 51, 59–63 (1971); R. Lillich, Forcible Self-Help Under International Law, 22 Naval War Coll. Rev. 56 (1970); R. Lillich, Forcible Self-Help by States to Protect Human Rights, 53 Iowa L. Rev. 325, 347–51 (1967); and B. Harlow, The Legal Use of Force Short of War, 1966 U.S. Naval Institute Proceedings 88 (Nov. 1966).

[29] See, e.g., McDougal and Feliciano, supra note 12, at 178–79, 196 and 200. This was also the Egyptian position in the Committee on Friendly Relations. UN Doc. A/AC.125/SR.25, at 12 (1966).

[30] Report of the International Law Commission (ILC), 4 UN GAOR, Supp. 10, at 7–10, UN Doc. A/925 (June 9, 1949).

[31] UN G.A. Res. 290(IV), 4 UN GAOR, UN Doc. A/1251, at 13 (Dec. 1, 1949).

[32] UN G.A. Res. 380(V), 5 UN GAOR, Supp. 20, at 13–14, UN Doc. A/1775, (Nov. 17, 1950).

[33] Report of the ILC, 9 UN GAOR, Supp. 9, at 11–12, UN Doc. A/2693, (July 28, 1954).

(e) The Declaration on Inadmissibility of Intervention Into the Domestic Affairs of States, 1965,[34]

(f) The Declaration on Principles of International Law Concerning Friendly Relations and Co-Operation Among States in Accordance With the Charter of the United Nations, 1970,[35]

(g) The resolution on Permanent Sovereignty over Natural Resources, 1973,[36]

as further explained and supplemented by:

(h) The Report by the Secretary-General of the United Nations on the Question of Defining Aggression, 1952,[37]

(i) The Soviet draft resolution on the Definition of Aggression, 1954,[38] and

(j) The Vienna Convention on the Law of Treaties, 1969.[39]

The General Assembly, for example, has authoritatively declared in the Declaration on Friendly Relations that it is "the duty of states to refrain in their international relations from military, political, economic or any other form of coercion aimed against the political independenec or territorial integrity of any state . . ."[40] In its exegesis of Article 2(4), it has also declared that every state has a duty to refrain from "any forcible action" which deprives certain peoples of self-determination, equal rights, and freedom and independence. The Declaration further states that "armed intervention and all other forms of interference or attempted threats against the personality of the state or against its political, economic, and cultural elements, are in violation of international law." Additionally it has been declared that:

> No state may use or encourage the use of economic, political or any other type of measures to coerce[41] another state in order to obtain

---

[34] UN G.A. Res. 2131, 20 UN GAOR, Supp. 14, at 11–12, UN Doc. A/6014 (Dec. 21, 1965).   [35] *Supra* note 1.

[36] UN G.A. Res. 3171, 28 UN GAOR (Dec. 17, 1973) (vote: 108–1–16).

[37] UN Doc. A/2211 (Oct. 3, 1952).

[38] 9 UN GAOR, Annexes, 51, at 6–7, UN Doc. A/C.6/L.332/Rev. 1 (Oct. 18, 1954).

[39] UN Doc. A/CONF.39/27 (May 23, 1969), *reprinted* at 63 AJIL 875 (1969).

[40] *Supra note 1.* We say "authoritatively" because it may be assumed that a unanimous consensus of the voting state elites in the General Assembly adequately reflects the generally shared expectations of the peoples of the United Nations. Regarding primary and representative authority, *see* J. Paust, *An International Structure for Implementation of the 1949 Geneva Conventions: Needs and Function Analysis*, 1 YALE STUDIES IN WORLD PUBLIC ORDER (1974) and J. Paust, *Human Rights and the Ninth Amendment: A New Form of Guarantee*, forthcoming.

[41] This sweeping condemnation of coercion or interference is not very useful by itself for the clarification of criterial distinctions between permissible and impermissible coercion. *See, e.g.*, McDOUGAL and FELICIANO, *supra* note 12, at 197, *passim*; and S. Schwebel, *Aggression, Intervention and Self-Defense in Modern International Law*, 2 REC. DES COURS 413, 453–54 (1972). Since the use of economic sanctions is regulated under Chapter VII of the UN Charter, it is useful to consider restraints upon the use of economic coercion in that Chapter in interpreting restraints upon all types of coercion under Article 2(4) of the Charter. Moreover, the fact that economic

from it the subordination of the exercise of its sovereign rights and to secure from it advantages of any kind.

By interpreting the preamble and Articles 1 and 2 of the UN Charter in light of this recent authoritative expression of the General Assembly we can identify and clarify the community expectation that a broad range of coercive conduct is impermissible. Through this clarified policy, it is now possible to see that the use of economic coercion can violate the Charter. A detailed study of trends in the Security Council and in other UN organs (not undertaken here) would also reinforce this expectancy. Moreover, UN decisions addressing questions of threats to the peace, breaches of the peace, and acts of aggression are relevant as indications of community expectations which are also useful for the interpretation of the dynamic content of Article 2(4) of the Charter.[42]

The General Assembly Declaration on the Inadmissibility of Intervention of 1965 [43] has articulated similar goals, including the free development of political status; the free pursuit of economic, social, and cultural development; the principle of "non-intervention" of states in the internal and external affairs of other states (declared to be "essential to the fulfillment of the purposes and principles of the United Nations"); and the interrelated ban on "economic, political or any other type of measures to coerce another State" from impermissible objectives of dominance or the extraction of "advantages." The final prohibition had also been incorporated in the Draft Code of Offences against the Peace and Security of Mankind of 1954 with respect to economic coercion which is utilized by a state or group against another state "in order to force its will and thereby obtain advantages of any kind." [44]

Even in the case where the objective of the initiator of coercion is couched in terms of permissible self-defense (or a claim is made on the basis of serving any other Charter policy), the international community has generally demanded and expected a proper deference to the two interrelated principles of *necessity* and *proportionality*, which seek to minimize coercion, violence, and the destruction of resource values, such as wealth, power, well-being, and skill. Both principles seek to minimize coercion in terms of permissible participants, arenas of interaction, inten-

---

forms of coercion are regulated under Chapter VII supplements the expectation that the term "force" in Article 2(4) includes measures of economic force. *See also infra* notes 43–47; and D. Bowett, *supra* note 11, at 2–3.

[42] The United Nations can respond to a "threat to the peace" (*e.g.*, under Article 39) which does not constitute a prohibited "threat or use of force" under Article 2(4). *See, e.g.*, M. McDougal, W. M. Reisman, *Rhodesia and the United Nations: The Lawfulness of International Concern*, 62 AJIL 1, 5–19 (1968). *See also*, McDOUGAL and FELICIANO, *supra* note 12, at 178–79 and 207 note 193, *passim.* Similarly, it is possible for the United Nations to respond to a "threat" of force prohibited under Article 2(4) which does not constitute, for example, an imminent armed attack within the broad meaning of Article 51 of the Charter which would justify a unilateral response.   [43] *Supra* note 34.

[44] Art. 2(9), *supra* note 33. *See also* UN Docs. cited *supra* notes 30–32. Similar prohibitory language appears in Art. 16 of the Charter of the OAS.

ities of coercion, and impacts. For example, the principle of proportionality requires that the use of coercion "be limited in intensity and magnitude to what is reasonably necessary promptly to secure the permissible objectives . . . under the established conditions of necessity." [45] And reasonableness should be tested by reference to the contextual features listed above with a view to minimizing coercion.

On a related point, some Arab spokesmen might put forth a claim that the oil found under Arab lands is their property and that it is their "right" to do whatever they wish with it. Although certain instruments adopted by the United Nations affirm the general community goal of allowing all states permanent control of their natural resources, recent General Assembly resolutions have reiterated the *priority* of other goals—that the natural resources be used or controlled in such a manner that international peace is served and the coercion of other states does not reach impermissible levels. A 1972 General Assembly resolution, adopted with nearly unanimous Arab approval, stated that states should control their natural resources, but then reaffirmed the Declaration on Principles of International Law Concerning Friendly Relations and Co-Operation Among States of 1970. It also expressly reiterated the prohibition on the use of "economic, political or any other type of measures to coerce another State" for impermissible objectives of dominance or "to secure from it advantages of any kind." [46] This seems sufficient in itself to make clear that the manipulation of natural resources is regulated by international law in certain cases. Natural resources are not always a matter of "domestic" concern or of complete "sovereignty," and a state cannot do whatever it wants with natural resources that happen to be under its control. [47] The 1972 resolution went on to declare "that actions, measures or legislative regulations by States aimed at coercing, directly or indirectly, other States engaged in . . . the exercise of *their* sovereign rights over *their* natural resources . . . are in violation of the Charter and of the Declaration contained in resolution 2625(XXV) and contradict the targets, objectives and policy measures of the International Strategy for Development for the Second United Nations Development Decade." [48] That strategy had

[45] *See* M. McDougal, *The Soviet-Cuban Quarantine and Self-Defense,* 57 AJIL 597, 598 (1963); and McDOUGAL and FELICIANO, *supra* note 12, at 241–44, *passim.*

[46] UN G.A. Res. 3016 (XXVII) (Dec. 18, 1972) (vote: 102–0–22).

[47] It also seems clear from Arts. 1(3) and 55(b), of the UN Charter that "international problems" of an economic nature can arise as matters of international concern. *See also* Washington Energy Conference Communique, 70 DEPT. STATE BULL. 220 (1974); Secretary Kissinger's speech to the Conference, *id.,* 201; and his joint news conference with Federal Energy Administrator, William Simon, *id.,* 109. *See also* T. F. Bradshaw, *Keeping the Energy Peace,* VISTA (Aug. 1973), at 20, predicting that an "inadequate flow of energy . . . can . . . provide more discord among nations than could all the ideological struggles of the past and present," and that developing countries stand to lose most. Professor R. N. Gardner, in testifying before the Subcommittee on International Economics of the Joint Economic Committee on December 13, 1973, disclosed an interesting anecdote in the remark of Cordell Hull: "if goods can't cross borders, armies will."

[48] *Supra* note 46 (emphasis added). UN G.A. Res. 2625, referred to in the resolu

been charted with a UN proclamation that "[e]conomic and social prog
ress is the common and shared responsibility of the entire internationa
community," and that "[e]very country has the right and duty to de
velop its human and natural resources, but the full benefit of its effort
can be realized only with concomitant and effective international action." [4]

On December 17, 1973 (just after the initiation of the Arab oi
"weapon"), an even stronger resolution (this time with full Arab approval)
expressly reiterated each of these major expectations and added that the
General Assembly:

> Deplores acts of States which use force, armed aggression, economic
> coercion or any other illegal or improper measures in resolving dis
> putes concerning the exercise of the sovereign rights [over natura
> resources].[50]

The General Assembly has emphasized the need for an inclusive and
peaceful approach to the overall problem of earth resource control and
usage in this era of a greater interdependence of peoples and an increasing scarcity of resources, as well as the need for an inclusive regulation
of the manipulation of resources for coercive impact. An inclusive approach, the General Assembly recognizes, is now necessary for the maximization of all interests or the "full benefit" of efforts to develop human
and natural resources in the context of interdependence and scarcity. This
critical recognition could be the beginning of an attempt by mankind
to avoid a global "tragedy of the commons" or, what may be worse, a war
for the "commons."

Secretary Kissinger has noted:

> If anything was needed to illustrate the interdependence of nations
> in this world, it is what has happened in the field of energy . . . It
> is a test of the proposition that the world has become truly interde-
> pendent, and that isolation and selfish approaches must be destructive
> for all concerned.[51]

tion, concerned the International Development Strategy. Here, the expectation seems
to encompass, at least, an international reflection of the general policy behind the
case of Rylands v. Fletcher, L.R. 3H.L. 330 (1868).

[49] See International Development Strategy, UN Doc. ST/ECA/139, at 3 (1970)
reproducing UN G.A. Res. 2625(XXV). See also UN Charter, preamble and Arts
1(3), 55, and 56; UN G.A. Res. 3172(XXVIII), Dec. 17, 1973 (vote: 123–0–0) concerning the growth of interdependence and the "urgent need for international co-
operation"; UN G.A. Res. 3082(XXVIII) (Dec. 6, 1973), Charter of Economic Rights
and Duties of States (adopted without objection); and R. FALK, C. BLACK, eds., 2
THE FUTURE OF THE INTERNATIONAL LEGAL ORDER: WEALTH AND RESOURCES (1970).

[50] UN G.A. Res. 3171(XXVIII), Dec. 17, 1973 (vote: 108–1–16).

[51] 70 DEPT. STATE BULL. 109 (1974). See also H. Kissinger, The Interrelation-
ships of Society, 1 THE INTERDEPENDENT (Apr., 1974) at 3.

Secretary-General Waldheim opened the sixth special session of the General Assembly on raw materials in April 1974 with the recognition of interdependence and
the need for a "just apportionment of natural resources" and the "optimum use of
the world's natural resources with the basic objective of securing better conditions of
social justice throughout the world." UN Doc. A/PV 2207, Apr. 9, 1974. This
necessarily infringes upon permanent control of resources by each individual state

Implicit here is the recognition that, by the "free" use or control of one's own resources, an impermissible interference with the "free" use or control of resources of others can result, and that a balance must be struck that best serves all relevant community goals in view of the actual context and policies at stake. In no other way can an individual or group maximize the enjoyment of freedom from fear and want,[52] or "the full benefit of its efforts."

This also explains the expectation in Article 1(2) of the International Covenant on Economic, Social and Cultural Rights of 1966 that the "free" disposal of natural wealth and resources must not prejudice "any obligations arising out of international economic co-operation, based upon the principle of mutual benefit, and international law," and "[i]n no case may a people be deprived of its own means of subsistence."[53] Undoubtedly, this statement is in effectuation of the purpose, set forth in the UN Charter, of achieving "international co-operation in solving international problems of an economic, social, cultural, or humanitarian character."[54] This is likewise the expectation behind the statement in the preamble of the Covenant on Economic, Social, and Cultural Rights recognizing that the Charter goal of equal rights for "all members of the human family is the foundation of freedom, justice and peace in the world." And each of these expectations should be considered in a rational effort to maximize

---

A position contrary to the inclusive approaches of Secretary Kissinger or the Secretary-General was taken by the People's Republic of China as disclosed in an opening speech at the special session. UN Doc. A/PV 2209, Apr. 10, 1974.

See also UN G.A. Res. 3085(XXVIII), Dec. 6, 1973 (adopted without objection), wherein the Assembly took notice of the Declaration adopted by the Fourth Conference of Heads of State or Government of Non-Aligned Countries (Algiers, Sept. 9, 1973) in which they expressed the belief that "the multilateral trade negotiations will . . . help in the establishment of a new system of world economic relations based on equality and the common interests of all countries." It has also become increasingly apparent that U.S. interests are best served with a more inclusive approach to economic matters. *See also* testimony of Professor Gardner, *supra* note 47, pointing out that Roosevelt and Churchill's Atlantic Charter had proclaimed the principle of "access, on equal terms, to the trade and to the raw materials of the world."

[52] *See* International Covenant on Economic, Social and Cultural Rights, preamble; adopted by UN G.A. Res. 2200, 11 UN GAOR, Supp. 16, at 49, UN Doc. A/6316 (Dec. 16, 1966). *See also* McDougal and Feliciano, *supra* note 12, at 376 (re: the maximization postulate); R. Falk, This Endangered Planet 247–49, 403–06, *passim* (1971) (offering an "ideology of economic humanism"); and W. Friedmann, *The Relevance of International Law to the Processes of Economic and Social Development*, 2 The Future of the International Legal Order 3 (Falk & Black *eds.*, 1970).

[53] *See also* preamble and Arts. 1(1), 1(3), 5, 24, 25. Withholding resources from another state in order to deprive its people of their own means of subsistence can constitute an egregious thwarting of these articulated policies and also constitute a threat to the peace as well as a violation of Article 2(4) of the Charter. *See also* UN G.A. Res. 3185(XXVIII) (Dec. 18, 1973) and Res. 3171(XXVIII) (Dec. 17, 1973).

[54] Art. 1(3), which is one of the "Purposes of the United Nations" that must not be thwarted by the threat or use of force against other states or peoples under Article 2(4). *See also* preamble and Arts. 55 and 56.

the serving of community policy, especially where freedom, justice, and peace are often interdependent.

International Trade Law.

The most important instrument governing international trade outside of the UN Charter itself is the General Agreement on Tariffs and Trade (GATT),[55] to which there are more than 76 parties, including Egypt,[56] Israel, Kuwait, Lebanon, and Syria. The purposes of the GATT include the raising of standards of living, provision of full employment, development of the full use of the resources of the world, and the elimination of discriminatory treatment in international commerce.[57]

Artcle 1 of the GATT provides for most-favored-nation treatment to assure the elimination of discriminatory measures (any "advantage, favour, privilege, or immunity granted") among the parties. Article 11 makes export prohibitions or restrictions unlawful; Article 13 prohibits discriminatory quantitative restrictions; and Article 20 lists certain general exceptions, but reiterates the basic denial of "arbitrary or unjustifiable discrimination" in the trade process.

Admittedly Article 21(b)(iii) of the GATT might seem to allow the Arab states at least a claim that the oil cuts were "necessary" measures to assure "essential security interests," taken in time of war or some other emergency in international relations. Such a claim, however, must be judged in terms of the general goals of the GATT and the UN Charter.[58]

[55] TIAS No. 1700; 55–61 UNTS.

[56] Egypt made a provisional accession in 1962 and a full accession in 1970. TIAS Nos. 5309 and 6916.   [57] Preamble and Arts. 1, 11, 13, and 20.

[58] UN Charter, Art. 103 and Vienna Convention on the Law of Treaties, Arts. 31(3)(c), 53, and 64, *supra* note 39.

The language in Article 21(b) of the GATT permitting a party to take "any action which it considers necessary for the protection of its essential security interests" should be interpreted as a recognition of that party's capacity for making an initial characterization of the matter, *i.e.* a provisional characterization. *See* McDougal and Feliciano, *supra* note 12, at 218–19 and M. McDougal, H. Lasswell, J. Miller, The Interpretation of Agreements and World Public Order (1967). Otherwise, the "obligations" of parties to the GATT would be meaningless for whatever the party "considers necessary" could not be questioned.

On this point, L. F. Ebb insightfully raised the question in 1964 whether the U.S. Supreme Court review of determinations of administrative agencies of "national security" factors, "in a purely domestic context . . . ," and its rationale does not "foreshadow any similar future exercise of judicial review of national security findings in the international sphere." L. F. Ebb, Regulation and Protection of International Business 816 (1964); and I.C.C. v. N.Y., N.H. & Hartford R.R., 372 U.S. 744, 761–64 (1963). For a recent questioning of the "necessity" of past U.S. restrictions of foreign oil imports which seems to rely upon the "rationale" referred to by Professor Ebb, *see* W. F. James, III, *The Mandatory Oil Import Program: A Review of Present Regulations and Proposals for Change in the 1970's,* 7 Tex. Int. L.J. 373, 391 and 410–11 (1972), *cf. id.* at 400–03.

On an interrelated point, the universally recognized principle of "good faith" would seem to require that a provisional characterization by one party to a treaty cannot stand in perpetuity after it has been questioned by other parties to the agreement. GATT, Arts. 22 and 23, require "sympathetic consideration" to counterassertions and

Moreover, the Arab statements that the oil would be restored to any country as soon as it complied with Arab demands appear to refute the basis in "necessity" for the claim, except possibly in relation to the overall effort to regain "Arab" territory.[59]   Even then, it has never been convincingly argued by any Arab spokesman that use of the oil "weapon" was actually necessary, as opposed to being merely helpful, to regain "Arab" lands.   There is no reason to assume that the use of the oil "weapon" against the United States, Japan, and the Netherlands, for example, was "necessary" in order to stimulate serious negotiations between Israel and the Arabs for the implementation of UN Security Council Resolution 242. Victories by the Arab armies seemed to have been sufficient for that purpose.   Nor can it be assumed that use of the "oil weapon" has changed Israel's basic position.

For reasons discussed below, we have concluded that: (1) Arab reliance on this exception in the GATT must fail in view of the actual context and relevant provisions of the UN Charter, which must be utilized as a guide to rational, policy-serving interpretation.   (2) The Arab oil cuts must be condemned as "arbitrary" in the sense of the purposes of the GATT and in light of the unilateral character of the Arab decisions.   (3) The oil cuts are also "unjustifiable" (even if not arbitrary) in that a joint Arab committee decided upon them in terms of the pro-Arab or anti-Arab posture of other states.   (4) The oil cuts are additionally "unjustifiable" in terms of serving the relevant goals of the international community as contained in the UN Charter.[60]

The bilateral trade agreements between the United States on the one hand, and Saudi Arabia, Oman, and Iraq, on the other contain most-favored-nation treatment clauses with respect to import, export, and other duties and charges affecting trade and similar principles with respect to any concession, regulation, advantage, prohibition, or restriction on imports or exports.[61]

No relevant exception appears in the Saudi Arabian agreement.   The agreement with Iraq, however, would seem to permit some discriminatory

"adequate opportunity for consultation."   The Arab threats against targeted countries which sought to stand up to the oil "weapon" or merely to meet for the formulation of joint approaches to the overall energy crisis were hardly conducive to an "adequate opportunity for consultation" and the actions of those Arab states parties to the GATT have, thus, also thwarted the goals contained in Articles 22 and 23.

[59] See, e.g., "Arabs Set Terms for Dutch," N.Y. Times, Dec. 1, 1973, at 11, col. 3; "5 Arab Ministers Confront Common Market Meeting," N.Y. Times, Dec. 15, 1973, at 1, col. 6; and The League of Arab States, "A Message to the American People," N.Y. Times, Nov. 29, 1973, at 49, col. 2, stating that "when American action to this effect is taken, we will be glad to resume oil shipments."

[60] Since under Article 103, Charter "obligations" must prevail in case of any conflict, the GATT should be interpreted so as to avoid such conflict.   Moreover, since there is no textual reference to the meaning of "unjustifiable," it is clear that general norms of international law shall apply to the full interpretation of the term.   See, e.g., Vienna Convention on the Law of Treaties, Art. 31(3)(c), supra note 39.

[61] 48 Stat. 1826; 142 LNTS 329, Art. 3 (Saudi Arabia).   TIAS No. 4530, 11 UST 1835, Arts. 4, 6, 8 (Oman).   54 Stat. 1790; TS 960, 203 LNTS 107, Art. 4 (Iraq).

action relating to "the adoption or enforcement of measures relating to neutrality or to rights and obligations arising under the Covenant of the League of Nations." Nevertheless, it would seem that joint Arab coercion designed to impose a pro-Arab stance in the context of a joint Arab initiated attack on Israeli forces does not properly fit within the meaning of the phrase "measures relating to neutrality." Certainly, the use of force to coerce other states into a non-neutral stance or conduct as well as a pro-Arab position on a Middle East settlement (such as Security Council Resolution 242) relates to neutrality; but since it plays havoc with the goal-values that underlie the principle of neutrality and also impairs other fundamental goal-values promulgated to regulate the use of force and the self-determination of states, the Arab coercion should not go unnoticed in interpreting the trade agreement.

It hardly needs to be pointed out that fundamental community policies should be taken into account in the interpretation of an international agreement to the extent that its precise meaning is unclear, that there is a gap in the disclosed intention of the agreement, or that peremptory norms would be impaired by one or more of several possible interpretations.[62] Moreover, an opposite conclusion would permit a party to create the very condition—a "necessity" or "security interest"—which would permit a derogation from the agreement. This would be in conflict with the import of the concomitant language in this agreement (as in the GATT) relating to the effort to fulfil obligations under the League of Nations Covenant, now presumptively the UN Charter. To say today that a state or group of states can initiate an armed attack upon another state and thus set up the very condition which allows a departure from trade obligations would permit a state to suspend performance of its obligations at will. Even if the armed attack were justifiable under the Charter, it does not automatically follow that any means of supplementing the attack are permissible or that the stability of world trade patterns and the serving of other Charter policies can be disregarded. Indeed, the serving of all relevant legal policy should be maximized.

The United States agreement with Oman contains a provision, as in the GATT, which allows a state to adopt a measure which is "necessary to protect its essential security interests"; however, the agreement with Oman, like the GATT, also refers to the fulfillment of UN Charter obligations.[63] A coercive strategy that is impermissible under the UN Charter cannot justify an exception to both the GATT and a trade agreement, which themselves contain provisions designed to assure the implementation of the law of the Charter. Moreover, what constitutes a state's "essential security interest" must be determined with comprehensive reference to all relevant legal policies and actual features of context. More specifically, the primary exceptions in the GATT and relevant bilateral trade

---

[62] See, e.g., Vienna Convention on the Law of Treaties, supra note 39, Arts. 31(3)(c), 53, and 64.

[63] Supra note 61, Art. 11(d). See also the GATT, Arts. 20(d), and 21(c).

agreements dealing with national "security interests" should be applied with reference to the full range of community policy to balance permissible national security interests with the UN Charter goals found in the preamble and Articles 1, 2, and 56. Moreover, Article 103 of the UN Charter clearly makes that instrument a peremptory set of norms which will prevail in case of any conflict between the obligations under the Charter and obligations under any other international agreement.

There is substantial authority to support this approach to interpretation.[64] The oil cuts are most assuredly discriminatory and contrary to the most-favored-nation treatment provisions of the GATT and the bilateral trade agreements.[65] Thus, the main remaining question of legal policy is whether the Arab oil "weapon" is permissible or impermissible under the UN Charter.

A CONSIDERATION OF THE ARAB STRATEGY

For present purposes, Arab strategy need not be considered in depth; it seems sufficient merely to indicate some of the most important and disturbing aspects of Arab use of the oil "weapon" and impairments of community policy under headings which are useful for systematic description of the coercive process: participants, objectives, situation, base values, strategies, outcomes, and effects.

Participants

Nearly all of the Arab states were joint initiators of this form of coercion, and nearly every state has been affected by the coercive process as instrumental target, primary target, or spillover victim. Moreover, specific targets included Japan, Western Europe, and the United States. Even though, in the words of Secretary Kissinger, one can "understand" the reasons that led some oil producing states to impose an embargo against the United States "at a time when they perceived us to be taking sides in a military conflict . . ."[66] the targeting of other countries is not understandable except with reference to the proclaimed Arab objectives, discussed below. Moreover, within targeted states the targets included

[64] See, e.g., Vienna Convention on the Law of Treaties, supra note 39, Arts. 31, 43, 53, and 64; M. McDOUGAL, H. LASSWELL, J. MILLER, supra note 60 especially on supplemental means of interpretation. On the use of economic coercion as a means of imposing a treaty, see also Final Act, Vienna Convention, UN Doc. A/CONF.39/ii, add. 2, at 285. Although many articles of the Convention prohibit coercion during the formation (pre-outcome) stage of agreement, the policy throughout clearly seems to prohibit coercion to force interpretations or exceptions at all stages, i.e., also during outcome and post-outcome stages. See McDOUGAL, LASSWELL, and MILLER, supra and J. Stone, supra note 2, commenting on Art. 52 of the Convention.

[65] See "Saudi Oil Embargo Is Termed Breach of '33 Treaty With U.S.," N.Y. Times, Dec. 19, 1973, at 12, col. 4 (quoting Professor R. N. Gardner).

[66] Joint news conference of Jan. 10, 1974, supra note 47, at 115. He added that "it is inappropriate to maintain the postures of confrontation that existed before" in the light of the major U.S. efforts to promote a settlement.

both combatant and noncombatant types of participants. Indeed, there seemed to be indiscriminate targeting of governmental, nongovernmental, military, economic, diplomatic, and other types of persons and institutions without proper deference to the basic principles of necessity and proportionality and the effects that such a strategy would have upon peoples and resources around the world.

Objectives

The use of this oil strategy was deliberate.[67] The stated objectives of the initiators were couched for the most part in terms of an overall effort to regain "occupied territory." But other objectives were also articulated by Arab spokesmen:

(1) To force an overall settlement upon Israel on terms satisfactory to the Arabs through the coercion of Israel itself or through the use of force to make others pay more attention to Arab claims and demands; [68]

(2) To seek a continued embargo against any country supporting Israel in any manner, with each country classified as either friendly to the Arabs, neutral, or supporting Israel; [69]

(3) To force other states to sever diplomatic and trade relations with Israel; [70]

[67] On the importance of this factor see, e.g., L. Chen, supra note 16, at 135–38.

[68] See, e.g., N.Y. Times, Mar. 1, 1974, at 5, col. 1; Dec. 11, 1973, at 34, col. 3; Dec. 29, 1973, at 2, col. 1; contra N.Y. Times, Feb. 25, 1974, at 1, col. 3. See also Dec. 1, 1973, at 11, col. 3; Dec. 15, 1973, at 1, col. 6; Feb. 5, 1974, at 2, col. 1, citing a pledge by Saudi Arabia and Kuwait that there would be no let up on the embargo until an agreement was reached on "Syrian terms"; Mar. 17, 1974, at 15, col. 1; and Mar. 19, 1974, at 20, col. 2.

The Algerian Minister of Energy, Belaid Abdesselam, also claimed a right of necessity to use "our oil weapon" in order "to call the world's attention to the injustices of the situation." U.S. NEWS & WORLD REPORT (Dec. 31, 1973), at 21. Egyptian Ambassador Ghorbal claimed that the oil weapon was used to gain attention to 25 years of suffering and demanded that it continue until the Israelis committed themselves to "total withdrawal." N.Y. Times, Jan. 7, 1974, at 1, col. 2. The Saudi Arabian Minister of Foreign Affairs, Omar Sakkaf, claimed, among other things, a right to use the oil weapon to "put" the "case" to the American people. N.Y. Times, Dec. 31, 1973, at 5, col. 1. See also The League of Arab States, "A Message to the American People," supra note 59.

The coercion continued far beyond a calling of "attention" to Arab demands, and it did not cease even after serious negotiations. President Sadat later declared that the oil weapon "was not blackmail. It was only a message to show the whole world that the Arabs after the 6th of October deserve to take their place under the sun." N.Y. Times, Feb. 25, 1974, at 1, col. 3.

[69] See Text of the Declaration After the Arab Leaders' Summit Meeting, N.Y. Times, Nov. 29, 1973, at 16, cols. 1 and 6.

This broad Arab objective did not confine itself to traditional distinctions in the law of neutrality but, in a sweeping approach, equated political and military "support." Even in the Vietnamese conflict, the United States did not regard political support for North Vietnam as a violation of neutrality.

[70] See supra notes 68 and 69 and N.Y. Times, Jan. 15, 1974, at 4, col. 1 noting that "a shift in Japanese policy in the Middle East was followed by a decision by the Arab countries to reclassify Japan as a friendly nation." See also N.Y. Times, Dec.

(4) To compel other states to extend economic aid to the Arab nations;[71]
(5) To compel other states to extend military aid to the Arab nations.[72]

These are attempts to control the foreign policies and conduct (international and domestic) of other states and peoples and to affect the free choice of such states and peoples through a manipulation of resources. They constitute an interference in domestic affairs and a thwarting of fundamental community policy, as some Arab spokesmen have stated, in order to "shape events."

Further, these objectives were being pursued unilaterally, with no known attempt to forewarn the international community of impending action.[73] There were no efforts to work through the United Nations—specifically created to maintain international peace and security, with its own built-in coercive strategy. Likewise, there were no Arab efforts to use any other peaceful and cooperative means or machinery to settle the underlying disputes. In fact, as the coercive strategy continued for the first four months, there were continuing threats made against any inclusive response to the oil "weapon" or to the arrogated oil prices by consumers and/or other producers.[74] Similarly, the Arab states refused to seek inclusive measures for settlement of the world energy crisis. As if to underline the unilateral approach of the Arabs to this whole matter, the embargo was continued despite the January 18th and other agreements, the Israeli pull back from occupied Egyptian territory, active U.S. involvement in the negotiating process as an accepted intermediary, and some five months of attention to Arab demands.[75] Even President Sadat appealed to other Arab leaders at the end of January for an end to the oil embargo.[76] By March 4, Sheik Zaki al-Yamani of Saudi Arabia openly agreed that the embargo against the United States should be lifted, and Saudi Arabia and Egypt were apparently prepared to do so by March 10, although Arab

---

13, 1973, at 4, col. 4 and Secretary Kissinger's speech to the Washington Energy Conference in which he criticized "the manipulation of raw material supplies in order to prescribe the foreign policies of importing countres" *supra* note 47, at 202.

[71] *See* N.Y. Times, Dec. 30, 1973, at 3, col. 1; Jan. 18, 1974, at 12, col. 2; Jan. 28, 1974, at 1, col. 6; Feb. 9, 1974, at 11, col. 2; Feb. 26, 1974, at 27, col. 2.

[72] *See supra* notes 68 and 71 and N.Y. Times, Jan. 26, 1974, at 3, cols. 2 and 3.

[73] N.Y. Times, Feb. 22, 1974, at 13, col. 1. To a certain extent the West might have been "warned" by some threats by certain Arab states in 1972 to use oil as a political weapon, but the actual cuts were very sudden. *See* J. E. Akins, *supra* note 3, and Sheehan, *supra* note 2, at 50 and 54.

[74] *See* N.Y. Times, Feb. 5, 1974, at 2, col. 2; Nov. 23, 1973, at 1, col. 6; Jan. 13, 1974, at 14, col. 4. Joint energy talks on February 11, 1974 in an effort to reach an inclusive response to an even greater global energy threat than the use of the oil weapon itself. *See* text of the President's invitation, 70 DEPT. STATE BULL. 123 (1974) and Secretary Kissinger's speech and news conferences, *supra* note 47.

[75] N.Y. Times, Jan. 28, 1974, at 19, col. 4; and Jan. 25, 1974, at 3, col. 1. The continuation of the embargo certainly leaves Arab claims of necessity in relation to *continued* use of the oil "weapon" in serious doubt. *See* REISMAN, *supra* note 1, at 842–43. *See also* N.Y. Times, Feb. 7, 1974, at 1, col. 4.

[76] *See* N.Y. Times, Jan. 28, 1974, at 19, col. 4 and Jan. 30, 1974, at 3, col. 1.

solidarity on this point proved elusive.[77]　In response, Secretary Kissinger warned as of early February that:

> Since October the United States first brought about the cease-fire, the six-point agreement, the disengagement between Israel and Egypt. To maintain an embargo now under these conditions must be construed as a form of blackmail, and would be considered highly inappropriate by the United States and cannot but affect the attitude with which we will have to pursue our diplomacy.[78]

These Arab actions are incompatible with the principles of the Charter which are designed to assure the adjustment or settlement of international disputes or situations that might lead to a breach of the peace by peaceful and inclusive means and the achievement of "international co-operation in solving international problems of an economic . . ." nature,[79] as recently supplemented by General Assembly resolution 3073(XXVIII).　In that resolution the General Assembly reiterated:

> Its appeal to all Member States to take full advantage of the framework and means provided by the United Nations in order to prevent the perpetuation of situations of tension, crisis and conflict, avert the creation of such new situations which endanger international peace and security, and settle international problems exclusively by peaceful means.[80]

Again, we must emphasize the General Assembly's condemnation of "economic coercion or any other illegal or improper means in resolving disputes concerning the exercise of the sovereign rights" of others over natural resources.[81]

In addition to the lack of a cooperative and inclusive approach, there seems to have been no attempt to offer any formal argument in favor of the necessity or legality of such action under the UN Charter or other international instruments (including trade agreements).　While we can appreciate and even applaud the new Arab confidence and solidarity,[82] the rise of this new confidence through the use of the oil "weapon" has tended to foster some of the very exclusive oriented perspectives that must be overcome if we are to have peace in the Middle East.　What the Arab states have included as some of their objectives and their unilateral approach to matters of international concern are the most alarming features

---

[77] N.Y. Times, Mar. 5, 1974, at 6, col. 8, and Mar. 12, 1974, at 1, col. 5.

[78] N.Y. Times, Feb. 7, 1974, at 1, col. 4 and joint news conference, *supra* note 47, at 117–18.

[79] *See* UN Charter, preamble and Arts. 1, 2, 55, and 56.

[80] *See also* UN G.A. Res. 3185(XXVIII) (Dec. 18, 1973); REISMAN, *supra* note 1, 842–43; McDOUGAL and FELICIANO, *supra* note 12, at 181–83; Bowett, *supra* note 11, at 11.　It should be recalled that the GATT also seeks a more inclusive conciliatory approach.　*See supra* note 58.

[81] UN G.A. Res. 3171(XXVIII) (Dec. 17, 1973) (vote: 108–1–16).

[82] For recent evidence of the new Arab confidence and sense of power, *see, e.g.,* "Arab Price and Power," NEWSWEEK, Feb. 18, 1974, at 40.　The article also explores certain psychological predispositions identified as "Arab traits."　*See also* N.Y. Times, Feb. 28, 1974, at 1, col. 7.

of context. This has also prompted Professor Julius Stone to declare:

Article 53 of the UN Charter expressly commands that "no enforcement action shall be taken under regional arrangements, or by regional agencies without the authorization of the Security Council."
This is exactly what present Arab state oil measures against the U.S.,
Netherlands, Japan and other states amount to, even if their demands
conformed (which they do not) to the Security Council resolutions
involved . . . This kind of unauthorized concerted plan by a group of
members to cripple the economies of other members for collateral
political ends obviously flouts the "purpose" and "principles" of articles one and two of the Charter . . . .[83]

While we agree with much of what Professor Stone has written, the Arab
embargo, properly speaking, cannot be considered as "enforcement action," for this implies a basic consistency between Arab objectives and
community interest. The oil cuts are unilateral efforts at coercion which,
even if claimed to be "enforcement action," are impermissible in terms
of serving all relevant legal policies. Thus, there is no conformity with the
basic requirements in Article 52 of the Charter. Moreover, the Arab
strategy would not meet the test of Article 53 in the absence of authorization by the Security Council. We do not seek to argue the illegality
of Arab actions against South Africa and the illegal regime of Southern
Rhodesia, which have been the subjects of United Nations sanctions. Such
action may constitute permissible self-help that seeks to serve overall community interest.[84]

[83] J. Stone, *supra* note 2.

[84] *See, e.g.,* UN Charter, Arts. 25 and 48–50; UN G.A. Res. 3055(XXVIII) (Oct.
28, 1973), 3115(XXVIII) (Dec. 12, 1973), and 3116 (XXVIII) (Dec. 12, 1973). *See
also* J. CAREY, UN PROTECTION OF CIVIL AND POLITICAL RIGHTS 23–26, *passim* (1971);
REISMAN, *supra* note 1, at 842–43; Bowett, *supra* note 11; and McDougal and Reisman, *supra* note 42.

A comprehensive policy and contextual analysis allows for a differentiation between
the Arab use of the oil weapon against a state like Japan or the Netherlands, with
global effects, from the selective use of trade measures against the emigration policies
of the Soviet Union by the United States, as proposed in the Jackson amendment.
The latter would promote a human rights objective and the fulfillment of Charter
obligations under Article 56, would be a highly selective response, and would be far
less coercive than in the case of the vital dependence of Japan and the Netherlands
on Middle East oil. *See also* REISMAN, *supra* note 1, at 836–39, 842–43, and 849–51.

It is not irrelevant to note that the Soviet Union advocated a continuation of the
oil weapon against the United States despite several U.S. efforts to obtain a viable
peace in the Middle East and almost in open defiance of norms on friendly relations,
cooperative action, and the peaceful settlement of disputes. *See* N.Y. Times, Mar.
13, 1974, at 24, col. 4.

On the imperfect Arab attempts to place the Jackson amendment and an earlier
"blockade" of Cuba in the same category as the Arab oil "weapon," *see* statement by
Belaid Abdesselam, *supra* note 68. In the Cuban case the U.S. refusal to trade with
Cuba was related to an OAS sanction against Cuban subversive activities in the
hemisphere that were allegedly violative of the norms of Article 2(4) of the UN
Charter. Moreover, the Cuban "blockade" has never cut off foreign trade. *See* N.Y.
Times, Jan. 9, 1974, at 6, col. 4.

We conclude that the five types of Arab objectives outlined above (despite claims concerning the recapture of territory or the desires to aid the Palestinian people) [85] are inconsistent with the UN Charter. More specifically, there is an impairment of both the "political independence" of states and of the prohibition of the use of force which thwarts the "Purposes" of the United Nations contained in Article 2(4) of the Charter; there appear to be no exculpating claims that may tip the balance against that impairment. The Arab objectives outlined above certainly affront the Charter goals of tolerance, friendly relations, cooperative effort to solve international economic problems, and the peaceful settlement of disputes. The Arab economic coercion is in contradiction with the principle contained in the Declaration on Friendly Relations and Co-Operation of 1970 which prohibits the use of coercion to impair the sovereign rights of other states (such as the right to determine foreign or domestic policy and actions relatively free of coercion) or "to secure from" them "advantages of any kind." As regards the Arab purpose of regaining territory or of acquiring territory for the Palestinians, the principles of necessity and proportionality have not been observed and the use of the oil "weapon" seems a highly unnecessary and disproportionate response to continued Israeli control of some Arab lands.

Moreover, as recognized in the Report of the Secretary-General in 1952 on the Question of Defining Aggression,[86] impermissible intervention or interference in the affairs of another state "may assume the most varied forms: e.g., encouraging a party, paying it funds, sending weapons, etc." Certainly the coercion of another state in an effort to force the payment of funds (e.g., economic aid) or the shipment of weapons would fit within that sort of prohibition, and there seems little doubt that the use of the Arab oil "weapon" is rendered illegal on these grounds alone.

Related to these issues was the Syrian refusal to comply with the basic humanitarian provisions of the Geneva Conventions of 1949 which require, among other things, that a list be provided to Israel of captured prisoners of war and that the International Committee of the Red Cross be given access to captured persons in order to assure their humane treatment.[87] We would not mention this violation of international law here, except for the fact that it became a central issue in regard to Israel and Syrian disengagement and was inextricably intertwined with the

[85] Professors Paust and Gardner addressed this and other issues at a board meeting of the International League for the Rights of Man (N.Y., Feb. 7, 1974). There Professor Gardner cogently argued that the Arab claim to use the oil weapon for the promotion of human rights of the Palestinians is "nearly hollow" in view of their past lack of "support" of Palestinian refugees with oil profits. *See also* remarks of the U.S. Representative before ECOSOC, "Oil Nations Scored on Aid to Poor," N.Y. Times, Jan. 18, 1974, at 12, col. 2.   [86]*Supra* note 37.

[87] *See* A. Blaustein and J. Paust, On POW's and War Crimes, 120 Cong. Rec. E37 (Jan. 31, 1974). For text of two Israeli complaints submitted to the ICRC and the UN Secretary-General in December, *see* 119 Cong. Rec. E8033–E8036 (Dec. 13 1973). Complaints were also forwarded to the ICRC by Egypt and Syria of Israel violations of the Geneva Conventions. N.Y. Times, Mar. 13, 1974, at 3, col. 6.

continuation of the Arab oil embargo even after repeated and generally effective U.S. efforts to bring about a peaceful settlement.[88] Egypt and other Arab states did not press the Syrians on this matter as they are required to do under Article 1 of the Geneva Conventions and Articles 1(3) and 56 of the UN Charter.[89] Other Arab states allowed this violation to continue for nearly five months. The oil embargo was extended, while Syria utilized prisoners of war as pawns in the negotiating process.[90]

Situation

The geographic area within which the Arabs utilized their oil strategy was global. There was no effort to minimize the destruction of values through a limitation of coercion to arenas of armed conflict between the Arab states and Israel, or even to arenas of active military involvement. Nor did the Arabs make the traditional criterial distinctions [91] between military and civilian objectives in their delineations of targets. The coercion was of substantial duration. Moreover, the continued use of the strategy long after agreements for military disengagement and the extensive efforts made by all parties to begin serious negotiations for an overall settlement plays even greater havoc with the principles of necessity and proportionality.

Bases of Power

The Arab states obviously possess ample resources of power and wealth to apply intense coercion through time and space. Saudi Arabia alone is thought to possess one quarter of the world's known oil resources and is the world's largest oil exporter.[92] Specific targets such as Japan, the Philippines, the Netherlands, and numerous Western European countries are extremely dependent upon oil and the maintenance of stable trade relations not only for wealth and well-being but for overall power, including the power to maintain their national defense and security. Japan, which is nearly 100 percent dependent upon oil imports, obtains some 88 percent of its oil from Arab states and Iran; Western European states in general depend on the Middle East for some 73 percent of their oil

[88] N.Y. Times, Feb. 25, 1974, at 1, col. 3.

[89] See, e.g., PAUST and BLAUSTEIN, supra note 21; and J. Paust, My Lai and Vietnam: Norms, Myths and Leader Responsibility, 57 MIL. L. REV. 99, 118–23 (1972). Subsequently Egypt did make efforts ot comply with an ICRC initiative to establish a special commission to investigate charges and countercharges of violations of the Geneva Conventions. N.Y. Times, Mar. 13, 1974, at 3, col. 6.

[90] Finally, on February 27, 1974, Syria provided Secretary Kissinger and the ICRC with a list of 65 prisoners of war and opened the way toward a multilateral Geneva conference on the settlement of Middle East conflict.

[91] By "criterial distinctions" we mean distinctions based upon criteria which are formulated in order to facilitate rational, policy-serving decision. See McDOUGAL and FELICIANO, supra note 12, at 15, 56–59, 152 n. 88, 158, passim; H. Lasswell, M. McDougal, Criteria For A Theory About Law, 44 S. CAL. L. REV. 362, 376, 384, passim (1971); H. LASSWELL, A PRE-VIEW OF POLICY SCIENCES 85–95 (1971).

[92] See N.Y. Times, Nov. 29, 1973, at 16, col. 1.

imports,[93] and are generally dependent upon foreign oil to make up about 98 percent of their needs.[94]

Strategies

While the primary strategy employed was economic, there was also a manipulation of the diplomatic and ideological instruments of corecion.[95] Diplomatic efforts included use of the economic instrument to communicate threats against "supporting Israel" and "joining the Americans" in any kind of countermeasures, "because your whole economy will definitely collapse all of a sudden." [96]   The use of this particular strategy, the oil "weapon," involved a choice of the sort of weapon that is far less capable of discriminate application than, for example, the embargo of military arms to another country. It is the type of strategy which will necessarily have a great impact upon the civilian economy and civilian participants. Thus, its use would seem to require a very strong showing of necessity.

Outcomes

It is clear that the outcomes of the use of the oil weapon involved intense coercion on target governments and peoples. The coercion met with some notable successes. Some states have changed their official diplomatic posture toward Israel, and states have also begun to change their domestic and international policies with respect to trade, emigration of foreign nationals, the supply of arms to Arab states, economic programs for Arab development, a Middle East settlement, and other matters. In the first four months of the coercive process, new trade and development agreements were "negotiated" involving a total of some six billion dollars for the Arabs, while another five billion dollars of benefits was being actively considered.[97]

Effects

A particularly important effect was the sudden disruption of normal trade patterns, which threatened and still threatens the stability of the

[93] N.Y. Times, Dec. 24, 1973, at 1, col. 8.   See also U.S. Dept. State, FOREIGN POLICY OUTLINES, "Oil and Energy," No. 33–99 (Nov. 1973); J. Dapray Muir, Legal and Ecological Aspects of the International Energy Situation, 8 INT. LAWYER 1, 2–4 (1974); and J. E. Akins, supra note 3.

[94] See chart, "Dependence on Imported Oil," N.Y. Times, Feb. 10, 1974, Sec. 3, at 2, col. 1.   Italy's Foreign Minister, Aldo Moro, has bluntly called for a pro-Arab policy and bilateral trade with oil exporters, adding: "The Arab peninsula and Iran are a complex that is essential to Italy and Europe."   N.Y. Times, Mar. 1, 1974, at 5, col. 1.

[95] The President of Algeria, at a 38-nation Islamic Conference in February, defended the use of oil as a "political" weapon. See N.Y. Times, Feb. 24, 1974, at 1, col. 3.   The text of the Arab statement in Vienna on the ending of the embargo declared that "its main objective" was to "draw the attention of the world to the Arab cause in order to create the suitable political climate . . ."   See supra note 10, at 20, col. 5.

[96] See N.Y. Times, Nov. 23, 1973, at 1, col. 6.

[97] See N.Y. Times, Jan. 28, 1974, at 1, col. 6.

world economy.[98] There was also a threatened destruction of resource values throughout the globe which would be disproportionate to the claimed necessity for realizing Arab objectives (even assuming that all of these objectives are otherwise proper in terms of legal policy and contextual factors).[99]

More specifically, we list some of the "disproportionate" effects of this strategy in terms of certain specific values affected: [100]

(a) *Wealth*: We note here the deleterious effects upon jobs, balance of payments, worldwide trade patterns, incentives for new development programs (national and international), general economic development (if not survival) of the developing countries of the Third World, and recessionary trends.[101] The interrelated price increases for oil could also result in a deficit of $29 billion for developing countries.[102] And there is an

---

[98] On the importance of this factor *see, e.g.,* L. Chen, *supra* note 16, at 135–38 and 159 and Washington Energy Conference Communique, *supra* note 47.

[99] *See, e.g.,* N.Y. Times, Dec. 31, 1973, at 2, col. 1.

[100] We utilize the eight value categories adopted by Professors McDougal and Lasswell for a more comprehensive and rational appraisal of aggregate value consequences (*i.e.,* wealth, well-being, power, skill, enlightenment, respect, affection, rectitude). The reader should note that these may not have been intended results, but they are, nevertheless, direct effects. For references to value analysis *see, e.g.,* Lasswell and McDougal, *supra* note 91, at 388; M. McDougal, H. Lasswell, W. M. Reisman, *Theories about International Law: Prologue to a Configurative Jurisprudence,* 8 VA. J. INT. L. 188 (1968); and J. N. Moore, *Prolegomenon to the Jurisprudence of Myres McDougal and Harold Lasswell,* 54 VA. L. REV. 662 (1968).

[101] *See, e.g.,* Washington Energy Conference Communique and News Releases, *supra* note 47; N.Y. Times, Dec. 31, 1973, at 2, col. 1; Mar. 3, 1974, at 10, col. 1 and Mar. 4, 1974, at 1, col. 4; D. Ottaway, "Black Africa Feels Arab Oil Cuts a Threat to Solidarity," The Guardian, Dec. 13, 1973 (London); "Kicking the Poor," The Economist, Dec. 8, 1973 (London). Economic disruption became evident with the 25 percent cut in oil production and colossal price increases.

[102] *See* N.Y. Times, Feb. 7, 1974, at 1, col. 4. The Shah of Iran's pledge of $1 billion to the World Bank and the International Monetary Fund in this regard is commendable but insufficient, and some day the Third World may come to view such resource profits as "windfall" profits from the earth's resources (a chance national distribution) despite certain trends toward "permanent control" over natural resources. *See* N.Y. Times, Feb. 25, 1974, at 14, col. 3. *See also* E. M. Borgese, "Who Owns the Earth's Resources–," VISTA (Aug. 1973) at 12, 46 and *infra* note 110. Instead of new patterns of ownership, however, it seems more likely in the near future that international cooperation between producers and major consumers of oil will result in international commodity agreements. *See* R. C. Longworth, *The Ecopolitics of Oil,* SAT. REV., WORLD (Jan 26, 1974) at 25, 27. A supplemental suggestion has been made by Dr. Abbas Zaki, head of an Abu Dhabi foreign aid fund, that 20 percent of the oil profits should be paid for in certificates issued by the World Bank and the Fund so that some profits can be directed toward global development. *See* E. Sheehan, *supra* note 2, at 68. Whatever the Arabs devise to offset the effects of higher oil prices for the Third World, it is probable that there will be some Arab controls on the use of available funds. Other means of meeting the problem of resource allocation might include agreements and institutions for the greater stabilization of trade and equal access to resources and markets or a breakdown of cooperative patterns and a North-South war. *See* the dichotomy between annihilation and economic humanism offered in FALK, *supra* note 52, at 415–37. During a lecture at Yale Law School in

overall danger of world depression if inclusive measures are not soon taken. The resultant $6 billion development programs for the Arabs stand in sharp contrast.

(b) *Well-being*: There have been devasting effects upon fertilizer production and consequential cuts in food production which have emphasized the warning that as many as 20,000,000 people could die in the Third World as a result of such scarcities.[103] Noticeable cutbacks in the production of medicines could also result in health problems and more deaths around the globe. The poorest of the earth will be the most seriously affected "victims" of the scarcity of oil, food, and fertilizer, and it has been estimated that an additional $3 billion in aid will be needed to save them from "catastrophe."[104] The scarcity of fertilizer could result in a loss of some five million tons of food for India alone. Surely, the Arabs could have foreseen the disastrous effects upon food production. It is the ready foreseeability of such consequences that is one of the most alarming aspects of the matter. Given the fact that the United States and Japan produce much of the world's fertilizer and that North America and Australia are the only food grain exporters in the entire world, it is difficult to escape the fact of predictable food scarcity over an extended period and an extended area of the globe—an effect which was neither "necessary" nor "proportionate" in terms of "legitimate military objectives" or the maximizing of all relevant community goals of world public order and human dignity.[105]

March, 1974, Professor Falk outlined additional possibilities including a great politico-military power dominance system which would control the primary war, power, and media systems and/or a geo-economic dominance system which would encourage a "businessman's peace" and an alignment of the superpowers and certain natural resource "have" states for the stabilization of markets and the relative value position of the wealth and power elites. Both of these possibilities would favor detente and world trade over any attempt to share earth resources and technology with an outside Fourth World or any attempt to promote human rights within particular states.

[103] N.Y. Times, Jan. 26, 1974, at 1, col. 1, quoting Dr. N. E. Borlaug, Rockefeller Foundation, that as many as 20 million may die because of crop shortages which will result in part from climate changes, but primarily from fertilizer cut backs. *See also* N.Y. Times, Mar. 11, 1974, at 10, col. 3, citing a report by the World Bank and Mar. 10, 1974, at 13, col. 1, on an F.A.O. report disclosing a doubling and tripling in fertilizer costs. *See also* N.Y. Times, Dec. 31, 1973, at 2, col 1, and Feb. 28, 1974, at 20, col. 1, noting the known interdependency of "virtually all parts of the agriculture industry" on electricity or oil.

[104] *See* N.Y. Times, Feb. 9, 1974, at 10, col. 3 and Feb. 24, 1974, at 4, col. 4.

[105] On the principles of "proportionality" and "necessity" in the use of weapons, *see* Panel on Human Rights and Armed Conflict, PROC. AMER. SOC. OF INT. LAW, 67 AJIL (No. 4), 141–68 (1973); J. Paust, *My Lai and Vietnam: Norms, Myths and Leader Responsibility, supra* note 89, and *Command Responsibility and Military Necessity*, 26 NAVAL WAR COLL. REV. 103 (Feb. 1973); E. Rosenblad, *Starvation as a Method of Warfare—Conditions for Regulation by Convention*, 7 INT. LAWYER 252 (1973); and Mudge, *Starvation as a Means of Warfare*, 4 INT. LAWYER 228 (1970). On more recent efforts to proscribe starvation and the ruination of food supplies and patterns of distribution for noncombatants, *see* ICRC BASIC TEXTS, Protocol I, Arts. 40–51 (Geneva 1972); and UN G.A. Res. 3102 (XXVIII) (Dec. 12, 1973) (vote: 107–

Evidence has been made public showing that cuts in oil imports to the United States (presumably a legitimate target for some sort of Arab coercion in response to military aid of Israel) would not have a deleterious effect upon the military capability of the United States.[106] It has, however, had an effect upon fertilizer and food production in an "indiscriminate" and "uncontrollable" manner. Not only have noncombatants in the United States suffered, but noncombatants in the Third World will be the primary victims of the oil "weapon." Moreover, the complex interdependence of oil, fertilizer, and food patterns throughout the globe now accentuate the unworkability and "impossible rigidity" of old "rules" that allowed the embargo of oil as contraband of war as well as the infeasibility of any "list theory" for the regulation of weapons in times of armed conflict.[107]

The laws of armed conflict, however, are not the only community goals at stake where a possible and foreseeable effect of economic coercion is the death of some twenty million people—equivalent in terms of lives lost to deaths from World War II atrocities. Articles 25 and 28 of the Universal Declaration of Human Rights state that everyone is entitled to an international order in which adequate food and medical care can be provided.[108] There is a great deal of room for disagreement whether the

---

0–6). UN S.C. Res. 253 (1968) excepted from the sanctions against the illegal regime of Southern Rhodesia those medical and other supplies needed for humanitarian purposes. In marked contrast to humanitarian efforts to limit the usages and impacts of violence have been the Soviet assertions that the Arabs have a "legitimate, inalienable right to use *all effective means* for liberation" of territories (emphasis added). This approach to "law" and social order, though shared by certain totalitarian ideologists and self-appointed terrorist elites, is completely indifferent to the principles of necessity and proportionality, to the authority of shared perspective and praxis, and to the human values inherent in human rights law. The Soviet-Syrian communique is reported in N.Y. Times, Mar. 15, 1974, at 8, col. 4. *See also* J. Paust, *Terrorism and the International Law of War,* and *Some Terroristic Claims Arising From the Arab-Israeli Context, supra* note 17; J. Paust, *Law in a Guerrilla Conflict: Myths, Norms and Human Rights,* 3 ISRAEL Y.B. ON HUMAN RIGHTS (1974); Y. Dinstein, *Terrorism and Wars of Liberation Applied to the Arab-Israeli Conflict, id.,* 78.

[106] *See* W. F. James, III, *supra* note 58, at 388–91, and references cited. Thus, no direct detriment to the United States was engendered by the Arab cuts in oil production and exports. *Cf.* R. C. Longworth, *supra* note 102, at 25, 26, disclosing some fuel problems for the U.S. Sixth Fleet due to Italian cuts in available oil. Secretary of Defense Schlesinger also stated that "the immediate effect of the oil embargo was the cutting off of our overseas forces from local sources of fuel," but that "bulk fuels in support of the Mediterranean forces was quickly available." See *Report of the Secretary of Defense to the Congress on the FY 1975 Defense Budget and FY 1975–1979 Defense Program* 233 (Mar. 4, 1974). He also noted that the Defense Department consumes only 3.5 percent of "the national petroleum usage." Thus, presumably, the oil embargo affected primarily the civilian population and the "weapon" was indiscriminate in impact.

[107] *See* J. Paust, remarks, 67 AJIL, *supra* note 105, at 163; and McDOUGAL and FELICIANO, *supra* note 12, at 479–80.

[108] UN G.A. Res. 217A, 3 GAOR, UN Doc. A/810, at 71 (1948). *See also* UN CHARTER, preamble and Arts. 1(3), 55(b), and 56; UN, THE UNITED NATIONS AND

actions of certain states sufficiently promote these goals "in such a way as to achieve the most efficient development and utilization of natural resources . . . [t]aking into account the problems of both food-importing and food-exporting countries, to ensure an equitable distribution of world food supplies in relation to need"—especially when equal distribution may not mean equal survival but equal starvation because there may not be enough to feed the present population of the globe.[109] But it seems obvious that the deliberate use of the oil "weapon" has substantially jeopardized the fulfillment of these policies. Because of the unnecessary, "disproportionate," and foreseeable effect of this economic form of coercion, it undermines any prospect of ensuring through cooperative action an equitable distribution of food and medicine to the world's needy. Moreover, this kind of effect will perpetuate, if not exacerbate, a general Third World inequality, perhaps as devastating to the Third World as Arab economic neglect has been to the Palestinian people.[110]

(c) *Power*: Commentators have stressed concern over the potential effect of the oil cuts on the combat capability of European allies of the

---

HUMAN RIGHTS 39–41 (1968); UN G.A. Res. 3121(XXVIII) (Dec. 13, 1973); and 3085(XXVIII) (Dec. 6, 1973).

[109] See International Covenant on Economic, Social, and Cultural Rights, preamble and Arts. 11 and 12; *cf. id.*, Art. 25. *See also* N.Y. Times, Feb. 17, 1974, at 13, col. 1; and R. FALK, *supra* note 52, at 177.

It has also been stated by Dr. J. Knowles, president of the Rockefeller Foundation, that among the 2½ billion people in less developed countries, 60 percent are malnourished and 20 percent (500 million people) are believed to be starving to death. *See* N.Y. Times, Mar. 15, 1974, at 34, col. 4. Certainly an important conditioning factor here is the population menace. *See, e.g.,* Falk, *supra*; and V. Nanda, *The Role of International Law and Institutions Toward Developing A Global Plan of Action on Population,* 3 DEN. J. INT. L. & POL. 1 (1973), and references cited.

[110] Exceptions might include increased economic strengths and dominance of certain Arab and other oil producers of the Third World such as Nigeria and Indonesia. *See* "Kicking the Poor," The Economist, Dec. 8, 1973 (London). The 1973 "Arab" contribution ($2.25 million) to the UN relief program for Palestinian refugees was only 9 percent of the U.S. pledge ($25 million), and the Arab contribution has been even smaller in proportion to the total contributed by the United States since 1950. With Saudi Arabia alone spending more than $1 billion on the 1973 Egyptian and Syrian war effort, one wonders why more Arab oil profits could not have gone to feed the Arab poor. Was the financing of peace and the greater well-being of other Arabs so significantly less desirable? And why did the Soviet Union, Eastern Europe, and the People's Republic of China (itself, the world's largest grain importer) contribute nothing to the UN relief efforts for the Palestinian people? *See Money to burn; time to kill,* THE INTERDEPENDENT (Apr. 1974) at 1, col. 3; and C. L. Cooper, N.Y. Times, Apr. 4, 1974, at 41, col. 1, pointing out that the United States and Western Europe have contributed nearly 66 percent of the aid to the starving people of the Sahelian area of Africa but the Arab oil exporters have, so far, contributed less than 1 percent. It hardly needs to be emphasized that an extremist policy of state control over national resources will exacerbate this situation; and, although it would allow a few of the "have" natural resource states to escape a Third World existence, it could entrench another group (some 30 states and one quarter of the earth's population at a minimum) into a permanent Fourth World status with the rather uncomforting and irrelevant "control" of nearly nothing.

United States and thus on detente in Europe.[111] Political analysts have already noted the effects of oil scarcity upon European unity.[112] The Arabs cannot be entirely blamed for the unilateral scrambling of others for oil but their strategy has certainly provoked a bilateralist approach and brought politico-economic turmoil to many European nations.

If there are threats to European unity, detente, and security, one can imagine the threats to the national security interests of the Third World countries that are hard hit by economic, food, and health problems. The effect on overall world peace could be substantial, as governmental elites face power depletions and their fellow countrymen face recession or depression.

(d) *Skill*: The economic, food, and health problems could reduce skill levels among all peoples either directly or through job training cuts and a lack of funds for general education programs. Unemployment has risen in the United States, Great Britain, and other countries and these types of deleterious impacts are likely to continue in European and Third World countries.

(e) *Respect*: Patterns of respect for international law and international institutions have been threatened.[113] If some organ of the United Nations does not inquire into the legality of the use of oil as a "weapon" by the Arabs, there may be not only a diminution of UN authority in general, but also an unregulated increase in the use of oil and numerous other resources as a "weapon" in international relations with, perhaps, a concomitant increase in military interventions.[114]

Conclusion

At stake are not only the Charter goals of tolerance, friendly relations, the peaceful settlement of disputes, cooperative effort to solve international economic and other problems, and peace in general, but also the relative independence of peoples and their own political, economic, and ideological self-determination (the full and free shaping and sharing of all values). Several declared objectives of the Arab states are incompatible with basic community goals and the actual use of the oil "weapon" was "unnecessary" and "disproportionate" in terms of legitimate objectives. Thus, both the scope and purpose of this coercive strategy were

---

[111] See R. C. Longworth, *supra* note 22, at 25, 27, disclosing the warning of British strategist Neville Brown and certain findings of a Princeton study for the U.S. Navy; N.Y. Times, Jan. 12, 1974; and S. M. Schwebel, *supra* note 23. *See also* N.Y. Times, Mar. 4, 1974, at 1, col. 4, on the European political crises.

[112] See N.Y. Times, Feb. 18, 1974, at 3, col. 4; C. L. Sulzberger, *id.*, Jan. 13, 1974, at E17, col. 8; and Washington Energy Conference Communique, *supra* note 47.

[113] See, e.g., U. Scheuner, The German Tribune, Jan. 10, 1974, at 4, col. 1. Professor Gardner also noted that "not a single voice has been raised in the United Nations to cite" the 1970 Declaration On Friendly Relations and Co-Operation in response to the oil "weapon." N.Y. Times, Dec. 19, 1973, at 12, col. 4.

[114] See N.Y. Times, Jan. 27, 1974, at E3, col. 3; and C. L. Sulzberger, *id.*, Jan. 9, 1974, at 35, col. 5.

unreasonable under the actual circumstances. The impact of the use of this form of economic coercion has been substantial in terms of the persons affected and the goals impaired. It was a coercion that threatened and might still impair not only the general wealth, well-being, and power of numerous nation-states and peoples, but also, more specifically, their national defense and security. Thus, the coercion was of such mounting intensity and efficacy that it can be authoritatively proscribed as a violation of basic Charter goals and of Article 2(4).

A cooperative effort is called for to obtain a more inclusive regulation of the economic instrument of coercion and a more inclusive and policy-serving use of the earth's resources—not for war and unilateral dominance, but for peace and for mankind.

Destination Embargo of Arab Oil:
Its Legality under International Law

IBRAHIM F. I. SHIHATA

I.

MEASURES APPLIED BY OIL EXPORTING ARAB STATES

The use of Arab oil as an instrument of pressure for the revival of dormant efforts to restore peace in the Middle East was already a popular demand in many Arab countries before the outbreak of Arab-Israeli hostilities in October 1973. The political argument was simple. Production of oil beyond certain limits did not make economic sense for many Arab countries. Their depleting crude was increasingly converted into depreciating dollars and pounds yielding in fact a lower economic return than that achieved by simply keeping it in the ground. Worse still, this conversion was taking place in countries with few alternative resources and with a rather limited absorption capacity for the generated funds. Unchecked production was thus an economic sacrifice that could only be interpreted as a political favor to the consuming countries. Instead of responding positively to such a favor, the United States and most of its Western allies continued to ignore the vital interests of the Arab states. In particular, they either acquiesced in or actually encouraged the continuation of Israel's territorial expansion at the expense of its neighboring Arab states,[1] and of its refusal to implement the United Nations resolutions on the rights of the Arab Palestinian people.[2] By continuing to extend its massive military, economic, and diplomatic support to Israel, the United States in particular opted for a partial position in the Middle East conflict

---

* Legal Advisor, Kuwait Fund for Arab Economic Development. Opinions expressed in this essay are those of the writer and do not necessarily represent the views of the Kuwait Fund.

[1] The "Jewish State" suggested in the Partition Plan of Palestine (adopted by the UN General Assembly by Resolution 181(II) Nov. 29, 1947, GAOR, 2nd Sess., Resolutions, 31–50, UN Doc. A/519) was to cover an area of about 5,655 sq. miles, compared to about 907 sq. m. owned by Jewish settlers and agencies at the time and to about 10,249 sq. m. which formed the total area of Palestine under British Mandate. Territories of Palestine controlled by Israel after the 1949 Armistice Agreements covered, however, 8,017 sq. m., while territories of Arab States occupied by Israel in June 1967 covered 26,476 sq. m., including 23,622 sq. m. in Egypt, 2,270 sq. m. in Jordan (other than the Arab city of Jerusalem) and 444 sq. m. in Syria. See THE MIDDLE EAST AND NORTH AFRICA 398 (19th ed., 1972).

[2] For a comprehensive list of these resolutions, see UNITED NATIONS RESOLUTIONS ON PALESTINE 1947–1972, at 176–79, 195–98 (Institute for Palestine Studies, Beirut & Center for Documentation and Studies, Abu Dhabi, 1973). These resolutions have affirmed, in particular, the right of the Palestinians to return to their homes, to compensation for those who opt not to return, to respect for their immovable properties in Palestine, for their human rights, self-determination, and the legitimacy of their struggle for it.

which was clearly anti-Arab. In such circumstances, Arab oil exporting
countries had no reason to continue to do political favors for the Western
consuming countries. It was time for them to act on the basis of economic
rationality only and to cutback their production to the limits justified by
their economic needs.

The weight of this simple argument carried its way after repeated warnings by Arab statesmen had proved futile. Shortly before the outbreak of
hostilities in October, 1973, officials of Saudi Arabia, the largest Arab oil
producer, were revealing plans to check the increase of their crude oil production if the United States did not take a more impartial position in the
Middle East conflict.[3] With the outbreak of hostilities the argument un-
surprisingly gained full momentum.[4] Less than 24 hours after the fighting
started on October 6, the Executive Committee of the Palestine Liberation
Organization called for an immediate halt of the pumping of all Arab oil.[5]
The Iraqi Government responded on the same day by nationalizing the
interests of two U.S. companies, Exxon and Mobil, in the Basrah Petroleum
Company.[6] Amidst the warnings issued in various Arab oil producing
countries, Kuwait took the initiative, on October 9, of calling for an emergency meeting of Arab Oil Ministers to discuss "the role of oil in the light
of current developments."

Held in Kuwait on 17 October and attended by 10 Arab countries,[7] the
meeting issued a communiqué [8] indicating that oil production would be
reduced by not less than 5 percent of the September 1973 level of output
in each Arab oil exporting country, with a similar reduction to be applied
each successive month, until such time as total evacuation of Israeli forces
from all Arab territory occupied during the June 1967 war is completed
and the legitimate rights of the Palestinian people are restored.[9] The

[3] See, e.g., statements of Saudi Arabia's Oil Minister Sheikh Zaki Yamani, Washington Post, April 17, 1973, at 1, confirmed by King Faisal, id., July 6, 1973, at 1 and
Newsweek, Sept. 10, 1973. In the latter magazine's interview, King Faisal explicitly
explained that "cooperation requires action on both sides: not sacrifices on one side
and negative, if not hostile attitudes on the other side."

[4] Ironically, however, the first cutback in Arab oil production was a direct result
of Israeli military action. Two of the four East Mediterranean terminals—Banias
and Tartus in Syria—were targets of Israeli air and sea raids which damaged considerably their loading facilities. A third terminal—Sidon in Lebanon—remained
open but was not visited by tankers. As a result, throughput from Saudi Arabia and
Iraq had to be reduced to a trickle before the cutback decisions on the Arab side
were actually issued. See 17 MIDDLE EAST ECONOMIC SURVEY (MEES), No. 1, Oct.
26, 1973, at 2. Israel also suspended operations at the Ashkelon terminal as of Oct.
6, 1973 thus halting a potential 500,000 b/d of exports. See Middle East Oil Emergency, 40 PETROLEUM PRESS SERVICE, No. 11, at 407, 408 (Nov. 1973).

[5] 16 MEES, No. 51, Oct. 12, 1973, at 4.

[6] Law No. 70, Oct. 7, 1973. English translation in id., at i–iii.

[7] Saudi Arabia, Kuwait, Iraq, Libya, Algeria, Egypt, Syria, Abu Dhabi, Bahrain, and
Qatar.

[8] 16 MEES, No. 52, Oct. 19, 1973, at iii–iv. The communiqué was signed by all
participants excepting the Oil Minister of Iraq.

[9] Coinciding with this step, a Ministerial Committee representing the six Gulf member states of OPEC (five Arab countries plus Iran) decided on October 16, 1973, to

meeting had in fact passed the following resolution which was unofficially released at a later date, and may be worth quoting here in full:

Considering that the direct goal of the current battle is the liberation of the Arab territories occupied in the June 1967 war and the recovery of the legitimate rights of the Palestinian people in accordance with the United Nations resolutions;

Considering that the United States is the principal and foremost source of the Israeli power which has resulted in the present Israeli arrogance and enabled the Israelis to continue to occupy our territories;

Recalling that the big industrial nations help, in one way or another, to perpetuate the status quo, though they bear a common responsibility for implementing the United Nations resolutions;

Considering that the economic situation of many Arab oil producing countries does not justify raising oil production, though they are ready to make such an increase in production to meet the requirements of major consumer industrial nations that commit themselves to cooperation with us for the purpose of liberating our territories;

Decided that each Arab oil exporting country immediately cuts its oil production by a recurrent monthly rate of no less than 5% to be initially counted on the virtual production of September, and thenceforth on the last production figure until such a time as the international community compels Israel to relinquish our occupied territories or until the production of every individual country reaches the point where its economy does not permit of any further reduction without detriment to its national and Arab obligations.

Nevertheless, the countries that support the Arabs actively and effectively or that take important measures against Israel to compel its withdrawal shall not be prejudiced by this production cut and shall continue to receive the same oil supplies that they used to receive prior to the reduction.   Though the cut rate will be uniform in respect of every individual oil exporting country, the decrease in the supplies provided to the various consuming countries may well be aggravated proportionately with their support to and cooperation with the Israeli enemy.

The Participants also recommend to the countries party to this resolution that the United States be subjected to the most severe cut proportionately with the quantities of crude oil, oil derivatives and hydrocarbons that it imports from every exporting country.

The Participants also recommend that this progressive reduction lead to the total halt of oil supplies to the United States from every individual country party to the resolution.[10]

---

abandon negotiations with oil companies on the price of crude and announced new posting pricse adding about 70 percent to the posting for Arabian light crude. *Id.*, at (i). This measure was already under consideration before the flare-up of Arab-Israeli hostilities and was particularly espoused by Iran, a non-Arab country. The establishment of its legality is therefore beyond the scope of this paper.

   [10] 17 MEES, No. 4, Nov. 16, 1973, at (iii).   First published as an advertisement, in The Guardian (London), Nov. 10, 1973.   The resolution was not signed by the Oil Minister of Iraq.

The communiqué and resolution defined their objective in no unclear terms,[11] combining escalating cutbacks in production with selective dis- crimination between friendly and unfriendly states. The "legitimacy" of such an objective was particularly emphasized, along with the concern of the participants for the economic welfare of the industrial world. Produc- tion of crude oil in the ten countries attending the meeting averaged in September 1973 around 19.5 million barrel/day. A 5–10 percent cut meant a reduction of 1 and 2 million, or roughly from 3 to 6 percent of the volume of oil exports then moving in world trade.[12]

On October 18, the Saudi Arabian Royal Cabinet decided to reduce oil production immediately (and until the end of November) by 10 percent and to continue reduction thereafter "month after month at a rate to be determined at the time in accordance with the [Arab Oil Minister's] de- cision." The Cabinet indicated also that efforts to get the U.S. Government to modify its stand vis-à-vis the on-going war and its military assistance to Israel were "currently in progress." It added the clear warning that "if these efforts do not produce tangible results soon, then the Kingdom will stop oil exports to the U.S." [13]

The embargo of Arab oil to the United States, already recommended at the October 17 meeting, was imposed unilaterally by Abu Dhabi on Oc- tober 18, by Libya on October 19, by Saudi Arabia and Algeria on October 20, by Kuwait and Qatar on October 21 and by Oman on October 25.[14] On October 19, it should be noted, the U.S. involvement in the military conflict then going on between Arab and Israeli forces reached such a magnitude that President Nixon requested that Congress appropriate $2,200 million in the current financial year for military assistance to Israel.

On October 21 Iraq, which had not concurred in the cutback decision of October 17, announced the nationalization of the 60 percent Dutch hold- ing in Shell's 23.75 percent interest in the Basra Petroleum Company as a "punitive measure against the Netherlands for its hostile stand towards the Arab Nation." [15] Two days later, Kuwait which had already adopted an

---

[11] See also the communiqué of Arab Oil Ministers dated March 18, 1974, where this objective is reiterated as quoted in note 30 infra. Other wild objectives propagated by the Western press and quoted in Paust and Blaustein, The Arab Oil Weapon—A Threat to International Peace, 68 AJIL 427ff. (1974) never figured in the original cutback decision or in subsequent official Arab joint statements.

[12] Estimates in 17 MEES, No. 4, Nov. 16, 1973, at 3–4.

[13] English translation of text in id., at iv.

[14] For the attitude of each Arab country see, 17 MEES, No. 1, Oct. 26, 1973, at 3–7.

[15] Law No. 90, Oct. 21, 1973. For English translation of the text, see id., at 12. The reasons stated by the Iraqi News Agency for this action include the use of Dutch territory as "a bridgehead for assistance sent to the enemy," the supply by the Nether- lands to Israel of crude oil from its imported stock, the continuous flights of KLM to "transport mercenaries and assistance to the enemy," the initial opposition of the Netherlands to the issue of an unbiased communiqué by EEC members, the declara- tion of the Dutch Foreign Minister to Arab Ambassadors of his country's support for Israel, the personal participation of the Dutch Minister of Defense in a demonstra- tion staged in the Dutch capital to express support for Israel during the war, and the participation of various Dutch establishments and companies in collecting contributions for the Israeli war effort. Id., at 13.

immediate 10 percent cut in production on October 21, embargoed oil shipments to the Netherlands for "its hostile attitude towards Arab rights and
its Pro-Israeli bias." [16]   Oil exports to that country were also curtailed by
Abu Dhabi, on October 23, by Qatar on October 24, by Oman on October
25, by Libya on October 30 and its curtailment was confirmed by Saudi
Arabia on November 2. [17]   With the beginning of November, oil production
had already been cut back by at least 25 percent in Kuwait, 10 percent in
Saudi Arabia, Algeria, and Qatar and by at least 5 percent in Libya,
Bahrain, Dubai, and Oman. [18]   Before the embargo went into effect, total
U.S. imports of Arab oil averaged, according to reliable estimates, around
1.8–1.9 million b/d equivalent to 28 percent of aggregate U.S. oil imports
and 10 percent of its total consumption. [19]   Dutch imports of Arab oil
reached, on the other hand, 1.47 million b/d or 71 percent of its overall
oil imports. [20]

After the cessation of military operations, Arab Oil Ministers held their
second meeting on November 4–5 in an attempt to enhance the use of oil
for accelerating the process of reaching a peaceful settlement of the Arab-
Israeli conflict.   They decided on escalation in the initial percentage reduction to 25 percent below the September 1973 level, including the volumes
deducted as a result of the embargo.   At that time Saudi Arabia had already reached a staggering 31.7 percent drop in production and Kuwait
25 to 30 percent. [21]   The decision was meant, however, to bring about a
similar decrease in production in Libya, Abu Dhabi, Algeria, and Qatar.
As a result, a total reduction of about 2,826,000 b/d or some 28.5 percent
below the September average became effective. [22]   The meeting decided
also to send the Arab Oil Ministers of Algeria and Saudi Arabia to Western
capitals "to explain the Arab point of view regarding the oil production
cutback measures."   As for future cutbacks, it was decided that a further
reduction amounting to 5 percent of the November output should follow
in December "provided that such reduction shall not affect the share that
any friendly state was importing from any Arab exporting country during
the first nine months of 1973." [23]

The trend towards escalation was soon to be reversed, however, partly in
view of the less biased attitudes which gradually developed in Western
Europe and Japan, and partly because of the relative success of the efforts
for reaching a peaceful settlement in the area.   On November 18, nine
Arab Oil Ministers convening in Vienna decided not to implement the 5
percent reduction for the month of December with respect to European
countries (meaning the nine EEC members with the exception of the

[16] *Id.*, at 5.
[17] *See id.*, at 6–7 and 17 *id.*, No. 2, Nov. 2, 1973, at 3–4.   It was later explained
however that the embargo did not cover oil shipped to Rotterdam for the purposes
of refining and reexportation to nonembargoed countries.
[18] *Ibid.*
[19] *Id.*, 16, No. 52, Oct. 19, 1973, at 4, and 17 *id.*, No. 22, March 18, 1974, at 13.
[20] *Id.*, No. 2, Nov. 2, 1973, at 1.
[21] *Id.*, Supp. Nov. 6, 1973, at 2, 5.
[22] *Id.*, at 2.   [23] *Id.*, at 4.

Netherlands) "in appreciation of the political stand taken by the Common Market countries in their communiqué of 19 November, 1973 regarding the Middle East crisis." [24] The Sixth Summit Arab Conference held in Algiers from November 26 to 28 further exempted Japan and the Philippines from the effects of the 5 percent cutback scheduled for December. It also qualified the progressive monthly reduction formula by adopting a ceiling for reductions in production "to the extent that reduction in income should not exceed one quarter on the basis of the 1972 income level of each producing country." [25] Consuming countries were also to be classified in three categories: friendly, neutral, or "supporting the enemy." The classification was to be applied and reviewed by a committee of the Ministers of Foreign Affairs and Oil of the Arab oil producing states. Any neutral country reclassified as friendly would receive the same quantities of oil as it imported in 1972, while re-export of oil from any country to a hostile state should be guarded against. In response to a decision of the OAU Ministerial Council held in Addis Ababa on November 21 and attended by 42 African countries,[26] the Arab Summit Conference decided also to impose an oil embargo against Portugal, South Africa, and Rhodesia.[27]

Subsequent to the Sixth Arab Summit Conference, Arab Oil Ministers convened in Kuwait and expressed a greater measure of flexibility. In their communiqué of December 8 they agreed to lift the oil embargo against the United States with the beginning of the implementation of a schedule of withdrawal of Israeli forces from Arab territories occupied since 1967. Furthermore, they decided that once a withdrawal schedule was reached, a schedule for the gradual return of oil production to its September 1973 level would be drawn up to go with the implementation of the stages of withdrawal. Supply of oil to "African countries and friendly Islamic States" was also to continue uninterrupted "to the extent that they have valid contracts even if it means an increase in production." These latter countries either had never established diplomatic relations with Israel or had severed such relations before or during the hostilities of October 1973 as an expression of support for the legitimacy of the Arab cause. African countries had further called upon all countries, Arab and non-Arab, to impose a total economic embargo and in particular an oil embargo against Israel, in the abovementioned decision of the OAU Ministerial Council.

Emphasizing that the use of oil by Arab states was an instrument of flexible persuasion meant only to ensure respect for the rules of interna-

[24] *Id.*, No. 5, Nov. 23, 1973, at 5. Iraq did not attend the meeting.

[25] Considering that oil prices (excluding dollar depreciation adjustments) have risen by 70 percent since 1972, this ceiling meant that oil producing Arab states could in fact reduce output to some 45 percent of the 1972 level before reaching the minimum 75 percent of 1972 revenue level. 17 MEES, No. 6, Nov. 30, 1973, at 1.

[26] OAU Doc., ECM/RES 21 (viii) Nov. 21, 1973.

[27] For an English translation of the Conference "Resolution on Oil," *see* 17 MEES, No. 6, Nov. 30, 1973, at 9. The Conference was attended by Heads of States of 16 Arab countries. Iraq and Libya were not represented, while Jordan sent a lower level delegation.

tional order in the Middle East, Arab Oil Ministers took further steps in their meeting in Kuwait on December 24–25 for the relaxation of oil production cutbacks. The 25 percent cutback was eased down to 15 percent of the September 1973 level of production with effect from January 1, 1974, while the extra 5 percent originally scheduled for January was dispensed with altogether. Japan, which had already issued two Foreign Ministry statements endorsing UN Security Council resolutions on the Middle East conflict, was allowed a "special treatment which would not subject it to the full extent of the across-the-board cutback measures." This was explicitly justified not only by "the change in Japan's policy towards the Arab cause," but also by "the deteriorating economic situation in Japan." It was also decided to resume oil supply to Belgium via Rotterdam, (up to the level of September 1973 imports) and to supply "certain friendly countries," presumably France, Britain, and Spain, with all their actual oil requirements even in excess of that level.[28] The embargo imposed against the Netherlands remained intact however, despite the earlier declaration of the Dutch Government spokesman on December 4 to the effect that his government "considers that the Israeli presence in occupied territories is illegal." [29] As for the United States, the Ministers' communiqué made a conciliatory gesture by expressing the hope that the "desire of the U.S. Government to participate in the search for a just and peaceful settlement of the problem will be fruitful and will lead to results beneficial to the peoples of the world and in particular to bilateral relations between the Arab and the American peoples."

This gesture was later followed by the much argued decision of Arab Oil Ministers, taken in Vienna on March 18, 1974, to lift the embargo of Arab oil to the United States, to treat both Italy and West Germany as "friendly countries," and to increase oil production in each Arab country to the extent needed to enable it to carry out that decision.[30]

As a result of the above decisions, countries importing Arab oil are, at the time of writing (May, 1974), classified as follows: [31]

(1). The "friendly states" which are allowed to import all their actual requirements of Arab oil;

(2). the "neutral states," including the United States, which are allowed to import the equivalent of their average imports of Arab oil during the

[28] Id., No. 11, Jan. 4, 1974, at 1.   [29] Id., No. 7, Dec. 7, 1973, at 13.

[30] Id., No. 22, March 22, 1974, at 1, 6. The Ministers' communiqué reiterated the "basic objective" of the Arab oil measures which is "to draw world attention to the Arab question in order to create an atmosphere conducive to the implementation of UN Security Council Resolution 242 calling for total withdrawal from the occupied Arab territories and the restoration of the legitimate rights of the Palestinian people" and referred to "the new direction" in American official policy toward the Arab-Israeli conflict. The communiqué provided however that the decision would be subject to review on June 1, 1974. Algeria expressed the view that the lifting of the embargo was "provisional in nature and limited to the period expiring 1 June 1974." Syria and Libya dissented to the decision altogether. See a translation of the text of the communiqué in Ibid.

[31] Compare a quadripartite classification in 17 id., No. 11, Jan. 4, 1974, at 1.

first nine months of 1973 or during the month of September 1973, whichever is greater; and

(3). "the embargoed States," the Netherlands, South Africa, Portugal, and Rhodesia, whose supplies of Arab oil are cut off completely, (although in the case of the Netherlands, supplies are allowed for purposes of refining and re-exportation to nonembargoed countries).

Measures applied by Arab oil producing countries have thus included nationalization of foreign assets (in Iraq), reduction of oil production, discrimination in oil exports, and embargo of oil shipments to certain countries. The arguments for and against the validity of discriminatory and politically motivated nationalizations are well known.[32] The imposition of limitations on the production of primary commodities is, on the other hand, obviously within the exclusive domestic jurisdiction of sovereign states. Such limitations have, at any rate, been imposed in the past by two Arab states [33] as a conservation measure in respect of oil production, without invoking any international legal controversy. The discussion in this article will therefore concentrate on the legality of the embargo of Arab oil shipments to certain foreign states and the politically motivated discrimination in the export of Arab oil. Since these measures are intrinsically tied to the Middle East conflict, a discussion of certain legal aspects of that conflict seems inescapable in this respect.

II.

ILLEGALITY OF ARMED ISRAELI PRESENCE ON EGYPTIAN AND SYRIAN TERRITORIES

The legal complexities of the Arab-Israeli conflict are many.[34] Although their details do not fall within the scope of this article, one issue has to be clearly established as a basis for the reasoning that follows: Israel has no legal right under contemporary international law to the occupation and, a fortiori, to the annexation of the territories of Egypt and Syria which it has occupied by force since June 1967.[35]

---

[32] See, e.g., 8 WHITEMAN, DIGEST OF INTERNATIONAL LAW 376–82 (1967); 3 HACKWORTH, DIGEST OF INTERNATIONAL LAW 555, 645 (1943); FATOUROS, GOVERNMENT GUARANTEES TO FOREIGN INVESTORS 249–51 (1962); S. FRIEDMAN, EXPROPRIATION IN INTERNATIONAL LAW 189–93 (1953); Charpentier, De la non-discrimination dans les investissements, 9 ANNUAIRE FRANÇAIS DE DROIT INTERNATIONAL 35–63 (1963).

[33] Kuwait limited the annual production of its crude oil to 3 million b/d as from 1972 (15 MEES, No. 25, April 14, 1972, at 12), while Libya introduced several successive cutbacks on the production of oil companies operating in its territory beginning in 1968 (12 id., No. 4, Nov. 22, 1968), and continuing in 1970 (13 id., No. 33, June 12, 1970) and in 1972 (15 id., No. 19, March 3, 1972).

[34] For enumeration of such legal issues, see QUINCY WRIGHT, THE MIDDLE EAST: PROSPECTS FOR PEACE (1969); Quincy Wright, Legal Aspects of the Middle East Situation, 33 L. & CONTEMP. PROB. 24 (1968). And see a comprehensive, but partisan, discussion of these issues, in MARTIN, LE CONFLIT ISRAELO-ARABE (1973).

[35] Occupied Jordanian territory and the Gaza Strip are excluded from discussion only because of their irrelevance to the topic of this article.

Israel has not denied the sovereignty of Egypt over the Sinai Peninsula [36] or that of Syria over the Golan Heights. Both territories were outside the international boundaries of "Palestine" before the establishment of Israel and have been part of the respective territories of Egypt and Syria since their independence. Israel's claim to their occupation has thus been "justified" only by alleged considerations of security and less overtly by the desire to gain territorial advantages in future negotiations.[37] Such considerations are obviously of a political, not legal, character. Foreign military occupation, which "cannot displace or transfer sovereignty," [38] may not be legally based on mere allegations by the occupying power of its self-appreciated security requirements. The prohibition of the use of force as a means for the settlement of international disputes and in particular for acquisition of territory, which seems to constitute the cornerstone of contemporary international law,[39] would otherwise be meaningless. Several partisan writers have attempted, however, to find legal bases for Israel's political claims to the occupation and even to the annexation of territories of neighboring Arab states. Four main arguments have been advanced in this respect: [40]

(1). Israel, it is alleged, was in a state of self-defense when it invaded Arab territories in June 1967.[41] This is based either on the assumption that

[36] The shaky arguments presented in L. M. BLOOMFIELD, EGYPT, ISRAEL AND THE GULF OF AQABA IN INTERNATIONAL LAW (1957) and reproduced in STONE, THE MIDDLE EAST UNDER CEASE FIRE 13 (1967) and in BLUM, SECURE BOUNDARIES AND MIDDLE EAST PEACE 8 (1971), disputing the long established Egyptian title over Sinai, were wisely not quoted by responsible Israeli officials.

[37] See, e.g., Israel's statement dated April 2, 1969 on its conception of secure and recognized boundaries in answer to Question No. 5 submitted by the UN Secretary-General's Special Representative, Ambassador Jarring, in UN Doc. S/10070, Annex 1, at 6; and its statement of February 26, 1971 in response to Ambassador Jarring's proposal of withdrawal of Israeli forces beyond the international boundaries of Egypt in UN Doc. S/10070, Add. 2, at 4. And see BLUM, supra note 36, at 63–70.

[38] McNAIR, LEGAL EFFECTS OF WAR 320 (3rd ed., 1958) where this doctrine is described as "the most important principle of law incident to belligerent occupation." See also, CASTREN, THE PRESENT LAW OF WAR AND NEUTRALITY 215–16 (1954); DEBBASCH, L'OCCUPATION MILITAIRE 10 (1962).

[39] See the first principle in the UN General Assembly Declaration of Principles of International Law concerning Friendly Relations and Co-operation among States in accordance with the Charter of the United Nations, GAOR, 25th Sess., SUPP. No. 28 (A/8028): Resolution 2625, Oct. 24, 1970. And see, e.g., BROWNLIE, INTERNATIONAL LAW AND THE USE OF FORCE BY STATES 410–23 (1963); JENNINGS, THE ACQUISITION OF TERRITORY IN INTERNATIONAL LAW (1963); Garner, Non-Recognition of Illegal Territorial Annexation and Claims to Sovereignty, 30 AJIL 679–88 (1936). For international documents establishing the principle, see 5 WHITEMAN, DIGEST OF INTERNATIONAL LAW 847–965 (1965).

[40] For a discussion and refutation of other minor arguments such as alleged "acquisitive prescription" or "general recognition" see WRIGHT, THE MIDDLE EAST, supra note 34, at 22–23. The argument that international practice knows precedents for annexation of territories for the purpose of guaranteeing the security of certain states, presented in particular by BLUM, supra note 36, at 24–45, simply ignores the development of international law under the UN system.

[41] See e.g., Higgins, The June War, the U.N. and Legal Background, 3 JOURNAL OF CONTEMPORARY HISTORY 271 (1968); STONE, No PEACE—No WAR IN THE MIDDLE

the measures taken by Egypt before that date (mainly its declaration on May 23, 1967 of the closure of the Straits of Tiran to Israeli shipping and its request for withdrawal of UN troops from Sharm El Sheikh) amounted in fact to an "armed attack" against Israel in the sense of Article 51 of the UN Charter,[42] or on the basis of the controversial theories of "anticipatory"[43] or even "interceptive"[44] self-defense. If such a "legitimate" exercise of force was so successful as to enable Israel to occupy vast territories of other states, it conferred on it, in that view, a right to continue its occupation of such territories until adequate security measures are instituted, and further gives it a better title to these territories, against their prior holder, to the extent that the holder had itself seized them unlawfully.[45] Territorial change could therefore properly result from the "lawful use of force" which is said to have been exerted by Israel in its invasion of Arab territories in 1967.[46] The alleged objective territorial title which vested in Israel as a result is thus based on the twofold assumption that Israel was exercising self-defense against states whose previous territorial sovereignty over the conquered areas was doubtful.

Such subjective assertions are not adequately substantiated by factual evidence. Despite initial claims to the contrary, it is now established beyond doubt that Israel initially attacked Egypt on June 5, 1967, that it continued its invasion of Egyptian, Syrian, and Jordanian territory until it achieved its war aims notwithstanding earlier appeals by the Security Council for a cease-fire, and that it has since refused to withdraw to the pre-June 5 lines.[47] Similar acts have been cited elsewhere as appropriate criteria for defining aggression, not self-defense.[48] The earlier Egyptian

---

EAST 39–40 (1969); ELIHU LAUTERPACHT, JERUSALEM AND THE HOLY PLACES 46 (Anglo-Israeli Association, Pamphlet No. 19, 1968); Schwebel, *What Weight to Conquest* 64 AJIL 344–47 (1970); Shapira, *The Six Day War and the Right of Self Defence* 6 ISRAEL L. REV. 65–80 (1971); MARTIN, *supra* note 34, at 153–70.

[42] *Id.*, at 165; Dinstein, *The Legal Issues of Para-War and Peace in the Middle East,* 44 ST. JOHN'S L. REV. 466 (1969–70).

[43] Schwebel, *supra* note 41, at 346. For the refutation of the doctrine of anticipatory self-defense, *see,* 2 OPPENHEIM, INTERNATIONAL LAW 156 (H. Lauterpacht ed., 7th ed., 1952); KELSEN, THE LAW OF THE UNITED NATIONS 269, 787–89 (1950); JESSUP, A MODERN LAW OF NATIONS 165–68 (1948); BROWNLIE, *supra* note 39, at 278; Brownlie, *The Use of Force in Self Defence,* 28 BYIL 232–47 (1961). *Compare* Schwebel, *Aggression, Intervention and Self-Defence in Modern International Law,* RECUEIL DES COURS 413, 478–83 (II, 1972).

And see an early insistence, on another occasion, by Israel's representative to the United Nations on the argument that self-defense presupposes an actual armed attack. In UN Security Council, Official Records, 6th Year, 551st Meeting, 10.

[44] Dinstein, *supra* note 42, at 466, 468–70.

[45] Schwebel, *supra* note 41, at 345–46.

[46] E. Lauterpacht, *supra* note 41, at 52; MARTIN, *supra* note 34, at 263. *And see* MEYROWITZ, LE PRINCIPE DE L'EGALITÉ DES BELLIGERENTS DEVANT LE DROIT DE LA GUERRE 296 *et seq.* (1970).

[47] For these developments see *Report of the Secretary-General presented pursuant to Security Council Resolution 331 (1973) dated 20 April 1973,* in UN Doc. S/10929, May 10, 1973.

[48] *See Report by the Secretary-General of the United Nations on the Question of Defining Aggression,* submitted to the General Assembly pursuant to its Resolution 599

acts, even if considered unjustified when taken, could not reasonably be construed as an actual "armed attack" that would justify Israel's resort to self-defense.[49] If, *arguendo*, Article 51 of the UN Charter were to be construed as extending the exercise of self-defense to response to measures which do not constitute "armed attack" and the Egyptian measures were such as to justify Israel's right to "anticipatory self defense," the exercise of such a right would not at any rate give rise to a subsequent right to occupation or annexation.[50] As the UN resolutions on this very matter have indicated, international law prohibits acquisition and occupation of territory by "war," [51] "force," [52] or "military conquest," [53] not only by "aggression" or "aggressive conquests." The General Assembly Declaration of the Principles of International Law concerning Friendly Relations and Co-operation among States,[54] as well as its subsequent Declaration on the Strengthening of International Security,[55] both declare that the forcible military occupation of the territory of any state is inconsistent with international law. The Security Council's declarations of the "invalidity" of Israel's annexation of Arab Jerusalem [56] and the deliberate abstention of all states from recognizing such annexation further confirm the weakness of the counterargument which was meant in particular to defend that step.

(2). The Armistice Demarcation Lines, agreed upon between Israel and its neighboring states in 1949, were provisional in character and did not prejudice the rights of the parties in respect of the ultimate peaceful settlement of the Palestine question.[57] This valid statement was construed in the pro-Israel literature to mean that the pre-June 5, 1967 lines were not "secure and recognized boundaries" for Israel and did not constitute polit-

---

(VI), Jan. 21, 1952, in GAOR, 7th Sess. Annex. Agenda Item 54 UN Doc. A/2211, at 17–86, Oct. 3, 1952. *And see,* 5 WHITEMAN, *supra* note 39, at 719–873; Wright, *The Concept of Aggression in International Law,* 29 AJIL 873 (1953).

[49] Wright, *Legal Aspects of the Middle East Situation, supra* note 34, at 27.

[50] *Accord.* Wright, *id.,* at 24. *See also,* Falk, *Quincy Wright on Legal Tests of Aggressive War,* 66 AJIL 560, 566 n. 22 (1972). *And see,* JENNINGS, *supra* note 39, at 52–67.

[51] *See,* Security Council Res. No. 242, Nov. 22, 1967, UN Security Council Official Records, 22nd Year, RESOLUTION AND DECISIONS, at 8.

[52] *See,* UN G.A. Res. 2628 (XXV), Nov. 4, 1970, GAOR, 25th Sess., SUPP. No. 28 (A/8028), at 5; Res. 2799 (XXVI), Dec. 13, 1971, *id.,* 26th Sess., SUPP. No. 29 (A/8429), at 82; Res. 2949 (XXVII), Dec. 8, 1972, *id.,* 27th Sess. (A/4548) Part I, at 24. In the three above resolutions the illegality of occupation is properly considered a corollary of the illegality of annexation as "the acquisition of territories by force is inadmissible and . . . consequently territories thus occupied must be restored."

[53] *See,* UN Security Council Res. 252, May 21, 1968, UN Security Council Official Records, 23rd Year, RESOLUTIONS AND DECISIONS, 8–12; Res. 267, July 3, 1969, *id.,* 24th Year, 4; Res. 271, Sept. 15, 1969, *id.,* 5; Res. 298, Sept. 25, 1971, *id.,* 26th year, 6.

[54] UN G.A. Res. 2625(XXV), Oct. 24, 1970, GAOR, 25th Sess., SUPP. No. 28 at 22–24 (A/8028).

[55] UN G.A. Res. 2734(XXV), Dec. 16, 1970, *id.,* at 22–24.

[56] Referred to in note 53 *supra.*

[57] *See,* The General Armistice Agreement between Israel and Egypt, Feb. 24, 1949 (Art. IV (3)), 42 UNTS 251; between Israel and Lebanon, March 23, 1949, *id.,* 287; between Israel and Jordan, April 3, 1949 (Art. II (2)), *id.,* 303; and between Israel and Syria, July 20, 1949 (Art. II (2)), *id.,* 327.

ical frontiers immune from alterations that "would render them more secur(
from a strategic viewpoint." [58] Such assertions are not only in contraven
tion of earlier Israeli official positions [59] but also ignore the important fac
that, with the exception of the lines separating Israeli and Jordanian forces
most of the armistice lines coincided with previously established interna
tional boundaries. The Armistice Agreements themselves distinguished be
tween two such types of line and carefully described the pre-establishe(
boundaries by their proper name. The explicit provisions of these agree
ments on the right of each party to assert territorial claims in the ultimat(
settlement were confined to claims on the territory of Palestine. As en
visaged in 1949, the settlement of the "Palestine question" could not hav(
included, by any stretch of imagination, reallocation of sovereignty ove
the territory of *other* Arab states in favor of Israel. Article IV(3) of th(
Egypt-Israel Armistice Agreement leaves no doubt in this respect as it rec
ognizes the right of the parties to assert rights, claims, or interests of ;
nonmilitary character only *"in the area of Palestine covered by this Agree*
ment." In fact, the only demarcation line under that agreement which wa
not part of the "Egyptian frontiers" was that which separated the Gaz(
Strip from the Israeli-held territory. That line was defined in the Agree
ment (Article VI(1)) in connection with "the Egyptian frontier." Th(
delimitation of the demilitarized zone (Article VIII(2)) as well as th(
withdrawal of Egyptian forces from Al-Faluja area (Article III(2)) wer(
also described in terms of "the Egypt-Palestine frontier." Likewise, Articl(
V(3) of the Israel-Syria Armistice Agreement explicitly provided tha
"where the existing truce lines run along the international boundary be
tween Syria and Palestine, the Armistice Demarcation Line shall follov
the boundary line."

The provisional character of the armistice lines could not in any cas(
have conferred on Israel lawful sovereignty over territories to which it wa
not otherwise legally entitled, even within the former boundaries of man
dated Palestine. The boundaries of the "Jewish State" adopted by the UN
General Assembly in 1947,[60] which are still "the only generally recognize(
boundaries for Israel," [61] included in fact only about two-thirds of the are:
which became subject to Israel's control after the 1949 armistices. Israel
expansion beyond the 1947 lines was itself an incident of its military suc
cesses in the 1948 war. The provisional character of the armistice line
should therefore have inspired, as it did in 1949, a return to the lines of th(
1947 Partition Plan, not further expansion beyond the armistice lines. State

[58] BLUM, *supra* note 36, at 23. *See also* MARTIN, *supra* note 34, at 280–81.

[59] *See, e.g.,* Statements of Israel's Permanent Representative to United Nations be
fore the Security Council during discussion of Israel's complaint concerning passag
through the Suez Canal, UN Security Council Official Records, 6th Year, 549th Meet
ing, at 2–7 (July 23, 1951). *And see generally,* FEINBERG, THE LEGALITY OF A STAT
OF WAR AFTER CESSATION OF HOSTILITIES 36 (1951).

[60] Resolution 81(II), Nov. 29, 1947, GAOR, 2nd Sess., RESOLUTIONS, 31–50, UN
Doc. A/519.

[61] Wright, *The Middle East Problem,* 64 AJIL 270, 277 (1970).

nents of Israeli officials issued after the conclusion of the Armistice Agreements confirmed that understanding.[62] The Israeli Government also accepted, in the Protocol of Lausanne of May 12, 1949, the use of a map of Palestine identical to the UN Partition Plan as the "basis for discussion" of the ultimate settlement [63] on the recommendation of the UN Conciliation Commission.[64] Even when Israel changed its attitude during the Lausanne negotiations of 1949, it did not extend its ambitious territorial claims beyond the territory of mandated Palestine. It suggested, on the contrary, the exclusion of "the middle area of Palestine under Jordanian occupation," i.e., the West Bank, from its immediate claims.[65] Israel's insistence at that time on new claims beyond the previously agreed-upon basis of the discussions was indeed the blow which brought negotiations to a halt. It was that attitude, perhaps more than any other factor, which reinforced the spirit of mistrust prompting Arab Governments to adopt in subsequent years a negative position towards further negotiations on the subject.

(3). Security Council Resolution 242 of 1967 [66] was repeatedly described by Israeli writers as merely a recommendation.[67] Doubts on the binding character of that resolution have probably been erased, however, by the text of Security Council Resolution 338 (1973) [68] which was equally "accepted" by Israel.

The meaning attributed to Resolution 242 in the standard pro-Israel argument is that it does not require withdrawal of Israeli forces from all Arab occupied territories but requires withdrawal only to such lines as would constitute "secure boundaries" for Israel.[69] Such an interpretation is based *first* on a certain reading of the English text of the resolution which affirmed that a just and lasting peace in the Middle East should include the application of the principle of "*withdrawal of Israeli forces from territories*

[62] *See, e.g.,* UN Doc. A/AC. 24/SR. 45–48, 50–51, May 5–9, 1949. And see earlier and more explicit statements of Israeli representatives in UN, GAOR, 3rd Sess., Pt. 1, 1st Comm., 640–43, 644–45, 832, 840–42.

[63] *See,* UN GAOR, 3rd Sess., Ad hoc Political Committee, Annex, vol. II, at 5, 8–9, UN Doc. A/927, June 21, 1949.

[64] *Ibid.*

[65] *Id.,* Supp. 18, at 3–4, 19–21, UN Doc. A/1367/Rev. 1 (1950).

[66] Res. No. 242, Nov. 22, 1967, UN Doc. S/PV 1382, at 36; UN Security Council Official Records, 22nd Year, Resolutions and Decisions at 8.

[67] *E.g.,* Blum, *supra* note 36, at 63, Dinstein, *supra* note 42, at 477, Shapira, *supra* note 41, at 235, 236; Rosenne, *Directions for a Middle East Settlement—Some Underlying Legal Problems,* 33 L. & Contem. Prob. 44, 57 (1968); Lapidoth, *La résolution du Conseil de Sécurité en date 22 Novembre 1967 au sujet du Moyen Orient,* 74 Rev. Gén. Dr. Int. Public 289, 292–4 (1970).

[68] S/Res./338 adopted by the Council in its 1747th Session, October 21/22, 1973. In paragraph 2, the Security Council "*calls* upon the parties concerned to start immediately after the cease-fire the implementation of Security Council Resolution 242 in all of its parts."

[69] *E.g.,* Blum, *supra* note 36, at 72–79; Lapidoth, *supra* note 67, at 300–01; Rosenne, *supra* note 67, at 60. *See also* Stone, *The "November Resolution" and Middle East Peace: Pitfall or Guidepost?,* University of Toledo L. Rev., Nos. 1 and 2, at 43 (1970); E. V. Rostow, *Legal Aspects of the Search for Peace in the Middle East,* Proc. Amer. Soc. Int. L., 64 AJIL, No. 4, 64, 69 (1970).

occupied in the recent conflict" (and not explicitly from *all the* said territories). It is based secondly on the resolution's provision for the right of each state in the area to live in peace "*within secure and recognized boundaries free from threats or acts of force*," a description which could not apply—says the argument—to the pre-June 5, 1967 lines.

The resolution, it is true, does not use the definite article in the withdrawal paragraph, but it amply describes the territories from which withdrawal is required as being those "occupied in the recent conflict" without any exception. Insistence on the relevance of the absence of the definite article in this respect would lead to the absurd conclusion that some Israeli forces could be maintained in any territories from which withdrawal is accomplished, as the resolution fails also to provide for withdrawal of "*all the*" Israeli forces from such territories.

The United Nations itself has understood the resolution to mean withdrawal for *all* occupied territories, as is evident from the language of the other official texts of the resolution [70] and from the subsequent resolutions of the General Assembly on the subject.[71] Other states and international organizations have also expressed on several occasions their understanding that the resolution requires "total withdrawal" and have called upon Israel to withdraw accordingly. Not less than thirty-five states have in fact severed their diplomatic relations with Israel because of the latter's failure to conform to that understanding. Even the United States, the real power behind the failure of the Security Council to adopt a stronger decision against Israel,[72] has indicated, through its former Secretary of State, that any alterations in the former armistice lines "should not reflect the weight of conquest."[73] The absurdity of the counterargument is demonstrated in fact by its insistence, against the consensus of the international community, on tying the destiny of sovereign states, their history, and geography, to the absence of a definite article which is not even needed grammatically to convey the required comprehensive meaning.

---

[70] *See, e.g.*, the French text: "*Retrait des forces armées israeliennes des territoires occupés lors du recent conflit;*" and the Spanish text "*Retiro des las fuerzas armadas isralies de los territorios que ocuparon durente el reciento conflicto*," UN Doc. S/INF. 22/REV. 2, at 4. Since the English text does not mean partial withdrawal there is no room for the argument that in case of conflict between the texts in different languages the one which was submitted to the vote prevails, or for the argument, advanced by MARTIN, *supra* note 34, at 256, that partial withdrawal is the common meaning in all texts.

[71] *See* resolutions referred to in note 52, *supra.*

[72] For a detailed account, *see,* LALL, THE UN AND THE MIDDLE EAST CRISIS, 1967, at 230–73 (1968).

[73] Text of Address of Mr. William Rogers, Dec. 9, 1969, *U.S. Mission to the U.N., Press Release* 371, Dec. 9, 1969; 62 DEPT. STATE BULL. 7 (1970). Mr. Rogers indicated that only "insubstantial alterations" may be introduced to ensure mutual security. Such alterations would be based, however, on the acceptance of the parties, not merely on the language of the Security Council resolution. *See also,* Wright *Legal Aspects of the Middle East Situation, supra* note 34, at 24; Wright, *The Middle East Problem, supra* note 61, at 274–75; Falk, *The Beirut Raid and the International Law of Retaliation,* 63 AJIL 415, 435, n. 55 (1969).

Withdrawal from occupied territories should not at any rate be mixed
with the establishment of secure boundaries. The resolution requires withdrawal *from* occupied territories and not *to* secure boundaries. The purpose of withdrawal is indeed the restoration of the *status quo ante,* while
the establishment of secure and recognized boundaries aims at the creation
of a *status juris* which understandably cannot admit the forcible acquisition
by one party of territory over which it does not otherwise have a valid title.
In this, the Security Council resolution may have been generous with Israel,
as noted by Quincy Wright,[74] since it did not extend the withdrawal paragraph to all the territories over which Israel lacked an established legal
title. The resolution indicates, however, in no less than four places, that
the creation of secure boundaries cannot result in the forcible acquisition
of territory. It emphasizes in its preamble "the inadmissibility of the
acquisition of territory by war." It also emphasizes the commitment of all
UN members to act in accordance with Article 2 of the Charter which
recognizes the sovereign equality of states and prohibits the threat or the
use of force in the settlement of international disputes. In its operative
paragraphs the resolution calls for "the respect for and acknowledgment of
the sovereignty, territorial integrity and political independence of every
State in the area." It also affirms the necessity for guaranteeing "the territorial inviolability" of every state in the area. To say that the proper application of such language should result in the forcible occupation or annexation of Arab territories by Israel, because the pre-June 5 lines did not
satisfy its self-appreciated security requirements, is, to say the least, an
anomaly in reading the text which goes beyond a partisan *petiti principii.*

One may finally wonder, in the light of the more recent events of October
1973, whether the pre-June 5 lines were in fact less secure than any other
possible frontiers for Israel. The lines, which were accused in the popular
argument of failing to prevent three previous wars, did not exist in fact at
the time of the first of these wars and were crossed and successfully conquered, in 1956 and 1967, by the Israeli, not the Arab, armed forces. Since
their establishment in 1949, they have never been crossed in the opposite
direction by regular forces under the authority of Arab states. When these
lines were replaced by the "natural barriers" reached in 1967, Israel proved,
despite its own security theories, less successful in "defending" the new
lines. Once again the quest for secure boundaries seemed to require a
search for proper guarantees and arrangements which would ensure their
continuity and stability, instead of providing an excuse for geographical
expansion.[75] The falsity of such an excuse, one may notice, is particularly

---

[74] Wright, *The Middle Eastern Crisis,* Proc. Amer. Soc. Int. L., 64 AJIL, No. 4,
71, 78 (1970).

[75] The history of Resolution 242 further confirms this truth. The phrase "secure and
recognized boundaries" in the British draft was taken from the earlier U.S. draft submitted to the Security Council on November 7, 1967 (UN Doc., S/8229). Security in
boundaries was envisaged by the sponsors of the latter draft as a condition in the
arrangements to be adopted, not in the geographic location, as is evident in the draft
resolution submitted by the United States on June 20, 1967 to the General Assembly

proved by the fact that the part of the occupied territories which has actually been annexed by Israel, *i.e.* Arab Jerusalem, is by no means an Israeli security issue.

(4). Some Israeli writers, while expressing respect for the principle of inadmissibility of acquisition of territory by war, have indicated that such a principle does not prohibit acquisition of territory by cession, *i.e.*, by an agreement between the victorious state and its occupied enemy.[76] In this argument, inadmissibility of annexation does not entail inadmissibility of occupation. On the contrary, it gives the victorious state the right to maintain control of the occupied territories until an agreement is reached with the former sovereign by means of which the latter relinquishes its rights and cedes them to the occupant power. In practical terms this view can have but one of two results: The occupant power may use its military occupation as an instrument of pressure and coercion to gain territorial concessions from the occupied country or, failing this, it may extend its occupation indefinitely. In both situations, the very principle of inadmissibility of acquisition of territory by war will definitely be sacrificed. The law which prohibits forcible annexation cannot therefore tolerate forcible occupation. Resolutions of the UN General Assembly have thus stipulated that the territory of a state should not be the object of *occupation or acquisition* by another state resulting from the threat or use of force,[77] and have explicitly considered the restoration of occupied territories a natural sequence of the inadmissibility of acquisition of territory by force.[78]

An agreement reached under alien military occupation through which an occupied sovereign state is forced to relinquish part of its territory is likely at any rate to be deemed null under modern international law. If not vitiated by coercion,[79] it would violate a *jus cogens* principle of the highest international order [80] and could be considered as inconsistent with the UN Charter and the Declaration of Principles of International Law concerning Friendly Relations and Co-operation among States.[81] The remote possibil-

---

(UN Doc., A/L 520). According to the last draft the proposed settlement was thus to include "recognized boundaries and *other arrangements that will give them security* against terror, destruction and war." (Emphasis added).

[76] *See, e.g.*, Blum, *supra* note 36, at 84, Rosenne, *supra* note 67, at 59; Lapidoth, *supra* note 67, at 295–96.

[77] *See* resolutions referred to in notes 52, 54, 55, *supra*.

[78] Res. 2628(XXV), Res. 2799 (XXVI), and Res. 2949(XXVII) referred to in note 52, *supra*.

[79] *Compare* Art. 52 of the Vienna Convention on the Law of Treaties opened for signature from May 23, 1969 until November 30, 1969 (UN Doc., A/CONF. 39/27, May 23, 1969). *And see*, 1 OPPENHEIM, *supra* note 43, at 891–92; McNAIR, THE LAW OF TREATIES 213–17 (1961); H. LAUTERPACHT, RECOGNITION IN INTERNATIONAL LAW 426, 429 (1947).

[80] *Compare* Art. 53 of the Vienna Convention, *supra* note 79. *And see*, McNair, *supra* note 79, at 213–17; BROWNLIE, PRINCIPLES OF PUBLIC INTERNATIONAL LAW 417–18 (1966); Verdross, *Jus Dispositivum and Jus Cogens in International Law*, 60 AJIL 55, 60 (1966).

[81] *See* in particular Art. 2(4) of the UN Charter and Principle I of the abovementioned Declaration, Res. No. 2625(XXV), Annex.

ty of reaching such an agreement could not therefore provide a valid pretext for continuing the military occupation of a territory against the will of its proper sovereign.

The case for the legality of Israel's forcible occupation and annexation of territories of neighboring Arab states was obviously presented to promote the short term political ends of Israel without regard to the advancement of *lex lata* international law or the purposes of the United Nations. Such a case can hardly serve the legitimate interests of other members of the international community, and fails to promote a settlement of the Arab-Israeli conflict just to both sides. It remains therefore void of the moral value which may have otherwise justified it *de lege ferenda*.

Egypt and Syria as the states vested with sovereignty, but illegally deprived of actual control, over territories occupied by Israel were thus entitled to seek redress for the protection of their territorial integrity. Under the UN system they were probably under the obligation to resort first to peaceful methods. This they have done in vain for more than six years. Egypt, in particular, expressed officially [82] its readiness to enter into a peace agreement with Israel containing all the obligations provided for in Security Council Resolution 242(1967) as broadly elaborated by the Special Representative of the UN Secretary-General.[83] In response, Israel defiantly insisted on territorial expansion.[84]

With such an intransigent Israeli position, encouraged in fact by the near total support of the U.S. Government and by the acquiescence of most other Western powers, little choice was left for Arab states to regain control over their occupied territories. Egypt and Syria finally managed, in October 1973, to exercise their territorial jurisdiction by employing forcible measures limited respectively to Egyptian and Syrian territories and aimed solely at restoring control over such territories. Governmental action taken by a state within its own territory for the restoration of legal order disrupted by unauthorized acts of others certainly falls within the inherent territorial jurisdiction of each sovereign state. Although such action may be based on the exercise of the state's traditional right to self-help under customary international law [85] or under a broad reading of the UN Charter

---

[82] See, Aide-Memoire presented to Ambassador Jarring by the United Arab Republic (now the Arab Republic of Egypt) on 15 February 1971, UN Doc. S/10929, Annex III, at 1–2.

[83] See, Aide-Memoire presented to Israel and the United Arab Republic by Ambassador Jarring on 8 February 1971, id., Annex II, at 1–2.

[84] See, Communication presented to Ambassador Jarring by Israel on 26 February 1971, id., Annex IV, at 1–2. In item 4 of that communication, it is bluntly stated that "Israel will not withdraw to the pre-5 June 1967 lines."

[85] See, e.g., Lillich, Forcible Self-Help under International Law, 22 NAVAL WAR COLL. REV. 56 (1970), where he refers also to a lecture given by Professor McDougal in 1968 in which the latter came to the conclusion that "in the absence of collective machinery to protect people against attack and deprivation . . . the principle of major purposes requires an interpretation which would honor self-help against a prior unlawfulness." Id., at 65.

provisions on self-defense,[86] one need not argue the relevance of such con-cepts in regard to the Egyptian and Syrian measures. The denial to Egypt and Syria, in the particular circumstances of the situation, of the right to take individual or collective action would have resulted in fact in depriving them indefinitely of their essential right to territorial integrity, guaranteed by the UN Charter.[87] Without such a right, state jurisdiction, let alone sovereignty, would be nothing but a sham. This obviously explains the fact that not a single state or international organization has characterized the Egyptian and Syrian measures of October 1973 as illegal or even unwarranted.

Whether these two states and the other Arab states bound with them by regional arrangements including mutual defense pacts [88] were entitled to use against third states such economic measures as those explained in detail in the previous section of this paper is a different question, however. The fact that such measures were taken on the whole as a complementary step in the legitimate struggle of Arab states to regain control of occupied Arab territories and to reach a final peaceful settlement of the Middle East con-flict is of great relevance. It remains to be proved, however, that the use of such measures by the Arab states applying them did not constitute a violation of general principles of customary international law or a breach of specific treaty commitments.

III.

LEGALITY OF ARAB OIL MEASURES UNDER CUSTOMARY INTERNATIONAL LAW

In applying the standards of customary international law to the measures adopted by Arab oil exporting countries the following points should be taken into consideration:

(1). The measures in question were initiated at a time when many of the states applying them were in an actual situation of war—Egypt and Syria as the major belligerents against Israel, with Iraq, Kuwait, and to a lesser extent, Algeria and Saudi Arabia as cobelligerents with them. This war situation was prompted, as shown above, by Israel's insistence on the forcible occupation of Egyptian and Syrian territories and the attempt by Egypt and Syria to regain control over their occupied territories after ex-haustion of peaceful means to achieve that result.

[86] That is, a reading which considers a continued forcible occupation following an armed intervention a prolonged "armed attack" under Article 51 of the Charter.

[87] Using the above argument in what is submitted to be the wrong context, Elihu Lauterpacht adds: "For if force can never be used to effect lawful territorial change, then, if territory has once changed hands as a result of an unlawful use of force, the illegitimacy of the position thus established is sterilized by the prohibition upon the use of force to restore the lawful sovereign." E. LAUTERPACHT, supra note 41, at 52.

[88] All Arab states are members of the Joint Arab Defense Council, an organ of the Arab League. For an English translation of some relevant inter-Arab joint military pacts, see, 2 KHALIL, THE ARAB STATES AND THE ARAB LEAGUE. A DOCUMENTARY RECORD. INTERNATIONAL AFFAIRS 101–05, 242–45, 250–53 (1962).

(2). The use of the measures was clearly tied, as shown above, to the achievement of the twofold objective of "withdrawal of Israeli forces from occupied Arab territories and restoration of the legitimate rights of the Palestinian people." They were aimed, in other words, at the establishment of two of the basic requirements of a lasting peace in the Middle East.

(3). The measures were also in complete conformity with the economic interests of the states applying them. As explained earlier, these measures meant, in fact, the termination by Arab oil exporting states of the practice of doing favors for countries whose foreign policy made them unworthy, in Arab eyes, of receiving such favors. Yet in taking these measures Arab states showed consideration for the welfare of the countries particularly affected, such as Japan, and modified their position towards them accordingly.

(4). The measures were taken, on the whole, pursuant to resolutions of the Oil Ministers of the states members of the Organization of Arab Petroleum Exporting Countries (OAPEC). With the exception of the "Resolution on Oil" issued by the Sixth Summit Arab Conference on 28 November, 1973,[89] such measures were adopted in meetings which were sponsored by OAPEC and were chaired in each case by the Minister from the country whose representative assumed chairmanship of the meetings of OAPEC's organs in each particular month. It is not clear, however, whether these resolutions should be treated as resolutions of OAPEC's Council of Ministers, or merely as the result of ad hoc meetings of the Ministers of Oil of member countries in their respective capacities. The OAPEC's Secretariat has not officially published them as resolutions of the organization. The "Resolution on Oil" issued by the Arab Summit Conference, on the other hand, is legally attributable to the League of Arab States. The Conference is the highest political organ of the League.

Identification of the standards of customary international law according to which the legality of the measures in question are to be tested requires a detailed scrutiny of state practice in the matter of the political uses of export controls. These standards will further be clarified by reference to the practice of those international organizations which have considered such uses, either by authorizing them in individual cases or by issuing general statements on the extent of their legitimacy.

A. STATE PRACTICE IN PEACETIME CONDITIONS

(1) *U.S. Practice.*

Special export controls over individual commodities have been long imposed by U.S. legislation for economic and strategic reasons.[90] General

---

[89] *See, supra,* note 27.

[90] *See,* e.g., The United States Shipping Act of 1916, as amended, 46 U.S.C. §808, 835, 46 C.F.R. §221.5 *et seq.* (sale and transfer to foreign registry of vessels owned by

U.S. export controls may be said to have begun, however, in 1940, as measures of national defense and economic warfare.[91] Such controls continued to apply after the termination of World War II, resulting in fact in the embargo on shipments of a great number of articles to a wide range of countries. Around the turn of the year 1947, the U.S. Administration began to revive some war regulations and to use them for control of exports to the Soviet bloc. By 1948 most exports to the Soviet Union and Eastern Europe were thus placed under control "in the interest of security." [92] This practice was further formalized in 1949 by the adoption of the Export Control Act which bluntly stated it to be U.S. policy to use export controls, *inter alia,* "to further the foreign policy of the United States." [93] According to that Act, the President of the United States was authorized to "prohibit or curtail the exportation from the United States, its territories and possessions of any articles, materials, or supplies . . . except under such rules and regulations as he shall prescribe." [94] Pursuant to the Act, such rules and regulations were to provide for the denial of any request for authority to export U.S. commodities "to any nation or combination of nations threatening the national security of the United States if the President shall determine that such exports make a significant contribution to the military or economic potential of such nation or nations which could prove detrimental to the national security and welfare of the United States." The Export Regulations actually issued under that Act had a wide extraterritorial effect.[95] They contained a detailed licensing system which required "validated licenses" for certain goods and "general licenses" for others and discriminated between different countries of destination.[96] A sophisticated system of discrimination developed accordingly, culminating in the classification of foreign destinations (excepting Canada) into eight

US citizens); the Act of October 6, 1917, 12 U.S.C. §95a, 95b; 31 C.F.R. §54.1 *et seq.* and the Gold Reserve Act of 1934, 31 U.S.C. §440 (export of gold); the Natural Gas Act of 1938, 15 U.S.C. §717b; 18 C.F.R. §153.1 *et seq.* (export of natural gas) The Tobacco Seed and Plant Exportation Act of 1940; 7 U.S.C. §576 (export of tobacco seed and live tobacco plants); the Agricultural Trade Development and Assistance Act of 1954, 7 U.S.C. §1691 *et seq.;* 68 Stat. 454 (export of subsidized U.S. agricultural commodities to the Sino-Soviet bloc); the Atomic Energy Act of 1954, 42 U.S.C. §2011 (export of atomic materials, facilities) etc.

[91] *See* Act of July 2, 1940, 54 Stat. 712, 714 (1940), as amended, 50 U.S.C. App. §701 (expired). For a historical account *see, Comment, Export Controls,* 58 YALE L.J. 1325 (1951).

[92] THE STRATEGIC TRADE CONTROL SYSTEM 1948–1956, Dept. of State, Ninth Report to Congress (1957) on Operations under the Mutual Defense Assistance Control Act of 1951, at 4–5 (excerpt republished in METZGER, LAW OF INTERNATIONAL TRADE. DOCUMENTS AND READINGS 1047, 1051 (1966)).

[93] The Export Control Act of 1949, Section 2, 19 U.S.C. §2021 (1949) as extended and amended by Public Law 89-63, 89th Cong.

[94] *Id.,* Sec. 3 (a).

[95] *See,* Silverstone, *The Export Control Act of 1949: Extraterritorial Enforcement,* 108 U.P.L.R. 337–43 (1959).

[96] *See,* SURREY AND SHAW (eds.), A LAWYER'S GUIDE TO INTERNATIONAL BUSINESS TRANSACTIONS 56–85 (1963).

groups, each with a different export control treatment.[97] A complete embargo of U.S. exports to the People's Republic of China, Hong Kong, and Macao was imposed on December 3, 1950 and continued in operation for over twenty years, while a similar embargo imposed on exports to Cuba on October 19, 1960 remains, with a few exceptions, in effect at the present time.[98]

Even when the Export Control Act of 1949 was finally replaced by the Export Administration Act of 1969 (in effect since January 1, 1970),[99] the latter Act, described as "the first significant trade liberalization measure passed by Congress since the end of World War II," [100] maintained the President's power to prohibit the export of materials under such rules and regulations as he may prescribe. This extensive power was again based on the declared policy to preserve "the national security" and to "further significantly the foreign policy of the United States and to fulfil its international responsibilities." As a result, many of the regulations adopted under the 1949 Act, including the grouping of countries of destination, remain in full force.[101]

This discriminatory trade control system is further reinforced by the Mutual Defense Assistance Act of 1951, commonly called the Battle Act.[102] In this Act the policy of the United States is stated to include an embargo on the shipment of a host of strategic supplies, *including petroleum,* to "nations threatening United States security, including the USSR and all countries under its domination." Such a legislatively sanctioned embargo is unabashedly stated to be imposed in order to "(1) increase the material strength of the United States and of the cooperating nations; (2) impede the ability of nations threatening the security of the United States to conduct military operations, and (3) to assist the people of the nations under the domination of foreign aggressors to reestablish their freedom." A classified list of items embargoed under the provisions of Title I of the Act was thus established and remains, after many amendments, in force to this date. Further steps were also adopted under the Act to strengthen and adjust the control of the export of other commodities which called for a lesser degree of control than outright embargo.[103]

[97] For these groups, *see* EXPORT CONTROL, 99th Rep., 1st Quarter 1972, by the Secretary of Commerce to the President, the Senate and the House of Representatives, 2–3. *And see* a description of an earlier classification in Metzger, *Federal Regulation and Prohibition of Trade with Iron-Curtain Countries,* 29 LAW & CONTEM. PROB. 1000, 1001 (1964).

[98] For a critical detailed account of these measures, *see* ADLER-KARLSSON, WESTERN ECONOMIC WARFARE 1947–1967—A CASE STUDY IN FOREIGN ECONOMIC POLICY, particularly at 201, 210 (Stockholm Economic Studies, New Series IX, 1968).

[99] 50 U.S.C. App. §§2401 *et seq.* as extended by Senate Joint Resolution 218, April 29, 1972, Public Law 92–284, 92nd Congress.

[100] Statement of Senator Mondale of Minnesota as quoted in, Berman, *The Export Administration Act of 1969: Analysis and Appraisal,* 3 AMER. REV. OF EAST-WEST TRADE 19 (Jan., 1970).

[101] *See* EXPORT CONTROL, *supra* note 97, at 1.

[102] 22 U.S.C. S1611 *et seq.;* 65 Stat. 644 (1951), as amended by 75 Stat. 424, approved Sept. 4, 1961.

[103] See, THE STRATEGIC TRADE CONTROL SYSTEM 1948–1956, *supra* note 92, at 11–14.

(2) *Practice of other States, including the Netherlands.*

(a) *Multilateral measures: Internationalization of the U.S. discriminatory practice:* Since the beginning of the implementation of its export control system, the U.S. Government has attempted to increase its effectiveness by securing similar action by other countries. It has succeeded in achieving this objective by two means. First, the United States put economic pressure on the countries which received assistance from it by relating, in the Cannon Amendment,[104] the Kem Amendment [105] and the Battle Act,[106] American foreign aid to export control action by the recipient countries against the Sino-Soviet bloc.[107] Secondly, it negotiated with other Western countries, first on a bilateral basis, then multilaterally, the establishment of strategic export controls on the pattern of the U.S. system. Early in 1949 the United Kingdom and France formulated an Anglo-French list of strategic items which was similar to the U.S. lists prepared earlier for the same purpose. Later in November of that year a Consultative Group was founded in Paris by the United Kingdom, France, Italy, the Netherlands, Belgium, Luxembourg, and the United States which was joined on later dates by Norway, Denmark, Canada, the Federal Republic of Germany, Portugal, Greece, Turkey, and Japan. Members of the Group formulated three lists of controlled goods covering items for embargo, for quantitative control, and for exchange of information and surveillance.[108] Thus, a detailed multilateral export control program was developed by fifteen Western states with a permanent organization and agreed lists continually updated by the "Coordinating Committee" and the "China Committee" in accordance with criteria for adding, deleting, upgrading, and downgrading the items involved. The objectives of such a multilateral system were identical to those of the U.S. program and, as in that program, more restrictive controls were applied to exports to China, North Korea, and North Vietnam.[109]

It should be particularly recalled that the countries which were intended to be adversely affected by such multilateral measures in many cases maintained normal diplomatic relations with the states applying those measures. The countries affected have not helped directly or indirectly in maintaining forcible occupation of American or Western European territories. Nor have they been involved in any manner in depriving the peoples of the United States or of the other cooperating Western nations of their right to self-determination. Some of the affected countries were accused, however, at the time of the Korean War, (December 17, 1950) of providing military assistance to regimes with which U.S. forces were involved in armed hostilities. Only North Korea and North Vietnam could be said to have been

---

[104] Sec. 1304 of Public Law 843, effective Sept. 27, 1950.

[105] Sec. 1302 of Public Law 45, effective June 2, 1951.

[106] Sec. 103(b), 104 and 105, 202 and 203 of the Mutual Defense Assistance Control Act of 1951, *supra* note 102.

[107] For the effect on the 61 countries then receiving military, economic, or financial assistance from the United States, *see* METZGER, *supra* note 92, at 1066.

[108] *See, id.,* at 1064.

[109] For further details, *id.,* at 1066-79.

ngaged in armed conflict with the United States during part of the period
n which shipment of all American and West European strategic goods to
:hese two countries was officially embargoed.

(b) *Domestic legislation:* The imposition of export control regulations
and discrimination in their application to different countries of destination
by no means constitute isolated instances in state practice. Although such
regulations are often meant to serve economic purposes, they have been
widely used as instruments of foreign policy to secure political advantages
for the states applying them, such as the denial to unfriendly countries of
badly needed strategic goods. Thus, the European countries cooperating
with the United States in the implementation of the multilateral program
met with no difficulty in finding a basis in their own domestic legal systems
for such a practice. A report submitted to the U.S. Congress in 1962 on
export controls in six European countries, including the Netherlands, found
that each of the six countries "maintains substantially the same controls on
strategic exports to countries of the Sino-Soviet bloc" as those imposed by
the United States.[110] It further confirmed that "controls over exports of
goods on the international embargo list . . . are carried out through their
own laws and regulations." [111]

In the Netherlands, the embargo of strategic goods to such destinations
as the Sino-Soviet bloc was executed under an export prohibition law issued
in 1935 along with some other supporting wartime regulations.[112] In 1962
a new law on foreign trade [113] was issued and further formalized the Dutch
participation in the Western embargo policy, which, it is reported, was
never officially treated in the parliamentary debates required by that law
as to all import and export regulations.[114]

The politically inspired export control of strategic goods may even be
traced in such countries as Sweden and Switzerland.[115] It is, of course, a
general practice in the Soviet Union [116] and, one may safely assume, in other
Socialist countries where the government exercises a monopoly over foreign

---

[110] *See,* REPORT ON EXPORT CONTROLS IN THE U.K., FRANCE, ITALY, FEDERAL RE-
PUBLIC OF GERMANY, BELGIUM AND THE NETHERLANDS, submitted by Senator Thomas J.
Dodd and Senator Kenneth B. Keating to the Sub-Comm. to Investigate the Adminis-
tration of the Internal Security Act and other Internal Security Laws of the Senate
Comm. on the Judiciary. 87th Cong. 2nd Sess., April 4, 1962 at 12.

[111] *Ibid.* Reference in the Report is made in particular to Law of June 30, 1931,
modified by Law of July 10, 1934, and Decree of January 17, 1955, in *Belgium;* Decree
of November 30, 1944 in *France;* Foreign Trade Circular No. 89154 in *Germany;* and
Tabella Esport dated July 22, 1957, amended on August 13, 1960, in *Italy.* No mention is made in the Report, however, of the *U.K.'s* Import, Export and Customs Powers
(Defence) Act 1939 or, quite obviously, of the Export of Goods (Control) order 1967
which was issued pursuant to the 1939 Act after the date of the Report. For text *see*
S.I. 1967 No. 675 reprinted in SCHMITTHOFF, THE EXPORT TRADE 429–33 (5th ed.,
1969). The Dutch Laws of 1935 and 1962, referred to *infra,* are also not mentioned
in the Report.

[112] *See,* ADLER-KARLSSON, *supra* note 98, at 68.

[113] STAATSBLAD, No. 295. [114] *See* ADLER-KARLSSON, at 68.

[115] *Id.,* at 75–77.

[116] *See, e.g.,* ALLEN, SOVIET ECONOMIC WARFARE (1960).

trade. A list of the "Laws and Regulations relating to Control of Import and Export Trade in Member Countries" of the Asian-African Legal Consultative Committee also confirms that such restrictive practices have found their way into the legal systems of developing countries.[117]   In short, as Adler-Karlsson concluded in his exhaustive study of the subject, "the embargo policy has been world-wide." [118]

B. STATE PRACTICE IN TIME OF WAR

The right of a belligerent state to resort to measures of economic warfare against its adversary and to apply economic sanctions against third states which violate their obligations of neutrality in this regard is so manifest that elaborate treatment is unnecessary. It should be pointed out, however, that neutral states (such as the United States and the Netherlands supposedly were during the Arab-Israeli hostilities of October 1973) are under the obligation of acting towards belligerents in accordance with their attitude of impartiality. This means, in particular, abstention from "the supply in any manner, directly or indirectly, by a neutral Power to a belligerent Power, of warships, ammunition or war material of any kind whatever." [119]   It means also that a neutral power should not allow a belligerent to transport war materials or supplies over its territory.[120]   As the Dutch Government itself admitted in the course of World War I, a neutral state is bound to prevent the transit of materials likely to strengthen a belligerent when such materials are connected with military operations.[121] A breach of such obligations of neutrality entitles affected belligerents to take retaliatory action in the nature of reprisals [122] (including maritime embargo in the technical sense). It enables them, a fortiori, to resort to retorsion against the delinquent neutral by taking unfriendly or unfair acts in its regard (such as the imposition of an embargo on shipment of strategic goods destined to its ports). Such measures of reprisal or retorsion [123] are

---

[117] [Asian-African Legal Consultative Committee], ECONOMIC LAWS SERIES No. 1: LAWS AND REGULATIONS RELATING TO CONTROL OF IMPORT AND EXPORT TRADE IN MEMBER COUNTRIES, DECEMBER 1965.

[118] ADLER-KARLSSON, *supra* note 98, at 3.

[119] Art. 6 of Hague Convention XIII(1907) Respecting the Rights and Duties of Neutral Powers in Naval War. 36 Stat. 2415; TS 545; 1 BEVANS 723. *See also* Art. 44 of the "Rules of Aerial Warfare, 1923," drafted by a Commission of Jurists at The Hague, Dec. 1922–Feb. 1923, reproduced in GREENSPAN, THE LAW OF LAND WARFARE 650 (1959). For the general character of the international custom codified in these provisions *see*, 2 OPPENHEIM, *supra* note 43, at 686; Greenspan, *supra*, at 548.

[120] *See* Art. 2 of Hague Convention V(1907) concerning the Rights and Duties of Neutral Powers and Persons in Case of War on Land. 36 Stat. 2310; TS 540; 1 BEVANS 654. *And see* 2 OPPENHEIM, *supra* note 43, at 690.

[121] *See* the argument presented by the Netherlands in answer to Great Britain's protest over the transit of metals from occupied Belgium to Germany and of sand and gravel from Germany to Belgium during World War I, as reported in 2, OPPENHEIM, *supra* note 43, at 690–91.

[122] *Accord*, Greenspan, *supra* note 119, at 584.

[123] For a clear distinction between the two terms, as used in the above context, *see* 2 OPPENHEIM, *supra* note 43, at 136.

not merely punitive retaliatory acts, but must also be considered as instruments for discouraging the offending nonbelligerent from committing further violations of international law with regard to the injured party.

Under the controversial concept of differential or qualified neutrality in its modern sense, a neutral power might be able to discriminate against the belligerent whose recourse to war is unlawful.[124] Such a concept cannot therefore be cited in defense of a neutral state which supplies or helps in supplying war materials to a belligerent in order to enable it to maintain forcible control over territories of other states.   This should be particularly so when the military operations during which the supply of such war materials takes place are restricted to the area of the illegally occupied territories, as was the case in the Arab-Israeli hostilities of 1973.

The practice of states, especially that of the United States, in the course of World War II reveals the extent of the use of economic warfare measures, not only among belligerents but also by or against neutrals.   The oil policy adopted by the major powers during that war is particularly significant.   "It was the general aim of British policy to create an oil famine in Europe." [125]   In accordance with that policy, Great Britain requested the United States, early in 1940, and the latter agreed, to complete arrangements to ensure that no U.S. flag tankers would carry oil from the Americas to such "adjacent neutrals" in Europe as Spain and Portugal.[126]   The U.S. Government went further by proposing to cutoff all supplies of oil to foreign countries including Japan.[127]   A presidential order issued on July 25, 1940 extended the application of the Defense Act so that licences would be required for the export of petroleum and its products, and of scrap.[128] Six days later, the U.S. President ordered that export of aviation petrol should be restricted to the countries of the Western Hemisphere.[129]   Meanwhile the Soviet and Japanese Ambassadors in Washington were informed that "it was the policy of the U.S. Government to give Great Britain every help short of war and that they intended to give licences for all British oil requirements." [130]   As a result of such measures, Japan, which at the time was not at war with either the United States or Britain, and which was believed to be "very short of aviation oil," was deprived of American oil imports on which it was dependent for about two-thirds of its total import requirements.[131]   Furthermore, on September 26, 1940, the United States, while still a "neutral" power, declared an embargo on the export of iron and steel scrap as from October 16, 1940 "except to countries of the Western Hemisphere and to Great Britain." [132]

The relevance of the above practice is clear.   As explained earlier, Arab oil exporting countries were either cobelligerents against Israel in the hos-

---

[124] *See, e.g., id.*, at 651.

[125] I Medlicott, The Economic Blockade 474 (1952).

[126] *Id.*, at 476, Furthermore, Medlicott reports that, with a minor exception, "the British and American oil policies were virtually identical" even before the U.S. entered the war.   *Id.*, at 481.

[127] *Id.*, at 477.   [128] *Id.*, at 478.

[129] *Id.*, at 479.   [130] *Ibid.*

[131] *Id.*, at 480.   [132] *Id.*, at 485.

tilities of October 1973 or were merely "nonbelligerents." Along with Egypt and Syria, Iraq, Kuwait, and to a lesser degree, Algeria and Saudi Arabia participated in the war. They were thus definitely entitled to take retaliatory measures against such neutral powers as the United States, which supplied Israel, in the course of operations, with massive quantities of war materials, some of which are reported to have been delivered directly in Arab occupied territories. Sanctions were also justified against such states as the Netherlands and Portugal, which allowed the use of their territory for the transit of some of these war materials to Israel. Other Arab oil exporting countries were following the example of the United States in 1940 by curtailing the exportation of their oil to unfriendly countries. A great many countries have taken similar steps even in peacetime conditions.

It is much too simple to dismiss such an impressive state practice and the special role of the United States in it, both in peacetime and in war conditions, by merely stating that "the United States itself has been one of the worst offenders in using trade controls in ways which have adversely affected other countries." [133] No general rule of international custom denying states the power to use export controls for political purposes could have developed against the overwhelming weight of such a state practice. The basic elements required for the emergence of such a general customary rule are not only absent, they are negated, as shown above, by impressive evidence to the contrary.

IV.

LEGALITY OF ARAB OIL MEASURES UNDER PERTINENT RESOLUTIONS OF INTERNATIONAL ORGANIZATIONS:

A. UN DECLARATIONS

The UN General Assembly's Declaration of the Principles of International Law concerning Friendly Relations and Co-operation among States, which is generally treated as declaratory of contemporary international law, includes the following statement:

> No State may use or encourage the use of economic, political or any other type of measures to coerce another State in order to obtain from it the subordination of the exercise of its sovereign rights and to secure from it advantages of any kind.[134]

The seemingly general language of such a statement which has figured in

---

[133] Testimony of Professor Richard N. Gardner to the Sub-committee on International Economics of the Joint Economic Committee of the United States Congress, December 13, 1973, at 3. Professor Gardner admitted, however, that "the present state of international law in this area is most unsatisfactory" and that there was a clear need for "new rules."

[134] UN G.A. Res. 2625(XXV), Oct. 24, 1970, GAOR, 25th Sess., SUPP. No. 28 at 122–24 (A/8028).

earlier UN declarations of a more political nature,[135] certainly represents a progressive development, not a mere codification of the international practice described above. It should be read in the light of the following considerations:

(1) The statement cannot be read in isolation from other parts of the Declaration. That instrument includes, in particular, the following principle:

> The territory of a State shall not be the object of military occupation resulting from the use of force in contravention of the provisions of the Charter. The territory of a State shall not be the object of acquisition by another State resulting from the threat or use of force. No territorial acquisition resulting from the threat or use of force shall be recognized as legal.[136]

The Declaration also states that subjection of peoples to alien domination is contrary to the Charter and that the peoples deprived by forcible action of their right to self-determination "are entitled to seek and to receive support in accordance with the purposes and principles of the Charter." When the principles embodied in the latter statements are violated in regard to a certain state, one may reasonably assume from the reading of the entire text of the Declaration that such a state will not be deprived of the right to resort to economic measures of self-defense or of reprisal [137] against the states responsible, directly or indirectly, for that violation.

(2) Prohibition of the use of economic measures to coerce another state in order to secure advantages from it cannot be absolute in any case. "[A] certain degree of coercion is inevitable in States' day-to-day interactions for values. Fundamental community policy does not seek to reach and prohibit this coercion. . . ." [138] It will be necessary, therefore, to characterize unlawful economic measures by their objective, not merely by their effect,[139] and to limit this characterization to measures involving the subordinating of sovereign rights of other states, and not merely seeking some advantage from them.

---

[135] *See, e.g.,* Declaration on the Inadmissibility of Intervention in Domestic Affairs of States and the Protection of their Independence and Sovereignty, UN G.A. Res. 2131, Feb. 21, 1965, GAOR, 20th Sess., Supp. No. 14 at 12 (A/6220), described by the U.S. representative to the General Assembly as "a political Declaration with a vital political message, not as a declaration or elaboration of the law governing non-intervention." *Id.,* 1st Committee, 143rd Meeting, A/C.1/PV.1422, at 12.

[136] *Supra* note 34.

[137] *Cf.,* Bowett, *Economic Coercion and Reprisals by States,* 13 Va. J. Int'l L. 1, 7–9 (1972). Mr. Bowett further maintains that "there has been no agreement within the United Nations that economic reprisals are illegal under the Charter. Indeed, given the rather low level of compliance accorded by States to the prohibition of armed reprisals (footnote omitted), *it would seem excessively optimistic to argue that economic reprisals are illegal per se*" (emphasis added).

[138] McDougal and Feliciano, Law and Minimum World Public Order 197 (1961).

[139] *Accord,* Bowett, *supra* note 137, at 5.

(3) The statement under consideration may not, at any rate, be interpreted as imposing an obligation on states to make economic sacrifices for the benefit of other states without receiving a proper consideration therefor. If a state chooses to do favors for other countries at the expense of its long term economic interests, it is for that state to decide what advantage it should receive in return, as long as the required consideration is permissible under international law. The legitimacy of the action of such a state becomes all the more evident, when the consideration required by it is simply the cooperation of the recipients in ensuring respect of international law in regard to itself or to other states.[140]

(4) Finally, the language of the above-quoted statement assumes normal peacetime conditions. It cannot apply in an actual war situation where belligerent states are ordinarily entitled, in accordance with the rules of the law of war, to use their economic power to coerce their adversaries and even to inflict damage on third parties violating their obligations of neutrality towards them.

The statement of the Friendly Relations Declaration should also be read in conjunction with other general UN declarations, especially the General Assembly's resolutions on state sovereignty over natural resources. In 1960, the Assembly upheld "the sovereign right of every State to dispose of its wealth and its natural resources." [141] Such a sovereign right to the free disposition of natural resources is confirmed by subsequent resolutions of the Assembly and of UNCTAD's Trade and Development Board.[142] It includes in particular the freedom of each state to develop rules and conditions which it considers "necessary or desirable with regard to the *authorization, restriction* or *prohibition*" of such activities as exploration, development, and disposition of natural resources.[143] More recently, the UN General Assembly deplored actions aimed at coercing states engaged in the exercise of their "sovereign rights over their natural resources" as violations of the Charter and of the Friendly Relations Declaration.[144]

---

[140] In the light of the above, one may differentiate between the U.S. practice under the Battle Act, where U.S. assistance is tied to the recipient's adoption of economic sanctions against third states which are not necessarily guilty of a breach of international law, and the Arab oil measures, which practically made the unlimited supply of oil dependent on the expression of friendly attitudes towards the Arabs' claim for the restoration of the *status juris* in the Middle East.

[141] UN G.A. Res. 1515(XV), GAOR, 15th Sess., Dec. 15, 1960.

[142] *See,* UNCTAD: Resolution on Permanent Sovereignty over Natural Resources, Oct. 19, 1972, UN Doc. TD/B/421 of Nov. 5, 1972 (335th meeting) where reference is made to all earlier UN General Assembly resolutions on this matter.

[143] *See,* e.g., UN G.A. Res. 1803(XVII), GAOR, 17th Sess., Dec. 14, 1962 (emphasis added). For a study of this and earlier UN resolutions in their application to Arab Oil, *see,* MUGHRABY, PERMANENT SOVEREIGNTY OVER OIL RESOURCES (1966).

[144] UN G.A. Res. 3016(XXVII), GAOR, 27th Sess., Dec. 18, 1972; Res. 3171 (XXVIII), GAOR, 28th Sess. Dec. 17, 1973. It is surprising therefore to see these two resolutions, which are obviously meant to strengthen the right of states over *their* natural resources against coercion from consuming countries, cited against Arab states, in Paust and Blaustein, *supra* note 11, at 420–21.

When Arab oil measures were in full force, the Assembly, far from condemning them, affirmed "the right of the Arab States and Peoples whose territories are under foreign occupation to permanent sovereignty over all their natural resources." [145]

The prohibition of "economic coercion" expressed in the Friendly Relations Declaration cannot therefore be an absolute injunction in the *lex lata* of international law. It is not a restatement of the wider and more controversial concept of "economic aggression." [146] The latter concept was found, early in 1952, to be "particularly liable to extend the concept of aggression almost indefinitely" [147]:

> The acts in question not only do not involve the use of force, but are usually carried out by a State by virtue of its sovereignty or discretionary power. Where there are no commitments a State is free to fix its customs tariff and to limit or prohibit exports and imports.[148]

In the above context, the prohibition of economic coercion should be realistically limited to the use by states of economic measures for achieving illegitimate purposes. According to this interpretation it is the objective of the measures that stands out as the most pertinent criterion for their legitimacy.

B. ACTION AUTHORIZED OR REQUESTED BY INTERNATIONAL ORGANIZATIONS

Economic coercion, including the embargo on shipments of strategic materials to countries in need of them, has also been stipulated by international organizations as an appropriate method for securing collective policy objectives of a noneconomic character. Sanctions of this type have by no means been confined to measures applied by the Security Council under Article 41 of the UN Charter or authorized by it for adoption by regional agencies, pursuant to Article 53(1) of the Charter.

The Security Council is certainly qualified, under these provisions, to employ coercive economic measures and to call upon states to apply them, as it has done in fact with regard to Rhodesia (general embargo on trade including specifically the supply of oil and oil products) [149] and to South

---

[145] UN G.A. Res. 3175(XXVIII), GAOR, 28th Sess., Dec. 17, 1973.

[146] Recent proposals in the United Nations on the definition of aggression seem content to leave out economic coercion at this stage at least. *See*, the USSR Draft in UN Doc. A/AC 134/L.12 (1969); Draft of the thirteen non-committed Powers in, *id.*, A/AC 134/L.16 (1969); and Add. 1 & 2; Draft of the eight Western Powers in, *id.* A/AC 134/L.17 (1969); and draft definition adopted by the Special Committee and forwarded to the General Assembly A/AC. 134/L.46 (1974).

[147] *See, Report by the Secretary-General of the United Nations on the Question of defining Aggression*, GAOR, 7th Sess., Agenda Item 54, UN Doc. A/2211, at 74.

[148] *Ibid. And see* Schwebel, *Aggression, Intervention and Self-Defence in Modern International Law*, RECUEIL DES COURS 413, 449–52 (II, 1972).

[149] *See*, S/Res/217 (1965), Nov. 20, 1965; S/Res/221 (1966), April 9, 1966; S/Res/ 232 (1966), Dec. 16, 1966; S/Res/253 (1968), May 29, 1968; S/Res/277 (1970), March 18, 1970; S/Res/314 (1972), Feb. 28, 1972; S/Res/318 (1972), July 28, 1972; S/Res/320 (1972), Sept. 29, 1972.

Africa (embargo on the supply of arms and ammunition).[150] Similar actions have also been authorized by the UN General Assembly. Early in 1951, the Assembly recommended that every state impose "an embargo on the shipment to areas under the control of the Central People's Government of the People's Republic of China and of the North Korean authorities" of many strategic materials including petroleum.[151] On other occasions, the Assembly has called upon states or Specialized Agencies to withhold financial, economic, and technical assistance from certain countries.[152] For instance, it has specifically invited "all States" to "avoid actions, including actions in the field of aid, that could constitute recognition of [Israel's] occupation" of Arab territories.[153]

Coercive economic measures were also authorized by the O.A.S. with regard to the Dominican Republic in 1961 and to Cuba in 1962 and 1964.[154] The O.A.U. has similarly assumed competence to authorize and request the adoption of such measures against such states as South Africa,[155] Portugal,[156] Rhodesia,[157] and, indeed, Israel.[158] The recent Resolution 21

---

[150] See, S/Res/181 (1963), Aug. 7, 1963; S/Res/182 (1963), Dec. 4, 1963; S/Res/191 (1964), June 18, 1964; S/Res/282 (1970), July 23, 1970; S/Res/311 (1972), Feb. 9, 1972.

[151] UN G.A. Res. 500(V), May 18, 1951, GAOR, 5th Sess., Supp., No. 20A, A/1775/Add.1 (1951), at 2.

[152] See, e.g., UN G.A., Res. 2107(XX), Dec. 21, 1965; UN G.A., Res. 2311(XXII), Dec. 14, 1967; UN G.A. Res. 2426(XXIII), Jan. 8, 1969 (with respect to South Africa and Portugal).

[153] UN G.A., Res. 2949(XXVIII), Dec. 8, 1972.

[154] See a discussion of these measures and of the question of the competence of a regional organization such as the O.A.S. to authorize them in the absence of a prior authorization from the Security Council in Claude, The OAS, The UN and the United States, 347 Int. Conciliation 1 (March 1964); Halderman, Regional Enforcement Measures and the United Nations, 52 Georgia L.J. 89 (1963).

[155] See, e.g., OAU Doc. CIAS/Plen.2/Rev.2, May 25, 1963 in Resolutions Adopted by the Conference of Heads of States and Governments of Independent African Countries 1963–1972 at 3, 5; AHG/Res. 5(1), 6(1), July 21, 1964, id., 20, 21; AHG/Res/34(11), Oct. 25, 1965, id., 49. Res. 6(1) of 1964 appealed to all oil producing countries to impose an embargo on shipment to South Africa of oil and oil products. See also the following resolutions of OAU Council of Ministers: CM/Res. 6(1), 11 August 1963, 1 Resolutions, Recommendations and Statements Adopted by the Ordinary and Extraordinary Sessions of the Council of Ministers 1963–1967 at 5 (May 1973); CM/Res. 31(III), July 17, 1964, id., 29; CM/Res. 48(IV), March 9, 1965, id., 50, CM/Res. 66(V), Oct. 21, 1965, id., 74; CM/Res. 68(VII), Nov. 4, 1966, id., 102; CM/Res. 102(IX), Sept. 10, 1967, id., 122; CM/Res/138(X), Feb. 24, 1968, 2 id., 1968–1973 at 7, CM/Res. 242/Rev. 1(XVII), June 19, 1971, id., 141; CM/Res. 269(XIX), June 12, 1972, id., 183.

[156] See, e.g., OAU Doc. CIAS/Plen. 2/Rev. 2 supra note 155; AHG/Res. 9(1), July 24, 1964, id., 26; AHG/Res. 35(11), Oct. 25, 1965, id., 52. And see, CM/Res. 6(1), supra note 155; CM/Res. 83(VII), Nov. 4, 1966, id., 99; CM/Res. 137(X), Feb. 24, 1968, 2 id., 5; CM/Res. 268(XIX), June 12, 1972, id., 178; CM/Res. 272(XIX), June 12, 1972, id., 193.

[157] See, OAU Doc. CM/Res. 62(V), Oct. 21, 1965, id. 70, ECM/Res. 13(VI), Dec. 5, 1965, id. 86; CM/Res. 78(VII), Nov. 4, 1966, id. 94; CM/Res. 102(IX), Sept. 10, 1967,

(1973) of the Council of Ministers of that organization specifically calls upon states to "impose a total economic embargo, particularly on the supply of oil, against Israel, Portugal, South Africa and the racist minority regime of Southern Rhodesia." [159]

With the exception of the 1951 UN General Assembly resolution on China and North Korea, these measures were authorized in peacetime. The measures recommended in the latter resolution were to be taken, on the other hand, by "every State" including nonbelligerents and thus were not meant to be a mere exercise of the rights of belligerents under the law of war.

Such precedents may well be cited in support of the Arab oil measures as a supplementary basis for their lawfulness. On the one hand, they further prove the prevailing trend in international practice, whereby the application of coercive measures is clearly differentiated from the use of armed force, which is subject to a much more restrictive set of rules. On the other hand, they do explain a certain aspect of the legal background of Arab oil measures. These measures were not only sanctioned by the Summit Arab Conference, the highest organ of the League of Arab States; they were also taken in compliance with previous resolutions of other international organizations in so far as they applied to Rhodesia, South Africa, and Portugal. Furthermore, the embargo on the supply of oil to Rhodesia is a legal obligation incumbent on Arab states by virtue of binding decisions of the Security Council.

V.

LEGALITY OF ARAB OIL MEASURES UNDER TREATY LAW

A. MULTILATERAL CONVENTIONS

Of all existing multilateral trade conventions, the General Agreement on Tariffs and Trade (GATT)[160] seems to be the only one that has some bearing on our discussion. Other multilateral trade conventions either do not regulate quantitative export controls, or do not include any of the Arab oil exporting countries among their parties. As for the GATT, Egypt and Kuwait are contracting parties to it while Algeria, Bahrain, and Qatar have accepted its *de facto* application to them.[161] These countries have participated, as shown above,[162] in the oil cutback and embargo resolutions.

---

id. 116; CM/Res/10(IX), Sept. 10, 1967, *id.* 133; CM/Res/207(XIV), March 6, 1970, 2 *id.* 86; CM/Res. 269(XVIII), Feb. 19, 1972, *id.* 164; CM/Res. 267(XIX), June 12, 1972, *id.* 175.

[158] *See,* OAU Doc., ECM/Res. 21(VIII), Nov. 21, 1973.

[159] *Ibid.,* para. 20.

[160] Signed at Geneva on Oct. 30, 1947, TIAS 1700; 55–61 UNTS.

[161] *See,* TREATIES IN FORCE. A list of Treaties and Other International Agreements of the United States in Force on January 1, 1974, at 330. (Dept. of State Pub. 8755).

[162] *See supra* note 7.

Article 11 of the GATT contains a general prohibition, subject to exceptions irrelevant to our discussion, on quantitative restrictions imposed on imports or exports "through quotas, import or export licences or other measures." Prohibition or restriction of imports and exports are also to be administered, pursuant to Article 13(1), without discrimination against "all third countries." Furthermore, Article 1, which is entitled "General Most-Favoured-Nation Treatment," provides for the automatic extension to like products imported from or exported to other parties, of any advantage granted by a party in respect of, *inter alia,* "all rules and formalities in connection with importation or exportation."

Such provisions, if read in isolation from other parts of the Agreement, may give the erroneous impression that contracting Arab states are under a general and absolute prohibition in the employment of discriminatory export controls against other contracting parties such as the United States and the Netherlands. The GATT, much like any other treaty, must, however, be read in its entirety.[163] Pursuant to other provisions of the GATT, the above-quoted general principles are subject to two types of exceptions. The "general exceptions" provided for in Article 20 include in particular the right of each party to take measures "relating to the conservation of exhaustible natural resources." Such measures must be made effective "in conjunction with restrictions on domestic production *or* consumption," and "should not apply in a manner which would constitute a means of arbitrary or unjustified discrimination between countries where the same conditions prevail or a disguised restriction on international trade . . ." These conditions obviously obtain in the case of production cutbacks employed for the purpose of conserving a depleting resource such as oil. More importantly, the "security exceptions" contained in Article 21 allow each contracting party to take "any action which *it considers* necessary for the protection of its essential security interests," if such an action is taken "in time of war or other emergency in international relations." It is significant to note that in the latter provision the Agreement maintains the freedom of each party to estimate the necessity of the action it takes in such exceptional circumstances. Even if necessity is to be judged by objective criteria, one may easily recognize its relevance in a wartime situation when the vital interests of the state are at stake. Discretion of the state in such matters is, indeed, a question of public policy,[164] which may restrict the application of the most favored-nation clause even in the absence of explicit provisions.[165]

It is true that Article 22(1) of the GATT requires each contracting party to accord "sympathetic consideration" to, and to afford "adequate opportu-

---

[163] *See,* H. Lauterpacht, *Restrictive Interpretation and the Principle of Effectiveness in the Interpretation of Treaties,* 26 BYIL 76 (1949). *And see* for possible exceptions, not warranted in the above context, McNair, *supra* note 79, at 474–84.

[164] *See,* T. FLORY, LE G.A.T.T.—DROIT INTERNATIONAL ET COMMERCE MONDIAL 83 (1968), where the security exceptions in GATT's Article 21 are also described as constituting matters within the "domestic jurisdiction" of each party.

[165] *See,* a discussion of this point in relation to bilateral trade agreements, *infra* pp. 623–25.

nity for consultation" with other parties. However, such an obligation is incumbent upon a contracting party only after it receives "such representations as may be made by another contracting party with respect to any matter affecting the operation of this Agreement." Consultation cannot therefore be a precondition for taking measures, but is merely a procedure devised in the GATT to secure satisfaction to the injured party in cases of alleged violations.[166] None of the contracting parties affected by the Arab oil measures has submitted representations under Article 22 of the GATT; nor have they resorted to the nullification or impairment procedure provided for in Article 23 of that Agreement.

Article 35 of the Agreement provides, on the other hand, for its non-application between any two contracting parties which have not entered into tariff negotiations with each other. No such negotiations were entered into, however, between the State of Kuwait, which is the only Arab oil exporting contracting party, and any other party to the GATT. It may also be relevant to note that the United States had long implemented an oil import program which gave practical preferences to such states as its neighbor Canada,[167] notwithstanding the above-quoted general principles of the GATT. These points need not be over emphasized, however, in view of the fact that Arab oil measures are perfectly justified under Article 21 of the Agreement, which effectively suspends its operation under emergency conditions.[168]

B. BILATERAL TREATIES

The relevant bilateral trade agreements concluded between Arab oil exporting countries and countries affected by the Arab oil embargo seem to be limited to three agreements[169] concluded between the United States and Saudi Arabia, Iraq, and Oman, respectively, before any of these latter countries was significantly involved in the export of oil. None of these agreements, it is submitted, presented a legal barrier to the implementation of the Arab oil measures vis-a-vis the United States. Although all agreements include a most-favored-nation clause, the special wording used in each agreement warrants its independent examination.

The U.S.-Saudi Arabia Agreement of 1933[170] confined the application of

[166] *Cf.*, DAM, THE GATT, LAW AND INTERNATIONAL ECONOMIC ORGANIZATION 221 (1970).

[167] *See* a description of U.S. practice in, James III, *Comment, The Mandatory Oil Import Program: A Review of Present Regulations and Proposals for Change in the 1970's*, 7 TEX. INT'L L.J. 373 (1972).

[168] *See also* the testimony of Prof. R. N. Gardner referred to in note 133 *supra*, where he emphatically states that all the GATT principles on discrimination are "effectively vitiated" by Article 21 thereof.

[169] The above statement is based on information obtained from some of the Foreign Offices of the Arab states involved, supported by the results of a review of the League of Nations Treaty Series, the United Nations Treaty Series, and the U.S. TREATIES IN FORCE referred to in note 161, *supra*.

[170] Provisional Agreement in regard to Diplomatic and Consular Representation, Judicial Protection, Commerce and Navigation, signed at London on Nov. 7, 1933, 48

the most-favored-nation clause included in its Article 3 to treatment "[i]n respect of import, export and other *duties* and *charges* affecting commerce and navigation, as well as in respect of *transit, warehousing* and *other facilities.*" Such a wording obviously excludes quantitative restrictions on exports from the scope of the clause. The same article mentions also "any . . . regulation affecting commerce or navigation," but this is only in stating that *concessions* with respect to them will be immediately reciprocated. Even if the oil measures applied by Saudi Arabia were to be characterized as involving "concessions," [171] a presumption in favor of an exception on grounds of national security interests can well be derived from a treaty of this type.[172] A similar presumption may also be established "in favor of the overriding character of exemptions on grounds of international public policy." [173] As explained earlier in this article, the Saudi oil embargo was applied in an attempt to secure an objective of the highest international order: The restoration to the lawful sovereigns of illegally occupied territories and the restoration of the rights of peoples deprived of self-determination.

The U.S.–Iraq Agreement of 1938 [174] explicitly provides, in Article 2, that "in all that concerns matters of prohibition or restrictions on importations and exportations each of the two countries will accord, whenever they may have recourse to the said prohibitions or restrictions, to the commerce of the other country, treatment equally favourable to that which is accorded to any other country . . ." Article 4 is equally explicit, however, in permitting exceptions relating to "the adoption or enforcement of measures relating to neutrality or to rights and obligations arising under the Covenant of the League of Nations." Such a codification of the "international public policy exception" could obviously be invoked by Iraq against the United States, which deviated from its obligations of neutrality in the course of the Arab-Israeli hostilities in which Iraqi forces were involved. It should be noted, however, that Iraq did not concur in the cutback and embargo resolutions of the Arab Oil Ministers, and that exportation of its oil through the East Mediterranean terminals was halted due to Israeli military action.[175]

Stat. 1826 (1933); 11 BEVANS 5456; 142 LNTS 329. The Agreement does not extend, pursuant to Article (4) thereof, to the treatment which the United States accords to the commerce of Cuba and the Panama Canal zone.

[171] As is implied in the testimony of Professor R. N. Gardner referred to in note 133 *supra*, and in his statement quoted in "Saudi Oil Embargo Termed Breach of '33 Treaty with U.S.," N.Y. Times, Dec. 19, 1973, at 12, col. 4.

[172] *Accord*, Schwarzenberger, *The Most-Favoured-Nation Standard in British State Practice*, 22 BYIL 96, 110, 111 (1945).

[173] *Id.*, at 111, 120.

[174] Treaty of Commerce and Navigation, signed at Baghdad, Dec. 3, 1938, 54 Stat. 1790 (1940); TS960; 9 BEVANS 7; 203 LNTS 107. According to the treaty, extension of advantages given by the United States does not include advantages accorded to Cuba, the Panama Canal Zone, border traffic zones, and states in Customs Unions (Art. 1).

[175] *See, supra* note 4.

Finally the trade agreement concluded in 1958 between the United States and the "Sultanate of Muscat and Oman and Dependencies" [176] prohibits, in Article 8, the imposition by either party of restrictions on the exportation of any product to the territories of the other party "unless the exportation of the like product to all third countries is similarly restricted or prohibited." Such a provision, which admittedly would preclude Oman under normal conditions from implementing discriminatory embargo measures on oil shipments to the United States, is restricted, however, by the text of Article 11(d) of the same Agreement. According to this latter article the agreement does not preclude the application of measures "necessary to fulfil the obligations of a Party for the maintenance or restoration of international peace and security, or necessary to protect its essential security interests." The internal security interests of that country would certainly have been further impaired had it deviated from the collective Arab stand adopted during the war crisis. It is unofficially reported, at any rate, that Oman, which is not an OAPEC member, has not participated in the meetings of Arab Oil Ministers, and was the last Arab country to declare an embargo on oil shipments to the United States, was quite lenient in applying that measure, and was the first to lift it.

It may be worth repeating in this respect that the United States has felt free in normal peacetime to impose a quota system for the import of oil, which discriminated in favor of oil imported from certain countries other than Saudi Arabia, Iraq, and Oman. The preferential treatment given under that system to certain countries, such as Canada, could hardly conform to the standards provided for in the above-mentioned agreements. It is not surprising, therefore, that the U.S. Government has not officially characterized the measures adopted by these Arab countries with respect to the export of their oil in a crisis situation as constituting a breach of treaty commitments on their part.

VI.

CONCLUSION

In the light of the above analysis, the destination embargo of Arab oil may now be viewed in its right perspective. Far from being a "weapon for blackmailing the West" or a "threat to international peace," it has been employed as an instrument for the respect and promotion of the rule of law in an area of international relations where such a rule has long been forsaken for the rule of superior military force. In their use of that instrument, Arab oil exporting countries were in fact following the steps of a great number of other states which have used their export regulations to

[176] Treaty of Amity, Economic Relations and Consular Rights (with Protocol) signed at Salalah on Dec. 20, 1958, 11 UST 1835; TIAS No. 4530; 380 UNTS 181. Each party reserved the right to accord special advantages to "adjacent countries" or by virtue of a customs union (Art VIII (4)). Application of the treaty does not extend to Cuba, the Philippines, trusteeship territories in the Pacific, and the Panama Canal Zone.

further their foreign policies.   Only the objective of the Arab states seems
to have been more legitimate.   The Arab states took that measure not to
weaken unfriendly countries but merely to discourage third countries from
violating their obligations of neutrality toward them and from continuing
their encouragement of, or their acquiescence in, an illegal situation.   The
Arab states have considered it their moral responsibility to keep the indus-
trialized nations fueled with Arab exhaustible oil, in spite of their awareness that such a policy may not serve their best selfish economic interests.
They were not to be expected, however, to do favors indefinitely for states
which had refused to cooperate with them in putting an end to the illegal
occupation and annexation of Arab territories and to the continuing denial
of the right of the Palestinian people to self-determination.

The oil measures taken by the Arab states were the result of the exercise
of their "sovereign right" to dispose of their natural resources in the manner
which best suits their legitimate interests.   In exercising that right, the
Arab states have not violated any established rule of international custom
or any prior treaty commitments.   To accuse them of abuses in the exercise
of that right by questioning its necessity and proportionality is to assume
a simplistic wisdom that does not befit the circumstances of the case.   After
all other measures had been exhausted in vain, it could hardly have been
deemed unnecessary for the Arab states to resort to economic pressure for
the restoration of Arab occupied homeland.   Such a pressure was readily
available in the field of oil supply as the Arab states had little influence
outside this field vis-a-vis the countries concerned.   When the pressure
proved to be particularly damaging to countries relatively remote from the
dispute, as in the case of Japan, or when affected countries showed a slight
concern for the legitimate demands of Arab states, the Arab oil measures
were almost immediately lifted with regard to them.   This is to be compared with the intransigent stand of Israel which—opposing the interests
of the international community in the uninterrupted supply of Arab oil—
has insisted in the face of these measures on the continuation of its forcible
occupation of territories of Arab states.

A general and absolute prohibition on the use of economic measures for
political purposes in the international sphere is still an idealist's dream.
Before it hardens into a rule of international law, enforcement machinery
must develop for the protection of the militarily weaker states, which may
happen to have a relatively great economic power.   Precluding such states
from the use of their economic power in the settlement of political disputes
before a general ban is imposed on armaments and in the absence of an
effective collective security system could not serve the interests of international justice.   It would only help the development of what President
Roosevelt once described as "a one-way international law which lacks
mutuality in its observance and therefore becomes an instrument of oppression." [177]

---

[177] The President's message to Congress of Jan. 6, 1941, cited in GREENSPAN, *supra*
note 119, at 519.

In retrospect, the Arab oil measures have proved to be an effective instrument for reestablishing concern for the long-awaited peace in the Middle East. The new direction in the U.S. policy in that area has no doubt been influenced by the U.S. energy needs and its dependence on Arab oil for meeting them. Inasmuch as that new direction is characterized by evenhandedness, it is likely to serve the general interests of the international community for peace and justice in an area where both elements have long been lacking. It should also serve the best interests of the United States itself. Arab oil limitation will also probably turn out to have been a blessing in disguise for the United States in another sense, "for without it a crash alternative source program would have come later, if at all." [178] Arab oil measures may even prove, in a wider perspective, to have been a blessing for all parties to the Middle East conflict, including Israel. To the extent that the application of these measures was a major factor in the efforts presently being undertaken for reaching a lasting and just settlement of the Arab-Israeli dispute, they should be partially credited for the outstanding results. It is this settlement, not the forcible occupation and the arrogance of power practiced by Israel since 1967, which is the best guarantee for the security of all the states of the Middle East and for the long term interests of their peoples.

[178] W. E. Griffith, *The Fourth Middle East War, the Energy Crisis and U.S. Policy,* 17 ORBIS 1161, 1185 n.23 (1974).

The Illegality of the Arab Attack on Israel of October 6, 1973

EUGENE V. ROSTOW

In part II of his article, *Destination Embargo of Arab Oil: Its Legality under International Law*,[1] Mr. Ibrahim F. I. Shihata defends the legality of the armed attack on Israel launched by many Arab states, with Soviet assistance, on October 6, 1973. "Egypt and Syria," he writes, "as the states vested with sovereignty, but illegally deprived of actual control, over territories occupied by Israel were . . . entitled to seek redress for the protection of their territorial integrity. Under the UN system they were probably under the obligation to resort first to peaceful methods. This they have done in vain for more than six years. Egypt, in particular, expressed officially its readiness to enter into a peace agreement with Israel containing all the obligations provided for in Security Council Resolution 242 (1967) as broadly elaborated by the Special Representative of the UN Secretary-General, Ambassador Jarring. In response, Israel defiantly insisted on territorial expansion."[2] Under these circumstances, he

---

* Sterling Professor of Law and Public Affairs, Yale University. As Undersecretary of State (1966–1969), I was Chairman of an Interdepartmental Control Group responsible for preparing, proposing, and supervising the execution of the plans of the United States Government for dealing with the Middle East crisis of that period. Perhaps I should add that while the views expressed in this article are those I have developed in the course of my teaching and study in the field during the last five years, they coincide with the official positions of the United States Government during the period of my service, and, it is believed, since that time.

[1] 68 AJIL 591, 598–608 (1974), hereafter cited as SHIHATA.

[2] SHIHATA, 607. It is important to note that Mr. Shihata correctly bases his argument on the only possible legal ground for his claim, the law of Article 51, and the relation between Article 51 and Article 2(4). He does not invoke the theories which seek to justify the international use of force in behalf of "Wars of National Liberation." Thus Mr. Shihata does *not* contend that the Arab armed attack of October 6, 1973, was justified in order to vindicate an alleged right of the Arab inhabitants of Palestine to use force internationally in behalf of their claims of self-determination, or pursuant to resolutions of the Arab League viewed as a regional arrangement under Chapter VIII of the Charter. Such arguments would justify the international use of force to destroy a state, and are incompatible with Article 2(4) of the Charter, its most fundamental principle, which assures each state protection against the threat or use of force against its territorial integrity or political independence, "or in any other manner inconsistent with the Purposes of the United Nations." The theory of such "Wars of National Liberation" has been consistently rejected by every authoritative process of international decisionmaking on many occasions since 1945.

The argument for a right to wage war internationally in behalf of the right of peoples to self-determination under Article 1(2) of the Charter was made by Yasir Arafat in his speech before the General Assembly on November 13, 1974. Mr. Arafat asserted that the Palestine Mandate and all the decisions and other resolutions of the Security Council flowing from it are null and void, and that the existence of Israel in

argues, both Egypt and Syria (which had never accepted any version of Security Council Resolution 242 or given any assurances to Ambassador Jarring) had an inherent right of self-help under customary international law, or of self-defense under "a broad reading" of Article 51 of the Charter, in what he asserts was no more than an attempt to recover those territories by force.[3]

Presumably Mr. Shihata would add that because in his view Egypt and Syria were legally exercising their right of self-defense in attacking the Israelis on October 6, 1973, states other than Egypt and Syria had the right under customary international law and under Article 51 to assist Egypt and Syria in the name of the principle of collective self-defense, until the Security Council decided otherwise.

Mr. Shihata's legal justification for the Arab attack of October 6, 1973, then, depends upon a chain of related propositions: (1) that in 1973, at

---

parts of the territory of the Palestine Mandate is therefore a deprivation of the rights of the Palestinian people to self-determination—a standing "armed attack" against those "rights." For this reason, he claimed a right to use force internationally to achieve a single unified state in the entire territory of Palestine. (In international law and international relations, the word "Palestine" can only mean the territory of the Palestine Mandate, which remained under British Administration until the end of the League, and the establishment of Transjordan and Israel as separate states.) New York Times, Nov. 14, 1974, at 22–23. On the status of these contentions in international law, see Rostow, Book Review, 82 Yale L. J. 829, 842–55 (1973); Q. Wright and M. Khadduri, The Palestine Conflict in International Law, in M Khadduri, ed., Major Middle Eastern Problems in International Law 25–26 (1972): "The recognition of a distinctive people, whether within a colony or the home territory of a state, or scattered throughout the world, is inconsistent with the rights of the state within whose territory they live. Such recognition involves political and legal change but, in accord with the Charter, must not involve the use of force by outside states." The General Assembly resolution defining aggression (UN Doc. A/Res 3314 (XXIX), Dec. 14, 1974) fully accepts the view that rights of self-determination can be vindicated only by methods which are in conformity with the Charter. Art. 7, Art. 3(f) and (g). For full text, see Official Documents section, infra p. 480.

[3] Shihata, 607–08. Mr. Shihata makes two inconsistent arguments on this point: (1) that the continued occupation by Israel of the territories it conquered in 1967 (in the course of exercising its own right of self-defense) is an "armed attack" for purposes of Article 51; and (2) that Article 51 is not in any event relevant, since Egypt and Syria should be deemed to have a right to use force to regain those territories, as an essential aspect of their right to territorial integrity. "Without such a right," Mr. Shihata says, "state jurisdiction, let alone sovereignty, would be nothing but a sham." Id., at 608.

I am unable to detect the difference between Mr. Shihata's two arguments in the perspective of the Charter, which authorizes states to use force internationally by their own unilateral decision only in cases of individual or collective self-defense, or in circumstances which do not constitute a breach of Article 2(4), i.e., humanitarian interventions, and interventions to assist a state in repressing a rebellion, an attempt at secession, or a rebellion supported from abroad. The Biafran case is the paradigm of the latter class: there Soviet, British, and Egyptian assistance to Nigeria was treated as obviously lawful, while any attempt to assist the Biafrans, asserting their "right" of national self-determination as a people, was treated as a violation of Article 2(4). See Rostow, supra, note 2. Thus each of Mr. Shihata's alternative arguments turns on the legality of Israel's presence in the disputed territory as the occupying power.

least, Israel was illegally in possession of the territories occupied in the course of the Six Day War in 1967; (2) that Israel had refused to follow the peacemaking procedures called for, under Chapter VI of the Charter, by the Security Council in 1967, which in his view Egypt (but not Syria) had accepted; (3) that no peaceful remedies were available, and the other criteria which have evolved in international law from the *Caroline* episode, the *Alabama* arbitration, and the *Corfu Channel* case had been satisfied; [4] (4) and therefore that Israel's presence in the Golan Heights and the Sinai as an occupying power constituted an "armed attack" on Egypt and Syria, and justified their large scale attack of October 6, 1973, as a legitimate act of self-defense. He implies that the same rationale would apply to the West Bank and the Gaza Strip as well, although neither Jordan nor Egypt could claim "sovereignty" over those disputed territories.

Mr. Shihata's chain of reasoning would be in error even if Israel's presence in the territories it occupied during the 1967 war did violate the Security Council's 1967 cease-fire resolutions and its Resolution 242. Many, many procedures of negotiation, mediation, "good offices," and conciliation, both within the United Nations and outside it, have been pressed upon Egypt and Syria by dozens of governments since 1967. All those attempts failed. The Syrian Government flatly refused to accept Security Council Resolution 242 in any form or to consider any other procedure for making peace. Until 1971, Egypt rejected many proposals that would have required it to make peace with Israel. In 1971, as Mr. Shihata notes, Egypt did agree to make peace, but only on terms which the Security Council had rejected when Resolution 242 was adopted. The heart of the dispute, nominally at least, has been whether Resolution 242 required Israeli commitment, in advance of negotiations, to withdrawal from *all* the occupied territories at issue.[5] Under Article 33 of the Charter, the parties, or the Security Council, could have sought a judicial interpretation of Resolution 242, or an arbitration, in order to determine its meaning. All procedures for the pacific settlement of the dispute based on Security Council Resolution 242 have been rejected by Egypt and Syria. The option of making peace in accordance with that resolution was always open to Syria, Jordan, Lebanon, and Egypt.

But Mr. Shihata's major premise—that Israel's presence in the occupied territories is illegal—is an assertion which cannot be made. For the present writer, who participated officially in the negotiations which led to the adoption of Security Council Resolution 242 in November, 1967, and in the unremitting efforts of the American Government between November, 1967, and January 20, 1969, to persuade Egypt to implement its terms, Mr.

---

[4] On the history of the *Caroline* episode, *see* 2 J. B. Moore, Digest of International Law 409–14 (1906); 11 M. Whiteman, Digest of International Law 211–36 (1968); for the *Alabama* arbitration, Papers Relating to the Treaty of Washington (1872–1873) 5 vols.; Corfu Channel Case, [1949] ICJ Rep. 4. *See* I. Brownlie, International Law and the Use of Force by States ch. 12–13 (1963); D. W. Bowett, Self-Defence in International Law (1958); M. McDougal and F. Feliciano, Law and Minimum World Public Order ch. 2–3 (1961).

[5] *See infra*, p. 283 *et seq.*

Shihata's argument is fantasy.[6] It rests on an erroneous interpretation of Resolution 242, which was confirmed and made mandatory under Article 25 as a "decision" by Security Council Resolution 338 of October 22, 1973.[7]

[6] Between November, 1967, and January 20, 1969, Egypt refused every proposal for a negotiating procedure that might permit the parties to carry out Resolution 242. Those involving Ambassador Jarring are reported by the Secretary-General on the activities of the Special Representatives to the Middle East, UN Doc. S/10070, Jan. 4, 1971, SECURITY COUNCIL OFFICIAL RECORDS (SCOR), SUPP. FOR JANUARY, FEBRUARY, AND MARCH, 1971, at 18 (1972) [hereafter referred to as the Secretary-General's Report]. There were many others. In the fall of 1968, the United States offered to support the terms Egypt professed to want as the price for peace, the return of the whole of the Sinai in accordance with an agreed timetable. The offer was rejected by the Egyptian Foreign Minister at the time, Mahmoud Riad. I am satisfied that the Egyptian official position on making peace, save for the abortive Jarring proposal of February 8, 1971, on which Mr. Shihata relies (discussed *infra*, at p. 285), remained the same until October 6, 1973.

[7] The texts of the two resolutions are as follows:

Resolution 242 (1967)

The Security Council,

Expressing its continuing concern with the grave situation in the Middle East,

Emphasizing the inadmissibility of the acquisition of territory by war and the need to work for a just and lasting peace in which every State in the area can live in security,

Emphasizing further that all Member States in their acceptance of the Charter of the United Nations have undertaken a commitment to act in accordance with Article 2 of the Charter,

1. *Affirms* that the fulfillment of Charter principles requires the establishment of a just and lasting peace in the Middle East which should include the application of both the following principles:

(i) Withdrawal of Israeli armed forces from territories occupied in the recent conflict;

(ii) Termination of all claims or states of belligerency and respect for and acknowledgement of the sovereignty, territorial integrity and political independence of every State in the area and their right to live in peace within secure and recognized boundaries free from threats or acts of force;

2. *Affirms further* the necessity

(a) For guaranteeing freedom of navigation through international waterways in the area;

(b) For achieving a just settlement of the refugee problem;

(c) For guaranteeing the territorial inviolability and political independence of every State in the area, through measures including the establishment of demilitarized zones;

3. *Requests* the Secretary-General to designate a Special Representative to proceed to the Middle East to establish and maintain contacts with the States concerned in order to promote agreement and assist efforts to achieve a peaceful and accepted settlement in accordance with the provisions and principles in this resolution;

4. *Requests* the Secretary-General to report to the Security Council on the progress of the efforts of the Special Representative as soon as possible.

Resolution 338 (1973)

The Security Council,

1. *Calls upon* all parties to the present fighting to cease all firing and terminate all military activity immediately, no later than 12 hours after the moment of the adoption of this decision, in the positions they now occupy;

2. *Calls upon* the parties concerned to start immediately after the cease-fire the implementation of Security Council resolution 242 (1967) in all of its parts;

3. *Decides* that, immediately and concurrently with the cease-fire, negotiations shall start between the parties concerned under appropriate auspices aimed at establishing a just and durable peace in the Middle East.

That the "just and durable peace" required by Resolution 338 is to be negotiated in

Its view of the diplomacy of the period is untenable. And it is contradicted by every precedent defining the law of the Charter regarding the use of force by states, and the responsibility of states for the use of force from their territories. It is contradicted also by the pattern of customary international law, if it be deemed more comprehensive in this regard than the law of the Charter.

I.

The central feature of Resolution 242, and of the Security Council's cease-fire resolutions which preceded it, is that Israel is legally entitled to remain on the cease-fire lines of 1967 as the occupying power until the parties themselves reach an agreement of peace in conformity with the principles and provisions of Resolution 242. This is the famous "package deal" on which Resolution 242 rests—withdrawal for peace, and no withdrawal without a binding agreement of peace. I can find no reference in Mr. Shihata's article to this crucial fact, which both the text and the context of Resolution 242 make unmistakably clear.[8]

Instead, Mr. Shihata sets up a strawman, which he then attempts to demolish. Israel's claim to the occupation of the Sinai Peninsula, the West Bank, the Gaza Strip, and the Golan Heights, he writes, has been justified "only by alleged considerations of security and less overtly by the desire to gain territorial advantages in future negotiations. Such considerations are obviously of a political, not legal, character." [9]

But Mr. Shihata's premise is incorrect. Israel's rights as the occupying power in the territories it held as a result of the Six Day War do not rest on political considerations, claims of annexation, or bargaining tactics. On the contrary, they derive from the Security Council's cease-fire resolutions which brought the Six Day War to an end and on Resolution 242 which prescribes both principles and procedures for terminating the cease-fire regime by making peace.

Until the states concerned in the dispute make peace in accordance with Resolution 242, the Security Council decided, Israel could remain in the

accordance with the princples and provisions of Resolution 242, see Secretary of State Kissinger, Statement before the Geneva Conference, Dec. 21, 1973, 70 DEPT. STATE BULL. 21, 23 (1974); News Conference of Nov. 21, 1973, 69 DEPT. STATE BULL. 701, 709 (1973).

[8] See Rostow, Legal Aspects of the Search for Peace in the Middle East [1970] PROC ASIL, 64 AJIL (No. 4) 64; Book Review, 67 AJIL 808, 809 (1973); America, Europe and the Middle East, 57 COMMENTARY 40, 52–54 (1974); LALL, THE UN AND THE MIDDLE EAST CRISIS, 1967, ch. 13–15 (1968); G. Rafael, UN Resolution 242: A Common Denominator, THE NEW MIDDLE EAST (June, 1973) 26; J. STONE, NO PEACE—NO WAR IN THE MIDDLE EAST (1969); The Cease Fire of 1967: The Legal Framework 3 THE BRIDGE 3 (Sydney, Australia, October, 1967); The "November Resolution" and Middle East Peace: Pitfall or Guidepost, 3 TOLEDO L. REV. 43 (1971).

The late Professor Quincy Wright also ignored this feature of Resolution 242 in his writing on the subject. See Wright, The Middle Eastern Crisis [1970] PROC ASIL, 64 AJIL (No. 4) 71, 73, 78–87, and Wright and Khadduri, supra, note 2, 27–36.

[9] SHIHATA, 599.

territories it held after the Six Day War as the occupying power. The legality and legitimacy of its presence as occupying power is thus certified by the Security Council. That right is fully protected by the law of Article 2(4), which the General Assembly attempted to summarize and restate in its Declaration on Principles of International Law concerning Friendly Relations and Co-operation among States, in the following terms:

> Every State has the duty to refrain from the threat or use of force to violate the existing international boundaries of another State or as a means of solving international disputes, including territorial disputes and problems concerning frontiers of States.

> Every State likewise has the duty to refrain from the threat or use of force to violate international lines of demarcation, such as armistice lines, established by or pursuant to an international agreement to which it is a party or which it is otherwise bound to respect. Nothing in the foregoing shall be construed as prejudicing the positions of the parties concerned with regard to the status and effects of such lines under their special regimes or as affecting their temporary character.[10]

The "purpose" of the Security Council in adopting Resolution 242 was unmistakable. It was confronted by a situation in which the Arabs feared that the Israelis would never withdraw from any lands they conquered and the Israelis feared that the Arabs would never make peace. The dispute over Israel's right to exist, exacerbated by Soviet political policies and programs of arms supply and military training, had already led to three major wars, a standing threat to the peace, and endless violations of the Charter through the failure of states to discharge their "duty to refrain from organizing or encouraging the organization of irregular forces or armed bands, including mercenaries, for incursion into the territory of another state." [11]

The Council therefore decided to link the two main themes of the dispute, by providing twin and reciprocal pressures both for withdrawal and for peace.

Every government involved in the negotiation and drafting of Resolu-

---

[10] GA Res. 2625, 25 UN GAOR SUPP. 28, at 122, UN Doc. A/8082 (1970). *See* Rusk, *The 25th UN General Assembly and the Use of Force, Symposium, Legal Regulation of the Use of Force*, 2 GEORGIA J. INT. AND COMP. LAW 19, 25 (Supp. 1, 1972): "The Declaration on Friendly Relations appears to say that, whatever the issues between the parties in the divided states, in Kashmir, the Middle East or other places where demarcation and armistice lines are not settled international boundaries, those issues are not to be settled by the threat or use of force." The Declaration on Friendly Relations is reaffirmed in the resolution defining aggression, *supra*, note 2, which characterizes military occupation as illegal only when undertaken "in contravention of the Charter," *i.e.*, when it is not justified under Article 51, or by the Security Council.

[11] Declaration on Principles of International Law concerning Friendly Relations and Co-operation among States, *supra* note 10, at 123. One should add that under Article 2(4) of the Charter, and the customary international law which is its matrix, the duty of states is broader than that stated in the Declaration: it is one of nearly absolute responsibility for the international use of force from its territory. *See* note 4, *supra*.

Articles 3(f) and (g) of the General Assembly's resolution defining aggression, *supra*, note 2, characterize such illegal uses of force as "aggression" if the Security Council finds them to be of sufficient gravity.

tion 242 accepted this basic principle as the foundation on which Resolution 242 was built. The Soviet Union itself took the position in 1967 and 1968 that Resolution 242 represented the first occasion in the experience of the Cold War in which the Soviets used the term "package deal" in a positive sense. This is still the position of all the governments directly responsible for the text. Some now profess to differ on one aspect of the resolution, but not on its fundamental principle that there should be no Israeli withdrawal without an agreement of peace. As P. M. Martin has correctly concluded, Israeli occupation was intended by the Security Council to be "the gage for peace." [12]

The reason for this principle in the resolution is well known, but bears repeating.

The Security Council has called on the parties to make peace many times between 1948 and October, 1973.[13] It has ruled twice that a state of war between Israel and the Arab states does not exist and therefore that the Arab states cannot legally claim the authority of "a state of belligerency" to justify the use of coercion or of armed force against Israel.[14] Throughout the long and bitter years between 1948 and 1973, however, the Arab states refused to make peace, and did claim that they had belligerent rights, standing on the policy which, at a later point, was summed up in the Khartoum Resolution of September 1, 1967 adopted by the Heads of State or Government of the Arab League members and the head of the Palestine Liberation Organization: "No peace with Israel, no recognition of Israel, no negotiations with it, and insistence on the rights of the Palestinian people in their own country." [15]

In 1957, in the aftermath of Suez, the United States, acting as go-between, persuaded Israel to withdraw from the Sinai in exchange for a number of assurances which were transmitted to Israel by the United States in behalf of Egypt: that Israel's maritime rights through the Suez Canal and the Strait of Tiran would be respected; that Egypt would meet its international responsibilities to prevent guerrilla attacks on Israel from

[12] P. M. Martin, Le Conflit Israelo-Arabe, ch. 7 (1973).

[13] E.g., SC Res. 54 (1948), July 15, 1948, para. 8; SC Res. 61 (1948), Nov. 4, 1948; SC Res. 62 (1948), Nov. 16, 1948; SC Doc. S/1152, SCOR, 3rd year Supp. for December, 1948, at 300; SC Res. 73 (1949), Aug. 11, 1949; SC Res. 89 (1950), Nov. 17, 1950; SC Res. 93 (1951), May 18, 1951.

[14] SC Res. 95 (1951), Sept. 1, 1951, 10 SCOR, 688th meeting, paras. 98–102, at 20; SC Res. 118 (1956), Oct. 13, 1956, 11 SCOR, 743d meeting, 18. See Q. Wright, Legal Aspects of the Middle East Situation, 33 L. and Contemp. Prob. 5, 20–22 (1968); United States Reply to the Arab States Representations concerning the Suez Canal and the Gulf of Aqaba, June 27, 1957, in United States Senate, Committee on Foreign Relations, 91st Cong., 1st Sess., A Select Chronology and Background Documents relating to the Middle East 179–82 (1st rev. ed., 1969). Professor Khadduri agrees that only the claim of belligerent rights could justify the closing of the Suez Canal or the Strait of Tiran to Israeli shipping—a claim rejected by the Security Council. Closure of the Suez Canal to Israeli Shipping, 33 L. and Contemp. Prob. 147, 154–55 (1968).

[15] The text appears in Y. Alexander and N. Kittrie, Crescent and Star, 427–29 (1973).

Egyptian territory; and that peace would be made in due course. It was explicitly understood that if force were used to close the Strait of Tiran to Israeli shipping, Israel would be entitled to use force in reply by way of self-defense under Article 51. Great Brtain, France, and the United States guaranteed the international character of the Strait of Tiran. And it was agreed as well that if Egypt should ever request the removal of UNEF forces from the Sinai, the Secretary-General would undertake negotiations, in accordance with a memorandum duly filed, to prevent that eventuality.

In deference to Egypt's political sensibilities, the international understanding of 1957 was embodied in an agreed series of statements, letters, memoranda, and silences, both in the General Assembly, at United Nations Headquarters, and in the several capitals.[16]

Between 1957 and June, 1967, Egypt broke every provision of the 1957 international understanding, finally obtaining the withdrawal of the UNEF forces, closing the Strait of Tiran, and mobilizing in the Sinai. A united Arab command was formed. The Arab armies were arrayed against Israel in Syria, Jordan, and the Sinai and rapidly increased in size and equipment. The Arab radio and the Arab press began to trumpet out the call for a Holy War to destroy Israel.[17]

This bitter experience was in every mind when the Six Day War broke out. On the first day of the fighting, President Johnson called for an immediate cease-fire and announced that the policy of the United States was to press for peace, and not a renewal of the 1949 Armistice.[18] This position rested on an extended and carefully considered review of Soviet policy in the area; one of the conclusions drawn from the study was that American policy in 1956 and 1957 had turned out to be a mistake, in that the United States had not insisted on an agreement of peace in exchange

[16] The full story of this negotiation and its outcome has not yet been published. One aspect of the understanding was officially disclosed in Rostow, *The Middle East Crisis and Beyond*, 59 DEPT. STATE BULL. 41, 45 (1968):

> Egypt's announcement that it would use force to close the strait had another set of consequences. In 1957 the United States had taken the lead in negotiating the withdrawal of Israeli troops from Sharm-al-Sheikh and the Sinai as a whole. At that time Israel made it clear that if force were used to close the strait, it would regard itself justified in responding with force as an act of self-defense authorized under article 51 of the United Nations Charter. This carefully considered formal statement was noted at the time as part of the process of settlement. The international understanding was that the Strait of Tiran would be kept open as an international waterway. The United Arab Republic, it is true, never took formal responsibility for this understanding, as it refused to recognize Israel or to deal directly with her. But in every other sense Egypt was a party to and beneficiary of this arrangement, through which Israeli withdrawal had been secured.

See also ROSTOW, LAW, POWER, AND THE PURSUIT OF PEACE 78 (1968) (also officially cleared); D. BEN-GURION, ISRAEL: A PERSONAL HISTORY 522–36 (1971); Rostow, *supra*, note 8; H. FINER, DULLES OVER SUEZ, ch. 16–18 (1964); T. DRAPER, ISRAEL AND WORLD POLITICS: ROOTS OF THE THIRD ARAB-ISRAELI WAR 19–22 (1968); Q. Wright, *supra*, note 8, at 72. The fullest treatment thus far is C. N. Rostow, Diplomatic Patchwork: The United States and the Settlement at Suez, 1956–1957 (unpublished student essay, 1972, on deposit at the Yale University Library).

[17] See Yost, *How the Arab-Israeli War Began*, 46 FOREIGN AFFAIRS 304 (1968); N. SAFRAN, FROM WAR TO WAR, ch. 6 (1969). [18] 56 DEPT. STATE BULL. 949 (1967).

for Israel's withdrawal from the Sinai. In June 1967, neither the Arab states nor the Soviet Union would consider a cease-fire until they realized how the tide of war was running. Against the background of these events, the Arab states and the Soviet Union could not persuade a majority to condemn Israel as the aggressor in 1967, either in the General Assembly or in the Security Council. After the war, five months of intense diplomacy achieved Resolution 242, proposed and sponsored by the British Government. All the resolutions finally considered by the Security Council in November, 1967, rested on the principle of "no withdrawal without peace." [19] They differed in other respects, but on this fundamental issue they were consistent. One of the things the international community said clearly in Resolution 242 was that this time Israel would not be required to withdraw without a prior agreement of peace. Unlike many Security Council cease-fire resolutions, there was no disposition in 1967 to call on one party to the hostlities to return to the position it occupied before hostilities broke out. [20]

Lord Caradon, the British representative at the United Nations, whose devoted and effective work was of critical importance to the negotiation of Resolution 242, explained the idea of the British draft in several statements before the Council.

> 10. We went to both sides. We know and respect their intense feelings. We well realize that the future security and progress and happiness of their peoples depends on what we do here. It is entirely understandable, therefore, that to each point, indeed to each word, they should attach the utmost importance. Nevertheless, the representatives of both sides have been ready to consider with the greatest patience and care the representations which we have put to them. Perhaps we cannot hope that full agreement between both sides can be secured. It may be too early for such a miracle. But there has been a readiness to go back over every word and phrase, and a readiness, too, to understand the needs and views of others.

[19] Draft resolutions were introduced by India, Mali, and Nigeria, UN Doc. S/8227, Nov. 7; the United States, UN Doc. S/8229, Nov. 7; the United Kingdom, UN Doc. S/8247, Nov. 16; the USSR, UN Doc. S/8253, Nov. 20. The Soviet draft resolution called for the simultaneous (1) withdrawal of Israeli forces to the lines of June 5, 1967, and (2) recognition by all states members of the United Nations in the area that each such state has a right to exist in peace and security under the Charter, and renunciation of all claims inconsistent therewith. 22 SCOR, 1381st meeting, Nov. 20, 1967, at 2. The other drafts were also based on the principle of linking withdrawal and peace.

[20] See Goldberg, *United Nations Security Council Resolution 242 and the Prospects for Peace in the Middle East*, 12 Colum. J. Transnational L. 187, 192 (1973):

> On the second day of the war, June 7, the U.N. Security Council, with the concurrence of Israel and Egypt (Syria later also agreed), unanimously voted a cease-fire. This cease-fire, however, was not conditioned upon the withdrawal of Israeli armed forces. They were, in effect, to stand in place, pending further developments. In U.N. history, this type of cease-fire is virtually unique. Generally, when a conflict breaks out, it is almost "boiler plate" for the United Nations to adopt a cease-fire resolution embracing withdrawal of the contending forces to the positions they occupied before the conflict.

Ambassador Tomeh, speaking for Syria, criticized the British draft, adopted as Resolution 242, because it provided no time limit for withdrawals, and because it made Israeli withdrawal subject to "conditions amounting to the liquidation of the whole Palestine question." 22 SCOR, 1382nd meeting, Nov. 22, 1967, at 2. No one disputed his view.

11. In the long discussion with representatives of Arab countries, they have made it clear that they seek no more than justice. The central issue of the recovery and restoration of their territories is naturally uppermost in their minds. The issue of withdrawal to them is all-important and, of course, they seek a just settlement to end the long suffering of the refugees.

12. The Israelis, on the other hand, tell us that withdrawal must never be to insecurity and hostility. The action to be taken must be within the framework of a permanent peace and withdrawal must be to secure boundaries. There must be an end of the use and threat and fear of violence and hostility. I have said before that their aims do not conflict; they are equal. They are both essential. There must be adequate provision in any resolution to meet them both, since to attempt to pursue one without the other would be foolish and futile.

13. So we have been guided by all the earlier work which has been done and by the eloquent statements which have been made by both sides, and we have endeavoured, with the help of my brother members of the Council, to set out in a draft resolution what I believe will be recognized as a sincere and fair and honest attempt both to meet the just claims of both sides and also to discharge the high responsibility of this Council.[21]

The Security Council fully recognized the difficulties of the undertaking, against the background of the tragic history of the problem. The agreements required by Resolution 242 will have to resolve many thorny and difficult controversies: security arrangements, including demilitarized zones; maritime rights; a fair and humane resolution of the refugee prob-

---

[21] 22 SCOR, 1379th meeting 2 (1967). Earlier Lord Caradon had stated:

37. The Arab countries insist that we must direct our special attention to the recovery and restoration of their territories. The issue of withdrawal is to them of top priority. The Arabs want not charity but justice. They seek a just settlement to end the long and bitter suffering of the refugees. There is a recognition on all sides that a new, comprehensive, imaginative plan, as we have advocated, to deal with this desperately urgent problem is essential.

38. The Israelis tell us that withdrawal must never be to the old precarious truce. It must be to a permanent peace, to secure boundaries, to a new era of freedom from the use or the threat or the fear of hostility and force.

39. Both are right. The aims of the two sides do not conflict. They converge. They supplement and they support each other. To imagine that one can be secured without the other is a delusion. They are of equal validity and equal necessity. The recent consultations which have been going forward so energetically and continuously strongly reinforce my conviction that we in this Council now have a supreme opportunity to serve the interests of all those concerned. Every day it is more clear what should be done. Every day it is more apparent that we are not dealing with conflicting interests but with complementary interests. Justice and peace are not in conflict; they are inseparable as they are indispensable. One must go hand in hand with the other.

22 SCOR, 1377th meeting 4–5 (1967). *See also id.*, 1381st meeting 4–5.

Ambassador Adebo of Nigeria said that under the resolution withdrawal "should take place in a context in which all the countries in the area, including Israel and all the Arab states, can feel and enjoy a sense of security. We therefore subscribe very heartily to what Lord Caradon said when he stated that the Resolution must be taken as a whole." *Id.*, 1382nd meeting, 8–9; Ambassador Ruda of Argentina commented that the road towards peace required "mutual concessions . . . this means the withdrawal of troops from the occupied areas on the one hand and the cessation of belligerency on the other . . . [P]eace could not be brought about by withdrawal pure and simple, but . . . such a step must of necessity be accompanied by measures assuring peace and security." *Id.*, 15–16.

lem; and the status of Jerusalem. That is why the resolution authorized the appointment of a Special Representative of the Secretary-General to assist the parties in reaching the peace agreement called for by paragraph 3 of the resolution. Israeli withdrawal and the emergence of peace cannot, as a practical matter, go "hand in hand" unless there is a prior agreement between the parties as to the stages and terms which would govern the twin process.

This fundamental aspect of Resolution 242 was summarized by Secretary of State Rogers on January 29, 1970, in these terms:

> We have never suggested any withdrawal until there was a final, binding, written agreement that satisfied all aspects of the Security Council resolution.

> In other words, we have never suggested that a withdrawal occur before there was a contractual agreement entered into by the parties, signed by the parties in each other's presence, an agreement that would provide full assurances to Israel that the Arabs would admit that Israel had a right to exist in peace.

> Now, that is what has been lacking in the past. The Arabs have never been willing to do that; and if that could be done, we think it would be a tremendous boon to the world.

> Now, we have also provided that the security arrangements would be left to the parties to negotiate, such as Sharm-al-Shaykh, and the Gaza Strip, the demilitarized zone, and so forth.[22]

II.

A second feature of Resolution 242, which Mr. Shihata does discuss, is whether "the secure and recognized boundaries" called for by the resolution—the boundaries to which Israel would withdraw after peace was agreed upon—had to be the same as the Armistice Demarcation Lines as they stood on June 5, 1967.

It should be recalled that the Armistice Agreements of 1949, save in the case of Lebanon, provide that the Armistice Demarcation Lines are not political boundaries, and can be changed by the agreement of the parties when they move from a state of armistice to one of peace.[23]   Mr. Shihata

---

[22] 62 DEPT. STATE BULL. 218–19 (1970). *See also* ROSTOW, *supra* note 17, at 81:

The essential idea of the President's statement [closely followed in Security Council Resolution 242] is that the continuation of claims of a right to wage war against Israel have become a burden to world peace. It is therefore a world responsibility, and a responsibility of the parties, to achieve an end to such claims—a condition of peace in the area. It should be a fair and dignified peace reached by the parties, not one imposed by conquest, or by the Great Powers. It should recognize each nation's right to live, and to live in security. And it should rest on the principle of the territorial integrity and political independence of all the nations of the area.

On the basis of such a peace, the other principal features of the Arab-Israeli controversy should be resolved by the parties through any procedure on which they can agree. Israeli forces should of course withdraw to agreed and secure boundaries, which should replace the fragile armistice lines of 1948 and 1949. Those armistice agreements expressly contemplated boundary adjustments when they were superseded by arrangements of peace.

[23] 42 UNTS 303, No. 656 (1949) (with Jordan); *id.*, 327, No. 657 (1949) (with Syria); *id.*, 251, No. 654 (1949) (with Egypt); *id.*, 287, No. 655 (1949) with Lebanon.

notes this aspect of the Armistice Agreements, but ingeniously contends
that it is a one-way street—that it authorizes only a withdrawal by Israel
to the boundaries set out for the Jewish state in the General Assembly's
resolution of November 29, 1947, which recommended to the Security
Council the partition of the western part of Palestine into an Arab and an
Israeli state, joined in economic union, and a special regime for Jerusalem.[24] The Security Council never acted on the Assembly's recommendation. Its mediation efforts at the time and its decisions of 1949 following the
Arab war against the 1947 resolution rested on quite different principles.
In insisting on the armistice, the Security Council necessarily ruled that
the Arab states had committed aggression in 1948–1949, and were being
punished for their 1948–49 aggression, and their refusal to make peace.[25]
The fundamental weakness of Mr. Shihata's one-way-street argument, beyond its errors and omissions, is that it would make aggression costless.
No system of law fails to provide penalties for its violation.

But Mr. Shihata does not rely on his highly idiosyncratic interpretation
of the Armistice Agreements and their relationship to the General Assembly's Partition Resolution of 1947. His basic contention is that the
hotly contested provision in the British draft resolution, requiring the
"withdrawal of Israeli forces from territories occupied in the recent conflict" really means withdrawal from "all the" territories occupied in the
course of that conflict. Mr. Shihata's serious contention is that Israel
should withdraw from the 1967 cease-fire lines to the 1949 Armistice Demarcation Lines, and not to the shadowy lines set forth in the General
Assembly's 1947 Partition plan. Like the Arab governments, Mr. Shihata
now treats the Armistice Demarcation Lines as political boundaries, defining the extent of "Arab" and "Israeli" territory. "The absurdity of the
counterargument," Mr. Shihata writes, "is demonstrated in fact by its
insistence, against the consensus of the international community, on tying
the destiny of sovereign states, their history, and geography, to the absence of a definite article which is not even needed grammatically to
convey the required comprehensive meaning." [26]

But the absence of the definite article in paragraph 1(i) of Resolution
242 was fully and carefully considered—and fully understood—in the debates of the Council. As Lord George-Brown, who was the British Foreign Minister in 1967, remarked, the omission of the word "the" was
deliberate.[27] The Soviet and Indian draft resolutions were both explicit

---

[24] Resolution 181(II) Nov. 29, 1947, GAOR, 2nd Sess. RESOLUTIONS, 31–50 (1947).

[25] Rostow, *America, Europe, and the Middle East, supra* note 8, at 50.

[26] SHIHATA, 604.

· [27] GEORGE-BROWN, IN MY WAY at 226–27 (1971, Pelican ed., 1972):

> This resolution set out in a most carefully balanced way what the Israelis and
> the Arabs would have to do to secure both peace in the Middle East and recog-
> nition of the State of Israel. I have been pressed many times to spell out exactly
> what the resolution meant, but I've always refused to go farther than what it says.
> It declares "the inadmissibility of the acquisition of territory by war" and it also
> affirms the necessity "for guaranteeing the territorial inviolability and political
> independence of every state in the area." It calls for "withdrawal of Israeli armed
> forces from territories occupied in the recent conflict" and also for "termination
> of all claims or states of belligerency."

in requiring Israeli withdrawal from *all* the territories in question. They did not prevail. Many, many attempts were made to persuade Lord Caradon and the British Foreign Minister to accept language which would require withdrawal to the Armistice Demarcation Lines. They all failed. In the end, the Council agreed unanimously on the British draft, knowing exactly what it meant: that is, that Resolution 242, resting on the Armistice Agreements of 1949, did permit the parties to make what President Johnson called "insubstantial" changes in the Armistice Demarcation Lines of 1949 as they moved from armistice to peace.[28]

The present writer conducted dozens if not hundreds of diplomatic conversations on the subject, in Washington, in New York, in Asia, and in Europe. He never encountered the slightest doubt, disagreement, or ambiguity on the point, or support in any quarter for the view of the matter Mr. Shihata takes, beyond the formal and often cynical registration of official positions, purporting to rely on the French text. As Ambassador Ruda of Argentina said, explaining his vote for the resolution, "With regard to the formula for the withdrawal of troops, which reads:

> It does *not* call for Israeli withdrawal from "the" territories recently occupied, nor does it use the word "all". It would have been impossible to get the resolution through if either of these words had been included, but it does set out the lines on which negotiations for a settlement must take place. Each side must be prepared to give up something: the resolution doesn't attempt to say *precisely* what, because that is what negotiations for a peace-treaty must be about. However unpromising it may look, the fact of the matter is that Resolution 242 is the *only* basis on which negotiations for a peace-treaty can ever be started. It is both interesting and important that, whatever is said by anybody, the one thing on which all parties are agreed is that they still claim to accept Resolution 242.

[28] Speech of Sept. 10, 1968, 59 DEPT. STATE BULL. 345, 348 (1968). President Johnson also said: "We are not the ones to say where other nations should draw lines between them that will assure each the greatest security. It is clear, however, that a return to the situation of June 4, 1967, will not bring peace. There must be secure and there must be recognized borders. Some such lines must be agreed to by the neighbors involved as part of the transition from armistice to peace." *See also* speech of Secretary of State Rogers, Dec. 9, 1969, 62 DEPT. STATE BULL. 7 (1970). This is still the policy of the United States. Secretary of State Kissinger, News Conference, *supra*, note 7, at 714–15. *See* testimony of J. L. Hargrove, Senior Adviser on International Law to the United States Mission to the United Nations, 1967–1970:

> The provision of Resolution 242 which bears most directly on the question which you raised, Congressman, is subparagraph (1) of paragraph 1 of the resolution, which envisages "withdrawal of Israeli armed forces from territories occupied in the recent conflict."
> The language "from territories" was regarded at the time of the adoption of the resolution as of high consequence because the proposal put forward by those espousing the Egyptian case was withdrawal from "the territories." In the somewhat minute debate which frequently characterizes the period before the adoption of a United Nations resolution, the article "the" was regarded of considerable significance because its inclusion would seem to imply withdrawal from all territories which Israel had not occupied prior to the June war, but was at the present time occupying.
> Consequently the omission of "the" was intended on our part, as I understood it at the time, and was understood on all sides, to leave open the possibility of modifications in the lines which were occupied as of June 4, 1967, in the final settlement.

Hearings on the Middle East before the Subcomm. of the House Comm. on Foreign Affairs, 92nd Cong., 1st Sess. 187 (1971). *See also* Y. BLUM, SECURE BOUNDARIES AND MIDDLE EAST PEACE (1971).

withdrawal of Israel armed forces from territories occupied in the recent conflict,' this does not, in our view reflect a fully rounded-off notion; and although my delegation voted for paragraph 1(i) of the draft, we would have preferred a clearer text . . ." [29]

Mr. Shihata makes much of the fact that the French translation of Resolution 242 reads "retrait des forces armées israeliennes des territoires occupés . . ." [30] When the French text appeared, the British and American Governments raised the matter at once with the United Nations Secretariat, and with the French Government, to be told that the French language offered no other solution for the problem. Since the question had been debated so long and so intensively and the decision of the Council was so clear, the matter was dropped, especially since none of the people involved could think of a more accurate French translation. Mr. Shihata's argument, based on the French and Spanish texts, does not reflect differences of policy, but the anomalies of translation. Whatever content it might be deemed to possess vanished on November 20, 1974, when the French Ambassador to the United Nations, supporting the enforcement of Resolution 242 pursuant to the Security Council's "decision" in Resolution 338, spoke of Resolution 242 as requiring a return to the Armistice Lines, save for "minor rectifications." [31]

It is quite true, as Mr. Shihata points out, that in 1971 Ambassador Jarring attempted to obtain agreement among the parties on the basis of an Israeli withdrawal from *all* the territories it had occupied in 1967. Ambassador Jarring's position was without foundation in Resolution 242. By going beyond the plain meaning of his mandate, he lost his capacity to act as an intermediary, and his mission ended in failure.[32]

[29] 22 SCOR, 1382nd meeting, Nov. 22, 1967, at 16. Statements by the Rt. Hon. Michael Stewart, H.C. (5th ser.) 791 PARL. DEB. 844–45 and 793 PARL. DEB. 253, 261 (1969). In the debate on the adoption of Resolution 242 Ambassador DeCarvalho Silva of Brazil remarked that the acceptance of the resolution "does not imply that borderlines cannot be rectified as a result of an agreement freely concluded among the interested states." 22 SCOR, 1382nd meeting 13 (1969).

[30] SHIHATA, 604, note 70.

[31] New York Times, Nov. 21, 1974, at 4, col. 1. Ambassador Berard, the French Representative at the United Nations, had confirmed this view of the French text in the Security Council at the time Resolution 242 was adopted (22 SCOR, 1382nd meeting, Nov. 22, 1967, at 12), when he said that the phrase "des territoires occupés" indisputably corresponds to the English expression "occupied territories."

[32] UN Doc. S/10929, May 18, 1973, at para. 46, Annex II.
Among the many unresolved mysteries of Middle Eastern diplomacy during the last seven years is why Ambassador Jarring never called a conference of the parties, or separate bilateral conferences of Israel with each of the other parties, to carry out the agreement announced by the Secretary-General of the United Nations on August 7, 1970, after the Government of Egypt had agreed to the proposals advanced by Secretary of State Rogers for ending Egypt's "war of attrition." Note by the Secretary-General on the Jarring Mission for the information of the Security Council, UN Doc. S/9902, Aug. 7, 1970. Ambassador Jarring had written to the Secretary-General:

The United Arab Republic, Jordan and Israel advise me that they agree:
(A) that having accepted and indicated their willingness to carry out resolution 242 in all its parts, they will designate representatives to discussions to be held under my auspices, according to such procedure and at such places and times as

The long, futile, and destructive debate over this feature of Resolution 242 was resolved on December 21, 1973, when the Egyptian, Syrian
and Jordanian representatives met at Geneva in the first session of the
Conference, convened under the presidency of the United States and the
Soviet Union, to implement Security Council Resolution 338. The Arab
states did not require Israel to accept their views on total withdrawal
from the territories occupied in 1967 as a condition of their attendance
at the Conference.

III.

The controversy, of course, is not a matter of grammar, but of principle, international law, and the national interests of many states, including
the United States. Israel had come into being in reliance on a long series
of entirely legal decisions by the international community. The Treaty
of Sèvres separated the Levant from Turkey, and a League Mandate authorized the establishment of a Jewish National Home in an area defined
legally as "Palestine" for the first time in modern history.[33] That decision
of the world community of the day was based on its recognition of the
historic connection of the Jewish people with that land. The immutable
character of the establishment of the Mandate and of the long cycle of
international decisions and events which has flowed from it is the predicate for Resolution 338 of October 22, 1973. Arab public opinion was—
and still is—profoundly convinced that the Mandate was an injustice to
the Arab people of Palestine, and a violation of the League Covenant.
They resisted the development of the Jewish National Home in the western
part of Palestine and went to war to prevent the implementation of the
General Assembly's 1947 resolution, upon which the Security Council had
failed to take effective action.

The debate between these two poignant arguments has been settled by
the authoritative decisions of the world community and by history. It is
unthinkable that the international community could stand idly by if
Israel were in danger of destruction. The moral and political convulsion
which such an event would engender, with the memory of Hitler's time
still fresh, is beyond calculation.

This is the ultimate thrust of Resolution 338, a binding decision of the

I may recommend, taking into account as appropriate each side's preference as
to method of procedure and previous experience between the parties.
   (B) that the purpose of the aforementioned discussions is to reach agreement
on the establishment of a just and lasting peace between them based on (1)
mutual acknowledgement by the United Arab Republic, Jordan and Israel of each
other's sovereignty, territorial integrity and political independence, and (2) Israeli
withdrawal from territories occupied in the 1967 conflict, both in accordance
with resolution 242.
The Secretary-General correctly characterized the agreement as "an important step
forward in the search for peace in the Middle East."
   [33] See, D. HALL, MANDATES, DEPENDENCIES AND TRUSTEESHIPS (1948); J. STOYANOV-
SKY, THE MANDATE FOR PALESTINE: A CONTRIBUTION TO THE THEORY AND PRACTICE OF
INTERNATIONAL MANDATES (1928); United States Department of State, Division of
Near Eastern Affairs, *Mandate for Palestine* (1927); United States Department of State,
Near Eastern Series No. 1, *Mandate for Palestine* (1931); J. ZASLOFF, GREAT BRITAIN
AND PALESTINE: A STUDY OF THE PROBLEM BEFORE THE UNITED NATIONS (1952).

Security Council, with all the power and prestige of the decisions of the International Court of Justice in the *Namibia* case behind it.[34] "Decisions" of the Security Council, like those for Rhodesia and Namibia, are rare and not lightly voted. Under Article 25, they are legally binding on all member states.

Yet the destruction of Israel, by stealth and by overwhelming force, was precisely what was ominously threatened on October 6, 1973. In the setting of history, it strains credulity to suppose that the Syrian and Egyptian forces, had they been successful in 1973, would have stopped at the Golan escarpment, and the Armistice Demarcation Lines generally. The dream of destroying Israel, as the Crusaders' Kingdom was destroyed, has been the express basis for the steadfast Arab policy of refusing to make peace with Israel, and of their assertion, firmly rejected by the Security Council, that they have a right to claim that a state of war continues to exist between them and Israel.[35] That is why Security Council Resolutions 242 and 338 insist that if the Arab states wish to recover most of the territories Israel seized in the course of the 1967 hostilities, they must make peace in accordance with the principles and provisions of Resolution 242.

Mr. Shihata argues that "an agreement reached under alien military occupation through which an occupied sovereign state is forced to relinquish part of its territory is likely at any rate to be deemed null under modern international law." [36] This is hardly an argument to command universal acceptance in a world society which has recently witnessed many transfers of territory by agreements made while the state ceding territory has had foreign troops on its soil. The cases of Poland, East Germany, Japan, Romania, and Czechoslovakia come to mind. In any event, the Security Council has a comprehensive power to deal with threats to the peace, breaches of the peace, and aggressions, even if they arise within states. Exercising that jurisdiction, the Council has now decided that the particular circumstances of the Middle Eastern situation, and in particular the fate of the 1957 settlement and the refusal of Egypt and Syria between 1967 and 1973 to implement Resolution 242, require the policies of Resolution 338 in order to obtain the agreements of peace which it has sought in vain since 1948.

Implicit in this decision is a judgment that the continuing threat to international peace in the region, and beyond, is the Arab policy of "no peace with Israel, no recognition, and no negotiations." That policy must be overcome, the Security Council has now decided, by the agreement of the parties pursuant to Resolution 242, in the name of the principal respon-

---

[34] Legal Consequences for States of the Continued Presence of South Africa in Namibia (South West Africa) notwithstanding Security Council Resolution 276 [1970], Advisory Opinion, ICJ REP. 1971, at 16. *See also*, Higgins, *The Advisory Opinion on Namibia: Which UN Resolutions are Binding under Article 25 of the Charter?* 21 INT. & COMP. L.Q. 270 (1972). The more controversial aspects of the court's Namibia judgment do not arise in connection with Security Council Resolution 338, which is addressed to a problem under Article 39, and is therefore binding under Article 25, according to all the authorities.

[35] *See* note 15, *supra.*   [36] SHIHATA, 606.

sibility of the United Nations—its responsibility for peace. The "parties" referred to in Resolution 242 are the states of the region.

This postulate is the basis for both Security Council resolutions, now embodied in the "decision" of October 22, 1973. For this reason, the Arab attack on Israel of October 6, 1973, was the least ambiguous violation of Article 2(4) of the Charter since the North Korean invasion of South Korea in 1950. The North Korean attack, like that of the Arabs in October, 1973, crossed a demarcation line which was not an international boundary. Like the Arabs, the North Koreans claimed an inherent right under international law to use force in order to unite two parts of a nation-state which was divided by political circumstance and by international agreement—in the Middle Eastern case, by an international agreement embodied in a series of Security Council resolutions; in the Korean case, by an international agreement embodied in great power understandings and General Assembly resolutions.[37]   In both cases, the decision of the international community was that the war was not a civil but an international war, an attack by one state against another. In the Korean case, the General Assembly and the Security Council found that the Republic of Korea was a state, "a lawfully established government." [38] In the Middle Eastern conflict, of course, the status of Israel as a state had long been established by the usual criteria of recognition under international law, and by its membership in the United Nations.

In the United Nations debates on the Middle Eastern war of October, 1973, there was a notable and deliberate silence concerning the illegality of the Arab attack on the part of the United States. That fact measures the ominous recent decline in the influence of international law on international politics. The decision of the Security Council embodied in Resolution 338 speaks for itself. The premises on which it necessarily rests reaffirm the principles of the Charter, as the Security Council has long sought to apply them to the facts of the dispute about Israel's right to exist. Resolution 338, adopted by the contemporary Security Council, authoritatively reaffirms the legitimacy of the Palestine Mandate, and the emergence of Israel and Jordan as the successor states to the sovereignty of Turkey in the territories included within the Palestine Mandate.

But Resolution 338 was not accompanied by speeches, statements, and articles elucidating the reasons on which it is based, and denouncing the Arab attack of October 6, 1973, as a breach of the peace and an aggression. Nor have the Security Council and the General Assembly made any attempt, as they did when South Korea was invaded in 1950, to rally other nations to assist Israel in the exercise of its inherent right of self-defense.

Mr. Shihata's argument, considered here, and Mr. Arafat's bolder argument, summarized in note 2, represent two phases of a disquieting rebellion against the norms of international law regarding the use of force by states, and from states. Those norms have taken on tangible and coherent form in a dozen or more cases since 1945. Security Council Reso-

[37] The documents are conveniently collected in 2 R. Higgins, United Nations Peacekeeping, 1946–1967 at 151–72 (1970).
[38] Id., at 159–60.

lutions 242 and 338 have been criticized, implicitly at least, in a number of General Assembly resolutions.[39] General Assembly resolutions of this kind are, it is true, no more than recommendations. They cannot qualify or overrule resolutions of the Security Council, especially those which invoke the authority of Article 25. Nonetheless, the trend represents a current in world opinion which should be taken seriously.

An essential feature of all systems of law is the principle that similar cases be decided alike, if, in full context, they are indeed similar. The reciprocal rules of Article 2(4) and Article 51 define relationships based on the nature of states. They elucidate conditions essential to the peaceful coexistence of states within an international society which is and will remain a society of states, not of peoples. These rules are more necessary than ever before in an age of revolutionary transition, characterized by the presence within the states system of nations organized under different social and political ideologies. No state could accept the application to itself of the rules urged by Mr. Shihata or Mr. Arafat.

The Soviet Union would vehemently oppose the proposition that West Germany and its NATO allies had a right under Article 51 to use force internationally to redeem the national territory of Germany. Yet Mr. Shihata's argument allows no escape from this proposition. At least until the recent East German treaties were ratified, the case of a hypothetical NATO liberation of that country, as sovereign German territory held by force, cannot be distinguished from the case Mr. Shihata makes. And his argument even suggests that the international agreements recognizing the German Democratic Republic are "null," because of the presence of the Red Army in East Germany and of NATO forces in the Federal Republic. This cannot be the law.

Mr. Arafat, of course, goes much further. His thesis would authorize the international use of force to liberate the Estonians, the Uzbeks, or the Ukrainians, and would recognize the "right" of France to send regular or irregular forces into Spain to help vindicate the right of the Basques or the Catalonians to self-determination. This, too, can hardly be the law.

Looking back over our experience with war since 1945 and the arguments advanced to justify the successive and prospective Arab wars against Israel, I conclude that Maxim Litvinov was right when he used to say, nearly forty years ago, that "peace is indivisible." Litvinov's thesis, which the Soviet Union once professed to support, is the fundamental idea of the Charter. In a world of small, weak states, and strong imperial ambitions, it is the only rule that could protect the interests of all states, Western and Eastern, capitalist and communist, developed and developing, large and small. A legal rule can survive as the compass for a legal system if it is not invariably and uniformly obeyed. But it cannot survive for long as a norm unless in the end it is respected reciprocally, and equally, by all those who participate in the political process it is intended to govern.[40]

[39] See SHIHATA, 601, note 52, and UN Doc. A/RES/3236 (XXIX), Nov. 23, 1974.
[40] Rostow, The Role of International Law in International Politics, an address before the Twentieth Anniversary Meeting of the Atlantic Treaty Association, The Hague, June 21, 1974, reprinted in 12 THE ATLANTIC COMMUNITY Q. 500 (Winter 1974–75).

II. THE SIX-DAY WAR, THE OCTOBER WAR, AND CONTINUED HOSTILITIES

B. *Human Rights for Contexts of Violence: The Geneva Conventions and the Protection of Civilians and Prisoners of War*

The Culprit, the Targets and the Victims*

M. BURHAN W. HAMMAD

THE Commission on Human Rights adopted resolution 6 (XV), concerning Israel's violation of human rights in the occupied Arab territories on March 4, 1969. This resolution is both generic and specific in its terms. It is generic in the sense that it recalls previous resolutions adopted by various organs of the United Nations relative to this matter; reaffirms the right of return to those inhabitants who have left since the outbreak of the 1967 hostilities; deplores Israel's continued violations of human rights in the occupied territories; and calls upon Israel fully to respect and apply the Geneva Convention of August 12 relative to the protection of civilian persons in time of war.

It is specific, in the sense that, in accordance with operative paragraph 4, it confers on the Special Working Group the following mandate:

To investigate allegations concerning Israel's violation of the Geneva Convention relative to the Protection of Civilian Persons in Time of War of August 12, 1949, in the territories occupied by Israel as a result of hostilities in the Middle East; receive communications, to hear witnesses, and use such modalities of procedure as it may deem necessary; report its conclusions and recommendations to the Commission's twenty-sixth session.

The competence of the Special Working Group is wide and extensive, as prescribed in section (b) of paragraph 4, and evidence regarding Israel's violation is also enormous and extensive. It may be found in statements of Israeli officials printed in both Israeli and foreign publications, in articles and books written by Israeli as well as non-Israeli correspondents and writers, in coverage of news items by the mass media—namely, television, radio, newspapers and magazines; in the reports of the Secretary-General based upon the observations of Mr. Gussing, his personal representative in the occupied territories; in the report of the Secretary-General based upon the observations of Ambassador Thalmann, his personal representative in Jerusalem, in

---

* Ed. Note: See also Mallison, "The Geneva Convention for the Protection of Civilian Persons: An Analysis of Its Application in the Arab Territories under Israeli Occupation," 15-16 *The Arab World* 16-22 (1970).

the two reports of the Commissioner-General of the United Nations Relief and Works Agency for Palestine Refugees in the Middle-East, known as UNRWA, to the twenty-second and twenty-third sessions of the General Assembly, and in his report to the International Conference on Human Rights held in Teheran; in the report of the deputation of three American Protestant clergymen who visited the occupied territories on a mandate extended to them by the National Council of Churches of Christ in the United States; in the numerous letters by the Permanent Representatives of Jordan, Syria and the United Arab Republic addressed to the President of the Security Council and to the Secretary-General and issued accordingly as official documents of the Security Council and the General Assembly; as well as in many other publications. There is no need here to enumerate the violations committed by Israel, or to submit evidence relating to each and all of them. Israel's record is well known and comprehensively documented.

The basic objective of this article is to discuss the applicability of the Geneva Convention in the occupied territories. It is necessary to state here that the host Arab states, as well as Israel, are signatories to the Convention. Lebanon became party to the Convention on April 10, 1951; Jordan, on May 29, 1951; the United Arab Republic on November 10, 1952; Syria, on November 2, 1953; and Israel, on July 6, 1951. I submit that the provisions of the Geneva Convention represent the shared expectations of the contracting parties, including Israel and the host Arab states, as to what type of authority governs specific events that may arise in the future—in other words, specific provisions in the Geneva Convention govern the behavior and attitude of Israel regarding events in the occupied Arab territories. A legal and policy-oriented approach to the applicability of the Geneva Convention should start with a study of the factual process of action initiated by the culprit against the targets and victims. Against this background it is necessary to articulate the various claims and counter-claims to authority made by the culprit, the targets and the victims, and other interested non-parties, concerning the policies that govern the action; finally, a study of the process of decision, in which authority is conjoined with effective control, in which decisions are both authoritative and controlling. After this general and brief review of the three processes, I shall try to examine the relevance and scope of each in regard to the issue of Israeli violations of human rights in the occupied territories.

As to the process of action, in one phase of this process, the participants are Israel—referred to here as the culprit—and the Arab states —referred to here as the targets. In another phase they are Israel— again the culprit—and the civilians in the occupied territories—referred to as victims. In the former phase, the mere fact that the four Arab states and Israel signed the Convention and became parties to it proves without any doubt that they all accepted its prescriptions to govern certain events that may arise among them. Those prescriptions represented their shared expectations as to what any of them should or should not do when it occupies part of the territory of the other.

Israel has resorted to various actions in administering the occupied territories. In resorting to such actions, Israel aims at the maximization of its own values and the utilization and exploitation of the *basic* values available in the occupied territories for its own benefit. In doing so, it disregarded the prescription of the Convention; its only *aspect* in such action being its own benefit. Of course, the targets of both maximization and utilization have been the host governments.

In the other phase of this process, Israeli actions have adversely affected the well-being, wealth and rectitude of the civilians living in the occupied territories, who have become victims of maltreatment torture, loss of means of livelihood, loss of property and the like.

With regard to the process of claim, in the course of the actions resorted to by Israel, by which it utilizes and exploits the basic values available in the occupied territories, continuous controversies have arisen relating to the deprivations occurring as a result of such actions. The parties to these controversies have made claims in various arenas of authority, both international and national, with respect to the unlawfulness of the value changes affected by such deprivations. These claims, in certain instances, embrace not only the parties' perspectives of the events precipitating controversy but also their demands for specific redress and all the justifications—technical and policy—which they invoke in support of their demands.

The claimants who invoke processes of authority in this context are the following:

(1) The Governments of Jordan, Syria and the United Arab Republic, whose territories are occupied by Israel. Their claims have been addressed to various organs of the United Nations.

(2) The individual civilians in the occupied territories. Their claims have been addressed to the authorities of the occupying power, and to the Commission on Human Rights.

(3) Local councils, such as city councils in the occupied territories. Their claims have been addressed to Israeli authorities and to various organs of the United Nations, such as the Security Council in the case of the Mayor of Jerusalem.

(4) Private associations in the occupied territories, such as chambers of commerce, bar associations, unions, and so on. Their claims have been addressed to Israeli authorities and to various United Nations organs.

(5) Private associations in Arab and non-Arab countries. Their claims have been addressed to United Nations organs.

(6) Other nation-states that have special interests in the occupied areas, such as Morocco, with regard to the destruction of the Magharba quarter in Jerusalem, and numerous Moslem states with regard to the Islamic sites and shrines in Jerusalem. Their claims have been addressed to various United Nations organs, especially the Security Council.

(7) Other nation-states that have no special interest in the occupied areas but are influenced by their concern for the protection of human rights. Certain Western powers are examples of such states. Their claims have been addressed to the Israeli authorities.

(8) International non-governmental organizations, such as the Moslem Congress. Their claims have been addressed to United Nations organs.

(9) Various organs of the United Nations, including the Security Council, the General Assembly, the Economic and Social Council, the International Conference on Human Rights held in Teheran and the Commission on Human Rights. These organs are both decision-makers and claimants. They enjoy dual functions: decision-makers when they render their decisions regarding the claims, but, because of their lack of enforcement, power, or their unwillingness to use it, when they appeal to or call upon Israel to respect the human rights of the civilians in the occupied territories, they are asserting claims to the arena of Israel's authority, and accordingly, they are considered claimants.

I turn now to the enumeration of the types of claims or controversies. In the context of Israel's actions in the occupied territories, it is more accurate to use the term "types of violations." Nevertheless, I shall for convenience of verbal usage and adherence to conventional use, not depart from the term "types of claims." A comprehensive but not exhaustive description of the claims relating to Israel's violation of the Geneva Convention and conditioned by the provisions of the Convention, is restricted to an investigation of the "allegations concerning Israel's violations of the Geneva Convention," and may be presented under the following headings.

(I) Claims Relating to Institutions
    (A) Claims against interference in religious matters
    (B) Claims against the promulgation of new laws
(II) Claims Relating to Population
    (A) Claims relating to the Arab population
        1. claims relating to humane treatment
        2. claims relating to torture and coercion
        3. claims relating to collective punishment and reprisals
        4. claims relating to transfers and deportations of persons
    (B) Claims relating to the Israeli population
        1. claims relating to the transfer of the occupant's civilian population into occupied territory
        2. claims relating to responsibility of individuals for grave breaches of the Convention
        3. claims against ignorance of individuals
(III) Claims Relating to Property
    (A) Claims relating to the destruction of real or personal property
    (B) Claims relating to looting of property
    (C) Claims relating to reprisals against property.

The process of authoritative decision established by the general community of states for resolving controversies arising from the Geneva Convention, as well as other similar prescriptions, exhibits in a very high degree the primitive, yet complex, development of organizational, jurisdictional and procedural structures and techniques generally characteristic of international law. Although the Convention prescribed certain modalities for resolving controversies, thus entitling certain authoritative decision-makers with competence to apply authority to the claims of others, and despite the fact that various organs of the United Nations have inherent competence to act as decision-makers, and have indeed acted as such with regard to the human rights of the civilians in the occupied territories, it is submitted that in this context, and in accordance with the relevant resolution of the Commission of Human Rights, the Special Working Group is the authoritative decision-maker.

Of course, the decisions of the Group will take into account the relevant decisions taken by the various other decision-makers, especially organs of the United Nations that have already dealt with the matter.

Before we turn to an examination of the various types of controversies outlined earlier, it is necessary to draw the reader's attention to the question of the duration of the provisions of the Convention, in totality or in part.

Article 6 provides:

> In the case of occupied territory, the application of the present Convention shall cease one year after the general close of military operations. However, the Occupying Power shall be bound for the duration of the occupation,

by a number of main articles in the Convention. The paragraph then reads:

> Protected persons whose release, repatriation or re-establishment may take place after such date shall meanwhile continue to benefit by the present Convention.

It is obvious that there is no problem regarding the applicability of the entire Convention on civilians with certain problems, as provided for in the last paragraph. The problem relates to the whole civilian population, after the passage of one year following the general close of military operations.

I submit that as long as there is no "general close of military operations," but, on the contrary, military operations continue to take place —which is the prevailing situation along the cease-fire line and inside the occupied territories—the Convention in its entirety is applicable to all civilians in the occupied territories.

I turn to the examination of that claim in the context of the relevant article in the Convention that governs it, and Israeli violations of that article starting with the first major type of claim, i.e., claims relating to institutions. The first is claims against interference in religious matters. Paragraph 1 of article 58 reads as follows: "The Occupying Power shall permit Ministers of Religion to give spiritual assistance to the members of their religious communities."

Israel violated this article by requiring that the text of the *Khutbat el-Jumma*—major speech of the mass prayer on the Moslem sabbath—

be censored by its officials before delivery in Jerusalem. It also violated it by denying spiritual assistance to the Moslem community in Jerusalem by exiling the Chairman of the Moslem *Sharia* to the east bank.

The second is claims against the promulgation and application of new laws. Articles 64 to 71 of the Convention confer certain protection on civilians in terms of requiring the application of certain laws and the prohibition of the application of new laws against them. Israel has disregarded these articles and promulgated various and numerous laws in the occupied territories.

As for the second major type of claim—claims relating to population —those relate to the Arab population. Under this, the first claim is: claims relating to humane treatment. Article 27 of the Convention provides: "Protected persons are entitled to . . ." after which various things are listed. The quotation continues: "They shall at all times be humanely treated and shall be protected especially against all acts of violence, or threats thereof, and against insults."

Israel has violated this article on various occasions. Shortly after the 1967 war, Arab women in Jerusalem were brutally attacked and maltreated by Israeli police; in August, 1968, Israeli mobs savagely attacked civilian Arabs in Jerusalem, seriously wounding scores of them. In September, 1968, Israeli mobs mercilessly attacked Arabs in Tel Aviv and Jaffa. In February, 1969, violence was directed against school girls in Gaza, requiring the hospitalization of many of them.

Second, there are claims relating to torture and coercion. Articles 31 and 32 of the Convention prohibit the occupying power from exercising physical or moral coercion against civilians, torturing them and taking any measures that cause physical suffering or extermination of civilians. Israel has repeatedly violated this article.

In one instance, Jewish prostitutes in an Israeli prison savagely attacked Arab female inmates. In another instance, leaders of the west bank sent a petition on July 20, 1968, to the military governor of the west bank, with copies to the United Nations Secretary-General U Thant, and the International Red Cross, containing illustrations of the tortures and intimidations of Arab detainees.

In a recent instance, an Arab owner of a cafeteria in Jerusalem was tortured to death. The Israeli authorities refused a demand made that an autopsy on the body be conducted by Arab or non-official Jewish doctors.

Third, there are claims relating to collective punishments and reprisals. Article 33 provides:

No protected person may be punished for an offence he or she has not personally committed. Collective penalties and likewise all measures of intimidation or of terrorism are prohibited. Reprisals against protected persons are prohibited.

These two provisions have been violated by Israel. The report of the Commissioner-General of UNRWA described Israeli measures in Gaza, which included, *inter alia*, curfews, interrogations, and detentions. Curfews have been imposed on numerous other west bank cities.

Fourth, there are claims relating to transfers and deportations of persons. Paragraph 1 of article 49 provides:

Individual or mass forcible transfers, as well as deportations of protected persons from occupied territory to the territory of the Occupying Power, or to that of any other country, occupied or not, are prohibited regardless of their motive.

Israel has continuously and systematically violated this article. Mass expulsion of Arabs to the east bank followed the June war. Complete evacuation and expulsion of individuals from thirteen areas were brutally executed. The tragedy of Yalu, Beit Nuba and Emmaus is a case in point. Expulsion of individuals likewise followed. The list of those expelled is too long to recount. It included, among others, the Mayor of Jerusalem, former ministers, lawyers, doctors, priests, teachers, and leaders of women's organizations.

I come now to the third major type of claim, or to the second part of the third type of claim, which is claims relating to population—namely, claims relating to the Israeli population. The first claim that comes under this heading is claims relating to transfers of the occupant civilian population in occupied territory. The last paragraph of article 49 reads: "The Occupying Power shall not deport or transfer parts of its own civilian population in the territory it occupies."

Israel has violated this paragraph by systematically establishing scores of Jewish settlements in the Golan Heights, the west bank and the Sinai Peninsula. Israeli citizens are transferred to these settlements as permanent occupants.

Second, there are claims relating to responsibility of individuals for grave breaches of the Convention. Paragraph 2 of article 146 provides:

Each High Contracting Party shall be under the obligation to search for persons alleged to have commited or to have ordered to be committed such grave breaches and shall bring such persons, regardless of their nationality, before its own courts.

Israel has violated this article by failing to bring any person in Israel, official or non-official, who has committed the breaches defined in this article, before Israeli courts.

The third type is claims against ignorance of individuals. Paragraph 1 of article 144 provides that "the Contracting Parties should disseminate the text of the Convention as widely as possible." Paragraph 2 provides that:

Any civilian, military, police or other authorities who in time of war assume responsibilities in respect of protected persons must possess the text of the Convention and be especially instructed as to its provisions.

Yet, an Israeli Colonel who assumed responsibilities in one of the occupied areas said when asked about the Geneva Convention, that "he had never heard of the Convention." This was reported in the British newspaper, *The Observer*, in January, 1968.

I come now to the third major type of claims—i.e., claims relating to property. The first claim under this heading is claims relating to the destruction of real or personal property. Article 53 provides:

And destruction by the Occupying Power of real or personal property belonging individually or collectively to private persons or to the State or to other public authorities, or to social or co-operative organizations, is prohibited except where such destruction is rendered absolutely necessary by military operations.

Israel has frequently violated this article in various instances. Destruction of property has taken place in the absence of military operations. The villages of Yalu, Beit Nuba and Emmaus were totally destroyed. Ninety per cent of the 400 houses in the village of Beit Huna in the Hebron area were destroyed. About 135 houses in the Magharba quarter in Jerusalem, in the area near the Wailing Wall, were dynamited and bulldozed in 1967. The remaining few houses near the Wall have recently been destroyed. Numerous houses in Jerusalem, Nablus, Hebron, Jenin and other cities and towns in the west bank were razed to the ground.

The second type of claim is claims relating to looting of property. Paragraph 2 of article 33 states: "Pillage is prohibited." Israel practiced looting of property in the occupied areas on a large scale. An example of that was the systematic looting of all houses and shops in the city of Kuneitra in the Syrian Golan Heights. Another is the looting of deserted as well as undeserted houses in Jericho in June, 1967. A third is the looting of UNRWA schools in the Gaza Strip, as was reported by the Commissioner-General of UNRWA.

The third type of claim under this heading is claims relating to reprisals against property. Paragraph 3 of article 33 provides: "Reprisals against protected persons and their property are prohibited." Israel has resorted to reprisals against personal property on numerous occasions. In Gaza, for example, houses were demolished in the aftermath of its occupation, in reprisal for the resistance of its citizens against the Israeli invasion. In Jerusalem, fifteen shops owned by prominent Arabs were confiscated in reprisal for the strike of the shopkeepers on November 2, 1968, the fifty-first anniversary of the Balfour Declaration. Houses in various cities and towns in the west bank were completely demolished under the pretext that their owners were relatives of resistance fighters or on the suspicion that they had harbored such persons or that their houses had been used to hide arms.

I have enumerated certain types of claims regarding the violations by Israel of the Geneva Convention, which are important in terms of law as the system of international law lacks an enforcement power. Only repeated indictments of Israel by organs of the United Nations are in a way an enforcement action that might compel Israel to respect the Convention and implement it.

The Observance of International Law in the Administered Territories*

MEIR SHAMGAR

I. *Application of Conventions*

THERE is certainly a wide awareness of the great difficulty in approaching problems connected with the actual implementation of the rules of warfare without being influenced by innate prejudices or by a subjective outlook. The difficulty is actually twofold: the lack of that unanimity and clarity which is a comparatively frequent characteristic of municipal law, and, over and above that, the difficulty posed by political predilection. It is perhaps not superfluous to be reminded, from the start, of the well-known special characteristics of international law as put succinctly by O'Connell:

> International law today is not so much a description of what States have done, as a complex intellectual construction, and it thus exhibits more affinity with the integrated exposition of the Grotian period than with the empiricism of the nineteenth century. The legal practitioner . . . is likely to be misled into supposing that rules of international law are more concrete and more absolute than they really are.

Before turning to the question of the observance of rules of international law, due consideration should be given to the difference between the questions connected with the observance of these rules and the prior question of the applicability of a certain set of rules to given circumstances. In other words, *de facto* observance of rules does not necessarily mean their applicability by force of law. There are cases of undisputed applicability of rules of law followed by no implementation, and even no protests or other censure, and there are, on the other hand, cases of the voluntary observance of certain rules unconnected with acceptance of their legal applicability.

There are abstract legal solutions to this point, and each and every

---

* Ed. Note: See also T. Meron, "Some Legal Aspects of Arab Terrorists' Claims to Privileged Combatancy," in S. SHOHAM, (ED.), OF LAW AND MAN, ESSAYS IN HONOR OF HAIM H. COHN 1-44 (1971).

political datum is of utmost importance, not only in relation to the question of the application of the Fourth Geneva Convention, but furthermore in relation to the rights in other far-reaching subjects. The interplay of political and legal data is conspicuous. Any attempt at separation of the legal and political problems involved, and rules of applicability, would create great difficulties *de lege late*. But, on the other hand, human problems demand immediate solution.

Humanitarian law concerns itself essentially with human beings in distress and victims of war, not States or their special interests. As Max Huber said: "The fate of human beings is independent of the legal character which belligerents wish to give to their struggle." It is, therefore, always important to seek ways and means by which humanitarian relief can be extended to victims of war without waiting for the international law to develop further and without subjecting the fate of the civilians to the political and legal reality. While political rights and the legal interpretation of a given set of factual circumstances are of far-reaching consequence for the fate of nations, and cannot be excluded from consideration, any possible separation between the decision on political issues and the pragmatic application of humanitarian rules should be considered positively. It must be borne in mind that this was also the underlying idea of Article 3, common to all four Geneva Conventions.

In my opinion there is no existing rule of international law according to which the Fourth Convention applies in each and every armed conflict whatever the status of the parties. Territory conquered does not always become occupied territory to which the rules of the Fourth Convention apply. It is apparently not so, for example, in cases of cessation of hostilities that lead to termination of war,[1] nor is it so in cases of subjugation,[2] although this question arose only before 1949.

The whole idea of the restriction of military government powers is based on the assumption that there had been a sovereign who was ousted[3] and that he had been a legitimate sovereign. Any other conception would lead to the conclusion that France, for example, should have acted in Alsace-Lorraine according to rules 42-56 of the Hague Rules of 1907,[4] until the signing of a peace treaty.

---

[1] [2] Oppenheim, *International Law* 596 (7th ed. Lauterpacht 1952).

[2] *Id.* 599.   [3] *Id.* 434.

[4] Annex to the Convention concerning the laws and customs of war on land, signed at The Hague, October 18, 1907.

As I mentioned before, I am aware of the theory of subjugation, which has been applied since World War II; if the Fourth Convention applies to every conflict, how do we adapt this theory to the Fourth Convention? In my view, *de lege late*, the automatic applicability of the Fourth Convention to the territories administered by Israel is at least extremely doubtful, to use an understatement, and automatic application would raise complicated juridical and political problems. I shall mention some of them.

Israel never recognized the rights of Egypt and Jordan to the territories occupied by them till 1967. Judea and Samaria and the Gaza Strip were part of the territory of the British Mandate of Palestine which ended on May 14, 1948. The war which started on that date never led to recognized boundaries. On the contrary, the Armistice agreements of 1948 explicitly stated that the Armistice demarcation line is not to be construed in any sense as a political or territorial boundary and is deliniated without prejudice to the rights, claims, or position of either party.

From 1948 till 1956 and again from 1956 till 1967 the Gaza Strip was, according to express U.A.R. statements, under Egyptian military occupation, ruled by a U.A.R. Military Governor. The inhabitants of the Gaza Strip were not nationals of the Occupying Power. They even needed a special permit to enter the U.A.R. Military courts were set up, curfew was declared, and administrative detention was carried out according to the orders of the Military Governor. It is worth noting that notwithstanding these facts, the question of the application of the Fourth Convention to this territory was never brought up or considered before 1967.

The history of the legal status of Judea and Samaria is also relevant. On May 13, 1948, a law was enacted in Transjordan[5] according to which the provisions of the Transjordan Defense Law apply to any country or place in which Jordan is responsible for the preservation of security and order. On May 18, 1948, General Ibrahim Pecha Hashem was appointed by King Abdullah as Military Governor of all territories which were held by the Transjordan Army. According to Proclamation No. 2 published by General Hashem:

All the laws and regulations which were in force in Palestine at the end of the Mandate on 15.5.48 shall remain in force in all areas in

5 Law No. 20 of 1948 [1948] *O.G.* 945.

which the Arab Jordan Army stays or in which it is responsible for the preservation of security and order, except the laws and regulations which are contrary to the Defense Law of Transjordan of 1935 or the Regulations and Orders published under this law.

On Sept. 16, 1950, the Law Regarding Laws and Regulations in Force in the Two Banks of the Hashemite Jordan Kingdom was published and entered into force. This law provided that the laws and regulations in each of the two banks should remain in force until unified laws for the two banks were promulgated with the consent of the national council and with the ratification of the King. The unification of the laws of the East and West Banks went on from 1950 to 1967, although by June 5, 1967, some laws still remained different.

In relation to the invasion and conquest by military force of parts of Palestine by Jordan and Egypt, it is interesting to quote Mr. Tarasenko, the representative of the Ukraine in the Security Council, who stated on May 13, 1948:

> None of the states whose troops have entered Palestine can claim that Palestine forms part of its territory. It is an altogether separate territory without any relationship to the territories of the states which have sent their troops into Palestine.

Senator Austin, the U.S. delegate, stated before the Security Council on May 22, 1948:

> These were questions addressed to him [King Abdullah], as a ruler who is occupying land outside his domain, by the Security Council, a body which is organized in the world to ask these questions of him. . . . The contumacy of the reply to the Security Council is the very best evidence of the illegal purpose of this Government in invading Palestine with armed forces and conducting the war which it is waging there. It is against the peace; it is not on behalf of peace. It is an invasion with a definite purpose. . . . Therefore here we have the highest type of the international violation of the law: the admission by those who are committing this violation.

There is no need to fully appraise the relative value and merit of the rights of the parties in this context. It should, however, be mentioned that in the interpretation most favorable to the Kingdom of Jordan her legal standing in the West Bank was at most that of a belligerent occupant following an unlawful invasion. In other words, following an armed invasion in violation of international law, the military forces of Jordan remained stationed in the West Bank and the Kingdom of Jordan then annexed the West Bank, after having agreed in the Armistice agreement of 1949 that it had no intention of prejudicing the rights, claims, and positions of the parties to the agreement. It is therefore not surprising to find the following conclusion as to the relative rights in the West Bank in Blum's article "Reflections on the Status of Judea and Samaria":

> . . . the traditional rules of international law governing belligerent occupation are based on a twofold assumption, namely, (a) that it was the legitimate sovereign which was ousted from the territory under occupation; and (b) that the ousting side qualifies as a belligerent occupant with respect to the territory. According to Glahn, "(b)elligerent occupation . . . as regulated by customary and conventional international law, presupposes a state of affairs in which the sovereign, the legitimate government of the occupied territory, is at war with the government of the occupying forces." This assumption of the concurrent existence in respect of the same territory of both an ousted legitimate sovereign and a belligerent occupant lies at the root of all those rules of international law, which, while recognizing and sanctioning the occupant's rights to administer the occupied territory, aim at the same time to safeguard the reversionary rights of the ousted sovereign. It would seem to follow that, in a case like the present where the ousted State never was the legitimate sovereign, those rules of belligerent occupation directed to safeguarding that sovereign's reversionary rights have no application.[6]

The same conclusion would apply to the Gaza Strip which was regarded even by the U.A.R. government as territory under military occupation, and that Government never even raised the claim that it had any legal rights to the territory.

The territorial position is thus *sui generis*, and the Israeli government tried therefore to distinguish between theoretical juridical and political problems on the one hand, and the observance of the humanitarian provisions of the Fourth Geneva Convention on the other hand. Accordingly, the Government of Israel distinguished between the legal problem of the applicability of the Fourth Convention to the territories

[6] *Israel Law Review* 279, 293 (1968).

under consideration which, as stated, does not in my opinion apply to these territories, and decided to act *de facto*, in accordance with the humanitarian provisions of the Convention.

II. *The Legal System*

Any judicial system involves continuing accommodation between the need to preserve a coherent set of ordering principles and the quest for tolerable results in individual disputes. One test of any system is the incidence of compatibility between dominating formal theory on the one hand and justice for the individuals affected on the other hand. Constant harmony between the two is an unattainable ideal, though an ideal nonetheless; yet a legal system is not judged in the main according to cases which are out of the ordinary course of things, but generally according to the ordinary ones. As to exceptional cases—cases of deviations—the system should not be judged according to them but mainly according to the character of the steps taken in order to remedy unwarranted deviation from the norm.

As aptly stated by Greenspan,[7] the basis of all military government lies in the necessity for the occupying force to exercise the functions of civil government and to restore and maintain public order and safety, where the military administration has substituted its authority for that of the sovereign or previous government or where the previous government is absent or unable to function properly. The restoration and maintenance of public order and safety, or, in other words, the orderly government of the country, is not an abstract matter. It is a mission in many and various areas of everyday life. The expression "restoration and maintenance of public order"—"*la vie publique*"—is, it would seem, a paraphrase of the words "normalization and rule of law." Rule of law, in its turn, is based on the defined norms of a given legal system. In our case, we have decided, rule of law means: (a) *de facto* observance of the humanitarian rules of the Hague Rules and of the Fourth Geneva Convention, and (b) observance of the basic principles of natural justice as derived from the system of law existing in Israel, whether or not these rules have found expression in the Fourth Convention.

In order to analyze the main spheres of activity in the Administered Territories, I shall use the following division for convenience: (a) the legal system; (b) safeguarding the various rights of the individual; (c)

[7] Greenspan, *The Modern Law of Land Warfare* 212 (1959).

security measures. Of course I do not intend to cover all areas, and, too, any division of topics, as proposed, is more or less arbitrary.

The legal system operative in the Territories as a whole may be viewed in terms of a layer of proclamation law enacted by the Military Commanders of the area, called "Security Enactments," which has been superimposed on the local law existing before the entry of the Israel Defense Forces (I.D.F.), with both types of law binding on all courts, whether military or indigenous. Both in the military courts, set up by order of the military commander, and in the local courts, the peacetime standards of justice prevail and are applied.

Proclamation No. 1, published on the day of entry of the I.D.F. into the area, declared the assumption of Government and the responsibility for order and security by the I.D.F. following the direction of Article 43 of the Hague Rules, according to which:

> The authority of the power of the State having passed de facto into the hands of the occupant, the latter shall do all in his power to restore, and ensure, as far as possible, public order and safety, respecting at the same time, unless absolutely prevented, the laws in force in the country.

I shall refer to Orders of Judea and Samaria, although similar orders have been published in the other areas too. Proclamation No. 2, published the same day, states:

> 2. The law which existed in the area on the 7th June, 1967, shall remain in force in so far as there is nothing therein repugnant to this proclamation, any other proclamation or order which will be enacted by me, and subject to such modifications as may result from the establishment of the rule of the I.D.F. in the area.
>
> 3. (a) All powers of government, legislation, appointment, and administration in relation to the area or its inhabitants shall henceforth vest in me alone and shall be exercised by me or by whomsoever shall be appointed by me in that behalf or act on my behalf.
>
> (b) Without derogating from the generality of the foregoing it is hereby provided that any duty to consult, obtain consent and the like, prescribed in any law as a condition—precedent for legislation, enactment or appointment, or as a condition for the entry into force of any legislation or appointment—is hereby repealed.
>
> 4. Immovable and movable property, including money, bank deposits, arms, ammunition, cars and other vehicles, and any other

military and civil supplies which were the property of or were registered in the name of the State or Government of Jordan or any governmental unit or subdivision or any part thereof, shall pass into my exclusive possession and be under my administration.

Article 2 of Proclamation 2 is the explicit expression of the proviso to Article 43 that the Military Government shall, unless absolutely prevented, respect the laws in force in the country. Furthermore, it is in agreement with Article 64 of the Fourth Geneva Convention which provides (*inter alia*):

The penal laws of the occupied territory shall remain in force, with the exception that they may be repealed or suspended by the Occupying Power in cases where they constitute a threat to its security or an obstacle to the application of the present Convention.

According to Proclamation No. 2, the civil and penal laws of the area continue, as a rule, to be valid; the courts which administer them are permitted to sit; and all offenses committed by the inhabitants which are not of a military nature or do not affect the safety of the army are left to their jurisdiction. The detailed provisions of the Fourth Convention in relation to the administration of criminal law within the territory and for stringent judicial safeguards for persons accused and convicted of crimes are respected in the Orders which followed Proclamation 2.

The penal laws of the territory remained in force. They were repealed or suspended only where they constituted a threat to security or an obstacle to the application of orderly government. As stated, if the exigencies of war, the maintenance of order, or the welfare of the population would so require, it is within the power of the I.D.F. to alter, suspend, or repeal any of the existing laws, or to promulgate new laws. Nevertheless, in those of the Territories possessing an adequate legal system in conformity with generally recognized principles of law, important changes were avoided as far as possible.

Article 3 of Proclamation 2, dealing with the assumption of legal and administrative powers, is an expression of the need to fill the vacuum created by the cessation of the ordinary legislative, executive, and administrative functions of the former Government, whatever its legal status.

Article 4 of Proclamation 2, dealing with Government property, represents the principles set out in Articles 53 and 55 of the Hague Rules and is supplemented by special General Staff Orders which deal with enemy public property along the same guidelines.

Returning to the general principles of the courts system, the local courts continue to function in Judea and Samaria, and in Gaza. Some changes, however, were found necessary, as follows:

(1) In Gaza, the President of the Supreme Court, who was an Egyptian, and some other Egyptian judges left the area. The Deputy President, a local Arab inhabitant, was appointed President, and vacancies were filled by other local jurists who submitted appropriate applications and were found suitable.

(2) Criminal justice in El-Arish and Sinai had been in the hands of military courts during Egyptian rule. An order of the Israel Military Commander turned it over to the regular civilian courts.

(3) The death penalty as a mandatory punishment was abolished in all Territories (Order 268) and the life sentence replaced it.

(4) In Judea and Samaria it was necessary to abolish the right of recourse to the fourth instance—the Court of Cassation which sits in Amman. In order to safeguard the rights of the inhabitants, its powers as a High Court of Justice were transferred to the third instance, namely the Appeal Court.

(5) Because of the strike of the Arab lawyers of Judea and Samaria, the local population remained without legal services. This could have brought the work of the local courts to a standstill, to the detriment of the civilian population. Order 145 authorized Israeli lawyers to appear before local courts. The object of this order was stated in its preamble, namely, that it was issued in order to facilitate the enforcement of the law and the activity of the local courts and to enable the inhabitants to receive the service of lawyers to this end. No similar order was needed in the Gaza Strip.

(6) In the Golan Heights another problem arose: no judges, lawyers, or law books had remained in the area. The judicial machinery of the previous administration was therefore totally disrupted and, according to the accepted principles of international law, it was the duty of the military administration to establish courts of its own.[8] A civil court manned by an Israeli judge was therefore set up in the Golan Heights by Order 185.

In summing up the activity of the local civil courts, it must be

---

[8] Compare "the Greek precedent" Thrace (Notarial Service) case, [1949] *Annual Digest and Reports of Public International Law Cases* (case No. 167) at 466 (ed. by Lauterpacht).

stressed that the military administration confined itself entirely to initiating the work of these courts, which are now run by their own judges and their own administrative staff. The legal officer at Military Government Headquarters representing the Ministry of Justice has no powers whatsoever in regard to adjudication or review of litigation, as practiced by many other countries in similar circumstances, and confines himself to supervision of the administration.

The military courts in the area deal with the trial of breaches of the Security Provisions Order (Order 3, now reissued as Order 378), other Security Enactments and criminal offenses against local law which, according to their facts, are in the nature of security offenses. Order 3 is the basic criminal security code of the area. This order, as the other orders, was published by poster and in the Official Gazette in Hebrew and Arabic. The Official Gazette is distributed free of charge to all local officeholders and is on sale to the general public.

The military courts are of two kinds: courts consisting of three officers, and courts consisting of a single judge. whose powers of punishment are limited. A Military Court is composed of a president, who has to be a legally qualified officer of the Israel Defense Forces of the rank of captain or above, and two judges who are officers. The court is constituted by the Military Commander, who also appoints the president and the judges. A single judge must be a legally qualified officer of the I.D.F. Trials before military courts are held in accordance with procedure obtaining in courts following the Anglo-Saxon system of law, and guarantees observance of the rules of natural justice.

Prior to a defendant being brought before a Military Court, the nature of the charge and its particulars are entered on a charge sheet which is filed in court by a Military Prosecutor. A copy of the charge sheet is delivered to the defendant at a reasonable time prior to his trial. At the commencement of the trial the charge sheet is read before the defendant. The defendant is asked whether or not he admits the charge or the facts. The defendant can reply to the question in one of the following ways: (a) that he admits the charge; (b) that he denies the charge; (c) that he denies the charge but admits the facts or some of the facts set out in connection with the act which is the subject of the charge. Where the accused does not reply in accordance with the foregoing to the question put, he is regarded as having denied the charge. By leave of the court the defendant may, at any stage of the hearings up to the judgment, withdraw the reply he has made.

Proceedings are held only in the presence of the accused. The proceedings are public. The entire proceedings are translated by an interpreter provided to the accused by the court, and the accused has the right to request the replacement of the interpreter, as provided for in Article 12:

> If the defendant does not understand Hebrew, the Military Court shall appoint an interpreter in order to translate to him what is said during the course of the hearing and the decisions of the Court, unless the defendant has voluntarily waived the translation in whole or in part. The defendant possesses the right to object to the interpreter and to request his replacement.

The accused has the right to produce witnesses and to testify himself, to examine witnesses, and to be represented by counsel of his choice. The rules of evidence are those obtaining in military courts which try soldiers, i.e., the rules of evidence are identical to the rules according to which the civil courts in Israel try criminal cases. The procedure is identical to the procedure in criminal cases in Israel.

No person shall be found guilty by a Military Court except by the unanimous decision of the President and members.

There is no appeal against judgment to a judicial forum but the convicted person may make appeal and application to the Commander of the Region or the Military Commander, as the case may be, concerning conviction or sentence. The Military Court which sentenced the defendant shall bring to his knowledge his right under this section.

As to the defense, a detailed order was published according to which a person charged before a military court is entitled to choose as his defense counsel a local advocate or an Israeli advocate, or conduct his defense himself. In certain cases specified in the order (grave offenses), the court must appoint a defense counsel for an accused if he consents to the appointment.

The death penalty may be imposed, as the maximum penalty only, for sabotage of military installations and for causing death with malice aforethought, but the order provides that it shall not be imposed in any event on an accused person under eighteen years of age. Moreover, sentence of death shall not be imposed upon a defendant in a Military Court unless at least two of its judges are legally qualified officers and the sentence is unanimous. It should be noted that the death penalty has so far not been imposed in a single case, despite the fact that saboteurs directly implicated in the killing of soldiers and civilians have been brought to trial and convicted in many instances.

The other penalties are imprisonment and fine. Imprisonment can be wholly or partly conditional (that is, suspended) and the Court may order, in addition to or instead of a penalty, an undertaking by the defendant to abstain from committing offenses.

III. *Various Rights of the Individual*

By General Staff Orders of the Israeli Army, every soldier is bound to act according to the Fourth Convention which has been published as part of these Orders. Every soldier is obliged to respect the person, honor, family rights, religious convictions and practices, and manners and customs of the inhabitants of the Territories, and any action against these rules of behavior is punishable by virtue of the Israeli Military Justice Law.

The right to religious worship has been explicitly and specially safeguarded and ensured by order of the Military Commanders of the Area (Orders 66 and 327 of Judea and Samaria), along with free access to places of worship. After the entry of the I.D.F. into the Territories, an order against pillage was published (Order 1), and the Army acted according to the provisions of the Military Justice Law in punishing pillage severely and prohibiting requisitions except those made with strict compliance to military orders strictly following Articles 42 and 43 of the Hague Rules. The rights of depositors in banks were ensured according to Order 21. No person was compelled to work, even not to the extent permitted by Article 40 of the Fourth Convention.

The status of public officials and judges was not altered, and no sanctions or measures of coercion or discrimination were applied to those public officials or judges who abstained from fulfilling their former functions. Public officials eligible for pensions receive their pensions according to an Order, including pensions for the period of service under the former Government, although no such defined legal duty exists under international law on this point.

Government property is held by a special custodian, appointed according to Order 59, who acts as administrator and usufructuary. In order to protect the rights of absentees, Order 58 was published, according to which property whose owner or possessor has left the territory is held and guarded by a special custodian. According to Article 14 of this order the custodian is obliged to return the property on the return of the owner or any other person having right to lawful possession. A person dissatisfied with the decision of one or other of the two custodians can appeal to an Appeals Committee presided over by a legally qualified officer, usually a senior member of the bar in reserve service (Order 172).

No political organization which was not active in inciting to terrorism was outlawed. Neither was any newspaper closed because of expression of criticism against the military government or for any other reason. According to Order 101, dealing with sedition and censorship, a license is required for a procession or for any assembly of more than twenty persons assembled for a political reason. Sedition is defined in this order similarly to its meaning in the common law. The number of trials of offenses against Order 101 has been minimal.

So far there have been no elections to the local councils, and the period of tenure of the existing local councils has been extended. As to unions and corporations, according to Orders 94 and 356 of the Military Commander, trade unions and corporative and other societies have the right to continue their activities. Inhabitants have the right to travel freely in the territory and, except in cases of personal security reasons, they can travel by permit to the neighboring Arab countries or to Israel. During the war a certain number of cars were requisitioned for military transport purposes, but after fighting was over all cars were returned. Full payment was made for lost cars and compensation was paid for damage to cars.

If damage is done to the property of the inhabitants because of military operations and movement of troops even after fighting has stopped, as occurs occasionally inside Israel, inhabitants can, according to Order 271, present claim for compensation. The claim is presented to the Staff Officer for Claims, and if the claimant is dissatisfied with the decision of this officer he can appeal to the Appeal Committee of Claims composed of three members, at least one of whom is a lawyer. These committees are today presided over by senior members of the bar, generally in reserve service. The decision of this Claims Committee is final.

In a number of cases, inhabitants of the Territories have applied to the Supreme Court of Israel, sitting as High Court of Justice, for orders nisi of the kind known in Great Britain as orders of mandamus, habeas corpus, or certiorari. Although according to legal precedents in municipal courts during the period between the two World Wars (the Military Administration of the Rhineland) and after World War II this legal procedure had been denied to inhabitants of territories under military administration, no objection to these applications has been raised in the Supreme Court by the representatives of the Attorney General, and the right of the inhabitants to apply for orders has not been questioned by the Court. The policy is not to hinder inhabitants of the territory in making use of the legal remedies available in Israel against acts of the administration. This principle was applied not only in relation to the High Court of Justice but also in other spheres. For example, claims for compensation for damage caused to private cars by military operations during the fighting have been brought by inhabitants of the Territories in the form of civil suits to the regular civil courts in Israel.

There has been no expropriation of private real estate for military use, although there have been cases where private real estate is being used in front line areas or has been seized for use as military establishments, in which cases rent for use and compensation for damage is being paid. In areas near the front line which have been closed, the declared intent is to compensate the owner on the close of hostilities when arrangements with the other party will be arrived at. Acquisition of land for the benefit of the local population, e.g., highways and housing projects, is made according to the laws in force in the territory, and compensation is paid according to these laws.[9] Such acquisitions are mostly made at the request of the local authorities. It is worth noting here that a large part of the budget of the local councils is provided by the Military Government.

IV. *Security Measures*

Two subjects which have been often mentioned in a pejorative way —deportations and demolitions—require consideration:

(1) DEPORTATIONS

Saboteurs, members of terrorist organizations, and persons actively engaged on behalf of the Arab Governments in actions against security and public order have been deported to the East Bank of Jordan since 1967 by order of the Military Commander of the Area, based on Regulation 112 (1) of the Defense (Emergency) Regulations, 1945,[10] still in

---

[9] This according to the accepted rules as applied, e.g., in the Krupp case.
[10] Regulation 112 (1) provides:

force in Judea and Samaria. Most of the persons deported had been in administrative detention until their deportation; they were in detention for a long time prior to their deportation, and it would have been impossible to release them because of imperative reasons of security. In other words, the only alternative to their deportation to Jordan was their continued detention. In Jordan they are free to go where they like.

Two questions arise in this context: Are these regulations still in force? Can they be enforced according to the rules of international law, presuming for the sake of this analysis that these rules apply?

As to the first question, the Regulations of 1945 had been in force in the West Bank on the eve of the invasion by the Jordanian forces in 1948, as mentioned above. They were part of the law of Palestine. Although the Jordanians immediately applied part of their internal Jordanian security regulations to the West Bank, by order of the Military Governor, the Defense Regulations of 1945 were never repealed, whether explicitly or impliedly. On the contrary, the Jordanian law of annexation of 1950 provided that the law existing in the West Bank shall continue to be in force, until repealed by unified laws. No such law repealing the Regulations of 1945 was ever passed.

As to the second problem, namely the examination of the question before us according to the rules of international law, Article 64 of the Fourth Geneva Convention provides that the penal laws in occupied territory shall remain in force. It remains to be seen, therefore, if there is a specific provision in the Conventions suspending such local law, which has priority over the general rule of Article 64 of the Convention. Article 49 of the Convention, which relates specifically to deportations, is worded as follows:

Individual or mass forcible transfers, as well as deportations of protected persons from occupied territory to the *territory of the Occupying Power* or to that of any other country, occupied or not, are prohibited, regardless of their motive. (Emphasis added.)

Deportation of a person to Jordan is, according to the conceptions of the persons deported, neither deportation to the territory of *the occu-*

The High Commissioner shall have power to make an order, under his hand (hereinafter in these regulations referred to as "a Deportation Order") for the deportation of any person from Palestine. A person in respect of whom a Deportation Order has been made shall remain out of Palestine so long as the Order remains in force.

pying power nor to the territory of *another* country. It is more a kind of return or exchange of a prisoner to the power which sent him and gave him its blessing and orders to act. There is no rule against returning agents of the enemy into the hands of the same enemy. Article 49, therefore, does not apply at all. Furthermore, let us examine the purpose of Article 49. It was included in the Convention against the background of the specific and terrible experiences of World War II. As stated in the official ICRC *Commentary*:[11]

> There is doubtless no need to give an account here of the painful recollections called forth by the "deportations" of the Second World War, for they are still present in everyone's memory. It will suffice to mention that millions of human beings were torn from their homes, separated from their families and deported from their country, usually under inhumane conditions. These mass transfers took place for the greatest possible variety of reasons, mainly as a consequence of the formation of a forced labour service.

I venture to say that any comparison between deportation for the purpose of slave labor and the release of a saboteur to his fellows and commanders is out of context. Immediately upon their arrival in the East Bank, some of the deportees have publicly boasted of their subversive activities in the West Bank. Indeed, the Government of Jordan, in recognition of their services, has promoted some of the deportees to its highest positions, including the Cabinet. This could not be compared to deportation for slave labor.

In conclusion, it seems that Article 49 does not apply either in terms of its wording or in terms of its intent and purpose. On the other hand, Article 64 of the Convention, according to which the Defense Regulations remained in force, is effective and permits the further use of Regulation 112 of the Defense Regulations according to local law and without contradicting any of the norms of the Geneva Convention.

(2) DEMOLITIONS

Demolitions have been applied as personal punitive measures against a person in whose house acts of terrorism against the Army or the civilian population have been prepared or committed, or arms caches found. Demolitions are of two kinds: (a) actual demolition, or

---

[11] *Commentary: IV Geneva Convention* under the general editorship of Pictet 278 (1958).

(b) eviction of a person from the building and closing of the building or flat, without destroying it. The latter occurs mainly when there are other inhabitants in the building who have no connection to the offense.

The Demolitions are based on Regulation 119 of the Defense (Emergency) Regulations, 1945, which are part and parcel of the penal law in the West Bank and Gaza. It is of some interest to note that Jordanian legislation expressly grants the Jordanian government the power and discretion to order the destruction of buildings if required by urgent needs of public security or defense.[12]

The idea that the existing law in the territory changes automatically by adopting itself to the rules of the Fourth Convention is not founded on the express wording of the Convention; it is necessary to determine if some other provision of the Convention or some other rule of international law expressly or impliedly changes the rule of existing local law on this point. Article 64 of the Convention leaves the penal provisions of the local law intact insofar as the local law includes rules permitting demolition. It has been asserted that if there is another rule of international law according to which the local law is regarded as inhumane or contrary to a basic norm of international law, this rule of international law supervenes the rule of the local law. The wording of Articles 64 and 68 of the Convention does not support this thesis, but if we assume this assertion to be well-founded we should turn to Article 53 of the Fourth Convention, which has been mentioned as the specific provision prohibiting demolition. This article provides:

> Any destruction by the Occupying Power of real or personal property belonging individually or collectively to private persons, or to the State, or to the public authorities, or to social or co-operative organizations, is prohibited, except where such destruction is rendered absolutely necessary by military operations.

Rule 23 (g) of the Hague Rules of 1907 provides similar provisions. The ICRC *Commentary* states, in connection with Article 53:

> The prohibition of destruction of property situated in occupied territory is subject to an important reservation: it does not apply in cases "where such destruction is rendered absolutely necessary by

---

[12] Article 2 (4) of the General Defense Regulations (No. 2), 1930, issued by the King of Transjordan under the Transjordan Defense Ordinance of 1935.

military operations." The occupying forces may therefore undertake the total or partial destruction of certain private or public property in the occupied territory when imperative military requirements so demand. Furthermore, it will be for the Occupying Power to judge the importance of such military requirements.[13]

In other words, even if Article 53 has priority over Article 64, demolition that is necessary because of military requirements is permitted.

Military requirement can be of two kinds: On the one hand, there is the necessity to destroy the physical base for military action when persons in the commission of a hostile military act are discovered. The house from which hand grenades are thrown is a military base, not different from a bunker in other parts of the world. On the other hand, there is the necessity to create effective military reaction. The measure under discussion is of utmost deterrent importance, especially in a country where capital punishment is not used against terrorists killing women and children. Since January, 1971, more than 70 Arab civilians have been brutally murdered in Gaza because they or members of their family worked in Israel or visited Israel.

In conclusion, it appears that even if Regulation 119 of the Defense (Emergency) Regulations, 1945, is regarded as suspended, demolition can be based, in appropriate circumstances, on Article 53 of the Convention.

V. *Conclusion*

I do not pretend that Israel has achieved perfection, and, furthermore, I have no tendency to find solace in comparisons with other systems of law and government, because we do not content ourselves with the norms followed by others. I believe that Israel's bona fide effort in many and various fields of activity in the Territories has greatly contributed to a change in relations and to an improvement of the general atmosphere. This should not weaken our alertness to our duty to continue and further promote the different expressions of the rule of law.

The significant achievements of the existing system, in my opinion, are the following: (a) the existence, since the first day of Military Government, of a military legal system based on the rule of law, a system in which even hostile critics abroad have detected no real flaws; (b) the speedy restoration of the normal functioning of the local courts, which

---

13 *Commentary op. cit. supra* note 11, at 302.

exercise their powers without interference; (c) the fact that the right of defense is ensured in both military and civil trials; (d) the avenue for criticism of the army authorities which has been voluntarily provided for by recourse to the High Court of Justice, in contrast to what has been customary in all other countries during military rule in occupied territory; (e) the existence of Appeals Committees on compensation for damage and on decisions of the Custodian, presided over by lawyers; (f) the fact that the rights of the population are ensured by a long series of legislative acts relating to protection of property, safeguarding of rights to property, social benefit rights, and freedom of worship.

The interplay of hope and fear, belief and doubt, determination and frustration demand, in the sphere before us, more than in normal times and conditions, the use of a compass that will guide our behavior according to clear-cut criteria. Turbulence destroys perspective and vision, and turbulent conditions demand repeated reflection and reappraisal of our performance. These in their turn demand well-defined legal and political criteria and the utmost restriction upon trial-and-error methods.

Legal criteria which are the expression of political and humane beliefs are not necessarily our permanent possession. Both external and internal pressures constantly assail them. It is easier to know how to combat a foreign enemy who challenges our right to our beliefs, than to subject ourselves to daily analysis and discipline for the purpose of preventing the erosion which can with equal effectiveness undermine our beliefs and norms.

We must therefore do our utmost not to waver in our effort to prove that *inter arms non silent leges.*

The United Nations and Human Rights
in the Middle East*

NIGEL S. RODLEY

Introduction

WITHIN a few days of the cessation of hostilities in the Middle East war of June 1967, the United Nations Security Council was to manifest a concern for the fate of civilians in the area of conflict which it and other United Nations organs have continued to demonstrate. During the period in question, Israel has been accused of refusal to permit the return of refugees, wholesale violations of human rights, forced removal of Arabs from their homes and even places of residence and various specific infractions of the Fourth Geneva Convention,[1] ranging from the imposition of collective punishments and the destruction of property to torture of individuals. Some of these charges, such as those regarding collective punishment and property destruction, are confirmed by statements of the highest officials of the Israeli government.

That the international community be concerned, and evidence a desire to secure compliance, with principles of human rights and standards of humanitarian behavior towards civilians affected by war is laudable. Indeed, to the extent that this article presents a bias, I trust that it is in the direction of precisely such a con-

* Ed. Note: See also Int'l Comm. of the Red Cross, "The Middle East Activities of the Int'l Committee of the Red Cross, June 1967—June 1970," *In't Review of the Red Cross,* (10th year, #113, Aug. 1970), pp. 424-59, (10th year, #114, Sept. 1970), pp. 485-511.

* AUTHOR'S NOTE—I wish to express my gratitude to my former colleague in the U.N. Secretariat, Dr. John P. Pace of the Human Rights Division, for his help in securing materials and for the willing sharing of his insight and experience. Needless to say, the opinions expressed herein are in no way attributable to him or to the U.N. Secretariat.

I am also anxious to record my debt to Professor Leland M. Goodrich who first stimulated my interest in international organization when I was a graduate student of Columbia University Law School in 1964-65.

1 The Geneva Convention Relative to the Protection of Civilian Persons in Time of War of August 12, 1947, 75 U.N.T.S. 287 (1950).

cern. It constitutes the premise upon which is based much of the criticism here levelled at particular aspects of United Nations practices regarding the matter under consideration. Accordingly, I do not challenge, for example, the legitimacy of the Human Rights Commission's interest in the application of the Fourth Geneva Convention, even though I am not aware of any previously established connection between the jurisdiction a concern for human rights would presuppose and that with respect to the application of the Geneva Conventions. It seems to me that the term "human rights" is broad enough to encompass the standards of protection established at least in the Fourth Geneva Convention, though I do not know of that Convention's having been cited more than once among the major documents in the realm of international protection of human rights.[2]

However, in analyzing the activities of the Security Council, General Assembly and the Human Rights Commission [3] with respect to the treatment of civilians in the Middle East, there has to be borne in mind the extreme sensitivity which international fact-finding, or, even more important, "quasi-judicial" investigations have evoked in countries subjected to such procedures.

The possibility of meaningful international action in the field of human rights has always stumbled against the obstacle of "domestic jurisdiction." [4] Within the United Nations context, this has meant the invocation of Article 2(7) of the Charter. Despite forceful arguments, suggesting that the powers of the United Nations with regard to the promotion of respect for, and the implementation of, human rights may not be unduly hampered by categorization as intervention "in matters which are essentially

---

[2] None of the Geneva Conventions for the Protection of War Victims appears, for example, in *Human Rights: A Compilation of International Instruments of the United Nations,* U.N. Doc. E/CONF. 324 (U.N. Pub. Sales No. E.68.XIV.6), prepared for International Human Rights Year, 1968.

[3] This paper does not purport to analyze the actual conduct of the investigations that have so far taken place. The following article by John Bender admirably accomplishes this task.

[4] H. Lauterpacht, *International Law and Human Rights* (1950), at 166–220 and *passim.*

in the domestic jurisdiction of any state," the Commission on
Human Rights was to adopt, with the approval of the Economic
and Social Council, a very limited view of its power of action.[5]
Thus the late Sir Hersch Lauterpacht, in a landmark work, was
moved to observe, with respect to the powers of U.N. organs, including the Commission on Human Rights:

> Nothing in the Charter excludes . . . , with the consent of the
> State concerned, an investigation undertaken in its territory and
> with its co-operation; or without the consent of the State in
> question, an investigation conducted outside its territory and not
> requiring its co-operation.[6]

Nevertheless, it was not until 1963, when the President of
the General Assembly sent a Fact-Finding Mission to South Vietnam to inquire into allegations concerning the persecution of
Buddhists, that the U.N. launched an official inquiry into a matter
concerning human rights outside South Africa or colonial territories.[7] Even though the President of South Vietnam had *invited*
this action by the President of the General Assembly, the Mission
was undertaken "without benefit of a General Assembly resolution
establishing its juridical foundations and mandate," and though
no action was taken on the Report of the Mission, the Soviet
Union still felt impelled to issue an official statement that the
sending of the Mission was not to be considered a precedent for
the future.[8]

The investigations into human rights in non-self-governing
territories by the Fourth Committee of the General Assembly,
the Special Committee on Colonialism (the "Committee of 24"
established by the General Assembly) and the Trusteeship Council can perhaps be justified in terms of Article 2(7) by the argument that events taking place in colonies are no longer "essentially within the domestic jurisdiction" of the metropolitan state,

---

[5] *Id.* at 225–227.

[6] *Id.* at 232.

[7] There have, of course, been several fact-finding missions to investigate political
situations.

[8] M. Moskowitz, *The Politics and Dynamics of Human Rights* (1968), C.VII,
note 4, at 253, 4.

at least since the passage of the General Assembly resolution on the Granting of Independence to Colonial Peoples. Nevertheless, this history led to the observation that "the new double standard is discriminatory in that a higher standard of human rights was created in colonial territories than in the territories of states recognized as fully independent." [9]

The various inquiries into the situation in South Africa [10] also constitute something of a special case. For it has been observed that U.N. resolutions relating to that country have been based on "[l]anguage uncomfortably close to that of Article 39." [11] But the Security Council has yet to make a clear determination, under Article 39, that there is a threat to international peace and security, justifying enforcement measures that would override Article 2(7). Of course, fact-finding or investigation can hardly be regarded as "enforcement measures" anyway. This all leads to the silly conclusion that the United Nations, or at any rate the Security Council, can override the protection afforded by Article 2(7) and use force once it has made an Article 39 determination, but that no organ of the organization can use the mild technique of investigation without running up against the claim of domestic jurisdiction. The point, clearly, is that it is nonsense to consider fact-finding and investigations as constituting "intervention" within the meaning of Article 2(7). Accordingly, we must come to the conclusion that a "double standard" has been applied to South Africa.[12] Yet, even in this case, it was not until 1967 that the Commission on Human Rights established its *Ad Hoc* Working Group of Experts "to investigate the continuing ill-treatment of prisoners, detainees and others in police custody in the Republic of South Africa." [13]   The ECOSOC was to show

[9] J. Carey, *U.N. Protection of Civil and Political Rights* (1970), at 152, quoting Lady Gaitskell of the United Kingdom in the Third Committee.

[10] As to which, see Carey, *op. cit. supra,* note 9, at 95–126.

[11] R. Ballinger, "U.N. Action on Human Rights in South Africa," in Luard, ed., *International Protection of Human Rights* (1967), 248, at 257.

[12] Carey, *op. cit.,* at 143–153.

[13] *Id.* at 98.

its approval by asking the *Ad Hoc* Working Group to consider allegations of infringements of trade union rights in South Africa.[14]

Indeed ECOSOC was to go even farther by authorizing the Human Rights Commission to "make a thorough study of situations which reveal a consistent pattern of violations of human rights," as well as "to examine information relevant to gross violations of human rights and fundamental procedures."[15] However, when the Sub-Commission on the Prevention of Discrimination and the Protection of Minorities urged the Commission, under this new ECOSOC authorization, to investigate charges of such violations, not only in Southern Africa but also in Greece and Haiti,[16] the Commission took no action.

Given the scarcity of past U.N. human rights investigations and the legal difficulties that have accompanied them, especially in the case of South Africa, the viciousness of whose regime is not patently relevant for establishing distinctions under Article 2(7), it would appear of the essence that international attempts at investigating the extent of a state's compliance with standards of human rights should be as little as possible tainted with charges of "ulterior motives," political manoeuvering or propaganda warfare. That the United Nations has not succeeded, in the case under discussion, in manifesting the requisite sensitivity to avoid such charges will appear. If this article emphasizes an analysis of legal questions and their political implications, it is because it seems to me that questions of legality are basic in establishing the kind of atmosphere that would be conducive to the scrupulous respect for those human or humanitarian standards here in question.

Security Council Resolution 237 (1967) and the Jewish Minorities in Arab Countries

Four days after the war ended, the first of the humanitarian resolutions under consideration was passed by the Security Coun-

---

[14] *Id.* at 110.

[15] E/RES/1235 (XLII).

[16] Carey, *op. cit.,* at 86.

cil. Resolution 237 (1967), adopted at the Council's 1361st meeting on 14 June 1967, *inter alia,* recommended "to the Governments concerned the scrupulous respect of the humanitarian principles governing the treatment of prisoners of war and the protection of civilian persons in time of war, contained in the Geneva Conventions of 12 August 1949." [17] It also requested the Secretary-General "to follow the effective implementation of this resolution and to report to the Security Council."

First of all, the Secretary-General relied on UNRWA and its Commissioner-General for information which he could report. He later came to feel that "practically," due to the heavy burden UNRWA was facing in the wake of hostilities, and "politically," presumably because, as an administrative agency, it would be insidious for it to scrutinize the activities of a government whose cooperation was essential to its humanitarian activities, he needed "a representative of suitable experience and rank to obtain for him on the spot information." [18] Accordingly, some three weeks after the passage of resolution 237, he appointed Mr. Nils-Göran Gussing, the then UNRWA representative to Greece, as his Special Representative and dispatched him to the Middle East.

[17] The resolution as a whole reads:
The Security Council,
Considering the urgent need to spare the civil populations and the prisoners of the war in the area of conflict in the Middle East additional sufferings,
Considering that essential and inalienable human rights should be respected even during the vicissitudes of war,
Considering that all the obligations of the Geneva Convention relative to the Treatment of Prisoners of War of 12 August 1949 should be complied with by the parties involved in the conflict,
1. *Calls upon* the Government of Israel to ensure the safety, welfare and security of the inhabitants of the areas where military operations have taken place and to facilitate the return of those inhabitants who have fled the areas since the outbreak of hostilities;
2. *Recommends* to the Governments concerned the scrupulous respect of the humanitarian principles governing the treatment of prisoners of war and the protection of civilian persons in time of war, contained in the Geneva Conventions of 12 August 1949;
3. *Requests* the Secretary-General to follow the effective implementation of this resolution and to report to the Security Council.
[18] U.N. Doc. S/8021, para. 6.

Upon Gussing's arrival, the Israeli government broached the question of the fate of Jews in Arab territories. Gussing, uncertain as to whether the resolution applied to "this particular humanitarian problem," sought a ruling from the Secretary-General. The latter responded that the resolution "might properly be interpreted as having application to the treatment . . . of both Arab and Jewish persons in the States which are directly concerned because of their participation in that war." [19] Accordingly, towards the end of his mission, Gussing took the matter up with the governments of the United Arab Republic and Syria. The former government denied the applicability of the resolution to the local Jewish minority,[20] but the Syrians informally "welcomed the chance" to co-operate,[21] giving Gussing a tour of Jewish shops in the shopping district of Damascus.[22]

Some five months after the publication of the Secretary-General's report of the Gussing mission, in October 1967,[23] the Secretary-General again sought to send a representative to the area. Israel and the Arab states had been trading accusations, and he felt a representative's visit would "make it possible for him to meet his reporting obligations under the relevant resolution." [24] The replies of Syria and Israel marked the beginning of a series of communications which were to lead to the abandonment of the Secretary-General's attempts to appoint a new representative. The Syrians agreed to his initiative, "provided that the mission did not go beyond the terms of reference contained in the two resolutions." [25] Israel, replying a month later, requested that the

19 U.N. Doc. S/8158–A/6797, para. 212.
20 Id. at para. 218.
21 Id. at para. 221.
22 Id. at para. 222.
23 U.N. Doc. S/8158–A/6797.
24 U.N. Doc. E/CN.4/999, para. 19.
25 Ibid. The second resolution to which the Syrians referred was General Assembly resolution 2252 (ES–V), passed on 4 July 1967, which welcomed Security Council resolution 237 (1967) and was concerned with the provision of humanitarian relief to "persons coming within [the] mandate" of the Commissioner-General of UNRWA and to "other persons . . . in serious need."

representative should "look into . . . the situation of the Jewish communities in the Arab countries situated in the area of conflict."[26]   The Secretary-General replied to Israel stating that "the provisions of the resolutions would delineate the terms of reference of his representative."[27]   Given the history of the Gussing mission, including the Secretary-General's interpretation to Gussing, no conflict appeared to obtain between Israel and the Secretary-General.   But in the light of the United Arab Republic's previous adamant refusal to interpret the resolution so as to permit an examination of the fate of Jews in that country and the possibility, subsequently to become fact, of Syria formulating a formal and negative view of it, Israel's attempt at clarification was not, at this stage, unreasonable.

In the event, two weeks later the Syrian Permanent Representative denied that the resolutions could be interpreted "in any way" to include the scope requested by the Israelis.[28]   He further insisted, in a subsequent letter, that any questions about "Syrian citizens of the Jewish faith in Syria" would not be accepted by his government.[29]   Three days after the date of the second Syrian letter, the Israeli Permanent Representative communicated orally with the Secretary-General, indicating Israel's desire "that the treatment of Jewish communities in Iraq and Lebanon be included in the proposed mission."[30]   After some further communications between Israel and the Secretary-General, the latter arguing against inclusion of Iraq and Lebanon in the proposed mission,[31] an exchange of legal views essentially solidified the dispute into an *impasse*.

Strangely, the Iraq and Lebanon questions were hardly debated in these legal exchanges.   The Secretary-General merely denied that his "precedent," regarding the Gussing mission's inquiry into

[26] U.N. Doc. E/CN.4/999, para. 19.
[27] *Ibid.*
[28] *Id.* at para. 25.
[29] *Ibid.*
[30] *Ibid.*
[31] *Ibid.*

the fate of Jews in Syria and the United Arab Republic, "could be extended to Iraq and Lebanon or any other Arab state whose territories lie outside the areas where military operations have taken place . . . " [32] The position of Israel, as advanced by Foreign Minister Abba Eban, was confined to the observation that "Iraq and Lebanon . . . were also directly involved in the conflict." It is true that Iraq and Lebanon considered themselves at war with Israel. Pilots of the former country claimed to have shot down an Israeli jet.[33] Iraq sent a division and a hundred and fifty tanks into Jordan, but did not fight, despite claiming, inaccurately, to have destroyed seven Israeli aircraft in a raid on a base and to have bombed Tel Aviv.[34] However, operative paragraph 2 of Security Council resolution 237 is addressed to the "Governments concerned" without geographic limitation. It may be that the term "area of conflict," in the first preambular paragraph, limits the scope of the resolution as a whole. Even so, it would not be overly stretching its ambit to conclude that Lebanon, a neighbor of Israel, and Iraq, belligerent and close, though not contiguous, fall within it.[35] The Secretary-General's reference to "areas where military operations have taken place" is taken from the first operative paragraph which is specifically addressed to Israel. The obligations of the "Governments concerned," mentioned in operative paragraph 2, of necessity cover more territory than that specified in the first operative paragraph and the Secretary-General's legal analysis. The sole fact that the Iraqi trials and executions, for example, occurred subsequently to the passage of the resolution does not affect the geographic scope of the inquiry, any

---

32 U.N. Doc. A/7149–(S/8699), at 17.

33 R. Churchill and W. Churchill, *The Six Day War* (1967), at 151.

34 *Ibid.*

35 An argument made later by the Secretary-General to the effect that the term "area of conflict" is narrower than "the territories of States parties to the conflict" (U.N. Doc. A/7149, at 31) is interesting but inconclusive, as admittedly is his observation that the debates "disclose no reference to the possible inclusion of the Jewish communities in the Arab States as a concern of the resolutions." (*Id.* at 30) My point is that the vagueness of the term "area of conflict" admits of more than one interpretation.

more than the absence of similarly adverse reports from Lebanon. The Secretary-General's task was to "follow the effective implementation of the resolution." If compliance was all he would be able to report, so much the better!

But the brunt of the legal exchanges went to the heart of the applicability of the resolution to Jewish minorities in the Arab countries. Here the Israeli legal position, while not without merit, was less convincing. Although he had earlier "sought to avoid legal analysis and interpretation," [36] the Secretary-General argued that Jews in the Arab territories were not "protected persons" within the meaning of Article 4 of the Fourth Geneva Convention,[37] and that, although the benefits of Part II of the Convention, which is not restricted to protected persons, might apply, the relevant articles refer primarily to humanitarian relief of those least able to fend for themselves. He also contended that, under Article 6, the Convention ceased to apply except for certain key articles applicable to protected persons in occupied territory for the duration of the occupation.[38]

Mr. Eban's position was that some members of the Jewish minorities in question were, by admission of the United Arab

[36] U.N. Doc. A/7149–(S/8699), at 16.

[37] Article 4 excludes from the category of "protected persons" nationals of a party to the conflict.

[38] U.N. Doc. A/7149–(S/8699), at 16, 17.

Article 6

The present Convention shall apply from the outset of any conflict or occupation mentioned in Article 2.

In the territory of Parties to the conflict, the application of the present Convention shall cease on the general close of military operations.

In the case of occupied territory, the application of the present Convention shall cease one year after the general close of military operations; however, the Occupying Power shall be bound, for the duration of the occupation, to the extent that such Power exercises the functions of government in such territory, by the provisions of the following Articles of the present Convention: 1 to 12, 27, 29 to 34, 47, 49, 51, 52, 53, 59, 61 to 77, 143.

Protected persons whose release, repatriation or re-establishment may take place after such dates shall meanwhile continue to benefit by the present Convention.

Republic,[39] stateless and, accordingly, protected by the Convention; that Part II of the Convention could not be summarily dismissed as insignificant to the position of Jewish families; that Part III applies to all the territories of the parties to the conflict, and that Article 6 (4) preserves the life of the Convention as a whole for persons who have been interned and have not yet been released, which he claimed was the case for some Jews in Arab countries.

The claim regarding stateless Jews is correct, though presumably they constitute a very small proportion of the Jewish inhabitants in Arab countries other than the United Arab Republic. As far as the applicability of Part II of the Convention is concerned, particularly Articles 24 to 26 covering children under fifteen who are separated from their families, the exchange of intra-family news and the renewal of contacts among members of families dispersed owing to war, it may be agreed that they might be "positively and generously interpreted," so as to apply to Jewish families, the heads of which have been incarcerated.[40] But the interpretation is far from obvious, and apart from the benefits accorded children under 15 (Article 24), the convention does not do much for the alleged beneficiaries. Some positive and generous teleology is required to establish the applicability of the Articles in question. The Israeli contention regarding the applicability of Part III is unfounded. It pertains, by its own title, "Status and Treatment of Protected Persons," to protected persons, who, as has been noted, include in this case only *stateless* Jewish persons. Similarly, Article 6(4) only preserves the Convention's safeguards for protected persons coming within its terms. With regard to stateless persons, it may be remembered that the Syrian statement excluded only Syrian citizens of Jewish faith. The United Arab Republic, in its discussions with Gussing, had insisted, with unwarranted restrictiveness, that such persons

---

[39] U.N. Doc. S/8158–A/6797, para. 218.
[40] U.N. Doc. A/7149– (S/8699), at 25.

came within the mandate of the U.N. High Commissioner for Refugees.[41]

More persuasive for Israel's point of view is the language of operative paragraph 2 of the Security Council resolution, calling, as it does, for "scrupulous respect of the humanitarian principles . . . contained in the Geneva Conventions." While the term "humanitarian principles" may be the product of Council rhetoric, it adds something to the meaning of the resolution, even though the determination of what those principles are may prove difficult. Perhaps, at least, a generous interpretation of the applicability of the Convention is called for. It particularly casts some doubt, especially since its passage followed the close of hostilities, on the Secretary-General's contention with respect to the exclusions under Article 6.

It is unfortunate that this inconclusive, but fundamental, debate overshadowed the more limited question of whether the resolutions applied to Iraq and Lebanon. In the event, the Security Council essentially dictated its own interpretation and demonstrated its own priorities by passing resolution 259, on 27 September 1968. It thereby requested the Secretary-General to send a special representative to "the Arab territories under military occupation by Israel" and to report on the implementation of its earlier resolution, at the same time requesting Israel to receive and co-operate with him. Israel backed down from its position with respect to Iraq and Lebanon, but agreed only to co-operate if the mandate were subject to the Secretary-General's "broad" interpretation of the Gussing mission's mandate.[42] The Secretary-General correctly rejected this approach as constituting a condition inconsistent with the terms of the new Security Council resolution.[43]

The mission never got started; the General Assembly passed resolution 2443 (XXIII), and the Human Rights Commission

---

[41] U.N. Doc. S/8158–A/6797, para. 218.
[42] U.N. Doc. E/CN.4/999, para. 27.
[43] *Ibid.*

passed resolution 6 (XXV).[44]   By the time Israel was prepared to
accept the Secretary-General's geographically restrictive, but substantively broad interpretation of resolution 237, all U.N. organs
were prepared to investigate the humanitarian practices of Israel
alone.   Given especially the view of the Security Council, as
evidenced in its resolution 259 (1968), of what needed to be investigated, perhaps the Secretary-General's view more closely reflected the intent of resolution 237 than that of Israel.   By the
same token, Israel can hardly be blamed for reacting to Iraqi
practices that were to culminate in mass public hangings.   Nor,
even if she foresaw the vigor with which the U.N. would continue
to investigate her own practices in the occupied territories, could
she be blamed for resisting the U.N.'s selective humanitarian
concerns.   However, she did successfully prevent an investigation
into her willingness to permit the return of Arab inhabitants of
the occupied territories who had fled during and directly after the
hostilities.   Such an investigation would have been of general
humanitarian concern.   The denial of Israel's none-too-unreason-
able demands, from a similarly humanitarian point of view, left
human rights and humanitarian concerns the losers.

*General Assembly Resolution 2443 (XXIII) and the Establish-
ment of the Special Committee of Three*

Given the inability of the Secretary-General to implement the
mandate assigned him by Security Council resolutions 237 (1967)
and 259 (1968), the former resolution having been welcomed by
General Assembly resolution 2252 (ES–V), the General Assembly,
at its twenty-third session, turned its attention again to the
problem.   Its deliberations culminated in the passage of resolution 2443 (XXIII), by which it decided "to establish a Special
Committee to investigate Israeli practices Affecting the Human
Rights of the Population of the Occupied Territories composed of
three member states" (hereinafter referred to as the "Special

---

44 For both of which, see the following sections.

Committee of Three"). The membership of the Special Committee was to be appointed by the President of the General Assembly, who was then Dr. Emilio Arenales of Guatemala. Israel was requested to receive it, co-operate with it and facilitate its work.[45]

While the number of states voting for resolution 2443 exceeded (by one) the number voting against it or abstaining, the number of positive votes (60) nevertheless represented a minority of the membership of the General Assembly. Twenty-four of them belonged to the Arab or "Socialist" groups. A large majority had either never had or had subsequently ruptured diplomatic relations with Israel. It may well be that a political body such as the General Assembly may be expected to deal with human rights questions, along with other issues, as part of the normal process of diplomacy. Still, where it purports to establish a quasi-judicial body, that body's difficulties can only be increased if it can be shown to owe its life to the pressures of political manoeuver rather than impartial concern for the subject-matter of the investigation.

Although the resolution did not directly make prejudicial assertions regarding Israeli policies and practices in the occupied territories, it did note resolution I of the Teheran Conference, especially citing those parts of that resolution where the Conference "[e]xpressed its grave concern at the violation of human rights in Arab territories occupied by Israel" and "[d]rew the attention of the Government of Israel to the grave consequences resulting from the disregard of fundamental freedoms and human rights in occupied territories." The prejudicial nature of resolution 2443 was not as pronounced as that of the Human Rights Commission was to be. It did, after all, merely *note* the Teheran Conference resolution. Nevertheless, the gratuitous and detailed insertions of its provisions could not have been conducive to Israeli confidence in the purpose of investigation.

[45] A subsequent General Assembly resolution 2546 (XXIV) referred to Israel's "reported repressive practices and policies" and requested the Special Committee of Three to take cognizance of its provisions. Accordingly, I use at several points the formulation "policies and practices."

After the death of General Assembly President Arenales, the question arose as to how his functions could be discharged with respect to the appointment of the Special Committee of Three. The Secretary-General circularized the membership, suggesting three possibilities, one of which was to find a procedure whereby one of the Vice-Presidents might perform the relevant tasks.[46] Israel resisted this proposal by arguing,[47] *inter alia,* that the President of the General Assembly was requested to appoint the committee members in his individual capacity, since his duties would otherwise be limited to his term of office, which by Article 21 of the Charter is the end of the session of the General Assembly.[48] She also contended that, since rule 31 of the Rules of Procedure of the General Assembly provides also that Vice-Presidents cease to hold office at the close of the session for which they are elected, there were no Vice-Presidents upon whom the President's functions could devolve, assuming such delegation were possible.[49] When, on the basis of an overwhelmingly positive response to this proposal, the Secretary-General announced his intention to call a meeting of Vice-Presidents to entrust one of their number with the task in question,[50] Israel dug her heels in further, arguing that "even during the session at which they are elected, the Vice-Presidents do not under the rules of procedure or existing practice constitute a collective body that can exercise any collective functions or take any collective decisions." [51] Accordingly, the Israeli government concluded that "any action taken in pursuance [of a mandate arrived at by such defective procedure] will be *ultra vires."* [52] The position of the Secretary-General was merely that the situation was "unprecedented," [53] that, accordingly, it is sound

---

[46] U.N. Doc. A/7495, at 1.

[47] *Id.* at 4.

[48] Article 21 of the Charter provides that the "General Assembly . . . shall elect its President *for each session."* (Emphasis supplied)

[49] U.N. Doc. A/7495, at 4.

[50] U.N. Doc. A/7495/Add. 1, at 3.

[51] *Id.* at 5.

[52] *Ibid.*

[53] U.N. Doc. A/7495/Add. 2, Annex I, paras. 1 and 5.

constitutional practice to devise procedures that serve the interests of the organization's members and do not endanger its purposes and principles, and that this was such a "reasonable procedure" that would give effect to the will of the majority of the membership.[54]   However, this position is only valid if there is nothing in the constitution in question which contradicts it.   There is no attempt to refute the specific Israeli charges against the legality of the procedure.   Yet the Secretary-General did "not believe that the legality of the preferred procedure can be convincingly contested." [55]

While not wishing to insist on the validity of the Israeli position, I suggest it deserved more than the summary treatment it received.   Clearly we are dealing with a technical matter.   The problem could have been deferred to the following session of the General Assembly and would no doubt have been rapidly resolved (such indeed was Israel's position).[56]   The vast majority of the membership approved the procedure and the General Assembly was subsequently implicitly to ratify the decision by addressing the terms of its resolution 2546 (XXIV) to the Special Committee of Three.   The point is that legal claims short of the frivolous ought not to be brushed aside as of no consequence, especially where the U.N. action in question concerns an assessment of the legality of the actions of one of its members.   Respect for law, as is all too evident these days, is not promoted by those who do not demonstrate a similar respect.

The composition of the Special Committee,[57] as it eventually emerged from these procedures, also left something to be desired. The Foreign Minister of Somalia has apparently stated that his

[54] *Id*. at paras. 8 and 9.
[55] *Id*. at para. 8.
[56] See U.N. Docs. A/7495 at 5 and 3/7495/Add. 1 at 4.   In the event, the Committee was not formed until 12 September 1969, that is, just prior to the convening of the twenty-fourth session of the General Assembly.
[57] Ceylon, Somalia and Yugoslavia.   Unlike the Special Working Group of Six discussed in the next section, the membership of the Special Committee is composed of governments represented by their nominees.

country considers itself "in a state of war against Israel." Yugoslavia, which, as will be noted in the next section, had severed
diplomatic relations with Israel at the time of the 1967 war, had
already sponsored resolution 6 (XXV) in the Human Rights Commission establishing the Group of Six, and its President had a
"special relationship" with the then President of the United Arab
Republic.   Ambassador Alvarado of Peru, who was ultimately
entrusted with the functions assigned to Dr. Arenales, cannot be
blamed for not predicting that a new Ceylonese government
would subsequently suspend diplomatic relations with Israel.
Nevertheless, all three countries had voted for the resolution, a
factor that, together with the others mentioned, would hardly
be expected to breed confidence in the intentions of the Special
Committee membership.

The question of Israeli denunciations regarding the inherent weakness of the support given to Resolution 2443 (XXIII), the deficiencies of the appointment procedures following the death of Dr.
Arenales and the presumed bias of the states represented on the
Special Committee, in addition to the refusal of the General Assembly to investigate the problem of Jewish minorities in Arab
countries, has permitted Israel once more to avoid a direct investigation of her treatment of Arab civilians in the occupied territories.   A real interest in human rights in the General Assembly
could have made such avoidance more difficult.

*Human Rights Commission Resolution 6 (XXV) and the Es-
tablishment of the Special Working Group of Six*

The question of Israeli treatment of civilians in the territories
it had occupied in the course of the war arrived before the Human
Rights Commission more or less by default.   The appointment of
a representative of the Secretary-General to carry on the work
started by Gussing had become stalled over whether the representative was empowered to investigate the fate of Jews in Arab
countries involved in the war, and Emilio Arenales, the President
of the General Assembly, had not succeeded in forming the

Special Committee of Three envisaged by General Assembly resolution 2443 (XXIII). Accordingly, the matter was brought up in the Human Rights Commission under its item of discussion, "Study of situations which reveal a consistent pattern of violations of human rights," [58] at its twenty-fifth session in March 1969.

The Commission considered two draft resolutions [59] on the question, the second of which was a general appeal to all governments "to spare no efforts . . . towards insuring respect in that region for the fundamental rights of all human beings . . ." [60] This resolution was passed unanimously. The first, offered by India, Mauritania, Pakistan and Yugoslavia, became, subject to a minor amendment, Resolution 6 (XXV) and it set up the Special Working Group of Experts (hereinafter referred to as the Working Group of Six) to "investigate allegations concerning Israel's violations of the [Fourth] Geneva Convention." [61] The sponsorship of this resolution was not above reproach in regard to bias. Yugoslavia had broken off diplomatic relations with Israel in the wake of the June 1967 war, while the other three countries had never had relations with the country whose conduct it was proposed to investigate.

The first paragraph of the draft resolution, which had nothing to do with the intended mandate of the Group of Six, was voted on separately.[62] It reaffirmed "the inalienable right of all the inhabitants who have left since the outbreak of hostilities to return," and called on the Israeli government to implement the various U.N. resolutions that had previously called on her to take the steps necessary to permit such a return. This paragraph had much more support than the rest of the resolution and was overwhelmingly approved, with only one country voting against

[58] This reflects the language of ECOSOC resolution 1235 (XLII) noted earlier in the introductory section.

[59] U.N. Doc. E/4621–E/CN.4/1007, paras. 191–197.

[60] *Id.* at para. 195.

[61] *Id.* at 183.

[62] *Id.* at para. 222.

it.[63]   The resolution as a whole had much less satisfactory backing.   It was passed by thirteen votes, with one negative vote and
sixteen abstentions.[64]   Thus a minority of the members of the
Commission had voted in favor of the resolution as a whole.   Of
these thirteen, four were "Socialist" states, three were Arab states
and the rest had Moslem majorities or substantial minorities.
Only two [65] have diplomatic relations with Israel.   While none of
these factors ought fairly to be construed as precluding a legitimate judgment regarding the appropriateness of any particular
U.N. action—should African states be precluded from urging
U.N. action with respect to South Africa?—in their totality and
in the local and global context of the Middle East question, in
particular, it may be wondered whether such support offers the
most durable basis for securing initial co-operation with machinery designed to achieve more reliable U.N. performance in the
effective implementation of human rights.

Since the members of the Working Group of Six were appointed in their personal capacity, even though four of them hold
senior positions in the foreign services of their countries of
nationality, it would be inappropriate to suggest that there may be
some a priori taint of bias, by virtue of their nationalities.   However, it could hardly contribute to Israel's sense of confidence in
the Group's mission, that the Group's previous investigative work
for the Human Rights Commission had been on the question of
South African prison conditions and alleged infringements of
trade union rights.[66]   Israel, which no longer has diplomatic
relations with South Africa, could not reasonably be sanguine
about being singled out for treatment similar to that accorded
the international pariah.

Furthermore, the resolution itself seemed to have prejudged
the Working Group's findings.   The Group was to investigate

[63] *Id.* at para. 223.
[64] *Id.* at para. 224.
[65] Nigeria and Tanzania.
[66] See the introductory section *supra.*

"allegations" regarding Israeli violations of the Fourth Geneva Convention. Yet the resolution expressed the Commission's "deep concern on Israel's *refusal* to abide by" [67] it. Whatever may be thought to be the validity of Israel's doubts regarding the binding force of the Convention, in the circumstances, to leave the question of its applicability "open" [68] is not the same thing as refusal to abide by it. In addition, the resolution deplored "Israel's continued violations of human rights in the occupied territories" (terminology broader than the rights protected in the Convention), singling out for special mention "acts of destroying homes of Arab civilian population, deportation of inhabitants and the resorting to violence against inhabitants expressing their resentment to occupation." [69]

More important, however, than the obviously prejudicial nature of the document establishing the Working Group's mandate is the nature of the inquiry itself. It may well be that there have been incidents constituting breaches of the Convention. Indeed, the policy, acknowledged by the Israeli Government, of destroying homes of suspected saboteurs and their collaborators probably violates Article 33 and 53 of the Convention. However, as the Israeli delegate to the Third Committee pointed out, Israeli occupation has been described as "the most humane and generous in modern history" and as "unique in the history of humanity." [70] Therefore, an inquiry into the nature of the occupation ought perhaps to be permitted to test the validity of Israel's claims of establishing a humane occupation. Such, as has been noted, would have been possible under the mandate the General Assembly established for the Special Committee of Three. This provided for an investigation into Israeli practices and policies affect-

[67] Emphasis supplied.

[68] At least this would seem to be Israel's current position; *International Review of the Red Cross*, No. 113, August 1970, at 427.

[69] The debate on the resolution contained observations relating to the prejudicial nature of the resolution; U.N. Doc. E/4621–E/CN.4/1007, para. 215.

[70] Third Committee Statement by Ambassador Lorch, November 9, 1970, supplied by the Permanent Mission of Israel to the United Nations, p. 8A.

ing the occupied territories.[71]   Such a mandate permits the balancing of the good, if any, against the bad.   The mandate of the Working Group of Six, on the other hand, was to investigate allegations of violations.   Either it could find nothing or it could find and announce infractions.   It could not set any infractions it might record against a more positive background, if the nature and tenor of the occupation would have merited such action. Admittedly a court of law does not, or ought not to, test the guilt or innocence of an accused on the basis of whether or not he is usually law-abiding.[72]   But the Working Group was not intended to be a court of law and the proponents of its mandate may reasonably have been expected precisely to avoid phrasing its purposes in such a way as to resemble those governing criminal proceedings.

In the circumstances, it may be wondered how serious the Human Rights Commission was in purporting to bring about a clarification of the situation of the civilian population under occupation.   Certainly, it is unfortunate that one state is able unilaterally to flout an investigative process aimed at testing severe doubts over allegations of a most serious nature.   However, it was unrealistic of the Commission to expect the Working Group of Six to conduct a full and exhaustive investigation in the light of its background.   Israel's position on the matter was already well known after the developments that accompanied the Gussing mission and the attempts to send out a second representative. Given the concern that was generated throughout 1967 and 1968 by the steady flow of allegations regarding Israel's practices in the occupied territories, the Commission, had it been really concerned effectively to examine the allegations, might have been expected to have looked for a formula that would have assuaged at least some of Israel's doubts as to the genuineness of the Commission's efforts.   It would then have had a better chance of success, if only by having made it more difficult to resist its initiative.   Only two

---

[71] See the preceding section *supra*.

[72] Though even this may affect the sentence and perhaps carry weight in the credibility to be given his testimony.

months earlier there had been the mass public execution of "Zionist spies" in Iraq. It is true that they were Iraqi citizens, while the subject matter of the Working Group's investigation had an international component. But if human rights investigations are to be promoted beyond previous restrictions, as permitted by ECOSOC resolution 1235 (XLII), the events in Iraq might have equally qualified for investigation. Instead resolution 6 (XXV), containing prejudicial assertions of fact, dubiously sponsored, weakly supported and permitting only an investigation into negatives, established a Working Group that, like its Special Committee of Three, has been able to investigate everywhere but on the spot.

Conclusions

The efforts of three organs of the United Nations on the question of human rights in the Middle East have been examined. All of them have, I believe, been shown to have been defective from various points of view. Security Council resolution 242 (1967) was vaguely worded. Here the question first arose regarding whether or not the U.N. was interested in the fate of Jewish minorities in Arab countries. The United Arab Republic and, subsequently, Syria took a restrictive view of the wording of the resolution, maintaining that only the human rights of Arabs in the "area of conflict" were to be investigated. The Secretary-General, who was required to report to the Security Council under the resolution (and to the General Assembly under its resolution 2252 ES–V), eventually arrived at a similarly restrictive legal interpretation. While I have tried to show that such restrictiveness was not necessary, the Security Council evidenced, by its later adoption of resolution 259 (1968), that this interpretation adequately reflects its intent. In any event, the Secretary-General was never able to appoint a successor to Gussing.

This led to the passage of General Assembly resolution 2443 (XXIII) whereby that organ, with an unconvincing majority, mandated the setting up of the Special Committee of Three. The death of Dr. Arenales permitted a legitimate challenge to the procedures subsequently adopted to implement the duties assigned to him. The objections constituting the basis of this challenge were never properly answered. Meanwhile, the three states nominated to the Special Committee suggested a bias which the nominees of those states could be expected to find an intolerable burden in the carrying out of their duties. These defects again permitted Israel to avoid an on-the-spot investigation of her policies and practices in the occupied territories.

During the delay attending the establishment of the Special Committee of Three, the Commission on Human Rights, a functional commission of the Economic and Social Council, passed resolution 6 (XXV) that set up the Special Working Group of Six. This resolution, too, was weakly supported, contained prejudicial assertions of fact and authorized an investigation formulated in terms indicating a quasi-judicial examination of alleged misconduct. Furthermore, its activities were to appear as a somewhat unseemly duplication of effort, once the Special Committee of Three was finally created.[73] Yet again, the very origins of the Special Working Group provided fodder for Israel's argument that she was being subjected to political manoeuvering, rather than being asked to co-operate with a genuine U.N. concern for the protection of human rights. Her consequent refusal to co-operate had a color of legitimacy.

Common to all three initiatives was a selective concern for human rights. None of the organs involved demonstrated any real concern for the fate of Jews in the Arab territories. It is true that the occupied territories constituted an area of international concern that was immune to the plea of domestic jurisdiction. Nevertheless, the fate of stateless Jews in Arab countries, at least, was within the ambit of the Fourth Geneva Convention. Yet the U.N. did not demonstrate a concern for their interests. More importantly, to rely on this "international" aspect of the situ-

---

[73] The debate had anticipated this problem; U.N. Doc. E/4621–E/CN.4/1007, para. 218.

ation is further to strengthen resistance to a growing movement in favor of re-assessment of the validity of the domestic jurisdiction barrier to human rights investigations.[74]   Support for a renewed challenge to the hegemony of Article 2 (7) in preventing such investigations will hardly be forthcoming as long as those organs authorized to undertake these activities reflect an interest in the human rights only of regimes with political muscle.   One suspects that, regardless of Article 2(7), no resolution requiring an investigation of human rights in Arab countries would have been adopted by any of the U.N. organs under consideration.   Should such political, if not jurisdictional, immunity persist, it will hardly be suprising to find the plea of domestic jurisdiction acquiring more vigor, with states other than Israel able to flout with impunity the *genuine* humanitarian concerns of the international community.

[74] The most recent ECOSOC resolution 1503 (XLVIII), of May 27, 1970, (U.N. Doc. E/4868 and Corr. 2) already has hedged in the Commission's powers of investigation under resolution 1235 (XLII) with various procedural and jurisdictional obstacles.

III. THE ROLE OF THE UNITED NATIONS
A. *General*

The June War: The United Nations and Legal Background

ROSALYN HIGGINS

In the spring of 1948 the Security Council of the United Nations took its first action on Palestine. It did so in the face of increasing violence in that country and a rapidly disintegrating political situation. The General Assembly had approved, by a large majority, a plan for the partition of Palestine, economic union, and the internationalization of Jerusalem. This had been supported by both Russia and the United States, and accepted by the Jewish Agency. But it was totally opposed by the Arab Higher Committee, and Britain, as the Mandatory, let it be known that it would not allow its troops to implement a solution which did not have the support of both Arabs and Jews. After the Assembly resolution on partition (Resolution 181 (II), 29 November 1947) violence in Palestine became even more widespread. Not only were the British troops having to contend with the activities of Jewish military organizations, but in January 1948 troops began to enter Palestine from neighbouring Arab states, and open fighting began.

The UN Truce Supervision Organization
In April 1948, exercising 'its primary responsibility for the maintenance of international peace and security', the Security Council called for a truce in Palestine (Resolution S/714). Two weeks later another resolution was adopted, in mandatory language, calling for specific measures to be taken to implement the truce (Resolution S/723). On 23 April a truce commission was established to supervise this truce (Resolution S/727). It consisted of those members of the Security Council which had career consular officers in Jerusalem – though Syria, which numbered among them, declined to serve. As the United Kingdom had now insisted that it would terminate its mandate on 15 May, and would not thereafter be

responsible for law and order, the truce commission met in conditions of great urgency. The General Assembly took parallel action, and at its second special session appointed a UN Mediator for Palestine, who was to cooperate with the Truce Commission, and arrange for the operation of common services in Palestine, assure the protection of Holy Places, and promote a peaceful solution to the problem (General Assembly resolution 186 (ES–II)). Count Folke Bernadotte carried out the mediator's tasks with skill and patience until his assassination by Jewish terrorists.

On 15 May 1948, the United Kingdom mandate for Palestine came to an end, and the State of Israel was at once proclaimed within the boundaries recommended by the original General Assembly partition plan. The armed forces of Egypt, Iraq, Transjordan, Syria, and Lebanon crossed the frontier, and widespread and intense fighting broke out.

The Truce Commission asked for military advisers and observers. When the Security Council succeeded, on 29 May 1948, in getting a four week ceasefire, it incorporated this request into the arrangements. The Security Council decided that the UN Mediator and the Truce Commission should jointly supervise the ceasefire, and 'they shall be provided with a sufficient number of military observers' (Security Council resolution S/801, 29 May 1948). Here then was the clause from which, eventually, were to spring the observers of the UN Truce Supervision Organization (UNTSO), who have remained in the Middle East for nearly twenty years. During the arguments that surrounded the withdrawal of the UN Emergency Force (UNEF) from Egypt in May 1967, few commentators seemed even aware of the existence of UNTSO, still less of the significance of the role it had sought to play throughout the years. Although UNTSO has always operated within the framework of a UN observer group, its precise functions have been somewhat modified to meet the need of the four main phases which the past two decades have marked: the truce of 1948–9; the Armistice Agreements of 1949–56; the post-Suez era of 1956–67; and the present period, following the six-day war of June 1967.

So far as the 1948 truce was concerned, the Security Council's order was obeyed by both parties, and the Truce Commission Observers examined alleged breaches of the truce, including attempts to get arms into the country. They engaged in reconnaissance and patrolling and kept a check upon entry into Palestine of men of military age.

Untso and the Armistice Agreements

Shortly before his death, Bernadotte had urged that it was necessary to proceed from the ceasefire ordered by the UN to an armistice between the parties, and it was to the achievement of this that Ralph Bunche, the new Acting Mediator, dedicated himself in the first half of 1949. It was a very substantial achievement to have conducted, successfully, separate armistice negotiations between the Provisional Government of Israel on the one hand, and the Governments of Egypt, Lebanon, Jordan, and Syria on the other. Under the terms of the four Armistice Agreements, the remnants of the Truce Commission Observers – now termed the UN Truce Supervision Organization – remained in Palestine. Their task was to serve the newly established Mixed Armistice Commissions in supervising the armistice. The duties of UNTSO were basically threefold: first, each of the Mixed Armistice Commissions – in which two Arabs and two Israelis were to meet regularly, face to face – required a fifth 'neutral' member. This was to be the Chief of Staff of UNTSO or an UNTSO officer designated by him. Second, each of the Agreements stipulated that UNTSO should provide observers to investigate alleged breaches of the agreed provisions. And third, in all save the Israel–Lebanon agreement, there were specific arrangements for demilitarized zones, which were to be controlled by United Nations personnel. Ralph Bunche summarized the continuing need for UNTSO by stating:

... a nucleus of such observers must be kept on the spot until the final peace settlements are made or until the Parties themselves agree to changes in the Armistice Agreements which would no longer make necessary the employment or the presence of such United Nations staff. [1]

Even by June 1967 no final peace treaty had been made between Israel and her Arab neighbours, and no agreement had been reached between them to alter the terms of the Armistice Agreements.

The Armistice Agreements – and UNTSO – met with different degrees of success. That between Israel and Lebanon (22 March

[1] Security Council Official Records, 4th yr., part 2, 435th meeting, pp. 8–9.

1949, S/1296) has operated very smoothly. The Israel–Jordan Armistice Agreement had to work within a situation where Palestinian refugees lived within sight of their former lands; where Israel insisted on its right to cultivate right up to the demarcation lines; and where King Hussain was under very considerable pressure from internal opponents, and – until May 1967 – relentless hostility from Cairo and Damascus. Arguments about the status of Mount Scopus, and the right of Israel to use arms to protect the outlying Hebrew University in the demilitarized sector of Jerusalem, were early – and continuing – difficulties. Various incidents, including the Jordanian ambush of an Israeli bus on the Scorpion pass in 1954, rapidly dashed hopes of an effective armistice. In spite of a clear obligation to do so, Jordan did not allow Israelis access to Jewish Holy Places in Jerusalem, and after 1956 Israel refused to attend plenary meetings of the Mixed Armistice Commission, asserting that what was required was Jordanian implementation of agreed matters, not 'a routine examination of incidents in the MAC'.

The Syrian armistice, like the Jordanian one (20 July 1949, S/1353), was bedevilled by disputes concerning the demilitarized zones. Each of the Armistices provided that the demilitarized zones were not to be used in such a way as to provide either party with a military advantage. Syria claimed that this prevented Israel from draining the Huleh marshes, for reclamation would be beneficial to Israel. Israel in turn claimed that the 'no military advantage' clause was never intended to be a charter for perpetual agricultural wasteland, but rather a guarantee against military fortification. Further, Israel argued that under Article 5 of the Armistice Agreement, the Chairman of the Mixed Armistice Commission, *and not the Commission itself*, was responsible for matters in the demilitarized zone. The purpose of this argument was to deny Syria any *locus standi*, as a member of the MAC, in the matter. The outcome of this conflict of views was the failure of the Mixed Armistice Commission to hold regular meetings after 1951. Since that time the UN had to resort increasingly to ad hoc and unofficial machinery to endeavour to get discussion between the parties.[2] By 1955 there had begun the pattern of Arab shooting from the Syrian heights upon Israeli boats on Lake Tiberias,

---

[2] All these questions are discussed in considerable detail, with accompanying documents, in the forthcoming work by the present author, *UN Peacekeeping:*

followed by retaliatory action from Israel. From the perspective of the United Nations, it was essential to establish the legal distinction between self defence and retaliation: and this was done in a variety of resolutions, and, specifically, by Hammarskjöld in a report to the Security Council in April 1956 (S/3596). While self defence is permissible – that is to say, proportionate defence against an illegal use of force – retaliation is not. Retaliation – subsequent, punitive military response, not necessarily strictly proportionate – was both contrary to general international law and damaging to the whole structure of the Armistice Agreements. Legally correct though this view is, it relies for its justness upon the effective working of the Security Council as an impartial arbiter. Major violations of the Armistice Agreements had been taken to the Security Council, which had at its disposal the reports of UNTSO. The United States had shown a willingness to condemn both initial violations of the Armistice and any acts of retaliation; but by 1953 the Soviet Union had changed its earlier policy, and decided to protect Syria against Security Council condemnation for breaches of the Armistice. The consequence was that after 1953 it continued to be possible to pass resolutions condemning Israel for initial breaches of the Armistice, or for impermissible acts of retaliation; but not to pass, because of the Soviet veto, any condemnation of Syrian attacks upon Israeli citizens, or even a resolution which condemned both parties.

This, then, was the background on the Syrian front by 1966. The new Ba'thist government in Syria was pursuing a militant policy and challenging Nasser for the leadership of the Arab world. The Soviet Union was being drawn even more heavily into support for Syria. The Syrian government, far from attempting to check al-Fatah raids into Israel territory, encouraged them. The Syrians stated at the United Nations that

... nor is Syria responsible for the rise of Palestinian Arab organizations striving to liberate their conquered and occupied territory ... Had the Israeli intention been sincere, Israel would have resorted to the Mixed

Documents and Commentary. The first volume – which covers both UNTSO and UNEF, including the events of 1967 – is to be published by the Oxford University Press for the Royal Institute of International Affairs in 1968. The three volumes together will provide all the relevant documentation, and an accompanying analysis, of every UN peacekeeping group.

Armistice Commission, the international organization created for such a purpose (S/7412, 18 July 1966).

At this moment of time the Chief of Staff of UNTSO was faced simultaneously with the fact of damaging terrorist raids and sabotage from Syrian territory; a Syrian air attack, witnessed by UNTSO observers, on Israeli fishing boats on Lake Tiberias; verified Israeli jet aircraft attacks on targets in Syria; the flaring up of the old dispute over cultivation in the demilitarized zone; and an inability to get the parties to use the Mixed Armistice Commission. In the Security Council, a six-power resolution (sponsored by Argentina, Japan, Holland, New Zealand, Nigeria, and Uganda) would have invited Syria to strengthen measures to prevent violations of the Armistice Agreements, invited Israel to cooperate fully with the Mixed Armistice Commission, and called upon both Syria and Israel to facilitate the work of UNTSO. The resolution was vetoed by the Soviet Union, and public opinion in Israel pressed Eshkol's insecure government for action in the face of the Security Council's inability to issue an effective warning against Syrian raids.

At Syrian instigation, but apparently without the approval of King Hussain, Jordanian territory was used as a base for further raids into Israeli territory in the autumn of 1966. Israel now retaliated massively – but against Jordan, not Syria. The Security Council was faced with the choice of not condemning the Israeli action, because of its inability to pass a resolution condemning Syria, or of condemning Israel and attempting to prevent a total erosion of the Armistice Agreement. It chose the latter course, and Ambassador Goldberg of the United States explained that Soviet protection of Syrian transgressions could not in law lead to protection of Israeli illegality by nations whose first duty was to uphold the Armistice Agreements. Israel was thus condemned by the Security Council, and hostility to the United Nations within Israel grew.

By early 1967 Israel was subjected to an almost continuous stream of border raids and harassment from Syria; and on 12 May Prime Minister Eshkol spoke his fateful words in which he threatened, if such acts continued, to strike at Damascus at a time of his own choosing. Syria now appealed to Nasser and started within Egypt the chain of events that were to lead to the withdrawal of UNEF and the June war.

Much of the early arguments about the Egyptian–Israel armistice revolved around the clause on refugees, with Israel taking a hard line on those – such as the Azazme beduin tribe – who it claimed were not in Israeli territory at the time of the signing of the Armistice. The Chairman of the MAC, however, considered that Israel had unjustifiably expelled these beduins and called for their repatriation. There began to be established the unhappy pattern of incidents along the Gaza strip, but until 1955 they remained comparatively minor. Then their nature changed, and a new pattern emerged of well organized sabotage by *fedayeen* far within Israeli territory. The Chief of Staff of UNTSO reported in September 1955 that the number and type of acts of sabotage by the *fedayeen* indicated that they were an organized and well trained group. At the same time, hostilities were flaring up between Egyptian outposts and Israeli border patrols. After May 1956, when the Suez Canal Company was nationalized, Israel took the opportunity offered by France and Britain's intention of using force against Nasser, and invaded Egypt on 29 October 1956. The Chief of Staff of UNTSO confirmed that Israeli troops had violated the armistice and crossed the international frontier. On 30 October, Britain and France issued their ultimatum to Egypt and Israel, calling on both sides to stop all warlike action and to withdraw to within ten miles of the Suez Canal. Israel accepted this ultimatum: she was not yet within ten miles of the Canal, and it permitted her to penetrate yet further into Egyptian territory. Egypt rejected the ultimatum. At dusk on 31 October a Franco-British air offensive began on Egyptian airfields.

The first emergency special session of the Assembly convened on 1 November, and from the series of resolutions condemning Britain and France, and demanding a ceasefire, emerged the United Nations Emergency Force, which was to play such a significant role in Israeli–Egyptian relations for the next ten years.

Most significantly, Israel announced at this session of the Assembly that she regarded the Israeli–Egyptian Armistice Agreement as dead. She contended that Egypt's deliberate promotion of *fedayeen* raids over the previous years had been in fundamental breach of the Agreement, and that Israel was now exercising its legal right in declaring itself no longer bound by its terms. Israel was at pains to point out that this did not mean that she regarded herself as at war with Egypt: on the contrary, she wished to move forward from a temporary armistice arrangement to a permanent peace. The Secretary-General let it be known, however, that from the United Nations point of view the Armistice Agreement was still legally alive and could not be voided by the unilateral action of either party. Nonetheless, the UN had to face the reality of Israel's refusal to deal further with the Egyptian–Israeli Mixed Armistice Commission, or its UNTSO personnel. Accordingly, the new United Nations Emergency Force came to assume, unofficially, many of UNTSO's supervisory functions.

It also bears reiteration that all parties – including Israel – continued to accept the continuing validity of the other three Armistice Agreements, even though the operation of the Mixed Armistice Commission machinery had, in the case of the Jordan–Israel and Syria–Israel Agreements, become very unsatisfactory. The core of UNTSO personnel remained in the Middle East. As mere observers it was beyond their capacity to prevent war in the area, but during the tumultuous events of May and June 1967 they were heavily relied on by the United Nations for accurate information about the fighting, and by all parties for achieving on the ground those ceasefires which were agreed in New York. UNTSO's headquarters in Government House, Jerusalem, fell first to Jordan, and then to Israel during the 1967 fighting; and once the war was over it took considerable pressure to get Israel to return Government House, with its communications, to UNTSO. UNTSO has been supervising and reporting on the Israel–Jordan and Israel–Syrian ceasefire, and its mandate was extended to provide observers along the Suez Canal. While the contribution of these UNTSO observers is necessarily limited, it is a very real and very useful one.

UNEF and the question of 'consent'

When in May 1967 Egypt requested UNEF to stand aside from its positions, and ultimately to withdraw altogether, the world was reminded sharply that UNEF was on Egyptian soil only with the consent of Egypt. Yet this principle of 'consent' requires, especially in the particular context, more detailed examination. For many of the comments made in May 1967 reveal either ignorance, or humbug, or both.

The United Nations Emergency Force was largely the creation

of Lester Pearson of Canada, brilliantly implemented by Secretary-General Hammarskjöld. The speed and efficiency with which UNEF was organized – and with which it operated from 1956–7 – cannot be gainsaid. Hammarskjöld worked around the clock to get suitable contingents from ten nations, as well as the necessary logistical support. The Secretary-General presented the Assembly, as requested, with a plan for UNEF, and made the following definitive statements about its role:

... there is no intent in the establishment of the Force to influence the military balance in the present conflict, and thereby, the political balance affecting efforts to settle the conflict ... There is an obvious difference between establishing the Force in order to secure the cessation of hostilities, and establishing the Force with a view to enforcing a withdrawal of forces ... [UNEF would] enter Egyptian territory with the consent of the Egyptian Government ... It would be more than an observers' corps, but in no way a military force temporarily controlling the territory in which it is situated. [3]

These views were approved by the Assembly and reiterated time and time again. It was plain for all to see – and governments were well aware of these facts – that UNEF was in Egypt with the consent of that country, and with limited powers. Israel sought, unsuccessfully, to obtain for UNEF powers relating to the government of the Gaza strip, the opening up of the Suez Canal to all traffic without discrimination, and the guarantee of passage through the Gulf of Aqaba. It was made clear to Israel that the withdrawal of her forces had to be unconditional. The sole tasks for UNEF were those laid down in the Assembly resolutions, and these concerned the ending of hostilities, the withdrawal of foreign forces from Egypt, and the patrolling of the armistice lines. UNEF could not contribute to a redress of these broader wrongs claimed by Israel. Although it is true that in February 1957 the United States proclaimed the Straits of Tiran as an international waterway to be kept open to all shipping, and that Israel read this pronouncement as a sufficient guarantee to withdraw its troops from Egypt, it nonetheless remained true that UNEF itself was not given the task of keeping the straits open. This remained so in spite of the fact that Hammarskjöld succeeded, in private negotiation, in getting Egypt to agree to UNEF being stationed at Sharm

---

[3] *UN Document* A/3302, 6 November 1956, paras. 8, 10, 12.

el Shaikh. The dismay expressed in May 1967 by many British
MPs, including the Foreign Secretary, that 'the umbrella was withdrawn as soon as the rain began' seems a little wide of the mark.
The British Government had known since 1956 that UNEF was
not an umbrella to be used against rain: rather it was a barometer
to give warning of imminent rainfall. The original Assembly
resolution urged that UNEF be stationed on both Israeli and
Egyptian soil; Israel's refusal and UNEF's limited powers made it
inevitable that it could stay in Egypt only as a welcome guest.

This is not the whole story, however: for it remains to ask
whether Egyptian consent – which was undoubtedly required for
UNEF's entry into that country – continued to be necessary at
every moment of time since it was originally given in 1956; and
whether Egypt herself had in any way waived such a claim. These
are the questions to which MPs could properly have addressed
themselves in May 1967 – but did not – rather than talking of
umbrellas being withdrawn in the rain. To look at these questions
it is necessary to go back to the resolutions under which UNEF
was established.

General Assembly resolution 1000 (ES–I), 5 November 1956,
established a United Nations Command 'for an emergency international force to secure and supervise the cessation of hostilities
in accordance with all the terms of General Assembly resolution
997 (ES–I) of 2 November 1956'. General Assembly resolution
997 (ES–I), to which reference is made, had urged the parties
to agree

to an immediate ceasefire and, as part thereof, halt the movement of
military forces and arms into the area . . . [and] promptly to withdraw all
forces behind armistice lines, to desist from raids across the armistice
lines into neighbouring territory, and to observe scrupulously the
provisions of the armistice agreements . . .

Egypt then agreed to an aide mémoire on the basis for the presence and functioning of UNEF in Egypt (A/3375, 20 November
1956, Annex), under which

The Government of Egypt declares that, when exercising its sove-
reign rights on any matter concerning the presence and functioning of
UNEF, it will be guided, in good faith, by its acceptance of General
Assembly resolution 1000 (ES–I) of 5 November 1956.

In asking for UNEF to be withdrawn, in order to be free to proceed to, and perhaps to cross, its borders with Israel, was Egypt indeed acting 'in good faith', bearing in mind 'its acceptance of General Assembly resolution 1000 (ES–I)' ? This was the relevant legal question in May 1967, and one that could not be avoided merely by reiterating that UNEF was not an enforcement force, and had entered Egypt with President Nasser's consent. Secretary-General U Thant avoided direct comment on this issue by declaring that the aide mémoire of 20 November was irrelevant. He stated that it referred to resolution 1000 (ES–I), which mentioned only the securing and supervising of the cessation of hostilities. This task had been successfully completed by early 1957, and it was only in February 1957 that UNEF was given the additional task of overseeing the observance of the Armistice, and the 'good faith' undertaking could therefore not apply to that later function. Since 1957 UNEF had been carrying out only tasks relating to the Armistice Agreement.

To many international lawyers this was a novel and worrying interpretation. The General Assembly resolution speaks not only of supervising the cessation of hostilities, but adds 'in accordance with all the terms of General Assembly resolution 997'. And General Assembly resolution 997 (ES–I), as we have seen, refers to the obligation on both parties to desist from raids across the armistice lines and to observe the armistice terms. UNEF thus appears to have had an armistice-observing function from the outset. General Assembly resolution 1125 (XI) of 2 February 1957, which U Thant regarded as the relevant one, merely states *where* UNEF is to be placed (on the Egyptian–Israeli demarcation line) in order to maintain the efficacy of the Armistice Agreement. It gave UNEF no new functions. This view has, this writer submits, been long held by most international lawyers, including those who made a particularly close study of UNEF before 1967;[4] moreover, there seems clear evidence that it was the view held by Hammarskjöld also. As early as 6 November 1956, Hammarskjöld indicated that UNEF had two broad functions: 'to enter Egyptian territory with the consent of the Egyptian Government, in order to help maintain quiet during and after the withdrawal of non-Egyptian troops, *and to secure compliance with the other terms established in the resolution of 2 November 1956*' (A/3302, para. 12, italics

[4] Eg. Rosner, *The United Nations Emergency Force* (Columbia University Press, 1963), 66–116.

mine). The resolution of 2 November was, of course, resolution 997, which includes reference to observance of the Armistice.

If Egypt had in fact agreed that UNEF should remain on its territory until its tasks were completed, was it for Egypt to decide when UNEF's mission had been accomplished? It is certainly clear from the records that Israel and a fairly wide group of nations insisted upon a negative answer, lest a hostile force could be built up behind the shield of UNEF, which Egypt could then declare to have fulfilled its tasks. Australia buttressed this argument by saying that if this discretion were left solely to Egypt, it would run counter to Hammarskjöld's directive that UNEF was not to affect the power balance in the area. These matters, therefore, were clearly seen – and foreseen – in 1956–7. But there is no clear secretariat guidance on this point in the documents – it was deliberately left imprecise. While this point was left unresolved, there were indications by the Secretary-General as to how he would regard it as legally proper to proceed if circumstances should arise in which Egypt asked for UNEF to withdraw. Hammarskjöld had notified the Assembly (A/3943, para. 158) that such a request would call for 'an exchange of views . . . towards harmonizing the positions'. He had also said, in reply to a question about a possible request for UNEF to be withdrawn from Sharm el Shaikh, that the 'indicated procedure would be for the Secretary-General to inform the Advisory Committee on the United Nations Emergency Force, which would determine whether the matter should be brought to the attention of the Assembly' (A/6370/Add.3., para. 37). In the event, U Thant announced before he flew to Cairo for consultations that UNEF would be withdrawn. This flowed from his view that once the request for withdrawal had been made, he had no legal – and no political – alternative but to comply. He did consult the Advisory Committee, which was divided within itself about UNEF's withdrawal, and apparently made no recommendation that a special session of the Assembly be convened. U Thant spoke frankly of his own reasons for deciding not to go to the Assembly himself, when he said that the Assembly would only have offered divided counsels. In any event, and this is the key point, he felt that once Egypt's consent was withdrawn, there was no recommendation that the Assembly could legally make save that of withdrawal. The correctness of this view depends upon one's interpretation of the 'consent' principle, and we have already indicated why we believe that although political reality would within a reasonable period of time have required UNEF's withdrawal, the legal obligations did not lead inexorably to the same conclusion. That being so, we return to the view that UNEF was a body established by the General Assembly as a subsidiary organ under Article 22 of the Charter, and that the Assembly, and not the Secretary-General alone, had the legal authority to terminate its existence.

May 1967: The legal arguments

Quite apart from the question of the withdrawal of UNEF, a cluster of legal arguments was heard about the respective merits of the Arab and the Israeli case, especially in relation to the closing of the Gulf of Aqaba, which followed UNEF's withdrawal.

The Status of the Straits of Tiran: It was claimed by Israel, and the great majority of western nations, that the entrance to the Gulf of Aqaba constituted international straits, and as such the Tiran waterway – the only navigable channel – was open to all shipping. Whether the Tiran channel is indeed an international strait is open to some debate. Until 1958 it was widely accepted that international straits were a narrow passage of water, running wholly or partly through a state or states' territorial waters, linking high seas at one end to high seas at the other. In 1958 there took place in Geneva the United Nations Conference on the Law of the Sea, and the idea was there advanced that the definition of an international waterway should be a narrow passage of water linking high seas to high seas, or high seas to territorial waters. This definition was vigorously opposed by the Arab nations, who saw the clear implications for the Gulf of Aqaba, but it was nonetheless eventually adopted as Article 16 (4) of the Convention on the Territorial Sea. Egypt has not become a party to that Convention.

It is certainly clear that there is a heavy duty upon a riparian state to maintain an international right of passage through a strait. The text of the 1958 Convention can even be read to mean that warships have a right of innocent passage through a strait, and the 1949 Judgment of the International Court of Justice in the Corfu Channel Case is also authority for this view. And, *a fortiori*, a right of passage through straits is available to merchant ships, and Article 16 (4) of the 1958 Convention confirms that this right may not be suspended by the coastal state.

Insofar as it speaks of these rights of passage, the 1958 Convention is merely declaratory, that is, it operates already well established points of law. In this context, therefore, Egypt's non-accession to the treaty is irrelevant: she was already bound by the pre-existing rule of general international law. But whether Article 16(4), with its reference to straits linking high seas to *territorial waters*, as well as to high seas, is merely declaratory of an already existing legal principle, is more open to doubt. If this clause was in fact *de lege ferenda* – making new law – then Egypt's non-accession is of some legal relevance. Even if so, however, lawyers also have to ask themselves the question whether, in the intervening years, this clause has so much passed into common usage that it is no longer a mere treaty clause but now represents a new norm of law by which all nations have now come to be bound, whether or not they are parties to the 1958 Convention. These are far from easy questions, and it can only be admitted that an element of doubt exists.

This does not, however, lead to the conclusion that Egypt may in fact have been entitled to shut the Straits of Tiran to Israeli shipping. Even if Egypt was able to claim that Tiran is *not* an international strait, but merely part of her ordinary territorial waters, it must be recalled that there still exists a right of innocent passage for foreign shipping through a state's territorial waters. A coastal state may, of course, suspend this passage temporarily if such suspension is essential for its security. However, the legal propriety of terminating free passage for Israeli merchant ships after ten years of uneventful passage is in doubt: it is far from clear that Egypt was exercising a bona fide security requirement.

There is a further, and major, point: whether or not the waterway of Tiran is an international strait, it is clear beyond doubt that the Gulf of Aqaba is, in the legal sense, a bay – that is to say, the area in the Gulf is as large as the semi-circle whose diameter is a line drawn across the mouth of the indentation which marks its entry point. And it has long been accepted that a bay with more than one coastal state may not be shut without the consent of all the coastal states. Article 7 of the Convention on the Territorial Sea does provide that if the distance between the low water marks of the natural entrance point of a bay is less than twenty four miles, the waters behind this line may be 'closed off' as internal waters. But it is clearly stated, in Article 7(1), that this provision refers only to bays 'the coasts of which belong to a single state'. The Arab nations have nonetheless claimed that Aqaba is internal Arab waters, and reference has been made to the Fonseca Case of 1916 as authority for the proposition that they are entitled to decide between them to close it. This case is, however, no authority for the stated proposition, for it concerned a demarcation agreement between Nicaragua, Salvador, and Honduras, the *only* riparians. To claim that the Aqaba situation is identical was not only to assume that Jordan was as willing as the other Arab states for Aqaba to be closed, but also to ignore Israel's existence as a state.

Israel's position as a Coastal state: This leads on to a related argument advanced by Egypt – namely that, quite apart from whether Israel 'existed' or not, it was not a riparian on the Gulf of Aqaba because it was not entitled to Eilat. The contention was that Israel seized Eilat after the conclusion of her Armistice with Egypt. It is correct that Israel was not in possession of Eilat on 24 February 1949, when the Armistice with Egypt was signed. However, the demarcation lines in that Agreement (S/1264) did not cover that portion of territory now known as Eilat. The relevant demarcation lines, within which this portion of territory fell, were those laid down in the Israel–Jordan Armistice, which was not signed until 3 April 1949. It was in the intervening period that Israel occupied this territory, during hostilities. Moreover, one may note that this portion of territory was allotted to Israel under the original General Assembly partition plan for Palestine: although Israel declared her independence within these boundaries she had not, at the time of independence, in fact effectively occupied all the land which had been recommended under the partition plan. Although the 1948 war led to Israel occupying more territory than was assigned to her in the partition plan, the outlet to Aqaba at Eilat was not part of this extra territory.

The argument was also heard in May 1967 that Israeli ships were in any event not entitled, under the terms of Article 2(2) of the Armistice Agreement, to sail within three miles of Egyptian land. Even the most cursory examination of the Armistice Agreement reveals that the prohibition in Article 2(2) refers to warships, and is part of a clause which prohibits passage to the land, sea, or air forces of each party, in the territory or territorial sea of the other.

The claim to rights of belligerency: Underlying each of these legal arguments advanced by the Arab nations was a more fundamental one: that Egypt retained belligerent rights against Israel. Rights of belligerency do not entail, as laymen sometimes suppose, the right to invade or wage war. They are concerned with more technical matters whereby a state seeks to protect its security by limited acts which would not otherwise be permitted. The right of visit and search of enemy vessels on the high seas is one example, and the seizure in prize of enemy ships in one's territorial waters is another. Israel claimed no such rights vis-à-vis Egypt, declaring that rights of belligerency are incompatible with the Armistice Agreements, which were meant to bring to an end all 'warlike or hostile act(s)' (Article 2(2)), and to facilitate 'the transition from the present truce to permanent peace'. Egypt, on the other hand, argued that belligerent rights may be retained under an armistice, and are prohibited only when there is a peace treaty. This argument has, of course, been important for Egypt particularly in the context of the Suez Canal, where passage has been denied to Israeli ships, or cargo bound to and from Israel. In 1967 it was advanced also in relation to the prohibition of passage in the Straits of Tiran.

Under traditional, pre-war international law, the general view was that belligerent rights were retainable under an armistice, up to the signature of the peace treaty. It is very doubtful, however, whether this traditional rubric is applicable either to the post-UN Charter world, or to these Armistices in particular. It used to be the case that armistices represented a brief period following the truce, when preparations were being made for the peace treaty which followed soon afterwards. Since the war, however, the signature of final peace treaties has often been delayed long after the conclusion of military hostilities – the length of time between the end of the second World War and the conclusion by the Allies of peace treaties is a case in point. The prolonged intervening 'armistice' period is effectively one of peace, in the context of which belligerent rights would seem to have no place. The nature and purpose of these prolonged armistices are different from those of the pre-1939 world.

Moreover, a system of armistices underwritten by the Security Council (as were the four Arab-Israel armistices) in performance of its task of maintaining international peace, are still less likely to entail the retention of belligerent rights. These particular armistices were clearly seen as an end to military hostilities, to which no subsequent return was to be permitted. The clauses referring to the cessation of hostile acts and the transition to peace are pointers in this direction. Further, the degree to which the armistices had moved away from the limited, quasi-military functions performed by traditional armistices, was shown by the use of them to draw demarcation lines, to set up demilitarized zones, to point to agreed solutions on a wide variety of problems. All these facts were before the Security Council when in 1951 it had to consider the question of belligerent rights in relation to the Suez Canal. The Security Council found (Security Council resolution S/2322, 1 September 1951) that there should be freedom of passage for all nations through the Canal, and that a claim to exercise belligerent rights was not compatible with the existence of the Egypt–Israel armistice. The principle seems clear – and applicable also to the problem of Aqaba. Subsequent confirmation of it, and further supporting action by the Security Council, proved impossible, because in 1953 the Soviet Union altered its Middle East policy to a militantly pro-Egyptian posture. By using its veto the Soviet Union in 1954 prevented reaffirmation by the Security Council of the principles which she herself had favoured in 1951.

After the June War: The major legal arguments

Since the ceasefires marking the end of the June war, different legal contentions have held the attention of the United Nations. They have been concerned with Israel's right to retain the territories which she obtained as a result of the fighting. The General Assembly agreed only on a resolution calling on Israel not to alter the status of Jerusalem. But a two-thirds majority was available on no resolution on the broader issues, including the next steps to be taken. The more extreme resolutions were rejected, and the two more moderate resolutions just failed to win the necessary majority. There was obviously a fairly widespread sympathy with the view on the one hand, that Israel must be entitled to the security and peace which is the due of any UN member, and on the other, that Israel should be required to withdraw from the additional territories which she now held.

It is perhaps not unfair to say that, with the passage of time, the pendulum has somewhat swung, and the view that Israel must withdraw has come to hold a place of greater importance in the minds of many governments than the view that she is entitled to security. Specifically, there seems to have been a movement away from the idea that the security to which it is agreed Israel is entitled can be achieved only by direct talks between Arab and Israeli. And at the heart of the problem there remains the dilemma of which must be required to come first in time: Israeli withdrawal, or Egyptian acceptance of peace and recognition of Israel. The intractability of these problems is all too apparent. But what is particularly disturbing to the lawyer is the way in which the notion of territorial aggression has become deliberately blurred with that of military occupation. Foreign Secretary George Brown, speaking to the General Assembly on 21 June 1967, stated:

> Article 2 of the Charter provides that 'All members shall refrain in their international relations from the threat or the use of force against the territorial integrity or the political independence of any State'. Here the words 'territorial integrity' have a direct bearing on the question of withdrawal, on which much has been said in previous speeches. I see no two ways about this, and I state our position very clearly. In my view, from the words in the Charter, war should not lead to territorial aggrandisement.

This statement appears as the first in a list of 'principles' which Mr Brown set out. (The 'right of all states in the area to exist' appeared some four paragraphs later, after reference to the question of Jerusalem and the refugee problem.) Several comments require to be made. In the first place, there is no mention in this passage, or elsewhere in Mr Brown's speech, of the equally important principle of self defence. Second, the welcome prohibition against 'territorial aggrandisement' was directed against the old, pre-1939 practice, of an aggressor being allowed to retain the fruits of his aggression. It provides no clear guidance on the problem of a state which has responded to a threat of annihilation, and in so doing has taken the fight into the enemy's own territory. Now it may well be, as Professor R. Y. Jennings has suggested in his book *The Acquisition of Territory* (pp. 52–67), that there are compelling policy reasons why, even in these circumstances, the victorious state should not be permitted permanently to retain these territories: but we cannot pretend that it is Article 2 of the Charter which answers this problem.

Moreover, the really central point is that Mr Brown's reference to 'territorial aggrandisement' (a term which does not appear in the

Charter) fails completely to distinguish between claiming title to territory and legitimate military occupation of it. Israel has now effectively annexed Jerusalem, though she has not termed the measures she has taken as annexation. This would not appear to be justified in international legal terms notwithstanding Jordan's failure in the past to meet her obligation to provide open access to Jewish places of worship. But a sharp distinction must be drawn between the situation in Jerusalem and the situation in the rest of the territories which are presently occupied, for in the latter there is no claim to annexation or title. And there is nothing in either the Charter or general international law which leads one to suppose that military occupation, pending a peace treaty, is illegal. The Allies, it will be recalled, did not claim title to Berlin in 1945; but neither did they withdraw immediately they had entered it. The law of military occupation, with its complicated web of rights and duties, remains entirely relevant, and until such time as the Arab nations agree to negotiate a peace treaty, Israel is in legal terms entitled to remain in the territories she now holds.

Virtually all speeches in the United Nations have chosen to ignore this elementary but basic distinction between acquisition and occupation. In the British resolution unanimously adopted on 23 November 1967 – a considerable diplomatic feat by Lord Caradon – the introductory clause says: 'Emphasizing the inadmissibility of the *acquisition* of territory by war . . .' and then, in operative paragraph 1, affirms that the Charter principles require, *inter alia*, '(i) Withdrawal of Israeli armed forces from territories *occupied* in the recent conflict.'[5] The blurring of the principles of acquisition and occupation thus continues.

The resolution, which commanded the support of the Soviet Union, France, the United Kingdom, and the United States, sees the withdrawal of Israel from occupied territories as balanced by the termination of any claims by the Arab states to rights of belligerency, and the acknowledgement of the sovereignty, territorial integrity, and political independence of every state in the area. The resolution does not, however, provide any guidance as to which of these concessions is to come first; nor does it suggest that these matters should be guaranteed in direct Arab–Israel talks, or in a firm peace treaty. The second main paragraph refers to the need

[5] Italics mine.

for freedom of navigation through international waterways, a just
settlement of the refugee problem, and guarantees for the integrity
and independence of all states in the area 'through measures including the establishment of demilitarized zones'. But the key
problems remain unsolved: does Israeli withdrawal come ahead of
Arab termination of claims of belligerency and acknowledgment of
Israel's sovereignty and right to live in peace? And is Israel correct in her deeply held belief that all Arab concessions are valueless
unless they are willing to negotiate directly, and move away from
middlemen and ad hoc solutions to a final peace?

George Brown's enthusiasm for repairing Britain's relations
with Nasser led to some anxiety in Israel that Britain would sym-
pathize with the Egyptian insistence that Israeli withdrawal must
precede any recognition, and direct talks were unrealistic. However, Lord Caradon has carefully refrained from publicly espousing either of these views, and there is reason to believe that
the United Kingdom has not committed itself to support the Arabs
on these two points.

The Security Council resolution of 23 November 1967 did succeed in getting a UN representative into the field, and since that
time Gunnar Jarring of Sweden – a widely respected diplomatist –
has been in the Middle East seeking some common ground between
Arabs and Israelis. At one stage there were hopes held that Egypt
and Jordan would agree to direct talks, under UN auspices, with
Israel in Cyprus, but these hopes have come to nothing. Pressure
from his own students, and from Syria, makes exceedingly difficult
such a move by Nasser; and Hussain cannot act alone. Jarring continues his search for an acceptable formula, but in the face of a
deteriorating situation on the Jordan–Israel ceasefire line. Unable
or unwilling to prevent saboteurs entering Israel from Jordan,
King Hussain has faced massive retaliation from Israel. The increase in numbers of UN observers along the Suez Canal has
contributed to a marked improvement in the situation in that area;
but neither Jordan nor Israel, each for its own reasons, wishes at
the moment to have its hands tied by a large and effective UN
presence along their common ceasefire line.

Though no solution is in sight, it is hard to see any alternative
to the UN's modest, but real, efforts in the Middle East. UNTSO
personnel – reinforced and enlarged since the sinking of the Eilat
and the bombing of the refineries at Port Suez – remain on the

Canal, and on all the Arab–Israel ceasefire lines. Gunnar Jarring endeavours to build upon the common ground marked out by last November's Security Council resolution; and refugee work, of course, continues to rely enormously on the United Nations. The long history of United Nations involvement in the Middle East seems certain to continue for some time yet: for both humanitarian and political reasons, its services are still needed.

The Role of the United Nations vis-à-vis the Palestine Question

MUHAMMAD H. EL-FARRA

I

A SHORT REVIEW OF THE MAIN PROBLEM

The present Middle East Crisis is part and parcel of the Palestine problem, which has defied all efforts for a solution for the past fifty years. This is because, in attempting to solve the problem, no adequate weight was given to the rule of law, which embodies the right of every people to self-determination.

A review of this question shows that from the very beginning the law of nations was disregarded. Its first defiance took place in 1897 when the leaders of the Zionist movement resolved at Basle, Switzerland, to establish a Jewish state in Palestine.[1] It was later defied in 1917 when Lord Balfour, British Secretary of State for Foreign Affairs, promulgated the Balfour Declaration,[2] promising to facilitate the establishment of a national home for the Jewish peoples on Arab land without reference to the will of the vast majority of the legitimate inhabitants. No matter how we look at this promise it came from one who was giving what he did not own.

I would like to emphasize in this connection that the phrase "a national home for the Jewish people" provoked much controversy.[3] But, regardless of whether it was intended to mean creating a Jewish state or a "homeland," it conflicted with Arab rights. In 1937, twenty years after the Declaration was issued, the Palestine Royal Commission, after a thorough examination of the records bearing upon the question, came to the conclusion that

> His Majesty's Government could not commit itself to the establishment of a Jewish State. It could only undertake to facilitate the growth of a Home. It would depend mainly on the zeal and enterprise of the Jews whether the Home would grow big enough to become a State.[4]

The Zionist leaders got the hint and planned for the usurpation of Palestine through their zeal, ability, and enterprise, reflected in an organized campaign of

* LL.B. 1950, Suffolk University; LL.M. 1951, Boston University; S.J.D. 1958, University of Pennsylvania. Ambassador Extraordinary and Plenipotentiary, Permament Representative of the Hashemite Kingdom of Jordan to the United Nations.
[1] See 1 PALESTINE: A STUDY OF JEWISH, ARAB, AND BRITISH POLICIES (Esco Foundation for Palestine, Inc.) 40-42 (1947); C. SYKES, CROSSROADS TO ISRAEL 10-11 (1965).
[2] The text of the declaration is officially quoted in PALESTINE ROYAL COMMISSION, REPORT, CMD. No. 5479, at 22 (1937).
[3] See references cited note 1 supra.
[4] CMD. No. 5479, supra note 2, at 24.

political action, fund-raising, and propaganda. This organized campaign ignored all Arab rights including the reservations embodied in the Balfour Declaration that:

[N]othing shall be done which may prejudice the civil and religious rights of existing non-Jewish communities in Palestine, or the rights and political status enjoyed by Jews in any other country.

The Arabs of Palestine own 94.6 per cent of Palestine, and it is obvious that any attempt to establish a state conflicts with existing Arab rights. The Zionists, therefore, turned to President Truman and other Americans to commit another injustice in defiance of the legitimate rights of the Arab people of Palestine.

Thus, again, international law was utterly ignored when the question of Palestine became an issue of domestic politics in the United States, and American governors, senators, congressmen, mayors, and every conceivable aspirant for public office, with a few notable exceptions, pledged the establishment of a Jewish state in Palestine.

It might be noted in this connection that President Wilson, in his address of 4 July 1918, laid down the following as one of the four great ends for which the associated peoples of the world were fighting:

The settlement of every question, whether of territory, of sovereignty, of economic arrangement, or of political relationship, upon the basis of the free acceptance of that settlement by the people immediately concerned, and not upon the basis of the material interest or advantage of any other nation or people which may desire a different settlement for the sake of its own exterior influence or mastery.[5]

It should be stressed that the Arab peoples were among the associated peoples who fought with the United States, as allies and friends, for this principle, and who were promised complete independence only to be betrayed later on by their very allies and friends.

What is more, international law was disregarded when duress and pressure took the place of law and equity during the United Nations debate of 1947 that led to the recommendation calling for the partition of Palestine against the will of its people in violation of their inherent right to self-determination. Indeed, international law was disregarded when the General Assembly in 1947 rejected a request of Sub-Committee II of its Ad Hoc Committee on the Palestinian Question to the effect that, before recommending any solution to the Palestine problem, the International Court of Justice should be requested to give an advisory opinion on certain legal questions connected with or arising from the problem, including questions concerning the competence of the United Nations to recommend or enforce any solution contrary to the wishes of the majority of the people of Palestine.[6]

Why has the United Nations side-stepped international law by refusing to submit

---

[5] W. WILSON, *Four Factors of World Peace*, in SELECTED ADDRESSES AND PUBLIC PAPERS OF WOODROW WILSON 266, 268 (A.B. Hart ed. 1918).

[6] 2 U.N. GAOR, Ad Hoc Comm. on the Palestine Question 203 (1947). *See* remarks by Sir Mohammed Zafrullah Khan, 2 U.N. GAOR 1373 (1947).

basic legal issues in the Palestine case to the International Court of Justice? Is it not because it was clear to all political forces at the United Nations that, like Lord Balfour, the United Nations could not grant sovereignty to a Jewish state since the United Nations itself does not possess the sovereignty in order to be able to dispose of it, and, therefore, usurpation through votes, force and politics should be the answer?

II

The Present Crisis

I have so far spoken about the past. But it is the past which makes and conditions the present, and it is the present which molds the future. Let us now turn to the present crisis.

On 5 June, 1967 Israel, in a surprise attack, destroyed the Egyptian air force as well as that of Syria and Jordan. It subsequently occupied all of Sinai, all of the Gaza Strip, all of the West Bank of Jordan and a part of Syrian territory.

This Israeli attack is in most respects no different from the Sinai Campaign of 1956. The one factual difference is that Israel this time occupied both Jordanian and Syrian territories in addition to Sinai and the Gaza Strip. In 1956 only Sinai and Gaza were occupied.

But despite the gravity and the nature of the Israeli attack, a short comparison between the action of political forces in the United Nations vis-à-vis the 1956 invasion and the present one would show a different behaviour on the part of some of the big powers vis-à-vis this crisis. Thus, international law which was upheld in 1956 was trampled on in 1967.

On the Sinai invasion of 1956, firm and strict adherence to the rule of the Charter was championed by the overwhelming majority of members of the United Nations. The United States played a leading role in this matter. Former President Eisenhower said to the nation: "[A]s I review the march of world events in recent years, I am ever more deeply convinced that the processes of the United Nations represent the soundest hope for peace in the world."[7] Neither Zionist pressure, in an American election year, nor any other consideration was able to prevail in substituting political expediency for accepted norms of international law.

The basic facts in the present crisis are the same—the invasion, the occupation, the designs, the tactics, the planning, and the election year. And both Israeli invasions were intended to bring about further expansion.

The 1956 Sinai Campaign was preceded by the Israeli attacks on Gaza in February 1955 which led to a United Nations resolution calling once more upon Israel to take all necessary measures to prevent the recurrence of such actions.[8]

The 1967 Israeli invasion of the three Arab territories was preceded by many

---

[7] PUBLIC PAPERS OF THE PRESIDENTS OF THE UNITED STATES: DWIGHT D. EISENHOWER, 1956, at 106.
[8] S.C. Res. 106 (1955).

acts of provocation culminating in the Israeli invasion of Es Samu' in 1966 which led to a United Nations resolution of condemnation censuring Israel for "this large-scale military action."[9]

In both the 1956 and the 1967 cases the attempt was made by Israel to retain control of occupied areas. In 1956 the attempt failed. The outcome of the 1967 attempt is still pending before the United Nations.

There is a risk today threatening the very integrity of the United Nations. It may not be an exaggeration to state that the future of the United Nations and the rule of law would be at stake if the practice of 1947 is repeated and political expediency, in an American election year, is allowed to play a role. One wonders whether it would be in the interest of the United States to be part of such an attempt, or lend its support to it.

International law today is facing a real test. So is the United Nations which is the organization created to uphold the rule of law and safeguard the values enshrined in its Charter. Members of the world organization, scholars, and students of law know what brought about the end of the League of Nations. The memory of the Italian occupation of Ethiopia and the action of the King of Italy in declaring himself Emperor, as a result of this conquest, is still very vivid in the minds of these people. They are rightly disturbed about the future of the United Nations.

International law on the present Middle East Crisis is very clear. It is axiomatic that, by an illegal act, no legal result can be produced, no right acquired; no fruits for aggression. No reminder is needed of the "Stimson Doctrine" of 1932, nor of the position of the United States regarding the invasion of China by Japan in 1932. Equally well known is the position of the American states which, in 1936, declared the following as an accepted principle in the "American Community of Nations": (a) "Proscription of territorial conquest and that, in consequence, no acquisition made through violence shall be recognized."[10] This is part of what is known as the Buenos Aires Declaration of 1936. Again in 1938 the American states adopted the Lima Declaration, in which they reiterated: "[T]he occupation or acquisition of territory or any other modification or territorial or boundary arrangement obtained through conquest by force or by non-pacific means shall not be valid or have legal effect."[11] The Charter of the Organization of American States[12] signed at Bogotá on 30 April, 1948 embodies in Article 17 thereof the following: "No territorial acquisitions or special advantages obtained either by force or by other means of coercion shall be recognized."

---

[9] S.C. Res. 228 (1966).

[10] Report of the Delegation of the United States of America to the Inter-American Conference for the Maintenance of Peace, Buenos Aires, 1936, pp. 227, 228, quoted in 5 M. WHITEMAN, DIGEST OF INTERNATIONAL LAW 880-81 (1965).

[11] Report of the Delegation of the United States of America to the Eighth International Conference of American States, Lima, 1938, pp. 132, 133, quoted in 5 M. WHITEMAN, *supra* note 10, at 881.

[12] 119 U.N.T.S. 3 [1948] 2 U.S.T. 2394; T.I.A.S. No. 2361.

In July 1967, while the Middle East situation was being debated in the General Assembly's Special Session, and before any action was taken, Israel proceeded nevertheless to take steps to annex the City of Jerusalem and face the United Nations with a *fait accompli*. The General Assembly met this challenge with a resolution No. 2253 (ES-V) on 4 July, 1967, adopted by 99 votes with abstentions unfortunately including that of the United States.[13] This resolution in effect affirmed the above principles of international law:

> *The General Assembly,*
> *Deeply concerned* at the situation prevailing in Jerusalem as a result of the measures taken by Israel to change the status of the City,
> 1. *Considers* that these measures are invalid;
> 2. *Calls upon* Israel to rescind all measures already taken and to desist forthwith from taking any action which would alter the status of Jerusalem;
> 3. *Requests* the Secretary-General to report to the General Assembly and the Security Council on the situation and on the implementation of the present resolution not later than one week from its adoption.[14]

In the face of Israel's defiance of this United Nations resolution, the General Assembly adopted another resolution on 14 July, 1967, deploring the failure of Israel to implement the first resolution and reiterating its request. The resolution reads as follows:

> *The General Assembly,*
> *Recalling* its resolution 2253(ES-V) of 4 July 1967,
> *Having received* the report submitted by the Secretary-General,
> *Taking note with the deepest regret and concern* of the non-compliance by Israel with resolution 2253 (ES-V),
> 1. *Deplores* the failure of Israel to implement General Assembly resolution 2253 (ES-V);
> 2. *Reiterates* its call to Israel in that resolution to rescind all measures already taken and to desist forthwith from taking any action which would alter the status of Jerusalem;
> 3. *Requests* the Secretary-General to report to the Security Council and the General Assembly on the situation and on the implementation of the present resolution.[15]

The Israeli answer was, in effect, that Jerusalem is not negotiable.[16]

At a later stage, Jordan raised the question of Jerusalem before the Security Council, and after lengthy deliberations the Council adopted resolution 252 (1968) of 21 May, 1968. It deplored the failure of Israel to comply with the above General Assembly resolutions. It considered all Israeli measures which tend to change the legal status of Jerusalem invalid, and requested the Secretary-General to report on the implementation of the present resolution.

---

[13] U.N. Doc. A/PV. 1548, at 102-05 (1967).
[14] G.A. Res. 2253 (ES-V), U.N. GAOR 5th Emer. Spec. Sess., Supp. 1, at 4, U.N. Doc. A/6798 (1967).
[15] *Id.*
[16] *Cf.* Jones, *The Status of Jerusalem: Some National and International Aspects,* in this symposium, p. 169.

This Security Council resolution reads as follows:

The Security Council,

Recalling General Assembly resolutions 2253 (ES-V) and 2254 (ES-V) of 4 and 14 July 1967,

Having considered the letter (S/8560) of the Permanent Representative of Jordan on the situation in Jerusalem and the report of the Secretary-General (S/8146),

Having heard the statements made before the Council,

Noting that since the adoption of the above-mentioned resolutions, Israel has taken further measures and actions in contravention of those resolutions,

Bearing in mind the need to work for a just and lasting peace,

Reaffirming that acquisition of territory by military conquest is inadmissible,

1. *Deplores* the failure of Israel to comply with the General Assembly resolutions mentioned above;

2. *Considers* that all legislative and administrative measures and actions taken by Israel, including expropriation of land properties thereon, which tend to change the legal status of Jerusalem are invalid and cannot change that status;

3. *Urgently calls upon* Israel to rescind all such measures already taken and to desist forthwith from taking any further action which tends to change the status of Jerusalem;

4. *Requests* the Secretary-General to report to the Security Council on the implementation of the present resolution.

III

THE JEWS AND THE WAILING WALL

An example of Zionist tactics and designs for expansion is afforded by consideration of the Wailing Wall Area. How did the Jewish claim to the area start? Did they have any title or any right of possession to the Wailing Wall and the adjacent area in the Arab City of Jerusalem?

The Government of Great Britain, the Administering Power, stated to Parliament in a White Paper, in November 1928, the following:

> The Western or Wailing Wall formed part of the western exterior of the ancient Jewish Temple; as such, it is holy to the Jewish community, and their custom of praying there extends back to the Middle Ages and possibly further. The Wall is also part of the Haram-al-Sharif; as such, it is holy to Moslems. Moreover, it is legally the absolute property of the Moslem community, and the strip of pavement facing it is Waqf property, as is shown by documents preserved by the Guardian of the Waqf.[17]

It is thus clear that the Mandatory Power never doubted the exclusive legal ownership of the Wall and the adjacent pavement by the Moslem community.

Moreover, in 1930 an ad hoc international tribunal was appointed to determine the rights and the claims of both the Moslems and the Jews in connection with that area. This Tribunal consisted of three jurists—from Sweden, Switzerland and the

---

[17] THE WESTERN OR WAILING WALL IN JERUSALEM: MEMORANDUM BY THE SECRETARY OF STATE FOR THE COLONIES, CMD. No. 3229, at 3 (1928).

Netherlands: Eliel Löfgren, formerly Swedish Minister for Foreign Affairs, member of the Upper Chamber of the Swedish Riksdag (to act as Chairman); Charles Barde, Vice-President of the Court of Justice at Geneva, President of the Austro-Roumanian Mixed Arbitration Tribunal, and C. J. van Kempen, formerly Governor of the East Coast of Sumatra, member of the States-General of the Netherlands.

The Tribunal held twenty-three meetings, during which it heard the arguments of both sides and engaged in hearing evidence. It heard fifty-two witnesses, twenty-one presented by the Jewish side, and thirty by the Moslem side and one British official called by the Tribunal.

In its verdict, the Tribunal emphasized that the "Jews do not claim any proprietorship to the Wall or to the Pavement in front of it."[18] But the Tribunal none-theless "considered it to be its duty to inquire into the question of legal ownership as a necessary basis for determining the legal position in the matter."[19] As a result of thorough investigation, it reached the conclusion that

> [T]he ownership of the Wall, as well as the possession of it and of those parts of its surroundings that are here in question, accrues to the Moslems. The Wall itself as being an integral part of the Haram-esh-Sherif area is Moslem property. From the inquiries conducted by the Commission [same Tribunal] partly in the Sharia Court and partly through the hearing of witnesses' evidence, it has emerged that the Pavement in front of the Wall, where the Jews perform their devotions, is also Moslem property.[20]

The Tribunal went a step further and ascertained that "the area that is coincident with the said Pavement was constituted a Moslem Waqf by Afdal, the son of Saladin, in about the year 1193 A.D."[21]

It was also found that, in about 1320 A.D., what is known as the Magharba Quarter buildings were put up "to serve as lodgings for Moroccan pilgrims, those buildings were also made Waqf by a certain Abu Madian."[22]

The Moslem inhabitants of Jersualem have always objected to any Jewish acts calculated to change the status quo whereby to allege legal possession or ownership.

In 1911, the Guardian of the Abu Madian Waqf, i.e., the Magharba Quarter, had complained that "the Jews, contrary to usage, had placed chairs on the pavement, and he requested that 'in order to avoid a future claim of ownership' the present state of affairs should be stopped."[23] The Administrative Council of Jerusalem thereupon decided that it was not permissible to place on the pavement any article that

---

[18] Report of the Commission appointed by His Majesty's Government . . . with the approval of the Council of the League of Nations, to determine the rights and claims of Moslems and Jews in connection with the Western or Wailing Wall at Jerusalem, Dec. 1930, at 5-6 (London, 1931) (distributed in the United Nations as U.N. Docs. S/8427/Add. 1 and A/7057/Add. 1).

[19] Id.

[20] Id. at 39-40.

[21] Id. at 40.

[22] Id.

[23] Id. at 45.

could be "considered as indications of ownership."[24] The Commission found that the evident motive for the petition and the decision was to prevent any future Jewish claim to ownership or possession.[25] It is this same Magharba Quarter which was recently bulldozed in utter disregard of law, equity, and indeed any moral or religious values and despite United Nations resolutions on this matter. It is clear now that the apparently innocent carrying of chairs, lamps and curtains by the Jewish worshippers was the first sinister step to deprive Arabs of their title. The present bulldozing of the whole Magharba Quarter proves that Arab apprehension was justified.

IV

OTHER ARAB TERRITORIES

What is more (and in pursuance of their theory that might gives right), the Israelis established Jewish settlements and expropriated lands in newly occupied Arab territories, with no legal basis for this other than force and conquest. But in international law, the present military supremacy cannot create new rights where none previously existed. The late Dag Hammerskjöld, as Secretary-General of the United Nations, said in a report concerning the 1956 crisis:

> The United Nations cannot condone a change of the *status juris* resulting from military action contrary to the provisions of the Charter. The Organization must, therefore, maintain that the *status juris* existing prior to such military action be re-established by a withdrawal of troops, and by the relinquishment or nullification of rights asserted in territories covered by the military action and depending upon it.[26]

It is evident that Israel cannot dictate its conditions for withdrawal. Military conquest cannot be the framework within which peace terms may be negotiated. How can Arabs be expected to accept any conditions for Israeli withdrawal from undisputed Arab territory? This has no justification in law or equity. It takes us to the law of the jungle. The Israeli request implies recognition of rights of conquest, and conquest conveys no right but imposes a duty. Yes, a duty on the conquered if no measures are taken by the world Organization to check this aggression, to liberate the homeland from the invaders. This Israeli behaviour should not be encouraged. Israel should receive no support in its dangerous and continued infringements on international law. The rule of law must be upheld, and, on this point, we entirely subscribe to the United States views, expressed on 16 November, 1956 by Mr. Herbert Hoover, the Under-Secretary of State, who reminded the Assembly that:

---

[24] Decision described *id.*

[25] *Id.* These findings about Moslem legal rights and property vis-à-vis the Western (Wailing) Wall and adajecent areas were incorporated under: "Palestine (Western or Wailing Wall) Order in Council 1931," which appeared in the *Official Gazette of the Government of Palestine* in an extraordinary gazette, Supplement No. 8/1931, 8 June, 1931. This Order came into force on 8th June, 1931.

[26] Report of the Secretary-General in pursuit of General Assembly Resolution 1123, 11 U.N. GAOR, Annexes, Agenda Item No. 66, at 47, U.N. Doc. A/3512 (1957).

The basic purpose of the Charter is peace with justice. The United States is convinced that the United Nations is the best instrument for achieving this end. Peace alone is not enough, for without justice, peace is illusory and temporary. On the other hand, without peace, justice would be submerged by the limitless injustices of war.[27]

The same theory was reaffirmed by another United States Representative, Ambassador Lodge, when he said:

We do not believe that any Member is entitled to exact a price for its compliance with the elementary principle of this Organization that: all Members shall refrain from the use of force against the territorial integrity of any State, or in any other manner inconsistent with the purposes of the United Nations.[28]

While debating the tripartite invasion before the General Assembly on 1 March, 1957, Mr. Lodge said:

[T]he United States has sought a solution which would be based on justice and which would take account of the legitimate interests of all the parties. The United States position was manifested from the very beginning in its draft resolution before the Security Council [S/3710], which called upon Israel to withdraw and which called for the withholding of assistance to Israel if it did not withdraw. The United States views in this respect have been steadfast. They were most recently and most authoritatively set forth by President Eisenhower in his public address of 20 February 1957. In this endeavour we have recognized that it is incompatible with the principles of the Charter and with the obligations of membership in the United Nations for any Member to seek political gains through the use of force or to use as a bargaining point a gain achieved by means of force.[29]

Thus, if this Israeli theory is permitted to prevail, it will destroy the United Nations, the effectiveness of its Charter and the sanctity of international law. It certainly leads to more tension, more complications and more invitations to war in the future.

The Arab point of view, in the current crisis, is not different from the stand which the United States adopted in 1956.

Ambassador Goldberg, the distinguished United States representative on the Security Council and permanent United States representative to the United Nations, while arguing the case for the United States prior to the Israeli victory, said in May 1967 that restoration of the status quo is the first essential to peace.

I said that the short-range problem was restoration of the *status quo ante* in the Strait of Tiran—the status which has existed for eleven years—so that the Council, enjoying the breathing spell, the cooling-off period that the Secretary-General has suggested, could consider the underlying problems and arrive at a fair, just and honourable solution of these problems.[30]

---

[27] 11 U.N. GAOR 91 (1956).
[28] *Id.* at 1052-53.
[29] *Id.* at 1277.
[30] U.N. Doc. S/PV. 1344, May 30, 1967, at 56.

Today, students of international law will certainly ponder the utter inconsistency between the United States policy announced in May and that announced in June of the same year, that is, after the Israeli victory, which said:

> What the Near East needs today are new steps toward real peace, not just a cease-fire, which is what we have today; not just a fragile and perilous armistice, which is what we have had for eighteen years; not just withdrawal which is necessary but insufficient.[31]

Prior to the hostilities, Ambassador Goldberg stated to the Security Council that meaningful peace negotiations could not take place unless the Gulf of Aqaba was reopened to Israeli shipping thereby restoring the *status quo ante*. He added that it would not be possible to negotiate and explore the underlying causes of the Arab-Israeli dispute in the tense atmosphere created by the closing of the Gulf of Aqaba.[32]

Following the Israeli victory the United States adopted an entirely contrary position. Ambassador Goldberg called the *status quo ante*, a "prescription for renewed hostilities."[33]

This attitude, to a great extent, brought about the inaction of the Security Council, which encouraged Israel to refuse to withdraw. Israel now even insists on individual negotiations, *i.e.* under duress and coercion. This is what the Rt. Hon. Anthony Nutting called the doctrine of "divide and conquer" and these are what he called "conquerors' terms."[34]

The Arab position is very clear. We maintain that a military solution or any forced solution is a "prescription for war." I need not remind the reader of the consequences of the Versailles Treaty, nor of the Munich Agreement, nor of what happened when Hitler became intoxicated by his victories. Where did his desire for expansion lead him? He occupied almost all of Europe. He reached Stalingrad and was on the outskirts of Moscow. His influence spread through North Africa and his troops reached the borders of Egypt. None of these territories accepted surrender as the solution or negotiations at gunpoint. His illegal occupation, conquest, and continued expansion did not improve his image. And where is Hitler now? Where is Nazism, and where is Fascism?

In our present case, then, should we accept the substitution of power for justice, might for right, or should justice and right and international law be our guiding principles?

---

[31] U.N. Doc. S/PV. 1358, June 13, 1967, p. 51.
[32] *See* U.N. Docs. S/PV. 1343, May 29, 1967, at 6-21, and S/PV. 1344, May 30, 1967, at 52-58.
[33] U.N. Doc. A/PV. 1527, June 30, 1967, at 16-17.
[34] Anthony Nutting, The Tragedy of Palestine from the Balfour Declaration to Today, address delivered at the annual conference of the American Council for Judaism, Nov. 2, 1967, at 6.

The United Nations and the Arab-Israel Conflict

YORAM DINSTEIN

I. *Introduction*

THE United Nations (U.N.) is a world-wide organization of States, established in 1945—in the wake of the Second World War—with a view, primarily, to maintaining international peace and security. Other purposes of the U.N. are to bring about cooperation among nations in the economic, social, cultural and humanitarian spheres. Most (though not all) countries are members of the U.N., which has become the most important international forum for exchanging views between States, conducting diplomatic negotiations and adopting resolutions calling for concerted action by the world community. As a medium of discussion and resolution the U.N. has been instrumental in the process leading to the creation of Israel as well as in the course of the State's on-going struggle for survival. The U.N. has also been utilized as a forum of debates on a number of issues pertaining to the plight of distressed Jewish communities in the Diaspora.

II. *The Partition Resolution*

At the inception of the U.N. Palestine was still a Mandate under the administration of the United Kingdom (U.K.). The U.N. Charter, adopted on June 26, 1945, set up (in Chapter XII) an international trusteeship system, designed to apply *inter alia* to territories subject to Mandate. The founding conference of the U.N., convened in San Francisco in April 1945, had before it a memorandum submitted by the Jewish Agency for Palestine, requesting that the special rights of the Jewish people under the Mandate be secured. To that end the Jewish Agency in fact proposed the inclusion in the Charter of a general stipulation safeguarding rights acquired under existing Mandates. Despite Arab objections a "conservatory clause" was indeed incorporated in Article 80 of the Charter, but it was circumscribed in terms of temporal applicability to the period pending the conclusion of trusteeship agreements. Article 79 made the whole transformation of a Mandate into a trusteeship dependent on the agreement of the Manda-

tory Power. For its part the U.K. did not choose to follow, with
to Palestine, the procedure envisaged in the Charter. Initial
U.K. insisted on awaiting the report of a Joint Anglo-American
mittee of Inquiry, appointed to examine the question of European
Jewry. On April 2, 1947, when the U.K. did finally transmit the Palestine issue to the U.N., it was done beyond the purview of Chapter XII.
Asserting that the Mandate had proved unworkable, the U.K. requested the U.N. to recommend a settlement of the problem.

A special session of the U.N. General Assembly (G.A.)—the first of
its kind—was summoned in April 1947. It decided, in Resolution 106
(S-1) of May 15, to establish the U.N. Special Committee on Palestine
(UNSCOP), consisting of the representatives of 11 States. UNSCOP
members visited Palestine, neighboring countries and camps of displaced persons in Europe. They heard oral testimonies, received written communications from individuals and organizations, and finally
submitted a report to the G.A. UNSCOP report (A/364) unanimously
recommended that the Mandate over Palestine be terminated and that
it be granted independence as soon as possible after a brief transitional period. The majority of UNSCOP proposed the political partition
(subject to an economic union) of Palestine into a Jewish State, an
Arab State and a separate City of Jerusalem. A minority of UNSCOP
urged the formation of a Federal State of Palestine. The report was
discussed by the G.A., at its second regular session, in an *Ad Hoc* Committee on the Palestinian Question. After a prolonged debate the *Ad
Hoc* Committee endorsed with modifications the UNSCOP majority
plan. Strong Arab opposition was countered by a unique alliance between the United States (U.S.) and the Soviet Union (U.S.S.R.), supported by many smaller countries. On November 29, 1947, the G.A. in
a plenary meeting adopted the *Ad Hoc* Committee's report (A/516)—
containing the scheme of the partition of Palestine—by a vote of 33
in favor, 13 against and 10 abstentions. This is the famous Partition
Resolution No. 181 (II).

It is all too often stated that Israel was created by the U.N. in the
Partition Resolution. That, however, is not the case. The resolution was
no more than an important historical link in a chain of events that
brought the State into being. Israel emerged as a State from the
throes of its War of Independence. It acquired Statehood not from a
technical motion in Flushing Meadow, but from an ordeal by battle in
Palestine. A State is a legal person deriving the viability—its very ex-

istence—from a superior legal system, *i.e.*, international law. Under international law a State comes into being only when four cumulative conditions precedent are met: (a) nation; (b) territory; (c) Government, and (d) independence. When the four prerequisites are fulfilled, a State is born irrespective of resolutions and declarations. When they are not, resolutions and declarations cannot create something out of nothing. Weizmann's famous statement about a State not being handed to a nation on a silver platter reflects not only political sagacity but also legal positivism. Israel became a State when the Jewish nation managed to hold on to a territory in Palestine, ruled by its own independent Government. The scales of Statehood were tipped by a sword.

III. *The War of Independence*

The Partition Resolution was hardly a matter of record when the Arab leadership in Palestine resolved to oppose it by force. Confronted with a challenge to its moral authority, the U.N. convened a second special session of the G.A. early in 1948. Some delegates felt that the partition plan could no longer be implemented and that a new approach to the Palestine problem should be sought. The U.S. accordingly put forward a proposal (A/C.1/277) for the establishment of a "temporary" trusteeship for Palestine, thereby discarding in effect the partition scheme. Initially, the new idea gained ground—against Jewish protests—and a special sub-committee (No. 9) was designated to formulate the necessary details. Still, when the State of Israel was proclaimed on May 14, 1948, the U.S. granted recognition, and the trusteeship project was abandoned.

The Partition Resolution constituted a Palestine Commission to supervise its implementation under the guidance of the Security Council (S.C.). The Commission indeed submitted several reports to the S.C., but on May 14, 1948, was relieved by the G.A.—in Resolution 186 (S-2)—from its responsibilities. Instead, the G.A. created the post of a U.N. Mediator on Palestine, to which Count Folke Bernadotte of Sweden was appointed on May 20.

The Partition Resolution requested the S.C. to take required action for its implementation, including enforcement measures within the scope of Chapter VII of the Charter. But it was the consideration of the Palestine Commission's reports that generated the constantly increasing involvement of the S.C. with the Palestine question. At the outset the S.C. proceeded in a gingerly manner, and on March 5, 1948, merely appealed in general to all concerned to prevent or reduce disorders in Palestine (S/691). On April 17 the S.C. already adopted a detailed truce resolution (S/723), and on April 23 set up a Truce Commission for Palestine (P.T.C.) (S/727). Following the armed attack by a number of Arab States against Israel on May 15, the S.C. resumed the debate. A call for cease-fire, within 36 hours, was issued only on May 22 (S/773). 36 hours passed, and the Arab Governments still refused to stop the fighting. The S.C. continued the discussion for several more days. Not before May 29 did the S.C. finally adopt a strong resolution (S/801), which called for a four-week cease-fire by June 1, instructed the Mediator on Palestine and the P.T.C. to supervise its observance, and—for the first time—made a reference to Chapter VII of the Charter by way of warning.

The June 1 deadline was also ignored by the Arab States who insisted that Jewish immigration to Israel discontinue in the course of the cease-fire. But after lengthy negotiations through the Mediators, cessation of hostilities—commonly known as the first truce—was accepted as of June 11. When the four-week duration of the truce drew to a close, the S.C., on July 7, addressed an appeal to the parties to accept its prolongation (S/867). As in previous cases Israel agreed but the Arabs did not, and hostilities were renewed. On July 15 the S.C. approved its most vigorous resolution of the war (S/902). Therein the S.C. took into account Arab rejection of appeals for the continuation of the truce; determined that the situation constituted a threat to the peace within the meaning of Chapter VII; declared that failure to comply with the resolution would demonstrate the existence of a breach of the peace entailing action under that chapter, and ordered a cease-fire "until a peaceful adjustment of the future situation of Palestine is reached." Cease-fire—commonly known as the second truce—took effect as of July 18.

The second truce was frequently violated, and the poignant phrasing of the resolution of July 15 had only an initial impact on the antagonists. On August 19 the S.C. passed another resolution (S–983) which is of particular interest as a precursor of things to come. Here it was stated that each party "is responsible for the actions of both regular and irregular forces operating under its authority or in territory under its control," and that violations of the truce on the ground of "reprisals or retaliation" were impermissible.

The observance of the cease-fire was supervised by the Mediator who, at the same time, attempted to find a solution of his own to the Palestine question. On September 16 Bernadotte prepared a progress report (A/648), in which he recommended a number of crucial changes in the partition plan, e.g., that the Israeli Negev "should be defined as Arab territory." The following day Bernadotte was assassinated in the Israel sector of Jerusalem. (*note*: The murderers were never apprehended and Israel paid reparations to the U.N. The question of *Reparation for Injuries Suffered in the Service of the United Nations* was laid before the International Court of Justice in 1949, and the Court gave an advisory opinion to the effect that the U.N. as such had the "capacity to maintain its rights by bringing international claims"). Ralph Bunche, a member of the staff of the U.N. Secretary-General (S.C.), was appointed Acting Mediator.

In October heavy fighting broke out between Israel and Egypt. The S.C. adopted a resolution on the 19th (S/1044) calling for restoration of the cease-fire and suggesting withdrawal of forces as well as negotiations between the parties either directly or through the U.N. The unheeded call was reiterated in essence by the S.C. on November 4 (S/1070), November 16 (S/1080) and December 29 (S/1169). Negotiations between Israel and Egypt, under the chairmanship of the Acting Mediator, opened at Rhodes in January 1949. An Armistice Agreement was signed on February 24, followed by a series of similar agreements between Israel and Lebanon (signed March 22), Jordan (signed April 3) and Syria (signed July 20). All the Armistice Agreements were concluded without prejudice to territorial rights, and it was specifically stated that the armistice demarcation lines were not to be construed as political boundaries. The agreements established certain demilitarized zones, and set up Mixed Armistice Commissions (MACs) to supervise the implementation of the truce. The Chairman of each MAC was the Chief of Staff of the U.N. Truce Supervision Organization (UNTSO).

On the whole, the role played by the U.N. in the course of the War of Independence is extremely disappointing. Faced for the first time in its history with a clear-cut case of a concerted armed attack in flagrant contravention of the Charter, the U.N. failed to discharge its ultimate peace-keeping responsibility. The collective security system, painstakingly structured in San Francisco, remained a dead letter, and it was left to the State of Israel to defend itself as best it could. In the

S.C. protracted discussions replaced action and words became a substitute for deeds. As the number of resolutions increased, the specific weight of additions to the record book decreased. When agreement was finally reached between Israel and the Arab States, it was due almost entirely to Arab defeat on the battlefield and to negotiations between the parties. The lesson of U.N. paralysis was not lost, however, on aggressors and victims of aggression in subsequent years.

IV. *Membership of Israel*

Israel applied for admission to membership in the U.N. in November 1948 (S/1093). Under Article 4 of the Charter such admission is effected by a decision of the G.A. upon the recommendation of the S.C. The latter did not initially endorse Israel's application. Yet when, in February 1949, Israel requested renewed consideration of the matter (S/1267), recommendation was granted by the S.C. (A/818). The G.A. considered the issue at great length, but finally accepted Israel to the fold, in Resolution 273 (III), on May 11, 1949.

Having been inducted to membership, Israel soon perceived that, as a result of the bloc system permeating every facet of life within the organization, it could scarcely take a major part in the affairs of the U.N. Indeed, being beyond the pale of all blocs, Israel failed to get elected even once in two decades to any of the U.N. Councils: the S.C., the Trusteeship Council (T.C.) or the Economic and Social Council (ECOSOC). The most important elective office that Israel ever held in the U.N. framework was Vice-Presidency of the G.A. during the eighth session in 1953. Resolutions sponsored by Israel were practically doomed to failure, and even cosponsorship was not sought by other States since Arab opposition was almost automatically guaranteed. Israel did extend through the U.N. aid to developing countries, and did receive technical assistance from the organization, but regional cooperation with the Arabs proved impossible.

In the beginning Israel at least enjoyed a relative thaw in the confrontation between the U.S. and the U.S.S.R. concerning the Middle East. In a short while, however, the U.S.S.R. changed its policy and started to support the Arab cause in the hope of penetrating and in time dominating the Middle East through them. Once the U.S.S.R. considered its strategic investment in the Arab world profitable, it lent the Arabs its veto power in the S.C. and the significant bargaining position that it had in every U.N. organ. As far as the Soviets were concerned, the Arabs—as of the mid-1950s—could do no wrong against Israel. As far as the U.N. was concerned, not one single pro-Israeli resolution was passed by the S.C. subsequent to 1951. Israel did make impressive efforts to win friends and influence new States, and consequently was able to thwart many pro-Arab resolutions aimed at undermining its political independence and stifling its economic development. But the atmosphere in the U.N. became increasingly hostile to Israel, and, particularly after the Six Day War, the State found itself frequently isolated and ostracized.

Israel's political insulation in the U.N. had its psychological impact on many officials of the organization (especially within UNTSO), some of whom flaunted their partiality to the Arab cause in more than one way. Jewish public opinion, which in 1947 had an almost preternatural belief in the U.N. as a *deus ex machina*, became disenchanted and sceptical in the 1950s and openly defiant by the late 1960s. Israel became determined that an international organization dedicated in effect to the proposition that political might equals moral right would not be accepted as divine oracle.

V. *Jerusalem*

The U.N. has had a special concern for the City of Jerusalem since 1947. The Partition Resolution prescribed a special international regime for the City as a *corpus separatum*, to be administered by the U.N. through the T.C. In line with the resolution the T.C., in December 1947, appointed a Working Committee on Jerusalem to elaborate a Statute for the City. The Committee formulated a draft, which was discussed and modified—but not completed—by the T.C. by the end of April 1948. In the course of the War of Independence many U.N. debates revolved around the fate of Jerusalem and the need to protect the Holy Places. At the second special session of the G.A., in April and May of 1948, a special sub-committee (No. 10) was set up to consider the question of Jerusalem. A resolution dealing with the temporary administration of the City was adopted by the sub-committee, but failed to be carried by the G.A. Specific clauses relating to the protection of Jerusalem were incorporated in the cease-fire resolutions of the S.C. on May 29 (S/801), and July 15 (S/902), 1948. G. A. Resolution 194 (III) of December 11 of that year declared that, "in view of its association with three world religions," Jerusalem should be placed under an international regime. Israel and Jordan, however, were equally opposed to the *corpus separatum* concept. Since the City in effect was divided between them by the War of Independence, the Armistice Agreement stabilized the situation along the lines of the *status quo*.

In 1949 the G.A., at its fourth session, adopted Resolution 303 (IV), which restated the case for an international regime in Jerusalem. Pursuant to this Resolution the T.C., in 1950, resumed its work on the Statute for the City and approved a new text (A/1286). Still, Jordan's and Israel's united opposition to the internationalization scheme was so strenuous—and the state of affairs in reality so far removed from the wistful atmosphere prevailing in the U.N.—that the efforts of the protagonists of *corpus separatum* began to flag. A proposal to initiate further study on the subject by the T.C. was introduced at the fifth session of the G.A., in 1950, and approved by the *Ad Hoc* Political Committee (A/1724), but did not obtain the required two-thirds majority in plenary. A Philippine amendment endorsing "the principle of the internationalization of Jerusalem" (A/L.134) was submitted in plenary at the seventh session of the G.A., in 1952, and once more fell short of the necessary majority. In the next 15 years the issue of Jerusalem remained dormant in the G.A.

In the S.C. questions pertaining to violations of the Armistice Agreement in Jerusalem engendered several debates over the years. Already in 1950 Israel complained about Jordan's non-compliance with Article VIII of the Agreement, which had accorded to Israel certain rights regarding access to Holy Places, normal functioning of the institutions on Mount Scopus, and free movement of traffic on vital roads. The S.C., however, adopted a noncommittal Resolution (S/1899), and the Article was never implemented by Jordan. Israel renewed the complaint in 1957 (S/3883), but to no avail.

The U.N. did help in the supervision of the observance of a special agreement for the demilitarization of Mount Scopus, concluded between Israel and Jordan on July 7, 1948. The agreement provided for the supply of Mount Scopus by special convoys, and occasionally Jordan suspended the line of communication. The S.C., late in 1957, paid a special visit to the Middle East, and in 1958 appointed a number of personal representatives to conduct negotiations between the parties with a view to the full implementation of the 1948 agreement.

In 1957 Jordan brought before the S.C. the issue of Israeli activities in the zone between the demarcation lines in Jerusalem, and the S.C.

called for their suspension (S/3942). In 1961 Jordan complained that Israel planned to hold a military parade in the City on Independence Day despite the disallowance of heavy armaments under the Armistice Agreement. Israel pointed out that the equipment was brought into Jerusalem for ceremonial purposes only, and that military parades had been conducted before in the City by both sides. The S.C. refused to accept Israel's explanation and urged it to comply with a MAC decision upholding the Jordanian position (S/4788). The question of the Independence Day military parade was raised again in the S.C. in April 1968 (after the reunification of the City). In Resolution 250 (1968) the S.C. called upon Israel to refrain from proceeding with the parade. When Israel went ahead and held it anyway, the S.C. adopted in May another Resolution—No. 251 (1968)—deeply deploring that action.

The reunification of Jerusalem in the Six Day War revived U.N. interest in establishing an international regime in the City. The idea was espoused in a Latin American draft resolution, submitted in June, 1967, to the fifth emergency special session of the G.A. (A/L.523), but not adopted, having failed to gain the necessary two-thirds majority. The G.A. did nevertheless approve, on July 4, a Moslem-sponsored Resolution—No. 2253 (ES-V)—calling upon Israel to rescind and desist from any measures to alter the status of Jerusalem, and considering such steps invalid. Israel did not participate in the vote, and ignored the call. On July 14 the G.A. voted in favor of a second Resolution—No. 2254 (ES-V)—deploring Israel's non-compliance and reiterating the demand. In May 1968 the S.C. joined the bandwagon with a Resolution of its own—No. 252 (1968)—in the same vein. In July 1969 the S.C. approved Resolution 267 (1969), which censured "in the strongest terms" the measures taken by Israel. In September of that year, after the arson committed at the Al Aqsa Mosque, the S.C. adopted Resolution 271 (1969) condemning Israel for its failure to carry out any of the previous pronouncements. In the midst of the spate of resolutions the S.G. sent to Jerusalem, in August 1967, Ernesto A. Thalman of Switzerland as his Personal Representative. Thalman's report (S/8146) tried to reflect impartially the conflicting viewpoints about a complicated matter, but it was swept aside by the descent of one-sided attacks against Israel.

The fact that Christianity and Islam, like Judaism, each has legitimate claims to its own Holy Places in Jerusalem is beyond controversy.

he notion that the U.N., representing the world community, should
erefore concern itself with the fate of the City has much to commend
Yet an organization which kept silent for 15 years of Jordanian total
sregard for Israel rights (guaranteed by the Armistice Agreement)
d general desecration of Jewish Holy Places, can hardly expect Is-
el to be overawed by its sudden, ardent, concern for law and order
Jerusalem. More particularly in view of the fact that, since the re-
ification of the City, Moslem and Christian religious rights have
en scrupulously observed. Workable arrangements are undoubtedly
sired in terms of establishing the proper way of control over the
oly Places of each religious denomination, but all too often the banner
faith is waved so as to change the political fate of Jerusalem.

VI. *The Arab Refugees*

The problem of the Arab refugees was spawned by the War of In-
pendence and augmented by a myopic and self-deluding approach
the subject by Arab Governments. The G.A., in the pace-setting
ragraph 11 of Resolution 194 (III), dated December 11, 1948, pro-
imed that "the refugees wishing to return to their homes and live at
ace with their neighbors should be permitted to do so at the earliest
acticable date, and that compensation should be paid for the proper-
of those choosing not to return." The Palestine Conciliation Com-
ssion (P.C.C.), established in the same resolution, was instructed to
ilitate repatriation, resettlement, rehabilitation and compensation.
Israel, having admitted back tens of thousands of Arab refugees on
e basis of a reunion of families project, and having agreed in prin-
le to the admission of others (sometimes the figure of 100,000 was
ed), has always emphasized that, on the whole, the solution to the
oblem lies in resettlement rather than repatriation. Israel has point-
out that the Arab refugees, far from willing to live at peace with
ir Jewish neighbors, have been subjected to a continuous propa-
nda campaign (starting in primary schools) based on hatred for
ael, and have always been regarded by the Arab States as a means
bring about the disintegration of Israel from within. Israel has
sed the issue of Jewish refugees, from Palestine as well as other Arab
ds, which also emanated from the War of Independence. Israel has
ays expressed its readiness to contribute to the payment of com-
nsation for Arab property abandoned in Israel, though it has also
awn attention to the seizure of Jewish property, in Iraq and else-

where in the Arab world, and indicated that a set-off is in order. As a gesture of good will Israel even agreed to release blocked accounts of Arab refugees. At times Israel insisted on dealing with the problem of the Arab refugees only as part and parcel of a comprehensive settlement with the Arab States, but on other occasions it agreed that solution was not contingent on an overall reconcilement. The Arab States for their part, have consistently repeated that repatriation of the refugees (as distinct from resettlement) is their only goal, and as of 1949 have turned this essentially humanitarian issue into their main political weapon against Israel. Since then not a single year passed without an acrimonious debate on the subject in the U.N.

In the beginning hectic negotiations relating to the Arab refugees were held between Israel and the Arab States under the auspices of the P.C.C. The latter set in motion in 1949 an Economic Survey Mission for the Middle East, headed by Gordon R. Clapp of the U.S. The Clapp Mission came up with the suggestion that the only immediate constructive step was to give the refugees an opportunity to work in their new locations (A/AC.25/6). The Arabs rejected the idea, and having failed to find an acceptable formula, the P.C.C. for a long time was inactive. Then, in 1961, the G.A., at its 15th session, requested the P.C.C.—in Resolution 1604 (XV)—to renew efforts to secure the implementation of paragraph 11 of Resolution 194 (III). Accordingly the P.C.C. appointed Joseph E. Johnson of the U.S. as its Special Representative, and sent him to the Middle East. The mission, however, came to naught, and Johnson resigned in 1963. For many years the P.C.C. conducted, through its Technical Office, a program of identification and assessment of individual parcels of refugee immovable property left in Israel. It was hoped that, once concluded, the project could serve as a basis for the initiation of a compensation scheme. But, inasmuch as the Arabs were interested in repatriation only, the endeavor fizzled.

In Resolution 212 (III) of 1948, the G.A., at its third session, decided to appoint a Director of U.N. Relief for Palestine Refugees. In 1949 the G.A., at its fourth session, in Resolution 302 (IV), established the U.N. Relief and Works Agency for Palestine Refugees in the Near East (U.N.R.W.A.).

The term "Palestine Refugees," used in the definition of U.N.R.W.A.'s mandate, covered not only Arabs but also Jews displaced as a result of the War of Independence. Indeed, originally U.N.R.W.A ealt also with thousands of cases of Palestine Jewish refugees. These, owever, were quickly absorbed in the economic life of Israel, and eeded no further assistance from the U.N. The problem of the Palesne Arab refugees, on the other hand, kept constantly inflating, with 1ildren and grandchildren of 1948 refugees—born and reared in ew homes—automatically joining the lists.

The Arab refugee problem did not expand as a result of the Sinai ampaign of 1956. But the Six Day War of 1967 sent new waves of rabs—some of them already refugees, others displaced for the first me—away from the territories coming under Israel control. Israel ermitted many thousands of these to return, and some of them— ut by no means all—availed themselves of the opportunity. The G.A., : its 23rd session in 1968, adopted Resolution 2452 A (XXIII), which illed upon Israel to take effective steps for the return without delay f those inhabitants who had fled the occupied areas since the outreak of hostilities.

Perhaps the greatest impact of the Six Day War on the Arab refugee roblem is reflected in the fact that most of the refugees (in the Gaza :rip and the West Bank) found themselves under Israel's administraon for an indefinite period of time. Instead of the refugees returning) their old homes in Israel, Israel control reached their new homes. .t long last Israel was given a chance to prove in practice that resettlelent, rehabilitation and compensation were a valid alternative to reatriation. Unfortunately, due to the preemptive requisites of the postVar war, Israel has not yet grasped the unique opportunity.

In the 1960s the Arabs endeavored to get through the G.A. a resoluon, safeguarding the property rights of the Arab refugees as well as ppointing a custodian to administer and protect them. On some occaons draft resolutions along these lines were submitted to the Special olitical Committee but not pressed to a vote (A/SPC/L.90 at the 17th ssion in 1962; A/SPC/L.99 at the 18th session in 1963), or rejected y the Committee (A/SPC/L.116 at the 20th session in 1965; A/SPC/ .128 at the 21st session in 1966; A/SPC/L.168 at the 23rd session in 968). On other occasions the drafts were approved by the Committee ut not put to a vote in plenary (A/SPC/L.157 at the 22nd session in 967), or failed to receive the necessary two-thirds majority in the final ote (A/SPC/L.61 at the 15th session in 1961; A/SPC/L.81 at the 16th ssion in the same year).

All these drafts, designed to undermine the sovereignty of Israel in

an implicit way, proved abortive. Yet, at the 24th session of the G.A.
in 1969, an explicit Resolution—No. 2535 (XXIV)—was accepted, reaf
firming "the inalienable rights of the people of Palestine," and request
ing the S.C. to take effective measures against Israel. This resolution
probably reflects Israel's greatest defeat to that date in the U.N. I
transformed the problem of the Arab refugees into the problem of the
so-called people of Palestine. Resolution 2535 (XXIV) is the antithesi
of Resolution 181 (II).

VII. Direct Negotiations

From the outset of the War of Independence Israel has always in
sisted on direct negotiations with the Arab Governments, as the onl
productive way of arriving at a peaceful settlement of outstanding
issues. The Armistice Agreements were in effect an outcome of direc
negotiations albeit under U.N. auspices. In 1950 Israel submitted to
the Ad Hoc Political Committee of the G.A., at its fifth session, a draf
resolution (A/AC.38/L.60) urging direct negotiations upon the partie
concerned. The draft was withdrawn prior to a vote but the Resolution
finally adopted—No. 394 (V)—did call upon the parties to seek agree
ment by negotiations conducted either with the P.C.C. "or directly.
At the seventh session of the G.A., in 1952, the Ad Hoc Political Com
mittee endorsed a resolution (A/AC.61/L.23/Rev. 4), urging the pa
ties "to enter at an early date, without prejudice to their respectiv
rights and claims, into direct negotiations," but the required two-third
majority was not obtained in plenary.

At the 16th session of the G.A., in 1961, Israel undertook what late
became known as "the initiative." It canvassed sponsors in the G.A
for a draft resolution appealing for direct negotiations, and manage
to get 16 States—most of them from Africa and Latin America—to sub
mit it to the Special Political Committee (A/SPC/L.80). Having faile
in the vote, the initiative was renewed with 21 sponsors at the 17t
session in 1962 (A/SPC/L.89), 19 sponsors at the 18th session in 196
(A/SPC/L.100), and the sole sponsorship of Israel at the 20th sessio
in 1965 (A/SPC/L.115), but another confrontation on the floor of th
Committee was avoided. Following the Six Day War Israel revived th
demand for direct negotiations, but when the S.G. appointed in 196
(in keeping with the instructions of the S.C. Resolution 242 [1967]) Gur
nar V. Jarring of Sweden as his Special Representative to the Middl
East, Israel was willing to cooperate. Jarring travelled extensively o

·veral missions, and submitted a number of reports, but could not ·ing the Arabs to accept anything remotely like a settlement with Is-el. Direct negotiations, while frequently a shibboleth in Israel for-gn policy, are indubitably a serious issue. They may not always be ·e most effective first step towards a détente between hostile States, ·ut in the final analysis they must need take place if the conflict is to ·e resolved.

VIII. *Armistice: The First Phase*

The P.C.C., established by the G.A. in Resolution 194 (III) of 1948, ·ntered with a great deal of zeal upon its task of looking for ways and ·eans of reconciling Israel and the Arab States. Its essay culminated ·n a conference convoked at Lausanne, in 1949, when a rather am-iguous Protocol was signed separately by the parties on May 12 ·\/927). In 1951 another conference was convened by the P.C.C. in ·aris. The P.C.C. suggested that a declaration of pacific intentions be ·ccepted; Israel agreed in principle, but the Arabs refused, and when ·rther attempts to bring the adversaries together failed, the P.C.C. ·ached the conclusion that it was unable to discharge its duties ·\/1985). Nevertheless, the G.A., at its sixth session in 1952, decided ·n Resolution 512 (VI) to keep the P.C.C. alive. Similar resolutions ·ere passed in later years, but to all intents and purposes the P.C.C. ·ased looming large in the political picture of the Middle East.

Once the Armistice Agreements were signed, in 1949, the Acting ·ediator was relieved of his assignment by the S.C., and the super-·sion of the truce was entrusted to UNTSO (S/1376). UNTSO and ·e MACs could not, however, maintain the armistice, and many meet-·gs of the S.C. were monopolized by the Middle East question.

In 1950 Israel complained to the S.C. about Egypt's interference ·ith passage through the Suez Canal of goods destined for Israel. On ·eptember 1, 1951, the S.C. resolved that such practice was illegal and ·alled upon Egypt to terminate the restrictions imposed on Israel-·ound shipping (S/2322). This is historically the most—perhaps the ·nly—decidedly pro-Israeli resolution to have emerged from the S.C. ·Vhen Egypt refused to conform and even extended its interference ·om the Canal to the Gulf of Aqaba, Israel—in January 1954—re-·ewed its complaint to the S.C. A New Zealand draft resolution ·S/3188), noting "with grave concern" Egypt's non-compliance and ·alling for the implementation of the 1951 resolution, foundered on a

Soviet veto in March. When, in September, the Israeli vessel *Bat Galim* was seized by Egypt at the entrance to Suez, Israel complained to the S.C. once more. The S.C. was unable, however, to surmount the veto obstacle. On October 13, 1956, after the nationalization by Egypt of th Suez Canal Company, the S.C. adopted a resolution (S/3675) statin; that any settlement of the Suez question should meet six "require ments," including "free and open transit through the Canal withou discrimination, overt or covert." These requirements were accepted b Egypt, but access to the Canal was denied to Israel and Israel-boun shipping until its closure at the time of the Six Day War.

In the early 1950s a pattern began to be moulded in the S.C. Backe by the U.S.S.R. the Arabs seized the initiative and started to bombar the S.C. with complaints about violations and alleged violations b Israel of the armistice. Israel also turned occasionally to the S.C., bu was generally rebuffed. Paradoxically enough many of the dispute before the S.C. related to the demilitarized zones, which thus becam a source of friction rather than a buffer. Such a clash happened i 1951, when fighting erupted between Syria and Israel concomitant t the drainage of the Huleh Marshes. The matter was brought before th S.C., which first issued a directive of cease-fire (S/2130), and then i effect called upon Israel to desist from all operations in the demil tarized zone (S/2157). When, in 1953, Israel commenced to constru a Jordan Canal, as part of a hydro-electric project, the S.C. quickl called for the temporary suspension of operations in the demilitarize zone (S/3128). The suspension became indefinite as a Western dra resolution (S/3151/Rev.2), containing a compromise formula, e countered a Soviet veto in 1954.

In 1953 the Qibya incident occurred, and the S.C. expressed "th strongest censure" of Israel's retaliatory action (S/3139/Rev.2). Th was the first among many resolutions in which the S.C. tried to cur Israeli reprisals without coming to grips in a meaningful way with th Arab attacks that had triggered them. Thus Israeli reprisals were co demned by the S.C. in 1955, subsequent to the Gaza incident (S/3378 and in January 1956, following the Lake Tiberias incident (S/3538).

By 1956 it became clear that the armistice structure was crumblin In March of that year, at the U.S. request, the S.C. took up the gener issue of compliance given to the Armistice Agreements and its ow resolutions. In April the S.C. requested the S.G. to arrange with th parties for the adoption of certain measures designed to reduce th ension (S/3562). The S.G. visited the Middle East and submitted a progress report (S/3594). In June the S.C. called for re-establishment of full compliance with the Armistice Agreements, and requested the .G. to continue his good offices (S/3605). The S.G. returned to the region in July, and transmitted to the S.C. two more reports (S/3632 and S/3659). Conditions continued, however, to deteriorate. On October 29, 1956, the Sinai Campaign was launched, and Israel announced that the Armistice Agreement with Egypt was valid no more.

All things considered, the early 1950s represented a travesty of armistice in the Middle East and a parody of justice in the U.N. The record of the S.C. presents such a surrealist picture that in retrospect it is hard to believe that distinguished delegates in New York were mindful of what was really happening in the Middle East. Not once did any S.C. resolution refer specifically to the operations of the *edayeen*. Hardly any distinction was made between real aggressor and victim. In fact, judging by the peculiar legerdemain of the U.N., which treated curative measures as worse than the disease, it would appear to the uninformed that Israel was continuously brewing trouble in the Middle East and endangering world peace. Of such misrepresentations are wars begotten.

IX. *The Sinai Campaign*

If the U.N. was slow to react to the War of Independence, it showed remarkable ability for alacrity when the Sinai Campaign broke out. By October 30, 1956, the S.C. was already in session. The same evening a vote was taken on a U.S.-sponsored draft resolution (S/3710), calling for immediate withdrawal of Israeli troops and urging other States not to assist Israel. The resolution was vetoed by France and the U.K., but an emergency special session of the G.A. was convened forthwith. On November 1, the G.A. met, and the following day, in Resolution 997 (ES-I), it appealed for immediate cease-fire and prompt withdrawal of forces. Another Resolution—No. 998 (ES-I)—restating the case more strongly, was approved on November 4. Still another, Resolution 1002 (ES-I), again urging immediate withdrawal of Israeli troops, was taken on November 7.

New grounds were broken at the emergency special session with the adoption on November 4 of Resolution 998 (ES-I), originally introduced by Canada. Here the S.G. was requested to present a plan for the creation of an emergency international U.N. force. The S.G. re-

sponded speedily to the idea, and in correspondence with his su
gestions the U.N. Emergency Force (UNEF) was established, c
November 5, in Resolution 1000 (ES-I), its purpose being "to secu
and supervise the cessation of hostilities." Resolution 1001 (ES-I
dated November 7, approved guidelines proposed by the S.G. for th
functioning of UNEF. The formation of UNEF was carried out again
strong protests from the U.S.S.R., which adhered to the view tha
only the S.C.—as distinct from the G.A.—was empowered to tak
such action. The U.S.S.R., as well as several other countries, refuse
to participate in covering UNEF's expenses, and in time this refusi
precipitated a financial and political crisis for the U.N. (note: Th
question was also brought before the International Court of Justic
which, in 1962, in the matter of *Certain Expenses of the United N*
tions [Article 17, paragraph 2 of the Charter], gave an advisory opinic
to the effect that these were "expenses of the organization" within th
meaning of Article 17 of the Charter).

The 11th regular session of the G.A. continued the deliberations tha
had begun in the first emergency special session. On November 24, i
Resolution 1120 (XI), it noted "with regret" that no withdrawal (
Israeli, French or U.K. troops had been effected and reiterated its ca
to comply with former resolutions on the subject. In Resolution 112
(XI)—adopted the same day—it noted the "basis for the presence an
functioning" of UNEF in Egypt, in line with points made by the S.C
in an *aide mémoire* (A/3375). The *aide mémoire*, based on conve
sations that the S.G. had held in Cairo, clearly established an Egyptia
undertaking to be guided by Resolution 1000 (ES-I) and to enab
UNEF to operate until its task had been completed. First UNEF cor
tingents arrived in the Middle East within a matter of days.

During all that period Israel was subjected to intense pressure, t
the U.S. and the S.G. in person, to commence withdrawal. Dag Han
marskjöld was a strong and hyperactive S.G., who interpreted h
authority in a way that led him to play a direct and major role in th
affairs of the Middle East. Gradual withdrawal of Israeli troops star
ed late in November, but Israel had a constant feud with the S.G. r
garding the schedule of the evacuation of Sinai and the Gaza Strip. O
January 19, 1957, pursuant to a report by the S.G., the G.A.—in Resc
lution 1123 (XI)—noted "with regret and concern" that withdrawa
had not yet been finished, and lent its support to the S.G. in his ur
compromising stand. Israel then put forward an *aide mémoire* (A

3511), in which it indicated that withdrawal from Sharm el Sheikh had to be accompanied by related measures ensuring free navigation in the Straits of Tiran and the Gulf of Aqaba. Furthermore, Israel propounded that certain steps be taken to ascertain that the Gaza Strip would not again be used as a springboard for attack, and raised practical questions pertaining to the conditions for the termination of UNEF's functions. The S.G. still insisted on total and immediate withdrawal (A/3512). The debate in the G.A. resumed, and on February 2, in Resolution 1124 (XI), it deplored non-compliance by Israel with former resolutions and urged the completion of Israeli withdrawal without delay. In a complementary Resolution—No. 1125 (XI)—the G.A., on the same day, also called for the scrupulous observance of the Armistice Agreement. Israel now had a new round of exchanges with the S.G. (A/3527 and A/3563). On March 1 Israel announced that it was prepared to proceed with full withdrawal on the basis of certain assumptions, founded in part on statements made by the U.S. Government. Withdrawal followed suit.

It was during the Sinai Campaign, and immediately thereafter, that the U.N. suddenly sprang to life as a formidable peace-keeping organization. Its eager and energetic pursuit of the goal of cease-fire and withdrawal had no precedent insofar as the Middle East was concerned. The same organization that remained aloof and unconcerned during weeks of bloodshed in 1948, and ignored the activities of the *fedayeen* in subsequent years, became agitated to a boiling point when Israeli pace of withdrawal from Sinai was not rapid enough. In the event, Israel knuckled under pressure from the U.N. and the U.S. Withdrawal did not, however, produce peace; and the moral of the story was engraved on Israel's collective memory.

X. *Armistice: The Second Phase*

The presence of UNEF contributed to the relative stability that characterized the southern border of Israel in the decade following the Sinai Campaign. But the attention of the S.C. was frequently drawn in that period to clashes between Israel and Syria (which, for a while, formed part of the United Arab Republic). Again most of the disputes involved the demilitarized zones.

In 1958 and 1959 the S.C. convened to discuss complaints by Israel against Syrian violations of the armistice (S/4123 and S/4151), but no resolution could be reached on account of the Soviet intransigent stand. Conversely, when Israel, in 1962, retaliated against Syria in the Lake Tiberias area, the S.C. adopted a resolution (S/5111), reaffirming the January 1956 condemnation of Israel (S/3538) and determining that the recent reprisal constituted a "flagrant violation" of that decision in 1963, after the Almagor incident, a Western draft resolution condemning the "wanton murder" of Israeli citizens (S/5407) was once again vetoed by the U.S.S.R. In 1964, when fighting erupted around Tel Dan, the S.C. rejected an Arab-sponsored draft resolution condemning Israel (S/6085), whereupon the Soviets cast their veto on a Western text which deplored the renewal of military action on both sides (S/6113). In July 1966, following a flare-up of fighting as a result of Syrian support of terrorist activities and attempt to divert the sources of the Jordan River, another Arab-sponsored draft resolution condemning Israel (S/7437) was rejected by the S.C. In October of that year Israel complained against the Syrian-backed terrorist attacks. A western resolution calling upon Syria to prevent the use of its territory by the terrorists (S/7568) was not even put to a vote. A weaker and broader draft (S/7575) was vetoed by the U.S.S.R. In November 1966, subsequent to the As-Samu reprisal action in Jordan, the S.C. approved a Resolution—No. 228 (1966)—which, for the first time, "censured" Israel for its action and emphasized that such retaliation "cannot be tolerated" and may entail "further and more effective steps."

The decade of relative quiet between Israel and Egypt, came to an abrupt end in May 1967. On the 16th Egypt demanded withdrawal of UNEF from observation posts along the border. By the 18th Egypt insisted on total evacuation by UNEF of Sinai and the Gaza Strip. S.G. U Thant immediately conceded that UNEF could remain in Egypt only as long as that country consented to its presence. On the same day the S.G. issued instructions to UNEF to withdraw, and merely reported his decision to the G.A. (A/6669). Without requesting permission from the G.A. or the S.C.; without consideration for Israel's views; without serious study of the legal right of Egypt unilaterally to terminate the presence of UNEF (in the light of the agreement reached in 1956 in Cairo with S.G. Hammarskjöld [A/3375] and endorsed by G.A. Resolution 1121 [XI]); and in circumstances amounting in effect to a U.N. emergency force, UNEF was ousted at the very moment when its presence was most needed. On May 19, after issuing the withdrawal instructions, the S.G. submitted a further report to the

S.C. (S/7896) and left for consultations in Cairo. On May 23—while U Thant was still in Egypt—Canada and Denmark requested an urgent meeting of the S.C. to examine the deteriorating situation. In the ensuing debates, held on May 24, the S.C. in all probability reached the nadir of its course in a quarter of a century. A fortnight before the Six Day War, the representatives of the U.S.S.R. and Bulgaria claimed that events in the Middle East were over-dramatized and that there was no reason in the first place for an urgent meeting of the S.C. Other representatives, from Asia and Africa, also contended that the discussion was untimely. A draft resolution, submitted by Canada and Denmark (S/7905)—merely requesting all Member States to refrain from steps which might worsen the situation—was not even put to a vote. On May 26 the S.G. returned from Cairo and put forth a new report (S/7906). On May 29 the S.C. reconvened, and purposeless discussions continued. While the S.C. was musing, cannons began thundering in the Middle East.

XI. *The Six Day War and After*

The S.C. met in emergency session on June 5, practically as soon as the news about the outbreak of fighting reached New York. The U.S. was immediately willing to adopt a resolution calling for cessation of hostilities, but, inasmuch as it was not yet clear at the time which one of the antagonists was having the upper hand, the U.S.S.R. preferred to await developments. Only on June 6, when the Egyptian military debacle became glaring, was the S.C. in a position to adopt Resolution 233 (1967) calling for immediate cease-fire. On June 7 a second Resolution—No. 234 (1967)—urging the discontinuance of all military activities (particularly between Israel and Jordan) was approved. On June 9 Resolution 235 (1967) demanded that hostilities between Israel and Syria come to an end immediately. On June 11 the S.C., in Resolution 236 (1967), condemned all violations of the cease-fire. On June 14, in Resolution 237 (1967), the S.C. called upon Israel to ensure the security of the inhabitants of the areas where military operations had taken place, and urged the Governments concerned to respect the humanitarian principles governing the treatment of prisoners of war and protection of civilians. However, a U.S.S.R.-sponsored draft resolution (S/7951/Rev.2)—condemning Israel as the aggressor and demanding immediate withdrawal—was rejected by the S.C. the same day.

Having failed to achieve the denunciation of Israel in the S.C., the U.S.S.R. took the initiative to convene the fifth emergency special session of the G.A. The session opened on June 17, and on the 19th the Chairman of the Council of Ministers of the U.S.S.R., Aleksei N. Kosygin, personally offered for consideration a draft resolution to the effect that the G.A. vigorously condemn Israel, demand immediate withdrawal of Israeli troops as well as compensation for damages inflicted on Arab countries, and appeal to the S.C. to take effective measures to eliminate all the consequences of Israel's aggression (A/L.519). This proposal was rejected by the G.A. on July 4. A similar draft, submitted by Albania, which also condemned the U.S. and the U.K. for their complicity in the aggression (A/L.521), was voted down on the same day. Yugoslavia introduced another text, ultimately sponsored by 17 mostly African and Asian States, which in the main restricted itself to a call for immediate withdrawal (A/L.522/Rev.3). An alternative Latin American draft resolution, sponsored by 20 States, made a request for withdrawal too, but coupled it with a call for end of belligerency: it also requested the S.C. to look into the questions of navigation and Arab refugees, and brought up the issue of Jerusalem (A/L.523/Rev.1). Both the Yugoslav and the Latin American proposals met the same fate on July 4, having failed to obtain the required two-thirds majority. The only Resolution adopted by the G.A. on that day —No. 2252 (ES-V)—related, like Resolution 237 (1967) of the S.C., to the need for respecting humanitarian principles.

By July 1967 the S.C. already had to convene with a view to examining complaints about breaches of the cease-fire along the Suez Canal, but no formal resolution was voted upon. The discussion resumed in October, after the sinking of the destroyer *Eilat*. On the 25th the S.C. approved Resolution 240 (1967), condemning violations of the cease-fire in general.

In November the S.C. reconvened. On the 22nd it adopted the famous Resolution 242 (1967)—initially proposed by the U.K.—which affirmed that the establishment of "a just and lasting peace in the Middle East" was based on both (a) withdrawal of Israeli forces and (b) termination or belligerency as well as respect for the right of every State in the area "to live in peace within secure and recognized boundaries." The resolution further affirmed the necessity for (1) guaranteeing freedom of navigation (2) achieving a just settlement of the refugee problem; and (3) guaranteeing the territorial inviolability and political independence of every State in the region. Finally, the resolution requested the S.G. to designate a Special Representative to proceed to the Middle East to promote a settlement between the parties.

Resolution 242 (1967) has become an important milestone in the post Six Day War period. Its precise meaning, however, is controversial, and its validity in later years—in view of the disintegration of the cease-fire on which it was based—subject to doubt (*note*: See Dinstein, "The Legal Issues of 'Para-War' and Peace in the Middle East," 44 *St. John's Law Review* [1970] 466, 467-482). It also reflects the low-water mark of Arab efforts after the war to bring about the adoption in the U.N. of unequivocally one-sided resolutions. From that point on the tide of resolutions, which practically challenged Israel's right to self-defense and self-preservation, proved too strong for the State to stem.

In March 1968, after the Karameh incident (in which Israel attacked an Arab terrorists' base in Jordan), the S.C. adopted Resolution 248 (1968), condemning the military action launched by Israel "in flagrant violation" of the Charter and the cease-fire, and declaring that it would have to consider more effective steps to ensure against repetition of such acts. The S.C. had to reconvene almost immediately for further debate about new violations of the cease-fire along the Israel-Jordan line, but no formal resolution was taken. The discussion resumed in August, and the S.C. approved Resolution 256 (1968), condemning Israel again, and reaffirming the warning that more effective measures may be taken. Once more the deliberation continued in March and April 1969, and the S.C. accepted Resolution 265 (1969), adding still another condemnation of Israel to the record while repeating the same warning.

In September 1968, the situation along the Suez Canal was brought up before the S.C., which insisted—in Resolution 258 (1968)—that the cease-fire "must be rigorously respected." In November 1968 the discussion recommenced, but no vote was taken.

In December 1968 the pendulum swung to Lebanon, and the S.C. met to examine Israel's reprisal action against the International Airport of Beirut. The S.C.—in Resolution 262 (1968)—condemned Israel adding "a solemn warning" about further steps that might be taken. The question of Lebanon was also raised in August 1969, when the S.C.—in Resolution 270 (1969)—condemned Israel again, as became the fashion. In May 1970, the same problem produced a similar resolution (S/9807), including condemnation of Israel and reiteration of the "solemn warning."

Condemnation of Israel by the S.C. in the post-war period has become practically par for the course. The most striking element in the rather repetitive discussions and resolutions of the S.C. is that so much of the same ground was covered before. Whole speeches and paragraphs in resolutions can in fact be lifted from the record of e.g., 1968 and inserted in that of, say, 1953, without more than slight modifications in terms of factual details. In the U.N., after three major wars in the Middle East, *plus ça change plus c'est la même chose.*

XII. *Anti-Semitism*

In 1959/60 a "swastika epidemic" swept through large parts of the world. Consequently several members submitted to the U.N. Sub-Commission on Prevention of Discrimination and Protection of Minorities (the Sub-commission), at its 12th session in January 1960, a draft resolution on condemnation of manifestations of anti-Semitism and other religious and racial prejudices (E/CN.4/Sub.2/L.159). There was a consensus in the Sub-Commission that it was necessary to take action against anti-Semitism, but some members had qualms about the explicit use of that term in the resolution. Finally a decision was taken to condemn anti-Semitism without resorting to euphemisms, and the Sub-Commission recommended to its parent body—the U.N. Commission on Human Rights (H.R.C.)—to do the same (Resolution 3 [XII]). The H.R.C. followed the recommendation, in a somewhat altered form, in Resolution 6 (XVI) adopted at its 16th session in March 1960. The matter was discussed later in the year in the Third Committee of the G.A., at its 15th session. The G.A., in Resolution 1510 (XV), condemned all manifestations of racial, religious and national hatred, but deleted a specific reference to anti-Semitism. The item of "manifestations of anti-Semitism and other forms of racial prejudice and religious intolerance of a similar nature" was placed on the agenda of the Sub-Commission at its 13th session in 1961. The Sub-Commission studied material on the subject obtained from Governments (E/CN.4/Sub.2/208) and Non-Governmental Organizations (N.G.O.s) (E/CN.4/Sub.2/L.216). The Sub-Commission discussed the nature of the manifestations of anti-Semitism as well as the causes and motivations for the occurrence of the swastika epidemic. It also examined public reaction to the incidents and measures taken by Governments. Again objections were raised to the spelling out of anti-Semitism in the merging resolution. Finally the term was relegated to the preamble of Resolution 5 (XIII); the operative paragraphs were of general character and dealt with the need to combat racial, religious and national hatred. At the 17th session of the H.R.C., in 1961, further evaluation of the manifestations of anti-Semitism was made, but Resolution 5 (XVII) practically ignored anti-Semitism as such. ECOSOC continued the trend in Resolution 826B (XXXII) of that year, calling for the eradication of racial prejudice and religious intolerance wherever they exist. The G.A. debated the subject at its 17th session, in 1962, when another Resolution—No. 1779 (XVII)—was adopted along the same lines.

As an outcome of the deliberations on the subject in the Third Committee, the G.A. also resolved in 1962 to initiate the drafting of a series of declarations and conventions on the elimination of all forms of racial discrimination (Resolution 1780 [XVII]) and religious intolerance (Resolution 1781 [XVIII]). The Declaration on the Elimination of All Forms of Racial Discrimination was adopted by the G.A. at its 18th session in 1963 (Resolution 1904 [XVIII]). In the course of the drafting of the accompanying Convention—at the 20th session of the H.R.C. —a representative of a Jewish N.G.O., Agudas Israel World Organization, suggested that a specific condemnation of anti-Semitism be incorporated in the document. The U.S. embraced the idea and officially proposed that Article 3 of the draft prepared by the Sub-Commission —condemning "racial segregation and apartheid"—be amended to include a condemnation of anti-Semitism too (789th meeting). Objection to the proposal was voiced on the ground that Article 3 dealt exclusively with segregation and apartheid and that anti-Semitism was out of place in this context. The U.S. therefore withdrew the amendment, and offered the addition of a new Article instead: "States parties condemn anti-Semitism and shall take action as appropriate for its speedy eradication in the territories subject to their jurisdiction" (E/CN.4/L.701, later revised). The U.S.S.R., for its part, proposed to expand the new article to cover also Nazism (including Neo-Nazism) and genocide (E/CN.4/L.710).

Most members of the Commission on Human Rights endorsed, in principle, the concept of the condemnation of anti-Semitism, but since the United States and the U.S.S.R. could not reach a mutually accepted formula, it was decided to transmit both versions to the General Assembly. The Third Committee debated the issue only at the 20th session, in 1965. By that time, opposition to the express mention of anti-Semitism had grown and congealed, particularly among Arab and Soviet bloc delegations. The U.S.S.R. was no longer satisfied merely with the joint listing of anti-Semitism and Nazism and now insisted on adding Zionism to the same category (A/C.3/L.1231). Many other delegations wanted to avoid a confrontation on the subject, inasmuch as they had reservations even about the direct reference to anti-Semitism. Therefore, at the suggestion of Greece and Hungary (A/C.3/L.1244), the Third Committee decided by an overwhelming majority—not to insert in the Convention "any reference to specific forms of racial discrimination," *i.e.*, to delete from the text all the "isms" (the condemnation of *apartheid* in Article 3 was left intact). The International Convention on the Elimination of All Forms of Racial Discrimination, adopted by the G.A. in Resolution 2106 (XX), thus does not condemn anti-Semitism in so many words (*note*: Still, there is good authority for the interpretation that anti-Semitism is covered by the general injunctions of the Convention. See Schwelb, "The International Convention on the Elimination of All Forms of Racial Discrimination," 15 *International and Comparative Law Quarterly* [1966] 996, 1011-1015).

Whereas progress in the U.N. codification relative to racial discrimination was very fast, many obstacles have impeded the drafting of the instruments regarding religious intolerance. The Declaration was in effect abandoned in the H.R.C. in favor of a Convention, and the latter does not seem to have good prospects of quick adoption by the G.A. In the process of drafting, however, at the 22nd session of the H.R.C. in 1966, Israel proposed to add in Article 5 (later enumerated as No. 6) of the text prepared by the Sub-Commission a specific reference to anti-Semitism (E/CN.4/L.791). This amendment was subsequently withdrawn in favor of a similar draft submitted by Chile (E/CN.4/L.797). The Chilean formulation was accepted by the H.R.C. (864th meeting), which once more did not reckon with the atmosphere prevailing in the G.A. In the 22nd session of the latter, in 1967, Libya having proposed in the Third Committee to add the words "Nazism, Fascism and Zionism" after anti-Semitism (A/C.3/L.1461), the G.A. adopted Resolution 2295 (XXII), which—even before discussion of

Article 6 as a whole was about to begin—decided not to mention in the Convention "any specific examples of religious intolerance."

Thus anti-Semitism, past or present, has become an accepted taboo in U.N. resolutions. Curiously enough, the closest that the U.N. ever got to denounce even the Holocaust was in a S.C. resolution, in 1960, in the case of Adolf Eichmann (S/4349). Here, in response to an Argentinian complaint against Israel re the abduction of Eichmann, the S.C. noted "the universal condemnation of the persecution of the Jews under the Nazis," and the concern that Eichmann should be brought to appropriate justice for his crimes. Nevertheless the S.C. requested Israel "to make appropriate reparation."

XIII. Distressed Jewish Communities

Israel, as the only Jewish Member State of the U.N., has always felt itself duty-bound to raise the voice of oppressed, sometimes silent, Jewish minorities in other countries. The same sense of responsibility has been shared by some Jewish N.G.O.s in consultative status with ECOSOC. The greatest efforts to appeal to the conscience of the world were made on behalf of Jews in Arab lands and in the U.S.S.R.

The plight of Jews in Arab lands, directly affected by the Middle East conflict, was first brought to the attention of the U.N., early in 1948, by the World Jewish Congress as an N.G.O. ECOSOC at that time thought it necessary to adopt two formal resolutions on the subject, admittedly bland in contents (Resolutions 133 [VI] H of March 1948 and 214 [VIII] B of February 1949). In future years formal resolutions proved beyond the reach of the Jewish N.G.O.s and Israel. The campaign was therefore confined to the debating ground.

Israel used the opportunity of the annual discussion in the G.A. on the subject of the Arab refugees to air in public the grievances against the Arab Governments in terms of their maltreatment of the Jews. Occasionally the need for more dramatic action was overpowering, and at the sixth session of the G.A., in January 1952, Israel publicly withdrew from meetings of the Ad Hoc Political Committee (57th meeting) and the Third Committee (398th meeting), as a protest against the hangings of Jews in Iraq following useless appeals to the U.N. to intercede on their behalf. When other hangings of Jews in Iraq occurred early in 1969, Israel proposed to the H.R.C., at its 25th session, to dispatch a special communication to the Baghdad Government, in an effort to prevent further summary executions (1013th meeting).

The H.R.C. was not responsive, even though the year before—when loss of Arab homes in the administered territories, rather than Jewish lives, was at issue—a telegram appealing to Israel "to desist forthwith from indulging in such practices" had been adopted at the 24th session without much ado (990th meeting).

The Sinai Campaign compounded the plight of the Jewish community in Egypt, and Israel brought the matter up in detail before the 11th session of the G.A. The Six Day War ignited an anti-Jewish campaign of unprecedented dimensions throughout the Arab world, and Israel strove to mobilize world public opinion on their behalf. A Special Representative of the S.G., Nils G. Gussing, was nominated in July 1967—pursuant to S.C. Resolution 237 (1967) relating to respect for humanitarian principles by "the Governments concerned"—and sought to obtain information with regard, *inter alia*, to the treatment of Jewish minorities in Egypt and Syria (A/6797). Israel requested that the condition of Jewish communities in the whole area of the conflict—including Iraq and Lebanon—be investigated by a projected second mission. But far from extending the terms of reference, the S.C.—in Resolution 259 (1968) of September 1968—called upon Israel alone to receive a Special Representative of the S.G. to examine the situation in the territories under its control. Israel, however, insisted that the assignment of the Special Representative include the issue of Jews in Arab countries. When this demand was denied, Israel refused to cooperate with any new mission. For the same reason Israel also expressed its unwillingness to cooperate with a Special Committee to Investigate Israeli Practices Affecting the Human Rights of the Population of the Occupied Territories, established in G.A. Resolution 2443 (XXIII) in 1968 and renewed in Resolution 2546 (XXIV) in 1969, as well as a special Working Group of Experts set up in H.R.C. Resolution 6 (XXV) in 1969 and renewed in Resolution 10 (XXVI) in 1970.

The plight of 3½ million Jews in the U.S.S.R. was generally kept off the U.N. forum in the 1950s. Israel felt inhibited *vis-à-vis* a hostile super-Power, and other States were not looking forward to a bitter exchange with the Soviets either. An exception to the rule was manifested in 1953, when Israel castigated in the First Committee of the G.A., at its seventh session, "the libel of an alleged world Jewish conspiracy" that had formed a sinister part of the notorious Doctors' Plot (597th meeting).

Only with the advent of the 1960s did the U.N. gradually become an important arena for exposing the deprivations suffered by Soviet Jewry. First N.G.O.s, then Israel, and eventually many other States from all five continents, raised their voice denouncing the denial of human rights and fundamental freedoms to the Jews of the U.S.S.R. Initially the accusations levelled at the U.S.S.R. were muted and circumspect—scarcely mentioning that country by name—but in time a systematic, sustained and poignant offensive developed. It has covered, under a variety of agenda items, almost every possible session of the Sub-Commission, the H.R.C., ECOSOC and the G.A.; since 1967 even the S.C. has been added to the roster.

The main objective of the campaign for Soviet Jewry in the U.N. has been to enlist world public opinion in an attempt to remind a defaulting Government of the human rights of an oppressed minority group, and to persuade it to mend its ways. Most of the critical statements at the U.N. have been hinged on the violations by the U.S.S.R. of fundamental freedoms proclaimed by the Universal Declaration of Human Rights and related instruments: communal Jewish activities that were not permitted; synagogues that were closed down; Jewish schools, religious facilities, publishing houses and cultural institutions that were practically non-existent; reunion of families torn asunder by the Second World War that was not made possible. Particularly since the Six Day War the focus of the philippics shifted from charges of discriminatory practices to an expression of shock at the virulent anti-Semitic propaganda spreading over the U.S.S.R. and the revival of the canard of "The Protocols of the Elders of Zion." In this respect special emphasis was made, on a number of occasions, on the poisonous writings of infamous Ukrainian anti-Semite Trofim Kichko. Thus his first book, "Judaism without Embellishment," was strongly reprehended by Israel already at the 20th session of the H.R.C. in 1964 (807th meeting). His later book, "Judaism and Zionism"—and, for that matter, the whole phenomenon of "Kichkoism"—was rebuked by Israel at the 25th session of the H.R.C. in 1969 (1024th meeting). As of November 1969 Israel has publicly raised the demand that Soviet Jews be permitted to go on *aliya*, and even circulated in the U.N. official communications on the subject, the first one containing a letter from a group of 18 families in Georgia who expressed the wish to live in the Jewish homeland (A/7762).

Soviet response to the statements made at the U.N. on behalf of Jews in the U.S.S.R. has been uneven. Frequently it did its utmost to muzzle such statements, contending that they were irrelevant to the agenda items under discussion. It took strong exception to the circulation by Israel of official documents on Soviet Jewry, and claimed that the procedure constituted "a gross violation" of the Charter, inasmuch as it intervened in the domestic jurisdiction of the U.S.S.R. (A/7787). The U.S.S.R. accused those who spoke out on behalf of Soviet Jews of slander and distortions, a smoke-screen to conceal their own violations of human rights, and even an attempt to undermine the whole Soviet social system. At times the U.S.S.R. also responded with elaborate statements, replete with statistics and quotes denying any discriminatory practices against Soviet Jews. It is noteworthy that whereas the Soviets consistently denied the existence of anti-Semitism in their country, they became the standard-bearers of the fight against the condemnation of that phenomenon by the U.N. Perhaps as a result, the general debate on anti-Semitism in the U.N. became synonymous with a debate on Soviet policies. With countries as with people guilt is sometimes branded on the brow.

Selective Bibliography

Israel and the United Nations, Report of a Study Group (1956).

J. Robinson, *Palestine and the United Nations* (1947).

N. Feinberg, *Submission of the Palestine Question to the United Nations, Palestine under the Mandate and the State of Israel* (1963) 172ff

E. Lauterpacht, *Jerusalem and the Holy Places* (1968).

Akzin, *Jewish Yearbook of International Law* (1948) 87ff.

Yearbooks of the United Nations, 1946 - to date.

III. THE ROLE OF THE UNITED NATIONS

B. *The United Nations Emergency Force and Its Withdrawal*

UNEF and Its Withdrawal

ARTHUR LALL

IN THE LIGHT OF the events of 1967, four points relating to the creation of UNEF ten years earlier acquire special significance.

First, UNEF was conceived as a temporary instrument but the duration of its use was neither determined nor laid down.

Second, its acceptance by Egypt—a vital element in the creation of the Force—was governed by a declaration of the government of that country to the effect that it would "be guided, in good faith, by its acceptance of General Assembly Resolution 1000 (ES-I) of 5 November 1956."[1] This meant that Egypt bound itself to observe strictly the provisions of the Egyptian-Israeli General Armistice Agreement of 1949, including desisting from raids across the armistice lines. It also undertook to refrain from introducing military goods into the area of hostilities. To a significant degree both Egypt and Israel were under a similar obligation of disengagement through Article VII of the Armistice Agreement, which limited "to defense forces only" both the Egyptian army in the forward areas of the Sinai and the Israeli forces in the areas bordering on the Sinai.

The original proposal made by Lester Pearson, then Foreign Minister of Canada, on November 1, 1956, was for a United Nations force "large enough to keep these borders at peace while a political settlement is being worked out."[2] Immediately after Pearson's speech, John Foster Dulles, U.S. Secretary of State,

[1] Annex to General Assembly Doc. A/3375, November 20, 1956.
[2] General Assembly Official Records, 562d plenary meeting, November 1, 1956, p. 36.

expressed his "complete agreement with what he said, and not only my personal agreement, but the feeling of President Eisenhower, with whom I talked a few hours ago about this aspect of the matter."[3] However, the draft resolution introduced by Pearson on November 3 did not mention the large problem of political settlement. It referred only to Resolution 997 (ES-I), the very first resolution of the First Emergency Special Session of the General Assembly, which confined its attention to a cease-fire, the withdrawal of forces, desistance from armed raids, scrupulous observance of the provisions of the Armistice Agreement, desistance from introducing military goods into the area, and the reopening of the Suez Canal. The General Assembly returned, somewhat obliquely, to the matter of the political settlement in its Resolution 1125 (XI) of February 2, 1957, which stated that the "scrupulous maintenance of the Armistice Agreement requires the placing of the UNEF on the Egyptian-Israeli armistice demarcation line and the implementation of other measures as proposed in the Secretary-General's report . . . with a view to assisting in achieving situations conducive to the maintenance of peaceful conditions in the area." In other words, side by side with the deployment of UNEF the United Nations was to proceed to the development of measures which would contribute to the stabilization of peaceful conditions between Israel and the Arab states. It should be noted that the Arab states and Israel abstained in the vote on this resolution although it was adopted by a large majority. For the United Nations as a whole, however, the continuing validity of this part of Resolution 1125 (XI) was emphasized by Secretary-General U Thant in his report of May 18, 1967. In paragraph 5 of that report he quotes the part of the resolution to which attention has just been drawn.[4] In February, 1957, the United Nations had taken upon itself the obligation to try to move toward a stable peace

[3] *Ibid.*   [4] A/6669, May 18, 1967.

in the Middle East and it had recognized that, as a practical matter, UNEF should continue till the attainment of this objective, or at any rate until it was in sight. This is the third point of significance.

Fourth, UNEF was created by the General Assembly in a series of resolutions adopted at its First Emergency Special Session and the Eleventh Regular Session. The Secretary-General's powers in regard to the Force were set out mainly in Resolution 1001 (ES-I) of November 7, which authorized him "to issue all regulations and instructions which may be essential to the effective functioning of the Force, following consultation with the Committee aforementioned, and to take all other necessary administrative and executive action." The committee referred to was the Advisory Committee, composed of one representative each from Brazil, Canada, Ceylon, Colombia, India, Norway, and Pakistan, with the Secretary-General as Chairman. This committee was to "undertake the development of those aspects of the planning for the Force and its operation not already dealt with by the General Assembly and which do not fall within the area of the direct responsibility of the Chief of the Command." The Secretary-General was to consult with it in all matters relating to the functioning of the Force, and provision was made that the Advisory Committee, "in the performance of its duties, shall be empowered to request, through the usual procedures, the convening of the General Assembly and to report to the Assembly whenever matters arise which, in its opinion, are of such urgency and importance as to require consideration by the General Assembly itself." [5]

The General Assembly made considerable delegations of

---

[5] The quotations on the powers of the Secretary-General and of the Advisory Committee are all from General Assembly Resolution 1001 (ES-I) of November 7, 1956. The author served on the Advisory Committee throughout the formative period of UNEF and for two years thereafter as the representative of India.

functions to the Secretary-General and the Advisory Committee, but it made no specific delegation of its power, such as it was, in regard to the extinguishing of the functioning of UNEF. It is, of course, a principle of jurisprudence that an authority which creates an institution retains the power to abolish its own creation unless it makes a specific delegation of that power. In this case, however, there was the complicating factor of the rights of Egypt as the state that had agreed to accept UNEF.

As noted above, it was envisaged that important matters concerning UNEF might arise which would warrant calling into session the General Assembly and that the Advisory Committee was given a delegation of power to this effect. Indeed, the first draft of the resolution did not contain the words "through the usual procedures" in regard to the convening of the Assembly. The Assembly's first thought was that the Advisory Committee should be given an extraordinary power, distinct from and in addition to all existing procedures, of convening the Assembly. However, this thought could not be implemented through a resolution of the Assembly, for it required an amendment of the Charter itself. Nevertheless, the essence of the idea remained in that the Assembly stood ready to convene to deal with important issues that might arise in the course of the life of the Force.

On the very day of the adoption of Resolution 1001 (ES-I) Dag Hammarskjöld, in one of his most important statements on UNEF, said:

I have been asked for an interpretation of what I have said about the length of the assignment of the Force being determined by the need arising out of the present conflict. I am sure the Members will appreciate that, in the still unclear situation, it would be premature for me to say how the needs might develop after the end of the immediate crisis. *However, the Force being under the ultimate authority of the General Assembly, I think that the point need not give rise to worries.*[6]

[6] General Assembly Official Records, 11th Session, 567th plenary meeting, November 7, 1956, p. 115. Italics added.

On February 25, 1957, Dag Hammarskjöld and the representative of Israel, Abba Eban, had a discussion on certain points relating to UNEF. On that occasion the Israeli representative raised the important question of the deployment of the Force in the Sharm el Sheikh area that commands the entrance to the Gulf of Aqaba. In raising this question what was at issue was not the total withdrawal of the Force but modification of deployment in a specific area which was not on the Egyptian-Israeli border. Therefore, the stationing of the Force in the Sharm el Sheikh area could perhaps, at some future date, be regarded as an action over and above what was originally contemplated in the General Assembly resolutions. Israel was especially anxious to seek clarification regarding this particular deployment of the Force. Its representative asked whether the Secretary-General would give notice to the General Assembly before UNEF would be withdrawn from this one area. Hammarskjöld's reply was interesting and correct:

On the question of notification to the General Assembly, the Secretary-General wanted to state his view at a later meeting. An indicated procedure would be for the Secretary-General to inform the Advisory Committee on the UNEF, which would determine whether the matter should be brought to the attention of the Assembly.[7]

In short, Hammarskjöld was referring to the mandate in Resolution 1001 (ES-I) and he was doing so on a matter of deployment as distinct from the question of the extinguishing or total withdrawal of UNEF.

To return to the birth of UNEF, the General Assembly's act of creation of the Force could not be completed unless it was followed by reciprocal action on the part of the parties to the conflict. One of them—Israel—refused to take such action and the Force remained stillborn on its side of the border. On the Egyptian side it came to life with the decision of the government

<hr />

[7] General Assembly Official Records, Agenda Item 66, Annexes, 11th Session, Doc. A/3563, February 26, 1957, p. 71.

of Egypt to give its consent to the stationing of the Force along its border and at other points within its territory. In practice there was, then, a duality in the act of creation which could, in fact, be undone by either party—the General Assembly or Egypt.

Two other points regarding the creation of UNEF must be borne in mind. First, although Egypt abstained in the vote on the first of the resolutions creating the Force, it telegraphed the Secretary-General on November 5, 1956, accepting Resolution 1000 (ES-I), the substantive resolution creating the Force and its Command. This resolution is integrally linked with "*all* the terms of General Assembly Resolution 997 (ES-I)." The significance of the word *all* calls for a brief explanation. When Lester Pearson introduced his draft resolution asking the Secretary-General to submit a plan for the setting up of an international force (Resolution 998 [ES-I]), he referred to the terms of Resolution 997 (ES-I). However, there seemed to be some possibility in this formulation that a selective process might come about whereby only some of the terms of Resolution 997 would be taken into account in the drawing up of the terms of reference of the Force. To make it quite clear that all the terms of that resolution should be engaged, I requested Lester Pearson, in my capacity as the representative of India at the 563d plenary meeting of the General Assembly, to "introduce the word 'all' into that phrase between the word 'with' and the words 'the terms' "[8] in his draft resolution.

Pearson made this amendment, which enabled India and a number of other countries to vote in favor of his proposal. One effect of the amendment was to bring within the terms of Egypt's acceptance of Resolution 1000 (ES-I) such matters as scrupulous observance of the provisions of the Armistice Agreement and refraining from introducing military goods into the

[8] General Assembly Official Records, 563d plenary meeting, November 4, 1956, p. 70.

area of hostilities. There is no time limit on these obligations, and their strict meaning would entail restraint by Egypt from deploying concentrations of forces close to the Israeli border in the Sinai and elsewhere. A corresponding obligation rests on Israel.[9] Egypt's obligation may be regarded as somewhat greater because it voted for Resolution 997 and signified its acceptance of Resolution 1000 (ES-I).

The second point to be taken into account concerns the position of the Soviet Union and by implication that of the other Communist members of the United Nations. These countries abstained on the resolutions creating UNEF. V. V. Kuznetsov, First Deputy Foreign Minister of the Soviet Union, on November 7, 1956, explained that his government regarded it to be the prerogative of the Security Council to create UN forces, but that taking into account that the "victim of aggression has been compelled to agree to the introduction of the international force, in the hope that this may prevent any further extension of the aggression, the Soviet delegation did not vote against the draft resolution, but abstained." [10] The words "has been compelled" did not, of course, relate to any action taken in the Assembly, but rather to the nature of the circumstances in which Egypt was placed at that time. However, and more importantly, Kuznetsov went on to state the following:

The Soviet Union is prepared to make its own contribution towards putting an end to the aggression against Egypt in the briefest possible space of time, towards a settlement of the Suez problem based on due regard for the interests of Egypt, a sovereign and independent State, and towards ensuring *freedom of navigation for all prospective users of the Canal.* Such a settlement of the Suez question would also serve the cause of world peace.[11]

[9] Article VII, pars. 4 and 5, of the Egyptian-Israeli General Armistice Agreement of February 24, 1949.
[10] General Assembly Official Records, 567th meeting, November 7, 1956, p. 128.
[11] *Ibid.* Italics added.

Here, then, the Soviet government states through one of its senior diplomats that it envisages navigation in the Suez Canal as being open to all users—a concept which obviously includes Israel—and that it would assist toward the attainment of this objective. The Soviet position is significant for the chances of success of future efforts in the United Nations to achieve a long-term settlement in the Middle East.

The withdrawal of UNEF, for which orders were issued on May 18, 1967, has to be viewed in the light of the foregoing remarks on the creation of the Force, the legal position regarding its continuance involving both the UN and Egypt, and Hammarskjöld's statement on the ultimate authority of the General Assembly. Among the significant factors relevant to the withdrawal, primacy of place rests with the general situation in the Middle East, to which attention has been drawn in Chapter I. The circumstances were such that U Thant characterized them as being "extremely menacing." [12] In such a situation the United Arab Republic's demand for withdrawal of the Force was, on the face of it, inconsistent with the terms and conditions of its own acceptance of the Force.

The Force had been created for the express purpose of assisting in the pacification of the Middle East. Even on a narrow interpretation of its functions the government of Egypt (as it then was) had bound itself "to be guided, in good faith, by its acceptance of General Assembly Resolution 1000 (ES-I) of 5 November 1956," to which Resolution 997 stands in an integral relationship. The obligations which Egypt accepted included strict observance of the Armistice Agreement, which, in its terms, included observance of "the injunction of the Security Council against resort to military force in the settlement of the Palestine question." [13] In spite of this injunction, on May

[12] Report by the Secretary-General, S/7896, May 19, 1967.
[13] Article I, par. 1, of the Egyptian-Israeli General Armistice Agreement, February 24, 1949: Security Council Official Records (4th Year), Special Supplement No. 3. Also published in United Nations, *Treaty Series*, Vol. 42, p. 251.

16 General I. J. Rikhye, the Commander of UNEF, was handed a letter signed by General M. Fawzy, Chief of Staff of the UAR armed forces, which stated: "I have my instructions to all United Arab Republic armed forces to be ready for action against Israel the moment it might carry out any aggressive action against any Arab country. Due to these instructions our troops are already concentrated in Sinai on our Eastern borders." [14] Here, the Egyptian Chief of Staff reveals concentration of forces on the borders of Israel. True, the claim is that military action was to be taken only in the event of aggression by Israel, but, Article 51 of the Charter notwithstanding, the Armistice Agreement, to which Egypt had again given its adherence in the context of the creation of UNEF, reiterates the Charter injunction against resort to military force in resolving the Palestine question. Egypt's action was an admission of default in its obligations under the Armistice Agreement. If it felt that Israel was about to attack any Arab country, then Egypt's obligations required it to ask for remedial action through the United Nations, such as an urgent convening of the Security Council with a view to obtaining measures to ensure the maintenance of peace. To ask instead for the withdrawal of UNEF in order to adopt an effective military posture in a situation that was already explosive was to negate the United Nations efforts to maintain peace in the area. It is true that UNEF could function only so long as Egyptian consent to the continuance of the Force was operative, but a demand for withdrawal of the Force in order to battle effectively with the adversary was in direct opposition to the whole series of actions comprising the creation of the Force and its deployment in the area. Situations in which the Force could and should have been withdrawn would have possessed characteristics directly opposite to those that had come to exist in the middle of May, 1967.

The failure of the Advisory Committee for UNEF to ask for

[14] A/6669, May 18, 1967, p. 4.

an immediate session of the General Assembly to deal with the situation is totally inexplicable in the light of the terms of its mandate contained in Resolution 1001 (ES-I).[15] That mandate clearly envisaged the calling of the Assembly in circumstances *falling short of* such a dramatic crisis as that engendered on May 16–18 by the United Arab Republic's demand. There was no question but that the UAR's demand for the extinguishing of the Force, in terms both of the principles of jurisprudence and of Hammarskjöld's statement to the Assembly on November 7, 1956, warranted the convoking of the General Assembly. But the Secretary-General reported that, when he met with the UNEF Advisory Committee on May 18, "no proposal was made that the Advisory Committee should exercise the right vested in it by General Assembly Resolution 1001 (ES-I) to request the convening of the General Assembly to take up the situation arising from the United Arab Republic communication."[16] U Thant went on to state:

At the conclusion of the meeting it was understood that the Secretary-General had no alternative other than to comply with the UAR's demand although some representatives felt the Secretary-General should previously clarify with that Government the meaning of its request that withdrawal should take place "as soon as possible."[17]

As a result of the failure of the Advisory Committee to act in accordance with its responsibilities, U Thant naturally felt that he had no alternative but to issue instructions for the withdrawal of the Force. In notifying the Foreign Minister of the United Arab Republic of his instructions, U Thant rightly cautioned Cairo as follows:

Irrespective of the reasons for the action you have taken, in all frankness, may I advise you that I have serious misgivings for, as I have said every year in my annual reports to the General Assembly

---

[15] See page 13 above.
[16] General Assembly Doc. A/6730/Add. 3, June 26, 1967, Report of the Secretary-General on the Withdrawal of the UNEF, p. 8.
[17] *Ibid.*

on UNEF, I believe that this Force has been an important factor in maintaining relative quiet in the area of its deployment during the past ten years and that its withdrawal may have grave implications for peace.[18]

It is evident that, since UNEF had been deployed on Egyptian territory with the consent of the UAR, the withdrawal of consent by the sovereign power would in fact extinguish an essential part of the basis for the continued deployment of the Force. However, if the full range of procedure implied and assumed at the time of the creation of the Force had been put into operation, either by some of the parties concerned or by the Advisory Committee, an opportunity would have been given to exert significant diplomatic pressures on the UAR to reconsider its request for withdrawal. At the same time, pressures could have been developed urging Israel to accept deployment of the Force on its side of the line, and it is not inconceivable that the crisis would have led to the strengthening of this United Nations activity rather than to its cessation. It was also open to the Advisory Committee to urge an immediate convening of the Security Council so as to impose restrictions on the conduct of all the parties at a time of dangerously mounting crisis. It is even conceivable that the Security Council would, at some stage, have considered altering the nature of UNEF into a Force with functions to maintain the peace in accordance with Chapter VII of the Charter. The point is that the failure to apply the full range of United Nations procedures curtailed gravely the diplomatic flexibilities upon which the peaceful resolution of dangerous situations must depend.

[18] *Ibid.,* p. 9.

The United Nations as Scapegoat*

U THANT

IN my own experience as secretary general, the most misunderstood misstated and deliberately distorted episode has been, without ques tion, the withdrawal of the United Nations Emergency Force (UNEF from the Middle East in 1967. I would hesitate to revert to this much publicized subject, were it not that totally misleading and fanciful ac counts of it continue to appear, sometimes emanating from people who have every reason to know the true facts and to understand the rea situation in the Middle East at that time. The full record has beer published by the United Nations, and I shall not go over it again in de tail. I merely wish to comment on it and on some of the mistaker judgments which persist in spite of that published record.

I may say that no one was more acutely aware than I was of the po tentially fateful consequences of the Egyptian demand for the with drawal of UNEF, and I was the first to point them out in no uncertair terms both to Cairo and to the Security Council, and to urge Presiden Nasser to reconsider his course of action. I did this first by urgen representations through the United Arab Republic permanent repre sentative in New York and, four days later, in personal conversation with President Nasser in Cairo. On neither occasion, unfortunately was I successful in persuading President Nasser to change his course or, in Cairo, to rescind his decision to blockade the Strait of Tiran which was announced while I was actually on my way to Cairo.

The hard facts of this very hard situation were as follows. The cen tral fact was that UNEF was stationed on United Arab Republic terri tory only, and that quite apart from the universally recognized sov ereign right of the United Arab Republic to request the withdrawal o UNEF at any time, we were faced, by the time I received the forma demand for UNEF's withdrawal on May 18, with a virtual *fait accom pli.* United Arab Republic forces had reoccupied the buffer zone which alone had made UNEF's function possible for 10 years, and had ousted UNEF from its posts on the line and at the entrance to the Gulf of Aqaba. Furthermore, the government which supplied the

* Excerpt from an address by the United Nations Secretary General on December 3, 1970

two largest contingents in UNEF had made it known that they had been approached by the United Arab Republic government and would immediately comply with its request for withdrawal of their troops. One of these contingents was manning all the posts in Sinai and on the Strait of Tiran. Furthermore, I knew all too well from UNEF's long experience that since the force was only stationed on the United Arab Republic side of the line, despite the original General Assembly intention that it be deployed on the Israel side as well, active United Arab Republic cooperation was indispensable both to maintain the force and to provide a reasonable measure of security for its personnel. If that cooperation was withdrawn by the United Arab Republic, the force could not subsist, let alone function.

It is sometimes forgotten or ignored, as was most recently the case in the memoirs of a former foreign minister of the United Kingdom, that UNEF was set up by the General Assembly, not the Security Council, and that its entry into Egypt was negotiated personally, and with great difficulty, with President Nasser by Secretary General Hammarskjold. The only provisos concerning withdrawal made in 1957 when UNEF was first stationed on the line between Israel and Egypt, were the so-called "good faith" agreement between Dag Hammarskjold and President Nasser, which I immediately drew to Cairo's attention when the question of withdrawal arose in 1967, and Hammarskjold's later undertaking that if Egypt requested the withdrawal of the force from Sharm el-Sheikh he would bring the matter to the attention of the UNEF Advisory Committee, which would determine whether the matter should be brought to the attention of the Assembly. The first of these provisos was a very brief agreement in which the government of Egypt and the secretary general agreed to be "guided in good faith" by the relevant Assembly resolutions in actions related to UNEF. This was as near as Hammarskjold could get to any commitment from Cairo concerning the maintenance of UNEF in Egypt.

In accordance with the latter proviso, I summoned the UNEF Advisory Committee on May 18, as soon as I received the formal United Arab Republic request for withdrawal. Although some of the members of the committee were most apprehensive, as I myself was, of the possible results of the withdrawal of UNEF and were reluctant to accede to the Egyptian demand, all recognized both the legal validity of the demand and the practical impossibility of insisting on UNEF's continuance in the face of Egyptian opposition. No member of the

Advisory Committee proposed bringing the matter to the General Assembly, and as a practical procedural matter it was highly unlikely that enough support could have been found to bring the problem before the Assembly. It was also obvious that the Security Council would be deadlocked in any discussion of the situation at that time. This was, I presume, the reason why no move was made by any member government to bring the matter before either body. Thus, since Israel was unwilling to accept the force on the Israel side of the line, an action which I proposed to the permanent representative of Israel on May 18, and which was rejected out of hand, there was literally no immediate practical alternative to acceding to Egypt's request for withdrawal, and no government at that time or since has been able to suggest any workable alternative.

This did not mean that the force was immediately to leave the area. In my reply to Cairo I made it clear that the force would be withdrawn in an orderly, deliberate and dignified manner, and for the time being it was simply to be concentrated in its unit areas behind the line, its functions on the line having in any case already been forcibly suspended by the United Arab Republic Army. In fact, it was not intended to move out any UNEF units for some weeks, and, with the exception of the Canadian contingent, they were all still there when Israel attacked in Gaza and Sinai on June 5, two contingents suffering casualties at that time. The fate of the Canadian UNEF contingent was indicative of the real difficulties of the actual situation. When, as a result of certain public statements by Canadian ministers and the publicized dispatch of two Canadian naval vessels to the eastern Mediterranean, the United Arab Republic government stated that it could no longer guarantee the safety of Canadian UNEF personnel and requested their immediate withdrawal, the Canadian government arranged for them to be flown out at once on May 31, some weeks earlier than the scheduled withdrawal date. This unfortunate development deprived UNEF of its air unit and its logistical services.

In the light of these facts, which have been on public record from the start, I have always been puzzled at the persistent use in some Western capitals of the word "precipitous"—surely "precipitate" was the word they were looking for—to describe my reply to President Nasser's demand for withdrawal. The implication that the troops had been "precipitously" withdrawn from the Middle East area was the opposite of the truth. They were not, in fact, scheduled to depart for some weeks. The hope, of course, was that in that time it would be possible to work out a formula by which the peacekeeping functions of UNEF could be resumed. Obviously the last way to persuade President Nasser to agree to such a course was to behave as if UNEF were an occupation force, which it very definitely was not, having neither the right nor the equipment to use force, but, unfortunately, many official statements in Western capitals did give precisely this impression and were deeply resented in Cairo. Such attitudes made it more difficult to argue for the continuation of UNEF.

I reported this sequence of events to the General Assembly on May 18, 1967, and on May 19 I also reported to the Security Council on the ominous situation in the Middle East as a whole. In that report I characterized the situation as "extremely menacing," and drew attention to the steady deterioration along the line between Israel and Syria, the increase in Al Fatah activities, the intemperate and bellicose public utterances on all sides, and the persistent rumors of troop movements. I drew attention to the new dangers which had arisen from the Egyptian request for the withdrawal of UNEF, but pointed out that UNEF was "a peacekeeping and not an enforcement operation" and had only been accepted by the United Arab Republic in the first place on this clear understanding. In stressing that UNEF's removal from the line had created a "brutally realistic and dangerous situation," I suggested that at least a limited United Nations presence on the Egypt-Israel line could be maintained if Israel would agree once again to participate in the Egypt-Israel Mixed Armistice Commission. I concluded by saying that the situation in the Middle East was "more menacing than at any time since the fall of 1956."

It has often been said that I should have tried to "negotiate." This, of course, is precisely what I did do, but I did not believe at the time and I still do not, that, after my first effort to get President Nasser to change his mind had met with an uncompromising refusal, a useful preliminary to further negotiations in Cairo would have been a public refusal to recognize Egypt's recognized sovereign rights in relation to UNEF, an attitude which in any case, as secretary general, I had no possible right to adopt toward a member state of the United Nations.

I arrived in Cairo on the afternoon of May 23, having learned only en route that President Nasser had announced his intention to reinstate the blockade of the Strait of Tiran. In response to my question as to the timing of this announcement, President Nasser explained that the decision to resume the blockade had been taken some time before, and that it was considered preferable to announce it before rather than after my visit to Cairo. This answer, incidentally, seems to dispose of the allegation which has since been frequently made that President Nasser was surprised by my acceptance of his demand to withdraw UNEF. Indeed, it would have been odd if he had been surprised, since his own troops, by moving up to the line and evicting UNEF posts on the line and on the Strait of Tiran on May 17 and 18, had removed the basis for UNEF's operation before I had even received the formal request for UNEF's withdrawal.

As I reported to the Security Council on my return from Cairo on May 26, my major concern was to try to gain time in order to lay the basis for a détente and in particular to avoid a clash between the United Arab Republic and Israel over the blockade, which Israel regarded as *casus belli*, and I urged that all parties practice special restraint to allow for a breathing spell and to let tension subside, suggesting various practical measures which might assist this process. Unfortunately, these measures were not adopted, nor did the Security Council achieve the necessary agreement, or even harmony, in its discussions on the Middle East in late May to influence effectively any of the parties to modify the collision course on which they appeared to be set. In Cairo, I had also suggested to President Nasser the appointment of a United Nations special representative in the Middle East to act as a go-between and moderator during this period of unusually dangerous tension. President Nasser agreed to this suggestion, but since it proved to be unacceptable to Israel, there was no point in going ahead with it.

"No Superior Wisdom"

In repeating all of this old history, it is not my intention to apportion blame for the Six Day War to any of the parties concerned. It would be utterly pointless and irrelevant to make such an attempt, for the Six Day War grew out of the underlying causes and tensions of the Middle Eastern conflict. Nor is it particularly relevant to try to assess in retrospect the failure of the United Nations to prevent this disastrous episode. The fact is that the Security Council in its meetings before June 5, 1967, despite all warnings and signs, displayed a cata-trophic, though predictable, lack of consensus concerning the ominous situation in the Middle East, and there was never any practical possibility of the General Assembly being called in, before war broke out, to consider the situation. I certainly can claim no superior wisdom or effectiveness in the days before the Six Day War. Like everyone else concerned, I was trying to deal with a situation in which the governments of the Middle East countries, in a state of tension heightened by misunderstanding, rumor, hatred, propaganda and a willful misreading of the portents of disaster, became set upon a collision course from which no one proved able to divert them.

UNEF was one of the breakwaters set up to control the tide of Middle East dissension, and it eventually collapsed because its constitutional basis, its geographical location and its very nature were not strong enough to withstand the pressure. I must confess that, second to the disasters of the war itself, what I found most disturbing about the 1967 situation was the eagerness of some governments, and important sections of world public opinion, to seize upon the withdrawal of UNEF as the main and primary cause of a disaster the real cause of which was the failure over the years to tackle the underlying problems of the Middle East conflict. It was apparently easier to pretend that UNEF was an enforcement operation which could, and should, have prevented by force the movement of Egyptian troops on Egyptian sovereign territory, than to face the tough realities of the Middle East situation and the true nature of UNEF as a peacekeeping instrument which had no right to use force and which, from the beginning, had operated entirely on the basis of the consent of Egypt to its presence.

The full record of this episode has been available to the press and public since June, 1967, but it is surprising how few of the people who make public statements on the subject seem to have bothered to read it. Those who *have* read it seem, for the most part, to have been convinced, if reluctantly, of the true nature of the situation. Some, including one of the most distinguished living French journalists, have even gone as far as to publish a reappraisal of their original attitude.

Naturally I dislike and resent some of the personal accusations leveled against me as the supposed author of the 1967 war, but I have spoken at length on this subject today rather to illustrate some of the difficulties of making the United Nations understood, and also because

I believe that the United Nations and its member states cannot suc ceed in the immensely difficult tasks which face us if problems, how ever disagreeable, are not faced squarely, and if in difficult times ther is a tendency to shift responsibility and find scapegoats rather than t face facts.

The October Middle East War: Lessons for UN Peacekeeping

MICHAEL HARBOTTLE

IT would be injudicious to predict that the re-establishment of a United Nations peacekeeping presence in the Middle East heralds a bright new era for international peacekeeping initiatives. One can, however, say with some confidence that the UN Emergency Force, and the factors that affected its constitution, give cause for hope that the instrument of peacekeeping will be used more often for the settlement of both inter-state and intra-state disputes. What had been written off in the majority of minds as having no viability after ten years in which no UN peacekeeping operations had been mounted, has suddenly become *de rigueur* and respectable once again. Much will depend upon geo-political attitudes towards third party interventions; in particular those of the two super-powers. But the Middle East war of October 1973 and the emergence of UNEF II, followed more recently by UNDOF (UN Disengagement Observer Force), is bound to encourage a more positive reaction by governments to the contribution that international forces can make to the peaceful settlement of disputes. More especially, it gives the Security Council a fresh opportunity to review the machinery and political procedures for mounting peacekeeping operations.

It cannot be right that one should have to justify a case for having peacekeeping institutions with third party capabilities. It is equally wrong that it should be necessary to justify the contribution that they can make and have made to the containment of violent conflict without recourse to counter-violence. But because of mistaken prejudices and misunderstanding of the function of peacekeeping forces and of the limitations on their objectives, they have tended to become the target of criticism and cynicism. Because of this, their undeniable potential has been ignored.

Why this misunderstanding and disregard? Fundamentally because the limitations and provisos under which such operations are undertaken are largely underestimated. Furthermore, the lack of political initiative coinciding with the peacekeeping presence, which has been the pattern of so many conflict crises since the Second World War, renders the single instrument of peacekeeping inconclusive and in certain instances counter-productive in the settlement of the dispute, despite the undeniable physical success of the operation itself. Since it is the peacekeeping that is providing the tangible on-stage effect while the political peace-making remains in the wings, it is not unnatural that it is the former that is the target of all the brickbats of condemnation and contempt. This lack of perception has done much to damage the image of the peacekeeping machine and to cause its potential as a contribution to conflict control and resolution to be rated so low that nation states do not take it seriously.

Confusion exists over its function—and its functional capacity. Over the years, the term *peacekeeping* has acquired many connotations—from exercises in oppression in Hungary and Czechoslovakia to more conventional military operations in Indo-china. So far as the United Kingdom is concerned, it has been the label by which all its internal security operations, including that in Northern Ireland, have been described. In this context the modus operandi has been enforcement, and the intervention has been second party in that it has invariably supported the established authority against those inclined towards over-throwing it. In no sense can these operations be described as *peacekeeping*; for peacekeeping by definition must be a third party intervention, peaceful and impartial—the task of a referee, equipped with a whistle rather than a gun with which to control the violence. UN peacekeeping is exactly that; an operation that is conducted without force, coercion or undue persuasion, but with tactful reasoning, quiet diplomacy and above all patient restraint. It is this difference in role between the unilateral and the United Nations' multinational approach that is so often forgotten when judgments are made of the effectiveness of UN peacekeeping.

The recent crisis in Cyprus illustrates very well what I mean. There were many who considered it ironic, to say the least, that the United Nations peacekeeping force was powerless to intervene, although its presence in Cyprus was to prevent fighting. Others, rather more scathing in their comments, cited it as yet another example of the inability of the United Nations effectively to rise to the occasion when a situation requires a positive response. Grandiose rather than modest achievements always seem to be expected from the United Nations, despite the obvious limitations under which it has to act. Since therefore the correct interpretation has a direct bearing on any discussion of the future of international peacekeeping, it is important to underline this vital point of concept so that the premise on which this attempt at defining prospects and possibilities is founded will be clear and understood.

For the past eighteen years the two salient principles that have governed the creation and implementation of United Nations peace-keeping operations have been (a) that they should be of a peaceful, not of an enforcement nature, and (b) that they should be mounted only at the request, or with the consent, of those who are a party to the dispute. Though not necessarily running contrary to the spirit of the UN Charter, these provisos do not square with the intentions or the visions of the founder members of the United Nations, who envisaged enforcement action as being the only collective measure by which to preserve international peace and security. This divergence from the fundamental principle of the Charter followed the controversy over the Korean War where, because of Russia's absence from the Security Council and its debates on account of its opposition to the seating of China's representative as president of the Council, it proved possible to mount a UN operation in exact accordance with the provisions of Chapter VII of the Charter. Such a circumstance is not likely to occur again, particularly in view of the appearance of the People's Republic of China at the United Nations; and therefore the Korean episode can be expected to be a single exception to the general rule for peacekeeping operations that has dictated their character ever since.

This change in the concept of peacekeeping has over the years polarised opinion as to its validity and acceptability, the chief protagonists being the United States and the Soviet Union. The super-powers have in the main argued the issues of procedure, and of command and control. Because of the divergence of opinion, the Special Committee on Peacekeeping Operations was set up by a General Assembly resolution in 1965, but has so far failed to agree on proposals for improving the machinery and procedural system for the conduct of peacekeeping operations. This impasse has had a significant effect on the attitudes of member states towards the intervention of international forces in conflict situations, with the result that there has been only inconclusive and often total inaction by the Security Council at times when international peace and security have been in jeopardy. It has also meant that the potential contribution that UN peacekeeping could make towards achieving a de-escalation and reduction in tension in violent conflict situations has too often been ignored. Hence the United Nations was powerless to intervene in the Nigeria-Biafra war and in Bangladesh. Although, under Article 2 (7) of the Charter, the United Nations had no call to intervene unless requested, the precedents of the Congo and Cyprus already existed to enable such a request to be made—had there been any inclination on the part of Nigeria and Pakistan to do so. Northern Ireland is another case in which a sovereign state could have sought help from the United Nations.

The prejudices that have often immobilised the Security Council's consideration of highly explosive international situations and restricted the use of international forces in dealing with them, stem from lack of confidence in the viability of such forces and suspicion that there is an ulterior imperialist design connected with their intervention. This has led to a definite polarisation of geopolitical attitudes, with the Third World particularly tending towards the latter belief. In the case of the big powers the United States, although generally in favour, will resist strongly any question of UN intervention whenever or wherever its own interests are involved—when they are it prefers to deal with the matter outside the framework of the United Nations as it did in Santo Domingo in 1964. The Soviet Union reacts to UN intervention in the same way, but has also maintained that peacekeeping as it is now practised by the United Nations does not accord with the Charter and does not therefore have a standing in international law. It is for this reason that Russia and France, which has taken the same view, have always refused to pay their legal dues towards the costs of peacekeeping as required by Article 17 (2). Russia, not unnaturally, tends to support the attitude of the Third World countries towards peacekeeping, while the People's Republic of China, which sees itself as the champion of the Third World, unequivocally opposes UN peacekeeping operations of any kind on the principle that they are an interference in conflicts which are the concern of the state or states involved and of no one else. With this array of opposites, it is surprising that the United Nations has been able to undertake the operations and missions that it has. It is even more significant that after a vacuum of nearly ten years in which no new UN peacekeeping operations were undertaken, the United Nations is once more in the peacekeeping business. Because of their implications in terms of future peacekeeping prospects and possibilities, the influences and considerations that created UNEF II are worth noting.

The role of the smaller powers in 1973

On the afternoon of October 6, 1973, the fourth war in twenty-five years of Middle East history broke out between Israel and its Arab neighbours. On October 7, the Security Council met to discuss the situation. Further meetings were held on October 9, 11 and 12, but no peace initiative emerged because of a lack of consensus among the Council's members. The United Nations appeared once again to be living up to its popular reputation for talking a lot but achieving nothing. In the meantime, the US Secretary of State, Henry Kissinger, had been holding an almost non-stop dialogue with Anatoly Dobrynin, the Soviet ambassador in Washington, which initiated a direct communication between President Nixon and Mr. Brezhnev. Even so, dangerous moves by both super-powers, involving Russia's declared intent to send troops to Egypt, and America's counter-action of placing its nuclear force on war alert, threatened to destroy the detente and with it any chance of peace in the Middle East. The storm passed and on October 20, Kissinger flew to Moscow for talks with the Russian leaders. From these overtures came the first glimmerings of a unity of purpose which crystallised in the joint resolution 338 on October 22. The resolution required a cease-fire *in situ* no later than twelve hours after the Security Council had adopted the resolution.

A number of factors may have influenced the super-powers to act in unison, but there seems little doubt that the primary consideration was that both had recognised that they were on an undesired collision course which, unless rectified, could lead to a direct confrontation between them. The consequences could have been catastrophic and to avoid them they had to act promptly and together—through the organs of the United Nations. Whatever the failings of the United Nations as an instrument for the peaceful settlement of disputes, and in spite of its dependence upon the vagaries and self-interests of the super-powers, it is the means by which super-power diplomacy and peace initiatives can be given effect; an instrument that even the super-powers find necessary to turn to on occasion in order to implement peace agreements. The United States and the Soviet Union could not by themselves have imposed the ceasefire on either Israel or the Arabs; it needed the sanction and authority of the Security Council.

This emphasis on the United Nations' role became even more evident a few days later on October 25, when with fighting continuing, the Security Council met to consider a resolution calling for the deployment of a peacekeeping force in Sinai (SC Res. 340). This resolution was brought by the eight non-permanent members of the Council—Guinea, India, Indonesia, Kenya, Panama, Peru, Sudan and Yugoslavia. When debated the permanent members, excluding China, supported the resolution. This initiative on the part of the smaller nations in creating a UN peacekeeping presence in the Middle East is an important illustration of how the United Nations can still take effective action in an international emergency when the big powers find themselves incapable of influencing events or achieving on their own the conditions that are required for the maintenance of peace and security. It is of course true that without the support of the big powers, the machinery of the Security Council is powerless to implement the resolutions placed before it—nor would it be seized with any such responsibility if it were not in the interests of the super-powers. No doubt on many occasions in the future self interest will prevail, but at least it is a hopeful sign that there are instances of world crisis, as in the Middle East in October 1973, where the interests of the big powers coincide.

The resolution for creating UNEF II was approved in the Security Council with no votes cast against—China simply dissociated itself from the debate and the voting. Initially, UNEF II was created by drawing on the peace force already in Cyprus and the first troops to arrive in the canal zone were the Austrian, Finnish and Swedish contingents from

UNFICYP, followed soon after by the Irish. Later this optimum force was strengthened by the arrival of contingents from Canada, Ghana, Indonesia, Nepal, Panama, Peru, Poland and Senegal. The physical mounting of the operation is a story in itself and is an impressive example of multi-national co-operation overcoming the incredibly complex problems arising out of the kind of ad hoc deployments which are the trademark of UN peacekeeping operations. Suffice it to say that the first troops of the United Nations were on the Canal negotiating ceasefire agreements within 36 hours of the order arriving at UNFICYP headquarters from New York. UNFICYP's presence close by was a fortuitous bonus in the creation of UNEF II and cannot be looked upon as a classic model for the future. There is, however, an important detail of the UNEF operation that should not be overlooked. The first contingents into Egypt were seasoned UN soldiers from countries that have had continuing experience of international peacekeeping. Although they came from what could at that time be called a sedentary role in Cyprus to a hot war in Egypt, they were mentally equipped to react immediately to their new roles and to assume their responsibilities within hours of their arrival. Had it been otherwise, the quick reaction on arrival in Egypt would have been lacking. Had the inexperienced arrived first the whole operation would have taken much longer to take effect— which might have had a fatal effect on its momentum and subsequent effectiveness. This is no criticism of the less experienced contingents; they themselves were well aware of their inadequacies and lack of preparation. Some individuals freely admitted that they had little or no idea of the role they were required to perform. They will learn, and learn fast, as their predecessors have done before them—but the hard way. Pre-education, preparation and preparedness would have done much to alleviate their deficiencies.

If the fault lies anywhere, it lies with the United Nations for not giving member states the information they need to prepare themselves. There is no UN handbook or guide to peacekeeping; the policy of the Secretariat has never been to publish evaluations or commentaries based on past experience of peacekeeping operations and missions. It is difficult to see, therefore, how the small member states can acquire the information they seek. Clearly, some kind of handbook is necessary, consolidating in one manual the essence of the information required; the peacekeeping provisions of the Charter, the peacekeeping machinery within the organs of the United Nations, the legal and broad political aspects of the Status of the Force, the mounting and functioning of forces, standing operating procedures and the use of force, as well as aids to preparation and training. The need for such a handbook is strongly supported by almost all those who have a wide experience of international peacekeeping, particularly those who have held senior command and staff appointments; an opinion borne out and confirmed during my visit to UNEF II, UNTSO and UNFICYP in January this year.[1]

In the Middle East we have seen UNEF II pass through two phases of what could and should be a three-phase operation. In the beginning it established a 'thin blue line' between two armies locked in battle. In January it moved into its second phase, the establishment of a narrow buffer zone to maintain a territorial vacuum between the Arab and Israeli forces, thereby providing a temporary safeguard against a renewal of hostilities. It will depend upon the progress made at Geneva towards reaching a peaceful settlement of the Middle East dispute whether or not a third phase will materialise; but if one does, the UN may be called upon to fulfil a more comprehensive role. If it is, then a more substantial ground buffer will be required than those which at present exist in Sinai and on the Golan Heights so that acceptable guaranteed safeguards can be offered. This implies demilitarised zones deep enough and strongly enough held to withstand infiltration or erosion.

The future role of UNEF II and UNDOF will not only depend upon the outcome of any peace conference, but also on any change of attitude that may occur among UN members as a result of this successful reactivation of the UN's peacekeeping machine. But the extent of the UN objective must not rest only upon keeping Arab and Jew apart; more important, it must be to bring together the parties to the dispute. This entails a positive political initiative of mediation and negotiation, as well as a major peace-building effort embracing social and economic reconciliation and reconstruction aimed at creating a peaceful inter-state co-existence on which a more stable and peaceful situation can be founded. This will be a hard and lengthy task but one which must be attempted; the absence of any determined peace initiative in the Middle East after the 1956 war made the 1967 war inevitable. This time peace-keeping, peacemaking and, most important, peacebuilding must go hand in hand.

Peacekeeping becomes a multi-professional commitment

What can be done to improve the United Nations' capability for keeping the peace? As at present politically structured, its pre-conflict action is likely to be limited to mediatory interventions of the kind introduced into the Iran-Iraq border dispute of February 1974, when the Secretary-General's special representative, Señor Luis Weckmann-Munoz of Mexico (now his special representative in Cyprus) was able to procure

---

[1] A handbook is shortly to be prepared by the International Peace Academy.

a solution to that problem before serious hostilities broke out between the two countries. Where hostilities of a major character break out, as in the Middle East in October 1973 and in Cyprus in July 1974, the problem of restoring order becomes much more complex—and generally involves top-level shuttle diplomacy by one or both of the super-powers before a ceasefire can be arranged. The level at which these negotiations are carried out is, in my view, of less significance than their subsequent endorsement and promulgation by the United Nations. The authoritative weight of the member states in the Security Council is more likely to achieve a continuing ceasefire and a reconstruction of both military and social stability than is a single state—even a super-power. It is therefore encouraging that in its resolutions in respect of the Middle East and Cyprus wars, the vote in the Security Council was a unanimous one (the People's Republic of China for the reasons already given took no part in either debate and did not cast a vote). In the case of the sending of a special representative to Iran and Iraq, the Security Council was equally unanimous in its vote.

If then there is a growing unanimity among permanent and non-permanent members of the Security Council that it should not only act forthrightly to stop wars, but that it should be the instrument through which initiatives towards this end should be taken, there is an urgent need to improve the procedural and physical machinery for developing peacekeeping techniques and the operational skills required in their practical application. This does not mean revising the Charter of the United Nations in order to embrace new innovative ideas. It means using the Charter as it stands and the organs existing in the UN organisation with greater flexibility. Even in the case of Article 43, which requires all member states to make available 'armed forces, assistance and facilities ... for the purpose of maintaining international peace and security', a more flexible approach is possible; it should involve a less formal and rigid agreement and allow nations more freedom of choice in deciding the kind of contribution and type of operational commitment they are prepared to undertake. A less demanding commitment than that set out in Article 43 could have the effect of encouraging member states to nominate options which they would be prepared to take up on behalf of the United Nations. In other ways too the machinery of the United Nations can be strengthened to meet the peacekeeping responsibility—a reactivation of the Military Staff Committee to a more positive and broadly based role in its relationship with the Security Council; a multi-professional advisory group including political, diplomatic, military, legal, economic and research members whose advice to the Secretary-General could be of some significant value in the preparation and conduct of peacekeeping operations; the creation of a data bank of case studies on conflict which could provide a form of early warning system for the

Security Council and alert it to the developing threat of potential conflict; the development of expertise and techniques directed at improving the overall capacity of member states to undertake commitments under a re-vamped Article 43. These and other related areas need to be examined if UN peacekeeping is to become a potent force in the settlement of disputes. But more than anything else it is the concept of international peacekeeping that requires to be re-examined. No longer is it enough to think of peacekeeping in terms of a purely military operation—it has become a multi-professional commitment.

The essence of peacekeeping is not only to separate the disputants and keep them apart, but ultimately to bring them together. All too often the United Nations and the concerned powers have limited themselves to the former objective. Peacekeeping alone, operating in a vacuum, will eventually become counter-productive, however physically successful it may have been at the start. To be productive it must be closely linked to an overall peace effort. Only in this way can a positive rather than a negative result emerge in the Middle East and Cyprus.

In the Middle East, as already indicated, the second phase of the UN operation is in progress. In Cyprus, where in a matter of days UN achievements over ten years may well have been negated, the long haul back has begun. If as a result of a Geneva settlement on the Middle East the role of UNEF II and UNDOF is enlarged, care must be taken to see that where demilitarised zones are established under UN control, these do not become military cantonments banning access to military and civilians alike. Rather they should assume the character of UN-supervised areas and become development areas in which a civilian community can live and work, cultivating the land, creating light industry, establishing co-operatives and building up private businesses. Hopefully, these protected zones would provide the opportunity for Arabs and Jews to live side by side and build up an inter-communal relationship. If this dual existence, constituting a kind of homogenous cocoon as a buffer around the state of Israel, comes about it will do more than anything else to establish the communication that is essential to reconciliation. In its creation the United Nations could play a significant role, providing a civilian administration as an interregnum for each zone until such a time as a joint community council was ready to take over. An interregnum is nothing new to the United Nations; one was set up in West Irian during 1962–63.

This may seem to be a giant step into the future, but if confidence can be kindled and fear allayed by such development projects, the reconciliation that could derive from inter-community relations within a demilitarised zone could make that significant difference to the strengthening of any peaceful settlement in the Middle East. The United Nations has a clear-cut role to see that once peace has been made at

Geneva, peacekeeping and peacebuilding go hand in hand in the Middle East.

In Cyprus restoration of the morale, confidence and trust of the two communities is as important as the prevention of fighting between them. Any progress that had been made towards peaceful co-existence has been washed away. The UN must recreate the incentive and this is going to require a major peace-building effort, linked and co-ordinated with the peacekeeping operation.

Peacekeeping is three dimensional in character and design, incorporating elements of peacemaking and peace building. Peacekeeping is a variation on a theme; adjusting to the character of the conflict for which it is required. It is like a doctor's treatment of a patient—the prescription applied must be appropriate to the complaint. Peacekeeping is nothing more than a relief operation for a man-made disaster and requires a broad range of professional skills and techniques. This should be the blueprint on which future operations should be constructed and developed. The Middle East and Cyprus give the United Nations the opportunity for that development. It would be most regrettable if the opportunity were missed; for peacekeeping, peacemaking and peace building are indivisible and represent a multi-professional commitment in the peaceful settlement of disputes.

IV. THOUGHTS ON SETTLEMENT

The Arab-Israeli Conflict and
the Obligation to Pursue Peaceful Settlement
of International Disputes

JOHN NORTON MOORE

The principal focus of international-legal analysis in the literature of major war-peace issues has been the permissibility of the contending belligerents' use of force. That is, whether each belligerent's use of the armed forces was in violation of Article 2(4) of the United Nations Charter, which proscribes "the threat or use of force against the territorial integrity or political independence of any state." In contrast, there has been little or no analysis of each belligerent's obligation under Articles 2(3) and 33(1) of the Charter to pursue peaceful settlement of international disputes. The resulting pattern is one of over-emphasizing the normative appraisal of initial use of coercion while woefully neglecting a continuing appraisal of each belligerent's efforts at peaceful settlement. The belligerent's positions on settlement, however, may be responsible for indefinite prolongation of conflict and as such may sometimes be a more meaningful indicator of compliance with Charter obligations than a single-barrelled focus on the appraisal of initiating coercion. Both the Indo-China and the Arab-Israeli conflicts, the principal contemporary war-peace issues, demonstrate this one-sided focus. A preoccupation in the Indo-China conflict has been whether the conflict could most meaningfully be characterized as an international or an internal conflict for purposes of assessing the lawfulness of initiating coercion. The negotiating positions of the contending belligerents, while a subject of generalized speculation, have not been the subject of normative analysis under the Charter.[1] Similarly, the principal focus in the Arab-Israeli conflict has been the lawfulness of the Arab and Israeli uses of force in the Six Day War and the consequences of that use of force with respect to retention of the occupied territories. There has been only sporadic attention paid to the "Charterability" of the negotiating positions of the belligerents.[2]

* This is a revised and updated version of a paper presented at a regional meeting of the American Society of International Law at the University of Kansas on November 20-21, 1970. I would like to thank Professor John Francis Murphy, the organizer of the meeting, for providing me with a forum to test and refine initial formulations. I would also like to thank Mr. Jacob Zemach for his helpful suggestions on an earlier draft. Any errors and infelicities are my own.

** Professor of Law and Director of the Graduate Program, the University of Virginia School of Law. B.A. 1959, Drew Univ.; LL.B. 1962, Duke Univ.; LL.M. 1965, Univ. of Illinois.

[1] There are more than 115 books and articles dealing with some aspect of the legal issues presented by the Indo-China War. None of these focus on appraisal of the principal belligerent's compliance with the Charter obligation to pursue peaceful settlement of international disputes. The only concession is an occasional article that mentions the Article 33 obligation to pursue peaceful settlement and briefly urges that one side or another is in violation of this obligation. What few materials have been published on efforts at settlement, such as D. KRASLOW & S. LOORY, THE SECRET SEARCH FOR PEACE IN VIETNAM (1968), have made no effort at international legal analysis. See the bibliography of writings on Indo-China and the legal order in J. N. MOORE, LAW AND THE INDO-CHINA WAR (to be published by the Princeton University Press in late 1971).

[2] In compiling a reader on THE ARAB-ISRAELI CONFLICT AND INTERNATIONAL LAW I recently collected more than 65 books and articles dealing with some aspect of the legal issues presented by the Arab-Israeli conflict. A number of these focus on the legal issues surrounding Security Council Resolution 242 of

The result in both conflicts has been that one or another party could stymie all efforts at conflict resolution simply by refusing to negotiate, by setting unreasonable preconditions to negotiation, or by insisting on an unreasonable substantive position for settlement.

Focus on efforts at settlement seems particularly important as limited war and interventionary activity become the predominant form of conflict in the international system. Settlement of such prolonged conflicts may well be a more important problem for the system than the prevention of initiating coercion leading only to short-lived and self-terminating conflict. That is, systemically, settlement of the Arab-Israeli and Indo-China conflicts is more critical than deterrence of the Indian invasion of Goa, even though the lawfulness of the Indian initiation of coercion in the Goan invasion is also a useful subject for inquiry. The prolonged continuation of both the Arab-Israeli and Indo-China conflicts suggests that the time has come to vitalize the Charter obligation to pursue peaceful settlement of international disputes. Normative appraisal of the settlement positions of contending belligerents should be as fundamental to legal analysis as the appraisal of initiating coercion. This is not to suggest substitution of a "justice of the cause" formula for the more advanced Charter framework for the regulation of coercion.[3] It is to urge that prolonged international conflict threatening international peace and security should be subjected to serious appraisal with respect to the efforts of both sides to seek peaceful settlement of the underlying dispute as well as to appraisal of the lawfulness of initiating coercion. Such an additional focus seems required on a major purposes rationale both by the provisions of the Charter regulating the use of force and by those regarding the obligation to pursue peaceful settlement of international disputes.

I. The Obligation to Pursue Peaceful Settlement of International Disputes

The principal difficulty in normative appraisal of the settlement positions of the participants in major world order disputes is the generality of the Charter provisions regarding the obligation to pursue peaceful settlement of international disputes and the resulting lack of criteria for appraisal. Article 1(1) provides that one of the purposes of the United Nations is "to bring about by peaceful means, and in conformity with the principles of justice and inter-

November 22, 1967, or on the illegality of maintaining a continuing state of belligerency against Israel, but none focus squarely on appraisal of the principal belligerent's compliance with the Charter obligation to pursue peaceful settlement of international disputes.

[3] For an analysis of the development of the international law of conflict management from the "just war" to the Charter see M. Kaplan & N. Katzenbach, *Resort to Force: War and Neutrality*, II R. Falk & S. Mendlovitz (eds.), The Strategy of World Order 276, 279-95 (1966); M. McDougal & F. Feliciano, Law and Minimum World Public Order, 121-55, 167-260 (1961); T. Taylor, *Just and Unjust Wars*, Nuremberg and Vietnam: An American Tragedy, ch. 3, at 58-77 (1970); Kunz, *Editorial Comment: Bellum Justum & Bellum Legale*, 45 Am. J. Int'l L. 528 (1951); Nussbaum, *Just War—A Legal Concept?*, 42 Mich. L. Rev. 453 (1943); Von Elbe, *The Evolution of the Concept of the Just War in International Law*, 33 Am. J. Int'l L. 665 (1939).

national law, adjustment or settlement of international disputes or situations which might lead to a breach of the peace." Article 2(3) provides: "All Members shall settle their international disputes by peaceful means in such a manner that international peace and security, and justice, are not endangered." And Article 33(1) provides: "The parties to any dispute, the continuance of which is likely to endanger the maintenance of international peace and security, shall, first of all, seek a solution by negotiation, enquiry, mediation, conciliation, arbitration, judicial settlement, resort to regional agencies or arrangements, or other peaceful means of their own choice." Taken together these three provisions indicate a positive obligation to pursue peaceful settlement of international disputes "the continuance of which is likely to endanger the maintenance of international peace and security." Goodrich and Hambro indicate that in this respect the Charter went beyond the Kellogg-Briand Pact "by which the parties agreed [only] that the settlement of their disputes should 'never be sought except by pacific means.' "[4]

It seems a fair inference that the obligation to pursue peaceful settlement of international disputes continues even during hostilities. The reference in Article 33 that the parties shall "first of all, seek a [peaceful] solution" seems to refer to action prior to referral to the Security Council pursuant to Article 37. And Articles 1(1) and 2(3) have no such temporal limitation.

Although there would seem to be an obligation to pursue some means of peaceful settlement in good faith, no particular means is required. On the substantive side, however, there is a strong implication from Article 1(1) that peaceful settlement is to be based on "the principles of justice and international law." Presumably the principles of the Charter would be among the most important of these principles of international law and as such are an important basis for appraisal of the negotiating positions of the parties. Interestingly, Resolution 242 of November 22, 1967,[5] by which the Security Council recommends general terms of settlement for the Arab-Israeli conflict, refers to "the fulfillment of Charter principles" when making recommendations concerning the principal terms of settlement.

In pouring content into the obligation to pursue peaceful settlement of international disputes it would seem helpful to specify these procedural and substantive obligations at a lower level of abstraction. The following principles of procedure and content are an effort to develop more specific standards for appraisal. Though they represent a personal extrapolation from the Charter they seem strongly inferable from the Charter obligation. Standards of procedure are those that concern the modalities by which settlement is reached. Standards of content are those that concern the content of the settlement.

---

[4] L. GOODRICH & E. HAMBRO, CHARTER OF THE UNITED NATIONS, COMMENTARY AND DOCUMENTS 237 (2d rev. ed. 1949).

[5] S.C. Res. 242, 22 U.N. SCOR, 1382d meeting 8 (1967).

Standards of Procedure

1. The extent to which the contending belligerents take the initiative in urging peaceful settlement.

2. The willingness of the belligerents to negotiate a settlement or at least to negotiate a modality for arriving at settlement: (a) willingness to negotiate at any time without preconditions; (b) willingness to negotiate with all de facto belligerents; (c) willingness to negotiate in direct talks; (d) willingness to negotiate with respect to all of the principal issues in dispute.

3. The willingness of the belligerents to publicly communicate general terms for settlement.

4. The willingness of the belligerents to suggest specific terms for settlement. Specific suggestions need not always be publicly communicated if public disclosure would inhibit the chances for acceptance.

5. The willingness of the belligerents to conclude a legally binding settlement, however arrived at, or to agree on a modality for settlement such as arbitration or judicial determination that implies a legally binding outcome.

Standards of Content

1. The reasonableness of suggested terms for settlement as appraised by reference to fundamental Charter principles including: (a) nonuse of force against the terrotorial integrity or political independence of any state; (1) cessation of all belligerent activities and claims of belligerency; (2) nonacquisition of territory (and other values) by force; (3) control of activities of terrorist or paramilitary forces; (4) measures to strengthen peace; (b) self-determination of peoples; (c) respect for fundamental human rights; (d) cooperation for economic and social progress.

2. The willingness of the parties to accept United Nations recommendations for settlement.

3. In situations in which fundamental Charter principles are uncertain or ambiguous, the willingness of the parties to enter into a compromise settlement.

It is not suggested that each of these standards gives rise under all circumstances to an independent legal obligation. Thus, there is a continuing debate about the legal effect of United Nations settlement recommendations.[6] Taken together, however, they provide a fair indication of compliance with the Charter obligation to pursue peaceful settlement of disputes. Moreover, these suggested principles of content and procedure are interrelated and in using them to appraise settlement positions they should be considered as a whole. For example, at least with respect to contemporary attacks,[7] a state that has

---

[6] See, e.g., Shapira, The Security Council Resolution of November 22, 1967—Its Legal Nature and Implications, 4 ISRAEL L. REV. 229 (1969).

[7] If the basic Charter principle that major coercion cannot be used as an instrument of national policy is to be preserved, at some point even the illegality of an initial acquisition of territory must yield to the overriding Charter judgment that unilateral force should not be employed to attempt to redress perceived past injustices. See the discussion of this point in part III(A) of this paper.

been subjected to an external armed attack in clear violation of fundamental Charter principles need not negotiate away its political territorial integrity. As this example illustrates, the content standard relating to the fundamental rights of the parties under the Charter is particularly important for appraisal of the obligation to pursue peaceful settlement of disputes. As such, appraisal might routinely begin by reference to the applicability of the Charter to the principal issues in the dispute.

The next sections of this paper will first briefly review the settlement positions of the principal belligerents in the Arab-Israeli conflict, will then analyze the conflict by reference to fundamental Charter principles and United Nations recommendations, and finally will appraise the settlement positions of the belligerents by reference to the suggested standards for determining compliance with the obligation to pursue peaceful settlement of disputes.

II. A Brief Review of the Settlement Positions of the Principal Belligerents in the Arab-Israeli Conflict

Assistant Secretary of State Joseph Sisco recently warned that "the Middle East . . . holds greater . . . risks for world peace than any other area in the world."[8] The warning should be heeded. The Arab-Israeli conflict is one that has defied solution since the commencement of the British Mandate for Palestine in 1922 and that since the termination of that Mandate in 1948 has precipitated three major wars. Yet in the aftermath of the third Arab-Israeli War of June, 1967, the conflict has become enormously more volatile. The principal factors responsible for this increased volatility have been a more active Soviet and American involvement, particularly an increased Soviet military presence in Egypt and the Mediterranean, the increasing sophistication of weapons systems on both sides, the rapid political and military growth of the various Palestine commando organizations, the joining of new Arab states in the conflict, and the destabilizing effect of the withdrawal of UNEF and the territorial dislocations of the Six Day War. Events during the past year, including an Egyptian "war of attrition" against Israeli positions in the Suez Canal area, Israeli deep penetration bombing raids against Egypt, the introduction in an operational capacity of Soviet advisors into Egypt, the continuing internal conflict in Jordan in which Syria militarily intervened on behalf of Palestinian insurgents and the United States considered counter-intervention, and the hijackings of commercial aircraft in international flight by the Popular Front for the Liberation of Palestine have underscored the present crisis proportions of the world order threat. The conflict seems clearly to be that kind of serious international dispute "the continuance of which is likely to endanger

---

[8] Sisco, *U.S. Objectives in the Middle East,* 63 Dept. State Bull. 175 (Aug. 10, 1970). Assistant Secretary of State Sisco recently reiterated this judgment in a speech before the Commonwealth Club of California. He urged: "[I]f Viet-Nam is our most anguishing problem, the Middle East is the most dangerous problem for the United States as we look ahead over the next decade." Sisco, *The Fluid and Evolving Situation in the Middle East,* 63 Dept. State Bull. 748 (Dec. 21, 1970).

the maintenance of international peace and security," which gives rise to an obligation to pursue peaceful settlement.

If efforts at peaceful settlement are obligatory, they are equally precarious. As I. F. Stone has written, the Arab-Israeli conflict is a tragedy in the classic sense. That is, it involves "a struggle of right against right."[9] From a Jewish perspective the establishment of the State of Israel represents fulfillment of the Jewish dream of a return to the homeland in which their spiritual, religious, and cultural identity were shaped after 2,000 years of dispersion. Yet as Israeli Premier Golda Meir has pointed out, continuing Arab threats against Israel have tragically drained the dream and forced the Israelis to be a people of war. From an Arab perspective a Jewish Israel is seen as an obstacle in the path of their dream of Arab unity and a denial of self-determination for the Arab Palestinians. Against this background Israelis doubt whether their adversaries really want to make peace, some Arabs doubt whether Israel is willing to withdraw from the occupied territories or to pursue a fair settlement of the refugee problem, and others refuse to accept the existence of Israel. These fundamental disagreements color every effort at settlement.

The starting point for review of post-Six Day War settlement efforts is Security Council Resolution 242 of November 22, 1967. The Resolution was adopted unanimously after five months of intense diplomatic effort and represents a delicately balanced compromise at a fairly high level of generalization.[10] Although the general understanding at the time it was hammered out was that the major parties should work to carry it out, not all of the belligerents have accepted it. The Resolution has been accepted by Egypt, Israel, Jordan, and Lebanon, among others. The principal nonaccepting parties have been Syria and the Palestine Liberation Organization, the conglomerate spokesman for the diverse Palestinian guerrilla organizations. But despite nonacceptance by several of the principal *de facto* belligerents, the resolution continues to be the focal point for serious efforts at settlement. Resolution 242 provides:

> *The Security Council,*
>
> *Expressing* its continuing concern with the grave situation in the Middle East,
>
> *Emphasizing* the inadmissibility of the acquisition of territory by war and the need to work for a just and lasting peace in which every State in the area can live in security,
>
> *Emphasizing further* that all Member States in their acceptance of the Charter of the United Nations have undertaken a commitment to act in accordance with Article 2 of the Charter,
>
> 1. *Affirms* that the fulfillment of Charter principles requires the establishment of a just and lasting peace in the Middle East which should include the application of both the following principles:

---

[9] Stone, *For a New Approach to the Israeli-Arab Conflict, reprinted from New York Review of Books* (Aug. 3, 1967), at 20. *See also* Goldmann, *The Future of Israel,* 48 FOREIGN AFFAIRS 443, 444 (1970).

[10] For a history of the diplomatic negotiations leading up to Resolution 242 see A. LALL, THE UN AND THE MIDDLE EAST CRISIS, 1967, 220-70 (1968).

(i) Withdrawal of Israel armed forces from territories occupied in the recent conflict;[11]

(ii) Termination of all claims or states of belligerency and respect for and acknowledgement of the sovereignty, territorial integrity and political independence of every State in the area and their right to live in peace within secure and recognized boundaries free from threats or acts of force;

2. *Affirms further* the necessity

(a) For guaranteeing freedom of navigation through international waterways in the area;

(b) For achieving a just settlement of the refugee problem;

(c) For guaranteeing the territorial inviolability and political independence of every State in the area, through measures including the establishment of demilitarized zones;

3. *Requests* the Secretary-General to designate a Special Representative to proceed to the Middle East to establish and maintain contacts with the States concerned in order to promote agreement and assist efforts to achieve a peaceful and accepted settlement in accordance with the provisions and principles in this resolution;

4. *Requests* the Secretary-General to report to the Security Council on the progress of the efforts of the Special Representative as soon as possible.[12]

The day after the passage of Resolution 242 Secretary-General U Thant announced the appointment of Dr. Gunnar V. Jarring, the Swedish Ambassador to the Soviet Union, as his Special Representative to promote agreement among the states concerned.[13] Dr. Jarring first met with the parties during December of 1967. Initial contacts indicated that Israel felt that the peaceful settlement required direct negotiations between the parties leading to bilateral peace treaties with Egypt and Jordan and that there could be no Israeli withdrawal from the occupied territories until such agreements had been signed. Accordingly Israel proposed that as a first step Israel should discuss an agenda for peace with Egypt and Jordan. Egypt and Jordan, however, felt that Israeli withdrawal from the occupied territories was a necessary precondition to negotiations.[14]

In an effort to circumvent their conflict, Ambassador Jarring sought assurance from each of the parties that they would implement Resolution 242. Israel's reply emphasized that Resolution 242 was a "framework for *agreement*" that could best be implemented by direct talks between the parties. Discussion with Israeli Foreign Minister Eban, however, indicated a willingness to participate in indirect talks if they were understood to be a prelude to direct talks and agreement. Egypt and Jordan, on the other hand, refused to agree to

---

[11] One semantically possible interpretation of the French version of this resolution is "the territories occupied" rather than simply "territories occupied." The validity of one or another interpretation has been much stressed in debate concerning whether Israel should withdraw from all or only some of the territories occupied during the Six Day War.

[12] S.C. Res. 242, 22 U.N. SCOR, 1382d meeting 8-9 (1967).

[13] Report by the Secretary-General on the Activities of the Special Representative to the Middle East, U.N. Doc. S/10070, at 2 (Jan. 4, 1971).

[14] *Id.* at 3-4.

direct negotiations but indicated a willingness to accept indirect talks. if Israel declared "in clear language" that it would implement Resolution 242.[15]

During March of 1968 Ambassador Jarring presented to the parties for their reactions a draft letter from himself to the Secretary-General, which in its key provision "invited the . . . Governments to meet with . . . [Ambassador Jarring], for conferences within the framework of the Security Council resolution, in Nicosia [on Cyprus]."[16] Contacts with the parties during March and April indicated disagreement with respect to the need for a prior Israeli statement of willingness to implement Resolution 242 and the phrasing of a Jordanian proposal to modify Dr. Jarring's letter to hold talks in New York rather than Nicosia. In general, the Arab states sought clear Israeli assurance that they would withdraw from the occupied territories, and Israel sought assurance that the Arab states intended to negotiate a peace agreement with Israel. According to the Arab interpretation Resolution 242 provided a plan for settlement and should be implemented by Israeli withdrawal from the occupied territories. According to the Israeli interpretation the Resolution was a framework for agreement and withdrawal should follow rather than precede agreement. Contacts in New York during May and June also foundered on this basic disagreement.[17] A second round of contacts during the spring and fall of 1968 in both the Middle East and New York reaffirmed this basic difference in interpretation of Resolution 242 and also clarified a difference in interpretation with respect to the term "territories occupied." The Arab states insisted that Resolution 242 required Israeli withdrawal from "all occupied territories" while Israel interpreted it as requiring withdrawal only to the extent required by agreement between the parties following a negotiated settlement.[18]

During March of 1969 Ambassador Jarring submitted a series of questions to Egypt, Jordan, Israel, and Lebanon concerning their settlement positions. The replies, delivered during March and April are one of the best sources of information about the positions of the parties. They continued to indicate the same major differences in interpretation that had prevented earlier agreement between the parties.[19]

Fearing that prolonged Israeli occupation of the territories seized in the Six Day War would lead to legitimation of the *de facto* borders, President Gamal Abdel Nasser of Egypt began a "war of attrition" against Israeli defenses along the Suez Canal in the Spring of 1969. The Egyptian offensive involved heavy bombardment of the Israeli line in the Suez Canal area. Accelerating mutual responses led to a level of hostilities that might appropriately

---

[15] *Id.* at 4-6.
[16] *Id.* at 6.
[17] *Id.* at 6-9.
[18] *Id.* at 9-10.
[19] *Id.* at 11-12. For the text of the questions submitted by Special Representative Jarring and the replies of Israel, Jordan, Egypt, and Lebanon see *id.* at Annex I. According to the Secretary-General's Report: "Unfortunately, the replies were in general a repetition of attitudes already expressed to Ambassador Jarring on numerous occasions from the beginning of his mission. They showed continued serious divergencies between the Arab States and Israel both as regards the interpretation to be given to the Security Council resolution and as to the procedures for putting its provisions into effect." *Id.* at 12.

be termed the fourth Arab-Israeli War. During January and February of 1970 he Israelis conducted deep penetration bombing raids against targets in Egypt. The intent of the raids seems to have been to lessen Egyptian pressure in the Suez Canal. In response to the raids a secret trip by Nasser to Moscow led to he introduction of Soviet SAM-3 ground-to-air missiles and substantial strengthening of Egyptian air defenses.[20] During the Spring of 1970 the situation deteriorated further with the introduction of Soviet military advisers into Egypt in an operational capacity, an intensification of the war along the Suez Canal, and a rise in the pattern of Palestinian guerrilla raids on Israeli settlements launched from within Jordan and Lebanon and Israeli responses against the guerrilla encampments within those countries.

On April 3, 1969 periodic four-power talks began between France, Great Britain, the United States, and the Soviet Union in an effort to assist in arriving at conditions for settlement.[21] Although the talks may have been helpful in narrowing the issues, they have not been able to significantly break the deadlock in conflicting interpretations.

In June of 1970 United States Secretary of State William Rogers initiated an "at least" 90-day standstill cease-fire between Israel, Egypt, and Jordan, which went into effect on August 7. After consulting with the parties Ambassador Jarring invited them to take part in discussions opening in New York on August 25. Because of Egyptian violation of the standstill cease-fire by continuing construction and emplacement of substantial numbers of Soviet anti-aircraft missiles in the Suez cease-fire zone, Israel informed Dr. Jarring that it would be unable to participate in the talks until the missiles installed in violation of the cease-fire were withdrawn.[22]

The Rogers initiative for an "at least" 90-day standstill cease-fire precipitated a rash of hijackings and attacks on commercial aircraft by the Popular Front for the Liberation of Palestine in order to focus attention on the Palestinian cause and to undermine efforts at peaceful settlement. Subsequently, there were a series of major clashes between Palestine Liberation Organization forces in Jordan and the army of King Hussain, culminating in an abortive Syrian intervention on behalf of the Palestinian guerrillas and a threatened United States counter-intervention. Although the level of external intervention in Jordan quickly receded, military clashes have continued to occur between Jordanian troops and Palestinian guerrilla forces. As an aftermath to these events, President Nasser died on September 28. He was succeeded as President of the United Arab Republic by Anwar el-Sadat.

---

[20] See N.Y. Times, Dec. 28, 1970, at 15, col. 1.

[21] Report by the Secretary-General on the Activities of the Special Representative to the Middle East, U.N. Doc. S/10070, at 12 (Jan. 4, 1971).

[22] Id. at 13-15. There may also have been Israeli violations in the form of overflights west of the canal into the Egyptian sector of the 50-kilometer standstill cease-fire zone. For a brief description of violations alleged against both sides see Sisco, *The Fluid and Evolving Situation in the Middle East*, 63 DEPT. STATE BULL. 748, 749-50 (Dec. 21, 1970). In appraising charges and countercharges concerning violations of the standstill cease-fire, it is useful to place them in chronological sequence. See particularly *The Middle East and American Security Policy*, REPORT OF SENATOR HENRY M. JACKSON TO THE SENATE COMMITTEE ON ARMED SERVICES, 91ST CONG., 2D SESS. 9-13 (Comm. Print 1970).

On November 4, 1970 the General Assembly passed a resolution requesting an additional three-month extension of the cease-fire.[23] Subsequently, on December 30, 1970, Abba Eban, the Foreign Minister of Israel, informed Ambassador Jarring that in view of "present political and military conditions" Israel was willing to resume talks.[24] During January and early February of 1971 an exchange of views between Egypt, Israel, and Jordan through Ambassador Jarring seemed to narrow the gap between them only slightly. Although Egypt had threatened not to continue the cease-fire beyond February 5 in the absence of substantial progress toward Israeli withdrawal from the occupied territories, on February 4 President el-Sadat announced that at the urging of Secretary-General U Thant he would agree to an extension of the cease-fire until March 7, 1971. President el-Sadat also suggested that the Suez Canal might be reopened if Israel would agree to a partial pullback from the Canal. Early indications were that Egypt and Israel might be in disagreement on whether Israeli shipping would be able to use the Canal following any such pullback or whether partial pullback meant a territorial pullback of all Israeli forces or merely a force reduction along the Suez Canal.[25]

According to the *New York Times,* on February 8, Ambassador Jarring put forward an initiative "in the form of a memorandum to both Israel and the United Arab Republic . . . [inviting] them to submit their formulations of the kind of peace settlement they envisioned."[26] The *Times* also reported that:

> Dr. Jarring's questions . . . framed the outline for an Israeli-Egyptian settlement without actually making a formal proposal.
>
> The gist of Dr. Jarring's reasoning . . . was that Israel should withdraw from the entire Sinai Peninsula, that an international peace force be established at Sharm el Sheik to insure Israeli maritime passage through the Strait of Tiran, that there should be a formal peace treaty between the two nations under which Egypt would end her state of war with Israel and recognize her sovereignty [sic] and borders, and that the international powers could provide some guarantees to underwrite the settlement.[27]

At this writing it is too early to assess whether the replies to the Jarring initiative will significantly narrow the gap between the principal belligerents. The indirect exchanges are continuing through the Jarring mission at the United Nations in an atmosphere of hope.[28]

The history of efforts at peaceful settlement on the basis of Resolution 242 demonstrates that, despite the compromise nature of the Resolution, varying

---

[23] G.A. Res. 2628 (XXV), U.N. Doc. A/RES/2628 (Nov. 4, 1970).

[24] Report by the Secretary-General on the Activities of the Special Representative to the Middle East, U.N. Doc. S/10070, at 15 & Annex II at 6 (Jan. 4, 1971).

[25] *See* N.Y. Times, Feb. 5, 1971, at 3, col. 3 (city ed.); N.Y. Times, Feb. 10, 1971, at 1, col. 5 (city ed.).

[26] N.Y. Times, Feb. 18, 1971, at 1, col. 5 (city ed.).

[27] N.Y. Times, Feb. 19, 1971, at 8, cols. 5-6 (city ed.).

[28] The New York Times reported that the Egyptian reply indicated a willingness to conclude a binding peace treaty with Israel rather than some other vague form of settlement. If so, this would be a significant departure from the position of the Arab heads of state at the Khartoum Conference of September, 1967, at which they agreed to a common policy toward Israel of no peace, no negotiations, and no recognition. *Id.* at 8, col. 4.

interpretations conceal wide differences between the parties. In attempting to sort out the competing positions it is helpful to keep in mind several general caveats. The first is that one ought not think of the Arab world as monolithic. The Arab world is composed of a politically diverse range of states ranging from traditional monarchies to revolutionary socialist regimes. It also includes an important nonstate participant, the Central Committee of the Palestine Liberation Organization, which itself reflects a wide range of political organizations.[29] Each of these participants, and Israel as well, is in turn the product of competing and sometimes shifting political forces. As a result, any statement of settlement position is likely to oversimplify or to become dated as political conditions change. Moreover, the diverse nature of the Arab camp and the competing political forces within each participant, including Israel, create internal pressures for an external settlement position that is deliberately vague in order to avoid the agony of internal political decision on highly charged issues. One suspects that this is particularly true of public as opposed to private proposals but that it may be shared in substantial degree by all external statements of position.

The second general caveat is that even when there is an internal consensus on position, international public relations and bargaining considerations may deter candid disclosure. Public statements of position, then, may not always reflect the genuine or complete position of the participants. The actual position may be either more or less conciliatory on the issues. Nevertheless, in most cases the public stance probably conveys at least a useful general image of the settlement posture of the participants. In any event the public record seems a fair basis for appraisal.

Perhaps partly as a result of these pressures, there is a dearth of public information about the negotiating positions of the principal participants. The major source of information is the January 4, 1971 Report by the Secretary-General on the Jarring Mission.[30] In addition, the New York Times has recently published accounts purporting to represent recent statements of position.[31]

With these caveats in mind, the range of issues and potential issues in the Arab-Israeli negotiations are or have been:

Issues of Procedure

1. Participants in the negotiations: (a) with respect to Israel and her immediately adjacent Arab neighbors, Egypt, Jordan, Syria, and Lebanon;

---

[29] See D. PERETZ, E. WILSON, & R. WARD, A PALESTINE ENTITY? 47-57 (Special Study Number One of the Middle East Institute 1970).
[30] Report by the Secretary-General on the Activities of the Special Representative to the Middle East, U.N. Doc. S/10070 (Jan. 4, 1971). There have also been a number of earlier reports by the Secretary-General on the Jarring mission.
[31] See the purported text of Israel's suggestions to Ambassador Jarring made during Jarring's visit to Israel on January 8, N.Y. Times, Jan. 19, 1971, at 10, col. 4 (city ed.), the purported Egyptian reply, N.Y. Times, Jan. 20, 1971, at 1, col. 2 (city ed.), and the purported text of the Jordanian reply, N.Y. Times, Jan. 26, 1971, at 6, col. 3 (city ed.).

(b) with respect to Israel and noncontiguous Arab states, Algeria, Libya, the Sudan, Saudi Arabia, Kuwait, and Iraq; (c) with respect to the Palestinian commando organizations.

2. Extension of the cease-fire during negotiations, including preconditions for extension and the modality of extension.

3. Strategies of negotiation: direct talks, indirect talks, "Rhodes formula," or United Nations mediation?

4. Location of talks: New York, Cyprus, or elsewhere.

5. Level of representation: foreign ministers, United Nations ambassador, or other.

6. Timing of agreement or implementation: (a) with respect to priority of Israeli withdrawal from occupied territories and Arab termination of belligerency and agreement on "secure and recognized boundaries;" (b) with respect to Israeli settlement with Egypt or Jordan followed by settlement with other major participants or simultaneous settlement with all major participants, *i.e.*, will settlement proceed state by state and if so in what order; (c) with respect to priority of issues of content such as Israeli passage through the Suez Canal or settlement of the refugee problem; (d) with respect to the possibility of a preliminary agreement to reopen the Suez Canal.

7. Form of final agreement: bilateral peace treaties registered with the United Nations, individual instruments addressed to and endorsed by the Security Council, or some other form.

Issues of Content

1. Status of Resolution 242: the settlement itself or a basis for negotiated agreement?

2. Withdrawal of Israeli armed forces from "territories occupied" or "all the occupied territories," and agreement on "secure and recognized boundaries": (a) with respect to the West Bank; (b) with respect to the Golan Heights; (c) with respect to the Gaza Strip; (d) with respect to the Sinai Peninsula; (e) with respect to Sharm el-Sheikh; (f) with respect to East Jerusalem.

3. The termination of all states of war and acts of belligerency including: (a) free navigation through waterways in the area including the Gulf of Aqaba, the Suez Canal, and the Strait of Tiran; (b) control of nongovernmental and paramilitary guerrilla forces operating from Arab States against Israel; (c) the protection of civilian populations; (d) cessation of economic boycotts and hostile propaganda; (e) annulment of reservations to international conventions stemming from an assumed state of belligerency; (f) nonadherence to political or military alliances directed against a neighboring state; (g) nonstationing on the territory of a nonbelligerent state of armed forces of a third state still maintaining belligerency; (h) recognition and diplomatic relations.

4. The specificity with which the Arab states terminate belligerency with Israel: termination of belligerency "with Israel" or "with any state in the area."

5. The location and extent of demilitarized zones: astride the borders or exclusively within the occupied territories.

6. The use of United Nations peacekeeping forces and other arrangements for insuring security.

7. "Just settlement" of the refugee problem: (a) arrangements for compensation and repatriation of Arab refugees from the 1948 and 1967 wars; (b) Arab Palestinian demands for self-determination including demands for a "secular democratic" State; (c) arrangements for compensation of Jewish refugees from the Arab states.

8. The status of Jerusalem and the Holy Places: (a) extent of Israeli, Arab, and international administration; (b) arrangements for protection of and access to the Holy Places within and without Jerusalem.

9. Recognition of the international status of waterways in the area including the Gulf of Aqaba, the Suez Canal, and the Strait of Tiran.

10. Arrangements for exchange of prisoners of war.

11. Arrangements for Jordan to have free port and transit facilities.

12. Guarantees of the terms of settlement and the role of the United Nations, the four powers, and the United States in implementing or guaranteeing the settlement.

The principal belligerents in the Arab-Israeli conflict are Israel, Egypt, Jordan, Lebanon, Syria, and the Palestine Liberation Organization. Other Arab states not bordering on Israel, including Saudi Arabia, Algeria, Libya, Iraq, Kuwait, and The Sudan, are to a greater or lesser extent also belligerents in the conflict. And as significant military suppliers to the region, the United States and the Soviet Union are also significantly caught up in the conflict.[32] For the most part, though, the greatest influence on settlement is exercised by Israel and the Arab states bordering on Israel, and more particularly by Israel and Egypt. The following discussion will focus on the settlement position of these principal belligerents.

Not all of the full range of issues in the Arab-Israeli conflict are of equal importance for each principal belligerent. At the risk of substantial oversimplification, there seem to be three basic positions: the first is the Israeli position; the second is that of Egypt, Jordan, and Lebanon; and the third is that of Syria and the Palestine Liberation Organization.

The principal concern of Israel is national security and the termination of all Arab states of belligerency against Israel, including cessation of guerrilla attacks on Israel launched from the sanctuary of neighboring states, and free navigation through the Gulf of Aqaba, the Suez Canal, and the Strait of Tiran. Accordingly, Israel seeks definitive bilateral peace treaties with her Arab

---

[32] For the United States position on settlement see Rogers, *A Lasting Peace in the Middle East: An American View*, 62 DEPT. STATE BULL. 7 (Jan. 5, 1970) (address of Dec. 9, 1969); Statement by United States Ambassador Charles W. Yost in the General Assembly Debate on the Situation in the Middle East, October 29, 1970, *reprinted in* 63 DEPT. STATE BULL. 656-61 (Nov. 23, 1970); Fulbright, *Old Myths and New Realities—II: The Middle East*, 116 CONG. REC. #147 (Aug. 24, 1970).

neighbors following direct negotiations on secure and recognized boundaries. Israeli withdrawal "from territories lying beyond positions agreed in the peace treaty" would occur only after conclusion of a general peace agreement terminating all states of belligerency. Israeli pronouncements suggest that the present *de facto* boundaries are subject to substantial alteration during negotiations but that Israel would not return to the exact pre-Six Day War boundaries. In support of this position Israel urges that Resolution 242 provides a basis for negotiated agreement rather than a final plan for settlement. Israel also points out that Resolution 242 speaks of withdrawal from "territories occupied" rather than "all the territories occupied" and that the legislative history of the Resolution supports an interpretation of this omission as a deliberate recognition that withdrawal need not be from *all* of the occupied territories. Although Israel has indicated willingness to discuss any issues, there have been strong intimations that Israeli administration of East Jerusalem and possibly of the Golan Heights and Sharm-el-Sheikh is not subject to change. Israel seeks a continuation of the ceasefire, preferably without additional Security Council action, which it fears might alter the delicate balance of Resolution 242, and at least for the present phase of the talks Israel has agreed to indirect talks through Ambassador Jarring at United Nations headquarters in New York. Israel also seeks specific Arab undertakings to control guerrilla activities launched from neighboring Arab territories, cessation of the Arab economic boycott against Israel, and an end to other manifestations of Arab belligerency. In turn, Israel indicates a willingness to terminate on a reciprocal basis all claims or states of belligerency, to discuss settlement of the refugee problem, arrangements concerning places of religious and historic significance, and arrangements for free port and transit facilities. Israel does not seem enthusiastic with respect to the possible role of United Nations peacemaking forces in the area. Nevertheless, it does not rule out discussion of such a presence "[i]n the context of peace providing for full respect for the sovereignty of States and the establishment of agreed boundaries."[33] With respect to the refugee problem, Israel urges that the humanitarian nature of the issues should not make agreement on these issues contingent on agreement on any other aspect of the Arab-Israeli conflict. Accordingly, Israel has proposed:

> [T]hat a conference of Middle Eastern States should be convened, together with the Governments contributing to refugee relief and the Specialized Agencies of the United Nations, in order to chart a five-year plan for the solution of the refugee problem in the framework of a lasting peace and the integration of refugees into productive life. This conference can be called in advance of peace negotiations.
>
> Joint refugee integration and rehabilitation commissions should be established by the governments concerned in order to work out agreed projects for refugee integration on a regional basis with international assistance.[34]

---

[33] Report by the Secretary-General on the Activities of the Special Representative to the Middle East U.N. Doc. S/10070, at Annex I p. 7 (Jan. 4, 1971).

[34] *Id.*

The position of Egypt (the United Arab Republic) centers on Israeli withdrawal from all of the territories occupied during the Six Day War. Egypt urges that Israel has expansionist aims and intends to annex East Jerusalem and maintain continued military occupation of the Syrian Heights, the West Bank, the Gaza Strip, Sharm-el-Sheikh, the Gulf of Aqaba area, and Eastern Sinai. Accordingly, Egypt indicates willingness to implement the obligations from Resolution 242 provided that Israel carries out its obligations, particularly withdrawal from all territories occupied as a result of the Six Day War. Egypt "agrees to pledge termination of all claims or state of belligerency . . . [to become] effective upon withdrawal of Israel's forces from all Arab territories occupied as a result of Israel's aggression of 5 June 1967."[35] It seems evident that Egypt regards Resolution 242 as the settlement itself rather than a basis for a negotiated agreement. There is also a strong intimation that Israel must first withdraw from all of the occupied territories prior to any Egyptian pledge to accept "the right of every State in the area to live in peace within secure and recognized boundaries free from threats or acts of force."[36] If there were prior Israeli withdrawal from all the occupied territories Egypt has indicated a willingness only to sign an instrument addressed to and endorsed by the Security Council rather than enter into a bilateral peace treaty with Israel.[37] In response to Ambassador Jarring's question "what is the conception of secure and recognized boundaries held by the United Arab Republic?,"[38] Egypt replied: "When the question of Palestine was brought before the United Nations in 1947, the General Assembly adopted its resolution 181 of 29 November 1947, for the partition of Palestine and defined Israel's boundaries."[39] Although this rather enigmatic response is ambiguous in a number of ways, it intimates that the "secure and recognized" boundaries to which Egypt would agree would be the 1947 partition boundaries rather than the pre-Six Day War boundaries. If so, this represents a very major divergence in the positions of the parties. Egypt's position also seems vague in a number of critical ways concerning termination of belligerency and recognition of Israel. Thus, because of its general policy of nonrecognition of Israel, Egypt prefers indirect talks through Ambassador Jarring rather than face-to-face talks. Similarly, Egypt seems committed, at least in public pronouncement, to continued assistance to the Palestine Liberation Organization, which seeks to replace the State of Israel with a secular democratic state of Arab design. In addition, Egypt's pledge of termination of belligerency is worded in terms of "the right of every State in the area to live in peace"[40] rather than referring to Israel by

---

[35] *Id.* at Annex I p. 15.

[36] *Id.* at Annex I p. 16.

[37] *Id.* at Annex I p. 17. According to the New York Times, however, in the reply to Ambassador Jarring's initiative of February 8, 1971, Egypt has indicated a willingness to conclude a binding peace treaty with Israel. At this writing the text of the Egyptian reply has not been made public. See N.Y. Times, Feb. 19, 1971, at 8, col. 4 (city ed.).

[38] Report by the Secretary-General on the Activities of the Special Representative to the Middle East, U.N. Doc. S/10070, at Annex I p. 2 (Jan. 4, 1971).

[39] *Id.* at Annex I p. 16.

[40] *Id.* at Annex I p. 16.

name. In this connection it is useful to note that President Anwar el-Sadat emphatically stated in an interview with James Reston and Raymond H. Anderson of the *New York Times* on December 23, 1970, that despite acceptance of Resolution 242 Egypt would never "make diplomatic relations" with Israel.[41] In the absence of a more definitive agreement between the parties specifically referring to termination of belligerency against Israel, Egypt might be tempted to continue belligerency under the guise that Israel is not a recognized state. With respect to navigation, Egypt has indicated willingness to implement all of the provisions of Resolution 242 including freedom of navigation in "international waterways" in the area provided that Israel implements all provisions of the Resolution. This position would seem to incorporate Egypt's general position concerning prior Israeli withdrawal from all of the occupied territories. There may also be some ambiguity in the parties interpretation of just which waterways in the area are "international waterways." For example, does Egypt's position with respect to freedom of navigation in "international waterways" include the Suez Canal?[42] Egypt does not indicate great enthusiasm for demilitarized zones but indicates a willingness to accept such zones "if they are astride the boundaries."[43] In case such zones are established Egypt "accepts that such zones be supervised and maintained by the United Nations."[44] With respect to the refugee problem, Egypt indicates that a "just settlement" is embodied in paragraph 11 of General Assembly Resolution 194 (III) of December, 1948 and that acceptance of a plan on the basis of that paragraph with adequate guarantees for implementation would justify implementation of the other provisions of Resolution 242.[45] Paragraph 11 of Resolution 194 (III) provides among other things that "the refugees wishing to return to their homes and live at peace with their neighbors should be permitted to do so at the earliest practicable date, and that compensation should be paid for the property of those choosing not to return and for loss of or damage to property which, under principles of international law or in equity, should be made good by the Governments or authorities responsible."[46] Following the November 4 General Assembly resolution requesting an extension of the United States-initiated August 7 cease-fire, Egypt agreed to an additional three-month extension to February 5, 1971. And on February 4 Egypt agreed to a further one-month extension to March 7. From an Egyptian perspective, however, the fear of legitimation of *de facto* Israeli control of the occupied territories places pressure on continued support of the

---

[41] N.Y. Times, Dec. 28, 1970, at 1, col. 1.

[42] For a discussion of the legal aspects of Israeli passage through the Suez Canal see R. BAXTER, THE LAW OF INTERNATIONAL WATERWAYS 221-37 (1964); Gross, *Passage Through the Suez Canal of Israel-Bound Cargo and Israel Ships,* 51 AM. J. INT'L L. 530 (1957); Huang, *Some International and Legal Aspects of the Suez Canal Questions,* 51 AM. J. INT'L L. 277 (1957); Khadduri, *Closure of the Suez Canal to Israeli Shipping,* 33 LAW & CONTEMP. PROB. 147 (1968).

[43] Report by the Secretary-General on the Activities of the Special Representative to the Middle East U.N. Doc. S/10070, at Annex I p. 16 (Jan. 4, 1971).

[44] *Id.* at Annex I p. 17.

[45] *Id.* at Annex I p. 16.

[46] G.A. Res. 194, U.N. Doc. A/810, 21 at 24 (1948).

cease-fire. Thus, should negotiations not be successful Egypt has threatened to renew hostilities.

The position of Jordan is closely identified with that of Egypt. In fact, the Egyptian and Jordanian replies to Ambassador Jarring's 14 points are in almost identical language.[47] The settlement situation of Jordan is different from that of Egypt, though, in a number of important ways. Problems of administration and religious freedom in East Jerusalem are of primary concern to Jordan rather than to Egypt. Similarly, the problem of control of paramilitary Palestinian guerrilla forces is greater for Jordan than for Egypt. And conversely, the questions of freedom of navigation through the Strait of Tiran and the Suez Canal are primarily Egyptian issues. Jordan might also be interested in free port and transit facilities in Israel. Because of these state-by-state differences it seems that settlement should take the form of individualized agreement with each accepting state. Although Jordan seeks the return of East Jerusalem to Jordanian administration, Jordan has indicated willingness to "guarantee free access to all religious and historical places to all concerned as well as freedom of worship."[48]

Lebanon is involved only indirectly. Lebanon did not take part in the Six Day War, and there is no territorial dispute between Lebanon and Israel. Perhaps the principal issue between Lebanon and Israel is Lebanese control of Palestinian guerrilla forces operating from Lebanese territory against Israel and the cessation of Israeli military activity directed against such forces within Lebanon. Lebanon has accepted Resolution 242, however, and in this respect has adopted the position of Egypt and Jordan. The Lebanese reply to Ambassador Jarring's 14 points stresses that the 1949 Armistice Agreement concluded between Lebanon and Israel remains valid and that the Armistice lines correspond with the internationally recognized boundaries of Lebanon. Lebanon also proclaims "Lebanon's support of the position of the Arab States whose territory has been occupied by Israel and which have accepted the Security Council's decision of 22 November 1967."[49]

There is perhaps a greater risk of distortion in grouping together the Syrian and Palestine Liberation Organization positions than in grouping together the Egyptian, Jordanian, and Lebanese positions. Nevertheless, both Syria and the Palestine Liberation Organization have rejected Resolution 242 as a basis for settlement, and both seem committed to some version of a Palestinian war of liberation against Israel that would substitute a "secular democratic" Palestinian State in place of the present State of Israel. Since Syria has not accepted Resolution 242, Ambassador Jarring's 14 points were

---

[47] Compare the reply of the Government of Jordan with the reply of the Government of the United Arab Republic reprinted in Report to the Secretary-General on the Activites of the Special Representative to the Middle East, U.N. Doc. S/10070, at Annex I pp. 9-11, 14-17 (Jan. 4, 1971). The omission of the first paragraphs of the Egyptian reply, which stressed Israeli expansionist aims, may evidence a generally more conciliatory attitude on Jordan's part.

[48] N.Y. Times, Jan. 26, 1971, at 6, col. 6 (city ed.).

[49] Report by the Secretary-General on the Activities of the Special Representative to the Middle East, U.N. Doc. S/10070, at Annex I pp. 12-13 (Jan. 4, 1971).

not even addressed to Syria. As such, the Syrian position on settlement is particularly vague. It seems a fair inference that Syrian nonacceptance of Resolution 242 means that they view settlement as peripheral to or inconsistent with their overriding objection to the existence of the State of Israel as a Jewish State. The Syrian rejection of Resolution 242 suggests again the importance of settlement proceeding state by state. One difficulty with this state-by-state solution is that Egypt has asserted that Israel must withdraw from all of the occupied territories, which would include the Syrian Heights prior to settlement with Egypt. In turn, Israeli withdrawal from the Heights seems unlikely in the absence of an agreement with Syria on "secure and recognized boundaries." The potential leverage of Syria in preventing settlement, then, is considerable as long as Egypt or Jordan insist on withdrawal from all of the occupied territories as a precondition to termination of belligerency. This also suggests that Egyptian insistence on Israeli withdrawal from Syrian territory as a precondition for settlement with Egypt is unreasonable in the absence of Egyptian ability to deliver on the other features of Resolution 242 for Syria, particularly Syrian termination of belligerency with Israel.

The Palestine Liberation Organization (PLO) is neither a state nor a particularly cohesive political arrangement. It exercises *de facto* control over areas of Jordan, Lebanon, and Syria and receives substantial financial support from a number of Arab states not bordering on Israel. It also receives more active military support from Syria. As such, it is a force to be reckoned with in settlement. To date the PLO has refused to accept Resolution 242 and seems committed to a sustained "war of liberation" against Israel. Beyond that, its precise program and objectives are vague.[50] Writing in early 1970 Don Peretz said of the PLO program:

> The commandos state categorically that they seek to destroy the government and state of Israel, its Zionist institutions and its exclusive Jewish character; they brook no compromise based on the pre-1967 borders or even the 1947 U.N. partition resolution. Some leaders have indicated that Palestine would become an Arab state; others have been more ambiguous. None has publicly recognized the possibility of coexistence between Arab and Hebrew nationalism . . . .
>
> Hebrew broadcasts of the commando organizations directed to Israel are listened to with derision rather than fear or hope of discovering any serious political intent. The recently announced objective of converting Palestine into a democratic secular state in which all Jews, Muslims and Christians will live in equity is not believed because of the long years in which the people as well as the state of Israel were threatened. The organizations have yet to define clearly the kind of government they propose, the status of minority groups, whether or not the country is to be an Arab state, or what is to become of its Hebrew-speaking residents who retain an attachment to their language and cultural, social and political institutions. . . .[51]

---

[50] For a description of the principal Palestinian guerrilla groups see D. PERETZ, E. WILSON, & R. WARD supra note 29, at 47-57. The Arab Palestine Organization (APO) and the Action Group for the Liberation of Palestine, two small Nasserite socialist guerrilla organizations did support the August 7 cease-fire. *Id* at 57.

[51] Peretz, *Arab Palestine: Phoenix or Phantom?*, 48 FOREIGN AFFAIRS 322, 331-32 (1970).

Whatever the program it would seem that all Pale÷inian organizations within the umbrella of the PLO would reject any political settlement that would retain a Jewish State of Israel. Their position, then, seems basically at variance with Resolution 242.

In summary, from the Israeli perspective the most important concern is the demand for clear and legally binding bilateral treaties with the Arab states by which the Arab states would effectively terminate all states of war and acts of belligerency against Israel and agree on "secure and recognized boundaries." Israeli withdrawal would then follow from the occupied territories beyond the agreed boundaries. From the Egyptian, Jordanian, and Lebanese perspectives Israeli withdrawal from all of the occupied territories including East Jerusalem is a precondition for termination of belligerency. Lastly, Syria and the Palestine Liberation Organization, both of which have refused to accept Resolution 242, seem committed to a Palestinian war of liberation against Israel for the purpose of creating a "secular democratic" State of Palestine. This wide divergence in position enormously complicates the problem of settlement.

III. An Appraisal of the Arab-Israeli Conflict By Reference to Fundamental Charter Principles and United Nations Recommendations

The major Charter principles applicable to appraisal of the Arab-Israeli conflict are nonuse of force against the territorial integrity or political independence of another state, self-determination of peoples, and respect for human rights. In addition, the United Nations has made important recommendations concerning partition of Palestine, refugees, control of terrorist activities, the status of Jerusalem, freedom of navigation through international waterways, and the protection of civilian populations.

A. *Nonuse of Force Against the Territorial Integrity or Political Independence of Another State*

Article 2(4) sets out what is perhaps the most important principles of the Charter. It provides: "All Members shall refrain in their international relations from the threat or use of force against the territorial integrity or political independence of any state, or in any other manner inconsistent with the Purposes of the United Nations." A major purpose of this provision is to incorporate and strengthen the judgment of the Kellogg-Briand Pact that major coercion could not be used as an instrument of national policy no matter how clear the justice of the cause. Instead, major coercion was restricted to individual and collective defense and enforcement action pursuant to a Security Council determination. In this respect the Charter and the Kellogg-Briand Pact before it made an evolutionary jump in the international law of conflict management from both the Augustinian "just war" doctrine that measured lawfulness by the justice of the cause and the 19th Century positivist notion that war was merely a "metajuristic phenomenon" between sovereign states and as such was neither legal nor illegal. The Charter principle was an advance over these earlier notions, particularly in focusing on the destructiveness of coercive strategies of change, in adopting a more objective test of permissible and impermissible coercion, and in focusing on the important difference between unilateral and community action.[52]

This basic Charter principle would seem to apply to the Arab-Israeli conflict in a number of important ways. First, the State of Israel has existed for more than 22 years within the 1949 Armistice boundaries; since 1949 it has been a member of the United Nations, and it is widely recognized among the community of nations, including long-term recognition by both the United States and the Soviet Union. As such, regardless of the legitimacy of Arab grievances with respect to the initial creation of the State of Israel, there is no right to use force to challenge the very existence of Israel. Israel clearly has a right to exist within "secure and recognized" borders as affirmed in Resolution 242. It is sometimes urged that the very existence of Israel constitutes a continuing attack on the Palestinian people or the Arab world. The argument is basically a rhetorical substitution of an armed attack claim in place of an underlying self-determination claim. The rhetorical claim, however, should not be confused with the factual reality of an armed attack by one state against another. A little reflection on the applicability of similarly broad claims in the Korean, China-Taiwan, Kashmir, German, and a host of other problem situations indicates its potential as a prescription for anarchy. The Charter principle proscribing the use of force against the territorial integrity or political independence of another state does not contain an exception permitting unilateral determination of denial of self-determination as a basis for lawful use of major coercion. If, of course, the argument is simply meant to announce a right of revolution of the Palestinian people against Israel (which is really the only meaningful referent) it is not a pronouncement of international law. But in this latter case it should be pointed out that international law does not recognize a right of revolution from the sanctuary of neighboring states. States have a legal duty to take measures within their means to control guerrilla attacks launched from their territory against third states.[53]

A second consequence of the principle of nonuse of force is that a continuing exercise of belligerent rights against another state is unlawful in the absence of a genuine need for individual or collective defense. If the Arab states are prohibited by international law from using force to challenge the existence of Israel as a Jewish state it would seem equally impermissible to

---

[52] For discussion of these points see the authorities cited at note 3 *supra*.

[53] The General Assembly Declaration of 1965 on the Inadmissibility of Intervention is representative of many authoritative pronouncements: "[N]o State shall organize, assist . . . or *tolerate* subversive terrorist or armed activities directed towards the violent overthrow of the régime of another State . . . ." G.A. Res. 2131, 20 U.N. GAOR, Supp. 14, at 11-12, U.N. Doc. A/6014 (1965) (emphasis added). For a general discussion of the problem of control of foreign intervention see Moore, *The Control of Foreign Intervention in Internal Conflict*, 9 VA. J. INT'L L. 205 (1969).

maintain a continuing state of belligerency for that purpose.[54] As a result, it would seem that the Arab states have a duty to terminate their continuing state of belligerency with Israel. As consequnces of this termination, Israel should enjoy security and freedom of navigation through the Gulf of Aqaba, the Suez Canal, and the Strait of Tiran. Resolution 242 would seem to support this analysis when it *"[a]ffirms* that the fulfillment of Charter principles requires ... [t]ermination of all claims or states of belligerency" and *"[a]ffirms further* the necessity . . . [f]or guaranteeing freedom of navigation through international waterways in the area."[55]

A third consequence of the principle of nonuse of force is the obligation to control guerrilla or private paramilitary forces operating from ones territory against a neighboring state. This principle has been frequently stated to be a requirement of international law and was recently reaffirmed in the 1970 General Assembly Declaration on Principles of International Law Concerning Friendly Relations and Co-operation Among States In Accordance With the Charter of the United Nations.[56] This principle would seem to require the Arab States to refrain from assisting the Palestine Liberation Organization or other Palestinian commando organizations and to take those measures within their ability to prevent guerrilla activities based in their territory and directed against Israel. The continuing civil conflict in Jordan between the army of King Hussain and the commandos of the Palestine Liberation Organization indicates that at least in some Arab countries effective control of Palestinian commando groups is difficult to achieve. It might also be noted that if Arab assistance to Palestinian resistance organizations were conceptualized as assistance to insurgents engaged in a civil war for Palestine, such assistance would still be unlawful. Despite the general uncertainty surrounding the law of nonintervention, international legal scholars are in substantial agreement that it is impermissible to provide assistance to insurgents attempting to overthrow a

---

[54] *See generally* N. FEINBERG, THE LEGALITY OF A "STATE OF WAR" AFTER THE CESSATION OF HOSTILITIES (1961); S. ROSENNE, ISRAEL'S ARMISTICE AGREEMENTS WITH THE ARAB STATES (1951). In this connection it might be noted that as early as September 1, 1951 the Security Council passed a resolution concerning passage of Israeli ships through the Suez Canal in which it pointed out: "[S]ince the armistice régime, which has been in existence for nearly two and a half years, is of a permanent character, neither party can reasonably assert that it is actively a belligerent or requires to exercise the right of visit, search, and seizure for any legitimate purpose of self-defence . . . ." 6 U.N. SCOR, 558th meeting 2 (1951).

[55] S.C. Res. 242, 22 U.N. SCOR, 1382d meeting 8-9 (1967). And with respect to the Suez Canal see the Security Council Resolution of September 1, 1951, which: *"Calls upon* Egypt to terminate the restrictions on the passage of international commercial shipping and goods through the Suez Canal wherever bound and to cease all interference with such shipping beyond that essential to the safety of shipping in the Canal itself and to the observance of the international conventions in force." 6 U.N. SCOR, 558th meeting 2 at 3 (1951).

[56] G.A. Res. 2625, 25th Sess., U.N. Doc. A/RES/2625 (Oct. 24, 1970). The Declaration states in pertinent part:
>   Every state has the duty to refrain from organizing or encouraging the organization of irregular forces or armed bands, including mercenaries, for incursion into the territory of another state.
>   Every state has the duty to refrain from organizing, instigating, assisting or participating in acts of civil strife or terrorist acts in another state or acquiescing in organized activities within its territory directed towards the commission of such acts, when the acts referred to in the present paragraph involve a threat or use of force.
See also the authorities cited at note 53 *supra*.

widely recognized government.[57] In any event, in view of the evidence that the principal base of Palestinian guerrilla activity is outside the State of Israel, this civil war characterization is not the most useful. With allowances for all of the imprecision of any analogy in international relations, the analogy most on point would seem to be the United States assistance to Cuban exiles in the Bay of Pigs invasion. Few would accept a characterization of that invasion as a civil war.

The meaning of the principle of nonuse of force is more difficult with respect to its corollary "the inadmissibility of the acquisition of territory by war," which is emphasized in Resolution 242 and its application to the territories occupied by Israel during the Six Day War. On the one hand, some scholars writing in support of the Arab position seem to suggest that since it is impermissible to acquire territory by war, Israel's continued occupation of the territories seized in the Six Day War constitutes a continuing armed attack against Arab territorial integrity justifying a defensive war of attrition against Israel until the territories are relinquished.[58] On the other hand, some scholars writing in support of the Israeli position urge that the principle is limited to aggressive as opposed to defensive wars and that Israel's use of force in the Six Day War was defensive. They then point out that with respect to the West Bank of Jordan, East Jerusalem, and the Gaza Strip, Israel's territorial claim following its defensive actions in the Six Day War should be at least as good as the Jordanian and Egyptian claims to those areas that were initially acquired aggressively by Jordan and Egypt during the 1948 Arab-Israeli War.[59] Both positions seem extreme. A more useful approach is to recognize that the doctrine of "the inadmissibility of the acquisition of territory by war" is being used in several different functional senses in the Arab-Israeli conflict. The first is the extent to which continued Israeli military occupation of the territories seized in the Six Day War is justified. The second is whether continued Israeli occupation of the territories seized in the Six Day War gives the Arab states a legal right to use force to recover the territories. And the third is the extent of "ownership" rights that Israel has in the occupied territories.

As announced in the Stimson Doctrine the basic purpose of the principle of "the inadmissibility of the acquisition of territory by war" was to discourage aggressive war by denying the spoils of war to the aggressor. Though an ineffective substitute for League action, the principle nevertheless embodied a useful deterrent by encouraging third states not to recognize claims to territories acquired by aggressive war. Under the United Nations Charter the basic distinction in determining whether initial military occupation is lawful is whether it is incident to unlawful aggression or lawful defense. It would seem, then, that the principle should be equally applicable under the Charter as

---

[57] See the authorities collected in Moore, *supra* note 53, at 242-46, 315-32.

[58] *See, e.g.,* Bassiouni, *Some Legal Aspects of the Arab-Israeli Conflict,* 14 THE ARAB WORLD 41, 44 (Special Issue on the Arab-Israeli Confrontation of June, 1967).

[59] *See, e.g.,* Schwebel, *What Weight to Conquest?,* 64 AM. J. INT'L L. 344 (1970).

applied to acquisition of territory by aggressive use of force. Even if incident to a defensive effort, however, to itself be lawful occupation of territory, like other defensive efforts, must be necessary and proportional to lawful defense objectives. Thus, a vast military occupation occasioned by an initial defensive effort but unnecessary for effective defense is probably unlawful. Although there is little authority on the issue it would seem that military occupation under the Charter confers a security interest only.[60] To the extent that continued occupation is necessary and proportional to lawful defense objectives it would be lawful. If military occupation is no longer needed for the protection of security, then it seems reasonable to require its termination. As applied in the Arab-Israeli conflict the first question is, was the Israeli action in the Six Day War aggressive or defensive, and the second is, if it was defensive was the resultant occupation of the territory necessary and proportional to lawful defense objectives. On the first question, although scholars are in disagreement about the lawfulness of Arab and Israeli actions in the Six Day War, the most persuasive assessment seems to be that the Israeli actions in the War were lawful defense actions.[61] And on the second question, Israeli seizure of the territories occupied in the Six Day War seems to have been reasonably necessary and proportional in relation to Israeli security needs. Moreover, at least most of the occupied territories seem to have a reasonable relation to continuing Israeli security needs. The Golan Heights and the Gaza Strip have been used repeatedly for launching attacks on Israel, and the Sinai and West Bank have an important strategic location in relation to overall Israeli security needs. As such, continued occupation until an overall peace agreement is negotiated or the security risk otherwise abates seems reasonable.

With respect to the second issue, the right of the Arab States to use force to recover the territories, whether the territories were occupied as a result of an aggressive or a defensive war would seem to be an important factor. An aggressive armed attack resulting in seizure of territory should, at least in the short run, give rise to a proportional right of defense. The distinction proves too much, though, as applied by some Arab spokesmen to the Arab-Israeli conflict. First, the most persuasive assessment seems to be that the Israeli actions in the Six Day War were lawful defense actions. Second, negotiations within the framework of Resolution 242, including cessation of Arab belligerent activities directed against Israel, would seem a preferable alternative to the use of force in recovering the territories even if the Israeli action had been aggressive action. Lawful defense action must be necessary and proportional,

---

[60] The 1970 General Assembly Declaration on Principles of International Law Concerning Friendly Relations and Co-operation Among States suggests a distinction between occupation and acquisition of territory by force. The test for lawful occupation is whether the use of force that gave rise to the occupation is consistent with the Charter. On the other hand, "[t]he territory of a state shall not be the object of *acquisition* by another state resulting from the threat or use of force. No territorial *acquisition* resulting from the threat or use of force shall be recognized as legal." G.A. Res. 2625, 25th Sess., U.N. Doc. A/RES/2625 (Oct. 24, 1970) (emphasis added).

[61] See, e.g., O'Brien, International Law and the Outbreak of War in the Middle East, 1967, 11 ORBIS 692, 713-23 (1968); Schwebel supra note 59, at 346; Wright, Legal Aspects of the Middle East Situation, 33 LAW & CONTEMP. PROB. 5, 26-27 (1968).

and the availability of a reasonable settlement alternative would seem to undercut the necessity for use of force. If the Arab States were to proclaim a willingness to immediately conclude peace agreements with Israel on condition that Israel would *subsequently* withdraw from the occupied territories, their case for use of force if Israel rejected the proposal would be much more plausible. Third, continued Arab attacks on Israel would seem inconsistent with the Security Council cease-fire resolutions of June, 1967.[62] Lastly, although the aggression-defense distinction is important in the short run, at some point *de facto* control of territory becomes sufficiently established that force can no longer be used to alter the situation whether or not occupation was initially lawful. Any other alternative would open up a pandora's box of claims to use force to redress ancient boundaries, and this would substantially emasculate Article 2(4) of the Charter. The suggestion of criteria for establishing when the point is reached at which the lawfulness of the initial occupation becomes unimportant in assessing responding coercion is one of the largely unexplored areas under the Charter. But at the least, this principle would seem to apply in the Arab-Israeli conflict to the boundaries resulting from the 1948 War. Just because force cannot be used to alter a *de facto* boundary, of course, does not indicate the lawfulness of continued occupation by an aggressor.

The third functional sense in which the principle of "the inadmissibility of the acquisition of territory by war" is invoked in the Arab-Israeli conflict is the extent of Israel's "ownership" rights in the occupied territories. It is reasonably clear that at least to the extent consistent with a security interest Israel is entitled to the normal rights and has the normal obligations of an occupying power under international law.[63] Such rights and obligations continue until a peace treaty is signed or the security interest abates. It is also clear that the parties concerned may fix the boundaries in the area by treaty in any way they see fit. It does not follow, however, that in the absence of a peace treaty Israel is entitled to greater rights in the occupied territories than an occupying power. An additional purpose of the doctrine of "the inadmissibility of the acquisition of territory by war" would seem to be to protect the self-determination of an indigenous population and the "ownership" expectations of a deprived state. Both purposes seem applicable with respect to the territories occupied during the Six Day War even though the occupation resulted from a defensive war.[64] It should be remembered that prior to the Six Day War the inhabitants of the occupied territories were largely Arab. The ownership expectations of Egypt and Jordan are perhaps less to the extent that they are based on Egypt's seizure of the Gaza strip from the territory of Palestine

---

[62] S.C. Res. 233, 22 U.N. SCOR, 1348th meeting 2 (1967); S.C. Res. 234, 22 U.N. SCOR, 1349th meeting 3 (1967); S.C. Res. 235, 22 U.N. SCOR, 1350th meeting 3 (1967); S.C. Res. 236, 22 U.N. SCOR, 1357th meeting 4 (1967).

[63] See Higgins, *The June War: The United Nations and Legal Background*, 3 J. CONTEMP. HISTORY 253, 270-73 (1968). With her usual perceptiveness Rosalyn Higgins is careful to separate the issue of occupation from that of acquisition.

[64] See R. JENNINGS, THE ACQUISITION OF TERRITORY 52-67 (1963). See also the excerpt from G.A. Res. 2625, *supra* note 60.

during the 1948 War and Jordan's seizure of East Jerusalem and the West Bank from Palestine during that War. Nineteen years of *de facto* control may nevertheless give rise to substantial expectations. In the absence of a solution that would provide for separate Palestinian-Arab self-determination in these territories, these expectations should be honored.

B. *Self-Determination of Peoples*

The second Charter principle applicable to appraisal of the Arab-Israeli conflict is the principle of self-determination of peoples. Article 1(2) of the Charter recognizes that a principal purpose of the United Nations is: "To develop friendly relations among nations based on respect for the principle of equal rights and self-determination of peoples . . . ." The principle is reasserted in Article 55. Self-determination of peoples is a notoriously slippery concept. The basic referent seems to be the freedom of a people to choose their own government and institutions and to share in the values of their society.[65] There is a wide range of potential kinds of self-determination claims. Most of these claims seem to arise from three basic situations. They are first, type I, the control by one nation of another's governmental structure or resources. Situations in this category are usually spoken of as colonialism or, in the case of control of resources other than governmental structures, neo-colonialism. A paradigm example is the Congo prior to independence. The second, type II, is a society that prevents a particular group within the society from sharing in authority structures or other value institutions of the society. A paradigm example is the system of apartheid in South Africa. And the third, type III, is an ethnic, religious, or other group within one or more societies that seeks to establish its own national identity. A paradigm example is the attempt of the Ibos to secede from Nigeria and set up a separate State of Biafra.

Applying these paradigms to the Arab-Israeli conflict, the Israeli claim to self-determination is an example of a type III claim. That is, a claim for the establishment (since 1948 the preservation) of a national homeland for the Jews where the Jewish cultural and religious heritage can be preserved. Internationally, Israel is supported in this claim by the 1947 decision of the General Assembly to partition Palestine into Arab and Jewish areas[66] and by the substantial expectations of a separate state resulting from the more than 22 year existence of the State of Israel, its admission to the United Nations, and its widespread international recognition and activity.

The Arab-Palestinian claim is not so readily apparent. In analyzing their claim it seems important to distinguish "moderate" from extreme claims. The "moderate" claim seems to be a demand for a unified, secular, democratic,

---

[65] See generally H. JOHNSON, SELF-DETERMINATION WITHIN THE COMMUNITY OF NATIONS (1967); R. Emerson, *Self-Determination* (unpublished paper prepared for the American Society of International Law Panel on Self-Determination, 1970); T. Mensah, *Self-Determination Under United Nations' Auspices* (unpublished J.S.D. dissertation in the Yale Law Library, 1963).

[66] G.A. Res. 181(II), U.N. Doc. A/519 at 131 (1947) (Recommending the Plan of Partition With Economic Union).

and multi-religious Palestinian State in which all Jews, Muslims, and Christians presently residing in the former mandate territory would be full citizens. Don Peretz indicates that this is a relatively recent formulation of the Palestinian position.[67] The extreme claim would exclude an indefinite number of "Zionist Jews," "persons who did not participate in the revolution," or "persons who did not accept the character of the state" from citizenship in the new state without stating where those excluded would go. There is a studied ambiguity in Palestinian pronouncements on this subject that makes it difficult to know precisely which claim is supported and what it means. For example, Article 6 of the 1968 Palestinian National Covenant provides: "Jews who were living permanently in Palestine until the beginning of the Zionist invasion will be considered Palestinians."[68] Dr. Harkabi, a lecturer in international affairs at Hebrew University, writes that this provision implies that only those Jews who lived permanently in Palestine before 1917 would be considered citizens of the Palestinian state.[69] That would, of course, exclude the bulk of the Jewish population of Israel, including more than half a million Jewish refugees who came to Israel from Arab countries. A recent survey of settlement efforts published in *International Conciliation* indicates as another formula that "leaders of the guerrilla movements have repeatedly stated that all the non-Zionist Israelis would be free to live in the 'secular and democratic' state they envision."[70] In the absence of a definition of what would be considered a "non-Zionist Israeli," this may mean the same thing or something different from Dr. Harkabi's interpretation of Article 6 of the 1968 Palestinian National Covenant. A partial explanation for this ambiguity, of course, is that there is a range of Palestinian views on the government, structure and composition of the new state. But the ambiguity of the Palestinian position on a critically important point suggests that it would not be unfair to appraise their position as if it were the extreme claim. Nevertheless, it seems useful first to analyze the "moderate" claim and then to analyze the extreme claim.

The Palestinian claim to a "secular democratic" Palestine does not readily

---

[67] See Peretz, *supra* note 51, at 332.

[68] *Reprinted* in Harkabi, *The Position of the Palestinians in the Israeli-Arab Conflict and Their National Covenant* (1968), 3 N.Y.U. J. INT'L L. & POLITICS 209, 230 (1970).

[69] *Id.* at 223, 230-31. Dr. Harkabi writes:
The . . . [1964 Palestinian National Covenant] can be interpreted to the effect that the Jews who lived in Palestine in 1947 would be recognized as Palestinians, that is, would be able to remain; whereas in the new text, as revised in the fourth session of the National Council (July, 1968), it is explicitly stated that only Jews who lived permanently in Palestine before 1917 would be recognized as Palestinians. This implies that the rest are aliens and must leave. It is indeed difficult to agree with the claim of some people, that the Arabs have become more realistic and their position more moderate, if a hallowed and authoritative document like the National Covenant specifies the aim of banishing almost two and a half million Jews.
Id. at 223.

[70] "Issues Before the 25th General Assembly," *International Conciliation* 17 (Sept. 1970). The full description of the Palestinian position given in *International Conciliation* is:
Palestinian guerrillas no longer insist that all those Jews who have migrated to Israel since 1948 have to be repatriated to the country of their origin. Since the adoption of the Palestinian National Covenant by the Palestinian National Council in 1968, leaders of the guerrilla movements have repeatedly stated that all the non-Zionist Israelis would be free to live in the "secular and democratic" state they envision.
Id.

fit any of the three paradigm self-determination situations. It is not a type I claim that Israel controls the governmental institutions or resources of another state or a type II claim that a class of citizens within Israel is denied self-determination as with apartheid in South Africa, although there may be overtones of both claims in the Arab position. And by its own terms it is not a type III claim for a separate Palestinian Arab national identity existing side by side with a Jewish Israel. Instead, it seems primarily a claim based on historical or territorial determinism. That is, historically the original territory and population of the Palestine mandate was largely Arab; therefore, a Jewish state within the mandate territory is a denial of self-determination. A principal difficulty with this position is that it fails to make clear why 1917 or 1922 is a more meaningful focus than the present for analyzing the demands of self-determination. Moreover, if history is the principal criterion then the Jews might also assert a plausible claim using an even older starting date.[71] But surely history is not the most meaningful referent of self-determination. To the contrary, it would seem more useful to refer to the demands and expectations of all of the people living in the former mandate territory today. That is, the starting place for self-determination is most meaningfully the demands and expectations of all of the people living in an area *now*, not merely the descendants of some group that at some time in the past were the principal inhabitants. This would include approximately two and one-half million Jews already organized in a separate Jewish state. Certainly their views on self-determination and the character of the state in which they would like to live are entitled to equal weight with the approximately equal number of Muslims and Christians in the area. It is hard to see, then, how in self-determination theory a separate Jewish state is any more unreasonable than a secular democratic state. To the contrary, it seems reasonable to take into account in support of the Israeli claim that the Jews have no national identity other than Israel,[72] that the United Nations recommended in 1947 after thorough study of what was already an intractable problem that Palestine should be partitioned into separate Jewish and Arab states, and that there is far greater assurance that the functioning democratic institutions of Israel represent its three million citizens than that the splintered Palestinian guerrilla organizations meaningfully represent the non-Israeli population of the area. In the real world the continued existence of the State of Israel would seem to have given rise to greater right than the rhetoric of the PLO.

The Palestinian claim also suggests a territorial determinism. That is, since the territory of Palestine was once united under the mandate it could not in 1948 or 1971 be divided into separate Jewish and Arab states. But as

---

[71] For an excursion into the historical arguments see, *e.g.*, W. LAQUEUR (ED.), THE ISRAEL/ARAB READER (1968); Feinberg, *The Recognition of the Jewish People In International Law*, JEWISH YEARBOOK OF INTERNATIONAL LAW 1 (1948); Mallison, *The Zionist-Israel Juridical Claims to Constitute "The Jewish People" Nationality Entity and to Confer Membership In It: Appraisal In Public International Law*, 32 GEO. WASH. L. REV. 983 (1964).

[72] This is, of course, also true of the Palestinian Arabs, but unlike the Palestinians the Israelis accepted the United Nations partition plan which would have created both Jewish and Arab states.

the reapportionment decisions should remind us, people, not territory, are the relevant standard. Moreover, there is no absolute of territorial determinancy in international law. French Togoland became Ghana and Togo, and the German Cameroons became the Cameroons and part of Northern Nigeria.[73] Interestingly, both examples share a colonial background as does Palestine. Although the principle of self-determination of peoples might support creation of a separate Arab Palestinian state side by side with Israel, as for example in the West Bank and Gaza, it does not readily support Palestinian demands for a unified "secular democratic" Palestine. Other principles, such as restitution for the Arab refugees, may support Arab claims, but if it proves anything, the principle of self-determination supports the continued existence of the State of Israel.

It might also be questioned whether the proposed Palestinian model of a "secular democratic" state is necessarily a preferable formula in terms of national development. Although there are many successful examples of a multi-religious state, including the United States, on the other hand Cyprus, Lebanon, Kashmir, the Sudan, and Northern Ireland suggest that at least some such models may lead to continued strife and retarded national and human development. Along these lines it is certainly reasonable to take into account that it would seem particularly hard to establish a secular multi-religious state in the Middle East, a part of the world where pressures are strong for an established religion.

Extreme Arab Palestinian claims are even more doubtful than the "moderate" claims. If the referent of self-determination is people, more precisely people currently residing in an area, then it would seem indefensible to exclude any of them either from the initial constitutive decision as to the preferred character of their state or from participation in the proposed state. But extreme Arab claims may do just that with respect to "Zionist Israelis," Jews not living permanently in Palestine at the "beginning of the Zionist invasion," or persons in some other equally vague category. Although these extreme claims may not be a formula for driving the Israelis into the sea, they are at least a formula for creating a massive new refugee problem for a people who do not have neighbors to receive them. As such, these extreme claims would seem to curtail rather than support genuine self-determination. One can understand the feeling of helplessness of the Arab Palestinian caught up in international decisions concerning the character of his homeland. One can also understand his sense of grievance at his substantial disenfranchisement from those decisions. To offer the same or worse to the Israeli, however, is but to compound the suffering.

C. *Respect for Human Rights*

Article 1(3) of the United Nations Charter focuses on "promoting and

---

[73] E. LAUTERPACHT, JERUSALEM AND THE HOLY PLACES 17 (Anglo-Israel Association Pamphlet No. 19, 1968).

encouraging respect for human rights and for fundamental freedoms." As is also the case with respect to self-determination, Article 55 reiterates this purpose. And pursuant to Article 56 the members of the United Nations pledge themselves to take action to promote the purposes set forth in Article 55. This pledge to promote basic human rights would seem applicable to the Arab-Israeli conflict in a number of important ways. First, both Israel and the Arab states have an obligation to alleviate the plight of the Arab and Jewish refugees.[74] Moreover, the refugee problem is a human rights problem that should not have to await a full political solution of the Arab-Israeli conflict. Israel has a responsibility to permit Arab refugees willing to live in peace in Israel to return to Israel. And the Arab states have a responsibility to assist Arab refugees not wishing to return to Israel to resettle elsewhere and to allow Jews in Arab countries who wish to emigrate to Israel to do so. Both sides have a responsibility to compensate Arab and Jewish refugees for lost property to the extent required under usual principles of international law.

Second, both Israel and the Arab states have an obligation to protect the human rights of Arabs and Jews living under their control. This means protection of Arab civilians in the Israeli occupied territories by applying at least the minimal standards of the 1949 Geneva Convention Relative to the Treatment of Civilians. As the report of the Special Working Group of Experts established by the Human Rights Commission[75] and the report of the Special Committee of the General Assembly[76] demonstrate, this has not always been the case. On the other hand, Arab states should protect Jews living in Arab countries. As the recent Baghdad trials demonstrate, this has also not always been the case.

Lastly, protection of basic human rights strongly suggests the importance of protection of free access for all religions to Jerusalem and the Holy Places.[77] One possible model is the Trusteeship Council Statute for the City of Jerusalem,[78] although both Israel and the Arab states seem to have rejected internationalization as a solution. A more likely possibility would leave the administration of the city jointly in the hands of the states in the area but would provide an international presence for guaranteed access to the Holy Places. Whatever the final solution it should not be unilaterally determined by either side and should adequately guarantee free access to the Holy Places.

---

[74] See generally on the refugee problem Louise W. Holborn, *The Palestine Arab Refugee Problem*, 23 INT'L J. 82-96 (1968).

[75] Report of the Special Working Group of Experts Established Under Resolution 6 (XXV) of the Commission on Human Rights, U.N. Doc. E/CN.4/1016 (Jan. 20, 1970), Adds. 1 & 2 (Feb. 11, 1970), Adds. 3 & 5 (Feb. 20, 1970), Add. 4 (Feb. 18, 1970).

[76] Report of the Special Committee to Investigate Israeli Practices Affecting the Human Rights of the Population of the Occupied Territories, U.N. Doc. A/8089 (Oct. 26, 1970).

[77] With respect to Jerusalem and the Holy Places see generally E. LAUTERPACHT, JERUSALEM AND THE HOLY PLACES 1-3, 5-85 (The Anglo-Israel Association Pamphlet No. 19, 1968); Jones *The Status of Jerusalem: Some National and International Aspects*, 33 LAW & CONTEMP. PROB. 169 (1968). It seems useful to keep separate the issues of administration of Jerusalem and free access to and preservation of the Holy Places.

[78] Trusteeship Council Statute for the City of Jerusalem, 5 U.N. GAOR, Supp. 9, at 19, U.N. Doc. A/1286 (1950).

D. *United Nations Recommendations*

There are a number of United Nations recommendations relevant to an appraisal of the Arab-Israeli conflict. One of the most important is General Assembly Resolution 181(II) of November 29, 1947, which recommended implementation of the United Nations Special Committee plan for partition with economic union.[79] The Resolution represents an important policy judgment that solution to the Arab-Israeli conflict should be a solution based on individual Jewish and Arab communities.

With respect to settlement of the refugee problem, General Assembly Resolution 242 of November 22, 1967, affirms the need "[f]or achieving a just settlement of the refugee problem"[80] as part of an overall settlement of the Arab-Israeli Conflict. General Assembly Resolution 194(III) of December 11, 1948, sets out a formula that has been repeatedly reaffirmed by the United Nations as a basis for just settlement. It provides that:

> the refugees wishing to return to their homes and live at peace with their neighbors should be permitted to do so at the earliest practicable date, and that compensation should be paid for the property of those choosing not to return and for loss of or damage to property which, under principles of international law or in equity, should be made good by the Governments or authorities responsible . . . .[81]

In a significant departure from this formula, General Assembly Resolution 2535 of December 10, 1969, speaks of "the inalienable rights of the people of Palestine."[82] The referent of "inalienable rights of the people of Palestine" is vague, but the Resolution seems to indicate a political shift in United Nations consideration of the refugee problem. In addition to considering the problem as a human rights problem, the resolution seems to be focusing on the self-determination dimensions of the Arab Palestinians' situation as well. As the previous discussion of self-determination illustrates, the potential difficulties concealed by this vague language are enormous.

With respect to the status of Jerusalem, General Assembly Resolution 194(III) of December 11, 1948,[83] and Resolution 303(IV) of December 9, 1949,[84] recommended that the City of Jerusalem be placed under United Nations control. Pursuant to these determinations a Draft Statute for the City of Jerusalem was drawn up by the Trusteeship Council and approved on April 4, 1950.[85] Although all parties in the area seem to reject an international solution, the Draft Statute provides a useful model for an internationalized city. More recently, during 1967, 1968, and 1969, the General Assembly and

---

[79] G.A. Res. 181(II), U.N. Doc. A/519 at 131 (1947).

[80] S.C. Res. 242, 22 U.N. SCOR, 1382d meeting 8 (1967).

[81] G.A. Res. 194(III), U.N. Doc. A/810, 21 at 24 (1948).

[82] G.A. Res. 2535, 24 U.N. GAOR, Supp. 30, U.N. Doc. A/7630 (1969). For a brief discussion of the debates leading up to the adoption of this resolution see "Issues Before the 25th General Assembly," *supra* note 70, at 29-30.

[83] G.A. Res. 194(III), U.N. Doc. A/810 at 21 (1948).

[84] G.A. Res. 303(IV), U.N. Doc. A/1251 at 25 (1949).

[85] Trusteeship Council Statute for the City of Jerusalem. 5 U.N. GAOR, Supp. 9, at 19, U.N. Doc. A/1286 (1950).

Security Council passed a series of four resolutions calling on Israel not to unilaterally alter the status of Jerusalem and to rescind measures already taken to change the status of the City.[86] With respect to freedom of navigation through international waterways in the area, a Security Council Resolution of September 1, 1951, calls on Egypt to permit the unrestricted passage of "shipping and goods through the Suez Canal wherever bound" and indicates that a continued state of belligerency is inconsistent with the 1949 Armistice agreements.[87] In addition, Resolution 242 of November 22, 1967, affirms the necessity "[f]or guaranteeing freedom of navigation through international waterways in the area"[88] as part of an overall settlement.

During 1967 the Security Council and the General Assembly called on all the parties to render humanitarian assistance to civilians and prisoners of war in the Arab-Israeli conflict and to "respect . . . the humanitarian principles governing the treatment of prisoners of war and the protection of civilian persons in time of war contained in the Geneva Conventions of 12 August 1949."[89] Most recently, a Special Committee of the General Assembly and a Committee of the Human Rights Commission have studied human rights problems in the occupied territories.[90] The composition and procedures of these Committees have been substantially politicized, and the resulting reports are correspondingly less useful. Nevertheless, the reports point up incidents of human rights violations that call for Israeli corrective action. A broadened study as requested by Israel that would also have examined the treatment of Jews in the Arab states would probably also have reported human rights violations requiring correction.

The most important United Nations recommendation on settlement is Resolution 242 of November 22, 1967. This resolution, set out in full earlier in this article,[91] outlines a carefully balanced package settlement. Most importantly, the outlines of that settlement include "[w]ithdrawal of Israel armed forces from territories occupied in the recent conflict" and "[t]ermination of all claims or states of belligerency and respect for and acknowledgement of the sovereignty, territorial integrity and political independence of every State in the area and their right to live in peace within secure and recognized bound-

---

[86] S.C. Res. 267, 24 U.N. SCOR, 1485th meeting 3 (1969); S.C. Res. 252, 23 U.N. SCOR, 1426th meeting 9 (1968); G.A. Resolutions 2253 (ES-V), 2254 (ES-V), U.N. GAOR (5th Emer. Spec. Sess. Supp. 1), 4 U.N. Doc. A/6798 (1967). Security Council Resolution 267 of July 3, 1969 was strongly worded. Among other strong clauses one "[c]ensures in the strongest terms all measures taken to change the status of the City of Jerusalem."
[87] S.C. Res. S/2322, 6 U.N. SCOR, 558th meeting 3 (1951).
[88] S.C. Res. 242, 22 U.N. SCOR, 1382d meeting 8 (1967).
[89] S.C. Res. 237, 22 U.N. SCOR, 1361st meeting 5 (1967); G.A. Res. 2252 (ES-V), U.N. GAOR (5th Emer. Spec. Sess. Supp. 1), 3 U.N. Doc. A/6798 (1967). Apparently the United States-sponsored truce accord of August 7 between Israel and Egypt also required both sides to abide by the Geneva Convention of 1949 Relative to the Treatment of Prisoners of War and to "accept the assistance of the International Committee of the Red Cross in carrying out their obligations under that convention." See "Treaty of Truce Accord," N.Y. Times, Aug. 14, 1970, at 7, col. 6.
[90] See the reports cited in notes 75-76 *supra*.
[91] See text at note 12 *supra*.

aries free from threats or acts of force."[92] Because of its careful balance, willingness to accept Resolution 242 would seem particularly important in assessing the settlement positions of the parties.

E. *The Outlines of a Reasonable Settlement as Suggested by Fundamental Charter Principles and United Nations Recommendations*

The outlines of a reasonable settlement as suggested by an analysis of these fundamental Charter principles and United Nations recommendations might be:

1. The Arab States should recognize the right of Israel to exist, terminate all claims of belligerency against Israel, and take effective measures to end fedayeen attacks on Israel launched from their territory.

2. The interest of Israel in the territories occupied as a result of the Six Day War is a functional interest limited to the protection of national security and the preservation of religious freedom in Jerusalem and the Holy Places. Except for freely negotiated border adjustments, the armed forces of Israel should withdraw from the occupied territories as the security threat abates and their religious freedom in Jerusalem and the Holy Places is assured. Under present conditions the nature of the security threat is such that it would not seem unreasonable to make peace agreements with the concerned Arab states a precondition for territorial withdrawal. In addition, demilitarized zones and arrangements for international supervision and major power guarantee might be employed to ensure the integrity of the agreed boundaries and freedom of passage through the Strait of Tiran. Demilitarized zones and some form of international supervision would seem particularly appropriate for the Golan Heights, Sharm-el-Sheikh, Jerusalem, the Gaza Strip, and border areas in the Sinai and the West Bank.

3. Any international supervisory forces should be under the continuing supervision of the United Nations. The agreement stationing such forces in the area should make it clear that they can be withdrawn only with the consent of the Security Council or other appropriate United Nations body.

4. As a consequence of termination of all states of belligerency Israeli shipping should be guaranteed free passage through the Strait of Tiran, the Gulf of Aqaba, a reopened Suez Canal, and the Strait of Bab-el-Mandeb.

5. There should be free access for all religions to the Holy Places in Jerusalem and elsewhere. In this connection it would seem appropriate that Jerusalem be demilitarized and that there be United Nations supervision of the Holy Places and guarantee of freedom of religious access within Jerusalem. Jerusalem could then be administered by some combination of Arab and Israeli control (*e.g.,* joint Israeli-Jordanian administration of the entire City or Israeli administration of West Jerusalem and Jordanian administration of East Jerusalem).

---

[92] S.C. Res. 242, 22 U.N. SCOR, 1382d meeting 8 (1967).

6. Settlement should be concluded by binding peace agreements between the principal parties that spell out in full the details of agreement, including the parties to be bound, secured boundaries for Israel and the Arab states, demilitarized zones, and any arrangements for international supervision and guarantee.

7. Settlement of the refugee problem should provide for voluntary repatriation and compensation to the extent consistent with security and economic viability of the states concerned. All of the states of the Middle East, the Arab states as well as Israel, have an obligation to assist in a meaningful permanent solution of the refugee problem. Solution to the refugee problem is an urgent human rights issue that need not await a final political settlement of the Arab-Israeli conflict.

8. Israel and the Arab States should take steps to afford greater protection for the human rights of Arabs in the occupied territories and Jews in the Arab states and to scrupulously observe the provisions of the 1949 Geneva Convention Relative to the Treatment of Prisoners of War.

9. Israel and the Arab states should cooperate for economic and social progress in the area. In this connection there should be a cessation of the Arab economic boycott against Israel. It might also be useful to arrange port facilities in Israel for Jordan and for Arab access between Gaza and the West Bank and to arrange for cooperative utilization of the resources of the Jordan River.

These proposals are by no means the only basis for a fair settlement of the Arab-Israeli conflict. A striking feature of the conflict is the wide range of reasonable compromise alternatives available if all participants were really dedicated to ending it. One creative suggestion demonstrating this wide availability of positive plans for peace is the proposal by Professor Michael Reisman, which features a Development Trust for the Sinai and a United Nations Trusteeship of the Golan Heights for the benefit of the indigenous Druze population.[93]

IV. COMPLIANCE OF THE PRINCIPAL BELLIGERENTS IN THE ARAB-ISRAELI CONFLICT WITH THE CHARTER OBLIGATION TO PURSUE PEACEFUL SETTLEMENT OF INTERNATIONAL DISPUTES

The three preceding sections have dealt with standards for appraisal of the obligation to pursue peaceful settlement of international disputes, the settlement positions of the contending belligerents in the Arab-Israeli Conflict, and the applicability of fundamental Charter principles and United Nations recommendations to that conflict. This final section will appraise the extent to which the parties settlement positions comply with their Charter obligation to pursue peaceful settlement. Since the record of settlement efforts is not wholly public,

---

[93] M. REISMAN, THE ART OF THE POSSIBLE: DIPLOMATIC ALTERNATIVES IN THE MIDDLE EAST (1970).

conclusions are necessarily tentative. Nevertheless, enough information seems available to make some useful judgments.

Fundamental Charter principles and United Nations recommendations strongly support the right of Israel to exist in peace within "secure and recognized boundaries." Pursuant to this obligation the Arab states should take effective measures to end fedayeen raids launched from their territory against Israel and should cease all acts of belligerency directed against Israel. Until the Arab states take steps to end their continuing state of belligerency against Israel, Israel will have a continuing security problem. As such, the Israeli position of no withdrawal from the occuped territories until a genuine peace is achieved seems not unreasonable under the Charter, at least with respect to those territories functionally necessary for Israeli security. If the Arab states were to agree to termination of belligerency on condition that Israel withdraw from the occupied territories and Israel refused to withdraw, the Arab states could simply resume belligerency and would not be seriously prejudiced. On the other hand, if Israel were to withdraw prior to Arab agreement to terminate belligerency and the Arab states then refused to terminate belligerency, Israel's security might be seriously impaired with no way of rectifying the situation short of another Six Day War. Since both sides mistrust the intentions of the other this is a useful comparison to make. On the other hand, it may also be true that the Arab states are put at a disadvantage in negotiations by virtue of Israel's continued occupation of the territories seized in the Six Day War. In order to comply with their Charter obligation to pursue peaceful settlement of disputes, though, the Arab states need not propose anything other than a reasonable settlement consistent with fundamental principles of the Charter and United Nations recommendations. If Israel then refused to accept the proposed settlement the burden of justification would rest on Israel rather than the Arab States.

If Israel's position is justifiable with respect to Arab termination of belligerency against Israel, in several other respects it has been less satisfactory. There have been indications that Israel would be unwilling to make concessions concerning the status of East Jerusalem and possibly the Golan Heights and Sharm-el-Sheikh. Moreover, the Israeli position even with respect to the other occupied territories has been ambiguous and has not clearly indicated that the interest of Israel in the occupied territories is a security interest only. Although Israel is entitled to retain the occupied territories until termination of Arab belligerency, it should make clear that its interest in the territories (other than East Jerusalem) is a security interest only. Israel might appropriately take the initiative in proposing territorial boundaries with only minor readjustments, pullback in exchange for unambiguous termination of belligerency, demilitarized zones, major power guarantees, and meaningful international supervision that would take account of the legitimate interests of both Israel and the Arab States as well as the indigenous population of the territories. Some minor boundary adjustments seem called for simply in terms of benefit to both sides from straightening out the accidents of the 1948 boundaries. But aside from freely negotiated readjustments in boundaries and in the status of Jerusalem, Israel should indicate clearly that its interest in the occupied territory is a security interest only.

Israel has a legitimate interest in orderly administration of and free access to Jerusalem and the Holy Places. In view of the past Jordanian refusal to comply with the intent of the 1949 Armistice Agreement permitting Israeli's access to the Holy Places in East Jerusalem, Israeli reluctance to negotiate the future of Jerusalem is understandable.[94] Nevertheless, the final status of Jerusalem should not be determined unilaterally by any state in the area. There are reasonable alternatives available to ensure free access to Jerusalem and the Holy Places. Israel should take the initiative in urging proposals that would recognize the substantial Arab, Israeli, and international religious concern for the status of Jerusalem. Perhaps the most realistic solution would be joint Israeli-Jordanian administration of the City with a limited international supervision to ensure free access to the Holy Places.

With respect to the Golan Heights, Israel should propose such arrangements as will recognize the very real security interests of Israel as well as the aspirations of the indigenous population, particularly the substantial Druze population of the area. Continued Syrian refusal to accept such arrangements or to terminate belligerency would justify continued occupation at least of those areas necessary for Israeli security.

Lastly, Israel should take the initiative in urging specific proposals for cooperative settlement of the refugee problem. Such initiatives should provide maximum free choice for refugees living in the occupied territories to return to Israel to the extent that such refugees are willing to live in peace with Israel.

Perhaps the central issue in the Arab-Israeli conflict is Arab willingness to accept the existence of Israel, to take steps to control fedayeen activities directed against Israel from Arab territory, and to end all acts of belligerency against Israel. Although both Egypt and Jordan have accepted Security Council Resolution 242, which implies all of this, in a number of important respects their settlement position fails to confirm that acceptance. Thus, they refuse to have direct talks with Israel, officially accept only the 1947 partition resolution boundaries, refuse (at least publicly) to accept a final settlement in the form of a binding peace agreement with Israel,[95] indicate that they will never have diplomatic relations with Israel, require pullback from Syrian as well as Egyptian and Jordanian territory as a precondition to settlement even though Syria has not accepted Resolution 242, and publicly proclaim support for the Palestine Liberation Organization, which is dedicated to a continuing armed

---

[94] See Article VIII of the General Armistice Agreement between the Hashemite Kingdom of Jordan and the State of Israel, 42 U.N.T.S. 304, 314 (April 3, 1949).

[95] The New York Times has reported that the Egyptian reply to Ambassador Jarring's initiative of February 8, 1970 indicates a willingness to conclude a binding peace treaty with Israel. If so this would be a significant shift in the Egyptian position. N.Y. Times, Feb. 19, 1971, at 8, col. 4 (city ed.).

struggle against the existence of Israel as a Jewish state. As a result, the ambiguity in their position raises serious doubt about good faith compliance with the Charter obligation to pursue peaceful settlement of disputes. Compliance with the Charter obligation suggests that the Arab states should be willing to negotiate directly with Israel for the purpose of concluding a definitive and legally binding settlement of the Arab-Israeli conflict. To that end they should take the initiative in proposing an agreement that would fully take account of Israel's right to exist within "agreed and recognized" boundaries approximating the pre-Six Day War boundaries, control of fedayeen raids from Arab territory directed against Israel, guarantees of free access through major waterways in the area, including the Strait of Tiran and the Suez Canal, and cessation of all acts of belligerency against Israel. They should also be willing to proceed state by state in settlement and not to link termination of belligerency with withdrawal from the territory of a State that has refused to accept Resolution 242. At least in the absence of such realistic proposals for ending belligerency, resumption of a "war of attrition" against Israel to force relinquishment of the occupied territories would seem in violation of the Charter.

Egypt and Jordan should also take the initiative in proposing cooperative settlement of the Jerusalem and refugee problems. If Israel should not unilaterally determine the status of Jerusalem neither should Jordan, even with respect to East Jerusalem. All states in the area have an obligation to recognize the substantial and legitimate Arab, Israeli, and international religious concern in Jerusalem and the Holy Places. If international administration is unacceptable, one possibility would be some form of joint Arab-Israeli administration of the City with international supervision of free access to the City and the Holy Places. Above all, however, Jerusalem should not be treated simply as a problem of territorial withdrawal like that of the other occupied territories. With respect to refugees, the Arab states should take steps to protect the human rights of Jews in Arab territories and should develop and provide meaningful opportunities for Palestinian refugees who would prefer assimilation in the Arab countries rather than to return to Israel. An appeal might be made to the United Nations or the four powers to provide the necessary financing for the plan. One of the great tragedies in the Arab-Israeli conflict has been the needless sacrifice of the human potential of the Palestinian refugees, a sacrifice now being passed along to a second generation. It is time for all sides to recognize that a genuine commitment to human rights transcends political causes.

Syria has refused to accept General Assembly Resolution 242 and seems committed to a continuing challenge to the existence of Israel. By any standards of content and procedure Syria is in fundamental violation of the Charter obligation to pursue peaceful settlement of disputes. Syria has not urged peaceful settlement, has not indicated a willingness to negotiate, has refused to terminate belligerency against Israel, provides substantial assistance and encouragement to the PLO, has refused to accept the most important United Nations recommendations for settlement, and seems unwilling to compromise.

The Palestine Liberation Organization is a revolutionary political and military front rather than a state. Accordingly, it may be somewhat anomalous to speak of its obligation under the Charter to pursue peaceful settlement of disputes. More precisely, the obligation is that of the states assisting the PLO and from whose territory the PLO operates. Nevertheless, it seems meaningful to appraise the PLO position by reference to fundamental Charter principles, particularly self-determination. As has been seen, the principle of self-determination of peoples does not readily support even "moderate" Palestinian demands for the replacement of Israel with a "secular democratic" State of Arab design. Even if it did, under the Charter principle restricting the use of force as an instrument of national policy, continuing third party assistance to the PLO would seem to violate the obligation to pursue peaceful settlement of disputes as well as the obligation to refrain from assisting insurgent movements directed against another state.

V. Conclusion

Appraisal of the Charter obligation to pursue peaceful settlement of international disputes has been virtually ignored by international-legal scholars concerned with major war-peace issues. Such appraisal is an important additional focus for legal analysis, particularly with respect to major recurring world order issues. One difficulty in such appraisal has been the lack of recognized standards. Analysis of the general Charter structure, however, suggests a range of useful standards of procedure and content. A particularly important criterion for appraisal is the consistency of the belligerents' settlement positions with respect to the fundamental Charter principles and United Nations recommendations.

Applying suggested standards of procedure and content to the positions of the major participants in the Arab-Israeli conflict indicates that all participants have room for improvement in complying with the Charter obligation to pursue peaceful settlement of disputes. Israel should clarify that its interest in the occupied territories is a security interest only and that its forces will withdraw as security in the area is guaranteed and a negotiated settlement is reached with respect to Jerusalem and the Holy Places. Egypt, Jordan, Syria, and Lebanon should unequivocally indicate their willingness to agree to a binding agreement with Israel recognizing the right of Israel to exist in peace within "secure and recognized boundaries," agreeing to take effective measures to control fedayeen raids on Israel launched from their territory, agreeing to a negotiated settlement of the problem of Jerusalem and the Holy Places, and terminating all acts of belligerency against Israel. That all parties have room for improvement does not indicate that all are in equal compliance with Charter obligations. Of the principal belligerents, Syria seems in open violation of the Charter obligation to pursue peaceful settlement of international disputes. Even with respect to the more moderate posture of Egypt, Jordan, and Lebanon, perhaps the most critical need is for unequivocal indication of Arab willingness to terminate belligerency against Israel.

The tortured history of efforts at belligerent solutions to the Arab-Israeli conflict strongly suggests that a peaceful solution is the only solution. Until all parties accept this fundamental truth time will probably be on the side of wider conflict. If, however, all parties to the conflict genuinely fulfill their Charter obligations to seek a peaceful solution, the present period of diplomatic activity could be a prelude to lasting peace.

Directions for a Middle East Settlement —Some Underlying Legal Problems

SHABTAI ROSENNE

I

Introduction

A. Legal Framework of Arab-Israeli Relations

The invitation to me to participate in this symposium suggested devoting attention primarily to the legal aspects and not to the facts. Yet there is great value in the civil law maxim: *Narra mihi facta,narrabo tibi jus.* Law does not operate in a vacuum or in the abstract, but only in the closest contact with facts; and the merit of legal exposition depends directly upon its relationship with the facts.

It is a fact that as part of its approach to the settlement of the current crisis, the Government of Israel is insistent that whatever solution is reached should be embodied in a secure legal regime of a contractual character directly binding on all the states concerned.

International law in general, and the underlying international legal aspects of the crisis of the Middle East, are no exceptions to this legal approach which integrates law with the facts. But faced with the multitude of facts arrayed by one protagonist or another, sometimes facts going back to the remotest periods of prehistory, the first task of the lawyer is to separate the wheat from the chaff, to place first things first and last things last, and to discipline himself to the most rigorous standards of *relevance* that contemporary legal science imposes. The authority of the International Court itself exists for this approach: the irony with which in 1953 that august tribunal brushed off historical arguments, in that instance only going back to the early feudal period, will not be lost on the perceptive reader of international jurisprudence.[1]

Another fundamental question which must be indicated at the outset relates to the very character of the legal framework within which the political issues are to be discussed and placed. A close study of presentations made by Arab spokesmen

---

* LL.B. 1938, University of London; Ph.D. 1959, Hebrew University of Jerusalem. Ambassador, Deputy Permanent Representative of Israel to the United Nations. Member of the Israel bar, and of the International Law Commission and the Commission on Human Rights of the United Nations. Associate of the Institute of International Law. Author, The Law and Practice of the International Court (1965), and various works on the law of Israel and on international law.

Insofar as a person holding an official and representative position can maintain personal views, the opinions expressed in this article are not necessarily those of the government which the author has the honor to represent.

[1] Minquiers and Ecrehos Case, [1953] I.C.J. 47, 56. Note its reference to "historical controversies." Likewise, in the *Temple of Preah Vihear Case,* the court refused to regard as legally decisive various arguments of a "physical, historical, religious and archaeological character." [1962] I.C.J. 6, 15.

may lead to the conclusion that very frequently they fall back not on objective and established principles and rules of contemporary international law, but on subjective, vague and, on the whole, discredited theories of natural law and natural justice, whatever those terms might mean—indeed it is never clear whether they have in mind the so-called *jus naturae* or the *jus naturale*. The word "discredited" is used not in a disparaging sense—the great importance which the very concept of natural law played in the primitive period of the history of international law and in its evolution as a branch of science distinct from theology, in which its roots were once embedded, is well known. The expression is employed in the sense that natural law and natural justice are undisciplined and highly subjective concepts or, at most, concepts of an exclusively philosophical character meaning all things to all men. *Quot homines, tot sententiae!* With all its vagueness and imperfections, positive international law today does provide the generally accepted standards of international conduct: it is to positive international law, both conventional and customary, and only to positive international law, that rights and obligations, whether synallagmatic or not, are traced. This is not to imply that natural law concepts and natural law approaches are of no value. Very frequently, they inspire the development of the law—both the creation of new law and the evolution of existing law—and even more frequently what might be called the natural sense of the lawyer is an essential element in the interpretation and application of the law. However, in the present case, the so-called natural law appears as a meta-juridical element. It is not the law, and it creates neither rights nor obligations. To some it would appear that reliance on natural law is a recognition that there is no case in law.

This factor is significant with regard to the Middle Eastern crisis because the more one probes into the matter, the more one is shocked by the absence of an accepted legal framework common to Israel and the Arab States within which debate is conducted and by the manner in which the Arab spokesmen reject received law as the standard-setting agent. Even the Charter of the United Nations is brushed aside or accorded perfunctory attention by the Arab diplomats, who prefer arbitrary interpretations unsupported by commonly accepted canons of legal workmanship. In fact, at times one is left with the impression that all that remains as a framework of the debate are the Rules of Procedure of whatever organ might be discussing the matter at a given moment, and even these are as often breached as observed.

B. Role of the International Court of Justice

Criticism is frequently advanced by these same proponents of a natural law approach to the case by reason of the fact that although, on several occasions since 1947, legal questions have been formulated for the purpose of seeking an advisory opinion from the International Court of Justice, neither the Security Council nor the General Assembly has ever decided to request an advisory opinion.[2] (Paren-

---

[2] For details, see 2 S. ROSENNE, THE LAW AND PRACTICE OF THE INTERNATIONAL COURT 665 (Gen-

thetically it may be observed that before World War II, the Jewish side felt that the Mandatory Government was not properly applying the Mandate and that certain legal issues ought to have been put by the competent organs of the League of Nations to the Permanent Court of International Justice and this, too, was never done.)

Several observations can be made on this criticism. As a matter of common practice, it is characteristic of the United Nations that the political organs have, in general, and probably wisely, refrained from submitting legal questions for advisory opinion in the course of their handling of political issues. The reasons for this are deep. They can be found in the whole structure of the United Nations and in the limited and ambiguous role which the Charter envisages for the advisory opinion in the course of political action by the Security Council and the General Assembly. Experience of the use of the advisory opinion in political circumstances seems to indicate two things at least: (*a*) that before the advisory procedure can be put to fruitful use, there has to be some measure of general agreement that the judicial pronouncement, *whatever it might be*, would facilitate the political decisions; and (*b*) that in the circumstances there is a reasonable measure of agreement between the states concerned that procedures available under the Statute of the International Court of Justice would be appropriate for the determination of given and agreed issues. Here, the United Nations presents no analogy with the League of Nations where the requirement of unanimity ensured that both these factors were thoroughly examined before the Council of the League decided to request an advisory opinion.[3] Examination of the questions which have been proposed for submission to the Court on the Palestine question since 1947 shows above all that those who sponsored them made no effort whatsoever to see if agreed formulations could be reached. They were one-sided, loaded questions and were treated as such by the competent political organs.

Since the question of the possible role of the Court in the Middle East crisis has been raised, it might be useful to reiterate that of all the states concerned only Israel has accepted the compulsory jurisdiction of the Court in its Declaration dated October 3, 1956 which is still in force.[4] It is an elementary principle of the law of the Court that the consent of the parties, whether expressed formally or in some informal manner, constitutes the only effective basis for judicial action; and this is as true of the contentious jurisdiction as it is of the advisory competence.

The Government of Israel has in the past expressed its reserves towards proposed references to the Court. The fundamental reason has always been the absence of

eral Assembly) and 668 (Security Council) (1965). Two cases arising out of the situation in Palestine have nevertheless been brought before the court, namely the Advisory Opinion on Reparation for Injuries Suffered in the Service of the United Nations, [1949] I.C.J. 174, and the Case Concerning the Protection of French Nationals in Egypt, [1950] I.C.J. 59.

[3] 2 S. ROSENNE, *supra* note 2, at 658.

[4] 252 U.N.T.S. 301.

the necessary consensual basis in fact. The proposals have not been seen as sincere attempts to obtain judicial determination of controverted issues which the parties have agreed should be judicially determined as part of the process of the pacific settlement of those issues, but rather as attempts to employ the judicial process for unilateral advantage. It may easily be the assumption that in such circumstances, the Court would have found it improper for it to have taken part in such an abuse of the judicial machinery.

C. Historic Issues

It is commonplace that, because of the central place it occupies in the history of human evolution, the Middle East evokes a host of mixed reactions. Their roots can be traced to many causes, but predominant among them are undoubtedly religious and psychological motives, the implications of the long and difficult history of the relations between the Jewish and the Christian worlds and the equally complex history of the relationships between the Christian and the Muslim worlds, this latter being symbolized by the spell which to this day the Crusades and all they stood for (and incidentally they were a very black period in Jewish history) cast upon the psychology of the peoples of the Middle East. One must also not ignore that the annals of Jewish-Muslim relations are not simply an uninterrupted succession of golden ages, as is sometimes inferred, but they, too, are characterized by episodic antisemitism of an extremely virulent character.

Thus questions frequently arise such as: the right of Great Britain to have disposed of the territory of Palestine during World War I; the legality of the Balfour Declaration, its interpretation, and its compatibility with other binding undertakings said to have been given by the British Government to others; the compatibility of the Mandate for Palestine with Article 22 of the Covenant of the League of Nations; the legality of the manner in which the Mandate was implemented; the appropriateness of the decision of the British Government in 1947 to remit the question of the future government of Palestine to the General Assembly of the United Nations; of the legitimacy of the decision then reached by the General Assembly and embodied in its well known resolution 181(II) of November 29, 1947, and so on. Much has been written and much no doubt will continue to be written on these and similar questions.

Although their existence as genuine and relevant legal questions may be open to doubt, a few general observations about some of these issues may be made.

Before the Peace Treaties that put an end to World War I, Palestine was part of the Ottoman Empire which, in 1914, in a manner fully in conformity with the international law of the epoch, joined the war as an active belligerent on the side of the Central Powers. During the war, the Allied Powers made certain arrangements between themselves regarding the disposition of various territories of the Ottoman Empire in the event they should be victorious. That was then and has remained a normal phenomenon of relations between allied belligerents. Ottoman sovereignty over the territory of Palestine, as over many other of its territories, was ceded to the Allied Powers in the Peace Treaty. No obvious ground is seen for challenging the title thus acquired by Great Britain as Mandatory on behalf of the League of Nations over Palestine.

The Balfour Declaration, contained in a letter dated November 2, 1917 from the British Foreign Secretary for the attention of the Zionist Federation, was also a part of the wartime political arrangements envisaged for the eventuality of the defeat of the Ottoman Empire.[5] Its precise legal status at the time it was made may be open to discussion but that problem is secondary in view of the fact that the Council of the League of Nations incorporated its text into the Preamble to the Mandate for Palestine[6] as follows:

> *Whereas* the Principal Allied Powers have also agreed that the Mandatory should be responsible for putting into effect the declaration originally made on November 2nd, 1917, by the Government of His Britannic Majesty, and adopted by the said Powers, in favour of the establishment in Palestine of a national home for the Jewish people, it being clearly understood that nothing should be done which might prejudice the civil and religious rights of existing non-Jewish communities in Palestine, or the rights and political status enjoyed by Jews in any other country; and
> *Whereas* recognition has thereby been given to the historical connection of the Jewish people with Palestine and to the grounds for reconstituting their national home in that country.

The formal and substantive validity of the Mandate for Palestine, as of all the other Mandates, is hardly a matter of discussion. As far back as 1924, the Permanent Court of International Justice interpreted and applied that Mandate and thus necessarily acknowledged its validity.[7] The International Court of Justice has pointed out in connection with the Mandate for South-West Africa, that a Mandate cannot be correctly regarded as embodying only an executive action by the Council of the League in pursuance of the Covenant but, in fact and in law, is an international agreement having the character of a treaty or convention.[8] This was carried into the Charter of the United Nations through the transitory provisions of Article 80 according to which "nothing . . . shall be construed in or of itself to alter in any manner the rights whatsover of any States or any peoples or the terms of existing international instruments to which Members of the United Nations may respectively be

---

[5] For text see CMD. No. 5479, at 22 (1937). See in general L. STEIN, THE BALFOUR DECLARATION (1961).

[6] CMD. No. 1785 (1922), reprinted in 2 U.N. GAOR, Supp. 11, U.N. Doc. A/364, Add. 1, at 18 (1947).

[7] See in particular the judgment of the Permanent Court of International Justice of August 30, 1924 in the Mavrommatis Palestine Concessions Case, [1924] P.C.I.J., Ser. A, No. 2.

[8] South-West Africa Cases, Preliminary Objections, [1962] I.C.J. 319, 330.

parties. . . ."[9] As the International Court of Justice said on another occasion, Article 80 "presupposes that the rights of States and peoples shall not lapse automatically on the dissolution of the League of Nations. It obviously was the intention to safeguard the rights of states and peoples under all circumstances and in all respects."[10]

II

ROLE OF THE UNITED NATIONS 1947-1967

In 1947 the question of the future Government of Palestine was submitted by the Mandatory Government to the General Assembly of the United Nations,[11] the only body competent under the Charter to deal with the future of the territories formerly under League of Nations Mandate, and, after exhaustive examination of the problem,[12] the General Assembly recommended the termination of the Mandate and the partition of Palestine into a Jewish and Arab state which, together with an internationalized Jerusalem, would be linked in a plan of economic union.[13]

In the course of its examination of the issue, the General Assembly made appropriate arrangements to acquaint itself fully with the position of all sides. Both the Jewish Agency for Palestine[14] (a body whose establishment was authorized by the Mandate for Palestine and from which it derived its status) and the Arab Higher Committee,[15] which was commonly regarded as representative of the Palestinian Arabs, were invited to participate in accordance with the Rules of Procedure in the General Assembly's deliberations, quite apart from the fact that several Arab states themselves were already at that time members of the United Nations. The partition plan constituted the General Assembly's compromise solution for the conflicting claims to self-determination of the Jews and of the Arabs. All the claims and counterclaims had been carefully weighed and all the different interests as they then existed had been balanced.

The Jewish side accepted the compromise. The Arab side rejected it[16] and almost

---

[9] On the relationship between Article 80 and the rights of the Jewish people under the Balfour Declaration and the Mandate, in the conception of the San Francisco Conference, see Gilchrist, *Colonial Questions at the San Francisco Conference*, 39 AM. POL. SCI. REV. 982, 990-91 (1945).

In view of the attitude adopted at the time, it is curious today to hear Arab spokesmen relying on parts of the Balfour Declaration and the Mandate. *Nemo potest venire contra factum proprium!*

[10] International Status of South-West Africa Case, [1950] I.C.J. 128, 134.

[11] See J. ROBINSON, PALESTINE AND THE UNITED NATIONS, PRELUDE TO SOLUTION (1947) on the first phase.

[12] For the report of the United Nations Special Committee on Palestine (UNSCOP), see 2 U.N. GAOR, Supp. 11, U.N. Doc. A/364 (1947).

[13] G.A. Res. 181(II), 2 U.N. GAOR, Resolutions 131, 132, U.N. Doc. A/519 (1947).

[14] G.A. Res. 104(S-1), 2 U.N. GAOR, 1st Spec. Sess., Resolutions at 6, U.N. Doc. A/310 (1947).

[15] G.A. Res. 105 (S-1), *id.* It might, however, be noted that on June 13, 1947 the Arab Higher Committee notified the Secretary-General of the United Nations that it would abstain from collaboration with UNSCOP. Report of UNSCOP, *supra* note 12, vol. 2, at 5. This was repeated on July 10, 1947. *Id.* at 8. And see paras. 32-34 of the Report of UNSCOP, *supra* note 12, vol. 1, at 4.

[16] *Cf.* the statements of the representatives of Saudi Arabia, Iraq, and Syria at the 128th Plenary meeting of the General Assembly on November 29, 1947, immediately after the adoption of resolution 181(II). 2 U.N. GAOR 1425-27 (1947).

from the outset openly used armed force to prevent its implementation. In its first special report to the Security Council of February 16, 1948, the United Nations Palestine Commission, which had been established to assist in the implementation of resolution 181(II), reported: "Powerful Arab interests, both inside and outside Palestine, are defying the resolution of the General Assembly and are engaged in a deliberate effort to alter by force the settlement envisaged therein."[17]

The Mandate over Palestine formally terminated at midnight of May 14-15, 1948 in conformity with the General Assembly's resolution and following the passing of the Palestine Act, 1948, by the British Parliament.[18] Simultaneously, the Jews of Palestine proclaimed the independence of Israel[19] which was immediately attacked not only by Arabs in Palestine but by the armed forces of the neighboring states. These forces rapidly advanced not only into the areas of Palestine which had been originally intended to form part of the Arab state, but beyond into parts of Palestine not destined for the Arab states, including Jerusalem. Thus at one and the same moment, the Mandate terminated, Israel proclaimed its independence, and the Arab-Israeli war began.

There is no formal declaration of war by the Arab states, it is true. A formal declaration of war in the sense of the third Hague Convention of 1907 would naturally have meant the recognition of Israel, something which the Arab states to this day have consistently avoided. But in lieu of the polite diplomatic communications customary even during World War II, there is a series of quite unambiguous statements made to different organs of the United Nations,[20] and these

---

[17] 3 U.N. SCOR, Spec. Supp. 2, at 11, U.N. Doc. S/676 (1948).

[18] Palestine Act of 1948, 11 & 12 Geo. 6, c. 27.

[19] For English translation, see 1 LAWS OF THE STATE OF ISRAEL 3 (authorized translation from the Hebrew). The principal operative paragraph of the Declaration contains the following sentence: "Accordingly, we . . . are here assembled . . . and, by virtue of our natural and historic right and on the strength of the resolution of the United Nations General Assembly hereby declare the establishment of a Jewish State . . . ." As Ben Gurion wrote later:

"[A] proposal was approved . . . to establish a Jewish state on the basis of the partition of the country. And once again the approved proposal was not acted upon until the Jews of the country proclaimed their independence, established their state, and defended it with their armed strength against all the Arab countries."

Jewish Survival, in ISRAELI GOVERNMENT YEAR-BOOK 1, at 32 (1953).

[20] See cablegram of May 15, 1948 from the Secretary-General of the League of Arab States to the Secretary-General of the United Nations, 3 U.N. SCOR, Supp., May 1948, at 83, U.N. Doc. S/745 (1948); cablegram of May 16, 1948 from the King of Transjordan to the Secretary-General of the United Nations, *id.* at 90, U.N. Doc. S/748 (1948); cablegram of May 15, 1948 from the Minister for Foreign Affairs of Egypt to the President of the Security Council, read into the record of the 292nd meeting of the Security Council on May 15, 1948. 3 U.N. SCOR, No. 66, at 2-3, U.N. Doc. S/743 (1948). Note, too, the answers given at the Council's 301st meeting on May 22, 1948 by the representatives of Egypt, Syria, Iraq and Lebanon to a questionnaire addressed to them by the Security Council. *Id.,* No. 72, at 6-17. For the questionnaire, see *id.,* Supp. May 1948, *supra,* at 90, U.N. Doc. S/753. For the reply by Saudi Arabia, see *id.* at 95 (U.N. Doc. S/772). For the refusal of Transjordan to reply, see U.N. Doc. S/760 (mimeographed only). Apparently the questionnaire was ignored by the Yemen. A similar questionnaire was addressed to the "Jewish Authorities in Palestine," and a reply, emanating from the Provisional Government of Israel, was given to the Security Council by a person designated in the *Official Records* as the representative of the Jewish Agency for Palestine, in the course of the 301st meeting. 3 U.N. SCOR, No. 72, at 8 (1948).

statements were accompanied by quite unambiguous actions. The Arab states have, each in its own way, made clear their position, that they regard themselves as being at war, in a state of belligerency with Israel. The absence of declarations of war is merely the absence of irrelevant formalities.

In that way, what Israel calls the War of Independence and which, as has regrettably transpired, was merely the first phase in a state of war which has now lasted for some twenty years, commenced. The Arab states partly succeeded in their objective. By dint of their efforts, they thwarted the implementation of that part of the General Assembly's resolution which aimed to give satisfaction to Arab aspirations and meet Arab claims for self-determination. Instead of Palestine being divided into an Arab state and a Jewish state, linked under the umbrella of an over-all economic union, the Arab parts of the country came under the occupation of Jordan and Egypt, respectively. This should be remembered today, when the right of the Arabs of Palestine to self-determination is asserted. It was they who rejected it in 1948. On the other hand, the Jews succeeded in beating off the Arab attacks on them.

This phase of the war was brought to an end by a series of armistice agreements negotiated directly by the parties under the chairmanship of a United Nations representative during the first seven months of 1949.[21] The central feature of those armistice agreements was their declared intention to form a transition to permanent peace, and their detailed provisions regarding the establishment and demarcation of the armistice lines to serve as a temporary expedient pending the drawing up of agreed frontiers. The armistice regime was a temporary stopgap measure which was supposed to bring an end to that military phase and constitute the basis for a peaceful settlement of all outstanding problems, including of course the Arab refugee problem.[22] The work of producing the peace settlement was conferred on the parties directly concerned, assisted by a three-power Palestine Conciliation Commission (United States, France, and Turkey), whose broad terms of reference were laid down by the General Assembly in its resolution 194 (III) of December 11, 1948.[22a]

It is not necessary now to trace in detail the tortuous paths followed by the Palestine Conciliation Commission. It is sufficient to state that by the end of 1951 it was leading nowhere.[23] Already by that time, the armistice agreements were coming under severe strain, and a very fundamental divergence of approach between

---

[21] See S. ROSENNE, ISRAEL'S ARMISTICE AGREEMENTS WITH THE ARAB STATES (1951); N. BAR-YAACOV, THE ISRAEL-SYRIAN ARMISTICE, PROBLEMS OF INTERPRETATION (1967). No comparable works of Arab provenance are known to us. For the official texts of the agreements, see 42 U.N.T.S. 251 (Egypt), 287 (Lebanon), 303 (Jordan), and 327 (Syria).

[22] Thus the Security Council, in its resolution 73 of August 11, 1949, after noting with satisfaction the conclusion of the agreements, expressed the hope that the governments concerned would by negotiations seek to extend their scope and seek agreement by negotiations on the final settlement of all outstanding questions.

[22a] 3 U.N. GAOR, pt. 1, Resolutions 21, U.N. Doc. A/810 (1948).

[23] Cf. Progress Report of the United Nations Conciliation Commission for Palestine covering the period from January 23 to November 19, 1951. 6 U.N. GAOR, Supp. 18, U.N. Doc. A/1985 (1951).

Israel and the Arab states—symptomatic of the fundamental differences on the very nature of the legal framework between them to which allusion has been made—began to make its presence felt as a matter of political reality. If this, which is ostensibly a question of interpretation, is mentioned now, it is because it seems that of all the many and complicated legal issues which lie behind the different strands of the Middle East situation, this is one of the most significant, both in terms of the concrete political situation which we face and in terms of the larger issues with which this symposium is concerned, namely, the test of international law in the contemporary world.

That difference of interpretation can be briefly summarized. I think it would be fair to the Arab states if their position were put in these words—it should be explained that the writer had the opportunity of discussing this very problem with an eminent lawyer in the service of Egypt in 1951, Mr. Waheed Raafat, at the time the greatest Egyptian authority on the law of the Suez Canal. He explained it in this way. Under the established law of nations, he said, an armistice is an incident of war, and the state of war continues until it is replaced by a peace treaty. The jural relations between the states concerned are governed by the laws of war. In support of this view, he adduced a number of learned authorities and many decisions of the Allied Prize Courts after the two World Wars. The only limitation on belligerent rights, the only contraction of the state of war which he could recognize, were those which flowed directly and specifically from the terms of the armistice agreement narrowly interpreted. This, in a nutshell, was the Arab view by 1951 and they seem to have held that view consistently all the time to this day, because a very similar doctrine was expounded by the representative of the United Arab Republic in the Security Council, at the end of last May.[24] Since then, the Khartoum Arab Summit Conference on September 1, 1967 reaffirmed the main principles of Arab policy, namely: no peace with Israel, no recognition of Israel, and no negotiations with it.[25] On the other hand, the Arab position does not apparently give any recognition to the principle of reciprocity, which occupies a central place in international legal relationships and one which is left untouched by the Charter.

Israel has not, as far as I am aware, expressed any views on what might have been the rules of international law before the League of Nations. What we do contest is that this is the law today, at all events as between members of the United Nations.[26] As a matter of principle we believe that the very existence of a state of war is utterly incompatible with membership in the United Nations and the obligations imposed by the Charter. We note that even the Council of the League took this view, in

---

[24] *Cf.* the statement of Ambassador El Kony at the 1343rd meeting of the Security Council on May 29, 1967. U.N. Doc. S/PV.1343, at 36 (1967).

[25] N.Y. Times, Sept. 2, 1967, at 1, col. 5.

[26] For an authoritative non-official Israeli exposition of that thesis, see N. FEINBERG, THE LEGALITY OF A "STATE OF WAR" AFTER THE CESSATION OF HOSTILITIES UNDER THE CHARTER OF THE UNITED NATIONS AND THE COVENANT OF THE LEAGUE OF NATIONS (1961).

connection with the dispute between Poland and Lithuania over Vilna,[27] and surely the Charter is not a retreat from the Covenant. That is a major premise. We go on to say that even regardless of that, the armistice agreements meant what they said and that they prohibited entirely any continuation of the state of war and any attempt to exercise belligerent rights on land, on sea or in the air, whether by regular military forces or by para-military forces and irregulars. This view, it seems to us, was forcefully upheld by the Security Council after a detailed discussion on this very issue, in its resolution 95 of September 1, 1951, as reaffirmed in a consensus decision of 1955.[28]

This is not a doctrinal refinement. It might be were it only a matter for academies and books. But when, on the one hand, it is juxtaposed with the subjective natural law concepts which are characteristic of so much of the Arab exposition on the legal and philosophical plane, and when, on the other hand, it is coupled with actions which under no circumstances are compatible with peaceful relations and are only to be explained as manifestations of claims of belligerency, of an *animus belligerendi*, it will be seen that the apparently technical issue of interpretation goes to the very roots of Arab-Israeli relations. For reduced to essentials, it is a symbol for the real crisis in the Middle East, a crisis which in substance has not changed from 1948 to this day. On the level of practical politics, the two theses are utterly irreconcilable and their existence side by side is a guarantee for political instability, to put it at its lowest, and a prescription for a fighting war when the tension reaches boiling point.

That is precisely what has happened. Scarcely was the ink dry on the armistice agreements when the old story of forays, raids, infiltration, acts of banditry and sabotage from across the armistice lines into Israel recommenced. The provocations were deliberate and were strong and when they became too much, Israel responded with deliberate but controlled force directed against the bases and centers from which the raiders and infiltrators proceeded. Whereas the Israeli Government acknowledged responsibility for its decisions and for the acts of its armed forces, the Arab Governments repeatedly disclaimed all responsibility for their decisions and for any of these acts emanating from their territories, under the pretext that they were perpetrated by irregulars and persons not amenable to their control. One result of this has been that in the Security Council, a number of resolutions have been adopted purportedly condemning Israel for this defensive use of her armed forces while the Arab states, behind the shield of the Soviet veto, have been virtually always protected against expressions of disapproval, even in the mildest of terms, by the organ responsible for the maintenance of international peace and security.[29] In

[27] 9 LEAGUE OF NATIONS OFF. J. 176-78 (1928).

[28] 10 U.N. SCOR, 688th meeting, paras. 98-102, at 20 (1955).

[29] As an example, see the proceedings of the 1319th meeting of the Security Council on November 4, 1966, when the Soviet veto prevented the adoption of a mild draft resolution which would have invited the Government of Syria to strengthen its measures for preventing that type of incident. Much

fact, in all the period from 1955 onwards, it was not until the Security Council's resolution 248, adopted on March 24, 1968, that the Security Council pronounced itself on these Arab acts and even then it used very indirect language.[30]

By 1956 the Israeli Government reached the conclusion that the constant violation of the armistice agreement by Egypt, its exploitation as a cover for perpetrating armed attacks against Israel on the basis of this continuation of the state of war doctrine, distorted the motive and purpose of the armistice agreement and deprived it of all its functions. The Egyptian attitude and actions constituted an unjustified repudiation of the agreement so that no useful purpose would be served by returning to it. It informed the Secretary-General of the United Nations of this and, through him, the Egyptian Government.[31] The arrangements which were then made to restore tranquility to the region took account of this at least in a *de facto* way. For instead of the armistice agreement and the special machinery for supervising its implementation, the UNEF was created and stationed along the sensitive areas of Sinai, that is, along the borders of the Gaza Strip and at the headland which forms the Strait of Tiran.[32] However, no direct agreement was then made between Israel and Egypt. All rested on indirect, and sometimes imprecise and unformulated, understandings, sometimes on a government-to-government basis, and sometimes on an individual basis.[33]

For several years the present Secretary-General of the United Nations had been drawing attention to the general fragility of the status of UNEF in the absence of progress towards the settlement of outstanding questions.[34] Furthermore, the question of UNEF, of its very constitutionality in United Nations terms, became entangled in another question which at the time loomed larger but in retrospect appears to have been of less long-term significance. I am referring to the question of the

---

earlier, in resolution 101 of November 24, 1953, the Security Council had admonished Jordan in those terms. In resolution 107 of March 30, 1955, it suggested ways in which "infiltration could be reduced to an occasional nuisance."

[30] See the discussion at the 1401st to 1407th meetings of the Security Council, between March 21 and 24, 1968. U.N. Docs. S/PV.1401-1407 (1968).

[31] Aide-mémoire of November 3, 1956. 11 U.N. GAOR, Annexes, Agenda Item No. 5, at 9, U.N. Doc. A/3279 (1956).

[32] *Cf.* UNEF, Report of the Secretary-General, 12 U.N. GAOR, Annexes, Agenda Item No. 65, at 1, U.N. Doc. A/3694 and Add. 1 (1957). Annual reports were submitted subsequently until 1966.

[33] The confusion over the legal basis for UNEF's operation was increased in 1967. The views of the present Secretary-General are contained in Report of the Secretary-General on the Withdrawal of the United Nations Emergency Force, U.N. GAOR, 5th Emer. Spec. Sess., Annexes, Agenda Item No. 5, at 4, 9, U.N. Doc. A/6730 and Add. 1-3 (1967). Nevertheless, the matter is still highly controversial.

[34] "It is an unhappy statement to have to make, but it is a reality all too apparent that, despite almost a decade of relative quiet along the long line on which UNEF is deployed, relations between the peoples on the opposite sides of the line are such that if the United Nations buffer should be removed, serious fighting would, quite likely, soon be resumed."
UNEF, Report of the Secretary-General, 21 U.N. GAOR, Annexes, Agenda Item No. 21, at 2, U.N. Doc. A/6406 (1966). That same year U Thant pointed out that the presence of a force like UNEF might actually free the parties "from any pressing obligation to exert a really serious effort towards a settlement of their differences." Introduction to the Annual Report of the Secretary-General on the Work of the Organization, June 16, 1965-June 15, 1966, *id.*, Supp. 1A, at 5, U.N. Doc. A/6301/Add. 1, at 17 (1966).

Congo and the issue of the interpretation of a number of cardinal provisions in the United Nations Charter which led to the crisis of the nineteenth session of the General Assembly in 1964.[35]

After a temporary but precarious respite, the same situation returned with even greater intensity, and already by 1965 it became evident that unless something was done crisis would again creep upon the Middle Eastern world. Yet nothing was done about it. The old story repeated itself. What is more the Arab states, and especially Syria and Egypt, encouraged by Soviet backing and by their own deteriorating relations with the West, and heavily armed, grew more arrogant and truculent. When the Egyptian Government decided in May 1967 to request the peremptory removal of UNEF,[36] the vacuousness of the settlement of 1957 as it related to Israel and Egypt and the shifting sands on which the pacification of the area rested became evident. The real and urgent threat posed to Israel's very existence by the massed armies of her immediate neighbors, backed by all the other Arab states, led straight to the third phase of the Arab-Israeli war, which goes by the name already of the Six Days War of June 1967.

III

THE SECURITY COUNCIL RESOLUTION OF NOVEMBER 22, 1967

A. Background and Scope

The principal events since then are fresh in everyone's mind. The fighting terminated after Israel, Egypt, Jordan, Iraq, Lebanon, and Syria had accepted on the basis of reciprocity a series of resolutions adopted by the Security Council calling for a cease-fire "as a first step." Although all the Arab states had in one way or another signified their participation in the Arabs' war on Israel, some of them even participating actively in it, it will be noted that the acceptance of the cease-fire was in fact limited to the four limitrophe states together with Iraq, which had been most actively concerned. Kuwait unabashedly rejected the cease-fire in a formal communication to the Secretary-General of the United Nations, and the other Arab states—including Algeria, from which country units had participated in the fighting and which is today a member of the Security Council—made no response at all.[37] The Security Council's call for a cease-fire was unconditional. Furthermore, the Council had rejected, as did the emergency special session of the General Assembly shortly thereafter, all attempts to attribute responsibility for the breakdown of peace to one side or another. All proposals tending to attribute to Israel

---

[35] Advisory Opinion on Expenses of the United Nations, [1962] I.C.J. 151.

[36] See Report of the Secretary-General on the Withdrawal of UNEF, *supra* note 33.

[37] On the status of the acceptance of the cease-fire resolutions, see U.N. Docs. S/7985 and S/8279, of June 15 and November 30, 1967, respectively. For the cease-fire resolutions themselves, see Security Council resolutions 233, June 6, 1967; 234, June 7, 1967; and 235, June 9, 1967. Iraq's acceptance of the cease-fire was couched in very roundabout terms. 22 U.N. SCOR, Supp. April-June 1967, at 260, U.N. Doc. S/7990. For the refusal of Kuwait, see U.N. Doc. S/7968 (mimeographed only).

responsibility for "aggression" were flatly rejected.[38] As a result, the cease-fire took effect on the basis of the military lines as they existed on the dates in question. It is unnecessary to describe those lines in detail: the Suez Canal with Egypt, the River Jordan with Jordan, and the Golan Heights with Syria.

The establishment of the cease-fire was followed by a long period of difficult negotiations which culminated in the Security Council's resolution 242 of November 22, 1967, adopted unanimously by all its fifteen members. Carefully drawn up in the English language,[39] after every word had been weighed, that resolution reads:

> *The Security Council,*
>
> *Expressing* its continuing concern with the grave situation in the Middle East,
>
> *Emphasizing* the inadmissibility of the acquisition of territory by war and the need to work for a just and lasting peace in which every State in the area can live in security,
>
> *Emphasizing further* that all Member States in their acceptance of the Charter of the United Nations have undertaken a commitment to act in accordance with Article 2 of the Charter,
>
> 1. *Affirms* that the fulfilment of Charter principles requires the establishment of a just and lasting peace in the Middle East which should include the application of both the following principles:
>
> (i) Withdrawal of Israeli armed forces from territories occupied in the recent conflict;
>
> (ii) Termination of all claims or states of belligerency and respect for and acknowledgment of the sovereignty, territorial integrity and political independence of every State in the area and their right to live in peace within secure and recognized boundaries free from threats or acts of force;
>
> 2. *Affirms further* the necessity
>
> (a) For guaranteeing freedom of navigation through international waterways in the area;
>
> (b) For achieving a just settlement of the refugee problem;
>
> (c) For guaranteeing the territorial inviolability and political independence of every State in the area, through measures including the establishment of demilitarized zones;
>
> 3. *Requests* the Secretary-General to designate a Special Representative to proceed to the Middle East to establish and maintain contacts with the States concerned in order to promote agreement and assist efforts to achieve a peaceful and accepted settlement in accordance with the provisions and principles in this resolution;
>
> 4. *Requests* the Secretary-General to report to the Security Council on the progress of the efforts of the Special Representative as soon as possible.

---

[38] See in particular the voting at the 1360th meeting of the Security Council on June 14, 1967 (U.N. Doc. S/PV.1360) and at the 1548th Plenary meeting of the General Assembly on July 4, 1967, A/PV.1548). See also the statement of the representative of Israel at the 1618th meeting of the General Assembly on December 4, 1967, U.N. Doc. A/PV.1618, at 133.

[39] For the original draft, see U.N. Doc. S/8247 (1967).

This resolution indicates the major problems the solution of which will, in the unanimous view of the members of the Security Council, lead to a just and lasting peace in the Middle East. It is an entity in itself and is not to be eroded away by selective and tendentious interpretations and choosiness. A few words about some of the legal aspects underlying it would now be appropriate.

In the first place, even if this smacks a little of legal technicalities, it may be mentioned that the resolution was proposed and adopted within the general framework of chapter VI of the United Nations Charter.[40] The significance of this would be that technically the resolution has the status of a recommendation of the Security Council. It is to be regarded essentially as a series of guidelines and signposts pointing in the direction of peace.

Looked at in more historical perspective, it is significant—a point which is often overlooked—that it is the first resolution in all the long history of the United Nations dealing with the Middle East situation that emphatically and deliberately calls for "a just and lasting peace." The political implications of the difference of interpretation to which allusion has been made, and the voting strength of the Arab states and their friends in the United Nations, had succeeded in keeping the word "peace" virtually unused in United Nations jurisprudence regarding the Middle East.[41] The body which has the primary responsibility for the maintenance of international peace in fact abdicated its function to maintain peace in the Middle East. It was content to let things drift, with the consequences all too familiar to us. Two major legal problems underlie this. In the first place it is often thought that multilateral diplomacy through common membership in a political organization such as the United Nations could provide an adequate general juridical framework for bilateral

---

[40] Cf. the reference by the sponsor, the representative of the United Kingdom, to chapter VI of the Charter when he introduced the draft resolution at the 1379th meeting of the Security Council on November 16, 1967. U.N. Doc. S/PV.1379, at 6.

[41] The relevant pronouncements make curious reading. The Security Council, in its resolution 62 of November 16, 1948, called upon the parties to negotiate the armistice agreements "in order to eliminate the threat to the peace in Palestine and to facilitate the transition from the present truce to permanent peace." In resolution 73 of August 11, 1949, taking note of the conclusion of the armistice agreements, it urged the parties to extend their scope and by negotiation to achieve agreement on the final settlement of all outstanding questions. In its resolution 89 of November 17, 1950, it reminded the parties of their obligations under the Charter and under the armistice agreements to settle their outstanding issues. In its resolution 93 of May 18, 1951, it expressed some concern at the lack of progress. In its resolution 95 of September 1, 1951, a similar reference appears. In its resolution 101 of November 24, 1953, it reaffirmed the necessity to make progress towards the settlement of outstanding questions. General Assembly resolution 186(S-2) of May 14, 1948 (U.N. GAOR, 2d Spec. Sess., Resolutions 5, U.N. Doc. A/555 (1948)) included among the terms of reference of the U.N. Mediator in Palestine to "promote a peaceful adjustment of the future situation of Palestine." Resolution 194(III) of December 11, 1948 called upon the parties to seek agreement with a view to the final settlement of all questions outstanding between them. For citation see note 22a supra. This sentiment was repeated in resolutions 394 of December 14, 1950 (5 id., Supp. 20, at 24, U.N. Doc. A/1775 (1950)) and 512 of January 26, 1952 (6 id., Supp. 20, at 11, U.N. Doc. A/2119 (1952)), which also considered that the governments concerned have the primary responsibility for reaching a settlement of their outstanding differences. Resolution 1125 of February 2, 1957 referred to "achieving situations conducive to the maintenance of peaceful conditions in the area." 11 id., Supp. 17, at 62, U.N. Doc. A/3572 (1957).

relations between individual members of the Organization. Israel's experience shows that this is not so. In a way it can be said that the armistice agreements attempted to fill this juridical need, and of course they did for a time. With their disappearance, which is now tacitly acknowledged by the Security Council—for not one of the resolutions adopted in 1967 makes any reference to them[42]—the void has become all the more glaring. The Charter of the United Nations may provide a series of general principles upon which the international relations of all states should be oriented. But these principles by themselves are not sufficiently closely woven together to provide an adequate juridical framework for any sort of bilateral relations, so long as neither general international law nor United Nations machinery provides other means of bridging the gap save negotiations and agreement *inter partes.* The question here cannot be assimilated to the more familiar situation in which states have temporarily broken off diplomatic relations with each other. In those circumstances, the general framework of international law, whether customary law or conventional law, operates to retain all the essential elements of juridical relationships despite the temporary obstacles of an essentially political character. In the Middle East situation, however, the general rules of international law have not been allowed to operate at all. This is symbolized on the general level by the refusal of the Arab states to recognize Israel,[43] and on the particular level by a series of carefully drawn reservations which the Arab states attach to their participation in general multilateral treaties, and intended to prevent any form of treaty relationship coming into force between them and Israel.[44]

In the second place, it must be recalled that one of the fundamental principles for the effective operation of international law in any circumstance is the principle of reciprocity. The rules of international law are abstractions until they come to be reciprocally applied in concrete circumstances. If one were to criticize the legal tenet of the Government of Israel in relation to the problem of interpretation of the armistice agreements mentioned earlier, it could fairly be said that it attached insufficient weight to this element of reciprocity. As a result of the events which led to the final collapse of the armistice system in the early part of 1967, it has become necessary to give greater weight to this element of reciprocity. So while we continue to hold that, in principle, the maintenance of a state of war is incompatible with obligations under the Charter, the principle of reciprocity, which is certainly not excluded by the Charter, leads to the conclusion that if the Arab states insist on placing their juridical relations with Israel on that basis, Israel for its part is entitled,

---

[42] The only comment on this was made by the Permanent Representative of Syria in his letter to the Secretary-General of the United Nations of July 25, 1967. U.N. Docs. S/8094, A/6775 (1967). Determining is the absence of reaction by any member of the Security Council.

[43] Reiterated in the Khartoum resolution of the Arab Summit Conference of September 1, 1967, referred to above. See note 25 *supra.*

[44] For a convenient illustration of this, compare *Depositary Practice in Relation to Reservations, Report of the Secretary-General,* 2 Y.B. INT'L L. COMM'N 74, 87, U.N. Doc. A/5687 (1965).

if not obliged, to meet them on the same ground. It cannot be accepted that one side is entitled to base its policies and actions on the law of war and on claims of belligerency, and the other side not.

B. Withdrawal of Forces

The Security Council's resolution commences with a reference to what it calls "the inadmissibility of the acquisition of territory by war." Something must be said about that because in one form or another this idea occupied a prominent place in the discussions of 1967.

Those words reformulate a Spanish expression which has become almost epigrammatic in United Nations circles, namely *"La victoria no da derechos."* This notion is one which, in that form, appears in a number of important treaties of Latin America. It lies behind the so-called Stimson Doctrine[45] and the Briand-Kellogg Pact of August 27, 1928,[46] and traces of it are also found in Article 2, paragraph 4, of the United Nations Charter. But the idea did not originate with them. In fact, it is nothing more than the established rule of international law that only a formal agreement, and more particularly after a war, usually a treaty of peace, is competent to transfer territory from one country to another. It is certainly in that sense, and in a juridical context that embodied the doctrine of *uti possidetis*, that the Spanish expression was first used by the Minister for Foreign Affairs of the Argentine, Sr. Mariano Varela, in his note of December 27, 1869 in connection with the war between Argentina, Brazil and Uruguay on the one hand and Paraguay on the other. The Argentine Government then argued that military victory by itself did not give rights to territory, and that the disposition of territory could only follow from an international agreement between the parties concerned, and the Spanish phrase, now aphoristic, is but a small part of a much longer contention.[47]

---

[45] See 26 Am. J. Int'l L. 342 (1932).

[46] 94 L.N.T.S. 57.

[47] For the text of that Note, see Republica Argentina, Memoria de Relaciones Exteriores de la Republica 164 (1870). The relevant passage reads as follows:

"La República Argentina cree y sostiene, apoyada en títulos incontestables, que el territorio que se cuestiona le pertenece esclusivamente, y que su posesion por parte del Paraguay ha sido una usurpacion á derechos nuestros. Residiendo ese territorio por la victoria del las armas aliadas, su ocupacion ha sido un hecho natural y lójico. Sin embargo, el Gobierno Argentino ha sostenido hace muy poco tiempo en discusiones con el representante de S.M. el Emperador del Brasil, que la victoria no dá derecho á las naciones aliadas, para declarar por sí, límites suyos los que el tratado señala.

"Cree mi Gobierno, hoy como entonces, que los limites deben ser discutidos con el Gobierno que se establezca en el Paraguay, y que su fijacion será establecida en los tratados que se celebren despues de exhibidas por las partes contratantes, los títulos en que cada uno apoye sus derechos."
In this connection, attention is called to the following:
The Special Committee on Principles of International Law Concerning Friendly Relations and Co-operation Among States in Accordance with the Charter of the United Nations at its 1967 session discussed the principle that states shall refrain in their international relations from the threat or use of force against the territorial integrity or political independence of any state or in any other manner inconsistent with the purposes of the United Nations, *i.e.*, the interrelationship, above all, of Article 2, paragraph 4, and Article 51 of the Charter. In the course of the discussion there was general agreement that the principle

In the context in which the Security Council used that expression, this seems to be the only possible meaning because it is immediately followed by an emphatic statement on the need to work for a just and lasting peace in which every state in the area can live in security.

As already indicated, the law does not operate in a vacuum. The Security Council was not throwing out maxims like the well-known maxims of equity, but was making a concrete recommendation to deal with a concrete set of circumstances. In doing that it seems to have recalled, in a form which in the particular circumstances was politically attractive, an established rule of international law which, as far as is known, is fully operative throughout the whole world up to the present day.

In point of fact any attempt to read too much into that assertion by the Security Council, or into the Spanish phrase from which it may have originated, is not likely to be fruitful in terms of advancing concrete solutions to concrete problems. If the acquisition of territory by war is inadmissible as a general proposition, it could be recalled that the United Arab Republic has no title to the Gaza Strip and the Kingdom of Jordan no title to the West Bank and the part of Jerusalem it formerly occupied. One could even go further and point to many defects in the political map of the world which would follow from any blind and unquestioning acceptance of the bald statement that victory does not give rights.

It is in that context that the question of the withdrawal of Israeli forces has to be viewed. The relevant portion of the English text of the Security Council resolution should be carefully scrutinized. It does not say "withdrawal of *the* Israeli armed forces from *the* territories occupied in the recent conflict" (even though that is a possible interpretation of some of the other language versions of the resolution). It refers to "withdrawal of Israeli armed forces from territories occupied in the recent conflict." It does not say *what* is to be withdrawn. It does not say to *where* the Israeli forces are to withdraw. It does not say *when* they are to withdraw. This is no accident. In the first place, and this remark is directed particularly to those who are attracted by the process of historical interpretation, it may be recalled that

---

applied in relation to present or existing boundaries of a state. On the other hand, a discussion arose as to whether international lines of demarcation were the equivalent of boundaries for this purpose. The difference was not reconciled, and the Committee's Report contains the following statement from the Report of the Working Group of the Drafting Committee:

"7. *Military occupation and non-recognition of situations brought about by the illegal threat or use of force*

"There was no agreement on the inclusion of a statement to the effect that the territory of a State may never be the object of military occupation or other measures of force on any grounds whatsoever.

"Nor was there agreement whether a statement should be included requiring that situations brought about by an illegal threat or use of force would not be recognized."

See the Committee's Report, to be published in the official records of the twenty-second session of the General Assembly, Annexes, Agenda Item No. 87, para. 107; for provisional version, see U.N. Doc. A/6799, at 62 (1967).

both the Security Council and the General Assembly had rejected all draft resolutions the intent of which was to require the withdrawal, immediate or otherwise, of all Israeli forces back to the lines they occupied on June 5, 1967.[48] There is widespread recognition that those lines are not satisfactory as permanent frontiers and that the establishment of just and lasting peace requires the establishment of new and more viable frontiers.[49] The Security Council did not attempt to spell out what those new frontiers should be. It left that to be elaborated by the normal free play of diplomatic processes. Here, it might be added, the Security Council was acting much in the way it had acted in 1948 when it adopted resolution 62 calling for negotiations for armistice agreements. Then, too, it did not attempt to spell out what the armistice lines should be. In fact the greater part of the negotiations for those armistice agreements consisted in detailed and direct discussion between the delegations as to what the appropriate lines should be, having regard to actual conditions on the ground.

In the structure of the Security Council's resolution the withdrawal of Israeli armed forces does not imply necessarily any corresponding advance of the armed forces of any Arab State, nor by itself does it imply the determination of territorial sovereignty over the affected areas. The resolution also refers specifically to the possibility of establishing demilitarized zones. This, too, follows the experience of the armistice agreements as well as more general international experience. The demilitarized zones created as a result of the armistice agreements were not notably successful. One of the reasons is that because at the time everybody concerned believed the armistice agreements would be of short duration, many of the practical details of the demilitarized zones were left unsettled, pending the peace treaty which was thought to be not far off. However, that unhappy experience does not preclude the establishment of new demilitarized zones as part of a wider agreement and settlement, but one of the essential conditions for this would be not again to leave more things unsaid than said.

In that way the Security Council indicates that what is required is, the establishment of secure and recognized boundaries in which all the states of the area can live in political independence and peace, free from threats and acts of force. This is to be accompanied by the termination of all claims and states of belligerency, and respect for the sovereignty, territorial integrity, and political independence of all states in the area. This points directly back to the element of reciprocity which, as already explained, is one of the linch-pins of international law.

The Security Council's resolution mentions certain other problems, although its list is by no means an exhaustive catalog of all the outstanding problems in the area.

---

[48] See in particular the meetings mentioned in note 38 *supra*.

[49] *Cf.* these words by President Johnson on June 19, 1967: "The nations of the region have had only fragile and violated truce lines for 20 years. What they now need are recognized boundaries that will give them security against terror, destruction and war." 57 DEP'T STATE BULL. 31, 33 (1967).

C. International Waterways

Foremost among these is the necessity for guaranteeing freedom of navigation through international waterways in the area.

This refers to three important international waterways, two of which have been much discussed, and the third of which has only recently come into international prominence. The first two are the Suez Canal and the Strait of Tiran, and the third is the Strait of Bab-el-Mandeb, where the Red Sea joins the Indian Ocean by Aden and the Island of Perim.[50]

[50] On the Gulf of Aqaba and the Strait of Tiran, see Kennedy, *A Brief Geographical and Hydrographical Study of Bays and Estuaries the Coasts of Which Belong to Different States*, 1 UNITED NATIONS CONFERENCE ON LAW OF THE SEA, OFFICIAL RECORDS, 198, at 208, U.N. Doc. A/CONF. 13/15 (1958). On Bab-el-Mandeb, see Kennedy, *A Brief Geographical and Hydrographical Study of Straits Which Constitute Routes for International Traffic, id.* at 114, 115, U.N. Doc. A/CONF. 13/6 and Add. 1 (1958). And see, more generally, the British Admiralty publication, RED SEA AND GULF OF ADEN PILOT (1955). At the 1382nd meeting of the Security Council on November 22, 1967, the Israeli Foreign Minister referred to the necessity for "guaranteeing free navigation for all shipping, including that of Israel, in all the waterways leading to and from the Red Sea." U.N. Doc. S/PV.1382, at 46.

One of the Arab arguments in relation to the Strait of Tiran is that Israeli possession of any part of the coastline of the Gulf of Aqaba constitutes a breach of the armistice agreement with Egypt. That Agreement distinguished between what it called the Western Front and the Eastern Front (see Article VII and Annex 2). It made provision for the Egyptian controlled and Israeli controlled parts respectively of the Western Front only but was completely silent regarding the Eastern Front. This means that the specifics of what is there called the Eastern Front, which included what became the southern part of Israel down to Eilat (except for the actual frontier of Egypt itself), were not covered by the Egyptian agreement but remained for settlement later when the Jordan agreement should be concluded.

Very shortly after the signing of the Israel-Egyptian agreement, early in March 1949, Israeli forces advanced south to the littoral. Jordan complained to the Acting Mediator that this advance was a breach of the truce of July 15, 1948. There was no breach of the Israel-Egyptian Agreement, and no complaints of any kind were made by Egypt.

In the Acting Mediator's report of March 23, 1949, after investigation by United Nations observers, the following appears:

"1. Since 8 March 1949 Israeli military forces at considerably more than normal patrol strength have moved into the area between the Dead Sea and the Gulf of Aqaba in Palestine, and have taken up positions at several points which they had not previously occupied.

"2. There has never been anything in the nature of a military line in this area. It appears that Arab forces in small strength have recently patrolled in parts of the area, as have small Israeli patrols, in violation of the truce in both cases.

"3. The main movement of Israeli troops has been down the road in the Wadi Araba, which road runs for its whole length inside Palestine but close to the Palestine-Transjordan frontier.

"4. The complaint that Israeli troops crossed the Transjordan border could not be verified. On 18 March, the senior United Nations observer at Amman reported that no Israeli post existed at that time on the Transjordan side of Wadi Araba.

"5. The report that one body of Israeli troops entered Umm Reshresh (MR 145 885) by a road from the Egyptian side of the frontier could not be verified. No complaint of such movement has been received from Egyptian authorities though it has been established by the observers that an Israeli force reached Umm Reshresh by way of Ras En Negeb on the Egyptian frontier. The Egyptian-Israeli General Armistice Agreement defines the western half of this area, *i.e.*, west of a line running midway between the Egyptian and Transjordan frontiers, as the western front, in which only Israeli defensive forces, based on the settlements, may be maintained. The eastern half of this area, or the eastern front, pending the conclusion of an armistice agreement with Transjordan, remains fully subject to the existing truce."

And

"It is clear on the evidence available to me as a result of the investigation by United Nations observers since 7 March that Israeli forces have effectively occupied this area since that date.

This is not the time or place to discuss the detailed legal questions of these international waterways. It is sufficient to recall that the Suez Canal regime is governed essentially by the Constantinople Convention of 1888,[51] and the two straits are

Previous to 7 March Transjordan forces had lightly patrolled at least parts of the area, and it is contended by Transjordan sources that they had maintained fixed positions at Gharandal, Bir Qattar (MR 137 890), Ain El Weinba and Meliha (MR 162 968). It has not been possible to verify on the basis of a check by United Nations observers when such positions were established by Transjordan forces, but it is established that no Transjordan forces are now on the Palestine side of the frontier in this area. No fighting ever having taken place in that area before and no significant forces of either side having been concentrated there, it had not been necessary to place it under close observation or to define any truce lines.

"I am quite convinced that, other than those at Aqaba, any positions established in this area either by Transjordan or by Israeli forces have all been established since the existing truce came into effect on 18 July 1948, with the possible exception of Transjordan positions at Ain Habd and Kurnub, and have, therefore, been established contrary to the terms of that truce. Similarly, patrolling activity and reinforcement of pre-truce forces on either side of the frontier in this sector are in conflict with truce conditions which have been accepted by both sides."
4 U.N. SCOR, Supp. March 1949, 44, 46-48, U.N. Doc. S/1295 & Corr. 1 (1949).

This position was consolidated by the armistice agreement with Jordan as appears clearly from Article V and the annexed map. See also the report by the Acting Mediator, after the conclusion on March 11, 1949 of a cease-fire agreement between Israel and Jordan, in U.N. Docs. S/1284 and S/1284/ Corr. 1 (1949) (mimeographed only).

On May 23, 1949, Egypt submitted a complaint to the Mixed Armistice Commission on the occupation of Umm Reshresh and Bir Qattar. On February 8, 1950 the Commission, by a majority vote, decided that "[t]he advance of Israeli Forces of 10 March 1949 to the Gulf of Aqaba area and the occupation of Bir Qattar is a violation of the Egyptian-Israeli General Armistice Agreement." However, the contention that the advance of Israeli Forces on March 10, 1949 and occupation of Umm Reshresh were another violation of the agreement, was rejected by a majority vote of the Commission. Both sides appealed against parts of the decision to the Special Committee established by Article X of the agreement. On March 20, 1950, the Special Committee, by a majority vote, confirmed the decision of the Mixed Armistice Commission. Under the provisions of the agreement, this decision was final, but the Israeli Government found unacceptable the decision about Bir Qattar mainly on the ground that it was based upon a misinterpretation of Article VII of the agreement. This interpretation placed the Bir Qattar in the area of the Western Front, covered by Article VII, para. 4, from which all Israeli Forces were excluded, apart from defensive forces based on the settlements. The views of the Government of Israel on this subject were formulated officially in a letter from the Minister for Foreign Affairs to the Chief of Staff of UNTSO of June 23, 1950. In spite of the fact that this issue was not mentioned in the original Egyptian complaint to the Security Council regarding expulsion of Arabs from the Negev (5 U.N. SCOR, Supp. Sept.-Dec. 1950, at 23, U.N. Doc. S/1790 (1950)), it was, nevertheless, discussed in the 511th, 514th, 517th, 518th, 522nd, and 524th meetings of the Council. In the course of the 522nd meeting of the Council, Mr. Eban explained that following the "assurances and clarifications" which emerged from conversations with the Chief of Staff securing Israel's interests, Israel was able to modify its attitude as regards Bir Qattar. Consequently, the Security Council, in its resolution 89 of November 17, 1950, inter alia took note of the Government of Israel's statement that "Israeli forces will evacuate Bir Qattar pursuant to the 20 March 1950 decision of the Special Committee . . . and that the Israeli Armed Forces will withdraw to positions authorized by the Armistice Agreement." In his letter dated March 12, 1951 to the President of the Security Council, the Chief of Staff informed the Security Council that "a United Nations observer visited Bir Qattar on January 3, 1951 and found no evidence of military positions there, and former defence works had been filled in." 6 U.N. SCOR, Supp. April-June 1951, at 11, U.N. Doc. S/2049 (1951).

Egypt did not pursue the question of Aqaba and Umm Reshresh any further and thus left the status of the area, including that of Umm Reshresh, outside the scope of the Israel-Egyptian armistice agreement, recognizing it to be within the area covered by the Israel-Jordan agreement.

[51] For the authentic French text, see 61 BRIT. & FOR. STATE PAPERS 293 (1887-88). For a contemporary English translation by the British Government, see Great Britain, Parliamentary Papers, 1889, Commercial No. 2, C. 5623. For a later translation by the United States Government, see THE SUEZ PROBLEM, JULY 26-SEPTEMBER 22, 1956, U.S. DEP'T OF STATE, PUB. No. 6392, at 16 (1956).

under the legal regime of international straits of customary international law or, which is much the same thing, the codified law particularly as embodied in Article 16 of the United Nations Convention on the Territorial Sea and Contiguous Zone of 1958.[52] Naturally these two sets of legal regimes are different in their details but they have in common an underlying conception which links back to the basic question of the juridical relationships *in toto* subsisting between Israel and the Arab States concerned. It is clear from all international experience that freedom of navigation through this type of international waterway cannot be guaranteed to anyone so long as any of the territorial states concerned adopts the subjective attitude that it is in a state of war with another state. It is in this respect that the Constantinople Convention of 1888 has proved inadequate because in practice the operation of the Canal has not been insulated from the politics of the territorial state;[53] and judging from the Tiran experience, much the same can be said regarding the general international law on the question of the innocent passage of ships through natural waterways linking two parts of the high seas or linking the high seas to the territorial sea of another state.

The issue of free navigation through international waterways of the Middle East has been one of the crucial issues of the smoldering Middle East crisis during the last twenty years. It twice provoked major outbreaks, in 1956 and in 1967. This aspect of the Middle East crisis may not be as spectacular as some of its other aspects. However, it it nonetheless real and pressing, and when I ponder on the problems which face us and direct my attention to the waterway problem, I cannot put out of my mind that the question of the freedom of the seas was a major issue in two world wars and found a place both in President Wilson's Fourteen Points[54] and in the Atlantic Charter.[55]

D. Refugees

The Arab refugee problem, too, is mentioned in the Security Council's resolution which affirmed the necessity for achieving a just settlement of the refugee problem.

Let it be stated quite frankly that this problem is not only tragic—there is an element of banality in that—but in some respects the most baffling of the individual problems which together combine to make up the crisis of the Middle East. It impinges pressingly on Israel's most vital interests.

Certain relatively secondary aspects of the problem may be disposed of first.

---

[52] 516 U.N.T.S. 205.

[53] S.C. Res. 118 (1956).

[54] The second of President Wilson's Fourteen Points referred to "[A]bsolute freedom of navigation upon the seas outside territorial waters, alike in peace and in war, except as the seas may be closed in whole or in part by international action for the enforcement of international covenants." 56 CONG. REC. 680 (1918).

[55] In the Atlantic Charter of August 14, 1941, the seventh of the common principles on which the future peace of the world should be based stated that "such a peace should enable all men to traverse the high seas and oceans without hindrance." 5 DEP'T STATE BULL. 125 (1941).

From the point of view of the existence of the problem, the question of how many refugees there are is not a matter of great moment because the fact remains that there are large numbers of refugees. Some of the exaggerated figures advanced from time to time may be contested, and some of the statistical data compiled by the United Nations or by other sources may be disputed. But that does not affect the broad political issue.

Again, while there may be technical distinctions between "old" and "new" refugees, the latter being those who became refugees after last June, it is doubtful if this goes to the fundamentals. Nevertheless, in both cases it has to be recognized that from one point of view the Arab refugee problem cannot be divorced from the general demographic problems of the State of Israel in which even before last June, Arab citizens constituted at least ten per cent of the total population and were increasing at a far higher rate than the Jewish majority. This, in turn, links it directly to the major problem of Israel-Arab relations.

That having been said, the refugee problem has two main aspects. The first is the welfare problem, which, serious though it is, should not be exaggerated and which is largely being handled by the United Nations Relief and Works Agency for Palestine Refugees with the assistance of governments including the Government of Israel. The second is the political problem, what the Security Council calls finding a "just settlement" of the refugee problem.

In brief, the Israeli view is that the just settlement of the refugee problem, which is earnestly desired, cannot be separated from the overall problem of the Middle East crisis. As far as I can understand the Arab position, it is based on two main elements. One is the so-called right of self-determination (of natural law origins) and the other is said to be based on the General Assembly resolution 194(III) of December 11, 1948.[56] Both these elements are an attempt to rationalize the refusal of the Arab governments, in which they have persisted since 1948, to cooperate in any manner, shape or form in the international efforts to produce a solution to the refugee problem through the traditional processes of resettlement in the different communities in which they now live. The Arab insistence on the absolute "right" of the refugees to return to their homes is regarded as a transparent attempt to win international support for the objective of planting a Trojan horse in Israel's midst. The Arab spokesmen, in their attempt to give legal verisimilitude to their approach, rely particularly on the following paragraph in General Assembly resolution 194(III):

> The General Assembly . . .
> *Resolves* that the refugees wishing to return to their homes and live at peace with their neighbours should be permitted to do so at the earliest practicable date, and that compensation should be paid for the property of those choosing not to return and for loss of or damage to property which, under principles of international law or in equity, should be made good by the Governments or authorities responsible;

---

[56] *Supra* note 22a.

Instructs the Conciliation Commission to facilitate the repatriation, resettlement and economic and social rehabilitation of the refugees and the payment of compensation, and to maintain close relations with the Director of the United Nations Relief for Palestine Refugees and, through him, with the appropriate organs and agencies of the United Nations.

Much could be said about that paragraph although probably all that there is to be said about it already appears in the records of the General Assembly. For that reason the present exposition will be limited to a few observations only.

It will, of course, be appreciated in the first place that this resolution as a whole has a status no different from that of any other resolution of the General Assembly. While there may be some ambiguity over the precise status, in legal terms, of a resolution of the General Assembly, one thing is, it is believed, generally accepted and that is that a General Assembly resolution is not legally a dispositive text. It neither creates rights nor does it take rights away. It is a political statement.

In the second place, Israel was not a member of the United Nations in 1948, although it participated in the committee meetings when the question was discussed. Those of the Arab states which then were members of the United Nations displayed little enthusiasm for that paragraph 11 and on some of the votes, even voted against it.

That paragraph itself is one paragraph out of a 15-paragraph resolution which established the Palestine Conciliation Commission and gave it broad terms of reference designed to carry through the transition to permanent peace initiated a little earlier by the Security Council when it called for the armistice negotiations. It was in that context that the two alternative solutions to the refugee problem, namely, return or resettlement with compensation, were placed. The assumption of the resolution was that the details would be elaborated by intergovernmental agreement. By a long process of erosion which is part and parcel of the whole Arab concept that their relations with Israel are relations of war, paragraph 11 became detached from its context. As a result the belief has been sedulously fostered that the Arab refugee problem exists and can be solved on its own, without intergovernmental agreement, and that paragraph 11 of the 1948 resolution, taken in an absolute fashion, indicates the only way in which the problem can be solved.

There is very little that the law can say on this. The Security Council's resolution of last November has recognized the real place of the refugee problem in the overall political context and it is in that context that its solution has been called for.

IV

CONCLUSION

This paper is confined to the major outstanding problems as they appear through the Security Council's resolution of last November. There are, of course, many others. I could mention by way of example all the questions of war damages, which are considerable; the question of compensation for the large numbers of Jewish refugees from the Arab states who have found refuge in Israel in a kind of population exchange and were forced to abandon their property in the Arab countries, in which, however, Israel accepted the moral and material responsibilities of a humane host-country and the Arab states did not; the questions of the Holy Places which give rise to extremely complex issues extending beyond the horizons of Israeli-Arab relations; and many technical questions relating to matters coming within the competence of the technical organs of the United Nations and of the Specialized Agencies. The list could be expanded *ad infinitum*. There is hardly a branch of international law or of United Nations law which does not come into play. But to do this would be a self-defeating task, because it would detract attention from the essentials.

The long drawn out crisis in the Middle East can be taken as a case study of the dangers to international peace which are created by a too loose and unthoughtful reliance on abstractions and general principles. It may come as a shock to realize that the principles of the United Nations Charter are of little value by themselves unless they are properly brought into a fully worked out context of political, military and legal relationships which correspond to the needs of the situation. It was too easily thought in the early days of the Middle East crisis that the United Nations Charter itself supplied a sufficiently taut legal regime which would be vigorous enough to protect all the states of the area from the threat or use of armed force against their political independence. It is this hope which has been disappointed. It is in this defect of contemporary international law and organization that the challenge to the international lawyer and political scientist lies. It is the inability of the contemporary legal order to provide any effective substitute for peaceful relations other than direct agreement between the states concerned that has led the government of Israel to the conviction that only full and direct-contractual relationships, freely arrived at, are the essential prerequisite for the establishment of a just and lasting peace in the area.

The "November Resolution" and Middle East Peace: Pitfall or Guidepost?

JULIUS STONE

Any serious hopes of settlement of the Arab-Israel dispute in the post-war years have centered on the Security Council Resolution 242[1] adopted on November 22, 1967, and the efforts of Dr. Gunnar Jarring as Special Representative to "promote agreement and assist efforts to achieve a peaceful and accepted settlement in accordance" with it.[2] The Resolution has been the focus of goodwill and sincere efforts to move the Middle East dispute to the conference table and the symbol of constructive compromise. It has also become a weapon of political warfare, against the hostile use of which the various Parties have also had to defend themselves.

The Resolution itself was presented by its British sponsor, under the dispute settlement provisions of Chapter 6 of the Charter, as a way of bridging the apparently unbridgeable opposing positions.[3] Its words and their order and composition are fertile in ambiguities, all no doubt important in securing its unanimous adoption. These ambiguities, and the "package" nature of all parts of the Resolution, were maintained into the vote by refusal of the British mover to allow the text of the Resolution to be tied to any particular interpretation offered by protagonists as a basis of their votes. Interpretation thus offered by a particular State as a basis of its acceptance of the Resolution may reserve some freedom to the State, but obviously cannot bind other States. The Resolution, in short,

---

* LL.M., Leeds, 1930; S.J.D., Harvard, 1932; D.C.L., Oxford, 1935. Challis Professor of International Law and Jurisprudence, University of Sydney.

1. S.C. Res. 242, 22 U.N. SCOR, 1382nd meeting 8-9 (1967).
2. *Id.* at para. 3.
3. *See* the United Kingdom representative's introduction on Nov. 16, 1967, 22 U.N. SCOR, 1379th meeting 6 (1967).

has to live its legal life with all the ambiguities of its birth; and only later substantive agreements of the Parties can redeem it from the pressures and twists of alternative possible meanings offered by partisans.

Professor Lall has given a vividly illuminating account of the complex off-stage diplomatic negotiations among the protagonists respectively of the "Afro-Asian," American, and British draft resolutions, which finally matured in the words as well as the silences of the November Resolution.[4] Even the very cautious optimism of diplomatic and political commentators concerning the chances of implementation may, against this kind of drafting background, appear oversanguine to the lawyer.[5]

I. THE ISSUES

The full text of the November Resolution[6] is as follows:

> *The Security Council,*
>
> *Expressing* its continuing concern with the grave situation in the Middle East,
>
> *Emphasizing* the inadmissibility of the acquisition of territory by war and the need to work for a just and lasting peace in which every State in the area can live in security,
>
> *Emphasizing further* that all Member States in their acceptance of the Charter of the United Nations have undertaken a commitment to act in accordance with Article 2 of the Charter,
>
> 1. *Affirms* that the fulfilment of Charter principles requires the establishment of a just and lasting peace in the Middle East which should include the application of both the following principles:
>
>   (i)   Withdrawal of Israel armed forces from territories occupied in the recent conflict;[7]
>
>   (ii)   Termination of all claims or states of belligerency and respect for and acknowledgement of the sovereignty, territorial integrity and political independence of every State in the area and

---

4.   A. LALL, THE U.N. AND THE MIDDLE EAST CRISIS, 1967, at 273 (1968).

5.   *Id.* at 230-71.

6.   S.C. Res. 242, 22 U.N. SCOR, 1382nd meeting 8-9 (1967).

7.   The French translation of the Resolution can be interpreted as referring to *"the* territories." On the other hand, the expression *"des territoires"* in that translation may be viewed merely as an idiomatic rendering into French, not intended to depart so substantially from the English text as to belie the above clear drafting history of the Resolution.

their right to live in peace within secure and recognized boundaries free from threats or acts of force;

    2.   *Affirms further* the necessity

        (a) For guaranteeing freedom of navigation through international waterways in the area;

        (b) For achieving a just settlement of the refugee problem;

        (c) For guaranteeing the territorial inviolability and political independence of every State in the area, through measures including the establishment of demilitarized zones;

    3.   *Requests* the Secretary-General to designate a Special Representative to proceed to the Middle East to establish and maintain contacts with the States concerned in order to promote agreement and assist efforts to achieve a peaceful and accepted settlement in accordance with the provisions and principles in this resolution;

    4.   *Requests* the Secretary-General to report to the Security Council on the progress of the efforts of the Special Representative as soon as possible.

Numerous legal questions have come into confused debate in the game of stop-go, and in the alternation of threats to resume fighting with self-righteous complaints of the other side's "noncompliance" or "refusal to implement" the November Resolution. All of these are related to the question whether, among any actions to be taken arising from the November Resolution, it can be said that any one specification must first be performed by one side or the other, without reference to progress in the performance of any other actions by its opponents. Two main, and opposed, theses of this kind will have to be considered. Though they have undergone varied formulations by both sides with the semantics of political warfare, and may do so in the future, an effort must be made to present fairly the continuing core elements of each. These core elements on each side will be called "the Israel threshold thesis" and "the Arab threshold thesis," respectively.

The Israel thesis seems to say that the entire November Resolution presupposes at least that each side acknowledges the legal standing and capacity of the other, and intends in good faith to agree and carry out the terms of peace. It would make nonsense of the Resolution, the thesis seems to say, if Israel, admitted as a "sovereign equal" State to the United Nations a generation ago, and so dealt with by most Members, could be deprived of such standing and rights by the conduct of Arab

States. Otherwise the November Resolution would legitimize an obvious illegality. For progress towards realizing the "principles" and "necessity" stated in the Resolution, therefore, the Arab States must, in this thesis, conform their conduct with this undoubted legal situation. And the best and most practical test of this conformity would be the Arab States' willingness to enter on a course leading to agreement on a genuine peace settlement with Israel, to what the Resolution terms a "just and lasting peace." The opposed Arab thesis, also to be examined here, is that Israel's withdrawal of all her armed forces from all the occupied territories must precede, in timing, action of the Arab States to change their present positions. Three main arguments, shortly to be elaborated, can be offered in support. The first is that (in the Arab view, of course) Israel occupied the territories concerned in consequence of aggression and that international law forbids her to retain any benefit flowing from this wrong. The second is that the "inadmissibility of the acquisition of territory by war" is recited in the preamble to the Resolution. The third is that the provision about withdrawal is also placed physically first in the body of the Resolution.

The November Resolution has become so much a weapon of political warfare, that its text and intention have faded from view behind interacting semantic exercises. For what can "acceptance" mean of so obviously a non-self-executing, interdependent and mutually delimiting set of guides towards a peace to be agreed? It is the more important to say at the outset that the operative part of the Resolution is predicated, beyond all doubt, on "the fulfilment" by both sides of Charter principles requiring "the establishment of a just and lasting peace in the Middle East . . . ." Whatever the other arguable matters to be considered later, the irreducible meaning of those words seems to preclude any party from basing its legal relations with another on such a motto as "no recognition, no negotiation, no peace."

II.   ACCEPTANCE OF THE "NOVEMBER RESOLUTION"

Before examining these opposed theses as to what obligation if any must be first carried out by one or other of the Parties, certain general legal points concerning the November Resolution must be clarified.

First, though that Resolution and indeed the various preceding draft resolutions do not on their face express whether they were to be adopted under Chapter 6 of the Charter concerning settlement of disputes, or with regard to threats to the peace, breaches of the peace or acts of aggression under Chapter 7, the British sponsor and other Members made clear that the former was the case.[8] The language of these resolutions, and of their protagonists in supporting them, implicitly but inescapably substantiates the Chapter 6 basis. The Afro-Asian position (India, Mali, Nigeria) in the Security Council, as introduced by Ambassador G. Parthasarathi, adopted the unsuccessful Latin American Draft which was presented to the Fifth Emergency Special Session of the General Assembly[9] as "the basic document of reference."[10] And the Latin American Draft did clearly refer, if not by number then by clear description, to Chapter 6. The Afro-Asian promotive Draft Resolution before the Assembly had urged action by the Security Council "guided by the principles of the Charter of the United Nations, in particular those contained in Articles 2 and 33."[11]

This means that the legal force of the November Resolution is only as a recommendation under Article 37(2), and not as a binding decision under Chapter 7 and Article 25. Indeed, it is probably the better view, which Egypt herself has from time to time invoked, that any resolution, even of the Security Council as to terms of settlement of disputes (as distinguished from action against threats to the peace, etc.) cannot, in any case, be legally binding on the parties, even if they purport to be "decisions" under Chapter 7. For under Article 25, only decisions "in accordance with the present

---

8. *See* his statement, 22 U.N. SCOR, 1373rd meeting 117(1967). *Cf.* statement of representative of Denmark, *id.* at 146; United States, 22 U.N. SCOR, 1377th meeting, 33-53 (1967); Canada, *id.* at 46; India, 22 U.N. SCOR, 1382nd meeting 23 (1967); Nigeria, 22 U.N. SCOR, 1373rd meeting 82 (1967).

9. U.N.G.A. Doc. A/4.523/Rev. 1 (1967).

10. 22 U.N. SCOR, 1373rd meeting 68 (1967).

11. *See* U.N.G.A. Doc. A/4.522/Rev. 1 (1967); A. LALL. *supra* note 4, at 153-68, 174 ff. *Cf.* as to Mr. Goldberg's statement on the United States Draft Resolution, 22 U.N. SCOR, 1373rd meeting 128-30 (1967); A. LALL, *supra* note 4, at 240-41.

Charter" are so made binding; and the Security Council's powers for the settlement of disputes given by Chapter 6 (Article 37) do not as to terms of settlement go beyond a power to "recommend."[12]

It is also quite clear from the post-voting statements by representatives of Israel and three Arab States (Egypt, Jordan and Syria) that none of them, for their part, regarded the November Resolution as binding on them.[13] Lall points out, however, that the Israel position at that stage showed the greater will to cooperate, the Arab States rather reverting to positions they had held long before the Resolution.

Second, whatever the legal force of the November Resolution, it cannot in any way qualify the obligation of all the States concerned to observe the cease-fire. No doubt, a successful outcome to negotiations could substitute some more satisfactory agreed order of legal relations than those based on the cease-fire undertaking. But until that is achieved, the cease-fire undertakings remain fully in force; and under international law a grave breach of them by one side is legal ground for the other to resume its freedom. All this applies, not only to Egypt and Jordan, but also to Syria which has openly rejected the November 22, 1967 Resolution.

Third, as already observed, the question of "acceptance" is central to the political warfare which surrounds the Resolution. This is the political aspect of the conflicting legal theses as to which side, if any, ought first of all to make some particular performance. Egypt, for example, has charged that Israel's refusal to withdraw from all the territories first was a rejection or "defiance" of the November Resolution as a whole. Israel, on the other hand, has seemed to assert that the Khartoum policies of no peace, no recognition, no negotiations, rendered Egyptian professions of "acceptance" rather spurious.

As to the more straightforward aspect of "acceptance" of the Resolution, the record shows that the Israel Government "acquiesced" at the time in the November Resolution as "a list

---

12.   See J.W. HALDERMAN, UNITED NATIONS AND THE RULE OF LAW 66-89, 167-72 passim (1967); J. STONE, LEGAL CONTROLS OF INTERNATIONAL CONFLICT 267-81 (1954).

13.   See the analysis with relevant quotations in A. LALL, supra note 4, at 263-65.

of principles on which the parties could base their agreement."
It later accepted "the call" in the November Resolution, "for
the promotion of agreement on the establishment of peace with
secure and recognized boundaries," and declared that it was
"prepared to negotiate on all matters included in the November
Resolution."[14] And on May 1, 1968, the Israel Representative
was instructed formally to confirm these positions and to
declare to the Security Council Israel's acceptance of the
November Resolution "for the promotion of agreement on the
establishment of a just and lasting peace" with each Arab State
and on all matters there dealt with.[15] On November 23, 1967,
President Nasser declared that while Egypt would give
consideration to the Resolution, Israel must first of all
withdraw from all the territories. And, moreover, Egypt would
still adhere to the Khartoum formula: No peace, no
recognition, no negotiation. Thereafter, the record also shows
that Egypt has from time to time declared "acceptance of," or
willingness to "implement" the Resolution. Yet as late as June
23, 1968, President Nasser still affirmed his understanding that
Egypt's "acceptance" of the Resolution was subject to her
continuing policies of "no negotiations . . . no peace with
Israel, no recognition of Israel . . . ."

Such a position, implying that withdrawal by Israel must
come first, before any assurance of movement towards a
genuine peace, was obviously unacceptable to Israel. The
Egyptian Foreign Minister's statement in the General Assembly
on October 10, 1968, though it showed no basic change in this
respect, did at that stage hint at willingness, in some unspecified
respect and degree, to leave the fixing of a timetable to Dr.
Jarring. On September 25, 1969, Foreign Minister Riad replied
to questions from the press in terms which implied that Egypt,
while rejecting direct negotiations so long as Israel remained in
occupation of Arab territories, might be willing to negotiate a
"package settlement" indirectly through Dr. Jarring, without
making prior Israel withdrawal a precondition of this. This was
shortly after Foreign Minister Eban had declared in the

---

14. Note to Dr. Jarring, Feb. 12, 1968, as reported in Foreign Minister Eban's
speech to the General Assembly of October 8, 1968. *See* U.N. Doc. A/PV. 1686 (1968).
15. U.N. Doc. S/PV. 1418 at 68-70 (1968).

Assembly that Israel was prepared for talks in which all issues were "negotiable." A Cairo spokesman on the next day seemed to suggest, however, that Mr. Riad's remarks of September 25, 1969, had not been accurately reported. It may conceivably be argued that Israel's acceptance of the Resolution covered a concealed rejection, parallel to Egypt's concealed rejection of it by coupling "acceptance" with reiteration of the Khartoum formula. The Resolution, as we have seen, spoke in the sponsor's English text of withdrawal of "Israel armed forces" from "territories, etc." But other language versions read "*the* Israel armed forces," "*the* territories" etc. In its ambiguity, therefore, it did not limit the territories from which withdrawal *might have to* be made; but it also *did not require* withdrawal from *all* the territories. It can be argued that Israel's declaration from time to time that she would not allow Jerusalem again to be divided attached to her acceptance a prejudgment of a matter on which the Resolution called for negotiation. As against this, three points must be considered.

One is that the Security Council, when it adopted the November Resolution, took no position on the Jerusalem question, although it was well-known. Second, insofar as some form of demilitarization, neutralization, or control by each religious denomination of its own Holy Places is not necessarily excluded by Israel's position, the inference of a concealed rejection of the Resolution seems less cogent.[16] (In the General Assembly on October 8, 1968, Foreign Minister Eban declared Israel's readiness to work out a regime for the Holy Places of Christianity, Islam and Judaism giving effect to their "universal character.") As late as September 1969, at a time when the impending general elections in Israel might have been expected to inhibit such an announcement, if annexation, as the General Assembly charged, had indeed taken place, Foreign Minister Eban declared explicitly that the East Jerusalem question remained "negotiable." In any case, East Jerusalem, though of course important, is but a small part of the territories from which Egypt demands a complete Israel withdrawal.

---

16. On this, and the legal effect of the various Israel pronouncements, and the related resolutions, see J. STONE, NO PEACE—NO WAR IN THE MIDDLE EAST 17-24 (1969, reprinted in 1970, Sydney, Maitland Publications).

III. ISRAEL THRESHOLD THESIS—SOVEREIGN EQUALITY OF ISRAEL AND THE OBJECTIVE OF GENUINE PEACE

A. The Israel Thesis Tested by the Charter

The threshold thesis of Israel, as spelled out, might proceed as follows. No sensible meaning can be given to the Security Council's adoption of the November Resolution except on the basis that all the States concerned, including Israel, are Members of the United Nations, bound by the Charter, and in particular by Article 2 (Resolution Preamble, paragraph 3). Refusal by a Member to acknowledge the *statehood*, and therefore implicitly *Membership* in the United Nations, of a State duly admitted is incompatible with the Charter, and in particular with Article 2(1) declaring the "sovereign equality" of all Members. This seems *a fortiori* so when the refusal carries with it the claim to be at liberty to destroy that State by force, despite Article 2(4) of the Charter. However wide or narrow be that last difficult text, the open claims of the Arab States since 1948 to destroy Israel and drive her people into the sea seem to violate its prohibitions against "threat or use of force," and the duties arising from Article 2(1) above, as well as those of Article 2(2), and 2(3) concerning the assurance to Israel of the benefits of Membership, and the peaceful settlement of disputes.[17]

Such claims were no less violative of the Charter before June 1967, than after the military defeat of the Arab States' designs. So far as persisted in after the cease-fire, the Israel thesis would be that they were doubly illegal. For *actual* force used against Israel *after the cease-fire* compounds illegality under the Charter with violation of the cease-fire. Genuine acceptance of the November Resolution, therefore, would on such a thesis require this chronic illegality to be desisted from. This would be reconfirmed by the fact that the Resolution itself draws the "principles" and "necessity" which constitute its substantive provisions from this same Article 2.

---

17. *Cf.* Wright, *Legal Aspects of the Middle East Situation*, 33 LAW & CONTEMP. PROB. 5, 17 (1968), in the valuable symposium, *The Middle East Crisis: Test of International Law* (J.W. Halderman ed.), 33 LAW & CONTEMP. PROB. 1-193 (1968) [hereinafter cited as J.W. Halderman, *Symposium*].

A more substantial objection to such an Israel thesis would be that it seems unreasonable thus to interpret the November Resolution as requiring Egypt to surrender, as it were, her most important bargaining counter at the very outset. For is not her refusal to recognize Israel and her claim of liberty to destroy Israel when she can, exactly such a counter? Of course, even if this objection were accepted, it would be two-edged. For it would apply even more powerfully to the demand for Israel's withdrawal from occupied territories, Israel's control of these being *her* most important bargaining counter.

The decisive point of differentiation is taken in Mr. Eban's criticism of the belated Soviet Draft Resolution of November 20, 1967. That Draft offered as a *quid pro quo* for Israel withdrawal the recognition that "every State must respect the political independence and territorial integrity of all other States in the area." But, in the Israel view, the Arab States' long-standing contrary postures towards her violated the Charter and were to be desisted from on that account.[18]

The outcome on the present matter, then, is not the mutual neutralization of the opposed theses. For insofar as Israel's bargaining stance, namely, her position in the territories, arose from lawful self-defense, international law by the applicable rule of *uti possidetis* leaves her lawfully in control, and therefore entitled to use this control as a position to bargain from until peace is attained.[19]

B.   The Israel Thesis Tested by Customary International Law

The principles of customary international law remain operative today, so far as consistent with the Charter. Those principles gave to States two broad alternatives in their mutual relations. One model was the relation of war, which however

---

18.   *See* U.N. Doc. S/8253 (1967). *See also* the discussion in A. LALL, *supra* note 4, at 259. The fact that the author is unable to see the point appears to be due to the political focus of his study. The point, though it also has political implications, is at its crux a legal one.

19.   We leave aside in the text the important *political* point often made that even if Egypt is playing with a hand of cards which appears to be Arab, the trumps in it are really drawn from a different pack of cards altogether. *Cf.* the witty title, Meyer-Ranke, *Arabisches Kartenspiel mit nicht arabischen Trumpfen (The Arab Card Game with the Use of Non-Arab Trump Cards)*, 10 AUSSENPOLITIK 173-83 (May 1968).

was reciprocal, and entitled the opponent to react in kind. Egypt has, indeed, claimed the liberty of belligerence against Israel, but she has also seemed to deny Israel's reciprocal liberty of response, appealing for protection to the United Nations against it. If Israel were to be held to the law of peace, however, so then must Egypt. And customary international law has long prescribed certain irreducible rights of States living at peace with one another.

These rights include the rights of each State to respect, to dignity, to the immunity of its territorial domain from intrusion and attack, and to the privileges of legation and intercourse—the right in short, in the very words also of the November Resolution, "to live in peace within secure and recognized boundaries free from threats or acts of force." This is so, even apart from the Charter, as clearly as it was three centuries ago under Vattel's famous doctrine of the "fundamental rights" of States. States, no doubt, can in fact, and sometimes do, flout these rights; but *they are not legally entitled to do so*, nor presumably to threaten continuance of these illegalities as a bargaining counter to extract concessions. In this light, too, insistence on normal State-to-State agreement leading to a treaty of peace, is a directive from basic legal principle and practice, rather than the mere matter of procedure to which U Thant has tried to reduce it.

Its charming irony in relation to the Middle East problem leads me to refer to the Soviet Union's Note of December 5 (or 3), 1929, in relation to her claims to take military action across the Soviet-Manchurian frontier, by way of "counter-measures" and "legitimate defense" against Russian counter-revolutionary bands, alleged by her to be operating "in accord" with units of the Nanking Government's Army for Chinese territory. This Note has become staple textbook material. It was addressed through France to the United States at a time when the Soviet Government was pressing, as Israel does today, for the renunciation by neighboring and other States of policies of nonrecognition and of sponsorship of terrorist activity of armed bands across her frontiers. The Soviet Government there declared "that the Soviet-Manchurian conflict can only be settled by way of direct pourparlers between the Soviet Union and China . . . ."[20] Nor, at the risk of straining history, can one resist noting the Soviet resentment at that time of the intrusion of the interests of the stronger Powers into her regional relations, when contrasted with her own present role in "keeping the Middle East pot boiling."

The Israel thesis, then, by its demand for negotiation looking towards a genuine peace, is also offering this as a simple way of ending a double anomaly. One is the *factual* anomaly of States refusing to treat with a proposed victim of their destructive designs who defeated them. The other is the *legal* anomaly of the at least implied claim of the Arab States to resume the liberty of attempting the destruction of Israel by force. The anomaly is no less under the customary law than under the Charter. As immemorial practice shows, and as a late work on negotiation has recently recalled,[21] negotiation *inter partes* is the normal way to the establishment of a just and lasting peace. And negotiation means direct discussions or talks between the parties, while mediation is but a transitional device to make such direct contact possible.

Israel's insistence on her threshold thesis cannot, of course, prevent future hostile designs against her, nor Soviet aid and abetment of such designs. But the truth remains that cessation of such unlawful designs of use of force is best and most easily evidenced by willingness to treat in pursuit of genuine peace.

C. The Israel Thesis as Related to the November Resolution

It is also part of the core elements constituting the Israel thesis that its demands are explicitly confirmed by the terms in which paragraph 3 of the November Resolution instructs the Special Representative to "promote agreement" for "the establishment of a just and lasting peace." The "agreement" thus to be promoted must mean agreement between the States in conflict. And this is reinforced by the references in the same paragraph 3 to "a peaceful and *accepted* settlement," and in paragraph 1(ii) to "secure and *recognized* boundaries." It does not seem possible to envisage movement towards such

---

20. *See* FOREIGN REL. U.S. 404-06 (1929). *Cf.* I. BROWNLIE, INTERNATIONAL LAW AND THE USE OF FORCE BY STATES 241-42 (1963).

21. A. LALL, MODERN INTERNATIONAL NEGOTIATION 9 (1966).

"agreement" unless the disputants acknowledge in each other at the very outset at least the *locus standi* and capacity to negotiate, and a shared will to seek the agreed terms of a genuine peace settlement.

This argument from the Resolution text, however, may prove too much. Paragraph 1(ii) of the Resolution contains the principle concerning "respect for and acknowledgement of the sovereignty, territorial integrity and political independence of every State in the area and their right to live in peace within secure and recognized boundaries free from threats or acts of force." Insofar as this is a matter towards agreement on which the Representative is to work, how can Egypt's termination of her posture of "belligerence" and nonrecognition be regarded as a threshold requirement, rather than part of the very "package" of terms of settlement? So, conversely, *as against Egypt*, insofar as paragraph 1(i) of the Resolution covers withdrawal of Israel armed forces as a principle on which agreement is to be sought, how can this be said to be a threshold matter to be performed first?

Some differentiations can be made here between the two threshold positions. First, in terms of the text of the Resolution itself, there is no *flat* inconsistency of the Israel argument with the fact that paragraph 1(ii) refers to wider matters, which include recognition and abandonment of belligerence against Israel. It refers also to secure and recognized frontiers, and to the entitlements in the various regards, not only of Israel but of "every State in the area." So that admission of the Israel threshold claim by no means renders paragraph 1(ii) redundant, in the way that admission of Egyptian claims for withdrawal first would so render paragraph 1(i). Second, if the legal position under the Resolution is taken as part of the overall position under the Charter and under customary international law, the Israel claim might be argued to rest on the overall illegality of the Egyptian positions on the matters in question[22] and on the legal and factual impossibility of negotiating a genuine peace, be it under the Resolution or otherwise, *until they are desisted from.*

On this basis, the Israel thesis would conclude, it is only after the much-tried Special Represesentative has persuaded the

---

22. *See* Wright, *supra* note 17, at 17.

Arab States to abandon the unlawful blocking stance, sufficiently at least to treat with Israel with the objective of reaching a just and lasting peace, that his other functions under the Resolution can bear fruit. It asserts that without this the implementation of the Resolution according to its terms cannot in fact or in law be approached.

IV. ARAB THRESHOLD THESIS—WITHDRAWAL TO COME FIRST

Were the charge well-based that Israel entered the occupied territories by an unlawful resort to war, rather than an act of lawful self-defense, then insistence on Israel withdrawal might have substance. This would not have flowed, as is sometimes argued, from the fact that it is withdrawal which is *first mentioned* in the substantive part of the November Resolution. As will be shown shortly, the structure of the Resolution does not permit its parts to be treated separately, much less permit the physical order of its provisions to determine the temporal order of performance. Nor would it have flowed merely from the preambulatory recital of the "inadmissibility of the acquisition of territory by war," the meaning of which will also shortly be reviewed. The consequence would flow rather from the assumed unlawfulness of the resort to war from which the occupation ensued, and from the application of the principle *ex iniuria non oritur ius* to the facts as thus hypothetically assumed.[23] Even then, however, there would have been the problem that the preceding Egyptian and Jordanian occupations, resulting, as these did, from their unlawful invasions of Palestine in 1948, were no less illegal.

But, of course, the actual facts of the June war were not as so assumed, but precisely the contrary. This author showed in *The Middle East Under Cease-Fire*[24] that according to commonly proposed criteria of aggression, unlawful initiatives were taken by Arab States before any Israel move across their

---

23. *See* 2 L. OPPENHEIM, INTERNATIONAL LAW 218 (7th ed. H. LAUTERPACHT 1952).

24. The Middle East Under Cease Fire, address by J. Stone, meeting of International Law Association (Australian Branch), Sydney, Oct. 18, 1967, published in 3 THE BRIDGE 3-18 (1967) (Box 4047 G.P.O. Sydney, 2001, Australia) [hereinafter cited as J. Stone, The Middle East Under Cease Fire].

frontiers on June 5, 1967. These initiatives included the naval blockade of the Straits of Tiran; the shelling from the Gaza Strip by Egypt; the air runs over Israel and bombardment from the Golan Heights by Syria; Egypt's persistent assertion of belligerent rights against Israel ships and cargoes in the Suez Canal in defiance of Security Council resolutions; and, Syria's systematic aid to incursion by armed bands into and against Israel in an openly avowed plan of "liberation" of "Palestine" by "guerrilla warfare." A remarkable number of these initiatives fell within the category of acts which, according to the definition of aggression promoted for thirty years by the Soviet Union, constitute acts, first commission of which constitutes aggression.[25] Such acts created for Israel a situation

---

25. It may be interesting to pinpoint here the paragraphs of the Soviet definition of aggression as revised in 1956 (U.N. Doc. A/AC 77/L4) under which acts committed by one or more of the Arab States before June 5, 1967, constituted "acts of aggression" by the State or States concerned. (The relevant paragraphs of the Soviet definition are indicated in parenthesis.)

(1) Declarations of general belligerence by Egypt and other Arab States against Israel continuing into the relevant period (para. 1(a)). (The declaration of belligerence of President Nasser of May 26, 1967, accompanying his announcement of the naval blockade in the Straits of Tiran, may also arguably be caught by this paragraph.)

(2) Syria's support of armed bands which invaded the territory of Israel, in accordance with an officially avowed plan of "liberation" of "Palestine" by "guerrilla warfare" (para. 1(f)).

(3) Repeated bombardments from Syrian gun emplacements in Golan against the territory and peaceable inhabitants of Israel in Galilee (para. 1(f)).

(4) Egypt's establishment of a naval blockade in May 1967, barring by force traffic to and from the coast and port of Israel in the Gulf of Aqaba through the Straits of Tiran. The warlike nature of these acts was accentuated by their inconsistency with the terms of Israel's withdrawal from Sharm el Sheikh and the Gaza Strip in 1957 (para. 1(e)).

(5) Specific threats and use of force by Egypt, in defiance of Security Council resolutions, against Israel ships and cargoes desiring to exercise international rights of navigation through the Suez Canal, and the invocation of prize law, applicable only to warlike relations, against them (para. 1(e), by arguable analogy only).

(6) Offensive mobilization by Egypt and other Arab States of forces of about 200,000 men around the frontiers of Israel, when seen in the light of Egypt's demands for withdrawal of UNEF, and of the declarations of intent by Egypt and some other of these Governments to "liquidate" Israel and "liberate" so-called "Palestine" (para. 1(a) and/or (b)).

(7) Various other declarations of belligerence of other Arab States, including Algeria, Iraq, Jordan, Lebanon, Syria, United Arab Republic (Egypt), in May and early June, 1967 (para. 1 (a)).

The above listing makes it unnecessary to consider further charges by the Israel Government that the Syrian Air Force crossed the frontier to attack targets in Galilee early on June 5, 1967 (para. 1 (c)); and that Jordan initiated hostilities in Jerusalem

of self-defense under Article 51 which at latest certainly matured at the point when Egypt and the other Arab States mobilized about 200,000 men around the frontiers of Israel, accompanying this by demands for withdrawal of the United Nations Emergency Force, and formal declarations of intent to liquidate Israel, as well as declarations of common belligerence by Algeria, Iraq, Jordan, Lebanon, and Egypt.[26] As against a State in the position of Israel, thus acting in lawful self-defense, the principle *ex iniuria non oritur ius* seems simply not applicable.[27] As between an unsuccessful aggressor whose territory falls under control of the prospective victim, the no less clear rule of international law of *uti possidetis* leaves the final outcome of the occupation to the negotiation of peace.[28] Lacking this the parties remain *in statu quo*, no principle requiring or even justifying any particular change.[29]

What then of the preambulatory recital in the November Resolution of the "inadmissibility of the acquisition of territory by war?" A first possibility is that the recital declares a broader rule than that of *ex iniuria non oritur ius*, requiring the Occupant to withdraw even if his entry were, as in the case of Israel, perfectly lawful. No doubt this is a *possible* meaning, but at least two other meanings are far more likely. A second possibility is that the recital was merely recalling, in the eloquently ambiguous style reconciling diverse standpoints apt in a preamble, the *ex iniuria* principle as it applies to war. Third, equally plausible, and to the same end, the recital may be a restatement of the rather technical and commonplace principle that mere military occupation does not transfer title,

---

on the same day despite an offer by Israel to Jordan to refrain (on a reciprocal basis) from hostilities between them (para. 1(c)).

It may be added that there may also have been (still in terms of the Soviet 1956 definition) a number of pre-1965 acts of "indirect aggression" (subversive activity, "acts of terrorism, diversionary acts, etc." (para. 2(a)), "economic aggression" (measures threatening "economic independence" (para. 3(a)), and "ideological agression" ("encouragement of war propaganda" (para. 4(a)), by various Arab States against the State of Israel.

26. *Cf.* the similar conclusions in O'Brien, *International Law and the Outbreak of War in the Middle East*, 11 ORBIS 692, 722-23 (1967), and (as to the Arab "armed attack" only) Wright, *supra* note 17, at 27.

27. Wright, *supra* note 17, at 27.

28. *See* text section III. A. *supra*.

29. *See* J. STONE, *supra* note 16, at 32-33.

this requiring some further act in the law, such as formal annexation or cession under a negotiated treaty of peace. Arab State supporters, no doubt, were confident that they could still charge Israel with agression. Israel and other States were no doubt also confident of the opposite effect, remembering that the majority of Members both of the Security Council and the General Assembly had repelled this charge. In any case as between the above meanings it is clear that the recital, in order to bear the first meaning, would have to be legislative in effect, rather than declaratory of existing international law.

This first possible meaning above, asserting *de lege ferenda* that an Occupant must withdraw even before peace terms are agreed, and even if he entered lawfully in self-defense against an aggressor, is worth further examination. A rule presented *de lege ferenda* must by definition be a rule the consequences of which would be regarded as desirable for members of the community generally. But it is apparent that *this proposed* rule would be disastrously undesirable. It would assure every prospective aggressor that, if he fails, he will be entitled to restoration of any territory he has lost. It would do this even if he still openly reserves the liberty to renew his aggressive design, and even if (as with Egypt in Gaza) the territories in question were formerly seized unlawfully and have been consistently used since then as a base for aggressive activity against the present Occupant. In short, it would underwrite unconditionally the risks of loss from any proposed agression. By such a rule an international law, which sets out by the *ex iniuria* principle to discourage aggressors, would end with a rule encouraging aggressors by insuring them in advance against the main risks involved in case of defeat. To offer such a rule *de lege ferenda* would sanctify a new and cynical legal maxim which might run: "If you cannot stop the aggressor, help him!" A meaning of the preamble yielding such a result cannot, therefore, be preferred when the two others mentioned above are available. It may perhaps be added that Soviet and Arab voting patterns in the West Irian and Goan affairs showed no particular support for a norm barring *simpliciter* acquisition of territory by force.[30]

---

30. *See* J. W. Halderman, *Some International Constitutional Aspects of the Palestine Case*, in J.W. Halderman, *Symposium, supra* note 17, at 79, 89-90.

Finally, as to this point, it must be added, as to Egypt in Gaza and as to Jordan on the West Bank, that even if their respective entries had not been unlawful, nor in defiance of the cease-fire and truce resolution of May 1948, the proposed rule would also negative any right of theirs to be in those territories, their claims also being purported "acquisitions . . . by war." So that even if the rule were now newly legislated with retrospective effect it could not improve *their* present legal position vis-à-vis Israel except by an entirely unprincipled discriminatory application of the new rule to one side and not the other.[31] Such an alleged rule, finally, would stand grotesquely with the Soviet Union's assertion on December 16, 1969, that its title to the Kurile Islands is based on the defeat and unconditional surrender of Japan. And that assertion, in turn, is inconsistent with positions which the Soviet Union presses against Israel.

There remains another possible basis for the Arab threshold thesis demanding prior and total Israel withdrawal. This is that the first enumerated "principle" (and indeed the first substantive provision altogether) in the November Resolution reads: "Withdrawal of Israel armed forces from territories occupied in the recent conflict." What stands first in the Resolution, the thesis would run, is first to be performed. The first difficulty with this is, of course, that the English text, which is that in which the sponsor drew up the Resolution, does not say precisely *what* forces are to withdraw, nor *from what* territories, nor indeed *when*.[32] Lord Caradon himself firmly though patiently withstood pressures from Arab and other States to employ in his draft their alternative formulation, namely, "*all the* territories." He also resisted the Indian delegate's argument, which was supported at one stage by the threat of a Russian veto, that the Indian understanding of the Resolution as, in effect, embodying the definite article would create a *binding* understanding as to the meaning of the Resolution.

The Indian delegate later agreed to vote for the British

---

31. *Cf.* A. LALL, *supra* note 4, at 247, quoting Foreign Minister Eban in the Security Council, 22 U.N. SCOR, 1375th meeting 28 (1967).

32. *Cf.* S. Rosenne, *Directions for a Middle East Settlement—Some Underlying Legal Problems*, in J.W. Halderman, *Symposium, supra* note 17, at 44, 60.

Draft, Lord Caradon in turn agreeing not to include in his remarks the otherwise projected sentence: "But the Indian interpretation is not binding on the Council." He said instead that "it will be recognized that it is only the resolution that will bind us, and we regard its wording as clear."[33] Ambassador Goldberg made a similar declaration and, of course, it is in any case clear that the adoption of a resolution affirms, not the diverse views and policies of individual members, but the contents of the resolution as stated. "For us," said Foreign Minister Eban, "the resolution says what it says. It does not say that which it has specifically and consciously avoided saying." Of course, recognition of these subtleties implies serious actual limits on the appearance of consensus. And it is always a question in each particular case whether more is gained than is lost by settling for the mere appearance, when the alternative is complete breakdown. Yet the actual limits still only await the occasion to show themselves. So that even Professor Arthur Lall's insightful account of these remarkable diplomatic maneuverings[34] shows far less concern about the effect of the absence of the definite article than later events have warranted. Professor Lall thinks[35] that the Arab States felt they could gain the point, that they had failed to gain in their unsuccessful attempt to insert the critical words "*all* the territories," by interpreting the unspecified word "territories" in paragraph 1(i) with the preambulatory reference to "inadmissibility of the acquisition of territory by war." This, of course, begs the very open question of the meaning of that reference, discussed above.[36]

Another way of testing such a "first-written, first-to-be-done" interpretation is to ask whether it could sensibly also be applied to the order in which the other provisions of the Resolution appear. Thus tested, it immediately falters. It must be supposed, for example, that the "necessity" for the establishment of "demilitarized zones," referred to in paragraph 2(c) of the Resolution, *may* be applicable to some or all of the territories in dispute. Such zones would therefore,

33. A. LALL. *supra* note 4, at 260.
34. *Id.* at 260-63.
35. *Id.* at 234.
36. *Id.* at 33-34.

in common prudence, have to be provided for simultaneously with the withdrawal of Israel forces, and before the reentry of the forces of the returning regime. Yet according to the physical order of the provisions, withdrawal comes first, and the demilitarized zones *fifth* and last. In between would lie the potentially long interval required to implement the intervening provisions, including notably the termination of Arab State belligerence, their acknowledgment of Israel "sovereignty, territorial integrity and political independence," the fixing of "secure" and "recognized" boundaries of all States in the area (paragraph 1(ii)), the guaranteeing of freedom of navigation to Israel through international waterways "in the area," certainly embracing the Straits of Tiran and the Suez Canal, and probably the Straits of Perim off Southern Yemen (paragraph 2(a)), and a "just settlement of the refugee problem" (paragraph 2(b)). Only thereafter would the task be approached of guaranteeing (presumably by the Permanent Members of the Security Council) the "territorial inviolability and political independence of every State in the area," of which the final provision for demilitarized zones is to be a part (paragraph 2(c)).

Finally, any claim that the references to withdrawal in the preamble to the November Resolution, or in paragraph 1(i), import automatic restoration of the former "boundaries" between Israel and the surrounding Arab States as at June 4, 1967, seems impossible to reconcile with the succeeding words of paragraph 1. These call *inter alia* for the right of Israel to "live in peace within secure and recognized boundaries." Since any ambiguity must be resolved in the light of other parts of the same paragraph, it becomes quite impossible to interpret either the preamble or paragraph 1(i) as proposing a return to the June 4, 1967 boundaries *as a first step.* We must perforce read these provisions together. They would then mean that the Special Representative, under paragraph 3, is to promote agreement between the Parties fixing "secure and recognized boundaries," and requiring the withdrawal of Israel forces behind the boundaries as thus fixed. Such agreement would also cut through the doubts affecting the sovereign title of Arab States, for instance, in Gaza and West Jordan.[37]

---

37. Such doubts affect most of the territories at present in controversy. As to the West Bank of the River Jordan, it is more than merely arguable that the State of

V. THE NOVEMBER RESOLUTION AS GUIDE-LINES FOR A "PACKAGE" PEACE

Any slight plausibility which survives the above methods of testing succumbs unfortunately to the even more basic test of reading all provisions of the Resolution in the context of the Resolution as a whole. This is a long sanctified and still rather undisputed general requirement of legal interpretation. Its applicability to the November Resolution is made even more imperative in view of the "package," that is, the "integral" nature of the Resolution as its sponsor offered it, and the Security Council finally accepted it. In view of this, so far from it being legally permissible to isolate one provision for temporal priority of performance, this is precisely what cannot be done. The truth is that all the above provisions serve as interdependent guidelines for the activities of the Special Representative under paragraph 3 of the Resolution, and not severable legal commands to the disputants. They are his terms of reference, within which he is "to promote *agreement* and

---

Jordan was in 1967 no more than a belligerent occupant. Moreover, the legality of its initial entry in 1948 was seriously challenged at that time in the Security Council; and the validity of her subsequent annexation of it was recognized by only two States, and denied even by other Arab States. Even, however, if the question of legality is disregarded, Israel's later entry and military occupation would legally displace the Jordanians. It is only a displaced sovereign and not a mere displaced military occupant who has a reversionary interest under international law. Similar analyses also affect Gaza and East Jerusalem vis-à-vis Egypt and Jordan respectively. *See* J. STONE, NO PEACE—NO WAR IN THE MIDDLE EAST, *supra* note 16, at 38-40; Blum, *The Missing Reversioner: Reflections on the Status of Judea and Samaria*, 3 ISRAEL L. REV. 279-312 (1968).

As to Sinai, this remained under the sovereignty of Turkey right until the Treaty of Lausanne, 1923, Article 16, by which Turkey renounced all titles thereto without however disposing of the sovereignty in favor of Egypt or any other particular State. What lay in Egypt after that time would appear to have been merely what was first accorded to the Khedivate of Egypt in 1892, and continued under the British protectorate until after World War I, namely, a grant of "administration." After 1923, and even after Egypt became independent, no other disposition, nor any new act of annexation by Egypt, is to be found. The only possible grounds for suggesting that Egypt had sovereignty over Sinai in 1967 would therefore have to be that her subsequent activities there sufficed for acquisitive prescription. Whether they sufficed to enlarge her "administration" into sovereignty, and whether indeed they were not all sufficiently explained in terms of "administration," remained a debatable question in 1967. This position might, for example, politically facilitate arrangements to ensure, for the future, the exclusively peaceful use of the Sinai Desert. See for further analysis, and citation to relevant literature, J. Stone, The Middle East Under Cease Fire, *supra* note 24.

assist efforts to achieve a peaceful and acceptable settlement *in accordance with the provisions and principles of this Resolution.*"[38]

It is to be noted that the word "principles" as used in this paragraph embraces not only the two "principles" the application of which to the Middle East paragraph 1 declares to be required by "Charter principles" (*sic*). It embraces also the three steps concerning freedom of navigation, refugees and territorial and political guarantees of which paragraph 2 declares the "necessity." Unless it does, the terms of reference would extend to the problems neither of navigation in international waterways, nor of refugees. It would obviously lack sense from either the Arab State or Israel point of view to exclude these two matters. This being so, no differentiation can be made, whether of importance or timetable, between "withdrawal," stated as a "principle" in paragraph 1, and the steps as to free navigation, refugees, and guarantees including "demilitarization" declared to be "necessary" in paragraph 2. The Special Representative is merely directed in omnibus terms, and with no indication of any preset priority or urgency as between them, to "the provisions and principles in this resolution."

It is now to be added, indeed, that the same paragraph 3 not only offers no support for the "first-written, first-to-be-done" theory; it also contains formidable counter-indications. For whatever other obligations the Resolution did or did not impose, paragraph 3 certainly imposed certain binding obligations upon the Secretary-General and the Special Representative. Among these was the obligation of the Special Representative "to establish and maintain contacts with the States concerned in order to promote agreement and assist efforts to achieve a peaceful and accepted settlement in accordance with the provisions and principles of this Resolution." It seems utterly impossible to read into an instruction "to promote agreement" between the opposed sides concerning all the provisions of the Resolution, a power of compelling one side, Israel, to carry out one of the provisions (that concerning withdrawal) *without such agreement.* Yet this,

---

38.   Italics supplied.

finally, would be the effect of admitting an Arab claim for priority of withdrawal of all Israel's armed forces from all occupied territories.

In summary then, I have already shown that this claim is without basis on the principle *ex iniuria non oritur ius*. I have also shown the same concerning the recital relied upon in the preamble to the November Resolution. And I have now had to conclude that the claim is without legal basis in the words or orders of words of the November Resolution, and, indeed, rather hard to reconcile either with particular provisions of the Resolution, with its very central provision, or with the effect of that Resolution as a whole.

Earlier sections of this article suggested the error of assuming that there is symmetry of legal merit between the Egyptian threshold thesis demanding prior Israel withdrawal, and Israel's claim that the Parties treat together with a shared basic objective of achieving agreement on the terms of a genuine, just and lasting peace. The present more direct examination has ended, it is believed, in disclosing further reasons why the Egyptian claim lacks legal support, and therefore why any appearance of symmetry of legal merit between the opposed theses is illusory.

I should now add, finally, that even if the legal merits are ignored, there is also no de facto symmetry between the two theses in the way they respectively affect the substantive bargaining positions of the Parties. Thus to satisfy the Egyptian thesis Israel would have to withdraw its forces at least to the pre-June 5, 1967 positions. She would then become exposed militarily as she was in May 1967, Egypt, Jordan and Syria having rearmed in the interim, and they continuing *ex hypothesi* their posture of nonrecognition and belligerence. Egyptian and Jordanian forces could again, as in 1967, concert an offensive advance against the narrow waist of Israel territory in the North Negev; Egyptian forces in Gaza could resume their menacing posture against Tel Aviv and Jerusalem; Syrian emplacements on the Golan Heights could resume bombardment of peaceful farms and fishing vessels in Galilee; East Jerusalem could again become an armed camp readied momentarily for assault against its civic neighbors of West Jerusalem; and the vital passage through the Straits of Tiran could again be blockaded by Egyptian forces. All this would be an irreversible relinquishment by Israel of essential elements of its present position, before either the Parties or the Special Representative have had an opportunity even to *seek* agreement on the other "principles" and "necessity" affirmed in the Resolution.

On the other hand, if we suppose that the Israel threshold thesis were accepted, all that would happen is that the Parties would face each other within the terms of the Resolution, implying to that extent Arab State recognition of Israel and the abandonment of belligerency. If we ignore (*as I do to strengthen the Arab argument*) the illegality of the positions in question, this too would be a renunciation of a main bargaining position, this time on the Arab side. But this renunciation, and here is where symmetry with the above assumed Israel withdrawal of forces breaks down, would still *in fact* be reversible *by the Arab States*. For when we ignore the illegalities of these Arab positions (as I am doing in order to strengthen the Arab argument) the question whether any recognition so accorded could not as a technical legal matter be withdrawn, and belligerency also resumed, would still leave ample room for maneuver to the Arab States. So that their momentary willingness on November 15, 1967, during the complex diplomacy which surrounded the abortive three Power resolution, to consider recognizing Israel's statehood in return for Israel's withdrawal from all the territories concerned, sometimes taken as betokening flexibility, may have rested merely on perception of this continuing freedom of action.[39]

Egypt would not (as would Israel after a postulated withdrawal) have a Hobson's choice of either getting the opponent's concurrence or winning another victory over superior military forces in order to retrieve its prenegotiation position. What Egypt momentarily conceded would be reversible by her with comparative ease. Insofar, moreover, as Israel's thesis would be met only implicitly by Egypt's entry into serious negotiation, this could be reversed more easily still. For by merely breaking off negotiation, Egypt could, if she so desired, largely cancel any such implication. Therefore this

---

39.   A. LALL, *supra* note 4, at 248.

concession, too, would be in fact reversible by decisions made wholly in Cairo. (I am still, of course, ignoring any illegalities involved; for these are a constant factor both before and after any supposed concession.)

All this seems equally true whether the terms of reference for negotiation are those of the November Resolution, or some version of them offered by either side, for example, King Hussein's paraphrase of its terms in 1969, which was interpreted by the mass media (erroneously as it appeared) as a moderation of what we have here termed the Arab threshold thesis; or Foreign Minister Eban's exposé on October 8, 1968, of "the nine principles by which peace can be achieved." Such proposals are all useful as items of an agenda to be approached in the search for terms of peace. In Mr. Eban's formulation, the first point as to the "establishment of peace" merely reaffirms the Resolution's expressed aim to replace the cease-fire with a "just and lasting peace" based on agreement of the Parties. The second point, agreement on "secure and recognized boundaries" compatible with the security and honor of both sides, is obviously at the core of such a peace. The proposals for nonaggression treaties, and for an "open frontier," are ancillary to the first two points. The fifth, sixth and seventh principles of guaranteed freedom of navigation in international waterways, of joint responsibility to agree and implement a five year plan for solving the refugee problem, and the establishment of a regime expressing the "universal interests" of Christianity, Islam and Judaism in their respective Holy Places in Jerusalem, must obviously be part of the subject for agreement. Each side would necessarily approach each matter in the light of its own interests, determining from moment to moment whether the mutual concessions offered merit persistence in effort. So that success in the ninth point, of regional cooperation, though it would, no doubt, be discussed concurrently, would have to be a crown to the success of all the rest. These nine principles went in certain respects (for instance, as to the call for nonaggression treaties, for "open frontiers," regional cooperation, and for the institutional expression of the "universal interests" of Christianity, Islam and Judaism in their respective Holy Places in Jerusalem) beyond the literal ambit of the November Resolution. But the extensions in these regards might be regarded as assurances rather than demands by Israel.

There seems to be no reason why such versions of what the November Resolution implies, or some other version offered, for example, by Egypt or Jordan, or by the Special Representative, should not be the basis of the sincere search for agreement. What is critical is that, in a positive sense, the version should cover the subject matter; and, in a negative sense, that it should not call for an unreciprocated and irreversible commitment by one side to accept the other's standpoint, independently of the overall conclusion of a "just and lasting peace."

VI.   PITFALL OR GUIDEPOST?

The present article has disclosed a number of current misconceptions concerning the binding import for the Arab States and Israel of the November Resolution, and concerning the substantive meaning of its provisions. To clarify or correct conflicting assertions concerning a contractual or decisional instrument is, of course, not necessarily to move disputes concerning them towards solution. Promotion of errors may, indeed, be part of a pattern of political warfare, so that convincing exposure will not lead a disputant to desist from this activity. Yet, of course, such promotion can rarely be the decisive element in a party's bargaining strength and waiting power. It will add little to the position unless that party does actually have the ability, *without the cooperation of the other side*, to stay in a desired actual position or move forward to another preferred position.

It is at the point when such cooperation is sought that the removal of misconceptions surrounding the agenda for peacemaking may become important *to both sides*. This is clearly so when the side asserting an error sincerely believes that it is right. But, of course, a side may also come by the mere repeated assertion of an error really to believe that it is right, even though the error was originally espoused for political advantage, and without much conviction. Generally, in these first two situations, once the wish emerges to seek mutually tolerable terms, it may become rather essential to discard errors which obstruct the exploration of these terms. There may be some cases, even then, when the Government concerned will refuse to discard an error. These are mainly where its refusal would decisively and irreversibly impair either its bargaining position internationally, or an image of itself on which, for example, continued popular support at home depends.

It is believed that the instant questions concerning the November Resolution fall under one or other of the former two, rather than the last, categories. For, as has been seen, none of the various alternative steps by which Egypt and her allies could participate in exploring the possible terms of settlement, would be an irreversible step. Nor would it seem more difficult for President Nasser to explain to Egyptian public opinion the tentativeness of such steps towards peace, than it has been for him to explain other events which have occurred since June 1967. In view of all this, a decision by Egypt not to stand on certain interpretations of the November Resolution, which have hitherto blocked procedures aimed at a peace settlement, would not seriously impair her bargaining strength in any way which she could not thereafter rather readily restore.

To break the present impasse, two broad alternatives lie before the States concerned. Either the Arab adversaries would have to prove themselves strong enough to subvert by force the rights vested in Israel under international law, or they, along with Israel, must move toward agreement on such terms as will permit each to live in peace and reasonable security, and even, hopefully, in cooperative dedication to regional tasks. Freed of errors and distortions which have too often made it appear but a pitfall in the path to peace, the November Resolution may yet prove a guidepost along that very path.

The Middle East Problem

QUINCY WRIGHT

The Security Council resolution of November 22, 1967,[1] seems to provide for a satisfactory solution of the Middle East controversy, and it is difficult to see how there can be a satisfactory settlement except on the basis of the principles on which that resolution is based. The preamble of that resolution states three fundamental principles.

First is "the inadmissibility of the acquisition of territory by war."[2] This principle goes beyond the principle "no fruits of aggression." It says there shall be no territorial fruits from war, using the latter term in the material sense of a considerable use of armed force. Its application, therefore, does not depend on determining who was the "aggressor" in the 1967 hostilities, a difficult question to answer.[3] There can be no doubt that, whether or not Israel was the aggressor, its occupations of territory were achieved by the use of armed force. This principle is well established. It is inherent in the rules of customary international law defining "military occupation" and permitting acquisition of occupied territory only by annexation following generally recognized "completed conquest" or cession by the former sovereign.[4] It was accepted in the form "no title by conquest" as a principle of American international law by most of the members of the Pan American Conference of 1890 reaffirmed in the Buenos Aires Declaration of 1936, the Lima Declaration of 1938 and the Bogotá Charter of the O.A.S. of 1948.[5] It was assumed in President Wilson's Fourteen Points and generally applied in the peace settlements of World War I which required plebiscites to justify territorial transfers. It was assumed by the League of Nations as a necessary implication of the Covenant's guarantee of the territorial integrity of all Members, and was particularly insisted upon by the United States in the Stimson Doctrine refusing to recognize any Japanese acquisitions by its invasion and occupation of Manchuria. Secretary Stimson considered it an implication of the Kellogg-Briand Pact of 1928 to which the United States,

° Of the Board of Editors.

[1] 62 A.J.I.L. 482 (1968).

[2] Reaffirmed in Security Council Res. 252 (May 21, 1968). See also Muhammud H. El Farra, Permanent Representative of Jordan to the U.N., "The Role of the U.N. vis-a-vis the Palestine Question," 33 Law and Contemporary Problems 68 ff. (Winter, 1968), and Cherif Bassiouni, "Some Legal Aspects of the Arab-Israeli Conflict," 14 The Arab World (Nos. 10–11) 44 (Arab Information Center, N.Y., 1967).

[3] This difficulty exists whether one takes, as the test for determining aggression, priority in initiating hostilities, refusal to accept or observe provisional measures proposed by the U.N. (Art. 40), or manifest unwillingness to accept fair and effective procedures to settle the dispute. See Q. Wright, "Legal Aspects of the Middle East Situation," 33 Law and Contemporary Problems 26 ff. (Winter, 1968); *idem*, "The Concept of Aggression in International Law," 29 A.J.I.L. 373 ff. (July, 1935); "The Prevention of Aggression," 50 A.J.I.L. 514, 526 ff. (July, 1956).

[4] Charles G. Fenwick, International Law 426, 681 ff. (4th ed., N.Y., 1965).

[5] 1 Moore, Digest of International Law 292; 7 *ibid.* 318; 5 Whiteman, Digest of International Law 880–881; 119 U.N. Treaty Series 3 (1948).

though not a Member of the League, was a party.[6] By this instrument nearly all states had renounced war as an instrument of national policy. The League of Nations accepted the Stimson Doctrine as a necessary implication of Article 10 of the Covenant. The United States insisted on this principle in the Atlantic Charter of 1941 before its entry into World War II, and in the settlements after that war. The Allies, it is true, made some territorial acquisitions as a result of their victory but sought to justify them, not very successfully in all cases, by the principle of self-determination of peoples. The principle has been considered an implication of the obligation in Article 2, paragraph 4, of the U.N. Charter to refrain from the use or threat of force against the territorial integrity of any state.

The General Assembly resolution of November 29, 1947, partitioning Palestine and establishing the state of Israel as demanded by Zionists is difficult to reconcile with this principle. Local hostilities between Zionist and Arab forces deprived the "peoples" in the mandated territory of rights explicitly protected by the Mandate and Article 80 of the Charter without their consent. This action, however, must be regarded as an act of international legislation which the General Assembly deemed necessary to meet the crisis situation which developed from the local hostilities and British resignation of its Mandate. The admission of Israel to the United Nations on May 11, 1949, and its recognition by most states, including the Arab states, with qualifications, in a declaration to the U.N. Conciliation Commission on May 12, 1949,[7] gave legal effectiveness to the partition resolution.[8]

The extension of Israel's occupation beyond the original U.N. grant as a result of the Arab-Israeli hostilities of 1948–49, and the armistices negotiated in 1949, were justified as temporary measures to end the hostilities. The principle of no acquisition of territory by war should, if strictly applied, require that cease-fire lines be at the frontiers before hostilities began, thus preventing military occupations as well as acquisitions by force, but the overriding responsibility of the United Nations to stop hostilities justified the acceptance of the armistices as temporary cease-fire lines to be soon superseded by permanent boundaries established by peaceful means.

The principle was strictly adhered to in the hostilities of 1956. Britain, France, and Israel, under pressure of the U.N. General Assembly supported by the United States and the U.S.S.R., were induced to withdraw to their positions before the hostilities.[9]

[6] Q. Wright, "The Stimson Note of January 7, 1932," 26 A.J.I.L. 342 ff. (1932).

[7] General Progress Report of U.N. Conciliation Commission for Palestine, 5 U.N. General Assembly, Official Records, Supp. 18, pp. 3–4, 19–21, U.N. Doc. A/1367, Rev. 1 (1950), and Third Progress Report, U.N. C.C.P., 4 General Assembly, Official Records, Vol. II, Doc. A/927 (1949).

[8] Wright, "Legal Aspects of the Middle East Situation," note 3 above, pp. 13–15.

[9] The U.N. insisted on withdrawal to the boundaries before hostilities began in the Kashmir (1948, 1965) and Korean (1950) situations. In the debate on the cease-fire resolution of June 6, 1967, the Soviet Union, France, India, the Arab states and others demanded immediate withdrawal from occupied territories, but the United States insisted that withdrawal must be contingent on Arab renunciation of belligerency and opening the waterways to Israeli shipping. U.N. Doc. S/PV.1358 (1967); Wright, loc. cit. note 3 above, pp. 24, 25.

The circumstances inducing the Security Council to accept cease-fire lines in June and July, 1967, on the boundary of Israeli occupation were similar to those in 1949. The resolutions were justified as necessary to end the hostilities, but could not be regarded as conferring any title to the territory occupied by Israel. It is unfortunate that the position taken in 1956, requiring Israel immediately to withdraw to its *de facto* frontiers before the hostilities, was not adhered to. If the United States and the U.S.S.R., supported by France and Great Britain—as they were not in 1956—had insisted in the Security Council, with support of the General Assembly, withdrawal might have been effected. The American preoccupation with Viet-Nam and its conflict with the Soviet Union on that and other problems, as well as its vulnerability to domestic Zionist pressure, were factors preventing the common position taken by the super-Powers in 1956.[10]

In any case the principle in question clearly required that Israel gain no political advantage, in respect to the establishment of a boundary with its Arab neighbors, by its occupation of territories administered and claimed by Egypt, Jordan, and Syria before the six-day war. Israel would certainly be at an advantage if it negotiated independently with each of its neighbors while it occupied the disputed territories.[11]

[10] For statistics indicating bias in news and editorials in the U. S. Press during May and June, 1967, see Michael W. Sullivan, in 14 The Arab World (note 2 above), p. 59 ff.

[11] By taking suitable means to prevent states from gaining advantages from resorts to force, states not only observe their legal obligation but serve the general purpose of the U.N. "to save succeeding generations from the scourge of war." (Preamble.) Such action assists the technological developments which have tended to make resorts to military force useless as an instrument of foreign policy. Appraisal of over forty instances of hostilities which have occurred since World War II (see Q. Wright, A Study of War 1518 ff. (Chicago, 1965)) suggests that, although peoples seeking self-determination from colonial or other domination have sometimes utilized force successfully, states have been less successful in such utilization than in earlier periods of history and have usually preferred other methods for implementing foreign policies such as diplomacy, propaganda, resort to the U.N., technical assistance, or "non-military intervention" not likely to involve them in hostilities (see Q. Wright, in Karl W. Deutsch and Stanley Hoffmann (eds.), The Relevance of International Law 5 ff. (Cambridge, Mass., 1963)). They have feared that under present technological conditions hostilities may escalate into suicidal nuclear war, or may lead to destructive stalemate or the quagmire of guerrilla hostilities. A state initiating hostilities against another state seems to have gained what it wanted, at least temporarily, in only five instances during this period (Soviet invasions of Hungary, 1956, and Czechoslovakia, 1948 and 1967; Indian invasion of Portuguese Goa, 1962, and Chinese invasion of India, 1962). A few other instances of international hostilities were inconclusive. Israel occupied Arab territory in 1948 and 1967 but it is uncertain which side initiated the hostilities. China invaded Tibet in 1959 but may have had title to it before. Most of the hostilities since World War II were civil or colonial, sometimes leading to foreign intervention, and the insurgents were usually successful (Wright, "Peace-keeping operations of the U.N.," 7 International Studies 174 ff. (Indian School of International Studies (Oct. 1965)). Arnold Toynbee has suggested that the few states which have always gained the objectives which they sought in their wars, especially Israel and the United States, are less aware of the disutility of war as an effective instrument of policy than states which have often been defeated. (Experiences, pp. 231–233 (Oxford University Press, 1969).)

The *second* principle stated in the preamble to the Council resolution of November 22, 1967, is the "need to work for a just and lasting peace in which every State in the area can live in security." This states the basic purpose of the United Nations set forth in Article 1 of the U.N. Charter and supported by the principles stated in Article 2 of that instrument requiring Members to settle all international disputes by peaceful means, to refrain from the use or threat of force in international relations, to assist the United Nations in maintaining these principles, and not to intervene in matters essentially within the domestic jurisdiction of any state.

The danger of the Middle East situation imposes a positive responsibility upon the United Nations, and especially on the Security Council and its permanent members. The Security Council has "primary responsibility for the maintenance of international peace and security" (Article 24). In the existing state of the world and with the great-Power veto in the Security Council, this responsibility can hardly be met unless the principal Powers, especially the United States and the U.S.S.R., work in close harmony within the Security Council.[12] Agreement to end arms shipments to the Middle East would contribute to end the arms race in that area, to relax tensions and to facilitate settlement.

The *third* principle asserts that "all Member States, in their acceptance of the Charter . . . have undertaken a commitment to act in accordance with Article 2 of the Charter." The statements in this article are designated "principles," but paragraph 2 makes it clear that they constitute positive "obligations" of international law, which the Members must "fulfill in good faith." It is therefore an obligation of all Members to "refrain in their international relations from the threat or use of force against the territorial integrity or political independence of any state, or in any other manner inconsistent with the purposes of the United Nations."[13] This leaves individual or collective self-defense against armed attack[14] and assistance to the United Nations in collective security action[15] as the only permissible uses of force by states in international relations. Economic and even military assistance to a foreign government to maintain internal order is per-

[12] The United States and the Soviet Union have been continuously negotiating since February, 1968, on the issues. The United States seems to have supported the Israeli position and the Soviet Union the Arab position on the interpretation of the Security Council resolution of November, 1967, in regard to Israeli withdrawal from occupied territory, but the ten points communicated to Egypt by Secretary of State William P. Rogers on Oct. 28, 1969, reported in the Washington Post, Dec. 10, 1969 (p. A 14), appear to have moved toward the Arab position. In his speech on Dec. 9, 1969, he denied any essential change in the United States position but affirmed the U. S. policy of implementing the Security Council resolution. (See comment by A. D. Horne, Washington Post, Dec. 25, 1969, p. A 15.) The apparent rejection of the ten-point proposal by Egypt, Israel, and the Soviet Union, and the failure of the Arab summit meeting in Morocco in December, 1969, to reach agreement on policy toward Israel indicates a possible relaxation of the deadlock. (See comments by A. D. Horne, cited above, and Washington Post, Dec. 24, 1969, p. 1; Rowland Evans and Robert Novak, *ibid.*, Dec. 25, 1969, p. A 23.)

[13] Art. 2(4).   [14] Art. 51.

[15] Art. 2(5). See also Arts. 25, 39, 42, 43, 45, 48.

missible only if requested by a government which is generally recognized and is not so beset by civil strife that its capacity to represent the state is in doubt.[16]

These provisions of the Charter "outlaw war" in the legal sense of a situation in which the belligerents have an *equal* right to engage in hostilities and other coercive actions permissible under the law of war, and in which other states are obliged to observe the law of neutrality requiring impartiality. Under the Charter this situation cannot exist among Members of the United Nations or, according to Article 2, paragraph 6, among non-member states. A state of war implies a continuing use or threat of force by each belligerent upon the other, forbidden by the Charter, and equality between the belligerents. In the two circumstances in which the use of force is permissible in international relations—self-defense and collective security action—the belligerents are *not equal*. The defenders and the states co-operating with the United Nations enjoy rights denied the aggressor. Other states need not be neutral but may assist the defender in collective self-defense [17] and must assist the United Nations in action against an aggressor.[18]

The outlawry of war by the Charter means not only that armed force may not be used as an instrument of foreign policy but that other powers of belligerents permissible during a state of war, such as blockades, property confiscations, visit and search at sea, etc., are not permissible. The Arab argument that the armistice of 1949, while forbidding uses of armed force contrary to its terms, permitted the utilization of other belligerent powers such as blockade of the Suez Canal with respect to Israeli shipping, has no basis. The armistices were made to end *de facto* but illegal hostilities and to establish temporary lines of occupation. They did not recognize a state of war. Neither party enjoyed belligerent powers.[19]

The first and third of these principles must be observed if the just and lasting peace called for by the second is to be achieved. Paragraph 1 of the Security Council resolution of November 22, 1967, is a balanced application of these principles to the Middle East situation.[20] Israel must with-

---

[16] Q. Wright, "United States Intervention in Lebanon," 53 A.J.I.L. 112 ff. (1959); *idem*, "International Law and Civil Strife," 1959 Proceedings, American Society of International Law 145 ff.; The Role of International Law in the Elimination of War 49 ff. (Manchester University Press, 1961).

[17] Art. 51. [18] Art. 2(5).

[19] Wright, *loc. cit.* note 3 above, p. 16; *idem*, "The Outlawry of War and the Law of War," 47 A.J.I.L. 365 ff. (July, 1953); "The New Law of War and Neutrality," 6 Netherlands International Law Review 412 ff. (Special issue, July, 1959).

[20] "The Security Council. . . .

1. *Affirms* that the fulfilment of Charter principles requires the establishment of a just and lasting peace in the Middle East which should include the application of both the following principles:

    (i) Withdrawal of Israeli armed forces from territories occupied in the recent conflict;

    (ii) Termination of all claims or states of belligerency and respect for and acknowledgement of the sovereignty, territorial integrity and political independence of every State in the area and their right to live in peace within secure and recognized boundaries free from threats or acts of force;"

draw its armed forces from the recently occupied territories and the Arab states must renounce the claim of a "state of war," recognize Israel as a sovereign state, and declare that they will respect the territorial integrity and political independence of that state within secure and recognized boundaries.

These mutual renunciations must be simultaneous. Israel will not withdraw until assured that the Arab states will respect its rights as a sovereign state under international law, and the Arab states will not give such assurance or accept a procedure for establishing permanent boundaries until Israel has withdrawn its occupation.

The action called for by paragraph 1 of the resolution seems clear. The Arab states adjacent to Israel, with exception of Syria, have accepted it.[21] As Israeli occupation continues, however, they appear to have been increasingly influenced by the demand of the "Palestine Liberation Organization" for elimination of Israel and establishment of an Arab state of Palestine as defined in the Mandate. This organization appears to control the operations of Arab commandos in the occupied territories and elsewhere.[22] Israel has attempted to interpret the phrase "from territories occupied in the recent conflict" as not including *all* such territories.[23] It has professed

[21] For Egypt's acceptance, see letter of March 19, 1968, from Mohamed El Kony, permanent representative of the U.A.R. (Egypt) to the U.N., to Secretary General U Thant, quoting statement by Egyptian Minister of Foreign Affairs, March 13, 1968 (U.N. Doc. S/8479, A/7074), and "Annual Report of Secretary General U Thant, 1967" (U.N. Doc. A/7201, Add. 1, par. 50). In a letter of Oct. 2, 1968, replying to my inquiry, Nabil El-araby, First Secretary to the Permanent Mission of the U.A.R. to the United Nations, wrote: "Jordan and the U.A.R. have declared several times their acceptance and complete readiness to discharge their obligations under that resolution." A. D. Horne states that Egypt and Jordan but not Syria had accepted the resolution (Washington Post, Dec. 25, 1969, p. A 15). This writer, while attending the conference on the Middle East crisis at Duke University in March, 1968, was informed by Arab diplomats that Lebanon had also accepted the resolution.

[22] See statement by representative of this Organization to the Special Committee of the General Assembly in December, 1968. 6 U.N. Monthly Chronicle 83–84 (Jan. 1969). A report from Palestine by Alfred Friendly in the Washington Post, Nov. 22, 1969, and a comment by Rowland Evans and Robert Novak, *ibid.*, Nov. 20, 1969, give evidence of increasing anxiety by the Israeli as the influence of this organization develops, not only in the Arab governments, but also among the refugees and other Arabs in the occupied territories and in Israel.

[23] Efforts are made to justify this interpretation by the Security Council's rejection of a draft resolution which would have made immediate withdrawal from all occupied territories more explicit. See Security Council Meeting, June 12, 1967, Doc. S/PV. 1360, and Shabtai Rosenne, "Direction for Middle East Settlement," 33 Law and Contemporary Problems 60 (Winter, 1968); see also note 9 above. The International Court has held that preliminary material needs to be consulted for treaty interpretation only when the text is not clear on its face. (Interpretation of the 1919 Convention concerning Employment of Women during the Night, P.C.I.J., Ser. A/B No. 50, Advisory Opinion, 1932.) See also Fenwick, International Law 536 (4th ed.); William Tung, International Law in an Organizing World 350 (New York, 1968). This is especially true of multilateral lawmaking treaties which resemble statutes more than contracts. Q. Wright, "The Interpretation of Multilateral Treaties," 23 A.J.I.L. 94 ff. (1929).

to annex old Jerusalem and has said it will not withdraw from this and other occupied areas such as the Golan heights in Syrian territory and the Gaza strip and portions of Sinai in territory occupied by Egypt before the six-day war. The Security Council might well insist that Syria and Israel accept the resolution and that Israel withdraw from "territories occupied in the recent hostilities." This is the requirement of international law and the Charter and is probably essential if the further steps toward a secure peace—those concerning determination of boundaries, navigation of waterways, just settlement of the refugees problem, and suitable guarantees—can be proceeded with. Even if accepted in principle, the first step presents difficulties in arranging stages of withdrawal, supervision, and timing in relation to Arab recognition of Israel, on which the United States and the Soviet Union have been negotiating since February, 1968.[24]

In view of the acceptance in principle of the resolution by the adjacent Arab states except Syria, the major obstacle to progress seems to be the refusal of Israel to do so and to agree to withdraw from occupied territories. This obstacle might be overcome by providing that the occupied territories, or those deemed critical by Israel, should not be re-occupied by Arab states after Israeli withdrawal, but by the United Nations. This might reduce Israel's reluctance to withdraw and would resemble the procedure by which the West Irian problem was dealt with.[25] It should be clear that such U.N. occupation should continue until the United Nations considers it no longer necessary and may not be terminated at discretion of the government claiming the territory, as was the U.N. occupation of Egyptian border areas which began in 1956 and was ended on the demand of Egypt in May, 1967.[26]

The essential components of a "just and lasting peace" are subjective. As stated in the UNESCO Constitution, "It is in the minds of men that peace must be constructed." The embittered and suspicious attitudes of Israel and its Arab neighbors must change, but such changes can only be induced and manifested by objective acts and utterances. The parties must formally recognize that each enjoys the rights of a sovereign state under international law and must accept procedures, first to establish permanent boundaries and later to solve other disputes. Each must affirm intent to observe its obligations under the Charter, especially to renounce the use or threat of force in its international relations. It must be appreciated especially by Israel that formal declarations or agreements induced by territorial occupation or other duress are not likely to last. A "just and lasting" peace does not mean that all disputes and claims have been settled, but only that all parties are confident that only peaceful methods, such as stated in Article 33 of the Charter, will be used to effect settlement.

[24] Note 12 above.

[25] Everyman's United Nations 124 ff. (8th ed., 1968).

[26] The justification for this withdrawal is discussed in the report of the Secretary General to the Security Council (U.N. Docs. S/7896, May 19, 1967, and S/7906, May 26, 1967) and to the General Assembly (U.N. Doc. A/6730/Add. 3, June 26, 1967). See also Q. Wright, *loc. cit.* note 3 above, p. 23; and J. I. Garvey, above, p. 241 *et seq.*

It is doubtful whether the problem of boundaries can be settled by bilateral negotiations of the parties as demanded by Israel. The Arabs will not negotiate until Israel has withdrawn from the recently occupied territories and Israel will not negotiate if areas which it deems essential are restored to the former Arab occupants.[27] If the occupied areas were controlled by the United Nations after Israel's withdrawal, the prospects of negotiation would be improved. Furthermore, the raids of Arab guerrillas in and from occupied areas, likely to be stimulated rather than ended by vigorous Israel reprisals, suggest an Israeli interest in genuine peace which would imply an obligation of the Arab states to end the guerrilla raids.[28]

The problem is one which the United Nations must deal with. Israel is a creation of the United Nations. The United Nations ignored the principle of self-determination of peoples and the rights of the Arab peoples in Palestine, under the Mandate and Article 80 of the United Nations Charter, in order to carry out the policy of a national home for the Jewish people in Palestine, stated in the Balfour Declaration of 1917, and generally accepted in the League of Nations Mandate. Under the disturbed conditions which existed in 1947, the original concept of a cultural home in Palestine for Jews, Moslems and Christians seemed unattainable. Consequently partition was accepted by the United Nations, modified by the provision for the internationalization of Jerusalem and surrounding territory, where it was thought the original idea of a cultural home for the three religious groups under international protection could be effected.[29]

The justifiability of the original Arab objection to partition can hardly be questioned. However, the recognition of Israel by most states, the willingness of the Arabs prior to the armistices of 1949 to accept Israel within the boundaries proposed in the original United Nations resolution of November 29, 1947, the admission of Israel as a Member of the United Nations, and its continued existence as such for a period of twenty years, indicate that it must now be considered a sovereign state under international law.[80]

In view, however, of its origin and the continued hostility of its neighbors, the United Nations has a special responsibility to restore peace in the area and to establish permanent boundaries accepted by the states in the area. It should be understood that Israel has no generally recognized boundaries beyond those provided for in the original United Nations resolution of 1947. The armistice lines of 1949 and 1967 established merely cease-fire lines. The armistices of 1949 have, however, served as de facto boundaries for twenty years, and so have a somewhat different status from those of 1967.

It is suggested that after the mutual renunciation of hostilities and withdrawal from occupations called for by the Security Council's resolution of November 22, 1967, have been effected, the United Nations should seek to obtain agreement by Israel and its Arab neighbors to negotiate permanent

---

[27] This is implied by Israel's refusal to withdraw from occupied territories until permanent boundaries are accepted in treaties negotiated with each of its Arab neighbors.

[28] Note 22 above. [29] Note 8 above.

[80] Notes 7 and 8 above.

boundaries, directly or through a mediator, and if agreement on boundaries is not reached within a year, to agree on a third-party forum, in which boundary claims can be debated and decided. This procedure would be similar to that by which the Mosul dispute between Turkey and Iraq (then under British mandate) was settled in 1926. The Lausanne Treaty of 1924 had provided that if the dispute was not settled by negotiation within a year, the League of Nations Council would give a definitive decision.[31]

Among the forums which might be considered for settling the boundaries are the Security Council, acting under Article 38, or the General Assembly, acting under Article 14, but in either case the parties should agree to give the agency power not merely to recommend but to *decide* the boundary. Another possible forum might be the International Court of Justice given authority by the parties to decide on the boundary *ex aequo et bono* as provided in Article 38, paragraph 2, of the Court Statute. The deciding authority should not be limited by existing international law, but should be free to consider all the factors—political, social, and cultural—which the parties might advance. In such decisions the opinion of the inhabitants of the disputed territory has often been given much weight. Plebiscites have been arranged to determine their wishes in accord with the principle of self-determination of peoples. In view, however, of the movements— forced and voluntary—of the population of Palestine, the opinion of neither the present population nor that at any particular moment of history would seem appropriate. If the inhabitants of Palestine at the time of partition had been allowed to determine, Israel would have received no more than the original partition proposal, or perhaps even less as suggested by Count Bernadotte's report shortly before his assassination. If the present population were to determine, Israel would probably get most of the territory within the armistice lines of 1949 and perhaps some of the territory occupied in 1967. The fate of the plebiscite proposed for the Tacna-Arica area between Chile and Peru in 1925, when each was shipping in population to assure its victory in the plebiscite, indicates the problem. This boundary was finally settled by agreement of the parties.[32] Claims other than the wishes of the present or past population would have to be considered in determining Israel boundaries.

Another possible forum to decide the boundary would be an *ad hoc* arbitral tribunal composed of neutral arbitrators. This was suggested as the final procedure by the General Act for the Pacific Settlement of International Disputes, originally signed by twenty-three states under auspices of the League of Nations in 1928, and brought up to date by the United Nations two decades later, but signed by only a few states.

Clearly the problem of negotiating a forum acceptable to the parties would be difficult, whether before or after a year of negotiation, and would require considerable pressure by the United Nations and the great Powers acting within the Security Council. United Nations occupation of the territory would assist, especially if it implied responsibility of the United

---

[31] Q. Wright, "The Mosul Dispute," 20 A.J.I.L. 263 ff. (1926).
[32] *Idem*, "The Tacna Arica Dispute," 10 Minnesota Law Review 28 ff. (1925).

Nations to partition the occupied territory if the parties failed either to agree on a boundary or on a forum with power to decide.

The remaining issues,[33] it is believed, can be settled if the major issues of Israeli withdrawal from the recently occupied areas, Arab renunciation of hostility to Israel, and establishment of permanent boundaries are resolved.

Israel should have free access to the Suez Canal. The intent of the Constantinople Convention of 1888 was to make all states third-party beneficiaries assuring them the right of navigation in time of peace and war. This privilege has been enjoyed by the United States and many other nonparties to the convention. The Egyptian right of defense and responsibility to protect the Canal, recognized by the 9th and 10th Articles of the convention, were expressly limited by Article 11, which said such measures "shall not interfere with the free use of the canal." If Egypt actually wishes a stable peace, it should be willing to accept the United Nations resolution of 1951 supporting Israel's right to navigate the Canal as provided for in the convention, and in any case should be ready to carry out its commitment of 1957 to submit to the International Court of Justice all issues concerning the interpretation and application of the Constantinople Convention.[34]

The same is true of the issue of access by Israel to the Straits of Tiran and the Gulf of Aqaba. The Gulf appears to be a portion of the high seas because four states, including Israel, front on it. Under the *Corfu Channel* decision of the International Court of Justice, and the Territorial Sea Convention of 1958, such waters are open to innocent passage of the vessels of all states.[35]

The problem of refugees has resisted settlement because of Arab desire to win sympathy for the human misery involved, and Israel's unwillingness to admit more hostile Arabs to its territory. United Nations resolutions have called for settlement or compensation of the refugees by Israel,[36] and, if both parties are genuinely desirous to bury the hatchet, Israel should be

[33] Part 2 of the resolution of Nov. 22, 1967, provides:
"The Security Council . . . .
    2. *Affirms further* the necessity:
      (a) For guaranteeing freedom of navigation through international waterways in the area;
      (b) For achieving a just settlement of the refugee problem;
      (c) For guaranteeing the territorial inviolability and political independence of every state in the area, through measures including the establishment of demilitarized zones;"

[34] Q. Wright, "Intervention, 1956," 51 A.J.I.L. 261–272 (1957); *idem, loc. cit.* note 3 above, p. 20.

[35] *Ibid.* p. 22.

[36] Security Council Res. 237, June 14, 1967, U.N. Security Council, 22nd Sess., Official Records, 1361st meeting; 62 A.J.I.L. 305 (1968); General Assembly Res. 2252, July 4, 1967, General Assembly, 5th Emergency Spec. Sess., Official Records, Supp. 1; 62 A.J.I.L. 305 (1968). See also George Tomeh, Syrian Permanent Representative to the U.N., "Legal Status of Arab Refugees," 33 Law and Contemporary Problems 110 ff. (Winter, 1968).

prepared to carry out this obligation in the spirit in which Germany has compensated Israel for Hitler's persecution and massacre of Jews. Israel should permit as many refugees as she deems possible to return to their homes, over a period of time to permit returning groups to accommodate themselves to Israeli citizenship before the number becomes so large as to endanger Israel's security. Full compensation should be given to those not permitted to return, the amount to be determined by the International Court of Justice or an arbitral tribunal.

The problem of Jerusalem presents difficulties. The original partition resolution, and several subsequent resolutions of the General Assembly, supported the internationalization of Jerusalem and surrounding areas to assure access to the holy places by the three religious groups.[37] Two General Assembly resolutions of July 4 and 14, 1967, denied Israel's right to annex old Jerusalem which it had occupied.[38] The division of the city from 1949 to 1967 and the refusal of Jordan to admit Jews was unfortunate. Israel's large investment in western Jerusalem, which it has occupied since 1949, makes internationalization of the large area contemplated improbable.

The problem is an aspect of the general boundary question and should be dealt with in the way suggested. Israel's annexation should not be accepted and, like the other occupations of 1967, eastern Jerusalem might be placed under United Nations control until a settlement is reached. Israeli administration of the whole of Jerusalem, with agreements placing the holy places under United Nations guarantee with a United Nations supervisory commission in the area, might be considered. Such agreements should prevent in the future such serious violations of Arab rights in Jerusalem as have occurred during the Israeli occupation.[39]

Settlement of the Palestine problem might be facilitated by general recognition of Palestine, outside of Israel, as an Arab state after permanent boundaries of Israel are established. Jordan, which was part of the original Palestine mandated territory but was recognized in 1922 as virtually independent and not subject to the Jewish national home requirement, might or might not be part of the Palestine Arab state. In any case close economic relations between this state and Israel should be agreed upon. Such an arrangement was provided in the original United Nations Partition resolution of November 29, 1947, and was recommended in 1967 by the Council of the Sephardic Community in Israel claiming to represent the Oriental, mainly Arabic-speaking, majority of Israel's Jewish population.[40] Such an

[37] Res. 194, Dec. 11, 1948, U.N. General Assembly, 3rd Sess., Official Records, Rev. 21, 23, U.N. Doc. A/810; and Res. 303, Dec. 4, 1949, U.N. General Assembly, 4th Sess., Official Records, Rev. 25, U.N. Doc. A/1251. See also Shepard Jones, "The Status of Jerusalem," 33 Law and Contemporary Problems 169 ff. (Winter, 1968).

[38] U.N. General Assembly, Res. 2253, 2254, 5th Emergency Spec. Sess., Official Records, Supp. 1, p. 4, U.N. Doc. A/6798 (1967); 62 A.J.I.L. 307 (1968).

[39] Such an arrangement, distinguishing territorial sovereignty vested in Israel and functional sovereignty administered by an international commission has been proposed by Elihu Lauterpacht, Jerusalem and the Holy Places (London, October, 1968).

[40] 3 Israel's Oriental Problem 4–5, 7–8 (No. 1, 1967). See also Amos Perlmutter, 48 Commentary 14 ff. (Sept., 1969).

arrangement would assist in settling the refugees and would give partial satisfaction to the Palestine Liberation Organization.

Whatever the procedures accepted to settle the major problems of boundaries, the results should be incorporated in a treaty signed by Israel and its Arab neighbors. The whole should be placed under guarantee of the United Nations. Separate agreements should probably be made in respect to the Canal, the Gulf, the refugees and other issues, including the use of Jordan waters, but they should also be guaranteed by the United Nations. It should be recognized that any complaint of violation of any of these agreements should immediately be placed before the Security Council, and if it failed to act because of a veto, the issue should go to the General Assembly as provided in the Uniting for Peace Resolution of 1950. This procedure proved effective in the hostilities of 1956.

Legal Aspects of the Search for Peace in the Middle East

EUGENE V. ROSTOW

The topic set for the discussion tonight—legal aspects of the search for peace in the Middle East—must of course be examined, like any other legal problem, in the context of history and policy. The processes of politics which have been at work in the Middle East for more than sixty years make the famous Near Eastern Question of the nineteenth century seem like a children's game. The Near East has in fact plagued world politics for centuries. Disraeli's celebrated remark could have been made by nearly all his predecessors, and by all his successors. Over and over again, local rivalries, conflicts and enmities, bitter in themselves, have become irreconcilable when linked to the conflicting aspirations and fears of world Powers.

Since the focal point of our concern is the present and the future, I shall do no more than recall the break-up of the Turkish Empire, and the rise of Zionism and of Arab nationalism, during the first World War; the dissolution of French and British security positions, during and after the second World War; the emergence of Soviet ambition in the area, and its connection first with the Zionist cause, as a device to drive the British out of the Eastern Mediterranean, and then with the Arab dream of destroying Israel, as the catalyst for transformations greatly in its interest; and the special rôle of the United Nations in the creation of Israel in 1947, and in the wars and controversies which have swirled around it ever since.

Against this background, and that of customary international law, the effort to achieve a condition of peace in the Middle East—or at least a condition of peace between Israel and its neighbors—is taking place within a sharply defined legal framework. Three sets of documents are of primary importance in delineating that framework: the Armistice Agreements of 1949;[1] the Cease-Fire Resolutions of the Security Council, of June,

* Sterling Professor of Law and Public Affairs, Yale University.

[1] 42 U.N. Treaty Series 303, No. 656 (1949) (with Jordan); ibid., 327, No. 657 (1949) (with Syria); ibid., 251, No. 654 (1949) (with Egypt); ibid., 287, No. 655 (1949) (with Lebanon).

1967;[2] and the Security Council Resolution of November 22, 1967.[3] Other documents and rules of law are germane—the Tripartite Declaration of 1950,[4] for example, and successor statements, including the Eisenhower Middle East Resolution of March 9, 1957, which was amended and reaffirmed in 1961;[5] the Security Council resolutions on belligerency, the Suez Canal, and many other subjects; and the 1958 Convention on the Territorial Sea.[6] But the three documents I first listed dominate the problem, because they represent and embody rare moments of agreement on basic issues, made by the parties, and supported by the great Powers.

In view of my involvement in these problems for a time as an official of our Government, let me make explicit what will in any event be plain: that I shall take a position here which represents not only my personal and professional opinions, but those of American policy as well—American policy, be it said, increasingly conscious of Soviet penetration of the Middle East, and necessarily concerned to prevent Soviet hegemony.

I shall start, if I may, with Security Council Resolution No. 242, of November 22, 1967, for I consider it to be primary. That resolution was achieved after more than five months of intensive diplomatic effort on the part of the United States, Great Britain, Denmark, Canada, and a number of other countries. The history of that effort gives the text a very plain meaning indeed.

It will be recalled that when large-scale hostilities erupted on June 5, 1967, the Soviet Union blocked American cease-fire proposals for several days, until it realized what was happening in the field. Then, when the Cease-Fire Resolutions were finally in place, a major diplomatic campaign, extending around the world, was brought into focus first in the Security Council; then in the General Assembly; then at Glassboro; and finally back in the Security Council.

A number of positions emerged. Their interplay, and the resolution of that interplay, is reflected in the resolution itself.

The Soviet Union and its chief Arab associates wished to have Israel declared the aggressor and required, under Chapter VII if possible, to withdraw to the Armistice Demarcation Lines as they stood on June 5th, in exchange for the fewest possible assurances [7]: that after withdrawal, Israeli maritime rights in the Strait of Tiran would be "no problem" (sometimes the same thought was expressed about the Suez Canal as well); and that after Israeli withdrawal the possibility could be discussed of a document that might be filed with the Secretary General, or of a Security Council resolution, that would finally end any possibility of claiming that a "state of belligerency" existed between Israel and her neighbors.

[2] Security Council Res. 233, 234, 235, 236 (1967); 62 A.J.I.L. 303–304 (1968).
[3] Security Council Res. 242 (1967); 62 A.J.I.L. 482 (1968).
[4] 22 Dept. of State Bulletin 886 (1950).
[5] 71 Stat. 5, P.L. 87–5, March 9, 1957; 75 Stat. 463, P.L. 87–195, Sept. 4, 1961.
[6] 15 U. S. Treaties 1606, T.I.A.S., No. 5639; 516 U.N. Treaty Series 205; 52 A.J.I.L. 834 (1958).
[7] See, e.g., U.N. Doc. S/PV.1351, pp. 21–27, June 8, 1967.

The Israeli position was that the Arab governments had repudiated the Armistice Agreements of 1949 by going to war; that the parties should meet alone, and draw up a treaty of peace; and that until negotiations for that purpose began, Israel would not weaken its bargaining position by publicly revealing its peace aims, although the Prime Minister and the Foreign Minister did state publicly and officially that Israel had no territorial claims as such, but was interested in the territorial problem only insofar as issues of security and maritime rights, and, of course, the problem of Jerusalem, were concerned. Meanwhile, Israel began its administration of Jerusalem, the West Bank, the Golan Heights, the Gaza Strip and Sinai as the occupying Power under the Cease-Fire Resolutions, justifying its policies "at the municipal level," and without annexations, in the perspective of that branch of international law.[8]

The United States, Canada, most of the West European and Latin American nations, and a large number of nations from other parts of the world, supported a different approach, which ultimately prevailed.

In view of the taut circumstances of May and June, 1967, no majority could be obtained, either in the Security Council or the General Assembly, to declare Israel the aggressor. The question of who fired the first shot, difficult enough to resolve in itself, had to be examined as part of a sequence of Byzantine complexity: the false reports of Israeli mobilization against Syria; the removal of U.N.E.F. forces from the Sinai and the Gaza Strip; the closing of the Strait of Tiran; the mobilization of Arab forces around Israel, and the establishment of a unified command; and the cycle of statements, propaganda, speeches and diplomatic efforts which marked the final weeks before June 5. Before that mystery, sober opinion refused to reach the conclusion that Israel was the aggressor. No serious attempt was made to obtain a resolution declaring the United Arab Republic to be the aggressor.

Secondly, the majority opinion both in the General Assembly and in the Security Council supported the American view, first announced on June 5, 1967,[9] and stated more fully on June 19, 1967,[10] that after twenty bitter and tragic years of "war," "belligerency," and guerrilla activity in the Middle East, the quarrel had become a burden to world peace, and that the world community should finally insist on the establishment of a condition of peace, flowing from the agreement of the parties.

Third, the experience of the international community with the understandings which ended the Suez Crisis of 1956–1957 led to the conclusion that Israel should not be required to withdraw from the cease-fire lines

[8] Stone, No Peace—No War in the Middle East 7–20 (1969); E. Lauterpacht, Jerusalem and the Holy Places 50–51 (1968); McNair and Watts, The Legal Effects of War, Ch. 17 (1966); Gutteridge, "The Protection of Civilians in Occupied Territory," The Yearbook of World Affairs 290 (1951); Stone, The Middle-East under Cease Fire 10–13 (1967); Gazit, Israel's Policy in the Administered Territories (1969); Government of Israel, Two Years of Military Government, 1967–1969, (1969).

[9] 56 Dept. of State Bulletin 949–953 (1967).

[10] President Johnson, "Principles for Peace in the Middle East," 57 Dept. of State Bulletin 31 (1967).

except as part of a firm prior agreement which dealt with all the major issues in the controversy: justice for the refugees; guarantees of security for Israel's border, and her maritime rights in the Gulf of Aqaba and the Suez Canal; a solution for Jerusalem which met the legitimate interests of Jordan and of Israel, and of the three world religions which regard Jerusalem as a Holy City; and the establishment of a condition of peace.

In 1957, in deference to Arab sensitivity about seeming publicly to "recognize" Israel, to "negotiate" with Israel, or to make "peace" with Israel, the United States took the lead in negotiating understandings which led to the withdrawal of Israeli troops from the Sinai, and the stationing of U.N.E.F. forces along the Sinai border, in the Gaza Strip, and at Sharm-el-Sheikh. The terms of that understanding were spelled out in a carefully planned series of statements made by the governments both in their capitals, and before the General Assembly. Egyptian commitments of the period were broken one by one, the last being the request for the removal of U.N.E.F., and the closing of the Strait of Tiran to Israeli shipping in May, 1967. That step, it was clear from the international understandings of 1957, justified Israeli military action under Article 51 as an act of self-defense.[11]

Fourth, while the majority approach always linked Israeli withdrawal to the establishment of a condition of peace through an agreement among the parties which would also resolve long-standing controversies about the refugees, maritime rights, and Jerusalem, the question remained, "To what boundaries should Israel withdraw?" On this issue, the American position was sharply drawn, and rested on a critical provision of the Armistice Agreements of 1949. Those agreements provided in each case that the Armistice Demarcation Line "is not to be construed in any sense as a political or territorial boundary, and is delineated without prejudice to rights, claims or positions of either Party to the Armistice as regards ultimate settlement of the Palestine question." [12] Many other provisions of each Agreement make it clear that the purpose of the Armistice was "to facilitate the transition from the present truce to permanent peace in Palestine" and that all such non-military "rights, claims, or interests" were subject to "later settlement" by agreement of the parties, as part of the transition from armistice to peace.[13] These paragraphs, which were put into the agreements at Arab insistence, were the legal foundation for the controversies over the wording of paragraphs 1 and 3 of Security Council Resolution 242, of November 22, 1967.[14]

---

[11] Many of the critical documents appear in Department of State, United States Policy in the Middle East, September, 1956–June, 1957 (1957, esp. pp. 332–342; United States Congress, Senate Committee on Foreign Relations, "A Select Chronology and Background Documents Relating to the Middle East," prepared by the Library of Congress, Legislative Reference Service (1967, rev. ed., 1969). See also H. Finer, Dulles over Suez (1964), Chs. 17 and 18.

[12] 42 U.N. Treaty Series, 256, Art. V, par. 2 (1949).

[13] Ibid., Preamble, p. 252; Art. I, p. 252; Art. IV, par. 3, p. 256; Art. XI and Art. XII, p. 268.

[14] "The Security Council . . .

That resolution, promulgated under Chapter VI of the Charter, finally received the unanimous support of the Council. It was backed in advance by the assurance of the key countries that they would accept the resolution and work with Ambassador Jarring to implement it.

It is important to recall what the resolution requires. It calls upon the parties to reach "a peaceful and accepted" agreement which would definitively settle the Arab–Israeli controversy, and establish conditions of "just and lasting peace" in the area in accordance with the "provisions and principles" stated in the resolution. The agreement required by paragraph 3 of the resolution, the Security Council said, should establish "secure and recognized boundaries" between Israel and its neighbors "free from threats or acts of force," to replace the Armistice Demarcation Lines established in 1949, and the cease-fire lines of June, 1967. The Israeli armed forces should withdraw to such lines, as part of a comprehensive agreement, settling all the issues mentioned in the resolution, and in a condition of peace.

On this point, the American position has been the same under both the Johnson and the Nixon Administrations. The new and definitive political boundaries should not represent "the weight of conquest," both Administrations have said; on the other hand, under the policy and language of the Armistice Agreements of 1949, and of the Security Council Resolution of November 22, 1967, they need not be the same as the Armistice Demarcation Lines.[15] The walls and machine guns that divided Jerusalem need not be restored. And adjustments can be made by agreement, under paragraph 2 of Security Council Resolution 242, to guarantee maritime rights "through international waterways in the area," and, equally, to guarantee "the territorial inviolability and political independence of every State in the area, through measures including the establishment of demilitarized zones."[16]

"(1) Affirms that the fulfilment of Charter principles requires the establishment of a just and lasting peace in the Middle East which should include the application of both the following principles:

   (i) Withdrawal of Israeli armed forces from territories occupied in the recent conflict;

   (ii) Termination of all claims or states of belligerency and respect for and acknowledgement of the sovereignty, territorial integrity and political independence of every State in the area and their right to live in peace within secure and recognized boundaries free from threats or acts of force;

"(2) Affirms further the necessity

   (a) For guaranteeing freedom of navigation through international waterways in the area;

   (b) For achieving a just settlement of the refugee problem;

   (c) For guaranteeing the territorial inviolability and political independence of every State in the area, through measures including the establishment of demilitarized zones."

[15] Speech by President Johnson, Sept. 10, 1968, 59 Dept. of State Bulletin 348 (1968); Speech by Secretary Rogers, Dec. 9, 1969, 62 Dept. of State Bulletin 7 (1970).

[16] See note 14 above.

This is the legal significance of the omission of the word "the" from paragraph 1 (i) of the resolution, which calls for the withdrawal of Israeli armed forces "from territories occupied in the recent conflict," and not "from *the* territories occupied in the recent conflict." Repeated attempts to amend this sentence by inserting the word "the" failed in the Security Council. It is therefore not legally possible to assert that the provision requires Israeli withdrawal from *all* the territories now occupied under the Cease-Fire Resolutions to the Armistice Demarcation Lines.

This aspect of the relationship between the Security Council Resolution of November 22, 1967, and the Armistice Agreements of 1949 likewise explains the reference in the resolution to the rather murky principle of "the inadmissibility of the acquisition of territory by war." [17] Whatever the full implications of that obscure idea may be, it would clearly permit the territorial adjustments and special security provisions called for by the Security Council resolution [18] and the Armistice Agreements of 1949.

The resolution provided that the Secretary General should appoint a representative to consult with the parties, and assist them in reaching the agreement required by paragraph 3 of the resolution.

I might add a word on the much mooted question of who has "accepted" the resolution. As I indicated earlier, this is not a real issue, since the key parties to the hostilities had given advance assurances that they would co-operate with the Secretary General's representative to promote the agreement called for by the resolution. Shortly after Ambassador Jarring had begun his consultations in the area, however, the question emerged, in the form of Arab insistence that Israel indicate its "acceptance" of the resolution, or its "implementation" of the agreement, before discussions could proceed. One version of these proposals would be that Israel withdraw to the Armistice Demarcation Lines, as they stood on June 4, 1967, in advance of negotiations on any other problems of the resolution. This position, of course, would violate the text of the resolution, and the experience of broken promises which the text reflects.

A good deal of the diplomatic history of this problem is reported in Foreign Minister Eban's comprehensive speech to the General Assembly on October 8, 1968.[19] The Israeli position is summarized in the statement of May 1, 1968, made to the Security Council by the Israeli Permanent Representative to the United Nations:

> In declarations and statements made publicly and to Mr. Jarring, my Government has indicated its acceptance of the Security Council resolution for the promotion of agreement on the establishment of a just and lasting peace. I am also authorized to reaffirm that we are willing to seek agreement with each Arab State on all matters included in that resolution.

On May 31, 1968, Foreign Minister Eban reiterated this statement in the Israeli Parliament.

[17] Security Council Res. 242 (1967), Preamble.
[18] See S. M. Schwebel, "What Weight to Conquest?", 64 A.J.I.L. 344 (1970).
[19] U.N. General Assembly, 230th Plenary Session, p. 1686.

Corresponding statements have been made publicly and privately by other parties to the conflict, but without specific reference to the requirement of "agreement" in paragraph 3 of the resolution. The Government of the United Arab Republic has repeatedly said that it accepts the resolution as requiring "a package deal," but it has thus far rejected procedures for consultation and negotiation accepted by other parties to the conflict.

There is great skepticism among the parties: a skepticism altogether natural against the background of more than twenty years of history. The Arabs fear that Israel has no intention of withdrawing, even to secure and recognized boundaries; Israel fears that the Arabs have no intention of making peace.

But Israel has said repeatedly and officially that it has no territorial claims as such; that its sole interest in the territorial problem is to assure its security, and to obtain viable guarantees of its maritime rights; and that, even on the difficult issue of Jerusalem, it is willing to stretch its imagination in the interest of accommodating Jordanian and international interests in the Holy City.

These assurances by Israel have been the foundation and the predicate of the American position in the long months since June, 1967. If the Arabs are skeptical of Israeli professions, their remedy is obvious: put them to the test of negotiation. They could be sure, as Prime Minister Golda Meir remarked the other day, that the position of the United States in the negotiating process would come more than half way to meet their claims.

To this point, however, it has proved impossible to initiate the final stages of the processes of consultation and negotiation which are necessary to the fulfillment of the resolution. The reason for the stalemate is simple. The Government of the United Arab Republic has refused to implement the resolution. And thus far it has been backed in that posture by the Soviet Union. President Nasser could not long persist in this stand against the will of the Soviet Union. Under these circumstances, and in the nature of Arab opinion, no other party to the conflict can move towards peace.

In this connection, Secretary Rogers' recent comment is illuminating. He stated:

> We have never suggested any withdrawal until there was a final, binding, written agreement that satisfied all aspects of the Security Council resolution.
> In other words, we have never suggested that a withdrawal occur before there was a contractual agreement entered into by the parties, signed by the parties in each other's presence, an agreement that would provide full assurances to Israel that the Arabs would admit that Israel had a right to exist in peace.
> Now, that is what has been lacking in the past. The Arabs have never been willing to do that; and if that could be done, we think it would be a tremendous boon to the world.

Now, we have also provided that the security arrangements would be left to the parties to negotiate, such as Sharm-al-Shaykh, and the Gaza Strip, the demilitarized zone, and so forth.[20]

It is easy to understand the Soviet position, and that of the United Arab Republic, in terms of a policy of political and military expansion which threatens not only Israel, but Jordan, Lebanon, Saudi Arabia and the states of the Persian Gulf. It is not, however, a posture easy to reconcile with the terms and purposes of the Security Council Resolution of November 22, 1967.

The Future of Israel

NAHUM GOLDMANN

AFTER more than 50 years of Zionist activities—among them many decades over the international diplomatic front—and on looking back on the experiences gained in the 20 years of the existence of the state of Israel, I am beginning to have doubts as to whether the establishment of the state of Israel as it is today, a state like all other states in structure and form, was the fullest accomplishment of the Zionist idea and its twofold aim: to save Jews suffering from discrimination and persecution by giving them the opportunity for a decent and meaningful life in their own homeland; second, to ensure the survival of the Jewish people against the threat of disintegration and disappearance in those parts of the world where they enjoy full equality of rights. In expressing and explaining these thoughts, I want to make it clear that I have no doubt as to the historical justification and moral validity of Zionism. The concentration of a large part of the Jewish people in their own national home, where they are masters of their destiny, seems to me to be the only way to solve what has been called for centuries "the Jewish problem."

The character both of the Jewish people and of Jewish history can alone explain and justify the Zionist idea, criticized today by many anti-Israel countries and groups as a form of aggressive colonialism which has robbed the Arab people of a part of their patrimony. Any definition of the Jews as a race, a people, a religion, is incomplete; it is the combination of all these elements which accounts for the singular character and the unique destiny of Judaism. There is no other example of a people which has lost its own state and country of origin, which is dispersed in countries all over the world, which has gone through hundreds of years of persecution—from simple discrimination and denial of equal rights to the barbaric annihilation of millions by the Nazis—and which not only survived these tragic periods, but has consistently made notable contributions to civilization. In our own generation, the three greatest figures, who may have influenced our present life and thinking more than any others— Marx, Freud and Einstein—have been Jews. With such a history, the Jewish people certainly deserves to be given the means for its survival; and humanity, having been responsible for hundreds of years of suffering and having failed to do anything radical to save the Jewish people in the Nazi period, owes this people a moral debt which can be discharged only by helping it to secure its survival.

Experience has shown that only a country of its own, however small, can serve this purpose. And only Palestine can be this country, in view of the religious, emotional and even mystical attachment of the Jews to "Eretz Israel," the Land of Israel, in which they made their greatest contribution to human civilization; which in no period of their history they were ready to forget; and for the return to which they prayed and longed for during thousands of years. Only because of this particular attachment of the dispersed people to its country of origin can the Jewish claim to Palestine be justified against the Arab argument that it belongs to them because they lived there as a majority for several centuries. Under normal rules of international life, there is no question that the Arab claim has meaning and substance, and it would be foolish and unfair to deny its justification. Dr. Chaim Weizmann repeatedly declared that the Arab-Jewish conflict with regard to Palestine is a clash between two rights, not between right and wrong, and that is what makes it so complex and difficult. Only if one understands the singularity of the Jewish people (which has nothing to do with any notion of superiority) and its tragic history can one presume that the Jewish claim is morally and historically superior. The Arab peoples possess immense territories in which they are masters of their destiny, and their survival and future are in no way endangered by their renunciation of their claim to a very small part of their overall territorial expanse; whereas tiny Palestine is for the Jewish people the only means of survival and the sole guarantee of a creative future. The fact that in a relatively short period of time most of the peoples of the world have recognized this claim and that, under the impact of the Nazi tragedy, more than two-thirds of the United Nations approved the idea of a Jewish state in a part of Palestine—the Soviet as well as the Western bloc voting in favor—proves realistically the validity of the Jewish right as against the Arab one.

II

It is the very uniqueness of the Jewish problem and of the

Zionist idea as its solution which, in the last analysis, makes me doubt whether the creation and existence of a Jewish state no different in structure and character from any other state can be the real implementation of Zionism. Even in those bygone years when I, with many other Zionist leaders, fought on the diplomatic front for the acceptance of the Jewish claim for a state in Palestine, I pondered whether we should not ask for a state of a specific character, more in conformity with the special nature of the Jewish people and Jewish history. Together with Dr. Weizmann, Ben Gurion and Moshe Sharett I was among the protagonists of the idea of a partition of Palestine as the inevitable condition for creating a Jewish state after the war. Even in those days I considered the possibility of asking for a specific form of state; but I felt then that, with all the difficulties inherent in getting the consent of the majority of nations for a Jewish state at all, it would be too much to ask at the same time for a unique character for this state.

More than 20 years have now gone by since the creation of the state of Israel. The experiences gained in these two decades have led me to the conviction that to guarantee its survival and to make sure that it fulfills its raison d'être as the main instrument of Jewish future, one must begin to think of a specific character and form for this state.

My growing skepticism as to the present form of Israel's existence is based on the two decisive conditions for its future and survival. These two conditions are, on the one hand, the relation between Israel and the Arab world in whose midst it exists, and on the other hand its relation with the Jewish people, in its large majority dispersed over the world. These two problems will decide the destiny of Israel. From a short-term point of view, it may seem that the United States and the Soviet Union are more important factors in Israel's international position, but seen from a long-term point of view, in the context of Jewish and general history, the Arab and the Jewish aspect of Israel's position is much more fundamental and decisive.

As far as the relations with the Arab world are concerned, it was one of the shortcomings of the Zionist movement that, in its early years, it did not fully realize the gravity and importance of this problem. Theodor Herzl, the author of the *Judenstaat* (the Jewish State) and founder of the Zionist movement, once said that the Zionist idea is a very simple one—that all it has to do is to "transport a people without a country to a country without a people." This formula, like all oversimplifications, was wrong in both its premises: a large part of the Jewish people after the Emancipation was already a people with a country, and Palestine, inhabited for centuries by the Arabs, was certainly not a country without a people. It is true at the same time that neither in ideology nor in practical political action Zionism ever thought of having to resort to an armed conflict with the Arab world in order to create the Jewish state. It was the— maybe naïve—hope and belief of the Zionist movement that it would be possible to get Arab consent to the creation of a Jewish homeland or a Jewish state by bringing the blessings of Western civilization into Palestine, which was then sparsely populated, by providing room for new immigrants through economic and social development of the country and through the fact of being part of the same Semitic race. Many Zionist leaders tried hard to bring about such a consent: from the negotiations of Dr. Weizmann after the First World War with Emir Faisal and his success in obtaining his agreement to a Jewish state, through all the years of endeavors by Ben Gurion, Sharett, myself (when I represented the Jewish Agency in Geneva at the League of Nations) and other Zionist leaders. All these attempts were unfortunately unsuccessful. And when the Arab states rejected the decision of the United Nations to partition Palestine and establish a Jewish state in part of it, and reacted to the creation of the state by the invasion of the country by their armies, it was inevitable that the state from its first days had to be defended by military action.

The inevitability of this development does not diminish its tragic character. The first War of Liberation was followed by two other major wars, and from all three Israel emerged victorious—most decisively from the 1967 Six Day War. But these victories have not, for the time being, brought nearer any solution of the Arab-Israeli conflict. Victories in themselves, however important they are psychologically both for the victor and the defeated, are meaningful only if they lead to stability and peace. The fact that nearly three years after the overwhelming victory of the Six Day War none of the Arab states is ready to negotiate directly with Israel and certainly not to sign a formal peace treaty indicates the depth of Arab resentment and the categorical Arab rejection of the Jewish state. The Arab world regards Israel as a foreign element in its midst and refuses to accept its existence. This feeling is growing with every new Israeli victory, so as to compensate for the Arab sentiment of humiliation and inferiority. The hope to impose peace on the Arab world, either by pressure of the big powers or by another Israeli victory, is more than slim. History proves that an imposed peace does not last long, even if a defeated people is forced for a certain time to accept a truce extracted by arms. In the case of Israel and the Arabs, this probability is much smaller in view of the tremendous numerical superiority of the Arab peoples which no Jewish immigration, however large, can hope to match and which must, particularly considering the much higher Arab birth rate, lead to an ever-growing numerical disproportion. At the moment, and probably for some time to come, the qualitative superiority of Israel is outstanding; it is unrealistic, however, to rely on it forever: the Arab peoples have created a brilliant civilization in the past and will no doubt one day acquire the technical know-how of the West, both in peaceful endeavors and in warfare.

III

For both parties to the conflict, the present state of affairs has disastrous consequences, by imposing on Israelis and Arabs alike the necessity to mobilize and strengthen their arms potential, by diverting their efforts to a large degree from social and economic progress to military efforts. For Israel these consequences are even more significant—in a negative way—than for the Arabs, because at least qualitatively it must maintain equality and even superiority against the many surrounding states and in view of the impact of the situation on its international position. The hope of some Israeli leaders that time is on their side and that the Arabs, recognizing Israel's military capability, will be more ready to accept the fait accompli of Israel's existence, seems to me based on very tenuous assumptions. The attitude of the Arab leaders, both of the conservative and the revolutionary type, and the state of mind of the new Arab generation, as reported by experts, show that rather than diminishing, their rejection of Israel and their determination not to accept it are growing.

The Arab peoples are characterized by an unusual capability of ignoring or discarding realities. When defeated they attach their hopes to a new war with a possible victory, and have been doing this, with regard to Israel, after three defeats. They draw an analogy with the Crusaders' state which, after long domination, was destroyed by Saladin. This fundamental psychological trait of the Arabs, which explains their seemingly unrealistic approach, is shared also by the Jews. If, in centuries of persecution, discrimination and misery, the Jewish people had accepted the realities of its fate, there would not be a Jewish people today; but against the tragedy of their situation, the Jews reacted with increasing faith and passionate hopes for the coming of the Messiah.

In addition to the growing hostility of the Arab world, from an international point of view, the political position of Israel is also becoming more difficult and isolated. It has lost much of the sympathy aroused by the brutal Arab threats of 1967 to annihilate the Jews in Israel physically in case of their victory, and by the admiration caused by Israel's brilliant victory. Today the whole communist world—with some exceptions—is fundamentally anti-Israel. France has changed its position from a friendly to an unfriendly one. Nobody can say whether England inclines more to the Arabs or to Israel. Over twenty Arab and Moslem states, and countries with large Moslem populations, like India, are hostile to Israel. The only real and decisive political support of Israel at the moment is supplied by the United States and a few smaller West European countries. But the experience of the last twenty years has shown that American backing cannot be taken for granted, as was demonstrated so dramatically in the wake of the Suez-Sinai campaign. The recent statements by Secretary of State Rogers, and the rejection of his proposals by the Israeli Government, indicate again the possibility of a deterioration of the fundamentally friendly policy of the United States toward Israel, and have caused serious worries and disquiet in Israel. One must realize that for a normal diplomat, whose policies are determined by day-to-day interests rather than by great visions or moral concepts, 80 to 90 million Arabs and many more million Moslems, in possession of the Middle Eastern lands with the richest oil resources in the world, weigh more heavily than the small state of Israel, even taking into account its Jewish periphery. In decades of political work I have nearly always found all foreign ministries to be anti-Zionist and anti-Israel. Only exceptional statesmen with a great historical outlook, like Lloyd George, Balfour, General Smuts, President Wilson, could overcome their prosaic, realistic concerns in favor of the moral concept underlying the Jewish claim for a country of their own.

Another negative consequence of this permanent state of war is the change of image of the young state of Israel, which is more admired in the world today for its military brilliance than for its spiritual achievements. Although the world justly admires the strength and the courage, the resourcefulness and the unexpected talents of Israel's army, this is certainly nothing either unique or specific to the Jewish people, nor have other peoples and civilizations been admired and remembered in history primarily for their military accomplishments. It is furthermore not to be underestimated that in many parts of the world it is the reactionary, nationalistic groups which have become the sponsors and admirers of Israel, whereas large parts of the progressive world have become disappointed and antagonistic to Israel. In its classical days, Zionism was a movement favored and supported by liberal, progressive and radical groups all over the world. This has changed considerably and may change even more if the present situation prevails.

From a Jewish point of view, too, the situation presents negative consequences of far-reaching importance. The large majority of the Jewish people lives outside the state of Israel and it must be taken for a fact that, despite all appeals, there is no reasonable expectation for very large immigration in the coming years. Israel had grown from its initial 650,000 to two and a half million inhabitants by absorbing the natural reservoir of Jews who had to come to the Jewish state as their only country of salvation—half a million Nazi victims from the camps after the war, hundreds of thousands of Jews in Moslem countries who were the first victims of Arab antagonism to Israel, and large numbers of Jews from Eastern Europe. The one remaining large community which could, in previous decades, have been an obvious source for large-scale immigration into Israel, Soviet Jewry, is unable to come as long as the U.S.S.R. is hostile. Even if one day this impediment should be overcome, I doubt whether a major part of Soviet Jewry would go to Israel; to count on a few hundred thousands may not be unrealistic, but there will certainly not be millions (and I refrain from speaking of the tremendous problem of their absorption). Unless something tragic and unexpected happens, like large-scale persecution of Jews in Western countries, it is unlikely that within the foreseeable future the large majority of Jews living outside the Jewish state will settle in Israel.

This too is characteristic of the specific situation and structure of the Jewish people, and it explains why the existence and development of Israel are so decisive for the survival of the Jewish people as a whole. The two great challenges—to use Toynbee's terminology—which account for the miracle of Jewish survival in the dispersion were, on the one hand, the permanent persecution, the impossibility for Jews to forget their Jewishness and the feeling of solidarity this generated and, on the other hand, the tremendous power of the Jewish religion, the set of laws which regulated the life of the Jewish individual and collectivity in the days of the ghetto and constituted, in Heinrich Heine's famous formula, the "portable fatherland" which every Jew carried along with him in all his migrations. (To give an example only of our days: the persecution and annihilation of millions of Jews by the Nazis made the survivors more conscious of their Jewishness, gave them a feeling of guilt for not having been able to save the victims and inspired them with the determination not to allow a similar tragedy to recur.)

Both these motivations have to a great degree lost their impact nowadays. Anti-Semitism is no more what it used to be in past centuries; Jews everywhere enjoy equality of rights and have become more and more integrated into the political, social, economic and cultural life of the countries in which they live. Simultaneously, the Jewish religion has ceased to be, at least for the larger part of the Jewish people, the great authoritative force which guides their daily life and guarantees their identity and distinctive character. It must be recalled that the Nazi holocaust destroyed precisely those great Jewish communities in Central and Eastern Europe which maintained fully the Jewish tradition and created all the ideas on which the Jewish people today bases its spiritual existence, and that they cannot be replaced by the Jewish communities in the free world of today, which do not lead their own separate cultural life. The existence of Israel as the new center where Jewish civilization can be continued and where new ideas will be created, as a source of challenge and inspiration for Diaspora Jewry, is therefore much more essential for Jewish survival today than was even envisaged by Zionist ideologists before the Nazi period.

IV

For the survival of the Jewish people as a whole, but also from the point of view of Israel's future, it is no exaggeration to say that the problem of Israel-Jewish relations, the ties which attach Jewish communities and individuals in the Diaspora to the state of Israel, is the number-one problem on which the success or failure of the Zionist solution of the Jewish question will finally depend. There are other peoples who have diasporas, sometimes counting millions, but these diasporas are unimportant in comparison with the vast majority of the peoples living in their own country and state. For example, if—as is probable—the German diaspora in the United States or in South America will assimilate and disappear as a distinct minority in the future, or if the same thing happens to the Italian minority on the American continent, this will in no way endanger the existence of the German or the Italian people and state. But if, for argument's sake, the Jewish Diaspora were to assimilate itself to such a degree that it would lose all interest in the state of Israel, the survival of the state would be nearly impossible. Without the solidarity and coöperation of world Jewry, the state of Israel would never have come into existence, because it is ludicrous to assume that 650,000 Jews without the millions of others backing them could have established a Jewish state in the midst of the Arab world. Without the economic, financial and political help of Jewish communities in the Diaspora, the state would have been unable to secure its existence, develop its economy, build up its brilliant army and provide possibilities for the immigration of more than a million and a half needy Jews. To strengthen this solidarity is therefore the *condition sine qua non* for the future of Israel.

The present character and structure of the state, however, endanger this basic precondition of Israel's survival. Its participation in international politics and its conflict with the Arab countries must inevitably bring Israeli policies into situations which clash with the political attitudes of many other states. This, in turn, in the present atmosphere of state nationalism, must lead to problems as far as the attachment and solidarity of Jews in the Diaspora with the state of Israel are concerned. A few examples of events in recent years illustrate this fact: hundreds of thousands of Jews had to leave the Moslem countries because of the Arab-Israeli wars; the Jewish communities of South Africa and above all Russia have to face serious problems partly because of the policies of Israel, which may be fully justified from the point of view of the state as it is today, but create difficulties for the Jews living in countries to which Israel is in opposition (what happened in France is a clear and additional manifestation of this problem). All this means that a Jewish state which requires the solidarity and the coöperation of the great majority of the Jewish people for its survival must have a character which can claim the sympathy of Jewish communities wherever they live.

Finally, the present situation has another and by far not the least negative consequence for the moral, spiritual and cultural character of Israel. This aspect is important if Israel is to fulfill its historical task of securing Jewish survival all over the world; it requires that Israel become a center of attraction, the greatest challenge for the best, most idealistic elements of the young generation, which is in great danger of largely being lost to the Jewish people within a few decades. An Israel at war, in permanent mobilization, cannot become this center. There are limits to the possibilities and capabilities of even the most gifted and purposeful people. The tremendous effort which Israel had to make in order to maintain its military strength and superiority, and which it will have to continue to make to an ever-increasing degree, naturally deflects a large part of its creative resources from cultural and spiritual endeavors. An Israel at war can attract thousands of volunteers, but it will not attract tens of thousands of young Jews who are dissatisfied with their present form of life—particularly in such rich countries as the United States —who look for more idealistic ways of existence and who would be natural candidates for immigration into Israel. One can but imagine what even in the very short lapse of 20 years could have been created by the dynamic genius of Israel—culturally, scientifically, spiritually—if its young, gifted and creative generation, with its tremendous energy and élan, not to speak of the billions of dollars, had been concentrated on science, literature, social experiments and similar tasks, instead of having had to build and maintain, as its greatest and most successful achievement, the brilliant army of the young state.

V

What is the answer to these questions? I belong, as my record proves, among the very first proponents of the idea of partition of

Palestine. I was always a political Zionist, in the sense that I believed that Jews must have a state of their own to secure their identity and civilization. More and more, however, I am coming to the conclusion that Israel cannot be one of the more than a hundred so-called sovereign national states as they exist today and that, instead of relying primarily and exclusively on its military and political strength, it should be not merely accepted but guaranteed, de jure and de facto, by all the peoples of the world, including the Arabs, and put under the permanent protection of the whole of mankind. This neutralization would certainly be an exception to the normal forms of modern states but, as I indicated before, the Jewish people and the Jewish history are unique. Their singular character and ceaseless suffering—particularly during the Nazi catastrophe—allow the Jewish state to demand from the world the right to establish its own national center in its old homeland and to guarantee its existence. How this guarantee should be practically formulated and implemented will have to be thought out and elaborated. There may be a slight precedent for it in the neutrality of Switzerland, which was guaranteed by the major powers more than 150 years ago, with lasting results. If Switzerland, because of its history and tradition, was and is entitled to claim and obtain the respect for its specific neutral character, the Jewish people and Israel certainly have an even greater moral claim to it.

This neutralization of Israel would naturally have important consequences for the character and the activities of the state. It would have to keep itself outside the sphere of power politics. Switzerland, for example, is not a member of the United Nations, because it is more than difficult to be in the United Nations and remain really neutral, abstaining from decisions which indicate a political position in favor of one or another of the groups and blocs in the world. Neutralization may even mean that a permanent symbolic international force may have to be stationed in the state of Israel, so that any attack on it would imply an attack on all the states guaranteeing Israel's existence and neutrality and participation in this international force. (To avoid misunderstandings, I would add that this does not signify the demilitarization of Israel and the abolition of its army, as long as there are no proof and experience to show the effectiveness of the international guarantee.) But by the nature of things, especially if this guarantee were tied up with a control of arms deliveries to the countries of the Middle East—a plan much discussed these days—the importance of the army and armaments would be reduced the more the guarantee and the neutralization become a reality, and this would allow Israel, as I said, to concentrate fully on its economic, cultural and spiritual efforts.

I can well imagine that such a neutralization could be the basis for an Arab-Israeli settlement and peace. Psychological and emotional motives are primarily at the root of the enduring Arab-Israeli conflict, as of most conflicts. All the factual problems—refugees, borders, etc.—could be solved without too great difficulties if there were goodwill and eagerness to reach an understanding. Seen from this aspect, the greatest hindrance in Arab-Israeli relations is the humiliation which the Arab world has suffered time and again by its military defeats. Whoever knows the Arabs, their history and character, agrees that pride is one of their most excessive virtues. But an appeal to the generosity of the Arabs, to be guarantors with the rest of the world for a Jewish state in a tiny part of the tremendous territories at their disposal—however unrealistic it may sound at the moment —may be more effective in the long run for an Arab-Israeli coexistence than one Israeli victory after another.

Neutralization would also do away with one of the major and understandable fears of the Arab world, namely the worry about possible Israeli territorial expansion on the one hand and, on the other, the obstacle which Israel, by its geopolitical position, represents to the ideal of a united policy for the Arab world. A guaranteed neutrality of Israel, including the guarantee of its boundaries after the settlement of the present conflict, would do away with the Arab fear of Israeli aggression and expansion. A neutralized Israel, outside the sphere of power politics, would not be a handicap for the policies of a united Arab world, which sooner or later will have to emerge in this period tending toward the creation of larger units comprising many sovereign states. I mention, in this regard, a conversation between Nasser and Dag Hammarskjöld, who tried several times in talks with him to find a basis for an Arab-Israeli agreement, and on which Hammarskjöld reported to me. Nasser, Hammarskjöld told me, had indicated that maybe the Arabs would acquiesce in the partition of Palestine and the establishment of a Jewish state in part of it, but they could never accept that Israel, by its location, partitions the whole Arab world—between Morocco and Iraq—and makes a united Arab policy very difficult. A neutralized Jewish state would do away with this fear.

The solution I suggest would depend on two preconditions. The first and obvious one is that the present crisis and war between Israel and the Arabs find an end by some kind of agreement between the parties, the exact nature of which this essay would not attempt to outline. Although nothing can be done concretely toward the implementation of my concept until this is achieved, if the concept should be accepted, it would naturally influence the character of the settlement of the present conflict.

The second precondition would be a basic settlement of the greatest human and emotional obstacle to Arab-Israeli understanding, namely the Arab refugee problem. Its main solution would have to consist in financing the settlement of the major part of the refugees in Cis- and Transjordan, which experts believe to be technically feasible; in Israel's acceptance, even as a matter of principle, of a limited number of Arab refugees; and possibly in yielding the Gaza Strip to Israel, on condition that it integrate the 200,000 Arabs living there as equal citizens.

There was a time when I advocated, privately and publicly, as a solution of the Arab-Israeli conflict, the establishment of a confederation of states of the Middle East in which Israel should be a member. In such a confederation the Arabs would naturally be the majority and Israel would have to adapt its world policies to their desires. When I negotiated the idea of partition in 1945 with Dean Acheson, the then Undersecretary of State, and got his agreement, followed later by the consent of President Truman to this idea, I submitted to him a memorandum on behalf of the Zionist Executive, formulating our proposal as twofold: a Jewish state in part of Palestine and this state as part of a confederation of Middle Eastern states. In view of the experience of the last 20 years, I am no longer convinced of the practicability of this solution. First of all, because of Arab individualism and the tremendous cleavage between the feudalistic Arab forces of yesterday and the revolutionary forces of today, it will take a very long time for the Arab world to unite and form such a confederation. Secondly, and even more decisively, if this day should come, Israel as the only Jewish state in such a confederation would be overwhelmed by the enormous numerical superiority of the Arabs, even if a few non-Arab states were to participate.

In the last two years, another solution suggested by certain Arabs as well as by some Israelis has been gaining the sympathy of Left-leaning pro-Arab groups in the free world. It proposes the recognition of the Palestinian people in Cis-jordan which (in the suggestion of El Fatah) would form one democratic Palestinian state together with Israel or (the solution favored by the Israeli proponents) would be recognized as a state of its own, linked in a federation with Israel. I do not regard this as practical, either from a Jewish or an Arab point of view.

From the Jewish aspect, such a unitarian Palestinian state would do away with the Jewish character of Israel. Had the purpose of Zionism been merely to save homeless and persecuted Jews, this concept might have been of value. But the Zionist ideal was to create a state which, beyond offering refuge to a number of suffering Jews, would be determined by its Jewish majority and would enable the Jewish people to maintain its traditions, develop its genius and contribute to world civilization. This aim could not be achieved by a binational Arab-Jewish Palestinian state, particularly in view of the higher birthrate of the Arab population, which would in a short while become the majority and do away with the Jewish character of this state— even if, as is the case in Lebanon, the equal position of both parts of the population, irrespective of their number, were to be guaranteed constitutionally. In addition, the Arab citizens of such a unitarian Palestinian state would, quite naturally, tend to side with the neighboring Arab states and would, consciously or unconsciously, constitute a "fifth column" within the state.

From an Arab point of view, genuine patriots will not agree to a Palestinian state which would imply their separation from the main body of the Arab world and would make them dependent on the superior strength and know-how of the Jewish citizens, with their greater technical and scientific knowledge and larger financial and economic means.

As for a federation between an Arab and a Jewish state, from an Arab point of view, the Israeli part would be economically and technologically so much superior that the Arab component would be practically a satellite of the Jewish one, which the Arab world would of course never accept.

For all these reasons, the idea seems to me—despite a certain attractiveness—unrealistic and unfeasible. I suggest, instead, the neutralization of the Jewish state of Israel.

VI

Let me now deal with the chances for this proposal which at first glance may seem utopian and not to be implemented. The emergence of the state of Israel shows that one must not be too hasty in characterizing radical, visionary proposals as quixotic and unrealistic. We are living in a great revolutionary period, probably the most revolutionary of human history, with tremendous events taking place again and again that even experts would have regarded as impossible a short while before. There are a number of arguments and facts which favor my solution and make it appear as practicable.

The Arab-Israeli conflict is a permanent grave worry to the world at large. It is one of the possible major causes of a world conflagration, in view of the geopolitical importance of the area, rich in oil resources, significant by its location among three continents and a center of interest for all major powers and the three major religions. It has already had great international consequences. It has facilitated Soviet penetration into the Middle East and into the Mediterranean. It has made the Middle East a place of unremitting tension and turbulence, and as the years go by without a settlement, the explosive character of the situation is increasing. This danger gives the Arab-Israeli conflict a much wider international significance than it would normally have, and makes any program for its solution important to the whole world. I believe that neither the United States nor the U.S.S.R., the decisive international powers for the Middle East problems, desire a war and both wish to avoid a confrontation because of the Arab-Israeli conflict; their attitude in the Six Day War proved it. Both are interested therefore in reaching a solution as soon as possible, especially if there is a chance for some general and global agreement between them, which would be impossible without a Middle East settlement. I am not sure that the United States is delighted with its primary responsibility for Israel's survival, nor that Russia is happy with its burden of protecting and rearming the Arabs without any certainty as to the usefulness and effectiveness of their rearmament. The U.S.S.R. has gained, because of the Arab-Israeli conflict, what Russia had tried to obtain for centuries without success, namely a firm position in the Middle East; and nothing in my view justifies the belief that it is interested in a permanent state of war in this area in order to maintain its position. I have been told by communist statesmen close to the Soviet Union that the Soviet position in the Middle East is so strong and deeply rooted—economically, financially and militarily—that it is genuinely interested now in stability and peace, especially in view of the much more important and difficult problems which it has to face in some of the nearer communist countries. I have reason to hope that the Soviet Union would be ready, in case of a satisfactory agreement, to guarantee the stability and territorial integrity of the countries of the Middle East, together with the United States or with the Big Powers or within the framework of the United Nations.

As for the Arabs, once they know that the Big Powers guarantee the stability of the Middle East and may agree to a limitation of arms deliveries to the area, the hope of the extremists among them of destroying Israel with the help of the U.S.S.R. would fade away. Furthermore, as I said, an appeal to them to be generous and magnanimous and accept the fait accompli of the existence of the tiny Jewish state and even be among its guarantors, could have a tremendous psychological impact on the Arabs who are a very emotional people, given to extremes, able to be cruel and brutal on the one hand, noble and large on the other. It is worthwhile to note here that in Jewish history, with its many encounters with countless peoples, states and civilizations, the Arab-Jewish rencontre was much more human and fair than the instances of Jewish-Christian relations. The great Arab-Jewish civilization in Spain, and the freedom of life and creativeness of Jewish communities in many Moslem countries in the past, may encourage the hope of a positive Arab reaction to this solution of the problem.

Israel would, I am sure, as a neutralized country quickly become a major international cultural center, especially in view of the special character of Jerusalem, to which all religions and peoples of the world would naturally have free access. I could see many international organizations, religious, cultural and social, being established in the city of Jerusalem which, as the capital of a neutralized state, could be a holy place and center for Christian and Moslem religious institutions. Israel would above all become the natural center of the creativeness of the Jewish people as a whole. It would attract many of the most gifted and idealistic elements of the Jewish community in the world. It would become the great new source of Jewish inspiration and challenges, and in the deepest sense of the word the spiritual center of the Jewish people.

One last observation. Zionism is a singular movement—the re-turn of a people to its ancient homeland after two thousand years —the result of the unique history of a unique people. Seen from a large historical point of view, which alone justifies, explains and validates the Zionist idea, I am convinced that the Jewish state, in order to survive, must represent the singularity of this people and its destiny. I cannot imagine that the thousands of years of Jewish suffering, persecution, resistance and heroism should end with a small state like dozens of others today, living continuously in peril of its annihiliation, bound to remain mo-bilized and armed to the teeth, and concentrating its major efforts on physical survival. Nor am I sure that the enthusiasm and loyalty of the Jewish people in the world will forever be secure for such a state. What I suggest here is something excep-tional, and therefore the fitting outcome of the exceptional Jew-ish history.

It may appear to hard-boiled politicians today as a quixotic vision. It is certainly no more quixotic by far than Herzl's *Judenstaat* seemed to the peoples of the world and to most of the Jews when it was published some 75 years ago. The history of the Zionist movement, as of many others, proves that the greatest real factors in history in the long run are neither armies nor physical, economic or political strength, but visions, ideas and dreams. These are the only things which give dignity and mean-ing to the history of mankind, so full of brutality, senselessness and crime. Jewish history certainly proves it: we survived not be-cause of our strength—physical, economic or political—but be-cause of our spirit. And therefore, seen from a historical point of view, this different concept of the character of a Jewish state as the solution of the Jewish problem may become not less real-istic than the original Zionist idea proved to be and could, I am inclined to think, be implemented in a much shorter period than it took for the *Judenstaat* to be carried into effect in the state of Israel.

The Arab-Israeli Conflict: An American Policy

JOHN C. CAMPBELL

THE purpose of recent American diplomatic initiatives in the Middle East is simply stated. It is to stop the fighting and bring the peace effort back to the point, now nearly three years ago, when Ambassador Gunnar Jarring was setting out on his mission to help bring about an agreed Arab-Israeli settlement on the basis of a unanimous U.N. resolution. It is a measure of the deterioration since that time that these modest proposals, the results of which are uncertain as these lines are written, have generated optimism by their initial success in breaking the fixed pattern of reliance on force alone. For they came at a time of gloom over the prospects for settlement and of alarm over military events which could bring major Soviet gains or grave risk of war. Participation of Soviet pilots and missile crews in military operations had already limited Israel's mastery of the skies over Egypt and might in time shift the balance of power which now favors Israel. Once that balance is upset, President Nixon has said, the United States "will do what is necessary" to restore it.

This is, many have said, a time for urgent American decision if we are to avoid bolder Soviet moves and a worse crisis later, or a desperate Israeli decision to launch a preventive war with incalculable consequences. In the background looms Israel's actual or potential atomic capability, not to be ignored even if it bears a "last resort" label. Precipitate action spurred by a sense of crisis may serve neither peace nor the national interest. But is the present initiative for Arab-Israeli negotiations enough? Weighing policies in the present atmosphere of mixed hope and alarm requires at the very least a perspective relating the past to the future.

Ever since the war of 1948 in Palestine there has been no peace between the Arab states and Israel, so it should be no surprise if peace cannot be found now. At no time have the Arab governments been able, even under the shock of defeat, to bring themselves to the point of talking directly with Israel. At no time has Israel been willing to make concessions which might induce the Arabs to make the peace that Israel wants. Each side has chosen to interpret the ambiguous U.N. resolution of November 1967 in accordance with its own views. So also in their gingerly acceptance of U.S. Secretary of State William Rogers' proposals made last June the U.A.R., Jordan and Israel took care not to retreat from basic positions which they have long preferred to the political risks lurking in substantive concessions for the sake of compromise.

Meanwhile, in the absence of a peace, Israel finds retention of the territories conquered in the 1967 war a military necessity, wholly aside from considerations of their political future. Abdel Nasser holds a door open to political settlement but will not give up recourse to force unless he finds that the kind of settlement he wants, including full satisfaction on Israeli withdrawal, can be won by other means. The more radical Arabs of Syria, Iraq and the Palestinian organizations will be looking for ways to discredit not only the effort for peace through diplomacy but also any Arab leader who goes along with it.

Thus the attempt to get a negotiated political settlement in the near future, encouraging as the initial indications may be, will probably have but an outside chance of success. Perhaps it makes more sense to concentrate on more immediate measures to contain the conflict and reduce the danger of further Soviet gains. In any case it will be necessary to have a sound estimate of the prospects for both sides, and of the aims and policies of the Soviet Union.

II

Israel's leaders count on the continuing success of their present strategy. If the Arab states will not negotiate peace, then let them suffer the consequences of the absence of peace. Israel's margin of military superiority, so runs the argument, can be maintained and even increased because the gap between Israeli and Arab technical proficiency will grow with time; whatever the quantity and type of weapons obtained by the Arabs, it will make no difference because they will not know how to make proper use of them. The Israeli reply to the question of when the Arabs may be able to reverse the military balance is a confident "Never."

This strategy depends for success, however, on factors outside Israel's control. First, Israel must be able to replace its advanced equipment, especially aircraft, and for the foreseeable future it must get such items from abroad, mainly from the United States.

Second, introduction of Soviet combat forces into the U.A.R. or other Arab states can cut down Israel's margin of superiority. Israeli strategy, accordingly, must rely heavily on American support both to retain its superiority over Arab enemies and to counterbalance the weight of Soviet intervention.

In the longer view, even if the Arabs prove unable to threaten Israel's security or to win back the lost territories, other serious questions will pose themselves for Israel. The prospect of unending war will compel spending a large percentage of resources for military purposes, a strain that will distort the economy and weigh heavily on the population. It may be a cliché to say that Israel will become a garrison state, but there is little doubt that its citizen army will be increasingly sacrificing civilian pursuits in favor of training for and waging war; that the demand for unity and full popular support for the nation in time of peril will limit the free atmosphere necessary to the working of the democratic political system; and that the great stress on military considerations will tend to inflate the power of those leaders who have the responsibility for the country's military security.

More serious for Israel, perhaps, will be the problem of handling the Palestinian Arabs now under its control in the occupied territories, plus predictable new difficulties in dealing with its old Arab minority. Caught between the Israeli authorities and the militant fedayeen, the Arab inhabitants are likely to be pushed into resistance, with the result that the cycle of violence and reprisal within the occupied territories will match the cycle of military operations across the borders. Even if Israel can control the Arabs fairly well by security measures, their mere presence under its jurisdiction will constitute a threat to the Israeli national state by the weight of their growing numbers. Unless they are allowed self-determination through Israeli withdrawal, Israel's choice lies between incorporating them into its political and social life or keeping them under control as a subject people. Neither choice is without grave forebodings for Israel's future.

Israel faces another dangerous prospect—increasing international isolation. Some of the admiration and goodwill in the world community gained at the time of its spectacular military victory under threat of extinction is no longer extended to a state which has taken on the role of a conquering and occupying power. Israel's uncoöperative and often contemptuous attitude toward the United Nations and its reluctance to coöperate with

outside powers seeking ways to move toward a political settlement have disillusioned and alienated public opinion in the
West. Even in the United States, the one power on which Israel
depends, enthusiasm for its cause has cooled outside the American
Jewish community. Despite the heavy support for Israel in the
Senate, the general mood of turning away from foreign involve-
ments, in the popular reaction against the Indochina war, makes
no exception for the Middle East.

All these factors, which are known to Israel's leaders and
people, have had but slight effect on their current policies. They
are either given an optimistic interpretation or pushed aside as
not convenient to talk about at the present time of struggle. The
few who have opposed the hard official line may some day win
more adherents to their thesis that total dependence on force as
the way to surmount growing dangers and reach the ultimate goal
of peace with the Arabs is self-defeating, and that the very
process of unending war is changing the character of Israeli
society in directions far from its original concepts. The recent
flurry over Nahum Goldmann, whose differing approach to
Israel's future was made manifest in these pages[1] and in his plan
for a dialogue with Nasser, raised the issue of the merits of conciliation at a time when Israel has considerable bargaining
power. But it was U.S. diplomacy, rather than a change of heart
in Jerusalem, that brought acceptance of the Rogers proposals.

III

That the future prospects for Israel are clouded with doubt
does not mean that Arab prospects are correspondingly bright.
Time is not working for anybody. The theory that Arab numbers,
economic growth and increasing competence in the use of arms
will eventually overwhelm Israel has no real substance, at least
not in this generation. If Arab leaders see a future more favorable
than the bleak short-term outlook, that is because they persist in
coloring the future with hopes and illusions.

The Arab states directly involved in the conflict are under
pressure from militant Palestinians and from their own public
opinion (which they did much to create) to look to force rather
than conciliation. They are reluctant or unwilling to establish
any durable ceasefire though they get the worst of the fighting. They concentrate their thoughts and resources on the armed

[1] "The Future of Israel," *Foreign Affairs*, April 1970.

struggle at the expense of many things which need to be done at home. The result is that they fail in both areas. King Hussein in Jordan and the government of Lebanon are unable to control the Palestinian fedayeen movements, with which they must negotiate as with sovereign powers. Even Nasser, though not directly threatened by the fedayeen, feels pressure to carry on the fight because he has clung to the role of leader of the Arab world.

What we are likely to see among the Arabs as time goes on is a turning of the forces of frustration and violence inward, into internal revolutions and intensification of inter-Arab strife. New governments appearing on the scene cannot be expected to be more moderate than those they replace. Certainly they will not be in Jordan and Lebanon if present trends continue. In Syria and Iraq it is established practice that each new revolutionary government promises ever more intense prosecution of the struggle against Israel. Saudi Arabia and Kuwait cannot be regarded as immune to these trends, especially after what has happened in Sudan and Libya. Their oil wealth and their economic relations with the West have given them a relatively high level of prosperity, and their financial support of the U.A.R. and Jordan and the Palestinian fedayeen may give them some insurance against radical forces, but over time they are bound to be vulnerable for the same reasons.

The Palestinian resistance organizations, judging by their methods and their ultimate aims, will only magnify the difficulties and increase the tension within the Arab world. The more radical of them are working to "liberate" not only Palestine from Zionism but Arab countries from their "reactionary" régimes, including Nasser's. These organizations feel they have nothing to lose from violence and turmoil; they gain encouragement from the continuing impotence of Arab governments and from increasing unrest among the Arabs under Israel's control.

It is often said that only the Palestinian Arabs and the Israeli can settle the Palestine problem, and this proposition may ultimately prove true. If a binational or federal solution was at least a possibility before 1948, however, it appears to have been buried under the events of the intervening years. Recently, similar ideas have been discussed in Israel and among Arab intellectuals in places like Tunis and Beirut. But the only effective leadership the Palestinian Arabs have lies in the fedayeen organizations. Probably it would take a series of cataclysmic events to make possible a real search on both sides for a basis for compromise. Meanwhile, the Palestinian Arabs have proved that they exist as a nation, or as a branch of the Arab nation, which will have to be taken into account by the Arab governments, by Israel, and by outside powers.

To sum up the Arabs' general plight, while they may take comfort in contemplating Israel's present and potential difficulties, they cannot expect alone to defeat Israel. So long as they cannot gain equality of military capability but continue to base policies on the illusion of doing so, they cannot break out of the cycle of thought and action which is self-destructive as well as inimical to reconciliation and peace. Probably it will take positive action on the part of others stronger and less tortured than themselves— say Israel, or the international community, or the Soviet Union —to turn them in more constructive directions. Of these the Soviet Union, which has fed Arab hopes but also at times restrained them, may have the crucial role to play.

IV

The Soviet role in the Middle East is indeed the question of the day. The commitment of Soviet combat personnel to the fighting in Egypt came as a rude shock to the United States. Coming on top of the build-up of Soviet naval power in the Mediterranean, the massive arms deliveries to Nasser, the sending of military advisers in the thousands to the U.A.R. and Syria, the use of naval facilities in those two countries and perhaps in Algeria, and the signs of Soviet interest in the Arabian Peninsula and the Indian Ocean, it added force to the arguments of those who had been pointing to those events as proof of a firm Soviet strategy to dominate the Middle East and as signs of forthcoming disaster for the United States and Western Europe if they did not wake up.

The remedies proposed range from massive aid to Israel, in order to keep the Arabs and Soviets at bay, to the virtual abandonment of Israel, in order to preserve and regain positions in the Arab world rapidly falling into Soviet hands. Mr. George W. Ball has advocated a showdown with the Soviet Union not unlike the Cuban affair of 1962, to call a halt to their recklessness and compel the withdrawal of their combat units from Egypt.[2] Israeli advocacy and inspired stories from Washington

[2] "Suez is the Front to Watch," *The New York Times Magazine*, June 28, 1970.

have harped on the same theme. Any proposals for American policy, particularly such drastic ones as these, should rest, of course, on the best estimate we can make of Soviet policies.

After the Six Day War, Moscow made the decision to restore its shaken position in the Arab world by rearming the U.A.R., Syria and Iraq, and by giving all-out political and diplomatic support to the Arab campaign for the unconditional withdrawal of Israel from the occupied territories. The main purpose behind that decision was the same that lay behind Soviet policy before 1967: to build a political base for influence in the Arab world and for the growth of Soviet power in the Middle East, taking advantage of the sapping effect of the Arab-Israeli conflict on the American position there. Soviet willingness to see a political settlement, as evidenced by support of the U.N. resolution of November 1967, by participation in later negotiations with the Western powers, and by many public statements, should be interpreted in the light of that purpose. The Soviet leaders have ideas of their own on what a reasonable settlement would be and are willing to talk about details but not to press on the Arab states (and particularly on Nasser) terms which the latter find objectionable. It is significant that Soviet terms include the two vital points of Israeli withdrawal and Arab acceptance of Israel's existence, but the withdrawal must be total and the nature of the acceptance is left vague.

Moscow's attitudes toward the Palestinian fedayeen organizations expose a Soviet dilemma. When the fedayeen leapt into the spotlight through raids and bombings and their growing influence in Arab countries, the Soviets gave them public praise but clearly preferred to see them under the control of Arab governments rather than acting as a freewheeling force unconcerned with Soviet interests and more inclined to look to Peking than to Moscow. More recently they have given greater recognition to the fedayeen movements, talked of support, established communication with some of their leaders, and may be dealing with them through communist channels, but they have neither established a program of direct arms aid nor backed the political aim of destroying the state of Israel. The ambivalence remains. The Soviet Union is conservative in wishing to base its influence on reasonably stable Arab governments rather than risk entanglement in the revolutionary and factional struggles of the unpredictable Palestinians. But it does not want to be left behind if

the latter carve out for themselves a significant role in determining the Arab future.

For the Soviets the main front in the Middle East is the battle-
line between the U.A.R. and Israel; that is one point on which
their view is in accord with Israel's. The entire Soviet position
in the region rests on the U.A.R. and the Nasser régime. Thus
in the situation of last spring when Israeli aircraft were ranging
at will over Egyptian territory, bombing within a few miles of
Cairo, the Soviet leaders on receiving Nasser's desperate plea
must have felt they had no alternative to use of their own combat units to prevent his total humiliation and possible fall. Was
this an essentially defensive move to stabilize a worsening situation or the first of a number of moves aimed at shifting the military balance, turning the tide of war against Israel, and forcing
the United States out of the Middle East? Their going along
with the ceasefire proposal is no solid proof either way.

Soviet policy since 1967 has been successful in that Soviet influence is stronger than ever in the U.A.R. and has made inroads in
surrounding Arab countries, all without great risk of a crisis or
threat of war with the United States. Yet the future holds no
assurance that events will move only in that same direction and
at no greater risk. The Soviets have used the Arabs but have also
been used by them, and have come to depend on them. They have
made heavy political and economic investments in Egypt, in
Syria and Iraq, and in radical and socialist elements in general.
They do not, however, dominate any Arab state. They have to
negotiate with Abdel Nasser, not just give him orders. They cannot control the upheavals of Arab politics; they cannot be sure
that pro-Soviet régimes or individuals will stay in power; they
cannot hope for immunity from the forces of Arab nationalism
which can assert themselves against Russia as they have against
the West; they may find themselves blamed for economic failures
despite the aid they have provided. They may also see their
involvement gradually, almost unwittingly, deepened to the
point of placing them at the mercy of decisions made not in
Moscow but in Jerusalem or Cairo. Above all, they do not wish
to be faced with the dilemmas another all-out Arab-Israeli war
would pose.

Soviet foreign policy, moreover, does not exist in isolated geographic compartments. The Middle East is not the center of
aspirations of the Soviet Union, to borrow the language of the

abortive Nazi-Soviet negotiations of 1940 often cited to prove that it is. It is important for security reasons, being located on Russia's doorstep, and as a route to the expansion of military and political influence to the regions beyond. But the Soviet régime throughout its history has been more vitally concerned with Europe and East Asia. It would not be likely to engage its power in the Middle East without regard to aims, risks, and possible setbacks on those other two fronts, any more than it would do so without regard to crucial aspects of the relationship with the United States.

As yet we have seen no specific evidence to the effect that the dispute with China or events in Europe or the status of relations with the United States on the Strategic Arms Limitation Talks (SALT) or Southeast Asia have put limits on Soviet activity in the Middle East. Yet such developments as a heightening of the conflict with China, a new challenge to Soviet authority in Eastern Europe, or a crisis with the West over Berlin should lead to greater caution in Soviet Middle East policy. At the least the need for a secure rear in coping with China weighs heavily in Kremlin thinking.

The Soviet leadership will change and Soviet policy in the Middle East will not be immune to change. Though we cannot predict such matters as the factional line-ups, the record of the past justifies the following conclusions on how Soviet political leaders have seen and probably will continue to see the situation in the Middle East: (a) they will take opportunities, and even make some, to reduce American positions and influence, and will push ahead with the expansion of their naval presence in the region and their political footholds in Arab countries; (b) they will play the game of competition, however, in the knowledge that they have neither local military superiority nor overall strategic superiority; (c) they will be sensitive to American moves which affect the local balance and the relative positions of the two great powers; and (d) while polarization of alignments has brought them benefits, they are wary of its passing the point where they are deprived of freedom of choice, and they will continually reassess their support and commitments to the Arabs in the light of Soviet rather than Arab interests.

At a time of apparent American uncertainty the Soviet leaders may not be inclined to show caution until events persuade them to do so. But it is hard to see any absolutes in Soviet policy—any imperatives derived from Leninism or the heritage of the tsars —driving them to the goal of domination of the Middle East. They have a sounder sense of their own limitations in coping with Middle Eastern nations and with rival powers than do observers in the United States who speak of imminent Soviet mastery of the Mediterranean, of a joint Soviet-Arab assault on Israel to destroy its independence, of the danger of Soviet control of all the oil of the Middle East and North Africa, and of Soviet domination of the Red Sea, the Persian Gulf and the Indian Ocean once the Suez Canal is reopened. Could the Soviets control the Arab world after a victory over Israel any more than they control it today? We should not underestimate Soviet gains, actual and potential, but the picture of a Middle East in which Turkey, Iran and all the Arab states are serving as docile instruments of the U.S.S.R., with no other power on the horizon, belongs in the realm of fantasy.

V

Putting the Soviet threat into realistic perspective does not mean that the present situation is not full of danger or that the United States can afford a policy of complacency or indifference. The present moment, because of the bold Soviet move in using its own combat forces in Egypt, requires a firmness and a specificity of policy which the United States has not previously shown. But it also requires a long-range approach in which current moves and proposals will logically fit.

First come the elements of a declaratory policy, points which the United States should put on the record as its views and positions for the future peace and security of the region. They have to do with the framework of an Arab-Israeli settlement, establishing an American position that will be there for both sides and for the world to see. It may seem paradoxical to admit that an early settlement is not likely and then in the same breath propose that the principles of a sound settlement guide our current policies, but it is the only way to avoid foreclosing the future and to take account of our interests on both sides. Some major points have been put forward in the Rogers speech of December 9, 1969, and elsewhere. With due regard to the state of negotiations under Jarring's auspices, they should be completed by new statements so that the picture would look something like this:

(a) Arab acceptance of Israel as a sovereign state and Israeli withdrawal o agreed state frontiers described below, set forth in binding obligations (the wo points being inseparably linked but with some flexibility in timing to nake it easier for both sides to carry them out).

(b) State frontiers to be the lines of June 4, 1967, with certain specific xceptions: minor adjustments in the border between Israel and the West 3ank (whether the latter is Jordan or Arab Palestine); special international tatus for East Jerusalem, the detailed legal and other aspects of which would e left to consideration among the many parties concerned; special status for he Gaza Strip (*e.g.* U.N. administration) for a period of about 10 years; the 3olan Heights to be returned to Syria, but only after Syrian acceptance of he U.N. resolution of November 1967 and of the other points of settlement.

(c) Demilitarized zones on both sides of the frontiers, including total de-nilitarization of the Golan Heights, the Gaza Strip and the Sharm-el-Sheikh rea; U.N. observers and peacekeeping forces in all demilitarized zones, sub-ect to withdrawal only with the consent of the Security Council.

(d) Acceptance of Israel's right to navigate the Suez Canal and the Strait f Tiran on a basis of equality with other states.

(e) Recognition of the right of the Arab people of Palestine to existence as nation and to compensation for their privations as refugees, within the ramework of a peace settlement as outlined here, but with no unlimited ight of return to Israel.

(f) International guarantees of the settlement, within the framework of hich there would be a U.S. guarantee to Israel.

By taking the role of advocate of a fair settlement not tied to ither side and obviously not based on tactical considerations, the Jnited States would be presenting to Israel, the Arabs and the oviet Union an alternative to their present policies. Let these erms sink into the minds of the respective leaderships and of hose in their societies who may make themselves heard in the uture. The vital points among the terms are the first and the last. he first gives us the best basis for decisions, policies and actions n such specific issues as cooling off the conflict, arms deliveries o the parties, and forward movement on disputed questions such s the Arab refugees. The last point stresses the international ramework necessary to any settlement, including the close in-olvement of the United Nations as has been the case since 1947; nd the added factor, an American guarantee, may be the one hing that would make possible Israel's acceptance.

So far as an approach to the Arabs is concerned, America has ess chance of influencing them than any of the other parties, but primary task is to keep in communication with them. It must pproach them against the background of a position on Israeli vithdrawal which is clear, is not tied to a set of known or un-nown Israeli conditions and procedures, and depends only on

explicit Arab acceptance of Israel. That last point is the on(
which Arab governments have found so difficult to swallow
although they admit they have accepted the existence of Israe
de facto since 1949. Some flexibility on how their formal ac
ceptance is expressed is possible, but there is no getting aroun(
the basic requirement. On the other side of the equation, the U.S
position on Israeli withdrawal should help put to rest Ara[
charges and fears concerning past or future American suppor
of Israeli expansion. Except for areas with special intcrnationa
status, Arab rights to all territories conquered in 1967 would b(
accepted; the "minor adjustments" would be reciprocal conces
sions to straighten the line as at Latrun, not cession of large piece
of territory on grounds of military security. And the Unite(
States should leave no doubt, while the question of withdrawa
is pending, of its total opposition to any extension of Israel
occupation into territory beyond the present ceasefire lines.

These considerations will make no impression on Palestinia1
resistance leaders and others dedicated to the destruction of th(
state of Israel. Yet it is important to see that the message gets t(
them and to all Palestinian Arabs, especially those living in th(
occupied territories. The message is a double one, half encourag
ing and half limiting: the United States recognizes their righ
to self-expression as a people, but it does not accept the proposi
tion of the disappearance of Israel. The implication is that th
Palestinian Arabs are entitled to find their future on that part o
the territory of Palestine which was not part of Israel before th
war of 1967.

While declarations will not present the Arabs with the fact o
Israeli withdrawal, such a clarification of its position might en
able the United States to widen and deepen its contacts in th
Arab world and to discuss such matters as economic coöperatio1
without raising the charge that it is trying to bribe the Arabs int(
acceptance of Israel's occupation or Israel's terms for peace
It is a way of giving Arab governments which may be looking fo
it some counterweight to overdependence on the Soviet Union

The danger is that revolutionary turmoil and general frustra
tion will deny to any outside power the ability to control th
situation, with the result that Arab irresponsibility will provok
heavy use of Israeli force and possible further outside interven
tion. We will not gain by encouraging strife or mixing int(
inter-Arab struggles, such as by backing the conservative Ara[

régimes against the radicals, a strategy which has been tried and found wanting before. It is not in our interest to see the Arab countries, including those whose governments now denounce us, sink into disorder. They should know that American coöperation toward a fair settlement and in coping with economic ills will be available to Arab leadership prepared to face up to those problems.

If the United States has to show the Arabs it is not 100 percent on the Israeli side, it also has to get the same point across in Israel. Israel's leaders regard the Arab governments (especially Nasser's) and the Soviet Union as pursuing a common policy aimed at undermining and probably destroying the security and even the existence of the Israeli state. Feeling the need of American support, they have an interest in polarization of the conflict, so that Israel and the United States stand on one side opposing the Arabs and Russia on the other; not wanting America to fight but merely to hold the ring. A strong case can be and has been made that this country can best serve peace and its own interests by accepting that situation as reality, like it or not, and providing Israel with the arms it needs to keep its superiority.

The main points of the argument are the following: it is hopeless to try to appease the Arabs or the Soviets, both of whom are trying to get us to put pressure on Israel to make concessions, which will only be followed by more pressure for further concessions; Israel is capable of keeping the present favorable balance and can continue to do so with American arms aid; in playing this role Israel blocks the U.S.S.R. and its Arab clients from expanding their power and dominating the Middle East, while it encourages pro-Western states like Iran, Saudi Arabia and Tunisia to hold their own; Israel is friendly to the United States and a democracy, thus a stronger reed to rely on than the Arab states are for anybody.

Such a policy, however, has pitfalls which far outweigh its possible advantages; sharp polarization of the conflict, leaving the Soviets little choice but further commitment and escalation on the Arab side; loss of control over decisions which could bring us to the brink of war; setbacks to the chances for agreement with the U.S.S.R. on arms limitation and other matters; loss of positions, interests and contacts throughout the Arab world; increasing international isolation on this issue and alienation from NATO partners, who are disturbed about Soviet penetration in the Mediterranean and Middle East but do not see all-out support of Israel as the answer to it.

Not that past policy is an infallible guide to the requirements of the future, but undivided support for one side in the conflict, especially in a phase of warfare of indefinite duration, would be a departure from the past quarter-century of American policy. It would forsake the approach not only of the Tripartite Declaration of 1950 and the Eisenhower-Dulles "impartiality," but also that of 1967–68 when we took Israel's side against those insisting on unconditional return to the status quo, taking it as a means of promoting a more durable settlement, not of establishing an alignment with Israel to protect its gains.

The crucial points of American policy toward Israel have to do with what kind of support and for what purpose. There is no denying that a balance exists in the Middle East in which Israel's power plays a part. The fact that a state friendly to the United States holds military superiority over states which have become clients of the Soviet Union has left us better off than if the balance had been reversed. Moreover, the United States has an interest in—some would say a commitment to—the independence of Israel, and if the latter's military position deteriorates, we may be confronted at a later time with desperate decisions on military intervention to rescue Israel which could have been avoided by timely support to enable the Israeli to hold their own. Faced by these factors and also by those counseling against a one-sided policy, the United States has not been sure of the principles and standards against which to measure its actions.

The soundest guidelines for that purpose are two: first, to keep in the forefront of thinking the basis on which a peaceful settlement in the Middle East must rest; and second, to move the level of military conflict downward and not upward. Thus, the United States will continue to be concerned about Israel's security, but it need not and should not give uncritical support to whatever Israel does to maintain it. Such actions as bombing close to Cairo or Damascus or heavy raids into Lebanon and Jordan achieved little other than increased Arab hostility, greater Soviet involvement, and alienation of world opinion. We are in a false position if we do not differentiate between support for Israel's survival and support for its existing strategy, between the need for a durable settlement and support of policies which by freezing the status quo make it impossible.

If the United States wishes to discourage Israel from a strategy
imed only at keeping existing advantages while trying to force
he Arabs into making peace, which is but a vain hope, it has
o be discriminating in its decisions on the supply of weapons.
'o fill Israel's periodic requests merely perpetuates a situation
n which Israel finds no reason to modify its political line or its
military strategy; the result is to bring the Soviets into the field
o redress the balance, and that in turn brings Israeli requests
or more effective weapons to contend with the Russians as well
s the Arabs. This cycle of escalation must be stopped short of
lisaster. To check it requires American influence and pressure
on the Russians and the Arabs, to the degree it can be exercised,
but also influence on Israel, which can be exerted through policy
n requests for arms. The United States can make some different
choices of weapons to be made available: for example, fewer
'hantoms and more shorter-range aircraft, antiaircraft missiles,
nd equipment for defense on the ground. It has already begun
o relate decisions on arms requests to its own estimates, rather
han Israel's, of the military balance in the area. There is no
cason not to relate them to general policy considerations as well.

Similar considerations apply to the effectiveness of a ceasefire.
t would certainly be desirable if the opposing forces will hold
heir fire and cool off a bit. But a fundamental difficulty con-
ronts any attempt to build a stable situation or a peacekeeping
ructure on the inviolability of the ceasefire lines. Agreement to
op the fighting on the basis of the status quo, unless there are
gns of progress in the peace talks, is bound to appear to the
.rabs as a confirmation of Israel's presence in the occupied
crritories for an indefinite period. The sound argument to be
1ade to them is not to accept formal stabilization of the status
uo, but to accept the existence of Israel as the only way they
an get back the occupied territories.

On the political side, matching a shift to a more defensive
1ilitary strategy, a turn in the direction of Israel's policy could
1ake a great contribution to the chances for settlement. It could
egin with an indication of willingness to withdraw from the
ccupied territories (with certain specific exceptions and safe-
uards such as those mentioned above), on condition of formal
ecognition and acceptance of Israel by the Arab states. Israeli
ttitudes to date should leave us in no doubt as to the reception
uch a suggestion from the United States would have in Jeru-

salem. But if our government can take the inevitable domesti
pressure, Israel would surely have to take full account o
American views whatever they may be. More important in th
longer run may be a growing discussion in Israel itself about th
wisdom of the current hard-line policies.

In its approach to Israel the United States must take ful
account of Israel's deep attachment to self-reliance and its lac
of faith in the international community when it comes to securit
and survival. Experiences with armistice arrangements and witl
the United Nations have been totally disillusioning to Israel, anc
the crises of 1956–57 and of 1967 have left its leaders highl
skeptical of counting on the United States. That is why the
put such value on the present "strategic frontiers," even thougl
it seems to others that Israel has less security now than it hac
with the old pre-1967 borders. And that is why this country, i
urging a settlement in which Israel would go back roughly t
the old borders, should be prepared to extend a treaty guarante
to defend Israel's independence and integrity within thos
borders. Neither a blanket guarantee of the settlement by th
U.N. Security Council nor an elaborate U.N. peacekeepin
structure, both of which are necessary and desirable, would b
sufficient. The U.S. government has long considered itself t
have a moral guarantee to Israel's independent existence. It i
quite likely that this vague commitment carries a greater risk o
dangerous military involvement than would a solemn specifi
obligation clear to Israeli, to Arabs, and to Russians alike.

VI

These considerations on dealing with the Arab-Israeli conflic
are obviously pertinent to the larger question of the threat t
American security from the intrusion of Soviet power into th
Middle East, and to the thesis that we are faced with a possibl
shift in the global balance of power, perhaps even a 1962 Cuba
crisis in reverse. The United States has three kinds of objective
in dealing with the Soviets in the Middle East. One is to limi
the growth of their power and keep a balance which prevent
their dominance. The second is to limit their participation ir
the Arab-Israeli conflict so that it does not threaten Israel'
independence or dangerously widen the war. The third is to pre
serve the channel for negotiation and the search for areas o
agreement. We should not put aside any of these objectives.

It is a natural reaction to see in Soviet military moves proof that the era of negotiation is over and the era of confrontation has begun, and to reply with positive action in order to preserve or right the balance. But it seems wiser to continue the attempts to establish priority for the common interest in avoiding wider war. The aim should be to combine warnings of what the United States cannot tolerate—Soviet participation in the war on the Arab side to defeat and destroy the state of Israel—with efforts to create a pattern of restraint by both powers that will temper the extreme aims of the local disputants.

We know that the Soviet Union has not filled Nasser's every request, just as the United States has limited its support of Israel. The Soviet government says that it favors a political settlement and that it accepts Israel's right to exist. That position should continue to be tested and not summarily dismissed. If the main difference between Soviet and U.S. positions lies in the exceptions and conditions surrounding Israeli withdrawal, that surely is a reasonable subject for discussion rather than a "breaking point." If it is necessary to give the Kremlin a sign of American seriousness and determination, the way to do it is not by directly pushing up the level of the Middle East war by large new deliveries of arms to Israel, but through independent and joint moves to strengthen American and NATO positions in nearby areas such as southern Europe, the Mediterranean, Turkey and the Indian Ocean. And Turkey, incidentally, holds the power to block the Straits to Soviet ships.

When we consider what to do to hold down the fighting if the ceasefire runs out or fails, the limits of diplomacy are obvious unless the two powers are able and willing to put pressure on the belligerents. If the United States can show that its attempts to persuade Israel are serious and will have some effect, it can argue strongly to the Soviets that reciprocal moderation must come from the Arab and the Soviet side; that there is no call for the use of Soviet combat personnel in defense of central Egypt when Israel has abandoned its attacks there; and that the restriction of the warfare in the Suez Canal area to essentially defensive operations, with no decisive struggle for control of the air and no attempt by either side to cross the Canal in force, will keep the situation tolerable for both great powers and for the disputants as efforts are made to move further toward political settlement. No formal agreement is necessary for such an understanding. Indeed, limitation of fighting by tacit agreement of all concerned may be more effective than a formally accepted ceasefire, which is almost bound to be violated by one side and then by the other amid general recrimination.

If and as negotiations go forward on ways of controlling and containing the conflict, the United States can buttress its arguments for Soviet disengagement by continuing to take the line that both powers should follow a policy of restraint in the supply of weapons, either by agreement or by reciprocal unilateral action. Past efforts to get Moscow to discuss the question have evoked nothing beyond statements that Israel must first withdraw from all Arab territory, and it may well be that the Soviet leaders must be faced with unpleasant alternatives before they will talk seriously. They have, however, even while maintaining the flow of arms to the U.A.R., held back on most weapons which could be called strictly offensive. The warnings and the talk should come first; increased deliveries of American aircraft for Israel or stronger demands in Moscow can come later if they prove necessary.

All these considerations essentially have to do with stopping hostilities short of the point of a big explosion while efforts toward a political settlement go forward. It is difficult enough in view of the interlocking of the local war with the big-power rivalry. It becomes almost impossible in the absence of a reasonable chance of progress toward a settlement. The idea of a comprehensive settlement, a package deal covering boundaries, guarantees, refugees, navigation rights and all the rest, has taken such firm root that governments give little thought to possibilities for partial settlement. One such possibility concerns the Suez Canal, on which a successful initiative might change some of the dimensions of the problem and jolt it out of the present impasse.

The Canal lies at the center of the conflict on the main front. Israel regards it as an essential strategic frontier, and the U.A.R. as the focus of the battle of attrition and a jumping-off place for regaining lost territory. Yet it remains symbolic not as a battle-front but as a closed international highway still important to the commerce of many nations. There has been talk of a mutual withdrawal of forces from the Canal to buttress the new ceasefire. So much the better if that can be accomplished. But why not go further and seek agreement on carrying out the clearance nd rehabilitation of the Canal under international auspices, with a demilitarized and internationally controlled zone some o miles wide on each side, the reopened Canal to be adminstered by the U.A.R. (which would get the revenues after the 'osts of rehabilitation had been met), and Israel to enjoy guaraneed freedom of passage along with other states?

The fact that the Soviet Union would gain the means to move hips easily from the Mediterranean into the Indian Ocean is ardly a strategic change of such magnitude as to outweigh the general benefits to many nations, not to mention the more important factor of a reduction of the fighting and stabilization on he most critical front. Israel would not lose the Canal as a defensive ditch since the Egyptian army would be withdrawn rom it on the other side. Egypt would have the satisfaction of eeing a limited pullback of Israeli forces, one which might be he start of a process.

Regardless of its merits and its chances of acceptance, which nay be minimal, such a proposal focuses attention on the main question of the American approach to the Middle East. Is Suez ur Thermopylae? Is the United States to move to a showdown vith the Soviet Union on such a point as maintenance of Israel's ir superiority over Egyptian territory west of the Canal as the ey to blocking Soviet domination of the Middle East? Or is it going to use the present critical situation to push toward widening areas of agreement between the Arab states and Israel and etween itself and the Soviet Union? If the showdown comes, et it be because the Soviets chose to wreck the chances of reonciliation and fair settlement.

Diplomacy has had a chance and has not succeeded, but it eeds more chances. Egypt's and Israel's acceptance of a temporary ceasefire and a new round with Jarring, difficult decisions vhich meant a break with extreme elements on both sides, may rovide some. In any case it is quite possible that some of the arties involved in the Middle East tangle—Israel and the oviet Union above all—may be near or at the crest of success ained by their policies since the Six Day War. It could be somevhat different when they look down the other side.

A Lasting Peace in the Middle East:
An American View*

WILLIAM P. ROGERS

I AM VERY HAPPY to be with you this evening and be a part of this impressive conference. The Galaxy Conference represents one of the largest and most significant efforts in the Nation's history to further the goals of all phases of adult and continuing education.

The State Department, as you know, has an active interest in this subject. It is our belief that foreign policy issues should be more broadly understood and considered. As you know, we are making a good many efforts toward providing continuing education in the foreign affairs field. I am happy tonight to join so many stanch allies in those endeavors.

In the hope that I may further that cause I want to talk to you tonight about a foreign policy matter which is of great concern to our nation.

U.S. POLICY IN THE MIDDLE EAST

I am going to speak tonight about the situation in the Middle East. I want to refer to the policy of the United States as it relates to that situation in the hope that there may be a better understanding of that policy and the reasons for it.

Following the third Arab-Israeli war in 20 years, there was an upsurge of hope that a lasting peace could be achieved. That hope has unfortunately not been realized. There is no area of the world today that is more important, because it could easily again be the source of another serious conflagration.

When this administration took office, one of our first actions in foreign affairs was to examine carefully the entire situation in the Middle East. It was obvious that a continuation

* An address by the Secretary of State on December 9, 1969.

of the unresolved conflict there would be extremely dangerous, that the parties to the conflict alone would not be able to overcome their legacy of suspicion to achieve a political settlement, and that international efforts to help needed support.

The United States decided it had a responsibility to play a direct role in seeking a solution.

Thus, we accepted a suggestion put forward both by the French Government and the Secretary General of the United Nations. We agreed that the major powers—the United States, the Soviet Union, the United Kingdom, and France—should cooperate to assist the Secretary General's representative, Ambassador Jarring, in working out a settlement in accordance with the resolution of the Security Council of the United Nations of November 1967. We also decided to consult directly with the Soviet Union, hoping to achieve as wide an area of agreement as possible between us.

These decisions were made in full recognition of the following important factors:

First, we knew that nations not directly involved could not make a durable peace for the peoples and governments involved. Peace rests with the parties to the conflict. The efforts of major powers can help, they can provide a catalyst, they can stimulate the parties to talk, they can encourage, they can help define a realistic framework for agreement; but an agreement among other powers cannot be a substitute for agreement among the parties themselves.

Second, we knew that a durable peace must meet the legitimate concerns of both sides.

Third, we were clear that the only framework for a negotiated settlement was one in accordance with the entire text of the U.N. Security Council resolution. That resolution was agreed upon after long and arduous negotiations; it is carefully balanced; it provides the basis for a just and lasting peace—a final settlement—not merely an interlude between wars.

Fourth, we believe that a protracted period of no war, no peace, recurrent violence, and spreading chaos would serve the interests of no nation, in or out of the Middle East.

U.S.–SOVIET DISCUSSIONS

For 8 months we have pursued these consultations in four-power talks at the United Nations and in bilateral discussions with the Soviet Union.

In our talks with the Soviets we have proceeded in the belief that the stakes are so high that we have a responsibility to determine whether we can achieve parallel views which would encourage the parties to work out a stable and equitable solution. We are under no illusions; we are fully conscious of past difficulties and present realities. Our talks with the Soviets have brought a measure of understanding, but very substantial diffences remain. We regret that the Soviets have delayed in responding to new formulations submitted to them on October 28. However, we will continue to discuss these problems with the Soviet Union as long as there is any realistic hope that such discussions might further the cause of peace.

The substance of the talks that we have had with the Soviet Union has been conveyed to the interested parties through diplomatic channels. This process has served to highlight the main roadblocks to the initiation of useful negotiations among the parties.

On the one hand, the Arab leaders fear that Israel is not in fact prepared to withdraw from Arab territory occupied in the 1967 war.

On the other hand, Israeli leaders fear that the Arab states are not in fact prepared to live in peace with Israel.

Each side can cite from its viewpoint considerable evidence to support its fears. Each side has permitted its attention to be focused solidly and to some extent solely on these fears.

What can the United States do to help to overcome these roadblocks?

Our policy is and will continue to be a *balanced* one.

We have friendly ties with both Arabs and Israelis. To call for Israeli withdrawal as envisaged in the U.N. resolution without achieving agreement on peace would be partisan toward the Arabs. To call on the Arabs to accept peace without Israeli withdrawal would be partisan toward Israel. Therefore, our policy is to encourage the Arabs to accept a permanent peace based on a binding agreement and to urge the Israelis to withdraw from occupied territory when their territorial integrity is assured as envisaged by the Security Council resolution.

BASIC ELEMENTS OF U.N. RESOLUTION

In an effort to broaden the scope of discussion we have recently resumed four-power negotiations at the United Nations.

Let me outline our policy on various elements of the Security Council resolution. The basic and related issues might be described as peace, security, withdrawal, and territory.

Peace Between the Parties

The resolution of the Security Council makes clear that the goal is the establishment of a state of peace between the parties instead of the state of belligerency which has characterized relations for over 20 years. We believe the conditions and obligations of peace must be defined in specific terms. For example, navigation rights in the Suez Canal and in the Strait of Tiran should be spelled out. Respect for sovereignty and obligations of the parties to each other must be made specific.

But peace, of course, involves much more than this. It is also a matter of the attitudes and intentions of the parties. Are they ready to coexist with one another? Can a live-and-let-live attitude replace suspicion, mistrust, and hate? A peace agreement between the parties must be based on clear and stated intentions and a willingness to bring about basic changes in the attitudes and conditions which are characteristic of the Middle East today.

Security

A lasting peace must be sustained by a sense of security on both sides. To this end, as envisaged in the Security Council resolution, there should be demilitarized zones and related security arrangements more reliable than those which existed in the area in the past. The parties themselves, with Ambassador Jarring's help, are in the best position to work out the nature and the details of such security arrangements. It is, after all, their interests which are at stake and their territory which is involved. They must live with the results.

Withdrawal and Territory

The Security Council resolution endorses the principle of the nonacquisition of territory by war and calls for withdrawal of Israeli armed forces from territories occupied in the 1967 war. We support this part of the resolution, including withdrawal, just as we do its other elements.

The boundaries from which the 1967 war began were established in the 1949 armistice agreements and have defined the areas of national jurisdiction in the Middle East for 20 years. Those boundaries were armistice lines, not final political borders. The rights, claims, and positions of the parties in an ultimate peaceful settlement were reserved by the armistice agreements.

The Security Council resolution neither endorses nor precludes these armistice lines as the definitive political boundaries. However, it calls for withdrawal from occupied territories, the nonacquisition of territory by war, and the establishment of secure and recognized boundaries.

We believe that while recognized political boundaries must be established and agreed upon by the parties, any changes in the preexisting lines should not reflect the weight of conquest and should be confined to insubstantial alterations required for mutual security. We do not support expansionism. We believe troops must be withdrawn as the resolution provides. We support Israel's security and the security of the Arab states as well. We are for a lasting peace that requires security for both.

ISSUES OF REFUGEES AND JERUSALEM

By emphasizing the key issues of peace, security, withdrawal, and territory, I do not want to leave the impression that other issues are not equally important. Two in particular deserve special mention: the questions of refugees and of Jerusalem.

There can be no lasting peace without a just settlement of the problem of those Palestinians whom the wars of 1948 and 1967 have made homeless. This human dimension of the Arab-Israeli conflict has been of special concern to the United States for over 20 years. During this period the United States has contributed about $500 million for the support and education of the Palestine refugees. We are prepared to contribute generously along with others to solve this problem. We believe its just settlement must take into account the desires and aspirations of the refugees and the legitimate concerns of the governments in the area.

The problem posed by the refugees will become increasingly serious if their future is not resolved. There is a new consciousness among the young Palestinians who have grown up since 1948 which needs to be channeled away from bitterness and frustration toward hope and justice.

The question of the future status of Jerusalem, because it touches deep emotional, historical, and religious wellsprings, is particularly complicated. We have made clear repeatedly in the past two and a half years that we cannot accept unilateral actions by any party to decide the final status of the city. We believe its status can be determined only through the agreement of the parties concerned, which in practical terms means primarily the Governments of Israel and Jordan, taking into account the interests of other countries in the area and the international community. We do, however, support certain principles which we believe would provide an equitable framework for a Jerusalem settlement.

Specifically, we believe Jerusalem should be a unified city within which there would no longer be restrictions on the movement of persons and goods. There should be open access to the unified city for persons of all faiths and nationalities. Arrangements for the administration of the unified city should take into account the interests of all its inhabitants and of the Jewish, Islamic, and Christian communities. And there should be roles for both Israel and Jordan in the civic, economic, and religious life of the city.

It is our hope that agreement on the key issues of peace, security, withdrawal, and territory will create a climate in which these questions of refugees and of Jerusalem, as well as other aspects of the conflict, can be resolved as part of the overall settlement.

FORMULAS FOR U.A.R.–ISRAEL ASPECT OF SETTLEMENT

During the first weeks of the current United Nations General Assembly the efforts to move matters toward a settlement entered a particularly intensive phase. Those efforts continue today.

I have already referred to our talks with the Soviet Union. In connection with those talks there have been allegations that we have been seeking to divide the Arab states by urging the U.A.R. to make a separate peace. These allegations are false. It is a fact that we and the Soviets have been concentrating on the questions of a settlement between Israel and the United Arab Republic. We have been doing this in the full understanding on both our parts that, before there can be a settlement of the Arab-Israeli conflict, there must be agreement between the parties on other aspects of the settlement—not only those related to the United Arab Republic but also those related to Jordan and other states which accept the Security Council resolution of November 1967.

We started with the Israeli-United Arab Republic aspect because of its inherent importance for future stability in the area and because one must start somewhere.

We are also ready to pursue the Jordanian aspect of a settlement; in fact the four powers in New York have begun such discussions. Let me make it perfectly clear that the U.S. position is that implementation of the overall settlement would begin only after complete agreement had been reached on related aspects of the problem.

In our recent meetings with the Soviets we have discussed some new formulas in an attempt to find common positions. They consist of three principal elements:

First, there should be a binding commitment by Israel and the United Arab Republic to peace with each other, with all the specific obligations of peace spelled out, including the obligation to prevent hostile acts originating from their respective territories.

Second, the detailed provisions of peace relating to security safeguards on the ground should be worked out between the parties, under Ambassador Jarring's auspices, utilizing the procedures followed in negotiating the armistice agreements under Ralph Bunche in 1949 at Rhodes. This formula has been previously used with success in negotiations between the parties on Middle Eastern problems. A principal objective of the four-power talks, we believe, should be to help Ambassador Jarring engage the parties in a negotiating process under the Rhodes formula.

So far as a settlement between Israel and the United Arab Republic goes, these safeguards relate primarily to the area of Sharm al-Shaykh controlling access to the Gulf of Aqaba, the need for demilitarized zones as foreseen in the Security Council resolution, and final arrangements in the Gaza Strip.

Third, in the context of peace and agreement on specific security safeguards, withdrawal of Israeli forces from Egyptian territory would be required.

Such an approach directly addresses the principal national concerns of both Israel and the U.A.R. It would require the

U.A.R. to agree to a binding and specific commitment to peace. It would require withdrawal of Israeli armed forces from U.A.R. territory to the international border between Israel [or Mandated Palestine] and Egypt which has been in existence for over a half century. It would also require the parties themselves to negotiate the practical security arrangements to safeguard the peace.

We believe that this approach is *balanced* and fair.

U.S. INTERESTS IN THE AREA

We remain interested in good relations with all states in the area. Whenever and wherever Arab states which have broken off diplomatic relations with the United States are prepared to restore them, we shall respond in the same spirit.

Meanwhile, we will not be deterred from continuing to pursue the paths of patient diplomacy in our search for peace in the Middle East. We will not shrink from advocating necessary compromises, even though they may and probably will be unpalatable to both sides. We remain prepared to work with others—in the area and throughout the world—so long as they sincerely seek the end we seek: a just and lasting peace.

A Legacy of Peace:
Our Responsibility to Future Generations*

WILLIAM P. ROGERS

PROGRESS is urgently required in the Middle East. Over several years, the United Nations has made determined and persistent efforts to achieve a lasting peace in that critical area. Nonetheless, the opportunities for success and the risks of failure remain in precarious balance.

Security Council Resolution 242,[7] establishing the principles for a durable peace, was the first major step toward reason after 18 years of belligerency and a fragile, often violated armistice.

The cease-fire along the Suez Canal, now nearing its 15th month, was the second major step away from war.

It is time for a third major step toward peace.

For 4 years Ambassador Jarring [U.N. Special Representative Gunnar Jarring] has worked diligently to secure the agreement called for in Security Council Resolution 242. We support his efforts. We believe his mission remains the best path to an overall settlement and to lasting peace. Our views on such a final peace settlement remain those expressed in President Nixon's foreign policy report earlier this year and in my statement of December 9, 1969.[8]

Both sides to the conflict are committed to the fundamental and reciprocal principles to which the Jarring Mission is dedicated: living in peace with each other and withdrawal from territories occupied in the 1967 conflict as set forth in Security Council Resolution 242. Despite those commitments, a deep gulf of suspicion and distrust remains.

Each side is convinced of the justice of its cause. Each is concerned about its future security. A political settlement based on mutual accommodation could assure both. An attempt to achieve these ends by force will destroy all possibilities for either.

* Excerpt from an address by the Secretary of State before the 26th session of the U.N. General Assembly on October 4, 1971.

7 For text of the resolution, see BULLETIN of Dec. 18, 1967, p. 843.

8 The complete text of President Nixon's foreign policy report to the Congress on Feb. 25 appears in the BULLETIN of Mar. 22, 1971; for Secretary Rogers' address at Washington on Dec. 9, 1969, see BULLETIN of Jan. 5, 1970, p. 7.

This is why we believe a third major step toward peace is essential:

—A step which can be taken now;
—A step that is practical;
—A step that could help create the confidence and trust which are now lacking;
—A step toward full and complete implementation of Resolution 242.

That step is an interim Suez Canal agreement. That is why the United States has welcomed the interest of both Egypt and Israel in such an agreement. That is why, at the request of the parties, the United States has undertaken to play a constructive role in the process of arriving at an agreement.

In order to explore the positions of each side, we have discussed concrete and specific ideas designed to meet the legitimate needs and concerns of both sides. Those ideas, given willingness and good intentions on both sides, could become the basis for a breakthrough. They require further quiet discussions with the parties, an undertaking we now hope can be expedited along the following lines:

A first point is the relationship between an interim agreement and an overall settlement. A fair approach should be founded on two basic principles:

—That a Suez Canal agreement is merely a step toward complete and full implementation of Resolution 242 within a reasonable period of time and not an end in itself. That has to be clearly established in any agreement.
—That neither side can realistically expect to achieve, as part of an interim agreement, complete agreement on the terms and conditions of an overall settlement. If it could, there would be no necessity for an interim agreement. Those final terms and conditions will have to be worked out through negotiations under Ambassador Jarring's auspices. And we would hope that if an interim agreement is reached, active negotiations under Ambassador Jarring's auspices could be renewed.

A second point is the matter of the cease-fire. Its maintenance is in the interest of all of us, of everyone concerned, of everyone in this room—in fact, in the interest of the whole world. The ultimate objective, of course, is a permanent end to belligerency as part of a final binding peace agreement. But such a commitment is not realizable in the context of an interim agreement. Neither would a cease-fire of short duration be realistic. With good will on both sides, it should be possible to find common understanding between the parties on this issue.

Third is the zone of withdrawal. There are, of course, very important strategic considerations involved in this key point. However, based on our discussions, we believe it should be possible to meet the principal concerns of both sides. Without going into the details, I would merely say that I believe that in the long run the most significant aspect of an interim agreement might prove to be that it established the principle of withdrawal looking to an overall settlement as a fact rather than as a theory.

Fourth is the nature of the supervisory arrangements. Both sides must have confidence that the agreement will not be violated and that adequate machinery will be provided for prompt detection of any infractions. We are confident that ways reassuring to both Israel and Egypt can be found for altering and strengthening the supervisory mechanisms that have existed in the area for the past two decades.

Fifth is the question of an Egyptian presence east of the Suez Canal. The reopening and operation of the Suez Canal would require Egyptian personnel east of the canal. It is understandable, too, that normal activities should be pursued in as much of the zone evacuated as possible. The question of an Egyptian military presence east of the canal is one on which the parties hold opposite views. But here, too, based on our discussion, we believe that there are possibilities for compromise on this issue.

Sixth is the use of the Suez Canal. The United States has long held that the canal should be open to passage for all nations without discrimination. This principle is clear in the Security Council resolution of November 1967. What is at present at issue in considering an interim agreement is principally the timing at which this right could be exercised. We believe an accommodation on this point is quite possible.

With those six points in mind let me say this: Because the parties have asked us, we intend to continue our determined effort to assist them in arriving at an interim agreement. This effort, we believe, is imperative because—and I think it is important to keep this in mind—there is no more realistic and hopeful alternative to pursue.

There are risks to peace; but the greater risk is inaction, unwillingness to face up to the hard decisions.

A practical step now—an interim agreement—would make the next step toward peace less difficult for all the parties to take.

It would restore the use of the Suez Canal as a waterway for international shipping.

It would reestablish Egypt's authority over a major national asset.

It would separate the combatants.

It would produce the first Israeli withdrawal.

It would extend the cease-fire.

It would diminish the risk of major-power involvement.

It would be an important step toward the complete implementation of Security Council Resolution 242.

I submit that the logic for such an agreement is overwhelming. If the leaders of the area would grasp this opportunity, they would give new hope to their peoples for tranquillity, for progress, and for peace.

In all of our efforts, both in the United Nations and elsewhere, we should recall that nothing we do matters so much as the legacy we leave to those who follow, the bridge that we build between the past and the future. There is a tendency, especially when tensions are high and tempers short, to regard the present as the focal point of all of man's history. But ours is only the latest generation, not the last generation; and nothing we leave to future generations will matter so much as a structure of enduring peace.

Peace must be achieved and maintained not by the decree of a few but by accommodation among many.

Each government, in upholding its people's particular interests, must also advance the world interest in a peace which will endure.

To that interest the United Nations, from its creation, has been dedicated.

To that interest the United States pledges anew its best efforts.

Soviet Proposal on the Middle East:
December 30, 1968*

Following in translation from the Arabic is the text of the Soviet proposal for peace in the Middle East as published in the Lebanese newspaper Al Anwar.

The main provisions of the action plan can be stated as follows:

Israel and those neighboring Arab states willing to participate in the implementation of such a plan shall confirm their acceptance of the Security Council resolution of Nov. 22, 1967. They shall also express their readiness to implement all its provisions.

This will signify their agreement that a timetable and method for withdrawal of the Israeli forces from the territories occupied in 1967 shall be determined through contacts with [Dr. Gunnar V.] Jarring.

At the same time a plan agreed on by both parties to implement the other Security Council provisions shall be drawn up. In drawing up this plan, consideration shall be given to the establishment of a just and lasting peace in the Middle East, enabling every state in the area to live in security.

The objective of these contacts [through Dr. Jarring] can be the holding of negotiations on definite steps to implement the Security Council resolutions.

[1]

The Governments of Israel and the Arabs states willing to participate in the implementation of the plan shall proclaim their joint willingness and readiness to end the state of war between them and to reach a peaceful settlement of the problem through withdrawal of the Israeli forces from the occupied Arab territories. In this respect Israel shall proclaim its readiness to begin on the fixed date the withdrawals of its forces from the Arab territories which it occupied in the conflict of the summer of 1967.

[2]

On the date of the Israeli forces' withdrawal, which shall take place in stages under supervision, the aforementioned states and Israel shall

---

* N. Y. *Times*, January 11, 1969, at 2 col. 4. The *New York Times* text of the Soviet proposal has been reprinted in 2 *New York University Journal of International Law & Politics* 215 (1969).

deposit with the U.N. documents ending the state of war and recognizing the sovereignity of each state in the region as well as each state's territorial integrity, political independence and right to live in peace and security within secure and recognized boundaries in accordance with the aforementioned Security Council resolution.

Under an agreement to be reached through the mediation of Dr. Jarring the following points must be agreed on: secure and recognized boundaries accompanied by relevant maps; freedom of navigation in the region's international waterways; a just solution of the refugee problem; the territorial integrity and political independence of each state in the region. This can be achieved by various means, including the establishment of demilitarized zones. It is assumed that this agreement—as defined by the Security Council resolution—will be one unit covering all aspects of a Middle East peaceful settlement; in other words as one integral question.

[3]

In the month (to be agreed on) the Israeli forces shall withdraw from the Arab territories to lines (to be agreed on) in the Sinai Peninsula; the west bank of the Jordan; and the "Quneitra area in Syria." When the armed forces have withdrawn to these agreed lines in the Sinai Peninsula—for instance 30-40 kilometers from the Suez Canal— the U.A.R. Government shall send its forces to the canal zone and begin clearing it for resumption of navigation.

[4]

In the month (to be agreed on) the Israeli forces shall withdraw to their pre-June, 1967 lines. Arab administration shall then be restored in the liberated areas and Arab army and police forces shall also return to these areas. During the second stage of the Israel forces withdrawal from the U.A.R., the U.A.R. and Israel—or the U.A.R. alone, if its Government agrees—shall announce acceptance of the stationing of U.N. forces near the pre-June 5 lines in the Sinai Peninsula, Sharm el Sheik and the Gaza sector. In other words, the situation that existed in May, 1967, shall be restored.

The Security Council shall adopt a resolution for the dispatch of U.N. forces under the U.N. Charter to guarantee freedom of navigation to the ships of all countries in the Tiran Strait and the Gulf of Aqaba.

[5]

Following the Israeli forces' withdrawal to the international boundaries to be demarcated by the Security Council, or through an agreement signed by all parties, the documents that were previously deposited [with the United Nations] by the Arab states and Israel shall
come into effect. Under U.N. Charter provisions the Security Council
shall adopt a resolution on special guarantees concerning the Arab-
Israeli borders. Guarantees by the four permanent member states of
the Security Council are not ruled out.

Soviet Proposals

YEVGENY PRIMAKOV

For more than three years now the Middle East conflict has remained unsettled, a factor which keeps not only that area but the entire world in a state of tension.

The Israeli Government, backed by the ruling political circles of the United States, continues its obstructive actions aimed at thwarting a political settlement of the Middle East conflict.

Many facts which determine developments in the Middle East are presented in the reactionary bourgeois press in an entirely different and sometimes conflicting light, others are juggled with, while still others are not mentioned at all. . . .

Israel, who attacked the Arab countries in June 1967, who is occupying extensive Arab territory in defiance of the United Nations resolution, and who is continuing to carry out piratical armed raids against the Arab states, is presented by US propagandists as a kind of 'defenceless islet' in a hostile Arab sea which is ready to swallow it up.

At the same time, certain people in Washington are perfectly well aware that the actions of Israel—in 1956 when, in retaliation for the nationalization of the Suez Canal Company, a piratical tripartite attack was made against Egypt, in 1967 when the extremist leadership in Tel Aviv, with US support, tried with one blow to get rid of progressive regimes in the United Arab Republic and Syria, and again at the present time, when the unbridled Israeli military command is dreaming of bringing 100 million Arabs to their knees—are aware that all those actions have nothing to do with a 'fight for existence.'

Whenever the Soviet Union's attitude to events in the Middle East is involved, such methods as distortions, insinuations and the suppression of the true facts are employed to a still greater degree in the American and the pro-Zionist West European press.

Essence of conflict

The Soviet Union's approach to these developments is based on its assessment of the essence of the Arab-Israeli conflict. The Soviet Union regards the Middle East crisis, not as a clash of national interests, but as an attempt by world imperialism, with the assistance of the Israeli leaders in pursuit of their own expansionist aims, to deal a blow at the national liberation movement in the Arab countries.

The right-wing bourgeois press spares no effort to impress upon public opinion the view that the United States has stepped up her diplomatic action, that it is seeking a political settlement in the Middle East. Any manoeuvre by Washington is called a 'new initiative.'

At the same time, this press maintains complete silence—as though they do not exist at all—over the Soviet proposals on the implementation of the UN Security Council resolution of 22 November 1967—proposals which are concrete, spelt out and capable of bringing peace and security to all the Middle East countries.

It should be pointed out that the Soviet proposals were worked out on the basis of an analysis of the Middle East situation, taking into account the positions of the parties to the conflict, as well as bilateral and quadripartite consultations on questions concerning a Middle East settlement. The Soviet plan was submitted in due course to the countries concerned and it was clarified and supplemented. . . .

So what is the Soviet plan for the normalization of the Middle East situation?

First, in drafting our proposals, we proceed from the need for a just and lasting peace in the Middle East. It is precisely a lasting peace that we have in mind, and not a precarious truce.

Israeli withdrawal

It is quite natural that peace of this order cannot be ensured by encouraging the aggressor and cannot be made stable unless Israeli troops are withdrawn from the extensive Arab territories which they have seized.

The Soviet Union has always proceeded, and continues to proceed, on the basis of the right of all Middle East states to a safe and autonomous national existence. . . .

A just solution to the Middle East crisis must be worked out not only because it is morally necessary—even though the moral factor is of extremely great importance. Without justice—that is to say, without the ending of the Israeli occupation of seized Arab territories, and not only without an end to the state of war, but also without the establishment of peace between states in this area and equally without recognition of the rights of the Palestinian Arabs—there will be no reasonably stable settlement.

Engels once wrote that the annexation of Alsace and Lorraine had made war a permanent factor in European politics. Is there any less reason to believe that Israel's present occupation of Arab territories turns war into an inevitable prospect in the Middle East?

Meanwhile, we know that there are a number of UN resolutions which provide for the repatriation of the Palestinian refugees or for compensation for their property. It is clearly necessary to decide the question of the Palestinian refugees in order to have a stable peace in the Middle East. All the more so do we regard as impermissible attempts to have 'self-determination' for one people or a set of peoples on the basis of other peoples being completely deprived of their national rights.

Secondly, our proposals provide not just for the simple proclamation of peace in the Middle East, but for an understanding between the sides which would impose commitments on both of them. A tangible way to this now could be provided by contacts through the UN Secretary-General's special envoy, Dr Gunnar Jarring.

The Soviet Union has been and is in favour of the implementation of the Jarring mission. But is this mission an aim in itself? Of course not. What is needed is to establish contacts between the sides through Dr Jarring; the Jarring mission is required to find concrete ways of implementing the UN Security Council resolution of 22 November 1967.

It should be remembered that this resolution provides for the evacuation of Israeli troops from occupied Arab territories, the ending of the state of war between the Arab countries and Israel, their right to live in peace within secure and recognized frontiers, the freedom of shipping along sea lanes and a solution to the problem of the Palestinian refugees.

In the Soviet view, for the Jarring mission to be successful it is first of all necessary for the two sides, straightforwardly and unequivocally, to declare their readiness to implement the UN Security Council resolution all along the line.

A statement of this kind has already been made by the Government of the United Arab Republic, which is contributing most to the effort to eliminate the consequences of Israeli aggression.

From the formal point of view Tel Aviv also seems to have consented to implement this resolution. However, this was done too indefinitely and in too general a form. Meanwhile, subsequent pronouncements by the Israeli leaders conflict with the provisions of the resolution to so great a degree that one cannot but doubt the sincerity of this Israel consent.

Thirdly, the Soviet proposals guarantee the practical implementation of the entire complex of provisions of this Security Council resolution

It is particularly important today to stand firm on the two main line of settlement, which are: Israeli evacuation from all Arab territorie occupied in 1967 and the simultaneous establishment of a just anc lasting peace in the Middle East. Both issues are organically fused anc must be viewed as one composite entity.

'Secure frontiers'

The Soviet proposals thus co-ordinate the solution of these questions the moment the final document, as co-ordinated through Dr Jarring, i deposited with the United Nations, the two sides must refrain from all action that would operate against the termination of the state of war; juridically, the termination of the state of war and the establishment of peace will begin the moment the first phase of the Israeli troop withdrawal from the territories occupied in June 1967 is completed—the evacuation may be carried out in two phases. . . .

It is absolutely plain that today, in this age when armaments are rapidly developing, the safety of this or that frontier is not at all ensured by shifting it a few miles away, but by having it universally recognized.

Were the present Israeli leaders really concerned about anything other than expansionist projects for territorial 'acquisitions,' Tel Aviv would pay closer heed to proposals guaranteeing the frontiers of the states in this area, including the frontiers of Israel, which would accord with the demarcation lines that existed on 4 June 1967.

As for guarantees for the frontiers of the Middle East states, the Soviet proposals ensure them by having the two sides adopt specific commitments to recognize, in conformity with the UN Security Council resolution of 22 November 1967, the impermissibility of acquiring territory through war, to respect one another's sovereignty, territorial integrity, inviolability and political independence, to do all in their power to prevent hostile acts against one another from their respective territories and mutually to refrain from interference in one another's internal affairs.

The Soviet proposals also stipulate demilitarized zones on either side of the frontier: such zones would give no advantage to either side, and their regime would incorporate restrictions of a purely military character, the introduction of UN troops at a number of points and direct guarantees from the Big Four Permanent Members of the Security Council or from the UN Security Council itself.

Such are the Soviet proposals. If the Israeli leaders, who are supported by the imperialist circles of the USA, had not blocked their adoption, a just and lasting peace would long ago have become an established fact in the Middle East. . . .

The Soviet position, which is one of full support for the Arab countries in their struggle to eliminate the consequences of Israeli aggression, remains unchanged as ever. . . .

Could it be that Tel Aviv or Washington thinks that the Soviet position will change following President Nasser's death? Empty, illusory hopes! The Soviet policy of all-round support for the Arab states which are the victims of Israeli aggression rests on objective and unchanging factors.

Hopes of achieving success by exerting pressure on the USSR— whether it is a question of alleged 'violations' of the cease-fire in the Suez Canal zone or Big Four meetings on the Middle East crisis—are equally shortsighted and without foundation.

Desiring a lasting and just peace in the Middle East—an area which is directly contiguous to its borders—the USSR is presenting a balanced, detailed programme for an Arab-Israeli settlement. It is in the interests of all peoples to make these proposals the groundwork for a basis that will lead to lasting peace in this part of the world, which is fraught with danger.

Toward a Democratic Palestine

THE Palestinian Revolution has officially adopted the creation of a democratic, non-sectarian Palestine where Christians, Jews and Moslems can live, work and worship without discrimination as the ultimate objective of its liberation struggle. Undoubtedly, the establishment of a progressive open society for all the Palestinians is the only humanitarian and permanent solution to the problem. It is certainly superior to "throwing the Arabs to the desert," or "throwing the Jews into the sea."

For the goal to be feasible, it must be acceptable to the parties concerned, as well as to the people of the world as an interested third party. It must be shown that it will work.

A revolutionary change of attitude on the part of the Palestinians may be observed in the fact that the revolutionary Palestinians do not see the Jews as monsters, supermen, pigmies or as eternal enemies. They clearly identify their enemy as the racist-colonialist State of Israel and its Western allies. Reading Jewish literature, joining hands with progressive Jews around the world, and acquiring self-confidence —all have helped the Palestinians change their attitudes. Racist-chauvinistic solutions epitomized by the "throw-the-Jews-in-the-sea" slogan have been categorically rejected, to be replaced by the goal of creating the new democratic Palestine.

On the part of the Jews, perceptions of the Palestinians as nomads, bloodthirsty terrorists and treacherous villains have persisted through Zionist propaganda, several Jews—especially those living outside Palestine—are changing their minds, and are rallying to the call for a progressive non-sectarian Palestine. *Changing the minds and attitudes of Jews in Palestine remains an important and unfulfilled task of the revolution.* A popular war of liberation aimed at the destruction of racism and imperialism will create new conditions that will make a new Palestine possible. In the process, the alternatives presented to the Jews of Palestine will be drastically changed. Instead of the fortress of Israel versus being thrown into the sea, the revolution offers a new set of alternates. The insecurity of an exclusive-racist Israel versus an open, safe and tolerant Palestine for all. *The Palestinian Revolution thus aims —in the long run—to recruit Jewish Palestinians as well as non-Jews n its liberation forces as an important step toward its final goal.* This requires a basic change in Jewish attitudes.

It is toward the fulfillment of such a goal that further elaboration on and clarification of a democratic Palestine is attempted. We will presently address ourselves to the question of what is really meant by a democratic, non-sectarian Palestine.

Difficulties and Limitations

It is both difficult and risky at this early stage of the revolution to make a clear and definitive statement about liberated Palestine. Realism, rather than romantic day-dreaming, should be the basic revolutionary approach. We do not believe that victory is around the corner. The revolution does not underestimate the enemy or its allies. What will happen during the years of hard struggle for liberation cannot be easily predicted. Will the attitude of Palestinian Jews harden or become more receptive and flexible? A further drift to the right, stepping up anti-Arab terrorism—in the Algerian O.A.S. tradition—followed by a voluntary mass exodus on the eve of liberation will pose, for example, a completely different problem.

On the other hand, joining the revolution and working with it will lay firmer growth for the New Palestine. The revolution is striving hard to achieve the second alternative. Guerrilla operations are basically directed at the military and economic foundations of the Zionist settler-state. *Whenever a civilian target is chosen, every effort is made to minimize loss of civilian life—though it is hard to distinguish between civilians and non-civilians in this modern Spartan militaristic society where every adult is mobilized for the war.* Hitting quasi-civilian areas has the psychological effect of shocking the Israelis into realization that a racist-militaristic state cannot provide them with security when it is conducting genocide against the exiled and oppressed Palestinian masses. In the Dizengoff Street bomb in Tel Aviv, Fateh guerrillas delayed the operation three times to choose a place (in front of a building under construction) and a time (12:30 after midnight) to maximize noise but minimize casualties. The result: few were injured, but thousands were shocked and made to engage in serious thinking.

In conclusion, despite all uncertainties, there is hope that the vision and the behavior of the Palestinian revolutionaries will achieve a better future for their oppressed countrymen. Answers must be thought out and found for myriad questions relating to this future. Even if the

answers are tentative, they will start a dialogue which will provide th
path toward maturity and fulfillment.

Profile of the Democratic Palestine

1. THE COUNTRY

Pre-1948, Palestine—as defined during the British Mandate—is th
territory to be liberated and it is there that a democratic, progressiv
state is to be created. This liberated Palestine will be part of the Ara
nation and will not be an alien state within it. The eventual unity o
Palestine with other Arab states will make boundary problems les
relevant and will end the artificiality of the present status of Israe
and possibly that of Jordan as well. The new country will be anti-im
perialist and will join the ranks of progressive revolutionary countries
Therefore, it will have to cut the present life line links with, and tota
dependence on, any of the Great Powers. Therefore, integration withir
the area will be a prerequisite.

It should be quite obvious at this stage that the New Palestine dis
cussed here is not simply the occupied West Bank or the Gaza Strip o
both; these are areas occupied by the Israelis since June, 1967. Th
homeland of the Palestinians usurped and colonized in 1948 is as dea
and important as the part occupied in 1967. Besides, the very existenc
of a racist State of Israel based on expansion, and the consequen
forced exile of part of the citizens is unacceptable by the revolution
Any arrangement accommodating an aggressor settler-state is unac
ceptable and temporary.

2. THE CONSTITUENTS

All Jews, Moslems and Christians living in Palestine or forcibly ex
iled from it will have the right to Palestinian citizenship. This guaran
tees the right of all exiled Palestinians to return to their land whethe
they were born in Palestine or in exile, and regardless of their presen
nationality.

Equally, this means that all Jewish Palestinians—at present Israeli
—have the same rights provided of course they reject Zionist racis
chauvinism and fully accept to live as Palestinians in the New Pales
tine. The Revolution therefore rejects the supposition that only Jew
who lived in Palestine prior to 1948 or 1914 and their descendants ar
acceptable.

In a recent interview, Fateh official "Abu Iyad" reasserted that not only progressive anti-Zionist Jews, but even present Zionists willing to abandon their racist ideology will be welcome as Palestinian citizens. *It is the belief of the revolution that all present Israeli Jews will change their attitudes and will subscribe to the New Palestine, once they are aware of its ideology.*

3. THE IDEOLOGY

During the process of liberation, the Palestinians will decide upon the system of government and the political-economic-social organization of their liberated country.

(One repeats at this juncture that the term *Palestinians* includes those in exile, those under occupation, and all Jewish settlers.)

A democratic and progressive Palestine, however, rejects a theocratic, feudalist, aristocratic, authoritarian or a racist-chauvinistic form of government. It will not allow oppression or exploitation of any group of people by any other group or individuals. The goal is to establish a state that provides equal opportunities for its people in work, worship, education, political decision-making, cultural and artistic expression.

This is no utopian dream. For, the very process of achieving the New Palestine inherently produces the requisite climate for its future system of government, i.e. a people's war of liberation brings about new values and attitudes that serve as guarantees of democracy after liberation.

Palestinians, after liberation, will not accept subjugation and will not reintroduce oppression against any group, for this will be a negation of their *raison d'être* and an abdication of their revolutionary existence. This is an obvious result of experiences in Palestinian refugee camps in Lebanon and Jordan. After twenty-two years of oppression, humiliation and manipulation, the camps have awakened. In the process, the exiles have instituted democratic self-management. Medical, educational and social services are being provided locally through the revolutionary organizations. Crime rates in these camps have drastically gone down to 10 per cent of pre-revolutionary magnitude. Self-discipline has replaced the police. The new militia is providing the link between the revolutionary *avant-garde* and the masses. Democratic checks are built in.

Newsmen and other foreign visitors have discovered that nowhere in the Arab world can they find equally mature and tolerant people vis-à-vis the Jews than in the camps in Jordan and Lebanon and especially among the *Ashbals*, the fighting lion cubs. These young Palestinians (8-16 years) are almost totally free of any anti-Jewish bias. They have a clearer vision of the new democratic Palestine than that held by bourgeois city-dwellers. These young people are the liberators of tomorrow. They will complete the dismantling of Israeli oppression and the rebuilding of the new Palestine.

If the democratic and progressive New Palestine is utopian, then the Palestinian guerrillas and camp-dwellers are practicing utopian living.

Two Misconceptions

Several interpretations of a democratic Palestine have sprung up in different quarters and these require clarification and some correction. An attempt will be made to discuss two vital issues:

1. The call for a non-sectarian Palestine should not be confused with a multi-religious, a poly-religious or a bi-national state. *The new Palestine is not to be built around three state religions or two nationalities. Rather, it will simply provide freedom from religious oppression and freedom to practice religion without discrimination.* No rigidification of religious lines is desired by the revolution. No hard and fast religious distribution of political offices and other important jobs is envisioned. The Lebanese model, where the reactionary, quasi-feudalist or commercial-capitalist hierarchy divides jobs and offices on the basis of sectarian lines to perpetuate its domination of the masses, is completely alien to the Revolution.

Abu Ammar has often reiterated that the President of liberated Palestine may be a Jew, a Moslem or a Christian, not because of his religion or sect, but on the basis of his merit as an outstanding Palestinian. Furthermore, religious and ethnic lines clearly cross in Palestine so as to make the term bi-national and the Arab-Jewish dichotomy meaningless, or at best dubious.

The majority of Jews in Palestine today are Arab Jews—euphemistically called "Oriental" Jews by the Zionists. Therefore, Palestine combines Jewish, Christian and Moslem Arabs as well as non-Arab Jews (Western Jews).

2. The new democratic Palestine is *not* a substitute for liberation. Rather, it is the ultimate objective of liberation. A client state in the

west bank and Gaza, an Avneri-style de-Zionized Israel or a Semitic Confederation are all categorically rejected by the Revolution. They are all racist blue-prints designed to prolong Israeli hegemony and Palestinian subjugation. They all assume the maintenance of the basic factors that led to the forced exile of Palestinians and the oppression of the people. The *sine qua non* of the New Palestine is the destruction of the political, economic and militarist foundations of a chauvinist-racist settler-state. The maintenance of a technologically-advanced military machine through a continuous Western capital flow and exchange of population has led the Zionist machinery to perpetuate one aggression after the other. Therefore, liquidation of such a machinery is an irreplaceable condition for the creation of the New Palestine. When the machinery of the Nazi state was liquidated, the German people were liberated together with other nations that were oppressed by Nazi Germany such as Poland, Hungary, Holland and France.

The Transition, and After

It is quite logical to expect specific transitional collective accommodations immediately after liberation, as well as some collective or group privileges. Jews or non-Jews for that matter would have the right to practice their religion and develop culturally and linguistically as a group, beside their individual political and cultural participation. It is quite logical for example to have both Arabic and Hebrew as official languages taught in governmental schools to all Palestinians, Jews and non-Jews.

The right of free movement within the country and outside it would be guaranteed. Palestinians desirous of voluntarily leaving the country would be allowed to do so. Immigration would be restricted in the transitional period to the return of all exiled Palestinians desirous of return. In a normal permanent state, however, immigration would be open without discrimination. Freedom of access, visits and extended pilgrimage and tourism would be guaranteed to all Jews, Moslems or Christians of the world who consider Palestine a holy place worthy of pilgrimage and meditation.

Is the New Palestine Viable?

Several well-intentioned critics maintain that even if the creation of the democratic Palestine is possible, it will not survive for long. Their basic contention is that the population and cultural balance will heavily favor the Jews in the new Palestine. This—in their view—will lead either to an explosive situation, or to the domination of New Palestine by the Jews and a possible reversion to a neo-Zionist state in disguise.

The argument is serious and looks quite plausible given the present setup, and the European dichotomy of the "Arabs" as a backward group and the "Jews" as a modern one.

As for population, the Jews in Palestine today number 2.5 million compared to 2.6 million Palestinian Arabs (Christians and Moslems) in the occupied territories before 1967 and after it, and those in exile.

Birth rates and natural growth rates are higher among Arab Palestinians.

Immigration, however, has been the major cause of growth in the Jewish ranks. Nevertheless, one must consider the fact that 250,000 Jews have permanently left Palestine—emigrated—since 1949 in a period where relative security prevailed. Most of the emigrants were European Jews. Most of the new immigrants were Arab Jews who found it very difficult to stay in the Arab states after the creation and survival of Israel.

The process of the revolution will inevitably increase the tempo of emigration especially of those beneficiaries of the racist state who will find it difficult to adapt to an open plural society. Parallel to that development will be the increasing modernization of the Arab countries and a growing toleration of all minorities including the Jewish. *Fateh is already engaged in serious negotiations with several Arab countries to allow Jewish emigrants back, to return their property, and guarantee them full and equal rights.*

The pace of social and educational development is rising rapidly among the Arab Palestinians as well. It is estimated that the number of university graduates among the Palestinians in exile exceeds 50,000.

Palestinians have successfully played the role of educators, professionals and technicians in several Arab countries, especially in the Arabian Peninsula and North Africa. Arab Palestinians faced this cultural challenge in pre-1948 Palestine and managed in the relatively short period of thirty years to compete effectively with the Jews in agriculture, industry, education, and even in the field of finance and banking. Hopeful in the comradeship of a significant number of Jews, the Arabs of Palestine will become effective and equal partners, in the building of the new country.

Integration of Palestine within the Arab region will add to its economic and political viability. Present Arab boycott will obviously be replaced by economic aid and trade, a goal which Israel completely failed to achieve, remaining thus an American ward and protégé during the entire existence.

Conclusion

The democratic, non-sectarian Palestine still lacks full clarity and elaboration, but this is the best that can be done at this stage of the struggle. The Palestinians have outgrown their bitterness and prejudice in a relatively short-time through rebirth of national pride. A few years ago, discussing this proposal would have been considered a complete sell-out or high treason. Even today, some Arabs still find it very difficult to accept the proposed goal and secretly—or publicly—hope that it is nothing more than a tactical propaganda move. It is definitely not so. The Palestinian revolution is determined to fight for the creation of the new democratic and non-sectarian Palestine as the long-term ultimate goal of liberation. Annihilation of the Jews or the Palestinian exiles, and the creation of an exclusive racist state in Palestine be it Jewish, Christian or Moslem is toally unacceptable and unworkable. The oppressed Palestinian people will fight and make all necessary sacrifices to demolish such a state, now and in the future.

The Israeli racists are greatly irritated by the idea of a democratic Palestine. It reveals the contradictions of Zionism and exposes the moral schizophrenia that has beset world Jewry since the creation of Israel. The adoption by several significant progressive Jews of the new goal threatens world Zionism. Israeli Jewish Professor Loebel and French Jewish writer Ania Francos were molested by Zionists for their sponsorship of the Democratic Palestine as the ultimate goal of liberation. The Zionists are stepping up their campaign to discredit the idea especially among the Jews. Their effort has been in vain. The force of logic and the effect of years of persecution in exclusive societies at the hands of racists are opening the eyes of Jews and others in the world to the only permanent solution that will bring lasting peace and justice to our Palestine: the building of a progressive, open, tolerant homeland for all of us.

Memorandum Submitted to the Big Powers and the Secretary-General of the United Nations by the Representative of the Arab Higher Committee for Palestine
(August 13, 1970)

Loose talk about "a lasting and just peace in the Middle East" is being made in the lobbies of the United Nations and the capitals of the big powers. We regret to say that negotiations for such a peace are not guided by the principles of justice, international law, or the United Nations Charter, but are made under duress with the object of upholding aggression and confirming the fruits of aggression.

It seems that the big powers and the United Nations are only guided by the rule of force and not by the rule of law. To base discussions for "a lasting and just peace in the Middle East" on the infamous Resolution of the Security Council of November 22nd, 1967, is to mock peace and mock justice.

The big powers and the United Nations are not interested in peace, or in justice, in the Middle East, but in furthering their selfish interests and protecting the interest of the international Zionist gangsters who control many of the Governments of the big powers, and thereby control the United Nations.

The negotiations which are being conducted by the Governments of the United Arab Republic and Jordan are being conducted under the duress of foreign occupation of their territories, and under undue influence, pressure, and maneuvering by the big powers, and therefore the result of such negotiations will not be binding on the governments and peoples of the United Arab Republic and Jordan, and are categorically rejected in advance by the Palestinians and all the Arab people in the Middle East.

The Zionist controlled press in America and Europe is conducting a smear campaign against Palestinians for rejecting the "Rogers Plan." Palestinians who are victims of Zionist war crimes, Zionist aggression and Zionist robbery are called "terrorists," "warmongers" and "murderers," terms which become and justly fit the international Zionist gangsters and war criminals. No people in the world yearn and pray for peace more than the Palestinians. They have been victims of wars of aggression, usurpation, exile, deprivation, and misery for a quarter of a century.

Any settlement of the Middle East problem which confirms Zionist aggression and illegal occupation in Palestine, and recognizes rights and sovereignty for the Zionist invaders, war criminals, and robbers is a sham peace. Such unjust, illegal and immoral settlement is a crime of genocide against the Palestinians and a negation of their right to self-determination and freedom. Such a settlement violates the principles of International law and justice and the United Nations Charter.

The insistence by the big powers and the United Nations on such a settlement displays moral bankruptcy and irresponsible disregard for human rights and human decency.

Although we are convinced that it is useless to submit to the big powers and the United Nations suggestions about what can lead to a lasting and just peace in the Middle East, we feel that it is our duty to place before the big powers and the United Nations the only proper guidelines for such a just and lasting peace.

The Security Council should revoke its Resolution of the 22nd November 1967, and should decide that a lasting peace in the Middle East can only be established by the just solution of the Palestine problem on the following lines:

1. A United Nations force must be sent to subdue the Military racists colonial Zionist regime in Palestine.
2. A United Nations Commission must be formed to enable the Muslim, Christian and Jewish indigenous citizens of Palestine to form a Constituent Assembly for drafting and adopting a Constitution for a democratic State of Palestine.

Should the big powers and the United Nations be unable to pursue this only just and honorable course then they should wash their hands of Middle East problems.

Extract from a Statement by the United Kingdom Secretary of State for Foreign and Commonwealth Affairs, Sir Alec Douglas-Home, Delivered to the Yorkshire Area Council of the British Conservative Party at Harrogate, October 31, 1970

An equilibrium is needed in the Middle East which both sides would be prepared to accept. The actual issues in dispute are of a kind which can be solved. The fabric of a settlement consistent with the Security Council Resolution of November 1967 which would be fair and should be workable can easily be produced. Agreed solutions in all the separate elements would have to be incorporated into a formal and binding agreement which would be endorsed by the United Nations Security Council. Like the Resolution of 1967, any such settlement must be based on two fundamental principles: the inadmissibility of the acquisition of territory by war, and the need for a just and lasting peace in which every state in the area could live in security. This means, as the Security Council Resolution said, that Israeli armed forces must withdraw from territories occupied in the conflict, and that, on the other hand the state of belligerency which has existed in the Middle East must be ended and the right of every state to live in peace within secure and recognised boundaries free from threats or acts of force, must be recognised.

Territorial Questions

I believe that a settlement should establish a definitive agreement on territorial questions. Such an agreement would be the answer both to Israel's fear for her existence and, at the same time, to Arab fear of Israeli expansionism. This is why the balance between the provisions for Israeli withdrawal and secure and recognised boundaries is so important. No outsider can prescribe exactly where these boundaries should be. If they are to be recognised they must first and foremost be agreed by the countries concerned.

Between Israel and Egypt, an international boundary has existed for a long time. I believe that this boundary should once again be recogised in a settlement, subject to whatever arrangements might be made to deal with the special problems of *Gaza*, problems that derive from the immense concentration of refugees in the Gaza area, whose future would have to be resolved by a settlement.

Between Israel and Jordan, the problem is more difficult. There has never been a recognised boundary between the two countries. But I believe that the Resolution implies that secure and recognised boundaries should be based on the armistice lines which existed before the war of 1967, subject to minor changes which might be agreed between the two countries.

Between Israel and Lebanon there is no problem; the present boundary, though troubled by fighting like so many other areas in this troubled region, has never been questioned and should remain.

Between Israel and Syria there is of course the very sensitive problem of the Golan Heights. Syria has not accepted the Security Council Resolution. It is therefore impossible yet to discuss how the dispute between Israel and Syria should be resolved. But I would expect that, once Syria accepted the Resolution, the general principles governing the location of the other boundaries would also govern the boundary between Israel and Syria.

Jerusalem

There is one special problem, which in some ways symbolizes the Arab/Israel problem as a whole. I mean the problem of *Jerusalem*. The complexity of this problem and the depth of feeling about the city are so great as to make any compromise between the positions of the two sides hard to conceive. Some agreement on the status of the city, some agreement providing for freedom of access to the holy places and for their protection will be an essential part of a settlement. But this may have to be almost the last problem to be tackled.

Commitments to Peace

The second main pillar of a settlement would be the binding commitments which the Arab countries and Israel would make to live at peace with one another. These would include the establishment of a formal state of peace. They should cover an obligation on all states to refrain from any act or threat of hostility and to do all in their power to prevent the planning or conduct of any such acts on their territory.

Refugees and Palestinian Aspirations

There are, of course, other problems. One, which I should like to emphasise, is that of the Arabs who were refugees from Palestine during and after the fighting of 1948. When I spoke earlier of the Arab/Israel dispute being a problem of people, it was above all of the refugees that I was thinking. For many years the international community as a whole has agreed on how this problem should be settled. It is agreed that those refugees who wish to return to their homes and are prepared to live in peace with their neighbours should be allowed to do so; and that those who choose not to should be enabled to resettle elsewhere with compensation. The need for a just settlement of the refugee problem is pressing, although it is unrealistic to suppose that a settlement will be reached before the other issues of which I have spoken are resolved. And we must not ignore the political aspirations of the Palestinian Arabs and their desire to be given a means of self-expression. We cannot support any political programme which would involve the disappearance of the state of Israel; this is what the Palestinian resistance organisations at present demand. But we must work for a settlement which will attract the agreement of all the peoples of the area, including the Palestinians, and which takes account of their legitimate aspirations.

Navigation

There is also the problem of freedom of navigation in the Straits of Tiran, the Gulf of Aqaba and the Suez Canal. Firm guarantees will be required for all three.

The Opportunity

All these are matters which are capable of solution. They are matters on which practical action can be taken, action which would remove the distrust which has so far stultified progress. Now that for a time the shooting has stopped, now that the fighting has ceased in Jordan, now that the four major powers and all the parties agree that peace should be made, now is the opportunity; and it should be seized. There are many problems ahead. There is the problem of how a settlement would be achieved. There is a more important problem of the charges and the counter-charges of violations of the military standstill on the Suez Canal. These are all problems which must be resolved. I believe that a simultaneous effort by all concerned, a simultaneous decision to grasp the opportunity of making peace which I think exists, would allow progress to be made. Britain launched the Resolution on which Dr. Jarring's peace mission rests. If this opportunity to relaunch him is lost, we may face another twenty years of tension and strife—twenty years or more in which the peace which the region so desperately needs will be lacking—and with the risks of confrontations between the major powers increasing. This is a price which I believe none of us, neither Arab nor Jew, neither Russian nor American, certainly not we in Britain, should be prepared to pay.

Statement by the United Kingdom
Permanent Representative, Sir Colin Crowe,
in the General Assembly on November 2, 1970

A GREAT deal of emotion and much passion has been expressed in the course of this debate, as indeed is bound to happen in any debate on the Middle East. Hard things have been said. But what is so interesting and encouraging is that practically everybody agrees on what we should be trying to do, both in the short term, and in the long. There is virtual unanimity.

We all agree on the same *immediate* objectives: to enable Dr. Jarring to make progress in his mission and to extend the observance of the ceasefire meanwhile.

We all agree too on the longer term objective: to establish a just and lasting peace in the Middle East. There is virtually unanimous agreement that Resolution 242 is the only basis for such a settlement.

After the dinner which the Secretary-General gave for the Foreign Ministers of France, the Soviet Union, the United States and the United Kingdom on 23 October, he issued the following statement. It has been referred to before in this debate but I think it is worth reading out in full.

The four Foreign Ministers had a useful exchange of views with the Secretary-General and Ambassador Jarring on the situation in the Middle East. They agreed to exert their utmost efforts
(i)   to enable Ambassador Jarring to resume his mission at the earliest possible date;
(ii) to search for possibilities through agreement of the parties directly concerned to extend the observance of the ceasefire for a period to be determined; and
(iii) to find a peaceful solution on the basis of Security Council Resolution 242.

The Four Powers will continue their consultations and their Permanent Representatives will meet again in New York on 28 October.

The points made in this statement are covered in the two draft resolutions we have before us. Both drafts call for Resolution 242 to be

arried out in all its parts. Both call for the early resumption of the
arties' discussions with Dr. Jarring. The draft resolution in A/L.603
alls for the extension of the ceasefire. Although the resolution con-
ained in document A/L.602 does not mention the ceasefire, we under-
tand from consultations in the United Nations that the sponsors may
e prepared to include a paragraph calling for the temporary exten-
ion of the ceasefire to facilitate Dr. Jarring's mission.

We all agree, but implementation of Resolution 242 still eludes us.
Ve seem unable to break through the miasma of distrust, of charge
nd countercharge. For three and a half years we have been talking
ithout success—but we must not, we cannot, give up—we must make
urther efforts to achieve a breakthrough, to reach success.

It may help us to move forward if I set out the issues as my Govern-
ent see them.

In doing this I am not saying anything new. I am merely bringing to
his wider forum some of the ideas which are within the range of
hose which the United Kingdom has been urging or supporting dur-
ng many months of discussions between the representatives of the
our Powers, permanent members of the Security Council, here in
ew York.

Let me make quite clear at the outset that we have never believed
hat a settlement should or could be imposed on the parties. We think
right however that the Assembly should know the sort of ideas which
e believe the parties and Dr. Jarring could work on to lay the basis
or a just and lasting peace in the area, taking account of the legitimate
terests of all concerned.

From the very beginning, it has been clear that the settlement will
ave to be a "package deal" and that this will have to be embodied in
n agreement or agreements which will be binding on all the parties in
ternational law and endorsed by the Security Council. The two main
ements in the package, as in Resolution 242, are commitments to
eace on the one hand and withdrawal and boundaries on the other.
hese elements are of equal importance and one cannot be taken with-
ut the other.

First, let me consider commitments to peace.

The Arab states, on the one hand, and Israel on the other, must
gree to establish a genuine state of peace between them. It is not suffi-
ient for them merely to undertake to terminate all states or claims of
elligerency which exist between them, though they must certainly do

this. They must also undertake to refrain from all acts inconsistent with a state of peace. In particular, they must respect and recognise the sovereignty, territorial integrity, inviolability and political independence of each other without resorting to threats or use of force. They must ensure that no act of belligerency or hostility originates within their respective territories. They must settle their international disputes by peaceful means and refrain from interfering in each other's domestic affairs for any reason.

Turning to the second main element of the package, the objective, again as set out in Resolution 242, must be to establish secure and recognised boundaries. In doing this, we must be guided by the principle of the inadmissibility of the acquisition of territory by war. This principle has been re-stated in the Declaration on Friendly Relations which we all adopted with acclamation a mere ten days ago. Thus there must be Israeli withdrawal from territories occupied in the war of 1967. But this should not preclude the possibility of minor rectifications of the frontiers, to be agreed between the parties.

In the case of *Jordan*, the lines which existed before June, 1967 were not boundaries and had never been recognised as international frontiers—they were only Armistice lines. In some areas they were impractical, dividing villages from their fields and even houses from their gardens. What is required is agreement on a definitive boundary. We believe that this should be based on the lines existing before 5 June, 1967 but that there could be minor rectifications to these lines. The criteria for determining such minor rectifications might be the suppression of anomalies which make difficult the maintenance of local security or impede interior surface communications or normal surveillance of the boundary.

In the case of the *U.A.R.*, we consider that the international boundary of the former mandated territory of Palestine should constitute the frontier between Israel and the U.A.R., except for the Gaza area for which special arrangements will have to be made and embodied in the agreement.

The frontier between Israel and *Lebanon* should be the international boundary of the former mandated territory of Palestine.

As for the boundary between Israel and *Syria*, we believe that the general principles governing the remainder of the settlement should also govern the settlement between Israel and Syria, once Syria has accepted the Security Council resolution.

There is one special problem which in some ways symbolised the Arab/Israel problem as a whole. I mean the problem of Jerusalem. The problem is so complex and feelings run so deep that it is difficult to see what compromise could emerge. But some agreement on the status of the City, some agreement providing for freedom of access to the Holy Places and for their protection, will be an essential part of a settlement.

I turn now to *guarantees.*

The best guarantee of the settlement would, of course, be its acceptability to all governments and peoples of the area. However, the probability is that more concrete guarantees will be required for some time to come. We believe that the Security Council should endorse the agreement. As an internal guarantee, we favour a United Nations presence both to supervise withdrawal and remain in the area thereafter. Another important element might be the formation of demilitarised zones, as provided for in Resolution 242. These might be supervised by the United Nations. In addition, consideration should be given to any forms of external guarantee which might be suggested.

Another important element of the package is freedom of navigation. The Resolution speaks in operative paragraph 2(A) of the necessity for "guaranteeing freedom of navigation through international waterways in the area." We recognise this necessity. We believe that there should be freedom of navigation for the ships and cargoes of all countries through the Suez Canal, the Gulf of Aqaba and the Strait of Tiran. This freedom of navigation should be guaranteed, as appropriate for each of these waterways since we recognise that they do not all have the same status.

And then there are the aspirations of the Palestinians. Any settlement which is to be fair and lasting must take account of the views of all the peoples of the area, including the Palestinians. But it is impossible for the international community to engage in negotiations with those who reject a settlement in accordance with Resolution 242 and who are determined to seek their objectives through the use of force and terrorism. It is for the Arab governments concerned to enlist the support of the Palestinians for a settlement. We should certainly not wish to oppose any new political or constitutional arrangements freely worked out by the Arab governments and the Palestinians within the framework of a settlement in accordance with Resolution 242.

The agreement should include provisions for a just settlement of the refugee problem. The parties should agree to co-operate in working out such a settlement under the auspices of Ambassador Jarring, in accordance with General Assembly Resolution 194 (III) and Security Council Resolution 237 (67). The settlement should reaffirm that the 1948 refugees wishing to return to their homes and to live at peace with their neighbours should be permitted to do so and should include mutually acceptable arrangements and annual programmes for repatriation and for the resettlement with compensation of those refugees who choose not to return. The parties should undertake to co-operate in the establishment and operation of machinery for consulting interested persons and governments and for giving effect to the provisions of the just settlement of the refugee problem. The parties should accept that implementation of all other provisions of the agreement need not await the full implementation of the settlement of the refugee problem.

As I have tried to indicate, the essence of any settlement is that we must create true peace and security which will ensure the area against a recurrence of conflict. Equally important is that the parties, as they move towards that settlement, must feel secure at each and every stage. Thus questions of timing and of the entry into force of specific mutual engagements will have cardinal importance and will have to be fully provided for.

We understand the reasons which prompted Arab Delegations to bring this problem to the Assembly this year. We have serious doubts about whether it is proper for the Assembly to attempt in any way to alter a Resolution of the Security Council. We should therefore not be able to support any resolution of the Assembly which sought to amplify, modify or alter the balance of Resolution 242, or which sought to do more than simply reaffirm Resolution 242 and appeal for early progress towards its implementation. But more important than our doubts about the legal position is the firm conviction that it is unwise for the Assembly to attempt to alter Resolution 242. As the authors of that Resolution, we are naturally proud of it. But even allowing for our pride of authorship, we believe that it does contain all the essential elements of a just and lasting peace in the area. But perhaps its greatest virtue is the fact that it was adopted unanimously and that it still commands the support of the very great majority of the members of the United Nations. We believe that we should therefore hang on to this Resolution and attempt to build on it.

Thus my Delegation would prefer that if any resolution was to emerge from this debate it should be quite short and simple—not much more than the Secretary-General's statement of 23 October.

As for the two draft resolutions before us in A/L.602 and 603 my comments have already covered that in L.602, the draft sponsored by certain Afro-Asian countries. We would not dissent from the draft in L.603 which follows the lines of the Secretary-General's statement. It has the heart of the matter, but its formulation may not be quite what is required if it is to secure unanimity.

It is nearly three years since Resolution 242 was adopted—we have reason to be disappointed at the lack of progress. Let us hope that out of the current debate there will come a move forward. If there is none and we have to take up the problem once more, we believe this should be done by the Security Council. We accept that if no progress can be made in a reasonable period of time it would be right for the Security Council to address itself to the problem once more.

Address by King Hussein to Jordanian and Palestinian Dignitaries on March 15, 1972 Concerning Basic Principles of a Plan to Establish a United Arab Kingdom of Palestine and Jordan

My dear brethren,
Dear Citizens,

It gives me great pleasure to meet with you today and to talk to you and to the nation about the affairs of the present, the past, its experiences and our aspirations and hopes for the future.

The establishment of the state of Jordan in 1921 was the most important step taken in the life of the Arab Revolution after the plot against it by its allies in the first World War was discovered. With the issue of the Balfour Declaration in 1917, the formation of the State of Jordan gained a new dimension, in that it made it possible to exclude the land east of the Jordan River from the application of the Declaration and thus save it from the Zionist schemes of that period.

In 1948 when the Arab armies entered into Palestine, the smallest among them was the "Jordan army"; yet it was able to save that part of Palestine which extends from Jenin in the north to Hebron in the south and from the Jordan River in the east to a point lying not more than 15 kilometers from the sea-shore in the west. The Jordan army was also able to save Jerusalem—the Holy Old City—in its entirety and other areas outside the city wall to the north, south and east, all of which came to be known later as Arab Jerusalem. That area which came to be known as the "West Bank" was all that remained to the Arabs from the whole of Palestine together with the narrow area now called the "Gaza strip."

After a brief period of temporary administration, the leaders of the West Bank, and a selected group of leaders and notables, representing the Arabs of Palestine who had left their homes in the occupied territories, found the union with the East Bank was a national demand and a guarantee in the face of the constantly expanding Israeli dangers. They therefore, called for two historic conferences, the first of which convened in Jericho on 1.12.1948 and the second in Nablus on 28.12.1948. Representatives of all sections of the population including leaders and men of thought, young and old, labourers and farmers, all, attended the two conferences. Resolutions were adopted requesting His Majesty King Abdallah ibn Al-Hussein to take immediate steps to unite the two Banks into a single state under his leadership. His Majesty responded to the appeal of the nation and ordered that constitutional and practical steps be taken to realize this important national desire, which steps included that elections be held to choose legal representatives of the people of the West Bank to sit in Parliament. On April 24, 1950 the new parliament representing both Banks with its senators and deputies, held a historic session in which the first real step in contemporary Arab history was taken on the road to unity, which the Arab Revolt proclaimed on the dawn of its inception. This was achieved by the declaration of the union of the two Banks and by their fusion into one independent Arab state with a democratic parliamentary monarchy to be known as the Hashemite Kingdom of Jordan.

The union sailed in seas which were neither calm nor smooth. There were many underhanded currents stirred up by external hands attempting to create tempests in the face of the ship to force it slowly towards the rocks. But the awareness of the people in both Banks, their firm belief in the unity of their land and their recognition of the dangers lurking behind the frontiers, were the basic guarantee for the safety of the union and for its salvation from all the evils that beset it.

Foremost among the realities which the union of both Banks evolved day after day was that those living therein are one people, not two peoples. This reality became first clear when the Ansars (the supporters)—the inhabitants of the East Bank—welcomed their brethren, the Muhajereen (the Emmigrants)—the refugees from the territories of Palestine in 1948—and shared with them the loaf of bread, the roof and both sweetness and bitterness of life. This fact of life was emphasized and deepened by every step the government took and was clearly reflected in everyone of its institutions: In the armed forces, in the ministries and the various government departments, this reality became clear, also in all sectors of life: be it economic, agricultural or social. . . . The day came when it was impossible for anybody to distinguish between one from the West and one from the East, unlike the way a Palestinian is distinguished from a non-Palestinian in other parts of the Arab World.

The unity of blood and destiny between the people of both Banks reached its summit in 1967 when the sons of both Banks stood on the soil of the West Bank as they did for over twenty years, kneading its sacred soil with their common blood. But the struggle was stronger than their power and circumstances were bigger than their courage. And the catastrophe occurred.

In the midst of this sea of suffering created by the June calamity the aims of the Jordan government in that period which followed the war, were summed up in two aims: the brave stand in the face of continuous and unceasing aggression against the East Bank, and the strong determination to liberate the occupied land and free our kin and brethren in the West Bank. All our efforts were directed to achieve both these goals in an atmosphere of confidence that the Arab States would support Jordan in its calamity, and with unlimited trust that the unity of Arab destiny had become a deeply rooted reality in the conscience of the whole Arab nation, a reality which cannot be shaken by regional interests however great and which cannot be reached by plans and intentions however underhanded.

And suddenly, Jordan found itself facing a new catastrophe, which if allowed to befall the country, would have resulted in the loss of the East Bank, and would have laid the stage for a final liquidation of the Palestinian case and forever. The forces setting this calamity had mobilized many elements to serve their purpose. Many other elements also fell into the nets of these forces. Many of these elements claimed the Palestinian identity of the sacred cause and thus played their roles under the guise of that name. The contradictions and conflicting currents prevailing in the world found their way into the ranks of these elements.

It was only natural that Jordan should rise up to confront the impending tragedy. The challenge was met by the stand of the unique combination of its people: the Muhajereen and the Ansars. This evil subversion was shattered on the rock of the firm national unity, as it was disintegrated by the awareness of the new man, born in 1950 who grew and flourished in the challenges which he had to face during the past twenty years.

During all that period, and specially after the June war in 1967 or even before it, the leadership of Jordan was thinking about the future of the state and was planning for it. The leadership based its thinking on its faith in the message of Jordan, which message found its roots in the great Arab Revolution and its confidence in the man living on both sides of the river and his ability to play his role in serving its message and its aims.

The manner in which the fulfillment of the Palestinian cause was viewed, carried in its folds, the far reaching scope of the Arab-Israeli conflict. Palestine had always been the first goal of Zionist plans. The people of Palestine were its first victims, and were to be followed by the people of both Banks. Even if Zionist expansionism was to end at some limit, Zionist interests would only rest by keeping the Arab world weak and disunited in order to be able to safeguard its territorial gains forever. Because the opposite camp stands as one united force, it thus becomes incumbent on all Arabs to stand united also. Even more, unity in itself is not sufficient unless it comprises a real understanding encompassing all modern methods and aspects of modern development.

Jordan had always understood the magnitude of the tragedy that befell the Palestinians. After the Zionist plot had dispersed them, in 1948 no country, Arab or non-Arab, offered the Palestinians what Jordan gave them in the way of honourable life and decent living. In Jordan, and under the auspices of the union of both Banks, the genuine Palestinian community was found among the overwhelming majority of the people who live in both Banks, and in it the Palestinian found the appropriate framework in which to live and move as well as the real starting point for the will of liberation and all its hopes.

The Palestinians had existed hundreds of years before 1948 and continue to exist since 1948. But the events which started to prevail throughout the Arab World and all the forces and currents which manipulate them started to overlook these facts and to ignore them in conformity with the state of indecision which our nation is undergoing since years. This artificial status was given further impetus by the various conferences, plots and attacks, we have been seeing and hearing of. It was as if the Palestinian was intended to dissociate himself from his national identity and to place himself in a small separate flask which could easily be destroyed at any moment. Surely, this appeared to be another plot being hatched in the long chain of plots against the people of Palestine and the whole of the Arab nation.

These suspicious movements were not directed only to the minority of the Palestinians living outside both Banks, but were also aimed at the majority here in the hope of forcing the people of the West Bank into a state which would separate them from all that surrounds them. If some of the powers that encourages these currents do not conceal their desire to abandon their responsibilities toward the Palestine cause and the Palestinian people, by pushing them into separation, yet its brilliance however attractive it may seem to them, should not conceal from us the danger of their reaching a situation which would make them an easy prey to Israel's unlimited greed. These suspicious movements try to make the Jordan rule appear as attempting to seek gains and benefits. They try to find their way into our unity in an attempt to weaken it and create doubts about it. Attempts are also being made to exploit some people's desire to obtain material gains to the extent of pushing them to play their roles to attain their ultimate vicious end.

The Israeli occupation of the West Bank and other Arab territories dear to us has managed to continue due to the disintegration of the Arab front, the lack of coordination, the struggle to establish opposing axes and camps, the abandonment of the essence of the Palestine cause and its needs, the concentration on talking in the name of the Palestine cause in place of consorted action, as well as the attempt by certain groups to attain power through internal strife. All this also led to deepen the suffering of the Palestine people and to push them into a state of utter confusion and loss. The talk about municipal elections in the West Bank is merely an example of such a tragedy which certain quarters are trying to exploit to their own interests.

And yet, Jordan has never ceased to call for a united front needing mobilization and coordination of efforts. Jordan has never hesitated to stretch its hand with all sincerity to all its Arab brethren in its belief in the unity of our cause and our destiny and future. Jordan did not spare any effort towards liberation, although the above realities in the Arab world retarded it. Yet the serious planning for the future of the state went on, as well the events and positions taken against this country have failed to weaken our belief in the imperativeness of our final victory in liberating the land and the people. This belief is based not only in our faith in the justice of our cause, but is also based on our faith in our country and people on both Banks of the river and in our nation as a whole.

Thus, it was decided to move with the state into a new stage based in its essence on liberation, its concept reflecting the aspiration of our people and embodying their belief in the unity of our nation and their sense of belonging to it. In addition to all that it is based on the absolute determination to regain the legitimate rights of the Palestinian people, and is directed to place them in a position which will enable them to regain and safeguard these rights.

This was the pledge we made to give our people the right of self-determination. It is our answer to all those who chose to doubt that pledge and void it from its essence. Today that pledge will find its way to every citizen in this country and to every individual in this nation and in the world. It is now expanding to exceed the limits of words in order to face every possibility of disunity and to embody all national aims and goals.

We wish to declare that planning for the new phase has come as a result of continuous meetings, discussions and consultations which were held with the representatives and leaders of both Banks. There was unanimous consensus that the main shape of the new phase should include the best and most developed concept of a modern democratic state. In addition to that, it will help to create a new society built by a new man to become the driving force which will put us on the way to victory, progress, unity, freedom and a better life.

We are pleased to announce that the basic principles of the proposed plan are:—

1.   The Hashemite Kingdom of Jordan shall become a United Arab Kingdom, and shall be thus named.

2.   The United Arab Kingdom shall consist of two regions:

   A.   The Region of Palestine, and shall consist of the West Bank and any other Palestinian territories to be liberated and where the population opts to join it.

   B.   The Region of Jordan, and shall consist of the East Bank.

3.   Amman shall be the central capital of the Kingdom and at the same time shall be the capital of the Region of Jordan.

4.   Jerusalem shall become the capital of the Region of Palestine.

5.   The King shall be the Head of the State and shall assume the central executive authority assisted by a Central Council of Ministers. The central legislative authority shall be vested in the King and in the National Assembly whose members shall be elected by direct and secret ballot. It shall have an equal number of members from each of the two regions.

6.   The Central Judicial Authority shall be vested in a "Supreme Central Court."

7.   The Kingdom shall have a single Armed Forces and its Supreme Commander shall be the King.

8.   The responsibilities of the Central Executive Power shall be confined to matters relating to the Kingdom as a sovereign international entity insuring the safety of the union, its stability and development.

9.   The Executive Power in each region shall be vested in a Governor General from the Region and in a Regional Council of Ministers also from the Region.

10. The Legislative Power in each Region shall be vested in "People's Council" which shall be elected by direct secret ballot. This Council shall elect the Governor General.

11. The Legislative Power in each region shall be vested in the courts of the region and nobody shall have any authority over it.

12. The Executive Power in each Region shall be responsible for all its matters with the exception of such matters as the constitution requires to be the responsibility of the Central Executive Power.

It is obvious that the implementation of this proposed plan will require the necessary constitutional steps and Parliament shall be asked to draw up the new constitution of the country.

This new phase to which we look will guarantee the rearrangement of the "Jordan-Palestinian home" in a manner that will insure for it additional innate strength and thus the ability to achieve our hopes and aspirations. This plan will strengthen the joint fabric of both Banks and will satisfy the requirements of their unity and brotherhood and shall lead to deepen the sense of responsibility in the individual in both regions of the Kingdom, to best serve our cause without prejudicing any of the acquired rights of any citizen of Palestinian origin in the Region of Jordan or any citizen of Jordanian origin in the Region of Palestine. For this plan collects but does not disperse; it strengthens but does not weaken; and it unifies but does not disintegrate. It does not allow any changes in the gains that our citizens have acquired as a result of twenty years of union. Any attempt to cast doubt on all this will be tantamount to treason against the unity of the Kingdom and against the cause, the nation and the homeland. The citizen in our country has passed such experience and has achieved a level of awareness and ability which qualify him to cope with coming responsibilities with greater confidence and determination.

If ability is a bliss which should grow to become man's responsibility toward himself and toward others, if his awareness is a weapon to be used for his own good and that of others, then the time has come for our man to stand face to face with his responsibilities, to discharge them with honesty and practice them with courage and honour.

Thus, the above formula becomes a title for a new page, brilliant and firmly believing in the history of this country. Every citizen has his role and his duties. As to the armed forces, which have marched right from the beginning under the banner of the great Arab Revolution, that included and will forever include among its ranks the best elements from among the sons of both Banks, these armed forces will remain ready to receive more of our sons from both Banks, based on the highest level of efficiency, ability and organization, it shall always be open to welcome any one who wishes to serve our nation and our cause with absolute loyalty to the eternal goals of our nation.

This Arab country is the home of the cause, just as it is from the Arabs and for the Arabs. Its record of sacrifice for our nation and our cause is full and well known. Its pages were inscribed by the blood of its gallant armed forces and its free people. The more the positions taken against it, change into more positive brotherly assistance and support, the easier it will be for it to continue its glorious march of sacrifices, with more ability and hope, until it regains for our nation its rights and attains victory.

This Arab Country is the country of all, Jordanians and Palestinians alike. When we say Palestinian we mean every Palestinian be he in the East or West of this great world on condition that he should be loyal to Palestine and should belong to Palestine. Our call is for every citizen in this country to rise and play his role and shoulder his responsibilities in this new phase, it is also addressed to every Palestinian outside Jordan to answer the call of duty, far from appearances and free from ailments and diversion and to proceed and join his kin and brethren along a single path based on this message, united in one front, clear in the aims, so that all should cooperate to reach the goals of liberation and to build up the structure to which we all aspire.

"GOD WILL AID THOSE WHO AID HIS CAUSE."

The Current Situation in the Middle East*

JOSEPH J. SISCO

As we view the Middle East today, the plausible argument could be made that the status quo in the area has improved over what it has been in the last several years:

—-The U.S.-negotiated cease-fire between Egypt and Israel is already in its 30th month. As uneasy as it is, nevertheless, it continues to hold.

—Second, contrasted with what the situation was in the crisis period of September 1970, the situation in Jordan is perhaps more stable today than it has been at any time since the June war of 1967.

—Third, along the Lebanese-Israeli border there has been a progressive reduction of the number of incidents, and our hope would be that in time this border can truly become a border of quiet and tranquillity. Even along the Syrian-Israeli border, where one reads from time to time about incidents, actions, counteractions, while we continue to view these incidents with concern, our hope and expectation is they will not mushroom into something which is more serious and which could embrace other elements in a Middle East imbroglio.

—And above all, I believe the possibility of confrontation between the United States and the Soviet Union over the Middle East has been sharply reduced. There are two reasons: first, the results of the discussions that were held with the Soviets at the summit last May; and second, the reduced Soviet presence in Egypt brought about by the decision taken by the Egyptian Government last summer in turn has reduced the likelihood of confrontation in the Middle East between the United States and the Soviet Union.

I mentioned the summit discussions last May. You will recall that at the end of those discussions a communique was issued which reaffirmed that both the United States and the Soviet Union continue to seek as an objective a political solution of the Arab-Israeli dispute based on the November 1967 Security Council resolution, a resolution that, you will recall, laid down not a blueprint for a solution but rather a framework

* Address before the national foreign policy conference for editors and broadcasters at the Department of State on March 29, 1973.

of principles within which an agreement presumably could be achieved on the basis of negotiations between the parties.[1] Alongside what appeared to be an anodyne communique limited largely to reaffirming the political objective of a peaceful solution was a declaration of principles which was adopted at that summit, the main principle of which was that both major powers should try to avoid any confrontation over such troubled areas as the Middle East.[2]

In practical terms what the communique meant was this: While there was not a meeting of the minds between ourselves and the Soviet Union as to what might constitute a fair settlement of the Arab-Israeli dispute, the fact of the matter is that both were agreed that the political objective should continue to be a resolution of the problem by peaceful means rather than by force and with emphasis on no confrontation between the major powers. In effect this meant that both powers were saying that both should do whatever they could to try to maintain the present cease-fire that exists in the area while further efforts are made to try to make some practical progress toward a solution. I believe the major powers were saying in that communique that whatever the differences might be regarding the substance of a settlement, both were agreed that the Middle East should not be an area over which there should be confrontation between us. This reflects a parallelism of interest between the United States and the Soviet Union that the present staus quo, as uneasy as it might be, should not become the focus of future confrontation between us.

Series of Discussions With Middle East Leaders

Now, I said that you could make a plausible argument that the status quo has been very considerably improved, and I believe it has despite the recent tragic occurrences in the area. However, it would be a mistake to view the current situation in the Middle East with a complacent attitude. It is true that the cease-fire is now in its 30th month, but if we need a cogent reminder of how fragile is the cease-fire we need only recall the recent shooting down of a Libyan aircraft and the recent murders of our diplomats in Khartoum. Moreover, from the point of view of the United States, as long as the "no war, no peace" situation

[1] For text of the resolution, see BULLETIN of Dec. 18, 1967, p. 843.

[2] For texts of the Basic Principles of Relations and of the joint communique issued at Moscow May 29, 1972, see BULLETIN of June 26, 1972, p. 898 and p. 899.

continues, with all of the instability, our national interests cannot be pursued with maximum effectiveness.

The United States, of course, has a special relationship with Israel. We have consistently supported the security of the State of Israel. At the same time we should bear in mind that the overall interests of the United States go beyond any one nation in the area. We have important political, economic, and strategic interests that broadly encompass the area. We will continue to support the security of the State of Israel. At the same time, we will continue to do everything feasible to develop and to nurture and to strengthen our relationships with the individual Arab states, because the present instability in the area is too risky, too fragile, too dangerous. The only entirely satisfactory answer is the eventual achievement of a stable, just, and durable peace—a peace in which both sides are committed on the basis of an exchange of obligations between them and both sides have adopted a fundamental attitude of coexistence and live-and-let-live.

What are the prospects? We have had an important series of discussions with various leaders of the Middle East during the month of February.

In the first instance King Hussein was here, and these discussions afforded us an oportunity for a full exchange of views on the current situation in the Middle East and a number of important aspects of our bilateral relationships. I can summarize these discussions in this way: Jordan made clear to us that it feels it has adopted and will continue to adopt a relatively flexible posture regarding the question of a solution and it would like to see the United States actively and constructively involved in helping to bring about a settlement.

Insofar as our discussions with the Egyptians, some of you may know we have had here in Washington a visit from the National Security Adviser of the Egyptian Government, [Hafez] Ismail. These discussions were useful and provided an excellent opportunity for an in-depth exchange of views regarding the situation in the Middle East and the possibilities for diplomacy which currently may exist. It is no secret that the Egyptian representative did not come with any new proposals. President Sadat confirmed this in his speech just 48 hours ago. But I believe, as the Egyptian representative himself indicated publicly, that the discussions did contribute to a better atmosphere in our relations. While no new doors were opened as a result of these in-depth discussions, I can report to you that no doors were closed either and the possibilities of diplomacy in the future remain open. I would also make this same judgment in the aftermath of the recent visit of the Israeli Prime Minister to this country just a couple of weeks ago.

Interim Suez Canal Agreement

Now, the impasse we face can be described very simply. In our judgment, the chasm on the overall settlement is too broad to bridge in the foreseeable future. The Egyptian position is: not one inch of territory by way of any concessions. The Israeli position is that in order for their security concerns to be met, substantial territorial adjustments are required. As long as both sides adhere firmly to these two positions, we frankly do not see the gap being bridged in the foreseeable future.

For this reason, we continue to believe that the approach must be a more modest approach, that the most feasible approach to peace continues to be a step-by-step approach. And for this reason we continue to feel that, with the doors of diplomacy remaining open, perhaps the most practical approach continues to be that of trying to achieve a so-called interim Suez Canal agreement. Such an intermediate agreement would involve the opening of the Suez Canal, an extended cease-fire, and some Israeli withdrawal east of the Canal.

With respect to an interim agreement, Israel has agreed to engage without preconditions in indirect negotiations between Israel and Egypt under the aegis of the United States. The Egyptian position is that before it could agree to engage in such indirect negotiations there must be a prior commitment by Israel to total evacuation from Egyptian territory. We have over the past 18 months tried to make clear that we feel that this kind of a prior commitment is unattainable.

We do understand and appreciate, however, the Egyptian view that any interim Suez Canal agreement should not become an end in itself. We understand this because an interim agreement obviously leaves unresolved not only a number of important territorial and security questions on the Egyptian-Israeli aspect of the settlement but it leaves untouched the multifarious and intricate and complex questions that relate to the Jordanian-Israeli aspect of the question. An interim agreement, for example, does not touch the fundamental question of the Palestine problem, and we don't believe any durable peace is achievable unless such a peace not only meets the legitimate concerns of both the established Arab and Israeli states but of the Palestinians as well; an interim agreement does not touch the crucial question of the West Bank; an interim agreement does not touch the crucial question of Jerusalem which is so complicated because there are so many interests involved.

And it is for this reason we feel that any interim agreement should and must be a step toward an overall settlement. In other words, we continue to maintain that the most practical and feasible approach is the step-by-step approach involving the modest objective of the opening of the Canal and some Israeli withdrawal, and we consider that such a step in fact would be a significant practical test of peace on the ground, a practical test of peace on the ground which would maximize the opportunities for further subsequent efforts toward an overall settlement. Our view that any interim agreement must be linked to the November 1967 Security Council resolution has long been the position of the United States. So it is a very modest approach we have in mind for the forseeable future.

Energy Needs and the Middle East

I will make one other overall observation because it is a matter that is on so many people's minds. I said that we have important and significant overall political, economic, and strategic interests in this area. And of course the question of oil inevitably comes up, and access to oil by the Western world, including the United States.

At the outset, in terms of the energy situation in the future, I believe it is important that we Americans bear in mind a couple of fundamentals.

First of all, in the long range—and I emphasize in the long range—I believe that we have the resources in this country on an all-resource basis to meet our future needs—and when I say this I mean oil, I mean gas, I mean fusion, I mean coal, I mean shale, and so on. So we have the capacity to develop whatever we need in the long range, and it is important for us to keep this in mind.

Second, it is not in the national interest of the United States to be overly reliant on any one source or any one area for our energy needs. It is not in our interest on security grounds; it is not in our interest on economic grounds, and specifically I have in mind the question of balance of payments. Now having said that, obviously we have some difficult decisions domestically as well as internationally that face us, and my expectation is that there will be at an appropriate time an overall statement of policy on this by the President.

But the question that inevitably arises is this: How does the question of oil get related to the whole question of the Arab-Israeli dispute? And here I think one can take either an overly optimistic or overly pessimistic view of the situation. You can dismiss this aspect out of hand, which I think would be foolhardy. On the other hand, I think you can overdraw the possible implications and distort what I consider to be the reality of the situation.

I believe there is a mutuality of interests that has been manifest over the past number of decades between producers and consumers of oil. Most of you know that there have been adjustments occurring in the financial arrangements between the producer and the consumer; for example, recently an agreement between Saudi Arabia and Kuwait and the oil companies on the basis of 25 percent participation, with 51 percent anticipated perhaps in the eighties sometime. There is also a new understanding being negotiated between the Government of Iran and the oil companies which embraces a so-called sales contract approach, with the Iranian Government doing a good deal more than it has in the past in the actual production and management of the oil installations.

I don't say that the economic relationships, the financial relationships, are not in flux and are not apt to change; they have been changing in the past and are likely to change in the future, and I think this adjustment will go on. But I have serious doubts that the mutuality of interests between the producer and the consumer will in fact be jeopardized on the basis of whatever differences there may or may not be over the question of the Arab-Israeli dispute and particularly if we in this country face up to the kind of decisions required to assure that in the long range we are not overly reliant on any one area or any one source for our energy needs.

A New Policy for Israel

STANLEY HOFFMANN

SINCE the end of the Yom Kippur War, the main attempt
resolving the Arab-Israeli conflict has been the step-by-step a]
proach initiated by Secretary of State Henry Kissinger. Eno
mous energy has been spent in Washington and in Israel on negoti
ting disengagement agreements with Egypt and with Syria, and (
preparing for a new limited agreement with Egypt. But whether
not the current effort succeeds, we are reaching the end of this pa
ticular road. The time has come to look at the long term, to lea
lessons from the obstacles the current method has met, and to resc
to a new diplomatic strategy.

My own conviction is that it is time for a sweeping Israeli initiati
aimed at a peace settlement. The United States will remain an ind
pensable participant in the effort. But instead of what is essentially
American policy groping to bring gradual peace to the parties, v
now need a decisive effort by the party whose future existence a
security are at stake, whose role in the Middle East has been the hea
of the matter since 1948, and which finds itself on the defensive. F
it is its destiny that is being shaped, and it has a vital interest both
remaining its own master and in reaching with its adversaries a sett
ment that cannot be seen as the result of an outside power's skill
exploiting temporary circumstances.

II

After 15 months of American efforts and after the successes
the Palestine Liberation Organization at Rabat and at the Uni
Nations, the leaders of Israel have had to face two serious problet

The first is the choice of a method toward a settlement. Here, th
is a serious division on how to proceed. But there are also some i
portant common features in their views. The first is a sense of dep
dence on Henry Kissinger, who is in a way the most important po
ical personality of Israel. This dependence is accepted with hope a

ititude by some; it breeds misgivings in others. But everybody, for
: time being at least, believes that—for better or worse—he has the
y to the locked door that separates Israel from the Arab world. A
ond common feature is a profound distrust of the Soviet Union,
n both as an intriguing great power pursuing great-power interests
1 as a potential force for social revolution and disruption in the
ab world. Not all Israeli Sovietologists agree with this view, but it
hat of the policy-makers. A third common feature is a set of con-
dictions, resulting from the sense of dependence on the United
ites and distrust of the Soviet Union. Concerning the United States,
n the officials who are most obviously converted to America's ap-
)ach are keen on avoiding telling Mr. Kissinger what Israel's
ws of an ultimate settlement should be. They are willing to entrust
n with the next step, because they feel that they have no choice,
t they do not want to reveal too much of their final hand, not only
ause they do not agree among themselves but also because they
not want to have their whole fate negotiated by the United States.
Finally, they note that there is a potential conflict of priorities.
nerican priorities in the Middle East are what could be called
at-power relations: how to keep the Soviet Union contained, or
; how to deal with the oil producers so that they do not strangulate
: industrial powers, provoke crises in the American alliance, etc.
d Israel fits in with that strategy. Israel's priorities are quite dif-
ent: essentially, its first concern is relations with the Arab world.
)m that conflict of priorities even the most pro-American Israelis
lize that there could come a clash in strategies later on. Also, even
>se who are most pro-American would not like to have superpower
ces stationed in the Middle East as the end result. But even those
o are most anti-Soviet realize that there will not be a settlement
hout including the Soviet Union somehow, and even those who ask
t Egypt drop its Soviet connection as a way of showing its good-
l toward peace would also, like Egypt, prefer to be able to play
h both superpowers, and to have diplomatic relations with Mos-
v, however much they distrust the Soviet Union.

The division on how to proceed opposes the partisans of the step-
step approach, who include the Prime Minister and the Foreign
nister, and those who would prefer the "Geneva method." The
p-by-step approach represented a blend of America's two earlier
irses between which Washington had oscillated since 1948: a
eat-power" approach which aimed at keeping the Arab-Israeli
flict local, and at trying to find a solution either through the action
he permanent members of the Security Council or through Soviet-

American cooperation; and a "strategy of commitment," which de
veloped after the Soviets' own shift of policy against Israel, and cor
sisted of firm American military and diplomatic support to Israe
Like the "strategy of commitment," the step-by-step approach stresse
American support to Israel and tried to contain the Soviets by shuttin
them out diplomatically. Like the "great-power" approach, it aime
at a settlement through outside efforts, and at restoring America
position in the Arab world. (Paradoxically, the blend also meant th
the United States is now to some degree arming both sides.)

Moreover, this policy represented a blend of necessity and interes
As for necessity, Kissinger, in November 1973, had discovered
President Sadat a man eager for American friendship and willing
move cautiously toward peace with Israel. But Sadat could not "b
tray the Arab cause" by making a separate deal with Israel. Step-b
step agreements could set in motion a process in which Egypt wou
gradually get its lost territory back. Israel, in turn, would obtain a
surances of nonbelligerence, in such a way that Sadat could not
accused of repudiating Nasser's ideal of Arab solidarity and wou
not have to grant Israel full recognition while other Arab states st
refused to recognize the existence of the Jewish state. Similarly, t
deadlocks of Israeli politics made it impossible for any Israeli gover
ment to shift abruptly from immobilism to a settlement involving
retreat from most of the occupied territories, at a moment when
Arab enemies were still unwilling to grant Israel formal recognitic

The approach was also likely to be beneficial both to the Unit
States and to Israel. For Israel what was involved was a gamble
the good effects of time. At home, it was in the interest of the Isra
government to dispose of a long period of peace during which pub
opinion would recover from the trauma of October 1973, regain cc
fidence in Israel's strength, accept the idea of gradual retreats, a
find in strength a reason for magnanimity. Externally, it was
Israel's interest not to engage in a global negotiation with the Ar
while they were elated by the success of their oil strategy. Isr
would benefit from dragging out matters until the time when K
singer's common front of the consumer countries, set up to deal b
with the problem of energy independence and with the problem
recycling the petrodollars, had restored the broken world balance.

A step-by-step approach was also in Washington's interest.
home, Kissinger had to deal with the powerful forces that had tra
tionally supported Israel—in the press and in Congress especia]
A return to the prewar White House policy of pro-Israeli passiv
was impossible. Merely to provide Israel with weapons without pr

ıg toward a settlement would have meant the certainty of more wars, ew confrontations with Moscow, a splendid opportunity for the So- iets to expand their influence in the Middle East, a widening breach ith Western Europe and Japan (i.e., no possibility of a common oil rategy under U.S. leadership), and the sacrifice of U.S. positions in iendly Arab countries. But a shift to maximum pressure on Israel ıward a full settlement involving a retreat from the occupied terri- ıries, concessions on Jerusalem, and an immediate tackling of that ıost difficult of all issues, that of the Palestinians—all of this in ap- arent collusion with Moscow—would have seriously weakened the ɔmestic base of Kissinger's foreign policy. He strenuously tried to ınvince Jewish leaders in the United States both that *some* move- ıent was unavoidable and that it would serve to protect rather than ndermine Israel. Externally, this approach allowed Kissinger to ploit Egypt's distaste for the Soviets, and to keep the Soviets—as ell as the Europeans—out of the bargaining; it was complicated ıough without additional outside interference. Moreover, only the nited States could "deliver the goods" to Egypt and Syria.

In Israel today, what still appears decisive to many is Egypt's situa- ɔn. Will Egypt define its national interest narrowly (as it did ırough the late 1930s) or will it continue to define it in a pan-Arab ay? The step-by-step approach is seen as the only one that might low one to find out. For most Israelis understand that Sadat cannot ıt his ties to the other Arab countries openly or rapidly, that there a need for a period of defusing and transition. Therefore the Israeli ıvernment is willing to sign an intermediate agreement which serves ıth sides. This of course also suits Israel's own psychological reluc- nce to think too much about the end of the road.

However, there are increasing doubts about the validity of this bet. irst of all, even if there is a new agreement with Egypt, what would ɘ the next? Nobody seems to see much room for a second disengage- ent agreement with Syria; here, the obstacle is geography. Sinai a huge desert; the Golan Heights are narrow and almost impossible slice up. Whoever controls its summits dominates either the Syrian the Israeli valleys. So there is not very much leeway in between last ar's disengagement and literally either war or peace with Syria.

Is there a Jordanian step? There was a hope that perhaps, after gypt, Israel might conclude an agreement with Jordan which would al not with the West Bank but with the other issues that concern ıth Israel and Jordan. With that view, there are two problems. One that these issues are entirely minor with the exception of Jerusalem, hich is crucial and cannot be handled only by Jordan and by Israel

in a partial agreement. Also, the requirement for good Israeli rela
tions with the King of Jordan is that they not be formalized, becaus
he cannot formalize them without exposing himself to charges an
threats.

Second, concerning a new agreement with Egypt itself, one neec
to find a devilishly clever formula. The agreement must be ambiguou
enough to protect Egypt from other Arab charges of treason (whic
would undoubtedly come if Egypt granted formal nonbelligerenc
or a promise of several years of nonaggression to Israel), yet clea
enough to protect Israel from new pressures from Cairo just a fe
months later on behalf of Egypt and of the other Arab states an
forces. Diplomacy is the art of reconciling irreconcilables, and histor
is full of agreements which are ambiguous enough to one side an
clear enough to the other, but normally there comes a moment or a
event or a person that is a terrible clarifier or simplifier, and at th
point agreement collapses. Moreover, finding the right formula
difficult in itself, for it means writing an agreement by which tl
Israelis give up very tangible territory and the Egyptians give u
something which is not so important politically as to weaken Egypt
position in the Arab world, yet consists of more than mere words th
almost everybody in Israel would denounce as meaningless.

In the negotiation of this difficult formula, there are beginning
be serious doubts about who is the cat and who is the mouse, or wf
is the salami. Mr. Kissinger may be applying salami tactics, but it
not entirely clear to whom. Is Egypt, is the Arab world the salam
Is this a process by which gradually the links among Egypt, Syri
the PLO, Saudi Arabia, are being loosened, so that Israel gains son
breathing space, or is it a process by which Israel is gradually pushe
back piece by piece without anything really tangible being given u
in exchange by the other side?

President Sadat, who has a way of hiding behind the smoke scree
of countless interviews, in each one of which he says something di
ferent so as to maximize his freedom of maneuver, is clever enoug
not only to tie the size of his concessions to the willingness of Isra
to move on other fronts—Syria and the PLO—as well, but also
suggest that his concessions will take the form of assurances, not
Israel, but to Kissinger. In effect, this puts the United States in tl
unhappy position both of having to pressure Israel for the kind
moves that will release those assurances *and* of answering for Israe
future good behavior so that no reason or pretext for an Egypti
cancellation of those assurances arises. Thus Sadat tries to expl
simultaneously America's mediating effort—in order to get back te

tories—and America's special link with Israel—in order to keep
Israel both retreating and restrained. Any significant disengagement
agreement with Cairo could therefore have the effect of forcing Israel
to renounce any possibility of preemptive action even against a fully
armed and mobilizing Syria—so as not to force Sadat to revoke his
concessions—and, in the event that Syria should attack Israel first, to
rely on the dubious hope that Egypt, faithful to its word, would remain passive.

Hence another debate which goes on in Israel: on whose side is
time? Many Israelis have come to fear that time may be on the Arabs'
side. If one looks at the past, one finds that the curve of inter-Arab
relations rises toward cooperation, if not unity; certainly Rabat suggests that time does not guarantee a weakening of the links in the Arab
chain. Moreover, on whom (as between Egypt and Israel) will there
be greater American pressure for concessions? The Israelis remember with some trepidation that in the second half of October 1973 it
was on Israel that the hardest pressure was put (in their own best
interest of course, as seen by Mr. Kissinger). This may happen again,
precisely because Mr. Kissinger argues that if Israel should demand
the impossible from Mr. Sadat, Mr. Sadat will not be able to demonstrate his goodwill. This, in turn, poses again the question of who is
manipulating whom.

There is still another reason why the step-by-step approach may
actually put time on the Arabs' side. For Israel, because of Egypt's
tactics, each new step entails, directly or obliquely, marginally or
importantly, dealing with the essential: security, i.e., giving away
part of the only Israeli trump: occupied territory. But the Arabs, in
return, are not giving away any part of their trump: nonrecognition.
That will have to wait for the final step, by which time Israel's bargaining power will have shrunk. Is trading territory for formulas the
best use of time? Does not the length of the process provide Israel's
adversaries with opportunities for tightening the noose, rather than
with occasions for falling apart?

A final argument against the step-by-step approach refers to domestic affairs within Israel. Again time is not necessarily an ally of the
policy. Small concessions for limited periods of time, leading only to
renewed demands for more concessions without peace, mean that
shortly before the period ends there is maximum pressure on Israel
to make a new concession in order to have a new agreement; there is
an artificial crisis aimed at creating the "right" international climate.
This, internally, increases psychological resistance and plays, in effect,
into the hands of the right-wing opposition, both outside and within

the government. Whereas the external effects of time can be the sub
ject of debate, there is now little doubt that within Israel any polic
that postpones a settlement has a very dangerous effect in two impo
tant respects.

First, there is a pressure for the establishment of new Jewish settl
ments in the occupied territories. On the whole, the government ha
resisted and rebuffed these on the West Bank. It has not resisted then
and in fact it has promoted and financed them in Jerusalem and on th
Golan Heights, perhaps because of the theory of bargaining chip
But we know from the field of arms control that bargaining chi
may complicate rather than facilitate agreements. Another intern
danger has to do with the new generation of Israelis, those who ha
come from Arab countries or from the Soviet Union, and are bein
integrated into Israeli society. If it has been difficult for Israel
make peace with the Arabs and to find accommodation with the Sovi
Union under the present establishment and leadership, it will be fi
more difficult when this establishment is largely or partly compose
of people who, because of what they have suffered in Arab countri
or in the Soviet Union, hate the Soviet Union and the Arab countri
with a perfectly understandable but flaming passion.

The debate over the step-by-step approach is accompanied by
debate about the alternative—a resumption of the Geneva conferenc
The opponents of Geneva rely on four arguments. First, when a
the Arab opponents of Israel are under the same roof, there is a pr
mium on intransigence. Today, Egypt can express its preference f
peace and its willingness to achieve it gradually despite Syria's ha
line and the PLO's recriminations. At Geneva, the toughest wou
set the norm—as they did at Rabat. Second, the step-by-step approa
postpones the most difficult problem—the PLO—which would be t
first to surface in Geneva, thus wrecking the conference or at le
putting Israel on the spot immediately, over an issue that is dom
tically explosive. Third, Geneva reintroduces the Soviet Union. O
of the great merits of the step-by-step approach, in Israeli eyes, is th
it keeps the Soviet devil out. Fourth, in Geneva, the difference
priorities between the United States and Israel (which is impli
already in the step-by-step process) would become explicit. T
United States, on good terms not only with Israel but with seve
Arab states, might put even stronger pressure on Israel in order
reach a settlement.

However, at present, there is a bizarre coalition of Israelis who a
favorable to a return to Geneva. Some would like to go to Gene
because they think that there is at least a chance for a general sett

ent there, which the step-by-step method squanders by running into
o many obstacles. These people think that leaping over those ob-
acles and facing the whole problem at once makes more sense than
ying to detach elements of a chain that seems to be increasingly
lid. But a return to Geneva is also favored by people, either outside
ie government on its Right or in the government, who believe that
Geneva would show once and for all that one cannot really reach
eace with the Arabs. The United States or the Soviet Union would
o longer be able to say to Israel: "If you are not cooperative, we may
ave to go to Geneva." Recent statements of Abba Eban and of the
Iinister of Defense, Shimon Peres, create the impression that Geneva
as become the refuge of both the prudent optimists and of the deep
essimists who want to demonstrate that there is no Geneva solution.

Then there is the specific problem of the Palestinians. Here again
sraeli opinion shows some common features. There has been a con-
derable evolution since 1973. There is no longer any attempt to deny
iat there is a Palestinian problem, or to deny that there is a Palestinian people, although there are many different views about what
ie Palestinian people is. However, there still is a common refusal
 deal with Palestinian organizations that do not recognize Israel's
vn existence and the legitimacy of the state of Israel. There is also
 fear that any Palestinian organization that would negotiate with
srael would be immediately outflanked by an extremist faction,
hich would then become the rallying point, so that negotiations
ould in fact not lead anywhere. The official policy comes close to
iat old French adage "it is urgent to do nothing," it is urgent to wait.

And what appears impossible—dealing with the PLO—is also ra-
onalized as undesirable. A negotiation with the PLO would under-
ine King Hussein, with whom there are many common interests,
icluding the interest in not having in between Israel and Jordan a
evolutionary state out to destroy both. Less convincing is the second
rgument: the hope that if one does not deal with the PLO long
nough, it will fade away—that it will lose its influence if it does not
chieve anything. In other words, the PLO may not really be repre-
entative, and if one just waits long enough and avoids building it up,
 will lose its aura of success, which any revolutionary movement
eeds. Hussein will then come back into the picture, and there is still
 preference for a solution negotiated with him rather than with
ie PLO, for a number of reasons. One of these is that there are about
s many Palestinians on the East Bank as on the West Bank, so that
ny separate Palestinian West Bank state would be a recipe for inability anyhow. Another reason is that one can perhaps demilitarize

part of a Jordanian state including the West Bank, but it is difficu
to demilitarize a whole state.

How realistic is the hope that the PLO will fade away? Washin
ton as well as Israel had hoped that Rabat would not consecrate th
PLO. The very fact that at Rabat it was Saudi Arabia which mor
or less imposed the final formula recognizing the PLO as represent:
tive of all Palestinians makes one a bit suspicious about the Israeli
reasoning. It may very well be that since Saudi Arabia has a pa
ticular interest in Jerusalem it has chosen to support the one organiz:
tion whose state, if it ever gets one, would have to have Jerusalem :
its capital because it could not be anywhere else, whereas a Jorda
with the West Bank would still have its capital in Amman an
could make compromises about Jerusalem more easily.

One must remember that a "Jordanian solution" was possible fc
many years, before the rise of the PLO, and that it failed to materia
ize. To be sure, Israel's terms for returning part or all of the We
Bank might now become more generous; but Hussein is less than ev
able to make a final deal before the other Arab states, and they ar
now pressing either entirely for a PLO monopoly or at least for
PLO role.

One can also ask oneself whether the Israeli policy of not doin
anything now is based on any real knowledge of what is actually ha
pening among the Palestinians. In Israel, one hears very conflictin
estimates. Some believe that what is happening on the West Bank
the gradual Jordanization of the Palestinians. Others think that wh:
one can expect on the East Bank in the long run is the gradual Pale
tinization of the Jordanians. It is clear that the inhabitants of th
West Bank, the notables and the people who follow them, are n
going to reveal their hands while they are still both a stake of inte
national politics and under military occupation. But there is no dou
that there is sympathy for the PLO, and one must remember, whe
one talks of the effect of failure, that the PLO's international eme
gence followed its crushing defeat by Jordan in 1970.

What are the alternatives suggested for the Palestinian problem
The most "dovish" is the one recommended by Nahum Goldman
the President of the World Jewish Congress.[1] It proposes the evacu:
tion of the West Bank by Israel, a temporary U.N. administratic
and plebiscite on independence vs. confederation with Jordan, an
meanwhile either the creation of a Palestinian government in exi
including but not limited to the PLO, or an invitation to Arafat t
come to Geneva on the basis of Resolution 242. This essentially a

[1] Interview in *Le Monde* (Paris), January 9, 1975, p. 5.

ımes the willingness of the Palestinians to moderate their position
ıd to accept merely a West Bank state. It is a proposal that prac-
cally nobody in Israel endorses. Some Israelis put forward a much
ıore limited and tactical notion: the idea that Israel should at least
ublicly recognize the right of the Palestinians to self-determination,
; long as the Palestinians recognize the Israeli right to self-deter-
ıination. This is not the policy adopted by the government, precisely
ecause it leaves the ultimate fate of the West Bank to decisions
ıong the Arabs; if the outcome should favor the PLO, the present
overnment would not accept it. It is also suggested that any prime
ıinister who would offer this formula (comparable to what de Gaulle
ad offered for Algeria in 1959) would find himself without a gov-
ʳnment.

As for the hawks' alternatives, the most extreme is the annexation
f the West Bank, for reasons in which strategy and Biblical references
ɾe mixed, while the most surprising is the notion of a Jordanian-
ʃraeli common market and common army on the West Bank. This
ıtter solution appears remarkably utopian, not only because it would
ʒquire between the Jordanians and the Israelis a degree of coopera-
on which even the Europeans have not achieved, but also because it
 very hard to imagine any Jordanian government accepting it and
ırviving.

III

Whether or not Secretary Kissinger succeeds in his current efforts,
 is essential for Israel to think about its ultimate goals. Success would
ıean one or more disengagement agreements, a more or less limited
eriod of assured non-war. But it would also mean a continuing arms
ʋildup, new Arab pressures for further Israeli withdrawals, and
ıe absence of recognition and peace. Failure would mean an immedi-
te or rapid danger of war. The difference between success and failure
 important—but not decisive, precisely insofar as the situation of
either-peace-nor-war, however stabilized new gradual agreements
ıight make it appear, would be no more than an armistice, with
ʋorried and partly demoralized Israelis, unsatisfied yet encouraged
ʌrabs. There would remain a choice between a resumption of war,
nd a new march to peace. Success of the gradual approach gives a
ʰance to the latter but is no substitute for it. It is merely a prelude.

The heart of the present Israeli strategy is the Israeli-American
onnection. When we turn to the long run, it is with that link that we
ıust begin. The present relationship, the present uneasy symbiosis
etween Premier Rabin and Secretary Kissinger, is fraught with

potential unhappiness. One does not have to be a Gaullist to believ
that there is a risk in entrusting somebody else with one's fate, eve
when one feels one has no choice. Furthermore, the conflict of prio
ities, already noted, breeds a constant and double risk of mutu
recrimination: the Israelis feeling that the United States because o
its priorities, of its need to have an Arab policy, may sacrifice (u
knowingly, of course) some essential Israeli interests, and the Unite
States becoming exasperated with the obstinacy of Israelis.

There are also risks of serious misunderstandings in the Israel
American association. Today, it is not always easy to know who is t
tail and who is the dog. Mr. Kissinger has a way of saying to h
visitors: "I have to propose the following steps, because they are t
only ones acceptable to Israel"; but one can hear from the Israe
officials that they are following the same course because they want
help Mr. Kissinger. Is the exclusion of the Soviet Union somethin
Mr. Kissinger has accepted because it is in Israel's interest? Is it som
thing Israel accepts because it's in Mr. Kissinger's strategy? Is t
refusal to do anything that might undermine Hussein primarily
American or primarily an Israeli interest? It is not always clea
Tomorrow, another misunderstanding is possible: Mr. Kissinger,
solo performer, is a master at flexibility; the one thing he cannot to
erate is failure. If the step-by-step approach leads nowhere—eith
because there is no next step or because it is clear that the next st
will not be followed by any more—he will go to Geneva. He h
already suggested this. It is not at all clear whether those Israel
whom he has so thoroughly convinced of all of the disasters of Gene
are ready for it. The people who are ready for Geneva are the peop
who most disagree with him, and the people who most agree with hi
are those who, in a rigid parliamentary and governmental situatio
have staked their careers on the avoidance of Geneva.

There is a long-range risk of misunderstanding also. The Israe
hard-liners—and this means not only members of the opposition c
alition Likud but very important members of the cabinet—wh
asked what they would like America's role to be (instead of the ste
by-step policy which they denounce) reply that they don't want t
much from Washington: the United States should just give Isra
weapons in numbers sufficient to compensate the Arab inflow of arm
America's diplomatic role is simply to neutralize the Soviet Unio
Behind that double shield, Israel would take care of itself.

This "American alternative" strikes me as untenable, first of
because of an inherent contradiction. If the United States wants
"neutralize" the Soviet Union, it has to have an Arab policy. It has

present in Egypt, in Saudi Arabia, in Jordan, and that means
itting pressure on Israel, which is precisely what hard-liners do not
ant. Furthermore, there is a built-in hopelessness in this policy.
xternally, it offers no prospect but continuing reliance on situations
 strength and risks of war. Also, it means that hard-liners put all
eir American hopes first of all in Senator Jackson, and second, in
e perpetuation of the cold war. They misread current American
)licy, by seeing in it an excessively "soft" and prudent course cor-
sponding to a post-Vietnam weakening of resolve and battle-fatigue
th world responsibility. Not only is this an inaccurate reading of
·cretary Kissinger, who does not suffer from the Munich syndrome,
d seems in fact haunted by the fear of a decline of the West. It is
so a mistake for Israelis to want to base their association with the
nited States on purely strategic and anti-Soviet arguments, and, in
rms of American politics, to want to associate only with the sector
presented by Senator Jackson.

If this is an Israeli alternative to the present U.S.-Israeli rela-
)nship, what alternatives have been offered by Americans? Richard
llman, in the last issue of *Foreign Affairs*,[2] argued for an American
ilitary guarantee to and military presence in Israel. But he did not
ake it clear whether it would be a guarantee after a settlement, or a
iarantee before, aimed at making Israelis more confident about
ithdrawals and concessions. If it is a guarantee after a settlement,
e are left with the problem of how to get the settlement. If it is a
iarantee aimed at facilitating a settlement, yet preceding it, it intro-
ices even more blackmail into Israeli-American relations than the
·esent relationship, while probably weakening United States lever-
·e in the Arab world. Ullman's argument that Sadat, Hussein and
iisal would welcome such a commitment as long as it was accom-
.nied by Israeli withdrawals may be correct, but only if the United
ates puts maximum pressure on Israel for withdrawals that may—
ce the present course—merely shrink Israeli-held territory without
iything tangible in return.

In short, his plan is not in Israel's long-term interest (unless it
imes *after* a settlement), for Israel's long-term interest is not merely
:terrence of an Arab attack, it is peace, i.e., a settlement. It would
it solve the problems extant between the Arab countries and Israel,
id especially not the PLO problem; it would exacerbate Arab per-
·ptions of Israel as a kind of Western spearhead; and, as some

---

2 Richard Ullman, "After Rabat: Middle East Risks and American Roles," *Foreign Affairs*,
nuary 1975, pp. 284 ff. *Editor's note:* further discussion of Mr. Ullman's article will be found
the Correspondence Section of this issue, at pp. 577–80.

Israelis put it, it would even complicate matters for Israel by limitir present Israeli freedom of movement in areas such as southern Le anon: if one is a military ally of the United States, every retaliatic will have to be checked with Washington, which may have goc reasons for not approving.

Nor would a guarantee before a settlement be desirable for tl United States, where it would be seen as giving Israel a kind of lien Washington's Middle Eastern policy and as facilitating the task the Soviet Union in Arab countries. For Moscow could point out th it had always told them that the Israelis are merely a tool of tl United States. The guarantee would become a substitute for a settl ment, and, as in so many alliances between a distant Protector and exposed small ally, there would remain a fundamental ambigui about who maneuvers whom. Every incident that occurred in the a sence or in the course of withdrawals would confront Washingt with the unwelcome choice of either carrying out its commitmei however reluctantly, or reneging on it. It is most unlikely that Co gress would undertake *this* kind of a formal commitment. Thu Washington would be reluctant to underwrite Israel too much, ai Israel would be reluctant to tie itself down too much.

Is there any other American alternative? Many Jewish America have argued that the basis of the American-Israeli relationship shou be an unassailable moral link resting in turn on an unassailable mor position of Israel. Such a link is indeed the best explanation of Ame ican support to Israel in the past. To maintain this bond we must ta a hard look both at the moral roots of Israel's position, and at t moral implications for its foreign policy.

Unquestionably, there *is* an Israeli right to existence and securi and an Israeli claim on other nations, not for the maintenance of t occupied territories, but for the survival and safety of Israel as a sta As Raymond Aron wrote shortly before the Six-Day War, any We erner, in fact anybody, who would let this country be destroyed cou not face himself anymore. Even if one believes that the creation of t state of Israel repaired one historical injustice at the cost of a nc one perpetrated on Palestine's Arabs, the reparation of that injusti cannot be allowed to threaten Israel's own right to live. Even the who believe that the ideal solution is a "binational state" in form Palestine should realize that this has no chance of leaping from t printed page to political reality as long as one side sees in this formu a pretext for its own annihilation as a self-governing entity, and t other sees in it a weapon against the other's existence.

On the other hand, the argument that Israel has a right to to

d unconditional support for whatever its policy, because of the
azi holocaust, I find impossible to accept, especially since a grue-
me, almost unprecedented moral and political tragedy is thus turned
to a source of political blackmail. Nor can we believe that there is
 Israeli monopoly on morality. There *is* a claim of the other side
so, which is precisely what makes the problem so difficult. There are
nflicting claims of justice on the same land. This means at a min-
1um that while there is a compelling Israeli right to its security and
rvival in its pre-1967 borders, there is no such right for the occupied
ritories.

It follows that the policy of Israel will be both more unassailable
orally and more persuasive if it includes a clear and categorical
llingness to return the occupied territories. (I shall state later what
rael is entitled to demand and receive in exchange.) It follows also
at Israeli policy should recognize the avoidance of another war as
 absolutely crucial priority.

Practically nobody in Israel wants war—people and leaders alike
ve known war in all its horror five times (for one must include the
var of attrition" with Egypt in 1969-70). But there is a reluctance
 envisage broad concessions to opponents suspected of wanting not
ite gains but the end of Israel. There is a belief that there may
ally be no choice other than that between war and surrender. And
t it is morally imperative that Israel not provide its opponents with
y reason for starting a new war to reconquer the territories lost in
67, or for obliging Israel to preempt.

For another war would surely be a disaster, even if it is "only" a
ir of attrition at the outset. Wars of attrition, even if they do not
:alate, *are* wars and cause heavy casualties. These also have a way,
oner or later, of escalating into full wars. If in the absence of a
:ond set of disengagement agreements—or indeed at any time—
ere should be a war between Egypt and Israel, or a war between
rael and Syria, which it would be very hard for Egypt not to join,
en one would face dismal prospects. This war, fought with the new
phisticated weapons accumulated by both sides, could be infinitely
ore destructive than anything in the past. More than in 1973, Israel's
te would depend on the American tie, and strains on that tie would
 among the immense hazards involved.

If the Arabs were to impose another oil embargo, the war could
so escalate geographically, providing Washington with the oppor-
nity that some American policy analysts or advisers seem to be pray-
g for, of seizing oil fields in the Persian Gulf. While this is not the
ice to argue in detail against such a course, it may be necessary to

summarize the main objections, precisely because some of Israe
supporters have come to believe that the only alternative to a show
force in the whole Middle East is a Munich-like appeasement at t
expense of Israel *and* of the industrial powers. On this view, a w
might seem to provide a way of cutting the entire Gordian knot in o
bold stroke.

However "easy" the military aspects may be, there are five hu
political drawbacks. The targets of our attack would be the mc
conservative pro-Western and anti-Soviet regimes in the Ar
world: they would in all likelihood be replaced by more extrer
ones. Also, inflicting new humiliations on the Arab world, whatev
it might do for resolving the world problem of oil and petrodolla
would not exactly be devised to enhance the chances for peace in t
Arab-Israeli conflict. Even if Western Europe and Japan might
the beneficiaries of an American "oil seizure," the operation itse
would strain the alliances more than any other American poli
since 1947. Even if the Soviets remain militarily passive or restraine
they would gain huge opportunities for influence in the Middle E.
(even conservative Middle Eastern regimes might not reject Sov
offers of cooperation any more than Churchill rejected an allian
with Moscow against the common enemy in World War II). Ev
though they are themselves victims of the rise in oil prices, natic
of the "Fourth World" would react against an American use of for
and the whole future of "North-South relations," the biggest comi
world issue, would be pushed in a disastrous direction. A policy th
avoids force, on the other hand, has far better chances of orienti
these relations in the direction of interdependence, of letting strai
between the "new rich" and the poor develop, and of leading to
gradual and sensible redistribution of world resources.

Finally, even if the next Arab-Israeli wars were like the previc
ones and did not escalate in any way, they would offer no prospect f
a political settlement achieved by Israel at the Arabs' expense. Eith
as after 1967, the defeated Arabs would merely rebuild their streng
until the next round, or else the great powers would do what th
have not done before: impose a settlement that would ipso fac
wound the pride of the Israelis and leave deep resentments throug
out the Middle East. If there are two things that Israel cannot affo
one is a defeat because it might indeed be destroyed (whereas
Arabs can suffer many defeats and anyhow hope to be rescued) a
the other is another major victory, because it would not lead to sett
ment but to headaches, problems, commitments, entanglements whi
would tie the Israeli body politic in knots.

Thus, our discussion of an unassailable moral position for Israel brings us to this question: what political risks should Israel accept in order to maximize the chances of avoiding war? How could Israel act in such a way that, if war breaks out nevertheless, the onus for it would be unassailably on the other side? The answer lies in a new, long-run Israeli strategy aimed at achieving a general settlement. The strategy should be based on the following considerations:

First, the idea of a settlement must confront a central paradox. Ultimately, it is *Israel,* not the United States, which has to live with the Arabs in the Middle East. It is Israel's future which is being discussed. It is Israel's integration into the area which must be achieved. For there is something absurd as well as dangerous in the present situation, which is one of isolation—physical and mental—of Israel from its neighbors, and indeed from much of the outside world. The United States is almost the only pipeline to the world. What goes on among the Arab neighbors is a matter of guesswork. This is the result largely of a recurrent state of war, of a protracted state of siege. It is imperative that the siege be lifted, and that Israel be able to get out of the Hobbesian universe, with its two chief features: obsession and uncertainty. It is imperative for Israel's own future that the weight of the state-of-war on the budget and balance of payments be reduced. The only alternative is a drastic reduction in the standard of living that would both provoke serious inner tensions if it goes too far and increase the appeal of "hawkish" solutions.

Therefore the policy to be followed, whether or not it succeeds in leading to peace, ought to be primarily Israel's policy rather than America's. Rather than letting concessions be squeezed out of them by the gentle coaxing and the subtle threats of Mr. Kissinger, the Israelis should—even if this does not lead anywhere at once—seize the initiative toward neighbors who will remain their neighbors just as France remains the neighbor of Germany, and with whom permanent war is as hopeless as was the prospect of permanent war in Algeria.

On the other hand, and this is why we are in the presence of a paradox, the settlement itself *cannot* be left to the parties alone. The Israelis have come to recognize this: they had waited from 1967 to 1973 for the direct talks that never came. The settlement itself will not be negotiable by the parties only; other powers will have to play brokers and put pressure on the parties. If there should be a settlement, it will require external enforcement and protection also. However, it *does* make a difference whether the outside world is there to help the parties reach their own agreements and stick to their word,

or whether it is there to impose its own views and exert its own tutelage. The latter is a formula for future trouble and instability.

Second, Israel cannot expect the United States to continue to be the
only outside power directly involved in the quest for a settlement.
After the next disengagement agreement with Egypt, if there is one,
the United States will have done about as much as it can do in dragging concessions out of both sides. After that, despite Mr. Kissinger's
apparent need to solve absolutely everything alone, it does not seem
that he can do it any more, partly because his leverage will have been
exhausted, and partly because there are other actors in the area over
whom his influence is small—such as the PLO. Indeed, any Egyptian-
Israeli agreement that is not linked to Israeli concessions to Syria and
the Palestinians is likely to make Syria and the Palestinians more dis-
trustful and uncooperative.

This brings us to the problem of the Soviet Union. There are as
many views about Soviet interests in the Middle East as there are
Sovietologists, and the Soviets themselves, unlike our own officials,
do not publish a yearly State of the World message in which they
describe their interests in sententious epigrams. We are obliged to
guess and to gamble. The present situation is not exactly ideal for
Moscow. One could have argued easily that between 1967 and 197?
the state of neither-peace-nor-war served Soviet interests. This may
not be the case any more. There are two major risks for Moscow: a
risk of loss of control and a risk of loss of influence. The two are no
the same. Even those countries in which there is a Soviet influence
such as Syria, are perfectly capable of following their own course and
of starting to move at moments when the Soviet Union would no
want it. Thus there is the danger, with which we are very familiar
of the superpower being dragged into the unknown or the unwantec
by its clients, something which the Soviet Union, even more than any
other great power, has always resisted. This may explain why it i
Moscow rather than Cairo which drags its feet in the Soviet-Egyptiar
controversy. Moscow holds back its more advanced weapons unles
they are accompanied by Soviet advisers and other assurances of So
viet control. Moreover, the present situation, it is clear, does not en
large the sphere of Soviet influence, which is strong in Iraq, rela
tively so in Syria and with the PLO—and that is all, in the main. O
course it might increase again if there is a war, but then we are back
to the issue of control: a war entails a danger of confrontation with
the United States.

If one analyzes the behavior of the Arabs since October 1973, on
gets the impression that here, too, arises the question of who is the tai

ıd who is the dog: the Arabs are able to use the Soviet Union at ast as much as the other way around. As for OPEC's oil strategy, is being waged without Soviet involvement, and increases the Arabs' ʊility to develop their own policies—including buying or building eapons—without relying too much on Moscow. The only thing hich could definitely sink or destroy Soviet influence in the Middle ast would be the disappearance of the state of Israel. If there were ɔ Israel, there would be many more Arabs turning to Washington ʊr their development needs and very few Arabs going to Moscow. his in itself creates a Soviet incentive for keeping that "minor irri- nt," Israel, alive.

On balance, what is known as a Geneva-type settlement would have ıe advantage of recognizing formally something which the Soviets ave all over the world tried to get consecrated as if this were the ʒy objective of their policy: to put on sacred, hallowed paper, known ҫ a treaty, the Soviet right to have a say in the area. It is not enough ʊr them to have a say de facto, just as they have had their glacis in ʊurope de facto; they also want it de jure.

This might be worth granting, since I do not think that the Soviets ʊuld by themselves really endanger the stability of the area as much ; seems feared all over Israel. The area does not need the Soviet ʻnion to have its stability endangered! Natural forces can take care f that extremely well—especially in the absence of peace. There is ery little to justify the fear that Geneva would somehow put the ,rab world, which is getting richer, under Soviet control.

There is a counterargument that in the absence of a settlement ʊviet influence would actually shrink: that the Arab states would get ҫonomically and financially involved with the West and Japan, ʻhereas Geneva, by giving to the U.S.S.R. an important position as ҽgotiator and guarantor, would reverse this trend. However, we are ıced with a vicious circle. This very Arab involvement only puts ıore pressure on the United States to use its influence in Israel in rder to push Israel back—without Israel obtaining a settlement in ҽturn. And should the United States refuse to carry such a burden, r fail to deliver the goods, there is nothing but the Sisyphean pros- ҽct of more wars—which inevitably re-injects Moscow into the pic- ıre, as protector of the Arabs against ignominious defeat, and as ҽssurer on Washington to stop Israeli advances.

IV

These reflections suggest some major guidelines. The first one is ıat Israel should take the initiative of demanding an overall peace

agreement, to be negotiated with its Arab opponents, and with t
help of outside powers. In order to make such an agreement possib
Israel should at the same time declare what, in its eyes, constitutes t
essential features of the agreement. There is, of course, a risk in inte
national negotiations that whatever are presented as maximum co
cessions and minimum demands become treated as minimum conce
sions and maximum demands. But there are greater risks in t
present stance: especially the risk that it leads nowhere or only
unmatched concessions by Israel. What is required is a willingness
the part of Israel, in exchange for its recognition and the signatu
of a peace treaty, to accept categorically and in specific terms
withdrawal from occupied territories. What Israel should emph
size is the creation of conditions under which this restitution wou
not threaten its security, instead of *subordinating* a recognition of t
Arab right to these territories to the prior creation of these conditioi
Thus, the emphasis would not be, let us say, on the strategic nee
for *Israel* to remain on the Golan Heights but on the danger th
would exist if *Syrian armies* were again on the Golan Heights.

Israel should present its final view, concealed until now, if only
order to avoid giving the Arabs the impression that it is making
gradual concessions and is retreating due to weakness and outsi
pressure, with its back to the wall. Since most people within Israel ai
outside assume that, at the end, something very much like a return
the 1967 borders will be unavoidable, an Israeli initiative would ha
the advantage of shifting attention and the burden of proof. Instead
Israel having to prove its willingness to withdraw and the Ara
mobilizing opinion in the world against Israeli occupation, Isra
could rally support behind its demand for recognition, and it wou
be up to the Arabs to meet Israeli security needs. To be sure, the ba
gaining would still be very tough, since the prize which the Ara
have withheld so far—recognition of Israel and a contractual peace-
could be held up by them until Israel has considerably reduced i
security demands or its demand for a change in the 1967 borde
around Jerusalem. But here we come to a second imperative.

It would be intensely desirable that Israel implicate in the negoti
tion as many external powers as possible, not only the United Stat
and the Soviet Union. Despite all of the disappointments which tl
Israelis have experienced with the West Europeans and the Japanes
once these countries no longer perceived Israeli immobility, or fe
that Israel was still placing all its eggs in the American basket, thi
would again be able to play a useful role in trying to moderate tl
Arabs and regain an interest in Israel's own security. In the specif

se of the West Europeans, it is their exclusion—by Israel and the
nited States jointly—their fear of seeing the Middle East become
erely a theater of the cold war, and their preference for something
ke the course suggested here, much more than their dependence on
rab oil, which explain their recent attitudes. All of them are on
cord on the subject of Israel's right to existence and recognition.

To be sure, in an overall negotiation, the risk of Arab extremist
ositions exists. Yet once the principle of a return to 1967 is estab-
hed, there is also a chance that the nuances among Arab parties
uld grow. A wider framework of bargaining would still leave room
r separate negotiations with each party. The present approach, on
e contrary, prevents those nuances from spreading and preserves a
rong joint Arab interest in pressure and maneuver. Moreover, the
esence of outside powers interested in a settlement would serve
ther to magnify these nuances or to create pressure toward a mod-
ate rather than an extreme Arab position.

Third, any agreement could be carried out in stages. A proposal has
en made by one Israeli scholar, Saul Friedländer, for a solution
nsisting of an Israeli statement of willingness to accept Resolution
2, and then to carry it out in stages.[3] His formula is "a little bit
territory against a little bit of peace." This is a fundamentally valid
proach, but *only* in the context of a general agreement. The kinds
steps which he demands of the Arabs in exchange for Israel's partial
ithdrawals are inconceivable for them unless they have already
anted Israel recognition. To suggest, as he does, that recognition
uld be the last Arab act, in exchange for the last piece of territory,
esupposes an agreement on a calendar in the absence of a contrac-
al settlement—something of a contradiction in terms—and in
fect makes the territories' return into a reward for good behavior:
psychological error, for, as Friedländer's Egyptian interlocutors put
"Arab opinion cannot bear any longer the notion that what's pos-
ble or not should be determined by Israel alone."[4]

Moreover, even in the framework of a settlement, the best that can
hoped for is a calendar of measures of two types: general measures
nefiting Israel but not involving overt cooperation (a reopening of
e Suez Canal, the passage of Israeli ships through it), and the end
hostile measures (propaganda, boycotts) that are obviously incom-
atible with peace. To be sure, one could theoretically link each stage
withdrawal to a cooperative Arab measure if one dragged out the

---

[3] See Saul Friedländer and Mahmoud Hussein, *Arabes et Israéliens*, Paris: Ed. du Seuil,
74, pp. 138 ff.
[4] *Ibid.*, p. 157.

process long enough. But to obtain Arab cooperation in trade, tou
ism, or joint patrols, by subordinating to such concessions the retu
of territory, would be resented by Arab countries as a patronizir
even blackmailing policy, and go against the very reasons for sugge
ing a new Israeli initiative.

Fourth, we come to the key question of security guarantees. Fo
long period, the sides will have to be militarily separated. The a
ought to be the stationing, in the Sinai, at Sharm-el-Sheikh, in t
Golan Heights, and in those portions of the West Bank that are ge
graphically closest to the Mediterránean, of international peace forc
not composed of soldiers of the superpowers. Should Washington a
Moscow insist on having their own soldiers there—as a way of unde
lining their guarantee of the settlement—there should at least
soldiers of other powers. And there must be an agreement by all t
parties, and all the contributors to the forces, against the arbitra
dismissal of the peace forces by one of the countries in which they a
stationed, or the arbitrary removal of a national contingent by t
country of origin. The tragic experience of UNEF in 1967 cann
be repeated. But a new status of U.N. peace forces can only be d
fined in the context of an overall agreement.

In addition, there is the problem of outside guarantees. Clear
every power in the area would prefer to be able to rely only
itself, and to have an agreement that is self-enforcing. Howeve
mutual security fears are likely to persist, as well as misunderstandin
about each other's intentions. The role of outside guarantees is
deter a new war.

Three sets of measures can be of help here. One is a guarantee
the borders by the powers involved in the negotiations. This wou
take the form of a collective guarantee given by them to all parti
but it could be supplemented by individual assurances given by o
great power to its closer friend(s) in the area, as an assurance
privileged support should the collective guarantee for any reason
paralyzed. (Until now, Washington has been most reluctant to e
visage such a guarantee—but this is precisely in order to retain leve
age over Israel in the step-by-step approach; should Israel call f
an overall settlement, it would be much more difficult for Washin
ton to withhold a guarantee in this context.) Also, the outside powe
should guarantee the provisions on demilitarization against unilater
repudiation by one of the parties, and commit their support to wh
ever state is the victim of such a repudiation. This would not be aim
at freezing the status quo, but at assuring that its revision would ha
to be agreed upon by all the interested parties in the area. Last but n

st, an agreement by outside powers to curb their arms sales to the
rties would be important. To be sure, Arabs and Israelis could still
nufacture their own weapons, but there would be a significant
alitative and quantitative difference.

Fifth, there is the problem of Jerusalem. There is no doubt that
gotiations will be difficult, if only because of the considerable ex-
nsion of the new Jewish Jerusalem into previously Arab territory.
 exception to the principle of a complete return to the pre-1967
rders will be necessary here. But Israel should declare its willing-
ss to return to the Arab part of Palestine the predominantly Arab
tions of north and east Jerusalem, currently included in the mu-
:ipal boundaries of the city, as well as the Arab sector of the Old
ty, and to place the holy places of the three religions under inter-
:ional jurisdiction. The entire area should be an open city, what-
:r the division of sovereignties. If, as Jean Giraudoux suggested in
yer at the Gates, law is the most powerful training ground for
agination, it should not be impossible to reconcile the demands of
th sides through a complex legal formula.

Sixth, we come to the most difficult issue: the specific problem of the
est Bank. Here, Israel should declare its willingness to grant to the
lestinians of the West Bank and the Gaza Strip the right to self-
termination. It will have to give up deciding who is the legitimate
)kesman of the Palestinians, even if this means foreclosing an in-
:asingly hypothetical "Jordanian solution." Such a declaration
uld throw the ball back into the Arabs' court. If—as is likely—
: Arabs designate the PLO, it will be up to Arafat to face a difficult
oice. Either he gives priority to setting up a state on the West Bank;
t this will mean negotiating, directly or indirectly, with Israel,
nich is not likely to withdraw unless it obtains security guarantees.
ch a negotiation would amount to de facto recognition. Or else
·afat will refuse to accept even this, declining to settle for less than
; "dream." But in that case, it is likely that other Arab states, and his
n-Arab supporters, will put strong, tangible pressure on him to
t him to stop preventing a settlement that entails a return to the
67 borders. The Israelis have been demanding de jure recognition
Israel by the PLO, as well as by other Arab states. But it would
 enough at first to obtain de facto recognition from the PLO
·ough the presence of a PLO delegation on the basis of Resolution
2 in Geneva, and its participation in a settlement.

It is foolish to expect, at this stage or in the near future, any West
ink state to give up on paper what Arafat calls his dream. It is
vays foolish to ask people to give up dreams. The essence of inter-

national relations simply consists in creating the conditions in whi
those dreams cannot be carried out, and the only way this can be dc
is a combination of Israeli strength, outside guarantees of Israc
borders, and some demilitarization of the West Bank state. The
are a few precedents in international law for neutral states with oi
limited military forces; one of them is Austria (although any rese
blance between the country of the waltz and Mr. Arafat's moveme
is a coincidence). To be sure, it would be courting failure to ask t
new state to be entirely without forces: it will have security fears
its own. But it can be partly protected by international peace forc
And the most decisive limitation would result from an agreement
the great powers present at the settlement not to sell arms to the Pal
tinian state, and to consider any presence of foreign armies, or t
entry of certain kinds of weapons, on the soil of the new state a;
violation of the settlement.

V

These are the outlines of the settlement which, in my opinion,
is in Israel's best interest to initiate. Three questions remain. What a
the assumptions behind this program? What are its chances of dom
tic success in Israel? What happens if it fails?

There are two major assumptions. The first one relates to the iss
of time. One can argue that such a settlement is quite unlikely a
moment when the Arabs ride the crest of a wave of wealth and si
cess; that it is imperative to postpone a global negotiation until t
combination of strains within OPEC, successes in the Americ
strategy on oil, and growing Arab concern for economic developme
results either in Arab disunity or in Arab moderation.

But while at present there exists a risk of Arab self-intoxicati
and intransigence, one has to weigh two factors on the other side. C
is that intra-Arab strains are likely to be subdued as long as a state
political war and a climate of anticipation of war exist between t
Arabs and Israel. While the concern for development is real, the n
Arab resources also allow the Arabs to buy weapons they need to
conquer what they lost: Egypt may want peace for reconstruction a
development, but not at the cost of sacrificing its claim on its ov
territory. Even though oil money will accelerate the development
the Arab countries, the notion that a richer Egyptian or a fatter Syri
is necessarily going to be less demanding of the Israelis strikes me
very debatable. The formidable social problems which developme
will create in Arab countries could all too easily be displaced on t
foreign enemy, and the gap between Israeli society and culture, a

ab society and culture, which is partly social, partly economic,
rtly psychological, will remain for a long time to come.
The other factor is the decline of support for Israel in the world,
d, if not the weakening of sympathy for and aid to Israel in the
iited States, at least the increasingly more conditional attitude of
: American Congress, the realization of the need for a more bal-
ced American policy in the Middle East. In the *long* run, time may
·ll be on Israel's side in one respect: Arab acceptance of its ex-
ence and irreversibility. But in the *middle* run, time is on the side
Arab pressures and drives toward Israeli withdrawals. Immobility
ids to war. Thus it is in Israel's interest to try to obtain sooner rather
an later its recognition as well as guarantees in exchange for what
will have to give up anyhow.
Another assumption refers to the nature of the peace to be negoti-
:d. Today, in Israel, there is a most striking confusion in the public
ind. On the one hand, there is profound pessimism about its Arab
ighbors ever accepting Israel, in the words of a distinguished reed general, as "a normal Jewish state." There is a fear that its neigh-
·rs will never consider that a Jewish state is normal, or that a normal
ite can be Jewish in that part of the world. On the other hand, there
e nevertheless various forms of wishful thinking. Retrospectively,
ere is some regret that the United States prevented Israel from in-
cting a "definitive" defeat on Egypt in October 1973. Now, peace
unlikely to result from a "sound" thrashing of the Arabs: 1967 did
·t bring them to Canossa. Prospectively, there is a belief that peace
ill come only when there has been a "change of heart" on the other
le. Without such a change, it cannot be "real peace." Hence a not-
·le contradiction. There is a strong emphasis on the strategic im-
·rtance of every piece of conquered territory (especially the West
ank: if it were given up to hostile hands, no plane could take off or
nd in Israel because it could be shot down from the West Bank, a
w miles away). And yet, there is also a perfectly genuine willing-
·ss to return almost everything in exchange for "real peace."
But "real peace" is conceived in terms that make it unrealistic.
·r what is called "real peace" is a set of attitudes and modes of behav-
·r that would normally *follow* from peace rather than precede it: ex-
·anges of tourists, of trade missions, of journalists, of sports teams,
·mmunications links. Now, if one has to wait for those modes of be-
·vior and attitudes in order to know that one has real peace, one will
ive to wait for a very long time indeed. As we have learned from
e history of the cold war, full reconciliation and exchanges are slow
come. Israelis must give up confusing peace and the ultimate bene-

fits from peace, just as they can no longer confuse military trium
and peace.

But does not that Israeli state of mind suggest the unlikeliness
the kind of initiative I have been suggesting here? There are, 1
deed, many reasons for pessimism. One lies in the conviction abc
Arab hostility, which explains why there are very few "doves," in t
sense in which the word was used here during the war in Vietna
Arab threats and imprecations, and Arab refusals to make visib
formal concessions are taken very seriously. This also becomes
alibi against initiatives, because of the fear that Arab dictatorshi
could always outdo Israel in pure propaganda, and because of t
fear that a domestic initiative could disrupt the Israeli body polit
thus weakening the nation. The millennial hope for a "change
heart" explains how an enormous concentration on the short run c
exists with strategic immobility. Another reason for pessimism is t
insulation of Israel from the outside world, already mentioned.
third is another contradiction between a proud emphasis on self-re
ance, and a recognition of dependence on the United States or, as o
important minister has suggested, of the fact that a nation of Israe
size has no foreign policy, only a policy of survival. Both facets of t
contradiction lead to fears of negotiation, which means both involv
ment with others, and the risk of replacing the relative certainties
the battle for survival and the reliance on the United States in tl
battle, with the uncertainties of diplomatic maneuver and concessio

Fourth, one may ask this question: to what extent has a 27-year-o
state of war, unwanted by all, nevertheless become functionally no
essary or useful, in order to assimilate the immigrants, to make c
of the many one, to get outside support; to what extent does this sta
of war play the useful role of displacing ideological and tactical d
ferences on the domestic scene, where they could be explosive, to t
foreign policy scene, where they remain in the realm of ideas, sin
there is a general immobility? Lastly, there is the political syste
Israel's parliamentary balance and governmental equilibrium remi
one of the Fourth Republic in 1957. Their delicacy is worthy of
watchmaker. There are within the government not only differe
parties, but different factions of the main party, the Labor Par
There is a formidable opposition outside, and of course the fear
either a disintegration of the cabinet or of new elections that cou
mean a reinforcement of the Right is constant.

But there are also some reasons for hope. The public may *drea*
about military victory, but most people *realize* that there is no "m
itary solution." There is a growing conviction that it is impossit

r Israel to achieve a political solution by military means, if only
cause the Soviet Union and probably the United States would save
e Arab countries from total defeat. Nor is there any Masada com-
ex. Even those who are most pessimistic about the possibility of
ace are convinced that somehow, through U.S. support or what-
er other means, they would "find a way." There is no grand roman-
ism about "us versus the rest of the outside world." There is a kind
tough realism—perhaps mistaken—about the consequences of what
e outside world seems to want Israel to give up or to do.

The confusions and contradictions I have stressed point to bewilder-
ent rather than extremism. The deepest obstacle to a change of
licy does not lie in the public but in the political system. The pub-
: would probably, as it has done before (for instance after Suez),
llow a strong leader willing to accept concessions in a way that sug-
sts Israeli mastery. The problem is that current leaders are either
luctant to change course, because they fear the collapse of the gov-
nment and the rupture of the parliamentary majority, or else—in
en or partial opposition—eager to equate strong leadership with
ughness, especially insofar as the West Bank is concerned.

But it is not absurd to believe that the present leaders would want
change course once they conclude that the present one leads Israel
to a dead end, and could then demand and receive a public vote of
nfidence for a new course. Nor is it too much to believe that if they
sitate or if the policy with which they are associated fails, they
ight be replaced by strong leaders, currently in semi-opposition to
semi-concurrence with the Rabin-Kissinger approach, who would
mper their toughness once in control. (I am obviously not thinking
the leaders of the Likud.)

And yet, even if this should happen, it is still possible that the
raeli initiative called for here would be rejected by the Arabs, or
at a complex negotiation would fail because of such intractable
oblems as the PLO, or because of irreconcilable clashes over secu-
ty and recognition. Such failure would indeed make war once again
kely, and probably remove for a long time any prospects of a settle-
ent. But the very fact that a general failure would not only be a set-
ck but a disaster explains why all the participants in the complex
ocess of negotiation I have suggested, and particularly the outside
wers, would have an interest in dragging out the Geneva process,
only in order to postpone the day of reckoning.

Moreover, from Israel's viewpoint, there are three decisive rea-
ns for trying, whatever the risks of failure. One is that a bold Israeli
itiative would restore Israel's diplomatic position, and make it far

more difficult for Israel's critics in the United States to argue that t
responsibility for deadlock in the Middle East is evenly divided
even largely Israel's. Again, this perspective of a restoration of Israe
position, and of less hesitant support in the U.S. Congress, wou
make the Arab states think twice before scuttling the negotiation. T
second reason has to do with Israel's own moral position. By offeri
a scheme that tries to reconcile the reasonable interests of all sid
replaces grudging small bargains with an overall conception, a
above all provides a home for the Palestinians, Israel would rever
a dangerous trend that equates conscience with good conscience, a
the latter with toughness alone. For without sacrificing its securi
it would offer a vision of peace and make it possible for the Pal
tinians to stop being—as refugees or exiles from former Palestir
and as pariahs of the other Arabs—a modern version of those d
placed persons the Jews themselves had suffered the fate of being un
the state of Israel was founded. One sometimes suspects that t
vehemence of Israeli fears about a Palestinian state is due not only
security concerns, but also to a half-repressed awareness of the dep
of the resentments created among the Palestinians outside the W
Bank by their tragic fate over the last 27 years. The equally veheme
Israeli denials of guilt prove, if not its presence, at least a fear of
justification. The initiatives suggested here could serve to drive su
doubts and demons away.

The third reason concerns Israel's destiny in the world. After tl
period of an intense and almost exclusive American connection, it
time for the Israelis to start thinking of a very distant, very ultimi
vision. It may seem terribly utopian at this point—another drea
this time of a Middle East in which all would live in peace, and
which Israel would not be the exclusive ally of one power, but a Je
ish state intent on good relations especially with the two countr
which have, and are likely to keep having, the greatest number of Je
outside of Israel, the United States and the Soviet Union. Israel a
partner in the development of the Middle East, yet neither a sta
for nor a party in the political and military competition of the gr
powers—this may appear as an irrelevant ideal today. But for the sa
of Israel's own spirit and promise, only the presence of an ideal su
as this can lift the hearts and inspire the minds of the Israelis beyo
the bitter sacrifices, the fears and the dreary prospect of the contin
ing state of siege.

A Mideast Proposal

M. CHERIF BASSIOUNI AND MORTON A. KAPLAN

THE NEED FOR INITIATIVE

Contrary to the opinions of many, a genuine peace in the Middle East between Israel and the Arab states has been possible for over a year. Yet, if this opportunity is missed, as now appears not unlikely, a similar one may not soon recur.

Although the prospects for war vary weekly and even daily, the secular trend toward war keeps rising. A new war would have horrendous consequences both for Israel and the Arab states. The impact of such a war on the economies of the parties concerned and the rest of the world, but particularly the western world, are potentially disastrous. Moreover, the risks of a catastrophic confrontation between the United States and the U.S.S.R. are implicit in the situation. War, therefore, should be in the classical phrase "unthinkable;" but such an eventuality is nonetheless possible.

The reason may well be found in the oft-proclaimed fears, suspicions, and misconceptions under which the parties labor. After more than twenty years of hostility, Israel finds it difficult to believe that the Arab states are ready for a peace that recognizes its existence as a Jewish state. Moreover, the internal political situation in Israel makes it difficult for any cabinet to proclaim a policy that would appear "weak" in the face of apparent external menace. On the other hand, the Arab states have their own internal difficulties. Indeed, for these states the issue is not only one of regaining national territory lost in the 1967 war but also the future of Palestine and the Palestinians.

Another element that is making the problem more rather than less difficult lies in the nature of the diplomacy that is being pursued. The first-stage disengagement of 1973 played a useful role in lowering tensions in the area but would have been more effective if it had been directly related to the search for a comprehensive peace. Unfortunately, the difficulty with step-by-step negotiations is that the stages are asymmetric. Israel gives up territory which it sees as useful for defense if the Arabs attack again. In return, it receives paper assurances that the Arab states can negate by a stroke of the pen. Israel, on the other hand, can retake the territory given up only by overt force. For their part, the Arab states are reluctant to provide the commitments that Israel wants, for the recognition of Israel as a state is their trump card for a return to the pre-1967 borders and a solution to the Palestinian question.

Thus, if one of the concerned states sees itself as giving up more of its bargaining advantages than does the other, it fears the future more, and even becomes increasingly reluctant to travel this road any further. On the other hand, the state that has gained asymmetric advantages will have greater difficulty in convincing its own constituents later on that it should make greater concessions that alone will produce further movement to a peace settlement, for it will already have gained much of what it wants at a far lower cost. In any event, it must be understood that although Israel can slice the Sinai and the Golan Heights in parcels to be bartered away, Egypt and Syria cannot parcel "peace" and "recognition." Thus, the parties do not have sufficient equivalent bartering chips to make that type of process work.

With the end of Secretary Kissinger's step-by-step diplomacy between Egypt and Israel, attention now begins to shift to the Geneva conference. Meanwhile the extensions by Egypt and Syria of the UN forces mandate are not likely to be further extended. When these deadlines expire, Egypt and Syria may be compelled either to take military actions or make military preparations that are likely to lead the Israelis to strike preemptively. Under these conditions anything can intentionally or accidentally trigger war.

Although such a war would probably end quickly as did the others, events may not be controllable this time. A prolonged oil boycott may affect the U.S. and Western Europe to the point that current ill-advised proposals for military intervention become a political reality that carries with it the prospects of a war involving the major powers.

Obviously, therefore, it is critical to prepare the Geneva negotiations in such a way as to maximize its chances of success. Without such preparations it is likely, given the current arrangements for Geneva, that it will fail in its purpose.

Geneva will likely fail because, unless Israel, the Arab states, and the Palestinians know in advance that they agree on certain basic principles, the "game" at Geneva will involve efforts to place the blame for failure on the other parties while reassuring publics and élites at home and abroad that important perceived interests will be protected. With no assurance of success, the effects of the encounter will bear upon regime and alliance interests that will assume greater importance than the peace Geneva is supposed to produce.

Therefore, it is essential to understand that Secretary of State Kissinger's failure was not a failure of mediation itself but a failure of mediation in step-by-step negotiations in which each step of the negotiations does not fit into an overall plan or at least an overall perception of the final product, as well as of basic asymmetries among the parties.

The real interests of the parties are not so far apart as they may at first appear. These interests are reinforced by both political and juridical considerations. The Arab states cannot make peace except on the condition of a return to the pre-1967 borders and a Palestinian settlement. The United States and the Soviet Union have a definite interest in reinforcing the political order that arose out of the settlements following World War II. Any violation of the principle of no territorial change by force would threaten this framework of world political order, the juridical system within which it is embodied, and other more specific and practical interests of the major powers (such as the existing boundaries of the East European states).

Israel, the existence of which is a product of the postwar settlements, also has an interest in the principle of no forcible change of territory. If Israel changes the pre-1967 borders by force, the Arabs could legitimate a forcible revision of any peace they sign with Israel. On the other hand, merely to return to the pre-1967 borders is obviously unacceptable to Israel even within the context of a peace treaty. The reasons that led Israel to shift in 1954 from its original second-strike strategy to a pre-emptive strategy are even stronger after the October 1973 War. Thus great power guarantees would not be considered sufficient to satisfy the security needs of either Israel or the Arab states. The use of United Nations forces would not be a primarily acceptable guarantee for Israel and would be in some ways objectionable to Egypt and Syria.

For these reasons also, it is essential that the road to Geneva be prepared in light of the interests of the parties and, in particular, of Israel, which must make territorial withdrawals and political concessions to the Palestinians if peace is to be achieved.

The first step, it is believed, is to reach agreement on certain basic principles, and then to allow all parties concerned to negotiate their specific claims within the framework of these principles. It is for these reasons that this proposal is made. Agreement on the basic principles of peace proposed herein might be negotiated among the parties privately prior to Geneva, or through the diplomacy of the United States and perhaps of the Soviet Union as well. It is essential that the parties communicate to each other their positions in such a manner that discussions over the proposed *Protocol on Principles of Peace* are fruitful. However, too great an effort to formulate "bargaining chip" positions on the *Principles* will likely be counterproductive.

The *Principles* formulated in the next section are designed to satisfy the minimal legitimate demands of the respective parties that are consistent with their reasonable concern for national security. The ensuing *Commentary* is illustrative of the application of these *Principles* in the Geneva negotiations.

The authors of this *Protocol on Principles of Peace*, concerned with the grave situation existing in the Middle East and its potentially disastrous consequences for all peoples in the area and for the world, and desirous of enhancing the opportunities for a just and lasting peace, hereby propose that this document be signed as an internationally binding agreement between Israel, Egypt, Syria, Jordan, and the Palestinian Liberation Organization on behalf of the Palestinian people, and that it be signed simultaneously by the respective parties in their capitals. The adoption of these *Principles* by the parties should precede their convening for a peace conference in Geneva and should constitute the framework of their negotiations for a just and lasting peace which can only begin to be attained by a permanent peace treaty.

PROTOCOL ON PRINCIPLES OF PEACE

The parties to this Protocol, desirous of insuring a just and lasting peace that is based on principles of international law, and concerned with the protection of the human rights of all peoples and persons in the area, hereby agree to the Principles enunciated herein as constituting the framework of their negotiations and agreements for a permanent peace between them.

1. The right of all peoples to live in peace, security, and dignity within a recognized state of their choice and under a form of government of their choice.

2. The right of the contracting parties to have secure and recognized boundaries not subject to forcible change and, consistent therewith, the recognition of the principle of non-acquisition of territory by use of force.

3. The restoration of the pre-1967 borders shall be effectuated. Concurrently boundary abutting conditions compatible with the reasonable defenses of the parties shall be established but only for as long as such needs realistically continue to exist. (See Article 9.)

4. Self-reinforcing security conditions shall be established as a result of agreements stemming from the principles of Article 3 and shall be overseen by a joint commission under United Nations auspices. Such commission shall prepare annual reports on their implementation. On the basis of such experience these security conditions shall be reviewed by the parties periodically but at least every five years with a view that in good faith such conditions be terminated as soon as practicable.

5. The right of self-determination of the Palestinian people is hereby expressly recognized, and, consistent therewith, the parties shall cooperate in the prompt establishment of a Palestinian state on the "West Bank" and "Gaza strip."

6. The future political relations between the State of Palestine and the State of Israel are a matter of concern for the peoples of these two states, including the possibility of a strictly peaceful evolution and transformation of their political ties or structures subject to the protection and preservation of the human rights of both communities and of their constituents.

7. The right of all the peoples from the region to return to their homes shall be recognized. That includes the return of Palestinians to Israel, and the return of those Jews who had lived in the Arab states to return thereto, subject to reasonable considerations of continued family ties, national security, and the integrity of national identity. To this end joint commissions, including a joint Israeli/Palestinian commission, shall be established to explore means of implementing this principle.

8. Where individuals in states of the region have been displaced from other states in the region and their property seized, confiscated, or sold at inadequate price, each state shall establish a commission to consider applications for adequate, just, and prompt compensation.

9. The boundary arrangements between Israel, Palestine, and Jordan shall include provisions for the peaceful passage of commerce and for civilian movement through Israel.

10. All parties shall have the right to free and innocent maritime passage in and through the Gulf of Aqaba, the Red Sea and the Suez Canal.

11. Maintenance of the substantial municipal unity of Jerusalem in a manner agreed upon by the parties and subject to the provisions of Article 2. The placement of the holy places in Jerusalem under guardianship acceptable to leaders of the faiths to which they belong and with international guarantees for free access to members of the respective faiths.

12. The parties shall cooperate in the preservation and restoration of the cultural heritage of the region.

13. After the previous principles have been implemented by incorporation in one or more treaties or agreements, good faith efforts shall be made to include, where feasible and consistent with national security and considerations of sovereignty, self-reinforcing procedures for conflict resolution such as, but not restricted to, resort to the International Court of Justice, arbitration, or mediation.

14. The Principles stated above shall be binding on the parties who sign

below for six months from the date of signature except that the parties agre
that if substantial and good faith efforts are being made to reach agreement
no fewer than two three-month extensions shall be granted.

Signed simultaneously this _____ day of _____197

_____

For the Arab Republic of Egypt, Done in Cairo, Egypt

_____

For the State of Israel, Done in Jerusalem, Israel

_____

For the Hashemite Kingdom of Jordan, Done in Amman, Jordan

_____

For the Palestine Liberation Organization, Done in Damascus, Syria

_____

For the Syrian Arab Republic, Done in Damascus, Syria

Commentary on the "Basic Principles of Peace"
and Implementation Proposals

The authors are aware that the principles stated above, although important
as an expression of intentions, may be insufficient to avoid dysfunctional
bargaining at Geneva unless there is also prior understanding on some
parameters of their implementation. The authors wish to emphasize that
these comments are illustrative of some of the ideas that would help implement the Principles stated above and that would help produce a viable peace
treaty. (The numbers hereinafter refer to the *Principles*.)

1. As members of the United Nations, the parties to this agreement should
assert their commitment to implement United Nations obligations concerning
the human rights of individuals regardless of race, creed, or color. To that
end the parties should consider signing, ratifying, or acceding to treaties
for the international protection of human rights and devise means for their
effective implementation. Additionally they may consider establishing in
the Old City of Jerusalem a Regional Supreme Court of Human Rights. At
least until such time as the contracting parties agree to extend its authority,
it shall be limited to hearing, investigating, and publishing complaints concerning the infringement of human rights in any of the contracting states.

2. The contracting parties should recognize that they have a duty to refrain from, or to permit their territory to be used for, force, the threat of
force, or harsh economic or political pressures or threats against each other.
Israel and the Palestinian state should establish a joint commission with a
secretariat that will hold regular meetings to discuss political and economic
cooperation. Such meetings will provide a forum for the exchange of views
and serve as means for exploring ideas between the parties.

3 & 4. Because of vast differences in territory, population, and resources,
defensive needs will be considerably different among the participating states.
Thus, for instance, if the Sinai is demilitarized, the demilitarization of all
of Israel would not be substantially equal. Moreover, even a proportional
demilitarization might be inconsistent with Israel's defense needs. Thus,
zonal demilitarization in Israel might be restricted to token areas for purposes of formal symmetry in exchange for substantial demilitarization of the
Sinai. Such demilitarization includes offensive weaponry and heavy military
equipment that may constitute a basis for offensive military action. It does
not exclude reasonable police, border, and customs forces or early warning
defensive systems and light weaponry. Since Israel and Egypt would bind
themselves to such mutual restrictions, these arrangements would be in the

category of arms control and limitations agreements such as the SALT agreements between the U. S. and the U.S.S.R. In that respect this region would lead in the progress toward world peace. All possible means of providing security should be explored at Geneva. These might include great power guarantees, great power forces, or United Nations forces under conditions in which they would be withdrawn only upon the consent of both sides or with adequate notice. The defect in UN forces is that, even if their mandate and the agreements specify that they cannot be withdrawn without the consent of all parties to the peace treaties, the states providing the forces nonetheless may withdraw them, particularly if a resolution of the General Assembly advocates it. For this reason, UN forces, unless modified in some important ways, are unlikely to be acceptable to all the parties. Some self-reinforcing type of agreement likely will be necessary. One possible type of self-reinforcing agreement might be acceptable to all parties. This type of arrangement has a precedent in the successful Rhodes agreement of 1949, although it will be adapted to the circumstances of the present case with respect to numbers, dispositions, and weaponry. The Sinai would be substantially demilitarized and be reinforced by a "plate glass window." This proposed "plate glass window" would consist of relatively small and lightly armed joint Egyptian/Israeli patrols or inspection teams. Additionally or alternatively the area could be monitored by agreed forms of aerial observation including the use of satellites. The same could be applied to certain parts of Israel to insure symmetry between the conditions of implementation. The Golan Heights would be demilitarized because of its importance to Israeli defense. Demilitarization shall not exclude lightly armed customs an border guards or police to an extent not inconsistent with the objectives of this type of self-reinforcing system. To insure Israel against Syrian military occupation of the Heights, the following arrangements are proposed: Israeli troops (about 500-1,000 in number) would be stationed below the eastern base of the Heights and Israeli troops of an equivalent size would be stationed at the top of the Heights, which would be returned to Syrian civilian control. Roughly 1,000-2,000 equivalently armed Syrian troops would be stationed on the Israeli side of Lake Galilee – (without interfering with Syrian and Israeli civilian control). These troops should be armed as lightly as possible, including, if this proves feasible upon examination, restrictions to hand guns and rifles. Arrangements would be made for relief of troops and for civilian police activities. Limits would be placed on Syrian and Israeli mobilization in the border area. Here also aerial observation can be very useful and can work to the mutual satisfaction of the parties. The West Ban area would be demilitarized – a status that does not exclude lightly armed police, customs, and border guards – but its citizens may be trained in military units stationed in Jordanian territory. This agreement could be monitored by small joint Israeli/Palestinian patrols. For purpose of symmetry, token demilitarized areas in Israel could be monitored similarly. Although this Article makes legally possible the mutual renunciation of the security arrangements of Article 3 at the end of five years, it is perhaps too optimistic to believe that adequate confidence among the parties will have occurred that early even if no incidents occur. Even if this should be the case, early reconsideration will increase the probability of future renunciation and the transformation of formal peace into good relations. Article 3 does not rule out minor territorial adjustments freely agreed to by the parties.

5. Developments to date make clear that only the Palestinian Liberation Organization is competent to negotiate and to sign a peace settlement. However, recognition of the P.L.O. as the bargaining agent for the Palestinians at Geneva should not preclude the right of the Palestinians to choose their government in free and democratic elections. Furthermore, the other Arab states will provide sufficient developmental assistance to the Palestinian state to sustain its economic viability.

6 & 2. Jointly, these two Articles mandate recognition of the sovereign independence of Israel and the Palestinian state; rule out external interference to change this state of affairs; but do not infringe on the right of the two states to explore, to the extent they so desire, peacefully and without resort to coercive or threatening measures, other possible future arrangements such as a federated state, a binational state, or a new amalgamated state as a successor to the existing states.

8. Possible models for the compensation provision may be found in the German war claims settlement, the World Bank model plan for the nationalization of foreign assets, and the U. S. Foreign Claims Settlement Commission.

9. For the Palestinian state this means reasonable and tax-free transit of goods and police personnel from the west bank area to Gaza and to a tax-free port in Israel on the Mediterranean.

11. In many ways the Jerusalem issue is the most difficult one for a peace treaty to solve. And yet, if the parties can agree on the other terms, good faith should produce a solution here also. There is little doubt that Jerusalem can hardly be severed municipally even though certain parts could be detached from it without affecting that concept. However, to include the Old City of Jerusalem within Israel would violate Article 2. Thus, a single city administration might be combined with some (obviously not complete) de-

centralization of police and courts in the Old City. National offices of a
Palestinian state might be placed there along with a small military guard.
Its national tax laws might be applied to inhabitants of the Old City (althou
a commission would be needed to deal with anomalies in economic legislation). Moreover, no customs or passport controls should exist to impede
travel within the City. Other alternatives might be considered such as turning over the Mount of Olives with the area up to the eastern walls of the Old
City to the Palestinian state. The walled city could be placed under control
of a commission of the major religions, although both Israel and the Palesti
ian state could pass national laws recognizing this status while claiming
concurrent sovereignty over it but subject to certain municipal restrictions.
The remainder of the City would be under Israeli control, although its inhabi
tants would have a choice of Israeli or Palestinian nationality.

   13. It is obviously to the interests of all parties to provide for self-
reinforcing methods of conflict resolution where disputes exist over interpre
tations of the Principles that do not involve vital questions of sovereign
national security. However, this problem is both so complex and subtle that
to consider it before the other means of implementing the Principles have
been agreed upon would be counterproductive. The following examples are
intended as possible illustrations of the complexity of the problem. Conside
the possibility of Israeli restrictions on traffic to permit repairs or impositic
of tariffs to compensate for the costs of providing transit or port facilities t
the Palestinian state. In the first case, a quick arbitral method would guara
tee the Palestinians against arbitrary Israeli restrictions that might damage
important Palestinian economic interests. In the latter case, quickness
would not be important. Funds could be placed in escrow and the matter decided by more formal procedures. On the other hand, consider a dispute ove
a characterization of the kinds of weapons deployed in the demilitarized
zone. A cooling off period during which mediation occurs might be feasible,
but such a matter may be close enough to sovereign considerations of
national security that arbitration or adjudication, although not mediation, is
likely to be ruled out. Some decisions concerning repatriation will come in
this latter category, for no state that believes it has valid reasons will
transfer to an external agency its sovereign right to exclude individuals it
deems likely to act in a manner injurious to its national security. Some
aspects of compensation may be subject to outside adjudication or arbitration. But at some point, the potential awards may threaten the economic
viability or national security of a state. In these latter instances, only
mediation may be possible. And, in some cases, even mediation during a

"cooling off" period may be inconsistent with considerations of sovereign national security as, for instance, those acts of remilitarization for which the "plate glass window" principle was designed.

The Arab-Israeli Dispute

U.S. DEPARTMENT OF STATE

Our Middle East policy rests on three pillars. All are essential for our policy to succeed.

• First, we have made a firm commitment to work for a just and lasting settlement of the Arab-Israeli conflict which takes into account the legitimate interests of all states and peoples in the area, including the Palestinians.

• Second, we seek in every possible way to improve our relations with all the states of the Middle East on a bilateral basis, maintaining our support for Israel's security while strengthening our relations with the Arab countries.

• Third, we seek to avoid the Middle East's becoming a sphere of influence of any outside power.

At the time of the October 1973 war between Israel and the Arab countries, we faced an Arab world convinced that the United States was one-sidedly supporting Israel and that there was a basic hostility between American objectives and Arab objectives. Our relations with Europe and Japan were under severe stress because of the emerging oil problem and the pressures for a rapid Middle East settlement. The Soviet Union was the principal friend of many Arab countries, and Israel was worried about its future.

Since then our diplomatic efforts have contributed to important steps toward peace. While we have maintained our steady and traditional support of Israel, we also have moved toward fundamental improvements in our relations with the Arab nations. Many of these countries have turned toward a more moderate course, giving up exclusive reliance on a single outside power and seeking a negotiated settlement through the good offices of the United States. This is in the interests of all peoples in the Middle East; it is clearly in our own interest.

The United States and the Soviet Union were joint sponsors of the Security Council resolution of October 22, 1973, which brought about the cease-fire at the end of the October war and also established the framework for what became the Geneva Peace Conference. The United States and the U.S.S.R. are cochairmen of that conference. We have had no desire to play an exclusive role or to try in any way to keep the Soviets from playing a legitimate role in the peacemaking process. If for a time we have played a particularly prominent role, it has been because the parties themselves wanted it.

The step-by-step approach to negotiations after the October war attempted to separate the Middle East problem into individual and, therefore, manageable segments. We proceeded according to the concept that peace could best be achieved by increments, rather than by trying to solve all problems at once. This approach led to disengagement-of-forces agreements between Egypt and Israel in January 1974 and subsequently, that May, between Syria and Israel. After a temporary setback in March 1975 when negotiations were suspended, the United States resumed its step-by-step effort at the request of both Egypt and Israel. The result was the Sinai agreement, which was signed in Geneva on September 4.

This important interim step in resolving the Arab-Israeli conflict has significantly advanced the prospects for peace in the Middle East. For the first time Israel and an Arab state have agreed not just to halt fighting or disengage forces, but to commit themselves to a peaceful settlement. Both have been scrupulous in implementing the various provisions of the agreement. The achievement owes much to the courage of leaders on both sides.

The challenge now is to build on the progress that has been made. The United States is prepared to work with all the parties toward a solution of all the issues yet remaining—including the issue of the future of the Palestinians. We stand ready to assist in negotiations between Syria and Israel, should the parties desire, and to consult with all concerned, including the Soviet Union, about the timing and substance of a reconvened Geneva Conference.

The path ahead will be difficult. But the United States will continue to pursue the goal of a just and lasting settlement. The peoples of the Middle East, be they Arab or Jew, have had enough of bloodshed; they cry out for peace. For the Arabs, there can be no peace without a recovery of territory and redress of grievances of a displaced people. For Israel, peace requires both security within internationally recognized boundaries and a recognition of its legitimacy as a state.

Israel and the United States

HENRY A. KISSINGER

The greatness of America has been not so much its physical strength as its moral significance. Since its birth this Nation has stood for something larger than itself. Americans have always had a sense of mission; we have been inspired by the knowledge that we were champions of liberty and progress for all mankind. We have been not only a refuge for those fleeing persecution, but the defense of democracy and bulwark for others in time of need, a feeder of the hungry, and a solace to the suffering. And history continues to present us these challenges and more. Today we bear a central responsibility for maintaining peace and shaping a global structure which can help realize mankind's dream of an end to conflict and hatred.

These are the qualities and responsibilities and hopes which tie America to Israel. No people knows more vividly than the Jewish people that morality must be more than a theory—it must be a quality of human conduct. No people yearns more for tranquillity than those who historically have been the first victims of its loss. And no people perceives more acutely that peace depends ultimately not on political arrangements but on the conscience of mankind.

History is often cruel, but the wisest are those who know that fate can be shaped by human faith and human courage. The true realists are those who recognize that all great achievements were a dream before they became a reality. These are qualities that have enabled the Jewish people to survive their tragedies. These are the qualities that brought about the State of Israel. These are qualities that guarantee the future of the people of Israel. And these are qualities which peoples and nations everywhere must possess if they are to be free.

The Moral Basis of Foreign Policy

History challenges us amid the world's ambiguities to shape events by our own purposes and ideals. If democratic societies like America and Israel are to prosper, we must summon the unity and resolve to be masters of our futures on the basis of our values.

The decisions that must be made are always difficult for foreign policy deals with the interaction of sovereign entities. No country, no matter how strong, can impose its will on the world. Today in a world of thermonuclear weapons, diffusion of power, and growing interdependence, foreign policy is more than ever an enterprise of incomplete and imperfect solutions. Tension is unavoidable between moral values, which are invariably cast in absolute terms, and efforts to achieve them, which of necessity involve compromise.

This accounts for much of the foreign policy debate in democratic societies, which to some extent is a rebellion against the contemporary world. In all democratic societies the temptation is great to deny the circumstances of the contemporary world and to blame them on individuals, to confuse optimism with the shallow projection of the desirable.

But we cannot escape the conditions around us. Morality without pragmatic action is empty, just as pragmatism without moral direction is like a rudderless ship. The true optimists are those who are prepared to face complexity and who have the faith that their people can master it by dedication and vision.

If democracies like America and Israel are to survive and flourish in a world of sovereign states and competing wills, they must stand firmly for their belief in human dignity; otherwise we will lose our bearings. There is no way to make these choices, and to navigate between the shoals of temptation and danger, without a strong inner moral conviction. Equally we need a mature and hardheaded understanding of the difficult choices that must be made lest we substitute wishful thinking for the requirements of survival.

For Americans foreign policy has always been more than the search for stability. Americans have a vision of a world of justice that drives all our efforts. A pragmatic policy alone would be empty of humanity; it would lack direction and roots and heart.

But equally if policy becomes excessively moralistic, it can turn quixotic or dangerous. A presumed monopoly on virtue can make impossible any solution or negotiation. Good results may be given up or sabotaged in the quest for the elusive ideal. Some of this country's most serious errors—of both involvement and abdication—were driven by misguided moral arguments. Some intervention began as crusades to reform other societies, and we were isolationist in the 1930's to preserve our purity and register our distaste for the balance of power.

Our responsibility to conduct a moral, farsighted, and realistic policy has grown in recent years. In a world made smaller by technology and communications, events anywhere are instantly known and have effects in distant places. Never before have the destinies of nations been more intertwined—not only practically but morally.

And so we have a stake in a peaceful world and an environment where man's aspirations for justice and liberty and dignity have the greatest chance of fulfillment. The ultimate safety of every minority, every oppressed people, lies in a world where respect for human dignity governs the affairs of nations. Peace can be said to exist only when the insecurity of nations is eased, the hopes of people for economic advance are fulfilled, international habits of restraint and conciliation are nurtured, and men experience at last the blessings of a world of justice and progress.

Peace in the Middle East

I have spoken at some length about the moral foundation of our foreign policy to this group which is so concerned and serious about the survival of Israel. For the relationship between America and Israel depends ultimately not on formal assurances but on the links of our peoples and the reality of our values.

The survival and security of Israel are unequivocal and permanent moral commitments of the United States. Israel is a loyal friend and a fellow democracy, whose very existence represents the commitment of all free peoples. The moral strength of the people of Israel, which has so often meant the margin of victory in war, gives us confidence that Israel will also win peace. No people have earned it more.

Time and events have brought us to a threshold in Middle East history—an unprecedented opportunity to realize the peace of which we all have dreamed; a peace in the interest of all the peoples of a region that has experienced enough anguish for this generation.

- Israel, having proven by its own courage that it is here to stay, has taken equally courageous steps toward peaceful resolution of the conflict.
- Some of its Arab neighbors, for the first time ever, are now speaking openly and wisely of making peace and ending generations of conflict.
- The United States has demonstrated to both

sides its commitment to continue to promote a just
and enduring solution.

● The relationships among the major outside
powers, if conducted with reason and firmness, can
create a global environment of restraint that will
enhance security and the possibilities of peaceful
settlement in the Middle East.

Israel obviously faces profound problems—not
the least of which is that in any negotiation with
its neighbors, it will be asked to yield the physical
buffers of territory in exchange for intangible
pledges. Indeed Israel's gains will be intangible even
as it achieves its own stated objectives of a formal
peace treaty and diplomatic recognition by its
neighbors. So the process of peace inevitably presents it with many anguishing decisions—and the
pain is shared by all of us who are friends of Israel
and who are dedicated to further progress toward
peace. Throughout this process we owe Israel our
compassion and support.

The risks and obstacles are many. Steps taken
must be carefully thought out and realistic. But we
must move together with courage and with a vision
of how reality can be shaped by a vision of peace.
And we must not paralyze ourselves by a suspi-
ciousness that deprives our relationship of dignity
and our cooperation of significance.

The United States will help keep Israel
strong—to insure that peace is seen clearly to be
the only feasible course. We will never abandon
Israel—either by failing to provide crucial assistance
or by misconceived or separate negotiations or by
irresolution when challenged to meet our own
responsibility to maintain the global balance of
power.

We will never forget that America's responsibility for peace includes, above all, responsibility
for the fate of smaller nations who rely upon us as

the ultimate defender of their survival and freedom
and that Israel's fate is inseparable from the future
of human dignity. America will not abandon a
friend because to do so in one part of the world
would shake confidence in every part of the world.
There will be no American weakness or abdication
for this can only tempt adversaries, confuse allies,
and undermine security in the world—ultimately to
the grave peril of our country.

Moral ideals and practical interest thus come
together. Peace in the Middle East is a goal shared
by Americans and by Israelis alike. The road
toward it will be a common one. And so, in truth,
as we pursue the course of peace, our guarantees
rest not so much in any formal agreements or reassurances endlessly repeated but in the deeper ties
of emotion and morality, history and principle,
that can never be sundered.

The dream of peace is the dream of the
prophet Isaiah—that "nation shall not lift up sword
against nation, neither shall they learn war any
more." It is written in the Book of Numbers that
"the Lord lift up his countenance upon thee,
and give thee peace." This dream is both an inspiration and a duty. And those who strive for it know
both the pain and the exhilaration of man's noblest
endeavor.

The United States and Israel will have the
courage and the faith to seek this dream and fulfill
it.

V. DOCUMENTS RELATING TO THE ARAB-ISRAELI CONFLICT

A. *Origins of the Conflict: 1897-1947*

1. The Basle Programme, August 1897[*]

[*] From ISRAEL COHEN, THE ZIONIST MOVEMENT 77 (1946).

"The aim of Zionism is to create for the Jewish people a home in Palestine secured by public law.

"In order to attain this object the Congress adopts the following means:

"1. The systematic promotion of the settlement of Palestine with Jewish agriculturists, artisans, and craftsmen.

"2. The organisation and federation of all Jewry by means of local and general institutions in conformity with the local laws.

"3. The strengthening of Jewish sentiment and national consciousness.

"4. Preparatory steps for the procuring of such Government assents as are necessary for achieving the object of Zionism."

2. The Sykes-Picot Agreement, May 16, 1916*

---

* [1919] IV DOCUMENTS ON BRITISH FOREIGN POLICY 1919-1939 244, 245-47 (First Series 1952).

Sir Edward Grey to M. Cambon
'(Secret.)
'Your Excellency,   'FOREIGN OFFICE, *May 15, 1916*
   'I shall have the honour to reply fully in a further note to your
Excellency's note of the 9th instant, relative to the creation of an Arab
State, but I should meanwhile be grateful if your Excellency could
assure me that in those regions which, under the conditions recorded in
that communication, become entirely French, or in which French
interests are recognised as predominant, any existing British concessions, rights of navigation or development, and the rights and privileges
of any British religious, scholastic, or medical institutions will be
maintained.
   'His Majesty's Government are, of course, ready to give a reciprocal
assurance in regard to the British area.
                                        'I have, &c.
                                        E. GREY'

Sir Edward Grey to M. Cambon
'(Secret.)
'Your Excellency,   'FOREIGN OFFICE, *May 16, 1916*
   'I have the honour to acknowledge the receipt of your Excellency's
note of the 9th instant, stating that the French Government accepts
the limits of a future Arab State, or Confederation of States, and of
those parts of Syria where French interests predominate, together with
certain conditions attached thereto, such as they result from recent
discussions in London and Petrograd on the subject.
   'I have the honour to inform your Excellency in reply that the
acceptance of the whole project, as it now stands, will involve the
abdication of considerable British interests, but, since His Majesty's
Government recognise the advantage to the general cause of the Allies
entailed in producing a more favourable internal political situation in
Turkey, they are ready to accept the arrangement now arrived at,
provided that the co-operation of the Arabs is secured, and that the
Arabs fulfil the conditions and obtain the towns of Homs, Hama,
Damascus, and Aleppo.
   'It is accordingly understood between the French and British
Governments—
   'I. That France and Great Britain are prepared to recognise and
protect an independent Arab State or a Confederation of Arab States in
the areas (A) and (B) marked on the annexed map [not here

reproduced] , under the suzerainty of an Arab chief. That in area (A) France, and in area (B) Great Britain, shall have priority of right of enterprise and local loans. That in area (A) France, and in area (B) Great Britain, shall alone supply advisers or foreign functionaries at the request of the Arab State or Confederation of Arab States.

'2. That in the blue area France, and in the red area Great Britain, shall be allowed to establish such direct or indirect administration or control as they desire and as they may think fit to arrange with the Arab State or Confederation of Arab States.

'3. That in the brown area there shall be established an international administration, the form of which is to be decided upon after consultation with Russia, and subsequently in consultation with the other Allies, and the representatives of the Shereef of Mecca.

'4. That Great Britain be accorded (1) the ports of Haifa and Acre, (2) guarantee of a given supply of water from the Tigris and Euphrates in area (A) for area (B). His Majesty's Government, on their part, undertake that they will at no time enter into negotiations for the cession of Cyprus to any third Power without the previous consent of the French Government.

'5. That Alexandretta shall be a free port as regards the trade of the British Empire, and that there shall be no discrimination in port charges or facilities as regards British shipping and British goods; that there shall be freedom of transit for British goods through Alexandretta and by railway through the blue area, whether those goods are intended for or originate in the red area, or (B) area, or area (A); and there shall be no discrimination, direct or indirect, against British goods on any railway or against British goods or ships at any port serving the areas mentioned.

'That Haifa shall be a free port as regards the trade of France, her dominions and protectorates, and there shall be no discrimination in port charges or facilities as regards French shipping and French goods. There shall be freedom of transit for French goods through Haifa and by the British railway through the brown area, whether those goods are intended for or originate in the blue area, area (A), or area (B), and there shall be no discrimination, direct or indirect, against French goods on any railway, or against French goods or ships at any port serving the areas mentioned.

'6. That in area (A) the Bagdad Railway shall not be extended southwards beyond Mosul, and in area (B) northwards beyond Samarra, until a railway connecting Bagdad with Aleppo via the Euphrates Valley has been completed, and then only with the concurrence of the two Governments.

'7. That Great Britain has the right to build, administer, and be sole owner of a railway connecting Haifa with area (B), and shall have a perpetual right to transport troops along such a line at all times.

'It is to be understood by both Governments that this railway is to facilitate the connexion of Bagdad with Haifa by rail, and it is further understood that, if the engineering difficulties and expense entailed by keeping this connecting line in the brown area only make the project unfeasible, that the French Government shall be prepared to consider that the line in question may also traverse the polygon Banias-Keis Marib—Salkhad Tell Otsda—Mesmie before reaching area (B).

'8. For a period of twenty years the existing Turkish customs tariff shall remain in force throughout the whole of the blue and red areas, as well as in areas (A) and (B), and no increase in the rates of duty or conversion from *ad valorem* to specific rates shall be made except by agreement between the two powers.

'There shall be no interior customs barriers between any of the above-mentioned areas. The customs duties leviable on goods destined for the interior shall be collected at the port of entry and handed over to the administration of the area of destination.

'9. It shall be agreed that the French Government will at no time enter into any negotiations for the cession of their rights and will not cede such rights in the blue area to any third Power, except the Arab State or Confederation of Arab States, without the previous agreement of His Majesty's Government, who, on their part, will give a similar undertaking to the French Government regarding the red area.

'10. The British and French Governments, as the protectors of the Arab State, shall agree that they will not themselves acquire and will not consent to a third Power acquiring territorial possessions in the Arabian peninsula, nor consent to a third Power installing a naval base either on the east coast, or on the islands, of the Red Sea. This, however, shall not prevent such adjustment of the Aden frontier as may be necessary in consequence of recent Turkish aggression.

'11. The negotiations with the Arabs as to the boundaries of the Arab State or Confederation of Arab States shall be continued through the same channel as heretofore on behalf of the two Powers.

'12. It is agreed that measures to control the importation of arms into the Arab territories will be considered by the two Governments.

'I have further the honour to state that, in order to make the agreement complete, His Majesty's Government are proposing to the Russian Government to exchange notes analogous to those exchanged by the latter and your Excellency's Government on the 26th April last. Copies of these notes will be communicated to your Excellency as soon as exchanged.

'I would also venture to remind your Excellency that the conclusion of the present agreement raises, for practical consideration, the question of the claims of Italy to a share in any partition or rearrangement of Turkey in Asia, as formulated in article 9 of the agreement of the 26th April, 1915, between Italy and the Allies.

'His Majesty's Government further consider that the Japanese Government should be informed of the arrangements now concluded.

'I have, &c.
E. GREY'

3. The Balfour Declaration, November 2, 1917*

---

* Photographic reproduction from the original in the archives of the British Museum of a letter of November 2, 1917, from Lord Arthur James Balfour, the British Foreign Secretary, to Lord Rothschild. See also the earlier Hussein-McMahon Letters, July 1915 – March 1916, *Correspondence Between Sir Henry McMahon, G.C.M.G., G.C.V.O., K.C.I.E., C.S.I., His Majesty's High Commissioner at Cairo, and the Sherif Hussein of Mecca*, COMMAND PAPER 5957 (1940), at 1-16, GREAT BRITAIN HOUSE OF COMMONS PARLIAMENTARY SESSIONAL PAPERS 1938-39, Vol. 27 (Accounts and Papers, Vol. 12); and the later interpretation of the Hussein-McMahon Correspondence by McMahon, Letter from A. Henry McMahon to *The Times*, July 23, 1937.

Foreign Office,
November 2nd, 1917.

Dear Lord Rothschild,

I have much pleasure in conveying to you, on behalf of His Majesty's Government, the following declaration of sympathy with Jewish Zionist aspirations which has been submitted to, and approved by, the Cabinet

'His Majesty's Government view with favour the establishment in Palestine of a national home for the Jewish people, and will use their best endeavours to facilitate the achievement of this object, it being clearly understood that nothing shall be done which may prejudice the civil and religious rights of existing non-Jewish communities in Palestine, or the rights and political status enjoyed by Jews in any other country".

I should be grateful if you would bring this declaration to the knowledge of the Zionist Federation.

Y. ing

Arthur James Balfour

4. The Anglo-French Declaration of November 7, 1918*

* 145 PARLIAMENTARY DEBATES H.C. (5th Series) 36 (1921).

"The object aimed at by France and Great Britain in prosecuting in
the East the War let loose by the ambition of Germany is the complete
and definite emancipation of the peoples so long oppressed by the
Turks and the establishment of national governments and administrations deriving their authority from the initiative and free choice of the
indigenous populations.

In order to carry out these intentions France and Great Britain are at
one in encouraging and assisting the establishment of indigenous
Governments and administrations in Syria and Mesopotamia, now
liberated by the Allies, and in the territories the liberation of which
they are engaged in securing, and recognising these as soon as they
are actually established.

Far from wishing to impose on the populations of these regions any
particular institutions they are only concerned to ensure by their
support any by adequate assistance the regular working of Governments
and administrations freely chosen by the populations themselves. To
secure impartial and equal justice for all, to facilitate the economic
development of the country by inspiring and encouraging local
initiative, to favour the diffusion of education, to put an end to
dissensions that have too long been taken advantage of by Turkish
policy, such is the policy which the two Allied Governments uphold in
the liberated territories."

5. Article 22 of the Covenant of the League of Nations, June 28, 1919*

*   Reprinted from *Report to the General Assembly of the United Nations Special Committee on Palestine,* Vol. II, *Annexes, Appendix and Maps* 22, U.N. Doc. A/364 Add. 1 (Sept. 9, 1947). See also L. SOHN, BASIC DOCUMENTS OF THE UNITED NATIONS 295, 301-2 (2nd edn. rev., 1968).

1. To those colonies and territories which as a consequence of the late war have ceased to be under the sovereignty of the States which formerly governed them and which are inhabited by peoples not yet able to stand by themselves under the strenuous conditions of the modern world, there should be applied the principle that the well-being and development of such peoples form a sacred trust of civilization and that securities for the performance of this trust should be embodied in this Covenant.

2. The best method of giving practical effect to this principle is that the tutelage of such peoples should be entrusted to advanced nations who by reason of their resources, their experience or their geographical position can best undertake this responsibility, and who are willing to accept it, and that this tutelage should be exercised by them as Mandatories on behalf of the League.

3. The character of the mandate must differ according to the stage of the development of the people, the geographical situation of the territory, its economic conditions and other similar circumstances.

4. Certain communities formerly belonging to the Turkish Empire have reached a stage of development where their existence as independent nations can be provisionally recognized subject to the rendering of administrative advice and assistance by a Mandatory until such time as they are able to stand alone. The wishes of these communities must be a principal consideration in the selection of the Mandatory.

5. Other peoples, especially those of Central Africa, are at such a stage that the Mandatory must be responsible for the administration of the territory under conditions which will guarantee freedom of conscience and religion, subject only to the maintenance of public order and morals, the prohibition of abuses such as the slave trade, the arms traffic and the liquor traffic, and the prevention of the establishment of fortifications or military and naval bases and of military training of the natives for other than police purposes and the defence of territory, and will also secure equal opportunities for the trade and commerce of other Members of the League.

6. There are territories, such as South West Africa and certain of the South Pacific Islands, which, owing to the sparseness of their population, or their small size, or their remoteness from the centres of civilization, or their geographical contiguity to the territory of the Mandatory, and other circumstances, can be best administered under the laws of the Mandatory as integral portions of its territory, subject to the safeguards above mentioned in the interest of the indigenous population.

7. In every case of mandate, the Mandatory shall render to the Council an annual report in reference to the territory committed to its charge.

8. The degree of authority, control, or administration to be exercised by the Mandatory shall, if not previously agreed upon by the Members of the League, be explicitly defined in each case by the Council.

9. A permanent Commission shall be constituted to receive and examine the annual reports of the Mandatories and to advise the Council on all matters relating to the observance of the mandates.

6. The Mandate for Palestine Confirmed by the Council of the League of Nations on July 24, 1922, and the Memorandum by the British Government Relating to Its Application to Transjordan Approved by the Council of the League on September 16, 1922*

*　Reprinted from *Report to the General Assembly of the United Nations Special Committee on Palestine*, Vol. II, *Annexes, Appendix and Maps* 18-22, U.N. Doc. A/364 Add. 1 (Sept. 9, 1947). For the French as well as the English text of the Mandate for Palestine and the British Memorandum Relating to Transjordan, see *Terms of League of Nations Mandates*, U.N. Doc. A/70 (Oct. 1946), at 2-7.

Mandate for Palestine

The Council of the League of Nations:

Whereas the Principal Allied Powers have agreed, for the purpose of giving effect to the provisions of Article 22 of the Covenant of the League of Nations, to entrust to a Mandatory selected by the said Powers the administration of the territory of Palestine, which formerly belonged to the Turkish Empire, within such boundaries as may be fixed by them; and

Whereas the Principal Allied Powers have also agreed that the Mandatory should be responsible for putting into effect the declaration originally made on November 2nd, 1917, by the Government of His Britannic Majesty, and adopted by the said Powers, in favour of the establishment in Palestine of a national home for the Jewish people, it being clearly understood that nothing should be done which might prejudice the civil and religious rights of existing non-Jewish communities in Palestine, or the rights and political status enjoyed by Jews in any other country; and

Whereas recognition has thereby been given to the historical connection of the Jewish people with Palestine and to the grounds for reconstituting their national home in that country; and

Whereas the Principal Allied Powers have selected His Britannic Majesty as the Mandatory for Palestine; and

Whereas the mandate in respect of Palestine has been formulated in the following terms and submitted to the Council of the League for approval; and

Whereas His Britannic Majesty has accepted the mandate in respect of Palestine and undertaken to exercise it on behalf of the League of Nations in conformity with the following provisions; and

Whereas by the aforementioned Article 22 (paragraph 8) it is provided that the degree of authority, control or administration to be exercised by the Mandatory, not having been previously agreed upon by the Members of the League, shall be explicitly defined by the Council of the League of Nations;

Confirming the said mandate, defines its terms as follows:

ARTICLE 1

The Mandatory shall have full powers of legislation and of administration, save as they may be limited by the terms of this mandate.

ARTICLE 2

The Mandatory shall be responsible for placing the country under such political, administrative and economic conditions as will secure the establishment of the Jewish national home, as laid down in the preamble, and the development of self-governing institutions, and also for safeguarding the civil and religious rights of all the inhabitants of Palestine, irrespective of race and religion.

ARTICLE 3

The Mandatory shall, so far as circumstances permit, encourage local autonomy.

ARTICLE 4

An appropriate Jewish agency shall be recognized as a public body for the purpose of advising and co-operating with the Administration of Palestine in such economic, social and other matters as may affect the establishment of the Jewish national home and the interests of the Jewish population in Palestine, and, subject always to the control of the Administration, to assist and take part in the development of the country.

The Zionist organization, so long as its organization and constitution are in the opinion of the Mandatory appropriate, shall be recognized as such agency. It shall take steps in consultation with His Britannic Majesty's Government to secure the co-operation of all Jews who are willing to assist in the establishment of the Jewish national home.

ARTICLE 5

The Mandatory shall be responsible for seeing that no Palestine territory shall be ceded or leased to, or in any way placed under the control of the Government of any foreign Power.

ARTICLE 6

The Administration of Palestine, while ensuring that the rights and position of other sections of the population are not prejudiced, shall facilitate Jewish immigration under suitable conditions and shall encourage, in co-operation with the Jewish agency referred to in Article 4, close settlement by Jews on the land, including State lands and waste lands not required for public purposes.

ARTICLE 7

The Administration of Palestine shall be responsible for enacting a nationality law. There shall be included in this law provisions framed so as to facilitate the acquisition of Palestinian citizenship by Jews who take up their permanent residence in Palestine.

ARTICLE 8

The privileges and immunities of foreigners, including the benefits of consular jurisdiction and protection as formerly enjoyed by capitulation or usage in the Ottoman Empire, shall not be applicable in Palestine.

Unless the Powers whose nationals enjoyed the aforementioned privileges and immunities on August 1st, 1914, shall have previously renounced the right to their re-establishment, or shall have agreed to their non-application for a specified period, these privileges and immunities shall, at the expiration of the mandate, be immediately re-established in their entirety or with such modifications as may have been agreed upon between the Powers concerned.

ARTICLE 9

The Mandatory shall be responsible for seeing that the judicial system established in Palestine shall assure to foreigners, as well as to natives, a complete guarantee of their rights.

Respect for the personal status of the various peoples and communities and for their religious interests shall be fully guaranteed. In particular, the control and administration of Wakfs shall be exercised in accordance with religious law and the disposition of the founders.

ARTICLE 10

Pending the making of special extradition agreements relating to Palestine, the extradition treaties in force between the Mandatory and other foreign Powers shall apply to Palestine.

ARTICLE 11

The Administration of Palestine shall take all necessary measures to safeguard the interests of the community in connection with the development of the country, and, subject to any international obligations accepted by the Mandatory, shall have full power to provide for public ownership or control of any of the natural resources of the country or of the public works, services and utilities established or to be established therein. It shall introduce a land system appropriate to the needs of the country, having regard, among other things, to the desirability of promoting the close settlement and intensive cultivation of the land.

The Administration may arrange with the Jewish agency mentioned in Article 4 to construct or operate, upon fair and equitable terms, any public works, services and utilities, and to develop any of the natural resources of the country, in so far as these matters are not directly undertaken by the Administration. Any such arrangements shall provide that no profits distributed by such agency, directly or indirectly, shall exceed a reasonable rate of interest on the capital, and any further profits shall be utilized by it for the benefit of the country in a manner approved by the Administration.

ARTICLE 12

The Mandatory shall be entrusted with the control of the foreign relations of Palestine and the right to issue exequaturs to consuls appointed by foreign Powers. He shall also be entitled to afford diplomatic and consular protection to citizens of Palestine when outside its territorial limits.

ARTICLE 13

All responsibility in connection with the Holy Places and religious buildings or sites in Palestine, including that of preserving existing rights and of securing free access to the Holy Places, religious buildings and sites and the free exercise of worship, while ensuring the requirements of public order and decorum, is assumed by the Mandatory, who shall be responsible solely to the League of Nations in all matters connected herewith, provided that nothing in this article shall prevent the Mandatory from entering into such arrangements as he may deem reasonable with the Administration for the purpose of carrying the provisions of this article into effect; and provided also that nothing in this mandate shall be construed as conferring upon the Mandatory authority to interfere with the fabric or the management of purely Moslem sacred shrines, the immunities of which are guaranteed.

ARTICLE 14

A special Commission shall be appointed by the Mandatory to study, define and determine the rights and claims in connection with the Holy Places and the rights and claims relating to the different religious communities in Palestine. The method of nomination, the composition and the functions of this Commission shall be submitted to the Council of the League for its approval, and the Commission shall not be appointed or enter upon its functions without the approval of the Council.

ARTICLE 15

The Mandatory shall see that complete freedom of conscience and the free exercise of all forms of worship, subject only to the maintenance of public order and morals, are ensured to all. No discrimination of any kind shall be made between the inhabitants of Palestine on the ground of race, religion or language. No person shall be excluded from Palestine on the sole ground of his religious belief.

The right of each community to maintain its own schools for the education of its own members in its own language, while conforming to such educational requirements of a general nature as the Administration may impose, shall not be denied or impaired.

ARTICLE 16

The Mandatory shall be responsible for exercising such supervision over religious or eleemosynary bodies of all faiths in Palestine as may be required for the maintenance of public order and good government. Subject to such supervision, no measures shall be taken in Palestine to obstruct or interfere with the enterprise of such bodies or to discriminate against any representative or member of them on the ground of his religion or nationality.

ARTICLE 17

The Administration of Palestine may organize on a voluntary basis the forces necessary for the preservation of peace and order, and also for the defence of the country, subject, however, to the supervision of the Mandatory, but shall not use them for purposes other than those above specified save with the consent of the Mandatory. Except for such purposes, no military, naval or air forces shall be raised or maintained by the Administration of Palestine.

Nothing in this article shall preclude the Administration of Palestine from contributing to the cost of the maintenance of the forces of the Mandatory in Palestine.

The Mandatory shall be entitled at all times to use the roads, railways and ports of Palestine for the movement of armed forces and the carriage of fuel and supplies.

ARTICLE 18

The Mandatory shall see that there is no discrimination in Palestine against the nationals of any State Member of the League of Nations (including companies incorporated under its laws) as compared with those of the Mandatory or of any foreign State in matters concerning taxation, commerce or navigation, the exercise of industries or professions, or in the treatment of merchant vessels or civil aircraft. Similarly, there shall be no discrimination in Palestine against goods originating in or destined for any of the said States, and there shall be freedom of transit under equitable conditions across the mandated area.

Subject as aforesaid and to the other provisions of this mandate, the Administration of Palestine may, on the advice of the Mandatory, impose such taxes and Customs duties as it may consider necessary, and take such steps as it may think best to promote the development of the natural resources of the country and to safeguard the interests of the population. It may also, on the advice of the Mandatory, conclude a special Customs agreement with any State the territory of which in 1914 was wholly included in Asiatic Turkey or Arabia.

ARTICLE 19

The Mandatory shall adhere on behalf of the Administration of Palestine to any general international conventions already existing, or which may be concluded hereafter with the approval of the League of Nations, respecting the slave traffic, the traffic in arms and ammunition, or the traffic in drugs, or relating to commercial equality, freedom of transit and navigation, aerial navigation and postal, telegraphic and wireless communication or literary, artistic or industrial property.

ARTICLE 20

The Mandatory shall co-operate on behalf of the Administration of Palestine, so far as religious, social and other conditions may permit, in the execution of any common policy adopted by the League of Nations for preventing and combating disease, including diseases of plants and animals.

ARTICLE 21

The Mandatory shall secure the enactment within twelve months from this date, and shall ensure the execution of a Law of Antiquities based on the following rules. This law shall ensure equality of treatment in the matter of excavations and archaeological research to the nationals of all States Members of the League of Nations.

(1)

"Antiquity" means any construction or any product of human activity earlier than the year 1700 A.D.

(2)

The law for the protection of antiquities shall proceed by encouragement rather than by threat.

Any person who, having discovered an antiquity without being furnished with the authorization referred to in paragraph 5, reports the same to an official of the competent Department, shall be rewarded according to the value of the discovery.

(3)

No antiquity may be disposed of except to the competent Department, unless this Department renounces the acquisition of any such antiquity. No antiquity may leave the country without an export licence from the said Department.

(4)

Any person who maliciously or negligently destroys or damages an antiquity shall be liable to a penalty to be fixed.

(5)

No clearing of ground or digging with the object of finding antiquities shall be permitted, under penalty of fine, except to persons authorized by the competent Department.

(6)

Equitable terms shall be fixed for expropriation, temporary or permanent, of lands which might be of historical or archaeological interest.

(7)

Authorization to excavate shall only be granted to persons who show sufficient guarantees of archaeological experience. The Administration of Palestine shall not, in granting these authorizations, act in such a way as to exclude scholars of any nation without good grounds.

(8)

The proceeds of excavations may be divided between the excavator and the competent Department in a proportion fixed by that Department. If division seems impossible for scientific reasons, the excavator shall receive a fair indemnity in lieu of a part of the find.

ARTICLE 22

English, Arabic and Hebrew shall be the official languages of Palestine. Any statement or inscription in Arabic on stamps or money in Palestine shall be repeated in Hebrew and any statement or inscription in Hebrew shall be repeated in Arabic.

ARTICLE 23

The Administration of Palestine shall recognize the holy days of the respective communities in Palestine as legal days of rest for the members of such communities.

ARTICLE 24

The Mandatory shall make to the Council of the League of Nations an annual report to the satisfaction of the Council as to the measures taken during the year to carry out the provisions of the mandate. Copies of all laws and regulations promulgated or issued during the year shall be communicated with the report.

ARTICLE 25

In the territories lying between the Jordan and the eastern boundary of Palestine as ultimately determined, the Mandatory shall be entitled, with the consent of the Coucil of the League of Nations, to postpone or withhold application of such provisions of this mandate as he may consider inapplicable to the existing local conditions, and to make such provisions for the administration of the territories as he may consider suitable to those conditions, provided that no action shall be taken which is inconsistent with the provisions of Articles 15, 16 and 18.

ARTICLE 26

The Mandatory agrees that, if any dispute whatever should arise between the Mandatory and another Member of the League of Nations relating to the interpretation or the application of the provisions of the mandate, such dispute, if it cannot be settled by negotiation, shall be submitted to the Permanent Court of International Justice provided for by Article 14 of the Covenant of the League of Nations.

ARTICLE 27

The consent of the Council of the League of Nations is required for any modification of the terms of this mandate.

ARTICLE 28

In the event of the termination of the mandate hereby conferred upon the Mandatory, the Council of the League of Nations shall make such arrangements as may be deemed necessary for safeguarding in perpetuity, under guarantee of the League, the rights secured by Articles 13 and 14, and shall use its influence for securing, under the guarantee of the League, that the Government of Palestine will fully honour the financial obligations legitimately incurred by the Administration of Palestine during the period of the mandate, including the rights of public servants to pensions or gratuities.

The present instrument shall be deposited in original in the archives of the League of Nations and certified copies shall be forwarded by the Secretary-General of the League of Nations to all Members of the League.

Done at London the twenty-fourth day of July, one thousand nine hundred and twenty-two.

Article 25 of the Palestine Mandate
Memorandum by the British Representative

Approved by the Council on September 16th, 1922
1. Article 25 of the Mandate for Palestine provides as follows:
"In the territories lying between the Jordan and the eastern boundary of Palestine as ultimately determined, the Mandatory shall be entitled, with the consent of the Council of the League of Nations, to postpone or withhold application of such provisions of this Mandate as he may consider inapplicable to the existing local conditions, and to make such provisions for the administration of the territories as he may consider suitable to those conditions, provided that no action shall be taken which is inconsistent with the provisions of Articles 15, 16 and 18."
2. In pursuance of the provisions of this article, His Majesty's Government invite the Council to pass the following resolution:
"The following provisions of the Mandate for Palestine are not applicable to the territory known as Transjordan, which comprises all territory lying to the east of a line drawn from a point two miles west of the town of Akaba on the Gulf of that name up the centre of the Wady Araba, Dead Sea and River Jordan to its junction with the River Yarmuk: thence up the centre of that river to the Syrian frontier.
"*Preamble.* Recitals 2 and 3.
"*Article 2.*
"The words 'placing the country under such political administration and economic conditions as will secure the establishment of the Jewish national home, as laid down in the Preamble, and . . .'
"*Article 4.*
"*Article 6.*

"*Article 7.*

"The sentence 'there shall be included in this law provisions framed so as to facilitate the acquisition of Palestinian citizenship by Jews who take up their permanent residence in Palestine.'

"*Article 11.*

"The second sentence of the first paragraph and the second paragraph.

"*Article 13.*

"*Article 14.*

"*Article 22.*

"*Article 23.*

"In the application of the Mandate to Transjordan, the action which, in Palestine, is taken by the Administration of the latter country will be taken by the Administration of Transjordan under the general supervision of the Mandatory."

3. His Majesty's Government accept full responsibility as Mandatory for Transjordan, and undertake that such provision as may be made for the administration of that territory in accordance with Article 25 of the Mandate shall be in no way inconsistent with those provisions of the Mandate which are not by this resolution declared inapplicable.

7. Congressional Resolution Favoring the Establishment in Palestine of a National Home for the Jewish People, September 21, 1922*

*   42 STAT. 1012 (Part I, 1922).

Resolved by the Senate and House of Representatives of the United States of America in Congress assembled, That the United States of America favors the establishment in Palestine of a national home for the Jewish people, it being clearly understood that nothing shall be done which may prejudice the civil and religious rights of Christian and all other non-Jewish communities in Palestine, and that the holy places and religious buildings and sites in Palestine shall be adequately protected.

Approved, September 21, 1922.

V. DOCUMENTS RELATING TO THE ARAB-ISRAELI CONFLICT

B. *Establishment of the State of Israel and the 1948 War: 1947-1949*

8. General Assembly Resolution 181 (II) Concerning the Future Government of Palestine, November 29, 1947*

* G.A. Res. 181 (II), 2 U.N. GAOR, Resolutions Sept. 16 - Nov. 29, 1947, at 131-32, U.N. Doc. A/519 (Jan. 8, 1948).

A

The General Assembly,

Having met in special session at the request of the mandatory Power to constitute and instruct a special committee to prepare for the consideration of the question of the future government of Palestine at the second regular session;

Having constituted a Special Committee and instructed it to investigate all questions and issues relevant to the problem of Palestine, and to prepare proposals for the solution of the problem, and

Having received and examined the report of the Special Committee (document A/364) including a number of unanimous recommendations and a plan of partition with economic union approved by the majority of the Special Committee,

Considers that the present situation in Palestine is one which is likely to impair the general welfare and friendly relations among nations;

Takes note of the declaration by the mandatory Power that it plans to complete its evacuation of Palestine by 1 August 1948;

Recommends to the United Kingdom, as the mandatory Power for Palestine, and to all other Members of the United Nations the adoption and implementation, with regard to the future government of Palestine, of the Plan of Partition with Economic Union set out below;

Requests that

(*a*) The Security Council take the necessary measures as provided for in the plan for its implementation;

(*b*) The Security Council consider, if circumstances during the transitional period require such consideration, whether the situation in Palestine constitutes a threat to the peace. If it decides that such a threat exists, and in order to maintain international peace and security, the Security Council should supplement the authorization of the General Assembly by taking measures, under Articles 39 and 41 of the Charter, to empower the United Nations Commission, as provided in this resolution, to exercise in Palestine the functions which are assigned to it by this resolution;

(*c*) The Security Council determine as a threat to the peace, breach of the peace or act of aggression, in accordance with Article 39 of the Charter, any attempt to alter by force the settlement envisaged by this resolution;

(*d*) The Trusteeship Council be informed of the responsibilities envisaged for it in this plan:

Calls upon the inhabitants of Palestine to take such steps as may be necessary on their part to put this plan into effect;

Appeals to all Governments and all peoples to refrain from taking any action which might hamper or delay the carrying out of these recommendations, and

Authorizes the Secretary-General to reimburse travel and subsistence expenses of the members of the Commission referred to in Part I, Section B, paragraph 1 below, on such basis and in such form as he may determine most appropriate in the circumstances, and to provide the Commission with the necessary staff to assist in carrying out the functions assigned to the Commission by the General Assembly.

B

The General Assembly

Authorizes the Secretary-General to draw from the Working Capital Fund a sum not to exceed $2,000,000 for the purposes set forth in the last paragraph of the resolution on the future government of Palestine.

Hundred and twenty-eighth plenary meeting on 29 November 1947.

At its hundred and twenty-eighth plenary meeting on 29 November 1947 the General Assembly, in accordance with the terms of the above resolution, elected the following members of the United Nations Commission on Palestine:

BOLIVIA, CZECHOSLOVAKIA, DENMARK, PANAMA and PHILIPPINES.

PLAN OF PARTITION WITH ECONOMIC UNION

Part I
Future constitution and government of Palestine

A. TERMINATION OF MANDATE, PARTITION AND INDEPENDENCE

1. The Mandate for Palestine shall terminate as soon as possible but in any case not later than 1 August 1948.

2. The armed forces of the mandatory Power shall be progressively withdrawn from Palestine, the withdrawal to be completed as soon as possible but in any case not later than 1 August 1948.

The mandatory Power shall advise the Commission, as far in advance as possible, of its intention to terminate the Mandate and to evacuate each area.

The mandatory Power shall use its best endeavours to ensure that an area situated in the territory of the Jewish State, including a seaport and hinterland adequate to provide facilities for a substantial immigration, shall be evacuated at the earliest possible date and in any event not later than 1 February 1948.

3. Independent Arab and Jewish States and the Special International Regime for the City of Jerusalem, set forth in part III of this plan, shall come into existence in Palestine two months after the evacuation of the armed forces of the mandatory Power has been completed but in any case not later than 1 October 1948. The boundaries of the Arab State, the Jewish State, and the City of Jerusalem shall be as described in parts II and III below.

4. The period between the adoption by the General Assembly of its recommendation on the question of Palestine and the establishment of the independence of the Arab and Jewish States shall be a transitional period.

B. STEPS PREPARATORY TO INDEPENDENCE

1. A Commission shall be set up consisting of one representative of each of five Member States. The Members represented on the Commission shall be elected by the General Assembly on as broad a basis, geographically and otherwise, as possible.

2. The administration of Palestine shall, as the mandatory Power withdraws its armed forces, be progressively turned over to the Commission; which shall act in conformity with the recommendations of the General Assembly, under the guidance of the Security Council. The mandatory Power shall to the fullest possible extent co-ordinate its plans for withdrawal with the plans of the Commission to take over and administer areas which have been evacuated.

In the discharge of this administrative responsibility the Commission shall have authority to issue necessary regulations and take other measures as required.

The mandatory Power shall not take any action to prevent, obstruct or delay the implementation by the Commission of the measures recommended by the General Assembly.

3. On its arrival in Palestine the Commission shall proceed to carry out measures for the establishment of the frontiers of the Arab and Jewish States and the City of Jerusalem in accordance with the general lines of the recommendations of the General Assembly on the partition of Palestine. Nevertheless, the boundaries as described in part II of this plan are to be modified in such a way that village areas as a rule will not

be divided by state boundaries unless pressing reasons make that necessary.

4. The Commission, after consultation with the democratic parties and other public organizations of the Arab and Jewish States, shall select and establish in each State as rapidly as possible a Provisional Council of Government. The activities of both the Arab and Jewish Provisional Councils of Government shall be carried out under the general direction of the Commission.

If by 1 April 1948 a Provisional Council of Government cannot be selected for either of the States, or, if selected, cannot carry out its functions, the Commission shall communicate that fact to the Security Council for such action with respect to that State as the Security Council may deem proper, and to the Secretary-General for communication to the Members of the United Nations.

5. Subject to the provisions of these recommendations, during the transitional period the Provisional Councils of Government, acting under the Commission, shall have full authority in the areas under their control, including authority over matters of immigration and land regulation.

6. The Provisional Council of Government of each State, acting under the Commission, shall progressively receive from the Commission full responsibility for the administration of that State in the period between the termination of the Mandate and the establishment of the State's independence.

7. The Commission shall instruct the Provisional Councils of Government of both the Arab and Jewish States, after their formation, to proceed to the establishment of administrative organs of government, central and local.

8. The Provisional Council of Government of each State shall, within the shortest time possible, recruit an armed militia from the residents of that State, sufficient in number to maintain internal order and to prevent frontier clashes.

This armed militia in each State shall, for operational purposes, be under the command of Jewish or Arab officers resident in that State, but general political and military control, including the choice of the militia's High Command, shall be exercised by the Commission.

9. The Provisional Council of Government of each State shall, not later than two months after the withdrawal of the armed forces of the mandatory Power, hold elections to the Constituent Assembly which shall be conducted on democratic lines.

The election regulations in each State shall be drawn up by the Provisional Council of Government and approved by the Commission. Qualified voters for each State for this election shall be persons over eighteen years of age who are: (a) Palestinian citizens residing in that State and (b) Arabs and Jews residing in the State, although not Palestinian citizens, who, before voting, have signed a notice of intention to become citizens of such State.

Arabs and Jews residing in the City of Jerusalem who have signed a notice of intention to become citizens, the Arabs of the Arab State and the Jews of the Jewish State, shall be entitled to vote in the Arab and Jewish States respectively.

Women may vote and be elected to the Constituent Assemblies.

During the transitional period no Jew shall be permitted to establish residence in the area of the proposed Arab State, and no Arab shall be permitted to establish residence in the area of the proposed Jewish State, except by special leave of the Commission.

10. The Constituent Assembly of each State shall draft a democratic constitution for its State and choose a provisional government to succeed the Provisional Council of Government appointed by the Commission. The constitutions of the States shall embody chapters 1 and 2 of the Declaration provided for in section C below and include *inter alia* provisions for:

(a) Establishing in each State a legislative body elected by universal suffrage and by secret ballot on the basis of proportional representation, and an executive body responsible to the legislature;

(b) Settling all international disputes in which the State may be involved by peaceful means in such a manner that international peace and security, and justice, are not endangered;

(c) Accepting the obligation of the State to refrain in its international relations from the threat or use of force against the territorial integrity or political independence of any State, or in any other manner inconsistent with the purposes of the United Nations;

(d) Guaranteeing to all persons equal and non-discriminatory rights in civil, political, economic and religious matters and the enjoyment of human rights and fundamental freedoms, including freedom of religion, language, speech and publication, education, assembly and association;

(e) Preserving freedom of transit and visit for all residents and citizens of the other State in Palestine and the City of Jerusalem, subject to considerations of national security, provided that each State shall control residence within its borders.

11. The Commission shall appoint a preparatory economic commission of three members to make whatever arrangements are possible for economic co-operation, with a view to establishing, as soon as practicable, the Economic Union and the Joint Economic Board, as provided in section D below.

12. During the period between the adoption of the recommendations on the question of Palestine by the General Assembly and the termination of the Mandate, the mandatory Power in Palestine shall maintain full responsibility for administration in areas from which it has not withdrawn its armed forces. The Commission shall assist the mandatory Power in the carrying out of these functions. Similarly the mandatory Power shall co-operate with the Commission in the execution of its functions.

13. With a view to ensuring that there shall be continuity in the functioning of administrative services and that, on the withdrawal of the armed forces of the mandatory Power, the whole administration shall be in the charge of the Provisional Councils and the Joint Economic Board, respectively, acting under the Commission, there shall be a progressive transfer, from the mandatory Power to the Commission, of responsibility for all the functions of government, including that of maintaining law and order in the areas from which the forces of the mandatory Power have been withdrawn.

14. The Commission shall be guided in its activities by the recommendations of the General Assembly and by such instructions as the Security Council may consider necessary to issue.

The measures taken by the Commission, within the recommendations of the General Assembly, shall become immediately effective unless the Commission has previously received contrary instructions from the Security Council.

The Commission shall render periodic monthly progress reports, or more frequently if desirable, to the Security Council.

15. The Commission shall make its final report to the next regular session of the General Assembly and to the Security Council simultaneously.

C. DECLARATION

A declaration shall be made to the United Nations by the provisional government of each proposed State before independence. It shall contain *inter alia* the following clauses:

The stipulations contained in the declaration are recognized as fundamental laws of the State and no law, regulation or official action shall conflict or interfere with these stipulations, nor shall any law, regulation or official action prevail over them.

CHAPTER 1

Holy Places, religious buildings and sites

1. Existing rights in respect of Holy Places and religious buildings or sites shall not be denied or impaired.

2. In so far as Holy Places are concerned, the liberty of access, visit and transit shall be guaranteed, in conformity with existing rights, to all residents and citizens of the other State and of the City of Jerusalem, as well as to aliens, without distinction as to nationality, subject to requirements of national security, public order and decorum.

Similarly, freedom of worship shall be guaranteed in conformity with existing rights, subject to the maintenance of public order and decorum.

3. Holy Places and religious buildings or sites shall be preserved. No act shall be permitted which may in any way impair their sacred character. If at any time it appears to the Government that any particular Holy Place, religious building or site is in need of urgent repair, the Government may call upon the community or communities concerned to carry out such repair. The Government may carry it out itself at the expense of the community or communities concerned if no action is taken within a reasonable time.

4. No taxation shall be levied in respect of any Holy Place, religious building or site which was exempt from taxation on the date of the creation of the State.

No change in the incidence of such taxation shall be made which would either discriminate between the owners or occupiers of Holy Places, religious buildings or sites, or would place such owners or occupiers in a position less favourable in relation to the general incidence of taxation than existed at the time of the adoption of the Assembly's recommendations.

5. The Governor of the City of Jerusalem shall have the right to determine whether the provisions of the Constitution of the State in relation to Holy Places, religious buildings and sites within the borders of the State and the religious rights appertaining thereto, are being properly applied and respected, and to make decisions on the basis of existing rights in cases of disputes which may arise between the different

religious communities or the rites of a religious community with respect to such places, buildings and sites. He shall receive full co-operation and such privileges and immunities as are necessary for the exercise of his functions in the State.

CHAPTER 2

Religious and minority rights

1. Freedom of conscience and the free exercise of all forms of worship, subject only to the maintenance of public order and morals, shall be ensured to all.

2. No discrimination of any kind shall be made between the inhabitants on the ground of race, religion, language or sex.

3. All persons within the jurisdiction of the State shall be entitled to equal protection of the laws.

4. The family law and personal status of the various minorities and their religious interests, including endowments, shall be respected.

5. Except as may be required for the maintenance of public order and good government, no measure shall be taken to obstruct or interfere with the enterprise of religious or charitable bodies of all faiths or to discriminate against any representative or member of these bodies on the ground of his religion or nationality.

6. The State shall ensure adequate primary and secondary education for the Arab and Jewish minority, respectively, in its own language and its cultural traditions.

The right of each community to maintain its own schools for the education of its own members in its own language, while conforming to such educational requirements of a general nature as the State may impose, shall not be denied or impaired. Foreign educational establishments shall continue their activity on the basis of their existing rights.

7. No restriction shall be imposed on the free use by any citizen of the State of any language in private intercourse, in commerce, in religion, in the Press or in publications of any kind, or at public meetings.[1]

8. No expropriation of land owned by an Arab in the Jewish State (by a Jew in the Arab State)[2] shall be allowed except for public purposes. In all cases of expropriation full compensation as fixed by the Supreme Court shall be paid previous to dispossession.

---

[1] The following stipulation shall be added to the declaration concerning the Jewish State: "In the Jewish State adequate facilities shall be given to Arabic-speaking citizens for the use of their language, either orally or in writing, in the legislature, before the Courts and in the administration."

[2] In the declaration concerning the Arab State, the words "by an Arab in the Jewish State" should be replaced by the words "by a Jew in the Arab State".

CHAPTER 3

Citizenship, international conventions and financial obligations

1. *Citizenship.* Palestinain citizens residing in Palestine outside the City of Jerusalem, as well as Arabs and Jews who, not holding Palestinian citizenship, reside in Palestine outside the City of Jerusalem shall, upon the recognition of independence, become citizens of the State in which they are resident and enjoy full civil and political rights. Persons over the age of eighteen years may opt, within one year from the date of recognition of independence of the State in which they reside, for citizenship of the other State, providing that no Arab residing in the area of the proposed Arab State shall have the right to opt for citizenship in the proposed Jewish State and no Jew residing in the proposed Jewish State shall have the right to opt for citizenship in the proposed Arab State. The exercise of this right of option will be taken to include the wives and children under eighteen years of age of persons so opting.

Arabs residing in the area of the proposed Jewish State and Jews residing in the area of the proposed Arab State who have signed a notice of intention to opt for citizenship of the other State shall be eligible to vote in the elections to the Constituent Assembly of that State, but not in the elections to the Constituent Assembly of the State in which they reside.

2. *International conventions.* (*a*) The State shall be bound by all the international agreements and conventions, both general and special, to which Palestine has become a party. Subject to any right of denunciation provided for therein, such agreements and conventions shall be respected by the State throughout the period for which they were concluded.

(*b*) Any dispute about the applicability and continued validity of international conventions or treaties signed or adhered to by the mandatory Power on behalf of Palestine shall be referred to the International Court of Justice in accordance with the provisions of the Statute of the Court.

3. *Financial obligations.* (*a*) The State shall respect and fulfil all financial obligations of whatever nature assumed on behalf of Palestine by the mandatory Power during the exercise of the Mandate and recognized by the State. This provision includes the right of public servants to pensions, compensation or gratuities.

(*b*) These obligations shall be fulfilled through participation in the Joint Economic Board in respect of those obligations applicable to

Palestine as a whole, and individually in respect of those applicable to, and fairly apportionable between, the States.

(*c*) A Court of Claims, affiliated with the Joint Economic Board, and composed of one member appointed by the United Nations, one representative of the United Kingdom and one representative of the State concerned, should be established. Any dispute between the United Kingdom and the State respecting claims not recognized by the latter should be referred to that Court.

(*d*) Commercial concessions granted in respect of any part of Palestine prior to the adoption of the resolution by the General Assembly shall continue to be valid according to their terms, unless modified by agreement between the concession-holder and the State.

CHAPTER 4

Miscellaneous provisions

1. The provisions of chapters 1 and 2 of the declaration shall be under the guarantee of the United Nations, and no modifications shall be made in them without the assent of the General Assembly of the United Nations. Any Member of the United Nations shall have the right to bring to the attention of the General Assembly any infraction or danger of infraction of any of these stipulations, and the General Assembly may thereupon make such recommendations as it may deem proper in the circumstances.

2. Any dispute relating to the application or the interpretation of this declaration shall be referred, at the request of either party, to the International Court of Justice, unless the parties agreed to another mode of settlement.

D. ECONOMIC UNION AND TRANSIT

1. The Provisional Council of Goverment of each State shall enter into an undertaking with respect to Economic Union and Transit. This undertaking shall be drafted by the Commission provided for in section B, paragraph 1, utilizing to the greatest possible extent the advice and co-operation of representative organizations and bodies from each of the proposed States. It shall contain provisions to establish the Economic Union of Palestine and provide for other matters of common interest. If by 1 April 1948 the Provisional Councils of Government have not entered into the undertaking, the undertaking shall be put into force by the Commission.

The Economic Union of Palestine

2. The objectives of the Economic Union of Palestine shall be:

(*a*) A customs union;

(*b*) A joint currency system providing for a single foreign exchange rate;

(*c*) Operation in the common interest on a non-discriminatory basis of railways; inter-State highways; postal, telephone and telegraphic services, and ports and airports involved in international trade and commerce;

(*d*) Joint economic development, especially in respect of irrigation, land reclamation and soil conservation;

(*e*) Access for both States and for the City of Jerusalem on a non-discriminatory basis to water and power facilities.

3. There shall be established a Joint Economic Board, which shall consist of three representatives of each of the two States and three foreign members appointed by the Economic and Social Council of the United Nations. The foreign members shall be appointed in the first instance for a term of three years; they shall serve as individuals and not as representatives of States.

4. The functions of the Joint Economic Board shall be to implement either directly or by delegation the measures necessary to realize the objectives of the Economic Union. It shall have all powers of organization and administration necessary to fulfil its functions.

5. The States shall bind themselves to put into effect the decisions of the Joint Economic Board. The Board's decisions shall be taken by a majority vote.

6. In the event of failure of a State to take the necessary action the Board may, by a vote of six members, decide to withhold an appropriate portion of that part of the customs revenue to which the State in question is entitled under the Economic Union. Should the State persist in its failure to co-operate, the Board may decide by a simple majority vote upon such further sanctions, including disposition of funds which it has withheld, as it may deem appropriate.

7. In relation to economic development, the functions of the Board shall be the planning, investigation and encouragement of joint development projects, but it shall not undertake such projects except with the assent of both States and the City of Jerusalem, in the event that Jerusalem is directly involved in the development project.

8. In regard to the joint currency system the currencies circulating in the two States and the City of Jerusalem shall be issued under the authority of the Joint Economic Board, which shall be the sole issuing authority and which shall determine the reserves to be held against such currencies.

9. So far as is consistent with paragraph 2 (*b*) above, each State may operate its own central bank, control its own fiscal and credit policy, its foreign exchange receipts and expenditures, the grant of import licenses, and may conduct international financial operations on its own faith and credit. During the first two years after the termination of the Mandate, the Joint Economic Board shall have the authority to take such measures as may be necessary to ensure that—to the extent that the total foreign exchange revenues of the two States from the export of goods and services permit, and provided that each State takes appropriate measures to conserve its own foreign exchange resources—each State shall have available, in any twelve months' period, foreign exchange sufficient to assure the supply of quantities of imported goods and services for consumption in its territory equivalent to the quantities of such goods and services consumed in that territory in the twelve months' period ending 31 December 1947.

10. All economic authority not specifically vested in the Joint Economic Board is reserved to each State.

11. There shall be a common customs tariff with complete freedom of trade between the States, and between the States and the City of Jerusalem.

12. The tariff schedules shall be drawn up by a Tariff Commission, consisting of representatives of each of the States in equal numbers, and shall be submitted to the Joint Economic Board for approval by a majority vote. In case of disagreement in the Tariff Commission, the Joint Economic Board shall arbitrate the points of difference. In the event that the Tariff Commission fails to draw up any schedule by a date to be fixed, the Joint Economic Board shall determine the tariff schedule.

13. The following items shall be a first charge on the customs and other common revenue of the Joint Economic Board:

(*a*) The expenses of the customs service and of the operation of the joint services;

(*b*) The administrative expenses of the Joint Economic Board;

(*c*) The financial obligations of the Administration of Palestine consisting of:

(*i*) The service of the outstanding public debt;

(*ii*) The cost of superannuation benefits, now being paid or falling due in the future, in accordance with the rules and to the extent established by paragraph 3 of chapter 3 above.

14. After these obligations have been met in full, the surplus revenue from the customs and other common services shall be divided in the following manner: not less than 5 per cent and not more than 10 per cent to the City of Jerusalem; the residue shall be allocated to each State by the Joint Economic Board equitably, with the objective of maintaining a sufficient and suitable level of government and social services in each State, except that the share of either State shall not exceed the amount of that State's contribution to the revenues of the Economic Union by more than approximately four million pounds in any year. The amount granted may be adjusted by the Board according to the price level in relation to the prices prevailing at the time of the establishment of the Union. After five years, the principles of the distribution of the joint revenues may be revised by the Joint Economic Board on a basis of equity.

15. All international conventions and treaties affecting customs tariff rates, and those communications services under the jurisdiction of the Joint Economic Board, shall be entered into by both States. In these matters, the two States shall be bound to act in accordance with the majority vote of the Joint Economic Board.

16. The Joint Economic Board shall endeavour to secure for Palestine's exports fair and equal access to world markets.

17. All enterprises operated by the Joint Economic Board shall pay fair wages on a uniform basis.

Freedom of transit and visit

18. The undertaking shall contain provisions preserving freedom of transit and visit for all residents or citizens of both States and of the City of Jerusalem, subject to security considerations; provided that each State and the City shall control residence within its borders.

Termination, modification and interpretation of the undertaking

19. The undertaking and any treaty issuing therefrom shall remain in force for a period of ten years. It shall continue in force until notice of termination, to take effect two years thereafter, is given by either of the parties.

20. During the initial ten-year period, the undertaking and any treaty issuing therefrom may not be modified except by consent of both parties and with the approval of the General Assembly.

21. Any dispute relating to the application or the interpretation of the undertaking and any treaty issuing therefrom shall be referred, at the request of either party, to the International Court of Justice, unless the parties agree to another mode of settlement.

E. ASSETS

1. The movable assets of the Administration of Palestine shall be allocated to the Arab and Jewish States and the City of Jerusalem on an equitable basis. Allocations should be made by the United Nations Commission referred to in section B, paragraph 1, above. Immovable assets shall become the property of the government of the territory in which they are situated.

2. During the period between the appointment of the United Nations Commission and the termination of the Mandate, the mandatory Power shall, except in respect of ordinary operations, consult with the Commission on any measure which it may contemplate involving the liquidation, disposal or encumbering of the assets of the Palestine Government, such as the accumulated treasury surplus, the proceeds of Government bond issues, State lands or any other asset.

F. ADMISSION TO MEMBERSHIP IN THE UNITED NATIONS

When the independence of either the Arab or the Jewish State as envisaged in this plan has become effective and the declaration and undertaking, as envisaged in this plan, have been signed by either of them, sympathetic consideration should be given to its application for admission to membership in the United Nations in accordance with Article 4 of the Charter of the United Nations.

Part II
Boundaries[3]

A. THE ARAB STATE

The area of the Arab State in Western Galilee is bounded on the west by the Mediterranean and on the north by the frontier of the Lebanon from Ras en Naqura to a point north of Saliha. From there the

---

[3] The boundary lines described in part II are indicated in Annex A. The base map used in marking and describing this boundary is "Palestine 1:250,000" published by the Survey of Palestine, 1946.

boundary proceeds southwards, leaving the built-up area of Saliha in the Arab State, to join the southernmost point of this village. Thence it follows the western boundary line of the villages of 'Alma, Rihaniya and Teitaba, thence following the northern boundary line of Meirun village to join the Acre-Safad sub-district boundary line. It follows this line to a point west of Es Sammu'i village and joins it again at the northernmost point of Farradiya. Thence it follows the sub-district boundary line to the Acre-Safad main road. From here it follows the western boundary of Kafr I'nan village until it reaches the Tiberias-Acre sub-district boundary line, passing to the west of the junction of the Acre-Safad and Lubiya-Kafr I'nan roads. From the south-west corner of Kafr I'nan village the boundary line follows the western boundary of the Tiberias sub-district to a point close to the boundary line between the villages of Maghar and Eilabun, thence bulging out to the west to include as much of the eastern part of the plain of Battuf as is necessary for the reservoir proposed by the Jewish Agency for the irrigation of lands to the south and east.

The boundary rejoins the Tiberias sub-district boundary at a point on the Nazareth-Tiberias road south-east of the built-up area of Tur'an; thence it runs southwards, at first following the sub-district boundary and then passing between the Kadoorie Agricultural School and Mount Tabor, to a point due south at the base of Mount Tabor. From here it runs due west, parallel to the horizontal grid line 230, to the north-east corner of the village lands of Tel Adashim. It then runs to the north-west corner of these lands, whence it turns south and west so as to include in the Arab State the sources of the Nazareth water supply in Yafa village. On reaching Ginneiger it follows the eastern, northern and western boundaries of the lands of this village to their south-west corner, whence it proceeds in a straight line to a point on the Haifa-Afula railway on the boundary between the villages of Sarid and El Mujeidil. This is the point of intersection.

The south-western boundary of the area of the Arab State in Galilee takes a line from this point, passing northwards along the eastern boundaries of Sarid and Gevat to the north-eastern corner of Nahalal, proceeding thence across the land of Kefar ha Horesh to a central point on the southern boundary of the village of 'Ilut, thence westwards along that village boundary to the eastern boundary of Beit Lahm, thence northwards and north-eastwards along its western boundary to the north-eastern corner of Waldheim and thence north-westwards across the village lands of Shafa 'Amr to the south-eastern corner of Ramat

Yohanan. From here it runs due north-north-east to a point on the Shafa 'Amr-Haifa road, west of its junction with the road to I'Billin. From there it proceeds north-east to a point on the southern boundary of I'Billin situated to the west of the I'Billin-Birwa road. Thence along that boundary to its westernmost point, whence it turns to the north, follows across the village land of Tamra to the north-westernmost corner and along the western boundary of Julis until it reaches the Acre-Safad road. It then runs westwards along the southern side of the Safad-Acre road to the Galilee-Haifa District boundary, from which point it follows that boundary to the sea.

The boundary of the hill country of Samaria and Judea starts on the Jordan River at the Wadi Malih south-east of Beisan and runs due west to meet the Beisan-Jericho road and then follows the western side of that road in a north-westerly direction to the junction of the boundaries of the sub-districts of Beisan, Nablus, and Jenin. From that point it follows the Nablus-Jenin sub-district boundary westwards for a distance of about three kilometres and then turns north-westwards, passing to the east of the built-up areas of the villages of Jalbun and Faqqu'a, to the boundary of the sub-districts of Jenin and Beisan at a point north-east of Nuris. Thence it proceeds first north-westwards to a point due north of the built-up area of Zir'in and then westwards to the Afula-Jenin railway, thence northwestwards along the district boundary line to the point of intersection on the Hejaz railway. From here the boundary runs south-westwards, including the built-up area and some of the land of the village of Kh Lid in the Arab State to cross the Haifa-Jenin road at a point on the district boundary between Haifa and Samaria west of El Mansi. It follows this boundary to the southernmost point of the village of El Buteimat. From here it follows the northern and eastern boundaries of the village of Ar'ara, rejoining the Haifa-Samaria district boundary at Wadi'Ara, and thence proceeding south-south-westwards in an approximately straight line joining up with the western boundary of Qaqun to a point east of the railway line on the eastern boundary of Qaqun village. From here it runs along the railway line some distance to the east of it to a point just east of the Tulkarm railway station. Thence the boundary follows a line half-way between the railway and the Tulkarm-Qalqiliya-Jaljuliya and Ras el Ein road to a point just east of Ras el Ein station, whence it proceeds along the rail-way some distance to the east of it to the point on the railway line south of the junction of the Haifa-Lydda and Beit Nabala lines, whence it proceeds along the southern border of Lydda airport to its south-west

corner, thence in a south-westerly direction to a point just west of the
built-up area of Sarafand el'Amar, whence it turns south, passing just to
the west of the built-up area of Abu el Fadil to the north-east corner of
the lands of Beer Ya'Aqov. (The boundary line should be so demarcated
as to allow direct access from the Arab State to the airport.) Thence the
boundary line follows the western and southern boundaries of Ramle
village, to the north-east corner of El Na'ana village, thence in a straight
line to the southernmost point of El Barriya, along the eastern
boundary of that village and the southern boundary of 'Innaba village.
Thence it turns north to follow the southern side of the Jaffa-Jerusalem
road until El Qubab, whence it follows the road to the boundary of
Abu Shusha. It runs along the eastern boundaries of Abu Shusha,
Seidun, Hulda to the southernmost point of Hulda, thence westwards
in a straight line to the northeastern corner of Umm Kalkha, thence
following the northern boundaries of Umm Kalkha, Qazaza and the
northern and western boundaries of Mukhezin to the Gaza District
boundary and thence runs across the village lands of El Mismiya, El
Kabira, and Yasur to the southern point of intersection, which is
midway between the built-up areas of Yasur and Batani Sharqi.

From the southern point of intersection the boundary lines run
north-westwards between the villages of Gan Yavne and Barqa to the
set at a point half way between Nabi Yunis and Minat el Qila, and
south-eastwards to a point west of Qastina, whence it turns in a south-
westerly direction, passing to the east of the built-up areas of Es Sawafi
Esh Sharqiya and Ibdis. From the south-east corner of Ibdis village it
runs to a point south-west of the built-up area of Beit 'Affa, crossing
the Hebron-El Majdal road just to the west of the built-up area of Iraq
Suweidan. Thence it proceeds southwards along the western village
boundary of El Faluja to the Beersheba sub-district boundary. It then
runs across the tribal lands of 'Arab el Jubarat to a point on the
boundary between the sub-districts of Beersheba and Hebron north of
Kh. Khuweilifa, whence it proceeds in a south-westerly direction to a
point on the Beersheba-Gaza main road two kilometres to the north-
west of the town. It then turns south-eastwards to reach Wadi Sab' at a
point situated one kilometre to the west of it. From here it turns north-
eastwards and proceeds along Wadi Sab' and along the Beersheba-
Hebron road for a distance of one kilometre, whence it turns eastwards
and runs in a straight line to Kh. Kuseifa to join the Beersheba-Hebron
sub-district boundary. It then follows the Beersheba-Hebron boundary
eastwards to a point north of Ras Ez Zuweira, only departing from it so

as to cut across the base of the indentation between vertical grid lines 150 and 160.

About five kilometres north-east of Ras ez Zuweira it turns north, excluding from the Arab State a strip along the coast of the Dead Sea not more than seven kilometres in depth, as far as Ein Geddi, whence it turns due east to join the Transjordan frontier in the Dead Sea.

The northern boundary of the Arab section of the coastal plain runs from a point between Minat el Qila and Nabi Yunis, passing between the built-up areas of Gan Yavne and Barqa to the point of intersection. From here it turns south-westwards, running across the lands of Batani Sharqi, along the eastern boundary of the lands of Beit Daras and across the lands of Julis, leaving the built-up areas of Batani Sharqi and Julis to the westwards, as far as the north-west corner of the lands of Beit Tima. Thence it runs east of El Jiya across the village lands of El Barbara along the eastern boundaries of the villages of Beit Jirja, Deir Suneid and Dimra. From the south-east corner of Dimra the boundary passes across the lands of Beit Hanun, leaving the Jewish lands of Nir-Am to the eastwards. From the south-east corner of Beit Hanun the line runs south-west to a point south of the parallel grid line 100, then turns north-west for two kilometres, turning again in a south-westerly direction and continuing in an almost straight line to the north-west corner of the village lands of Kirbet Ikhza'a. From there it follows the boundary line of this village to its southernmost point. It then runs in a southerly direction along the vertical grid line 90 to its junction with the horizontal grid line 70. It then turns south-eastwards to Kh. el Ruheiba and then proceeds in a southerly direction to a point known as El Baha, beyond which it crosses the Beersheba-El 'Auja main road to the west of Kh. el Mushrifa. From there it joins Wadi El Zaiyatin just to the west of El Subeita. From there it turns to the north-east and then to the south-east following this wadi and passes to the east of 'Abda to join Wadi Nafkh. It then bulges to the south-west along Wadi Nafkh, Wadi Ajrim and Wadi Lassan to the point where Wadi Lassan crosses the Egyptian frontier.

The area of the Arab enclave of Jaffa consists of that part of the town-planning area of Jaffa which lies to the west of the Jewish quarters lying south of Tel-Aviv, to the west of the continuation of Herzl street up to its junction with the Jaffa-Jerusalem road, to the south-west of the section of the Jaffa-Jerusalem road lying south-east of that junction, to the west of Miqve Yisrael lands, to the north-west of Holon local council area, to the north of the line linking up the north-west corner of

Holon with the north-east corner of Bat Yam local council area and to the north of Bat Yam local council area. The question of Karton quarter will be decided by the Boundary Commission, bearing in mind among other considerations the desirability of including the smallest possible number of its Arab inhabitants and the largest possible number of its Jewish inhabitants in the Jewish State.

B. THE JEWISH STATE

The north-eastern sector of the Jewish State (Eastern Galilee) is bounded on the north and west by the Lebanese frontier and on the east by the frontiers of Syria and Transjordan. It includes the whole of the Hula Basin, Lake Tiberias, the whole of the Beisan sub-district, the boundary line being extended to the crest of the Gilboa mountains and the Wadi Malih. From there the Jewish State extends north-west, following the boundary described in respect of the Arab State.

The Jewish section of the coastal plain extends from a point between Minat et Qila and Nabi Yunis in the Gaza sub-district and includes the towns of Haifa and Tel-Aviv, leaving Jaffa as an enclave of the Arab State. The eastern frontier of the Jewish State follows the boundary described in respect of the Arab State.

The Beersheba area comprises the whole of the Beersheba sub-district, including the Negeb and the eastern part of the Gaza sub-district, but excluding the town of Beersheba and those areas described in respect of the Arab State. It includes also a strip of land along the Dead Sea stretching from the Beersheba-Hebron sub-district boundary line to Ein Geddi, as described in respect of the Arab State.

C. THE CITY OF JERUSALEM

The boundaries of the City of Jerusalem are as defined in the recommendations on the City of Jerusalem. (See Part III, Section B, below).

Part III
City of Jerusalem

A. SPECIAL REGIME

The City of Jerusalem shall be established as a *corpus separatum* under a special international regime and shall be administered by the United Nations. The Trusteeship Council shall be designated to discharg the responsibilities of the Administering Authority on behalf of the United Nations.

B. BOUNDARIES OF THE CITY

The City of Jerusalem shall include the present municipality of Jerusalem plus the surrounding villages and towns, the most eastern of which shall be Abu Dis; the most southern, Bethlehem; the most western, Ein Karim (including also the built-up area of Motsa); and the most northern Shu'fat, as indicated on the attached sketch-map (annex B).

C. STATUTE OF THE CITY

The Trusteeship Council shall, within five months of the approval of the present plan, elaborate and approve a detailed Statute of the City which shall contain *inter alia* the substance of the following provisions:

1. Government machinery; special objectives.

The Administering Authority in discharging its administrative obligations shall pursue the following special objectives:

(*a*) To protect and to preserve the unique spiritual and religious interests located in the city of the three great monotheistic faiths throughout the world, Christian, Jewish and Moslem; to this end to ensure that order and peace, and especially religious peace, reign in Jerusalem;

(*b*) To foster co-operation among all the inhabitants of the city in their own interests as well as in order to encourage and support the peaceful development of the mutual relations between the two Palestinian peoples throughout the Holy Land; to promote the security, well-being and any constructive measures of development of the residents, having regard to the special circumstances and customs of the various peoples and communities.

2. Governor and administrative staff.

A Governor of the City of Jerusalem shall be appointed by the Trusteeship Council and shall be responsible to it. He shall be selected on the basis of special qualifications and without regard to nationality. He shall not, however, be a citizen of either State in Palestine.

The Governor shall represent the United Nations in the City and shall exercise on their behalf all powers of administration, including the conduct of external affairs. He shall be assisted by an administrative staff classed as international officers in the meaning of Article 100 of the Charter and chosen whenever practicable from the residents of the city and of the rest of Palestine on a non-discriminatory basis. A detailed plan for the organization of the administration of the city shall be submitted by the Governor to the Trusteeship Council and duly approved by it.

3. Local autonomy.

(a) The existing local autonomous units in the territory of the city (villages, townships and municipalities) shall enjoy wide powers of local government and administration.

(b) The Governor shall study and submit for the consideration and decision of the Trusteeship Council a plan for the establishment of special town units consisting, respectively, of the Jewish and Arab sections of new Jerusalem. The new town units shall continue to form part of the present municipality of Jerusalem.

4. Security measures.

(a) The City of Jerusalem shall be demilitarized; its neutrality shall be declared and preserved, and no para-military formations, exercises or activities shall be permitted within its borders.

(b) Should the administration of the City of Jerusalem be seriously obstructed or prevented by the non-co-operation or interference of one or more sections of the population, the Governor shall have authority to take such measures as may be necessary to restore the effective functioning of the administration.

(c) To assist in the maintenance of internal law and order and especially for the protection of the Holy Places and religious buildings and sites in the city, the Governor shall organize a special police force of adequate strength, the members of which shall be recruited outside of Palestine. The Governor shall be empowered to direct such budgetary provision as may be necessary for the maintenance of this force.

5. Legislative organization.

A Legislative Council, elected by adult residents of the city irrespective of nationality on the basis of universal and secret suffrage and proportional representation, shall have powers of legislation and taxation. No legislative measures shall, however, conflict or interfere with the provisions which will be set forth in the Statute of the City, nor shall any law, regulation, or official action prevail over them. The Statute shall grant to the Governor a right of vetoing bills inconsistent with the provisions referred to in the preceding sentence. It shall also empower him to promulgate temporary ordinances in case the Council fails to adopt in time a bill deemed essential to the normal functioning of the administration.

6. Administration of justice.

The Statute shall provide for the establishment of an independent judiciary system, including a court of appeal. All the inhabitants of the City shall be subject to it.

7. Economic union and economic regime.

The City of Jerusalem shall be included in the Economic Union of Palestine and be bound by all stipulations of the undertaking and of any treaties issued therefrom, as well as by the decisions of the Joint Economic Board. The headquarters of the Economic Board shall be established in the territory of the City.

The Statute shall provide for the regulation of economic matters not falling within the regime of the Economic Union, on the basis of equal treatment and non-discrimination for all Members of the United Nations and their nationals.

8. Freedom of transit and visit; control of residents.

Subject to considerations of security, and of economic welfare as determined by the Governor under the directions of the Trusteeship Council, freedom of entry into, and residence within, the borders of the City shall be guaranteed for the residents or citizens of the Arab and Jewish States. Immigration into, and residence within, the borders of the city for nationals of other States shall be controlled by the Governor under the directions of the Trusteeship Council.

9. Relations with the Arab and Jewish States.

Representatives of the Arab and Jewish States shall be accredited to the Governor of the City and charged with the protection of the interests of their States and nationals in connexion with the international administration of the City.

10. Official languages.

Arabic and Hebrew shall be the official languages of the city. This will not preclude the adoption of one or more additional working languages, as may be required.

11. Citizenship.

All the residents shall become *ipso facto* citizens of the City of Jerusalem unless they opt for citizenship of the State of which they have been citizens or, if Arabs or Jews, have filed notice of intention to become citizens of the Arab or Jewish State respectively, according to part I, section B, paragraph 9, of this plan.

The Trusteeship Council shall make arrangements for consular protection of the citizens of the City outside its territory.

12. Freedoms of citizens.

(*a*) Subject only to the requirements of public order and morals, the inhabitants of the City shall be ensured the enjoyment of human rights and fundamental freedoms, including freedom of conscience, religion and worship, language, education, speech and Press, assembly and association, and petition.

(*b*) No discrimination of any kind shall be made between the inhabitants on the grounds of race, religion, language or sex.

(*c*) All persons within the City shall be entitled to equal protection of the laws.

(*d*) The family law and personal status of the various persons and communities and their religious interests, including endowments, shall be respected.

(*e*) Except as may be required for the maintenance of public order and good government, no measure shall be taken to obstruct or interfere with the enterprise of religious or charitable bodies of all faiths or to discriminate against any representative or member of these bodies on the ground of his religion or nationality.

(*f*) The City shall ensure adequate primary and secondary education for the Arab and Jewish communities respectively, in their own languages and in accordance with their cultural traditions.

The right of each community to maintain its own schools for the education of its own members in its own language, while conforming to such educational requirements of a general nature as the City may impose, shall not be denied or impaired. Foreign educational establishments shall continue their activity on the basis of their existing rights.

(*g*) No restriction shall be imposed on the free use by any inhabitant of the City of any language in private intercourse, in commerce, in religion, in the Press or in publications of any kind, or at public meetings.

13. Holy Places.

(*a*) Existing rights in respect of Holy Places and religious buildings or sites shall not be denied or impaired.

(*b*) Free access to the Holy Places and religious buildings or sites and the free exercise of worship shall be secured in conformity with existing rights and subject to the requirements of public order and decorum.

(*c*) Holy Places and religious buildings or sites shall be preserved. No act shall be permitted which may in any way impair their sacred character. If at any time it appears to the Governor that any particular Holy Place, religious building or site is in need or urgent repair, the Governor may call upon the community or communities concerned to carry out such repair. The Governor may carry it out himself at the expense of the community or communities concerned if no action is taken within a reasonable time.

(*d*) No taxation shall be levied in respect of any Holy Place, religious building or site which was exempt from taxation on the date of the creation of the City. No change in the incidence of such taxation shall be made which would either discriminate between the owners or occupiers of Holy Places, religious buildings or sites, or would place such owners or occupiers in a position less favourable in relation to the general incidence of taxation than existed at the time of the adoption of the Assembly's recommendations.

14. Special powers of the Governor in respect of the Holy Places, religious buildings and sites in the City and in any part of Palestine.

(*a*) The protection of the Holy Places, religious buildings and sites located in the City of Jerusalem shall be a special concern of the Governor.

(*b*) With relation to such places, buildings and sites in Palestine outside the city, the Governor shall determine, on the ground of powers granted to him by the Constitutions of both States, whether the provisions of the Constitutions of the Arab and Jewish States in Palestine dealing therewith and the religious rights appertaining thereto are being properly applied and respected.

(*c*) The Governor shall also be empowered to make decisions on the basis of existing rights in cases of disputes which may arise between the different religious communities or the rites of a religious community in respect of the Holy Places, religious buildings and sites in any part of Palestine.

In this task he may be assisted by a consultative council of representatives of different denominations acting in an advisory capacity.

D. DURATION OF THE SPECIAL REGIME

The Statute elaborated by the Trusteeship Council on the aforementioned principles shall come into force not later than 1 October

1948. It shall remain in force in the first instance for a period of ten years, unless the Trusteeship Council finds it necessary to undertake a re-examination of these provisions at an earlier date. After the expiration of this period the whole scheme shall be subject to re-examination by the Trusteeship Council in the light of the experience acquired with its functioning. The residents of the City shall be then free to express by means of a referendum their wishes as to possible modifications of the regime of the City.

Part IV
Capitulations

States whose nationals have in the past enjoyed in Palestine the privileges and immunities of foreigners, including the benefits of consular jurisdiction and protection, as formerly enjoyed by capitulation or usage in the Ottoman Empire, are invited to renounce any right pertaining to them to the re-establishment of such privileges and immunities in the proposed Arab and Jewish States and the City of Jerusalem.

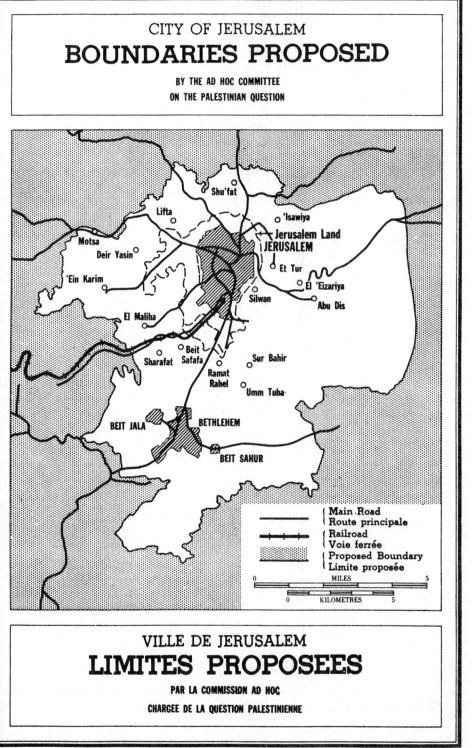

CITY OF JERUSALEM
BOUNDARIES PROPOSED
BY THE AD HOC COMMITTEE
ON THE PALESTINIAN QUESTION

VILLE DE JERUSALEM
LIMITES PROPOSEES
PAR LA COMMISSION AD HOC
CHARGEE DE LA QUESTION PALESTINIENNE

9. Declaration of the Establishment of the State of Israel, May 14, 1948*

*I Laws of the State of Israel 3-5 (1948).

ERETZ-ISRAEL[1] was the birthplace of the Jewish people. Here their spiritual, religious and political identity was shaped. Here they first attained to statehood, created cultural values of national and universal significance and gave to the world the eternal Book of Books.

After being forcibly exiled from their land, the people kept faith with it throughout their Dispersion and never ceased to pray and hope for their return to it and for the restoration in it of their political freedom.

Impelled by this historic and traditional attachment, Jews strove in every successive generation to re-establish themselves in their ancient homeland. In recent decades they returned in their masses. Pioneers, *ma'pilim*[2] and defenders, they made deserts bloom, revived the Hebrew language, built villages and towns, and created a thriving community, controlling its own economy and culture, loving peace but knowing how to defend itself, bringing the blessings of progress to all the country's inhabitants, and aspiring towards independent nationhood.

In the year 5657 (1897), at the summons of the spiritual father of the Jewish State, Theodore Herzl, the First Zionist Congress convened and proclaimed the right of the Jewish people to national rebirth in its own country.

This right was recognised in the Balfour Declaration of the 2nd November, 1917, and re-affirmed in the Mandate of the League of Nations which, in particular, gave international sanction to the historic connection between the Jewish people and Eretz-Israel and to the right of the Jewish people to rebuild its National Home.

The catastrophe which recently befell the Jewish people—the massacre of millions of Jews in Europe—was another clear demonstration of the urgency of solving the problem of its homelessness by re-establishing in Eretz-Israel the Jewish State, which would open the gates of the homeland wide to every Jew and confer upon the Jewish people the status of a fully-privileged member of the comity of nations.

Survivors of the Nazi holocaust in Europe, as well as Jews from other parts of the world, continued to migrate to Eretz-Israel, undaunted by difficulties, restrictions and dangers, and never ceased to assert their right to a life of dignity, freedom and honest toil in their national homeland.

In the Second World War, the Jewish community of this country contributed its full share to the struggle of the freedom and peace-loving

---

[1] *Eretz-Israel* (Hebrew)—the Land of Israel, Palestine.
[2] *Ma'pilim* (Hebrew)—immigrants coming to Eretz-Israel in defiance of restrictive legislation.

nations against the forces of Nazi wickedness and, by the blood of its soldiers and its war effort, gained the right to be reckoned among the peoples who founded the United Nations.

On the 29th November, 1947, the United Nations General Assembly passed a resolution calling for the establishment of a Jewish State in Eretz-Israel; the General Assembly required the inhabitants of Eretz-Israel to take such steps as were necessary on their part for the implementation of that resolution. This recognition by the United Nations of the right of the Jewish people to establish their State is irrevocable.

This right is the natural right of the Jewish people to be masters of their own fate, like all other nations, in their own sovereign State.

ACCORDINGLY WE, MEMBERS OF THE PEOPLE'S COUNCIL, REPRESENTATIVE OF THE JEWISH COMMUNITY OF ERETZ-ISRAEL AND OF THE ZIONIST MOVEMENT, ARE HERE ASSEMBLED ON THE DAY OF THE TERMINATION OF THE BRITISH MANDATE OVER ERETZ-ISRAEL AND, BY VIRTUE OF OUR NATURAL AND HISTORIC RIGHT AND ON THE STRENGTH OF THE REVOLUTION OF THE UNITED NATIONS GENERAL ASSEMBLY, HEREBY DECLARE THE ESTABLISHMENT OF A JEWISH STATE IN ERETZ-ISRAEL, TO BE KNOWN AS THE STATE OF ISRAEL.

WE DECLARE that, with effect from the moment of the termination of the Mandate, being tonight, the eve of Sabbath, the 6th Iyar, 5708 (15th May, 1948), until the establishment of the elected, regular authorities of the State in accordance with the Constitution which shall be adopted by the Elected Constituent Assembly not later than the 1st October 1948, the People's Council shall act as a Provisional Council of State, and its executive organ, the People's Administration, shall be the Provisional Government of the Jewish State, to be called "Israel."

THE STATE OF ISRAEL will be open for Jewish immigration and for the Ingathering of the Exiles; it will foster the development of the country for the benefit of all its inhabitants; it will be based on freedom, justice and peace as envisaged by the prophets of Israel; it will ensure complete equality of social and political rights to all its inhabitants irrespective of religion, race or sex; it will guarantee freedom of religion, conscience, language, education and culture; it will safeguard the Holy Places of all religions; and it will be faithful to the principles of the Charter of the United Nations.

THE STATE OF ISRAEL is prepared to cooperate with the agencies and representatives of the United Nations in implementing the resolution of the General Assembly of the 29th November, 1947, and will take steps to bring about the economic union of the whole of Eretz-Israel.

WE APPEAL to the United Nations to assist the Jewish people in the building-up of its State and to receive the State of Israel into the comity of nations.

WE APPEAL—in the very midst of the onslaught launched against us now for months—to the Arab inhabitants of the State of Israel to preserve peace and participate in the upbuilding of the State on the basis of full and equal citizenship and due representation in all its provisional and permanent institutions.

WE EXTEND our hand to all neighbouring states and their peoples in an offer of peace and good neighbourliness, and appeal to them to establish bonds of cooperation and mutual help with the sovereign Jewish people settled in its own land. The State of Israel is prepared to do its share in a common effort for the advancement of the entire Middle East.

WE APPEAL to the Jewish people throughout the Diaspora to rally round the Jews of Eretz-Israel in the tasks of immigration and upbuilding and to stand by them in the great struggle for the realization of the age-old dream—the redemption of Israel.

PLACING OUR TRUST IN THE ALMIGHTY, WE AFFIX OUR SIGNATURES TO THIS PROCLAMATION AT THIS SESSION OF THE PROVISIONAL COUNCIL OF STATE, ON THE SOIL OF THE HOMELAND, IN THE CITY OF TEL-AVIV, ON THIS SABBATH EVE, THE 5TH DAY OF IYAR, 5708 (14TH MAY, 1948).

David Ben-Gurion

Daniel Auster	Rachel Cohen	David Zvi Pinkas
Mordekhai Bentov	Rabbi Kalman	Aharon Zisling
Yitzchak Ben Zvi	Kahana	Moshe Kolodny
Eliyahu Berligne	Saadia Kobashi	Eliezer Kaplan
Fritz Bernstein	Rabbi Yitzchak	Abraham Katznelson
Rabbi Wolf Gold	Meir Levin	Felix Rosenblueth
Meir Grabovsky	Meir David	David Remez
Yitzchak Gruenbaum	Loewenstein	Berl Repetur
Dr. Abraham	Zvi Luria	Mordekhai Shattner
Granovsky	Golda Myerson	Ben Zion Sternberg
Eliyahu Dobkin	Nachum Nir	Bekhor Shitreet
Meir Wilner-Kovner	Zvi Segal	Moshe Shapira
Zerach Wahrhaftig	Rabbi Yehuda Leib	Moshe Shertok
Herzl Vardi	Hacohen Fishman	

10. Cablegram from the Secretary-General of the League of Arab States to the Secretary-General of the United Nations, May 15, 1948*

*U.N. Doc. S/745, reprinted in 3 U.N. SCOR, Supp. for May 1948, at 83-88.

15 May 1948

On the occasion of the intervention of Arab States in Palestine to restore law and order and to prevent disturbances prevailing in Palestine from spreading into their territories and to check further bloodshed, I have the honour to request your Excellency to bring following statement before General Assembly and Security Council.

1. Palestine was part of the Ottoman Empire subject to its rule of law and enjoying full representation in its parliament, the great majority of its population was composed of Arabs with a small minority of Jews enjoying all rights alike with all the remaining citizens and liable only to such charges as all others were. Never were they as minority the subject of any discrimination on account of their creed. Holy Places were protected and accessible to all without distinction.

2. The Arabs have constantly been seeking their freedom and independence; when the Second World War broke out and the Allies declared that they were fighting to restore freedom to the nations the Arabs sided with the Allies and placed all their means at their disposal and in fact fought with them for the realization of their national aspirations and their independence. Great Britain took upon herself the recognition of the independence of the Arab countries in Asia including Palestine. The Arabs' effort was felt and duly appreciated in winning victory.

3. Great Britain issued a declaration in 1917 in which expression was made of its sympathy with the establishment of a Jewish National Home in Palestine. When this was brought to the knowledge of the Arabs they did not fail to express their resentment and opposition to such expression of policy and when they protested formally to Great Britain the latter made the necessary reassurances with a confirmation of the view that such a declaration did not affect in any degree their rights nor their freedom and independence, and that the said declaration did not prejudice the political position of the Arabs of Palestine notwithstanding the illegality of the said declaration. The British Government's interpretation of it was that it meant no more than the establishment of a spiritual abode for the Jews in Palestine without there being any ulterior political motives such as the creation of a Jewish State, that being further the expressed views of the Jewish leaders at the time.

4. When the war ended Great Britain did not fulfil its pledges. Instead Palestine was placed under a Mandate entrusted to Great Britain. The terms of the Mandate provided for the safeguarding of the interests of the inhabitants of Palestine and their preparation for eventual independ-

ence to which they were entitled by virtue of the Covenant of the League of Nations which admitted that the inhabitants of Palestine were fit for it.

5. Great Britain however placed Palestine in such a position as made it possible for the Jews to flood the country with waves of immigrants and factually helped their establishment on the soil despite the saturation of the land with its population which did exceed the absorptive capacity of the country economically and otherwise, thereby neglecting the provided for interests and the rights of its lawful inhabitants. The Arabs used all means at all times to express their deep concern and anxiety at such a policy which they felt was undermining their future and their very existence. But at all such times they were met with utter disregard and harsh treatment such as jail, exile, etc.

6. And whereas Palestine is an Arab country falling in the heart of the Arab countries and attached to the Arab world with all bonds spiritual, historical, economical and strategical, the Arab States as well as Eastern countries, whether through their people or governments, could not but concern and interest themselves with the fate of Palestine. This is why they took upon themselves the task of handling its case before the international institutions generally and particularly before Great Britain, insisting upon a solution for the problem based upon undertaking given to them and upon democratic principles. A round-table conference was held early in 1939 in London in which the Arab States took part asking for the safeguarding of the independence of Arab Palestine as a whole. That conference resulted in the issue of the well-known White Paper in which Great Britain defined its policy towards Palestine, admitting its right to independence while laying down at the same time certain provisions for the exercise of such independence. Great Britain did therein further declare that its obligations regarding the establishment of the Jewish National Home have been completely fulfilled as the said National Home had been established. But unfortunately the underlying policy of the White Paper was not carried out, which led to an increasingly bad situation and, in fact, resulted in complete prejudice and disregard to Arab interests.

7. During the time that the Second World War was raging the respective Governments of the Arab States began to co-ordinate their views and actions for the useful purpose of better securing co-operation regarding not only their present and future but for playing their part in the establishment of lasting world-wide peace. The problem of Palestine did not at any time during their mutual consultations fail to absorb its due

share of attention and interest. It was a result of those consultations that then emerged the present Arab League as instrument for the realization of their own peace, security and welfare. The Arab League Charter declared that Palestine had become an independent country since its separation from the Ottoman Empire, but that all the appertaining external rights and privileges attendant upon formal independence had to be subdued temporarily for reasons beyond the will of its people. It was a happy coincidence which gave rise to the hopes of the Arab States then that at that time the United Nations was brought to existence soon after. And accordingly the Arab States unhesitatingly participated in its creation and membership out of deep belief in that institution, its ideals, and high aims.

8. Since then the Arab League, through its member States, unceasingly endeavoured by all its means, whether with the Mandatory or with the United Nations, to find a fair and just solution for the problem of Palestine, based on democratic principles and consistent with the provisions of the League of Nations Covenant as well as of the United Nations Charter, a solution which would be lasting and would ensure peace and security in the land leading to prosperity, but such solution invariably conflicted with opposition from Zionists and with their demands as they then started to openly declare their insistence upon a Jewish State and in fact bent upon full preparations with arms and fortifications to impose their own solution by force.

9. When the General Assembly made its recommendations on 29 November 1947 for the solution of the Palestine problem on the basis of partition providing for the establishment of two States, one Arab and one Jewish, with an international regime of trusteeship for the City of Jerusalem, the Arab States expressed the warning that such a solution was prejudicial to the rights of the Arab inhabitants of Palestine to independence and was contradictory to democratic principles and to the League of Nations as well as the United Nations Charter. The Arabs then rejected such a scheme declaring that it was not susceptible of execution by peaceful means and that its imposition by force constituted a threat to peace and security in this area.

The apprehensions of the Arab States proved to be well founded as the disturbances of which they had warned soon swept the country, and armed conflict took place between its two peoples who started to combat against each other and shed each other's blood. Consequently, the United Nations realized the mistake upon which the recommendation of partition was made and turned to search for an outlet.

10. Now that the Mandate over Palestine has come to an end, leaving no legally constituted authority behind in order to administer law and order in the country and afford the necessary and adequate protection to life and property, the Arab States declare as follows:

(*a*) The right to set up a Government in Palestine pertains to its inhabitants under the principles of self-determination recognized by the Covenant of the League of Nations as well as the United Nations Charter;

(*b*) Peace and order have been completely upset in Palestine, and, in consequence of Jewish aggression, approximately over a quarter of a million of the Arab population have been compelled to leave their homes and emigrate to neighbouring Arab countries. The prevailing events in Palestine exposed the concealed aggressive intentions of the Zionists and their imperialistic motives, as clearly shown in their acts committed upon those peaceful Arabs and villagers of Deer Yasheen, Tiberias, and other places, as well as by their encroachment upon the building and bodies of the inviolable consular codes, manifested by their attack upon the Consulate in Jerusalem.

(*c*) The Mandatory has already announced that on the termination of the Mandate it will no longer be responsible for the maintenance of law and order in Palestine except in the camps and areas actually occupied by its forces, and only to the extent necessary for the security of those forces and their withdrawal. This leaves Palestine absolutely without any administrative authority entitled to maintain, and capable of maintaining, a machinery of administration of the country adequate for the purpose of ensuring due protection of life and property. There is further the threat that this lawlessness may spread to the neighbouring Arab States where feeling is already very tense on account of the prevailing conditions in Palestine. The respective members of the Arab League, and as Members of the United Nations at the same time, feel gravely perturbed and deeply concerned over this situation.

(*d*) It was the sincere wish of the Arab States that the United Nations might succeed in arriving at a fair and just solution of the Palestine problem, thus establishing a lasting peace for the country under the precepts of the democratic principles and in conformity with the Covenant of the League of Nations and the United Nations Charter.

(*e*) They are responsible in any . . . by virtue of their responsibility as members of the Arab League which is a regional organization within the meaning of Chapter VIII of the Charter of the United Nations. The recent disturbances in Palestine further constitute a serious and direct threat to peace and security within the territories of the Arab States themselves. For these reasons, and considering that the security of Palestine is a sacred trust for them, and out of anxiousness to check the further deterioration of the prevailing conditions and to prevent the spread of disorder and lawlessness into the neighbouring Arab lands, and in order to fill the vacuum created by the termination of the Mandate and the failure to replace it by any legally constituted authority, the Arab Governments find themselves compelled to intervene for the sole purpose of restoring peace and security and establishing law and order in Palestine.

The Arab States recognize that the independence and sovereignty of Palestine which was so far subject to the British Mandate has now, with the termination of the Mandate, become established in fact, and maintain that the lawful inhabitants of Palestine are alone competent and entitled to set up an administration in Palestine for the discharge of all governmental functions without any external interference. As soon as that stage is reached the intervention of the Arab States, which is confined to the restoration of peace and establishment of law and order, shall be put an end to, and the sovereign State of Palestine will be competent in co-operation with the other States members of the Arab League, to take every step for the promotion of the welfare and security of its peoples and territory.

The Governments of the Arab States hereby confirm at this stage the view that had been repeatedly declared by them on previous occasions, such as the London Conference and before the United Nations mainly, the only fair and just solution to the problem of Palestine is the creation of United State of Palestine based upon the democratic principles which will enable all its inhabitants to enjoy equality before the law, and which would guarantee to all minorities the safeguards provided for in all democratic constitutional States affording at the same time full protection and free access to Holy Places. The Arab States emphatically and repeatedly declare that their intervention in Palestine has been prompted solely by the considerations and for the aims set out above and that they are not inspired by any other motive whatsoever. They are, therefore, confident that their action will receive the support of the United Nations as tending to further the aims and ideals of the United Nations as set out in its Charter.

11. General Assembly Resolution 194 (III) Concerning the Progress Report of the United Nations Mediator, December 11, 1948*

---

*G.A. Res. 194 (III). *Palestine—Progress Report of the United Nations Mediator*, 3 U.N. GAOR, Resolutions, at 21-25, U.N. Doc. A/810 (1948).

The General Assembly,

Having considered further the situation in Palestine,

1. *Expresses* its deep appreciation of the progress achieved through the good offices of the late United Nations Mediator in promoting a peaceful adjustment of the future situation of Palestine, for which cause he sacrificed his life; and

Extends its thanks to the Acting Mediator and his staff for their continued efforts and devotion to duty in Palestine;

2. *Establishes* a Conciliation Commission consisting of three States Members of the United Nations which shall have the following functions:

(*a*) To assume, in so far as it considers necessary in existing circumstances, the functions given to the United Nations Mediator on Palestine by resolution 186 (S-2) of the General Assembly of 14 May 1948;

(*b*) To carry out the specific functions and directives given to it by the present resolution and such additional functions and directives as may be given to it by the General Assembly or by the Security Council;

(*c*) To undertake, upon the request of the Security Council, any of the functions now assigned to the United Nations Mediator on Palestine or to the United Nations Truce Commission by resolutions of the Security Council; upon such request to the Conciliation Commission by the Security Council with respect to all the remaining functions of the United Nations Mediator on Palestine under Security Council resolutions, the office of the Mediator shall be terminated;

3. *Decides* that a Committee of the Assembly, consisting of China, France, the Union of Soviet Socialist Republics, the United Kingdom and the United States of America, shall present, before the end of the first part of the present session of the General Assembly, for the approval of the Assembly, a proposal concerning the names of the three States which will constitute the Conciliation Commission;

4. *Requests* the Commission to begin its functions at once, with a view to the establishment of contact between the parties themselves and the Commission at the earliest possible date;

5. *Calls upon* the Governments and authorities concerned to extend the scope of the negotiations provided for in the Security Council's resolution of 16 November 1948 and to seek agreement by negotiations conducted either with the Conciliation Commission or directly, with a view to the final settlement of all questions outstanding between them;

6. *Instructs* the Conciliation Commission to take steps to assist the Governments and authorities concerned to achieve a final settlement of all questions outstanding between them;

7. *Resolves* that the Holy Places—including Nazareth—religious buildings and sites in Palestine should be protected and free access to them assured, in accordance with existing rights and historical practice; that arrangements to this end should be under effective United Nations supervision; that the United Nations Conciliation Commission, in presenting to the fourth regular session of the General Assembly its detailed proposals for a permanent international regime for the territory of Jerusalem, should include recommendations concerning the Holy Places in that territory; that with regard to the Holy Places in the rest of Palestine the Commission should call upon the political authorities of the areas concerned to give appropriate formal guarantees as to the protection of the Holy Places and access to them; and that these undertakings should be presented to the General Assembly for approval;

8. *Resolves* that, in view of its association with three world religions, the Jerusalem area, including the present municipality of Jerusalem *plus* the surrounding villages and towns, the most eastern of which shall be Abu Dis; the most southern, Bethlehem; the most western, Ein Karim (including also the built-up area of Motsa); and the most northern, Shu'fat, should be accorded special and separate treatment from the rest of Palestine and should be placed under effective United Nations control;

Requests the Security Council to take further steps to ensure the demilitarization of Jerusalem at the earliest possible date;

Instructs the Conciliation Commission to present to the fourth regular session of the General Assembly detailed proposals for a permanent international regime for the Jerusalem area which will provide for the maximum local autonomy for distinctive groups consistent with the special international status of the Jerusalem area;

The Conciliation Commission is authorized to appoint a United Nations representative, who shall co-operate with the local authorities with respect to the interim administration of the Jerusalem area;

9. *Resolves* that, pending agreement on more detailed arrangements among the Governments and authorities concerned, the freest possible access to Jerusalem by road, rail or air should be accorded to all inhabitants of Palestine;

Instructs the Conciliation Commission to report immediately to the Security Council, for appropriate action by that organ, any attempt by any party to impede such access;

10. *Instructs* the Conciliation Commission to seek arrangements among the Governments and authorities concerned which will facilitate the economic development of the area, including arrangements for

access to ports and airfields and the use of transportation and communication facilities;

11. *Resolves* that the refugees wishing to return to their homes and live at peace with their neighbours should be permitted to do so at the earliest practicable date, and that compensation should be paid for the property of those choosing not to return and for loss of or damage to property which, under principles of international law or in equity, should be made good by the Governments or authorities responsible;

Instructs the Conciliation Commission to facilitate the repatriation, resettlement and economic and social rehabilitation of the refugees and the payment of compensation, and to maintain close relations with the Director of the United Nations Relief for Palestine Refugees and, through him, with the appropriate organs and agencies of the United Nations;

12. *Authorizes* the Conciliation Commission to appoint such subsidiary bodies and to employ such technical experts, acting under its authority, as it may find necessary for the effective discharge of its functions and responsibilities under the present resolution;

The Conciliation Commission will have its official headquarters at Jerusalem. The authorities responsible for maintaining order in Jerusalem will be responsible for taking all measures necessary to ensure the security of the Commission. The Secretary-General will provide a limited number of guards for the protection of the staff and premises of the Commission;

13. *Instructs* the Conciliation Commission to render progress reports periodically to the Secretary-General for transmission to the Security Council and to the Members of the United Nations;

14. *Calls upon* all Governments and authorities concerned to cooperate with the Conciliation Commission and to take all possible steps to assist in the implementation of the present resolution;

15. *Requests* the Secretary-General to provide the necessary staff and facilities and to make appropriate arrangements to provide the necessary funds required in carrying out the terms of the present resolution.

Hundred and eighty-sixth plenary meeting, 11 December 1948.

. . .

At the 186th plenary meeting on 11 December 1948, a committee of the Assembly consisting of the five States designated in paragraph 3 of the above resolution proposed that the following three States should constitute the Conciliation Commission:

FRANCE, TURKEY, UNITED STATES OF AMERICA.

The proposal of the Committee having been adopted by the General Assembly at the same meeting, the Conciliation Commission is therefore composed of the above-mentioned three States.

12. General Armistice Agreement between Israel and Egypt, February 24, 1949*

* 42 U.N.T.S. 251-70 (1949). Annexes have been omitted. See also the General Armistice Agreement between Israel and Lebanon, March 23, 1949, 42 U.N.T.S. 287-98 (1949); General Armistice Agreement between Israel and Jordan, April 3, 1949, 42 U.N.T.S. 303-20 (1949); General Armistice Agreement between Israel and Syria, July 20, 1949, 42 U.N.T.S. 327-40 (1949); Statements by Saudi Arabia and Iraq on the Armistice Agreements, February 8, 1949, in *A Select Chronology and Background Documents Relating to the Middle East, Senate Committee on Foreign Relations*, 90th CONG., 1st SESS., 56-57 (Comm. Print, 1967).

Preamble

The Parties to the present Agreement, responding to the Security Council resolution of 16 November 1948 calling upon them, as a further provisional measure under Article 40 of the Charter of the United Nations and in order to facilitate the transition from the present truce to permanent peace in Palestine, to negotiate an Armistice; having decided to enter into negotiations under United Nations Chairmanship concerning the implementation of the Security Council resolutions of 4 and 16 November 1948; and having appointed representatives empowered to negotiate and conclude an Armistice Agreement;

The undersigned representatives, in the full authority entrusted to them by their respective Governments, have agreed upon the following provisions:

Article I

With a view to promoting the return to permanent peace in Palestine and in recognition of the importance in this regard of mutual assurances concerning the future military operations of the Parties, the following principles, which shall be fully observed by both Parties during the Armistice, are hereby affirmed:

1. The injunction of the Security Council against resort to military force in the settlement of the Palestine question shall henceforth be scrupulously respected by both Parties.

2. No aggressive action by the armed forces—land, sea, or air—of either Party shall be undertaken, planned, or threatened against the people or the armed forces of the other; it being understood that the use of the term "planned" in this context has no bearing on normal staff planning as generally practiced in military organizations.

3. The right of each Party to its security and freedom from fear of attack by the armed forces of the other shall be fully respected.

4. The establishment of an armistice between the armed forces of the two Parties is accepted as an indispensable step toward the liquidation of armed conflict and the restoration of peace in Palestine.

Article II

1. In pursuance of the foregoing principles and of the resolutions of the Security Council of 4 and 16 November 1948, a general armistice between the armed forces of the two Parties—land, sea and air—is hereby established.

2. No element of the land, sea or air military or para-military forces of either Party, including non-regular forces, shall commit any warlike or hostile act against the military or para-military forces of the other Party, or against civilians in territory under the control of that Party; or shall advance beyond or pass over for any purpose whatsoever the Armistice Demarcation Line set forth in Article VI of this Agreement except as provided in Article III of this Agreement; and elsewhere shall not violate the international frontier; or enter into or pass through the air space of the other Party or through the waters within three miles of the coastline of the other Party.

Article III

1. In pursuance of the Security Council's resolution of 4 November 1948, and with a view to the implementation of the Security Council's resolution of 16 November 1948, the Egyptian Military Forces in the AL FALUJA area shall be withdrawn.

2. This withdrawal shall begin on the day after that which follows the signing of this Agreement, at 0500 hours GMT, and shall be beyond the Egypt-Palestine frontier.

3. The withdrawal shall be under the supervision of the United Nations and in accordance with the Plan of Withdrawal set forth in Annex I to this Agreement.

Article IV

With specific reference to the implementation of the resolutions of the Security Council of 4 and 16 November 1948, the following principles and purposes are affirmed:

1. The principle that no military or political advantage should be gained under the truce ordered by the Security Council is recognized.

2. It is also recognized that the basic purposes and spirit of the Armistice would not be served by the restoration of previously held military positions, changes from those now held other than as specifically provided for in this Agreement, or by the advance of the military forces of either side beyond positions held at the time this Armistice Agreement is signed.

3. It is further recognized that rights, claims or interests of a non-military character in the area of Palestine covered by this Agreement may be asserted by either Party, and that these, by mutual agreement being excluded from the Armistice negotiations, shall be, at the discretion of the Parties, the subject of later settlement. It is emphasized

that it is not the purpose of this Agreement to establish, to recognize, to strengthen, or to weaken or nullify, in any way, any territorial, custodial or other rights, claims or interests which may be asserted by either Party in the area of Palestine or any part or locality thereof covered by this Agreement, whether such asserted rights, claims or interests derive from Security Council resolutions, including the resolution of 4 November 1948 and the Memorandum of 13 November 1948 for its implementation, or from any other source. The provisions of this Agreement are dictated exclusively by military considerations and are valid only for the period of the Armistice.

Article V

1. The line described in Article VI of this Agreement shall be designated as the Armistice Demarcation Line and is delineated in pursuance of the purpose and intent of the resolutions of the Security Council of 4 and 16 November 1948.

2. The Armistice Demarcation Line is not to be construed in any sense as a political or territorial boundary, and is delineated without prejudice to rights, claims and positions of either Party to the Armistice as regards ultimate settlement of the Palestine question.

3. The basic purpose of the Armistice Demarcation Line is to delineate the line beyond which the armed forces of the respective Parties shall not move except as provided in Article III of this Agreement.

4. Rules and regulations of the armed forces of the Parties, which prohibit civilians from crossing the fighting lines or entering the area between the lines, shall remain in effect after the signing of this Agreement with application to the Armistice Demarcation Line defined in Article VI.

Article VI

1. In the GAZA-RAFAH area the Armistice Demarcation Line shall be as delineated in paragraph 2.B (i) of the Memorandum of 13 November 1948 on the implementation of the Security Council resolution of 4 November 1948, namely by a line from the coast at the mouth of the Wadi Hasi in an easterly direction through Deir Suneid and across the Gaza-Al Majdal Highway to a point 3 kilometres east of the Highway, then in a southerly direction parallel to the Gaza-Al Majdal Highway, and continuing thus to the Egyptian frontier.

2. Within this line Egyptian forces shall nowhere advance beyond

their present positions, and this shall include Beit Hanun and its surrounding area from which Israeli forces shall be withdrawn to north of the Armistice Demarcation Line, and any other positions within the line delineated in paragraph 1 which shall be evacuated by Israeli forces as set forth in paragraph 3.

3. Israeli outposts, each limited to platoon strength, may be maintained in this area at the following points: Deir Suneid, on the north side of the Wadi (MR 10751090); 700 SW of Sa'ad (MR 10500982); Sulphur Quarries (MR 09870924); Tall-Jamma (MR 09720887); and KH AL Ma'in (MR 09320821). The Israeli outpost maintained at the Cemetery (MR 08160723) shall be evacuated on the day after that which follows the signing of this Agreement. The Israeli outpost at Hill 79 (MR 10451017) shall be evacuated not later than four weeks following the day on which this Agreement is signed. Following the evacuation of the above outposts, new Israeli outposts may be established at MR 08360700, and at a point due east of Hill 79 east of the Armistice Demarcation Line.

4. In the Bethlehem-Hebron area, wherever positions are held by Egyptian forces, the provisions of this Agreement shall apply to the forces of both Parties in each such locality, except that the demarcation of the Armistice Line and reciprocal arrangements for withdrawal and reduction of forces shall be undertaken in such manner as may be decided by the Parties, at such time as an Armistice Agreement may be concluded covering military forces in that area other than those of the Parties to this Agreement, or sooner at the will of the Parties.

Article VII

1. It is recognized by the Parties to this Agreement that in certain sectors of the total area involved, the proximity of the forces of a third party not covered by this Agreement makes impractical the full application of all provisions of the Agreement to such sectors. For this reason alone, therefore, and pending the conclusion of an Armistice Agreement in place of the existing truce with that third party, the provisions of this Agreement relating to reciprocal reduction and withdrawal of forces shall apply only to the western front and not to the eastern front.

2. The areas comprising the western and eastern fronts shall be as defined by the United Nations Chief of Staff of the Truce Supervision Organization, on the basis of the deployment of forces against each other and past military activity or the future possibility thereof in the

area. This definition of the western and eastern fronts is set forth in Annex II of this Agreement.

3. In the area of the western front under Egyptian control, Egyptian defensive forces only may be maintained. All other Egyptian forces shall be withdrawn from this area to a point or points no further east than El Arish-Abou Aoueigila.

4. In the area of the western front under Israeli control, Israeli defensive forces only, which shall be based on the settlements, may be maintained. All other Israeli forces shall be withdrawn from this area to a point or points north of the line delineated in paragraph 2.A of the Memorandum of 13 November 1948 on the implementation of the resolution of the Security Council of 4 November 1948.

5. The defensive forces referred to in paragraphs 3 and 4 above shall be as defined in Annex III to this Agreement.

Article VIII

1. The area comprising the village of El Auja and vicinity, as defined in paragraph 2 of this Article, shall be demilitarized, and both Egyptian and Israeli armed forces shall be totally excluded therefrom. The Chairman of the Mixed Armistice Commission established in Article X of this Agreement and United Nations Observers attached to the Commission shall be responsible for ensuring the full implementation of this provision

2. The area thus demilitarized shall be as follows: From a point on the Egypt-Palestine frontier five (5) kilometres north-west of the intersection of the Rafah-El Auja road and the frontier (MR 08750468), south-east to Khashm El Mamdud (MR 09650414), thence south-east to Hill 405 (MR 10780285), thence south-west to a point on the Egypt-Palestine frontier five (5) kilometres south-east of the intersection of the old railway tracks and the frontier (MR 09950145), thence returning north-west along the Egypt-Palestine frontier to the point of origin.

3. On the Egyptian side of the frontier, facing the El Auja area, no Egyptian defensive positions shall be closer to El Auja than El Qouseima and Abou Aoueigila.

4. The road Taba-Qouseima-Auja shall not be employed by any military forces whatsoever for the purpose of entering Palestine.

5. The movement of armed forces of either Party to this Agreement into any part of the area defined in paragraph 2 of this Article, for any purpose, or failure by either Party to respect or fulfil any of the other

provisions of this Article, when confirmed by the United Nations representatives, shall constitute a flagrant violation of this Agreement.

Article IX

All prisoners of war detained by either Party to this Agreement and belonging to the armed forces, regular or irregular, of the other Party shall be exchanged as follows:

1. The exchange of prisoners of war shall be under United Nations supervision and control throughout. The exchange shall begin within ten days after the signing of this Agreement and shall be completed not later than twenty-one days following. Upon the signing of this Agreement, the Chairman of the Mixed Armistice Commission established in Article X of this Agreement, in consultation with the appropriate military authorities of the Parties, shall formulate a plan for the exchange of prisoners of war within the above period, defining the date and places of exchange and all other relevant details.

2. Prisoners of war against whom a penal prosecution may be pending, as well as those sentenced for crime or other offence, shall be included in this exchange of prisoners.

3. All articles of personal use, valuables, letters, documents, identification marks, and other personal effects of whatever nature, belonging to prisoners of war who are being exchanged, shall be returned to them, or, if they have escaped or died, to the Party to whose armed forces they belonged.

4. All matters not specifically regulated in this Agreement shall be decided in accordance with the principles laid down in the International Convention relating to the Treatment of Prisoners of War, signed at Geneva on 27 July 1929.[1]

5. The Mixed Armistice Commission established in Article X of this Agreement shall assume responsibility for locating missing persons, whether military or civilian, within the areas controlled by each Party, to facilitate their expeditious exchange. Each Party undertakes to extend to the Commission full co-operation and assistance in the discharge of this function.

[1] League of Nations, *Treaty Series*, Volume CXVIII, page 303; Volume CXXII, page 367; Volume CXXVI, page 460; Volume CXXX, page 468; Volume CXXXIV, page 431; Volume CXXXVIII, page 452; Volume CXLII, page 376; Volume CXLVII, page 351; Volume CLVI, page 229; Volume CLX, page 383; Volume CLXIV, page 388; Volume CLXXII, page 413; Volume CLXXVII, page 407; Volume CLXXXI, page 393; Volume CXCIII, page 270; Volume CXCVI, page 417; Volume CXCVII, page 316; Volume CC, page 511; and Volume CCIV, page 448, and United Nations, *Treaty Series*, Volume 31, page 497.

Article X

1. The execution of the provisions of this Agreement shall be supervised by a Mixed Armistice Commission composed of seven members, of whom each Party to this Agreement shall designate three, and whose Chairman shall be the United Nations Chief of Staff of the Truce Supervision Organization or a senior officer from the Observer personnel of that Organization designated by him following consultation with both Parties to this Agreement.

2. The Mixed Armistice Commission shall maintain its headquarters at El Auja, and shall hold its meetings at such places and at such times as it may deem necessary for the effective conduct of its work.

3. The Mixed Armistice Commission shall be convened in its first meeting by the United Nations Chief of Staff of the Truce Supervision Organization not later than one week following the signing of this Agreement.

4. Decisions of the Mixed Armistice Commission, to the extent possible, shall be based on the principle of unanimity. In the absence of unanimity, decisions shall be taken by a majority vote of the members of the Commission present and voting. On questions of principle, appeal shall lie to a Special Committee, composed of the United Nations Chief of Staff of the Truce Supervision Organization and one member each of the Egyptian and Israeli Delegations to the Armistice Conference at Rhodes or some other senior officer, whose decisions on all such questions shall be final. If no appeal against a decision of the Commission is filed within one week from the date of said decision, that decision shall be taken as final. Appeals to the Special Committee shall be presented to the United Nations Chief of Staff of the Truce Supervision Organization, who shall convene the Committee at the earliest possible date.

5. The Mixed Armistice Commission shall formulate its own rules of procedure. Meetings shall be held only after due notice to the members by the Chairman. The quorum for its meetings shall be a majority of its members.

6. The Commission shall be empowered to employ Observers, who may be from among the military organizations of the Parties or from the military personnel of the United Nations Truce Supervision Organization, or from both, in such numbers as may be considered essential to the performance of its functions. In the event United Nations Observers should be so employed, they shall remain under the command of the United Nations Chief of Staff of the Truce Supervision Organization. Assignments of a general or special nature given to

United Nations Observers attached to the Mixed Armistice Commission shall be subject to approval by the United Nations Chief of Staff or his designated representative on the Commission, whichever is serving as Chairman.

7. Claims or complaints presented by either Party relating to the application of this Agreement shall be referred immediately to the Mixed Armistice Commission through its Chairman. The Commission shall take such action on all such claims or complaints by means of its observation and investigation machinery as it may deem appropriate, with a view to equitable and mutually satisfactory settlement.

8. Where interpretation of the meaning of a particular provision of this Agreement is at issue, the Commission's interpretation shall prevail, subject to the right of appeal as provided in paragraph 4. The Commission, in its discretion and as the need arises, may from time to time recommend to the Parties modifications in the provisions of this Agreement.

9. The Mixed Armistice Commission shall submit to both Parties reports on its activities as frequently as it may consider necessary. A copy of each such report shall be presented to the Secretary-General of the United Nations for transmission to the appropriate organ or agency of the United Nations.

10. Members of the Commission and its Observers shall be accorded such freedom of movement and access in the areas covered by this Agreement as the Commission may determine to be necessary, provided that when such decisions of the Commission are reached by a majority vote United Nations Observers only shall be employed.

11. The expenses of the Commission, other than those relating to United Nations Observers, shall be apportioned in equal shares between the two Parties to this Agreement.

Article XI

No provision of this Agreement shall in any way prejudice the rights, claims and positions of either Party hereto in the ultimate peaceful settlement of the Palestine question.

Article XII

1. The present Agreement is not subject to ratification and shall come into force immediately upon being signed.

2. This Agreement, having been negotiated and concluded in

pursuance of the resolution of the Security Council of 16 November 1948 calling for the establishment of an armistice in order to eliminate the threat to the peace in Palestine and to facilitate the transition from the present truce to permanent peace in Palestine, shall remain in force until a peaceful settlement between the Parties is achieved, except as provided in paragraph 3 of this Article.

3. The Parties to this Agreement may, by mutual consent, revise this Agreement or any of its provisions, or may suspend its application, other than Articles I and II, at any time. In the absence of mutual agreement and after this Agreement has been in effect for one year from the date of its signing, either of the Parties may call upon the Secretary-General of the United Nations to convoke a conference of representatives of the two Parties for the purpose of reviewing, revising or suspending any of the provisions of this Agreement other than Articles I and II. Participation in such conference shall be obligatory upon the Parties.

4. If the conference provided for in paragraph 3 of this Article does not result in an agreed solution of a point in dispute, either Party may bring the matter before the Security Council of the United Nations for the relief sought on the grounds that this Agreement has been concluded in pursuance of Security Council action toward the end of achieving peace in Palestine.

5. This Agreement supersedes the Egyptian-Israeli General Cease-Fire Agreement entered into by the Parties on 24 January 1949.

6. This Agreement is signed in quintuplicate, of which one copy shall be retained by each Party, two copies communicated to the Secretary-General of the United Nations for transmission to the Security Council and to the United Nations Conciliation Commission on Palestine, and one copy to the Acting Mediator on Palestine.

IN FAITH WHEREOF the undersigned representatives of the Contracting Parties have signed hereafter, in the presence of the United Nations Acting Mediator on Palestine and the United Nations Chief of Staff of the Truce Supervision Organization.

DONE at Rhodes, Island of Rhodes, Greece, on the twenty-fourth of February nineteen forty-nine.

For and on behalf of the Government of Egypt:	For and on behalf of the Government of Israel:
(Signed)	(Signed)
Colonel Seif El Dine	Walter Eytan
Colonel El Rahmany	Colonel Yigael Yadin
	Elias Sasson

13. General Assembly Resolution 273 (III) Admitting Israel to Membership in the United Nations, May 11, 1949*

---

* G.A. Res. 273 (III), 3 U.N. GAOR, Pt. II, Resolutions April 5, - May 18, 1949, at 18, U.N. Doc. A/900 (May 31, 1949).

273 (III). Admission of Israel to
membership in the United Nations

Having received the report of the Security Council on the application of Israel for membership in the United Nations,[1]

Noting that, in the judgment of the Security Council, Israel is a peace-loving State and is able and willing to carry out the obligations contained contained in the Charter,

Noting that the Security Council has recommended to the General Assembly that it admit Israel to membership in the United Nations,

Noting furthermore the declaration by the State of Israel that it "unreservedly accepts the obligations of the United Nations Charter and undertakes to honour them from the day when it becomes a Member of the United Nations,"[2]

Recalling its resolutions of 29 November 1947[3] and 11 December 1948[4] and taking note of the declarations and explanations made by the representative of the Government of Israel[5] before the *ad hoc* Political Committee in respect of the implementation of the said resolutions,

THE GENERAL ASSEMBLY,

Acting in discharge of its functions under Article 4 of the Charter and rule 125 of its rules of procedure,

1. *Decides* that Israel is a peace-loving State which accepts the obligations contained in the Charter and is able and willing to carry out those obligations;

2. *Decides* to admit Israel to membership in the United Nations.

Two hundred and seventh plenary meeting,
11 May 1949.

---

[1] See document A/818.

[2] See document A/1093.

[3] See *Resolutions adopted by the General Assembly* during its second session, pages 131-132.

[4] See *Resolutions adopted by the General Assembly* during Part I of its third session, pages 21-25.

[5] See documents A/AC.24/SR.45-48, 50 and 51.

V. DOCUMENTS RELATING TO THE ARAB-ISRAELI CONFLICT

C. *From Armistice to War: 1949-1956*

14. Statute for the City of Jerusalem Approved by the Trusteeship Council on April 4, 1950*

---

* *Question of an International Regime For the Jerusalem Area and Protection of the Holy Places, Special Report of the Trusteeship Council,* 5 U.N. GAOR, Supp. 9, at 19-27, U.N. Doc. A/1286 (1950). See also the Draft Statute for the City of Jerusalem Prepared by the Trusteeship Council, April 21, 1948, U.N. TRUSTEESHIP COUNCIL OFFICIAL RECORDS, 2nd Sess., 3rd Part, Annex at 4-24, U.N. Doc. T/118/Rev. 2 (1948); The United Nations Conciliation Commission Draft Instrument Establishing a Permanent International Regime for the Jerusalem Area, September 1, 1949, 4 U.N. GAOR, Ad Hoc Political Committee, Annex at 10-14, U.N. Doc. A/973 (1949); General Assembly Resolution 303 (IV) Concerning an International Regime for Jerusalem and the Protection of the Holy Places, December 9, 1949, G.A. Res. 303 (IV), 4 U.N. GAOR, Resolutions Sept. 20-Dec. 10, 1949, at 25, U.N. Doc. A/1251 & Corrs. 1 & 2 (Nov. 28, 1950).

Preamble

Whereas the General Assembly of the United Nations in its resolution 181 (II) of 29 November 1947, laid down that the City of Jerusalem, as delimited in that resolution, should be established as a *corpus separatum* under a special international regime and should be administered by the United Nations,

Whereas the General Assembly designated the Trusteeship Council to discharge the responsibilities of the Administering Authority on behalf of the United Nations:

Whereas the special objectives to be pursued by the United Nations in discharging its administrative obligations were set forth in the aforesaid resolution as follows:

"(*a*) To protect and to preserve the unique spiritual and religious interests located in the City of the three great monotheistic faiths throughout the world, Christian, Jewish and Moslem; to this end to ensure that order and peace, and especially religious peace, reign in Jerusalem;

"(*b*) To foster co-operation among all the inhabitants of the City in their own interests as well as in order to encourage and support the peaceful development of the mutual relations between the two Palestinian peoples throughout the Holy Land; to promote the security, well-being and any constructive measures of development of the residents, having regard to the special circumstances and customs of the various peoples and communities,"

Whereas the General Assembly in the aforesaid resolution directed the Trusteeship Council to elaborate and approve a detailed Statute for the City and prescribed certain provisions, the substance of which should be contained therein,

Whereas the Trusteeship Council prepared on 21 April 1948 the draft Statute for the City of Jerusalem (T/118/Rev.2),

Whereas the General Assembly of the United Nations, in its resolution 194 (III) of 11 December 1948, resolved that a special treatment separate from that accorded to the rest of Palestine should be accorded to the Jerusalem area and that it should be placed under effective United Nations control,

Whereas the General Assembly of the United Nations, in its resolution 303 (IV) of 9 December 1949 re-stated "its intention that Jerusalem should be placed under a permanent international regime, which should envisage appropriate guarantees for the protection of the Holy Places, both within and outside Jerusalem," and requested the Trusteeship

Council to "complete the preparation of the Statute of Jerusalem, omitting the now inapplicable provisions" and, "without prejudice to the fundamental principles of the international regime for Jerusalem set forth in the General Assembly resolution 181 (II) of 29 November 1947 introducing therein amendments in the direction of its greater democratization, approve the Statute, and proceed immediately with its implementation,"

The Trusteeship Council,
In pursuance of the aforesaid resolutions,
Approves the present Statute for the City of Jerusalem.

Article 1

SPECIAL INTERNATIONAL REGIME

The present Statute defines the Special International Regime for the City of Jerusalem and constitutes it as a *corpus separatum* under the administration of the United Nations.

Article 2

DEFINITIONS AND INTERPRETATIONS

In this Statute unless the contrary is stated or the context otherwise requires:

(*a*) "City" means the territory of the *corpus separatum;*

(*b*) "Governor" means the Governor of the City, and includes, to the extent of his authority, any officer authorized by or in pursuance of this Statute to perform the functions of the Governor;

(*c*) "Instructions of the Trusteeship Council" means any instructions, whether of a general or special character, which are given by the Trusteeship Council in relation to the application of this Statute;

(*d*) When a duty is imposed or a power is conferred, the duty shall be performed and the power may be exercised from time to time as occasion requires;

(*e*) When a power is conferred to make any order, or to enact any legislation, or to give any instruction or direction, the power shall be construed as including a power to rescind, repeal, amend or vary the order, legislation, instruction or direction;

(*f*) When a duty is imposed or a power is conferred on the holder of an office, the duty shall be performed and the power may be exercised by the holder of the office or by a person duly appointed to act for him.

Article 3

AUTHORITY OF THE STATUTE

This Statute shall prevail in the City. No judicial decision shall conflict or interfere with its provisions, and no administrative act or legislative measure which conflicts or interferes with its provisions shall be valid.

Article 4

BOUNDARIES OF THE TERRITORY OF THE CITY

1. The territory of the City shall include the municipality of Jerusalem, as delimited on 29 November 1947, together with the surrounding villages and towns, the most eastern of which is Abu Dis; the most southern Bethlehem; the most western Ein Karim (including also the built-up area of Motsa) and the most northern Shu'fat.

2. The precise boundaries of the City shall be delimited on the ground by a Commission to be nominated by the Trusteeship Council. A description of the boundaries so delimited shall be transmitted to the Trusteeship Council for its approval and a description of the approved boundaries shall be annexed to this Statute.

Article 5

FUNCTIONS OF THE TRUSTEESHIP COUNCIL

The Trusteeship Council, by virtue of the authority conferred upon it by General Assembly resolutions 181 (II) of 29 November 1947 and 303 (IV) of 9 December 1949, shall discharge the responsibilities of the United Nations for the administration of the City in accordance with this Statute.

Article 6

TERRITORIAL INTEGRITY

1. The territorial integrity of the City and the special regime as defined in this Statute shall be assured by the United Nations.

2. The Governor, appointed by the Trusteeship Council in accordance with the provisions of article 12 of this Statute, shall inform the Trusteeship Council of any situation relating to the City the continuance of which is likely to endanger the territorial integrity of the City, or of any threat of aggression or act of aggression against the

City, or of any other attempt to alter by force the special regime as defined in this Statute. If the Trusteeship Council is not in session and the Governor considers that any of the foregoing contingencies is of such urgency as to require immediate action by the United Nations, he shall bring the matter to the immediate attention of the Security Council through the Secretary-General of the United Nations.

Article 7

DEMILITARIZATION AND NEUTRALITY

1. The City shall be, and remain, neutral and inviolable.
2. The City shall be demilitarized and no para-military formations, exercises or activities shall be permitted within its borders. No armed forces, except as may be provided under article 15 of this Statute or under the authority of the Security Council, shall be allowed in the City.

Article 8

FLAG, SEAL AND COAT OF ARMS

The Legislative Council, constituted in accordance with the provisions of article 21 of this Statute, may approve a flag, a seal and a coat of arms for the City.

Article 9

HUMAN RIGHTS AND FUNDAMENTAL FREEDOMS

1. All persons are entitled to all the rights and freedoms set forth in this Statute, without distinction of any kind, such as race, colour, sex, language, religion, political or other opinion, national or social origin, property, birth or other status.
2. All persons shall enjoy freedom of conscience and shall, subject only to the requirements of public order, public morals and public health, enjoy all other human rights and fundamental freedoms, including freedom of religion and worship, language, education, speech and Press, assembly and association, petition (including petition to the Trusteeship Council), migration and movement.

Subject to the same requirements no measure shall be taken to obstruct or interfere with the activities of religious or charitable bodies of all faiths.

3. All persons have the right to life, liberty and security of person.

4. All persons are equal before the law and are entitled without any discrimination to equal protection of the law. All persons are entitled to equal protection against any discrimination in violation of this Statute and against any incitement to such discrimination.

5. No person may be arrested, detained, convicted or punished, except according to due process of law.

6. No person or property shall be subjected to search or seizure, except according to due process of law.

7. All persons are entitled in full equality to a fair and public hearing by an independent and impartial tribunal, in the determination of their rights and obligations and of any criminal charge against them.

8. All persons charged with a penal offence have the right to be presumed innocent until proved guilty according to law in a public trial at which they have had all the guarantees necessary for their defence.

No person shall be held guilty of any penal offence on account of any act or omission which did not constitute a penal offence, under national or international law, at the time when it was committed. Nor shall a heavier penalty be imposed than the one that was applicable at the time the penal offence was committed.

9. No person shall be subjected to arbitrary interference with his privacy, family, home or correspondence, nor to attacks upon his honour and reputation. All persons have the right to the protection of the law against such interference or attacks.

10. All persons have the right to freedom of thought, conscience and religion; this right includes freedom to change their religion or belief, and freedom, either alone or in community with others, either in public or in private, to manifest their religion or belief in teaching, practice, worship and observance.

11. All persons have the right to freedom of opinion and expression; this right includes freedom to hold opinions without interference and to seek, receive and impart information and ideas through any media.

12. The legislation of the City shall neither place nor recognize any restriction upon the free use by any person of any language in private intercourse, in religious matters, in commerce, in the Press or in publications of any kind, or at public meetings.

13. The family law and personal status of all persons and communities and their religious interests, including endowments, shall be respected.

14. All persons, as members of society, have the right to social

security and are entitled to realization, through national effort and international co-operation and in accordance with the organization and resources of the City, of the economic, social and cultural rights indispensable for their dignity and the free development of their personalities.

15. Without prejudice to the provisions of the preceding paragraphs, the Universal Declaration of Human Rights shall be accepted as a standard of achievement for the City.

16. At such time as the proposed United Nations Covenant of Human Rights shall come into force the provisions of that Covenant shall enter into force also in the City in accordance with the provisions of article 37 of this Statute.

Article 10

DEFINITION OF RESIDENTS

For the purposes of articles 11, 17, 21, 22 and 42 of this Statute, the following persons shall be deemed to be residents of the City:

(*a*) Persons who were ordinarily resident in the City on 29 November 1947 and have remained ordinarily so resident since that date;

(*b*) Persons ordinarily resident in the City on 29 November 1947, who, having left the City as refugees, subsequently return for the purpose of residing there;

(*c*) Persons who do not qualify as residents under paragraphs (*a*) or (*b*) of this article but who, after 29 November 1947 have been ordinarily resident in the City for a continuous period of not less than three years, and have not ceased to be ordinarily so resident: provided that the legislation of the City may make provision for the registration of persons ordinarily resident in the City, and that subject to such exceptions as are provided for in that legislation, persons shall be deemed not to be ordinarily resident in the City for the purposes of paragraphs (*a*), (*b*) and (*c*) of this article during any period in which they are in default in complying with the requirements of the legislation as to registration.

Article 11

CITIZENSHIP

1. All persons who at the date of coming into force of this Statute are residents of the City within the meaning of article 10 of this Statute

shall become *ipso facto* citizens of the City: provided that:

(*a*) All such residents who, at the date of coming into force of this Statute, are citizens of any State and who give notice in such manner and within such period as the Governor shall by order prescribe of their intention to retain the citizenship of that State shall not be deemed to be citizens of the City;

(*b*) Unless a wife gives notice on her own behalf within the period prescribed by order of the Governor, she shall be bound by the decision of her husband in either submitting or not submitting notice as prescribed by sub-paragraph (*a*) above;

(*c*) A notice given by a parent or legal guardian in accordance with the provisions of sub-paragraph (*a*) above shall bind his or her children of minor age of whom he or she has custody: provided that such a minor, on attaining his majority, may opt for the citizenship of the City by giving notice in such manner as the Governor may by order prescribe.

2. Subject to the provisions of paragraph 1 of this article, the conditions for the acquisition of citizenship of the City by persons who become residents after the date of the coming into force of this Statute and for the loss of citizenship of the City shall be laid down by legislation.

Article 12

SELECTION AND TERM OF OFFICE OF THE GOVERNOR

1. The Governor shall be appointed by and responsible to the Trusteeship Council.

2. The term of office of the Governor shall be three years from the time of his appointment: provided that:

(*a*) The Trusteeship Council may extend the term of office of the Governor in any particular case for such period as it may deem fit;

(*b*) The Governor may resign his appointment upon due notice to the Trusteeship Council and the Trusteeship Council may terminate his appointment for due cause at any time.

3. At the expiration of his term of office a Governor shall be eligible for re-appointment.

Article 13

GENERAL POWERS OF THE GOVERNOR

1. The Governor shall be the representative of the United Nations in the City.

2. The Governor, on behalf of the United Nations, shall exercise executive authority in the City and shall act as the chief administrative officer thereof, subject only to the provisions of this Statute and to the instructions of the Trusteeship Council. He shall be responsible for ensuring the peace, order and good government of the City in accordance with the special objectives set out in the Preamble to this Statute.

3. The Governor shall be responsible for exercising such supervision over religious or charitable bodies of all faiths in the City as may be required for the maintenance of public order, public morals and public health. He shall exercise such supervision in conformity with existing rights and traditions.

4. The Governor shall negotiate with the States concerned agreements to ensure, in conformity with the resolutions of the General Assembly, the protection of the Holy Places located in the Holy Land outside the City.

5. The Governor and his official and private property shall not be in any way subject to the jurisdiction of the Legislative Council or of the Courts of the City.

Article 14

POWER OF PARDON AND REPRIEVE

The Governor may grant to any offender convicted of any offence in any Court of the City a pardon, either free or conditional, or may grant remission of the sentence passed on such offender, or any respite of the execution of such sentence, for such period as the Governor deems fit, and may remit any fines, penalties or forfeitures which may accrue or become payable to the City by virtue of the judgment of any Court of the City or of the operation of any legislation of the City.

Article 15

PRESERVATION OF ORDER

1. The Governor shall be responsible for the organization and direction of the police forces necessary for the maintenance of internal law and order.

2. The Governor shall organize and direct a special police force, of such numbers as he may deem necessary, for the maintenance of internal law and order, and especially for the protection of the Holy Places, religious buildings and sites.

Article 16

EMERGENCY POWERS OF THE GOVERNOR

1. If, in the opinion of the Governor, the administration is being seriously obstructed or prevented by the non-co-operation or interference of persons or groups of persons, the Governor, during the period of the emergency, shall take such measures and enact by order such legislation as he may deem necessary to restore the effective functioning of the administration, and such orders shall have effect notwithstanding anything to the contrary in any legislation in force.

2. The circumstances in which the Governor may have exercised any power conferred on him by this article shall be reported to the Trusteeship Council as soon as may be practicable.

Article 17

ORGANIZATION OF THE ADMINISTRATION

1. The Governor shall be assisted by a Chief Secretary who shall be appointed by the Trusteeship Council on the recommendation of the Governor.

2. The Governor shall appoint an administrative staff, including an Attorney General, the members of which shall be selected on a non-discriminatory basis for their competence and integrity and, whenever practicable, from among the residents of the City. Subject to any instructions of the Trusteeship Council and to any legislation of the City, the appointments of members of the administrative staff may be terminated by the Governor at any time.

3. There shall be a Council of Administration consisting of the Chief Secretary and such other principal officers and residents as the Governor may appoint. The Governor may also, if he considers it desirable, add to the Council other persons chosen by him..The Council of Administration shall advise and assist the Governor in the administration of the City.

4. In the performance of their duties, the Governor, the members of the Council of Administration and administrative staff, including members of the police forces, shall not seek or receive any instructions from any Government or any authority other than the Government of the City or the Trusteeship Council.

Article 18

DISQUALIFICATION FROM PUBLIC OFFICE

A person shall be disqualified from holding any public office, central or local, in the City, including membership of the Council of Administration and of the Legislative Council, if he holds any office under any other Government: provided that the Governor may appoint to any public office in the City for a limited period any person seconded from the service of another Government.

Article 19

OATHS OF OFFICE

The Governor, the Chief Secretary, members of the Judiciary, members of the Council of Administration, members of the Legislative Council, members of the special police force and such other officers as the Governor may determine, shall take such oaths and make such affirmations as are specified in the instructions of the Trusteeship Council.

Article 20

ACTING GOVERNOR

If the office of Governor is vacant, or if the Governor is absent from the City or is unable to exercise his powers or perform his duties, the officer holding substantively the appointment of Chief Secretary, or, if there is no such officer or he is absent from the City or unable to act, such persons as may have been authorized to act in the circumstances by the instructions of the Trusteeship Council, may exercise all the powers and perform all the duties of the Governor so long as the office of Governor is vacant or the Governor is absent from the City or unable to exercise his powers or perform his duties.

Article 21

THE LEGISLATIVE COUNCIL

1. A Legislative Council, consisting of a single chamber, shall have power to legislate, consistent with the provisions of this Statute, upon all matters affecting the interests of the City, except such matters as are

included within powers specifically granted by this Statute to the Trusteeship Council or to any other authority.

2. The Legislative Council shall be composed of citizens or residents of the City, twenty-five years of age and over, elected or designated in accordance with the provisions of this article and of article 22 of this Statute.

3. The Legislative Council shall consist of twenty-five elected members and of not more than fifteen non-elected members.

The twenty-five members shall be elected by four electoral colleges: a Christian college, a Jewish college, a Moslem college and a college which shall be composed of the residents of the City who declare that they do not wish to register with any of the other three colleges. The Governor shall make all the necessary arrangements for opening and keeping the electoral registers in each of these four colleges.

The first three colleges shall each elect eight members to the Legislative Council and the fourth college one member.

The non-elected members of the Council shall be designated by the Heads of the principal religious communities of the City: the number of these members representing the Christian religion, the Jewish religion and the Moslem religion being equal. The Governor shall submit to the Trusteeship Council a plan for the number and allocation of the non-elective seats.

4. The legislation of the City may make provisions as to the disqualifications from, election to, and membership of, the Legislative Council, resulting from loss of legal capacity.

5. The legislation of the City shall provide for the remuneration of the members of the Legislative Council.

Article 22

ELECTIONS TO THE LEGISLATIVE COUNCIL

1. The elected members of the Legislative Council shall be elected by residents of the City, twenty-one years of age and over, irrespective of nationality or sex, on the basis of universal and secret suffrage and proportional representation in each electoral college. For this purpose every resident of the City may register with the college of his own community, or with the fourth college; he may be registered at only one college.

2. The legislation of the City shall provide for an electoral law and make provisions regarding disqualifications from voting resulting from loss of legal capacity.

Article 23

DURATION OF THE LEGISLATIVE COUNCIL

1. The term of the Legislative Council shall be four years from the date of its election, unless it is earlier dissolved.

2. If, at the end of a four-year term of the Legislative Council, it is the opinion of the Governor that circumstances are inappropriate for the conduct of a general election, the Legislative Council may vote the prolongation of its term for a period not exceeding one year. The Governor shall forthwith submit a report to the Trusteeship Council which may issue such instructions as it may deem necessary.

3. If a serious political crisis arises in the City and if, in the opinion of the Governor, the dissolution of the Legislative Council would be justified, he shall report the circumstances to the Trusteeship Council which may, after examining the Governor's report, order such dissolution and at the same time fix a date for holding of new elections.

Article 24

LEGISLATION AND RESOLUTIONS

1. Bills and resolutions may be introduced in the Legislative Council by any member thereof.

2. The Governor, or any officer appointed by him, may make statements or answer questions before the Legislative Council, introduce any bill or resolution and participate without vote in all deliberations of the Legislative Council.

3. A bill adopted by the Legislative Council shall become law only upon promulgation by the Governor.

At any time within a period of thirty days after the transmission to him of any bill the Governor may disapprove the bill if, in his opinion, it is in conflict with the provisions of this Statute or it would impede the Administration of the City or inflict undue hardship on any section of the inhabitants of the City and he shall then inform both the Legislative Council and the Trusteeship Council of the reasons for his disapproval.

If, at the expiration of the period of thirty days, the Governor has not disapproved the bill, he shall forthwith promulgate it as a law.

Article 25

LEGISLATION BY ORDER OF THE GOVERNOR

1. At any time when there is no Legislative Council, the Governor may legislate by order which shall have the force and effect of law. All such orders shall be laid before the Legislative Council as soon as may be practicable and shall remain in force until and unless repealed or amended in accordance with the provisions of paragraph 3 of article 24 of this Statute.

2. When the Legislative Council is in session but fails to adopt in time a bill deemed essential to the normal functioning of the Administration the Governor may make temporary orders.

3. The Governor shall forthwith report to the Trusteeship Council any action taken by him in accordance with the provisions of this article and the Trusteeship Council may issue such instructions as it may deem necessary.

Article 26

STANDING ORDERS OF THE LEGISLATIVE COUNCIL

1. The Legislative Council shall adopt such standing orders for the conduct of its business, including the election of a President (who may or may not be a member of the Legislative Council), as it may deem appropriate.

2. The Governor shall convene the first session of each Legislative Council and may at any time convene an extraordinary session.

3. Subject to the provisions of article 23 of this Statute, subsequent sessions of the Legislative Council shall be convened in accordance with the standing orders of the Legislative Council.

4. Subject to the provisions of article 23 of this Statute, the Governor shall convene an extraordinary session of the Legislative Council upon the request of a majority of the members.

5. A majority of the members of the Legislative Council shall form a quorum.

6. Decisions of the Legislative Council shall be taken by a majority of those present and voting. Members who abstain from voting shall not be counted as voting.

Article 27

IMMUNITY OF MEMBERS OF THE LEGISLATIVE COUNCIL

1. No member of the Legislative Council shall be liable to any judicial or administrative penalty, or be called to account in any other way outside the Legislative Council, by reason of anything which he may have said, or of any vote which he may have cast, in the course of his duties as a member of the Legislative Council.

2. No member of the Legislative Council shall be liable during the sessions of the Council to criminal, administrative or disciplinary proceedings, nor shall he be deprived of his liberty without the permission of the Legislative Council: provided that he may be apprehended in the act of committing a crime and detained if his detention is or becomes imperative in the interests of justice, but in any such case his apprehension shall be reported as soon as may be practicable to the Legislative Council and he shall be released without delay should the Legislative Council so request.

Article 28

JUDICIAL SYSTEM

1. There shall be a Supreme Court which shall consist of such number of judges, not being less than three or more than five, as the Trusteeship Council may determine, of whom one shall be President and shall be styled Chief Justice. They shall be appointed by, and their appointments shall be terminated only by, the Trusteeship Council.

2. The legislation of the City shall provide for an independent judicial system for the City, including such subordinate and other Courts as may be deemed appropriate. Such legislation shall establish the jurisdiction of the Courts and provide for their organization.

3. All persons shall be subject to the jurisdiction of the City, except and in so far as such persons may enjoy immunity as provided for in this Statute.

4. Judicial personnel of subordinate Courts shall be appointed by and may be suspended or dismissed by, the Chief Justice with the approval of the Governor, in accordance with any instructions of the Trusteeship Council.

5. Subject to the special objectives set out in the preamble to this Statute and to social evolution in the City, the existing status and jurisdiction of religious Courts in the City shall be respected. In the case of any conflict regarding jurisdiction between religious Courts or

between religious Courts and civil Courts, the Supreme Court shall consider the case and decide in which Court the jurisdiction shall lie.

6. Decisions by the Supreme Court shall be made by a majority of its members: provided that, if in any case the opinion of the Court be equally divided, the opinion of the Chief Justice shall prevail.

Article 29

CONSTITUTIONALITY OF LEGISLATION AND ADMINISTRATIVE ACTS

1. In cases brought before the Courts of the City this Statute shall prevail over any legislation or administrative act. The Supreme Court shall have original and appellate jurisdiction in all cases involving claims that such legislation or act is incompatible with the provisions of this Statute.

2. In any case in which the Supreme Court decides that any legislation or administrative act is incompatible with the provisions of this Statute such legislation or administrative act shall be void and of no effect.

Article 30

ACCESS TO AND IMMIGRATION INTO THE CITY

1. Subject only to the requirements of public order, public morals and public health:

(a) Freedom of entry into and of temporary residence in and of exit from the City shall be ensured to all foreign pilgrims and visitors without distinction as to nationality or faith;

(b) The legislation of the City shall make special provisions to facilitate entry and exit from the City for inhabitants of adjoining areas.

2. Immigration into the City for the purposes of residence shall be controlled by order of the Governor under the instructions of the Trusteeship Council having regard to the absorptive capacity of the City and the maintenance of equality between the various communities.

Article 31

OFFICIAL AND WORKING LANGUAGES

Arabic and Hebrew shall be the official and working languages of the City. The legislation of the City may adopt one or more additional working languages as may be required.

Article 32

EDUCATIONAL SYSTEM AND CULTURAL AND BENEVOLENT INSTITUTIONS

1. All persons have a right to education. Education shall be directed to the full physical, intellectual, moral and spiritual development of the human personality and to the strengthening of respect for human rights and fundamental freedoms. It shall be directed to the promotion of understanding, tolerance and friendship among all national, racial and religious groups. It shall in particular be directed to the furtherance of the activities of the United Nations, to the establishment of peace and to the attainment of the special objectives set out in the preamble to this Statute.

2. Education, in its elementary stages, shall be free and compulsory. In its secondary stages, it shall in so far as may be practicable be free. Technical and professional educational facilities shall be provided in so far as may be practicable and those supported by public funds shall be equally accessible to all on the basis of merit.

3. The City shall maintain or subsidize and supervise a system of primary and secondary education on an equitable basis for all communities in their respective languages and in accordance with their respective cultural traditions: provided that such communities have a sufficient number of pupils to justify a separate school.

4. Subject to the provisions of paragraph 1 of this article and to such educational requirements of a general nature as the legislation of the City may impose, any community or any specific group within any community may maintain its own institutions for the education of its own members in its own language according to its own cultural traditions.

5. Subject to the provisions of paragraph 1 of this article and to the legislation of the City, private or foreign educational establishments may be maintained in the City: provided that existing rights shall continue unimpaired.

6. Educational and cultural establishments, charitable institutions and hospitals already in existence or founded after the coming into force of this Statute shall enjoy the fiscal privileges provided for in paragraph 6 of article 38 of this Statute.

7. At the request of a parent or legal guardian, any child may be exempted from religious instruction in any school supported in whole or in part by public funds.

Article 33

BROADCASTING AND TELEVISION

1. Radio broadcasting and television shall be reserved to the City administration and shall be controlled by a Joint Broadcasting Council which shall be appointed by, and shall be responsible to, the Governor and which shall include an equal number of representatives of each of the three principal religions: Christian, Jewish and Moslem.

2. Representatives of the Christian, Jewish and Moslem religions shall have equal opportunities of access to the broadcasting and television facilities of the City.

3. The principle of freedom of expression shall apply to broadcasting, but it shall be the responsibility of the Joint Broadcasting Council to ensure that the radio is used to further the interests of peace and mutual understanding between the inhabitants of the City and of the objectives of this Statute and of the Charter of the United Nations.

Article 34

ECONOMIC PROVISIONS

1. The plan for the economic and financial organization of the City adopted by the Trusteeship Council in accordance with the provisions of paragraph 4 of article 43 shall form an annex to this Statute.

2. In the economic and social fields the rights and interests of the inhabitants shall be considered as of primary importance. Subject to this provision, all economic, industrial and commercial matters shall be regulated on the basis of equal treatment and non-discrimination for all States, nationals, and companies or associations controlled by their nationals; and an equal treatment and non-discrimination shall be ensured in respect of freedom of transit, including transit and navigation by air, acquisition of property, both movable and immovable, protection of persons and property and the exercise of professions and trades.

Article 35

BUDGETS

1. The Governor shall be responsible for the preparation of the annual and supplementary budgets of the City and only the Governor or any officer appointed by him shall introduce budgets in the Legislative Council.

2. The financial provision made by the Governor in the budgets for the maintenance of the special police force shall not be altered by the Legislative Council. The Trusteeship Council may determine other services for which the financial provision made by the Governor in the budgets shall not be altered by the Legislative Council.

3. The Governor may authorize, in anticipation of approval by the Legislative Council, expenditure for which there is no provision in the budgets, if in his opinion such expenditure becomes a matter of urgency.

Article 36

LOCAL AUTONOMY

1. Existing local autonomous units and such new local autonomous units as may be created shall enjoy wide powers of local government and administration in accordance with the legislation of the City.

2. The plan for local autonomy adopted by the Trusteeship Council in accordance with the provisions of paragraph 5 of article 43 shall form an annex to this Statute.

Article 37

EXTERNAL AFFAIRS

1. Subject to the provisions of this Statute and to the instructions of the Trusteeship Council, the Governor shall conduct the external affairs of the City.

2. The Governor may ensure by means of special international agreements, or otherwise, the protection abroad of the interests of the City and of its citizens.

3. The Governor may accredit representatives of foreign States for the protection of the interests of the City and its citizens in those States.

4. Representatives may be accredited to the Governor by any State if he so permits.

5. The Governor, on behalf of the City, may sign treaties which are consistent with this Statute and shall adhere to the provisions of any international conventions and recommendations drawn up by the United Nations or by the specialized agencies referred to in article 57 of the Charter of the United Nations which may be appropriate to the particular circumstances of the City, or would conduce to the achievement of the special objectives set out in the preamble to this Statute.

6. Such treaties and international undertakings entered into by the

Governor shall be submitted for ratification to the Legislative Council. If the Legislative Council does not ratify any such treaties or international undertakings within six months of the date of signature by the Governor, the matter shall be referred to the Trusteeship Council which shall have the power to ratify them.

7. Foreign Powers shall enjoy immunities no less than those in force on 29 November 1947 in respect of their property within the City.

Article 38

HOLY PLACES, RELIGIOUS BUILDINGS AND SITES

1. The protection of Holy Places, religious buildings and sites shall be the special concern of the Governor.

2. The Governor shall decide any question which may arise as to whether any place, building or site, not hitherto regarded as a Holy Place, religious building or site, is to be regarded as such for the purpose of this Statute. For the purpose of deciding any such question, the Governor may appoint a Committee of Inquiry to assist him.

3. If any dispute arises between different religious communities or between different confessions and faiths in connexion with any Holy Place, religious building or site, the Governor shall decide on the basis of existing rights. For the purpose of deciding any such dispute, the Governor may appoint a Committee of Inquiry to assist him. He may also, if he shall deem fit, be assisted by a consultative council of representatives of different denominations acting in an advisory capacity.

4. At the request of any party to a dispute under paragraphs 2 or 3 of this article, the Governor shall seek an advisory opinion of the Supreme Court on points of law, before he takes a decision.

5. If at any time it appears to the Governor that any Holy Place, religious building or site is in need of urgent repairs, he may call upon the community or denomination or section of the community concerned to carry out such repairs. If the repairs are not carried out, or are not completed within a reasonable time, the Governor may arrange for repairs to be carried out or completed and the expenses of so doing shall be a charge on the revenues of the City but may be recovered from the community or denomination or section of the community concerned, subject to existing rights.

6. No form of taxation shall be levied in respect of any Holy Place, religious building or site which was exempted from taxation of that

form on 29 November 1947. No change in the incidence of any form of taxation shall be made which would either discriminate between the owners or occupiers of Holy Places, religious buildings and sites, or would place such owners or occupiers in a position less favourable in relation to the general incidence of that form of taxation than existed on 29 November 1947.

7. The Governor shall ensure that the property rights of churches, missions and other religious or charitable agencies shall be confirmed and respected. He shall ensure, further, that all such property which, since the outbreak of the Second World War had been seized without equitable compensation but which has not already been returned or, for one reason or another, could not be returned to its original owners, shall either be restored to them or be transferred to another church, or mission or other religious or charitable agency representative of the same confession.

8. The Governor shall by order ensure that:

(a) His decisions taken in accordance with the provisions of paragraphs 2 and 3 of this article are carried into effect and that provision is made for the recovery of sums recoverable in accordance with the provisions of paragraph 5 of this article;

(b) Existing rights in respect of Holy Places, religious buildings and sites shall not be denied or impaired;

(c) Subject to the requirements of public order, public morals and public health, free access is maintained to Holy Places, religious buildings and sites and that free exercise of worship therein is secured in conformity with existing rights;

(d) Holy Places, religious buildings and sites are preserved;

(e) No act is committed which may in any way impair the sacred character of Holy Places, religious buildings or sites;

(f) Provisions of this article generally, and the special objectives set out in the Preamble to this Statute in so far as they relate to Holy Places, religious buildings and sites, are carried into effect.

9. An order made in accordance with the provisions of paragraph 8 of this article may contain penal provisions and shall have effect notwithstanding anything to the contrary in any legislation.

10. The Governor shall transmit a copy of every order made in accordance with the provisions of paragraph 8 of this article to the Trusteeship Council as soon as may be practicable and the Trusteeship Council may give such instructions to the Governor in relation thereto as it may deem fit.

Article 39

PROTECTION OF ANTIQUITIES

Legislation of the City shall provide for the protection of antiquities.

Article 40

CAPITULATIONS

Foreign Powers whose nationals have in the past enjoyed in the City the privileges and immunities of foreigners, including the benefits of consular jurisdiction and protection as formerly enjoyed by capitulation or usage in the Ottoman Empire, are invited to renounce, if they have not already renounced, any right pertaining to them as regards the re-establishment of such privileges and immunities in the City. Any privileges and immunities which may be retained shall be respected.

Article 41

ENTRY INTO FORCE OF THE STATUTE

This Statute shall come into force at a date to be determined by a resolution of the Trusteeship Council.

Article 42

RE-EXAMINATION OF THE STATUTE

1. This Statute shall remain in force, in the first instance, for a period of ten years, unless the Trusteeship Council amends it before the expiration of this period.
2. On the expiration of this period of ten years, the whole Statute shall be subject to re-examination by the Trusteeship Council. The residents of the City shall then be free to express by means of a referendum their wishes as to possible modifications of the regime of the City. The Trusteeship Council shall in due course lay down the procedure by which this referendum shall be conducted.

Article 43

TRANSITORY PROVISIONS

1. FLAG

Unless the Legislature of the City decides otherwise, the flag of the United Nations shall be flown from official buildings.

2. FIRST ELECTIONS TO THE LEGISLATIVE COUNCIL

The first elections of members to the Legislative Council shall be held as soon as possible after the entry into force of this Statute at such date and in such manner as shall be provided by order of the Governor in accordance with the provisions of articles 21 and 22 of this Statute and of the instructions of the Trusteeship Council.

3. PROVISIONAL PRESIDENT OF THE LEGISLATIVE COUNCIL

The Provisional President of the Legislative Council shall be appointed by the Governor and shall remain in office until the election of a President by the Legislative Council.

4. ECONOMIC PROVISIONS

The Governor shall take prompt steps to formulate, with the advice and help of such experts as may seem to him desirable, the economic and financial principles upon which the government of the City is to be based. In doing so he shall take into consideration the desirability of meeting the costs of the administration of the City from rates, taxes and other local revenues, and the possibility that any advances from the United Nations towards such expenditure will be in the form of loans. The Governor, within six months of the date of his appointment, shall submit to the Trusteeship Council for its consideration a plan for the economic and financial organization of the City.

Pending a decision by the Trusteeship Council in this matter, the Governor may temporarily take such economic and financial measures as he may deem necessary for the proper administration of the City.

Commercial concessions, or concessions in respect of public services, granted in the City prior to 29 November 1947 shall continue to be valid according to their terms, unless modified by agreement between the Governor and the concession holder.

5. LOCAL AUTONOMY

The Governor, after consultation with the Legislative Council and, if possible, within six months of the date of his appointment, shall submit to the Trusteeship Council for its consideration a plan for dividing the City into local autonomous units and for the allocation of powers between the City authorities and the authorities of those autonomous units.

6. CONTINUITY OF LEGISLATION

The legislation in force in the City on the day preceding the termination of the Mandate, in so far as it is not inconsistent with the provisions of this Statute, shall be applicable in the City until such time as it may be amended or repealed by legislation.

7. REFUGEES

Having regard to any decisions or recommendations which have been, or may be, made by organs of the United Nations or to any agreements which have been accordingly concluded between the States concerned regarding the problem of the Palestine refugees, the Governor of the City, as soon as this Statute enters into force, shall facilitate the repatriation, resettlement and economic and social rehabilitation of persons who, on 29 November 1947, were ordinarily resident in the City and have left the City as refugees, as well as the payment of any indemnities which may be due to them.

15. Tripartite Declaration Regarding Security in the Near East: Three-Power Statement Released May 25, 1950, and Statement by President Truman Released May 25, 1950*

* 22 DEPT. STATE BULLETIN 886 (June 5, 1950).

Three-Power Statement

[RELEASED TO THE PRESS MAY 25]

The Governments of the United Kingdom, France, and the United States, having had occasion during the recent Foreign Ministers meeting in London to review certain questions affecting the peace and stability of the Arab states and of Israel, and particularly that of the supply of arms and war material to these states, have resolved to make the following statements:

1. The three Governments recognize that the Arab states and Israel all need to maintain a certain level of armed forces for the purposes of assuring their internal security and their legitimate self-defense and to permit them to play their part in the defense of the area as a whole. All applications for arms or war material for these countries will be considered in the light of these principles. In this connection the three Governments wish to recall and reaffirm the terms of the statements made by their representatives on the Security Council on August 4, 1949, in which they declared their opposition to the development of an arms race between the Arab states and Israel.

2. The three Governments declare that assurances have been received from all the states in question, to which they permit arms to be supplied from their countries, that the purchasing state does not intend to undertake any act of aggression against any other state. Similar assurances will be requested from any other state in the area to which they permit arms to be supplied in the future.

3. The three Governments take this opportunity of declaring their deep interest in and their desire to promote the establishment and maintenance of peace and stability in the area and their unalterable opposition to the use of force or threat of force between any of the states in that area. The three Governments, should they find that any of these states was preparing to violate frontiers or armistice lines, would, consistently with their obligations as members of the United Nations, immediately take action, both within and outside the United Nations, to prevent such violation.

Statement by the President

[RELEASED TO THE PRESS BY THE WHITE HOUSE MAY 25]

During the recent meeting in London, the Foreign Ministers of the United States, the United Kingdom, and France had an opportunity to review the security and armaments situation in the Near East and to consider what action their Governments might take to provide greater stability in the area. As a result of this consultation, a 3-power declaration is being issued. This is another of the many valuable results of the London meeting.

The participation of the United States Government in the declaration emphasizes this country's desire to promote the maintenance of peace in the Near East. It is the belief of the United States Government that the declaration will stimulate, in the Arab states and Israel, increased confidence in future security, thus accelerating the progress now being made in the Near East and contributing toward the well-being of the peoples there.

16. The Law of Return, 1950, as Amended in 1954 and 1970*

---

*. An unofficial translation incorporating the 1954 and 1970 •
Amendment Laws. For the official version of the Law of Return, see 4
LAWS OF THE STATE OF ISRAEL 144 (1950), as amended by 8 LAWS OF THE
STATE OF ISRAEL 144 (1954), *Sefer Hahukim* [Israeli Statutes] of 5730
(Hebrew Year) at 34 (March 10, 1970).

1. Every Jew has the right to immigrate to this country.

2. (a) Immigration shall be by immigrant's visa.

(b) An immigrant's visa shall be given to every Jew who has expressed his desire to settle in Israel, unless the Minister of the Interior is satisfied that the applicant—

> (1) is engaged in an activity directed against the Jewish people; or
>
> (2) is liable to endanger public health or the security of the State; or
>
> (3) is a person with a criminal past liable to endanger public welfare.

3. (a) A Jew who comes to Israel and subsequently expresses his desire to settle may, whilst still in Israel, receive an immigrant's certificate.

(b) The exceptions set out in section 2(b) shall also apply to the grant of an immigrant's certificate, provided that a person shall not be considered as endangering public health on account of an illness contracted after his arrival in Israel.

4. Every Jew who immigrated to this country before the commencement of this Law and every Jew born in the country, whether before or after the commencement of this Law, is in the same position as one who immigrated under this Law.

4A. (a) The rights of a Jew under this Law, the rights of an immigrant under the Nationality Law, 1952 and the rights of an immigrant under any other legislation are also granted to the child and grandchild of a Jew, to the spouse of a Jew and to the spouse of the child and grandchild of a Jew—with the exception of a person who was a Jew and willingly changed his religion.

(b) It makes no difference whether or not the Jew through whom a right is claimed under sub-section (a) is still alive or whether or not he has immigrated to this country.

(c) The exceptions and conditions appertaining to a Jew or an immigrant under or by virtue of this Law or the legislation referred to in sub-section (a) shall also apply to a person claiming any right under sub-section (a).

4B. For the purpose of this Law, "a Jew" means a person born to a Jewish mother or converted to Judaism and who is not a member of another religion.

5. The Minister of the Interior is charged with the implementation of this Law and may make regulations as to any matter relating to its

implementation and as to the grant of immigrants' visas and certificates to minors up to the age of 18.

Regulations regarding sections 4A and 4B require the approval of the Constitution, Law and Justice Committee of the Knesset.

17. Security Council Resolution Concerning the Passage of Israeli Shipping Through the Suez Canal, September 1, 1951*

---

* 6 U.N. SCOR, 558th meeting, at 2-3, U.N. Doc. S/2322 (1951).

The Security Council,

1. *Recalling* that in its resolution of 11 August 1949 (S/1376) relating to the conclusion of Armistice Agreements between Israel and the neighbouring Arab States it drew attention to the pledges in these Agreements 'against any further acts of hostility between the Parties',

2. *Recalling* further that in its resolution of 17 November 1950 (S/1907 and Corr. 1), it reminded the States concerned that the Armistice Agreements to which they are parties contemplate 'the return of permanent peace in Palestine', and therefore urged them and other States in the area to take all such steps as will lead to the settlement of the issues between them,

3. *Noting* the report of the Chief of Staff of the Truce Supervision Organization to the Security Council of 12 June 1951 (S/2194),

4. *Further noting* that the Chief of Staff of the Truce Supervision Organization recalled the statement of the senior Egyptian delegate in Rhodes on 13 January 1949, to the effect that his delegation was 'inspired with every spirit of co-operation, conciliation and a sincere desire to restore peace in Palestine', and that the Egyptian Government has not complied with the earnest plea of the Chief of Staff made to the Egyptian delegate on 12 June 1951, that it desist from the present practice of interfering with the passage through the Suez Canal of goods destined for Israel,

5. *Considering* that since the armistice regime, which has been in existence for nearly two and a half years, is of a permanent character, neither party can reasonably assert that it is actively a belligerent or requires to exercise the right of visit, search, and seizure for any legitimate purpose of self-defence,

6. *Finds* that the maintenance of the practice mentioned in paragraph 4 above is inconsistent with the objectives of a peaceful settlement between the parties and the establishment of a permanent peace in Palestine set forth in the Armistice Agreement;

7. *Finds further* that such practice is an abuse of the exercise of the right of visit, search and seizure;

8. *Further finds* that that practice cannot in the prevailing circumstances be justified on the ground that it is necessary for self-defence;

9. *And further noting* that the restrictions on the passage of goods through the Suez Canal to Israel ports are denying to nations at no time connected with the conflict in Palestine valuable supplies required for their economic reconstruction, and that these restrictions together with sanctions applied by Egypt to certain ships which have visited Israel ports represent unjustified interference with the rights of nations to

navigate the seas and to trade freely with one another, including the Arab States and Israel,

10. *Calls upon* Egypt to terminate the restrictions on the passage of international commercial shipping and goods through the Suez Canal wherever bound and to cease all interference with such shipping beyond that essential to the safety of shipping in the Canal itself and to the observance of the international conventions in force.

V. DOCUMENTS RELATING TO THE ARAB-ISRAELI CONFLICT

D. *The Suez Crisis, the 1956 War, and the Decade of UNEF: 1956-1967*

18. The Constantinople Convention Respecting the Free Navigation of the Suez Maritime Canal, October 29, 1888*

* English translation from *The Suez Canal Problem, July 26 - September 22, 1956*, at 16-20 (Dept. State Publication No. 6392, 1956). See also BRITISH COMMAND PAPER 5623, at 4-7, GREAT BRITAIN HOUSE OF COMMONS SESSIONAL PAPERS 1889, Vol. 87. The authoritative French text of the Convention may be found in 79 BRITISH AND FOREIGN STATE PAPERS 18-22 (1887-1888).

Convention Between Great Britain, Austria-Hungary, France, Germany, Italy, the Netherlands, Russia, Spain, and Turkey, Respecting the Free Navigation of the Suez Canal

In the name of Almightly God,

Her Majesty the Queen of the United Kingdom of Great Britain and Ireland, Empress of India; His Majesty the German Emperor, King of Prussia; His Majesty the Emperor of Austria, King of Bohemia, etc., and Apostolic King of Hungary; His Majesty the King of Spain, and in His Name the Queen Regent of the Kingdom; the President of the French Republic; His Majesty the King of Italy; His Majesty the King of the Netherlands, Grand Duke of Luxemburg, etc.; His Majesty the Emperor of all the Russias; and His Majesty the Emperor of the Ottomans, being desirous of establishing, by a Conventional Act, a definitive system intended to guarantee, at all times and to all the Powers, the free use of the Suez Maritime Canal, and thus to complete the system under which the navigation of this canal has been placed by the Firman of His Imperial Majesty the Sultan, dated February 22, 1866 (2 Zilkadé, 1282), and sanctioning the Concessions of His Highness the Khedive, have appointed as their plenipotentiaries, to wit:

Her Majesty the Queen of the United Kingdom of Great Britain and Ireland, Empress of India, the Right Honorable Sir William Arthur White, Her Ambassador Extraordinary and Plenipotentiary;

His Majesty the German Emperor, King of Prussia, His Excellency Joseph de Radowitz, His Ambassador Extraordinary and Plenipotentiary;

His Majesty the Emperor of Austria, King of Bohemia, etc., and Apostolic King of Hungary, His Excellency Baron Henri de Calice, His Ambassador Extraordinary and Plenipotentiary;

His Majesty the King of Spain and in His Name the Queen Regent of the Kingdom, Mr. Miguel Florez y Garcia, His Chargé d'Affaires;

The President of the French Republic, His Excellency Gustave Louis Lannes, Count de Montebello, Ambassador Extraordinary and Plenipotentiary of France;

His Majesty the King of Italy, His Excellency Baron Albert Blanc, His Ambassador Extraordinary and Plenipotentiary;

His Majesty the King of the Netherlands, Grand Duke of Luxemburg, etc., Mr. Gustave Keun, His Chargé d'Affaires;

His Majesty the Emperor of all the Russias, His Excellency Alexandre de Nélidow, His Ambassador Extraordinary and Plenipotentiary;

His Majesty the Emperor of the Ottomans, Mehemmed Saïd Pasha,
His Minister of Foreign Affairs;

Who, having communicated to each other their respective full powers,
found in good and due form, have agreed upon the following articles:—

ART. I. The Suez Maritime Canal shall always be free and open, in
time of war as in time of peace, to every vessel of commerce or of war,
without distinction of flag.

The Canal shall never be subject to the exercise of the right of
blockade.

ART. II. The High Contracting Parties, recognizing that the Fresh-
Water Canal is indispensable to the Maritime Canal, take cognizance of
the engagements of His Highness the Khedive towards the Universal
Suez Canal Company as regards the Fresh-Water Canal; which engagements are stipulated in a Convention dated March 18, 1863, containing
a preamble and four Articles.

They undertake not to interfere in any way with security of that
Canal and its branches, the working of which shall not be the object of
any attempt at obstruction.

ART. III. The High Contracting Parties likewise undertake to respect
the equipment, establishments, buildings and work of the Maritime
Canal and of the Fresh-Water Canal.

ART. IV. The Maritime Canal remaining open in time of war as a free
passage, even to ships of war of the belligerents, under the terms of
Article I of the present Treaty, the High Contracting Parties agree that
no right of war, act of hostility or act having for its purpose to interfere
with the free navigation of the Canal, shall be committed in the Canal
and its ports of access, or within a radius of 3 nautical miles from those
ports, even though the Ottoman Empire should be one of the
belligerent Powers.

Warships of belligerents shall not take on fresh supplies or lay in stores
in the Canal and its ports of access, except in so far as may be strictly
necessary. The transit of the said vessels through the Canal shall be
effected as quickly as possible, in accordance with the regulations in
force, and without stopping except for the necessities of the service.

Their stay at Port Saïd and the roadstead of Suez shall not exceed 24
hours, except in case of putting in through stress of weather. In such
case, they shall be bound to depart as soon as possible. A period of 24
hours shall always elapse between the sailing of a belligerent ship from
a port of access and the departure of a ship belonging to the enemy
Power.

ART. V. In time of war, belligerent powers shall not discharge or take on troops, munitions, or war matériel in the Canal and its ports of access. In case of an accidental hindrance in the Canal, however, troops broken up into groups not exceeding 1000 men, with a corresponding amount of equipment, may be embarked or disembarked at the ports of access.

ART. VI. Prizes shall in all respects be subject to the same rules and regulations as the warships of belligerents.

ART. VII. The Powers shall not keep any warship in the waters of the Canal (including Lake Timsah and the Bitter Lakes).

They may, however, have warships, the number of which shall not exceed two for each Power, stationed in the ports of access of Port Saïd and Suez.

This right shall not be exercised by belligerents.

ART. VIII. The Agents in Egypt of the Signatory Powers of the present Treaty shall be charged to see that it is carried out. In any circumstance threatening the security and free passage of the Canal, they shall meet at the summons of three of them and under the presidency of their Doyen, to make the necessary verifications. They shall inform the Khedivial Government of the danger perceived, in order that it may take proper steps to assure the protection and the free use of the Canal. In any case, they shall meet once a year to take note of the due execution of the Treaty.

These latter meetings shall be presided over by a Special Commissioner appointed for that purpose by the Imperial Ottoman Government. A Khedivial Commissioner may also take part in the meeting, and may preside over it in case of the absence of the Ottoman Commissioner.

They shall demand, in particular, the removal of any work or the dispersion of any assemblage on either bank of the Canal, the purpose or effect of which might be to interfere with the freedom and complete safety of navigation.

ART. IX. The Egyptian Government shall, within the limits of its powers based on the Firmans, and under the conditions provided for in the present Treaty, take the necessary measures for enforcing the execution of the said Treaty.

In case the Egyptian Government should not have sufficient means at its disposal, it shall appeal to the Imperial Ottoman Government, which shall take the necessary measures for responding to such appeal, give notice thereof to the other Signatory Powers of the Declaration of

London of March 17, 1885, and, if necessary, consult with them on the matter.

The provisions of Articles IV, V, VI, and VII shall not stand in the way of the measures taken by virtue of the present Article.

ART. X. Likewise, the provisions of Articles IV, V, VII, and VIII shall not stand in the way of any measures which His Majesty the Sultan and His Highness the Khedive in the name of His Imperial Majesty, and within the limits of the Firmans granted, might find it necessary to take to assure by their own forces the defense of Egypt and the maintenance of public order.

In case His Imperial Majesty the Sultan or His Highness the Khedive should find it necessary to avail himself of the exceptions provided for in the present Article, the Signatory Powers of the Declaration of London would be notified thereof by the Imperial Ottoman Government.

It is also understood that the provisions of the four Articles in question shall in no case stand in the way of measures which the Imperial Ottoman Government considers it necessary to take to assure by its own forces the defense of its other possessions situated on the eastern coast of the Red Sea.

ART. XI. The measures taken in the cases provided for by Articles IX and X of the present Treaty shall not interfere with the free use of the Canal. In the same cases, the erection of permanent fortifications contrary to the provisions of Article VIII is prohibited.

ART. XII. The High Contracting Parties, by application of the principle of equality as regards free use of the Canal, a principle which forms one of the bases of the present Treaty, agree that none of them shall seek, with respect to the Canal, territorial or commercial advantages or privileges in any international arrangements that may be concluded. Furthermore, the rights of Turkey as the territorial Power are reserved.

ART. XIII. Aside from the obligations expressly provided for by the clauses of the present Treaty, the sovereign rights of His Imperial Majesty the Sultan and the rights and immunities of His Highness the Khedive based on the Firmans are in no way affected.

ART. XIV. The High Contracting Parties agree that the engagements resulting from the present Treaty shall not be limited by the duration of the Acts of Concession of the Universal Suez Canal Company.

ART. XV. The stipulations of the present Treaty shall not interfere with the sanitary measures in force in Egypt.

ART. XVI. The High Contracting Parties undertake to bring the present Treaty to the knowledge of those States which have not signed it, inviting them to accede thereto.

ART. XVII. The present Treaty shall be ratified, and the ratifications thereof shall be exchanged at Constantinople within one month or sooner if possible.

In witness whereof the respective Plenipotentiaries have signed the present Treaty, and have affixed thereto the seal of their arms.

Done at Constantinople, on the 29th day of the month of October, of the year 1888.

For	Great Britain	(L.S.)	W. A. White
	Germany	(L.S.)	Radowitz
	Austria-Hungary	(L.S.)	Calice
	Spain	(L.S.)	Miguel Florez y Garcia
	France	(L.S.)	G. de Montebello
	Italy	(L.S.)	A. Blanc
	Netherlands	(L.S.)	Gus. Keun
	Russia	(L.S.)	Nélidow
	Turkey	(L.S.)	M. Said

19. Security Council Resolution Concerning the Question of the Suez Canal, October 13, 1956*

*   11 U.N. SCOR, Suppl. for Oct., Nov., and Dec. 1956, 47-48 (1956).

The Security Council,

Noting the declarations made before it and the accounts of the development of the exploratory conversations on the Suez question given by the Secretary-General of the United Nations and the Foreign Ministers of Egypt, France and the United Kingdom,

Agrees that any settlement of the Suez question should meet the following requirements:

1. There should be free and open transit through the Canal without discrimination, overt or covert—this covers both political and technical aspects;

2. The sovereignty of Egypt should be respected;

3. The operation of the Canal should be insulated from the politics of any country;

4. The manner of fixing tolls and charges should be decided by agreement between Egypt and the users;

5. A fair proportion of the dues should be alloted to development;

6. In case of disputes, unresolved affairs between the Universal Suez Maritime Canal Company and the Egyptian Government should be settled by arbitration with suitable terms of reference and suitable provisions for the payment of sums found to be due.

20. General Assembly Resolution 1001 (ES-I) Concerning the Establishment of the United Nations Emergency Force, November 7, 1956*

* G.A. Res. 1001 (ES-I), U.N. GAOR, Resolutions adopted by the General Assembly during its First Emergency Special Session from 1 to 10 November 1956, Supp. 1, at 3, U.N. Doc. A/3354 (1956). See also G.A. Res. 997 (ES-I), G.A. Res. 998 (ES-I), G.A. Res. 999 (ES-I), G.A. Res. 1000 (ES-I), and G.A. Res. 1002 (ES-I), U.N. GAOR, Resolutions adopted by the General Assembly during its First Emergency Special Session from 1 to 10 November 1956, Supp. 1, at 2-4, U.N. Doc. A/3354 (1956).

The General Assembly,

Recalling its resolution 997 (ES-I) of 2 November 1956 concerning the cease-fire, withdrawal of troops and other matters related to the military operations in Egyptian territory, as well as its resolution 998 (ES-I) of 4 November 1956 concerning the request to the Secretary-General to submit a plan for an emergency international United Nations Force,

Having established by its resolution 1000 (ES-I) of 5 November 1956 a United Nations Command for an emergency international Force, having appointed the Chief of Staff of the United Nations Truce Supervision Organization as Chief of the Command with authorization to him to begin the recruitment of officers for the Command, and having invited the Secretary-General to take the administrative measures necessary for the prompt execution of that resolution,

Noting with appreciation the second and final report of the Secretary-General[1] on the plan for an emergency international United Nations Force as requested in General Assembly resolution 998 (ES-I), and having examined that plan,

1. *Expresses its approval* of the guiding principles for the organization and functioning of the emergency international United Nations Force as expounded in paragraphs 6 to 9 of the Secretary-General's report;

2. *Concurs* in the definition of the functions of the Force as stated in paragraph 12 of the Secretary-General's report;

3. *Invites* the Secretary-General to continue discussions with Governments of Member States concerning offers of participation in the Force, toward the objective of its balanced composition;

4. *Requests* the Chief of the Command, in consultation with the Secretary-General as regards size and composition, to proceed forthwith with the full organization of the Force;

5. *Approves provisionally* the basic rule concerning the financing of the Force laid down in paragraph 15 of the Secretary-General's report;

6. *Establishes* an Advisory Committee composed of one representative from each of the following countries: Brazil, Canada, Ceylon, Colombia, India, Norway and Pakistan, and requests this Committee, whose Chairman shall be the Secretary-General, to undertake the development of those aspects of the planning for the Force and its operation not already dealt with by the General Assembly and which do not fall within the area of the direct responsibility of the Chief of the Command;

[1] *Official Records of the General Assembly, First Emergency Special Session, Annexes,* agenda item 5, document A/3302.

7. *Authorizes* the Secretary-General to issue all regulations and instructions which may be essential to the effective functioning of the Force, following consultation with the Committee aforementioned, and to take all other necessary administrative and executive action;

8. *Determines* that, following the fulfilment of the immediate responsibilities defined for it in operative paragraphs 6 and 7 above, the Advisory Committee shall continue to assist the Secretary-General in the responsibilities falling to him under the present and other relevant resolutions;

9. *Decides* that the Advisory Committee, in the performance of its duties, shall be empowered to request, through the usual procedures, the convening of the General Assembly and to report to the Assembly whenever matters arise which, in its opinion, are of such urgency and importance as to require consideration by the General Assembly itself;

10. *Requests* all Member States to afford assistance as necessary to the United Nations Command in the performance of its functions, including arrangements for passage to and from the area involved.

567th plenary meeting,
7 November 1956.

21. *Aide Mémoire* Handed to Israeli Ambassador Abba Eban on February 11, 1957, by Secretary of State Dulles*

* 36 DEPT. STATE BULLETIN 392-93 (March 11, 1957).

The United Nations General Assembly has sought specifically, vigorously, and almost unanimously, the prompt withdrawal from Egypt of the armed forces of Britain, France and Israel. Britain and France have complied unconditionally. The forces of Israel have been withdrawn to a considerable extent but still hold Egyptian territory at Sharm el Shaikh at the entrance to the Gulf of Aqaba. They also occupy the Gaza Strip which is territory specified by the Armistice arrangements to be occupied by Egypt.

We understand that it is the position of Israel that (1) it will evacuate its military forces from the Gaza Strip provided Israel retains the civil administration and police in some relationship to the United Nations; and (2) it will withdraw from Sharm el Shaikh if continued freedom of passage through the Straits is assured.

With respect to (1) the Gaza Strip—it is the view of the United States that the United Nations General Assembly has no authority to require of either Egypt or Israel a substantial modification of the Armistice Agreement, which, as noted, now gives Egypt the right and responsibility of occupation. Accordingly, we believe that Israeli withdrawal from Gaza should be prompt and unconditional, leaving the future of the Gaza Strip to be worked out through the efforts and good offices of the United Nations.

We recognize that the area has been a source of armed infiltration and reprisals back and forth contrary to the Armistice Agreement and is a source of great potential danger because of the presence there of so large a number of Arab refugees—about 200,000. Accordingly, we believe that the United Nations General Assembly and the Secretary General should seek that the United Nations Emergency Force, in the exercise of its mission, move into this area and be on the boundary between Israel and the Gaza Strip.

The United States will use its best efforts to help to assure this result, which we believe is contemplated by the Second Resolution of February 2, 1957.

With respect to (2) the Gulf of Aqaba and access thereto—the United States believes that the Gulf comprehends international waters and that no nation has the right to prevent free and innocent passage in the Gulf and through the Straits giving access thereto. We have in mind not only commercial usage, but the passage of pilgrims on religious missions, which should be fully respected.

The United States recalls that on January 28, 1950, the Egyptian

Ministry of Foreign Affairs informed the United States that the
Egyptian occupation of the two islands of Tiran and Senafir at the
entrance of the Gulf of Aqaba was only to protect the islands
themselves against possible damage or violation and that "this occupation being in no way conceived in a spirit of obstructing in any way
innocent passage through the stretch of water separating these two
islands from the Egyptian coast of Sinai, it follows that this passage, the
only practicable one, will remain free as in the past, in conformity with
international practice and recognized principles of the law of nations."

In the absence of some overriding decision to the contrary, as by the
International Court of Justice, the United States, on behalf of vessels of
United States registry, is prepared to exercise the right of free and
innocent passage and to join with others to secure general recognition of
this right.

It is of course clear that the enjoyment of a right of free and innocent
passage by Israel would depend upon its prior withdrawal in accordance
with the United Nations Resolutions. The United States has no reason
to assume that any littoral state would under these circumstances
obstruct the right of free and innocent passage.

The United States believes that the United Nations General Assembly
and the Secretary General should, as a precautionary measure, seek that
the United Nations Emergency Force move into the Straits area as the
Israeli forces are withdrawn. This again we believe to be within the con-
templation of the Second Resolution of February 2, 1957.

(3) The United States observes that the recent resolutions of the
United Nations General Assembly call not only for the prompt and unconditional withdrawal of Israel behind the Armistice lines but call for
other measures.

We believe, however, that the United Nations has properly established
an order of events and an order of urgency and that the first requirement is that forces of invasion and occupation should withdraw.

The United States is prepared publicly to declare that it will use its influence, in concert with other United Nations members, to the end that,
following Israel's withdrawal, these other measures will be
implemented.

We believe that our views and purposes in this respect are shared by
many other nations and that a tranquil future for Israel is best assured
by reliance upon that fact, rather than by an occupation in defiance of
the overwhelming judgment of the world community.

22. Address by President Eisenhower on the Situation in the Middle East, February 20, 1957*

* 36 DEPT. STATE BULLETIN 387-91 (March 11, 1957).

I come to you again to talk about the situation in the Middle East. The future of the United Nations and peace in the Middle East may be at stake.

In the 4 months since I talked to you about the crisis in that area, the United Nations has made considerable progress in resolving some of the difficult problems. We are now, however, faced with a fateful moment as the result of the failure of Israel to withdraw its forces behind the armistice lines, as contemplated by the United Nations resolutions on this subject.

I have already today met with leaders of both parties from the Senate and the House of Representatives. We had a very useful exchange of views. It was the general feeling of that meeting that I should lay the situation before the American people.

Now, before talking about the specific issues involved, I want to make clear that these issues are not something remote and abstract but involve matters vitally touching upon the future of each one of us.

The Middle East is a land bridge between the Eurasian and African continents. Millions of tons of commerce are transmitted through it annually. Its own products, especially petroleum, are essential to Europe and the Western World.

The United States has no ambitions or desires in this region. It hopes only that each country there may maintain its independence and live peacefully within itself and with its neighbors and, by peaceful cooperation with others, develop its own spiritual and material resources. But that much is vital to the peace and well-being of us all. This is our concern today.

So tonight I report to you on the matters in controversy and on what I believe the position of the United States must be.

When I talked to you last October,[1] I pointed out that the United States fully realized that military action against Egypt resulted from grave and repeated provocations. But I said also that the use of military force to solve international disputes could not be reconciled with the principles and purposes of the United Nations. I added that our country could not believe that resort to force and war would for long serve the permanent interests of the attacking nations, which were Britain, France, and Israel.

So I pledged that the United States would seek through the United Nations to end the conflict. We would strive to bring about a recall of the forces of invasion and then make a renewed and earnest effort

[1] BULLETIN of Nov. 12, 1956, p. 743.

through that organization to secure justice, under international law, for all the parties concerned.

Since that time much has been achieved and many of the dangers implicit in the situation have been avoided. The Governments of Britain and France have withdrawn their forces from Egypt. Thereby they showed respect for the opinions of mankind as expressed almost unanimously by the 80 nation members of the United Nations General Assembly.

I want to pay tribute to the wisdom of this action of our friends and allies. They made an immense contribution to world order. Also they put the other nations of the world under a heavy obligation to see to it that these two nations do not suffer by reason of their compliance with the United Nations resolutions. This has special application, I think, to their treaty rights to passage through the Suez Canal, which had been made an international waterway for all by the treaty of 1888.

The Prime Minister of Israel, in answer to a personal communication, assured me early in November[2] that Israel would willingly withdraw its forces if and when there should be created a United Nations force to move into the Suez Canal area. This force was, in fact, created and has moved into the canal area.

Subsequently, Israeli forces were withdrawn from much of the territory of Egypt which they had occupied. However, Israeli forces still remain outside the armistice lines. They are at the mouth of the Gulf of Aqaba, which is about 100 miles from the nearest Israeli territory. They are also in the Gaza Strip, which, by the Armistice Agreement, was to be occupied by Egypt. These facts create the present crisis.

Efforts To Bring About Israeli Withdrawal

We are approaching a fateful moment when either we must recognize that the United Nations is unable to restore peace in this area or the United Nations must renew with increased vigor its efforts to bring about Israeli withdrawal.

Repeated, but, so far, unsuccessful, efforts have been made to bring about a voluntary withdrawal by Israel. These efforts have been made both by the United Nations and by the United States and other member states.

Equally serious efforts have been made to bring about conditions designed to assure that, if Israel will withdraw in response to the repeated requests of the United Nations, there will then be achieved a

[2] *Ibid.*, Nov. 19, 1956, p. 797.

greater security and tranquillity for that nation. This means that the United Nations would assert a determination to see that in the Middle East there will be a greater degree of justice and compliance with international law than was the case prior to the events of last October-November.

A United Nations Emergency Force, with Egypt's consent, entered that nation's territory in order to help maintain the cease-fire which the United Nations called for on November 2. The Secretary-General, who ably and devotedly serves the United Nations, has recommended a number of measures which might be taken by the United Nations and by its Emergency Force to assure for the future the avoidance by either side of belligerent acts.

The United Nations General Assembly on February 2 by an overwhelming vote adopted a pertinent resolution.[3] It was to the effect that, after full withdrawal of Israel from the Gulf of Aqaba and Gaza areas, the United Nations Emergency Force should be placed on the Egyptian-Israeli armistice lines to assure the scrupulous maintenance of the Armistice Agreement. Also the United Nations General Assembly called for the implementation of other measures proposed by the Secretary-General. These other measures embraced the use of the United Nations Emergency Force at the mouth of the Gulf of Aqaba, so as to assure nonbelligerency in this area.

The United States was a cosponsor of this United Nations resolution. Thus the United States sought to assure that Israel would, for the future, enjoy its rights under the armistice and under international law.

In view of the valued friendly relations which the United States has always had with the State of Israel, I wrote to Prime Minister Ben-Gurion on February 3. I recalled his statement to me of November 8 to the effect that the Israeli forces would be withdrawn under certain conditions, and I urged that, in view of the General Assembly resolutions of February 2, Israel should complete that withdrawal.

However, the Prime Minister, in his reply, took the position that Israel would not evacuate its military forces from the Gaza Strip unless Israel retained the civil administration and police. This would be in contradiction to the Armistice Agreement. Also, the reply said that Israel would not withdraw from the Straits of Aqaba unless freedom of passage through the straits was assured.

It was a matter of keen disappointment to us that the Government of Israel, despite the United Nations action, still felt unwilling to withdraw.

[3] *Ibid.*, Feb. 25, 1957, p. 327.

Statement of U.S. Policy

However, in a further effort to meet the views of Israel in these respects, Secretary of State Dulles, at my direction, gave to the Government of Israel on February 11 a statement of United States policy. This has now been made public. It pointed out that neither the United States nor the United Nations had authority to impose upon the parties a substantial modification of the Armistice Agreement which was freely signed by both Israel and Egypt. Nevertheless, the statement said, the United States as a member of the United Nations would seek such disposition of the United Nations Emergency Force as would assure that the Gaza Strip could no longer be used as a source of armed infiltration and reprisals.

The Secretary of State orally informed the Israeli Ambassador that the United States would be glad to urge and support, also, some participation by the United Nations, with the approval of Egypt, in the administration of the Gaza Strip. The principal population of the strip consists of about 200,000 Arab refugees, who exist largely as a charge upon the benevolence of the United Nations and its members.

With reference to the passage into and through the Gulf of Aqaba, we expressed the conviction that the gulf constitutes international waters and that no nation has the right to prevent free and innocent passage in the gulf. We announced that the United States was prepared to exercise this right itself and to join with others to secure general recognition of this right.

The Government of Israel has not yet accepted, as adequate insurance of its own safety after withdrawal, the far-reaching United Nations resolution of February 2, plus the important declaration of United States policy made by our Secretary of State on February 11.

Israel seeks something more. It insists on firm guaranties as a condition to withdrawing its forces of invasion.

This raises a basic question of principle. Should a nation which attacks and occupies foreign territory in the face of United Nations disapproval be allowed to impose conditions on its own withdrawal?

If we agree that armed attack can properly achieve the purposes of the assailant, then I fear we will have turned back the clock of international order. We will, in effect, have countenanced the use of force as a means of settling international differences and through this gaining national advantages.

I do not, myself, see how this could be reconciled with the charter of the United Nations. The basic pledge of all the members of the United

Nations is that they will settle their international disputes by peaceful means and will not use force against the territorial integrity of another state.

If the United Nations once admits that international disputes can be settled by using force, then we will have destroyed the very foundation of the organization and our best hope of establishing a world order. That would be a disaster for us all.

I would, I feel, be untrue to the standards of the high office to which you have chosen me if I were to lend the influence of the United States to the proposition that a nation which invades another should be permitted to exact conditions for withdrawal.

Justice and Conformity With International Law

Of course, we and all the members of the United Nations ought to support justice and conformity with international law. The first article of the charter states the purpose of the United Nations to be "the suppression of acts of aggression or other breaches of the peace, and to bring about by peaceful means, and in conformity with . . . justice and international law, adjustment or settlement of international disputes." But it is to be observed that conformity with justice and international law are to be brought about "by peaceful means."

We cannot consider that the armed invasion and occupation of another country are "peaceful means" or proper means to achieve justice and conformity with international law.

We do, however, believe that upon the suppression of the present act of aggression and breach of the peace there should be greater effort by the United Nations and its members to secure justice and conformity with international law. Peace and justice are two sides of the same coin.

Perhaps the world community has been at fault in not having paid enough attention to this basic truth. The United States, for its part, will vigorously seek solutions of the problems of the area in accordance with justice and international law. And we shall in this great effort seek the association of other like-minded nations which realize, as we do, that peace and justice are in the long run inseparable.

But the United Nations faces immediately the problem of what to do next. If it does nothing, if it accepts the ignoring of its repeated resolutions calling for the withdrawal of invading forces, then it will have admitted failure. That failure would be a blow to the authority and influence of the United Nations in the world and to the hopes which humanity placed in the United Nations as the means of achieving peace with justice.

I do not believe that Israel's default should be ignored because the United Nations has not been able effectively to carry out its resolutions condemning the Soviet Union for its armed suppression of the people of Hungary. Perhaps this is a case where the proverb applies that two wrongs do not make a right.

No one deplores more than I the fact that the Soviet Union ignores the resolutions of the United Nations. Also no nation is more vigorous than is the United States in seeking to exert moral pressure against the Soviet Union, which by reason of its size and power, and by reason of its veto in the Security Council, is relatively impervious to other types of sanction.

The United States and other free nations are making clear by every means at their command the evil of Soviet conduct in Hungary. It would indeed be a sad day if the United States ever felt that it had to subject Israel to the same type of moral pressure as is being applied to the Soviet Union.

There can, of course, be no equating of a nation like Israel with that of the Soviet Union. The people of Israel, like those of the United States, are imbued with a religious faith and a sense of moral values. We are entitled to expect, and do expect, from such peoples of the free world a contribution to world order which unhappily we cannot expect from a nation controlled by atheistic despots.

It has been suggested that United Nations actions against Israel should not be pressed because Egypt has in the past violated the Armistice Agreement and international law. It is true that both Egypt and Israel, prior to last October, engaged in reprisals in violation of the Armistice Agreements. Egypt ignored the United Nations in exercising belligerent rights in relation to Israeli shipping in the Suez Canal and in the Gulf of Aqaba. However, such violations constitute no justification for the armed invasion of Egypt by Israel which the United Nations is now seeking to undo.

Failure to withdraw would be harmful to the long-term good of Israel. It would, in addition to its injury to the United Nations, jeopardize the prospects of the peaceful solution of the problems of the Mid-East. This could bring incalculable ills to our friends and indeed to our nation itself. It would make infinitely more difficult the realization of the goals which I laid out in my Middle East message of January 5th to the

Congress[4] seeking to strengthen the area against Communist aggression, direct or indirect.

The United Nations must not fail. I believe that—in the interests of peace—the United Nations has no choice but to exert pressure upon Israel to comply with the withdrawal resolutions. Of course, we sti'l hope that the Government of Israel will see that its best immediate and long-term interests lie in compliance with the United Nations and in placing its trust in the resolutions of the United Nations and in the declaration of the United States with reference to the future.

Egypt, by accepting the six principles adopted by the Security Council last October in relation to the Suez Canal,[5] bound itself to free and open transit through the canal without discrimination and to the principle that the operation of the canal should be insulated from the politics of any country.

We should not assume that, if Israel withdraws, Egypt will prevent Israeli shipping from using the Suez Canal or the Gulf of Aqaba. If, unhappily, Egypt does hereafter violate the Armistice Agreement or other international obligations, then this should be dealt with firmly by the society of nations.

The Tasks of the United Nations

The present moment is a grave one, but we are hopeful that reason and right will prevail. Since the events of last October-November, solid progress has been made, in conformity with the charter of the United Nations. There is the cease-fire, the forces of Britain and France have been withdrawn, the forces of Israel have been partially withdrawn, and the clearing of the canal nears completion. When Israel completes its withdrawal, it will have removed a definite block to further progress.

Once this block is removed, there will be serious and creative tasks for the United Nations to perform. There needs to be respect for the right of Israel to national existence and to internal development. Complicated provisions insuring the effective international use of the Suez Canal will need to be worked out in detail. The Arab refugee problem must be solved. As I said in my special message to Congress on January 5, it must be made certain that all the Middle East is kept free from aggression and infiltration.

Finally, all who cherish freedom, including ourselves, should help the nations of the Middle East achieve their just aspirations for improving the well-being of their peoples.

[4] BULLETIN of Jan. 21, 1957, p. 83.
[5] Ibid., Oct. 22, 1956, p. 616.

What I have spoken about tonight is only one step in a long process calling for patience and diligence, but at this moment it is the critical issue on which future progress depends.

It is an issue which can be solved if only we will apply the principles of the United Nations.

That is why, my fellow Americans, I know that you want the United States to continue to use its maximum influence to sustain those principles as the world's best hope for peace.

23. Statement by Golda Meir, Israeli Minister for Foreign Affairs, before the United Nations General Assembly, March 1, 1957*

* 11 U.N. GAOR, 666th plenary meeting, at 1275-76 (1957).

1. Mrs. MEIR (Israel): The Government of Israel is now in a position to announce its plans for full and prompt withdrawal from the Sharm el Sheikh area and the Gaza strip, in compliance with General Assembly resolution 1124 (XI) of 2 February 1957.

2. We have repeatedly stated that Israel has no interest in the strip of land overlooking the western coast of the Gulf of Aqaba. Our sole purpose has been to ensure that, on the withdrawal of Israel forces, continued freedom of navigation will exist for Israel and international shipping in the Gulf of Aqaba and the Straits of Tiran. Such freedom of navigation is a vital national interest for Israel, but it is also of importance and legitimate concern to the martime Powers and to many States whose economies depend upon trade and navigation between the Red Sea and the Mediterranean Sea.

3. There has recently been an increasingly wide recognition that the Gulf of Aqaba comprehends international waters, in which the right of free and innocent passage exists.

4. On 11 February 1957, the Secretary of State of the Ambassador of the United States of America handed to the Ambassador of Israel in Washington a memorandum dealing, among other things, with the subject of the Gulf of Aqaba and the Straits of Tiran. This statement discusses the rights of nations in the Gulf of Aqaba and declares the readiness of the United States to exercise those rights on its own behalf and to join with others in securing general recognition of those rights.

5. My Government has subsequently learned with gratification that other leading maritime Powers are prepared to subscribe to the doctrine set out in the United States memorandum of 11 February and have a similar intention to exercise their rights of free and innocent passage in the Gulf and the Straits.

6. General Assembly resolution 1125 (XI) of 2 February 1957 contemplates that units of the United Nations Emergency Force will move into the area of the Straits of Tiran on Israel's withdrawal. It is generally recognized that the function of the United Nations Emergency Force in that area includes the prevention of belligerent acts.

7. In this connexion, my Government recalls the statements by the representative of the United States in the General Assembly on 28 January 1957 [645th meeting] and 2 February [650th meeting], with reference to the function of the United Nations Emergency Force units which are to move into the area of the Straits of Tiran on Israel's withdrawal. The statement of 28 January, repeated on 2 February, said:

"... It is essential that units of the United Nations Emergency Force be stationed at the Straits of Tiran in order to achieve there the separation of Egyptian and Israel land and sea forces. This separation is essential until it is clear that the non-existence of any claim to belligerent rights has established in practice the peaceful conditions which must govern navigation in waters having such an international interest." [*645th meeting, para. 4.*]

8. My Government has been concerned with the situation which would arise if the United Nations Emergency Force, having taken up its position in the area of the Straits of Tiran for the purpose of assuring non-belligerency, were to be withdrawn in conditions which might give rise to interference with free and innocent navigation and, therefore, to the renewal of hostilities. Such a premature cessation of the precautionary measures taken by the United Nations for the prevention of belligerent acts would prejudice important international interests and threaten peace and security. My Government has noted the assurance embodied in the Secretary-General's note of 26 February 1957 [*A/3563, annex*], that any proposal for the withdrawal of the United Nations Emergency Force from the Gulf of Aqaba area would first come to the Advisory Committee on the United Nations Emergency Force, which represents the General Assembly in the implementation of its resolution 997 (ES-I) of 2 November 1956. This procedure will give the General Assembly an opportunity to ensure that no precipitate changes are made which would have the effect of increasing the possibility of belligerent acts. We have reason to believe that in such a discussion many Members of the United Nations would be guided by the view expressed by Mr. Lodge, representative of the United States, on 2 February in favour of maintaining the United Nations Emergency Force in the Straits of Tiran until peaceful conditions were in practice assured.

9. In the light of these doctrines, policies and arrangements by the United Nations and the maritime Powers, my Government is confident that free and innocent passage for international and Israel shipping will continue to be fully maintained after Israel's withdrawal.

10. It remains for me now to formulate the policy of Israel both as a littoral State and as a country which intends to exercise its full rights of free passage in the Gulf of Aqaba and through the Straits of Tiran.

11. The Government of Israel believes that the Gulf of Aqaba comprehends international waters and that no nation has the right to prevent free and innocent passage in the Gulf and through the Straits giving access thereto, in accordance with the generally accepted definition of those terms in the law of the sea.

12. In its capacity as a littoral State, Israel will gladly offer port facilities to the ships of all nations and all flags exercising free passage in the Gulf of Aqaba. We have received with gratification the assurances of leading maritime Powers that they foresee a normal and regular flow of traffic of all cargoes in the Gulf of Aqaba. Israel will do nothing to impede free and innocent passage by ships of Arab countries bound to Arab ports or to any other destination. Israel is resolved on behalf of vessels of Israel registry to exercise the right of free and innocent passage and is prepared to join with others to secure universal respect of this right. Israel will protect ships of its own flag exercising the right of free and innocent passage on the high seas and in international waters.

13. Interference, by armed force, with ships of Israel flag exercising free and innocent passage in the Gulf of Aqaba and through the Straits of Tiran, will be regarded by Israel as an attack entitling it to exercise its inherent right of self-defence under Article 51 of the United Nations Charter and to take all such measures as are necessary to ensure the free and innocent passage of its ships in the Gulf and in the Straits.

14. We make this announcement in accordance with the accepted principles of international law under which all States have an inherent right to use their forces to protect their ships and their rights against interference by armed force. My Government naturally hopes that this contingency will not occur.

15. In a public address on 20 February 1957, President Eisenhower stated: "We should not assume that, if Israel withdraws, Egypt will prevent Israel shipping from using the Suez Canal or the Gulf of Aqaba." This declaration has weighed heavily with my Government in determining its action today.

16. Israel is now prepared to withdraw its forces from the regions of the Gulf of Aqaba and the Straits of Tiran in the confidence that there will be continued freedom of navigation for international and Israel shipping in the Gulf of Aqaba and through the Straits of Tiran.

17. We propose that a meeting be held immediately between the Chief of Staff of the Israel Defence Army and the Commander of the United Nation Emergency Force in order to arrange for the United Nations to take over its responsibilities in the Sharm el Sheikh area.

18. The Government of Israel announces that it is making a complete withdrawal from the Gaza strip in accordance with General Assembly resolution 1124 (XI). It makes this announcement on the following assumptions:

(*a*) That on its withdrawal the United Nations forces will be deployed in Gaza and that the take-over of Gaza from the military and civilian control of Israel will be exclusively by the United Nations Emergency Force.

(*b*) It is, further, Israel's expectation that the United Nations will be the agency to be utilized for carrying out the functions enumerated by the Secretary-General, namely:

". . . safeguarding life and property in the area by providing efficient and effective police protection; as will guarantee good civilian administration; as will assure maximum assistance to the United Nations refugee programme; and as will protect and foster the economic development of the territory and its people." [*659th meeting, para. 29.*]

(*c*) It is, further, Israel's expectation that the aforementioned responsibility of the United Nations in the administration of Gaza will be maintained for a transitory period from the take-over until there is a peace settlement, to be sought as rapidly as possible, or a definitive agreement on the future of the Gaza strip.

19. It is the position of Israel that, if conditions are created in the Gaza strip which indicate a return to the conditions of deterioration which existed previously, Israel would reserve its freedom to act to defend its rights.

20. Accordingly, we propose that a meeting be held immediately between the Chief of Staff of the Israel Defence Army and the Commander of the United Nations Emergency Force in order to arrange for the United Nations to take over its responsibilities in the Gaza area.

21. For many weeks, amidst great difficulty, my Government has sought to ensure that on the withdrawal from the Sharm el Sheikh and the Gaza areas, circumstances would prevail which would prevent the likelihood of belligerent acts. We record with gratitude the sympathetic efforts of many Governments and delegations to help bring about a situation which would end the insecurity prevailing for Israel and its neighbours these many years. In addition to the considerations to which I have referred, we place our trust in the vigilant resolve of the international community that Israel should, equally with all Member States, enjoy its basic rights of freedom from fear of attack, freedom to sail the high seas and international waterways in peace, freedom to pursue its national destiny in tranquillity without the constant peril which has surrounded it in recent years. In this reliance we are embarking upon the course which I have announced today.

22. May I now add these few words to the States in the Middle East area and, more specifically, to the neighbours of Israel. We all come from an area which is a very ancient one. The hills and the valleys of the region have been witnesses to many wars and many conflicts. But that is not the only thing which characterizes that part of the world from which we come. It is also a part of the world which is of an ancient culture. It is that part of the world which has given to humanity three great religions. It is also that part of the world which has given a code of ethics to all humanity. In our countries, in the entire region, all our peoples are anxious for and in need of a higher standard of living, of great programmes of development and progress.

23. Can we, from now on—all of us—turn a new leaf and, instead of fighting with each other, can we all, united, fight poverty and disease and illiteracy? Is it possible for us to put all our efforts and all our energy into one single purpose, the betterment and progress and development of all our lands and all our peoples?

24. I can here pledge the Government and the people of Israel to do their part in this united effort. There is no limit to what we are prepared to contribute so that all of us, together, can live to see a day of happiness for our peoples and see again from that region a great contribution to peace and happiness for all humanity.

24. Congressional Resolution on the Middle East of March 9, 1957, as Amended by the Foreign Assistance Act of September 4, 1961*

* 71 STAT. 5 (March 9, 1957) as amended by 75 STAT. 424 (Sept. 4, 1961). Reprinted from *Collective Defense Treaties*, 90th CONG., 1st SESS., at 199-200 (Comm. Print, April 10, 1967). See also the Letter of March 12, 1970, from H. G. Torbert, Jr., Acting Assistant Secretary for Congressional Relations, to Senator J. William Fulbright, Chairman of the Senate Committee on Foreign Relations, Concerning State Department Views on Proposals to Repeal Certain Congressional Resolutions Including the Middle East Resolution, 62 DEPT. STATE BULLETIN 468-69, 470, 471 (April 6, 1970).

JOINT RESOLUTION To promote peace and stability in the Middle
   East.

*Resolved by the Senate and House of Representatives of the United
States of America in Congress assembled*, That the President be and
hereby is authorized to cooperate with and assist any nation or group of
nations in the general area of the Middle East desiring such assistance in
the development of economic strength dedicated to the maintenance of
national independence.

SEC. 2.   The President is authorized to undertake, in the general area
of the Middle East, military assistance programs with any nation or
group of nations of that area desiring such assistance. Furthermore, the
United States regards as vital to the national interest and world peace
the preservation of the independence and integrity of the nations of the
Middle East. To this end, if the President determines the necessity
thereof, the United States is prepared to use armed forces to assist any
nation or group of such nations requesting assistance against armed
aggression from any country controlled by international communism:
Provided, That such employment shall be consonant with the treaty
obligations of the United States and with the Constitution of the United
States.

SEC. 3.   The President is hereby authorized to use during the balance
of fiscal year 1957 for economic and military assistance under this joint
resolution not to exceed $200,000,000 from any appropriation now
available for carrying out the provisions of the Mutual Security Act of
1954, as amended, in accord with the provisions of such Act: *Provided,*
That, whenever the President determines it to be important to the
security of the United States such use may be under the authority of
section 401(a) of the Mutual Security Act of 1954, as amended (except
that the provisions of section 105(a) thereof shall not be waived), and
without regard to the provisions of section 105 of the Mutual Security
Appropriation Act, 1957: *Provided further*, That obligations incurred
in carrying out the purposes of the first sentence of section 2 of this
joint resolution shall be paid only out of appropriations for military
assistance, and obligations incurred in carrying out the purposes of the
first section of this joint resolution shall be paid only out of appropriations other than those for military assistance. This authorization is in
addition to other existing authorizations with respect to the use of such
appropriations. None of the additional authorizations contained in this
section shall be used until fifteen days after the Committee on Foreign

Relations of the Senate, the Committee on Foreign Affairs of the House of Representatives, the Committees on Appropriations of the Senate and the House of Representatives and, when military assistance is involved, the Committees on Armed Services of the Senate and the House of Representatives have been furnished a report showing the object of the proposed use, the country for the benefit of which such use is intended, and the particular appropriation or appropriations for carrying out the provisions of the Mutual Security Act of 1954, as amended, from which the funds are proposed to be derived: *Provided*, That funds available under this section during the balance of fiscal year 1957 shall, in the case of any such report submitted during the last fifteen days of the fiscal year, remain available for use under this section for the purposes stated in such report for a period of twenty days following the date of submission of such report. Nothing contained in this joint resolution shall be construed as itself authorizing the appropriation of additional funds for the purpose of carrying out the provisions of the first section or of the first sentence of section 2 of this joint resolution.

SEC. 4. The President should continue to furnish facilities and military assistance, within the provisions of applicable law and established policies, to the United Nations Emergency Force in the Middle East, with a view to maintaining the truce in that region.

SEC. 5. The President shall whenever appropriate[1] report to the Congress his action hereunder.

SEC. 6. This joint resolution shall expire when the President shall determine that the peace and security of the nations in the general area of the Middle East are reasonably assured by international conditions created by action of the United Nations or otherwise except that it may be terminated earlier by a concurrent resolution of the two Houses of Congress.

[1] Sec. 705 of the Foreign Assistance Act of 1961 substituted the words "whenever appropriate" in lieu of the words "within the months of January and July of each year".

25. Security Council Resolution 228 Concerning Military Action by Israel on the Territory of Jordan, November 25, 1966*

* S.C. Res. 228, 21 U.N. SCOR, Resolutions and Decisions of the Security Council 1966, at 11, U.N. Doc. S/INF/21/Rev. 1 (1968).

The Security Council,

Having heard the statements of the representatives of Jordan and Israel concerning the grave Israel military action which took place in the southern Hebron area on 13 November 1966,

Having noted the information provided by the Secretary-General concerning this military action in his statement of 16 November [17] and also in his report of 18 November 1966,[18]

Observing that this incident constituted a large-scale and carefully planned military action on the territory of Jordan by the armed forces of Israel,

Reaffirming the previous resolutions of the Security Council condemning past incidents of reprisal in breach of the General Armistice Agreement between Israel and Jordan [19] and of the United Nations Charter,

Recalling the repeated resolutions of the Security Council asking for the cessation of violent incidents across the demarcation line, and not overlooking past incidents of this nature,

Reaffirming the necessity for strict adherence to the General Armistice Agreement,

1. *Deplores* the loss of life and heavy damage to property resulting from the action of the Government of Israel on 13 November 1966;

2. *Censures* Israel for this large-scale military action in violation of the United Nations Charter and of the General Armistice Agreement between Israel and Jordan;

3. *Emphasizes* to Israel that actions of military reprisal cannot be tolerated and that, if they are repeated, the Security Council will have to consider further and more effective steps as envisaged in the Charter to ensure against the repetition of such acts;

4. *Requests* the Secretary-General to keep the situation under review and to report to the Security Council as appropriate.

Adopted at the 1328th meeting by 14 votes to none, with 1 abstention (New Zealand).

V. DOCUMENTS RELATING TO THE ARAB-ISRAELI CONFLICT

E. *The Six-Day War and the Search for Peace: 1967-1973*

26. Speech by President Nasser on Closing of the Gulf of Aqaba, May 22, 1967*

* *N.Y. Times*, May 26, 1967, at 16, cols. 2-5, reprinted in A SELECT CHRONOLOGY AND BACKGROUND DOCUMENTS RELATING TO THE MIDDLE EAST, COMMITTEE ON FOREIGN RELATIONS OF THE UNITED STATES SENATE, 90th CONG., 1st SESS., at 131-35 (Comm. Print, 1967).

The entire country looks up to you today. The entire Arab nation supports you. It is clear that in these circumstances the entire people fully support you and consider the armed forces as their hope today. It is definite that the entire Arab nation also supports our armed forces in the present circumstances through which the entire Arab nation is passing.

What I wish to say is that we are now in 1967, and not in 1956 after the tripartite aggression. A great deal was said and all the secrets were ambiguous. Israel, its commanders and rulers, boasted a great deal after 1956. I have read every word written about the 1956 events, and I also know exactly what happened in 1956.

On the night of Oct. 29, 1956, the Israeli aggression against us began. Fighting began on Oct. 30. We received the Anglo-French ultimatum which asked us to withdraw several miles west of the Suez Canal.

On Oct. 31, the Anglo-French attack on us began. The air raids began at sunset on Oct. 31. At the same time, all our forces in Sinai were withdrawn completely to inside Egypt. Thus in 1956 we did not have an opportunity to fight Israel. We decided to withdraw before the actual fighting with Israel began.

Despite our decision to withdraw, Israel was unable to occupy any of our positions except after we left them. But Israel created a big uproar, boasted and said a great deal about the Sinai campaign and the Sinai battle.

Every one of you knows all the rubbish that was said. They probably believed it themselves.

Today, more than 10 years after Suez, all the secrets have been exposed. The most important secret concerns Ben-Gurion, when the imperialists brought him to France to employ him as a dog for imperialism to begin the operation.

Ben-Gurion refused to undertake anything unless he was given a written guarantee that they would protect him from the Egyptian bombers and the Egyptian Air Force. All this is no longer secret. The entire world knows.

It was on this basis that France sent fighter planes to Ben-Gurion, and it was also on this basis that Britain pledged to Ben-Gurion to bomb Egyptian airfields within 24 hours after the aggression began.

This goes to show how much they took into account the Egyptian forces. Ben-Gurion himself said he had to think about the Haifa-Jerusalem-Tel Aviv triangle, which contains one-third of Israel's population. He could not attack Egypt out of fear of the Egyptian Air Force and bombers.

At that time we had a few Ilyushin bombers. We had just acquired them to arm ourselves. Today we have many Ilyushins and others. There is a great difference between yesterday and today, between 1956 and 1967.

Why do I say all this? I say it because we are in a confrontation with Israel. Israel today is not backed by Britain and France as was the case in 1956. It has the United States, which supports it and supplies it with arms. But the world cannot again accept the plotting which took place in 1956.

Israel has been clamoring since 1956. It speaks of Israel's competence and high standard of training. It is backed in this by the West and the Western press. They capitalized on the Sinai campaign, where no fighting actually took place because we had withdrawn to confront Britain and France.

Today we have a chance to prove the fact. We have, indeed, a chance to make the world see matters in their true perspective. We are now face to face with Israel. In recent days Israel has been making threats of aggression and it has been boasting.

On May 12 a very impertinent statement was made. Anyone reading this statement must believe that these people are so boastful and deceitful that one simply cannot remain silent. The statement said that the Israeli commanders have announced they would carry out military operations against Syria in order to occupy Damascus and overthrow the Syrian Government.

On the same day, Israeli Premier Eshkol made a strongly threatening statement against Syria. At the same time, the commentaries said that Israel believed Egypt could not make a move because it was bogged down in Yemen.

Of course they say that we are bogged down in Yemen and have problems there. We are in Yemen. But they seem to believe the lies they have been saying all these years about our existence in Yemen. It is also possible that the Israelis believe such lies.

We are capable of bearing our duties in Yemen, and at the same time doing our national duty here in Egypt in defending our borders and in attacking if Israel attacks Arab country.

On May 13 we received accurate information that Israel was concentrating on the Syrian border huge armed forces of about 11 to 13 brigades. These forces were divided into two fronts, one south of Lake Tiberias and the other north of the lake.

The decision made by Israel at this time was to carry out an aggression against Syria as of May 17. On May 14 we took our measures, discussed the matter and contacted our Syrian brothers. The Syrians also had this information.

On this basis, Lieut. Gen. Mahmud Fawzi left for Syria to coordinate matters. We told them that we had decided that if Syria was attacked, Egypt would enter the battle from the first minute. This was the situation May 14. The forces began to move in the direction of Sinai to take up normal positions.

News agencies reported yesterday that these military movements must have been the result of a previously well-laid plan. And I say that the sequence of events determined the plan. We had no plan before May 13, because we believed that Israel would not dare attack any Arab county and that Israel would not have dared to make such an impertinent statement.

On May 16 we requested the withdrawal of the United Nations Emergency Force (U.N.E.F.) in a letter from Lieut. Gen. Mahmud Fawzi. We then requested the complete withdrawal of U.N.E.F.

A big worldwide campaign, led by the United States, Britain and Canada, began opposing the withdrawal of U.N.E.F. from Egypt. Thus we felt that there were attempts to turn U.N.E.F. into a force serving neoimperialism.

It is obvious that U.N.E.F. entered Egypt with our approval and therefore cannot continue to stay in Egypt except with our approval. Until yesterday, a great deal was said about U.N.E.F.

A campaign is also being mounted against the United Nations Secretary General because he made a faithful and honest decision and could not surrender to the pressure brought to bear upon him by the United States, Britain and Canada to make U.N.E.F. an instrument for implementing imperialism's plans.

It is quite natural—and I say this quite frankly—that had U.N.E.F. ignored its basic mission and turned to achieving the aims of imperialism, we would have regarded it as a hostile force and forcibly disarmed it. We are definitely capable of doing such a job.

I say this now not to discredit the U.N.E.F. but to those who have neoimperialist ideas and who want the United Nations to achieve their aims: There is not a single nation which truly respects itself and enjoys full sovereignty which could accept these methods in any form.

At the same time I say that the U.N.E.F. has honorably and faithfully carried out its duties. And the U.N. Secretary General refused to succumb to pressure. Thus he issued immediate orders to the U.N.E.F to withdraw. Consequently, we laud the U.N.E.F., which stayed 10 years in our country serving peace.

And when they left—at a time when we found that the neoimperialist forces wanted to divert them from their basic aim—we gave them a cheerful sendoff and saluted them.

Our forces are now in Sinai, and we are in a state of complete mobilization in Gaza and Sinai. We note that there is a great deal of talk about peace these days. Peace, peace, international peace, international security, U.N. intervention and so on and so forth, which appears daily in the press.

Why is it that no one spoke about peace, the United Nations and security when on May 12 the Israeli Premier and the Israeli commanders made their statements that they would occupy Damascus, overthrow the Syrian region, strike vigorously at Syria and occupy a part of Syrian territory?

It was obvious that they approved of the statements made by the Israeli Premier and commanders.

There is talk about peace now. What is peace? If there is a true desire for peace, we say that we also work for peace.

But does peace mean that we should ignore the rights of the Palestinian people because of the lapse of time? Does peace mean that we should concede our rights because of the lapse of time? Nowadays they speak about a "U.N. presence in the region for the sake of peace." Does "U.N. presence in the region for peace" mean that we should close our eyes to everything?

The United Nations adopted a number of resolutions in favor of the Palestinian people. Israel implemented none of these resolutions. This brought no reaction from the United States.

Today U.S. Senators, members of the House of Representatives, the press and the entire world speak in favor of Israel, of the Jews. But nothing is said in favor of the Arabs.

The U.N. resolutions which are in favor of the Arabs were not implemented. What does this mean? No one is speaking in the Arab's favor. How does the United Nations stand with regard to the Palestinian people? How does it stand with regard to the tragedy which has continued since 1958?

The peace talk is heard only when Israel is in danger. But when Arab rights and the rights of the Palestinian people are lost, no one speaks about peace, rights or anything.

Therefore it is clear that an alliance exists between the Western powers—chiefly represented by the United States and Britain—and

Israel. There is a political alliance. This political alliance prompts the Western powers to give military equipment to Israel.

Yesterday and the day before yesterday the entire world was speaking about Sharm el Sheik, navigation in the Gulf of Aqaba, the Elath port. This morning I heard the B.B.C. say that in 1956 Abdel Nasser pledged to open the Gulf of Aqaba.

Of course this is not true. It was copied from a British paper called The Daily Mail. No such thing happened. Abdel Nasser would never forfeit any U.A.R. right. As I said, we would never give away a grain of sand from our soil or our country.

The armed forces' responsibility is now yours. The armed forces yesterday occupied Sharm el Sheik. What is the meaning of the armed force's occupation of Sharm el Sheik? It is an affirmation of our rights and our sovereignty over the Aqaba Gulf. The Aqaba Gulf consti tutes our Egyptian territorial waters. Under no circumstances will we allow the Israeli flag to pass through the Aqaba Gulf.

The Jews threatened war. We tell them: You are welcome, we are ready for war. Our armed forces and all our people are ready for war, but under no circumstances will we abandon any of our rights. This water is ours.

War might be an opportunity for the Jews—for Israel and Rabin [Maj. Gen. Itzhak Rabin, the Chief of Staff]—to test their forces against ours and to see that what they wrote about the 1956 battle and the occupation of Sinai was all a lot of nonsense.

Of course there is imperialism, Israel and reaction. Reaction casts doubt on everything, and so does the Islamic alliance.

We all know that the Islamic Alliance is now represented by three states: the kingdom of Saudi Arabia, the kingdom of Jordan, and Iran. They are saying that the purpose of the Islamic Alliance is to unite the Moslems against Israel.

I would like the Islamic Alliance to serve the Palestine question in only one way: by preventing the supply of oil to Israel. The oil which now reaches Israel through Elath comes from one of the Islamic Alliance states. It goes to Elath from Iran.

Who is supplying Israel with oil? The Islamic Alliance-Iran, an Islamic Alliance state.

Such is the Islamic Alliance. It is an imperialist alliance, and this means it sides with Zionism because Zionism is the main ally of imperialism.

The Arab world, which is now mobilized to the highest degree, knows all this. It knows how to deal with the imperialist agents, the allies of Zionism and the fifth column. They say they want to coordinate their plans with us. We cannot at all coordinate our plans with the Islamic Alliance members because it would mean giving our plans to the Jews and to Israel.

This is a serious battle. When we said we were ready for the battle, we meant that we would indeed fight if Syria or any other Arab state was subjected to aggression.

The armed forces are now everywhere. The army and all the forces are now mobilized, and so are the people. They are all behind you, praying for you day and night and feeling that you are the pride of their nation, of the Arab nation. This is the feeling of the Arab people in Egypt and outside Egypt. We are confident that you will honor the trust.

Every one of us is ready to die and not give away a grain of his country's sand. This, for us, is the greatest honor. It is the greatest honor for us to defend our country. We are not scared by imperialist, Zionist or reactionary campaigns.

We are independent and we know the taste of freedom. We have built a strong national army and achieved our objectives. We are building our country.

There is currently a propaganda campaign, a psychological campaign and a campaign of doubt against us. We leave all this behind us and follow the course of duty and victory.

May God be with you!

27. Security Council Resolution 236 Concerning Implementation of the Cease-Fire, June 11, 1967*

* S.C. Res. 236, 22 U.N. SCOR, Resolutions and Decisions of the Security Council 1967, at 4, U.N. Doc. S/INF/22/Rev. 2 (1968). See also S.C. Res. 233, S.C. Res. 234, and S.C. Res. 235, 22 U.N. SCOR, Resolutions and Decisions of the Security Council 1967, U.N. Doc. S/INF/22/Rev. 2 (1968), at 2-3.

The Security Council,

Taking note of the oral reports of the Secretary-General on the situation between Israel and Syria, made at the 1354th, 1355th, 1356th and 1357th meetings and the supplemental information supplied in documents S/7930 and Add. 1-3,

1. *Condemns* any and all violations of the cease-fire;

2. *Requests* the Secretary-General to continue his investigations and to report to the Council as soon as possible;

3. *Affirms* that its demand for a cease-fire and discontinuance of all military activities includes a prohibition of any forward military movements subsequent to the cease-fire;

4. *Calls for* the prompt return to the cease-fire positions of any troops which may have moved forward subsequent to 1630 hours GMT on 10 June 1967;

5. *Calls for* full co-operation with the Chief of Staff of the United Nations Truce Superversion Organization and the observers in implementing the cease-fire, including freedom of movement and adequate communications facilities.

*Adopted unanimously at the
1357th meeting.*

28. *Aide Mémoire* by Secretary-General Dag
Hammarskjöld on Conditions Governing Withdrawal
of UNEF, dated August 5, 1957, and made public
on June 12, 1967*

---

*   The Editorial Note and *Aide Memoire* are reprinted from 6 INT'L
LEGAL MATERIALS 593-602 (May-June 1967).

Editorial Note:

On June 12, 1967, Ernest A. Gross transmitted to the Editor a photocopy of a carbon copy of an *aide memoire* prepared by Secretary-General Dag Hammarskjold, dated August 5, 1957, from which the copy on the following pages is reproduced. Mr. Gross noted:

"1. The document, to which the late Secretary-General gave the formal title, "Aide Memoire," was considered by him to be an authoritative statement of the events and transactions leading to the agreement embodied in his report of November 20, 1956 (A/3375), and accepted by the General Assembly on November 24 of the same year. On August 7, 1957, Mr. Hammarskjold personally placed a copy of the Aide Memoire in my hands, making it explicitly clear that it was intended for the record and for such possible future use and interest as circumstances might require.

"2. The substance of the Aide Memoire was set out in great detail in my book, "*The United Nations: Structure for Peace*," published by the Council on Foreign Relations in 1962. In a footnote on page 31, reference is made to the fact that the "discussion is based upon authentic, though unpublished, sources," I did not consider it necessary at that time to identify the author. No question was ever raised, to my knowledge, of its validity or accuracy.

"3. The basic principle underlying the agreement was that an international force could not and should not be placed at the disposal of a national government, merely to serve the convenience of the latter or be subject to a unilateral and peremptory right to demand withdrawal.

"4. The agreement on the part of the United Nations "to maintain UNEF until its task was completed" (Document A/3375) was a reciprocal, rather than a unilateral undertaking. This is made clear by the clause in the same context: "understanding this to correspond to the wishes of the Government of Egypt."

"5. The task envisaged for UNEF, and the basis for its operations— at least as understood by the United States Government— appears from the following excerpt from the Report by the President of the United States to the Congress for the year 1957, covering U.S. Participation in the U.N. (Department of State Publication 6654, released June 1958, pp. .82-83) as follows:

'Following the recess of the 11th session of the General
Assembly on March 8, 1957, the United Nations Emergency
Force (UNEF) continued to play a vital role in maintaining
peace and relative stability along the armistice demarcation
line between Egypt and Israel and at Sharm el-Sheikh on the
Straits of Tiran. Its operations were based upon the resolution
adopted by the first emergency special session of the General
Assembly on November 5, 1956, which established UNEF "to
secure and supervise the cessation of hostilities" in accordance with all the terms of the General Assembly's resolution
of November 2, 1956, as well as upon the Assembly's resolution of February 2, 1957, which stipulated that, "after full
withdrawal of Israel from the Sharm el-Sheikh and Gaza
areas, scrupulous maintenance of the Armistice Agreement
requires the placing of the United Nations Emergency Force
on the Egyptian-Israel armistice demarcation line.'

"6. The "good faith" agreement which is central to Mr. Hammarskjold's conclusion continued to govern the treatment of UNEF
after adoption of the Assembly's resolution of February 2,
1957. This is shown also by the following quotation from an
aide memoire of U Thant of May 17, 1967 (A/6669, p. 7),
which records that:

'The Minister for Foreign Affairs of Egypt, in concluding on
behalf of the Government of Egypt the agreement of 8 February 1957 concerning the status of the United Nations Emergency Force in Egypt, recalled:

". . . the declaration of the Government of Egypt that,
when exercising its sovereign powers on any matter concerning the presence and functioning of the United Nations
Emergency Force, it would be guided, in good faith, by its
acceptance of the General Assembly resolution of 5 November 1956. . . ." ' "

5 August 1

Aide Memoire

As the decision on the UNEF was taken under Chapter VI, it was
obvious from the beginning that the resolution did in no way limit
the sovereignty of the host state. This was clear both from the resolution of the General Assembly and from the Second and Final Report
on the Emergency Force. Thus, neither the General Assembly nor the
Secretary-General, acting for the General Assembly, created any right

for Egypt, or gave any right to Egypt, in accepting consent as a condition for the presence and functioning of the UNEF on Egyptian territory. Egypt had the right, and the only problem was whether that right in this context should and could in some way be limited.

My starting point in the consideration of this last mentioned problem—the limitation of Egypt's soveriegn right in the interest of political balance and stability in the UNEF operation—was the fact that Egypt had spontaneously endorsed the General Assembly resolution of 5 November and by endorsing that resolution had consented to the presence of the UNEF for certain tasks. They could thus not ask the UNEF to withdraw before the completion of the tasks without running up against their own acceptance of the resolution on the Force and its tasks.

The question arose in relation to Egypt first in a cable received 9 November from Burns, covering an interview the same day with Fawzi. In that interview Egypt had requested clarification of the question how long it was contemplated that the Force would stay in the Demarcation Line area. To this I replied the same day: "A definite reply is at present impossible, but the emergency character of the Force links it to the immediate crisis envisaged in the resolution of 2 November and its liquidation. In case of different views as to when the crisis does not any longer warrant the presence of the troops, the matter will have to be negotiated with the parties." In a further cable to Burns the same day I said, however, also that "as the United Nations Force would come with Egypt's consent, they cannot stay nor operate unless Egypt continues to consent."

On 10 November Ambassador Loutfi, under instruction, asked me "whether it was recognized that an agreement is necessary for their (UNEF's) remaining in the Canal area" once their task in the area had been completed. I replied that it was my view that such an agreement would then be necessary.

On 11 November Ambassador Loutfi saw me again. He then said that it must be agreed that when the Egyptian consent is no more valid, the UN Force should withdraw. To this I replied that I did not find that a withdrawal of consent could be made before the tasks which had justified the entry, had been completed; if, as might happen, different views on the degree of completion of the tasks prescribed proved to exist, the matter should be negotiated.

The view expressed by Loutfi was later embodied in an Aide Memoire, dated the same day, where it was said: "The Egyptian Government takes note of the following: *A*. It being agreed that consent of Egypt is indispensable for entry and presence of the UN Forces in any part of its territory. If such consent no longer persists, these forces shall withdraw."

I replied to this in a memo dated 12 November in which I said: "I have received your Aide Memoire setting out the understanding on the basis of which the Egyptian Government accepts my announcing today that agreement on the arrival in Egypt of the United Nations Force has been reached. I wish to put on record my interpretation of two of these points.* Regarding the point quoted above in the Egyptian Aide Memoire, I then continued: "I want to put on record that the conditions which motivate the consent to entry and presence, are the very conditions to which the tasks established for the Force in the General Assembiy Resolution, 4 November, are directed. Therefore, I assume it to be recognized that as long as the task, thus prescribed, is not completed, the reasons for the consent of the Government remain valid, and that a withdrawal of this consent before completion of the task would run counter to the acceptance by Egypt of the decision of the General Assembly. I read the statement quoted in the light of these considerations. If a difference should develop, whether or not the reasons for the arrangements are still valid, the matter should be brought up for negotiation with the United Nations."

This explanation of mine was sent to the Egyptian Mission after my telephone conversation in the morning of the 12th with Dr. Fawzi where we agreed on publication of our agreement on the entry of the UNEF into Egypt. In view of the previous exchanges, I had no reason to believe that my statement would introduce any new difficulty. I also counted on the fact that Egypt probably by then was so committed as to be rather anxious not to reopen the discussion. However, I recognized to myself that there was an element of gambling involved which I felt I simply had to take in view of the danger that further delays might cause Egypt to change its mind, accept volunteers and throw our approaches overboard.

However, the next morning, 13 November, I received a message from Dr. Fawzi to the effect that the Government of Egypt could not subscribe to my interpretation of the question of consent and withdrawal, as set out on 12 November, and therefore, in the light of my communication of that date, "felt impelled to consider that the announced agreements should remain inoperative until all misunderstandings were cleared up." The Government reiterated in this context its view that if its consent no longer persisted, the UNEF should withdraw.

* [Should read: points." *Ed.*]

I replied to this communication—which caused a further delay of the transportation of troops to Egypt by at least 24 hours—in a cable sent immediately on receipt of the communication. In drafting my reply I had a feeling that it now was a must to get the troops in and that I would be in a position to find a formula, saving the face of Egypt while protecting the UN stand, once I could discuss the matter personally with President Nasser.

In the official reply 13 November I said that my previous statement had put forward my personal opinion that "the reasons" for consent remained valid as long as the task was not completed. I also said that for that reason a withdrawal of consent leading to the withdrawal of the Force before the task was completed (as previously stated) in my view, "although within the rights of the Egyptian Government would go against its acceptance of the basis resolution of the General Assembly." I continued by saying that my reference to negotiation was intended to indicate only that the question of withdrawal should be a matter of discussion to the extent that different views were held as to whether the task of the General Assembly was fulfilled or not. I referred in this respect to my stand as explained already in my message of 9 November, as quoted above.

I commented upon the official reply in a special personal message to Fawzi, sent at the same time, where I said that we "both had to reserve our freedom of action, but that, all the same, we could go ahead, hoping that a controversial situation would not arise." "If arrangements would break down on this issue" (withdrawal only on completion of the tasks), "I could not avoid going to the General Assembly" (with the conflict which had developed between us on this question of principle) "putting it to their judgment to decide what could or could not be accepted as an understanding. This situation would be a most embarrassing one for all but I would fear the political repercussions, as obviously very few would find it reasonable that recognition of your freedom of action should mean that you, after having permitted the Force to come, might ask it to withdraw at a time when the very reasons which had previously prompted you to accept were still obviously valid." I ended by saying that I trusted that Fawzi on the basis of this personal message could help me by "putting the stand I had to take on my own rights, in the right perspective." The letter to Fawzi thus made it clear that if the Government did not accept my stand on withdrawal as a precondition for further steps, the matter would be raised in the Assembly.

On the basis of these two final communications from me, Egypt gave green lights for the arrival of the troops, thus, in fact, accepting my stand and letting it supersede their own communication 13 November.

In my effort to follow up the situation, which prevailed after the exchange in which different stands had been maintained by Egypt and by me, I was guided by the consideration that Egypt constitutionally had an undisputed right to request the withdrawal of the troops, even if initial consent had been given, but that, on the other hand, it should be possible on the basis of my own stand as finally tacitly accepted, to force them into an agreement in which they limited their freedom of action as to withdrawal by making a request for withdrawal dependent upon the completion of the task—a question which, in the UN, obviously would have to be submitted to interpretation by the General Assembly.

The most desirable thing, of course, would have been to tie Egypt by an agreement in which they declared, that withdrawal should take place only if so decided by the General Assembly. Put in this naked form, however, the problem could never have been settled. I felt that the same was true of an agreement to the effect that withdrawal should take place upon "agreement on withdrawal" between the UN and the Egyptian Government. However, I found it worthwhile to try a line, very close to the second one, according to which Egypt would declare to the United Nations that it would exert all its sovereign rights with regard to the troops on the basis of a good faith interpretation of the tasks of the Force. The United Nations should make a reciprocal commitment to maintain the Force as long as the task was not completed. If such a dual statement was introduced in an agreement between the parties, it would be obvious that the procedure in case of a request from Egypt for the withdrawal of UNEF would be as follows. The matter would at once be brought before the General Assembly. If the General Assembly found that the task was completed, everything would be all right. If they found that the task was not completed and Egypt, all the same, maintained its stand and enforced the withdrawal, Egypt would break the agreement with the United Nations. Of course Egypt's freedom of action could under no circumstances be limited but by some kind of agreement. The device I used meant only that instead of limiting their rights by a basic understanding requesting an agreement *directly concerning withdrawal*, we created an obligation to reach agreement on the fact that the tasks were completed and, thus, *the conditions for a withdrawal established.*

I elaborated a draft text for an agreement along the lines I had in mind during the night between 15 and 16 November in Capodachino. I showed the text to Fawzi at our first talk on 16 November and I discussed practically only this issue with Nasser for 7 hours in the

evening and night of 17 November. Nasser, in this final discussion,
where the text I had proposed was approved with some amendments,
showed that he very fully understood that, by limiting their freedom of
action in the way I proposed, they would take a very serious step, as
it would mean that the question of the extent of the task would become
decisive for the relations between Egypt and the United Nations and
would determine Egypt's political freedom of action. He felt, not without justification, that the definition given of the task in the UN texts
was very loose and that, tying the freedom of action of Egypt to the
concept of the task—which had to be interpreted also by the General
Assembly—and doing so in a written agreement, meant that he accepted
a far-reaching and unpredictable restriction. To shoot the text through
in spite of Nasser's strong wish to avoid this, and his strong suspicion of
the legal construction—especially of the possible consequences of differences of views regarding the task—I felt obliged, in the course of the
discussion, to threaten three times, that unless an agreement of this type
was made, I would have to propose the immediate withdrawal of the
troops. If any proof would be necessary for how the text of the agreement was judged by President Nasser, this last mentioned fact tells the
story.

It is obvious that, with a text of the content mentioned approved by
Egypt, the whole previous exchange of views was superseded by a
formal and explicit recognition by Egypt of the stand I had taken all
through, in particular on 9 and 12 November. The previous exchange of
cables cannot any longer have any interpretative value as only the text
of the agreement was put before the General Assembly and approved by
it with the concurrence of Egypt and as its text was self-contained and
conclusive. All further discussion, therefore, has to start from the text
of the agreement, which is to be found in Document A/3375. The
interpretation of the text must be the one set out above.

29. Statement of Secretary-General U Thant on the Hammarskjöld *Aide Mémoire*, June 19, 1967*

* *N.Y. Times*, June 20, 1967, at 19, cols. 2-7. See also the Report of the Secretary-General on the Withdrawal of the United Nations Emergency Force, June 26, 1967, U.N. GAOR, Annexes, Fifth Emergency Special Session, at 9-21, U.N. Doc. A/6730/Add. 3 (June 26, 1967).

I have noted press reports on the morning of 19 June relating to a paper or memorandum which I am told was written by Dag Hammarskjold in August, 1957, setting forth certain of his views about the presence of U.N.E.F. in the U.A.R. The plain fact is there is little that is new in the memorandum and it makes no revelations which would warrant the special significance being attributed to it in some quarters. In any case, such a paper could not alter the basis for the presence of U.N.E.F. on the soil of the U.A.R., as set out in the official documents.

I wish to make the following specific comments on this memorandum:

1. It is not an official document, is not in the official files of the Secretary General's Office, and its existence has never been reported in any way to any organ of the United Nations, including the U.N.E.F. Advisory Committee. It was thus of a purely private character and although supposedly secret in nature, is said to have been given by him to one or more of Mr. Hammarskjold's friends. To say the least, the release of such a paper at this time would seem to raise some questions of ethics and good faith.

2. It can be said with full confidence that this paper was never conveyed to President Nasser or to the Government of the U.A.R. That Government knew nothing about it and was in no way bound by it.

3. I, however, had been made aware of the substance of the paper before my visit to Cairo to talk with President Nasser.

4. The crux of the matters dwelt upon in the Hammarskjold paper is the understanding between Mr. Hammarskjold and President Nasser, which sometimes has been referred to as the "good faith" accord. There is, in fact, nothing new about this. In my special report to the General Assembly of 18 May (A/6669, Paragraph 7) I gave the text of an aide-memoire which I had immediately sent to the Government of the United Arab Republic on the "good faith" accord. No response to it was received.

5. It is puzzling to me, however, that those who attempt to read so much into the Hammarskjold paper, and particularly into the "good faith" accord, do not see—or do not choose to see—the clear fact that the "good faith" accord, having been reached in November, 1956, had a more limited scope and could not possibly have envisaged or have had any relevance to the later function defined for U.N.E.F. by the General Assembly in February, 1957.

In OPI [Office of Public Information] background Release EMF/449 of 3 June 1967, entitled "Notes on Withdrawal of United Nations Emergency Force (U.N.E.F.)" this point was clearly stated in Paragraph 17 of that paper in the following words:

"It has been asserted that the so-called 'good faith' accord (see Document A/6669 of 18 May 1967, Para. 7) implied that Egypt's acceptance of General Assembly Resolution 1000 (ES-I) of 5 November 1956 would oblige Egypt to continue to accept the presence of U.N.E.F. until the task of the force was completed.

"Such a view, which reads more into the 'good faith' understanding than is justified, also ignores the fact that this understanding was reached in mid-November 1956 and therefore could relate only to General Assembly Resolution 1000 (ES-I) of 5 November 1956 which defined the task of U.N.E.F. in very general terms as being 'to secure and supervise the cessation of hostilities.'

"At that early stage the purpose of the force in reality was to replace the withdrawing forces of France, Israel and the United Kingdom, and to be, in fact, the condition for the withdrawal of those forces. Hostilities ceased, automatically in fact, once U.N.E.F. was deployed and thus its task at that time was completed.

"It was not until its resolution of 2 February 1957 that the General Assembly broadened the function of U.N.E.F. in its resolution 1125 (XI) by stating that:

" 'The scrupulous maintenance of the armistice agreement requires the placing of the United Nations Emergency Force on the Egyptian-Israeli armistice demarcation line and the implementation of other measures as proposed in the secretary-general's report.'

"'That broader task, clearly, is not completed, and it would be impossible to say at present when it will or can be completed. The armistice has already endured for over 18 years. But this was not the task envisaged or defined for U.N.E.F. when Secretary General Hammarskjold and President Nasser reached the 'good faith' understanding.

6. There is also a failure by many to recognize another central and decisive point which is not touched upon at all in the Hammarskjold paper. This point is that from the time of the development of U.N.E.F. along the lines between Israel and the United Arab Republic in pursuance of the General Assembly resolution of 2 February 1957, 1125 (xi)—although only on the U.A.R. side because of Israel's firm refusal to accept it on the Israel side—U.N.E.F.'s effective discharge of its buffer function depended completely upon the voluntary action of the U.A.R. in keeping its troops away from the line, thus leaving U.N.E.F. in a buffer position and avoiding a direct military confrontation between the armed forces of Israel and the United Arab Republic.

Indeed, Israel has never observed a buffer zone on its side of the line and Israel troops have always patrolled directly alongside it.

On the other hand, no one could possibly question the full right of the United Arab Republic to move its troops to the line whenever it might choose to do so. Once its troops began to make such a move, as they did in fact on the morning of 17 May—more than 24 hours before I received the request from the Government of the United Arab Republic for the withdrawal of the force—U.N.E.F. could no longer perform any useful function in maintaining quiet and its continuing presence on U.A.R. territory lost any real significance.

30. Security Council Resolution 237 Concerning Humanitarian Protection for Civilians and Prisoners of War in the Area of the Middle East Conflict, June 14, 1967*

---

* S.C. Res. 237, 22 U.N. SCOR, Resolutions and Decisions of the Security Council 1967, at 5, U.N. Doc. S/INF/22/Rev. 2 (1968). See generally the Geneva Convention Relative to the Treatment of Prisoners of War of August 12, 1949, and the Geneva Convention Relative to the Protection of Civilian Persons in Time of War of August 12, 1949, 79 UNTS Nos. 972 and 973, at respectively 135-287 and 287-419 (1950).

The Security Council,

Considering the urgent need to spare the civil populations and the prisoners of the war in the area of conflict in the Middle East additional sufferings,

Considering that essential and inalienable human rights should be respected even during the vicissitudes of war,

Considering that all the obligations of the Geneva Convention relative to the Treatment of Prisoners of War of 12 August 1949[1] should be complied with by the parties involved in the conflict,

1. *Calls upon* the Government of Israel to ensure the safety, welfare and security of the inhabitants of the areas where military operations have taken place and to facilitate the return of those inhabitants who have fled the areas since the outbreak of hostilities;

2. *Recommends* to the Governments concerned the scrupulous respect of the humanitarian principles governing the treatment of prisoners of war and the protection of civilian persons in time of war contained in the Geneva Conventions of 12 August 1949;[2]

3. *Requests* the Secretary-General to follow the effective implementation of this resolution and to report to the Security Council.

*Adopted unanimously at the
1361st meeting.*

Decisions

At its 1365th meeting, on 8 July 1967, the Council decided to invite the representatives of Israel, the United Arab Republic, Syria, Jordan, Lebanon, Iraq, Morocco, Saudi Arabia, Kuwait, Tunisia, Libya and Pakistan to participate, without vote, in the discussion of the item entitled:

"Letter dated 23 May 1967 from the Permanent Representatives of Canada and Denmark addressed to the President of the Security Council (S/7902);

"Complaint of the representative of the United Arab Republic in a letter to the President of the Security Council dated 27 May 1967 entitled 'Israel aggressive policy, its repeated aggression threatening peace and security in the Middle East and endangering international peace and security' (S/7907);

"Letter dated 29 May 1967 from the Permanent Representative of the United Kingdom addressed to the President of the Security Council (S/7910);

[1] United Nations, *Treaty Series*, vol. 75 (1950), No. 972.
[2] United Nations, *Treaty Series*, vol. 75 (1950), Nos. 970-973.

"Letter dated 9 June 1967 from the Permanent Representative of the Union of Soviet Socialist Republics addressed to the President of the Security Council concerning an item entitled 'Cessation of military action by Israel and withdrawal of the Israel forces from those parts of the territory of the United Arab Republic, Jordan and Syria which they have seized as a result of an aggression' (S/7967);

"Letter dated 8 July 1967 from the Permanent Representative of the United Arab Republic addressed to the President of the Security Council (S/8043);

"Letter dated 8 July 1967 from the Permanent Representative of Israel addressed to the President of the Security Council (S/8044)."

At its 1366th meeting, on 9 July 1967, the Council decided to invite the representative of Algeria to participate, without vote, in the discussion of the question.

At the same meeting, the President read the following statement as representing the consensus of the views of the members of the Council:

"Recalling Security Council resolutions 233 (1967) of 6 June, 234 (1967) of 7 June, 235 (1967) of 9 June and 236 (1967) of 11 June 1967, and emphasizing the need for all parties to observe scupulously the provisions of these resolutions, having heard the statements made by the Secretary-General and the suggestions he has addressed to the parties concerned, I believed that I am reflecting the view of the Council that the Secretary-General should proceed, as he has suggested in his statements before the Council on 8 and 9 July 1967, to request the Chief of Staff of the United Nations Truce Supervision Organization, General Odd Bull, to work out with the Governments of the United Arab Republic and Israel, as speedily as possible, the necessary arrangements to station United Nations military observers in the Suez Canal sector under the Chief of Staff of the United Nations Truce Supervision Organization."

At its 1369th meeting, on 24 October 1967, the Council decided to invite the representatives of Israel, the United Arab Republic, Jordan and Syria to participate, without vote, in the discussion of the item entitled "The situation in the Middle East: (a) Letter dated 24 October 1967 from the Permanent Representative of the United Arab Republic addressed to the President of the Security Council (S/8207); (b) Letter dated 24 October 1967 from the Permanent Representative of Israel addressed to the President of the Security Council (S/8208)."

31. General Assembly Resolution 2252 (ES-V) Concerning Humanitarian Assistance to Civilians and Prisoners of War, July 4, 1967*

---

* G.A. Res. 2252 (ES-V), U.N. GAOR, Resolutions adopted by the General Assembly during its Fifth Emergency Special Session 17 June-18 September 1967, Supp. 1, at 3-4, U.N. Doc. A/6798 (1967). See also the *Note by the Secretary-General Under Security Council Resolution 237 (1967) and General Assembly Resolution 2252 (ES-V) July 31, 1968,* 23 U.N. SCOR, Supp. for July, Aug., and Sept. 1968, at 73-95 (1969), U.N. Doc. S/8699 & A/7149 (1969); *Report of the Secretary-General Under General Assembly Resolution 2252 (ES-V) and Security Council Resolution 237 (1967),* 22 U.N. SCOR, Supp. for Oct., Nov., and Dec. 1967, at 80-154 (1968), U.N. Doc. S/8158 & A/6797 (Oct. 2, 1967). This 1967 report includes detailed information compiled by Mr. Nils-Goran Gussing, the Special Representative of the Secretary-General, on conditions affecting civilian populations and prisoners of war in the aftermath of the 1967 war.

The General Assembly,

Considering the urgent need to alleviate the suffering inflicted on civilians and on prisoners of war as a result of the recent hostilities in the Middle East,

1. *Welcomes with great satisfaction* Security Council resolution 237 (1967) of 14 June 1967, whereby the Council:

(*a*) Considered the urgent need to spare the civil populations and the prisoners of war in the area of conflict in the Middle East additional sufferings;

(*b*) Considered that essential and inalienable human rights should be respected even during the vicissitudes of war;

(*c*) Considered that all the obligations of the Geneva Convention relative to the Treatment of Prisoners of War of 12 August 1949[1] should be complied with by the parties involved in the conflict;

(*d*) Called upon the Government of Israel to ensure the safety, welfare and security of the inhabitants of the areas where military operations had taken place and to facilitate the return of those inhabitants who had fled the areas since the outbreak of hostilities;

(*e*) Recommended to the Governments concerned the scrupulous respect of the humanitarian principles governing the treatment of prisoners of war and the protection of civilian persons in time of war, contained in the Geneva Conventions of 12 August 1949;[2]

(*f*) Requested the Secretary-General to follow the effective implementation of the resolution and to report to the Security Council;

2. *Notes with gratitude and satisfaction* and endorses the appeal made by the President of the General Assembly on 26 June 1967;[3]

3. *Notes with gratification* the work undertaken by the International Committee of the Red Cross, the League of Red Cross Societies and other voluntary organizations to provide humanitarian assistance to civilians;

4. *Notes further with gratification* the assistance which the United Nations Children's Fund is providing to women and children in the area;

5. *Commends* the Commissioner-General of the United Nations Relief and Works Agency for Palestine Refugees in the Near East for his efforts to continue the activities of the Agency in the present situa-

---

[1] United Nations, *Treaty Series,* vol. 75 (1950), No. 972.
[2] United Nations, *Treaty Series,* vol. 75 (1950), Nos. 970-973.
[3] See *Official Records of the General Assembly, Fifth Emergency Special Session, Plenary Meetings,* 1536th meeting, paras. 29-37.

tion with respect to all persons coming within his mandate;

6. *Endorses,* bearing in mind the objectives of the above-mentioned Security Council resolution, the efforts of the Commissioner-General of the United Nations Relief and Works Agency for Palestine Refugees in the Near East to provide humanitarian assistance, as far as practicable, on an emergency basis and as a temporary measure, to other persons in the area who are at present displaced and are in serious need of immediate assistance as a result of the recent hostilities;

7. *Welcomes* the close co-operation of the United Nations Relief and Works Agency for Palestine Refugees in the Near East, and of the other organizations concerned, for the purpose of co-ordinating assistance;

8. *Calls upon* all the Member States concerned to facilitate the transport of supplies to all areas in which assistance is being rendered;

9. *Appeals* to all Governments, as well as organizations and individuals, to make special contributions for the above purposes to the United Nations Relief and Works Agency for Palestine Refugees in the Near East and also to the other intergovernmental and non-governmental organizations concerned;

10. *Requests* the Secretary-General, in consultation with the Commissioner-General of the United Nations Relief and Works Agency for Palestine Refugees in the Near East, to report urgently to the General Assembly on the needs arising under paragraphs 5 and 6 above;

11. *Further requests* the Secretary-General to follow the effective implementation of the present resolution and to report thereon to the General Assembly.

1548th plenary meeting,
4 July 1967.

32. Law of Israel Amending the Municipalities Ordinance to Empower the Minister of the Interior to Enlarge a Particular Municipality to Include an Area Designated by the Government by Order, June 27, 1967*

* 21 LAWS OF THE STATE OF ISRAEL 75 (passed by the Knesset on June 27, 1967). For the implementing proclamation under this amendment extending the municipality of Jerusalem, see Jerusalem Proclamation (Extension of Municipality Borders), 5727-1967, KOVETZ-HATAKANOT of 5727, p. 2634 (proclaimed by the Minister of the Interior, June 28, 1967). For the implementing order under this enabling act applying Israeli law to East Jerusalem, see Law and Administration Order No. 1, 5727-1967, KOVETZ-HATAKANOT of 5727, p. 2690 (Ordered by the Government [the Cabinet] of Israel, June 28, 1967). See also the Law of Israel amending the Municipalities Ordinance to Empower the Minister of the Interior to enlarge a particular municipality to include an area designated by the Government by order, 22 LAWS OF THE STATE OF ISRAEL 75 (passed by the Knesset on June 27, 1967), and the implementing proclamation under this amendment extending the municipality of Jerusalem, Jerusalem Proclamation (Extension of Municipality Borders), 5727-1967, KOVETZ-KATAKANOT of 5727, p. 2634 (proclaimed by the Minister of the Interior, June 28, 1967).

Municipalities Ordinance (Amendment No. 6)
Law, 5727-1967

1. In the Municipalities Ordinance), the following section shall be inserted after section 8:

8A. (a) The Minister may, at his discretion and without an inquiry under section 8 being made, enlarge, by proclamation, the area of a particular municipality by the inclusion of an area designated by order under section 11B of the Law and Administration Ordinance, 5708-1948).

(b) Where the Minister has enlarged the area of a municipality as aforesaid, he may, by order, appoint additional councillors from among the inhabitants of the newly-included area. A councillor appointed as aforesaid shall hold office so long as the council holds office: Provided that the Minister may, by order, appoint another person in his stead."

2. This Law shall come into force on the date of its adoption by the Knesset.

LEVI ESHKOL
Prime Minister

HAIM MOSHE SHAPIRO
Minister of the Interior

SHNEUR ZALMAN SHAZAR
President of the State

33. Law of Israel Concerning Protection of the Holy Places, June 27, 1967*

* 21 LAWS OF THE STATE OF ISRAEL 76 (passed by the Knesset on June 27, 1967).

Protection of Holy Places Law, 5727-1967

1. The Holy Places shall be protected from desecration and any other violation and from anything likely to violate the freedom of access of the members of the different religions to the places sacred to them or their feelings with regard to those places.

2. (a) Whosoever desecrates or otherwise violates a Holy Place shall be liable to imprisonment for a term of seven years.

(b) Whosoever does anything likely to violate the freedom of access of the members of the different religions to the places sacred to them or their feelings with regard to those places shall be liable to imprisonment for a term of five years.

3. This Law shall add to, and not derogate from, any other law.

4. The Minister of Religious Affairs is charged with the implementation of this Law, and he may, after consultation with, or upon the proposal of, representatives of the religions concerned and with the consent of the Minister of Justice make regulations as to any matter relating to such implementation.

5. This Law shall come into force on the date of its adoption by the Knesset.

LEVI ESHKOL
Prime Minister

ZERACH WARHAFTIG
Minister of Religious Affairs

SHNEUR ZALMAN SHAZAR
President of the State

34. General Assembly Resolution 2253 (ES-V) Concerning Measures Taken by Israel to Change the Status of the City of Jerusalem, July 4, 1967*

---

* G.A. Res. 2253 (ES-V) U.N. GAOR, Resolutions adopted by the General Assembly during its Fifth Emergency Special Sessions 17 June-18 September 1967, Supp. 1, at 4, U.N. Doc. A/6798 (1967).

The General Assembly,

Deeply concerned at the situation prevailing in Jerusalem as a result of the measures taken by Israel to change the status of the City,

1. *Considers* that these measures are invalid;

2. *Calls upon* Israel to rescind all measures already taken and to desist forthwith from taking any action which would alter the status of Jerusalem;

3. *Requests* the Secretary-General to report to the General Assembly and the Security Council on the situation and on the implementation of the present resolution not later than one week from its adoption.

1548th plenary meeting,
4 July 1967.

35. Report of the Secretary-General on Measures Taken by Israel to Change the Status of the City of Jerusalem, Including a Letter from Abba Eban, the Israeli Minister for Foreign Affairs, to the Secretary-General Concerning the Status of Jerusalem, July 10, 1967*

* *Report of the Secretary-General on Measures Taken by Israel to Change the Status of the City of Jerusalem,* 22 U.N. SCOR, Supp. July-Sept. 1967, at 73, U.N. Doc. S/8052 (July 10, 1967).

[10 July 1967]

1. The General Assembly, in paragraph 3 of its resolution 2253 (ES-V) adopted on 4 July 1967, requested the Secretary-General "to report to the General Assembly and the Security Council on the situation and on the implementation of the present resolution not later than one week from its adoption."

2. In a letter dated 5 July 1967 addressed to the Minister for Foreign Affairs of Israel, the Secretary-General requested the Minister to draw the above-mentioned resolution to the attention of his Government as a matter of urgency.

3. On 10 July the Secretary-General received the following reply from the Minister for Foreign Affairs, transmitted by the Permanent Representative of Israel to the United Nations.

Letter addressed to the Secretary-General by the Minister
for Foreign Affairs of Israel

My Government has given careful consideration to your letter of 5 July 1967, concerning resolution 2253 (ES-V) of the General Assembly. Israel's position on Jerusalem was explained by me at the plenary meetings of the General Assembly on 21 and 29 June 1967.[1] In response to your letter, the Government of Israel now takes the opportunity of reviewing recent developments in the City.

As a result of aggression launched by the Arab States against Israel in 1948, the section of Jerusalem in which the Holy Places are concentrated had been governed for nineteen years by a regime which refused to give due acknowledgement to universal religious concerns. The City was divided by a military demarcation line. Houses of worship were destroyed and desecrated in acts of vandalism. Instead of peace and security there was hostility and frequent bloodshed. The principle of freedom of access to the Holy Places of all the three monotheistic religions was violated with regard to Jews, but not to them alone. The Jordan Government informed the *Ad Hoc* Political Committee at the fourth and fifth sessions of the General Assembly, on 6 December 1949 [58th meeting] and 11 December 1950 [77th meeting], that it would not agree to any special arrangements for the Holy Places. This policy was the subject of a reference by the President of the Trusteeship Council, M. Roger Garreau, in his report [T/681][2] on the mission entrusted

[1] See *Official Records of the General Assembly, Fifth Emergency Special Session, Plenary Meetings,* 1529th and 1541st meetings.

[2] *Ibid., Fifth Session, Supplement No. 9,* annex III.

to him by virtue of the Trusteeship Council resolution [232 (VI)] of 4 April 1950, in which he stated:

"... I have to state with the deepest regret that up to yesterday, when my term as President of the Trusteeship Council came to an end, the Government of the Hashemite Kingdom of Jordan had not seen fit to break its silence.

"The Government of Israel showed a spirit of conciliation which led it to submit to the Trusteeship Council certain new proposals which ... represent a considerable advance towards a settlement of the various aspects of the problem of Jerusalem and the Holy Places ..."

On 5 June 1967, the Jordanian forces launched a destructive and unprovoked armed assault on the part of Jerusalem outside the walls. This attack was made despite Israel's appeals to Jordan to abstain from hostilities. Dozens of Jerusalem citizens were killed and hundreds wounded.

Artillery bombardment was directed against synagogues, the Church of Dormition, hospitals, centres of secular and religious learning, the Hebrew University and the Israel Museum. Intensive fire was directed against institutions and residential centres from positions in and near the Holy Places themselves, which were thus converted into military positions for shelling Jerusalem.

Since 7 June, the entire City of Jerusalem has experienced peace and unity. The Holy Places of all faiths have been open to access by those who hold them sacred.

The resolution presented on 4 July by Pakistan and adopted on the same date evidently refers to measures taken by the Government of Israel on 27 June 1967. The term "annexation" used by supporters of the resolution is out of place. The measures adopted relate to the integration of Jerusalem in the administrative and municipal spheres, and furnish a legal basis for the protection of the Holy Places in Jerusalem.

I now come to specify the character and effect of the measures adopted of 27 June:

(1) THE HOLY PLACES

The Protection of Holy Places Law, 5727-1967, provides that "the Holy Places shall be protected from desecration and any other violation and from anything likely to violate the freedom of access of the members of the different religions to the places sacred to them or their feelings with regard to those places. Whoever desecrates or otherwise violates a Holy Place shall be liable to imprisonment for a term of seven years. . . ."

During the previous nineteen years there had been no such legislation to
to protect the Holy Places in Jerusalem. Since 27 June, sacred buildings
desecrated since 1948 have been restored, and houses of worship
destroyed during the Jordanian occupation are being rebuilt.

(2) CIVIC CO-OPERATION

One of the most significant results of the measures taken on 27 June
is the new mingling of Arabs and Jews in free and constant association.
The Arab residents within the walls had been cut off for nineteen years
from all contact with the residents of the newer parts of the City. Today
they are free to renew or initiate contacts with their Jewish neighbours
in Jerusalem and elsewhere.in Israel. The residents of the City outside
the walls now visit the Old City. There is a profound human and
spiritual significance in the replacement of embattled hostility by
normal and good neighbourly relations. It is especially appropriate that
oecumenical habits of thought and action should take root in the City
from which the enduring message of human brotherhood was proclaimed
with undying power in generations past.

(3) MUNICIPAL SERVICES

In the hills of Judea, where Jerusalem is situated, there is an acute
shortage of water. The Old City is now connected with the general water
supply system, and all houses are receiving a continuous supply of
water, double the quantity available to them in the past.

All hospitals and clinics are already functioning. In the past no health
services existed for the young within the framework of the school
system, nor were there any health stations for mother and child care.
These services are now being established.

There was no social welfare system in the Old City. Today all the
inhabitants of Jerusalem now enjoy the same welfare rights. The
municipality has already begun extending its welfare services to those
for whom none were available in the past.

School buildings are being prepared for the resumption of studies at
the beginning of the new school year. Teachers are being located and
arrangements made for them to return to their work. Their salaries are
paid by the municipality.

Compulsory education regulations have been extended to all parts of
the City. None of those arrangements affect the existing private education network.

If these measures had not been taken, the Holy Places would be without legal protection. The unified public utilities services would not exist. Municipal and administrative facilities would not be extended to some sections of the City, and Jerusalem's residents would still be divided, hermetically confined in separate compartments.

THE UNIVERSAL INTEREST

The measures taken by my Government to secure the protection of the Holy Places are only a part of Israel's effort to ensure respect for universal interests in Jerusalem. It is evident from United Nations discussions and documents that the international interest in Jerusalem has always been understood to derive from the presence of the Holy Places. Israel does not doubt her own will and capacity to secure the respect of universal spiritual interests. It has forthwith ensured that the Holy Places of Judaism, Christianity and Islam be administered under the responsibility of the religions which hold them sacred. In addition, in a spirit of concern for historic and spiritual traditions, my Government has taken steps with a view to reaching arrangements to assure the universal character of the Holy Places. In pursuance of this objective, the Government of Israel has now embarked on a constructive and detailed dialogue with representatives of universal religious interests. If these explorations are as fruitful as we hope and expect, the universal character of the Holy Places will for the first time in recent decades find effective expression.

The change which have affected Jerusalem's life and destiny as a result of the measures recently adopted may therefore be summarized as follows: where there was hostile separation, there is now harmonious civic union. Where there was a constant threat of violence, there is now peace. Where there was once an assertion of exclusive and unilateral control over the Holy Places, exercised in sacrilegious discrimination, there is now a willingness to work out arrangements with the world's religious bodies—Christian, Moslem and Jewish—which will ensure the universal religious character of the Holy Places.

The Government of Israel is confident that world opinion will welcome the new prospect of seeing this ancient and historic metropolis thrive in unity, peace and spiritual elevation.

(*Signed*) Abba EBAN
Minister for Foreign Affairs of Israel

36. Excerpt from a Statement by United States Representative Arthur J. Goldberg at the Fifth Emergency Special Session of the United Nations General Assembly Concerning the United States Position on Jerusalem, July 14, 1967*

* 57 DEPT. STATE BULLETIN 148 (1967); reprinted in UNITED STATES POLICY IN THE NEAR EAST CRISIS (Dept. of State Publication No. 8269 Aug. 1967), 22-24.

Statement by Ambassador Goldberg

Mr. President, the goal of the United States in the Middle East, one we believe shared by the great preponderance of the world community, is a durable peace and enduring settlement. We conceive of this goal as requiring throughout the area far more than a return to the temporary and fragile truce which erupted into tragic conflict on June 5.

We are convinced, both by logic and the unforgettable experience of a tragic history, that there can be progress toward the durable peace in the entire area only if certain essential steps are taken. One immediate, obvious, and imperative step is the disengagement of all forces and the withdrawal of Israeli forces to their own territory. A second and equally immediate, obvious, and imperative step is the termination of any claims to a state of war or belligerency on the part of Arab states in the area.

These two steps are essential to progress toward a durable peace. They are equally essential if there is to be substance and concrete meaning to the basic charter right of every state in the area, a right to which the United States remains firmly committed: the right to have its territorial integrity and political independence respected by all and free from the threat or use of force by all.

The United States stands ready to give its full support to practical measures to help bring about these steps—withdrawal of forces and the termination of belligerent acts or claims as soon as possible.

But if our goal is a durable peace, it is imperative that there be greater vision both from this organization and from the parties themselves. It is imperative that all look beyond the immediate causes and effects of the recent conflict. Attention must also be focused, and urgently:

—on reaching a just and permanent settlement of the refugee problem, which has been accentuated by recent events;

—on means to insure respect for the right of every member of the United Nations in the area to live in peace and security as an independent national state;

—on arrangements so that respect for the territorial integrity and political independence of all states in the area is assured;

—on measures to insure respect for the rights of all nations to freedom of navigation and of innocent passage through international waterways;

—on reaching agreement, both among those in the area and those outside, that economic development and the improvement of living standards should be given precedence over a wasteful arms race in the area.

In each and every one of the separate but related imperatives of peace, we recognize fully that agreement cannot be imposed upon the parties from outside. At the same time, we also believe that the machinery, experience, and resources of the United Nations can be of immeasurable help in implementing agreements acceptable to the parties.

The offer of such assistance by this organization is dictated not only by the roots of United Nations responsibility and involvement in the Middle East, which have grown deep and strong over two decades; it is also dictated by our common determination, even duty, under the charter to save succeeding generations in the Middle East from the scourge of another war.

It is against the background of this overall policy that my Government has developed its attitudes toward the question of Jerusalem, and I wish to make that attitude very explicit. The views of my Government on Jerusalem have been expressed by the President of the United States and other high-level officials.

On June 28, the White House released the following statement:[1]

The President said on June 19 that in our view "there . . . must be adequate recognition of the special interest of three great religions in the holy places of Jerusalem."[2] On this principle he assumes that before any unilateral action is taken on the status of Jerusalem there will be appropriate consultation with religious leaders and others who are deeply concerned. Jerusalem is holy to Christians, to Jews, and to Moslems. It is one of the great continuing tragedies of history that a city which is so much the center of man's highest values has also been, over and over, a center of conflict. Repeatedly the passionate beliefs of one element have led to exclusion or unfairness for others. It has been so, unfortunately, in the last 20 years. Men of all religions will agree that we must now do better. The world must find an answer that is fair and recognized to be fair. . . .

The second statement, released on the same day by the Department of State, read:[3]

The hasty administrative action taken today cannot be regarded as determining the future of the holy places or the status of Jerusalem in relation to them.

The United States has never recognized such unilateral actions by any of the states in the area as governing the international status of Jerusalem. . . .

[1] For text, see BULLETIN of July 17, 1967, p. 60.
[2] *Ibid.*, July 10, 1967, p. 31.
[3] For text, see *ibid.*, July 17, 1967, p. 60.

During my own statement to the General Assembly on July 3,[4] I said that the "safeguarding of the holy places, and freedom of access to them for all, should be internationally guaranteed; and the status of Jerusalem in relation to them should be decided not unilaterally but in consultation with all concerned." These statements represent the considered and continuing policy of the United States Government.

With regard to the specific measures taken by the Government of Israel on June 28, I wish to make it clear that the United States does not accept or recognize these measures as altering the status of Jerusalem. My Government does not recognize that the administrative measures taken by the Government of Israel on June 28 can be regarded as the last word on the matter, and we regret that they were taken. We insist that the measures taken cannot be considered other than interim and provisional, and not prejudging the final and permanent status of Jerusalem. Unfortunately and regrettably, the statements of the Government of Israel on this matter have thus far, in our view, not adequately dealt with this situation.

Many delegations are aware that we were prepared to vote for a separate resolution on Jerusalem which would declare that the Assembly would not accept any unilateral action as determining the status of Jerusalem and calling on the Government of Israel to desist from any action purporting to define permanently the status of Jerusalem. However, the sponsors made clear then, as was their right, that they preferred to proceed with their own text in document A/2253,[5] and now with their resolution in A/L.528/Rev.2.

The latter draft does include changes which we consider represent a improvement over the original version, particularly in that it no longer tends to prejudge action in the Security Council. Nevertheless, since the resolution just adopted expressly builds on Resolution 2253 on which we abstained for reasons which we stated publicly, consistent with that vote we also abstained today.

Even as revised, the resolution does not fully correspond to our views, particularly since it appears to accept by its call for recision of measures that the administrative measures which were taken constitute annexation of Jerusalem by Israel, and because we do not believe the problem of Jerusalem can realistically be solved apart from the other related aspects of Jerusalem and of the Middle Eastern situation. Therefore, the United States abstained.

[4] For text, see *ibid.*, July 24, 1967, p. 108.
[5] For a statement made by Ambassador Goldberg on July 4 in explanation of the U.S. abstention on A/RES/2253 (ES-V) and text of the resolution, see *ibid.*, pp. 112 and 113.

We have, of course, recently expressed ourselves in a more formal sense by voting for a resolution dealing with the question of Jerusalem. This was the Latin American resolution contained in document A/L.523/Rev.1,[6] which dealt with Jerusalem as one of the elements involved in a peaceful settlement in the Middle East.

It is in the treatment of one aspect of the problem of Jerusalem as an isolated issue, separate from the other elements of Jerusalem and of a peaceful settlement in the Middle East, that we were unable to support Resolution 2253. Certainly, Jerusalem, as has been pointed out universally, I think, by every speaker, is an important issue and, and in our opinion, one which must necessarily be considered in the context of a settlement of all problems arising out of the recent conflict. In Jerusalem there are transcendent spiritual interests. But there are also other important issues. And we believe that the most fruitful approach to a discussion of the future of Jerusalem lies in dealing with the entire problem as one aspect of the broader arrangements that must be made to restore a just and durable peace in the area. And we believe consistent with the resolution we were ready to sponsor, that this Assembly should have dealt with the problem by declaring itself against any unilateral change in the status of Jerusalem.

Mr. President, since we are approaching the end of this session on this important subject, in which remarks were made not relating specifically to Jerusalem but ranging very broadly on other subjects, I cannot let this occasion pass without reference to some of the allegations made regarding my Government's role in the recent conflict in the Middle East. The charges that the United States instigated, encouraged, or in any way participated in this tragic struggle are too unfounded to dignify by individual comment. I dealt with many of these falsehoods explicitly in the Security Council and will not take the time of the Assembly to go over the same ground here. I reaffirm what I said to the Security Council with respect to each and every one of these charges.[7]

I will merely say that one positive note in this session has been the abandonment of the most vicious falsehood of all—which could have been productive of the most disastrous consequences—that United States planes and military personnel participated in the war on the side of Israel. Before the war broke out, we sought to prevent it by all means at our command. And once it began, we did everything in our power to bring it to an early end. The record of our diplomacy is very clear in this

[6] For background, see *ibid.*, p. 108.

[7] For background, see *ibid.*, June 19, 1967, p. 920; June 26, 1967, p. 934; and July 3, 1967 p. 3.

matter, despite comments which have been read from newspapers which scarcely characterize that diplomacy. And the record of the Security Council is plain and clear for everyone to read as to the actions we took, supported, and initiated in the Security Council to bring the conflict to an end.

There is one charge about our position to which I believe no nation in this hall faithful to the charter would feel any necessity to plead. That is the charge that we support the right of every sovereign state member of the United Nations to an independent national existence, its right to live in a spirit of peaceful coexistence and good neighborliness with all in the area. That is a charge which the Charter of the United Nations places on us all and which we should all readily accept and acknowledge.

Our view has remained steadfast—before, during, and now after the conflict. We extend the hand of friendship to all states in the Middle East and express the fervent hope that as time heals the scars of war, we can soon again join our common efforts in helping build a better, more enduring order in every state and throughout the area, with peace, justice, security, and liberty for all.

Mr. President, so much vituperation has taken place in this Assembly, so unseemly in a world forum, that I could not help recalling today a statement made by my distinguished predecessor, who died 2 years ago today in the cause of peace, Adlai Stevenson. Adlai Stevenson, talking about our beloved Eleanor Roosevelt, said, "She would rather light candles than curse the darkness." And I share that spirit. I do not see that anything is gained in the cause of peace in the Middle East by the vituperation which has taken place, vituperation not only against my country but against other, small countries, vituperation which has no place in this forum.

The time has come—indeed, the time is long overdue—for vituperation and bitterness to be tempered by sober realization of the difficulties ahead and the willingness to face them squarely and to do something about them.

What is needed is the wisdom and statesmanship of all those directly concerned and the members of the United Nations so that conditions of hate, too much ventilated in this hall, can be eventually replaced by conditions of good neighborliness.

What is needed, above all, in the area is a spirit of reconciliation which will someday hopefully make possible a peace of reconciliation. I fervently hope that all in the area and all in this hall will approach the days ahead in this spirit.

37. General Assembly Resolution 2254 (ES-V) Concerning Measures Taken by Israel to Change the Status of the City of Jerusalem, July 14, 1967*

* G.A. Res. 2254 (ES-V), U.N. GAOR, Resolutions adopted by the General Assembly during its Fifth Emergency Special Session 17 June-18 September 1967, Supp. 1, at 4, U.N. Doc. A/6798 (1967). See also the *Report of the Secretary-General Under General Assembly Resolution 2254 (ES-V) Relating to Jerusalem,* 22 U.N. SCOR, Supp. for July, Aug., and Sept. 1967, at 232, U.N. Doc. S/8146 & A/6793 (Sept. 12, 1967); *Report of the Secretary-General in Pursuance of Security Council Resolution 252, Concerning the Status of Jerusalem,* 24 U.N. SCOR, Supp. for April, May, and June 1969, at 106-13, U.N. Doc. S/9149 and Add. 1 (April 11 and June 30, 1969).

The General Assembly,

Recalling its resolution 2253 (ES-V) of 4 July 1967,

Having received the report submitted by the Secretary-General,[1]

Taking note with the deepest regret and concern of the non-compliance by Israel with resolution 2253 (ES-V),

1. *Deplores* the failure of Israel to implement General Assembly resolution 2253 (ES-V);

2. *Reiterates* its call to Israel in that resolution to rescind all measures already taken and to desist forthwith from taking any action which would alter the status of Jerusalem;

3. *Requests* the Secretary-General to report to the Security Council and the General Assembly on the situation and on the implementation of the present resolution.

1554th plenary meeting,
14 July 1967.

[1] A/6753. For the printed text of this document, see *Official Records of the Security Council, Twenty-second Year, Supplement for July, August and September 1967,* document S/8052.

38. Summary of Resolution of Arab Summit Conference, Khartoum, Sudan, September 1, 1967*

* 13 ARAB NEWS AND VIEWS, No. 13 (Sept. 1967), reprinted in 2 NEW YORK UNIVERSITY JOURNAL OF INTERNATIONAL LAW AND POLITICS 209-10 (1969).

The eight Arab Heads of State who attended the Conference were from the UAR, Saudi Arabia, Sudan, Jordan, Lebanon, Kuwait, Iraq and Yemen. Morocco, Libya, Tunisia and Algeria were represented by their Prime Ministers. Syria, who did not attend, was represented by her Foreign Minister, Dr. Ibrahim Makhous, at the Foreign Ministers' Conference which preceded the Summit and drew up its agenda.

First, the Conference affirmed Arab solidarity and the unification of Arab joint action in a cordial atmosphere of coordination and conciliation.

The Heads of State reaffirmed their commitment to the Charter of Arab Solidarity issued at the Third Arab Summit Conference in Casablanca.

Second, the Conference affirmed the necessity of concerted joint efforts in the elimination of all traces of aggression on the basis that the recovery of all occupied Arab territory is the joint responsibility of all Arab countries.

Third, the Arab Heads of State agreed on unifying their efforts in joint political and diplomatic action at the international level to ensure the withdrawal of Israeli forces from the occupied Arab territory. This is within the framework of the basic Arab commitment, which entails non-recognition of Israel, no conciliation nor negotiation with her and the upholding of the rights of the Palestinian people to their land.

Fourth, the Ministers of Finance, Economy and Oil recommended the possibility of using oil as a weapon in the struggle. The Summit Conference, after careful study, sees that oil export could be used as a positive weapon which would be directed toward the strengthening of the economies of the Arab countries that suffered directly from the aggression.

Fifth, the Conference approved the proposal submitted by Kuwait to establish an Arab Economic and Social Development Bank in accordance with the recommendations of the Arab Finance, Economy and Oil Ministers' Conference which met in Baghdad.

Sixth, the Conference decided that it is necessary to take all steps to consolidate military preparedness to face the consequences of the situation.

Seventh, the Conference decided to speed up the liquidation of foreign bases in the Arab countries.

39. Security Council Resolution 242 Concerning Principles for a Just and Lasting Peace in the Middle East, November 22, 1967*

---

* S.C. Res. 242, 22 U.N. SCOR, 1382d meeting, at 8-9 (1967).
** The French version of section 1(i) of this Resolution provides:
"Retrait des forces armees israeliennes des territoires occupes lors du recent conflit." The English and French versions are equally authoritative.
For a summary of the Security Council Debate on Resolution 242, see *Report of the Security Council 16 July 1967-15 July 1968*, 23 U.N. GAOR, Supp. 2, at 13-23, U.N. Doc. A/7202 (1968).

The Security Council,

Expressing its continuing concern with the grave situation in the Middle East,

Emphasizing the inadmissibility of the acquisition of territory by war and the need to work for a just and lasting peace in which every State in the area can live in security,

Emphasizing further that all Member States in their acceptance of the Charter of the United Nations have undertaken a commitment to act in accordance with Article 2 of the Charter,

1. *Affirms* that the fulfilment of Charter principles requires the establishment of a just and lasting peace in the Middle East which should include the application of both the following principles:

(i) Withdrawal of Israel armed forces from territories occupied in the recent conflict;**

(ii) Termination of all claims or states of belligerency and respect for and acknowledgement of the sovereignty, territorial integrity and political independence of every State in the area and their right to live in peace within secure and recognized boundaries free from threats or acts of force;

2. *Affirms further* the necessity

(*a*) For guaranteeing freedom of navigation through international waterways in the area;

(*b*) For achieving a just settlement of the refugee problem;

(*c*) For guaranteeing the territorial inviolability and political independence of every State in the area, through measures including the establishment of demilitarized zones;

3. *Requests* the Secretary-General to designate a Special Representative to proceed to the Middle East to establish and maintain contacts with the States concerned in order to promote agreement and assist efforts to achieve a peaceful and accepted settlement in accordance with the provisions and principles in this resolution;

4. *Requests* the Secretary-General to report to the Security Council on the progress of the efforts of the Special Representative as soon as possible.

*Adopted unanimously at the
1382nd meeting.*

40. The Palestinian National Charter of 1968*

* LEILA S. KADI, BASIC POLITICAL DOCUMENTS OF THE ARMED PALESTINIAN
RESISTANCE MOVEMENT 137-42 (Palestine Books No. 27, Palestine Libera-
tion Organization Research Center, 1969). See also the Palestinian National
Charter of 1964.

THE PALESTINIAN NATIONAL CHARTER

(Palestine Liberation Organization)*

Article 1: Palestine is the homeland of the Arab Palestinian people; it is an indivisible part of the Arab homeland, and the Palestinian people are an integral part of the Arab nation.

Article 2: Palestine, with the boundaries it had during the British mandate, is an indivisible territorial unit.

Article 3: The Palestinian Arab people possess the legal right to their homeland and have the right to determine their destiny after achieving the liberation of their country in accordance with their wishes and entirely of their own accord and will.

Article 4: The Palestinian identity is a genuine, essential and inherent characteristic; it is transmitted from parents to children. The Zionist occupation and the dispersal of the Palestinian Arab people, through the disasters which befell them, do not make them lose their Palestinian identity and their membership of the Palestinian community, nor do they negate them.

Article 5: The Palestinians are those Arab nationals who, until 1947, normally resided in Palestine regardless of whether they were evicted from it or have stayed there. Anyone born, after that date, of a Palestinian father—whether inside Palestine or outside it—is also a Palestinian.

Article 6: The Jews who had normally resided in Palestine until the beginning of the Zionist invasion will be considered Palestinians.

(*) Decisions of the National Congress of the Palestine Liberation Organization held in Cairo from 1-17 July 1968.

Article 7:   That there is a Palestinian community and that it has material, spiritual and historical connection with Palestine are indisputable facts. It is a national duty to bring up individual Palestinians in an Arab revolutionary manner. All means of information and education must be adopted in order to acquaint the Palestinian with his country in the most profound manner, both spiritual and material, that is possible. He must be prepared for the armed struggle and ready to sacrifice his wealth and his life in order to win back his homeland and bring about its liberation.

Article 8:   The phase in their history, through which the Palestinian people are now living, is that of national struggle for the liberation of Palestine. Thus the conflicts among the Palestinian national forces are secondary, and should be ended for the sake of the basic conflict that exists between the forces of Zionism and of imperialism on the one hand, and the Palestinian Arab people on the other. On this basis the Palestinian masses, regardless of whether they are residing in the national homeland or in diaspora, constitute—both their organizations and the individuals—one national front working for the retrieval of Palestine and its liberation through armed struggle.

Article 9:   Armed struggle is the only way to liberate Palestine. Thus it is the overall strategy, not merely a tactical phase. The Palestinian Arab people assert their absolute determination and firm resolution to continue their armed struggle and to work for an armed popular revolution for the liberation of their country and their return to it. They also assert their right to normal life in Palestine and to exercise their right to self-determination and sovereignty over it.

Article 10:   Commando action constitutes the nucleus of the Palestinian popular liberation war. This requires its escalation, comprehensiveness and the mobilization of all the Palestinian popular and educational efforts and their organization and involvement in the armed Palestinian revolution. It also requires the achieving of unity for the national struggle among the different groupings of the Palestinian people, and between the Palestinian people and the Arab masses so as to secure the continuation of the revolution, its escalation and victory.

Article 11:   The Palestinians will have three mottoes: national unity, national mobilization and liberation.

Article 12: The Palestinian people believe in Arab unity. In order to contribute their share towards the attainment of that objective, however, they must, at the present stage of their struggle, safeguard their Palestinian identity and develop their consciousness of that identity, and oppose any plan that may dissolve or impair it.

Article 13: Arab unity and the liberation of Palestine are two complementary objectives, the attainment of either of which facilitates the attainment of the other. Thus, Arab unity leads to the liberation of Palestine; the liberation of Palestine leads to Arab unity; and work towards the realization of one objective proceeds side by side with work towards the realization of the other.

Article 14: The destiny of the Arab nation, and indeed Arab existence itself, depends upon the destiny of the Palestine cause. From this interdependence springs the Arab nation's pursuit of, and striving for, the liberation of Palestine. The people of Palestine play the role of the vanguard in the realization of this sacred national goal.

Article 15: The liberation of Palestine, from an Arab viewpoint, is a national duty and it attempts to repel the Zionist and imperialist aggression against the Arab homeland, and aims at the elimination of Zionism in Palestine. Absolute responsibility for this falls upon the Arab nation — peoples and governments — with the Arab people of Palestine in the vanguard. Accordingly the Arab nation must mobilize all its military, human, moral and spiritual capabilities to participate actively with the Palestinian people in the liberation of Palestine. It must, particularly in the phase of the armed Palestinian revolution, offer and furnish the Palestinian people with all possible help, and material and human support, and make available to them the means and opportunities that will enable them to continue to carry out their leading role in the armed revolution, until they liberate their homeland.

Article 16: The liberation of Palestine, from a spiritual point of view, will provide the Holy Land with an atmosphere of safety and tranquillity, which in turn will safeguard the country's religious sanctuaries and guarantee freedom of worship and of visit to all, without discrimination of race, color, language, or religion. Accordingly, the people of Palestine look to all spiritual forces in the world for support.

Article 17:   The liberation of Palestine, from a human point of view, will restore to the Palestinian individual his dignity, pride and freedom. Accordingly the Palestinian Arab people look forward to the support of all those who believe in the dignity of man and his freedom in the world.

Article 18:   The liberation of Palestine, from an international point of view, is a defensive action necessitated by the demands of self-defence. Accordingly, the Palestinian people, desirous as they are of the friendship of all people, look to freedom-loving, justice-loving and peace-loving states for support in order to restore their legitimate rights in Palestine, to re-establish peace and security in the country, and to enable its people to exercise national sovereignty and freedom.

Article 19:   The partition of Palestine in 1947 and the establishment of the state of Israel are entirely illegal, regardless of the passage of time, because they were contrary to the will of the Palestinian people and to their natural right in their homeland, and inconsistent with the principles embodied in the Charter of the United Nations, particularly the right to self-determination.

Article 20:   The Balfour Declaration, the mandate for Palestine and everything that has been based upon them, are deemed null and void. Claims of historical or religious ties of Jews with Palestine are incompatible with the facts of history and the true conception of what constitutes statehood. Judaism, being a religion, is not an independent nationality. Nor do Jews constitute a single nation with an identity of its own; they are citizens of the states to which they belong.

Article 21:   The Arab Palestinian people, expressing themselves by the armed Palestinian revolution, reject all solutions which are substitutes for the total liberation of Palestine and reject all proposals aiming at the liquidation of the Palestinian problem, or its internationalization.

Article 22:   Zionism is a political movement organically associated with international imperialism and antagonistic to all action for liberation and to progressive movements in the world. It is racist and fanatic in its nature, aggressive, expansionist and colonial in its aims, and fascist in its methods.

Israel is the instrument of the Zionist movement, and a geographical base for world imperialism placed strategically in the midst of the Arab homeland to combat the hopes of the Arab nation for liberation, unity and progress. Israel is a constant source of threat *vis-à-vis* peace in the Middle East and the whole world. Since the liberation of Palestine will destroy the Zionist and imperialist presence and will contribute to the establishment of peace in the Middle East, the Palestinian people look for the support of all the progressive and peaceful forces and urge them all, irrespective of their affiliations and beliefs, to offer the Palestinian people all aid and support in their just struggle for the liberation of their homeland.

Article 23: The demands of security and peace, as well as the demands of right and justice, require all states to consider Zionism an illegitimate movement, to outlaw its existence, and to ban its operations, in order that friendly relations among peoples may be preserved, and the loyalty of citizens to their respective homelands safeguarded.

Article 24: The Palestinian people believe in the principles of justice, freedom, sovereignty, self-determination, human dignity, and in the right of all peoples to exercise them.

Article 25: For the realization of the goals of this Charter and its principles, the Palestine Liberation Organization will perform its role in the liberation of Palestine in accordance with the Constitution of this Organization.

Article 26: The Palestine Liberation Organization, representative of the Palestinian revolutionary forces, is responsible for the Palestinian Arab people's movement in its struggle—to retrieve its homeland, liberate and return to it and exercise the right to self-determination in it—in all military, political and financial fields and also for whatever may be required by the Palestine case on the inter-Arab and international levels.

Article 27: The Palestine Liberation Organization shall cooperate with all Arab states, each according to its potentialities; and will adopt a neutral policy among them in the light of the requirements of the war of liberation; and on this basis it shall not interfere in the internal affairs of any Arab state.

Article 28:   The Palestinian Arab people assert the genuineness and independence of their national revolution and reject all forms of intervention, trusteeship and subordination.

Article 29:   The Palestinian people possess the fundamental and genuine legal right to liberate and retrieve their homeland. The Palestinian people determine their attitude towards all states and forces on the basis of the stands they adopt *vis-à-vis* the Palestinian case and the extent of the support they offer to the Palestinian revolution to fulfill the aims of the Palestinian people.

Article 30:   Fighters and carriers of arms in the war of liberation are the nucleus of the popular army which will be the protective force for the gains of the Palestinian Arab people.

Article 31:   The Organization shall have a flag, an oath of allegiance and an anthem. All this shall be decided upon in accordance with a special regulation.

Article 32:   Regulations, which shall be known as the Constitution of the Palestine Liberation Organization, shall be annexed to this Charter. It shall lay down the manner in which the Organization, and its organs and institutions, shall be constituted; the respective competence of each; and the requirements of its obligations under the Charter.

Article 33:   This Charter shall not be amended save by (vote of) a majority of two-thirds of the total membership of the National Congress of the Palestine Liberation Organization (taken) at a special session convened for that purpose.

41. General Assembly Resolution 2443 (XXIII) Concerning Respect for and Implementation of Human Rights in Occupied Territories, December 19, 1968*

* G.A. Res. 2443 (XXIII), U.N. Doc. A/RES/2443 (XXIII) (Jan. 13, 1969).

The General Assembly,

Guided by the purposes and principles of the Charter of the United Nations and by the Universal Declaration of Human Rights,

Bearing in mind the provisions of the Geneva Convention relative to the Protection of Civilian Persons in Time of War of 12 August 1949,[1]

Mindful of the principle embodied in the Universal Declaration of Human Rights regarding the right of everyone to return to his own country, and recalling Security Council resolution 237 (1967) of 14 June 1967, General Assembly resolutions 2252 (ES-V) of 4 July 1967 and 2341 B (XXII) of 19 December 1967, Commission on Human Rights resolution 6 (XXIV) of 27 February 1968[2] and Economic and Social Council resolution 1336 (XLIV) of 31 May 1968, in which those United Nations organs called upon the Government of Israel, *inter alia*, to facilitate the return of those inhabitants who have fled the area of military operations since the outbreak of hostilities,

Recalling the telegram dispatched by the Commission on Human Rights on 8 March 1968, calling upon the Government of Israel to desist forthwith from acts of destroying homes of the Arab civilian population in areas occupied by Israel,[3]

Recalling also Security Council resolution 259 (1968) of 27 September 1968, in which the Council expressed its concern for the safety, welfare and security of the inhabitants of the Arab territories under military occupation by Israel, and deplored the delay in the implementation of Council resolution 237 (1967),

Noting resolution I on respect for and implementation of human rights in occupied territories, adopted by the International Conference on Human Rights on 7 May 1968,[4] in which the Conference, *inter alia*:

(*a*) Expressed its grave concern at the violation of human rights in Arab territories occupied by Israel,

(*b*) Drew the attention of the Government of Israel to the grave consequences resulting from the disregard of fundamental freedoms and human rights in occupied territories,

(*c*) Called upon the Government of Israel to desist forthwith from acts of destroying homes of the Arab civilian population inhabiting areas occupied by Israel and to respect and implement the Universal

---

[1] United Nations, *Treaty Series*, Vol. 75 (1950), No. 973.

[2] See *Official Records of the Economic and Social Council, Forty-fourth Session, Supplement No. 4* (E/4475), chapter XVIII.

[3] *Ibid.,* para. 400.

[4] See *Final Act of the International Conference on Human Rights* (United Nations publication, Sales No.: E.68.XIV.2) p. 5.

Declaration of Human Rights and the Geneva Conventions of 12
August 1949[5] in occupied territories,

(d) Affirmed the inalienable rights of all inhabitants who have left
their homes as a result of the outbreak of hostilities in the Middle
East to return home, resume their normal life, recover their property
and homes, and rejoin their families according to the provisions of the
Universal Declaration of Human Rights,

1. *Decides* to establish a Special Committee to Investigate Israeli
Practices Affecting the Human Rights of the Population of the Occupied
Territories composed of three Members States;

2. *Requests* the President of the General Assembly to appoint the
members of the Special Committee;

3. *Requests* the Government of Israel to receive the Special
Committee, co-operate with it and facilitate its work;

4. *Requests* the Special Committee to report to the Secretary-General
as soon as possible and whenever the need arises thereafter;

5. *Requests* the Secretary-General to provide the Special Committee
with all the necessary facilities for the performance of its task.

1748th plenary meeting,
19 December 1968.

[5] United Nations, *Treaty Series,* Vol. 75 (1950), Nos. 970-973.

42. Security Council Resolution 262 Concerning Military Action by Israel against the Beirut International Airport, December 31, 1968*

* S.C. Res. 262, 23 U.N. SCOR, Resolutions and Decisions of the Security Council 1968, at 12, U.N. Doc. S/INF/23/Rev. 1 (1970).

The Security Council,

Having considered the agenda contained in document S/Agenda/1462,

Having noted the contents of the letter of the Permanent Representative of Lebanon (S/8945),

Having noted the supplementary information provided by the Chief of Staff of the United Nations Truce Supervision Organization contained in documents S/7930/Add.107 and Add.108,

Having heard the statements of the representative of Lebanon and of the representative of Israel concerning the grave attack committed against the civil International Airport of Beirut,

Observing that the military action by the armed forces of Israel against the civil International Airport of Beirut was premeditated and of a large scale and carefully planned nature,

Gravely concerned about the deteriorating situation resulting from this violation of the Security Council resolutions,

Deeply concerned about the need to assure free uninterrupted international civil air traffic,

1. *Condemns* Israel for its premeditated military action in violation of its obligations under the Charter and the cease-fire resolutions;

2. *Considers* that such premeditated acts of violence endanger the maintenance of the peace;

3. *Issues* a solemn warning to Israel that if such acts were to be repeated, the Council would have to consider further steps to give effect to its decisions;

4. *Considers* that Lebanon is entitled to appropriate redress for the destruction it has suffered, responsibility for which has been acknowledged by Israel.

*Adopted unanimously at the
1462nd meeting.*

43. Statement by Ambassador Charles W. Yost, United States Representative to the United Nations, in the Security Council, on the Situation in Jerusalem, July 1, 1969*

* United States Mission to the United Nations, Press Release USUN-70 (69) July 1, 1969.

Once again the Council has been summoned to deal with certain
actions taken by the Government of Israel in Jerusalem. We have
listened carefully to the statements of the Permanent Representative
of Jordan and other Arab Ambassadors, as well as the reply of the
Representative of Israel.

The discussion thus far has made amply clear that the status of
Jerusalem is not an isolated problem, but, rather, an integral part of a
whole complex of issues in the current Middle Eastern conflict which
must be resolved. This is not a novel conclusion. The Council clearly
recognized that fact in Resolution 242, which treats the entire Middle
Eastern situation as a package. This resolution remains the basis of our
approach to a just and lasting peace in the area. You are all well aware
of the strenuous efforts my own Government is making to help
Ambassador Jarring promote a peaceful settlement. Progress in these
efforts has, admittedly, been slow. This is perhaps not surprising when
one reflects on how deep the roots of the conflict go. But the
important thing is that some progress is being made. The fact that it
has not been crowned with dramatic success should not give grounds
for despair. Nor should it be exploited as justification for actions, which
will make greater progress even more difficult. This applies to actions
in Jerusalem as elsewhere in the area. Indeed, Jerusalem occupies a very
special place in all our minds and all our hearts as one of the holiest
cities in the entire world. For Jerusalem is a sacred shrine to three of
the world's largest and oldest religious faiths: Islam, Christianity and
Judaism. By virtue of that fact the United States has always
considered that Jerusalem enjoys a unique international standing and
that no action should be taken there without full regard to Jerusalem's
special history and special place in the world community. Unfortunately
there have been acts of many kinds which have broken the peace in
Jerusalem and which are of deep concern to my Government and to
the international community. Mr. President, we understand the deep
emotional concerns which move all parties to the Arab-Israeli dispute
on the subject of Jerusalem. We do not believe, however, that any of
these concerns are served by what is now taking place in East Jerusalem,
whether it be actions by those now exercising authority there or by
individuals considering themselves aggrieved and therefore justified in
resorting to violence. The expropriation or confiscation of land, the
construction of housing on such land, the demolition or confiscation
of buildings, including those having historic or religious significance,
and the application of Israeli law to occupied portions of the city are
detrimental to our common interests in the city. The United States

considers that the part of Jerusalem that came under the control of Israel in the June war, like other areas occupied by Israel, is occupied territory and hence subject to the provisions of international law governing the rights and obligations of an occupying power. Among the provisions of international law which bind Israel, as they would bind any occupier, are the provisions that the occupier has no right to make changes in laws or in administration other than those which are temporarily necessitated by his security interest, and that an occupier may not confiscate or destroy private property. The pattern of behavior authorized under the Geneva Convention and international law is clear: the occupier must maintain the occupied area as intact and unaltered as possible, without interfering with the customary life of the area, and any changes must be necessitated by immediate needs of the occupation. I regret to say that the actions of Israel in the occupied portion of Jerusalem present a different picture, one which gives rise to understandable concerns that the eventual disposition of East Jerusalem may be prejudiced and the rights and activities of the population are already being affected and altered.

My Government regrets and deplores this pattern of activity, and it has so informed the Government of Israel on numerous occasions since June 1967. We have consistently refused to recognize these measures as having anything but a provisional character and do not accept them as affecting the ultimate status of Jerusalem.

I have explained in some detail the opposition of the United States to certain measures taken by the Government of Israel in Jerusalem, since this is the precise object of the complaint brought before us by the Government of Jordan. But, as I suggested earlier, we cannot logically and intelligently consider the problem of Jerusalem without putting it in its proper perspective—the Middle East situation as a whole. In this connection, I would recall that one of the first major policy decisions taken by President Nixon after assuming office this year was that the United States Government should take new initiatives in helping to try to bring peace in the Middle East. For the past several months we have been devoting our best efforts to this task. We shall continue to do so but for these efforts to succeed we will require the goodwill and cooperation of the parties themselves. A just and lasting peace in the Middle East is long and tragically overdue. It will not be found through terror bombings, which inevitably harm innocent civilians, any more than through unilateral attempts to alter the status of Jerusalem. It will be found only through the instruments and processes of negotiation, accommodation and agreement. It will come only through the exercise by the parties of the utmost restraint—not just along the cease-fire lines or in public statements, but also on the ground in Jerusalem itself.

In treating the problem of Jerusalem, since we deal with it in the context of the total situation in the Middle East, my Delegation will subject any proposal for Council action, first of all, to the test of whether that proposal is likely to help or hinder the peaceful settlement process. I hope all members will do likewise. For example, one constructive move the Council might make would be to request the parties to lay aside their recriminations, to desist from any action—in Jerusalem or elsewhere—that might be construed as prejudicing or prejudging a final, comprehensive settlement, a just and lasting peace. Thus, our consideration of the situation in Jerusalem could provide a fitting occasion on which to insist once more that the parties to a dispute which keeps the world's Holiest City in turmoil act responsibly to resolve the whole dispute and, until it is resolved, that they take no action anywhere which could further jeopardize its resolution.

44. Security Council Resolution 271 Concerning Measures and Actions by Israel Affecting the Status of the City of Jerusalem, September 15, 1969*

* S.C. Res. 271, 24 U.N. SCOR, Resolutions and Decisions of the Security Council 1969, at 5, U.N. Doc. S/INF/24/Rev. 1 (1970).

The Security Council,

Grieved at the extensive damage caused by arson to the Holy Al Aqsa Mosque in Jerusalem on 21 August 1969 under the military occupation of Israel,

Mindful of the consequent loss to human culture,

Having heard the statements made before the Council reflecting the universal outrage caused by the act of sacrilege in one of the most venerated shrines of mankind,

Recalling its resolutions 252 (1968) of 21 May 1968 and 267 (1969) of 3 July 1969 and the earlier General Assembly resolutions 2253 (ES-V) and 2254 (ES-V) of 4 and 14 July 1967, respectively, concerning measures and actions by Israel affecting the status of the City of Jerusalem,

Reaffirming the established principle that acquisition of territory by military conquest is inadmissible,

1. *Reaffirms* its resolutions 252 (1968) and 267 (1969);

2. *Recognizes* that any act of destruction or profanation of the Holy Places, religious buildings and sites in Jerusalem or any encouragement of, or connivance at, any such act may seriously endanger international peace and security;

3. *Determines* that the execrable act of desecration and profanation of the Holy Al Aqsa Mosque emphasizes the immediate necessity of Israel's desisting from acting in violation of the aforesaid resolutions and rescinding forthwith all measures and actions taken by it designed to alter the status of Jerusalem;

4. *Calls upon* Israel scrupulously to observe the provisions of the Geneva Conventions[1] and international law governing military occupation and to refrain from causing any hindrance to the discharge of the established functions of the Supreme Moslem Council of Jerusalem, including any co-operation that Council may desire from countries with predominantly Moslem population and from Moslem communities in relation to its plans for the maintenance and repair of the Islamic Holy Places in Jerusalem;

5. *Condemns* the failure of Israel to comply with the aforementioned resolutions and calls upon it to implement forthwith the provisions of these resolutions;

6. *Reiterates* the determination in paragraph 7 of resolution 267 (1969) that, in the event of a negative response or no response, the

---

[1] Geneva Conventions of 12 August 1949 (United Nations, *Treaty Series*, vol. 75 (1950), Nos. 970-973).

Security Council shall convene without delay to consider what further action should be taken in this matter;

7. *Requests* the Secretary-General to follow closely the implementation of the present resolution and to report thereon to the Security Council at the earliest possible date.

Adopted at the 1512th meeting by 11 votes to none, with 4 abstentions (Colombia, Finland, Paraguay, United States of America).

45. Cease-Fire-Standstill Agreement between Israel and the United Arab Republic Effective August 7, 1970*

---

* Obtained from the United States Department of State and available to the general public. See also 63 DEPT. STATE BULLETIN 178-79 (1970) and the nearly identical text set out in the remarks of Israel Foreign Minister Eban in the United Nations General Assembly debate on September 28, 1970, *General Assembly Provisional Verbatim Record of the Eighteen Hundred and Fifty-First Meeting*, U.N. Doc. A/PV 1851 (Sept. 28, 1970), 56, at 66.

A. Israel and the UAR will observe ceasefire effective at 2200 GMT Friday, August 7.

B. Both sides will stop all incursions and all firing, on the ground and in the air, across the ceasefire line.

C. Both sides will refrain from changing the military status quo within zones extending 50 kilometers to the east and the west of the ceasefire line. Neither side will introduce or construct any new military installations in these zones. Activities within the zones will be limited to the maintenance of existing installations at their present sites and positions and to the rotation and supply of forces presently within the zones.

D. For purposes of verifying observance of the ceasefire, each side will rely on its own national means, including reconnaissance aircraft, which will be free to operate without interference up to 10 kilometers from the ceasefire line on its own side of that line.

E. Each side may avail itself as appropriate of all UN machinery in reporting alleged violations to each other of the ceasefire and of the military standstill.

F. Both sides will abide by the Geneva Convention of 1949 relative to the treatment of Prisoners of War and will accept the assistance of the ICRC (International Committee of the Red Cross) in carrying out their obligations under that Convention.

46. General Assembly Resolution 2727 (XXV) Concerning the Report of the Special Committee to Investigate Israeli Practices Affecting the Human Rights of the Population of the Occupied Territories, December 15, 1970*

* G.A. Res. 2727 (XXV), U.N. Doc. A/RES/2727 (XXV) (Jan. 20, 1971). See also G.A. Res. 2546 (XXIV), 24 U.N. GAOR, Supp. 30, at 54, U.N. Doc. A/7630 (1969). See also the *Report of the Special Committee to Investigate Israeli Practices Affecting the Human Rights of the Population of the Occupied Territories,* 8 U.N. Doc. A/8089 (Oct. 26, 1970); *Report of the Special Working Group of Experts Established Under Resolution 6 (XXV) of the Commission on Human Rights,* U.N. Doc. E/CN. 4/1016 (Jan. 20, 1970), Adds. 1 and 2 (Feb. 11, 1970), Adds. 3 and 5 (Feb. 20, 1970), Add. 4 (Feb. 18, 1970); and *Report of the Special Committee to Investigate Israeli Practices Affecting the Human Rights of the Population of the Occupied Territories,* U.N. Doc. A/8389 (Oct. 5, 1971), and U.N. Doc. A/8389/Corr. 1 (Oct. 15, 1971).

The General Assembly,

Guided by the purposes and principles of the Charter of the United Nations,

Bearing in mind the provisions of the Universal Declaration of Human Rights and the provisions of the Geneva Convention relative to the Protection of Civilian Persons in Time of War of 12 August 1949,[1]

Recalling Security Council resolutions 237 (1967) of 14 June 1967 and 259 (1968) of 27 September 1968,

Recalling also its resolutions 2252 (ES-V) of 4 July 1967, 2443 (XXIII) of 19 December 1968, 2452 A (XXIII) of 19 December 1968, 2535 B (XXIV) of 10 December 1969 and 2672 D (XXV) of 8 December 1970.

Further recalling Commission on Human Rights resolutions 6 (XXIV) of 27 February 1968,[2] 6 (XXV) of 4 March 1969[3] and 10 (XXVI) of 23 March 1970,[4] the telegram of 8 March 1968 dispatched by the Commission to the Israeli authorities,[5] the relevant resolutions of the International Conference on Human Rights,[6] held at Teheran in 1968, draft resolution VII of the Commission on the Status of Women of 9 April 1970[7] and the relevant resolutions of the Economic and Social Council, the United Nations Educational, Scientific and Cultural Organization and the World Health Organization,

Having considered the report of the Special Committee to Investigate Israeli Practices Affecting the Human Rights of the Population of the Occupied Territories,[8]

Noting with regret that the provisions of these resolutions have not been implemented by the Israeli authorities,

Gravely concerned for the safety, welfare and security of the inhabitants of the Arab territories under military occupation by Israel.

1. *Expresses its sincere appreciation* to the Special Committee to Investigate Israeli Practices Affecting the Human Rights of the Popula-

---

[1] United Nations, *Treaty Series,* vol. 75 (1950), No. 973.

[2] See *Official Records of the Economic and Social Council, Forty-fourth Session, Supplement No. 4* (E/4475), chapter XVIII.

[3] *Ibid., Forty-sixth Session,* document E/4621, chapter XVIII.

[4] *Ibid., Forty-eighth Session, Supplement No. 5* (E/4816), chapter XXIII.

[5] *Ibid., Forty-fourth Session, Supplement No. 4* (E/4475), para. 400.

[6] *Final Act of the International Conference on Human Rights* (United Nations publication, Sales No.: E.68.XIV.2), chapter III.

[7] See *Official Records of the Economic and Social Council, Forty-eighth Session, Supplement No. 6* (E/4831), chapter XIII. The draft resolution was later adopted by the Economic and Social Council on 28 May 1970 as resolution 1515 (XLVIII).

[8] A/8089.

tion of the Occupied Territories and to its members for their efforts in performing the task assigned to them;

2. *Calls upon* the Government of Israel immediately to implement the recommendations of the Special Committee embodied in its report and to comply with its obligations under the Geneva Convention relative to the Protection of Civilian Persons in Time of War of 12 August 1949, the Universal Declaration of Human Rights and the relevant resolutions adopted by the various international organizations;

3. *Requests* the Special Committee, pending the early termination of the Israeli occupation of Arab territories, to continue its work and to consult, as appropriate, with the International Committee of the Red Cross in order to ensure the safeguarding of the human rights of the population of the occupied territories;

4. *Urges* the Government of Israel to receive the Special Committee, co-operate with it and facilitate its work;

5. *Requests* the Special Committee to report to the Secretary-General as soon as possible and whenever the need arises thereafter;

6. *Requests* the Secretary-General to provide the Special Committee with all the necessary facilities for the continued performance of its tasks;

7. *Decides* to inscribe on the provisional agenda of its twenty-sixth session an item entitled "Report (or reports) of the Special Committee to Investigate Israeli Practices Affecting the Human Rights of the Population of the Occupied Territories."

1931st plenary meeting,
15 December 1970

47. Comments by the Government of Israel Concerning the Report of the Special Committee to Investigate Israeli Practices Affecting the Human Rights of the Population of the Occupied Territories, November 2, 1970*

---

* Submitted to Secretary-General U Thant by Yosef Tekoah, Permanent Representative of Israel to the United Nations, on November 13, 1970. See U.N. Doc. A/8164 (Nov. 13, 1970).

Letter dated 13 November 1970 from the Permanent Representative of Israel to the United Nations addressed to the Secretary-General

I have the honour to refer to the note by the Secretary-General (A/8089) transmitting to the Members of the General Assembly for their information a report which was submitted to the Secretary-General in accordance with paragraph 4 of General Assembly resolution 2443 (XXIII) of 19 December 1968.

On instructions of my Government, I should like to request you to be so good as to transmit to the Members of the General Assembly, likewise for their information, the attached statement, dated 2 November 1970, which contains some comments by the Government of Israel on that report.

I have the honour to request that this letter and the attached statement be circulated as an official document of the General Assembly.

(*Signed*) Yosef TEKOAH
Permanent Representative of Israel
to the United Nations

Statement

The "Special Committee to Investigate Israeli Practices Affecting the Human Rights of the Population of the Occupied Territories" is a body tainted with political bias and procedural irregularity. Since its inception, it has merely served as a tool of Arab propaganda.

The basis for its creation is General Assembly resolution 2443 (XXIII) of 19 December 1968, which was supported by a minority of Member States, almost all Arab or pro-Arab. In view of the one-sided character of the resolution and as it prejudged the issues the Special Committee was to investigate, all uncommitted States that were approached refused to serve on the Committee. The only countries willing to become members of the Committee were Somalia, Yugoslavia and Ceylon. All three have no diplomatic relations with Israel and have identified themselves with Arab hostility towards Israel. Somalia even denies Israel's right to independence and sovereignty.

The activities of the Committee have been in line with its composition. Passing over the fact that objective Governments and organizations were generally unwilling to co-operate with it, the Committee proceeded to organize a spectacle of hearing "evidence" from witnesses, most of whom were supplied by the Arab Governments and organizations. The result is a compilation of dated and already refuted Arab propaganda allegations and distortions.

The long list of pre-selected, coached and rehearsed witnesses presented to the Committee produced lurid and often pathological tales of alleged ill-treatment and atrocity.

As an illustration it is enough to mention the evidence of Mohammed Derbas, who appeared before the Committee in Cairo on 23 April 1970. He described very vividly how, following the 1967 war, he was forced into an Israeli hospital in Haifa and there castrated by an Israeli doctor, who was assisted by an Israeli nurse. What in fact happened was that for medical reasons Derbas had undergone two operations for the removal of his testicles. These were performed by Arab surgeons, in the Gaza Strip, in 1965 and 1966, respectively (that is, prior to the 1967 hostilities). Already in July 1966, he had arrived in Egypt in an illusory hope of a remedy by transplantation, as recorded in a medical report by an Egyptian professor dated 28 July 1966. The report, signed by Professor Muhamad Safawat, is in this Mission's possession. This episode clearly demonstrates how human misfortune is exploited for cheap propaganda.

The Committee was not in a position to evaluate any evidence, to expose fabrications or to punish perjury. It is clear that this was an organized propaganda exercise, wanting in minimal judicial guarantees. No valid conclusions can be drawn from it, least of all against a State Member of the United Nations, and the inclusion of such material in a United Nations document does a grave disservice to the Organization itself. Fact finding on disputed matters requires the highest standards of objectivity. Otherwise, as in this case, the results are not entitled to belief, and the United Nations is converted into a vehicle for political warfare.

It has been the consistent policy of the Government of Israel, in accordance with the existing legal procedures, to investigate every complaint of abuse or improper conduct by members of the Defence Forces or other authorities in the Israel-administered territories. Such investigations can be conducted only if proper complaints are lodged and the possibilities created of taking evidence with due safeguards.

Israel has nothing to conceal in the discharge of its responsibilities for the safety and welfare of the inhabitants in Israel-administered territories. These areas are open to the outside world. Hundreds of thousands of visitors move freely around in them and can observe conditions for themselves.

The "Special Committee" report cannot blur the true situation of the civilian population in areas under Israel's administration. Israel's liberal policy, the freedoms enjoyed by the inhabitants of these areas to a degree unparalleled in most Arab States, the normalcy of life and the economic progress achieved in the last three years are a matter of record. This is attested, among others, by the fact that, during this summer alone, over 55,000 tourists from Arab countries entered Israel and the administered areas to visit relatives and friends. These Arab visitors would not have come had they given any credence to the official Arab propaganda of the kind contained in the Committee's report.

No amount of falsification can dim the truth that the Israel administration is as humane, equitable and constructive as can be conceived in the situation and that—notwithstanding intimidation and incitement, such as are diffused by the Committee's report and its records of testimony—the population as a whole leads a remarkably tranquil and prosperous life, with schools open, services functioning, work available, agriculture and commerce flourishing, marketing organized, health cared for and movement uninhibited.

Israel and other Member States rejected the resolution setting up the so-called "Special Committee." Not only did that resolution dictate to the Special Committee in advance the very conclusions that the Committee was to reach, but it deliberately ignored the real problem of discrimination and violation of human rights which exists in the Middle East, namely, the mistreatment of Jewish communities in Arab lands. The plight of those communities was deliberately excluded from the Special Committee's terms of reference. It is a matter of common knowledge that innocent Jews in certain Arab countries are maltreated in gaols and concentration camps, deprived of their liberty, human dignity and property, held as hostages and denied the right to depart. No United Nations organ has concerned itself with their fate.

For these reasons, the Government of Israel did not find it possible to extend its co-operation or facilities to the Special Committee, and has no intention of entering upon a debate on the details of the "evidence" taken or the conclusions reached by the Special Committee.

A peaceful settlement in the Middle East will be attained through the incessant search for understanding between the parties to the conflict and not by acrimonious propaganda manoeuvres.

2 November 1970

48. General Assembly Resolution 2672 (XXV) Concerning the Palestine Refugees, December 8, 1970*

* G.A. Res. 2672 (XXV), U.N. Doc. A/RES/2672 (XXV) (Jan. 4, 1971). See also General Assembly Resolution 2649 (XXV) Concerning the Universal Realization of the Right of Peoples to Self-Determination, November 30, 1970, G.A. Res. 2649 (XXV), 25 U.N. GAOR, Supp. 28, at 73, U.N. Doc. A/8028 (1970).

A

The General Assembly,

Recalling its resolutions 194 (III) of 11 December 1948, 302 (IV) of 8 December 1949, 393 (V) and 394 of 2 and 14 December 1950, 512 (VI) and 513 (VI) of 26 January 1952, 614 (VII) of 6 November 1952, 720 (VIII) of 27 November 1953, 818 (IX) of 4 December 1954, 916 (X) of 3 December 1955, 1018 (XI) of 28 February 1957, 1191 (XII) of 12 December 1957, 1315 (XIII) of 12 December 1958, 1456 (XIV) of 9 December 1959, 1604 (XV) of 21 April 1961, 1725 (XVI) of 20 December 1961, 1856 (XVII) of 20 December 1962, 1912 (XVIII) of 3 December 1963, 2002 (XIX) of 10 February 1965, 2052 (XX) of 15 December 1965, 2154 (XXI) of 17 November 1966, 2341 (XXII) of 19 December 1967, 2452 (XXIII) of 19 December 1968 and 2535 A (XXIV) of 10 December 1969,

Noting the annual report of the Commissioner-General of the United Nations Relief and Works Agency for Palestine Refugees in the Near East, covering the period from 1 July 1969 to 30 June 1970,[1]

1. *Notes with deep regret* that repatriation or compensation of the refugees as provided for in paragraph 11 of General Assembly resolution 194 (III) has not been effected, that no substantial progress has been made in the programme endorsed in paragraph 2 of Assembly resolution 513 (VI) for the reintegration of refugees either by repatriation or resettlement and that, therefore, the situation of the refugees continues to be a matter of serious concern;

2. *Expresses its thanks* to the Commissioner-General and the staff of the United Nations Relief and Works Agency for Palestine Refugees in the Near East for their continued faithful efforts to provide essential services for the Palestine refugees, and to the specialized agencies and private organizations for their valuable work in assisting the refugees;

3. *Directs* the Commissioner-General of the United Nations Relief and Works Agency for Palestine Refugees in the Near East to continue his efforts in taking such measures, including rectification of the relief rolls, as to assure, in co-operation with the Governments concerned, the most equitable distribution of relief based on need;

4. *Notes with regret* that the United Nations Conciliation Commission for Palestine was unable to find a means of achieving progress in the implementation of paragraph 11 of General Assembly

---

[1] *Official Records of the General Assembly, Twenty-fifth Session, Supplement No. 13* (A/8013).

resolution 194 (III), and requests the Commission to exert continued efforts towards the implementation thereof;

5. *Directs attention* to the continuing critical financial position of the United Nations Relief and Works Agency for Palestine Refugees in the Near East, as outlined in the Commissioner-General's report;

6. *Notes with concern* that, despite the commendable and successful efforts of the Commissioner-General to collect additional contributions to help relieve the serious budget deficit of the past year, contributions to the United Nations Relief and Works Agency for Palestine Refugees in the Near East continue to fall short of the funds needed to cover essential budget requirements;

7. *Calls upon* all Governments as a matter of urgency to make the most generous efforts possible to meet the anticipated needs of the United Nations Relief and Works Agency for Palestine Refugees in the Near East, particularly in the light of the budgetary deficit projected in the Commissioner-General's report and therefore urges non-contributing Governments to contribute and contributing Governments to consider increasing their contributions.

1921st plenary meeting,
8 December 1970.

B

The General Assembly,

Recalling its resolutions 2252 (ES-V) of 4 July 1967, 2341 B (XXII) of 19 December 1967, 2452 C (XXIII) of 19 December 1968 and 2535 C (XXIV) of 10 December 1969,

Taking note of the annual report of the Commissioner-General of the United Nations Relief and Works Agency for Palestine Refugees in the Near East, covering the period from 1 July 1969 to 30 June 1970,[2]

Bearing in mind also the letter dated 13 August 1970 from the Secretary-General addressed to States Members of the United Nations or members of specialized agencies,[3]

Concerned about the continued human suffering resulting from the · June 1967 hostilities in the Middle East,

1. *Reaffirms* its resolutions 2252 (ES-V), 2341 B (XXII), 2452 C (XXIII) and 2535 C (XXIV);

[2] *Ibid.*
[3] A/8040.

2. *Endorses*, bearing in mind the objectives of those resolutions, the efforts of the Commissioner-General of the United Nations Relief and Works Agency for Palestine Refugees in the Near East to continue to provide humanitarian assistance, as far as practicable, on an emergency basis and as a temporary measure, to other persons in the area who are at present displaced and in serious need of continued assistance as a result of the June 1967 hostilities;

3. *Strongly appeals* to all Governments and to organizations and individuals to contribute generously for the above purposes to the United Nations Relief and Works Agency for Palestine Refugees in the Near East and to the other intergovernmental and non-governmental organizations concerned.

1921st plenary meeting,
8 December 1970.

C

The General Assembly,

Recognizing that the problem of the Palestinian Arab refugees has arisen from the denial of their inalienable rights under the Charter of the United Nations and the Universal Declaration of Human Rights,

Recalling its resolution 2535 B (XXIV) of 10 December 1969, in which it reaffirmed the inalienable rights of the people of Palestine,

Bearing in mind the principle of equal rights and self-determination of peoples enshrined in Articles 1 and 55 of the Charter of the United Nations and more recently reaffirmed in the Declaration on Principles of International Law concerning Friendly Relations and Co-operation among States in accordance with the Charter of the United Nations,[4]

1. *Recognizes* that the people of Palestine are entitled to equal rights and self-determination, in accordance with the Charter of the United Nations;

2. *Declares* that full respect for the inalienable rights of the people of Palestine is an indispensable element in the establishment of a just and lasting peace in the Middle East.

1921st plenary meeting,
8 December 1970.

[4] General Assembly resolution 2625 (XXV).

D

The General Assembly,

Recalling Security Council resolution 237 (1967) of 14 June 1967,

Recalling also its resolutions 2252 (ES-V) of 4 July 1967, 2452 A (XXIII) of 19 December 1968, calling upon the Government of Israel to take effective and immediate steps for the return without delay of those inhabitants who had fled the areas since the outbreak of hostilities, and 2535 B (XXIV) of 10 December 1969,

Gravely concerned about the plight of the displaced persons,

Convinced that the plight of the displaced persons could best be relieved by their speedy return to their homes and to the camps which they formerly occupied,

Emphasizing the imperative of giving effect to its resolutions for relieving the plight of the displaced persons,

1. *Considers* that the plight of the displaced persons continues since they have not been able to return to their homes and camps;

2. *Calls once more upon* the Government of Israel to take immediately and without any further delay effective steps for the return of the displaced persons;

3. *Requests* the Secretary-General to follow the implementation of the present resolution and to report thereon to the General Assembly.

1921st plenary meeting,
8 December 1970.

49. Report by the Secretary-General on the Activities of the Special Representative to the Middle East, January 4, 1971*

* U.N. Doc. S/10070 (Jan. 4, 1971).

Introduction

1. On 22 November 1967, the Security Council adopted resolution 242 (1967), which reads as follows:

"*The Security Council,*

"*Emphasizing further* that all Member States in their acceptance of the Charter of the United Nations have undertaken a commitment to

"*Emphasizing* the inadmissibility of the acquisition of territory by war and the need to work for a just and lasting peace in which every State in the area can live in security,

"*Emphasizing further* that all Members States in their acceptance of the Charter of the United Nations have undertaken a commitment to act in accordance with Article 2 of the Charter,

"1. *Affirms* that the fulfilment of Charter principles requires the establishment of a just and lasting peace in the Middle East which should include the application of both the following principles:

(*i*) Withdrawal of Israel armed forces from territories occupied in the recent conflict;

(*ii*) Termination of all claims or states of belligerency and respect for and acknowledgement of the sovereignty, territorial integrity and political independence of every State in the area and their right to live in peace within secure and recognized boundaries free from threats or acts of force;

"2. *Affirms further* the necessity

(*a*) For guaranteeing freedom of navigation through international waterways in the area;

(*b*) For achieving a just settlement of the refugee problem;

(*c*) For guaranteeing the territorial inviolability and political independence of every State in the area, through measures including the establishment of demilitarized zones;

"3. *Requests* the Secretary-General to designate a Special Representative to proceed to the Middle East to establish and maintain contacts with the States concerned in order to promote agreement and assist efforts to achieve a peaceful and accepted settlement in accordance with the provisions and principles in this resolution;

"4. *Requests* the Secretary-General to report to the Security Council on the progress of the efforts of the Special Representative as soon as possible."

2. On 23 November 1967 I reported to the Council (S/8259) that I had invited Ambassador Gunnar V. Jarring of Sweden to accept the

designation as the Special Representative mentioned in paragraph 3 of the Council's above-mentioned resolution. Ambassador Jarring accepted this designation and arrived at United Nations Headquarters on 26 November, where he entered into consultation with the representatives of Israel, Jordan, Lebanon and the United Arab Republic (Syria, the other State concerned, did not at that state or later accept the Security Council resolution). After those consultations with the parties, Ambassador Jarring established the headquarters of the United Nations Middle East Mission in Cyprus.

3. In reports dated 22 December 1967, 17 January 1968, 29 March 1968, 29 July 1968 and 3 December 1968 (S/8309 and Add. 1 to 4, respectively), I reported to the Security Council on the progress of the efforts of Ambassador Jarring. On 7 August 1970, I was able to inform the Security Council (S/9902) that Israel, Jordan and the United Arab Republic had agreed to take part in discussions under Ambassador Jarring's auspices for the purpose of reaching agreement on a just and lasting peace between them. Unfortunately and for well known reasons those discussions were interrupted immediately after they began. The Members of the Security Council will have been able to observe that in the last few days it has become possible to arrange for the resumption of the discussions. I hope that these resumed discussions will be fruitful. However, it seems appropriate at this time to provide the Security Council with a somewhat fuller account of the activities of the Special Representative than heretofore.

I. Activities of the Special Representative during the Period 9 December 1967 to 26 November 1968

4. When the Special Representative first met with the parties in December 1967, he found that the Israeli Government was of the firm view that a settlement of the Middle East question could be reached only through direct negotiations between the parties culminating in a peace treaty and that there could be no question of withdrawal of their forces prior to such a settlement. On 27 December, the Minister for Foreign Affairs of Israel, Mr. Abba Eban, communicated to the Special Representative a proposal that Israel and the United Arab Republic representatives should, as a first step, discuss an agenda for peace. The Israeli proposals for such an agenda were:

"1. *Political and juridical problems:* The replacement of cease-fire arrangements by peace treaties ending the state of belligerency,

ending all hostile acts and threats and embodying a permanent
undertaking of mutual non-aggression.

"2. *Territorial and security problems:* The determination of agreed
territorial boundaries and security arrangements. Agreement on this
measure would determine the deployment of armed forces after the
cease-fire.

"3. *Navigation problems:* Practical methods should be discussed for
ensuring free navigation for all states including Israel in the Suez
Canal and the Gulf of Aqaba when the cease-fire is replaced by
peace. In the light of tragic experience, it is evident that international
declarations cannot by themselves solve this problem. Concrete
measures and guarantees are required.

"4. *Economic problems:* Proposals for terminating boycott practices
and instituting normal economic relations."

5. The United Arab Republic and Jordan, for their part, insisted that
there could be no question of discussions between the parties until the
Israeli forces had been withdrawn to the positions occupied by them
prior to 5 June 1967. Reacting specifically to the Israeli proposals for
discussing an agenda for peace, the Minister for Foreign Affairs of the
United Arab Republic, Mr. Mahmoud Riad, stated that the withdrawal
of Israel's forces to the positions held prior to June 1967 was a basic
and preliminary step to a peaceful settlement in the Middle East.

6. An Israeli proposal for discussions on an agenda for peace with
Jordan was submitted to the Special Representative on 7 January 1968.
It followed the same general lines as the proposal for the United Arab
Republic but contained more detailed suggestions for economic co-
operation, as well as the following new topics:

"*Humanitarian problems:* In the proposed negotiation, high priority
should be given to a solution of the refugee problem with international and regional co-operation.

"*Religious and historical sites:* Access to sites of special religious
significance should be discussed. The Government of Israel clarified
its views on this subject in several verbal and written communications to the United Nations."

It was also stated:

"In the meantime, it is urgent that breaches of the cease-fire and
activities by El Fatah and other such organizations should be
suppressed and every effort made on both sides to avoid exchanges of
fire."

7. The proposals, when communicated to the Jordanian authorities

by the Special Representative, were objected to in the same way as the
proposals to the United Arab Republic had been.

8. Faced with these conflicting positions, the Special Representative
sought to obtain from the parties an assurance that they would
implement Security Council resolution 242 (1967), in the hope that
such a declaration would be regarded as a basis for subsequent
discussions between the parties. The Special Representative received
from Foreign Minister Eban a number of formulations of Israel's
position on the Security Council resolution, of which the last, dated 19
February 1968, read as follows:

"1. The Government of Israel, out of respect for the Security
Council's resolution of 22 November 1967 and responding affirmatively thereto, assures you of its full co-operation in your efforts
with the States concerned to promote agreement and to achieve an
accepted settlement for the establishment of a just and lasting peace,
in accordance with your mandate under the resolution.

"2. Israel's position has throughout been that the best way to achieve
the objective of the Security Council resolution is through direct
negotiations. However, as a further indication of Israel's co-operation,
we are willing that this be done in a meeting convened by the Special
Representative of the Secretary-General.

"3. On 12 February 1968, I informed you of Israel's acceptance of
the Security Council's call in its resolution of 22 November 1967 for
the promotion of agreement on the establishment of peace. The
United Arab Republic is also aware of Israel's willingness as explained
on 1 February to negotiate on all matters included in the Security
Council's resolution. We accept the sponsor's view that the principles
recommended for inclusion in the peace settlement are integrally
linked and interdependent.

"4. We have noted the United Arab Republic's willingness to
'implement' the Security Council's resolution and fulfil its obligations
thereunder. It is a matter of concern that the United Arab Republic
statements, unlike those of Israel, do not specifically use the precise
terms of the resolution in such crucial matters as 'agreement' and the
'establishment of a just and lasting peace,' and that the United Arab
Republic has not yet agreed to a process of negotiation without
which, of course, a declaration of willingness to fulfil the resolution
is of no substantive effect. The resolution is a framework for
agreement. It cannot be fulfilled without a direct exchange of views
and proposals leading to bilateral contractual commitments. The
United Arab Republic position is, therefore, still deficient in

important respects. We are, however, conscious of the importance of the fact that the United Arab Republic and Israel have both responded affirmatively to the call for co-operating with you in the mission laid upon you by the Security Council. At the same time, it would be unrealistic to ignore that there have been sharp differences of interpretation of what the resolution entails. To subscribe to similar declarations does not of itself solve practical issues at stake.

"5. It is accordingly urgent to move forward to a more substantive stage and to embark on a meaningful negotiation for achieving the just and lasting peace called for by the Security Council."

In discussions with the Special Representative, Foreign Minister Eban stated that Israel would not object to an indirect approach to negotiations provided that it was designed to lead to a later stage of direct negotiations and agreement.

9. The United Arab Republic Foreign Minister gave repeated assurances that the United Arab Republic was ready to implement the Security Council resolution as a whole and to fulfil its obligations under it, but stated that it would not accept direct negotiations. The United Arab Republic has not yet agreed to a process of negotiation without an Israeli declaration "in clear language" that it would implement the Security Council resolution.

10. The Jordanian authorities expressed a similar point of view to the Special Representative.

11. The Special Representative then proceeded to United Nations Headquarters for consultations with the Secretary-General. Returning to the area at the beginning of March, he informally presented to the parties, to ascertain their reactions, a draft letter from himself to the Secretary-General, which would be worded as follows:

"The Governments of Israel and the United Arab Republic [Jordan] have both indicated to me that they accept Security Council resolution 242 (1967) of 22 November 1967 for achieving a peaceful and accepted settlement of the Middle East question and intend to devise arrangements, under my auspices, for the implementation of the provisions of the resolution.

"The two Governments have expressed their willingness to co-operate with me in my capacity as Special Representative of the Secretary-General in the discharge of my tasks of promoting agreement and achieving such a settlement.

"In view of the urgency of the situation and with a view to expediting efforts to reach settlement, I have invited the two Governments to meet with me, for conferences within the framework of the

Security Council resolution, in Nicosia. I have pleasure in informing you that the two Governments have responded favourably to this invitation."

12. When Ambassador Jarring presented this text to the United Arab Republic Foreign Minister on 7 March 1968, the latter stated that recent statements by Israeli leaders showed that they were following an expansionist line. It was no longer sufficient to have Israel give an assurance of intent to implement the resolution; the Arabs had to be satisfied that the Israelis were going to "implement it for action." If the Israelis withdrew completely from the occupied territories, peace could be arrived at by the implementation of the other provisions of the Security Council resolution under the Council's guidance.

13. In a meeting on 10 March, the Special Representative informed the Israeli Foreign Minister of the United Arab Republic attitude. He then informally showed his draft letter to the Foreign Minister, who expressed the personal view that it would be fully acceptable to the Israeli authorities if it was also accepted by the other side and led to contacts between them. Subsequently the Special Representative was informed of Israel's official acceptance, without conditions, of the text.

14. In a meeting on 14 March, the Jordanian authorities stated that they were ready to accept the proposed meeting in principle provided that the text was modified to read that the parties had "declared their readiness to implement the resolution."

15. During the following weeks, Ambassador Jarring paid repeated visits to the countries concerned in an endeavour to obtain from the Israelis a more precise formulation of their acceptance of the resolution and from the two Arab States acceptance of the idea of meetings between the parties under his auspices.

16. At a meeting in Amman on 16 April 1968, the Jordanian authorities stated that they were prepared to accept the text of the Special Representative's draft letter provided that the third paragraph was amended to read as follows:

"In view of the urgency of the situation and with a view to expediting efforts to reach settlements, I will meet with representatives of Israel and Jordan for conferences within the framework of the Security Council resolution, in New York. I have pleasure in informing you that the two Governments have responded favourably hereto."

The acceptance was based on the assumption that the United Arab Republic would accept an identical text.

17. The Israeli authorities found difficulties in the Jordanian amended text. They had accepted meetings at Nicosia, on the understanding that the Special Representative's invitation would lead to joint meetings. The new text appeared to give the impression that only meetings between the parties and the Special Representative were intended. The change of venue, while not objectionable in principle, tended to create the impression that only discussions with the permanent missions in the scope of normal United Nations activities would take place; a change from Nicosia to a European city would be acceptable.

18. The United Arab Republic Foreign Minister at first continued to insist on a prior declaration by Israel of its intention to implement the Security Council resolution. Finally, however, on 9 May, on the eve of the Special Representative's departure from the area (see following paragraph), he replied to the Special Representative's proposed invitation in the form amended by Jordan in the following written statement:

"With reference to your indication to me today of your desire to meet with a representative of the United Arab Republic in New York, I wish to reaffirm the readiness of our Permanent Representative to the United Nations in New York to meet with you to continue the contacts which you have been conducting with the parties concerned in accordance with Security Council resolution 242 (1967) of 22 November 1967 for the implementation of that resolution.

"I have referred in the course of our previous meetings to the importance of the setting of a timetable for the implementation of the resolution of the Security Council, and offered you several alternatives towards that end, one of which, that you present a timetable prepared by yourself for the implementation of the resolution. These suggestions emanate from the United Arab Republic's indication to you of its acceptance and readiness to implement the above-mentioned resolution.

"I wish to express anew our willingness to co-operate with you in your capacity as Special Representative of the Secretary-General in the discharge of your tasks as defined in the Council's resolution of the 22nd of November 1967."

The United Arab Republic Foreign Minister repeated that the United Arab Republic was ready to implement the resolution as a whole and as a "package deal." It insisted, however, that Israel should do likewise, including complete withdrawal.

19. Ambassador Jarring was faced with a position where there was now agreement, though clearly with considerable differences of interpretation, on the first two paragraphs of his proposed invitation, but where

there was disagreement on the third paragraph containing the actual invitation. Further journeying backwards and forwards between the various countries was unlikely to be productive. In consultations with me, he considered issuing a formal invitation along the lines of his proposal, but with the venue at New York, but it was felt that a forced acceptance obtained by such an invitation would not be helpful. Instead it was decided that the talks in New York should begin without a formal invitation by the Special Representative or a letter from the Special Representative to the Secretary-General but on the basis of a short statement to the press in which it would be announced that the Special Representative was arriving in New York for consultations in continuation of his mission.

20. During his stay in the area, the Special Representative visited Beirut on three occasions. The Lebanese Government expressed its full support for a solution according to Security Council resolution 242 (1967). Lebanon, however, had no territory under occupation and therefore did not have the same detailed involvement in the settlement as the United Arab Republic and Jordan. The Special Representative did not visit Syria, whose Government, as noted above, had not accepted the Security Council resolution.

21. Ambassador Jarring left the area on 10 May 1968 and arrived at Headquarters on 15 May 1968.

22. In the five weeks following his arrival at New York, Ambassador Jarring pursued actively his contacts with the permanent representatives of the parties at both a formal and informal level. Unfortunately these contacts did not serve in any way to break the dead-lock between the parties concerning the interpretation of the Security Council resolution and the manner in which it should be implemented. In that regard, the Permanent Representative of Israel had stated in the Security Council on 1 May 1968:

> "In declarations and statements made publicly and to Mr. Jarring, my Government has indicated its acceptance of the Security Council resolution for the promotion of agreement on the establishment of a just and durable peace. I am also authorized to reaffirm that we are willing to seek agreement with each Arab State on all the matters included in that resolution."

This statement was not regarded as acceptable by the Arab representatives.

23. Returning to New York on 22 July after a short stay in Europe during which he had met in various capitals the Foreign Ministers of

the United Arab Republic, Israel and Jordan, Ambassador Jarring
decided, with my approval, to return to the Middle East and resume his
direct contacts with the parties. This second round of discussions, which
began on 16 August 1968, took the form of an exchange of questions
and of comments between the parties through the Special Representative.
Some progress in the clarification of the respective positions of the
parties had been made when the opening of the twenty-third session of
the General Assembly caused the venue of the discussions to be transferred to New York, where they could be carried out with greater
convenience. With the arrival of the foreign ministers of the parties for
the session toward the end of September, Ambassador Jarring began a
series of frequent meetings with them individually, which were at first
mainly of an informal nature but which, following the delivery by the
foreign ministers of their speeches in the general debate, assumed a more
formal character and concluded with written communications from the
Foreign Ministers of Israel and of the United Arab Republic restating
the positions of their respective Governments. Those written statements
were in amplification of the positions of the parties as publicly stated
in the General Assembly and made clear the essential differences
between them. On the one hand, Israel regarded the Security Council
resolution as a statement of principles in the light of which the parties
should negotiate peace and, on the other hand, the United Arab Republic considered that the resolution provided a plan for settlement of the
Middle East dispute to be implemented by the parties according to
modalities to be established by the Special Representative. It was also
abundantly clear that there was a crucial difference of opinion over the
meaning to be attached to the withdrawal provisions of the Security
Council resolution, which according to the Arab States applied to all
territories occupied since 5 June 1967 and according to Israel applied
only to the extent required when agreement had been reached between
the parties on secure and recognized borders between them.
24. Discouraging though the prospects seemed, Ambassador Jarring
decided to carry out another brief round of discussions in the Middle
East. As he explained in a letter to me, dated 26 November 1968, he
had in mind inviting the parties to a new round of discussions in the
middle of January 1969 in order to give them time for reflection and
for careful consideration of their respective positions.[1]

---

[1] For the texts of the letter from Ambassador Jarring and the reply by the Secretary-General,
see S/8309/Add.4.

II. *Activities of the Special Representative from* *27 November 1968 to June 1970*

25. Ambassador Jarring departed from Headquarters on 27 November 1968 and met with representatives of Israel in Nicosia on 2 and 3 December, of the United Arab Republic in Cairo on 4 December and of Jordan in Amman on 7 December. Unfortunately, these meetings did not reveal a change of position in the attitude of the parties that would have made it expedient for Ambassador Jarring to convene a meeting of the parties in the middle of January 1969, as envisaged in his letter of 26 November 1968.

26. After resuming for a time his duties as Ambassador of Sweden to the Union of Soviet Socialist Republics, Ambassador Jarring returned to Headquarters on 29 January 1969. He there undertook a series of personal contacts with the Permanent Representatives of the parties and the representatives of other Member States.

27. At that stage, Ambassador Jarring concluded, with my concurrence, that the best contribution which he could make to breaking the existing deadlock was to make a further tour of the Middle East in which he would submit formally to the parties a series of questions designed to elicit their attitude towards Security Council resolution 242 (1967). He accordingly left New York on 21 February 1969 for the Middle East. At meetings with the Foreign Ministers of the United Arab Republic on 5 March, of Jordan on 8 March, of Israel on 9 March and of Lebanon on 14 March, he submitted the questions which he had previously prepared. The replies of the parties were received by Ambassador Jarring as follows:

Israel: handed to Ambassador Jarring in Jerusalem by the Minister for Foreign Affairs on 2 April 1969.

Jordan: received by Ambassador Jarring in Nicosia on 24 March 1969.

Lebanon: received by Ambassador Jarring in Moscow on 21 April 1969.

United Arab Republic: handed to Ambassador Jarring in Cairo by the Minister for Foreign Affairs of the United Arab Republic on 27 March 1969.

The questions and replies are reproduced in annex I.

28. It had been the hope of Ambassador Jarring, in submitting his questions, that the replies might show certain encouraging features which might make it possible to invite the parties for a series of meetings between them and him at some mutually convenient place. Unfortunately, the replies were in general a repetition of attitudes already

expressed to Ambassador Jarring on numerous occasions from the beginning of his mission. They showed continued serious divergencies between the Arab States and Israel both as regards the interpretation to be given to the Security Council resolution and as to the procedures for putting its provisions into effect.

29. Ambassador Jarring was regretfully forced to conclude, with my agreement, that the conditions for convening a useful series of meetings at that time did not exist and that there was no further move which he could usefully make at that stage. He therefore returned on 5 April 1969 to Moscow, where he resumed his duties as Ambassador of Sweden to the Union of Soviet Socialist Republics.

30. Ambassador Jarring continued to keep in close touch with me and with representatives of the parties and of other interested States.

31. Ambassador Jarring returned to Headquarters from 12 September to 8 October 1969 and from 10 to 26 March 1970, but found no new elements which would permit him to organize active discussions with the parties. On each occasion he returned to his post in Moscow.

32. On 3 April 1969, the Permanent Representatives of France, the Union of Soviet Socialist Republics, the United Kingdom of Great Britain and Northern Ireland and the United States of America began a series of meetings on the Middle East question, which have continued at various intervals up to the present time. After each such meeting, the Chairman reported to me on the substance of the discussions and I kept Ambassador Jarring informed.

III. The Attempt to Hold Discussions under the Special Representative's Auspices
(June 1970–4 January 1971)

33. In June 1970, the Government of the United States of America proposed to the Governments of Israel, Jordan and the United Arab Republic that they should each advise Ambassador Jarring as follows:

(a) that having accepted and indicated their willingness to carry out resolution 242 in all its parts, they will designate representatives to discussions to be held under his auspices, according to such procedure and at such places and times as he may recommend, taking into account as appropriate each side's preference as to method of procedure and previous experience between the parties;

(b) that the purpose of the aforementioned discussions is to reach agreement on the establishment of a just and lasting peace between them based on (1) mutual acknowledgement by the United Arab Republic, Jordan and Israel of each other's sovereignty, territorial integrity and political independence, and (2) Israeli withdrawal from territories occupied in the 1967 conflict, both in accordance with resolution 242;

(c) that, to facilitate his task of promoting agreement as set forth in resolution 242, the parties will strictly observe, effective 1 July at least until 1 October, the cease-fire resolutions of the Security Council.

34. Having been informed by the United States Government that the States concerned had accepted its peace initiative, I invited Ambassador Jarring to return immediately to Headquarters, where he arrived on 2 August. I informed the Security Council in a note dated 7 August (S/9902) that Ambassador Jarring had received confirmation from the Permanent Representatives of those States of their acceptance and that he had addressed to me a letter as described above. I was informed by the United States representative that his Government had received the acceptance of the Governments of the United Arab Republic and Israel to a standstill cease-fire for a period of ninety days from 2200 GMT on the same day. Ambassador Jarring and I had previously been informed by Secretary of State Rogers that his Government would take responsibility for organizing the standstill cease-fire.

35. Ambassador Jarring at once entered into contact with the parties and, after considering their views on the time and place of the discussions, on 21 August 1970 addressed to them invitations to take part in discussions opening at New York on 25 August 1970. He met on the appointed day with representatives of each of the parties. However Ambassador Tekoah, who had been designated by Israel as its representative for the initial phase of the talks, then stated that he had been instructed by his Government to return to Israel for consultations. On his return on 8 September, he communicated to Ambassador Jarring the following decision of his Government:

"Israel's acceptance of the United States peace initiative according to its decision of 4 August 1970, and the appointment of a representative to the talks under the auspices of Ambassador Jarring are still in effect.

"The Government of Egypt has gravely violated the ceasefire-standstill agreement, and this violation is continuing without letup.

"The strictest observance of the ceasefire-standstill agreement is one of the central elements of the American peace initiative and of the talks under the auspices of Ambassador Jarring. Therefore, so long as the ceasefire-standstill agreement is not observed in its entirety, and.

the original situation restored, Israel will not be able to participate in these talks.

"Ambassador Tekoah, who is returning to his post as head of the permanent delegation of Israel at the United Nations, has been authorized to bring this decision of the Government of Israel to the attention of Ambassador Jarring."

The Special Representative thus found himself precluded for the time being from holding formal meetings with the Israeli representatives, and his talks with the representatives of the Arab States, though they continued, could not be productive because of the lack of contact with the Israeli representative. After a brief visit to Moscow from 6 to 14 October to attend to his affairs as Ambassador of Sweden there, the Special Representative returned to New York and had a wide range of contacts with representatives of the parties and of other Member States during the commemorative session of the General Assembly and the debate on the Middle East, which followed that session.

36. Immediately following the adoption of General Assembly resolution 2628 (XXV), Ambassador Jarring entered into contact with the representatives of the parties in order to invite them to re-enter into talks under his auspices for the purpose of reaching agreement on the establishment of a just and lasting peace. The representatives of Jordan and the United Arab Republic informed him that their Governments continued to to be willing to do so; the representative of Israel stated that the matter was under consideration in the Israeli Cabinet.

37. On 19 November and pending a decision by the Israeli Cabinet, Ambassador Jarring returned to Moscow. On the eve of his departure, he addressed a letter to the Israeli Minister for Foreign Affairs, in which he formally invited the Israeli Government to resume its participation in the discussions, as well as letters to the Permanent Representatives of Jordan and the United Arab Republic, in which he took note of the position of their Governments. These letters, together with replies from the Permanent Representative of the United Arab Republic and the Israeli Foreign Minister, are reproduced in annex II.

38. On 30 December, Ambassador Jarring received in Moscow a message from the Foreign Minister of Israel in which the latter informed him of the readiness of the Government of Israel to resume its participation in the talks. The message is also reproduced in annex II.

Annex I

Questions submitted in March 1969 by the Special Representative to the Governments concerned and their Replies

Note: Ambassador Jarring submitted his questions to the States concerned in the form of separate lists specifically addressed to each Government. Those lists were, however, prepared from a general list applicable to all the parties and that list is, to save repetition, reproduced here. As some questions related to provisions of Security Council resolution 242 (1967) which applied to only one or some of the parties, the numbers of questions in the specific lists were not always the same as those in the general list. Where the number of the answer differs from that of the question in the general list, the latter number is added in square brackets.

Specific lists of questions based on the following general list were submitted by Ambassador Jarring to the Governments of the United Arab Republic on 5 March, of Jordan on 8 March, of Israel on 9 March and of Lebanon on 14 March 1969.

A. QUESTIONS SUBMITTED BY THE SPECIAL REPRESENTATIVE

Security Council resolution 242 (1967) sets out provisions and principles in accordance with which a peaceful and accepted settlement of the Middle East Question should be achieved. Some of these provisions would impose obligations on both sides, some on one side, and some on the other. It has generally been accepted that they should be regarded as a whole. The following questions designed to elicit the attitude of the parties towards the provisions of the Security Council resolution are based on this assumption and are to be understood in the context that each provision is regarded as part of a "package deal."

1. Does Israel (Jordan, Lebanon, United Arab Republic) accept Security Council resolution 242 (1967) for implementation for achieving a peaceful and accepted settlement of the Middle East Question in accordance with the provisions and principles contained in the resolution?

2. Does Israel (Jordan, Lebanon, United Arab Republic) agree to pledge termination of all claims or states of belligerency with Jordan, Lebanon and the United Arab Republic (Israel)?

3. Does Israel (Jordan, Lebanon, United Arab Republic) agree to pledge respect for and acknowledgement of the sovereignty, territorial integrity and political independence of Jordan, Lebanon and the United Arab Republic (Israel)?

4. Does Israel (Jordan, Lebanon, United Arab Republic) accept the right of Jordan, Lebanon and the United Arab Republic (Israel) to live in peace within secure and recognized boundaries free from threats or acts of force?

5. If so, what is the conception of secure and recognized boundaries held by Israel (Jordan, Lebanon, United Arab Republic)?

6. Does Israel agree to withdraw its armed forces from territories occupied by it in the recent conflict?

7. Does the United Arab Republic agree to guarantee freedom of navigation for Israel through international waterways in the area, in particular:

  (*a*) through the Straits of Tiran, and

  (*b*) through the Suez Canal?

8. Does Israel (Jordan, Lebanon, United Arab Republic) agree that, if a plan for the just settlement of the refugee problem is worked out and presented to the parties for their consideration, the acceptance in principle of such a plan by the parties and the declaration of their intention to implement it in good faith constitute sufficient implementation of this provision of the Security Council resolution to justify the implementation of the other provisions?

9. Does Israel (Jordan, Lebanon, United Arab Republic) agree that the territorial inviolability and political independence of the States in the area should be guaranteed:

  (*a*) by the establishment of demilitarized zones;

  (*b*) through additional measures?

10. Does Israel agree that such demilitarized zones should include areas on its side of its boundaries?

11. Does Jordan agree that a demilitarized zone should be established in Jordanian territory from which Israel armed forces have been withdrawn?

12. Does the United Arab Republic agree that a demilitarized zone should be established:

  (*a*) at Sharm-el-Sheikh;

  (*b*) in other parts of the Sinai peninsula?

13. Does Israel (Jordan, Lebanon, United Arab Republic) agree that demilitarization of such zones should be supervised and maintained by the United Nations?

14. Would Israel (Jordan, Lebanon, United Arab Republic) accept as a final act of agreement on all provisions a mutually signed multilateral document which would incorporate the agreed conditions for a just and lasting peace?

B. REPLY OF THE GOVERNMENT OF ISRAEL

(Handed to Ambassador Jarring in Jerusalem by the Minister for
Foreign Affairs on 2 April 1969)

Jerusalem, 2 April 1969

Dear Ambassador Jarring,

Israel's position on all the subjects raised in your eleven questions has
been stated in detail in my address to the General Assembly of 8
October 1968, and in the memoranda presented to you on 15 October
1968 and 4 November 1968.

I now enclose specific replies in an affirmative spirit to the questions
as formulated. It is my understanding that on the basis of the answers
received from the three governments you propose to pursue further
mutual clarifications in an effort to promote agreement on all the
matters at issue in accordance with your mandate. We are ready to join
in this process at any appropriate place.

Israel's statements of attitude, including her replies to these questions,
has taken into account recent developments in Arab policy including the
speeches recently delivered by President Nasser and other Arab leaders.
We have noted the specific and emphatic reiteration of their refusal to
make peace with Israel, to recognize Israel, to negotiate with Israel, to
cease terrorist attacks on Israel or to admit the possibility of sovereign
co-existence in any field. It would appear at this time that the effective
negation by the UAR of the principles of the Charter and of the
Security Council's Resolution is obvious and vehement. We hope that
this policy, to which effect is given every day, will change; but these
authoritative statements have caused deep concern and have intensified
the tension which we would have wished to see relieved.

It is also our view that highly publicized encounters by four member
States have weakened the attention which should have been
concentrated on the efforts of the parties themselves to move towards
agreement. They are causing a duplication and dispersal of effort. They
have also encouraged a wrong impression in some quarters that a
solution can be sought outside the region and without its governments.
Israel recognizes your mission as the authoritative international framework within which peace between the States in the Middle East should
be promoted.

I recall the idea which we discussed some weeks ago that the Foreign
Ministers of the three governments should meet with you soon at a

suitable place to pursue the promotion of agreement. As you will
remember, I reacted positively to this idea. I wish to reaffirm that Israel
will continue to co-operate with you in the fulfilment of your mission.

Yours sincerely,

(*Signed*) Abba EBAN

Answer to Question One:

Israel accepts the Security Council resolution (242) for the promotion
of agreement on the establishment of a just and lasting peace, to be
reached by negotiation and agreements between the governments concerned. Implementation of agreements should begin when agreement
has been concluded on all their provisions.

Answer to Question Two:

It is the Arab States, not Israel which claimed and originated states of
belligerency. They declared themselves for two decades to be in a state
of unilateral war with Israel. It is therefore primarily incumbent upon
them to terminate the state of war with Israel.

On the establishment of peace with her Arab neighbours, Israel agrees
to the termination, on a reciprocal basis, of all claims or states of
belligerency with each State with which peace is established. A declaration specifying each State by name would be made by Israel in each
case.

The corresponding statement by any Arab State must specifically
renounce belligerency "with Israel" and not "with any state in the
area." Legal obligations must be specific in regard to those by whom
they are bound.

Renunciation of belligerency includes the cessation of all maritime
interference, the cessation of boycott measures involving third parties;
the annulment of reservations made by Arab States on the applicability
to Israel of their obligations under international conventions to which
they have adhered; non-adherence to political and military alliances and
pacts directed against Israel or including States unwilling to renounce
claims or states of belligerency with Israel and maintain peaceful
relations with it; the non-stationing of armed forces of such other States
on the territory of the contracting States and the prohibition and
prevention in the territory of Arab States of all preparations, actions or
expeditions by irregular or para-military groups or by individuals
directed against the lives, security or property of Israel in any part of
the world.

The last stipulation is without prejudice to the fact that the responsibility of Arab governments for preventing such activities is legally binding under the cease-fire established by the parties in June 1967.

Answer to Question Three:

Israel agrees to respect and acknowledge the sovereignty, territorial integrity and political independence of neighbouring Arab States; this principle would be embodied in peace treaties establishing agreed boundaries.

Answer to Question Four:

Israel accepts the right of Jordan, Lebanon, the United Arab Republic and other neighbouring States to live in peace within secure and recognized boundaries, free from threats or acts of force. Explicit and unequivocal reciprocity is Israel's only conditions for this acceptance. "Acts of force" include all preparations, actions or expeditions by irregular or para-military groups or by individuals directed against the life, security or property of Israel in any part of the world.

Answer to Question Five:

Secure and recognized boundaries have never yet existed between Israel and the Arab States; accordingly, they should now be established as part of the peace-making process. The cease-fire should be replaced by peace treaties establishing permanent, secure and recognized boundaries as agreed upon through negotiation between the governments concerned.

Answer to Question Six:

When permanent, secure and recognized boundaries are agreed upon and established between Israel and each of the neighbouring Arab States, the disposition of forces will be carried out in full accordance with the boundaries determined in the peace treaties.

Answer to Question Seven: [general question 8]

The refugee problem was caused by the wars launched against Israel by Arab States, and has been perpetuated through the refusal of Arab States to establish peaceful relations with Israel. In view of the human problems involved in this issue Israel has expressed its willingness to give priority to the attainment of an agreement for the solution of this problem through regional and international co-operation. We believe that agreement could be sought even in advance of peace negotiations. We suggest that a conference of Middle Eastern States should be convened, together with the Governments contribution to refugee relief and the Specialized Agencies of the United Nations, in order to chart a five-year plan for the solution of the refugee problem in the framework of a lasting peace and the integration of refugees into productive life. This conference can be called in advance of peace negotiations.

Joint refugee integration and rehabilitation commissions should be established by the governments concerned in order to work out agreed projects for refugee integration on a regional basis with international assistance.

In view of the special humanitarian nature of this issue we do not make agreement on plans for a solution of the refugee problem contingent on agreement on any other aspect of the Middle Eastern problem. For the same reason it should not be invoked by Arab States to obstruct agreement on other problems.

Answer to Question Eight: [general question 9]

The effective guarantee for the territorial inviolability and political independence of States lies in the strict observance by the governments of their treaty obligations. In the context of peace providing for full respect for the sovereignty of States and the establishment of agreed boundaries, other security measures may be discussed by the contracting governments.

Answer to Questions Nine and Ten: [general questions 10 and 13]

Without prejudice to what is stated in answer to Question Eight, it is pointed out that experience has shown that the measures mentioned in Questions Nine and Ten have not prevented the preparation and carrying out of aggression against Israel.

Answer to Question Eleven: [general question 14]

Peace must be juridically expressed, contractually defined and reciprocally binding in accordance with established norms of international law and practice. Accordingly, Israel's position is that the peace should be embodied in bilateral peace treaties between Israel and each Arab State incorporating all the agreed conditions for a just and lasting peace. The treaties, once signed and ratified, should be registered with the Secretariat of the United Nations in accordance with Article 102 of the United Nations Charter.

2 April 1969

C. REPLY OF THE GOVERNMENT OF JORDAN

(Received by Ambassador Jarring in Nicosia on 24 March 1969)

23 March 1969

Your Excellency,

Following are the answers of my Government to the questions which you presented to us in Amman, on Saturday, 8 March 1969. The answers as numbered, hereunder, correspond to your questions.

These answers explain my Government's position, which position has repeatedly been stated to Your Excellency throughout our past meetings.

May I take this opportunity to express to you my continued sincere wishes for your success in the important mission with which you are entrusted.

Yours sincerely,

(*Signed*) Abdul Monem RIFA'I
Minister of Foreign Affairs

His Excellency,
Ambassador Gunnar Jarring
Special Representative to
  The Secretary-General of
  The United Nations.

Answer (1)

Jordan, as it has declared before, accepts the Security Council resolution 242 (1967) and is ready to implement it in order to achieve a peaceful and accepted settlement in accordance with the provisions and principles contained in the resolution.

Answer 2

Jordan agrees to pledge termination of all claims or states of belligerency. Such a pledge becomes effective upon withdrawal of Israeli forces from all Arab territories which Israel occupied as a result of its aggression of 5 June 1967.

A pledge by Israel to terminate the state of belligerency would be meaningful only when Israel withdraws its forces from all Arab territories it occupied since 5 June 1967.

Answer (3)

On 5 June 1967 Israel launched its aggression against three Arab States, violating their sovereignty and territorial integrity. Agreement to pledge respect for and acknowledgement of the sovereignty, territorial integrity and political independence of every State in the area requires the termination by Israel of its occupation and the withdrawal of its forces from all the Arab territories it occupied as a result of its aggression of 5 June.

Answer (4)

Jordan accepts the right of every State in the area to live in peace within secure and recognized boundaries free from threats or acts of force, provided that Israel withdraws its forces from all Arab territories it occupied since 5 June 1967, and implements the Security Council resolution of 22 November 1967.

Answer (5)

When the question of Palestine was brought before the United Nations in 1947, the General Assembly adopted its resolution 181 (II) of 29 November 1947 for the partition of Palestine and defined Israel's boundaries.

Answer (6) [general question 8]

It has always been our position that the just settlement of the refugee problem is embodied in paragraph 11 of the General Assembly resolution 194 of December 1948 which has been repeatedly reaffirmed by each and every General Assembly session ever since its adoption.

If a plan on the basis of that paragraph is presented for consideration to the parties concerned, its acceptance by the parties and the declaration of their intention to implement it in good faith, with adequate guarantees for its full implementation, would justify the implementation of the other provisions of the resolution.

Answer (7) (8) [general questions 9 and 11]

We do not believe that the establishment of demilitarized zones is a necessity. However, Jordan shall not oppose the establishment of such zones if they are astride the boundaries.

Answer (9) [general question 13]

In case demilitarized zones are established Jordan accepts that such zones be supervised and maintained by the United Nations.

Answer (10) [general question 14]

In view of our past experience with Israel and her denunciation of four agreements signed by her with Arab States we consider that the instrument to be signed by Jordan engaging her to carry out her obligations, would be addressed to the Security Council. Israel would likewise sign and address to the Security Council an instrument engaging her to carry out her obligations emanating from the Security Council resolution of 22 November 1967. The endorsement by the Security Council of these documents would constitute the final multilateral act of agreement.

D. REPLY OF THE GOVERNMENT OF LEBANON

(Received by Ambassador Jarring in Moscow on 21 April 1969)

[Translated from French]

. . .

In reply to the questionnaire which Your Excellency addressed to me on 14 March 1969, I have the honour, on behalf of the Lebanese Government, to inform you of the following:

Lebanon is essentially involved in the general context of the Israeli-Arab conflict—and, therefore, in the consequences of the war launched by Israel on 5 June 1967—because of its brotherly solidarity with the Arab States and of the threats which are constantly directed at it by Israel.

Lebanon is justified in considering, however, that the armistice agreement which it concluded with Israel on 23 March 1949 remains valid, as indicated in its message of 10 June 1967 to the Chairman of the Mixed Armistice Commission and as confirmed by U Thant, Secretary-General of the United Nations, in his report to the General Assembly of 19 September 1967. In that report, Mr. Thant, referring to the actual text of the agreement, said that it could be revised or suspended only by mutual consent. In view of Lebanon's circumstances, now and in the past, the armistice lines have, of course, never been changed. These lines, it should be noted, correspond to the frontiers of Lebanon which have always been internationally recognized in bilateral and multilateral diplomatic instruments as well as by the League of Nations and the United Nations. Lebanon participated actively in the drafting of the United Nations Charter and was admitted in its present form and structure to membership in the Organization. Its frontiers have not undergone any *de facto* or *de jure* alteration as a result of the cease-fire decisions taken by the Security Council after 5 June 1967.

It may be appropriate to state the above-mentioned facts, more particularly with a view to explaining the nature and character of the only reply which we are in a position to give to the questionnaire sent to us by Your Excellency on 14 March 1969.

In this reply, which reflects the position taken by Lebanon at inter-Arab conferences, we proclaim Lebanon's support of the position of the the Arab States whose territory has been occupied by Israel and which have accepted the Security Council's decision of 22 November 1967.

The present note is consistent with the spirit of the talks which you have already held with various Lebanese officials.

Accept, Sir, the assurances of my highest consideration.

(*Signed*) Yousset SALEM
Minister for Foreign Affairs

E. REPLY OF THE GOVERNMENT OF THE UNITED ARAB REPUBLIC

(Handed to Ambassador Jarring in Cairo by the Minister for Foreign Affairs of the United Arab Republic on 27 March 1969)

The memorandum handed to you on 5 March 1969 during your recent visit to Cairo clearly expresses the realities of the present situation. In its items 1 to 7, the memorandum gives a clear restatement of the position of the United Arab Republic which is based on the acceptance of the Security Council resolution 242 of 22 November 1967, and its readiness to carry out the obligations emanating therefrom.

The memorandum also clearly expounds Israel's persistence in rejecting the Security Council resolution and its refusal to carry out its obligations emanating from it as well as Israel's plans for annexation of Arab lands through war; a policy not only prohibited by the Charter of the United Nations but also violates the Security Council resolution which specifically emphasizes the inadmissibility of the acquisition of territory by war. It has become obvious that Israel, in its endeavour to realize its expansionist aims, is no longer satisfied with the actual rejection of the Security Council resolution but actively works against it.

The same memorandum also states Israel's expansion plan as revealed by the quoted statements of Israeli leaders. This plan aims at:

1. Annexation of Jerusalem;
2. Keeping the Syrian Heights under its occupation;
3. Occupation of the West Bank in Jordan and its complete domination, practically terminating Jordan's sovereignty in that part;
4. Economic and administrative integration of the Gaza strip into Israel and the systematic eviction of its inhabitants;
5. Occupation of Sharm El-Sheikh and the Gulf of Aqaba area as well as the continued military presence in eastern part of Sinai;
6. The establishment of Israeli settlements in occupied territories.

This Israeli position constitutes a flagrant violation and clear rejection of the Security Council resolution of 22 November 1967 and of the peaceful settlement for which it provides.

In the light of these undeniable facts, I find it incumbent upon me to state categorically, at the outset of the replies to the specific questions you addressed to the United Arab Republic on 5 March 1969, that all the answers of the United Arab Republic, which reaffirm its acceptance of the Security Council resolution and its readiness to carry out the obligations emanating from it require, likewise, that Israel accept the resolution and carry out all its obligations emanating from it and in particular withdrawal from all Arab territories it occupied as a result of its aggression of 5 June 1967.

Question (1)

The United Arab Republic, as it has declared before, accepts the Security Council resolution 242 (1967) and is ready to implement it in order to achieve a peaceful and accepted settlement in accordance with the provisions and principles contained therein.

Question (2)

The United Arab Republic agrees to pledge termination of all claims or state of belligerency. Such a pledge becomes effective upon withdrawal of Israel's forces from all Arab territories occupied as a result of Israel's aggression of 5 June 1967.

A declaration by Israel terminating the state of belligerency would be meaningful only when Israel withdraws her forces from all Arab territories it occupied since 5 June 1967.

Question (3)

On 5 June 1967, Israel launched its aggression against three Arab States violating their sovereignty and territorial integrity. Acceptance by the United Arab Republic to pledge respect for and acknowledgement of the sovereignty, territorial integrity and political independence of every State in the area requires the termination by Israel of its occupation and the withdrawal of its forces from all the Arab territories it occupied as a result of its aggression of 5 June, and the full implementation of the Security Council resolution of 22 November 1967.

Question (4)

The United Arab Republic accepts the right of every State in the area to live in peace within secure and recognized boundaries free from threats or acts of force, provided that Israel withdraws its forces from all Arab territories occupied as a result of its aggression of 5 June 1967, and implements the Security Council resolution of 22 November 1967.

Question (5)

When the question of Palestine was brought before the United Nations in 1947, the General Assembly adopted its resolution 181 of 29

November 1947, for the partition of Palestine and defined Israel's boundaries.

Question (6) [General question 7]

We have declared our readiness to implement all the provisions of the Security Council resolution covering, *inter alia,* the freedom of navigation in international waterways in the area; provided that Israel, likewise, implements all provisions of the Security Council resolution.

Question (7) [General question 8]

It has always been our position that the just settlement of the refugee problem is embodied in paragraph 11 of the General Assembly resolution 194 of December 1948, which has been unfailingly reaffirmed by each and every General Assembly session ever since its adoption.

If a plan on the basis of that paragraph is presented for consideration to the parties concerned, its acceptance by the parties and the declaration of their intention to implement it in good faith, with adequate guarantees for its full implementation would justify the implementation of the other provisions of the Security Council resolution.

Questions (8), (9) [General questions 9 and 12]

We do not believe that the establishment of demilitarized zones is a necessity. However, the United Arab Republic will not oppose the establishment of such zones if they are astride the boundaries.

Question (10) [General question 13]

In case demilitarized zones are established the United Arab Republic accepts that such zones be supervised and maintained by the United Nations.

Question (11) [General question 14]

In view of our past experience with Israel and her denunciation of four agreements signed by her with Arab States, we consider that the instrument to be signed by the United Arab Republic engaging her to carry out her obligations, should be addressed to the Security Council. Israel should, likewise, sign and address to the Security Council an instrument engaging her to carry out her obligations emanating from the Security Council Resolution of 22 November 1967. The endorsement by the Security Council of these documents would constitute the final multilateral document.

Cairo, 27 March 1969

Annex II

Correspondence Relating to the Resumption of the Discussions

A. LETTER DATED 18 NOVEMBER 1970 ADDRESSED TO THE MINISTER FOR FOREIGN AFFAIRS OF ISRAEL

I have the honour to refer to my letter of 7 August 1970 addressed to the Secretary-General, referred to in document S/9902, in which I informed him of the agreement of your Government and of the Goverrments of Jordan and the United Arab Republic to the holding of discussions under my auspices for the purpose of reaching agreement on on the establishment of a just and lasting peace between the parties.

As you will recall, I issued on 21 August 1970 an invitation to the parties to take part in discussions opening at New York on 25 August 1970. Ambassador Tekoah, who was Israeli representative for the initial stage of the discussions, met with me twice on the opening date, but was recalled to Israel for consultations. On his return on 8 September he communicated to me the decision of your Government, for reasons which were explained to me and have been publicly announced by your Government, to suspend its participation in the talks.

I am definitely of the view that the time has come for me once again to invite your Government to participate in discussions for the purpose of reaching agreement on the establishment of a just and lasting peace in accordance with Security Council resolution 242 (1967).

When I met you last on 5 November 1970, to consider the question of Israel's return to the discussions, I noted your concern about the influence of the debate of the General Assembly on the Middle East question and of its resolution 2628 (XXV). I wish to assure you in this connexion that I am proceeding on the basis that there is no change in my mandate, which I continue to regard as having been defined in Security Council resolution 242 (1967).

You will understand, I know, my desire to make a positive report to the Secretary-General about the progress of our discussions. I am accordingly inviting your Government to reconsider its position on the question and to resume its participation in the discussions. In this connexion, I wish to state that I have already been informed by the Governments of Jordan and the United Arab Republic of their continued willingness to participate.

I take this opportunity to inform you that, pending a reply from your Government to this appeal, I am returning to my post in Moscow. I

hope that your Government will find it possible in the near future to
respond favourably to this invitation, in which case I shall be available
to return to New York at twenty-four hours' notice.

(Signed) Gunnar JARRING

B. LETTER DATED 18 NOVEMBER 1970 ADDRESSED TO THE PERMANENT REPRESENTATIVE OF JORDAN*

I have the honour to inform you that I have today addressed a letter
to the Israeli Minister for Foreign Affairs in which I once again appealed
to his Government to resume participation in discussions for the purpose
of reaching agreement on the establishment of a just and lasting peace
in accordance with Security Council resolution 242 (1967).

In that connexion, I keep in mind the willingness of the Governments
of Jordan and the United Arab Republic, as expressed to me by yourself and your colleague from the United Arab Republic, to continue to
participate in such discussions.

I take this opportunity to inform you that, pending the receipt of a
reply from Israel, it is my intention to return to my post in Moscow. I
wish to emphasize, however, that I am ready to return here at twenty-
four hours' notice on receipt of the Israeli reply.

(Signed) Gunnar JARRING

C. LETTER DATED 18 NOVEMBER 1970 FROM THE PERMANENT REPRESENTATIVE OF THE UNITED ARAB REPUBLIC

With reference to your letter of today in which you inform me of
your imminent return to your post in Moscow, I note with appreciation
your reference to the readiness of the United Arab Republic to co-
operate fully with you.

I wish to emphasize that, conscious of its obligations under the
Charter and in abiding by the Security Council resolution 242 (1967),
the United Arab Republic has for the last three years consistently co-
operated with you, in the sincere hope that you will successfully
achieve the targets entrusted, by the Secretary-General, to you in
accordance with the aforementioned resolution.

Since my Government designated me last August to enter into discussions with you, I have during several meetings restated my Government's
belief in a lasting peace based on the faithful implementation of the

* An identical letter *mutatis mutandis* was sent to the Permanent Representative of the United
Arab Republic.

aforementioned Security Council resolution in all its parts and consequently the restoration of all Arab lands occupied by Israel since June 5, 1967, as well as ending the injustices inflicted so far on the Arab people of Palestine.

I am sure that Your Excellency's report to the Secretary-General on your mission which would be transmitted by him to the Security Council before 5 January 1971, will be of great benefit to the members of the Security Council and would assist them in taking whatever steps they may deem necessary in carrying out the responsibility entrusted to them by the Charter.

(*Signed*) Mohamed H. EL-ZAYYAT

D. LETTER DATED 1 DECEMBER 1970 FROM THE MINISTER FOR FOREIGN AFFAIRS OF ISRAEL

I have received your letter of 18 November 1970 in which you invite the Government of Israel to participate in discussions under your auspices for the purpose of reaching agreement on the establishment of a just and lasting peace in accordance with Security Council resolution 242 (1967). I note your assurance in reply to my comments on General Assembly resolution 2628 (XXV) that you are proceeding on the basis that there is no change in your mandate, which you continue to regard as having been defined in Security Council resolution 242.

On 6 August 1970 Ambassador Tekoah conveyed to you Israel's position on the United States peace initiative. This communication remains valid as the expression of Israel's policy. Concerning the discussions which we have agreed to hold under your auspices, I also draw attention to the Israel Government's decision of 6 September 1970 which was conveyed to you by Ambassador Tekoah.

On 22 November 1970 the Government of Israel adopted and published the following decision:

"The Government will act in accordance with the policy expressed in the Prime Minister's statement to the Knesset on 16 November 1970, for the creation of conditions which will justify implementation of the Government's resolution of 4 August 1970 which was approved by the Knesset—concerning the holding of talks under the auspices of Ambassador Jarring including consolidation and extension of the cease-fire agreement with the aim of progressing from a cease-fire to a complete end to the war and to lasting peace."

We are now holding discussions on the creation of conditions which would justify a decision by the Government of Israel to hold talks with the United Arab Republic under your auspices, in accordance with our decision of 4 August 1970 conveyed to you by Ambassador Tekoah on 6 August. I shall keep you in touch with developments on this matter as they arise.

We have publicly announced that we are ready for discussions with Jordan whose Government has informed you on its continued willingness to participate in such talks.

We are also willing to hold discussions on the establishment of permanent peace with Lebanon which has announced its adherence to Security Council resolution 242.

(Signed) Abba EBAN

E. MESSAGE FROM THE MINISTER FOR FOREIGN AFFAIRS OF ISRAEL

Further to my letter of 1 December 1970 I have the honour to inform you that the Government of Israel decided on 28 December 1970 as follows:

The present political and military conditions enable and justify the termination of the suspension of Israel participation in the talks under the auspices of Ambassador Jarring. The Government decided to authorize the Minister for Foreign Affairs to inform those concerned of the readiness of the Government of Israel to resume its participation in the Jarring talks in accordance with the basic principles of the Government policy and on the basis of its decisions of 31 July and 4 August 1970 as approved by the Knesset concerning Israel's affirmative reply to the peace initiative.

In view of this decision I would like to meet you in Jerusalem at your earliest convenience and my intention is to survey the situation, to acquaint you with the basic views of my Government and to discuss steps necessary to ensure the fulfilment of your mission for the promotion of agreement on the establishment of peace.

Abba EBAN

50. Ambassador Jarring's *Aide Mémoire* to Israel and the United Arab Republic, February 8, 1971*

* Obtained from the United States Department of State and available to the general public.

I have been following with a mixture of restrained optimism and growing concern the resumed discussions under my auspices for the purpose of arriving at peaceful settlement of the Middle East question. My restrained optimism arises from the fact that in my view the parties are seriously defining their positions and wish to move forward to a permanent peace.

My growing concern is that each side unyieldingly insists that the other make certain commitments before being ready to proceed to the stage of formulating the provisions to be included in a final peace agreement. There is, as I see it, a serious risk that we shall find ourselves in the same deadlock as existed during the first three years of my mission.

I therefore feel that I should at this stage make clear my views on what I believe to be the necessary steps to be taken in order to achieve a peaceful and accepted settlement in accordance with the provisions and principles of Security Council Resolution 242 (1967), which the parties have agreed to carry out in all its parts.

I have come to the conclusion that the only possibility to break the imminent deadlock arising from the differing views of Israel and the United Arab Republic as to the priority to be given to commitments and undertaking—which seems to be the real cause for the present immobility—is for me to seek from each side the parallel and simultaneous commitments which seem to be inevitable prerequisites of an eventual peace settlement between them. It should thereafter be possible to proceed at once to formulate the provisions and terms of a peace agreement not only for those topics covered by the commitments but with equal priority for other topics and in particular the refugee question.

Specifically, I wish to request the Government of Israel and the United Arab Republic to make to me at this stage the following prior commitments simultaneously and on condition that the other party makes its commitments, and subject to the eventual satisfactory determination of all other aspects of peace settlement, including in particular a just settlement of the refugee problem:

Israel:

would give a commitment to withdraw its forces from occupied United Arab Republic territory to the former international boundary between Egypt and the British mandate of Palestine on the understanding that satisfactory arrangements are made for:

A. Establishing demilitarized zones,

B. Practical security arrangements in the Sharm el-Sheikh area for guaranteeing freedom of navigation through the Straits of Tiran, and

C.   Freedom of navigation through the Suez Canal.

The United Arab Republic:

would give a commitment to enter into a peace agreement with Israel and to make explicit therein to Israel, on a reciprocal basis, undertakings and acknowledgements covering the following subjects:

A.   Termination of all claims or states of belligerency;

B.   Respect for and acknowledgement of each other's sovereignty, territorial integrity and political independence;

C.   Respect for and acknowledgement of each other's right to live in peace within secure and recognized boundaries;

D.   Responsibility to do all in their power to ensure that acts of belligerency or hostility do not originate from or are not committed from within their respective territories against the population, citizens or property of the other party; and

E.   Non-interference in each other's affairs.

In making the above mentioned suggestions I am conscious that I am requesting both sides to make serious commitments but I am convinced that the present situation requires me to take this step.

51. The United Arab Republic Reply to Ambassador Jarring's *Aide Mémoire*, February 15, 1971*

---

* Obtained from the United States Department of State and available to the general public.

The United Arab Republic has informed you that it accepts to carry out, on a reciprocal basis, all its obligations as provided for in Security Council Resolution 242 (1967) with a view to achieving a peaceful settlement in the Middle East. Consequently, Israel should carry out all its obligations contained in this resolution.

The United Arab Republic, in accordance with your memorandum, submitted on 8 February 1971, would give a commitment covering the following:

1. Termination of all claims or states of belligerency,
2. Respect for and acknowledgement of each other's sovereignty, territorial integrity and political independence,
3. Respect for and acknowledgement of each other's right to live in peace within secure and recognized boundaries,
4. Responsibility to do all in their power to ensure that acts of belligerency or hostility do not originate from or are not committed from within the respective territories against the population, citizens or property of the other party and,
5. Non-interference in each other's domestic affairs.

The United Arab Republic would also give a commitment that:

6. It ensures freedom of navigation in the Suez Canal in accordance with the 1888 Constantinople Convention,
7. It ensures freedom of navigation in the Straits of Tiran in accordance with the principles of international law,
8. It accepts the stationing of UN peacekeeping force in Sharm el Sheikh,
9. And to guarantee the peaceful settlement and the territorial inviolability of every state in the area, the United Arab Republic would accept:
   A. The establishment of demilitarized zones astride the borders with equal distances,
   B. The establishment of a UN peacekeeping force in which the four permanent members of the Security Council participate.

Israel should likewise give a commitment to implement all the provisions of Security Council Resolution 242 (1967). Hence Israel should give a commitment covering the following:

1. Withdrawal of its armed forces from Sinai and the Gaza Strip,
2. Achievement of a just settlement for the refugee problem in accordance with UN resolutions,
3. Termination of all claims or states of belligerency,
4. Respect for and acknowledgement of each other's sovereignty, territorial integrity and political independence,

5. Respect for and acknowledgement of each other's right to live in peace within secure and recognized boundaries,
6. Responsibility to do all in their power to ensure that acts of belligerency or hostility do not originate from or are not committed from within the respective territories against the population, citizens or property of the other party and,
7. Non-interference in each other's domestic affairs, and
8. To guarantee the peaceful settlement and the territorial inviolability of every state in the area, Israel would accept:
   A. The establishment of demilitarized zones astride the borders with equal distances,
   B. The establishment of a UN peacekeeping force in which the four permanent members of the Security Council participate.

When Israel gives these commitments the United Arab Republic will be ready to enter into a peace agreement with Israel containing all the aforementioned obligations as provided for in Security Council Resolution 242.

The United Arab Republic considers that the just and lasting peace cannot be realized without the full and scrupulous implementation of Security Council Resolution 242 (1967) and the withdrawal of the Israeli armed forces from all the Arab territories occupied since 5 June 1967.

52. Document Transmitted by the Israel Ambassador to the United Nations, Mr. Yosef Tekoah, to Ambassador Gunnar Jarring, February 26, 1971*

* Obtained from the United States Department of State and available to the general public.

Pursuant to our meetings on 8 February and 17 February, I am instructed to convey to you, and through you to the UAR, the following:

Israel views favorably the expression by the UAR of its readiness to enter into a peace agreement with Israel and reiterates that it is prepared for meaningful negotiations on all subjects relevant to a peace agreement between the two countries.

The Government of Israel wishes to state that the peace agreement to be concluded between Israel and the UAR should—*inter alia*—include the provisions set out below.

A) Israel would give undertakings covering the following:

1. Declared and explicit decision to regard the conflict between Israel and the UAR as finally ended, and termination of all claims and states of war and acts of hostility or belligerency between Israel and the UAR.

2. Respect for and acknowledgement of the sovereignty, territorial integrity and political independence of the UAR.

3. Respect for and acknowledgement of the rights of the UAR to live in peace within secure and recognized boundaries.

4. Withdrawal of Israel Armed Forces from the Israel-UAR cease-fire line to the secure, recognized and agreed boundaries to be established in the peace agreement. Israel will not withdraw to the pre-June 5, 1967 lines.

5. In the matter of the refugees and the claims of both parties in this connection, Israel is prepared to negotiate with the Governments directly involved on:

    a) The payment of compensation for abandoned lands and property.

    b) Participation in the planning of the rehabilitation of the refugees in the region. Once the obligations of the parties towards the settlement of the refugee issue have been agreed neither party shall be under claims from the other inconsistent with its sovereignty.

6. The responsibility for ensuring that no warlike act, or act of violence, by any organization, group or individual originates from or is committed in the territory of Israel against the population, armed forces or property of the UAR.

7. Non-interference in the domestic affairs of the UAR.

8. Non-participation by Israel in hostile alliances against the UAR and the prohibition of stationing of troops of other parties which maintain a state of belligerency against the UAR.

B) The UAR undertakings in the peace agreement with Israel would include:

1. Declared and explicit decision to regard the conflict between the UAR and Israel as finally ended and termination of all claims and states of war and acts of hostility or belligerency between the UAR and Israel.

2. Respect for and acknowledgement of the sovereignty, territorial integrity and political independence of Israel.

3. Respect for and acknowledgement of the right of Israel to live in peace within secure and recognized boundaries to be determined in the peace agreement.

4. The responsibility for ensuring that no warlike act or act of violence, by any organization, group or individual originates from or is committed in the territory of the UAR against the population, armed forces or property of Israel.

5. Non-interference in the domestic affairs of Israel.

6. An explicit undertaking to guarantee free passage for Israel ships and cargoes through the Suez Canal.

7. Termination of economic warfare in all its manifestations, including boycott, and of interference in the normal international relations of Israel.

8. Non-participation by the UAR in hostile alliances against Israel and the prohibition of stationing of troops of other parties which maintain a state of belligerency against Israel.

The UAR and Israel should enter into a peace agreement with each other to be expressed in a binding treaty in accordance with normal international law and precedent, and containing the above undertakings.

The Government of Israel believes that now that the UAR has, through Ambassador Jarring, expressed its willingness to enter into a peace agreement with Israel, and both parties have presented their basic positions, they should now pursue their negotiations in a detailed and concrete manner without prior conditions so as to cover all the points listed in their respective documents with a view to concluding a peace agreement.

53. Further Report by the Secretary-General on the Activities of the Special Representative to the Middle East, March 5, 1971*

---

* U.N. Doc. S/10070/Add. 2 (March 5, 1971). See also the Report of the Secretary-General on the Jarring Mission, U.N. Doc. S/10070/Add. 1 (Feb. 1, 1971).

1. On 1 February 1971 I submitted to the Security Council a report (S/10070/Add.1) on the activities of Ambassador Jarring, my Special Representative to the Middle East, since the resumption on 5 January 1971 of the discussions under his auspices with the parties to the Middle East conflict for the purpose of reaching agreement on a just and lasting peace between them. In that report, I found grounds for cautious optimism in the fact that there had been some progress in the definition of the position of the parties and I appealed to them to pursue their role in the discussions in a constructive manner, to co-operate with Ambassador Jarring with a view to the carrying out of Security Council resolution 242 (1967) and, in that very difficult and crucial stage of the discussions, to withhold fire, to exercise military restraint and to maintain the quiet which had prevailed in the area since August 1970.

2. In response to that appeal, the Foreign Ministry of Israel, in a communiqué released in Jerusalem on 2 February, announced that Israel would preserve the cease-fire on a mutual basis; in a speech to the National Assembly on 4 February, the President of the United Arab Republic declared the decision of the United Arab Republic to refrain from opening fire for a period of thirty days ending on 7 March.

3. In pursuing his mandate to promote agreement between the parties, Ambassador Jarring, while sharing my cautious optimism that the parties were seriously defining their positions and wished to move forward to a permanent peace, noted with growing concern that each side was insisting that the other should make certain commitments before being ready to proceed to the stage of formulating the provisions of a final peace settlement.

4. On the Israeli side there was insistence that the United Arab Republic should give specific, direct and reciprocal commitments towards Israel that it would be ready to enter into a peace agreement with Israel and to make towards Israel the various undertakings referred to in paragraph 1 (*ii*) of Security Council resolution 242 (1967). When agreement was reached on those points, it would be possible to discuss others, including the refugee problem; such items as secure and recognized boundaries, withdrawal and additional arrangements for ensuring security should be discussed in due course.

5. The United Arab Republic continued to regard the Security Council resolution as containing provisions to be implemented by the parties and to express its readiness to carry out its obligations under the resolution in full, provided that Israel did likewise. However it held that Israel persisted in its refusal to implement the Security Council resolution, since it would not commit itself to withdraw from all Arab

territories occupied in June 1967. Furthermore in the view of the
United Arab Republic Israel had not committed itself to the implementation of the United Nations resolutions relevant to a just settlement to
the refugee problem.

6. The papers received by Ambassador Jarring from Israel and Jordan
relating to peace between these two countries showed a similar
divergence of views. Israel stressed the importance of Jordan's giving
an undertaking to enter into a peace agreement with it which would
specify the direct and reciprocal obligations undertaken by each of
them. Jordan emphasized the inadmissibility of the acquisition of
territory by war and expressed the view that the essential first step
towards peace lay in an Israeli commitment to evacuate all Arab
territories.

7. Ambassador Jarring felt that at this stage of the talks he should
make clear his views on what he believed to be the necessary steps to be
taken in order to achieve a peaceful and accepted settlement in accordance with the provisions and principles of Security Council resolution
242 (1967), which the parties had agreed to carry out in all its parts.
He reached the conclusion, which I shared, that the only possibility to
break the imminent deadlock arising from the differing views of Israel
and the United Arab Republic as to the priority to be given to commitments and undertakings—which seemed to him to be the real cause for
the existing immobility in the talks—was for him to seek from each side
the parallel and simultaneous commitments which seemed to be
inevitable prerequisites of an eventual peace settlement between them.
It should thereafter be possible to proceed at once to formulate the
provisions and terms of a peace agreement not only for those topics
covered by the commitments, but with equal priority for other topics,
and in particular the refugee question.

8. In identical aide-mémoires handed to the representatives of the
United Arab Republic and Israel on 8 February 1971 Ambassador
Jarring requested those Governments to make to him certain prior
commitments. Ambassador Jarring's initiative was on the basis that the
commitments should be made simultaneously and reciprocally and
subject to the eventual satisfactory determination of all other aspects of
a peace settlement, including in particular a just settlement of the
refugee problem. Israel would give a commitment to withdraw its forces
from occupied United Arab Republic territory to the former international boundary between Egypt and the British Mandate of Palestine.
The United Arab Republic would give a commitment to enter into a
peace agreement with Israel and to make explicitly therein to Israel, on

a reciprocal basis, various undertakings and acknowledgements arising directly or indirectly from paragraph 1 (*ii*) of Security Council resolution 242 (1967).

9. On 15 February, Ambassador Jarring received from the representative of the United Arab Republic an aide-mémoire in which it was indicated that the United Arab Republic would accept the specific commitments requested of it, as well as other commitments arising directly or indirectly from Security Council resolution 242 (1967). If Israel would give, likewise, commitments covering its own obligations under the Security Council resolution, including commitments for the withdrawal of its armed forces from Sinai and the Gaza Strip and for the achievement of a just settlement for the refugee problem in accordance with United Nations resolutions, the United Arab Republic would be ready to enter into a peace agreement with Israel. Finally the United Arab Republic expressed the view that a just and lasting peace could not be realized without the full and scrupulous implementation of Security Council resolution 242 (1967) and the withdrawal of the Israeli armed forces from all the territories occupied since 5 June 1967.

10. On 17 February, Ambassador Jarring informed the Israeli representative of the contents of the United Arab Republic reply to his aide-memoire.

11. On 26 February, Ambassador Jarring received a paper from the representative of Israel, in which, without specific reference to the commitment which he had sought from that Government, Israel stated that it viewed favourably "the expression by the United Arab Republic of its readiness to enter into a peace agreement with Israel" and reiterated that it was prepared for meaningful negotiations on all subjects relevant to a peace agreement between the two countries. Israel gave details of the undertakings which in its opinion should be given by the two countries in such a peace agreement, which should be expressed in a binding treaty in accordance with normal international law and precedent. Israel considered that both parties having presented their basic positions should now pursue the negotiations in a detailed and concrete manner without prior conditions.

12. On the crucial question of withdrawal on which Ambassador Jarring had sought a commitment from Israel, the Israel position was that it would give an undertaking covering withdrawal of Israeli armed forces from "the Israeli-United Arab Republic cease-fire line" to the secure, recognized and agreed boundaries to be established in the peace agreement; Israel would not withdraw to the pre-5 June 1967 lines.

13. On 28 February; Ambassador Jarring informed the United Arab Republic representative of the contents of the Israeli paper.

14. Ambassador Jarring has been very active over the past month and some further progress has been made towards a peaceful solution of the Middle East question. The problems to be settled have been more clearly identified and on some there is general agreement. I wish more-over to note with satisfaction the positive reply given by the United Arab Republic to Ambassador Jarring's initiative. However, the Govern-ment of Israel has so far not responded to the request of Ambassador Jarring that it should give a commitment on withdrawal to the inter-national boundary of the United Arab Republic.

15. While I still consider that the situation has considerable elements of promise, it is a matter for increasing concern that Ambassador Jarring's attempt to break the deadlock has not so far been successful. I appeal, therefore, to the Government of Israel to give further consid-eration to this question and to respond favourably to Ambassador Jarring's initiative.

16. To give time for further consideration and in the hope that the way forward may be reopened, I once more appeal to the parties to with-hold fire, to exercise military restraint and to maintain the quiet which has prevailed in the area since August 1970.

54. Security Council Resolution 298 Concerning Measures and Actions by Israel to Change the Status of the City of Jerusalem, September 25, 1971*

---

* S.C. Res. 298, U.N. Doc. S/Res/298 (Sept. 25, 1971).

The Security Council,

Recalling its resolutions 252 (1968) and 267 (1969) and the earlier General Assembly resolutions 2253 (ES-V) and 2254 (ES-V) of July 1967 concerning measures and actions by Israel designed to change the status of the Israeli-occupied section of Jerusalem,

Having considered the letter of the Permanent Representative of Jordan on the situation in Jerusalem (S/10313) and the reports of the Secretary-General (S/8052, S/8146, S/9149 and Add.1, S/9537 and S/10124 and Add.1 and 2), and having heard the statements of the parties concerned on the question,

Reaffirming the principle that acquisition of territory by military conquest is inadmissible,

Noting with concern the non-compliance by Israel with the above-mentioned resolutions,

Noting with concern further that since the adoption of the above-mentioned resolutions Israel has taken further measures designed to change the status and character of the occupied section of Jerusalem,

1. *Reaffirms* Security Council resolutions 252 (1968) and 267 (1969);

2. *Deplores* the failure of Israel to respect the previous resolutions adopted by the United Nations concerning measures and actions by Israel purporting to affect the status of the City of Jerusalem;

3. *Confirms* in the clearest possible terms that all legislative and administrative actions taken by Israel to change the status of the city of Jerusalem including expropriation of land and properties, transfer of populations and legislation aimed at the incorporation of the occupied section are totally invalid and cannot change that status;

4. *Urgently calls upon* Israel to rescind all previous measures and actions and to take no further steps in the occupied section of Jerusalem which may purport to change the status of the City, or which would prejudice the rights of the inhabitants and the interests of the international community, or a just and lasting peace;

5. *Requests* the Secretary-General, in consultation with the President of the Security Council and using such instrumentalities as he may choose, including a representative or a mission, to report to the Security Council as appropriate and in any event within 60 days on the implementation of this resolution.

55. Statement by the Government of Israel Concerning Security Council Resolution 298, September 26, 1971*

* Press Release of the Government of Israel, September 28, 1971.

In answer to questions from the press on Israel's position with regard to Security Council resolution 298 (1971) of 25 September 1971, a spokesman for Mr. Abba Eban, the Minister for Foreign Affairs, drew attention to the following statement issued by the Government of Israel on 26 September 1971:

The Government of Israel considers that there was no justification whatever for raising the issue of Jerusalem in the Security Council, nor for the resolution adopted. The Government of Israel will not enter into any discussion with any political organ on the basis of this resolution. Israel's policy on Jerusalem will remain unchanged. Israel will continue to ensure the development of the city for the benefit of all its inhabitants, the respect of the religious rights of all communities, and the scrupulous protection of the Holy Places of all faiths and the freedom of access to them. This policy has contributed to the development of fruitful relations between all sections of the population.

56. Further Report by the Secretary-General on the Activities of the Special Representative to the Middle East, November 30, 1971*

---

*   *Report of the Secretary-General on the Activities of the Special Representative to the Middle East*, U.N. Doc. A/8541 & S/10403 (Nov. 30, 1971). Annexes I, II, and III reprinting the Jarring *aide-mémoire* of February 8, 1971, the UAR response of February 15, 1971, and the Israel communication to Ambassador Jarring on February 26, 1971, have been omitted from the Report as they are set out above.

Introduction

1. By its resolution 242 (1967) of 22 November 1967, the Security Council affirmed the principles and provisions which should be applied in establishing a just and lasting peace in the Middle East and requested me to designate a special representative to establish and maintain contacts with the States concerned in order to promote agreement and assist efforts to achieve a peaceful and accepted settlement in accordance with these provisions and principles. I designated Ambassador Gunnar V. Jarring of Sweden as my Special Representative and submitted progress reports from time to time to the Security Council on his efforts (S/8309 and Add.1-5 and S/9902).

2. By its resolution 2628 (XXV) of 4 November 1970, the General Assembly, after expressing its views on the principles which should govern the establishment of a just and lasting peace in the Middle East, called upon the parties directly concerned to resume contact with the Special Representative of the Secretary-General with a view to giving effect to Security Council resolution 242 (1967) and requested me to report to the Security Council within a period of two months, and to the General Assembly as appropriate, on the efforts of the Special Representative and on the implementation of Security Council resolution 242 (1967).

3. In accordance with my responsibilities under Security Council resolution 242 (1967) and with the request contained in General Assembly resolution 2628 (XXV), I submitted to the Security Council on 4 January 1971 a comprehensive report (S/10070) on the activities of the Special Representative up to that date. Subsequently, on 1 February and 5 March, I submitted further progress reports (S/10070/-Add.1 and Add.2) on his activities.

4. In view of the fact that the General Assembly is about to debate again the situation in the Middle East and of the request contained in General Assembly resolution 2628 (XXV) that I should report to it as appropriate on the efforts of the Special Representative and on the implementation of Security Council resolution 242 (1967), I am arranging to have my report of 4 January 1971 (S/10070) available to the Members of the General Assembly; I am also submitting the present report on the implementation of Security Council resolution 242 (1967) to both the Security Council and the General Assembly in order to give a more comprehensive account of the activities of the Special Representative at the beginning of 1971 than that given in documents S/10070/Add.1 and Add.2 and to bring that account up to date.

I. The Holding of Discussions Under the Special Representative's Auspices (January-March 1971)

5. It will be recalled that at the close of 1970 it was possible to arrange for the resumption of the discussions under the auspices of Ambassador Jarring with Israel, Jordan and the United Arab Republic[1] for the purpose of reaching agreement on a just and lasting peace between them.

6. Ambassador Jarring resumed his discussions with the parties at Headquarters on 5 January 1971 and pursued them actively. He held a series of meetings with the representatives of Israel (including meetings with the Prime Minister and Foreign Minister during a brief visit to Israel made from 8 to 10 January 1971 at the request of that Government), of Jordan, and of the United Arab Republic. In addition, he held meetings with the Permanent Representative of Lebanon, which is also one of the States directly concerned with the Middle East settlement.

7. At an early stage in these meetings Israel presented to Ambassador Jarring, for transmission to the Governments concerned, papers containing its views on the "Essentials of Peace." Subsequently, the United Arab Republic and Jordan having received the respective Israeli views, presented papers containing their own views concerning the implementation of the provisions of Security Council resolution 242 (1967).

8. During the remainder of January, Ambassador Jarring held further meetings with the representatives of Israel, Jordan and the United Arab Republic, in the course of which he received further memoranda elaborating the positions of the parties. Unfortunately, these indicated that the parties held differing views on the order in which items should be discussed. More importantly, each side was insisting that the other should be ready to make certain commitments before being ready to proceed to the stage of formulating the provisions of a peace settlement.

9. On the Israeli side there was insistence that the United Arab Republic should give specific, direct and reciprocal commitments towards Israel that it would be ready to enter into a peace agreement with Israel and to make towards Israel the various undertakings referred to in paragraph 1 (*ii*) of Security Council resolution 242 (1967). When agreement was reached on those points, it would be possible to discuss others, including the refugee problem; such items ensuring security should be discussed in due course.

---

[1] The name of the United Arab Republic was changed to the Arab Republic of Egypt on 2 September 1971.

10. The United Arab Republic continued to regard the Security Council resolution as containing provisions to be implemented by the parties and to express its readiness to carry out its obligations under the resolution in full, provided that Israel did likewise. However it held that Israel persisted in its refusal to implement the Security Council resolution, since it would not commit itself to withdraw from all Arab territories occupied in June 1967. Furthermore in the view of the United Arab Republic Israel had not committed itself to the implementation of the United Nations resolutions relevant to a just settlement to the refugee problem.

11. The papers received by Ambassador Jarring from Israel and Jordan relating to peace between these two countries showed a similar divergence of views. Israel stressed the importance of Jordan's giving an undertaking to enter into a peace agreement with it which would specify the direct and reciprocal obligations undertaken by each of them. Jordan emphasized the inadmissibility of the acquisition of territory by war and expressed the view that the essential first step towards peace lay in an Israeli commitment to evacuate all Arab territories.

12. Ambassador Jarring felt that at this stage of the talks he should make clear his views on what he believed to be the necessary steps to be taken in order to achieve a peaceful and accepted settlement in accordance with the provisions and principles of Security Council resolution 242 (1967), which the parties had agreed to carry out in all its parts. He reached the conclusion, which I shared, that the only possiblity of breaking the imminent deadlock arising from the differing views of Israel and the United Arab Republic as to the priority to be given to commitments and undertakings—which seemed to him to be the real cause for the existing immobility in the talks—was for him to seek from each side the parallel and simultaneous commitments which seemed to be inevitable prerequisites of an eventual peace settlement between them. It should thereafter be possible to proceed at once to formulate the provisions and terms of a peace agreement not only for those topics covered by the commitments, but with equal priority for other topics, and in particular the refugee question.

13. In identical aide-memoires handed to the representatives of the United Arab Republic and Israel on 8 February 1971 Ambassador Jarring requested those Governments to make to him certain prior commitments. Ambassador Jarring's initiative was on the basis that the commitments should be made simultaneously and reciprocally and subject to the eventual satisfactory determination of all other aspects of

a peace settlement, including in particular a just settlement of the refugee problem. Israel would give a commitment to withdraw its forces from occupied United Arab Republic territory to the former international boundary between Egypt and the British Mandate of Palestine. The United Arab Republic would give a commitment to enter into a peace agreement with Israel and to make explicitly therein to Israel, on a reciprocal basis, various undertakings and acknowledgements arising directly or indirectly from paragraph 1 (*ii*) of Security Council resolution 242 (1967). (For the full text of the aide-mémoires, see annex I.)

14. On 15 February, Ambassador Jarring received from the representative of the United Arab Republic an aide-memoire in which it was indicated that the United Arab Republic would accept the specific commitments requested of it, as well as other commitments arising directly or indirectly from Security Council resolution 242 (1967). If Israel would give, likewise, commitments covering its own obligations under the Security Council resolution, including commitments for the withdrawal of its armed forces from Sinai and the Gaza Strip and for the achievement of a just settlement for the refugee problem in accordance with United Nations resolutions, the United Arab Republic would be ready to enter into a peace agreement with Israel. Finally the United Arab Republic expressed the view that a just and lasting peace could not be realized without the full and scrupulous implementation of Security Council resolution 242 (1967) and the withdrawal of the Israeli armed forces from all the territories occupied since 5 June 1967. (For the full text of the United Arab Republic reply, see annex II.)

15. On 17 February, Ambassador Jarring informed the Israeli representative of the contents of the United Arab Republic reply to his aide-memoire.

16. On 26 February, Ambassador Jarring received a communication from the representative of Israel, in which, without specific reference to the commitment which he had sought from that Government, Israel stated that it viewed favourably "the expression by the United Arab Republic of its readiness to enter into a peace agreement with Israel" and reiterated that it was prepared for meaningful negotiations on all subjects relevant to a peace agreement between the two countries. Israel gave details of the undertakings which in its opinion should be given by the two countries in such a peace agreement, which should be expressed in a binding treaty in accordance with normal international law and precedent. Israel considered that both parties, having presented

their basic positions, should now pursue the negotiations in a detailed and concrete manner without prior conditions.

17. On the crucial question of withdrawal on which Ambassador Jarring had sought a commitment from Israel, the Israeli position was that it would give an undertaking covering withdrawal of Israeli armed forces from "the Israeli-United Arab Republic cease-fire line" to the secure, recognized and agreed boundaries to be established in the peace agreement; Israel would not withdraw to the pre-5 June 1967 lines. (For the full text of the Israeli paper, see annex III.)

18. On 28 February, Ambassador Jarring informed the United Arab Republic representative of the contents of the Israeli communication. The latter held that it was improper for the Israeli authorities to have responded to his Government's reply, which had been addressed to Ambassador Jarring and would have full effect only if the Israeli authorities would give the commitment requested of them by Ambassador Jarring.

19. In accepting the United States proposal for renewed discussions under Ambassador Jarring's auspices (see S/10070, paras. 33 and 34), the parties had agreed that they would observe strictly, for a period of 90 days from 7 August 1970, the cease-fire resolutions of the Security Council. In response to the recommendation of the General Assembly in resolution 2628 (XXV), the cease-fire had been extended for a further period of three months. In my report of 1 February submitted as that period was expiring, I appealed to the parties at that stage of the discussions, to withhold fire, to exercise military restraint and to maintain the quiet which had prevailed in the area since August 1970.

20. In response to that appeal, the Foreign Ministry of Israel, in a communique released in Jerusalem on 2 February, announced that Israel would observe the cease-fire on a mutual basis; in a speech to the National Assembly on 4 February, the President of the United Arab Republic declared the decision of the United Arab Republic to refrain from opening fire for a period of 30 days ending on 7 March.

21. In submitting my report of 5 March 1971, I commented as follows:
    "Ambassador Jarring has been very active over the past month and
    some further progress has been made towards a peaceful solution of the
    Middle East question. The problems to be settled have been more
    clearly identified and on some there is general agreement. I wish
    moreover to note with satisfaction the positive reply given by the
    United Arab Republic to Ambassador Jarring's initiative. However,

the Government of Israel has so far not responded to the request of Ambassador Jarring that it should give a commitment on withdrawal to the international boundary of the United Arab Republic.

"While I still consider that the situation has considerable elements of promise, it is a matter for increasing concern that Ambassador Jarring's attempt to break the deadlock has not so far been successful. I appeal, therefore, to the Government of Israel to give further consideration to this question and to respond favourably to Ambassador Jarring's initiative.

"To give time for further consideration and in the hope that the way forward may be reopened, I once more appeal to the parties to withhold fire, to exercise military restraint and to maintain the quiet which has prevailed in the area since August 1970."[2]

II. Further Developments (March-November 1971)

22. In response to my appeal, the Israeli Government once again made clear its willingness to continue to observe the cease-fire on a basis of reciprocity. The President of the United Arab Republic, in a statement to the nation on 7 March 1971, declared that his country no longer considered itself further committed to a cease-fire or to withholding fire. This did not, however, mean that political action would cease.

23. On 11 March, the Israeli representative informed Ambassador Jarring that his Government was awaiting the reaction of the United Arab Republic Government to the Israeli invitation in its reply of 26 February to enter into detailed and concrete discussions (see paragraph 16 above). When that statement of the Israeli representative was brought to the attention of the United Arab Republic representative, he maintained that his Government was still awaiting an Israeli reply to Ambassador Jarring's aide-memoire.

24. Subsequently, the talks under Ambassador Jarring's auspices lapsed. He therefore left Headquarters to resume his post as Ambassador of Sweden in Moscow on 25 March.

25. Although he returned to Headquarters from 5 to 12 May and from 21 September to 27 October and has held certain consultations elsewhere, he has found himself faced with the same deadlock and with no possibility of actively pursuing his mission.

26. Indeed, during much of this time the promotion of agreement between the parties was the object of two separate initiatives, first, an

[2]S/10070/Add.2, paras. 14-16.

effort by the United States of America to promote an interim agreement providing for the reopening of the Suez Canal, which has not, so far, achieved any positive results, and, secondly, a mission of inquiry conducted by certain African Heads of States on behalf of the Organization of African Unity, which is still in progress as this report is being prepared. Both initiatives were described to Ambassador Jarring and myself by the sponsors as designed to facilitate the resumption of Ambassador Jarring's mission. Nevertheless, while they were being pursued, they obviously constituted an additional reason for him not to take personal initiatives.

27. In the introduction to my report on the work of the Organization (A/8401/Add.1 and Add.1/Corr.1), I expressed certain views on the situation in the Middle East. After recalling the responses of the United Arab Republic and Israel to Ambassador Jarring's initiative of 8 February, I said that I continued to hope—as I still do—that Israel would find it possible before too long to make a response that would enable the search for a peaceful settlement under Ambassador Jarring's auspices to continue.

28. After noting the relative quiet which has continued to exist in the area, I went on to say:

"It is not possible to predict how long this quiet will last, but there can be little doubt that, if the present impasse in the search for a peaceful settlement persists, new fighting will break out sooner or later. Since the parties have taken advantage of the present lull to strengthen considerably their military capabilities, it is only too likely that the new round of fighting will be more violent and dangerous than the previous ones, and there is always the danger that it may not be possible to limit it to the present antagonists and to the confines of the Middle East.

"I see no other way to forestall such a disastrous eventuality than by intensifying the search for a peaceful and agreed settlement. I believe there is still a chance of achieving such a settlement. I do not overlook the formidable difficulty of the problems to be tackled, but there exist several important assets on the side of peace efforts as well. The Security Council's cease-fire resolutions of June 1967 and its resolution 242 (1967) of 22 November 1967, if implemented simultaneously and fully, should provide the framework for achieving a peaceful and agreed settlement of the present conflict. To promote agreement for such a settlement, we are fortunate to have the services of Ambassador Jarring, who is uniquely qualified for this almost impossible task.

"Ambassador Jarring has clearly defined the minimum conditions that are required to move the peace talks ahead and, until those conditions are met, it is hard to see what else he can do to further his efforts. Steps to ensure that those conditions are met must be taken by the parties concerned and, failing this, by the Security Council itself or by States Members of the United Nations and, particularly, the permanent members of the Security Council, both because of their special responsibility within the United Nations and of their influence on the parties concerned."[3]

29. Recent developments have added to the urgency of my remarks. It therefore seems to me that the appropriate organs of the United Nations must review the situation once again and find ways and means to enable the Jarring mission to move forward.

[3] A/8401/Add.1, paras. 221-223.

57. General Assembly Resolution 2799 (XXVI) Concerning the Situation in the Middle East and Reaffirming Principles for the Establishment of a Just and Lasting Peace, December 13, 1971*

* G.A. Res. 2799 (XXVI). RESOLUTIONS OF THE GENERAL ASSEMBLY AT ITS TWENTY-SIXTH REGULAR SESSION 21 SEPTEMBER-22 DECEMBER 1971, U.N. PRESS RELEASE GA/4548 (Dec. 28, 1971), at Part I, pp. 22-24.

The General Assembly,

Deeply concerned at the continuation of the grave situation prevailing in the Middle East, particularly since the conflict of June 1967, which constitutes a serious threat to international peace and security,

Convinced that Security Council resolution 242 (1967) of 22 November 1967 should be implemented immediately in all its parts in order to achieve a just and lasting peace in the Middle East in which every State in the area can live in security,

Determined that the territory of a State shall not be the object of occupation or acquisition by another State resulting from the threat or use of force, which is contrary to the Charter of the United Nations and to the principles enshrined in Security Council resolution 242 (1967) as well as in the Declaration on the Strengthening of International Security adopted by the General Assembly on 16 December 1970,[1]

Expressing its appreciation of the efforts of the Commission of Heads of African States undertaken in pursuance of the resolution adopted on 23 June 1971 by the Assembly of Heads of State and Government of the Organization of African Unity,

Gravely concerned at the continuation of Israel's occupation of the Arab territories since 5 June 1967,

Having considered the item entitled "The situation in the Middle East,"

1. *Reaffirms* that the acquisition of territories by force is inadmissible and that, consequently, territories thus occupied must be restored;

2. *Reaffirms* that the establishment of a just and lasting peace in the Middle East should include the application of both the following principles:

(*a*) Withdrawal of Israeli armed forces from territories occupied in the recent conflict;

(*b*) Termination of all claims or states of belligerency and respect for and acknowledgement of the sovereignty, territorial integrity and political independence of every State in the area and its right to live in peace within secure and recognized boundaries free from threats or acts of force;

3. *Requests* the Secretary-General to take the necessary measures to reactivate the mission of the Special Representative of the Secretary-General to the Middle East in order to promote agreement and assist efforts to reach a peace agreement as envisaged in the Special Representative's aide-mémoire of 8 February 1971:[2]

[1] General Assembly resolution 2734 (XXV).
[2] A/8541-S/10403, annex I.

4. *Expresses its full support* for all the efforts of the Special Representative to implement Security Council resolution 242 (1967) of 22 November 1967;

5. *Notes with appreciation* the positive reply given by Egypt to the Special Representative's initiative for establishing a just and lasting peace in the Middle East;

6. *Calls upon* Israel to respond favourably to the Special Representative's peace initiative;

7. *Further invites* the parties to the Middle East conflict to give their full co-operation to the Special Representative in order to work out practical measures for:

(*a*) Guaranteeing freedom of navigation through international waterways in the area;

(*b*) Achieving a just settlement of the refugee problem;

(*c*) Guaranteeing the territorial inviolability and political independence of every State in the area;

8. *Requests* the Secretary-General to report to the Security Council and to the General Assembly, as appropriate, on the progress made by the Special Representative in the implementation of Security Council resolution 242 (1967) and of the present resolution;

9. *Requests* the Security Council to consider, if necessary, making arrangements, under the relevant Articles of the Charter of the United Nations, with regard to the implementation of its resolution.

58. Security Council Resolution 316 Concerning Israeli Military Acts Against Lebanon, June 26, 1972*

---

* S.C. Res. 316, U.N. PRESS RELEASE SC/3329 (Sec. Council 1650th meeting, June 26, 1972).

The Security Council,

Having considered the agenda contained in document S/Agenda/1650/Rev. 1,

Having noted the contents of the letter of the Permanent Representative of Lebanon (S/10715), of the letter of the Permanent Representative of Israel (S/10716), and of the letter of the Permanent Representative of the Syrian Arab Republic (S/10720),

Recalling the consensus of the members of the Security Council of 19 April 1972 (S/10611),

Having noted the supplementary information provided by the Chief of Staff of the United Nations Truce Supervisory Organization contained in the relevant documents S/7930/Add.1584 of 26 April 1972 to S/7930/Add.1640 of 21 June 1972, and particularly S/7930/Add. 1641 to 1648 of 21, 22, 23 and 24 June 1972,

Having heard the statements of the representatives of Lebanon and of Israel,

Deploring the tragic loss of life resulting from all acts of violence and retaliation,

Gravely concerned at Israel's failure to comply with the previous resolutions of the Security Council calling on her to desist forthwith from any violation of the sovereignty and territorial integrity of Lebanon (resolutions 262 (1968), 270 (1969), 280 and 285 (1970) and 313 (1972),

1. *Calls upon* Israel to strictly abide by the aforementioned resolutions and to refrain from all military acts against Lebanon;

2. *Condemns*, while profoundly deploring all acts of violence, the repeated attacks of Israeli forces on Lebanese territory and population in violation of the principles of the United Nations Charter and Israel's obligations thereunder;

3. *Expresses* the strong desire that appropriate steps will lead, as an immediate consequence, to the release in the shortest possible time of all Syrian and Lebanese military and security personnel abducted by Isareli armed forces on 21 June 1972 on Lebanese territory;

4. *Declares* that if the abovementioned steps do not result in the release of the abducted personnel or, if Israel fails to comply with the present resolution, the Council will reconvene at the earliest to consider further action.

59. Senate Resolution 358 Expressing the Sense of the Senate on the Killings of Israeli Olympic Team Members at the Twentieth Olympiad, September 6, 1972*

---

* S. Res. 358, 92d U.N. CONG. 2d SESS. (Sept. 6, 1972). The House of Representatives agreed to an essentially identical resolution the same day. See H. Res. 1106, 92d CONG. 2d SESS. (Sept. 6, 1972).

Expressing the sense of the Senate on the tragic killings of Israeli
  Olympic team members at the Twentieth Olympiad at Munich.
Whereas with profound sorrow and deep alarm the Senate is informed
  of the events surrounding the killing of eleven members of the
  Israeli Olympic team participating in the Twentieth Olympiad at
  Munich; and
Whereas such actions are to be condemned as inimical to the interests and aspirations of the civilized world: Be it hereby
    Resolved, That the United States joins with the world in mourn-
  ing the loss of Israel's athletes and extends its deepest sympathy to
  the people of Israel and to the families of those so tragically lost;
  and be it further
Resolved, That all means be sought by which the civilized world
may cut off from contact with civilized mankind any peoples or
any nation giving sanctuary, support, sympathy, aid or comfort to
acts of murder and barbarism such as those just witnessed at Munich
and that the Secretary of the Senate be directed to communicate
these sentiments and expressions to the Secretary of State for appropriate transmittal.

V. DOCUMENTS RELATING TO THE ARAB-ISRAELI CONFLICT

F. *The October War and the Continuing Search for Peace: 1973-*

60. Statement by Ambassador John Scali, United States Representative to the United Nations, on the Middle East Situation, October 21, 1973*

* Press Release USUN-96 (73), Oct. 21, 1973.

Mr. President: The United States, together with the U.S.S.R., has called for this meeting of the Security Council with one purpose in mind: to take joint action and to present a joint proposition to the Council whose aim is to bring an immediate ceasefire in place and to begin promptly negotiations between the parties under appropriate auspices looking toward a just and durable peace based on the November 1967 Security Council Resolution.

As the members of this Council know, the tragic fighting over the past 17 days has been both furious and costly. We believe that the prolongation of the war is not in the interests of the parties or the peoples in the area, and that its continuance carries grave risks for the peace of the world. Because of this, President Nixon agreed that Secretary of State Kissinger should fly to Moscow, in response to an invitation of Secretary General Brezhnev. As a result of these discussions the Council has before it the Resolution agreed jointly by the United States and the Soviet Governments on which both our governments request immediate action on the part of the Security Council. The Resolution has already been circulated to the members of the Council.

Let me make a few brief remarks regarding the three short paragraphs of the Resolution, for they all stand clearly on their own words and speak for themselves.

The first paragraph calls for an immediate ceasefire. In our view as well as that of the Soviet Union, this applies not only to the parties directly concerned but also to those who have joined in the fighting by sending units. This paragraph calls for the stopping of fighting in the positions presently occupied by the two sides. We believe that 12 hours should allow ample time to achieve the practical implementation of this paragraph.

The second paragraph calls for the implementation of the Security Council Resolution in all of its parts after the ceasefire. The members of this Council as well as the parties concerned are fully familiar with Security Council Resolution 242 and it needs no elaboration here. The paragraph is linked to paragraph 3 which calls for the immediate beginning of negotiations between the parties concerned under appropriate auspices aimed at establishing a just and durable peace in the Middle East. We believe that from the tragic events of the past seventeen days there must be a new resolve, a new attempt to remove the fundamental causes that have brought war to the Middle East so frequently and so tragically. Another respite between two wars is just not good enough. And for our part, both the United States and the Soviet Union are ready to make our joint good offices available to the parties as a means to facilitate the negotiating process.

Finally, I want to report to the Council that both the Soviet Union and the United States believe that there should be an immediate exchange of prisoners of war.

Mr. President, we believe this is an historic moment for the Council. We believe that this Council, in exercising its primary responsibility in the field of peace and security, can make a major contribution to this end by adopting this Resolution promptly.

61. Security Council Resolutions 338, 339, 340, and 341 Concerning the October War, October 22-27, 1973*

* S.C. Res. 338, 339, 340, and 341, U.N. Doc. S/RES/338, 339, 340, 341 (1973) respectively. U.N. Security Council Resolutions 338-341 were adopted by a vote of 14 to 0, with the People's Republic of China not taking part in the vote.

Resolution 338 (October 22, 1973)

The Security Council

1. .*Calls upon* all parties to the present fighting to cease all firing and terminate all military activity immediately, no later than 12 hours after the moment of the adoption of this decision, in the positions they now occupy;

2. *Calls upon* the parties concerned to start immediately after the cease-fire the implementation of Security Council resolution 242 (1967) in all of its parts;

3. *Decides* that, immediately and concurrently with the cease-fire, negotiations start between the parties concerned under appropriate auspices aimed at establishing a just and durable peace in the Middle East.

Resolution 339 (October 23, 1973)

The Security Council

Referring to its resolution 338 (1973) of 22 October 1973,

1. *Confirms* its decision on an immediate cessation of all kinds of firing and of all military action, and urges that the forces of the two sides be returned to the positions they occupied at the moment the cease-fire became effective;

2. *Requests* the Secretary-General to take measures for immediate dispatch of United Nations observers to supervise the observance of the cease-fire between the forces of Israel and the Arab Republic of Egypt, using for this purpose the personnel of the United Nations now in the Middle East and first of all the personnel now in Cairo.

Resolution 340 (October 25, 1973)

The Security Council·

Recalling its resolutions 338 (1973) of 22 October and 339 (1973) of 23 October 1973,

Noting with regret the reported repeated violations of the cease-fire in non-compliance with resolutions 338 (1973) and 339 (1973),

Noting with concern from the Secretary-General's report that the United Nations military observers have not yet been enabled to place themselves on both sides of the cease-fire line,

1. *Demands* that immediate and complete cease-fire be observed and that the parties return to the positions occupied by them at 1650 hours GMT on 22 October 1973;

2. *Requests* the Secretary-General, as an immediate step, to increase the number of United Nations military observers on both sides;

3. *Decides* to set up immediately under its authority a United Nations Emergency Force to be composed of personnel drawn from States Members of the United Nations except the permanent members of the Security Council, and requests the Secretary-General to report within 24 hours on the steps taken to this effect;

4. *Requests* the Secretary-General to report to the Council on an urgent and continuing basis on the state of implementation of the present resolution, as well as resolutions 338 (1973) and 339 (1973);

5. *Requests* all Member States to extend their full co-operation to the United Nations in the implementation of the present resolution, as well as resolutions 338 (1973) and 339 (1973).

Resolution 341 (October 27, 1973)

The Security Council

1. *Approves* the report of the Secretary-General on the implementation of Security Council resolution 340 (1973) contained in document S/11052/Rev.1 dated 27 October 1973;

2. *Decides* that the force shall be established in accordance with the above-mentioned report for an initial period of six months, and that it shall continue in operation thereafter, if required, provided the Security Council so decides.

62. Declaration of the European Community on the Middle East, November 6, 1973*

* *Texts Relating to European Political Co-operation*, Press and Information Office of the Federal Republic of Germany, p. 57, vol. 1974. The text also appears in *Intl. Legal Materials* at 1531 (1973).

The nine Governments of the European Community have continued their exchange of views on the situation in the Middle East. While emphasizing that the views set out below are only a first contribution on their part to the search for a comprehensive solution to the problem, they have agreed on the following:

They strongly urge that the forces of both sides in the Middle East conflict should return immediately to the positions they occupied on October 22 in accordance with Resolutions 339 and 340 of the Security Council. They believe that a return to these positions will facilitate a solution to other pressing problems concerning prisoners-of-war and the Egyptian Third Army.

They have the firm hope that, following the adoption by the Security Council of Resolution No. 338 of October 22, negotiations will at last begin for the restoration in the Middle East of a just and lasting peace through the application of Security Council Resolution 242 in all of its parts. They declare themselves ready to do all in their power to contribute to that peace. They believe that those negotiations must take place in the framework of the United Nations. They recall that the Charter has entrusted to the Security Council the principal responsibility for international peace and security—the Council and the Secretary-General have a special role to play in the making and keeping of peace through the application of Council Resolutions Nos. 242 and 338.

They consider that a peace agreement should be based particularly on the following points:

(1) The inadmissibility of the acquisition of territory by force.

(2) The need for Israel to end the territorial occupation which it has maintained since the conflict of 1967.

(3) Respect for the sovereignty, territorial integrity and independence of every state in the area and their right to live in peace within secure and recognized boundaries.

(4) Recognition that in the establishment of a just and lasting peace account must be taken of the legitimate rights of the Palestinians.

They recall that according to Resolution No. 242 the peace settlement must be the object of international guarantees. They consider that such guarantees must be reinforced, among other means, by the dispatch of peacekeeping forces to the demilitarized zones envisaged in Article 2(c) of Resolution No. 242. They are agreed that such guarantees are of primary importance in settling the overall situation in the Middle East in conformity with Resolution No. 242, to which the Council refers in Resolution No. 338. They reserve the right to make proposals in this connection.

They recall on this occasion the ties of all kinds which have long linked them to the littoral states of the South and East of the Mediterranean. In this connection they reaffirm the terms of the Declaration of the Paris Summit of October 21, 1972 and recall that the Community has decided, in the framework of a global and balanced approach, to negotiate agreement with those countries.

63. Cease-Fire Agreement between Egypt and Israel, November 11, 1973*

* U.N. Doc. S/11056/Add. 3, Annex (1973).

The military representatives of the Arab Republic of Egypt and of Israel, acting on behalf of their Governments, and with a view to implementing paragraph 1 of the United Nations Security Council resolution 338 (1973) and paragraph 1 of United Nations Security Council resolution 339 (1973), have agreed as follows:

A. Egypt and Israel agree to observe scrupulously the cease-fire called for by the United Nations Security Council.

B. Both sides agree that discussions between them will begin immediately to settle the question of the return to the October 22 positions in the framework of agreement on the disengagement and separation of forces under the auspices of the United Nations.

C. The town of Suez will receive daily supplies of food, water and medicine. All wounded civilians in the town of Suez will be evacuated.

D. There shall be no impediment to the movement of non-military supplies to the East Bank.

E. The Israeli checkpoints on the Cairo-Suez Road will be replaced by United Nations checkpoints. At the Suez end of the road, Israeli officers can participate with the United Nations to supervise the non-military nature of the cargo at the bank of the Canal.

F. As soon as the United Nations checkpoints are established on the Cairo-Suez Road, there will be an exchange of all prisoners of war, including wounded.

In witness whereof the undersigned military representatives, in the presence of the interim Force Commander of the United Nations Emergency Force (UNEF), have signed the present agreement, which shall forthwith enter into force.

Done at kilometre marker 101 on the Cairo-Suez road this eleventh day of November 1973 in the English language, in three originals, one for each of the signatories and the third for the United Nations.

(*Signed*) Major-General Mohamed El-Gamasy

(*Signed*) Major-General A. Yaariv

(*Signed*) Ensio Siilasvuo, Major-General

64. Letter from the Secretary-General to the President of the Security Council Concerning the Egyptian-Israeli Agreement on Disengagement of Forces in Pursuance of the Geneva Peace Conference, January 18, 1974*

---

* U.N. Doc. S/1198/Rev. 1 /Add. 1 (1974).

The Commander of the United Nations Emergency Force, Lieutenant-General Ensio Siilasvuo, has reported to me that at 1025 hours GMT on 18 January 1974, at a meeting held at kilometre 101 on the Cairo-Suez road, an Agreement on the disengagement of forces in pursuance of the Geneva Peace Conference was signed by the Chief of Staff of the Egyptian Armed Forces, Major-General Mohammad Abdel Ghani El-Gamasy, and the Chief of Staff of the Israel Defence Forces, Lieutenant-General David Elazar, and by the Force Commander as witness.

The text of the Agreement is attached to this letter. The map mentioned in the Agreement has not yet been received. I shall, of course, send a copy of this map to you as soon as it is available at United Nations Headquarters.

I should be grateful if you would bring this matter to the attention of the members of the Security Council.

(Signed) Kurt WALDHEIM

Annex

EGYPTIAN-ISRAELI AGREEMENT ON DISENGAGEMENT OF FORCES IN PURSUANCE OF THE GENEVA PEACE CONFERENCE

A. Egypt and Israel will scrupulously observe the cease-fire on land, sea and air called for by the United Nations Security Council and will refrain from the time of the signing of this document from all military or paramilitary actions against each other.

B. The military forces of Egypt and Israel will be separated in accordance with the following principles:

1. All Egyptian forces on the east side of the canal will be deployed west of the line designated as line A on the attached map. All Israeli forces, including those west of the Suez Canal and the Bitter Lakes, will be deployed east of the line designated as line B on the attached map.

2. The area between the Egyptian and Israeli lines will be a zone of disengagement in which the United Nations Emergency Force (UNEF) will be stationed. The UNEF will continue to consist of units from countries that are not permanent members of the Security Council.

3. The area between the Egyptian line and the Suez Canal will be limited in armament and forces.

4. The area between the Israeli line (B on the attached map) and the line designated as line C on the attached map, which runs along

the western base of the mountains where the Gidi and Mitla Passes are located, will be limited in armament and forces.

5. The limitations referred to in paragraphs 3 and 4 will be inspected by UNEF. Existing procedures of the UNEF, including the attaching of Egyptian and Israeli liaison officers to UNEF, will be continued.

6. Air forces of the two sides will be permitted to operate up to their respective lines without interference from the other side.

C. The detailed implementation of the disengagement of forces will be worked out by military representatives of Egypt and Israel, who will agree on the stages of this process. These representatives will meet no later than 48 hours after the signature of this Agreement at kilometre 101 under the aegis of the United Nations for this purpose. They will complete this task within five days. Disengagement will begin within 48 hours after the completion of the work of the military representatives and in no event later than seven days after the signature of this Agreement. The process of disengagement will be completed not later than 40 days after it begins.

D. This Agreement is not regarded by Egypt and Israel as a final peace agreement. It constitutes a first step toward a final, just and durable peace according to the provisions of Security Council resolution 338 and within the framework of the Geneva Conference.

For Egypt:

Mohammad Abdel Ghani El-Gamasy
Major-General
Chief of Staff of the Egyptian
Armed Forces

For Israel:

David Elazar
Lieutenant-General
Chief of Staff of the Israel
Defence Forces

Witness:
Ensio P. H. Siilasvuo
Lieutenant-General
Commander of the United Nations
Emergency Force

65. Agreement on Disengagement between Israeli and Syrian Forces, May 31, 1974*

U.N. Doc. S/11302/Add. 1/Annex 1 (1974).

AGREEMENT ON DISENGAGEMENT
BETWEEN ISRAELI AND SYRIAN FORCES

A. Israel and Syria will scrupulously observe the cease-fire on land, sea and air and will refrain from all military actions against each other, from the time of the signing of this document, in implementation of United Nations Security Council resolution 338 dated 22 October 1973.

B. The military forces of Israel and Syria will be separated in accordance with the following principles:

1. All Israeli military forces will be west of the line designated as Line A on the Map attached hereto,* except in the Quneitra area, where they will be west of Line A-1.

2. All territory east of Line A will be under Syrian administration, and Syrian civilians will return to this territory.

3. The area between Line A and the line designated as Line B on the attached Map will be an area of separation. In this area will be stationed the United Nations Disengagement Observer Force established in accordance with the accompanying protocol.

4. All Syrian military forces will be east of the line designated as Line B on the attached Map.

5. There will be two equal areas of limitation in armament and forces, one west of Line A and one east of Line B as agreed upon.

6. Air forces of the two sides will be permitted to operate up to their respective lines without interference from the other side.

C. In the area between Line A and Line A-1 on the attached Map there shall be no military forces.

D. This Agreement and the attached Map will be signed by the military representatives of Israel and Syria in Geneva not later than 31 May 1974, in the Egyptian-Israeli Military Working Group of the Geneva Peace Conference under the aegis of the United Nations, after that group has been joined by a Syrian military representative, and with the participation of representatives of the United States and the Soviet Union. The precise delineation of a detailed Map and a plan for the implementation of the disengagement of forces will be worked out by military representatives of Israel and Syria in the Egyptian-Israeli Military Working Group who will agree on the stages of this

---

* Ed Note: The map could not be reproduced here owing to its size and complexity. It was signed by the military representatives of Israel and Syria at the meeting of the Military Working Group of the Geneva Peace Conference on June 5, 1974. A simplified version has been included at page xxvi. The official map can be found in U.N. Doc. S/11032/Add. 3 (1974).

process. The Military Working Group described above will start their work for this purpose in Geneva under the aegis of the United Nations within 24 hours after the signing of this Agreement. They will complete this task within five days. Disengagement will begin within

24 hours after the completion of the task of the Military Working Group. The process of disengagement will be completed not later than 20 days after it begins.

E. The provisions of paragraphs A, B and C shall be inspected by personnel of the United Nations comprising the United Nations Disengagement Observer Force under this agreement.

F. Within 24 hours after the signing of this Agreement in Geneva all wounded prisoners of war which each side holds of the other as certified by the ICRC will be repatriated. The morning after the completion of the task of the Military Working Group, all remaining prisoners of war will be repatriated.

G. The bodies of all dead soldiers held by either side will be returned for burial in their respective countries within 10 days after the signing of this Agreement.

H. This Agreement is not a Peace Agreement. It is a step towards a just and durable peace on the basis of Security Council resolution 338 dated 22 October 1973.

PROTOCOL TO AGREEMENT ON
DISENGAGEMENT BETWEEN ISRAELI AND SYRIAN FORCES

CONCERNING THE UNITED NATIONS
DISENGAGEMENT OBSERVER FORCE

Israel and Syria agree that:

The function of the United Nations Disengagement Observer Force (UNDOF) under the Agreement will be to use its best efforts to maintain the cease-fire and to see that it is scrupulously observed. It will supervise the Agreement and Protocol thereto with regard to the areas of separation and limitation. In carrying out its mission, it will comply with generally applicable Syrian laws and regulations and will not hamper the functioning of local civil administration. It will enjoy freedom of movement and communication and other facilities that are necessary for its mission. It will be mobile and provided with personal weapons of a defensive character and shall use such weapons only in self-defense. The number of the UNDOF shall be about

1,250, who will be selected by the Secretary-General of the United Nations in consultation with the parties from members of the United Nations who are not Permanent Members of the Security Council.

The UNDOF will be under the command of the United Nations, vested in the Secretary-General, under the authority of the Security Council.

The UNDOF shall carry out inspections under the Agreement, and report thereon to the parties, on a regular basis, not less often than once every 15 days, and, in addition, when requested by either party. It shall mark on the ground the respective lines shown on the Map attached to the Agreement.

Israel and Syria will support a resolution of the United Nations Security Council which will provide for the UNDOF contemplated by the Agreement. The initial authorization will be for six months subject to renewal by further resolution of the Security Council.

66. General Assembly Resolution 3236 (XXIX) Concerning the Question of Palestine, November 22, 1974*

* U.N. Doc. A/RES/3236 (XXIX) (1974).

The General Assembly,

Having considered the question of Palestine,

Having heard the statement of the Palestine Liberation Organization, the representative of the Palestinian people, [1]

Having also heard other statements made during the debate,

Deeply concerned that no just solution to the problem of Palestine has yet been achieved and recognizing that the problem of Palestine continues to endanger international peace and security,

Recognizing that the Palestinian people is entitled to self-determination in accordance with the Charter of the United Nations,

Expressing its grave concern that the Palestinian people has been prevented from enjoying its inalienable rights, in particular its right to self-determination,

Guided by the purposes and principles of the Charter,

Recalling its relevant resolutions which affirm the right of the Palestinian people to self-determination,

1. *Reaffirms* the inalienable rights of the Palestinian people in Palestine, including:

(a) The right to self-determination without external interference;

(b) The right to national independence and sovereignty;

2. *Reaffirms also* the inalienable right of the Palestinians to return to their homes and property from which they have been displaced and uprooted, and calls for their return;

3. *Emphasizes* that full respect for and the realization of these inalienable rights of the Palestinian people are indispensable for the solution of the question of Palestine;

4. *Recognizes* that the Palestinian people is a principal party in the establishment of a just and durable peace in the Middle East;

5. *Further recognizes* the right of the Palestinian people to regain its rights by all means in accordance with the purposes and principles of the Charter of the United Nations;

6. *Appeals* to all States and international organizations to extend their support to the Palestinian people in its struggle to restore its rights, in accordance with the Charter;

7. *Requests* the Secretary-General to establish contacts with the Palestine Liberation Organization on all matters concerning the question of Palestine;

---

[1] A/PV.2282.

8. *Requests* the Secretary-General to report to the General Assembly at its thirtieth session on the implementation of the present resolution;

9. *Decides* to include the item entitled "Question of Palestine" in the provisional agenda of its thirtieth session.

2296th plenary meeting
22 November 1974

67. Senate Resolution 214 Expressing Concern over Attempts to Expel Israel from the United Nations, July 18, 1975*

---

* S. Res. 214, 94th CONG., 1st SESS. (July 18, 1975).

To express concern over attempts to expel Israel from the United Nations.

Whereas the United Nations Charter implores its members to "practice tolerance and live together in peace with one another as good neighbors, and to unite our strength to maintain international peace and security, and ... to employ international machinery for the promotion of the economic and social advancement of all peoples," and

Whereas any action to expel members for political reasons violates the spirit of the United Nations Charter: Now, therefore, be it

1   *Resolved*, That the United States Senate looks with dis-

2   favor and concern over persistent attempts by some nations

3   among the so-called nonalined nations of the Third World

4   to expel Israel from membership in the United Nations; and

5   be it further

6   *Resolved*, That if Israel is expelled from the United

7   Nations the Senate will review all present United States

8   commitments to the Third World nations involved in the

9   expulsion, and will consider seriously the implication of

10 continued membership in the United Nations under such

11 circumstances.

68. Agreement between Egypt and Israel with Annex and United States Proposal for an Early Warning System in Sinai, September 1, 1975*

* Department of State News Release, Sept. 1, 1975.

AGREEMENT BETWEEN
EGYPT AND ISRAEL

The Government of the Arab Republic of Egypt and the Government of Israel have agreed that:

ARTICLE I

The conflict between them and in the Middle East shall not be resolved by military force but by peaceful means.

The Agreement concluded by the Parties January 18, 1974, within the framework of the Geneva Peace Conference, constituted a first step towards a just and durable peace according to the provisions of Security Council Resolution 338 of October 22, 1973.

They are determined to reach a final and just peace settlement by means of negotiations called for by Security Council Resolution 338, this Agreement being a significant step towards that end.

ARTICLE II

The Parties hereby undertake not to resort to the threat or use of force or military blockade against each other.

ARTICLE III

The Parties shall continue scrupulously to observe the ceasefire on land, sea and air and to refrain from all military or para-military actions against each other.

The Parties also confirm that the obligations contained in the Annex and, when concluded, the Protocol shall be an integral part of this Agreement.

ARTICLE IV

A. The military forces of the Parties shall be deployed in accordance with the following principles:

(1) All Israeli forces shall be deployed east of the lines designated as Lines J and M on the attached map.

(2) All Egyptian forces shall be deployed west of the line designated as Line E on the attached map.

(3) The area between the lines designated on the attached map as Lines E and F and the area between the lines designated on the attached map as Lines J and K shall be limited in armament and forces.

(4) The limitations on armaments and forces in the areas described by paragraph (3) above shall be agreed as described in the attached Annex.

(5) The zone between the lines designated on the attached map as Lines E and J, will be a buffer zone. In this zone the United Nations Emergency Force will continue to perform its functions as under the Egyptian-Israeli Agreement of January 18, 1974.

(6) In the area south from Line E and west from Line M, as defined on the attached map, there will be no military forces, as specified in the attached Annex.

B. The details concerning the new lines, the redeployment of the forces and its timing, the limitation on armaments and forces, aerial reconnaissance, the operation of the early warning and surveillance installations and the use of the roads, the United Nations functions and other arrangements will all be in accordance with the provisions of the Annex and map which are an integral part of this Agreement and of the Protocol which is to result from negotiations pursuant to the Annex and which, when concluded, shall become an integral part of this Agreement.

ARTICLE V

The United Nations Emergency Force is essential and shall continue its functions and its mandate shall be extended annually.

ARTICLE VI

The Parties hereby establish a Joint Commission for the duration of this Agreement. It will function under the aegis of the Chief Coordinator of the United Nations Peacekeeping Missions in the Middle East in order to consider any problem arising from this Agreement and to assist the United Nations Emergency Force in the execution of its mandate. The Joint Commission shall function in accordance with procedures established in the Protocol.

ARTICLE VII

Non-military cargoes destined for or coming from Israel shall be permitted through the Suez Canal.

ARTICLE VIII

This Agreement is regarded by the Parties as a significant step towards a just and lasting peace. It is not a final peace agreement.

The Parties shall continue their efforts to negotiate a final peace agreement within the framework of the Geneva Peace Conference in accordance with Security Council Resolution 338.

ARTICLE IX

This Agreement shall enter into force upon signature of the Protocol and remain in force until superseded by a new agreement.

Done at _____ on the _____ 1975, in four original copies.

For the Government of the Arab Republic of Egypt   For the Government of Israel

_____   _____

WITNESS

_____

ANNEX TO THE AGREEMENT

Within 5 days after the signature of the Egypt-Israel Agreement, representatives of the two Parties shall meet in the Military Working Group of the Middle East Peace Conference at Geneva to begin preparation of a detailed Protocol for the implementation of the Agreement. The Working Group will complete the Protocol within 2 weeks. In order to facilitate preparation of the Protocol and implementation of the Agreement, and to assist in maintaining the scrupulous observance of the ceasefire and other elements of the Agreement, the two Parties have agreed on the following principles, which are an integral part of the Agreement, as guidelines for the Working Group.

1. Definitions of Lines and Areas

The deployment lines, Areas of Limited Forces and Armaments, Buffer Zones, the area south from Line E and west from Line M, other designated areas, road sections for common use and other features referred to in Article IV of the Agreement shall be as indicated on the attached map

(1:100,000—U.S. Edition).

2. Buffer Zones

(a) Access to the Buffer Zones will be controlled by the United Nations Emergency Force, according to procedures to be worked out by the Working Group and the United Nations Emergency Force.

(b) Aircraft of either Party will be permitted to fly freely up to the forward line of that Party. Reconnaissance aircraft of either Party may fly up to the middle line of the Buffer Zone between Lines E and J on an agreed schedule.

(c) In the Buffer Zone between Lines E and J, there will be established under Article IV of the Agreement an Early Warning System entrusted to United States civilian personnel as detailed in a separate proposal, which is a part of this Agreement.

(d) Authorized personnel shall have access to the Buffer Zone for transit to and from the Early Warning System; the manner in which this is carried out shall be worked out by the Working Group and the United Nations Emergency Force.

3. Area South of Line E and West of Line M

(a) In this area, the United Nations Emergency Force will assure that there are no military or para-military forces of any kind, military fortifications and military installations; it will establish checkpoints and have the freedom of movement necessary to perform this function.

(b) Egyptian civilians and third-country civilian oil field personnel shall have the right to enter, exit from, work, and live in the above indicated area, except for Buffer Zones 2A, 2B and the United Nations Posts. Egyptian civilian police shall be allowed in the area to perform normal civil police functions among the civilian population in such numbers and with such weapons and equipment as shall be provided for in the Protocol.

(c) Entry to and exit from the area, by land, by air or by sea, shall be only through the United Nations Emergency Force checkpoints. The United Nations Emergency Force shall also establish checkpoints along the road, the dividing line and at other points, with the precise locations and number to be included in the Protocol.

(d) Access to the airspace and the coastal area shall be limited to unarmed Egyptian civilian vessels and unarmed civilian helicopters and transport planes involved in the civilian activities of the area as agreed by the Working Group.

(e) Israel undertakes to leave intact all currently existing civilian installations and infrastructures.

(f) Procedures for use of the common sections of the coastal road along the Gulf of Suez shall be determined by the Working Group and detailed in the Protocol.

4. Aerial Surveillance

There shall be a continuation of aerial reconnaissance missions by the United States over the areas covered by the Agreement (the area between Lines F and K), following the same procedures already in practice. The missions will ordinarily be carried out at a frequency of one mission every 7 - 10 days, with either Party or the United Nations Emergency Force empowered to request an earlier mission. The United States Government will make the mission results available expeditiously to Israel, Egypt and the Chief Coordinator of the United Nations Peacekeeping Missions in the Middle East.

5. Limitation of Forces and Armaments

(a) Within the Areas of Limited Forces and Armaments (the areas between Lines J and K and Lines E and F) the major limitations shall be as follows:

(1) Eight (8) standard infantry battalions.

(2) Seventy-five (75) tanks.

(3) Seventy-two (72) artillery pieces, including heavy mortars (i.e., with caliber larger than 120 mm.), whose range shall not exceed twelve (12) km.

(4) The total number of personnel shall not exceed eight thousand (8,000).

(5) Both Parties agree not to station or locate in the area weapons which can reach the line of the other side.

(6) Both Parties agree that in the areas between Lines J and K, and between Line A (of the Disengagement Agreement of January 18, 1974) and Line E, they will construct no new fortifications or installations for forces of a size greater than that agreed herein.

(b) The major limitations beyond the Areas of Limited Forces and Armaments will be:

(1) Neither side will station nor locate any weapon in areas from which they can reach the other line.

(2) The Parties will not place anti-aircraft missiles within an area of ten (10) kilometres east of Line K and west of Line F, respectively.

(c) The United Nations Emergency Force will conduct inspections in order to ensure the maintenance of the agreed limitations within these areas.

6. Process of Implementation

The detailed implementation and timing of the redeployment of forces, turnover of oil fields, and other arrangements called for by the Agreement, Annex and Protocol shall be determined by the Working Group, which will agree on the stages of this process, including the phased movement of Egyptian troops to Line E and Israeli troops to Line J. The first phase will be the transfer of the oil fields and installations to Egypt. This process will begin within 2 weeks from the signature of the Protocol with the introduction of the necessary technicians, and it will be completed no later than 8 weeks after it begins. The details of the phasing will be worked out in the Military Working Group.

Implementation of the redeployment shall be completed within 5 months after signature of the Protocol.

For the Government of the Arab Republic of Egypt   For the Government of Israel

WITNESS

PROPOSAL

In connection with the Early Warning System referred to in Article IV of the Agreement between Egypt and Israel concluded on this date and as an integral part of that Agreement, (hereafter referred to as the Basic Agreement), the United States proposes the following:

1. The Early Warning System to be established in accordance with Article IV in the area shown on the map attached to the Basic Agreement will be entrusted to the United States. It shall have the following elements:

a. There shall be two surveillance stations to provide strategic early warning, one operated by Egyptian and one operated by Israeli personnel. Their locations are shown on the map attached to the Basic Agreement. Each station shall be manned by not more than 250 technical and administrative personnel. They shall perform the functions of visual and electronic surveillance only within their stations.

b. In support of these stations, to provide tactical early warning and to verify access to them, three watch stations shall be established by the United States in the Mitla and Giddi Passes as will be shown on the map attached to the Basic Agreement. These stations shall be operated by United States civilian personnel. In support of these stations, there shall be established three unmanned electronic sensor fields at both ends of each Pass and in the general vicinity of each station and the roads leading to and from those stations.

2. The United States civilian personnel shall perform the following duties in connection with the operation and maintenance of these stations:

a. At the two surveillance stations described in paragraph 1 a. above, United States civilian personnel will verify the nature of the operations of the stations and all movement into and out of each station and will immediately report any detected divergency from its authorized role of visual and electronic surveillance to the Parties to the Basic Agreement and to the United Nations Emergency Force.

b. At each watch station described in paragraph 1 b. above, the United States civilian personnel will immediately report to the Parties to

Accepted by:

the Basic Agreement and to the United Nations Emergency Force any movement of armed forces, other than the United Nations Emergency Force, into either Pass and any observed preparations for such movement.

c. The total number of United States civilian personnel assigned to functions under this Proposal shall not exceed 200. Only civilian personnel shall be assigned to functions under this Proposal.

3. No arms shall be maintained at the stations and other facilities covered by this Proposal, except for small arms required for their protection.

4. The United States personnel serving the Early Warning System shall be allowed to move freely within the area of the System.

5. The United States and its personnel shall be entitled to have such support facilities as are reasonably necessary to perform their functions.

6. The United States personnel shall be immune from local criminal, civil, tax and customs jurisdiction and may be accorded any other specific privileges and immunities provided for in the United Nations Emergency Force Agreement of February 13, 1957.

7. The United States affirms that it will continue to perform the functions described above for the duration of the Basic Agreement.

8. Notwithstanding any other provision of this Proposal, the United States may withdraw its personnel only if it concludes that their safety is jeopardized or that continuation of their role is no longer necessary. In the latter case the Parties to the Basic Agreement will be informed in advance in order to give them the opportunity to make alternative arrangements. If both Parties to the Basic Agreement request the United States to conclude its role under this Proposal, the United States will consider such requests conclusive.

9. Technical problems including the location of the watch stations will be worked out through consultation with the United States.

Henry A. Kissinger
Secretary of State

69. Statement of Secretary of State Kissinger before the Senate Foreign Relations Committee on the Egyptian-Israel Agreement, October 7, 1975*

* "Early Warning System in Sinai," *Hearings Before the Committee on Foreign Relations of the U.S. Senate*, 94th CONG., 1st SESS. (Oct. 6-7, 1975), at pp. 212-15. See also "Middle East Agreements and the Early Warning System in Sinai," *Hearings of the Committee on International Relations House of Representatives*, 94th CONG., 1st SESS. (Sept. 8, 11, 18, and 25, 1975).

PREPARED STATEMENT OF SECRETARY OF STATE KISSINGER BEFORE THE SENATE
FOREIGN RELATIONS COMMITTEE ON THE EGYPTIAN-ISRAELI AGREEMENT

Mr. Chairman, Members of the Committee:

I welcome this opportunity to appear before your Committee to testify on the
recent agreement between Israel and Egypt. That agreement— if carried out in
good faith by both parties—may well mark an historic turning point away from
the cycle of war and stalemate that has for so long afflicated Israelis and Arabs
and the world at large. I am here to urge prompt and positive Congressional action to help further the prospects for peace in the Middle East.

For more than thirty years the issues in dispute in that troubled region have
been recognized by successive American Administrations as having profound consequences for America's own interests. The United States' diplomatic role in the
Middle East is a matter of vital national importance:

We have an historic and moral commitment to the survival and security of
Israel.

We have important interests in the Arab world with its 150 million people and
the world's largest oil reserves.

We know that the world's hopes, and our own, for economic recovery and
progress could be dashed by another upheaval in the Middle East.

We must avoid the severe strains on our relations with our allies in Europe and
Japan that perpetual crisis in the Middle East would almost certainly entail.

We face the dangers of a direct US-Soviet confrontation, with its attendant nuclear risk if tension in the Middle East should increase.

The October War of 1973 brought home to every American, in concrete and
dramatic ways, the price we pay for continued Arab-Israeli conflict. The oil embargo triggered by that war cost us 500,000 jobs, more than $10 billion in national
production, and a rampant inflation. The 1973 crisis put our alliances with Western Europe and Japan under the most serious strain they had ever known. And it
brought us to the verge of a confrontation with the Soviet Union requiring us to
place our military forces on a global alert.

Thus for the most basic reasons of national policy we owe it to the American
people to do all we can to ensure that the Middle East moves towards peace and
away from conflict.

If the past two years of vigorous diplomatic endeavor have promoted the
prospects of peace—as I believe they have—the United States has made the
difference. We have maintained our special relationship with Israel, while at
the same time dramatically improving our relations with the Arab world. It is
the United States alone among the world's nations that both Israel and its Arab
neighbors have been prepared to trust. This link of confidence must be maintained. Without it the Middle East will have lost the key element of its stability.
Without it the period ahead—difficult at best—may well grow unmanageable.

It is our strong conviction that the Sinai Agreement is indispensable to the
process of peace. Were I here today to report that we had failed to obtain a Sinai
Agreement, I would have to tell you, as well, that the prospects of still another
Arab-Israeli war were infinitely and imminently greater. Instead, I can state
that the prospects for peace in the Middle East have been significantly advanced,
and that good chances exist for even further progress—if we have the wisdom
and the national will to seize the opportunity before us.

Hailed by both Prime Minister Rabin and President Sadat as a possible turning point, the Sinai Agreement represents the most far-reaching, practical test of
peace—political, military, and psychological—in the long and tragic history of
the Arab-Israeli conflict. For the first time in more than two decades, Israel and
an Arab state have agreed, not just to disentangle their forces in the aftermath
of war, but to commit themselves to the peaceful resolution of the differences
that for so long have made them mortal enemies.

Thus, what we are proposing to the Congress—as we seek approval for the
stationing of no more than 200 technicians in the Sinai—is an investment in
peace. But we must never forget that the most precarious part of the road

toward a just and lasting peace still lies ahead. We will require national unity and a sympethetic understanding for the delicacy of the process if we are to continue the journey.

With these considerations in mind, Mr. Chairman, I urge this Committee and the Congress to respond promptly and sympethetically to the President's request for approval of the stationing of up to 200 Americans in the Sinai—a request that has now been before the Congress for more than four weeks.

The proposed American presence is a limited but crucial American responsibility. It is not a role we sought; it is a role we accepted reluctantly at the request of both sides—and only when it was clear that there would be no agreement without it. The American personnel will be volunteers, and they will be civilian Their function is to assist in an early warning system in the small areas of the Sinai passes in the UN buffer zone. They are not combat personnel or advisers for one side; they will serve both sides at their request. They will complement the UN military contingents already there from such countries as Canada, Sweden, Austria and Finland whose responsibility it is to protect the buffer zone. Nor is our own presence in the area new—thirty-six Americans are serving there at this moment with the United Nations Truce Supervisory Organization. Americans have been serving in this capacity for over 25 years.

The proposal we ask you to approve provides that the President may withdraw these volunteer technicians if we believe them to be in jeopardy or are no longer necessary. We are prepared, as well, to accept the Congressional proposal to make: withdrawal mandatory in the event of hostilities.

Mr. Chairman, I am well aware of, and respect, this Committee's desire to be certain that it has before it all undertakings relevant to its consideration and approval of the proposal for U.S. participation in the Sinai early warning system.

We have made an unprecedented effort to meet the Committee's concerns. Within days of my return from the Middle East we voluntarily supplied to the Committees of Congress, on a classified basis, highly sensitive material relevant to the negotiations of the Sinai Accord. Included in this material was information from the record of the negotiations of the very category which President Washington declined to furnish to the House of Representatives in 1794, and which no Administration has supplied since.

Four weeks ago, we provided four sets of documents to the appropriate Congressional Committees. They are:

First, the United States Proposal for stationing technicians in the Sinai.

Second, the unclassified Agreement between Israel and Egypt, and its military annex.

Third, the classified documents which the Administration has certified include all of the assurances, undertakings, and commitments which we consider to be legally binding upon the United States. These documents also contain many provisions which are not considered legally binding; they were submitted because they were contained in documents which include binding clauses and which were initialed or signed by the United States and one of the parties.

Fourth, extracts from other classified documents in the negotiating record which the Administration believes are legally binding assurances, undertakings, or commitments. We have included in this category certain provisions which, although not regarded by the Administration as binding, might be so regarded by others.

Finally, the Legal Adviser of the State Department submitted yesterday to this Committee on a classified basis a memorandum which provides his assessment of the legal character of all the documents previously given to the Congress.

We presented these classified documents on the assumption that they would be treated as if they had been transmitted under the Case Act, which provides for submission of executive agreements to the Congress, but with "an appropriate injunction of secrecy to be removed only upon due notice from the President."

Mr. Chairman, the Executive Branch has complied with both the letter and spirit of the Committee's resolution requesting the President to inform the Committee "of all the assurances and undertakings by the United States on which Israel and Egypt are relying in entering into the Sinai Agreement. . . ." I am authorized on behalf of the President to state that there are *no other* assurances or undertakings, beyond those already submitted to the Congress, which are binding upon the United States. We will make no contrary claim in the future; nor can any other government.

Mr. Chairman, if there has been a disagreement between this Committee an the Executive Branch over the past several weeks, it has concerned not 'is-closure to the Congress—which has been complete—but the *form* of disclosure to the public.

We had hoped that a summary could be worked out with the Committee which could have been certified as containing all commitments so that the full Senate would feel free to vote unreservedly on the U.S. technicians. This procedure was intended as a means of satisfying the needs of the Congress and the rights of the American people to know, while at the same time maintaining the integrity and confidentiality of the diplomatic process. We believed that we were following the precedents set in previous negotiations in the Middle East when classified documents were submitted to the Congress but not made public. Our purpose was to avoid a situation in which other governments would feel compelled to take a public position and to protect our ability to act as a mediator in the future.

This plan became problematical when the confidential documents were leaked. This created a new and very difficult situation. The Administration disagrees with the decision of the Committee to publish these documents and maintains that it in no way sets a precedent. We consider that the provisions of the Case Act regarding classification remains valid; they should be respected in the future.

We recognize that the Committee faced an unusual problem to which no good answer existed. We are prepared to work with this Committee to develop procedures for future negotiations which will permit ground rules to be clearly established in advance so that all parties will know what to expect.

With regard to the U.S. undertakings, the Administration is particularly concerned about two points:

First, that Congressional approval of the proposal on the technicians not link the Sinai Agreement to the U.S. undertakings—which are distinct and separate; and

Second, that U.S. statements of intention not be given a legally binding character which was never intended and is not inherent in them.

The Administration is convinced that Congressional approval of the proposal to station technicians in the Sinai does not import or imply approval of anything more.

The United States is not a party to the Sinai Agreement. That Agreement is between Israel and Egypt; they are the only signatories and the only states bound by it. The Agreement repeatedly speaks of the obligations of "the parties"; it is beyond dispute that "the parties" are Egypt and Israel, and *not* the United States.

The Agreement provides, in an annex, that in the buffer zone between Egypt and Israel—in which the United Nations Emergency Force will continue to perform its functions—there will be established an early warning system entrusted to United States civilian personnel. The proposal of the United States, for which approval of the Congress is being sought, provides details of that early warning system. That proposal is described as a *part* of the Agreement between Egypt and Israel, but that does not imply that the United States is party to this Agreement. By the same token, the U.S. assurances and undertakings before this Committee, while given on the occasion of, and concordant with, the conclusion of the Sinai Agreement between Egypt and Israel, are not in any sense part of the Sinai Agreement.

Thus, even if the United States were unable to fulfill all of the intentions we have expressed, the parties—Egypt and Israel—would nonetheless remain bound by the Sinai Agreement. The obligations of the Egyptian-Israeli Agreement are clear, direct and unqualified; they stand on their own.

A vote in favor of the specific, limited U.S. role in the early warning system will not thereby commit the Congress to a position on any other issue—whether it be the question of undertakings and assurances to the parties involved; our continuing relations with various countries of the area; a given level of budget support; or our policies and programs in the Middle East. Those are separate issues which you will want to consider carefully at the appropriate time. Many will come up in the normal authorization and appropriation process; they are not an integral part of the Egyptian-Israeli Agreement.

Let me turn now to the question of the nature of American assurances and undertakings to Israel and Egypt.

The special position of trust enjoyed by the United States inevitably means that both sides attach great significance to our views. Statements of our intentions, therefore, served as a lubricant in this most recent negotiation just as they have in every previous mediation effort. But they must be seen in perspective and in the light of historical practice. It is extremely important, therefore, that in approving the sending of U.S. technicians the Congress should take care not inadvertently to create commitments that were never intended.

We have submitted all documents containing U.S. commitments. Not all provisions in these documents amount to binding undertakings. They include:

First, assurances by the U.S. of our political intentions. These are often statements typical of diplomatic exchange; in some instances they are merely formal reaffirmations of existing American policy. Other provisions refer to contingencies which may never arise and are related—sometimes explicitly—to present circumstances subject to rapid change.

Second, undertakings or assurances by the U.S. which are conditional on existing or prior authorization and appropriation of the Congress or which fall within the constitutional authority of the President to conduct the foreign relations of the United States.

Thus to speak of Memoranda of Agreement as Executive Agreements is by no means to say that each of their individual provisions is binding upon the United States. That depends entirely upon the content of the specific provisions in question. Moreover, nothing in these particular documents constrains Congressional action in any issue involving the future legislative process.

The fact that many provisions are not by any standard international commitments does not mean, of course, that the United States is morally or politically free to act as if they did not exist. On the contrary, they are important statements of diplomatic policy and engage the good faith of the United States so long as the circumstances that gave rise to them continue. But they are not binding commitments of the United States.

Mr. Chairman, I should like to conclude with this thought: the Sinai Accord could prove to be an historic milestone. It is not a peace agreement, but it can be an important step in that direction.

The United States remains committed to helping bring a just, durable and comprehensive peace to the Middle East. We do not consider the Sinai Agreement permitting stagnation in the process of negotiation; its purpose is to give impetus to that process. We are prepared to work with *all* the parties toward a solution of *all* the issues yet remaining—including the issue of the future of the Palestinians.

Whether the Sinai Agreement fulfills its promise depends crucially on the confidence and trust America inspires. Yet we cannot gain—nor retain—confidence abroad if we lack it at home. Whether there will be peace or war in the Middle East depends importantly on whether America is at peace with itself; whether America is united in its purpose.

The challenge now is to build on the progress that has been made. So let us get on with the job, for there will be no Sinai Accord unless the Congress of the United States takes positive action to approve the proposal to place up to 200 technicians in the Sinai. And if there is no accord, then all that America has worked for, and all that the Middle East has hoped for, may well be lost.

So, Mr. Chairman, I respectfully ask that this Committee act now to approve the resolution before it, so that Israel and Egypt can get on with the business of implementing the Sinai Accord, and so that the march toward peace can be resumed in the Middle East.

CERTIFICATION

I hereby certify on behalf of the President and the Administration that the documents on the Sinai disengagement which we have provided to the Committee in connection with the United States proposal for stationing technicians in the Sinai, include all the undertakings, commitments, and assurances which the United States regards as legally binding or which will become legally binding upon signature of the two Memoranda of Agreement. It also includes all the undertakings, commitments, and assurances upon which either Israel or Egypt is legally entitled to rely.

HENRY A. KISSINGER.

October 7, 1975.

70. Appendix from Senate Foreign Relations Committee Report Concerning Memoranda of Agreements between Israel and the United States, October 7, 1975*

* "Early Warning System in Sinai," *Hearings Before the Committee on Foreign Relations of the U.S. Senate*, 94th CONG., 1st SESS. (Oct. 6-7, 1975), at pp. 249-53. For discussion of the status of any such memoranda see the Hearing Record.

MEMORANDUM OF AGREEMENT BETWEEN THE GOVERNMENTS OF ISRAEL
AND THE UNITED STATES

The United States recognizes that the Egypt-Israel Agreement
initialed on September 1, 1975, (hereinafter referred to as the Agreement), entailing the withdrawal from vital areas in Sinai, constitutes
an act of great significance on Israel's part in the pursuit of final
peace. That Agreement has full United States support.

UNITED STATES-ISRAELI ASSURANCES

1. The United States Government will make every effort to be
fully responsive, within the limits of its resources and Congressional
authorization and appropriation, on an on-going and long-term basis
to Israel's military equipment and other defense requirements, to its
energy requirements and to its economic needs. The needs specified in
paragraphs 2, 3 and 4 below shall be deemed eligible for inclusion
within the annual total to be requested in FY76 and later fiscal years.

2. Israel's long-term military supply needs from the United States
shall be the subject of periodic consultations between representatives
of the United States and Israeli defense establishments, with agreement reached on specific items to be included in a separate United
States-Israeli memorandum. To this end, a joint study by military
experts will be undertaken within 3 weeks. In conducting this study,
which will include Israel's 1976 needs, the United States will view
Israel's requests sympathetically, including its request for advanced
and sophisticated weapons.

3. Israel will make its own independent arrangements for oil supply to meet its requirements through normal procedures. In the event
Israel is unable to secure its needs in this way, the United States Government, upon notification of this fact by the Government of Israel,
will act as follows for five years, at the end of which period either
side can terminate this arrangement on one-year's notice.

   (a) If the oil Israel needs to meet all its normal requirements
for domestic consumption is unavailable for purchase in circumstances where no quantitative restrictions exist on the ability of
the United States to procure oil to meet its normal requirements,

the United States Government will promptly make oil available for purchase by Israel to meet all of the aforementioned normal requirements of Israel. If Israel is unable to secure the necessary means to transport such oil to Israel, the United States Government will make every effort to help Israel secure the necessary means of transport.

(b) If the oil Israel needs to meet all of its normal requirements for domestic consumption is unavailable for purchase in circumstances where quantitative restrictions through embargo or otherwise also prevent the United States from procuring oil to meet its normal requirements, the United States Government will promptly make oil available for purchase by Israel in accordance with the International Energy Agency conservation and allocation formula as applied by the United States Government, in order to meet Israel's essential requirements. If Israel is unable to secure the necessary means to transport such oil to Israel, the United States Government will make every effort to help Israel secure the necessary means of transport.

Israeli and United States experts will meet annually or more frequently at the request of either party, to review Israel's continuing oil requirement.

4. In order to help Israel meet its energy needs, and as part of the overall annual figure in paragraph 1 above, the United States agrees:

(a) In determining the overall annual figure which will be requested from Congress, the United States Government will give special attention to Israel's oil import requirements and, for a period as determined by Article 3 above, will take into account in calculating that figure Israel's additional expenditures for the import of oil to replace that which would have ordinarily come from Abu Rodeis and Ras Sudar (4.5 million tons in 1975).

(b) To ask Congress to make available funds, the amount to be determined by mutual agreement, to the Government of Israel necessary for a project for the construction and stocking of the oil reserves to be stored in Israel, bringing storage reserve capacity and reserve stocks now standing at approximately six months, up to one-year's need at the time of the completion of the project. The project will be implemented within four years. The construction, operation and financing and other relevant questions of the project will be the subject of early and detailed talks between the two Governments.

5. The United States Government will not expect Israel to begin to implement the Agreement before Egypt fulfils its undertaking under the January 1974 Disengagement Agreement to permit passage of all Israeli cargoes to and from Israeli ports through the Suez Canal.

6. The United States Government agrees with Israel that the next agreement with Egypt should be a final peace agreement.

7. In case of an Egyptian violation of any of the provisions of the Agreement, the United States Government is prepared to consult with Israel as to the significance of the violation and possible remedial action by the United States Government.

8. The United States Government will vote against any Security Council resolution which in its judgment affects or alters adversely the Agreement.

9. The United States Government will not join in and will seek to prevent efforts by others to bring about consideration of proposals which it and Israel agree are detrimental to the interests of Israel.

10. In view of the long-standing United States commitment to the survival and security of Israel, the United States Government will view with particular gravity threats to Israel's security or sovereignty by a world power. In support of this objective, the United States Government will in the event of such threat consult promptly with the Government of Israel with respect to what support, diplomatic or otherwise, or assistance it can lend to Israel in accordance with its constitutional practices.

11. The United States Government and the Government of Israel will, at the earliest possible time, and if possible, within two months after the signature of this document, conclude the contingency plan for a military supply operation to Israel in an emergency situation.

12. It is the United States Government's position that Egyptian commitments under the Egypt-Israel Agreement, its implementation, validity and duration are not conditional upon any act or developments between the other Arab states and Israel. The United States Government regards the Agreement as standing on its own.

13. The United States Government shares the Israel position that under existing political circumstances negotiations with Jordan will be directed toward an overall peace settlement.

14. In accordance with the principle of freedom of navigation on the high seas and free and unimpeded passage through and over straits connecting international waters, the United States Government regards the Straits of Bab-el-Mandeb and the Strait of Gibraltar as international waterways. It will support Israel's right to free and unimpeded passage through such straits. Similarly, the United States Government recognizes Israel's right to freedom of flights over the Red Sea and such straits and will support diplomatically the exercise of that right.

15. In the event that the United Nations Emergency Force or any other United Nations organ is withdrawn without the prior agreement of both Parties to the Egypt-Israel Agreement and the United States before this Agreement is superseded by another agreement, it is the United States view that the Agreement shall remain binding in all its parts.

16. The United States and Israel agree that signature of the Protocol of the Egypt-Israel Agreement and its full entry into effect shall not take place before approval by the United States Congress of the United States role in connection with the surveillance and observation functions described in the Agreement and its Annex. The United States has informed the Government of Israel that it has obtained the Government of Egypt agreement to the above.

YIGAL ALLON,
Deputy Prime Minister and
Minister of Foreign Affairs
(For the Government of Israel).

HENRY A. KISSINGER,
Secretary of State
(For the Government of
the United States).

MEMORANDUM OF AGREEMENT BETWEEN THE GOVERNMENTS OF ISRAEL AND THE UNITED STATES

THE GENEVA PEACE CONFERENCE

1. The Geneva Peace Conference will be reconvened at a time coordinated between the United States and Israel.

2. The United States will continue to adhere to its present policy with respect to the Palestine Liberation Organization, whereby it will not recognize or negotiate with the Palestine Liberation Organization so long as the Palestine Liberation Organization does not recognize Israel's right to exist and does not accept Security Council Resolutions 242 and 338. The United States Government will consult fully and seek to concert its position and strategy at the Geneva Peace Conference on this issue with the Government of Israel. Similarly, the United States will consult fully and seek to concert its position and strategy with Israel with regard to the participation of any other additional states. It is understood that the participation at a subsequent phase of the Conference of any possible additional state, group or organization will require the agreement of all the initial participants.

3. The United States will make every effort to ensure at the Conference that all the substantive negotiations will be on a bilateral basis.

4. The United States will oppose and, if necessary, vote against any initiative in the Security Council to alter adversely the terms of reference of the Geneva Peace Conference or to change Resolutions 242 and 338 in ways which are incompatible with their original purpose.

5. The United States will seek to ensure that the role of the cosponsors will be consistent with what was agreed in the Memorandum of Understanding between the United States Government and the Government of Israel of December 20, 1973.

6. The United States and Israel will concert action to assure that the Conference will be conducted in a manner consonant with the objectives of this document and with the declared purpose of the Conference, namely the advancement of a negotiated peace between Israel and each one of its neighbors.

YIGAL ALLON,
*Deputy Prime Minister and
Minister of Foreign Affairs*
(For the Government of Israel).
HENRY A. KISSINGER,
Secretary of State
(For the Government of
the United States).

ASSURANCES FROM USG TO ISRAEL

On the question of military and economic assistance to Israel, the following conveyed by the U.S. to Israel augments what the Memorandum of Agreement states.

The United States is resolved to continue to maintain Israel's defensive strength through the supply of advanced types of equipment, such as the F-16 ircraft. The United States Government agrees to an early meeting to undertake joint study of high technology and sophisticated items, including the Pershing ground-to-ground missiles with conventional warheads, with the view to giving a positive response. The U.S. Administration will submit annually for approval by the U.S. Congress a request for military and economic assistance in order to help meet Israel's economic and military needs.

Assurances From USG to Egypt

1. The United States intends to make a serious effort to help bring about further negotiations between Syria and Israel, in the first instance through diplomatic channels.

2. In the event of an Israeli violation of the Agreement, the United States is prepared to consult with Egypt as to the significance of the violation and possible remedial action by the United States.

3. The United States will provide technical assistance to Egypt for the Egyptian Early Warning Station.

4. The U.S. reaffirms its policy of assisting Egypt in its economic development, the specific amount to be subject to Congressional authorization and appropriation.

HAJJI A.R. AHMAD
5825 Walton Ave.,
Philadelphia, Pa., October 1, 1975.

Chief Clerk, Arthur M. Kuhl,
COMMITTEE ON FOREIGN RELATIONS
Washington, D.C.

DEAR SIR: Please include this letter in the public record of hearings, to be published in opposition to the Sinai Agreement with particular regard to aid to Israel.

We are opposed to the Agreement on the grounds that:

(1) Aid to Israel is prohibited by 18 U.S.C. 960 which prohibits aid of any sort to any Expedition against a government or people with whom the United States is at peace. Violations of this criminal statute by the President and Congress of the United States since 1948 is the cause of the delicate situation now existing in the Middle East.

(2) The Zionist and some Officials of the United States Government through aid to Israel constitute such a conspiracy as is described in 18 U.S.C. 956 with particular regard to PALESTINE.

(3) Aid to any parties in this Agreement further violates 18 U.S.C. Sections 961,962, et al.

(All aid to Israel being exported from the United States is therefore illegal and subject to seizure under 22 U.S.C. 401, and the President of the United States is in violation of his oath of office for failure to execute faithfully these Laws.)

Sincerely,

HAAJJI A. R. AHMAD.

P.S. Please submit these allegations of criminal violations by the President and Congress of the United States to the Supreme Court of the United States for a ruling and let us know of their decision.

71. House Joint Resolution 683 Implementing a United States Proposal for an Early Warning System in Sinai, October 9, 1975*

---

* H. J. Res. 683, 94th CONG., 1st SESS. (Oct. 9, 1975).

To implement the United States proposal for the early-warning system in Sinai.

Whereas an agreement signed on September 4, 1975, by the Government of the Arab Republic of Egypt and the Government of Israel may, when it enters into force, constitute a significant step toward peace in the Middle East;

Whereas the President of the United States on September 1, 1975, transmitted to the Government of the Arab Republic of Egypt and to the Government of Israel identical proposals for United States participation in an early-warning system, the text of which has been submitted to the Congress, providing for the assignment of no more than two hundred United States civilian personnel to carry out certain specified noncombat functions and setting forth the terms and conditions thereof;

Whereas that proposal would permit the Government of the United States to withdraw such personnel if it concludes that their safety is jeopardized or that continuation of their role is no longer necessary; and

Whereas the implementation of the United States proposal for the early-warning system in Sinai may enhance the prospect of compliance in good faith with the terms of the Egyptian-Israeli agreements and thereby promote the cause of peace: Now, therefore, be it

Resolved by the Senate and House of Representatives

of the United States of America in Congress assembled,

That the President is authorized to implement the "United

State Proposal for the Early-Warning System in Sinai":

Provided, however, That United States civilian personnel

assigned to Sinai under such proposal shall be removed im-

mediately in the event of an outbreak of hostilities between

Egypt and Israel or if the Congress by concurrent resolution

determines that the safety of such personnel is jeopardized

or that continuation of their role is no longer necessary.

Nothing contained in this resolution shall be construed as

granting any authority to the President with respect to the

introduction of United States Armed Forces into hostilities

or into situations wherein involvement in hostilities is clearly

indicated by the circumstances which authority he would not
have had in the absence of this joint resolution.

SEC. 2. Any concurrent resolution of the type described
in the first section of this resolution which is introduced in
either House of Congress shall be privileged in the same
manner and to the same extent as a concurrent resolution of
the type described in section 5(c) of Public Law 93-148
is privileged under section 7 of such law.

SEC. 3. The United States civilian personnel participating in the early-warning system in Sinai shall include only
individuals who have volunteered to participate in such
system.

SEC. 4. Whenever United States civilian personnel, pursuant to this resolution, participate in an early-warning system, the President shall, so long as the participation of such
personnel continues, submit written reports to the Congress
periodically, but no less frequently than once every six
months, on (1) the status, scope, and anticipated duration
of their participation, and (2) the feasibility of ending or
reducing as soon as possible their participation by substituting nationals of other countries or by making technological
changes. The appropriate committees of the Congress shall
promptly hold hearings on each report of the President and
report to the Congress any findings, conclusions, and
recommendations.

SEC. 5. The authority contained in this joint resolution
to implement the "United States Proposal for the Early
Warning System in Sinai" does not signify approval of the

Congress of any other agreement, understanding, or commitment made by the executive branch.

Passed the House of Representatives October 8, 1975.

Attest: W. PAT JENNINGS,
                                                    Clerk.

Passed the Senate October 9 (legislative day, September 11), 1975

Attest: FRANCIS R. VALEO,
                                                    Secretary.

72. Security Council Resolution 378 Concerning Settlement of the Middle East Problem, October 23, 1975*

* U.N. Doc. S/RES/378 (1975).

The Security Council,

Recalling its resolutions 338 (1973), 340 (1973), 341 (1973), 346 (1974), 362 (1974), 368 (1975) and 371 (1975),

Having considered the report of the Secretary-General on the United Nations Emergency Force (S/11849),

Having noted the developments in the situation in the Middle East,

Having further noted the Secretary-General's view that any relaxation of the search for a comprehensive settlement covering all aspects of the Middle East problem could be especially dangerous in the months to come and that it is his hope, therefore, that urgent efforts will be undertaken by all concerned to tackle the Middle East problem in all its aspects, with a view both to maintaining quiet in the region and to arriving at the comprehensive settlement called for by the Security Council in its resolution 338 (1973),

1. *Decides*

(a) To call upon all the parties concerned to implement immediately Security Council resolution 338 (1973);

(b) To renew the mandate of the United Nations Emergency Force for a period of one year, that is, until 24 October 1976;

(c) To request the Secretary-General to submit at the end of this period a report on the developments in the situation and the steps taken to implement Security Council resolution 338 (1973);

2. *Expresses its confidence* that the Force will be maintained with maximum efficiency and economy.

73. General Assembly Resolution 3375 (XXX) Calling for an Invitation to the Palestine Liberation Organization to Participate in Efforts for Peace in the Middle East, November 10, 1975*

* U.N. Doc. A/RES/3375 (XXX) (1975). See also "Statements by Ambassador Moynihan," 74 *Dept. of State Bulletin* 21-26 (1976).

The General Assembly,

Having considered the item entitled "Question of Palestine",

Reaffirming its resolution 3236 (XXIX) of 22 November 1974, in which it recognized the inalienable national rights of the Palestinian people,

Recognizing the necessity of achieving a just and lasting peace in the Middle East at the earliest possible time,

Believing that the realization of the inalienable rights of the Palestinian people in accordance with the purposes and principles of the Charter of the United Nations is a prerequisite to achieving a just and lasting peace in the area,

Convinced that the participation of the Palestinian people is essential in any efforts and deliberations aiming at the achievement of a just and lasting peace in the Middle East,

1. *Requests* the Security Council to consider and adopt the necessary resolutions and measures in order to enable the Palestinian people to exercise its inalienable national rights in accordance with General Assembly resolution 3236 (XXIX);

2. *Calls* for the invitation of the Palestine Liberation Organization, the representative of the Palestinian people, to participate in all efforts, deliberations and conferences on the Middle East which are held under the auspices of the United Nations, on an equal footing with other parties, on the basis of resolution 3236 (XXIX);

3. *Requests* the Secretary-General to inform the Co-Chairmen of the Peace Conference on the Middle East of the present resolution and to take all necessary steps to secure the invitation of the Palestine Liberation Organization to participate in the work of the Conference as well as in all other efforts for peace;

4. *Requests* the Secretary-General to submit a report on this matter to the General Assembly as soon as possible.

2399th plenary meeting
10 November 1975

74. General Assembly Resolution 3376 (XXX) Concerning the Question of Palestine, November 10, 1975*

* U.N. Doc. A/RES/3376 (XXX) (1975).

The General Assembly,

Recalling its resolution 3236 (XXIX) of 22 November 1974,

Taking note of the report of the Secretary-General on the implementation of that resolution,[1]

Deeply concerned that no just solution to the problem of Palestine has yet been achieved,

Recognizing that the problem of Palestine continues to endanger international peace and security,

1.   *Reaffirms* its resolution 3236 (XXIX);

2.   *Expresses its grave concern* that no progress has been achieved towards:

(*a*) The exercise by the Palestinian people of its inalienable rights in Palestine, including the right to self-determination without external interference and the right to national independence and sovereignty;

(*b*) The exercise by Palestinians of their inalienable right to return to their homes and property from which they have been displaced and uprooted;

3.   *Decides* to establish a Committee on the Exercise of the Inalienable Rights of the Palestinian People composed of twenty Member States to be appointed by the General Assembly at the current session;

4.   *Requests* the Committee to consider and recommend to the General Assembly a programme of implementation, designed to enable the Palestinian people to exercise the rights recognized in paragraphs 1 and 2 of Assembly resolution 3236 (XXIX), and to take into account, in the formulation of its recommendations for the implementation of that programme, all the powers conferred by the Charter upon the principal organs of the United Nations;

5.   *Authorizes* the Committee, in the fulfillment of its mandate, to establish contact with, and to receive and consider suggestions and proposals from, any State and intergovernmental regional organization and the Palestine Liberation Organization;

6.   *Requests* the Secretary-General to provide the Committee with all the necessary facilities for the performance of its tasks;

[1] A/10265.

7. *Requests* the Committee to submit its report and recommendations to the Secretary-General no later than 1 June 1976 and requests the Secretary-General to transmit the report to the Security Council;

8. *Requests* the Security Council to consider, as soon as possible after 1 June 1976, the question of the exercise by the Palestinian people of the inalienable rights recognized in paragraphs 1 and 2 of resolution 3236 (XXIX);

9. *Requests* the Secretary-General to inform the Committee of the action taken by the Security Council in accordance with paragraph 8 above;

10. *Authorizes* the Committee, taking into consideration the action taken by the Security Council, to submit to the General Assembly, at its thirty-first session, a report containing its observations and recommendations;

11. *Decides* to include the item entitled "Question of Palestine" in the provisional agenda of its thirty-first session.

2399th plenary meeting
10 November 1975

75. General Assembly Resolution 3379 (XXX) Determining that Zionism Is a Form of Racism, November 10, 1975*

* U.N. Doc. A/RES/3379 (XXX) (1975).

The General Assembly,

Recalling its resolution 1904 (XVIII) of 20 November 1963, proclaiming the United Nations Declaration on the Elimination of All Forms of Racial Discrimination, and in particular its affirmation that "any doctrine of racial differentiation or superiority is scientifically false, morally condemnable, socially unjust and dangerous" and its expression of alarm at "the manifestations of racial discrimination still in evidence in some areas in the world, some of which are imposed by certain Governments by means of legislative, administrative or other measures",

Recalling also that, in its resolution 3151 G (XXVIII) of 14 December 1973, the General Assembly condemned, *inter alia*, the unholy alliance between South African racism and zionism,

Taking note of the Declaration of Mexico on the Equality of Women and their Contribution to Development and Peace,[1] proclaimed by the World Conference of the International Women's Year, held at Mexico City from 19 June to 2 July 1975, which promulgated the principle that "international cooperation and peace require the achievement of national liberation and independence, the elimination of colonialism and neo-colonialism, foreign occupation, zionism, apartheid and racial discrimination in all its forms, as well as the recognition of the dignity of peoples and their right to self-determination",

Taking note also of resolution 77 (XII) adopted by the Assembly of Heads of State and Government of the Organization of African Unity at its twelfth ordinary session,[2] held at Kampala from 28 July to 1 August 1975, which considered "that the racist régime in occupied Palestine and the racist régimes in Zimbabwe and South Africa have a common imperialist origin, forming a whole and having the same racist structure and being organically linked in their policy aimed at repression of the dignity and integrity of the human being",

Taking note also of the Political Declaration and Strategy to Strengthen International Peace and Security and to Intensify Solidarity and Mutual Assistance among Non-Aligned Countries,[3] adopted at the Conference of ministers for Foreign Affairs of Non-Aligned Countries held at Lima from 25

[1] E/5725, part one, sect. I.
[2] See A/10297, annex II.
[3] A/10217 and Corr. 1, annex, p. 3.

to 30 August 1975, which most severely condemned zionism as a threat to world peace and security and called upon all countries to oppose this racist and imperialist ideology,

Determines that zionism is a form of racism and racial discrimination.

2400th plenary meeting
10 November 1975

76. Statement by Ambassador Daniel P. Moynihan, United States Representative to the United Nations, in Plenary, in Explanation of Vote on the Resolution Equating Zionism with Racism and Racial Discrimination, November 10, 1975*

* Press Release, U.S. Mission to the United Nations, USUN-141 (75) (November 10, 1975).

The United States rises to declare before the General Assembly of the United Nations, and before the world, that it does not acknowledge, it will not abide by, it will never acquiesce in this infamous act.

Not three weeks ago, the United States Representative in the Social, Humanitarian, and Cultural Committee pleaded in measured and fully considered terms for the United Nations not to do this thing. It was, he said, "obscene." It is something more today, for the furtiveness with which this obscenity first appeared among us has been replaced by a shameless openness.

There will be time enough to contemplate the harm this act will have done the United Nations. Historians will do that for us, and it is sufficient for the moment only to note one foreboding fact. A great evil has been loosed upon the world. The abomination of anti-semitism — as this year's Nobel Peace Laureate Andrei Sakharov observed in Moscow just a few days ago — the abomination of anti-semitism has been given the appearance of international sanction. The General Assembly today grants symbolic amnesty — and more — to the murderers of the six million European Jews. Evil enough in itself, but more ominous by far is the realization that now presses upon us — the realization that if there were no General Assembly, this could never have happened.

As this day will live in infamy, it behooves those who sought to avert it to declare their thoughts so that historians will know that we fought here, that we were not small in number — not this time — and that while we lost, we fought with full knowledge of what indeed would *be* lost.

Nor should any historian of the event, nor yet any who have participated in it, suppose that we have fought only as governments, as chancelleries, and on an issue well removed from the concerns of our respective peoples. Others will speak for their nations: I will speak for mine.

In all our postwar history there has not been another issue which has brought forth such unanimity of American opinion. The President of the United States has from the first been explicit: This must not happen. The Congress of the United States, in a measure unanimously adopted in the Senate and sponsored by 436 of 437 Representatives in the House, declared its utter opposition. Following only American Jews themselves, the American trade union movement was first to the fore in denouncing this infamous undertaking. Next, one after another, the great private institutions of American life pronounced anathema on this evil thing — and most particularly, the Christian churches have done so. Reminded that the United Nations was born in the struggle against just such abominations as we are committing today – the wartime alliance of the United Nations dates from 1942 – the United Nations Association of the United States has for the first time in its history appealed directly to each of the 141 other delegations in New York not to do this unspeakable thing.

The proposition to be sanctioned by a resolution of the General Assembly of the United Nations is that "Zionism is a form of racism and racial discrimination." Now this is a lie. But as it is a lie which the United Nations has now declared to be a truth, the actual truth must be restated.

The very first point to be made is that the United Nations has declared Zionism to be racism – without ever having defined racism. "Sentence first – verdict afterwards," as the Queen of Hearts said. But this is not wonderland, but a real world, where there are real consequences to folly and to venality. Just on Friday, the President of the General Assembly, speaking on behalf of Luxembourg, warned not only of the trouble which would follow from the adoption of this resolution but of its essential irresponsibility – for, he noted, members have wholly different ideas as to what they are condemning. "It seems to me," he said, and to his lasting honor he said it when there was still time, "It seems to me that before a body like this takes a decision they should agree very clearly on what they are approving or condemning, and it takes more time."

Lest I be unclear, the United Nations has in fact on several occasions defined "racial discrimination." The definitions have been loose, but recognizable. It is "racism," incomparably the more serious charge – racial discrimination is a practice; racism is a doctrine – which has never been defined. Indeed, the term has only recently appeared in United Nations General Assembly documents. The one occasion on which we know its meaning to have been discussed was the 1644th meeting of the Third Committee on December 16, 1968, in connection with the report of the Secretary-General on the status of the international convention on the elimination of all forms of racial discrimination. On that occasion – to give some feeling for the intellectual precision with which the matter was being treated – the question arose, as to what should be the relative positioning of the terms "racism" and "Nazism" in a number of the "preambular paragraphs." The distinguished delegate from Tunisia argued that "racism" should go first because "Nazism was merely a form of racism ....." Not so, said the no less distinguished delegate from the Union of Soviet Socialist Republics. For, he explained, "Nazism contained the main elements of racism within its ambit and should be mentioned first." This is to say that racism was merely a form of Nazism.

The discussion wound to its weary and inconclusive end, and we are left with nothing to guide us, for even this one discussion of "racism" confined itself to word orders in preambular paragraphs, and did not at all touch on the meaning of the words as such. Still, one cannot but ponder the situation we have made for ourselves in the context of the Soviet statement on that not so distant occasion. *If*, as the distinguished delegate declared, racism is a form of Nazism — and *if*, as this resolution declares, Zionism is a form of racism — *then* we have step by step taken ourselves to the point of proclaiming — the United Nations is solemnly proclaiming — that Zionism is a form of Nazism.

What we have here is a lie — a political lie of a variety well known to the twentieth century, and scarcely exceeded in all that annal of untruth and outrage. The lie is that Zionism is a form of racism. The overwhelmingly clear truth is that it is not.

The word "racism" is a creation of the English language, and relatively new to it. It is not, for instance, to be found in the Oxford English Dictionary. The term derives from relatively new doctrines — all of them discredited — concerning the human population of the world, to the effect that there are significant biological differences among clearly identifiable groups, and that these differences establish, in effect, different levels of humanity. Racism, as defined by Webster's Third New International Dictionary, is "The assumption that ... traits and capacities are determined by biological race and that races differ decisively from one another." It further involves "a belief in the inherent superiority of a particular race and its right to domination over others."

This meaning is clear. It is equally clear that this assumption, this belief, has always been altogether alien to the political and religious movement known as Zionism. As a strictly political movement, Zionism was established only in 1897, although there is a clearly legitimate sense in which its origins are indeed ancient. For example many branches of Christianity have always held that from the standpoint of the biblical prophets, Israel would be reborn one day. But the modern Zionist movement arose in Europe in the context of a general upsurge of national consciousness and aspiration that overtook most other people of Central and Eastern Europe after 1848, and that in time spread to all of Africa and Asia. It was, to those persons of the Jewish religion, a Jewish form of what today is called a national liberation movement. Probably a majority of those persons who became active Zionists and sought to emigrate to Palestine were born within the confines of Czarist Russia, and it was only natural for Soviet Foreign Minister Andrei Gromyko to deplore, as he did in 1948, in the 299th meeting of the Security Council, the act by Israel's neighbors of "sending their troops into Palestine and carrying out military operations aimed" — in Mr. Gromyko's words — "at the supression of the national liberation movement in Palestine."

Now it was the singular nature — if I am not mistaken, it was the unique nature — of this national liberation movement that in contrast with the movements that preceded it, those of that time, and those that have come since, it defined its members in terms not of birth, but of belief. That is to say, it was not a movement of the Irish to free Ireland, or of the Polish to free Poland, not a movement of Algerians to free Algeria, nor of Indians to free India. It was not a movement of persons connected by historic membership in a genetic pool of the kind that enables us to speak loosely but not meaninglessly, say, of the Chinese people, nor yet of diverse groups occupying the same territory which enables us to speak of the American people with no greater indignity to truth. To the contrary, Zionists defined themselves merely as Jews, and declared to be Jewish anyone born of a Jewish mother or — and this is the absolutely crucial fact — anyone who converted to Judaism. Which is to say, in the terms of the International Convention on the Elimination of All Forms of Racial Discrimination, adopted by the 20th General Assembly, anyone — regardless of "race, colour, descent, or national or ethnic origin...."

The State of Israel, which in time was the creation of the Zionist Movement, has been extraordinary in nothing so much as the range of "racial stocks" from which it has drawn its citizenry. There are black Jews, brown Jews, white Jews, Jews from the Orient and Jews from the West. Most such persons could be said to have been "born" Jews, just as most Presbyterians and most Hindus are "born" to their faith, but there are many Jews who are converts. With a consistency in the matter which surely attests to the importance of this issue to that religious and political culture, Israeli courts have held that a Jew who converts to another religion is no longer a Jew. In the meantime the population of Israel also includes large numbers of non-Jews, among them Arabs of both the Muslim and Christian religions and Christians of other national origins. Many of these persons are citizens of Israel, and those who are not can become citizens by legal procedures very much like those which obtain in a typical nation of Western Europe.

Now I should wish to be understood that I am here making one point, and one point only, which is that whatever else Zionism may be, it is not and cannot be "a form of racism." In logic, the State of Israel could be, or could become, many things, theoretically including many things undesirable, but it could not be and could not become racist unless it ceased to be Zionist.

Indeed, the idea that Jews *are* a "race" was invented not by Jews but by those who hated Jews. The idea of Jews as a race was invented by nineteenth century anti-semites such as Houston Steward Chamberlain and Edouard Drumont, who saw that in an increasingly secular age, which is to say an age which made for fewer distinctions between people, the old religious grounds for anti-semitism were losing force. New justifications were needed for excluding and persecuting Jews, and so the new idea of Jews as a race — rather than as a religion — was born. It was a contemptible idea at the beginning, and no civilized person would be associated with it. To think that it is an idea now endorsed by the United Nations is to reflect on what civilization has come to.

It is precisely a concern for civilization, for civilized values that are or should be precious to all mankind, that arouses us at this moment to such special passion. What we have at stake here is not merely the honor and the legitimacy of the State of Israel — although a challenge to the legitimacy of any member nation ought always to arouse the vigilance of all members of the United Nations. For a yet more important matter is at issue, which is the integrity of that whole body of moral and legal precepts which we know as human rights.

The terrible lie that has been told here today will have terrible consequences. Not only will people begin to say, indeed they have already begun to say, that the United Nations is a place where lies are told, but far more serious, grave and perhaps irreparable harm will be done to the cause of human rights itself. The harm will arise first because it will strip from racism the precise and abhorrent meaning that it still precariously holds today. How will the peoples of the world feel about racism, and about the need to struggle against it, when they are told that it is an idea so broad as to include the Jewish national liberation movement?

As this lie spreads, it will do harm in a second way. Many of the members of the United Nations owe their independence in no small part to the notion of human rights, as it has spread from the domestic sphere to the international sphere and exercised its influence over the old colonial powers. We are now coming into a time when that independence is likely to be threatened again. There will be new forces, some of them arising now, new prophets and new despots, who will justify their actions with the help of just such distortions of words as we have sanctioned here today. Today we have drained the word "racism" of its meaning. Tomorrow, terms like "national self-determination" and "national honor" will be perverted in the same way to serve the purposes of conquest and exploitation. And when these claims begin to be made — as they already have begun to be made — it is the small nations of the world whose integrity will suffer. And how will the small nations of the world defend themselves, on what grounds will others be moved to defend and protect them, when the language of human rights, the only language by which the small can be defended, is no longer believed and no longer has a power of its own?

There is this danger, and then a final danger that is the most serious of all. Which is that the damage we now do to the idea of human rights and the language of human rights could well be irreversible.

The idea of human rights as we know it today is not an idea which has always existed in human affairs. It is an idea which appeared at a specific time in the world, and under very special circumstances. It appeared when European philosophers of the seventeenth century began to argue that man was a being whose existence was independent from that of the State, that he need join a political community only if he did not lose by that association more than he gained. From this very specific political philosophy stemmed the idea of political rights, of claims that the individual could justly make against the State; it was because the individual was seen as so separate from the State that he could make legitimate demands upon it.

That was the philosophy from which the idea of domestic and international rights sprang. But most of the world does not hold with that philosophy now. Most of the world believes in newer modes of political thought, in philosophies that do not accept the individual as distinct from and prior to the State, in philosophies that therefore do not provide any justification for the idea of human rights and philosophies that have no words by which to explain their value. If we destroy the words that were given to us by past centuries, we will not have words to replace them, for philosophy today has no such words.

But there are those of us who have not forsaken these older words, still so new to much of the world. Not forsaken them now, not here, not anywhere, not ever.

The United States of America declares that it does not acknowledge, it will not abide by, it will never acquiesce in this infamous act.

77. Senate Concurrent Resolution 73 Condemning General Assembly Resolution 3379 (XXX), November 11, 1975*

---

* S. Con. Res. 73, 94th CONG., 1st SESS. (Nov. 11, 1975). See also S. Res. 288, 94th CONG., 1st SESS. (Oct. 28, 1975).

Whereas the United States, as a founder of the United Nations Organization, has a fundamental interest in promoting the purposes and principles for which that organization was created; and

Whereas in Article 1 of the Charter of the United Nations the stated purpose of the United Nations include:

"To achieve international cooperation in solving international problems of an economic, social, cultural, or humanitarian character, and in promoting and encouraging respect for human rights and for fundamental freedoms for all without distinction as to race, sex, language, or religion;" and

Whereas the General Assembly of the United Nations decided to launch on December 10, 1973, a Decade of Action to Combat Racism and Racial Discrimination and a program of action which the United States supported and in which it desires to participate; and

Whereas the United Nations General Assembly on November 10, 1975, adopted a resolution which describes Zionism as a form of racism, thereby identifying it as a target of the Decade for Action to Combat Racism and Discrimination; and

Whereas the extension of the program of the Decade to include a campaign against Zionism brings the United Nations to a point of encouraging anti-Semitism, one of the oldest and most virulent forms of racism known to human history: Now, therefore, be it

Resolved by the Senate (the House of Representatives concurring), That the Congress sharply condemns the resolution adopted by the General Assembly on November 10, 1975, in that said resolution encourages anti-Semitism by wrongly associating and equating Zionism with racism and racial discrimination, thereby contradicting a fundamental purpose of the United Nations Charter; and be it

Resolved, That the Congress strongly opposes any form of participation by the United States Government in the Decade for Action to Combat Racism and Racial Discrimination so long as that Decade and program remain distorted

and compromised by the aforementioned resolution naming
Zionism as one of the targets of that struggle; and be it

Resolved, That the Congress calls for an energetic effort
by all those concerned with the adherence of the United
Nations to the purposes stated in its charter to obtain reconsideration of the aforementioned resolution with a view to
removing the subject of Zionism, which is a national but in
no way a racist philosophy, from the context of any programs
and discussions focusing on racism or racial discrimination;
and be it further

Resolved, That the Committee on Foreign Relations and
the Committee on International Relations begin hearings
immediately to reassess the United States' further participation in the United Nations General Assembly.

78. General Assembly Resolution 3414 (XXX) Concerning the Situation in the Middle East, December 5, 1975*

* U.N. Doc. A/RES/3414 (XXX) (1975). See also "Statement by Ambassador Bennett," 74 *Dept. of State Bulletin* 26-28 (1976).

The General Assemby,

Having considered the item entitled "The situation in the Middle East",

Guided by the purposes and principles of the Charter of the United Nations and resolutions of the United Nations as well as those principles of international law which prohibit the occupation or acquisition of territory by the use of force and which consider any military occupation, however temporary, or any forcible annexation of such territory, or part thereof, as an act of aggression,

Gravely concerned at the continuation of the Israeli occupation of Arab territories and Israel's persistent denial of the inalienable national rights of the Palestinian people,

Recalling relevant resolutions of the General Assembly and the Security Council, particularly those concerning the inalienable national rights of the Palestinian people and its right to participate in any efforts for peace,

Convinced that the early reconvening of the Peace Conference on the Middle East with the participation of all the parties concerned, including the Palestine Liberation Organization, is essential for the realization of a just and lasting settlement in the region,

Convinced that the present situation prevailing in the Middle East continues to constitute a serious threat to international peace and security, and that urgent measures should be taken in order to ensure Israel's full compliance with relevant resolutions of the General Assembly and the Security Council on the questions of Palestine and the Middle East,

Recognizing that peace is indivisible and that a just and lasting settlement of the question of the Middle East must be based on a comprehensive solution under the auspices of the United Nations, which takes into consideration all aspects of the Middle East conflict, including, in particular, the enjoyment by the Palestinian people of its inalienable national rights, as well as the total withdrawal from all the Arab territories occupied since June 1967,

1. *Reaffirms* that the acquisition of territory by force is inadmissible and therefore all territories thus occupied must be returned;

2. *Condemns* Israel's continued occupation of Arab territories in violation of the Charter of the United Nations, the principles of international law and repeated United Nations resolutions;

3. *Requests* all States to desist from supplying Israel with any military or economic aid as long as it continues to occupy Arab territories and deny the inalienable national rights of the Palestinian people;

4. *Requests* the Security Council, in the exercise of its responsibilities under the Charter, to take all necessary measures for the speedy implementation, according to an appropriate time-table, of all relevant resolutions of the General Assembly and the Security Council aiming at the establishment of a just and lasting peace in the region through a comprehensive settlement, worked out with the participation of all parties concerned, including the Palestine Liberation Organization, and within the framework of the United Nations, which ensures complete Israeli withdrawal from all the occupied Arab territories as well as full recognition of the inalienable national rights of the Palestinian people and the attainment of those rights;

5. *Requests* the Secretary-General to inform all concerned, including the Co-Chairmen of the Peace Conference on the Middle East, and to follow up the implementation of the present resolution and report thereon to the Security Council and to the General Assembly at its thirty-first session.

2429th plenary meeting
5 December 1975

Contributors

M. CHERIF BASSIOUNI, Professor of Law, De Paul University College of Law.

ALBERT P. BLAUSTEIN, Professor of Law, Rutgers University, Camden.

JOHN C. CAMPBELL, Senior Fellow, Council on Foreign Relations.

HENRY CATTAN, Barrister-at-Law of the Middle Temple; formerly member of the Palestine Bar and the Palestine Law Council and Delegate of the Palestine Arabs at the United Nations.

SIR COLIN T. CROWE, Permanent Representative of the United Kingdom to the United Nations.

YORAM DINSTEIN, Senior Lecturer in Law, Tel Aviv University; formerly Consul of Israel in New York.

SIR ALEC DOUGLAS-HOME, The United Kingdom Secretary of State for Foreign and Commonwealth Affairs.

MUHAMMAD H. EL-FARRA, Ambassador Extraordinary and Plenipotentiary, Permanent Representative of the Hashemite Kingdom of Jordan to the United Nations.

NATHAN FEINBERG, Professor Emeritus of International Law and Relations, Hebrew University of Jerusalem.

NAHUM GOLDMANN, President of the World Jewish Congress.

M. BURHAN W. HAMMAD, Deputy Permanent Observer of the League of Arab States to the United Nations; formerly Senior Adviser to the Permanent Mission of the Hashemite Kingdom of Jordan to the United Nations.

MICHAEL HARBOTTLE, Visiting Senior Lecturer at the School of Peace Studies, University of Bradford, England; formerly Chief of Staff of the United Nations Force in Cyprus.

JOHN LAWRENCE HARGROVE, Director of Studies, The American Society of International Law; formerly Senior Adviser for International Law, United States Mission to the United Nations.

Y. HARKABI, Lecturer in International Affairs, Hebrew University of Jerusalem; formerly Brigadier General and Head of the Strategic Research Department of the Ministry of Defense of Israel.

ROSALYN HIGGINS, Specialist on International Law and United Nations Affairs, The Royal Institute of International Affairs.

STANLEY HOFFMANN, Professor of Government, Harvard University.

LOUISE W. HOLBORN, Professor of Government, Radcliffe Institute.

HIS MAJESTY, KING IBN TALAL HUSSEIN, King of the Hashemite Kingdom of Jordan.

GUNNAR V. JARRING, Swedish Ambassador to the Soviet Union and Special Representative of the Secretary-General to the Middle East.

D. H. N. JOHNSON, Professor of International and Air Law, The University of London.

S. SHEPARD JONES, Burton Craige Professor of Political Science, The University of North Carolina.

MORTON A. KAPLAN, Professor of Political Science, Chairman of the Committee on International Relations, and Director of the Faculty Arms Control and Foreign Policy Seminar, The University of Chicago.

MAJID KHADDURI, Director of the Center for Middle East Studies, and Professor, The School of Advanced International Studies, The Johns Hopkins University.

HENRY KISSINGER, Secretary of State of the United States.

ARTHUR LALL, Professor of International Relations, Columbia School of International Affairs.

JOHN NORTON MOORE, Professor of Law and Director of the Graduate Program, The University of Virginia School of Law. On leave since 1972 as The Counselor on International Law to the Department of State (1972-73) and Chairman of the National Security Council Interagency Task Force on the Law of the Sea and Deputy Special Representative of the President for the Law of the Sea Conference with rank of Ambassador (1973-   ).

ISSA NAKHLEH, Permanent Representative of the Arab Higher Committee for Palestine in New York and Chairman of the Palestine Arab Delegation.

JORDAN J. PAUST, Associate Professor of Law, University of Houston School of Law.

DON PERETZ, Professor of Political Science and Director of the Southwest Asian and North African Program, State University of New York at Binghamton.

RICHARD H. PFAFF, Associate Professor of Political Science, The University of Colorado.

YEVGENY PRIMAKOV, reporter for *Pravda* and author and commentator on the Arab-Israeli conflict.

NIGEL S. RODLEY, Research Fellow, The New York University Center for International Studies and Visiting Lecturer of Political Science, The Graduate Faculty of the New School; formerly Associate Economic Affairs Officer, United Nations.

WILLIAM P. ROGERS, former Secretary of State of the United States.

SHABTAI ROSENNE, Ambassador, Permanent Representative of Israel to the United Nations Office in Geneva; formerly Legal Adviser to the Israel Ministry for Foreign Affairs.

EUGENE V. ROSTOW, Sterling Professor of Law and Public Affairs, Yale University; formerly Under Secretary of State for Political Affairs, United States Department of State.

NADAV SAFRAN, Professor of Government, Harvard University.

CARL F. SALANS, Deputy Legal Adviser, United States Department of State.

STEPHEN M. SCHWEBEL, Executive Vice President of the American Society of International Law and Professor of International Law at the School of Advanced International Studies, The Johns Hopkins University; formerly Assistant Legal Adviser of the United States Department of State.

MEIR SHAMGAR, Attorney General of Israel.

IBRAHIM F. I. SHIHATA, Legal Advisor, Kuwait Fund for Arab Economic Development.

JOSEPH J. SISCO, Under Secretary of State for Political Affairs, United States Department of State.

JULIUS STONE, Challis Professor of International Law and Jurisprudence, The University of Sydney.

GEORGE J. TOMEH, Ambassador Extraordinary and Plenipotentiary, Permanent Representative of the Syrian Arab Republic to the United Nations.

U THANT, Secretary-General of the United Nations.

QUINCY WRIGHT, Professor Emeritus of International Law, The University of Chicago; formerly President of the American Society of International Law.

CHARLES W. YOST, Senior Fellow on the permanent staff of the Council on Foreign Relations; formerly United States Representative to the United Nations.

Permissions

HENRY CATTAN, "Sovereignty over Palestine," reprinted with the permission of the author and publisher, the Longman Group Limited, from HENRY CATTAN, PALESTINE, THE ARABS & ISRAEL 242-75, Appendix XI (1969).

NATHAN FEINBERG, "The Question of Sovereignty over Palestine," reprinted with the permission of the author and publisher from NATHAN FEINBERG, ON AN ARAB JURIST'S APPROACH TO ZIONISM AND THE STATE OF ISRAEL 7-34 (1971).

DON PERETZ, "Arab Palestine: Phoenix or Phantom?," reprinted with the permission of the author and publisher from *Foreign Affairs*, Vol. 48, 1970, pp. 322-33. Copyright by the Council on Foreign Relations, Inc., New York, New York.

Y. HARKABI, "The Position of the Palestinians in the Israeli-Arab Conflict and Their National Covenant (1968)," reprinted with the permission of the author and publisher from *New York University Journal of International Law & Politics*, Vol. 3, 1970, pp. 209-44.

ISSA NAKHLEH, "The Liberation of Palestine Is Supported by International Law and Justice," reprinted with the permission of the author and publisher from ISSA NAKHLEH, THE LIBERATION OF PALESTINE IS SUPPORTED BY INTERNATIONAL LAW AND JUSTICE (Pamphlet published by the Palestine Arab Delegation, 2nd edn., March 1969), 3-17.

JULIUS STONE, "Peace and the Palestinians," reprinted with the permission of the author and publisher from *New York University Journal of International Law & Politics*, Vol. 3, 1970, pp. 247-62. (A longer but less documented account is Julius Stone, "Self-Determination and the Palestinian Arabs," *The Bridge*, Dec. 1970, pp. 3-14.)

LOUISE W. HOLBORN, "The Palestine Arab Refugee Problem," reprinted with the permission of the author and publisher from *International Journal*, Vol. 23, 1968, pp. 82-96.

GEORGE J. TOMEH, "Legal Status of Arab Refugees," reprinted with the permission of the author and publisher from *Law and Contemporary Problems*, Vol. 33, 1968, pp. 110-24.

*Permissions are listed to correspond to the sequence of the materials included in this volume.

WILLIAM P. ROGERS, "A Lasting Peace in the Middle East: An American View," reprinted with the permission of the author from *Department of State Bulletin*, Vol. 62, Jan. 5, 1970, pp. 7-11 (an address by Secretary of State Rogers before the 1969 Galaxy Conference on Adult Education at Washington, D. C., on December 9, 1969).

WILLIAM P. ROGERS, "A Legacy of Peace: Our Responsibility to Future Generations" (excerpt from an address by Secretary of State William P. Rogers before the 26th session of the U.N. General Assembly on October 4, 1971), reprinted from *Department of State Bulletin*, Vol. 65, 1971, p. 437, at 442-44.

NEW YORK TIMES, "Soviet Proposal on the Middle East: December 30, 1968," reprinted with the permission of the publisher from *N. Y. Times*, January 11, 1969, at 2, col. 4. Copyright 1968 by the New York Times Company.

YEVGENY PRIMAKOV, "Soviet Proposals," reprinted with the permission of *Pravda* from *Survival*, Vol. 13, #1, Jan. 1971, pp. 19-22.(This is a slightly abridged version of an article originally published in *Pravda* [Moscow] on October 15, 1970.)

FATEH, "Toward a Democratic Palestine," reprinted with the permission of the publisher from *Fateh*, Vol. 1, No. 6, 1970. Also reprinted in *The Arab World*, Vol. 16, Nos. 5 & 6, May-June 1970, pp. 30-32; and in *Arab Views*, Vol. 16, No. 2, Feb. 1970, pp. 4-6. Copyright 1970 by Fateh, Beirut, Lebanon.

MEMORANDUM SUBMITTED TO THE BIG POWERS AND THE SECRETARY-GENERAL OF THE UNITED NATIONS BY THE REPRESENTATIVE OF THE ARAB HIGHER COMMITTEE FOR PALESTINE, press release of August 13, 1970, reprinted with the permission of the Palestine Arab Delegation, New York, New York.

SIR ALEC DOUGLAS-HOME, "Extract from a Statement delivered to the Yorkshire Area Council of the British Conservative Party at Harrogate on Saturday, October 31, 1970," reprinted with the permission of the author from Information Release #79, The United Kingdom Mission to the United Nations, November 2, 1970.

SIR COLIN CROWE, "Statement by the United Kingdom Permanent Representative in the General Assembly on November 2, 1970," reprinted with the permission of the author from Information Release #80, The United Kingdom Mission to the United Nations, November 2, 1970.

His Majesty, King ibn Talal Hussein, "Address to Jordanian and Palestinian Dignitaries on March 15, 1972, Concerning Basic Principles of a Plan to Establish a United Arab Kingdom of Palestine and Jordan," reprinted with the permission of the author from a copy supplied by the Personal Secretary to His Majesty.

Joseph J. Sisco, "The Current Situation in the Middle East" (address before the National Foreign Policy Conference for Editors and Broadcasters at the Department of State on March 29, 1973), reprinted from *Department of State Bulletin*, Vol. 68, 1973, pp. 484-87.

Stanley Hoffmann, "A New Policy for Israel," reprinted with the permission of the author and publisher from *Foreign Affairs*, Vol. 53, 1975, pp. 405-31. Copyright 1975 by the Council on Foreign Relations, Inc., New York, New York.

M. Cherif Bassiouni and Morton A. Kaplan, "A Mideast Proposal," reprinted with the permission of the authors and publisher from Faculty Arms Control and Foreign Policy Seminar, The University of Chicago, May 20, 1975.

Department of State, "The Arab-Israeli Dispute," reprinted from United States Foreign Policy: An Overview, January 1976, pp. 29-31.

Henry A. Kissinger, "Israel and the United States," reprinted from Department of State pamphlet, April 4, 1976.

The Sykes-Picot Agreement, May 16, 1916, reprinted with the permission of Her Majesty's Stationery Office.

The Balfour Declaration, November 2, 1917, reprinted with the permission of the British Museum.

The Anglo-French Declaration of November 7, 1918, reprinted with the permission of Her Majesty's Stationery Office.

Speech by President Nasser on Closing of the Gulf of Aqaba, May 22, 1967, reprinted with the permission of *The New York Times*. Copyright 1967 by the New York Times Company.

AIDE MÉMOIRE BY SECRETARY-GENERAL DAG HAMMARSKJOLD ON CONDITIONS GOVERNING WITHDRAWAL OF UNEF, DATED AUGUST 5, 1957 AND MADE PUBLIC ON JUNE 12, 1967, reprinted with the permission of *International Legal Materials*.

STATEMENT OF SECRETARY-GENERAL U THANT ON THE HAMMARSKJOLD AIDE MÉMOIRE, JUNE 19, 1967, reprinted with the permission of *The New York Times*. Copyright 1967 by The New York Times Company.

SUMMARY OF RESOLUTION OF ARAB SUMMIT CONFERENCE, KHARTOUM, SUDAN, SEPTEMBER 1, 1967, reprinted with the permission of *Arab News and Views*. Permission has also been obtained from *The New York University Journal of International Law and Politics*.

THE PALESTINIAN NATIONAL CHARTER OF 1968, reprinted with the permission of the Palestine Liberation Organization Research Center.

STATEMENT BY THE GOVERNMENT OF ISRAEL CONCERNING SECURITY COUNCIL RESOLUTION 298, SEPTEMBER 26, 1971, reprinted with the permission of the Permanent Mission of Israel to the United Nations.

SELECTED BIBLIOGRAPHY ON
THE ARAB-ISRAELI CONFLICT AND
INTERNATIONAL LAW

prepared by
Mrs. Helen Philos
Librarian of the American Society
of International Law

I. *General Background and Context*

A. HISTORICAL SETTING

Bentwich, Norman D. ENGLAND IN PALESTINE. London, Kegan Paul, 1932. 358

Esco Foundation for Palestine, Inc. PALESTINE: A STUDY OF JEWISH, ARAB AND BRITISH POLICIES. New Haven, Yale University Press, 1947. 2 vols.

Feinberg, Nathan. SOME PROBLEMS OF THE PALESTINE MANDATE. Tel Aviv, Shoshani, 1936. 125 p.

Finch, George A. "Post-mortem on the Suez debacle," 51 *AJIL*, 376 (1957)

Gellner, Charles R. THE PALESTINE PROBLEM: AN ANALYSIS, HISTORICAL AND CONTEMPORARY. Washington, Library of Congress, Legislative Reference Service, Public Affairs Bulletin No. 50, 1947. 188 p.

Hadawi, Sami. BITTER HARVEST: PALESTINE BETWEEN 1914-1967. New York, New World Press, 1967.

Halpern, Ben. "The drafting of the Balfour Declaration," 7 *Herzl Year Book* 255 (1971).

Hurewitz, Jacob C. THE STRUGGLE FOR PALESTINE. New York, Norton, 1950. 404 p.

Hyamson, Albert M. PALESTINE UNDER THE MANDATE, 1920-1948. London, Methuen, 1950. 210 p.

Israel. Office of Information. ISRAEL'S STRUGGLE FOR PEACE. New York, 1960. 187 p.

Khalidi, Walid, ed. FROM HAVEN TO CONQUEST: READINGS IN ZIONISM AND THE PALESTINE PROBLEM UNTIL 1948. Beirut, Institute for Palestine Studies, 1971. 839 p.

Kimche, Jon, and David Kimche. A CLASH OF DESTINIES: THE ARAB-JEWISH WAR AND THE FOUNDING OF THE STATE OF ISRAEL. New York, Praeger, 1960. 287 p.

Kirk, G. E. A SHORT HISTORY OF THE MIDDLE EAST FROM THE RISE OF ISLAM TO MODERN TIMES. London, Methuen, 1966.

Lenczowski, George. THE MIDDLE EAST IN WORLD AFFAIRS. Ithaca, Cornell University Press, 1952.

Leonard, Leonard L. "The United Nations and Palestine," 454 *International Conciliation* 603 (1949).

Lorch, N. THE EDGE OF THE SWORD: ISRAEL'S WAR OF INDEPENDENCE, 1947-1949. New York, Putnam, 1961. 475 p.

Lumer, H. "On the origins of the State of Israel," 49 *Political Affairs* 52 (1970)

Neher-Bernheim, Renée. "Fronteres du Sinai: Un siecle de diplomatie au Moyen-Orient 1940-1948," 36 *Politique etrangere* 147 (1971)

Parkes, James W. A HISTORY OF PALESTINE FROM 135 A.D. TO MODERN TIMES. New York, Oxford University Press, 1949. 391 p.

Rose, Norman. "The debate on partition, 1937 - 38: the Anglo-Zionist aspect. I. The proposal," 6 *Middle Eastern Studies* 297 (1970). "II. The withdrawal," 7 *Middle Eastern Studies* 3 (1971)

Rosenne, Shabtai. ISRAEL'S ARMISTICE AGREMENTS WITH THE ARAB STATES: A JURIDICAL INTERPRETATION. Tel Aviv, Published for Israel Branch, International Law Association, by Blumstein's Bookstores, 1951. 98 p.

Royal Institute of International Affairs. GREAT BRITAIN AND PALESTINE 1915-1945. London, Oxford University Press, 1946.

Sakran, F. C. PALESTINE DILEMMA: ARAB RIGHTS VERSUS ZIONIST ASPIRATIONS. Washington, Public Affairs Press, 1948.

Wright, Quincy. "Intervention, 1956," 51 *AJIL* 257 (1957)

B. INTERNATIONAL AND POLITICAL SETTING

1. GENERAL

Bloomfield, L. P. "The United States, the Soviet Union, and the prospects for peacekeeping," 24 *International Organization* 548 (1970)

Carlson, Sevinc. "The explosion of a myth: China, the Soviet Union and the Middle East," No. 27 *New Middle East* 32 (Dec. 1970)

Draper, Theodore. "Israel and world politics," *Commentary* 19 (Aug. 1967)

Giniewski, Paul. "La politique européenne et américaine d'Israël," 36 *Politique Étrangère* 69 (1971)

Hurewitz, J. C. DIPLOMACY IN THE NEAR AND MIDDLE EAST. Princeton, N.J., Van Nostrand, 1956. 2 vols.

Kent, George. "Foreign policy analysis: Middle East," 14 *Papers of the Peace Research Society* 95 (1970)

Kimche, Jon. THE SECOND ARAB AWAKENING. New York, Holt. Rinehart & Winston, 1970. 288 p.

Lavergne, B. "Le problème d'Israel et l'iniquite des grandes puissances," 43 *L'Année politique et économique* 388 (1970)

Lewis, Bernard. "The great powers, the Arabs and the Israelis," 47 *Foreign Affairs* 642 (1968)

Newcombe, Hanna. "The case for an arms embargo," 11 *War/Peace Report* 17 (1971)

Rafael, Gideon. "The role of the two super-powers in the Middle East," *In* ISRAEL YEARBOOK, 1971. Tel Aviv, Israel Yearbook Publications, 1971, pp. 59-62.

Rostow, Eugene V. "The Middle Eastern crisis in the perspective of world politics," 47 *International Affairs* (London) 275 (1971)

2. SOVIET POLICY

Alexeyev, V., and V. Ivanov. "Zionism at the service of imperialism," No. 6 *International Affairs* (Moscow) 57 (1970)

Cottrell, Alvin J. "The Soviet Union in the Middle East," 14 *Orbis* 588 (1970)

Cox, Frederick J. "The Russian presence in Egypt," 22 *Naval War College Review* 44 (1969-70)

Curtis, Michael. "Soviet-American relations and the Middle East crisis," 15 *Orbis* 403 (1971)

Dmitriev, Y. "The Arab world and Israel's aggression," No. 9 *International Affairs* (Moscow) 20 (1970)

Forsythe, David P. "The Soviets and the Arab-Israeli conflict," 134 *World Affairs* 132 (1971)

Guriel, Boris. "The Mediterranean in Soviet strategic thinking; gateway to the Atlantic," No. 26 *New Middle East* 20 (Nov. 1970)

Kompansev, I. "The Soviet Union and the Middle East crisis," 23 *Pakistan Horizon* 287 (1970)

Laptev, V., and V. Alexeyev. "The Middle East: time for decision," No. 3 *International Affairs* (Moscow) 42 (March 1971)

Lindner, Robert. "Die Sowjetunion in Nahost. Politische Taktik und tatsächlichen Einfluss," 21 *Osteuropa* 305 (1971)

Shwadran, Benjamin. "The Soviet role in the Middle East crisis," 60 *Current History* 1 (1971)

Tolley, Rear Adm. Kemp. "The bear that swims like a fish," 97 *U.S. Naval Institute Proceedings* 41 (1971)

Touma, Emile. "The assault detachment of world Zionism and imperialism," No. 5 *International Affairs* (Moscow) 60 (1971)

U.S.S.R. Embassy, Washington, D.C. "Middle East peace plan," press release, Oct. 1970.

Zoppo, Ciro. "Soviet ships in the Mediterranean and the U.S.-Soviet confrontation in the Middle East," 14 *Orbis* 109 (1970)

3. UNITED STATES POLICY

Campbell, John C. "The Arab-Israeli conflict: an American policy," 49 *Foreign Affairs* 51 (1970-71)

Hart, P. "An American policy toward the Middle East," 390 *Annals of the American Academy of Political and Social Science* 98 (July 1970)

Johnson, Lyndon B. "Principles for peace in the Middle East," 57 *Department of State Bulletin* 31 (July 10, 1967)

Madadi, Hamid. "United States involvement in Middle East politics," 23 *Pakistan Horizon* 293 (1970)

Nixon, Richard. "U.S. foreign policy for the 1970's; building for peace. A report to Congress," 64 *Department of State Bulletin* 389 (March 22, 1971)

Reich, Bernard. "United States policy in the Middle East," 60 *Current History* 1 (1971)

Rogers, William P. "A legacy of peace: our responsibility to future generations," 65 *Department of State Bulletin* 437 (Oct. 25, 1971)

Sisco, Joseph J. "The fluid and evolving situation in the Middle East," 63 *Department of State Bulletin* 748 (Dec. 21, 1970)

Yost, Charles. "U.S. gives views in U.N. General Assembly debate on the situation in the Middle East," 63 *Department of State Bulletin* 656 (Nov. 23, 1970)

4. *OTHER COUNTRIES*

Buzzard, Sir Anthony. "Israel, the Arabs, and British responsibilities," 27 *World Affairs* 310 (1971)

Deutschkron, Inge. BONN AND JERUSALEM: THE STRANGE COALITION. Philadelphia, Chilton Book Co., 1970. 357 p.

Heradstveit, Daniel. "Norwegian policy in the Middle East crisis of 1967," 6 *Cooperation and Conflict* 1 (1971)

Japhet, M. D., and P. K. Rajiv. THE ARAB-ISRAEL CONFLICT: AN INDIAN POINT OF VIEW. Bombay, Pearl Publications, 1967.

"Notes on Israel," NONALIGNED THIRD WORLD ANNUAL, 1970. St. Louis, Mo., Books International of DH-TE International, 1971.

Radovanović, Ljubomir. "The question of Palestine," No. 502 *Review of International Affairs* (March 5, 1971)

Roughton, R. A. "Algeria and the June 1967 Arab-Israeli War," 23 *Middle East Journal* 433 (1969)

C. GENERAL

Abu-Lughod, Ibrahim. THE TRANSFORMATION OF PALESTINE: ESSAYS ON THE ORIGIN AND DEVELOPMENT OF THE ARAB-ISRAELI CONFLICT. Evanston, Ill., Northwestern University Press, 1971. 544 p.

"The Arab-Israeli conflict," 7 *Trans-Action* (Special issue, July-Aug. 1970)

Bassiouni, M. Cherif. "The Middle East: the misunderstood conflict," 19 *Kansas Law Review* 373 (1971)

Cattan, Henry. PALESTINE, THE ARABS AND ISRAEL: THE SEARCH FOR JUSTICE. London, Longman, 1969. 281 p.

"Christian faith and the Palestine problem," 46 *Middle East Forum* 63 (1970)

"The coming decade in the Middle East—a symposium," 3 *Interplay* 8 (1970)

Davis, John H. THE EVASIVE PEACE. London, John Murray, 1968.

Dodd, C. H., and Mary Sales, eds. ISRAEL AND THE ARAB WORLD. London, Routledge and Kegan Paul, 1970. 233 p.

Elkordy, Abdul-Hafez M. CRISIS OF DIPLOMACY: THE THREE WARS AND AFTER. San Antonio, Texas, Naylor, 1971. 296 p.

Ellis, H. B. THE DILEMMA OF ISRAEL. Washington, D. C., American Enterprise Institute for Public Policy Research, 1970. 110 p.

International Association of Democratic Lawyers. THE MIDDLE EAST CONFLICT—NOTES AND DOCUMENTS, 1915 - 1967. Brussels, 1968.

Khouri, Fred J. THE ARAB-ISRAELI DILEMMA. Syracuse, N.Y., Syracuse University Press, 1968. 436 p.

Macmoolson, H. J. "Middle Eastern dilemma," 217 *Contemporary Review* 175 (1970)

Middle East Institute, Washington, D. C. 24th Conference on Middle Eastern Affairs, 1970. VIOLENCE AND DIALOGUE IN THE MIDDLE EAST: THE PALESTINE ENTITY AND OTHER CASE STUDIES. A SUMMARY RECORD. Washington, D. C., The Institute, 1970. 75 p.

Murphy, C. F., Jr. "The Middle East crisis," 44 *St. John's Law Review* 390 (1970)

Nutting, Anthony. THE TRAGEDY OF PALESTINE FROM THE BALFOUR DECLARATION TO TODAY. London, Arab League Office, 1969. 15 p.

Peretz, Don. "Israel and the Arab nations," 19 *Journal of International Affairs* 100 (1965)

Richmond, Sir John C. B. "The changing Middle East" (Special issue), *International Affairs* (London) 34 (1970)

Rodinson, M. "Israel: the Arab options," 22 *Yearbook of World Affairs* 80 (1968)

Rosen, Harry M. THE ARABS AND JEWS IN ISRAEL: THE REALITY, THE DILEMMA, THE PROMISE. Jerusalem, Israel Office, Foreign Affairs Department, 1970. 114 p.

Sluyters, B. "A clash of destinies," 50 *Advocatenblad* 261 (1970)

II. The Relevance of International Law

American Society of International Law. INTERNATIONAL LAW AND THE MIDDLE EAST CRISIS: A SYMPOSIUM. New Orleans, Tulane Studies in Political Science, 1957. (Papers presented at a regional meeting of ASIL).

Boals, Kathryn. "Rhetoric and reality: a study of contemporary official Egyptian attitudes toward the international legal order," 62 *AJIL* 335 (1968)

Falk, Richard A. "Law, lawyers, and the conduct of American foreign relations," 78 *Yale Law Journal* 919 (1969)

––––––. "New approaches to the study of international law," 61 *AJIL* 477 (1967)

Fisher, Roger. "Law and legal institutions may help," *In* INTERNATIONAL CONFLICT FOR BEGINNERS. New York, Harper & Row, 1969, pp. 151-177.

––––––. "Bringing law to Bear on Governments." *In* Falk & Mendlovitz, eds. II THE STRATEGY OF WORLD ORDER. New York, World Law Fund, 1966, pp. 75-85.

Halderman, John W., ed. THE MIDDLE EAST CRISIS: TEST OF INTERNATIONAL LAW. Dobbs Ferry, N. Y., Oceana, 1969. Originally published as 33 *Law and Contemporary Problems* (1968)

Henkin, Louis. "The law works: Suez (I)" and "The law fails but is vindicated: Suez (II)," *In* HOW NATIONS BEHAVE: LAW AND FOREIGN POLICY. New York, Praeger, 1968, pp. 186-205.

Malawer, S. A. "Juridical paradigm for classifying international law in the foreign policy process: the Middle East war, 1967," 10 *Virginia Journal of International Law* 348 (1970)

McDougal, Lasswell & Reisman. "Theories about international law: prologue to a configurative jurisprudence," 8 *Virginia Journal of International Law*, 188 (1968)

Moore, John Norton. "The Arab-Israeli conflict and the obligation to pursue peaceful settlement of international disputes," 19 *University of Kansas Law Review* 403 (1971)

––––––. "The role of law in the management of international conflict," *In* LAW AND THE INDO-CHINA WAR. Princeton, N. J., Princeton University Press, 1972.

Neuman, Robert H. "Legal issues in the Middle East." Address delivered October 27, 1970, to American Foreign Law Association, New York.

Rosenne, Shabtai. "Directions for Middle East settlement – some underlying legal problems," 33 *Law and Contemporary Problems* 44 (1968)

Wright, Quincy. "Legal aspects of the Middle East situation," 33 *Law and Contemporary Problems* 5 (1968)

III. *Underlying Issues*

A. ARAB AND JEWISH NATIONALISM AND THE RIGHTS OF REFUGEES
Material included in the Abridged Edition:

Cattan, Henry. "Sovereignty over Palestine," *In* PALESTINE, THE ARABS & ISRAEL, London, Longman, 1969, Appendix XI, pp. 242-75.

Feinberg, Nathan. "The Question of Sovereignty over Palestine," *In* ON AN ARAB JURIST'S APPROACH TO ZIONISM AND THE STATE OF ISRAEL, Jerusalem, Magnes Press, 1971, pp. 7-34.

Peretz, Don. "Arab Palestine: phoenix or phantom?" 48 *Foreign Affairs* 322 (1970)

Harkabi, Y. "The position of the Palestinians in the Israeli-Arab conflict and their national Covenant (1968)," 3 *New York University Journal of International Law and Politics* 209 (1970)

Nakhleh, Issa. "The liberation of Palestine is supported by international law and justice," pamphlet issued by the Palestine Arab Delegation, 2nd edn., March 1969, pp. 3-17.

Stone, Julius. "Peace and the Palestinians," 3 *New York University Journal of International Law and Politics* 247 (1970)

Holborn, Louise W. "The Palestine Arab refugee problem," 23 *International Journal* 82 (1968)

Tomeh, George J. "Legal status of Arab refugees," 33 *Law and Contemporary Problems* 110 (1968)

Alroy, Gil Carl, ed. ATTITUDES TOWARD JEWISH STATEHOOD IN THE ARAB WORLD. New York, American Academic Association for Peace in the Middle East, 1971. 187 p.

———. "Semitic cousins' 'amity' before the Jewish state — the Arab myth of Zionism," 4 *Patterns of Prejudice* 1 (Nov.-Dec. 1970)

American Zionist Council. ISRAEL AND THE ARAB STATES, THE ISSUES IN DISPUTE: ISRAEL'S FRONTIERS AND THE ARAB REFUGEES. New York, American Zionist Council, 1941. 30 p.

Anabtawi, Samir N. "The Palestinians as a political entity," 60 *The Muslim World* 47 (1970).

Avineri, S. "The Palestinians and Israel," 49 *Commentary* 30 (1970).

Baehr, K. ARAB AND JEWISH REFUGEES: PROBLEMS AND PROSPECTS. New York, American Christian Palestine Committee, 1953.

Bassiouni, M. Cherif. "The Palestinians: refugees or a people?" *Catholic World* 257 (Sept. 1970)

Bassiouni, M. Cherif, and Eugene M. Fisher, "The Arab-Israeli conflict — real and apparent issues: an insight into its future from the lessons of the past," 44 *St. John's Law Review* 399 (1970)

Buchrig, E. THE UN AND THE PALESTINE REFUGEES: A STUDY IN NON-TERRITORIAL ADMINISTRATION, 1971, 215 p.

Brown, N. "Palestinian nationalism and the Jordanian state," 26 *World Today* 370 (1970)

Cattan, Henry. "The partition of Palestine from the juridical standpoint." Unpublished translation of an address delivered in French at the University of Bern on November 30, 1970.

"Conflict in Jordan highlights importance of UNRWA," *Palestine Refugees Today*, UNRWA 12 (Sept./Oct. 1970)

Davis, J. "Why and how the Palestinians fled from Palestine," No. 2 *Middle East International* 34 (May 1971)

Dubois, J. P. "Le conflit israelo-palestinien: Nationalisme et idéologie," *Politique aujourd'hui* 49 (février 1971)

Feinberg, Nathan. THE ARAB-ISRAEL CONFLICT IN INTERNATIONAL LAW. Jerusalem, Magnes Press, 1970, pp. 7-84, 96-120.

———. "The recognition of the Jewish people in international law," *from* JEWISH YEARBOOK OF INTERNATIONAL LAW, Jerusalem, Ruben Mass, 1948, pp. 1-26.

Frankenstein, Ernst. "The meaning of the term 'National Home for the Jewish People'," *In* JEWISH YEARBOOK OF INTERNATIONAL LAW 27 (1948)

Grahl-Madsen, Atle. THE STATUS OF REFUGEES IN INTERNATIONAL LAW. Leyden, Sijthoff, 1966. 499 p.

Halpern, Ben. THE IDEA OF THE JEWISH STATE. 2nd edn. Cambridge, Harvard University Press, 1970.

Hashem, Zaki. "Some international law aspects of the Palestine question," 23 *Revue Égyptienne de Droit International* 63 (1967)

Hillel, S. "The Palestinians must have a state where they are a majority," *New Middle East* 14 (Dec. 1970)

Hudson, Michael. "The Palestinian Arab resistance movement: its significance in the Middle East crisis," 23 *Middle East Journal* 291 (1969)

Khadduri, Majid. POLITICAL TRENDS IN THE ARAB WORLD: THE ROLE OF IDEAS AND IDEALS IN POLITICS. Baltimore, Johns Hopkins Press, 1970. 298 p.

Krenz, Frank E. "The refugee as a subject of international law," 15 *International and Comparative Law Quarterly* 90 (1966)

LaSablière, B. de. "Le problème des refugiés de Palestine," *Revue des daux mondex* 53 (mars 1971)

Mallison, W. T., Jr. "The Zionist-Israel juridical claims to constitute 'the Jewish people' nationality entity and to confer membership in it: appraisal in public international law," 32 *George Washington Law Review* 983 (1964)

Merhav, Peretz. "Arabs and Jews in Palestine: alternatives for sovereignty," 11 *War/Peace Report* 14 (Aug.-Sept. 1971)

"Notes on refugees," *In* NONALIGNED THIRD WORLD ANNUAL, 1970. St. Louis, Mo., Books Int'l. of DH-TE Int'l., 1971.

Peres, Yochanan. "Modernization and nationalism in the identity of the Israeli Arab," 24 *Middle East Journal* 479 (1970)

Peretz, Don. "The Arab-Israeli war: Israel's administration and Arab refugees," 47 *Foreign Affairs* 336 (1968)

———. "The Arab refugee dilemma," 33 *Foreign Affairs* 134 (1954)

Rosenne, Shabtai. "The Israel nationality law, 5712-1952 and the law of return, 5710-1950," 81 *Journal du droit international* 5 (1954)

Seminar of Arab Jurists on Palestine, Algiers, July 22-27, 1967. THE PALESTINE QUESTION. Monograph #18, Institute for Palestine Studies, 1968, pp. 15-136, 183-196.

Sherman, Alfred. "The Palestinians: a case of mistaken national identity?" 27 *World Today* 104 (1971)

Shihadeh, Aziz. "Must history repeat itself? The Palestinian entity and its enemies," No. 28 *New Middle East* 36 (Jan. 1971)

Stone, Julius. SELF-DETERMINATION, JEWS AND PALESTINE ARABS. (Paper presented to the Australian Society of Legal Philosophy on September 3, 1970.)

U.S. 90th Congress session House. Committee on Agriculture. Subcommittee on Foreign Agricultural Operation. REFUGEE SITUATION IN THE MIDDLE EAST. October 1967. 6 p.

"What future for the Palestine Arabs?" 10 *War/Peace Report* 3 (June-July 1970)

Zarhi, S. "Economics of refugee settlement," 10 *Middle East Monthly* 31 (Dec. 1967)

B. FREEDOM OF NAVIGATION THROUGH THE STRAITS OF TIRAN, THE GULF OF AQABA, AND THE SUEZ CANAL

Material included in the Abridged Edition:

Salans, Carl F. "Gulf of Aqaba and Strait of Tiran: troubled waters," 94 *United States Naval Institute Proceedings* 56 (Dec. 1968)

Johnson, D.H.N. "Some legal problems of international waterways, with particular reference to the Straits of Tiran and Suez Canal," 31 *Modern Law Review* 153 (1968)

Khadduri, Majid. "Closure of the Suez Canal to Israeli shipping," 33 *Law and Contemporary Problems* 147 (1968)

1. *SUEZ CANAL*

"Aspects du problème du canal de Suez," 13 *Revue Égyptienne de Droit International* 99 (1957)

Avran, Benno. THE EVOLUTION OF THE SUEZ CANAL STATUS FROM 1869 UP TO 1956: A HISTORICO-JURIDICAL STUDY. Geneva, Droz, 1958. 170 p.

Badr, G.M. "Israel and the Suez Canal — a new approach," 23 *Revue Égyptienne de Droit International* 63 (1967)

Bassiouni, M. Cherif. "The nationalization of the Suez Canal and the illicit act in international law," 14 *DePaul Law Review* 258 (1965)

Baxter, R.R. THE LAW OF INTERNATIONAL WATERWAYS. Cambridge, Mass., Harvard University Press, 1964, pp. 205-236.

Bechtoldt, Heinrich. "Suezkanal; Brücke zum Interessenausgleich? 22 *Aussenpolitik* 65 (1971)

Boutros-Ghali, B., et Youssef Chlala. LE CANAL DE SUEZ (1854-1957) Alexandrie, Société égyptienne de droit international, 1958. 211 p.

Dehaussy, J. "La déclaration égyptienne de 1957 sur le canal de Suez," 6 *Annuaire français de droit international* 169 (1960)

Delson, R. "Nationalization of the Suez Canal Co.; issues of public and private international law," 57 *Columbia Law Review* 755, 772 (1957)

Dinitz, S. "The legal aspects of the Egyptian blockade of the Suez Canal," 45 *Georgetown Law Journal* 169 (1956-57)

Etzioni, Amitai. "A buffer zone at the Suez: some generic questions," 13 *New Outlook* 30 (Nov. 1970)

Evron, Y. "Talking about disengagement: the Suez Canal as a factor," No. 28 *New Middle East* 20 (Jan. 1971)

Generales, Minos D. "Suez: national sovereignty and international waterways," 29 *World Affairs* 177 (1958)

Gross, Leo. "The Geneva Conference on the Law of the Sea and the right of innocent passage through the Gulf of Aqaba," 53 *AJIL* 564 (1959)

————. "Passage through the Suez Canal of Israel-bound cargo and Israel ships," 51 *AJIL* 530 (1957)

Hammad, M. Burhan W. "The right of passage in the Gulf of Aqaba," 15 *Revue Égyptienne de Droit International* 118 (1959)

Huang, Thomas T.F. "Some international and legal aspects of the Suez Canal question," 51 *AJIL* 277 (1957)

"International control of the Suez Canal; a symposium," 2 *International Lawyer* 27 (1967)

Lee, Luke T. "Legal aspects of internationalization of inter-oceanic canals," 33 *Law and Contemporary Problems* 158 (1968)

Love, Kennett. SUEZ: THE TWICE-FOUGHT WAR. New York, McGraw-Hill, 1969. 767 p.

Matthews, Robert O. "The Suez Canal dispute: a case study in peaceful settlement," 21 *International Organization* 79 (1967)

Obieta, Joseph A. THE INTERNATIONAL STATUS OF THE SUEZ CANAL. 2nd edn. The Hague, Nijhoff, 1970. 164 p.

Sick, G.G. "The U.S.S.R. and the Suez Canal closure," 12 *Mizan* 91 (Nov. 1970)

Siverson, Randolph M. "International conflict and perceptions of injury: the case of the Suez crisis," 14 *International Studies Quarterly* 157 (1970)

Stauffer, T. "Who needs the Suez Canal?" 10 *Middle East* 18 (Oct. 1970)

Stillman, A.M. THE UNITED NATIONS AND THE SUEZ CANAL. Ann Arbor, Mich., University Microfilms, 1965. 238 p.

Strange, S. "Suez and after," 11 *Yearbook of World Affairs* 76 (1957)

Thomas, Hugh. THE SUEZ AFFAIR. New York, Harper & Row, 1967. 261 p.

Wolf, J. "A qui profite la paralysie du canal de Suez?" 13 *Rémarques africaines* 78 (10 avril 1971)

Yahuda, Solomon. "The *Inge Toft* controversy," 54 *AJIL* 398 (1960)

2. *GULF OF AQABA AND STRAITS OF TIRAN*

"The Aqaba question and international law," 13 *Revue Égyptienne de Droit International* 86 (1957)

Bloomfield, L.M. EGYPT, ISRAEL AND THE GULF OF AQABA. Toronto, Carswell, 1957, pp. 109-143, 164-167.

Brown, T.D. "World war prize law applied in a limited war situation: Egyptian restrictions on neutral shipping with Israel," 50 *Minnesota Law Review* 849 (1966)

Bruel, Erik. INTERNATIONAL STRAITS: A TREATISE ON INTERNATIONAL LAW. London, Sweet & Maxwell, 1947. 2 vols.

Cagle, Malcolm W. "The Gulf of Aqaba — trigger for conflict," 85 *U.S. Naval Institute Proceedings* 75 (1959)

de La Pradelle, R. de G. "Il n'existe pas actuellement de statut juridique du golfe d'Akaba," *Le Monde*, 25 May 1967.

Döll, B. "Die Rechtslage des Golfes von Akaba," 15 *Jahrbuch für internationales Recht* 225 (1969)

Eckert, Robert J. "The straits of Tiran: innocent passage or an endless war?" 22 *University of Miami Law Review* 873 (1968)

Ghobashy, O.Z. "The Gulf of Aqaba and the Straits of Tiran," 45 *Islamic Review* 31 (1957)

———. "Tiran and Aqaba," 5 *Egyptian Economic and Political Review* (2nd ser.) 18 (1959)

Gross, Leo. "Passage through the Strait of Tiran and in the Gulf of Aqaba," 33 *Law and Contemporary Problems* 125 (1968)

———. "Passage through the Suez Canal of Israel-bound cargo and Israel ships," 51 *AJIL* 530 (1957)

Hashem, Z. "Rationale of the theory of historic bays with special reference to the international status of the Gulf of Aqaba," 25 *Revue Égyptienne de Droit International* 1 (1969)

Lapidoth, Ruth. "Passage par le détroit de Tiran," 73 *Revue Générale de Droit International Public* 30 (1969)

Melamid, Alexander. "Legal status of the Gulf of Aqaba," 53 *AJIL* 412 (1959)

Moser, M. "A survey of the definition of international straits and the issue of 'status mixtus'," 3 *Israel Law Review* 50 (1968)

Murti, B.S.N. "The legal status of the Gulf of Aqaba," 7 *Indian Journal of International Law* 201 (1967)

el-Oteifi, G. "The Gulf of Aqaba and Israel," 18 *Review of International Affairs* 5 (July 1967)

Porter, Paul A. THE GULF OF AQABA: AN INTERNATIONAL WATERWAY. ITS SIGNIFICANCE TO INTERNATIONAL TRADE. Washington, Public Affairs Press, 1957. 18 p.

Rabbath, Edmon. MER ROUGE ET GOLFE D'AQABA DANS L'EVOLUTION DU DROIT INTERNATIONAL. Cairo, Société égyptienne de droit international, Brochure no. 16, 1962.

Sayegh, F. "The status of the Straits of Tiran," 10 *Middle East Economic Survey*, supplement to no. 3 (1967)

Selak, Charles B., Jr. "A consideration of the legal status of the Gulf of Aqaba," 52 *AJIL* 660 (1958)

Speyer, J.M. "The Gulf of Aqaba: a political problem of juridical status," 11 *Internationale Spectator* 315 (1957)

Strohl, Mitchell P. THE INTERNATIONAL LAW OF BAYS. The Hague, Nijhoff, 1963. 426 p.

Whetten, L.L. "Legal aspects of the Egyptian blockade of the Gulf of Aqaba," 45 *Revue de Droit International et de Sciences Diplomatiques et Politiques* 339 (1967)

C.   JERUSALEM AND THE HOLY PLACES

Material included in the Abridged Edition:

Jones, S. Shepard. "The status of Jerusalem: some national and international aspects," 33 *Law and Contemporary Problems* 169 (1968)

Pfaff, Richard H. JERUSALEM: KEYSTONE OF AN ARAB-ISRAELI SETTLEMENT. Washington, American Enterprise Institute for Public Policy Research, 1969, pp. 1-54.

Berman, S.M. "Territorial acquisition by conquest in international law and the unification of Jerusalem," 7 *International Problems* 11 (Nos. 1-2 [13] May 1968)

———. "Recrudescence of the 'bellum justum et pium' controversy and Israel's reunification of Jerusalem," 7 *International Problems* 29 (Nos. 1-2 [15] May 1969)

Bovis, H. Eugene. THE JERUSALEM QUESTION: 1917-1968. Stanford, Hoover Institution Press, 1971.

"Christian religious courts and the unification of Jerusalem. *Hanzalis* v. *Greek Orthodox Patriarchate Religious Court* (1969 [I] 23 P.D. 260)" 5 *Israel Law Review*

Fitzgerald, W. "An international regime for Jerusalem," 37 *Royal Central Asian Journal* 273 (1950)

Golden, H. "Israel and the Christian shrines," *Saturday Review*, Dec. 19, 1970, pp. 15-16.

Israel. Office of Information. JERUSALEM AND THE UNITED NATIONS. New York, 1953. 27 p.

Karzarov, C. "L'internationalisation de la ville de Jerusalem," 28 *Revue de Droit International des Sciences Diplomatiques et Politiques* 400 (1950)

Lauterpacht, Elihu. JERUSALEM AND THE HOLY PLACES. London, Anglo-Israel Association Pamphlet #19, 1968, pp. 5-85.

Mansour, A., and E. Stock. "Arab Jerusalem after the annexation," 14 *New Outlook; Middle East Monthly* 22, 46 (January, February 1971)

Meron, Theodor. "The demilitarization of Mount Scopus: a regime that was," 3 *Israel Law Review* 501 (1968)

Mohn, Paul. "Jerusalem and the United Nations," 464 *International Conciliation* 421 (Oct. 1950)

"The new Jewish Jerusalem," *Appendix III, Report of the Executive of the Jewish Agency* submitted to the Palestine Partition Commission, July 22, 1938, pp. 46-56.

Peretz, Don. "Jerusalem, a divided city," 18 *Journal of International Affairs* 211 (1964)

THE RIGHTS AND CLAIMS OF MOSLEMS AND JEWS IN CONNECTION WITH THE WAILING WALL AT JERUSALEM. Beirut, Institute for Palestine Studies, Basic Documents Series No. 4, 1968.

Sayegh, S. "Le statu quo des Lieux-Saints. Nature juridique et portée internationale. Solution du statu quo," 43 *Apollinaris* 177 (1970)

Wilson, Evan M. JERUSALEM, KEY TO PEACE. Washington, Middle East Institute, 1970. 176 p.

———. "The internationalization of Jerusalem," 23 *Middle East Journal* 1 (1969)

D. JORDAN WATERS

American Jewish Committee. WATER AND POLITICS IN THE MIDDLE EAST. New York, The Committee, Dec. 1964. 15 p.

Arab League. THE ARAB PLAN FOR DEVELOPMENT OF THE WATER RESOURCES IN THE JORDAN VALLEY. Cairo, March 1964. 13 p.

Boals, Kathryn. "Jordan waters conflict," 553 *International Conciliation* 3 (May 1965)

Feinberg, Nathan. THE ARAB-ISRAEL CONFLICT IN INTERNATIONAL LAW. Jerusalem, Magnes Press, 1970. "Utilization of the waters of the River Jordan," pp. 88-96.

Ghobashy, O.Z. THE DEVELOPMENT OF THE JORDAN RIVER. New York, Arab Information Center, 1961.

Ionides, M.G. "The disputed waters of Jordan," 7 *Middle East Journal* 153 (1953)

Israeli, S. "Jordan waters," 3 *International Problems* 13 (Nos. 3-4, Dec. 1965)

Nakhleh, Issa. THE DIVERSION OF WATERS FROM THE INTERNATIONAL WATER SYSTEM OF THE JORDAN VALLEY BY ZIONIST AUTHORITIES IN OCCUPIED PALESTINE... Memorandum submitted by the Arab Higher Committee for Palestine to the Ministries of Foreign Affairs of Member States of the United Nations, Jan. 1964. 30 p.

Peretz, Don. "Development of the Jordan Valley waters," 9 *Middle East Journal* (1955)

Rizk, Edward A. THE JORDAN WATERS. London, Arab Information Centre, 1964. 24 p.

Rosenne, Shabtai, "Some legal aspects of Israel's Lake K inert-Negev water project." An expanded version of an unpublished lecture delivered in Jerusalem in February 1964.

Saliba, Samir N. THE JORDAN RIVER DISPUTE. The Hague, Nijhoff, 1968.

Seminar of Arab Jurists on Palestine, Algiers, July 22-27, 1967. Beirut, Institute for Palestine Studies, Monograph #18, 1968. "Diversion of the Jordan waters by Israel," pp. 137-151.

Stevens, Georgiana G. "The Jordan River Valley," 506 *International Conciliation* (1956)

————. JORDAN RIVER PARTITION. Stanford, Hoover Institution Studies No. 6, 1965.

IV. *The Six-Day War, The October War, and Continued Hostilities*

A. BACKGROUND AND SETTING

Material included in the Abridged Edition:

Yost, Charles W. "The Arab-Israeli war: how it began," 46 *Foreign Affairs* 304 (1968)

Abu-Lughod, Ibrahim. THE ARAB-ISRAELI CONFRONTATION OF JUNE, 1967: AN ARAB PERSPECTIVE. Evanston, Ill., Northwestern University Press, 1970. 201 p.

————, ed. "The Arab-Israeli confrontation of June 1967." Special issue 14 *Arab World* (1968)

Akhtar, S. "Arab-Israeli conflict since the June war," 23 *Pakistan Horizon* 138 (1970)

ARAB AREAS OCCUPIED BY ISRAEL IN JUNE, 1967. North Dartmouth, Mass., Association of Arab-American University Graduates, Inc., 1970. Information papers No. 2. 37 p.

Aruri, Naseer, ed. THE PALESTINIAN RESISTANCE TO ISRAELI OCCUPATION. Wilmette, Ill., Medina University Press International, 1970. 167 p.

Bar-Yaacov, N. THE ISRAEL-SYRIAN ARMISTICE: PROBLEMS OF IMPLE-MENTATION, 1949-1966. Jerusalem, Magnes Press, 1967. 377 p.

Blum, Yehuda Z. "The missing reversioner: reflections on the status of Judea and Samaria," 3 *Israel Law Review* 279 (1968). (Revised and with post-script by the author.)

Churchill, Randolph S., and Winston S. Churchill. THE SIX DAY WAR. Boston, Houghton Mifflin, 1967. 250 p.

Dayan, Moshe. "Israel's border and security problem," 33 *Foreign Affairs* 250 (1954/55)

Draper, Theodore. ISRAEL AND WORLD POLITICS: ROOTS OF THE THIRD ARAB-ISRAELI WAR. New York, Viking, 1968. 278 p.

Glubb, J.B. "Violence on the Jordan-Israel border," 32 *Foreign Affairs* 552 (1953/54)

Harkabi, Y. FEDAYEEN ACTION AND ARAB STRATEGY. London, Institute for Strategic Studies, Adelphi Paper No. 53, Dec. 1968.

Howard, M., and R. Hunter. ISRAEL AND THE ARAB WORLD: THE CRISIS OF 1967. London, Institute for Strategic Studies, Adelphi Paper No. 41, Oct. 1967.

Hurewitz, J.C. MIDDLE EAST POLITICS: THE MILITARY DIMENSION. New York, Praeger, for the Council on Foreign Relations, 1969. 550 p.

ISRAEL'S OCCUPATION OF PALESTINE AND OTHER ARAB TERRITORIES. North Dartmouth, Mass., Association of Arab-American University Graduates, Inc., 1970. Information papers No. 1. 47 p.

Kanovsky, Eliyahu. THE ECONOMIC IMPACT OF THE SIX-DAY WAR: ISRAEL, THE OCCUPIED TERRITORIES, EGYPT, JORDAN. New York, Praeger, 1970. 438 p.

Keesing's Research Report. THE ARAB-ISRAELI CONFLICT — THE 1967 CAMPAIGN. New York, 1968.

Laqueur, Walter. THE ROAD TO JERUSALEM: THE ORIGINS OF THE ARAB-ISRAELI CONFLICT. New York, Macmillan, 1968. 368 p.

Lewis, Bernard. "The consequences of defeat," 46 *Foreign Affairs* 321 (1968)

Little, Selby F., Jr. "Fedayeen: Palestinian commandos," *Military Review* 49 (Nov. 1970)

Safran, Nadav. FROM WAR TO WAR: THE ARAB-ISRAELI CONFRONTATION, 1948-1967. New York, Pegasus, 1969. 464 p.

Stone, Julius. "The Middle East under cease-fire," 3 *The Bridge* 3 (1967)

Tlass, M. "La lutte armée et la résistance palestinienne," 18 *Syrie et Monde Arabe* 36 (1971)

Toynbee, Arnold, and J.L. Talmon. "The argument between Arabs and Jews: an exchange," *Encounter* (Oct. 1967)

U.S. 91st Cong. 1st sess. House. Committee on Foreign Affairs. Subcommittee on the Near East. THE CONTINUING NEAR EAST CRISIS. BACKGROUND INFORMATION. Washington, GPO, Jan. 10, 1969.

————. 2nd sess. House. Committee on Foreign Affairs. Subcommittee on the Near East. THE NEAR EAST CONFLICT: HEARINGS. Washington, GPO, 1970. 383 p.

Wolf, John B. "The Palestinian resistance movement," 60 *Current History* 26 (1971)

Young, Oran R. "Intermediaries and interventionists: third parties in the Middle East crisis," 23 *International Journal* 52 (1968)

B. LEGAL ISSUES CONCERNING THE USE OF FORCE AND ITS
    CONSEQUENCES

Material included in the Abridged Edition:

Stone Julius. NO PEACE — NO WAR IN THE MIDDLE EAST. Sydney, Maitland Publications for the International Law Association (Australian Branch)
1970, pp. 1-7, 17-24, 38-40.

Bassiouni, M. Cherif. "The 'Middle East': the misunderstood conflict," 19
Kansas Law Review 373 (1971)

Schwebel, Stephen M. "What weight to conquest?" 64 *AJIL* 344 (1970)

Hargrove, John Lawrence. "Abating the Middle East crisis through the United
Nations (and vice versa)" 19 *Kansas Law Review* 365 (1971)

Safran, Nadav. "The war and the future of the Arab-Israeli conflict," 52
Foreign Affairs 215 (1974).

Paust, Jordan J., and Albert P. Blaustein. "The Arab oil weapon — a threat
to international peace," 68 *AJIL* 410 (1974).

Shihata, Ibrahim F.I. "Destination embargo of Arab oil: its legality under
international law," 68 *AJIL* 591 (1974).

Rostow, Eugene V. "The illegality of the Arab attack on Israel of October 6,
1973," 69 *AJIL* 272 (1975).

Ahmad, E. "Revolutionary war and counterinsurgency," 25 *Journal of International Affairs* 1 (1971)

Alexander, Yonah, and Miriam Lesly Sweet. "The 'just war' concept and its
application to the 1967 Arab-Israeli War," 9 *International Problems* 34 (1970)

"American Council for Judaism's statements on the Middle East crisis and
war of May-June 1967," 21 *Issues* (1967)

"The Arab-Israeli war and international law," 9 *Harvard International Law
Journal* 232 (1968)

Bassiouni, M.O., and E.M. Fisher. "The Arab-Israeli conflict — real and
apparent issues: an insight into its future from the lessons of the past," 44
St. John's Law Review 399 (1970)

"The Beirut retaliation — a case study of the use of force in time of peace,"
2 *New York University Journal of International Law and Politics* 105 (1969)

Blum, Yehuda Z. "The Beirut Raid and the international double standard: a
reply to Professor Richard A. Falk," 64 *AJIL* 73 (1970)

Dinstein, Yoram. "The legal issues of 'para-war' and peace in the Middle
East," 44 *St. John's Law Review* 466 (1970)

Falk, Richard A. "The Beirut Raid and the international law of retaliation,"
63 *AJIL* 415 (1969)

———, and Julius Stone. "Exchange of correspondence," 64 *AJIL* 161 (1970)

Feinberg, Nathan. THE LEGALITY OF A "STATE OF WAR" AFTER THE
CESSATION OF HOSTILITIES. Jerusalem, Magnes Press, 1961, pp. 7-71.

Goodhart, A.L. ISRAEL, THE UNITED NATIONS AND AGGRESSION. London,
Anglo-Israel Association, 1968, Pamphlet No. 17.

Greenwald, H. "International law and Israel's 'occupied' territories," 61
American Zionist 43 (1971)

Khadduri, Majid. "Some legal aspects of the Arab-Israeli conflict of 1967,"

In Lepowski, ed. FESTSCHRIFT FOR PROFESSOR QUINCY WRIGHT. New York, Appleton-Century-Crofts, 1971.

Koch, Howard, Jr. "June 1967: the question of aggression," 15 *Arab World* 10 (June 1969)

Levie, Howard. "The nature and scope of armistice agreements," 50 *AJIL* 880 (1956)

Malawer, S.S. "Anticipatory self-defence under Article 51 of the United Nations Charter and the Arab-Israeli War 1967," 8 *International Problems* 14 (Nos. 1-2, 1970)

Mushkat, M. "Some legal and political problems of the Arab war against Israel," 6 *International Problems* 51 (Nos. 4-5, 1967)

O'Brien, William V. "International law and the outbreak of war in the Middle East, 1967," 11 *Orbis* 692 (1968)

Pinto, R. "Aspects juridiques du conflit entre les Etats arabes et Israël," *In* MELANGES OFFERTS A MONSIEUR LE DOYEN LOUIS TROTABAS, Paris, 1970, pp. 401-422.

Rotman, R.B. "Conflito de titulos territoriales sobre Palestina," 135 *Revista Jurídica Argentina La Ley* 1507 (1969)

Schwebel, Stephen M. "The Middle East crisis: prospects for peace," *In* THE MIDDLE EAST: PROSPECTS FOR PEACE, Background Papers and Proceedings of the Thirteenth Hammarskjold Forum. Dobbs Ferry, N. Y., Oceana, 1969, pp. 70-74.

Shapira, Amos. "The Six-Day War and the right of self-defence," 6 *Israel Law Review* 65 (1971)

"The significance of the June, 1967 Arab-Israeli war: a symposium," by Jacob Neusner, Anthony Nutting, Leonard Binder, and others. 21 *Issues* (1967-68)

Stone, Julius. "Between cease-fires in the Middle East," 6 *Israel Law Review* 165 (1971)

Wright, Quincy. "The Middle East crisis," *In* THE MIDDLE EAST: PROSPECTS FOR PEACE, Background Papers and Proceedings of the Thirteenth Hammarskjold Forum. Dobbs Ferry, N. Y., Oceana, 1969, pp. 13-35 and 42-49.

C. HUMAN RIGHTS FOR CONTEXTS OF VIOLENCE

Material included in the Abridged Edition:

Hammad, M. Burhan W. "The culprit, the targets and the victims," 15 *Arab World* 3 (1969)

Shamgar, Meir. "The observance of international law in the administered territories," *In* I Y. Dinstein, ed. ISRAEL YEARBOOK ON HUMAN RIGHTS, 1971.

Rodley, Nigel S. "The United Nations and human rights in the Middle East," 38 *Social Research* 217 (1971)

Bender, John C. "Ad hoc committees and human rights investigation: a comparative case study in the Middle East," 38 *Social Research* 241 (1971)

Dershowitz, A.M. "Terrorism and preventive detention — the case of Israel," 50 *Commentary* 67 (Dec. 1970)

Dib, George, and Fuad Jabber. ISRAEL'S VIOLATION OF HUMAN RIGHTS IN THE OCCUPIED TERRITORIES. 3rd rev. edn. Beirut, Institute for Palestine Studies, April 1970.

Farer, T. "Humanitarian law and armed conflicts: toward the definition of 'international armed conflict'," 71 *Columbia Law Review* 37 (1971)

Hewitt, W.E. "Respect for human rights in armed conflicts," 4 *New York University Journal of International Law and Politics* 41 (1971)

International Committee of the Red Cross. "The Middle East activities of the International Committee of the Red Cross — June 1967-June 1970," 10 *International Review of the Red Cross* 424-459; 485-511 (1970)

ISRAEL AND THE GENEVA CONVENTIONS. Beirut, Institute for Palestine Studies, Anthology Series No. 3, 1968.

LAW AND COURTS IN THE ISRAEL-HELD AREAS. Institute for Legislative Research and Comparative Law of the Faculty of Law of the Hebrew University of Jerusalem, Jan. 1970.

Mallison, W.T., Jr. "The Geneva Convention for the Protection of Civilian Persons: an analysis of its application in the Arab territories under Israeli occupation," 15 *Arab World* 3 (1969)

Meron, Theodor. "Some legal aspects of Arab terrorists' claims to privileged combatancy," *In* S. Shoham, ed. OF LAW AND MAN, ESSAYS IN HONOR OF HAIM H. COHN, New York and Tel Aviv, Sabra Books, 1971, pp. 225-268.

Raphaeli, N. "Problems of military administration in the controlled territories," 8 *Public Administration in Israel and Abroad, 1967* 48 (1968)

"Red Cross relief action in Jordan," 10 *International Review of the Red Cross* 621 (1970)

Stone, Julius. "Behind the cease-fire lines: Israel's administration in Gaza and the West Bank," *In* S. Shoham, ed. OF LAW AND MAN, ESSAYS IN HONOR OF HAIM H. COHN, New York and Tel Aviv, Sabra Books, 1971, pp. 79-107.

V. *The Role of the United Nations*

A. GENERAL

Material included in the Abridged Edition:

Higgins, Rosalyn, "The June War: the United Nations and legal background," 3 *Journal of Contemporary History* 253-273 (1968)

El-Farra, Muhammad H. "The role of the United Nations vis-à-vis the Palestine question," 33 *Law and Contemporary Problems* 68-77 (1968)

Dinstein, Yoram. "The United Nations and the Arab-Israel conflict," *In* ENCYCLOPAEDIA JUDAICA, Vol. 15, 1971, p. 1543.

Anabtawi, Samir N. "The United Nations and the Middle East conflict of 1967," 14 *Arab World* 53 (Nos. 10-11, 1968)

Bowett, D.W. UNITED NATIONS FORCES: A LEGAL STUDY. New York, Praeger, 1964.

————. "United Nations peace-keeping," 3 *International Relations* 756 (Nov. 1970)

Boyd, J.M. UNITED NATIONS PEACE-KEEPING OPERATIONS: A MILITARY AND POLITICAL APPRAISAL. New York, Praeger, 1971. 261 p.

Buehrig, E. THE UN AND THE PALESTINIAN REFUGEES: A STUDY IN NON-TERRITORIAL ADMINISTRATION. 1971. 215 p.

Burns, A.L., and N. Heathcote. PEACE-KEEPING BY UNITED NATIONS FORCES: FROM SUEZ TO CONGO. New York, Praeger, 1963.

Castaneda, Jorge. "Certain legal consequences of the Suez crisis," 19 *Revue Égyptienne de Droit International* 1 (1963)

Cattan, H. "The U.N. General Assembly must redress its wrongs," No. 2 *Middle East International* 41 (May 1971)

Cox, Arthur M. PROSPECTS FOR PEACEKEEPING. Washington, Brookings Institution, 1967. 178 p.

Eagleton, Clyde. "Palestine and the constitutional law of the United Nations," 42 *AJIL* 397 (1948)

Egyptian Society of International Law. EGYPT AND THE UNITED NATIONS. New York, Manhattan, 1957.

Elarby, Nabil. "Some legal implications of the 1947 partition resolution and the 1949 armistice agreements," 33 *Law and Contemporary Problems* 97 (1968)

Farajallah, S.B. "The United Nations peace-keeping operations," *In* 1968 DAG HAMMARSKJOLD SEMINAR ON THE STRUCTURE, ROLE AND FUNCTIONS OF THE U.N. SYSTEM. Essays 119, 1968.

Gillon, D. "The prospects for the Jarring talks," 27 *World Today* 50 (1971)

Goldberg, Arthur. "A basic Mideast document – its meaning today," 8 *International Problems* 10 (Nos. 1-2, June 1970)

Gordenker, Leon, ed. THE UNITED NATIONS IN INTERNATIONAL POLITICS. Princeton, N. J., Princeton University Press, 1971. 241 p.

Graber, D.A. "Perceptions of Middle East conflict in the United Nations 1953-1965," 13 *Journal of Conflict Resolution* 454 (1969)

Greenwald, H. "Israel and the United Nations," 61 *American Zionist* 36 (1971)

Hadawi, Sami, ed. THE CASE OF PALESTINE BEFORE THE 23RD SESSION OF THE UNITED NATIONS, OCTOBER-DECEMBER 1968. New York, Arab Information Center, 1969.

Halderman, John W. "Some international constitutional aspects of the Palestine case," 33 *Law and Contemporary Problems* 78 (1968)

Hamzeh, F.S. INTERNATIONAL CONCILIATION, WITH SPECIAL REFERENCE TO THE WORK OF THE UNITED NATIONS CONCILIATION COMMISSION FOR PALESTINE. The Hague, Pasmans, 1963. 177 p.

Higgins, Rosalyn. UNITED NATIONS PEACEKEEPING, 1946-1967: DOCUMENTS AND COMMENTARY. Vol. I. THE MIDDLE EAST. London, Oxford University Press, 1969.

Howard, Harry N. "The United Nations in the Middle East," 60 *Current History* 7 (1971)

ISRAEL AND THE UNITED NATIONS. Report of a study group of Hebrew University, Jerusalem. New York, Manhattan, 1956. 322 p.

James, Alan. THE POLITICS OF PEACE-KEEPING. New York, Praeger, 1969. 452 p.

Kimche, J. "Palestine and the United Nations – two victims in search of a viable alternative," *New Middle East* 4 (Oct. 1970)

Lapidoth, Ruth. "La résolution du Conseil de Securité en date du 22 novembre

1967 au sujet du Moyen-Orient," 74 *Revue Générale de Droit International Public* 289 (1970)

———. "The Security Council in the May 1967 crisis: a study in frustration," 4 *Israel Law Review* 3 (1969)

Liang, Yuen-li. "The Palestine Commission," 42 *AJIL* 649 (1948)

Mezerik, A.G. THE ARAB-ISRAEL CONFLICT AND THE UNITED NATIONS. New York, International Review Service, 1969.

"The Middle East," *In* "Issues before the twenty-sixth session of the General Assembly," 579 *International Conciliation* (Sept. 1971). See also the September issues of previous years for earlier reports.

"1949-1969 — Israel and the United Nations," 16 *Review of Contemporary Law* 41 (1969)

Nakhleh, Issa. "The United Nations and peace in the Middle East. *In* John Norton Moore, ed. II THE ARAB-ISRAELI CONFLICT AND INTERNATIONAL LAW. Princeton, N. J., Princeton University Press, 1974.

"Peace-keeping: review and prospects of development," *In* 1968 DAG HAMMARSKJOLD SEMINAR ON THE STRUCTURE, ROLE AND FUNCTIONS OF THE U.N. SYSTEM. Essays 133, 1968.

Perazić, Gavro. "Third anniversary of the Security Council Resolution on the Middle East," 21 *Review of International Affairs* 23 (Dec. 5, 1970)

Potter, Pitman B. "The Palestine problem before the U.N.," 42 *AJIL* 859 (1948)

Sayegh, F.A. THE RECORD OF ISRAEL AT THE U.N. London, Arab Information Center, 1957.

Seyersted, Finn. UNITED NATIONS FORCES IN THE LAW OF PEACE AND WAR. Leyden, Sijthoff, 1966. 447 p.

Shapira, Amos. "The Security Council Resolution of November 22, 1967 — its legal nature and implications," 4 *Israel Law Review* 229 (1969)

U Thant. "The story of the Jarring Mission," No. 29 *New Middle East* 30 (Feb. 1971)

Yost, Casimir. ARABS, ISRAELIS, AND THE UNITED NATIONS: A STUDY OF PEACE THWARTED. New York, Americans for Middle East Understanding, Sept. 1970. 86 p. Mimeographed.

B. THE UNITED NATIONS EMERGENCY FORCE AND ITS WITHDRAWAL

Material included in the Abridged Edition:

Lall, Arthur. THE UNITED NATIONS AND THE MIDDLE EAST CRISIS 1967. New York, Columbia University Press, 1968. "UNEF and its withdrawal," pp. 11-21.

U Thant, "The United Nations as scapegoat," 11 *War/Peace Report* 9 (1971)

Harbottle, "The October Middle East war: lessons for UN peacekeeping," 50 *Int'l Affairs* 544 (1974).

Abi-Mershed, W. ISRAELI WITHDRAWAL FROM SINAI. Beirut, Institute for Palestine Studies, n.d.

Armstrong, Hamilton Fish. "The U.N. experience in Gaza," 35 *Foreign Affairs* 600 (1957)

Burns, E.L.M. BETWEEN ARAB AND ISRAELI. London, G.G. Harrap, 1962.

————. "The withdrawal of UNEF and the future of peacekeeping," 23 *International Journal* 1 (1968)

Chapman, Dudley H. "The U.N. Emergency Force: legal status," 57 *Michigan Law Review* 56 (1958)

Cohen, Maxwell. "The demise of UNEF," 23 *International Journal* (Toronto) 18 (1967-68)

————. "The U.N. Emergency Force: a preliminary view," 12 *International Journal* (Toronto) 109 (1957)

Elaraby, Nabil. "United Nations peacekeeping by consent: a case study of the withdrawal of the United Nations Emergency Force," 1 *New York University Journal of International Law and Politics* 149 (1968)

Galtung, I. and J. "Some factors affecting local acceptance of U.N. forces," 4 *International Problems* (Nos. 1-2, 1966)

Garvey, Jack Israel. "United Nations peacekeeping and host state consent," 64 *AJIL* 241 (1970)

Goodrich, L.M., and G.E. Rosner. "The U.N.E.F.," 11 *International Organization* 413 (1957)

Halderman, John W. "Legal basis for U.N. armed forces," 56 *AJIL* 976 (1962)

International Law Association. Committee on the Charter of the United Nations. "Problems of a U.N. force," 49 *International Law Association Report* 126 (Hamburg, 1960)

Kay, Z. "The United Nations forces in Korea and Sinai," 2 *International Relations* 168 (1961)

Malawer, S.S. "The withdrawal of UNEF and a new notion of consent," 4 *Cornell International Law Journal* 25 (1970)

Miller, R.I. "Suez — UNEF and after," *In* DAG HAMMARSKJOLD AND CRISIS DIPLOMACY. New York, Oceana, 1962, pp. 59-125.

Mushkat, M. "The Middle East conflict and some problems of peace-keeping operations and disarmament," 7 *International Problems* (Nos. 1-2, 1969)

Sohn, Louis B. "The authority of the U.N. to establish and maintain a permanent UN force," 52 *AJIL* 229 (1958)

Tandon, Yashpal. "UNEF, the Secretary-General, and international diplomacy in the third Arab-Israeli war," 22 *International Organization* 529 (1968)

U Thant. "The withdrawal of UNEF. Report of June 26, 1967," 4 *UN Monthly Chronicle* 135 (July 1967)

"Withdrawal of United Nations Emergency Force — some questions answered," 4 *UN Monthly Chronicle* 87 (June 1967)

VI. Thoughts on Settlement

Material included in the Abridged Edition:

Moore, John Norton. "The Arab-Israeli conflict and the obligation to pursue peaceful settlement of international disputes," 19 *Kansas Law Review* 403 (1971)

Rosenne, Shabtai. "Directions for a Middle East settlement — some underlying legal problems," 33 *Law and Contemporary Problems* 44 (1968)

Stone, Julius. "The 'November Resolution' and Middle East peace: pitfall or guidepost?" 1971 *University of Toledo Law Review*, 43-69 (1971).

Wright, Quincy. "The Middle East problem," 64 *AJIL* 270 (1970)

Rostow, Eugene V. "Legal aspects of the search for peace in the Middle East," No. 4 *Proceedings of the American Society of International Law*, 64 *AJIL* 64 (1970)

Goldmann, Nahum. "The future of Israel," 48 *Foreign Affairs* 443 (1970)

Campbell, John C. "The Arab-Israeli conflict: an American policy," 49 *Foreign Affairs* 51 (1970)

Rogers, William P. "A lasting peace in the Middle East: an American view," 62 *Department of State Bulletin* 7 (Jan. 5, 1970)

———. "A legacy of peace: our responsibility to future generations," 65 *Department of State Bulletin* 437 (1971).

"Soviet proposal on the Middle East: December 30, 1968," *New York Times*, January 11, 1969, p. 2, col. 4.

Primakov, Yevgeny. "Soviet proposals," 13 *Survival* 19-22 (Jan. 1971). (See also *Pravda*, October 15, 1970.)

"Toward a democratic Palestine," *Fateh* (1970)

"Memorandum submitted to the big powers and the Secretary-General of the United Nations by the representative of the Arab Higher Committee for Palestine" (press release of August 13, 1970)

Douglas-Home, Sir Alec. "Extract from a Statement delivered to the Yorkshire Area Council of the British Conservative Party at Harrogate on Saturday, October 31, 1970," INFORMATION RELEASE NO. 79, United Kingdom Mission to the United Nations, Nov. 2, 1970.

Crowe, Sir Colin. "Statement by the United Kingdom Permanent Representative in the General Assembly on November 2, 1970," INFORMATION RELEASE NO. 80, The United Kingdom Mission to the United Nations, Nov. 2, 1970.

His Majesty, King ibn Talal Hussein. "Address to Jordanian and Palestinian dignitaries on March 15, 1972, concerning basic principles of a plan to establish a United Arab Kingdom of Palestine and Jordan." Copy supplied by the Personal Secretary to His Majesty.

Sisco, Joseph J. "The current situation in the Middle East," 68 *Department of State Bulletin* 484 (1973)

Hoffmann, Stanley. "A new policy for Israel," 53 *Foreign Affairs* 405 (1975)

Bassiouni, M. Cherif, and Morton A. Kaplan. "A Mideast proposal," Faculty Arms Control and Foreign Policy Seminar, The University of Chicago, May 20, 1975

Department of State. "The Arab-Israeli Dispute," *In* UNITED STATES FOREIGN POLICY: AN OVERVIEW. January 1976, pp. 29-31.

Kissinger, Henry A. "Israel and the United States." Department of State, April 4, 1976.

American Friends Service Committee. SEARCH FOR PEACE IN THE MIDDLE EAST. Rev. edn. Philadelphia, 1970.

Arieli, Yehoshua. "Principles for peace negotiations," 13 *New Outlook* 34 (Nov. 1970)

Bassiouni, M. Cherif. "The Middle East in transition — from war to war: a proposed solution," 4 *International Lawyer* 379 (1970)

Berque, J. "Palestine 1971 — the future outlook," 4 *Interplay* 21 (1971)

Blum, Yehuda Z. "Secure boundaries and Middle East peace," *From* SECURE BOUNDARIES AND MIDDLE EAST PEACE. Jerusalem, Hebrew University, Faculty of Law, 1971. (Foreword by Julius Stone, and pp. 63-109)

Brzezinski, Zbigniew, François Duchêne, and Kiichi Saeki. "Peace in an international framework," 19 *Foreign Policy* 3 (1975)

"Can Arab and Jew live together in Palestine?" No. 2 *Middle East International* 23 (May 1971). Dialogue with Nabel Shaath, Uri Avnery and David Hirst.

Caradon, Lord. "A plan for Middle East peace," 10 *War/Peace Report* 7-11 (December 1970)

————. "A road from war in the Middle East," 11 *War/Peace Report* 10 (June-July 1971)

Cattan, Henry. "A new peace formula," *In* PALESTINE: THE ROAD TO PEACE, London, Longman, 1971. pp. 53-59.

Comay, Michael. "Peace in the Middle East," 9 *International Problems* 14 (1970)

"The coming decade in the Middle East: a symposium," 3 *Interplay* 8 (Nov. 1970) and following issues.

Dmitriyev, E. "Middle East settlement," No. 12 *International Affairs* (Moscow) 59 (Dec. 1970)

Eban, Abba. "The key to the future," *In* ISRAEL YEARBOOK, 1971. Tel Aviv, Israel Yearbook Publications, 1971, pp. 37-45.

Etzioni, A. "A buffer zone at the Suez," 13 *New Outlook* 30 (No. 8, Nov. 1970)

Fellowes, P. "Can peace be guaranteed? The ultimate enigma," No. 30 *New Middle East* 11 (March 1971)

Fulbright, J. William. "The Middle East: perspectives for peace," 12 *Survival* 360 (Nov. 1970)

————. "Old myths and new realities — II: The Middle East," 116 *Congressional Record* S 14022-S 14023, S 14029-S 14036 (Aug. 24, 1970)

Goldberg, Arthur J. "The context of peace efforts in the Middle East," 6 *Vista* 34 (1971)

Gottlieb, Gidon. "Of Suez, withdrawal and Jarring: the search for a compromise," No. 1 *New York University Center for International Studies Policy Papers* 4 (1971)

————. "A Palestine Commonwealth," 7 *Vista* 36 (1971)

Hartzberg, A. "Palestine: the logic of partition today," 13 *Columbia Forum* 17 (1970)

Hudson, Richard. "Middle East — peace is just, maybe, barely possible," 11 *War/Peace Report* 3 (Feb. 1971)

Jackson, Henry M. "The Middle East and American security policy," *In* REPORT OF SENATOR HENRY M. JACKSON TO THE SENATE COMMITTEE ON ARMED SERVICES, 91st Cong. 2nd sess. Dec. 21, 1970, pp. 1-19, 22-23.

Meir, Golda. "Israel and Arabs must achieve peace themselves," *In* ISRAEL YEARBOOK, 1971. Tel Aviv, Israel Yearbook Publications, 1971, pp. 15-18.

Murphy, John F. "Neutralization of Israel," 65 *AJIL* 167 (1971)

Peretz, Don. "A binational approach to the Palestine conflict," 33 *Law and Contemporary Problems* 32 (1968)

————, Evan Wilson, and Richard J. War. A PALESTINE ENTITY? Washington, Middle East Institute, 1970. 117 p. (Middle East Special Study No. 1.)

Petkovic, Ranko. "Toward settlement of the Middle East crisis," No. 502 *Review of International Affairs* (March 5, 1971)

Prlja, A. "The Rogers plan and the chances for peace," Nos. 488-489 *Review of International Affairs* (Aug. 5-20, 1970)

Reisman, Michael. THE ART OF THE POSSIBLE: DIPLOMATIC ALTERNATIVES IN THE MIDDLE EAST. Princeton, N. J., Princeton University Press, 1970.

Rogers, William P. "Peace and stability in the Middle East and Asia," 64 *Department of State Bulletin* 61 (Jan. 11, 1971)

Roots, John McCook. "David Ben-Gurion talks about Israel and the Arabs ... 'Peace is more important than real estate'," 14 *Saturday Review* (April 3, 1971)

Rosenne, Shabtai. "On multi-lingual interpretation," 6 *Israel Law Review* 360 (1971)

Rubinstein, Amnon. "A plan for Sinai — something less than peace in return for something less than total withdrawal," *New York Times Magazine* 13 (Jan. 17, 1971)

Sayegh, Fayez A. PALESTINE, ISRAEL AND PEACE. Palestine Essays No. 17. Palestine Liberation Organization, 1969.

Schwebel, Stephen M. "A solution for Sinai," *New York Times*, November 22, 1971.

Singh, K.R. "Rogers' proposals and Arab reactions," 19 *Foreign Affairs Report* 60 (1970)

Smart, Ian M.F. "Military insecurity and the Arab-Israel conflict: there is an effective alternative to the United Nations," No. 26 *New Middle East* 28 (Nov. 1970)

Taylor, Alan R., and Richard N. Tetlie, eds. PALESTINE: A SEARCH FOR TRUTH. Washington, Public Affairs Press, 1970. 284 p.

Tessler, M.A. "A cultural basis for Arab-Israeli accommodation," 133 *World Affairs* 183 (1970)

"War in the Middle East," 1 *Bulletin of Peace Proposals* 362 (1970). Articles from eleven sources.

Weil, Prosper. "Le reglement territorial dans la resolution du 22 novembre 1967," *Les Nouveaux Cahiers* 4-8 (Hiver 1970)

Wright, Quincy. "The Middle Eastern crisis," No. 4 *Proceedings of the American Society of International Law*, 64 *AJIL* 71 (1970)

Yost, Charles W. "Last chance for peace in the Middle East," 6 *Vista* 33 (1971)

VII. Collections of Documents and Bibliographies

A. DOCUMENTS*

American Journal of International Law. "Official Documents" section, esp. Vols. 50 (1956), 51 (1957), 52 (1958), 54 (1960), 62 (1968), and 63 (1969)

*Official United Nations publications have not been included here, i.e., UNITED NATIONS YEARBOOK (Annual); ANNUAL REPORT OF THE SECRETARY-GENERAL; *UN Monthly Chronicle*; Security Council OFFICIAL RECORDS, etc.

British Institute of International and Comparative Law. THE SUEZ CANAL. A SELECTION OF DOCUMENTS RELATING TO THE INTERNATIONAL STATUS OF THE SUEZ CANAL AND THE POSITION OF THE SUEZ CANAL COMPANY, NOV. 30, 1854 – JULY 25, 1956. London, Society of Comparative Legislation, 1956, 76 p.

Conference on the Suez Canal, London, 1956. THE SUEZ CANAL CONFERENCE: SELECTED DOCUMENTS. London, H.M.S.O., 1956. 18 p. CMD. 9853.

DOCUMENTS RELATING TO THE PALESTINE PROBLEM. New York, Jewish Agency for Palestine, 1945.

Eayrs, James G., ed. THE COMMONWEALTH AND SUEZ: A DOCUMENTARY SURVEY. New York, Oxford University Press, 1964. 483 p.

Higgins, Rosalyn. UNITED NATIONS PEACEKEEPING, 1946-1967: DOCUMENTS AND COMMENTARY: Vol. I. THE MIDDLE EAST. London, Oxford University Press, 1969.

Institute for Palestine Studies. UNITED NATIONS RESOLUTIONS ON PALESTINE, 1947-1965. Beirut, The Institute, 1965. 157 p.

International Legal Materials: Current Documents, esp. Vols. 6 (1967) and 7 (1968)

Jabber, F.A., ed. INTERNATIONAL DOCUMENTS ON PALESTINE, 1967. Beirut, Institute for Palestine Studies, 1970. (Continuation of an annual documentary volume entitled PALESTINE BEFORE THE UNITED NATIONS.)

Khalil, Muhammad. THE ARAB STATES AND THE ARAB LEAGUE. A DOCUMENTARY RECORD. Vol. II. International Affairs. Beirut, Khayats, 1962. 1019 p.

Laquer, Walter, ed. *The Israel-Arab Reader*. Rev. Bantam matrix edn. 1970. 511 p.

Lauterpacht, E., ed. THE SUEZ CANAL SETTLEMENTS: A SELECTION OF DOCUMENTS RELATING TO THE SETTLEMENT OF THE SUEZ CANAL DISPUTE, THE CLEARANCE OF THE SUEZ CANAL AND THE SETTLEMENT OF DISPUTES BETWEEN THE UNITED KINGDOM, FRANCE AND THE UNITED ARAB REPUBLIC, OCTOBER 1856 – MARCH 1959. London, Stevens; New York, Praeger, 1960. 82 p.

Magnus, Ralph H., ed. DOCUMENTS ON THE MIDDLE EAST. Washington, American Enterprise Institute for Public Policy Research, July 1969.

Mezerik, A.G., ed. THE UNITED NATIONS EMERGENCY FORCES. New York, International Review Service, 1958.

———. THE UNITED NATIONS EMERGENCY FORCE (UNEF) 1956 – CREATION, EVOLUTION, END OF MISSION, 1967. New York, International Review Service, 1969.

Palestine Arab Refugee Office, New York. OFFICIAL DOCUMENTS, PLEDGES AND RESOLUTIONS ON PALESTINE, BEGINNING WITH THE HUSAIN-MCMAHON CORRESPONDENCE 1916; DOCUMENTS OF SPECIAL INTEREST IN ANY STUDY OF THE PALESTINE CASE. New York, 1959. 161 p.

THE PALESTINIAN REFUGEES: A COLLECTION OF U.N. DOCUMENTS. Beirut, Institute for Palestine Studies, 1970. 641 p.

Sohn, Louis B. CASES AND MATERIALS ON WORLD LAW. Brooklyn, Foundation Press, 1950.

———. CASES ON UNITED NATIONS LAW. Brooklyn, Foundation Press, 1st edn., 1956. 2nd edn., 1967.

Tannous, Izzat, ed. UNITED NATIONS RESOLUTIONS ON PALESTINE
1947-1961. Palestine Arab Refugee Office, 1961.

U.S. 90th Cong. 1st sess. Senate Committee on Foreign Relations. A SELECT
CHRONOLOGY AND BACKGROUND DOCUMENTS RELATING TO THE
MIDDLE EAST. Washington, G.P.O., 1967. 1st rev. edn., May 1969, 91st
Cong. 1st sess.

U.S. Department of State, Pub. 6506. UNITED STATES POLICY IN THE
MIDDLE EAST, SEPTEMBER 1956 — JUNE 1957: DOCUMENTS. Washington, G.P.O., 1957.

————. AMERICAN FOREIGN POLICY: CURRENT DOCUMENTS, 1947,
1956, 1957.

Watt, Donald C., ed. DOCUMENTS ON THE SUEZ CRISIS, 26 JULY TO 6
NOVEMBER 1956. New York, Oxford University Press, 1957. 88 p.

B.   BIBLIOGRAPHIES

Arab-Israeli Research and Relations Project (AIRRP) ANNOTATED BIBLI-
OGRAPHY ON ARAB-ISRAELI RELATIONS. New York (1865 Broadway,
New York 10023) 1971.

Cottrell, A. "The Soviet Union as a major power in the Middle East: a review
of recent literature," 133 *World Affairs* 315 (1970-71)

Grech, Anthony P., comp. "Selected Bibliography on the Middle East Crisis,"
In THE MIDDLE EAST: PROSPECTS FOR PEACE. THIRTEENTH
HAMMARSKJOLD FORUM. Dobbs Ferry, N. Y., Oceana, 1969, pp. 87-107.

Johnsen, Julia E., comp. PALESTINE: JEWISH HOMELAND? New York,
H.W. Wilson, 1946. 342 p.

Shapira, Amos. LEGAL ASPECTS OF THE ARAB-ISRAEL CONFLICT: A
SELECT BIBLIOGRAPHY. Tel Aviv University, Overseas students' unit,
1971. Unpublished.

United Nations. Geneva. *Monthly List of Books catalogued in the Library of
the United Nations*, esp. the section "Special questions" under "Political,
historical and geographical questions."

United Nations. Geneva. *Monthly List of Selected Articles*, esp. the sections
"United Nations, International Peace, and Political questions."

United Nations. New York. *Current bibliographical information*, 1971 — "Middle
East Situation." This publication replaces *Current issues: a selected
bibliography on subjects of concern to the United Nations*, 1965-1970.

Library of Congress Cataloging in Publication Data
Main entry under title:

The Arab-Israeli conflict.

    Bibliography: p.
    1. Jewish-Arab relations--1917-   --Addresses,
essays, lectures. 2. Jewish-Arab relations--
1917-   --Sources. I. Moore, John Norton,
1937-   II. American Society of International
Law.
DS119.7.A6718 1977   956'.04   76-45905
ISBN 0-691-01066-8

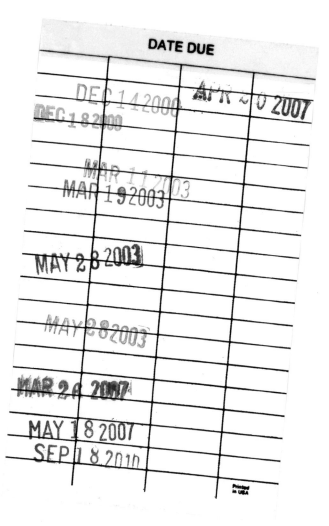